Handbook of Personal Relationships

Handbook of Personal Relationships

Theory, Research and Interventions

Edited by

STEVE DUCK
Daniel and Amy Starch Research Professor
Communication Studies Department
University of Iowa, USA

Sections Edited By

STEVE DUCK
DALE F. HAY, *Institute of Psychiatry, London, UK*
STEVAN E. HOBFOLL, *Kent State University, USA*
WILLIAM ICKES, *University of Texas at Arlington, USA*
BARBARA M. MONTGOMERY, *University of New Hampshire, USA*

JOHN WILEY & SONS
Chichester · New York · Brisbane · Toronto · Singapore

Library of Congress Cataloging in Publication Data:

Handbook of personal relationships: theory, research, and
  interventions / edited by Steve Duck.
    p.   cm.
  Bibliography: p.
  Includes index.
  ISBN 0 471 91491 6
  1. Interpersonal relations. I. Duck, Steve.
HM132.H3325 1988
302.3'4—dc19

87–22168
CIP

British Library Cataloguing in Publication Data:

Handbook of personal relationships: theory, research and interventions.
  1. Interpersonal relations
  I. Duck, Steve
  302   HM132
ISBN 0 471 91491 6

Phototypeset by Input Typesetting Ltd, London SW19 8DR
Printed and bound in Great Britain by
Anchor Brendon Ltd, Essex

Contributors

TERRY F. ADLER, *Department of Psychology, University of Denver, Colorado, USA*

LESLIE A. BAXTER, *Communications Department, Lewis and Clark College, Portland, Oregon, USA*

CHARLES R. BERGER, *Department of Communication Studies, Northwestern University, Evanston, Chicago, Illinois, USA*

FRANK BOSTER, *Department of Communication, Michigan State University, East Lansing, Michigan, USA*

JOSEPH N. CAPPELLA, *Department of Communication Arts, Vilas Hall, University of Wisconsin, Madison, Wisconsin, USA*

RODNEY M. CATE, *Department of Child and Family Studies, Washington State University, Pullman, Washington, USA*

J. ALLAN CHEYNE, *Department of Psychology, University of Waterloo, Ontario, Canada*

JAMES P. DILLARD, *Department of Communication Arts, Vilas Hall, University of Wisconsin, Madison, Wisconsin, USA*

STEVE DUCK, *Daniel and Army Starch Research Professor, 151 CSB Communication Studies, University of Iowa, Iowa, USA*

JUDITH DUNN, *Department of Individual and Family Studies, Pennsylvania State University, Pennsylvania, USA*

WYNDOL FURMAN, *Department of Psychology, University of Denver, Colorado, USA*

G. P. GINSBURG, *Interdisciplinary Program in Social Psychology, University of Nevada, Reno, Nevada, USA*

IAN H. GOTLIB, *Department of Psychology, University of Western Ontario, London, Ontario, Canada*

BENJAMIN H. GOTTLIEB, *Department of Psychology, University of Guelph, Ontario, Canada*

JOAN E. GRUSEC, *Department of Psychology, University of Toronto, Scarborough, Ontario, Canada*

JOHN H. HARVEY, *Department of Psychology, University of Iowa, Iowa, USA*

DALE F. HAY, *Department of Child Psychiatry, Institute of Psychiatry, London, UK*

ROBERT B. HAYS, *Department of Psychology, George Washington University, Washington DC, USA*

CLYDE HENDRICK, *Department of Psychology, Texas Tech University, Lubbock, Texas, USA*

SUSAN S. HENDRICK, *Department of Psychology, Texas Tech University, Lubbock, Texas, USA*

STEVAN E. HOBFOLL, *Applied Psychology Center, Kent State University, Kent, Ohio, USA*

JILL M. HOOLEY, *Department of Psychology and Social Relations, Harvard University, Cambridge, Massachusetts, USA*

WILLIAM ICKES, *Department of Psychology, University of Texas at Arlington, Texas, USA*

DAVID KENNY, *Department of Psychology, University of Connecticut, Storrs, Connecticut, USA*

SALLY A. LLOYD, *Family and Consumer Studies, University of Utah, Salt Lake City, Utah, USA*

SUSAN P. LOLLIS, *Department of Psychology, University of Waterloo, Ontario, Canada*

DAN P. MCADAMS, *Department of Psychology, Loyola University of Chicago, Illinois, USA*

GEORGE MCCALL, *Department of Sociology, University of Missouri, St Louis, Missouri, USA*

FRANK E. MILLAR, *Department of Communication, University of Wyoming, Laramie, Wyoming, USA*

GERALD R. MILLER, *Department of Communication, Michigan State University, East Lansing, Michigan, USA*

KATHERINE I. MILLER, *Department of Communication, Michigan State University, East Lansing, Michigan, USA*

ROSEMARY S. L. MILLS, *Department of Psychology, University of Waterloo, Ontario, Canada*

BARBARA M. MONTGOMERY, *Department of Communication, Paul Creative Arts Center, University of New Hampshire, Durham, New Hampshire, USA*

ALISON NASH, *Department of Psychology, State University of New York at New Paltz, New Paltz, New York, USA*

ROBERT W. NORTON, *Department of Communication, Memphis State University, Tennessee, USA*

KATHRYN A. PARK, *Department of Psychology, University of Denver, Colorado, USA*

MILES L. PATTERSON, *Department of Psychology, University of Missouri, St Louis, Missouri, USA*

HARRY T. REIS, *Department of Psychology, University of Rochester, New York, USA*

L. EDNA ROGERS, *Communication Department, University of Utah, Salt Lake City, Utah, USA*

KAREN S. ROOK, *Department of Social Ecology, University of California, Irvine, California, USA*

HILDY S. ROSS, *Department of Psychology, University of Waterloo, Ontario, Canada*

PHILLIP SHAVER, *Psychology Department, State University of New York at Buffalo, Buffalo, New York, USA*

JOSEPH P. STOKES, *Department of Psychology, University of Illinois at Chicago, Chicago, Illinois, USA*

WILLIAM TOOKE, *Department of Psychology, State University of New York, Plattsburgh, New York, USA*

KAREN TUCKER, *Counselling Center, Memorial Union, Ohio State University, Columbus, Ohio, USA*

EVERETT WATERS, *Department of Psychology, State University of New York at Stony Brook, New York, USA*

Contents

Introduction xiii
  Steve Duck

Section One   Conceptualizations and Methods

Overview 3
  William Ickes

1 Personal Needs and Personal Relationships 7
   Dan P. McAdams

2 Rules, Scripts and Prototypes in Personal Relationships 23
   G. P. Ginsburg

3 Functions of Nonverbal Behavior in Close Relationships 41
   Miles L. Patterson

4 The Analysis of Data from Two-Person Relationships 57
   David A. Kenny

5 The Observational Method: Studying the Interaction of Minds and
   Bodies 79
   William Ickes and William Tooke

6 Self-Report Methods in Studying Personal Relationships 99
   John H. Harvey, Susan S. Hendrick and Karen Tucker

Section Two   Developmental/Life Cycle

Overview 117
  Dale F. Hay

7 Ontogeny, Phylogeny, and Relationships 121
   Alison Nash

8   Defining and Studying Reciprocity in Young Children 143
    Hildy S. Ross, J. Allan Cheyne and Susan P. Lollis

9   Traits and Relationships in Developmental Perspective 161
    Kathryn A. Park and Everett Waters

10 Socialization from the Perspective of the Parent–Child Relationship . 177
    Rosemary S. L. Mills and Joan E. Grusec

11 Relations among Relationships 193
    Judith Dunn

12 A Model for Children's Relationships and Relationship Dysfunctions 211
    Terry F. Adler and Wyndol Furman

Section Three   Communication

Overview 233
    Barbara Montgomery

13 Uncertainty and Information Exchange in Developing Relationships   239
    Charles R. Berger

14 A Dialectical Perspective on Communication Strategies in
    Relationship Development 257
    Leslie A. Baxter

15 Persuasion in Personal Relationships 275
    Gerald R. Miller and Frank Boster

16 Relational Communication 289
    L. Edna Rogers and Frank E. Millar

17 Communicator Style Theory in Marital Interaction: Persistent
    Challenges 307
    Robert W. Norton

18 Personal Relationships, Social Relationships and Patterns of
    Interaction 325
    Joseph N. Cappella

19 Quality Communication in Personal Relationships 343
    Barbara M. Montgomery

Section Four   Social Psychology/Sociology

Overview 363
    Steve Duck

20 Intimacy as an Interpersonal Process 367
    Harry T. Reis and Phillip Shaver

21 Friendship 391
    Robert B. Hays

22 Courtship 409
    Rodney M. Cate and Sally A. Lloyd

23 Roles and Gender in Relationships 429
    Clyde Hendrick

24 Intimate Relationships in Task Environments 449
    James P. Dillard and Katherine I. Miller

25 The Organizational Life Cycle of Relationships 467
    George J. McCall

Section Five   Community and Clinical

Overview 487
    Stevan E. Hobfoll

26 The Processes and Mechanics of Social Support 497
    Stevan E. Hobfoll and Joseph P. Stokes

27 Support Interventions: A Typology and Agenda for Research 519
    Benjamin H. Gottlieb

28 Depression and Marital Distress: Current Status and Future
    Directions 543
    Ian H. Gotlib and Jill M. Hooley

29 Towards a More Differentiated View of Loneliness 571
    Karen S. Rook

References 591

Index of First Authors 685

Subject Index 698

Introduction

It is now commonplace to point to the obvious fact that the field of research in personal relationships has begun to emerge in the last ten years or so. I do not intend merely to add to the claims that the field is emerging and is just around the corner: indeed, authors and editors are finding that we have just about exhausted the ways of reminding readers of the fact anyway! The field is now here, and the viability of a Handbook such as this is testament to that fact, just as much as are the other monuments to the existence of the field, such as the flourishing *Journal of Social and Personal Relationships*, the developing series of *Advances in Personal Relationships* (Jones and Perlman, 1987), and the various groups and subgroups of people who meet regularly to hold conferences on relationships, whether these are international or are associated with a particular local centre for work on relationships, such as the Iowa Conferences on Personal Relationships. The field has been given form and life and must be recognized as already existing, even if the vigour of that existence to some extent dumbfounds its creators.

It is also now trite to point out just how much the field has developed: in truth it has expanded at an almost incredible rate since 1978. While before that time there were only a couple of academic books with words like 'personal relationships', 'social relationships', 'close relationships' or 'human relationships' in the title (e.g. Lowe, 1969; Duck, 1973), in the ten years since 1978 there have been published at least another *twenty-five* such books (e.g. Burgess and Huston, 1979; Hinde, 1979; Kelley, 1979; Foot, Chapman and Smith, 1980; Asher and Gottman, 1981; Duck and Gilmour, 1981a, b, c; Duck, 1982b; Berger and Bradac, 1982; Kelley *et al.*, 1983; Duck, 1983; Hendrick and Hendrick, 1983; Derlega, 1984; Duck 1984c; Knapp, 1984; Argyle and Henderson, 1985; Brehm, 1985; Duck and Perlman, 1985; Duck, 1986; Derlega and Winstead, 1986; Gilmour and Duck, 1986; Perlman and Duck, 1987; Burnett, McGhee and Clarke, 1987; Burnett and Clarke, 1988). In addition to this, the *Review of Personality and Social Psychology* will have its Volume 10 assigned to work on close relationships and had some 57 submissions of proposals for chapters. Other measures of the field's size and growth likewise confirm its burgeoning, whether these be bibliographic records (see Duck and Perlman, 1985; Perlman and Fehr, 1987) or indications of numbers of persons now working in the field.

Those of us who have devoted our academic lives to the field have grounds for feeling gratified, since it is rather like buying a house in an unpopular neighbourhood that suddenly becomes fashionable. It appears that many people in several different disciplines were waiting for some spark to set fire to their latent wishes to study the topic that had always interested them at a distance.

Some of them may have felt that the area was not somehow quite challenging enough while the view persisted that 'it's all common sense', or were wary of admitting the topic's importance in social life. Others perhaps opined that the area was not exciting enough or useful enough while it was still so clearly associated in people's minds with laboratory work on attraction to strangers or reactions to impression formation tasks. By contrast with the previous state of affairs, the list of research topics in personal relationships is now impressively respectable, lengthy and realistic, as the contents list of this Handbook shows. For instance, there are chapters here on Personal needs and personal relationships; on Relations among relationships; Persuasion in personal relationships; Intimate relationships in task environments; and Depression and marital distress. These are relatively new and developing topics, not usually found in earlier books in the field.

What is also evident from the chapters in the Handbook (especially, but not limited to, the chapters in Section One, Conceptualizations and Methods) is that there has been a remarkable development in the means of investigating relevant issues recently and also in the complexity of the theoretical questions that are being scrutinized. In place of studies of reactions to strangers are detailed considerations of intimacy in long-term relationships (e.g. Helgeson, Shaver and Dyer, 1987 and the Reis and Shaver chapter here). Where one previously saw studies of the effects of attractiveness of confederates on self-esteem in dating choice one now observes good research into the progress of courtship (e.g. Lloyd and Cate, 1985a and the Cate and Lloyd chapter here). Instead of reactive studies of nonverbal cues in structured laboratory situations, one is now challenged to consider the ways in which such nonverbal communication is relevant to relationship change (e.g. Cappella, 1984, and Cappella's chapter here). Where strangers were once given structure by the experimenter and had little freedom to represent real life in their laboratory interaction, there are now well-established methods for observing strangers' spontaneous interactions unobtrusively (e.g. Ickes, 1983, and the Ickes and Tooke chapter here). Where researchers had despaired of studying social participation in real life or everyday communication in relationships, there are now techniques for doing so (e.g. Wheeler and Nezlek, 1977) and they have been used to study real life relationship development and decline to good effect (e.g. Baxter and Wilmot, 1986; Duck and Miell, 1986, and Baxter's chapter here).

With the temporal extension of research to long-term relationships and the redirection of studies to new or different foci in all topic areas has come a simultaneous and quite remarkable concentration of workers from different disciplines who now interact together through scholarly channels and share the fruits of their expertise with others from different backgrounds. What remains to be established with greater certainty and clarity in some quarters is the extent to which the field of research in personal relationships is *inherently and necessarily* a cross-disciplinary enterprise. It can grow in scholarship and application only if the different disciplines continue to feed one another with their insights and own special contributions. No one discipline has all the answers and we must recognize that fact from the start (Duck and Perlman, 1985). This Handbook is therefore divided into sections that reflect and describe the inputs of the different disciplines: Communication; Community and Clinical Psychology; Developmental and Life-Cycle Psychology; Social Psychology and Sociology; and the overarching Conceptualizations and Methods, that also includes chapters from the tradition of research into issues of personality theory.

The Handbook thus reflects my view that the field of research in personal relationships is not created nor sustained by the efforts of only one section of the community of scholars alone, but instead feeds and grows from the interaction of many different schools of thought, all of which need to be informed about the work of the others.

Against this background of change, innovation and incipient cohesion in the field, the emergence of the present Handbook is itself an exciting event and a momentous opportunity. Handbooks can be of two sorts: predominantly forward looking or predominantly backward looking. The latter sort presents a comprehensive and historically based account of the work that has been done up until that point, establishing and identifying longitudinal and programmatic development and occasions for congratulation and intensification of past efforts. There is clearly a need for such kinds of volumes, particularly once a field is well established and can look back with satisfaction on its accumulated achievements. The other sort of volume, by contrast, focuses on the future and emphasizes the continuous development of the research by analysing the past and present in order to extract the trends that must be encouraged. As such it provides a whetstone for the cutting edge of future research and a stimulus for dismissal of complacency, even about the good work that has been carried out.

It is my intention and my hope that the present volume will be seen to be one of the latter sorts of volume. Indeed, contributors were asked to challenge rather than merely to report, to be selective and guiding rather than merely comprehensive, and to indicate future lines of promise rather than merely to applaud the accomplishments of the past. The field of research in personal relationships is now growing fast enough that it needs such direction and stimulation to encourage and continue its future growth.

Given these remarks, I do not believe that readers benefit by ploughing through long introductions by editors when they can instead see the products of the editing work in the structure, content, and, indeed, the very existence of the Handbook itself. I do not therefore intend to summarize the volume at length, but to give some background for the choice of topic groups that was made in its construction in the context of the foregoing remarks. The sections were chosen to reflect those areas where the new styles of research are most evident.

Exciting research is developing, and can be classified, in many ways, but I chose to label the groupings: Communication, Community and Clinical Psychology, Conceptualizations and Methods, Developmental/Life-Cycle Psychology, Social Psychology and Sociology. There are many ways to cut the particular cake of research into personal relationships and to structure the volume. At first sight my choice of the present labels may seem paradoxical in light of my advocacy of an interdisciplinary approach to the field. The decision to section the volume this way partly reflects the fact that the traditional disciplinary groupings are an inevitable fact of academic life, however undesirable their rigid influence may be, and partly reflects the desire to show that, within their own groupings, the different disciplines have much to say to one another.

This optimism is borne out in the volume itself, for while the various sections each have their own character, ably described by the section editors separately, the overarching plan presents a clear view of the general flavour of the many styles of research so that readers are given a clear picture of the diversity of the field while yet appreciating the common threads that will ultimately form the core of the discipline. Since one major theme in recent work seems to be the increased attention to temporal factors in the long-term lives of relationships, all the sections place emphasis there. While strict experimental work focuses on very short interactions, the authors in the Handbook are often dealing with extensive processual issues, whether these relate to ways in which intimacy is created by interpersonal processes (Reis and Shaver), the development of one sort of relationship in the context of others in the life cycle (Dunn), the creation of a sense of quality in a relationship (Norton; Montgomery), the long-term interaction of depressed persons with their spouses (Gotlib and Hooley), or the best means of conceptualizing social relationships in statistical terms (Kenny).

Because of the common threads in the work, there are some intriguingly natural cross-references between chapters that vindicate the foregoing remarks on the volume. When, for example, a social psychological chapter on the nature of intimacy acknowledges chapters in the developmental psychology section and the chapter by a sociologist refers extensively to work in the communication section, which itself makes frequent reference to the statistical and observational work in the methodological section, or work in the clinical and community psychology section draws on experimental work in the social psychology section, then there is good cause for sustained optimism about scholarly intercourse in this field.

In the course of the production of the manuscript for the Handbook, the desired, the predictable and the undesired all occurred. In creating the individual chapters in the volume, a number of remarkably insightful and impressive pieces of work were developed and produced by the contributors, who rose with vigour to the task set them in their invitation letters. Their universal enthusiasm for the project made it easier for the section editors and myself to extend our editorial demands, and all chapters were refined in exacting ways during the section editors' and editor's work on the pieces. Some chapters were put through four drafts and all went through at least one major revision and at least one minor one. The consequent high quality of the volume overall is a significant indicator of the future potential of the field, as much as it is a monument to their own endeavours. As a set, the chapters present a good overview of the key issues and research in the many corners of the field.

Of course, there were some disappointments. Some people who had agreed to produce chapters were unable to do so in the event, and when this happened very close to the deadlines it was impossible to replace them. Some people produced chapters that were not representative of their best work and these were dropped from the Handbook rather than compromise on the overall quality of the volume. There are therefore some gaps in the Handbook and some topics that both I and readers might have expected and hoped to see covered. For example, we have no chapter on involuntary relationships and none specifically on social networks or on intergenerational relationships. These gaps were unintentional. Others were the result of choices taken in the light of pressures on space or of editing priorities. Thus, for example, I did not include a section on marriage and the family, which justifies a handbook of its own. I also included no chapter on emotion as such, since I take the view that it is an intriguing general topic in social behaviour rather than one specific to research on relationships, even though it has great relevance there. Rather I have chosen to invite a chapter on one specific instance of the 'emergent' emotions that operate specifically in personal relationships, namely intimacy. Neither is there, for example, a chapter on fathering, since the developmental psychology section, as do most of the other sections, focuses on general principles of relating rather than on specific instances of relationships.

It may seem unnecessary to make these points and it may be adequate merely to point to the size and complexity of the field and raise one's hands to heaven. Yet a Handbook is a special sort of book and needs to cover the ground more thoroughly than other collections of chapters, even though no single volume could expect to provide utterly comprehensive coverage of so vast a field. The coverage here is extensive but cannot be regarded as complete—the more so as the field continues its rapid expansion. Nevertheless, the present mapping of the research terrain is likely to serve scholars for many years and to provide the academic leadership and direction that the field now needs.

ACKNOWLEDGEMENTS

I am grateful to Chris Brenneman for her superhuman efforts in coordinating the secretarial work, correspondence and reference list compilation for this volume. It really could not have been done without her unstinting and prodigiously efficient help. I am also grateful to Joanna Lawson for her help with the preparation of the final manuscript.

STEVE DUCK

Section One

Conceptualizations and Methods

Section Editor   *William Ickes*

Overview

The chapters in this first section of the *Handbook of Personal Relationships* concern some of the major conceptual and methodological frameworks that relationship researchers have used to structure their inquiries and investigations. These chapters tend to have a broader focus than those encountered later in this volume. They also tend to consider more explicitly such basic questions as 'What are the best ways to think about relationships?' and 'What are the best ways to study relationships?'

CONCEPTUAL FRAMEWORKS

In Chapter 1, Dan McAdams discusses several theories of relationships that stress the importance of personal needs. McAdams proposes that the theorists and researchers in this tradition can be ordered along a continuum that reflects the extent to which their theoretical formulations emphasize one as opposed to many personal needs whose fulfilment is sought in relationships. At one end of this continuum are theorists such as Rogers, Jung, Kelly, and Sternberg, whose work seems to emphasize a single, unitary need such as the need for self-realization or the need for love. At the other end are theorists such as Murray, Maslow, and Hendrick and Hendrick, who have specified a plurality of needs (in Murray's case, at least 20, including the needs for abasement, affiliation, aggression, dominance, exhibition, and nurturance). Between these two extremes, occupying the midrange of the continuum, are still another group of theorists who have emphasized two general classes of needs that the participants in relationships presumably seek to fulfill. Theorists in this group, such as Angyal, Bakan, Freud, and McAdams himself, focus on such dualistic motives as autonomy and surrender, agency and communion, eros and thanatos, or power and intimacy.

With clarity and economy of expression, McAdams presents a useful overview of the entire range of theories that account for various aspects of human relationships in terms of personal needs. He makes note of the existing and potential points of convergence and divergence in these theories and cites relevant research evidence to support his arguments. McAdams' chapter makes

3

an important contribution to our understanding of relationships by providing the groundwork for an integration of the various theories focusing on personal needs and motivations.

Gerald Ginsburg, in Chapter 2, attempts a similar conceptual integration of three theoretical approaches that are currently ascendant in cognitive social psychology: rules, scripts and prototypes. Rules are defined as 'the equivalent of statements which prescribe, proscribe or explicitly permit a particular type of behavior'. In human relationships, they are assumed to regulate and coordinate social behavior, facilitate individual autonomy and responsibility, provide justification for the legitimacy of one's actions, and even promote some misunderstanding, miscues, and confusion in situations in which they have been insensitively applied.

Scripts and prototypes, both regarded as variants of schemata, are stereotyped cognitive representations of temporally extended action episodes (scripts) and of 'best' or 'most central' categorical exemplars (prototypes). In social life, scripts are assumed to guide both the selection and sequencing of situationally appropriate behaviors, thereby facilitating the coordination of action, reducing the effort of interaction, and facilitating the maintenance of social order and social rituals. In contrast, prototypes are assumed to constrain the cognitive representations people have about others or about relationships, and thereby constrain the actual relationships that develop. Ginsburg reviews studies that illustrate the relevance of rules, scripts and prototypes to the study of personal relationships, and concludes by admonishing researchers in this area to give 'increased attention to the world that a person's head is in and somewhat less to what is in the person's head'.

There is an interesting difference between Chapter 3, by Miles Patterson, and the preceding chapters by McAdams and by Ginsburg. Whereas McAdams and Ginsburg focus on specific theoretical approaches to relationships that fall under the general headings of *motivational theories* or *cognitive theories*, Patterson focuses instead on the metatheoretical research strategies that investigators have used to study relationships. His chapter begins by reviewing two such strategies: (1) the analysis of 'the core components or processes that sustain relationships', and (2) 'the developmental analysis of the changing stages of relationships'. Patterson regards both strategies as useful and capable of complementing each other. He proposes, however, that a third research strategy is also needed—one that provides a functional analysis of the behaviors 'exchanged' in ongoing social interaction.

Patterson's own functional analysis of nonverbal behavior is offered as a prototypic example of this third research strategy. He proposes that the various functions served by nonverbal behavior in relationships can be subsumed under the broad and partially overlapping categories of (1) providing information, (2) regulating interaction, (3) expressing intimacy, (4) exerting social control, (5) engaging in self-presentation, (6) managing affect, and (7) performing a task or service. Patterson offers detailed examples of each function and suggests (a) how different behaviors can serve the same function, and (b) how the same behavior can serve different functions. He concludes that because the 'meaning' and function of a given pattern of behavior can vary greatly according to the physical and social context in which it occurs, the functional strategy provides an essential complement to the component/process and developmental strategies for the study of personal relationships.

METHODOLOGICAL FRAMEWORKS

By presenting a metatheoretical perspective, Patterson's chapter marks the transition between a primary concern with theoretical/conceptual issues and a primary concern with methodological issues. Although both sets of issues are implicated in all of the chapters in Section One, the last three chapters reflect a special emphasis on methodology.

The rapid expansion of research on personal relationships has been accompanied by a growing disenchantment with many of the statistical and methodological procedures traditionally employed in the social and behavioral sciences. Statistical and methodological procedures which for decades have been successfully applied to the study of single subjects performing highly structured laboratory tasks have frequently proved inadequate when applied to the study of human relationships. Fortunately, the long-standing challenge to develop more appropriate statistical procedures and research methodologies is no longer being ignored.

For at least a decade, David Kenny has been the major proponent and originator of a 'family' of new statistical techniques designed to address many of the special problems inherent in the study of social interaction. In Chapter 4, Kenny outlines these special problems and discusses an impressive range of statistical solutions. The special problems he describes include (1) the interdependence of behavior in dyadic relationships and the resulting nonindependence of the dyad members' responses, (2) the difficulty of establishing causal priority in such interdependent exchanges, (3) the problem of testing statistical relationships and establishing their generality at both the individual and dyad levels of analysis, and (4) the problem that it is often arbitrary which dyad member's response is used as the X or Y variable when correlating paired responses from heterogeneous ('similar partners') dyads.

According to Kenny, all but the second of these problems can be addressed through the application of special statistical techniques that range from the relatively simple intraclass correlation to the more complicated analyses of the social relations model (Kenny and La Voie, 1984; Malloy and Kenny, 1986). Kenny offers an authoritative guide to all of these techniques, suggesting which ones are appropriate to use in analyzing the data from time-series dyadic designs or from standard dyadic designs in which dyad members interact with single or multiple partners. His chapter is likely to become required reading for researchers interested in the study of dyadic interaction.

During the years that Kenny and his colleagues were developing new statistical procedures for the analysis of dyadic interaction data, William Ickes and his colleagues were developing a new research paradigm for the study of unstructured dyadic interaction. The most recent version of 'the dyadic interaction paradigm' is described by Ickes and Tooke in Chapter 5. Throughout its twelve-year history, the paradigm has proved to be effective as an observational method for studying the naturally occurring behavior of dyad members during a period of unstructured social interaction. In recent years, the paradigm has been extended to include the study of subjective thoughts and feelings in addition to the study of objectively coded behavior.

Ickes and Tooke cite empirical support for their claim that the covert thoughts and feelings of subjects engaged in naturalistic interactions can—like the subjects' overt behavior—be studied in a reliable and nonreactive way. Their procedures for assessing the actual and inferred thoughts and feelings of interaction partners have opened up several novel lines of inquiry for relationship research. In particular, these procedures enable the study of *naturalistic social cognition* (Ickes *et al.*, 1986) and can be used to investigate phenomena such as metaperspective taking, intersubjectivity, and empathic accuracy. As the title of Chapter 5 suggests, the observational method can be extended to study the interactions of the 'minds' as well as the 'bodies' of interaction partners.

A more traditional approach to studying the minds of interaction partners is the topic of Chapter 6 by Harvey, Hendrick and Tucker. These authors provide a cogent review and evaluation of the self-report methods most commonly used in the study of personal relationships. They contend that the heavy reliance on these methods is due to the desire of researchers to investigate the *meaning* that individuals impute to their relationships, a meaning that may or may not be congruent with the overt behavior displayed. Because 'forms of overt behavior, whether verbal or nonverbal, may have different meanings to people depending on the context of the behavior, the audience, the nature of the ongoing relationship, etc.,' it is necessary to study subjects' covert thoughts and feelings as well. In addition, self-report methods are typically less costly and more convenient to use than methods requiring behavioral observation.

Among the variety of self-report methods the authors discuss are questionnaires, interviews, behavioral self-reports, diaries and accounts. All of these techniques can be applied to study aspects of personal relationships such as liking and love, communication, conflict, sexuality, and relationship satisfaction. On the other hand, they are all susceptible to a common set of problems. These include a number of subject-related problems such as idiosyncratic interpretations of the meanings of various constructs or behaviors, respondent reactivity, egocentric and other forms of self-presentation bias, memory lapses and distortions, errors in the calculation of events, and so on. They also include a number of problems associated with either the researcher or the researcher–subject relationship. Because of these problems, the authors recommend that subjective self-report data be supplemented, whenever possible, with more objective data such as behavioral self-report, observational, or even physiological measures.

Handbook of Personal Relationships
Edited by S. W. Duck
© 1988 John Wiley & Sons Ltd

1

Personal Needs and
Personal Relationships

DAN P. MCADAMS
Loyola University of Chicago, Illinois, USA

ABSTRACT

The chapter reviews a number of different approaches to understanding personal relationships as expressions of personal needs. Needs revolving around the general tendency towards *agency* in human lives have been studied in research on the function of social control in relationships, masculinity, the power motive, and shyness. Needs revolving around the contrasting tendency towards *communion* have been examined in studies of the function of intimacy in relationships, femininity, the intimacy motive, and loneliness.

Our most significant personal relationships serve many masters. As Freud (1900) would have it, personal relationships of love and friendship—like our dreams, symptoms, and masterpieces of art—are richly *overdetermined* products of a myriad of contrasting and contradictory forces and factors. Through personal relationships, we may find our most profound experiences of security and anxiety, power and impotence, unity and separateness. Friendships and love affairs may gratify basic needs, fulfill fundamental values, meet developmental tasks, further instrumental pursuits, appease environmental demands, or merely fill up free time. Gender, age, intelligence, personality traits, cognitive schemas, life goals, social class, hormones, and luck all play roles in shaping the structure, content, and style of our personal relationships—and these constitute but a small subset of the shaping factors.

It is with this caveat in mind that the central question of this chapter may be posed: how do we play out *fundamental personal needs* in our most significant personal relationships? While realizing that relationships of love and friendship function in many different ways, many theorists and researchers assume that these personal relationships serve, in part, to fulfill internal needs or motives that are central to healthy personality functioning. Individual needs and motives are but one of a large number of factors that must be taken into consideration in understanding social interaction. Yet, they constitute an important, and sometimes overlooked, class of relatively stable, internal person variables that help to account for certain individual differences in how we conceive our social worlds and live our most significant personal relationships.

NEEDS AND RELATIONSHIPS

Personality Theories

Many traditional personality theories frame all interpersonal interaction as the expression of personal needs in the context of environmental opportunities and constraints. For instance, Murray (1938) conceived of personality and interpersonal relationships in terms of the intricate interplay of *needs and press*. According to Murray (1938, p. 124), a need is 'an internal force' 'which organizes perception, apperception, intellection, conation and action' in order to produce a recurrently desired end state. A press is an obstacle or opportunity in the environment for need expression. Murray delineated at least 20 psychological needs that regularly interact with press (plural) to shape human thought and action. Particularly important for personal relationships appear to be the needs for abasement, affiliation, aggression, dominance, exhibition, nurturance, order, play, sex, succorance, and understanding—all readily assessed on personality inventories developed by Edwards (1959) and Jackson (1967). Before Murray, McDougall (1908) developed a list of twelve human instincts and five 'nonspecific innate tendencies' that the individual repeatedly plays out in interpersonal relations. More recently, Maslow (1968) conceptualized personality and interpersonal behavior as functioning according to a hierarchy of personal needs, ranging from basic security needs up through more advanced needs for belonging, esteem, and self-actualization.

Whereas Murray, McDougall, and Maslow argue that personal relationships function in the service of a large number of basic needs, theorists such as Jung (1961), Rogers (1961), and Kelly (1955) boil it all down to one primary tendency that is hypothesized to pervade all of human life. According to Jung and Rogers, personal relationships ultimately promote, or interfere with, the individual's quest for *self-realization*. Healthy love and friendship facilitate the individual's explorations of the self, serving as catalysts for becoming a more fully functioning and integrated person. For Kelly, personal relationships enhance the individual's ability to *predict* and to *control* events in his or her world. According to Kelly, each of us is primarily a quasi-scientist seeking regularity and order in our daily lives. Thus, we may find in friendship and love further elaboration, articulation, and consensual validation of our own systems for making sense of subjective human experience. Therefore, Rogers and Jung imply that personal relationships should, and often do, help us to discover and understand ourselves while Kelly suggests that personal relationships help us to predict, control, and understand the world.

Six Types of Love

While many traditional personality theories imply that certain needs play themselves out in love and friendship, investigations of the actual experience of personal relationships provide a more direct view of how such relationships may be expressions of needs. The empirical and theoretical work of Hendrick and Hendrick (1986a) is a case in point. Integrating ancient and modern conceptions with a rigorous research program aimed at developing accurate measures of love, Hendrick and Hendrick argue for Lee's (1973) six conceptually independent and empirically discernible dimensions of love: eros, ludus, storge, pragma, mania, and agape.

Hendrick and Hendrick assess the six types of love via a 42-item self-report questionnaire entitled Attitudes About Love and Sex. Subjects who are currently involved in a romantic relationship are asked to complete the questionnaire with their 'current love partner in mind' (Hendrick and Hendrick, 1986a, p. 394). If the subject is not currently involved in a romantic relationship, he or she is asked to answer the questionnaire with reference to a previous love partner. If the subject reports that he or she has never been in love, then he or she is instructed to 'answer in terms of what you think your responses would most likely be' (p. 394). Factor analysis of the Attitudes About Love and Sex yields the hypothesized six separate dimensions of love with six corresponding subscales. Internal consistency of the subscales is adequate and intercorrelations between subscales are low.

Matching Walster and Walster's (1978) 'passionate love', the first dimension assessed on Hendrick and Hendrick's measure is eros. *Eros* is suffused with physical desire and intense longing for the other, as tapped in questionnaire items such as 'My lover and I were attracted to each other immediately after we first met' and 'Our lovemaking is very intense and satisfying.' *Ludus* is a coy 'game-playing' form of love, often idealized in both Shakespearean and prime-time-television comedy. Lovers are combatants in a generally light-hearted duel, as epitomized in the questions 'I believe that what my lover doesn't know about me won't hurt him/her' and 'I enjoy playing the "game of love" with a number of different partners.' *Storge* taps into the friendship dimension of romantic love, as described by Walster and Walster (1978) in 'companionate love'. Questionnaire items include 'Genuine love first requires *caring* for awhile' and 'Love is really a deep friendship, not a mysterious, mystical emotion.'

The fourth style of loving assessed is *pragma*, a practical and logical style represented in Kelley's (1983) conception of love as a pragmatic sharing of resources and implied in Blau's (1964) exchange theory of love: 'It is best to love someone with a similar background' and 'I try to plan my life carefully before choosing a lover.' *Mania* is the possessive, dependent style of loving described by Maslow (1968) as 'deficiency-love'. In mania, the person is obsessed with thoughts of the lover and fears of being rejected: 'I cannot relax if I suspect that my lover is with someone else' and 'When my lover doesn't pay attention to me, I feel sick all over.' Finally, *agape* is the altruistic form of love idealized by many religions across the world, expressed in a particularly compelling form in the caregiver–infant attachment bond (Bowlby, 1969; Harlow, 1958), and described by Clark and Mills (1979) as a selfless, 'communal' form of love. Agape is represented in the items 'I would rather suffer myself than let my lover suffer' and 'I would endure all things for the sake of my lover.'

Lee's (1973) typology is akin to a periodic table of love, with each type representing an element. Real-world love affairs, therefore, are seen as compounds containing various proportions of love elements and each partner in a love relationship may emphasize different dimensions of love. Thus, Hendrick *et al.* (1984) found that among 800 students completing a questionnaire similar to the Attitudes About Love and Sex, men tended to emphasize ludus more than women whereas women scored higher than men on pragma, storge, and mania.

With respect to personal needs, the work of Hendrick and Hendrick implies that our love relationships serve at least six different motivational masters. Eros may tap mainly into sexual needs and, perhaps, what Murray (1938) saw as a need for exhibition. Ludus suggests that love draws on the human tendency towards play and games, noted by motivational psychologists such as Murray (the need for play) and many developmental psychologists who consider play and simulative behavior to be a keystone of human nature (Garvey, 1977; Vygotsky, 1978). Storge appears to draw on what Murray called the need for affiliation: the recurrent desire 'to draw near and enjoyably co-operate or reciprocate with an allied other; to adhere and remain loyal to a friend' (1938, p. 174). Pragma is somewhat consistent with Kelly's (1955) cognitive view, that human beings use relationships for generally rational purposes of prediction and control, and it is also reminiscent of Murray's concepts of the needs for order and understanding. Mania ties into Murray's need for succorance and what many psychoanalysts have traditionally termed 'oral dependency needs' (Masling, 1986; Sears, 1963). Finally, the selfless love of agape suggests that a basic altruistic tendency, like that described in Hoffman's (1981) theory of empathically mediated human altruism, may be a prominent motivator in some love relationships. Agape is also implied in Murray's concept of the need for nurturance.

Sternberg's Model of Love

A very different view of love suggests a more unitary quality. Sternberg and Grajek's (1984) model posits that the structure of love is quite similar across the various close relationships in which one engages. Conceptualizing love in terms of structural models borrowed from psychometric theories of intelligence, Sternberg and Grajek argue that love is a unifactorial entity with possible subfactors. Like the 'g' factor of intelligence, much of the variance in love may be accounted for by an underlying general factor which represents the overlap of a large number of 'affective, cognitive, and motivational bonds that, in the experience of love, are jointly sampled' (p. 312).

Sternberg and Grajek administered a battery of psychological measures to adults ranging in age from eighteen to 70. Included were self-report scales of love from Rubin (1970), Levinger, Rands and Talaber (1977), and Lasswell and Lobsenz (1980) (a measure of the six types of love identified by Lee) applied to close relationships with fathers, mothers, siblings, same-sex best friends, and spouses and lovers. A series of factor analyses suggested that while the intensity of love varied greatly, the structure or pattern of love was quite similar across the various domains of close relationships. The possible exception to this uniformity was the love reported for same-sex best friend, whose factor structure was somewhat discrepant from the others.

What, exactly, enters into the general factor that cuts across the various love domains? Sternberg and Grajek claim that the factor 'is well identified as one of interpersonal communication, sharing, and support'. They write, 'Its aspects include especially (a) deep understanding of the other, (b) sharing of ideas and information, (c) sharing of deeply personal ideas and feelings, (d) receipt and provision of emotional support to the other, (e) personal growth through the relationship and helping the other in his or her personal growth, (f) giving help to the other, (g) making the other feel needed and needing the other, and (h) the giving and receiving of affection in the relationship' (p. 327). Sternberg and Grajek imply, therefore, that the experience of love in personal relationships draws mostly upon a single personal need or motive—what might be termed a general *love* or *intimacy motive*.

Two General Classes

In between the personality theorists and relationship researchers who argue for uniformity (Rogers, Jung, Kelly; Sternberg) and those who argue for plurality (Murray, McDougall, Maslow; Hendrick and Hendrick) in personal needs and personal relationships lies a diverse group of scholars who conceptualize the domain in terms of a basic *dualism*. With respect to the personal needs that play themselves out in personal relationships, personality theorists such as Freud (1920), Angyal (1941), Rank (1936), Bakan (1966), Hogan (1982), Tomkins (1979), and McAdams (1985a) have posited two central tendencies in human lives that shape and are shaped by the most significant relationships with others. Though the dualism is described in many different ways, it is generally understood as a distinction between a general motivational tendency towards *agency/power/excitement* and a contrasting tendency towards *communion/intimacy/joy*. Similarly, M. L. Patterson (1984; see also Patterson's chapter in this Handbook) and other investigators focusing on interpersonal relationships, rather than general personality functioning *per se*, suggest two basic *functions* of interpersonal involvement: *social control* and *intimacy*.

That two basic needs should play themselves out in significant personal relationships is an ancient idea, over 2000 years old. The preSocratic philosopher Empedocles argued that *strife* and *love* were the two great organizing principles of the universe (Russell, 1945). Earth, air, fire, and water were forced apart by strife and drawn together through love. Love and strife, therefore, corresponded to the forces of separation and union in realms as diverse as the movements of clouds and human relationships, and as the great cosmic motivators, they accounted for all motion and change. Empedocles' idea was translated into twentieth-century thought by Freud (1920) in his dualistic motivational theory of the death (*aggressive*) and the life (*erotic*) instincts. Bearing resemblance to Empedocles' ancient and Freud's more recent vision are many arguments for a basic duality in human motivation delineated in terms of opposing needs for *autonomy* and *surrender* (Angyal, 1941), the *fear of life* (which motivates one to separate from others) and the *fear of death* (which motivates one to unite with others) (Becker, 1973; Rank, 1936), the *striving for superiority* and *social interest* (Adler, 1927), the 'psychologics' of *independence* and *inclusion* (Kegan, 1982), the ethics of *individuation* and *interdependence* (Gilligan, 1982), the evolutionarily adaptive tendencies towards gaining *status* and *acceptance* in social groups (Hogan, Jones and Cheek, 1985), the 'psychological magnification' of *excitement/interest* and *joy/enjoyment* (Izard, 1977; Tomkins, 1979), the motives of *power* and *intimacy* (McAdams, 1985a), and the tendencies towards *agency* and *communion* (Bakan, 1966).

Though all of the theorists mentioned above bring something unique to the understanding of personal needs, they converge on a central dualism that is probably best and most generally described by Bakan (1966) in his concepts of agency and communion. According to Bakan, agency and communion are 'two fundamental modalities in the existence of living forms' (p. 14). Agency refers to the organism's striving to consolidate its individuality, to separate from other organisms, to master the surround, to assert, protect, and expand the self. Communion, on the other hand, refers to the organism's striving to lose its individuality by merging with others and the surrounding environment, to participate in a 'larger organism' of which it is a part, to surrender the self through contact, openness, and cooperation.

Agency and communion are exceedingly broad and multidimensional tendencies in human living that might best be conceived as *integrative themes in lives* (McAdams, 1985a). They encompass, among other things, dimensions of interpersonal style (traits), personal values and beliefs (schemata), and personal needs and motives. For instance, the theme of agency connects conceptually to personality traits such as Machiavellianism (Christie and Geis, 1970) and aggressiveness (Olweus, 1977), personal and societal beliefs and values concerning courage and a strong national defense (Rokeach, 1973), assertive human motives such as the need for achievement (McClelland, 1961) and the power motive (Winter, 1973), and the sex-role orientation of masculinity (Bem, 1974). Communion, on the other hand, connects thematically to stylistic personality traits such as sociability and friendliness (Guilford, 1959), belief and value clusters such as those centered around equality and peace on earth (Rokeach, 1973), human social motives such as the intimacy motive (McAdams, 1982a), and the sex-role orientation identified as femininity (Bem, 1974). Let us explore further Bakan's duality of personal needs as it pertains to personal relationships.

THEMES OF AGENCY IN PERSONAL RELATIONSHIPS

Social Control and Shyness

In his functional model of nonverbal behavior, M. L. Patterson (1982a, 1984, also this Handbook, Chapter 3) ascribes two general purposes to the display of nonverbal behavior in social interaction: social control and intimacy. In keeping with Bakan's conception of agency, social control is achieved through various nonverbal behaviors such as smiling, eye contact, and speech style that function in a given situation to change the behavior of another or create a particular impression. Through the judicious display of nonverbal behavior, the person may be able to control social situations, attain desired levels of status, influence the behavior of others, and generally master and manipulate the world for the ends of the self.

With respect to love, friendship, and the like, Patterson (1984) writes, 'a variety of social control motives may also determine involvement patterns in close relationships' (p. 129). Though social control may manifest itself in a Machiavellian way in certain situations, as when a person seeks to manipulate another who is disliked (Ickes et al., 1982), it can also take on a somewhat more innocent cast, as when lovers and friends seek to present desired images or impressions of the self to each other (Goffman, 1967). In his socioanalytic theory of personality and interpersonal relations, Hogan (1982) argues that impression management is a *sine qua non* of all social interaction, including the closest personal relationships. Rather than lamenting that concerns for social control sully or undermine 'spontaneous' personal relationships, Hogan insists that they lead to highly adaptive strategies for living (and loving) and reflect a biologically rooted human tendency towards seeking *status* in groups. The agentic desire to control the self and the social world, Hogan maintains, plays itself out in our most trivial social encounters and in our most profound affairs of the heart.

Problems in agency can appear in a number of different forms, but one pervasive difficulty, argues Hogan, is the fairly common phenomenon of 'shyness' (Hogan, Jones and Cheek, 1985; Jones, Briggs and Smith, 1986). Hogan regards shyness to be the paradigmatic 'psychopathology of everyday life' in the realm of agency—a common but sometimes debilitating problem in seeking status in groups (Hogan, Jones and Cheek, 1985). Persistent shyness is associated with greater levels of fearfulness in social groups, heightened levels of self-consciousness, and lower self-esteem (Cheek and Buss, 1981; Jones and Russell, 1982). Shy persons report that they lack the confidence and skill necessary to perform as effective agents in the many roles and rituals necessary for 'getting ahead' in everyday life. They are ineffective and reluctant impression managers, repeatedly failing to exert enough social control in their relationships in order to fulfil agentic needs.

Masculinity

One perspective on how agentic needs may play themselves out in personal relationships comes from the empirical literature on masculinity, typically described as a 'sex-role orientation' or 'gender schema'. Usually assessed via self-report checklists and questionnaires such as those designed by Bem (1974) and Spence (Spence, Helmreich and Stapp, 1975), masculinity is 'defined in terms of an active, controlling, and instrumental approach to social interaction' (Ickes, 1981, p. 96). A man or woman scoring high on measures of masculinity, therefore, attributes to the self a large number of traits traditionally associated with stereotypes of masculine behavior: assertiveness, aggression, dominance, achievement orientation, etc. A highly agentic (Bakan, 1966) and instrumental (Parsons and Bales, 1955) orientation to self and other, masculinity subsumes 'characteristic motivational tendencies' and 'related sets of specific capacities by which these motivational tendencies can be expressed in behavior' (Ickes, 1981, p. 97). In other words, while measures of masculinity sample a wide range of conscious self-attributions, they may tap into general agentic motivational tendencies (needs, desires, wants) as well as related agentic capacities (skills, competencies, abilities).

Masculinity in both men and women has been consistently related to a wide range of personal characteristics including traits of assertiveness and dominance, leadership skills, extraversion, emotional stability, and self-esteem (Cook, 1985). Contrary to the generally positive correlates of high masculinity, Rusbult (1987) reports that higher masculinity is related to tendencies to respond to problems in personal relationships in a destructive manner. When confronted with serious problems in love relationships, men and women scoring high in masculinity tend either to 'neglect' the problem—refusing to discuss the area of concern, criticizing the partner for things unrelated to the problem—or 'exit' the problem situation—formally separating, moving out of a joint residence, actively terminating the relationship, etc.

Most studies on sex-role orientation cross-classify subjects according to scores on both masculinity and femininity. Investigating the quality of communication in dyads, Ickes (1981) has paired subjects who are 'sex-role stereotyped' (men high in masculinity *and* low in femininity; women high in femininity *and* low in masculinity) or 'psychologically androgynous' (men or women high in both masculinity and femininity). In general, androgynous men and women show more flexibility and spontaneity in dyadic exchange, assumedly because they are able to draw on both agentic and communal skills and motivations. With respect to personal relationships, Shaver, Pullis and Olds (1980) found that marital satisfaction was (1) relatively high in dyads in which both partners were androgynous and (2) relatively low in sex-role stereotyped dyads, containing highly masculine husbands and highly feminine wives.

The Power Motive

Assessed through content analysis of imaginative stories written in response to pictures on the Thematic Apperception Test (TAT), the power motive is defined as a *recurrent preference or readiness for experiences of feeling strong and having impact on others* (McAdams, 1985a; Winter, 1973). The power motive is a relatively stable individual-difference dimension of personality that is assumed to *energize, direct, and select* behavior in certain situations (McClelland, 1985). A substantial empirical literature on the power motive attests to its validity in predicting thought and behavior that are generally *agentic* in quality. A number of studies, for instance, have linked power motivation to (1) seeking and attaining political offices and other positions of prestige in organizations; (2) speaking out and taking risks in order to attain visibility and have an impact; (3) adopting authoritative rather than egalitarian leadership strategies; (4) collecting prestige possessions; and (5) formulating a personal identity around central themes of strength, adventure, and conquest (Fodor and Smith, 1982; McAdams, 1982b, 1985a; McClelland, 1975; Winter and Stewart, 1978).

Power motivation, marriage, and dating

A few studies on power motivation and heterosexual relationships suggest that a highly agentic motivational orientation may lead to problems and conflicts in romantic love for men, but apparently not for women. Stewart and Rubin (1976) conducted a longitudinal study of dating couples living in Boston. Upon an initial assessment, high power motivation in the male members of the couples was associated with greater expressed dissatisfaction with the relationship on the part of both partners and greater anticipation of future problems among the men. In other words, when the man scored high in power motivation, he was more likely to predict serious problems in the relationship for the future, and both he and his partner were more likely than couples in which the man scored low in power motivation to express dissatisfaction with the present state of the romantic relationship. In general, power motivation scores among female members of the couples did not predict dissatisfaction.

Two years later, 50 per cent of the couples in which the man originally scored high in power motivation had broken up and 9 per cent had married. This contrasts markedly with the couples in which men scored low in power motivation, of whom only 15 per cent broke up after two years and 52 per cent married. Additionally, males high in power motivation were more likely to report that during the two years before the beginning of the study, they had been seriously involved in a romantic relationship that eventually terminated. Stewart and Rubin (1976) concluded that men high in power motivation manifest marked instability in romantic relationships, moving from one serious involvement to another in relatively rapid succession. Bolstering their claims are the findings of Winter (1973), in which power motivation among college men was positively associated with number of sexual partners and frequency of sexual activity. According to Winter, the archetypal representation of the high-power-motive man in Western folklore is Don Juan, the expansive and profligate womanizer.

Other studies have associated high power motivation in married men with a significantly higher divorce rate (McClelland *et al.*, 1972). In a nationwide sample, Veroff and Feld (1970) found high power motivation in men to be associated with reports of greater marital dissatisfaction. At the root of the high-power man's apparent dissatisfaction and instability in romantic relationships may be a latent fear of women and the control they exert. Slavin (1972) has shown that men high in power motivation express more themes of feminine evil in their fantasies than do men low on the motive. These themes include females harming men through physical contact, females exploiting men, females rejecting men, females proving unfaithful in relationships, and females triumphing over men. In keeping with this image of feminine evil, Winter and Stewart (1978) report that men high in power motivation, when asked to draw pictures of women, produce sometimes frightening and bizarre sketches of females with exaggerated sexual characteristics.

Winter, Stewart and McClelland (1977) found that high power motivation in married men was negatively associated with the career levels attained by their wives. In other words, men high in power motivation tended to marry women who, in the early 1970s, tended not to pursue professional careers. A contrasting study undertaken with women (Winter, McClelland and Stewart, 1981) found a reversal, in that well-educated women high in power motivation tended to marry successful men. Finally, in contrast to the general findings with men, Veroff (1982) reports that high power motivation in women is associated with *greater* levels of marital satisfaction.

Power motivation and friendship

Research into the power motive and friendship converges on an *agentic style* in friendship patterns manifested by both men and women scoring high in power motivation. This particular style of relating to friends can be highly adaptive and rewarding and, in contrast to findings on power motivation (among men) and romantic relationships, is *not* necessarily associated with dissatisfaction, frustration, or instability in friendships.

Two central themes of Bakan's conceptualization of agency are self-expansion and self-display. The agentic individual is a doer who makes things happen in his or her environment. Further, his or her doing is observed and remarked upon by others. An agentic style of friendship involves, therefore, opportunities for self-expansion and self-display among friends, friends with whom one *acts* assertively and proceeds to *do* things rather than merely *be*. The agentic actions of friends are applauded and affirmed as legitimate exercises in self-expansion and display that come to bring the friends closer together and strengthen their friendship.

McAdams, Healy and Krause (1984) collected accounts of naturally occurring 'friendship episodes' in the lives of college students. Male and female students high in power motivation reported a greater number of friendship episodes in which they interacted with a large group of friends (five friends or more at a time) compared to students low in power motivation. Presumably, more friends make for a larger audience for agentic action. Content analysis of the subjects' accounts of friendship episodes revealed a strong positive correlation between power motivation and number of episodes in which the individual reported 'agentic striving', whereby he or she adopted an active, assertive, or controlling role in the episode. Examples of agentic striving included taking charge of a situation, assuming responsibility, making a point in an argument or debate, giving advice, making plans, organizing activities, attempting to persuade others, and, quite frequently, *helping* others.

In a retrospective study of the history of one's 'best friendship', McAdams (1984) found that helping was a central theme in an agentic style of friendship. Students high in power motivation overwhelmingly described concrete incidents in which they and their best friend 'grew closer' in terms of one friend helping or rescuing the other. Helping—whether a heroic act or quiet counsel—is an active assertion of the self, an agentic act *par excellence*. Helping temporarily transforms a relationship into one between relative unequals. For the moment, the helper is dominant; the helped, submissive. With role reversals, helping relationships afford the opportunity for mutual self-assertion and self-display, as the previous helper becomes the object of help.

McAdams (1984) also collected accounts of negative experiences with best friends. In describing incidents in which their friendships had been tested or weakened, students high in power motivation emphasized scenes of *public disgrace* wherein the friend violated a general norm of social behavior. Examples included fighting, boasting, and other behaviors that were observed by others to be rude or boorish and which, therefore, lowered the prestige of all people associated with the transgressor. The agentic individual's concern that self-display be accepted and applauded rather than criticized by others is further reflected in the students' descriptions of the 'greatest fears' they experienced when with their best friends (McAdams, 1984). Subjects high in power motivation tended to emphasize fears of *conflict* with friends, such as arguments or fights. In fearing conflict, the agentic person expresses concern over a possible clash between active agents. Similarly, Winter (1973) reported that men scoring high in power motivation tend to avoid carefully the possibility of conflict in their relationships with their peers.

THEMES OF COMMUNION IN PERSONAL RELATIONSHIPS

Intimacy and Loneliness

In comparing the functions of intimacy and social control, M. L. Patterson (1984) argues that social interaction in general, and personal relationships in particular, may function to promote intimacy through relatively spontaneous and affectively positive patterns of behavior. Social control, on the other hand, may be better served in interactions and relationships that are highly scripted or structured according to roles and when certain negative emotions, like anger and fear, are elicited. Drawing on Tomkins' (1979) theory of emotions, on the other hand, McAdams (in press) links interpersonal experiences of intimacy with the positive emotion of joy–enjoyment and interpersonal experiences of power with the equally positive emotion of excitement–interest. Whether social

control (as an expression of agency) is seen in a relatively negative or positive
light, however, researchers and theorists typically cast intimacy (as an
expression of communion) in highly favorable terms, emphasizing themes of
spontaneity, closeness, sharing, and joy.

Perlman and Fehr (1987) write that the word intimacy derives from *intimus*,
the Latin term for 'inner' or 'inmost'. Although many different definitions of
intimacy have been offered (see chapter in this Handbook by Reis and Shaver),
most converge on the central idea of *sharing that which is inmost* with others.
In his interpersonal theory of psychiatry, Sullivan (1953) argues that the 'need
for interpersonal intimacy' and experiences of *loneliness* emerge in tandem in
the human life cycle. During the developmental stage of preadolescence,
suggests Sullivan, the person is motivated to take major risks in interpersonal
relations in order to ally him- or herself with a same-sex 'chum'—a friend who
is as much like the self as possible and whose welfare comes to be considered
as important as one's own.

When a person is repeatedly unable to share inner thoughts and feelings with
a 'chum' or some other special person, he or she may experience what Weiss
(1973) terms 'emotional isolation'—one particularly painful form of loneliness.
Though a person may be involved in an extensive network of friendships and
social relations, he or she may still experience the loneliness of emotional
isolation if no single personal relationship affords the opportunity for intimacy
(Shaver and Rubenstein, 1980; Weiss, 1973). Being able to share that which is
inmost in a highly intimate relationship, on the other hand, may not quell all
forms of loneliness. Weiss identifies a second form of loneliness, called 'social
isolation', in which a person feels alienated from a larger social network of
supportive friends and community involvements.

Integrating research on loneliness with Bowlby's (1969, 1973) attachment
theory, Shaver and Rubenstein (1980) show that early separations from attachment objects may lead to loneliness in later life. Living through the divorce of
one's parents, for example, especially when one is very young, seems to predispose a person to later loneliness and low self-esteem, distrust of others, health
problems, and doubts about one's own marriage. A rapidly growing research
literature has linked loneliness to a number of personality problems and interpersonal deficits (see chapters by Rook and Reis and Shaver in this volume).
As shyness is to agency, then, loneliness could be considered a paradigmatic
'psychopathology of everyday life' in the realm of human communion—a
pervasive problem in intimacy that commonly results from a failure in meeting
communal needs (Hogan, Jones and Cheek, 1985).

Femininity

Ickes (1981) defines femininity as a relatively 'reactive, emotionally responsive,
and expressive' sex-role orientation (p. 96). A man or woman scoring high on
femininity attributes to the self a number of characteristics that have traditionally been associated with the female sex role: compassionate, gentle, yielding,
interpersonally oriented, etc. Like masculinity, femininity is assumed to incor-

porate certain motivational tendencies and capacities that can be expressed in behavior, tapping into Bakan's general construct of communion.

Femininity has also been positively associated with adopting constructive approaches to solving problems in personal relationships. Rusbult (1987) found that partners high in femininity were more likely than those scoring lower to engage in 'voice' and 'loyalty' strategies to solve problems and less likely to show 'neglect'. When confronting a crisis in the relationship, individuals high in femininity tended to discuss problems, to seek help from clergy or therapists, to support the partner and remain committed to the relationship, and to try, in general, to work actively for change and improvement.

Remember John's class— there are problems w/ this research.

The Intimacy Motive

Like the power motive, intimacy motivation is assessed through content analysis of imaginative stories written to TAT pictures. The intimacy motive is defined as a *recurrent preference or readiness for experiences of warm, close, and communicative interaction with others*—interpersonal exchange perceived as an end in itself rather than a means to another end (McAdams, 1982a). A number of studies support the validity of intimacy motivation as a predictor of *communal* thought and behavior. Intimacy motivation has been positively associated with (1) peer ratings of 'loving', 'sincere', and 'natural'; (2) more time spent on an average day thinking about people and interpersonal relationships, conversing with others, and feeling positive emotions in the presence of others; (3) greater levels of eye contact, smiling, and laughter in friendly dyadic interviews; (4) engendering positive affect and interpersonal harmony in groups; and (5) formulating a personal identity around central themes of caregiving, loyalty, deep love, and service to others (McAdams, 1980, 1982b, 1985a, b; McAdams and Constantian, 1983; McAdams, Jackson and Kirshnit, 1984; McAdams and Powers, 1981). Though the differences are not always large, women generally score higher than men on intimacy motivation (McAdams *et al.*, 1987). Correlations between intimacy and power motivation tend to be slightly negative and nonsignificant.

Intimacy motivation, dating, and marriage

Very little research has been done on intimacy motivation and heterosexual love relationships. Only two studies speak to the issue, and their results are limited in scope. McAdams (1980) analyzed TAT stories written by heterosexual dating couples who participated in Stewart and Rubin's (1976) study of power motivation and dating. Couples in which both partners scored high on Rubin's (1970) 'love scale'—a nine-item self-report measure assessing intensity of love expressed and experienced in the relationship—scored significantly higher in intimacy motivation than other subjects of the same age who were not involved in intense romantic relationships.

In a longitudinal study of men graduating from Harvard College in the early 1940s, McAdams and Vaillant (1982) found a positive correlation between intimacy motivation, assessed through content analysis of TAT stories written by the men at age 30, and a single index of marital enjoyment determined seventeen years later, when the men were in midlife. Men high in intimacy motivation at age 30, therefore, were more likely to report happiness and stability in their marriages in their mid-40s. Intimacy motivation was also positively associated with job enjoyment and an overall index of psychosocial adaptation. Power motivation was unrelated to these variables.

Intimacy motivation and friendship

Bakan writes that communion involves an opening up of the self to the environment. In communion, the vulnerable self risks even greater vulnerability by surrendering control in interpersonal relations and offering the self up as a kind of gift, awaiting the reciprocal gift-giving of the other. Bakan's communion mandates intimate self-disclosure in the presence of a listener who receives the disclosure as a gift, cherishing it as a token of an ever-developing closeness and responding to the gift as if it were an integral 'Thou' (Buber, 1970)—an end in itself, rather than a means to something else, worthy of unswerving attention and consideration. In the communal 'I–Thou' encounter, intimate self-disclosure should beget intimate self-disclosure as the interaction unfolds spontaneously in the dyad, outside the control of either participant.

Persons high in intimacy motivation tend to display a *communal style* of friendship emphasizing dyadic, as opposed to large-group, interaction and high levels of *self-disclosure* and listening. In McAdams, Jackson and Kirshnit (1984), students high in intimacy motivation described a greater number of friendship episodes in their lives that involved their interaction with a single other person, rather than friendship interactions in large groups as was the case for students high in power motivation. Content analysis of the accounts of friendship episodes showed that intimacy motivation was strongly positively associated with (1) greater levels of self-disclosure in conversations with friends and (2) adopting the role of 'listener' with friends. In keeping with Bakan's description of communion, both men and women high in intimacy motivation compared to their peers scoring lower tended to open themselves up with their friends, risking vulnerability in intimate self-disclosure while affirming the reciprocal disclosure of their friends through careful listening. Power motivation was unrelated to self-disclosure and listening.

The centrality of self-disclosure in the friendships of individuals high in intimacy motivation is underscored in McAdams' (1984) study of students asked to recount the history of their best friendship. Asked to describe a specific incident in which they and their best friend 'grew closer', students high in intimacy motivation overwhelmingly portrayed scenes of intimate self-disclosure in which they and the friend shared highly personal information with each other. When asked to describe a specific incident in the friendship history in which the friendship was tested or weakened, subjects high in intimacy motivation emphasized a *private betrayal* of trust, as when one of the partners broke a promise, disclosed a secret to a third party, or failed to show the expected warmth and understanding to the other. Asked to describe their greatest fears in friendship, subjects with high intimacy motivation singled out fears of *separation*.

McAdams (1985c) found that among midlife men and women intimacy motivation was positively associated with ratings of how meaningful and satisfying one's friendships were. Power motivation was not significantly related to these ratings. In a study of fourth- and sixth-grade children, McAdams and Losoff (1984) scored imaginative stories written in response to pictures according to a simplified intimacy motivation scoring system. Children scoring high on this measure—termed in the study 'friendship motivation'—answered a greater number of factual questions about their best friends, suggesting perhaps that they had done more listening to their friends and engaged in more conversations of self-disclosure. In addition, children scoring high in friendship motivation were rated by their teachers as significantly more 'sincere', 'cooperative', and 'affectionate' than children scoring lower. In both grades, girls scored higher than boys on friendship motivation.

CONCLUSION

Table 1 summarizes the distinction between agency and communion as it applies to personal relationships from a number of different perspectives. Bakan's general distinction points to two broad classes of personal needs that are played

Table 1   Themes of agency and communion in personal relationships

	Agency	Communion
1. Two integrative themes in human lives (Bakan, 1966)	Agency	Communion
2. Two central functions of interpersonal relations (Patterson, 1984)	Social control	Intimacy
3. Two basic 'instinctual tendencies' adaptive for living in social groups (Hogan, Jones and Cheek, 1985)	Attaining status (getting ahead)	Being accepted (getting along)
4. Two common 'psychopathologies of everyday life' (Hogan, Jones and Cheek, 1985)	Shyness	Loneliness
5. Two fundamental positive emotions experienced in personal relationships (Izard, 1977; Tomkins, 1979)	Excitement/interest	Joy/enjoyment
6. Two personal needs assessed on the Thematic Apperception Test (McAdams, 1985a)	The power motive	The intimacy motive
7. Two styles of friendship		
(a) Positive hallmarks of friendships	Helping	Self-disclosure
(b) Transgressions in friendships	Public disgrace	Private betrayal
(c) Fears in friendships (McAdams, 1984)	Conflict	Separation
8. Two sex-role orientations (Bem, 1974; Ickes, 1981)	Masculinity	Femininity

out in personal relationships in important and predictable ways. How this motivational dichotomy relates to other theories of love and personal relationships, such as Hendrick and Hendrick's (1986a) six types of love and Sternberg and Grajek's (1984) unifactor model, remains an open question. It would appear that Sternberg and Grajek's model taps into a broad conception that resembles certain features of McAdams' intimacy motivation—a general communal tendency in lives emphasizing 'interpersonal communication, sharing, and support' (Sternberg and Grajek, 1984, p. 327). By contrast, Bakan's duality appears to cut across each of the six types of love measured by Hendrick and Hendrick. Each of the six appears to incorporate elements of both agency and communion, though ludus seems to be the most agentic and agape the most communal.

Personal relationships are highly complex phenomena whose many functions and determinants have escaped scientific scrutiny until quite recently. Personal needs such as those centered around agency and communion appear to inform and be informed by personal relationships in a few measurable ways. Findings and conclusions at this point, however, are rather sketchy and tentative, as we await further systematic exploration of the relations between personal relationships and basic personal needs.

Handbook of Personal Relationships
Edited by S. W. Duck
© 1988 John Wiley & Sons Ltd

2

Rules, Scripts and Prototypes in Personal Relationships

G. P. GINSBURG
University of Nevada, Reno, Nevada, USA

ABSTRACT

The chapter examines the theoretical and investigative utility of 'rules', 'scripts' and 'proto-types' for the study of personal relationships. Although there are only a few examples of deliberate application of these concepts to the study of personal relationships, their potential utility is very high. It is recommended that effort be devoted to discovery of culturally shared rules which pertain to the actions of people in relationships, to the discovery of invariant features of types of relationships which reveal the relationship for the type it is, and to the discovery of stereotypic action sequences commonly performed within particular types of relationship.

No man shall interrupt a companion before his speech has ended, nor speak before a man of higher rank; each man shall speak in his turn.

> From the *Book of Discipline* of the Qumran community ('Dead Sea Scrolls'), *ca* 125 BC (Vermes, 1975)

Put the toilet seat down when you're done.

No going through Mom and Dad's bedroom to go to the bathroom.

> From a collection of family rules supplied by readers to *USA Weekend* (Sunday newspaper supplement), 2–4 January 1987

Rules have guided the activities and relationships of people from antiquity, often dealing with prosaic aspects of mundane, daily life. But these are important features of our existence. The turn-taking rules of the Qumran community facilitate coordinated interaction and are unusual only in being written; the two modern rules regulate, respectively, a source of potential interpersonal conflict and the maintenance of personal privacy. As we will see later, these are among several functions that rules serve in the conduct of personal relationships. However, rules often apply differentially to different relationships and different situations, and usually they are not written or even discussed explicitly. Instead, they seem to be part of our background knowledge of how to engage in particular acts in particular kinds of circumstances and with particular categories of persons. Thus, an understanding of the operation of rules in personal relationships requires an understanding as well of the ways in which personal relationships are construed and action routines are guided. In recent social psychology, the major conceptual vehicles providing for this extended understanding are forms of schemata, especially prototypes and scripts. Therefore, in the limited space available, this chapter will examine the roles of three concepts in our understanding of the conduct of personal relationships—rules, scripts and prototypes.

RULES

The Nature of Rules

An examination of the use of 'rules' by social psychologists makes them the equivalent of statements which prescribe, proscribe or explicitly permit a particular type of behavior (Argyle, 1986; Argyle, Furnham and Graham, 1981; Argyle and Henderson, 1984; Collett, 1977; Semin and Manstead, 1983). Moreover, some rules apply very broadly, whereas others are specific to particular situations (Argyle, Furnham and Graham, 1981) or particular types of relationships (Argyle, 1986; Davis and Todd, 1982). Rules vary widely in their content, also. Some pertain to emotions and feelings, in that they prescribe, proscribe or permit the expression and even the experience of specified feelings and emotions on the parts of particular categories of persons on particular occasions and in particular relationships (Hochschild, 1979). Others deal with action and comportment, some involving social conventions and others specifying procedures which must be followed if the objective of the activity is to be achieved. Also, the rules of social convention can be distinguished from moral rules (Turiel, 1979), as is clear in the reactions of others to violations of each of the two types. Evaluations of conventions and their violations usually are a function of the social context, while evaluations of moral rules and their transgressions typically are a function of the consequences of the violations for others (Shantz, 1983).

The rules discussed above are largely regulative—they regulate activities and may be prescriptive, proscriptive or permissive. But regulative rules logically entail constitutive rules which are definitional and specify whether the event to which a regulative rule is being applied is one to which it *should* be applied (Collett, 1977). The learning of rules and their conditions of application occurs as part of the socialization process (McCall and Simmons, 1982; Shantz, 1983; Turiel, 1979), and may start very early (McClintock, 1983). For example, Bruner and Sherwood (1976) describe the acquisition of procedural rules by infants of nine to twelve months in repetitive games such as peek-a-boo. On the other hand, people are not just rule followers (Harré and Secord, 1972); they also create rules, often through negotiation (Shotter, 1984), and may behave in a rule-fitting fashion for reasons other than the rule (Collett, 1977; Sabini and Silver, 1981).

In addition, rules usually have an aura of sanction. Often, the possibility of sanction for rule violations is unstated and merely part of background understandings; but in formal specifications of rules, especially in laws and regulations, the associated sanctions typically are made explicit. For example, the *Book of Discipline* of the Qumran community was very explicit in its assignment of sanctions to breakage of its written rules (Vermes, 1975). If a man was dressed so carelessly that a gust of wind revealed his 'nakedness', he lost 25 per cent of his rations for the next 30 days; and if he unnecessarily stood fully naked before another person, he suffered that loss for six months. A 25 per cent reduction in rations was also imposed for other threats to interpersonal relations: deliberate lies (six months), deliberate insults (one year), deliberate deception (six months), slander (one year), unjust malice (six months–one year), not caring for another person (three months). Other punishable infractions pertained to coordinated interactions: interrupting a speaking person (ten days), speaking foolishly (three months), foolish guffawing (30 days). As will be seen later, these rules appear to have served social functions comparable to those found by Argyle and his colleagues in their recent studies of the rules of personal relationships (Argyle, 1986; Argyle and Henderson, 1984).

The Uses and Functions of Social Rules

Rules serve a variety of functions in social life. For example, they facilitate the coordination of interpersonal exchanges and relationships. This is accomplished at a microanalytic level through such rules as those of turn-taking (Duncan and Fiske, 1979) and sequence regulation (Bruner and Sherwood, 1976; McClintock, 1983) and at a more macroanalytic level through rules that protect privacy and confidences and ensure interpersonal support (Argyle, 1986), as well as rules that specify and coordinate the expression and exchange of emotional states (Hochschild, 1979). Rules also reduce the need for direct expression of influence and power in personal relationships, thereby avoiding a variety of interpersonal costs (Thibaut and Kelley, 1959; McClintock, 1983; Peplau, 1983).

Rules also facilitate the responsible autonomy of the individual (Shotter, 1984). Constant surveillance of all members of a community is physically impossible, and in many cultures morally repugnant, but at the same time a community must be able to rely on its members to act in ways that maintain and recreate the social order. Rules constitute one of the important devices through which community members can be relied upon to act responsibly even in the absence of surveillance.

In addition, rules are used as part of accounting processes (Semin and Manstead, 1983). They are cited in support of the legitimacy of an action and in support of challenges to an action's legitimacy. A closely related function of rules concerns the achievement of social control through sanctions: rules are used both to guide and to justify their application.

Finally, rules also have an interference effect. That is, attendance to a rule can interfere with a person's sensitivity to the actual contingencies of the situation (Hayes *et al.*, 1986a, b). If a rule has been mistakenly applied, or if it is no longer applicable to the situation, acting in accord with it is likely to be dysfunctional—reinforcements will be fewer and misunderstandings more likely.

Space precludes an extended discussion of these functions and effects of social rules, but the selected research examples described below will illustrate some of them.

Research Examples

There are few explicit applications of the rules concept to the study of personal relationships. Furthermore, much of the research on rules focuses on the person's understanding of a rule, a cognitive topic interesting in its own right but less directly relevant to this chapter (see Shantz, 1983, for a good example; also Turiel, 1979). Over the years, Kelley has developed the importance of interpersonal norms in the regulation of interpersonal relationships (Thibaut and Kelley, 1959) and especially interpersonal conflict (Braiker and Kelley, 1979); and his concept of norms is a behavioral rule shared by both parties in the dyad (for a review, see Peplau, 1983). Mills and Clark (1982) also deal with rules in their summary of research which distinguishes between communal and exchange relationships. Three illustrations will be given of research that focused deliberately on the operation of rules in the conduct of personal relationships.

The first illustration is the work by Argyle and Henderson (1984; see also Argyle, 1986). Based on earlier studies of rules as components of social situations (Argyle, Furnham and Graham, 1981), Argyle and Henderson construed rules as shared beliefs of group members regarding behaviors which should, should not or may be performed in particular situations. A series of interview and questionnaire studies was conducted which yielded ratings of the importance of each of a large number of mundane rule statements (e.g. should not reveal confidences to others, should share news with the other party) in each of a variety of relationships which ranged from casual or formal to intimate. The research was conducted in four different cultural milieux: England, Italy, Japan and Hong Kong.

Examining the rules of friendship, Argyle and Henderson (1984) found that respondents distinguished current from lapsed friendships largely in terms of rules regulating intimacy and rules pertaining to the provision of social support. The respondents also attributed the breakdown of an actual friendship mainly to violations of 'third-party' rules (not criticizing a friend in public, standing up for a friend in the friend's absence, keeping confidences) and 'coordination' rules (rules which regulated conflict and competition within the dyad). Very close friendships were distinguished from casual ones primarily in terms of the differential importance of rules governing personal support and regulation of intimacy, a finding consistent with the conceptualization of communal relation-

→ FRED—
FEW STUDIES
LOOK AT THIS

(disengagement of
Friendship)

ships by Mills and Clark (1982) and of friendships by Davis and Todd (1982). There also was some indication that the dissolution of a friendship is itself rule-guided, especially since most people maintain some contact with formerly close friends. Argyle and Henderson propose that general rules of personal relationships, such as those dealing with privacy and criticism, continue to guide the altered relationship, whereas the importance of intimacy and support rules declines.

More generally, based on the same series of studies, Argyle (1986) distinguished between rules of intimate and of nonintimate relationships; rules which maintain interpersonal distance through the proscription of expression of personal feelings, attitudes and affection are more commonly endorsed for the latter. These distinctions were made by respondents from all four cultural milieux; but there were also cultural differences. English respondents endorsed more rules, gave greater emphasis to repayment of debts and favors and to standing up for another person in his or her absence, and rated teasing and joking as often desirable; Hong Kong respondents understandably placed great emphasis on rules regulating privacy; Italians gave less emphasis to the proscription of sex in a variety of relationships; and Japanese respondents emphasized the avoidance of public criticism, and gave only weak endorsement to rules regulating privacy and the defense of others in their absence.

The questionnaire data of Argyle and Henderson reveal cross-cultural differences in rules involved in the conduct of interpersonal relationships; they also reveal cross-cultural constancies in some rules, perhaps reflecting problems and sources of potential conflict that are inherent in all close personal relationships; and they differentiate between a variety of personal relationships. On the other hand, the relationship of the endorsement patterns to the actual conduct of relationships in mundane daily life is unknown. This is not an error in their work but a topic for further research which is given explicit content and direction by their results. It is also unclear whether the endorsements reflect grounds for evaluation and sanction or guides for relationship conduct. Finally, Argyle and Henderson do not take a stand on whether rules are generative mechanisms or conditions under which particular behaviors are performed or evaluated, although in his earlier work Argyle did state that rules can be generative in a manner analogous to the generativity of grammar (Argyle, Furnham and Graham, 1981).

It is worth noting that the types of relationship rules extracted by Argyle (1986)—interpersonal exchange and emotional support, intimacy control, coordination, third-party rules—conform well to those of the Qumran community mentioned earlier. This, too, implies the existence of inherent sources of interpersonal conflict which rules serve to moderate.

Another study in the tradition of Argyle's work was conducted by Fusso (1985), who studied the relationships and interactions of paraplegic and quadriplegic patients with noninjured persons. He examined the rated importance of a variety of rules in sixteen situations identified by patients and by health professionals as problematic for spinal cord patients. The results clearly revealed that problematic situations were characterized by a lack of consensus between patients and nonpatients about the importance of various situated rules. This study offers many leads for skills training, for education of family and professionals working with spinal injury patients, and for further research on the role of rules in the situated conduct of problematic relationships. However, it is unclear whether rule dissensus produces situational problems, or the situational problems give rise to rule dissensus, or both occur because of some third factor (such as differences in the goals which the situation affords for injured versus noninjured persons).

STUDY THREE

A different approach was taken by Baxter (1986) in a study of rules implicated in the dissolution of heterosexual relationships. She analyzed the accounts provided by 157 respondents about romantic, heterosexual relationships which had been broken at their initiative. Eight primary rules were extracted from the accounts: obligation to grant autonomy outside the relationship, expectation of similarity, obligation to be supportive, to be open, to be loyal, expectation of shared time, of equity, and of some magical quality to the romantic relationship. Female respondents more frequently than males cited lack of autonomy, openness and equity as reasons for initiating the break-up, whereas males more frequently than females cited a lack of magical quality. Also, females cited more rules in general than did males. Baxter properly points out that there may be gender-role differences in judged importance of specific rules, but that there may also be differences in the skills of rule implementation. Also, the break-up account may be an attempted repair which justifies the respondent's disengagement initiative (Duck, 1982).

Baxter's study is informative and suggestive, but it is important to note that the rules extracted from the break-up accounts actually reflect grounds for dissolution rather than mechanisms for maintenance of the relationship. For example, the 'autonomy' rule actually reflects *constraint*—the partner constrained the respondent, which was a ground for termination of the relationship. Similarly, the absence of similarity implies *dis*similarity, which is a ground for termination. Although the rules cited could serve as components of a *model about* romantic relationships, it is questionable whether they can be construed as *rules of* relationships. Perhaps they should be taken as rules governing relationship dissolution, a process in its own right (Duck, 1982), in that specification of a rule the violation of which justifies the termination of the relationship is indeed part of that dissolution process. It is not necessarily reflective of either the formation or maintenance of romantic relationships.

SCRIPTS

The Nature of Scripts

Scripts are a form of schema, one of the more popular concepts in contemporary social psychology. In turn, schemata are a form of cognitive representation. Each of these constructs requires some comment, and the interested reader is urged to pursue them in detail in the recent treatments by Fiske and Taylor (1984) and Markus and Zajonc (1985).

Scripts are hypothesized cognitive and performative structures which organize a person's comprehension of situated events and guide a person's performance of a situated set of actions (Abelson, 1981; also see Schank and Abelson, 1977). They pertain to shared understandings of what typically happens on specific types of occasions, and it is important to note their 'shared' nature and 'typical' content (Fiske and Taylor, 1984). The activation of a script is a contingent matter; it is brought about by a variety of conditions under which the person is or becomes committed to participating in the script. In addition, scripts vary in 'strength'—that is, in the extent to which they contain not only scenes but sequences. Furthermore, a script can vary in content from one instantiation to the next due to several factors. First, some actions are equifinal—substitutable, leading to the same end; second, some aspects of scripts are variables, as in a choice between coffee and tea; third, scripts contain different paths at branch points; fourth, in weak scripts without clear sequential structure, different scenes can be selected; fifth, scripts have various tracks (e.g. a fast-food versus fancy restaurant track), each embodying some different scenes, paths, and props; sixth, different interferences, obstacles, errors, might arise from one instantiation to the next; seventh, distractions will vary across instantiations; and eighth, the incidental content may vary from one instantiation to the next— free behaviors that are allowed within the script but not required by it. Scripts can also differ in their concreteness or specificity, ranging in generality to 'metascripts' that contain a variety of more specific scripts, analogous to the various tracks that a single script might contain.

Scripts can be described in terms of their distinctiveness and internal coherence. A funeral has high internal coherence and high distinctiveness, so that a funeral script will be an efficient knowledge and action structure. On the other hand, going to a particular supermarket may entail a script with high internal coherence but low distinctiveness which would be inefficient as an individual knowledge structure, although it could be combined with other such scripts into a single, efficient script concerning supermarket shopping. This also bears upon the use of affects and emotions as organizing themes of episodes, and thereby as a basis for scripts. A given affect could organize a script with high internal coherence, such as an 'angry at authority' script (Abelson, 1981), but that script would have very low distinctiveness (if it were organized solely on the basis of anger) because it would share so many features with other episodes of anger, including anger at a recalcitrant lawnmower, and therefore would be an inefficient knowledge and action structure.

As noted above, scripts are *stereotyped* representations of action episodes (Markus and Zajonc, 1985); they are shared by members of a community or culture, and they refer to typical episodes within that community. Thus, they are neither necessary nor sufficient conditions for action, but should be increasingly likely to play important roles as the situation at hand becomes more familiar and routinized. This should apply to routinized situated episodes in personal relationships as well as to situations and rituals in the community at large. One arena of personal relationships in which this has been demonstrated is sexual scripts (Gagnon, 1977; Gagnon and Simon, 1973; Reed and Weinberg, 1984; Weinberg, Swensson and Hammersmith, 1983), as we will see later.

The Uses and Functions of Scripts

In their role as knowledge structures, scripts function much the same way as other schemata. They have an active quality in that they allow a person to reduce a presumably unmanageably complex environment to manageable proportions but also to go beyond the information provided by the environment, if necessary (Markus and Zajonc, 1985). In addition to these 'simplification' and 'filling-in' functions, they also operate as interpretive frameworks, although their influence is greatest during evaluation and inference; schemata do not appear to induce serious distortions of memory or of initial perception of stimuli. Scripts are concerned particularly with sets of events and especially with their temporal sequence, so that their organizational and memory effects are revealed in facilitated recall and recognition of script-consistent events and sequences. Furthermore, events in a narrative or passage which *interrupt* a script are recalled very well; events which are congruent with the script are recalled moderately well; and script-irrelevant events are recalled least well—they do not benefit from the presence of an activated script (Bower, Black and Turner, 1979). However, since scripts are stereotypic, if a script is activated but the events in the narrative occur in an order discrepant from the stereotypic sequence, they are likely to be recalled in the scripted rather than the actual order (Bower, Black and Turner, 1979; Wyer and Bodenhausen, 1985).

There is much less information about the functions of scripts as *performative* structures, especially with respect to the conduct of personal relationships. In general, they can be expected to facilitate the coordination of action, reduce the effort of interaction, reduce the necessity of attention to small details and allow joint action to be organized in large rather than minute chunks. Scripts also facilitate the maintenance of social order and social rituals, and strengthen one's ability to depend on other competent members of one's culture to coordinate with oneself in the performance of social routines. The shared nature of scripted routines also provides the opportunity for deliberate variations on the script, since the actor can assume that other parties in the interchange will detect the variations and respond to them (provided the variations are not so great as to destroy the identity of the scripted episode).

Little of this has been applied explicitly to the study of personal relationships, but extrapolation seems direct. It has been suggested (Rose and Serafica, 1986) that scripts influence the conduct of personal relationships by defining roles and establishing actions within them, but that over time the relationship can modify relevant scripts by influencing the parties' conceptions of the relationship. In addition, changes in the status of a personal relationship are likely to be occasions for script changes, as when couples move from a dating to an engaged relationship and concomitantly withdraw from the friendship network and enter the family network more actively (Johnson and Leslie, 1982). Alterations in the verbal content of scripts also would be expected as the relationship changed, based on extrapolations from research on 'role schemata' (Fiske and Taylor, 1984). When two individuals become a couple, one of the first signs that they wish to be taken as such may be their shift in speech from singular indexical pronouns ('I', 'me', 'him') to plural indexicals ('we', 'us'), indicative of ingroup status; comparably, if dissolution is under way, a script shift from plural to singular would be expected, reflecting an outgroup polarization process at the level of the personal relationship.

Finally, when evaluation, interpretation and inference enter into the moment-to-moment conduct of a personal relationship, activated scripts may obstruct rather than facilitate the smooth and coordinated flow of the interchange. Evaluation and inference are especially likely during conflicts (Braiker and Kelley, 1979) and disenchantment (Duck, 1982), and it is at evaluative and inferential stages of information processing that schemata, including scripts, may have a distorting effect.

Research Examples

The most sophisticated and informative research on scripts has to do with text processing and memory (Bower, Black and Turner, 1979; Wyer et al., 1985) and bears upon personal relationships only in the distant sense that some of the text passages contain information about people in relationships. Somewhat greater focus on relationships is found in studies of episode cognition (Forgas, 1982), but the connection to scripts is indirect. In this section, some recent studies by Wyer et al. (1985) will be summarized briefly, since they have clear potential for deliberate extension to personal relationships. Then an example will be given of the study of sexual scripts.

Wyer et al. (1985) conducted two experiments to explore differences between memory for the temporal order of actions in scripted in contrast to nonscripted (nonstereotypic) but coherent sequences of action. However, the investigators were interested only in the time taken to make judgements, not in the accuracy of those judgements. Subjects were given one or two printed narratives to read which described the activities of a person on a particular day. Pairs of actions selected from the narratives were then shown, one pair at a time, on a computer terminal, preceded by either 'Which occurred sooner?' or 'Which occurred later?' Judgements were faster when the paired actions occurred near the middle rather than at either end of the situation to which they pertained, when the three situations making up the narrative were unrelated to each other than when they were thematically related, when the paired actions occurred in different situations rather than in the same situation, and when the paired actions were far apart in the narrative. Evidence was also obtained which implied that memory for scripted action events (ordered a meal) entailed a different process from memory for situation-specific, particularized action sequences (salted his French fries). For example, judgements were faster for early items when the question was 'Which occurred sooner?', and for later items when the question was 'Which occurred later?'; but this difference obtained only for scripted items. Wyer et al. raise the possibility (as did Bower, Black and

Turner, 1979) that scripted actions are not coded in the primary representation of the observed episode; instead, only the more informative, particularized actions are coded there. The scripted acts are redundant with the particularized actions and are coded elsewhere, perhaps in the form of larger action units. Thus, a person might be expected to remember most readily the actions of another person which *stood out* on a particular occasion, rather than the other person's stereotypic actions on that occasion.

Wyer *et al.* also offer a trenchant discussion of the problems which must be resolved when applying their findings and proposed model to daily, real-time activities, and interested readers will benefit from their analysis. But the explicit extension of their experimental approach to the study of relationship scripts remains to be done. On the other hand, the work described below does deal directly with relationship scripts, but its nonexperimental format precludes the drawing of strong inferences.

The concept of sexual scripts was developed at length and in rich detail by Gagnon and Simon (1973; Gagnon, 1977), and by the very nature of the topic those scripts pertained to close personal relationships—albeit on occasion of short duration. Weinberg and his colleagues have used the notion of sexual scripts to further our understanding of changes in patterns of sexual behavior within the US over the last few decades. In a study of the content of 49 sex manuals from 1950 to 1980, Weinberg, Swenson and Hammersmith (1983) found three different models of female sexuality: the sexuality of women is different from that of men and not equivalent to it, a humanistic view of female sexuality but still within the context of a loving relationship, and an autonomous model which imposes no necessary or 'healthy' context. Each model has different assumptions and values, and different social and political implications; since 1975, the sexual autonomy model has been the most common. Weinberg *et al.* argue that changes in attitudes about sex influence the marketability of new sexual scripts, and as those scripts become accepted they appear in the sex manuals and provide evidence of the legitimacy of redefinitions of women's roles and sexuality.

The actual process of script change and development was examined in more detail by Reed and Weinberg (1984) in a path analysis of interview responses of 301 college students, male and female, drawn from Kinsey's 1967 sample of 1177 respondents. Reed and Weinberg selected only those respondents who were engaged or going steady or dating serially (one person at a time, but more than one over an extended period), and who had not engaged in coitus before college. Using input variables of religiosity, fraternity or sorority affiliation, dating frequency, and beliefs about sexual experience of their close friends, they predicted differential path relations on the basis of presumed availability of sexual scripts. Specifically, for males a sexual script presumably existed (casual sex is all right; control of the encounter is the woman's responsibility); and for engaged females and males a marital script existed, and the influence of friends should be reduced due to the withdrawal from the friend network (Johnson and Leslie, 1982). Thus, for none of these groups should it be necessary to turn to close friends for help in the development of a sexual script, and to the extent that the coital activities of these respondents are influenced by the input variables, that influence should be direct. But for the other women a script of greater premarital sexual freedom was just beginning to form (it did not actually emerge until the 1970s); and those women should have developed individual sexual scripts by reference to the behaviors of others who were situationally and socially close. Moreover, the development of a script should have been more likely as the woman became more committed to the relationship. Therefore, only for women who were going steady but not engaged should the path structure indicate that they turned to their close friends for assistance in script development; that is, the perceived behavior of close friends should be the exclusive mediator of the influences of all other input variables, and only the close friends variable should have a direct effect on coital behavior. This is exactly the pattern obtained.

In sum, these research examples demonstrate that the script notion can be applied profitably to the study of personal relationships, and that our understanding would be enhanced by the deliberate use of personal relationship material—text or video—as the stimuli in script experiments. Furthermore, the use of experimental designs would supplement the rich field data of the sort described above and would allow for much stronger inferences to be drawn.

PROTOTYPES

The Nature of Prototypes

Prototypes are generally considered synonymous with schemata (Markus and Zajonc, 1985; Mayer and Bower, 1986), but they can be distinguished conceptually (Fiske and Taylor, 1984, pp. 146–148). All uses of such terms embody the notion that the organism—or in current jargon, the cognitive system—abstracts a best example from the patterns it encounters or produces (Bartlett, 1932; Head, 1926; Medin and Schaffer, 1978; Neisser, 1976; Posner, 1973; Solso and Raynis, 1979). Prototypes are the 'best example' of a set of exemplars that is defined in terms of family resemblances (e.g. see Rosch, 1978) rather than criterial or necessary and sufficient attributes. When a distinction is made (Fiske and Taylor, 1984), schemata are defined as abstract representations in which some features are unspecified, whereas prototypes are construed to resemble *instances* which are complete with all their attributes, even those that are irrelevant to category membership. An examination of the conceptual treatments of prototypes would not uphold the distinction, since prototypes are also considered by their proponents to be abstractions; but most of the operations by which prototypes are investigated do indeed involve complete instances ('the "prototype"'), although there are some exceptions (Mayer and Bower, 1986). In social cognition, a prototype ordinarily is a list of the features common to a category, and commonly associated with the members of the category. They have been demonstrated for persons, groups, episodes, and situations (Markus and Zajonc, 1985), and under other names for some types of personal relationships such as friends and romantic partners (Davis and Todd, 1982; Serafica,

1983). In cognitive psychology, however, prototype formation has been demonstrated across a much wider range of modalities and procedures than just verbal lists of features: faces, auditory tones, sentence structure, motor responses, and geometric forms, among others. Prototypes formed in one modality (e.g. active tracing of geometric patterns) even cross to other modalities (e.g. imaged geometric patterns; see Solso and Raynis, 1982), suggesting the formation of higher-order isomorphisms that reflect an invariance in the relations between internal representations and their external referent object, regardless of the modality of perception.

There is some disagreement over the processes of prototype acquisition, but a simple 'feature frequency' model has received strong support (e.g. Mayer and Bower, 1986; Solso and Raynis, 1982). According to that model, prototypes form through repeated exposure to the features common to a variety of exemplars. Procedurally, prototypes are indicated when research subjects falsely identify the prototype as a previously seen exemplar *and* when they are at least as confident of that judgement as they are about exemplars which they actually had seen previously. Thus, the major evidence for prototype formation and operation comes from false recognition and confidence data—the same sorts of data obtained from schemata studies in general.

The Uses and Functions of Prototypes

Prototype research has emphasized their role in the categorization process, and little attention has been paid to their possible roles in the structuring of action and relationships. They allow persons to distinguish among categories, and between members or instances of categories; and they facilitate recall and discrimination among items and yield speedier reactions in experimental assessments. In common with other forms of presumed cognitive representations, they can lead to false positive recognition errors. Their major functions, theoretically, pertain to the *cognitive* acquisition, organization and operation of knowledge, although, as noted above, motor prototypes have also been demonstrated (Solso *et al.*, 1986). Moreover, there is no question that the prototype concept could be applied to the conduct of personal relationships; events and partners presumably would be classified on prototypical grounds, and subsequent actions would be based on those classifications. Since relationships exist as socially defined, discriminable 'entities' within a culture, and exemplars of those relationships are frequently perceived and engaged, relationship prototypes can be presumed to exist as part of our set of 'natural categories' (Rosch, 1978).

Research Examples

In this section, three examples of prototype research will be described briefly. My objective is to give the reader a flavor of prototype research in areas close to the study of personal relationships. The first example is a series of studies by Cantor, Mischel and Schwartz (1982) in which they found that subjects had readily available situation prototypes, and that those situation prototypes were

STUDY ONE

richer and more readily available than their person prototypes or person-by-situation prototypes. Cantor *et al.* noted that the '. . . accessibility of situation knowledge is especially interesting given the prevailing view of the lay perceiver as persistently categorizing the world in terms of persons rather than situations' (pp. 61–62).

Prototypes in the Cantor *et al.* research were lists of features generated by naive subjects as typical of the type of target situation. There was no actual identification of a prototype; instead, 'prototype' was an abstraction operationalized in terms of features mentioned by two or more out of ten subjects as typical, with an average of fifteen such features for each of the 36 'prototypes' (lists of features). This is different from research in which a prototype is established *a priori* and used as a basis for generating exemplars which differ from it in varying degrees. In the latter studies, subjects are familiarized with the exemplars then shown a new set of stimuli which include the prototype (not previously seen); the subjects typically make false recognition errors about having seen the prototype before (e.g. Solso and McCarthy, 1981). Such studies do not test the central proposition that people will form prototypes through contact with environmental stimuli, but the studies do incorporate an identifiable prototype. The Cantor *et al.* study does not, although it is interesting on other grounds and certainly implicates prototypicality.

A set of studies that comes much closer to a demonstration of prototype formation and at the same time includes identifiable prototypes has been published recently by Mayer and Bower (1986). They presented subjects with 60 paragraphs, each describing a hypothetical person in terms of sixteen features. Each subject had his or her own assigned prototype, randomly generated from the sixteen categories of feature information, and the subject's task was to specify whether the person described in the given paragraph was a member of the prototype set. Of course, no subject knew the content of his or her prototype; but each was given immediate feedback after making a judgement. If repeated exposure to complex stimuli is sufficient for prototype formation, the subjects should show a learning curve over the 60 paragraphs, and this is exactly what Mayer and Bower obtained. Roughly 75 per cent of the last 20 instances were correctly classified by the subjects. Also, the paragraphs varied in the number of prototypical features they contained (with a maximum of all sixteen of the features being prototypical), and the probability of classification of the person described by a paragraph as prototypical increased monotonically with the number of prototypical features in the paragraph.

In another study, Mayer and Bower compared the 'arbitrary prototype' procedure with an evaluative prototype. Some subjects received the procedures described above, while others received paragraphs generated from evaluatively pleasant, unpleasant or neutral prototypes. Both groups of subjects showed prototype acquisition, as reflected in the large proportion of correct classifications of the last 20 paragraphs (68 per cent for the arbitrary group, 78 per cent for the evaluative group). The authors interpret their findings as indicating that prototype formation can occur simply by observation—that *a priori* schemata are not necessary; the detectable common features of repeatedly contacted types of stimuli may be sufficient for prototype acquisition.

The preceding two examples could be applied to the study of personal relationships directly, requiring only a change in the task content or stimulus content from person descriptions to relationship descriptions. But in both cases, we would be relying implicitly on cultural commonalities inherent in our language. The cultural relativity of linguistically based person prototypes is demonstrated nicely in another recent study (Hoffman, Lau and Johnson, 1986). Three groups of subjects were given parallel English or Chinese language descriptions of four hypothetical persons; two of the described characters had ready labels (prototype labels) in English but not in Chinese, and two had ready labels in Chinese but not in English. One group of subjects comprised English monolinguals who received the material and responded in English, another comprised Chinese–English bilinguals who received the material and responded in Chinese, and the third comprised Chinese–English bilinguals who received the material and responded in English. All subjects were asked to form impressions of the four characters, and five days later they were given four tasks: to give a written impression of each character, to recall actual statements from the original material, a recognition task involving old and new person-description statements, and an inference task in which they had to judge the likelihood that various statements would be characteristic of each of the four stimulus persons.

The availability of the prototype in the language did have effects, especially in the free impression and inference tasks, and to a lesser degree in the recognition task. In general, the usual prototype and schema effects were found for those character descriptions which had a ready prototype in the language in which the task was being implemented. Thus, the lexicon may facilitate or obstruct the formation and implementation of different kinds of prototypes about persons—and by extension, about personal relationships; and this in turn could facilitate or obstruct the formation and implementation of different kinds of relationships themselves. That is, how we can talk about personal relationships can influence what kinds of relationships we are likely to produce and maintain; our language may provide many of our prototypes.

INTEGRATION AND RECOMMENDATIONS

The central concepts reviewed in this chapter—rules, scripts and prototypes—clearly are applicable to the study of the conduct of personal relationships; but deliberate and explicit application has been rare. Such application might be facilitated by an examination of the links between the concepts, and of some of the problems associated with them.

Rules, scripts and prototypes are interwoven through the classification of actions and events and the unfolding of action sequences. Constitutive rules specify whether an event or act is a type to which particular regulative rules apply; but prototypes also are part of the classification process. Once an event or act or person is prototypically classed as an instance of a set, the members of which share a family resemblance, certain actions are implied. For example, a 'best friend' prototype sets the context in which intimacy can be expressed and experienced (Serafica, 1983). Moreover, the component features of the prototype imply the kinds of actions that would violate the relationship, the kinds that would be expressive of it, and even the sorts of situations which should be sought to affirm the relationship or avoided to hide it (Davis and Todd, 1982). Scripts, too, pertain both to classification and performance of situated actions, as indicated in the earlier discussion of their dual identity as knowledge structures and performative structures. Thus, precise boundaries cannot be established between the three. On the other hand, they do vary in emphases.

Most uses of 'rule' in social psychology deal with regulative rules which are equivalent to prescriptive, proscriptive or permissive statements shared by the members of a group. The emphasis is on the shared nature of the rule, and this suggests a means for avoiding the concept's major difficulty. Specifically, it is very difficult to demonstrate that a person knows a rule, regardless of whether the person's behavior conforms to it; and derivatively, it is difficult to establish the link, if any, between the person's rule knowledge and the person's behavior. These issues have been discussed in detail by Collett (1977), and also by Argyle, Furnham and Graham (1981), but there is no easy resolution. However, the difficulties arise because of an unnecessary theoretical step—construing rules as items of knowledge. If they were to be conceptualized as features of the social world—of situations, and of relationships—the problem of demonstrating that an individual *knew* the rule and that his or her behavior was influenced by that *knowledge* would not exist. This is the conceptual shift taken by Argyle and his colleagues (Argyle, Furnham and Graham, 1981; Argyle and Henderson, 1984). The deliberate construal of rules as social rather than psychological entities differentiates them from the other two concepts and simultaneously augments their utility as explanatory tools. In the study of personal relationships, investigators should try to discover the rules shared by a culture with respect to how people in a particular relationship should or should not act, feel and appear, given the type of relationship, the career stage of the relationship, its qualitative state, and the context (Ginsburg, 1986).

Scripts and prototypes are less readily distinguished. However, the emphasis of scripts is on culturally stereotyped sequences of action, whereas the emphasis of prototypes is on categorization into fuzzy sets. Action is *implied* by a prototype (see Davis and Todd, 1982), but it is *specified* by a script—although not necessarily in detail. Acknowledgement of these different emphases allows the two concepts to be used in complementary fashion in the study of personal relationships. A prototype can be construed as a set of the common, invariant features of a family of instances, and it can be studied as a discriminative stimulus complex; that is, if we construe prototypes as reflections of detectable, invariant features of a set of instances, then it behoves us to discover those features. We would attempt to identify the cues available in the situated behaviors of relationally linked persons which are detected by others, often unwittingly, and which identify the relationship as the sort that it is. Detection

of such invariants is socially important, since it indicates reinforcement contingencies: the reception a person gets from a couple will depend on whether that
person acts towards them in a manner consistent with the kind of relationship
they express. Tie signs (Goffman, 1971; see also Fine, Stitt and Finch, 1984),
for example, are likely to serve as discriminative stimuli about relationships and
can be construed as invariant features of a prototypic set. Enduring affective
tone may be a candidate invariant, too, since it can be a basis for a prototype
(Mayer and Bower, 1986), and Clarke and his colleagues have demonstrated
that different kinds of personal relationships are characterized by different
affective tones (Clarke, Allen and Dickson, 1985).

Scripts, too, reflect common, invariant features of a family of instances, but
the instances are extended sequences of situated actions. The primary research
task is to discover those invariant features which are detectable and thereby
inform participants and observers about what acts are under way, which in turn
will imply what personal relationship is being expressed. This puts a different
interpretation on the 'gap-filling' function of scripts. That is, if in a restaurant
script it was stated that a patron ordered lobster but not that he ate it, a
subject who is asked what the patron ate will answer, 'Lobster'. That usually is
interpreted as inference—going beyond the information given. But alternatively
it can be seen as a meaning change brought about by the question itself. The
question, 'What did the patron eat?' transforms the narrative from a description
of what the patron ordered to one of what the patron ate. This would occur
easily because the *act* described in the narrative is 'going to a restaurant for
dinner', which normatively involves eating what one orders as an invariant
feature.

This illustration emphasizes the importance of context; the nature of the
script had to be interpreted by taking into account the 'story-in-the-context-of-
the-*question*'. Our research procedures are conversational or quasi-conver-
sational practices, and our data reflect the conversational conventions of our
culture. In accord with the contention of Markus and Zajonc (1985) that further
advance in our understanding will require increased attention to the stimulus
environment, the social context, and the role of dialogue and discourse, we
probably should shift our research orientation in personal relationships, with less
emphasis on 'cognition' and more on the detectable structure of relationships as
they are expressed in social situations. That would include attending to what
people say and how they talk to and about each other.

One line of work that meets the above prescription and can be extended
directly to relationship research is the study of discourse and conversational
pragmatics (H. H. Clark, 1985). Examples include the demonstration by Brown
and Fish (1983) of psychological causality implicit in English verbs and adjectives, the analysis by McGuire and McGuire (1986) of differences in the kinds
of verbs people use to talk about themselves *versus* others, the earlier work by
Kanouse (1971) and the more recent work by Hilton and Slugoski (1986)
and by Turnbull and Slugoski (in press) on conversational processes in causal
attribution, and a conversational pragmatics interpretation of the attitude
concept (Lalljee, Brown and Ginsburg, 1984). Each of these emphasizes the

pragmatic implications inherent in the words and phrases that people use in their conversations with each other; those implications structure relationships, often just for the moment but sometimes enduringly. Of equal potential is the study of accounts people use to justify their entry into and termination of personal relationships (Baxter, 1986; Duck, 1982; Harvey *et al.*, 1986; Rose and Serafica, 1986).

Davis and Todd (1982) contend that clear instances of various kinds of relationships do exist and are directly detectable. This, too, suggests that much effort be devoted to the discovery of detectable structure in the situated expression of personal relationships, especially over time. Such a view is compatible with Gibson's (1966) 'ecological perception' position, and applications of the argument to social perception can be found in papers by Knowles and Smith (1982), McArthur and Baron (1983) and Smith and Ginsburg (1987). Empirical evidence of its applicability to personal relationships has been offered by Smith (1977), who found that there are invariant features of such complex social routines as pick-up episodes which allow them to be known for what they are directly and without reflective thought, even when other noncentral actions in the episode are randomly rearranged.

An underlying purpose of this chapter was to challenge the reader to consider a shift in orientation that would facilitate the applicability of three important concepts to the study of the conduct of personal relationships. The discovery of those rules which are shared by members of a culture and pertain to the actions of people in relationships will enhance our understanding of people's behaviors in their relationships and of their talk about their relationships. The discovery of the invariant features that reveal a relationship for what is, across the wide variety of phenotypic forms that it can take in any situated instantiation, similarly will enhance our understanding of the relationship and of other people's reactions to it. Much the same can be said with respect to scripts: discovery of the stereotypic action sequences commonly performed within a given type of situation by people in a particular type of relationship will further our understanding of internal dynamics of relationships and of their modes of situated manifestation. And if our discoveries include emotion rules and affective prototypes, we may even gain insight into the joys, trials and tribulations of human personal relationships.

Handbook of Personal Relationships
Edited by S. W. Duck
© 1988 John Wiley & Sons Ltd

3

Functions of Nonverbal Behavior in Close Relationships

MILES L. PATTERSON
University of Missouri, St Louis, Missouri, USA

ABSTRACT

Component and developmental approaches to analyzing close relationships are briefly reviewed and an alternative approach that focuses on patterns of interactive behavior is described. The patterns of nonverbal exchange and the functions served by those patterns provide insight into the intimacy and quality of close relationships.

There are a variety of ways of describing and analyzing close relationships. The extensive literature on relationships reviewed in this volume is testimony to that variety. Perhaps one way of classifying the various theoretical approaches to close relationships is in terms of an emphasis on either: (1) the core components or processes that sustain relationships or (2) the developmental analysis of the changing stages of relationships. Of course, one may start with an analysis of the components or processes basic to close relationships and, building on that, come to an assessment of specific relationship stages, just as the developmental approach does. Conversely, the differentiation among developmental stages may be discussed in terms of changes in the core component processes. In effect, these two categories may simply reflect different strategies for studying relationships. In this first section of this chapter I will present a brief overview of these two approaches. This overview is not comprehensive, but it should provide a representative picture of the manner in which relationships have been studied. In the second section of the chapter I propose an alternative means of analyzing close relationships—one that emphasizes the various functions of nonverbal behavior that are reflected in close relationships.

Two general advantages of this functional analysis of nonverbal behavior in close relationships may be suggested. First, nonverbal behavior is typically more important in most face-to-face interactions than is verbal behavior. Consequently, understanding the patterns of social exchange characteristic of different kinds of relationships requires attention to the nonverbal components. Second, the functional approach towards nonverbal behavior in close relationships stresses the processes underlying social exchange. Such an orientation is consistent with the view that relationships are themselves processes and not stable states (Duck and Sants, 1983). In the first section of this chapter, the overview of the more traditional approaches to the study of close relationships will set the context for the discussion of this functional analysis of nonverbal exchange.

COMPONENT ANALYSES

Individual Perspectives

Relationship analyses that focus on critical components or processes can emphasize the roles played by the individual participants in the relationship, the joint or interactive qualities of the relationship, or both. Representative of the individual orientation are McAdams' (1980, 1984, see also McAdams' chapter in this volume) motivational approach and Sternberg's (1986) triangular theory of love. McAdams' analysis of relationships is based on a contrast between the motives of intimacy and power. He suggests that intimacy and power reflect the same kinds of fundamental properties of life that are represented by Bakan's (1966) dimensions of communion and agency, respectively.

In McAdams' approach, the motives of intimacy and power are assessed by means of thematic coding of story descriptions to pictures on the Thematic Apperception Test (TAT). In general, the intimacy motive is characterized by themes such as positive affect between individuals, commitment or concern, union, harmony, and surrender of control. In contrast, power is characterized by themes such as control, conflict, influence, and concern about one's prestige or reputation. In his research on dating and marriage, McAdams (1984) reported that the power motive, especially in men, was associated with greater relationship dissatisfaction and instability, a higher rate of divorce, and marriages in which the wife assumes a more traditional role. In contrast, the intimacy motive was associated with reports of intense love in dating couples and marital satisfaction in men. In McAdams' research on friendships, the power motive was related to themes of influence, disagreement, and fear of conflict, whereas the intimacy motive was related to themes reflecting a larger number of dyadic friendship interactions, increased self-disclosure and listening to friends, and fear of separation from friends. The contrast between the power and intimacy motives is also likely to be reflected in different patterns of nonverbal behavior. Later, the discussion of the intimacy and social control functions of nonverbal behavior will specify some of those differences.

Sternberg (1986) has proposed a component model of love that has direct application to the study of close relationships. Sternberg identifies intimacy, passion, and decision/commitment as the basic components in his triangular theory of love. Intimacy refers to feelings that promote closeness and attachment towards a loved one. Passion refers to the motives and drives that lead to physical attraction, romance, and sexual fulfilment. Decision/commitment is assumed to have both a short-term and a long-term aspect. For the short term, there is the decision that one loves a specific other. For the long term, there is a commitment to maintain that love. Sternberg notes that although all three components are necessary to describe and understand love, different love relationships will vary considerably in the strengths of the three components. For example, developing romantic love might be heavily weighted on the passion and intimacy components, but less on the decision/commitment component. In contrast, love for a best friend may be highly weighted on decision/commitment and possibly intimacy, but it would have little or no passion component.

By comparing the perceptions of the two individuals in a relationship along the dimensions of intimacy, passion, and decision/commitment, it is possible to assess the degree to which they match one another. There is some evidence that, across partners, increased similarity in the perceived pattern of the three components is predictive of increased satisfaction with a relationship (Sternberg and Barnes, 1985).

Dyadic Perspectives

McAdams' analysis of motives and Sternberg's triangular model of love both focus on the perspective of the individual. In other component approaches to relationships, the focus is more directly on the dynamics of the relationship itself. Representative of this dyadic perspective are the equity theory (Hatfield and Traupmann, 1981; Hatfield et al, 1985; Walster, Walster and Berscheid, 1978) and communication analysis (Fitzpatrick, 1984; Gottman, 1979; Noller, 1984) approaches to relationships. Equity theory assumes that a basic concern about one's own behavior is that it leads to a fair outcome relative to one's own inputs and to the inputs and outcomes of others (Perlman and Fehr, 1987). Equity theory proposes that equitable relationships are those in which each party perceives his or her input-to-outcome ratio as comparable to that of the partner. Inequity is perceived as aversive and leads individuals to attempt to restore equity by changing their inputs, their outcome, or their perception of these elements. In general, equitable relationships are assumed to be more stable and more likely to progress to greater intimacy, whereas inequitable relationships are more stressed (Hatfield et al., 1985; Perlman and Fehr, 1987). Furthermore, if attempts to restore equity are not successful, the prognosis for the relationship becomes more negative.

In the communication approach to relationships, the emphasis is on assessing the quality or quantity of communication in relationships. This approach has been widely used in the study of marital relationships. Noller (1984) reviewed research designed to study a number of dimensions that are presumably related to marital adjustment, including: (1) the quality or valence of communication,

(2) accuracy of communication, (3) communication awareness, and (4) consistency of messages.

An alternative way of analyzing communication in marital relationships is in terms of the styles of communication (Fitzpatrick, 1984; Gottman, 1979). For example, Gottman (1982b) proposed that closeness (and presumably satisfaction) in marriages is facilitated by symmetry in the partners' emotional responsiveness, particularly in low-intensity affective interactions. Fitzpatrick (1984) has offered a typology of marital partners that is based on the patterns of messages of control or influence that are made between them. Fitzpatrick's categories include the following types: (1) *traditionals* who have relatively few disagreements but who do confront one another on important issues; (2) *independents* who tend to avoid discussing important issues of disagreement but frequently try to control the course of their conversations; (3) *separates* who tend to talk less, avoid conflict, and appear less spontaneous than the other types; and (4) *mixed* types composed of husbands and wives who define their relationship differently from one another and whose behavior shows selective overlap with the styles of other types. By classifying styles of communication in couples, Fitzpatrick has moved beyond the simple description of self-report indices of marital satisfaction to a consideration of behavioral styles. This emphasis on patterns of interaction is consistent with the functional approach of this chapter.

Overview of Component Approaches

In summary, the various component approaches all try to identify, either at the individual or at the dyadic level, the central processes that underlie close relationships. McAdams' (1980, 1984) motivational approach and Sternberg's (1986) triangular theory of love focus on the nature of each person's strong affective attachment to his or her partner. Equity theory proposes that relationships will move either towards the maintenance of equity between the partners or towards instability and dissolution. Although the communication approach does recognize the importance of self-disclosure in relationships, just as McAdams and Sternberg do, a more general concern is the style of communication (Fitzpatrick, 1984; Gottman, 1979; Noller, 1984). Of course, one could probably make a good case for the interrelatedness of these presumably independent factors. Specifically, the greater the love or intimacy in a relationship, the greater the incentive for equity and for communicating effectively and accurately. Conversely, the greater the equity and the more sensitive the communicative styles, the greater the resulting intimacy or love. Ultimately, love, intimacy, sensitivity, and equity (or their absence) are communicated behaviorally. In particular, the patterns of nonverbal exchange and the functions underlying those patterns are especially important for understanding close relationships.

DEVELOPMENTAL ANALYSES

Developmental approaches emphasize the changing course of relationships over time. These changes are usually described in terms of relatively distinct stages. One example of such a stage analysis is Altman and Taylor's (1973) social penetration theory. This theory emphasizes the critical role of changing patterns of communication in the development of close relationships. One important factor is the breadth and depth of disclosure between partners in a relationship. A second important factor is the manner in which interactions take place. That is, interactions in more intimate relationships are assumed to be more efficient and spontaneous, qualities that are reflected in the patterns of nonverbal behavior.

Altman and Taylor posit the existence of the four following stages in intimate relationships: (1) orientation, (2) exploratory affective exchange, (3) affective exchange, and (4) stable exchange. Orientation refers to the initial phase of a relationship in which only limited and peripheral aspects of the personality are accessible to a partner. Interactions at this stage tend to be stereotyped and, usually, considerable care is taken to make sure that these contacts are relatively pleasant ones. In exploratory affective exchange, increasing breadth and depth of personality is made accessible to the partner. Relationships at this stage are typically characterized as friendly, relaxed, and casual, but commitments are often limited (Altman and Taylor, 1973, pp. 138–139). At the stage of affective exchange, partners get to know more about the more central areas of each other's personality and, consequently, each is more vulnerable to the other. This sharing and mutuality is also reflected in the manner and the quality of the interactions themselves. In particular, mutual patterns of nonverbal behavior are likely to be smoother, more synchronous and more efficient. At the final stage, stable exchange, partners feel free to express spontaneously both intermediate and core elements of the personality. That is, there is a desire and willingness to share very private feelings and experiences.

Altman and Taylor caution that the stages are not static levels of achievement but, rather, are open to change over time. Furthermore, Altman and Taylor (1973, pp. 173–180) assume that unresolved conflict over various issues, particularly those in the more intimate areas of a partner's personality, can lead to a deterioration in the relationship. The deterioration in a relationship is assumed to follow the direction opposite that of developing relationships. That is, over time interpersonal exchange will be limited to more superficial areas of the relationship.

A different stage approach to close relationships has been proposed by Levinger (1980, 1983). Levinger's model has been characterized as the ABCDE model, with A standing for *acquaintance*, B for *buildup*, C for *continuation*, D for *deterioration*, and E for *ending*. In contrast to social penetration theory, Levinger places a greater emphasis on the asymmetry of developing and deteriorating relationships. Not all close relationships proceed through continuation to deterioration and ending; however, for those that do, there is a decrease in interdependency and mutual satisfaction. These changes, in turn, promote comparative evaluations and the eventual development of new relationships to replace the old ones.

Perlman and Fehr (1987), in reviewing these and other developmental theories, offer two observations about the developmental approach. Their first point concerns the lack of agreement on (1) the stages themselves, (2) the crucial antecedents of attraction, and (3) the order of importance of the predictor variables. Second, citing Hinde (1979), Perlman and Fehr note that the division of any continuous process—like a relationship—into discrete phases is bound to be somewhat arbitrary. In spite of these limitations, thinking of relationships in terms of stages can be a quite useful way of generating hypotheses about them.

A FUNCTIONAL APPROACH

At the start of this chapter, it was proposed that the component and developmental analyses, though different, might in fact be quite complementary. The pursuit of critical component processes of relationships naturally leads to questions of change over time, whereas the pursuit of developmental changes naturally leads to questions about critical component processes. The preceding discussion of these two approaches has included some examples of the role of nonverbal behavior in relationships. Nevertheless, patterns of nonverbal behavior have received relatively little attention in the research literature. One exception is Cappella's (1984) discussion of behavior styles as an index of relationship quality (cf. Cappella's chapter in the present volume). From Cappella's discussion, at least three important observations about relationships and behavioral patterns may be identified. First, general impressions of and attraction towards others are systematically related to patterns of nonverbal, vocal, and verbal characteristics. Second, individuals exhibit consistency in their behavior to different partners. Third, the study of specific behavioral patterns in interaction facilitates an understanding of the interpersonal functions of behavior. In turn, these interpersonal functions can provide a means for generating theory and research on interpersonal relationships.

The first of Cappella's points is relevant to both the initiation of relationships and the early expectancies that one has about a partner. The second point recognizes the existence of stable individual differences in behavior, but also emphasizes the potential for adjustments in behavior that may create greater meshing of the joint behavioral patterns between partners. The third point, the emphasis on a functional analysis of nonverbal behavior in relationships, is the focus of the remainder of this chapter. Specifically, an analysis of the functional patterns in close relationships can provide a means of evaluating the quality of those relationships.

The first consideration in that discussion is to present a classification of functions of nonverbal behavior. In recent years, I have developed a theoretical framework for explaining patterns of nonverbal behavior in social interaction. This framework was built around a classification of the functions of nonverbal behavior (Patterson, 1982a, 1983). Earlier classifications included categories that related either to *managing social interaction* (synchronizing speech, providing feedback, and expressing intimacy) or *providing communicative content* (e.g. Argyle, 1972; Argyle, Lalljee and Cook, 1968; Ekman and Friesen, 1969; Harrison, 1973; Kendon, 1967).

The classification system that is presented here develops out of the earlier distinctions of other researchers, but it also expands the range of functions. The following five functions were discussed in the original treatments of the sequential functional model (Patterson, 1982a, 1983): (1) providing information, (2) regulating interaction, (3) expressing intimacy, (4) attempting social control, and (5) engaging the service–task function. Later, two additional functions, the presentational function and the affect management function, were proposed (Patterson, 1987). In the remainder of the chapter, I will describe these functions and discuss their relevance for a behavioral analysis of close relationships. Table 1 identifies these categories, provides a brief description of each one, and offers an example of each category in close relationships.

FUNCTIONAL PATTERNS AND QUALITY OF RELATIONSHIP

In the beginning of this chapter it was noted that a functional approach to close relationships stresses the processes underlying interactive behavior. More specifically, a functional analysis is one way of studying the motives and goals of behavior. In the following discussion it is assumed that a given pattern of nonverbal behavior may serve different functions (e.g. a discreet touch can signal simple affection or, in contrast, be very manipulative) and, conversely, different patterns of nonverbal behavior can serve the same function (e.g. both increased gaze and discreet touch can signal affection). In applying a functional analysis, it is important to differentiate between the actor's behavioral manifestation of the function (an encoding approach) and the partner's evaluation or reaction to the behavior pattern (a decoding approach). Because there has been relatively little research conducted specifically on the links between the functions and relationship intimacy, much of what is offered here will be speculative in nature.

Providing Information

The function of providing information may be a universal category in the sense that all publicly observable behavior is potentially informative. That is, such behavior can provide the observer with information about the actor's states, traits, or specific isolated reactions to self, to other people, or to the environment. Informative behavior that is spontaneous or reactive can be described as *indicative*, in that it indicates something about the actor's underlying states, traits, or judgements. Informative behavior that is purposeful or managed may be described as *communicative*, in line with MacKay's (1972) definition of communication. Specifically, MacKay defined communication as behavior that is goal oriented or purposeful in its intent. The distinction between indicative

Table 1 Categories of functions in close relationships

Category	Description	Example
Providing information	Actor's behavior patterns permit an observer to make inferences about the actor's states, traits, or reactions to people or to the environment.	A subtle change in a husband's facial expression may lead his wife to judge that he is upset, but the same cues would not be useful to a stranger.
Regulating interaction	Changes in nonverbal behavior serve as cues to regulate the efficient give-and-take of interactions.	Close friends and family members are more likely than mere acquaintances to anticipate when a partner will start or stop speaking by knowing the partner's idiosyncratic pattern of gaze changes or postural adjustments.
Expressing intimacy	Increased intimacy between partners is indicated by higher levels of nonverbal involvement.	Lovers are more likely to stand close, touch, and gaze towards one another more than do mere acquaintances.
Social control	Social control involves goal-oriented behavior designed to influence another person.	As a person requests a favor from his close friend, he leans forward, touches him on the arm, and gazes intently.
Presentational function	A behavior pattern is managed by an individual, a couple, to create or enhance an image.	When a quareling couple arrive at a party, they may cover their conflict by holding hands and smiling at one another.
Affect management	The experience of affect, especially strong affect, leads to changing patterns of nonverbal involvement.	Unexpected good fortune (winning the lottery) leads to sharing the news with family and friends. Hugs, kisses, and other forms of touching are likely in celebrating the good fortune with others.
Service-task function	Patterns of nonverbal involvement are determined primarily by service or task goals in an interaction.	The close approach, touch and gaze initiated by a physician towards a patient does *not* reflect interpersonal affect.

and communicative behavior is an important one in differentiating among the other functions to be described.

Even though all behavior is potentially informative, the ease of gaining information from the verbal and nonverbal behavior of others undoubtedly increases as a function of relationship intimacy. Thus, individuals in more intimate relationships are likely to become better or more efficient decoders of their partner's behavior because of their experience with a specific partner. In the example in Table 1, the wife's familiarity with her husband's range of facial expressions makes it possible for her to infer accurately his changing feelings from a minimum of cues. In contrast, a broader sampling of behavior may be necessary in less intimate relationships.

At the same time, however, attention to the informational value of a partner's behavior probably decreases with increasing intimacy in the relationship. Presumably, in the early stages of a relationship, when there may be greater ambiguity about the nature and quality of the relationship, one must attend more carefully to the meaning of the partner's behavior. As the relationship becomes more intimate and stable, there is generally less need to monitor the partner's behavior as closely as there was earlier. That is, expectancies about the relationship have probably crystallized enough so that less attention is required. Increasing instability and/or conflict would, again, increase the utility of the inferences made from the partner's behavior and greater attention to the partner's behavior would result. An example might be the increased attention to a spouse's behavior if he or she is suspected of being unfaithful.

Interaction Regulation

The focus of interaction regulation is generally on the momentary changes in nonverbal behavior that are associated with instances of initiating interactions, greeting, turn-taking, interruptions, and terminating interactions (Cappella, 1985a; Duncan and Fiske, 1977; Feldstein and Welkowitz, 1978; Kendon, 1967; Rosenfeld, 1978). Behaviors such as gaze, touch, smiling, head nods, postural shifts, gestures, and paralinguistic cues often combine to signal concurrent or impending changes in the state of an interaction. Interaction regulation usually operates in an automatic fashion, outside of awareness, and, consequently, would be indicative. When expectations about appropriate interactive behavior are violated, however, individuals may deliberately initiate, change, or intensify specific behaviors in order to bring the exchange more in line with expectations. For example, if a conversation partner failed to react to a speaker's comments, either verbally or nonverbally (e.g. a head nod or a smile), then the speaker might repeat the comment, say 'Well?', or initiate a quizzical expression at the listener. Presumably, one of these tactics would be likely to get a reaction from the partner and move the interaction back on track again.

Across different types of relationships there are a number of communalities in the give-and-take of conversational sequences. For example, in terminating a speaking turn, speakers typically show the following behaviors: (1) decreased pitch or loudness, (2) termination of gestures, (3) drawl or stretching out of the

last word, and (4) the use of comments such as 'you know' (Duncan, 1972). In
addition, gaze directed towards a listener may become more likely at the end
of a speaker's turn (Kendon, 1967), although such a pattern may be even more
likely when one is asking a question than when finishing a statement (Thomas
and Bull, 1981). Listeners, in contrast, are far more likely to nod or even offer
reinforcing comments (e.g. mm hmm, uh huh, yeh) when they wish the speaker
to continue. When listeners are trying to initiate a turn, they are more likely
to (1) shift the head towards the speaker; (2) inhale audibly; and (3) initiate a
gesture (Duncan and Niederehe, 1974).

Even though the elements involved in the regulation of interaction may be
relatively constant across individuals and relationships, the efficiency of regulating interaction probably increases in more intimate relationships. Altman and
Taylor (1973, pp. 138–140) suggest that, as relationships move from the early
orientation stage to more developed stages, interactions become more predictable and synchronized. In the example in Table 1, the increased contact between
partners in close relationships makes it possible to predict and anticipate their
styles of interacting. Obviously, not all of this increased efficiency is due to
increased sensitivity to nonverbal patterns of behavior. Vocal and verbal
patterns also become more predictable and, consequently, contribute to the
degree to which exchanges are synchronous. Practically, this increased efficiency
might be reflected in a lower incidence of accidental interruptions between
partners and a decreased latency of pauses in turn-taking. Relationship intimacy
might also contribute to another indicator of mutual influence, postural congruence. Postural congruence or matching might take the form of either 'carbon
copies' or 'mirror images'. Scheflen (1963, 1964, 1974) has reported in his
analysis of psychotherapeutic exchanges that increased postural congruence is
indicative of increased rapport between therapist and client. Other research
suggests that high levels of postural congruence in initial meetings may actually
signal concern over the absence of adequate rapport (LaFrance and Ickes,
1981). It is possible that such an initial concern may actually promote the later
development of rapport and a closer relationship. There are currently not a
great deal of data on this issue, but it appears that postural congruence may be
one indicator of closer relationships.

Expressing Intimacy

Intimacy might be described as a bipolar dimension reflecting the degree of
union with or openness towards another person. The function of expressing
intimacy is manifested when a person's level of nonverbal involvement towards
a partner spontaneously flows from the intimacy felt towards that person.
Characteristic of increased involvement as a function of increased intimacy are
higher levels of mutual gaze among couples in love (Rubin, 1970) and more
frequent affectionate touches in pairs having close relationships (Jones and
Yarbrough, 1985). At the other end of the continuum, decreased intimacy may
be expected to produce lower levels of nonverbal involvement. Even though

this function is typically spontaneous or indicative in character, the behavioral expression of intimacy is necessarily constrained by the social setting.

Although more intimate relationships are usually characterized by higher levels of nonverbal involvement, this pattern probably holds more strongly for romantic relationships than for most other types of relationships. This difference may help to explain the greater frequency of research on patterns of nonverbal behavior in romantic relationships. For example, in couples scoring higher on a self-report measure of love, mutual gaze was greater than for those scoring lower on such a measure (Rubin, 1970). Similarly, individuals who reported being in love showed higher levels of mutual gaze when matched with their partners than when matched with a stranger (Goldstein, Kilroy and Van de Voort, 1976). In addition, higher levels of reciprocated gaze in pairs lead observers to infer stronger liking between partners (Kleinke, Meeker and LaFong, 1974) and higher levels of sexual involvement (Thayer and Schiff, 1977).

For couples in intimate relationships, the level of nonverbal involvement can provide an important indicator of the quality of the relationship. For example, Beier and Sternberg (1977) interviewed newlywed couples who varied in their degree of agreement/disagreement. Compared to those showing high levels of disagreement, those low in disagreement showed the following patterns: (1) sitting closer to one another; (2) displaying higher levels of gaze; (3) more frequent touching of the partner; (4) touching themselves less often; and (5) having more open leg positions.

Touch in close relationships may be used in a number of ways to signal positive affect. Jones and Yarbrough (1985) identified several categories of touch that are characteristic of close relationships, including the following: (1) support, (2) appreciation, (3) inclusion, (4) sexual involvement, and (5) affection. These categories evolved out of self-reports of touch by participant–observers who were students in upper-level courses on nonverbal communication. Support touches served to nurture, reassure, or promise protection to another person. Appreciation touches signaled gratitude from the toucher, often accompanied by a verbal expression of 'Thanks'. Inclusion touches, such as holding hands or putting an arm around a partner, emphasized the closeness or intimacy between partners. Sexual touches signaled physical attraction or sexual interest between intimates in cross-sex relationships and usually involved holding or caressing of the partner in the chest, pelvis or buttocks areas. Affection touches expressed general positive regard towards the partner.

In general, it seems that the characteristic patterns of nonverbal involvement in relationships can indicate the intimacy level of relationships. Close relationships obviously provide more opportunities for high involvement exchanges than do less close relationships. Perhaps more importantly, however, patterns of nonverbal involvement can also signal the quality of the relationship. Conflict or even apathy in a relationship might be reflected in decreased nonverbal involvement between partners (Beier and Steinberg, 1977).

At least two cautions should be mentioned regarding the interpretation of relationship quality from the patterns of nonverbal exchange. First, as partners become more intimate, there may often be less pressure to focus their full attention in interacting with one another. That is, each partner may be engaged in a solitary activity while in the presence of the other and only occasionally direct a gaze or a comment towards the other person. It is as though relationship intimacy gives individuals some license to ignore their partner by engaging in a separate activity while in the presence of the partner. The second caution will be mentioned only briefly here, but will be considered more fully under the presentational function. Specifically, because nonverbal involvement can be managed, just as verbal content can, one or both members of a pair may initiate high levels of involvement to create a specific impression for observers.

Social Control

The fourth function, social control, is characterized by goal-oriented behavior designed to influence another person. For example, behaviors such as distance, gaze, touch, facial affect, and paralinguistic cues may be important in: (1) exercising power and dominance over others, (2) initiating persuasive communication, (3) providing feedback and reinforcement, (4) deceiving others, and (5) engaging in impression management (Edinger and Patterson, 1983; Patterson, 1985). In general, the initiation of the social control function might be expected when a person has an identifiable purpose in influencing his or her interaction partner. In the example in Table 1, the pattern of high nonverbal involvement in seeking a favor is likely to increase the effectiveness of the request. This particular tactic may facilitate compliance if the pattern of high involvement leads either to increased liking or, simply, to increased pressure on the friend. It is assumed that the person who engages in social control has some general awareness of his or her behavioral agenda (e.g. to be assertive or to be especially attentive), even though the person may be unaware of managing specific behaviors to achieve those ends. Consequently, social control behavior is typically communicative.

Even in the ideal, close relationship, it is naive to assume that interpersonal behavior is always spontaneous. Partners frequently attempt to influence the judgements, feelings, decisions, and behavior of one another, often for the best of reasons. Such attempts typically include some management of nonverbal behavior. Touch and direct gaze may be especially important in inducing compliance to simple requests in strangers (e.g. Kleinke, 1977, 1980; Patterson, Powell and Lenihan, 1986; Willis and Hamm, 1980). Such tactics are, undoubtedly, components of successful influence among intimates too.

A comparison between the intimacy and social control functions in relationships can provide some insight into the quality of these relationships. McAdams' (1984) distinction between the intimacy and power motives in relationships is especially relevant here, and runs parallel to my contrast between the intimacy and social control functions. According to McAdams, the intimacy motive reflects commitment or concern, harmony, union, and *surrender of control*. In contrast, the power motive is characterized by *control*, conflict, and influence. McAdams (1984) notes that the intimacy motive was related to reports of intense love and greater satisfaction in couples. Greater intimacy in relationships is likely to be reflected in higher levels of nonverbal involvement, but the converse is not necessarily true. Isolated instances and, in some cases, habitual patterns of high involvement can be managed for social control reasons. In fact, the actor may want his or her partner to infer that the managed behavior is really a spontaneous manifestation of love or concern. Thus, the *form* of both intimacy and social control patterns may be similar but the motives of the actors could be very different.

How does one differentiate between the intimacy and social control functions? Basically, comparisons with the actor's behavior in different situations and behavior of other actors in the same situation have to be considered. In effect, one is applying Kelley's (1971) principle of covariation. If the actor rarely behaves in a highly involved, friendly, or loving way except when he or she is seeking something from a partner, a social control inference is likely to be correct. In addition, if most actors in the same situation behave in a similar highly involved fashion with a partner, then a unique inference of love or intimacy is less likely.

The very existence of a close relationship probably entails an expectancy of both mutual influence and mutual openness to influence. Consequently, social control patterns are not necessarily inconsistent with a positive, intimate relationship. As social control patterns become more pervasive and/or more deceptive, however, those changes may signal a decrease in the intimacy and/or quality of a relationship.

Presentational Function

The fifth category may be termed a *presentational* function because the focus of the individual's behavior is to present or enhance an identity or image, at either the individual or the relationship level. Presentational behavior patterns, like social control patterns, are often purposeful or communicative, designed to influence the reactions of other people. The basic difference between the social control and presentational patterns is in the target of the influence attempt. In social control, the individual's nonverbal behavior is focused on a partner in order to gain compliance, change attitudes, or create a favorable impression. In the presentational function, the purpose is not to influence the partner or even to show liking or love towards the partner (characteristic of the intimacy function) but, rather, to create an identity or image for third-party observers. In Goffman's (e.g. 1959, 1963, 1967, 1971) terminology, the actor is 'performing' for a surrounding 'audience'. In such a circumstance the behavior is necessarily directed towards the interaction partner, but the purpose of that behavior is to fashion an image for a group of observers. A person who wished to be seen as the loving spouse, the considerate parent, or the patient and understanding friend might exaggerate the degree of nonverbal involvement so that observers would form the desired impression.

This function has been termed presentational rather than self-presentation because some presentations are designed to create a relationship or unit identity.

Such performances are often, though not always, collusive in nature. In the example cited in Table 1, the couple may be feuding, but they do agree on trying to present an image of harmony when they are in more public situations. In this function, mutual involvement (in the form of holding hands, mutual gaze, or shared orientations) is not merely interactive but also serves to identify and promote the image of a certain type of a relationship.

Goffman (1971) used the term 'tie-signs' to describe such behaviors when they serve to identify a relationship, whereas Scheflen (1974; Scheflen and Ashcraft, 1976) used the term 'withness cues' to describe similar types of behaviors. The interactive behaviors of partners in close relationships are more likely to become presentational when they enter more public social settings. Holding hands, standing close, or sharing a common focus of attention can signal that the partners have a relational identity. Scheflen (1974, pp. 58–60) proposed that withness cues facilitate order in the larger social group by identifying the specific subgroup boundaries. To the extent that a particular pair is less well known in a given setting, we might expect that there would be greater pressure to initiate tie-signs or withness signals. More extensive involvement, that might include additional touch or gaze between partners, may also reflect a different aspect of the presentational function. Specifically, such close involvement may signal that a given pair is not only a 'couple', but also that they have an intimate relationship. Of course, such behavior can be conveniently managed for an audience that may value such relationships. If such high levels of behavioral involvement are seen only on important 'public' occasions, then such patterns are likely to reflect the presentational function and not the intimacy function.

Presentational patterns may often be initiated mutually in the form of a scripted routine, but they can also be initiated by just one member of a pair. For example, if a person is concerned about his or her own image as the 'loving' spouse, such a person is more likely to touch, gaze, or attend to the partner than *vice versa*. Similarly, the jealous individual may stake his or her claim to the partner by initiating a high level of nonverbal involvement towards the partner. Deliberate avoidance or indifference towards a partner is also an example of the presentational function. That is, exaggerated noninvolvement may be designed to show observers that the relationship is not a close one. A presentational pattern of indifference can be a negative indicator of the quality of the relationship, but it may also be a response to what the individual feels is appropriate or desirable to observers.

Affect Management

This function identifies adjustments in interactive behavior that regulate the experience of affect, especially that of strong affect. In most cases, affect management patterns are spontaneous or indicative. Negative affective reactions such as embarrassment, shame and social anxiety that are characterized by high levels of public self-consciousness often result in decreased gaze or some other form of avoidance (Buss, 1980; Chapters 8 and 9). Stronger negative affect might even lead to turning away and increasing distance from others. Other types of negative affect may literally induce a need for contact with others. Affective reactions such as fear often bring individuals together to support or comfort one another (Schachter, 1959). In a similar fashion, grieving individuals may be consoled by hugs or embraces from others. Consequently, one set of negative reactions, such as embarrassment, shame, and guilt, typically leads to greater avoidance of others, whereas fear and grief typically lead to greater involvement with others.

In contrast, the highly positive affect, described in the example in Table 1, leads people to share the news with others and celebrate it with hugs, kisses, and laughter. Even our most masculine sports heroes share embraces or 'fanny-slapping' after scores or other important plays. More generally, the surprise, excitement, or happiness that may result from success, achievement, or good fortune frequently lead to intense, if only brief, exchanges with surrounding others, especially if they are friends or loved ones. Such intense exchanges may be the result of attempting to 'share' one's feelings. In this case, as in the case of negative affects such as fear and grief, inhibitions against public displays of intimate involvement are typically reduced.

The relevance of affect management for close relationships is substantial. First, in the cases of fear and grief, more support and consolation might be expected from loved ones than from friends or acquaintances. Furthermore, such support and consolation are likely to lead to greater behavioral involvement than that expressed by those with whom we are less intimate. The experience of positive affective states such as happiness, joy, or simple good fortune is likely to be intensified if shared with loved ones. In turn, such exchanges are likely to include hugs, kisses, or other forms of behavioral involvement. In a similar fashion, guilt, embarrassment, and shame are likely to be experienced more intensely with loved ones than with strangers. In such instances, behavioral avoidance is likely to be more intense in a close relationship than in other relationships. Of course, in close, positive relationships the person's partner may offer support to overcome the intense negative feelings.

In effect, intense affect in the presence of others often leads to behavioral adjustments that serve to maximize the positive affect and minimize the negative affect. Furthermore, it is assumed that the partner in a close relationship is more likely to complement the actor's behavior in managing the affect, i.e. sharing the positive affect and providing support or comfort to help alleviate the negative affect.

Service–Task

The service–task function concerns those instances in which service or task goals primarily determine patterns of nonverbal involvement. Consequently, the variable involvement required across different types of service relationships or determined by various task requirements is essentially impersonal. For example, a physician's high level of tactile involvement with a patient in a physical examination is an integral part of that professional service. Task or activity constraints may require that individuals position themselves in very close arrangements in one situation or very distant arrangements in another situation. For the most part, behavior determined by service or task constraints is not directly relevant for close relationships. Nevertheless, service or task settings may be important because they often provide the context in which people meet and relationships form.

CONCLUSIONS

This chapter started with an overview of approaches to analyzing close relationships. It was suggested that most theoretical approaches could be identified as emphasizing either the critical components or the developmental stages of close relationships. In contrast, the approach outlined in this chapter emphasized an analysis of interactive behavior in close relationships. If there is utility in viewing relationships, not as states, but as interactive processes (Duck and Sants, 1983), then those processes will be reflected in the way in which partners *behave* towards one another. Furthermore, nonverbal behavior, more than verbal behavior, becomes the subtle, yet efficient, vehicle for transmitting affect and intention to one's partner.

Although nonverbal behavior is usually relatively spontaneous, like verbal behavior it can also be quite deliberate. Consequently, it is important to examine not only the form or pattern of behavior, but also the apparent functions served by that behavior. In this chapter, it was proposed that comparative information, both within an individual over time and across individuals in similar situations, may permit inferences about the functions served by nonverbal behavior. The relative efficiency of different functional patterns may also be a useful indicator of the quality of relationships. For example, in close relationships, fewer nonverbal cues, either spontaneous or deliberate in nature, will be needed to transmit specific feelings or reactions. In addition, the efficiency of nonverbal cues in regulating interaction should increase with increasingly closer relationships. Perhaps more importantly, the relative frequency of spontaneous (expressing intimacy, affect management) versus deliberate (social control, presentational) functions may provide insights into the quality and health of relationships. If there is a great deal of interpersonal behavior that is managed and deliberate, then that might suggest that the partners do not feel comfortable being spontaneous or that there is little communality from which spontaneity might flow. On the other hand, it is probably naive to assume, even in the closest relationships, that partners can always be spontaneous and always expect 'automatic' compatibility. The functional approach, focusing on patterns of nonverbal behavior, provides a new and potentially useful means for examining these and other important issues in close relationships.

Handbook of Personal Relationships
Edited by S. W. Duck
© 1988 John Wiley & Sons Ltd

4

The Analysis of Data from Two-Person Relationships

DAVID A. KENNY
University of Connecticut, Storrs, Connecticut, USA

ABSTRACT

Data from dyads can either be comparative (different dyads are compared) or time series (the same dyad is studied over time). Comparative designs can either be standard or each person can interact with multiple partners. Methods for measuring nonindependence and covariation are presented for comparative designs. Measures of mutual influence and cycling are presented for time-series designs.

Those of us interested in studying dyadic or two-person relationships have been forced to rely on methods that were developed for the study of agricultural problems. Analysis of variance was developed by statisticians primarily to study methods of improving crop yields. These methods were adapted for experimental psychology and survey research. Unfortunately, they are inadequate for the study of interpersonal relations. As a result, all too often some of the more interesting questions in two-person social interaction cannot be adequately addressed by mainstream statistical methods. For this reason, researchers are often forced to translate their interesting research questions into rather boring, mundane issues. There are, however, new techniques reflecting the structure of the questions that we really want to answer.

There are unique aspects of two-person social interaction that make standard methods difficult to apply. First, and perhaps foremost, social relationships are two-sided. It cannot be claimed that one person is the stimulus person and the other the subject. Or to use the jargon of accuracy research, that one is the perceiver and the other the target. Persons in social interaction play both roles, and to pretend that they do not is to avoid studying social relationships as they occur naturally. Of course, one can design a confederate study so that only one person can influence the other, but such studies have limited generalizability as well as many other problems (Duncan and Fiske, 1985, pp. 6–13).

The second key aspect of social interaction is the difficulty of determining who influences whom even if the interaction is one-sided. If husbands tend to smile more often after their wives gaze at them, are the wives controlling the smiling behavior of their husbands? Or are the husbands' smiles reinforcing and so controlling the gazing behavior of their wives? This example illustrates how issues of causality can become quite murky when studying interpersonal behavior (cf chapter by Mills and Grusec on parent–child interaction). Causal priority issues, which are difficult to resolve in other disciplines, are virtually insoluble in the study of two-person relationships.

A third aspect of dyadic interaction is that the members can often be distinguished only by some arbitrary means. Say a researcher wants to measure reciprocity of attraction in roommates. To compute the correlation between two roommates' liking scores, it is arbitrary which roommate's score is used as the X variable and which is used as the Y variable. This indistinguishable aspect of the dyad members can greatly complicate the analysis of dyadic data. If dyad members can be distinguished only by some arbitrary means (as opposed to a nonarbitrary distinction such as race or sex), the dyad members will be said to be *indistinguishable*.

A fourth difficulty in dyadic research is the level of analysis. Should the person or the dyad be treated as the unit of analysis? It may not be possible to use person as the unit because the two scores within each dyad are not independent (an issue that will be discussed in the next section). However, there may still be a need to generalize the results to the individual level. So statistical considerations may make it difficult to test theories that operate at a certain level of analysis.

Unfortunately, many of the standard statistical tools do not adequately address these and other special questions posed by social relationship data. The more recent methods described in this chapter were designed to be responsive to these special problems.

There are two major approaches to the study of dyads. One can either study many dyads, or intensively study a single or a few dyads over time. I will call the former design a *comparative* design and the latter a *time-series* design. While the two strategies can be blended (e.g. Gottman, 1979), most dyadic research focuses on one to the other's exclusion. This chapter will consider both of these strategies. I shall first consider comparative designs and then time-series designs.

In a comparative design, one studies a set of persons who are in different dyads. There are two major classes of design: the *standard dyadic design* in which each person has one and only one partner (by far the most frequent type) and the *multiple partner design* in which each person rates or interacts with more than one partner. An important type of data structure resulting from multiple partner designs is a set of sociometric ratings.

I will not consider designs in which all persons interact with the same partner. Such studies are typically confederate studies and are handled by standard methods. Also, when the dyad produces a joint score (e.g. productivity), standard methods can be used. Finally, studies in which only one of the two dyad members is measured will not be considered.

THE STANDARD DYADIC DESIGN

For the standard dyadic design, two topics will be discussed: independence of the two persons' responses and covariation between variables. The independence question concerns the relationship between two persons' scores on the same variable. The covariation question concerns the effect of some external or 'predictor' variable (often called the independent variable) on the other variable.

Before I detail how to analyze this type of data, I want to discuss a common practice that should be avoided if possible. One should avoid taking the two scores from each dyad and combining them to form an index. Examples of such indices are similarity, agreement, and accuracy. It is best to consult the classic paper by Cronbach (1955), which details the problems with these type of scores. The major problem is that a single global score often contains within it various components and it is not known to which component the result refers. It is almost always better to compute scores across a set of dyads instead of within each dyad. For instance, if one wishes to assess how similar a husband and a wife are, one should not create a discrepancy score (the absolute value of the difference between husband and wife), but rather correlate, across dyads, the husband's score with the wife's. There may be cases in which a dyadic index offers the only reasonable alternative, but the researcher should first consider alternative strategies that do not involve creating a global dyadic index. Cronbach *et al.* (1972) say the following:

> The claim that an index has validity as a measure of some construct carries a considerable burden of proof. There is little reason to believe and much empirical reason to disbelieve the contention that some . . . weighted function of . . . variables will properly define a construct. More often, the profitable strategy is to use the . . . variables separately in the analysis to allow for more complex relationships. (p. 339)

Assessing Nonindependence

If both members of the dyad are measured, it is likely that their scores are correlated or not independent. If person is used as the unit of analysis and dyad is ignored in the analysis, the independence assumption is likely to be violated and the significance test results are likely to be misleading. The error of using person as the unit of analysis when the data are nonindependent is unfortunately quite common. For instance, Sarason *et al.* (1985), in studying the interactions between socially skilled and unskilled persons, used person as the unit, as did Worobey, Laub and Schilmoeller (1983) in studying how fathers and mothers soothed their infant children.

As Kenny and Judd (1986) show, the bias stemming from using person as the unit of analysis when the data are nonindependent can be considerable. In some cases the test is too liberal (too many Type I errors) while in other cases the test is too conservative (too many Type II errors). Table 1 shows the conditions in which Type I and Type II errors are obtained. Consider a study of married couples involving ten distressed couples and ten nondistressed couples. Say the researcher wants to measure the effects of distress and gender on marital satisfaction. It is likely that the satisfaction scores for each pair of spouses are nonindependent: if the husband is satisfied, the wife tends also to be satisfied. The direction of the correlation between the satisfaction scores is likely to be positive. Examining Table 1, it can be seen that if the effect of distress is tested and person is used as the unit, the F statistic will be too large. If, however, the effect of gender is tested (are husbands more satisfied than wives?), the bias results in too small an F value.

Table 1   Consequences of nonindependence on the test statistic (e.g. F)

Type of variable	Direction of correlation*	
	Positive	Negative
Between-dyad factor†	Too large	Too small
Within-dyad factor‡	Too small	Too large

*For example, the correlation between husband's score and wife's score.
†For example, distressed *versus* nondistressed couples.
‡For example, gender.

In contrast, if there is a negative correlation between dyad members' scores on the dependent variable, the results would reverse. For instance, if the dependent variable is amount of housework done, it is likely that the correlation is negative. That is, although women typically do more housework than men, in marriages in which the man does more than other husbands it is reasonable to expect that his wife does less than other wives. Using Table 1, the test of gender would be too liberal and so F would be too large, and the test of distress would be too conservative and so F would be too small.

There are a number of possible responses to the nonindependence problem that are detailed in Kenny and Judd (1986) and Malloy and Kenny (1986). Briefly, throwing out the data of one person (see for example, Jones, Hobbs and Hockenbury, 1982) is not only wasteful, but it also precludes the examination of various important questions (e.g. reciprocity). Experimental strategies such as using confederates or phantom others prevent persons from interacting.

The analysis of the standard dyadic design should always begin with an analysis of the degree of nonindependence. (The procedures for doing this will be presented shortly.) If the data are independent, then person can be used as the unit of analysis and dyad can be ignored. If the data are not independent, then dyad must be considered in the analysis. Doing so would avoid the most common error in dyadic data analysis: using person as the unit when the data are nonindependent.

Nonindependence is more than a statistical nuisance. An assessment of nonindependence can often answer an important theoretical issue. Consider the variable of gaze: if Alice gazes at Barbara, does Barbara gaze at Alice? Ques-

Why nonindependent as: opp to dependent?

Bill- no particular reason

tions of reciprocity are also referred to as questions of matching, adjustment, coordination, and synchrony. If the direction of the correlation is negative, the nonindependence is usually described as compensation. All of these important theoretical issues can be viewed as issues of nonindependence.

Sometimes the failure to realize that the data may be nonindependent prevents the researcher from asking (and answering) some interesting questions. For instance, Worobey, Laub and Schilmoeller (1983) measured the amount of fussing and crying in infants when they were cared for by both their father and their mother. But by not correlating the child's behavior across partners, the researchers were not able to test whether stable individual differences emerged in the infant's behavior at two weeks of age.

To measure nonindependence when dyad members are distinguishable is straightforward. Consider opposite-sex dyads. The researcher correlates the male's dominance with the female's. So the male's score serves as the X variable and the female's as the Y variable.

However, in dyads with indistinguishable members, there is a problem. It is not clear whose score should be treated as the X variable and whose score should be treated as the Y variable. Behavioral geneticists have the same problem when dealing with data from identical twins when they attempt to measure how correlated the twins are on some phenotype. To solve the problem, behavioral geneticists use the *intraclass correlation* (see below), and this measure should be increasingly used by investigators of social relationships.

Because the intraclass correlation is not well known, I will detail its computation. Consider the data in Table 2 which were taken from Warner *et al.* (1987). They measured the number of cycles in a person's speech, which can be taken as measure of how rhythmic a person's speech is. In this study there were a total of twelve (symbolized by n) dyads and the scores for dyad i are denoted as X_{i1} and X_{i2}. The two scores are said to be *indistinguishable* because it is arbitrary in each dyad whose score is assigned to X_{i1} and whose is assigned to X_{i2}. If the data of those designated as person 1 in Table 2 are correlated with person 2, the correlation is 0.654. But if for the last dyad the scores of persons 1 and 2 are reversed, the correlation changes to 0.722. (As will be seen, both of these values are different from the appropriate value of 0.674.) To avoid the problem of the correlation changing depending on which person is assigned a 1 or 2, the intraclass correlation is used.

For each dyad the following are computed: $m_i = (X_{i1} + X_{i2})/2$ and $d_i = X_{i1} - X_{i2}$. The term M equals the average of all the scores, or in terms of a formula $\Sigma m_i/n$. Next computed is $a = 2\Sigma (m_i - M)^2/(n - 1)$ and $b = \Sigma d^2/(2n)$. For the example in Table 2, a equals 13.920 and b equals 2.708. The intraclass correlation equals $(a - b)/(a + b)$ which is 0.674 for the example. Using analysis of variance terms, the term a is called the mean square between-dyads and b is called the mean square within-dyads.

Like an ordinary correlation, the intraclass correlation for dyads varies from -1 to $+1$. It equals 1 when each dyad member has the same score and the dyad means differ. It equals -1 when the dyad means are the same for every

62

DAVID A. KENNY

Table 2 Intraclass correlation example taken from Warner *et al.* (1987)

dyad *difference* (handwritten)

Dyad	Person 1	2	m *mean for each dyad*	d
1	10	11	10.5	−1
2	9	10	9.5	−1
3	8	6	7.0	2
4	5	5	5.0	0
5	7	2	4.5	5
6	8	5	6.5	3
7	3	3	3.0	0
8	9	9	9.0	0
9	5	5	5.0	0
10	9	9	9.0	0
11	6	10	8.0	−4
12	1	4	2.5	−3

mean of all 24 observations (handwritten)   79.5 (handwritten)

$$M = \frac{79.5}{12} = 6.625$$

# of dyads (handwritten)

to find out whether there is dependence or independence of the data when you have nondistinguishable data (handwritten)

$$a = \frac{2\Sigma (m - M)^2}{n - 1} = \frac{(2)(76.563)}{11} = 13.920$$

estimate of the between dyad variance (handwritten)

$$b = \frac{\Sigma d^2}{2n} = \frac{65}{(2)(12)} = 2.708$$

within dyad variance (handwritten)

$$\text{Intraclass } r = \frac{a - b}{a + b} = \frac{13.920 - 2.708}{13.920 + 2.708} = 0.674$$

$$F = \frac{a}{b} = \frac{13.920}{2.708} = 5.14$$

dyad, but the scores vary within dyads, and so if one dyad member scores high the other scores low.

The intraclass correlation can be tested for statistical significance by an F test. One computes a/b (or b/a if the intraclass correlation is negative) and assigns $n - 1$ and n degress of freedom (or n and $n - 1$ if b/a is computed). Because the test is two-sided, the standard tabled p values of F are divided in half. The F for the example in Table 2 is 5.14 with eleven degrees of freedom on the numerator and twelve on the denominator, a value which is statistically significant at the 0.02 level. The significant intraclass correlation indicates nonindependence. A test that compares two intraclass correlations for different groups is given by Kraemer (1975).

The intraclass correlation illustrates the two sources of variation in dyadic data. The first is variation within-dyads, which is indicated by the difference score. The second is variation between-dyads, which is indicated by the average score. Given normality, these two sources of variance are independent.

Single Dichotomous Independent Variable

Assuming that the test of intraclass is significant, person should not be used as the unit of analysis. Now considered is the problem of measuring covariation between two variables given nonindependence. To simplify the discussion, the independent variable is assumed to be a dichotomy. The independent variable can either be entirely between-dyads, entirely within-dyads, or mixed. Consider the independent variable sex. Sex is between-dyads if all dyads are same sexed, e.g. half are male–male and half are female–female. Sex is a within-dyad variable if in each dyad, one person is male and the other female. Sex is a mixed variable if some of the dyads are same-sex and others are opposite-sex. More precisely, for a between-dyad variable each dyad member has exactly the same score. For a within-dyad variable the sum of the two persons' scores is the same for each dyad.

Another way to define within- and between-dyad variables is by the intraclass correlation. A between-dyad variable (dummy coded if necessary) has an intra-class correlation of $+1$ and a within-dyad variable has an intraclass correlation of -1. A mixed variable has a value somewhere between -1 and $+1$. An examination of the intraclass correlations is useful in determining how a variable should be analyzed.

How can the effects of variables be estimated and tested if there is a single independent variable that is a dichotomy? The specific approach that is taken depends on whether the independent variable is between-dyads, within-dyads, or mixed. For a within-dyad independent variable, difference scores are computed. The difference score is always computed in the same way; for instance, if sex is the within-dyad variable, the sample being married couples, then the male's score is always subtracted from the female's. The test of the within-dyad effect is that the mean of the difference scores equals zero. One should use a matched-pairs t test for interval dependent variables, a sign test for ordinal dependent variables, and a McNemar test (Kenny, 1987) for dichot-omous dependent variables.

If the independent variable is between-dyads, then the averages of the two scores are computed. [Computing averages and differences does not violate the rule presented earlier about computing a dyadic index. The average and differ-ence contain exactly the same information as the two raw scores because the raw scores can be derived from the sum and the difference.] To evaluate whether the scores differ as a function of dyad type, one should use a two-group t for interval dependent variables, a Mann-Whitney test for ordinal dependent variables, or a chi square test of independence for nominal depen-dent variables.

If the independent variable is mixed, the analysis becomes more complicated. The appropriate analysis strategy is to employ a method developed by Kraemer and Jacklin (1979). Because of the importance of their contribution and because most researchers are not familiar with their method (and because there are a few typographical errors in their example), I will extensively detail the procedure using their example.

If the design is mixed, there are three dyad types. To use child's gender (B and G) as an example, each person is a member of one of three dyad types: GG, GB, and BB. Dyads are designated as type 1 (GG), type 2 (GB), and type 3 (BB), as in Table 3. The dependent variable is frequency of offering one's partner a toy. For each dyad, an average score is computed. Then the mean of these averages is computed for each dyad type. So m_1 is the mean of the GG averages, m_2 the mean of the GB averages, and m_3 the mean of the

Table 3   Kraemer and Jacklin illustration

G G	m_{1i}	G B	m_{2i}	d_{2i}	B B	m_{3i}
3,10	6.5	1,2	1.5	−0.5	2,1	1.5
5,0	2.5	0,0	0.0	0.0	2,1	1.5
2,2	2.0	0,9	4.5	−4.5	1,1	1.0
1,5	3.0	3,2	2.5	0.5	3,3	3.0
3,0	1.5	5,2	3.5	1.5	0,2	1.0
2,3	2.5	2,3	2.5	−0.5	2,0	1.0
2,3	2.5	5,5	5.0	0.0	1,4	2.5
3,0	1.5	0,1	0.5	−0.5	5,4	4.5
2,7	4.5	3,3	3.0	0.0	1,1	1.0
2,3	2.5	5,5	5.0	0.0	1,0	0.5
1,5	3.0	4,3	3.5	0.5	1,4	2.5
5,8	6.5	2,0	1.0	1.0	0,0	0.0
		1,2	1.5	−0.5		
		3,14	8.5	−5.5		
		4,1	2.5	1.5		
		7,2	4.5	2.5		
		0,0	0.0	0.0		
		0,0	0.0	0.0		
		0,0	0.0	0.0		
		3,1	2.0	1.0		
		1,2	1.5	−0.5		
Mean	3.208		2.524	−0.190		1.667
Variance	2.975		4.662	3.212		1.561

Estimates

Actor $= 0.25 \{3.208 + 2(-0.190) - 1.667\} = 0.290$
Partner $= 0.25 \{3.208 - 2(-0.190) - 1.667\} = 0.480$
Interaction $= 0.25 \{3.208 - 2(2.524) + 1.667\} = -0.043$

Standard errors

$$\text{Actor \& partner} = 0.25\sqrt{\frac{2.975}{12} + \frac{4(3.212)}{21} + \frac{1.561}{12}} = 0.249$$

$$\text{Interaction} = 0.25\sqrt{\frac{2.975}{12} + \frac{4(4.662)}{21} + \frac{1.561}{12}} = 0.281$$

Z tests

Actor   1.16
Partner   1.92
Interaction   −0.15

BB averages. The variances of the averages can also be computed and are designated as s_1^2, s_2^2, and s_3^2. For the GB dyads a difference score is computed and is divided by two. The difference involves subtracting the B score from the F score, or more generally type 3 from type 1. The mean of these differences divided by two is designated as d_2 and the variance of the differences as s_4^2.

The Kraemer–Jacklin model has three parameters. Again using the example in Table 3, the variable is child's gender and girls will be compared to boys. First, the *actor* effect measures girls' tendency, relative to boys, to offer a toy to their partner. The *partner* effect measures the tendency for the girls to be offered a toy more than boys are offered. The *interaction* effect involves the interaction of actor and partner. It measures whether same-sex dyads have more toy offers than opposite-sex interactions. The interaction is a between-dyad variable whereas actor and partner are mixed variables.

A second example might help. If the dependent variable is interruptions and the independent variable is sex (as in Dindia, 1987) and men are compared to women, the actor effect measures whether men interrupt more than women, the partner effect measures whether men are interrupted more than women, and the interaction measures whether there are more interruptions in same *versus* opposite-sex interactions.

The estimates of the parameters of the Kraemer–Jacklin model are:

Actor: $(m_1 + 2d_2 - m_3)/4$

Partner: $(m_1 - 2d_2 - m_3)/4$

Interaction: $(m_1 - 2m_2 + m_3)/4$

So for the example in Table 3, the actor and partner effects are positive. Girls are more likely than boys to offer a toy and to be offered a toy. The interaction is negative but small; it indicates slightly fewer toy offers in same- versus opposite-sex dyads. The Kraemer–Jacklin standard error for both the actor and partner effect is:

$$0.25\sqrt{\frac{s_1^2}{n_1} + \frac{4s_4^2}{n_2} + \frac{s_3^2}{n_3}}$$

and for interaction, the standard error is:

$$0.25\sqrt{\frac{s_1^2}{n_1} + \frac{4s_2^2}{n_2} + \frac{s_3^2}{n_3}}$$

To test the null hypotheses of no effect, a Z is formed by taking each estimate and dividing by its standard error. If the absolute value of Z exceeds 1.96, the estimate is deemed statistically significant at the 0.05 level. For other significance levels, a Z table can be consulted. For the example in Table 3, none of three terms are significant, although the partner effect is marginally significant. These tests are not exact and hold only for large samples.

There is a small sample test of interaction because it is a between dyad variable and not mixed. The interaction effect when divided by the following expression has a t distribution with $n_1 + n_2 + n_3 - 3$ degrees of freedom:

$$0.25\sqrt{\left(\frac{1}{n_1} + \frac{4}{n_2} + \frac{1}{n_3}\right)\left(\frac{(n_1 - 1)\,s_1{}^2 + (n_2 - 1)\,s_2{}^2 + (n_3 - 1)\,s_3{}^2}{n_1 + n_2 + n_3 - 3}\right)}$$

This test presumes that the variances of the dyad means are the same for three dyad types, the usual homogeneity of variance assumption.

A necessary consideration is the effect of sample allocation on power. Like the ordinary between-dyad test, power is maximized for a fixed overall sample size when n_1 equals n_3. To maximize power of the interaction test, n_2 should equal $2n$ where $n = n_1 = n_3$. But to maximize the power of the test of actor and partner effects, $n_2/2n$ should equal $(1 - r)/(1 + r)$ where r is the correlation between dyad member scores which is assumed to be the same for the three dyad types. Note that if $r = 0$, then $n_2 = 2n$. So a simple rule of thumb is to have about twice as many type 2 dyads as type 1 or type 3 dyads, and if r is large then the number of type 2 dyads should be lessened, but if r is negative then have more than twice as many type 2 dyads.

Seay and Kay (1983) discuss an extension of the Kraemer and Jacklin model to include an additional within-dyad factor, and Mendoza and Graziano (1982) provide a multivariate test. Wasserman and Iacobucci (1986) have modified the analysis for nominal and ordinal dependent variables.

Multiple Independent Variables

Despite all the complications of the preceding section, only a relatively simple case in the analysis of dyads was presented—one with a single independent variable which is a dichotomy. Most studies of dyads contain multiple independent variables, some of which are not dichotomies. The analysis strategies for these cases are briefly sketched below. At issue for each are within- and between-dyad analyses.

No within-dyad variables

If there are no within-dyad variables and so all the independent variables are between-dyads, one can treat dyad as the unit of analysis. One then treats the mean score of the two persons as the dependent variable. If the between-dyad independent variables are continuous, then multiple regression can be used to estimate effects. If the between-dyad independent variables are categorical, analysis of variance can be used.

For instance, Berndt (1981) studied 114 grade school children. He created 57 dyads by pairing a child with either a friend or an acquaintance. Between-dyad factors were sex, grade, and relationship (friend *versus* acquaintance). There were no within-dyad factors. Because the between-dyad factors are all categorical, analysis of variance can be used.

Single within-dyad variable

Ickes (1984) studied same-sexed interracial dyads. Only one variable varied within dyads and that was race. Between-dyad factors were sex of the dyad members, race of the emperimenter, and racial attitude of the white member. For this type of design, two analyses are done. In the first, the difference score is used as the dependent variable and the between-dyad variables are used as independent variables. The test that the mean of the difference score equals zero evaluates the effect of the within-dyad variable. The interactions of the within-dyad variable with the between-dyad variables are the 'main effects' of the between-dyad variables in this analysis. The second analysis uses the dyad average as the dependent variable and from this analysis the effects of the between-dyad variables can be estimated and tested.

Repeated measures analysis of variance can simultaneously accomplish these two analyses. Dyad is the unit in the analysis, and the within-dyad variable is the repeated measure. So if sex is within-dyads, then sex would be treated as the repeated measure with dyad as the 'subject'.

Continuous mixed variable

Say that age, continuously measured, is the independent variable. Age may then vary between- and within-dyads and so would be a mixed independent variable. The within-dyad effects can be estimated by computing difference scores of both age and the dependent variable and then regressing the latter on the former. The between-dyad effects are estimated by regressing the dyad average of the dependent variable on the mean age of the dyad.

To estimate the terms of the Kraemer and Jacklin model, one proceeds as follows:

Actor: (between + within)/2
Partner: (between − within)/2

where *between* refers to the between-dyad regression coefficient and *within* to the within-dyad coefficient. Continuing with the age example, the actor effect measures whether a person engages in more of a behavior if he or she is older. The partner effect measures the effect of the age of one's partner on one's behavior. One would need to pool the between and within standard errors by a method described by Erlebacher (1977) to test these effects. The measurement of the actor–partner interaction would involve computing a product term: a person's age times his or her partner's age.

Two Random Variables

The previous discussion presumes that the independent variable is fixed. Fixed variables, in this context, are variables not affected by dyadic processes. Variables such as sex, age, and experimental condition can be safely treated as fixed. Also, variables whose values are set before the dyad is formed can be treated as fixed, for example, personality variables. But if one seeks to measure the correlation between what are essentially two dependent variables, then complications arise. For instance, if one wished to correlate gaze duration with smile duration, neither variable is fixed and both are random. Kenny (1985) discusses the distinction between fixed and random variables in this context.

More complicated procedures must be used to estimate the effects of random variables, especially for the between-dyad analysis. Kenny and La Voie (1985) present the details for these analyses. The within-dyad or person-level analyses are essentially the same as in the previous analyses. Within each dyad, the dyad mean is subtracted from each person's score. It is these adjusted scores that are used to compute the within-dyad correlations. This analysis is virtually the same as creating a difference score for each dyad.

The between-dyad or group analysis is more complicated. For each dyad, the group means are created. In a fixed variable analysis, these means would be correlated and interpreted. But in a random variable analysis, the between-dyad correlations are adjusted by the within-dyad correlations. The reason for this is that when variables are random, person-level variation is contained in the dyad means. To return to the gaze example, variation between dyads in gaze is due, in part, to individual differences. Even if persons are randomly assigned to dyads, persons in some dyads will have a disposition to gaze more than persons in other dyads. The proper dyad-level correlation needs to remove chance, individual-level variation. The formulas for these adjusted dyad-level correlations are given in Kenny and La Voie (1985) and a computer program was developed by Kenny and Stigler (1983). (The program can be used to estimate correlations at both the within- and between-dyad levels. It also computes intraclass and partial intraclass correlations.)

Although the correlations are legitimate estimates of the dyad-level correlations, they are not ordinary, computed product-moment correlations. Because of this, the correlations have some unusual properties. First, the between-dyad correlations cannot be tested for significance by the standard test of significance. Even more troubling, these correlations can be out of range, larger in absolute value than 1. To avoid the out-of-range problem, one should compute between-dyad correlations only if both variables have significant between-dyad variance which is indicated by a significant positive intraclass correlation. Kenny (1985) and Kenny and La Voie (1985) contain more information on these matters. A third problem is that the dyad-level correlations, even if they are not out of range, are often very large, in the 0.70s and 0.80s. This happens because the dyad-level correlations have little or no measurement error and because the variables that we often study have relatively poor discriminant validity.

There are no published examples using the method that was developed for the correlation of random variables. As this brief review indicates, there are many computational and interpretational complexities. This is an area where we need statistical work that will give us a dyad-level test of significance and better understanding of why the correlations are often too large. Perhaps too, if we had stronger theories that would predict different processes for persons and dyads, the method would have a chance to prove itself by uncovering subtle yet theoretically meaningful results.

Correlational Structure

If there is a single within-dyad variable (for instance, all the dyads are opposite-sex pairs), tests of the difference between the correlational structure of the two types of persons can be made. Normally one would want to evaluate whether the covariance matrices are equal. Alternatively, the correlation matrices can be compared. Tests of the difference in correlational structure can be accomplished by LISREL VI (Jöreskog and Sörbom, 1986).

In Table 4 is a set of correlations of five intimacy variables from husbands and wives. The five intimacy variables are taken from a measure developed by Schaefer and Olson (1981). The intimacy measures are emotional, social, sexual, intellectual, and recreational. The data, gathered by Acitelli (1986), are taken from 42 couples. Using LISREL VI, the test that the correlations for husbands are not equal to those for wives is $\chi^2 (10) = 5.18$. Because the chi square is not significant, the set of correlations for husbands do not significantly differ from the set for wives. The test that the covariance matrices are equal is $\chi^2 (15) = 7.26$, which is also not significant.

One can also compare the correlation matrices by a test developed by Kenny and Harackiewicz (1979) for longitudinal data. Their test allows for the fact that the correlations may differ because of difference in communality across dyad members. For instance, there may be more reliable variance in the husbands' data than in the wives'. Also possible is the more complicated pattern that some variables have more communality for husbands and some have more for wives. Using the Kenny and Harackiewicz test, the correlation matrices corrected for changes in communality are not significantly different,

Table 4 Correlations and standard deviations (on the diagonal) for five intimacy variables (42 married couples). Data taken from Acitelli (1986)

	1	2	3	4	5	1	2	3	4	5
Husband										
1	16.17									
2	0.329	19.50								
3	0.550	0.139	18.60							
4	0.662	0.270	0.465	17.42						
5	0.268	0.336	0.309	0.296	13.32					
Wife										
1	0.492	−0.138	0.356	0.344	0.132	16.39				
2	0.396	0.543	0.172	0.098	0.217	0.175	16.93			
3	0.433	−0.203	0.579	0.377	0.091	0.514	0.016	17.80		
4	0.411	−0.075	0.306	0.454	0.218	0.675	0.037	0.471	16.17	
5	0.171	−0.099	0.113	0.159	0.481	0.327	0.064	0.145	0.388	14.08
	1	2	3	4	5	1	2	3	4	5
		Husband					Wife			

1 = Emotional, 2 = Social, 3 = Sexual, 4 = Intellectual, 5 = Recreational.

$\chi^2 (5) = 2.83$. (The communality ratios, while not significant, show that husbands had higher communalities for Social and Sexual while for Intellectual and Recreational the communalities were higher for wives.) So regardless of how the test is done for this data set, the matrices do not appear to differ significantly.

MULTIPLE PARTNER DESIGNS

In a multiple partner design, each person is paired with more than one person. The prototypical multiple partner design is the round robin design. In a round robin design, persons rate or interact with all possible partners. For example, if there is a set of ten six-person groups, in every six-person group each person would rate or interact with the five other persons in his or her group. An example of a round robin design is presented in Table 5. Six persons state their attraction on a 20-point scale. John's liking of Bill is 15 while Bill's liking of John is 11. The rows of the table can be called *actors* and the columns are called *partners*.

A second type of multiple partner design is the block design. In a block design persons are put in two groups and each person interacts with every person in the other group. Referring to Table 5, the design would be a block design if the first three actors (John, Paul, and Mike) rated the second three (Bill, Dave, and Phil) and *vice versa*, but there were no 'ingroup' ratings. An important special case of the block design is the checkerboard design. In this design, the two persons rate or interact with two other persons. Referring to Table 5, the design would be a checkerboard if the first two actors (John and Paul) rated the second two (Mike and Bill) and *vice versa*. Checkerboard designs are especially useful in social interaction studies because persons need only interact with two partners.

There are a number of advantages that are provided by multiple partner designs. First, the consistency of a person's behavior across interaction partners can be examined. For instance, looking across the rows of Table 5, it can be determined whether some persons generally like the others that they meet. It appears that John generally likes his partners whereas Dave does not. Second, the effect of a person on his or her interaction partners can be measured. For instance, looking down the columns of Table 5, it can be determined whether some persons are liked more than others. It appears that Bill is liked by others and that Phil is not. Finally and most importantly for those of us interested in

Table 5. Round robin example. From Kenny (1986a, p. 306)

Actor	Partner John	Paul	Mike	Bill	Dave	Phil
John		12	12	15	15	10
Paul	9		4	13	11	4
Mike	14	9		15	15	9
Bill	11	8	7		9	7
Dave	6	8	7	8		4
Phil	12	10	8	15	13	

relational phenomena, it can be asked whether in a given dyad, one person likes his partner more than would be expected given the two previous effects: that is, more than the tendency for the one person to like others in general and more than the tendency for the partner to be generally liked by others. In Table 5, it appears that Bill and Dave do not like each other very much even though other people like them.

These three effects embody the social relations model (Kenny and La Voie, 1984; Malloy and Kenny, 1986). Assume that one measures how much Alice smiles when interacting with Betty. According to the model, Alice's smiling is a function of how much she smiles at others in general (Alice's actor effect), how much people in general smile when interacting with Betty (Betty's partner effect), and how much Alice uniquely smiles when interacting with Betty (Alice's relationship effect with Betty). To separate relationship effects from error, the behavior must be observed on two or more occasions or measured by two or more indicators.

A major use of the social relations model is to apportion variance into actor, partner, and relationship. An example of variance partitioning from Montgomery and Kenny (1987) is given in Table 6. One hundred and twenty-eight undergraduates taking a course were assigned to one of 29 groups. Group sizes were four and five. In each group, persons rated each other three times during the semester on effectiveness and leadership. Because persons rated every one in the group, the design is round robin. Also, because the ratings were made using two measures, there are replications and the combined measure will be referred to as *competence*. The results in Table 6 show declining actor variance. Thus, the tendency for some persons to see all their partners as competent and other persons to see all their partners as incompetent declined over time. There is substantial partner variance at all three times, and this variance increases over time. That is, some persons appear to be competent to all their interaction partners whereas others appear to be incompetent. There is relationship variance at all three times. So a person tended to view a partner as competent (and others did not necessarily) at all three times.

A second major use of the model is to measure reciprocity. Consider again the data in Table 5. If the data are considered as belonging to fifteen different dyads, reciprocity of attraction can be measured by an intraclass correlation. For the data in the table, the intraclass correlation is -0.38. But that correlation actually measures a combination of individual and dyadic reciprocity. The individual-level correlation relates the actor and partner effects. For attraction it measures whether persons who generally like others are liked, in turn, by

Table 6   Per cent variance of competence at three times. Data from Montgomery and Kenny (1987)

Time	Actor	Partner	Relationship
I	27	37	36
II	9	40	51
III	8	48	44

others. The dyadic-level correlation correlates relationship effects. It measures the extent to which if a person likes a particular partner, the partner returns that liking. The dyadic correlation more closely corresponds to reciprocity than does the individual-level correlation. The dyadic correlation can be viewed as an intraclass correlation of the relationship effects; that is, the actor and partner effects have been removed. The dyadic correlation for the data in Table 5 is 0.65, which is quite impressive because if actor and partner effects are ignored the correlation is −0.38.

The model has been applied to data concerning reciprocity of attraction (Kenny and La Voie, 1982) and reciprocity of self-disclosure (Miller and Kenny, 1986). Other applications have been in the areas of interpersonal perception (Kenny, 1988a), small group process (Montgomery, 1984c), accuracy (DePaulo et al., 1987; Kenny and Albright, 1988), and marital dyads (Sabatelli, Buck and Kenny, 1986).

Currently a major focus is applying the social relations model to the study of close, two-person relationships. Three different approaches are being developed. First, Kenny (1988b) shows how special dyads differ from ordinary dyads in terms of the social relations model. A special dyad would be a married couple or best friends, while an ordinary dyad would be an unmarried couple or acquaintances. Second, Stevenson et al. (1988) have applied the model to the study of families. In their study they created dyads in which fathers and mothers played with two of their children. Third, Kenny and Acitelli (1987) have developed a method by which couple measures of accuracy, agreement, or similarity can be studied by forming such indices using both real and pseudo couples.

Social relations analyses, while very informative, do have their limitations. First, they require extensive data collection because of the requirement of multiple partners. Second, the data analysis requires specialized software (Kenny, 1986b, c). Third, because the terms are new, it can be very difficult to understand and interpret the results. In spite of all these difficulties, the model should be increasingly applied.

SOCIOMETRIC DATA

One special form of multiple partner data is a sociometric data set. With sociometric data, the response variable is typically a dichotomy. Table 7 gives

Table 7. Sociometric data (artificial data)

Actor	Target A	B	C	D	E	F
A	—	1	1	0	1	0
B	1	—	1	1	0	0
C	1	1	—	1	0	1
D	0	1	1	—	1	1
E	1	0	0	1	—	1
F	0	1	1	1	0	—

1, like; 0, dislike.

an example of a sociometric data set. Liking is indicated by a 1, while a zero indicates dislike. For instance, actor A likes targets B, C, and E and does not like D and F. Although the usual sociometric relation is liking, many other possible relations such as status, dependency, and familiarity can be examined.

The modern analysis of sociometric data uses log linear models. Considered here is one illustration, how to measure reciprocity. The matrix of zeros and ones as in Table 7 is converted to an $n \times n \times 2 \times 2$ table where n is the number of actors. The four variables are denoted as A through D. Variable A can be called actor, variable B partner, variable C denotes whether the actor likes the partner, and variable D denotes whether the partner likes the actor. An entry in the table is either zero or 1. Formally, an entry into the table, f_{ijkm}, is defined as follows:

$f_{ij11} = 1$ if person i likes j and j likes i
$f_{ij12} = 1$ if person i likes j and j does not like i
$f_{ij21} = 1$ if person i does not like j and j likes i
$f_{ij22} = 1$ if person i does not like j and j does not like i

Started to get lost here ↓

If a cell entry is not 1 it is zero. It follows that for every actor–partner pair only one of their four entries equals 1 and the other three are zero. More formally: $f_{ij11} + f_{ij12} + f_{ij21} + f_{ij22} = 1$. Since for each dyad one can be considered the actor and the other the partner, each dyad is entered twice and it follows that $f_{ijkm} = f_{jimk}$. The diagonals of the four $n \times n$ tables are set *a priori* to zero.

In log linear models subtables of the full table are fitted. To test for reciprocity, two log linear models are fitted:

Model I: AB, AC, AD, BC, BD
Model II: AB, AC, AD, BC, BD, CD

The adequacy of each model can be evaluated by the usual chi square goodness of fit test. However, for various reasons the likelihood ratio test is used. It can be interpreted like an ordinary chi square and is usually symbolized by G^2. Because each dyad is used twice, the G^2 from computer programs must be divided by two.

The degree of association in the CD table measures the degree of reciprocity. Note that it is a 2×2 table whose cells contain the number of pairs who reciprocate either liking or disliking.

The test of reciprocity is given by the difference between the G^2 values of model I from model II, which is a G^2 with one degree of freedom. If this chi square difference is significant, then reciprocity is indicated. For the data in Table 7, the G^2 for model I is 39.45, and for model II the G^2 is 31.06. Differencing the two chi squares, the test of reciprocity is 8.39. Since this G^2 with one degree of freedom is significant, reciprocity is indicated. An examination of the CD effect under model II shows that reciprocity is positive: if A likes B, B likes A, or if A dislikes B, B dislikes A.

There are other possible measures and tests that one can perform with socio-metric data: dominance hierarchies and cliques. Fienberg and Wasserman (1981) and Reitz (1982) should be consulted for detail concerning these and other tests.

TIME-SERIES DESIGNS

While not as frequently used in the study of two-person relationships as comparative designs, time-series designs have provided us with important insights into interpersonal behavior. I need only mention the work by Gottman (1979) on marital dyads, Gottman and Parker (1986) on children's friendship, Duncan and Fiske (1985) on turn-taking, Street and Cappella (1985) on interpersonal communication, Jaffe and Feldstein (1970) on conversations in dyads, and Dabbs and Ruback (1987) on groups, to illustrate the importance of these designs. I will only briefly sketch a few methods that use them. I refer the reader to more detailed sources in this area: Bakeman and Gottman (1986), Gottman (1981), Gottman and Roy (1987), and Bakeman and Dabbs (1976).

Mutual Influence Models

Imagine a researcher who observes a husband and wife interacting over a period of 40 minutes. Every ten seconds the researcher observes whether the husband is smiling and whether the wife is smiling. The 240 data points (six observations a minute times 40 minutes) can be denoted as H_t for husband smiling and W_t for wife smiling. A first-order model presumes that the effect of smiling at any given time is dependent upon the presence or absence of smiling in the previous time period. Once the previous time period is controlled, there remains no relationship between the past and the present. In equation form, the following model is estimated:

$$H_t = aH_{t-1} + bW_{t-1} + U_t$$
$$W_t = cW_{t-1} + dH_{t-1} + V_t$$

The first equation simply states that a husband's smiling at a given time is a function of whether he and his wife were smiling in the previous time period. If b is positive, it would mean that men are more likely to smile at a given time when their wives were smiling at the previous time. The second equation treats the wife's smiling as the dependent variable. The U_t and V_t terms are residual or error terms.

If H and W are continuously measured variables, the estimation could proceed using regression analysis. That is, H_t is regressed on H_{t-1} and W_{t-1}; and W_t is regressed on W_{t-1} and H_{t-1}. Such time-series regressions do require special assumptions (Gottman, 1981). The major difficulty centers around the fact that most data points are used twice, once as a predictor and once as a criterion score in the regression equation. This nonindependence will tend to distort significance test results. There are complicated techniques for controlling for each subject but these methods require either long time series (over 50 observations) or that the type of nonindependence be known in advance.

An alternative, simple procedure is, for each dyad, to use multiple regression to *estimate* (not to test) the coefficients and then do a between-dyad analysis on the within-dyad data. That is, one estimates for each dyad the regression coefficient b (see the above equation) which measures the lagged effect of the wife's behavior on the husband's. Then one does a simple t test to evaluate whether the mean of the bs is significantly different from zero. Such an approach represents a blending of the comparative and time-series approaches.

For dichotomous variables, the model is called a first-order Markov model. Log linear or logistic models are used to estimate such models. There are four variables, H_{t-1}, H_t, W_{t-1}, and W_t. Those four variables give rise to a $2 \times 2 \times 2 \times 2$ table ($H_{t-1}W_{t-1}H_tW_t$) of frequencies as in Table 8. (Data in the table are artificial.) To estimate the first-order Markov model, two log linear models are fitted. First, using the $H_{t-1}W_{t-1}W_t$ table, the $H_{t-1}W_{t-1}$, $H_{t-1}H_t$, and $W_{t-1}H_t$ subtables are fitted. The $W_{t-1}H_t$ parameter measures the effect of the wife on the husband. For the data in Table 8, only the $H_{t-1}H_t$ effect is significant, which indicates that the husband's behavior is stable over time and is not influenced by his wife's prior behavior.

The second model uses the $H_{t-1}W_{t-1}H_t$ table. The $H_{t-1}W_{t-1}$, $W_{t-1}W_t$, and $H_{t-1}W_t$ subtables are fitted. The $H_{t-1}W_t$ parameter measures the effect of husband on wife. In this analysis, using the data in Table 8, both the $W_{t-1}W_t$ and $H_{t-1}W_t$ parameters are significant. So both stability (if the wife smiles at time 1, she smiles at time 2) and influence (if the husband smiles at time 1, the wife tends to smile at time 2) are indicated. Alison and Liker (1982) present a test of difference between the $W_{t-1}H_t$ and $H_{t-1}W_t$ parameters for logistic analysis.

In log linear terms, the model represents fitting all the two-way tables of a three-way table. If these models do not fit then a two-factor interaction is indicated. For instance, it may be that the lagged effect of husband's smiling on his wife's smiling may depend on whether or not the wife is smiling at time 1. For the data in Table 8, neither of these interactions is significant.

Table 8   Husband (H) and wife (W) smiling at times $t - 1$ and t (artificial data)

Time t		Time $t - 1$ H smile				
		Yes		No		
H Smile	W Smile	W Yes	Smile No	W Yes	Smile No	Total
Yes	Yes	25	8	15	6	54
Yes	No	6	15	7	12	40
No	Yes	14	12	18	4	48
No	No	15	8	15	60	98
Total		60	43	55	82	240

Detecting Cycles

In Markov models, the data have limited memories in that current behavior is a function of the immediate past and is not related to the distant past after the immediate past is controlled. An alternative formulation is to examine cycles in the data which have, in a sense, an eternal memory. With time-series data, one can detect regular cycles or rhythms in behavior. For continuous variables, a spectral analysis can be conducted (Gottman, 1981). In such an analysis, the time series is assumed to be a weighted average of sines and cosines. In spectral analysis there is a special type of graph called a *power spectrum*, which shows what cycles are present in the data. In this graph, the X-axis is the *frequency*, which is defined as the number of cycles completed in a given unit of time. So if the cycle length is 30 seconds, the frequency would be two per minute. A frequency of 30 would correspond to a cycle of two seconds. The longer the cycle, the less the frequency. The Y-axis can be interpreted as a measure of how important each frequency is. For instance, if speech data measured in minutes are used and the graph spikes at a frequency of 0.25, then a four-minute cycle would be indicated.

A less elegant but easier method to detect cycles is the *autocorrelagram*. The X-axis of an autocorrelagram is lag length. The Y-axis is the autocorrelation, which is very similar to a correlation. If the time unit is minutes and there is a ten-minute cycle, then there should be large autocorrelation for lag lengths of 10, 20, 30, and so on.

For discrete data, the analog of the autocorrelation function is a graph of conditional probabilities. One graphs $P(A_t A_{t-k})$ as a function of k (Bakeman, 1983). If there are peaks at multiples of some integer, cycling is indicated. Kraemer, Hole and Anders (1984) present various nonparametric methods to detect cycles.

With dyadic data the logical question concerns whether two persons' cycles are synchronized or coordinated. The previous discussion is limited to a single time series, while in social interaction there are two parallel time series. Warner, Waggener and Kronauer (1983) describe in detail how this question can be addressed. They propose the following two criteria. First, if behavior is synchronized, the power spectra of the two persons should be similar. So if one person has three-minute cycles, so should the other. Second, the two cycles should be coordinated. The peaks and valleys of the two cycles should co-occur.

CONCLUSION

Quite a number of techniques have been described. One unfortunate common denominator is that most of these techniques are not available in standard computer packages. If they are available, the analysis must be done in an awkward and inefficient manner. For instance, to compute intraclass correlations one needs to trick the program by treating dyads as groups and then doing an analysis of variance of the group effect. We need a complete, mainframe computer package tailored to dyadic data. The lack of such software is a major reason for the many errors that are made in the analysis of dyadic data.

A major issue is whether to use a comparative or a time-series design. Although the two methods appear to be addressing the same question, they may give different answers. This is especially clear when questions of reciprocity are concerned. Reciprocity in a comparative design asks whether some dyads have high scores and others have low scores; in time-series designs, the question is whether for a given dyad at some times both members score high whereas at other times they both score low. It has been argued that time-series designs are superior to comparative designs (Duncan and Fiske, 1985). Certainly, comparative designs cannot be used to draw inferences about temporally extended processes. However, temporally aggregated data are not necessarily inferior to a fine-grained, moment-by-moment analysis. More data are not always better than fewer data and the different designs can be used to complement each other. For instance, it is not usually recognized that a between-dyad analysis can be done on effects estimated from a within-dyad analysis.

Another emphasis in this chapter is an avoidance of issues of causality. We should avoid issues of who influences whom. This is not to say we should not study dominance or status effects in two-person behavior. But the measures of dominance should not be statistical but should be given by the variables: for example, time speaking, observer ratings, topic control, and interruptions.

Finally, we need to educate researchers studying interpersonal relations about the many important questions they could be answering. All too often we fail to ask many interesting, answerable questions. We fail to utilize fully the interesting data that we collect. While the area is full of methodological landmines, we may have to take our chances of stepping on a few if we are to understand the complexities of dyadic social interaction. We need to encourage methodologists and statisticians to develop and extend methods for the study of personal relationships. Although our data may seem messy and difficult to analyze, the many fascinating things they can tell us would be well worth the effort.

ACKNOWLEDGEMENTS

I would like to thank Linda Acitelli for providing me with data. Special thanks are due to the following persons who provided me with extensive feedback on a prior draft: Linda Acitelli, Roger Bakeman, William Cook, Steve Duck, Nancy Eisenberg, William Ickes, John Gottman, Helena Kraemer, Thomas Malloy, Barbara Montgomery, Rebecca Warner, Stanley Wasserman, Carol Werner, and Stephen West. Support was provided in part by a National Institute for Health Grant RO1 MH4029501.

Handbook of Personal Relationships
Edited by S. W. Duck
© 1988 John Wiley & Sons Ltd

5

The Observational Method: Studying the Interaction of Minds and Bodies

WILLIAM ICKES and WILLIAM TOOKE*
University of Texas at Arlington, Texas, USA

ABSTRACT

An observational method, the dyadic interaction paradigm, can be used to study both the overt behavior and the covert thoughts and feelings of dyad members during a period of unstructured interaction. The paradigm can also be used to assess the dyad members' inferences about each other's thoughts and feelings in order to study aspects of naturalistic social cognition such as metaperspective taking, intersubjectivity, and empathic accuracy.

The observational method has been used extensively in the study of personal relationships. Indeed, if the term 'personal relationships' is defined broadly enough, there are entire disciplines in which the observational method is not only the preferred method for studying such relationships but is the *only viable method* for doing so. Studies by ethologists of the dominance hierarchies found in free-ranging nonhuman primates such as Barbary macaques (Deag, 1977) provide one such example, but we need not look outside the domain of human relationships to find others. The study of the earliest and most fundamental type of human relationship—that of the parent and the infant—has been almost entirely dependent on the use of the observational method (e.g. Ainsworth *et al.*, 1978; Lamb and Gilbride, 1985; Lewis and Rosenblum, 1974; Pedersen, 1980; Stern, 1977).

Even if we restrict our use of the term 'personal relationships' to include only those of human beings who are capable of speech, the range of relationships studied by means of the observational method would still be impressively large. To cite just a few representative examples, the observational method has been applied to the study of children's quarrels (Dawe, 1934) and children's friend-

---

* William Tooke is now at the State University of New York, Plattsburgh.

ships (Gottman and Parker, 1986). It has been used to explore the interactions of poker players (Hayano, 1980), police officers (Rubenstein, 1973), prison inmates (Jacobs, 1974), distressed and nondistressed married couples (Gottman, 1979), and the families of schizophrenics (Cheek and Anthony, 1970). In clinical and counseling psychology, its most common application has been to the study of therapist–client relationships (Jones, Reid and Patterson, 1975; Scheflen, 1974).

The diversity in the types of relationships studied has necessitated a corresponding diversity in the settings for observational research. Although many observational studies are conducted in the psychological laboratory (e.g. Gottman, Markman and Notarius, 1977), others are conducted in settings as varied as an auction (Clark and Halford, 1978), a party (Reisman and Watson, 1964), a playground (Dawe, 1934), a high school (Barker and Gump, 1964), a hospital delivery room (Leventhal and Sharp, 1965), a geriatric ward (Sommer and Ross, 1958), a police station (Holdaway, 1980), a subway train (Fried and DeFazio, 1974), an ocean-going research vessel (Bernard and Killworth, 1973), and the United Nations building (Alger, 1966).

The range of methodologies employed in systematic observational research is similarly large and diverse. As Weick (1985) has noted:

> A staggering variety of procedures and assumptions for inquiry can be assembled loosely under the category of systematic observational methods: participant observation, systematic observational surveys, field research, naturalistic methods, qualitative investigations, ethnography, case study, ecological psychology, professional social inquiry (Lindblom and Cohen, 1979), qualitative evaluation, unobtrusive measures, behavioral ecology, subjective inquiry, Verhesten tradition, ethnomethodology, field experiments, precision journalism, ethology, and behavioral assessment. (p. 568)

We will not attempt to review such methodologies here. Excellent reviews can be found in Weick's (1968, 1985) chapters in the second and third editions of *The Handbook of Social Psychology* and in a variety of other sources (e.g. Barker, 1968; Brandt, 1972; Cone and Hawkins, 1977; Haynes and Wilson, 1979; Hutt and Hutt, 1970; Irwin and Bushnell, 1980; Sechrest, 1979; Willems and Raush, 1969; Wright, 1967). The point of departure for our inquiry begins not with an assessment of the differences among these methodologies, but with the question: what do they all have in common?

The common, and perhaps defining, feature of observational methodologies is the observation and 'selective' recording (Weick, 1968, p. 361) of naturally occurring behavior in social situations. In the typical observational study, the individuals who are doing the observing are trained research personnel, and the behaviors they are selectively recording are the overt, naturally occurring behaviors of people whose responses are not overly biased by the knowledge that they are being studied. The range of methodologies able to meet these conditions is at least as large as that described by Weick (1985). In fact, as he has noted, it is difficult to define the term 'observational method' in a way that excludes very much (Weick, 1968, p. 360).

From this perspective, it may seem a bit ironic that the major point we wish to make in this chapter is that the term 'observational method' should not be defined too narrowly in the study of personal relationships. While we agree that the observational method is typically used to obtain 'objective' data from trained observers about the overt behavior of human subjects, we propose that it can also be used to obtain 'subjective' data from the subjects themselves about their own covert thoughts and feelings. This proposition is based on the notion that subjects, under optimal conditions, can make reliable 'observations' about their own subjective states in a manner analogous to the way that observers, under optimal conditions, can make reliable observations about the subjects' behavior.

It is one thing to claim that the observational method can be used to assess not only the overt behavior displayed by the participants in a relationship but their covert thoughts and feelings as well. It is another thing to document such a claim. In order to do so, we begin by describing the most recent version of an observational paradigm that the first author developed for the unobtrusive study of unstructured dyadic interaction (Ickes, 1982, 1983). Since its inception in 1975, the original version of the 'dyadic interaction paradigm' has repeatedly proved to be an effective means of studying the unstructured, naturally occurring behavior of dyad members in a reliable and unobtrusive way. In the most recent version of the paradigm, procedures have been added that permit the actual thoughts and feelings of the dyad members to be assessed in a manner that is similarly reliable and nonreactive (cf. Cacioppo and Petty, 1981).

After providing a brief overview of the current version of the dyadic interaction paradigm, we continue with a detailed description of its methodological features. We then consider how the recent addition of the thought–feeling assessment procedures has extended the paradigm's capabilities beyond the study of naturalistic social behavior to the study of naturalistic social cognition—in particular, to the study of phenomena such as metaperspective taking, intersubjectivity, and empathic accuracy. Our discussion of the paradigm concludes with a summary of its perceived advantages and disadvantages.

OVERVIEW OF THE DYADIC INTERACTION PARADIGM

Because the dyadic interaction paradigm is used to study a short-term interaction occurring in many separate dyads, it is most appropriately applied in what Kenny (Chapter 4) has referred to as the *standard dyadic design*. In a typical study, the members of each dyad are led into a 'waiting room' and left there together in the experimenter's absence. During this interval while the subjects are ostensibly waiting for the experiment to begin, their verbal and nonverbal behaviors are unobtrusively audio- and videotaped over the course of a five-minute observation period. Any interaction that occurs during this period is essentially spontaneous since the subjects have been given no instruction to interact. When the experimenter returns at the end of the observation period, the subjects receive a partial debriefing. They are then asked for their signed consent to (a) release the tape of the interaction for use as data in the study, and (b) participate in a second part of the study that concerns their thoughts and feelings during the interaction.

If consent is given, the subjects are seated in separate but identical cubicles where they are each instructed to view a videotaped copy of the interaction. By stopping the videotape with a remote start/pause control at those points where they remember having had a particular thought or feeling, each subject makes a written, time-logged listing of these *actual thought–feeling entries*. The subjects are then instructed to view the videotape a second time, during which the experimenter or an assistant stops the tape for them at each of those points at which their interaction partner reported a thought or feeling. The subjects' task during this pass through the tape is to infer the content of their partner's thoughts and feelings and provide a written, time-logged listing of these *inferred thought–feeling entries*. When both subjects have completed this task and have filled out a short post-test questionnaire, they are debriefed more completely and then thanked and released.

To the initiated, this brief overview of the dyadic interaction paradigm will appear deceptively simple and straightforward. The job of making this series of events 'work' inside the laboratory requires a relatively elaborate and sophisticated methodology—one that has slowly evolved over the course of nearly twelve years of research. Our intent is to provide some insight into the details of this methodology without losing the reader in the midst of them. The following section represents what we hope is a reasonable attempt to balance these two concerns.

METHODOLOGY

Subjects

In many of our studies, the subjects are preselected on the basis of relevant personality or sociodemographic variables and are recruited by telephone to participate in dyads of predetermined composition (e.g. Ickes and Barnes, 1977, 1978; Ickes, Schermer and Steeno, 1979; Rajecki, Ickes and Tanford, 1981; Ickes and Turner, 1983). In other studies, two separate sign-up sheets are used to schedule non-preselected volunteer subjects, who thus become more or less randomly paired as the dyad members for a given session (e.g. Ickes, Reidhead and Patterson, 1986; Ickes *et al.*, 1986). The separate sign-up sheets, which not only bear the names of different experiments and different experimenters but also direct subjects to report to different waiting areas, are used to help ensure (a) that two friends or previously acquainted individuals will not sign up for the same session and (b) that each scheduled pair of subjects will be unlikely to meet and interact before their session begins. Obviously, in studies of the interactions of dyads whose members already have an established relationship (e.g. friends, roommates, dating or married couples), the precautions just described are unnecessary and can be dispensed with.

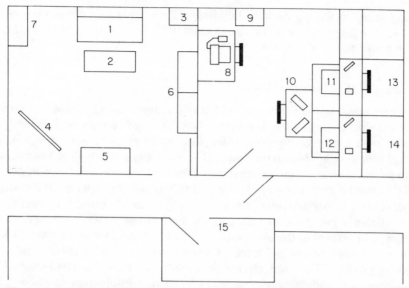

Figure 1. Schematic diagram of the setting for the dyadic interaction paradigm

Setting and Equipment

As indicated in Figure 1, the observation room in which the dyad members' interaction is recorded is furnished with a long couch (1) and an accompanying coffee table (2) that conceals an FM wireless microphone. A video camera focused on the area of the couch and coffee table is concealed in a darkened storage room (15) across a hallway from the observation room. This arrangement permits the dyad members' interaction to be recorded through the open doorways of the storage and observation rooms with minimal likelihood of the camera being detected.

Adjacent to the observation room is a control room used to house the video and audio equipment operated by the experimenter or by a research assistant. Along one wall of the control room is the experimenter's control station. Here the experimenter can sit in front of a single table (10) that supports a microphone, an intercom system, and two identical videocassette recorders that are both connected (by means of a Y-adaptor) to the video camera in the storage room across the hall. Each VCR is also connected, respectively, to one of two 25 in. color TV monitors (11 and 12) that are oriented to face through one-way mirrors into identical test cubicles. The test cubicles (13 and 14) are each equipped with an intercom speaker, a remote start/pause switch connected to the VCR and TV monitor system unique to each cubicle, and a supply of 'Thought and Feeling Coding Forms'.

Procedure

Following the directions given on the telephone or on their respective sign-up sheets, the two subjects who are scheduled for each session report to different waiting areas in the psychology building. These areas are physically isolated from each other but are both in reasonably close proximity to the suite of research rooms just described.

Collection of the videotape data

After activating and checking the video equipment, the experimenter collects the two subjects from their respective waiting areas, conducts them into the observation room, asks them to place their belongings on the table (5), and directs them to be seated on the couch (1). When the subjects have been seated, the experimenter arranges to leave the room, ostensibly to obtain additional copies of the informed consent forms. At this point, an experimental assistant in the control room activates the video equipment (10) and the videotaping begins. Exactly five minutes later, at the end of the observation period, the experimenter returns to the observation room and the videotaping is terminated.

After probing for any evidence of suspicion, the experimenter conducts a partial debriefing. The subjects are told that they have been videotaped for the purpose of studying their naturally occurring interaction behavior. The experimenter describes the videotaping procedure, explains the methodological importance of not telling them about the taping in advance, and informs them that their written consent is required for the tape to be used as data. To assure the subjects that their rights to privacy have been protected, the experimenter explains that the video camera was activated before they entered the observation room and recorded their interaction automatically. If one or both exercise the right to have the tape erased immediately instead of releasing it for use as data, the content of the interaction will remain their own private concern. (Of the hundreds of subjects run in the dyadic interaction paradigm, only one has ever requested to have the tape erased.)

Collection of the thought and feeling data

Once the subjects' written consent has been obtained, the experimenter describes the next part of the study. In this part, the subjects are asked to view the videotape and make a written record of the thoughts and feelings they experienced during the five-minute interaction period. When the subjects have been seated in their individual cubicles (13 and 14), the experimenter uses the intercom in the control room to give them detailed instructions regarding the thought–feeling data collection procedure. The two VCRs are then activated, and the subjects use their start/pause controls to independently start and stop their respective copies of the videotape.

Consistent with the instructions they have received, the subjects stop the videotape at each point during the interaction that they recall having had a specific thought or feeling. They record each thought or feeling on a 'Thought and Feeling Coding Form' by entering (a) the time the thought or feeling occurred (available as a digital readout on the upper-left part of the videotape). (b) the specific content of the thought–feeling entry (to be written in sentence form on the coding sheet), and (c) whether the entry was a thought or a feeling (to be coded T or F on the coding sheet). The coding forms were modelled on ones described by Cacioppo and Petty (1981).

Collection of the empathic accuracy data

When both subjects have made a complete pass through the videotape and have finished listing all of the thoughts and feelings they recall having had, the experimenter collects their respective thought–feeling coding forms. The experimenter then returns to the station in the control room, and instructs the subjects via intercom that they will now each view the videotape a second time. On this second pass through the videotape, however, the subjects will no longer use their remote start/pause control to start and stop the tape. Instead, the experimenter (aided by a research assistant) will start and stop each subject's copy of the videotape during the second viewing.

Using their own video-synchronized 'logs' of the times at which each dyad member's *partner's* thoughts and feelings were reported during the first viewing of the videotapes, the experimenter and the research assistant independently present their respective copies of the tape to the two dyad members, stopping them at each of those points at which the partner's thoughts and feelings were recorded. The subjects' instructions are in most respects analogous to those of the previous thought-listing task. Each time the tape is stopped for them, the subjects are required to make an inference about the nature of the specific thought or feeling reported by their partner at that point. Then, using the same type of coding form on which they had previously recorded their own thoughts and feelings, the subjects code *the inferred content of their partner's thoughts and feelings* by entering (a) the time the thought or feeling occurred (available from the digital readout on the videotape), (b) the specific content of the thought–feeling entry (to be written in sentence form on the coding sheet), (c) whether the entry is presumed to be a thought or a feeling (to be coded T or F on the coding sheet), and (d) whether the entry is presumed to be positive, neutral, or negative in its overall affective tone (to be coded as +, 0, or − on the coding sheet).

Collection of the final self-report measures

In the final part of the study, the subjects are asked to remain in their respective cubicles long enough to complete a brief paper-and-pencil post-test questionnaire. The items on the questionnaire, which may vary from study to study, typically assess the subjects' perceptions of (a) the quality of their interaction, and (b) the degree to which they like each other. When each subject has completed the questionnaire and returned it to the experimenter, the subjects are then debriefed more fully, are asked not to discuss the study with potential future subjects, and are then thanked and released.

DEPENDENT MEASURES

At least two types of behavioral data and three types of self-report data can be generated in the dyadic interaction paradigm. The different types of data, the specific measures that comprise them, and the methods employed to code, compute, or transform these measures, are described in some detail below.

Behavioral Measures

Two types of behavioral data, 'static' behaviors and 'dynamic' behaviors, are coded from the videotapes by two independent judges who are kept blind, insofar as possible, with respect to any independent or predictor variables being studied. The static behaviors, which either occur only once or do not vary much across time, are represented by measures of interpersonal distance (shoulder-to-shoulder), body orientation, and openness of body posture. The more temporally variable dynamic behaviors include the total frequency and duration of verbalizations (i.e. speaking turns), directed gazes, mutual gazes, expressive gestures, and expressions of positive affect (i.e. smiles and laughter). Also included are measures of the number of conversation sequences initiated and the number of back-channel responses or verbal reinforcers provided by each dyad member during the course of the interaction. In the studies conducted to date, the interrater reliabilities of these behavioral measures have typically been in the 0.80–0.99 range. (For the operational definitions of these behaviors, see Ickes and Turner, 1983, pp. 214–215.)

Five of the dynamic behaviors just cited—frequency of verbalizations, directed gazes, positive affect, expressive gestures, and verbal reinforcers—have consistently proven useful in defining the overall levels of *interactional involvement* displayed by the members of the dyads we have studied over the past twelve years. A recent factor analysis of these five behaviors yielded a single interactional involvement factor accounting for 74 per cent of the total factor variance (Ickes *et al.*, 1986, p. 76).

As important as these behaviors are, however, there are obviously many other interesting behaviors one might choose to code from the videotapes, depending on the specific nature of the hypotheses being tested. For example, there are additional nonverbal behaviors such as postural mirroring (LaFrance and Ickes, 1981); there are contingency-based measures of recurring behavior patterns and exchanges (e.g. Gottman, 1979); and there are more specific features of the verbal interaction such as personal pronoun usage (Ickes, Reidhead and Patterson, 1986).

Self-Report Measures

With the recent addition of the thought–feeling and empathic inference assessment procedures, at least three types of self-report data can now be obtained by means of the dyadic interaction paradigm. These include (a) the dyad members' own reported thoughts and feelings, (b) their inferences about their partner's reported thoughts and feelings, and (c) their responses to the items on the post-test questionnaire. We have already commented briefly on the third type of self-report data, the post-test questionnaire measure, but we need to elaborate a little more on each of the first two types, the thought–feeling measures and the empathic accuracy measures.

Thought–feeling measures

The subjects' own thought–feeling data are coded by two independent judges who are also kept blind with respect to any independent or predictor variables being studied. These judges code (a) the total number of entries (thoughts + feelings) for each subject, and (b) the emotional valence of the entry (+, 0, or −). They also record, in terms suggested by Laing, Phillipson and Lee (1966), (c) whether the entry represents a direct perspective (subject's own perspective) or a metaperspective (subject's adoption of his or her partner's perspective), and (d) the target or object of the perception expressed by the entry (self, partner, other person(s), environmental object, event or circumstance; see Table 1).

Table 1 Direct and metaperspective perceptions of self, partner, other(s), and environment

Direct perspectives		Metaperspectives	
S > S	S's perception of S	S > P > S	S's perception of P's perception of S
S > P	S's perception of P	S > P > P	S's perception of P's perception of P
S > O	S's perception of O	S > P > O	S's perception of P's perception of O
S > E	S's perception of E	S > P > E	S's perception of P's perception of E

S, subject; P, partner; O, other person(s); E, environmental object, event or circumstance.

Clearly, these categories are not the only ones possible (subjects might, for example, adopt the experimenter's or a roommate's perspective or even the 'group perspective' of the interacting dyad (Wegner and Giuliano, 1982) in considering the various targets or objects of perception. In practice, however, we have found that these categories are sufficient to categorize over 98 per cent of the thought–feeling entries, with the frequency of the remaining entries being too low to justify using them as data in any event. Moreover, these categorical judgements can be made quite reliably, with the judges' rates of agreement within each category ranging from 91 to 100 per cent.

The coded thought–feeling data for the subjects within each dyad are then entered into a microcomputer as the input to a software program called COLLECT YOUR THOUGHTS. COLLECT YOUR THOUGHTS is an Applesoft Basic program written by William Ickes specifically for this program of research. Within two years of its development, a Pascal version of COLLECT

YOUR THOUGHTS was written by one of our colleagues, Victor Bissonnette. Both versions produce as output various summary indexes that represent simple aggregations (i.e. counts) of the frequency of occurrence of entries in specific thought–feeling categories. These summary indexes (and the corresponding percentage measures derived from them) are used as the primary dependent measures in analyses of the thought–feeling data.

As its standard output, COLLECT YOUR THOUGHTS yields relatively general, single-category measures of the number and percentage of each subject's entries that are coded as thoughts, feelings, positive entries, neutral entries, negative entries, direct perspective entries, metaperspective entries, self (-relevant) entries, partner entries, other entries, or environment entries. The program can be modified, however, to yield a much larger number of more specific measures that represent the entries' classification on two or more categories (e.g. number and percentage of positive partner-relevant entries, negative self feelings, neutral metaperspective thoughts). Although the more general, single-category measures will typically be the more reliable, due to their greater level of aggregation (cf. Epstein, 1979; Jaccard, 1974; Snyder and Ickes, 1985), the use of more specific, multiple-category measures may be preferred, or even necessitated, in tests of certain *a priori* hypotheses (for examples, see Ickes *et al.*, 1986, pp. 70–73).

Empathic accuracy measures

Two measures of empathic accuracy are computed from comparisons of the actual and inferred thought–feeling entries. The first measure, *valence accuracy*, is an index of the percentage of instances in which a dyad member's inference about the overall emotional tone of his or her partner's entry (positive, neutral or negative) matches the actual valence label assigned to the entry during the data-coding process. The second measure, *content accuracy*, is an index of the degree to which a dyad member's written description of the inferred content of his or her partner's entry matches the actual content of the sentence that the partner had written to describe the entry.

The valence accuracy measure is computed with the aid of a specialized utility program that Victor Bissonnette has written to support the Pascal version of COLLECT YOUR THOUGHTS. This program accesses the relevant 'raw' data from a master data file created by COLLECT YOUR THOUGHTS. The number of matches and mismatches in the rated valence of the actual entries and the corresponding inferred entries is computed for the members of each dyad, and the resulting percentage measures of valence accuracy are written to a diskette data file. The data on this file are then uploaded to a mainframe computer and merged with other data files for analysis.

A different procedure is used to derive the content accuracy measure because of the need for subjective judgements to be made about the degree of similarity in the written content of the actual and inferred thought–feeling entries. First, a transcript of all the thought–feeling entries reported in the study, both actual and inferred, is created with the aid of a word processor. The printed copy of this transcript is structured such that each dyad member's actual thought–feeling entries appear on the left side of the page with the corresponding inferred entries appearing directly beside them on the right. Then, separate copies of the transcript are given to six independent judges. Their task is to compare the written content of each actual entry with that of the corresponding inferred entry and rate the degree of similarity (i.e. content accuracy) using a three-point scale ranging from 0 (essentially different content) through 0.5 (somewhat similar, but not the same, content) to 1 (essentially the same content).

In the first study in which this scoring procedure was employed, the internal consistency of the six judges' content accuracy ratings was 0.94. The high reliability of these ratings indicated that the six raters were using essentially the same criteria to judge the degree of similarity in the content of the actual and the inferred entries. It also justified the decision to use the mean of the ratings as our empirical measure of content accuracy.

In summary, by means of the procedures just described, it is possible to operationally define and measure empathic accuracy in a highly objective and reliable way. Moreover, the measures of empathic accuracy thus obtained are not just 'distant cousins' of the phenomenon of empathic accuracy as it naturally occurs in ongoing social interaction. They are instead compellingly faithful representations of the degree to which each dyad member can accurately infer the emotional tone and specific content of his or her partner's actual thoughts and feelings. In the absence of a metaphysical aid such as telepathy, procedures of the type we have developed may provide the best means available of studying the phenomenon of empathic accuracy.

APPLICATIONS OF THE DYADIC INTERACTION PARADIGM

The dyadic interaction paradigm has a wide range of applications (for other reviews, see Ickes, 1982, 1983). Its most recent applications are those resulting from the extension of the original paradigm to incorporate procedures for measuring the actual and inferred thoughts and feelings of the dyad members. Because all of these newer applications have not previously been described, they are given special attention here. We begin by reviewing a number of phenomena implicated by our thought–feeling assessment procedure and consider the relevance of these phenomena to the study of *naturalistic social cognition* (Ickes *et al.*, 1986). We then offer some comments on the broader range of problems to which the dyadic interaction paradigm can be applied.

Applications to the Study of Naturalistic Social Cognition

In the research reported by Ickes *et al.* (1986), we employed the first stage of the paradigm's thought–feeling assessment procedure. By having the members of each dyad make a written record of their own thoughts and feelings during the interaction period, we were able to study a number of different aspects of naturalistic social cognition. These included (a) thought–feeling correlates of perceived interaction quality and liking for one's interaction partner, (b) thought–feeling correlates of personality traits and dispositions, (c) thought–feeling correlates of interactional involvement, (d) variables moderating the relations between covert affect and overt behavior, and (e) individual-difference correlates of metaperspective taking. In more recent studies, we have employed either one or both stages of the thought–feeling assessment procedure to investigate such additional aspects of naturalistic social cognition as (f) intersubjectivity and (g) empathic accuracy.

Thought–feeling correlates of interaction quality and liking

In tests of the concurrent validity of certain thought–feeling indexes, we predicted that self-reported discomfort in the interaction would be positively correlated with the number and percentage of negative self entries (direct perspective). We further predicted that self-reported liking for one's interaction partner would be positively correlated with the number and percentage of positive partner entries, Both of these predictions were confirmed (see Ickes *et al.*, 1986, pp. 70–71).

Thought–feeling correlates of traits and dispositions

In tests of the convergent and discriminant validity of certain thought–feeling indexes, we predicted that the trait measures of private self-consciousness, public self-consciousness and social anxiety (Fenigstein, Scheier and Buss, 1975) would be positively correlated, respectively, with the number and percentage of (a) direct perspective self entries, (b) metaperspective self entries, and (c) negative self entries (summed across both perspectives—direct and meta). We further predicted that the trait measure of internal correspondence (Brickman, 1978; Ickes and Teng, 1987) would be positively correlated with the number and percentage of (d) feeling entries. The predictions for private self-consciousness, social anxiety, and internal correspondence were largely confirmed; the prediction for public self-consciousness was not.

Thought–feeling correlates of interactional involvement

Behavioral measures of the degree of interactional involvement in the dyad (e.g. frequency of verbalizations, directed gazes, positive affect, expressive gestures, and verbal reinforcers) were found to be correlated with a number of thought–feeling indexes. Specifically, these behaviors were positively correlated with (a) the total number of thought–feeling entries, (b) the percentage of positive partner entries, and (c) the percentage of all positive entries. In addition, they were negatively correlated with (d) the percentage of negative thought–feeling entries (Ickes *et al.*, 1986, pp. 73–74). The positive correlations were typically in the range 0.30–0.60; the negative in the range −0.20–−0.50.

Variables moderating the affect/behavior relationship

The relationships between interactional involvement and the percentages of positive, neutral, and negative thought–feeling entries were found to be moderated by the personality variables of private self-consciousness (Fenigstein, Scheier and Buss, 1975) and internal correspondence (Brickman, 1978; Ickes and Teng, 1987). These two personality variables were found to exert both independent and interactive influences on the degree of correlation between interactional involvement and the relevant thought–feeling indexes. For a complete description and interpretation of these somewhat complex findings, see Ickes *et al.*, 1986, pp. 74–78.

Individual-difference correlates of metaperspective taking

The frequency and percentage of the metaperspective entries reported by the dyad members was found to vary according to their gender. Men tended to report fewer metaperspective entries than did women, and appeared to adopt their partners' perspective in a less spontaneous, more instrumental way. Subjects high in both private self-consciousness and internal correspondence appeared to deliberately adopt their partner's perspective in order to regulate the behavioral expression of their own thoughts and feelings. For these subjects, metaperspective taking was associated with expressing only their positive and neutral thoughts and feelings in behavior while suppressing their negative ones (Ickes *et al.*, 1986, pp. 77–79).

Intersubjectivity

In the second and third studies employing the thought–feeling assessment procedure, we and our colleagues have begun to examine other aspects of naturalistic social cognition that can be addressed by means of the dyadic interaction paradigm. One of these aspects, the phenomenon of intersubjectivity, can be assessed by determining the degree to which dyad members' scores are correlated on each of the primary thought–feeling indexes. Patterns of significant positive correlations on these indexes can be used to identify the specific categories of thought–feeling content that both dyad members are likely to report to a similar degree as a function of having interacted together.

An example of such patterns of intersubjectivity correlations is provided in Table 2. These data reveal that, in both an original study and a replication study, dyads comprised of two previously unacquainted men displayed a different pattern of intersubjectivity than did dyads comprised of two previously unacquainted women. Specifically, the male dyad members in both studies were similar in the numbers and percentages of thoughts and feelings they reported that concerned (a) their interaction partners and (b) their own affective states. In contrast, the female dyad members in both studies were similar in the extent to which their thoughts and feelings (a) reflected the adoption of their partner's perspective and (b) concerned 'other people' outside of the interaction.

Table 2   Intraclass correlations in the set of thought–feeling measures for the male–male and female–female dyads in studies 1 and 2

Thought–feeling measure	Male–male dyads		Female–female dyads	
	Study 1 (n = 18)	Study 2 (n = 28)	Study 1 (n = 18)	Study 2 (n = 28)
# thought entries	0.30*	0.22†	0.03	−0.06
% thought entries	0.32*	0.43***	−0.03	−0.23†
# feeling entries	0.31*	0.32*	−0.38*	−0.14
% feeling entries	0.32*	0.43***	−0.03	−0.23†
# positive entries	0.22†	0.49***	0.02	0.07
% positive entries	0.29†	0.49***	0.31*	−0.05
# neutral entries	0.42*	0.08	0.27†	−0.05
% neutral entries	0.56***	0.46***	0.11	−0.17†
# negative entries	0.47**	0.23†	0.32*	0.08
% negative entries	0.17	0.30*	0.66****	−0.14
# self entries	0.27†	0.06	−0.26†	−0.09
% self entries	−0.02	0.23†	0.07	0.02
# partner entries	0.43*	0.28*	0.22†	0.05
% partner entries	0.23†	0.37*	0.13	0.26*
# others entries	−0.01	0.12	0.29†	0.40**
% others entries	−0.09	−0.01	0.14	0.18†
# environment entries	0.04	−0.15	−0.06	−0.07
% environment entries	0.11	−0.16	−0.10	0.08
# direct perspective entries	0.38*	0.09	−0.21†	−0.02
% direct perspective entries	−0.08	−0.24*	0.67****	0.27*
# metaperspective entries	0.11	−0.29*	0.42*	0.14
% metaperspective entries	−0.08	−0.24*	0.67****	0.27*

†$p < 0.10$.
*$p < 0.05$.
**$p < 0.01$.
***$p < 0.005$.
****$p < 0.001$.

Behavioral differences in the interactions of male–male versus female–female strangers help to provide an interpretation of these distinctly different patterns of intersubjective thought–feeling content. Because the initial interactions of two men are typically less pleasant and involving than those of two women (e.g. Ickes and Barnes, 1977; Ickes, Schermer and Steeno, 1979), men may have greater cause to monitor their own affective states and engage in mutual social comparison with their interaction partners. In contrast, because women can generally assume that their initial same-sex interactions will be affectively pleasant and involving, they are freed from being concerned about the quality of their affective states and can focus instead on their mutual willingness to see the world—and, in particular, other people—through each other's perspective. This interpretation would lead us to predict that the patterns of intersubjectivity in the dyadic interactions of male friends would more closely resemble those of female strangers than of male strangers.

Empathic accuracy

In a study currently in progress, we and our colleagues have employed both stages of the paradigm's thought–feeling assessment procedure. By having the members of each dyad make a written record of (a) their own thoughts and feelings and (b) the inferred thoughts and feelings of their interaction partners, we can now study the phenomenon of *empathic accuracy* in unstructured social interaction. Although most of the data from this study have yet to be analyzed, some preliminary findings suggest that our empirical measures of empathic accuracy—valence accuracy and content accuracy—are positively correlated with relevant personality predictors such as Davis's (1982) measure of perspective taking.

General Applications to the Study of Social Interaction

Broadly defined, there are two major paths for research using the dyadic interaction paradigm. These two paths are represented by *structural* versus *external variable* studies of social interaction (Duncan, 1969; Duncan and Fiske, 1977).

Regarding the first of these paths, the paradigm seems to be ideally suited to structural studies of social interaction. It permits the researcher to study not only the overt behavioral structure of the interaction but its covert cognitive structure as well. A particular advantage of the paradigm in such structural studies is the capability to specify the precise time location of both subjects' thoughts and feelings as the events of their behavioral interaction unfold. This capability may enable the relationship's infrastructure, defined as 'the causal interconnections between the partners' activity chains' (Berscheid, 1985a; Kelley *et al.*, 1983), to be explored in detail.

Regarding the second of these paths, the paradigm is also well suited to external variable studies of social interaction. The general categories of external variables whose influence on social interaction can be studied include (a) personality and individual-difference variables, (b) cultural and role variables, (c) environmental and situational variables, and (d) social–cognitive variables such as attributions, preinteraction expectancies, and stereotypes.

For example, the paradigm has been used to study such personality variables as locus of control (Rajecki, Ickes and Tanford, 1981), Machiavellianism (Ickes, Reidhead and Patterson, 1986), self-monitoring (Ickes and Barnes, 1977), and sex-role orientation (Ickes and Barnes, 1978; Ickes, Schermer and Steeno, 1979; Ickes, 1982, 1985). It has been used to study such cultural and role-relevant phenomena as interracial interactions (Ickes, 1984) and the interaction styles of firstborn versus lastborn men and women (Ickes and Turner, 1983). It has been used to study the effect of the larger 'social context' in which initial dyadic interactions can take place (Ickes, 1984). And it has been used to study how the course of such interactions can be determined by preinteraction expectancies (Ickes *et al.*, 1982) and social stereotypes (Ickes, 1984).

In summary, the dyadic interaction paradigm has a wide range of applications in both structural and external variable studies of social interaction.

ADVANTAGES AND DISADVANTAGES OF THE DYADIC INTERACTION PARADIGM

Advantages

The dyadic interaction paradigm offers many advantages to relationship researchers. Several of its advantages were apparent even before the addition of procedures for the assessment of the dyad members' own thoughts and feelings and their inferences about the thoughts and feelings of their interaction partners (Ickes, 1982, 1983). With these newer procedures added, the paradigm's advantages can be summarized as follows.

1. *Flexibility*. The paradigm is highly flexible in application. It can be used to conduct studies of dyadic interaction that are fully experimental (e.g. Ickes *et al.*, 1982), fully correlational (e.g. Ickes *et al.*, 1986), or that combine the two approaches (e.g. Ickes, 1984).

2. *Levels of analysis*. Within the framework of the dyadic interaction paradigm, the researcher can study the effects of independent variables that are either manipulated or systematically varied at two levels of analysis: within dyads and between dyads. Moreover, with the recent availability of a family of new statistical techniques specifically designed for the study of social interaction (for a review, see the chapter by Kenny in this volume), effects at both the within-dyad and between-dyad levels of analysis can be estimated with reasonable accuracy in studies employing a wide range of possible research designs.

3. *Controlled observation*. The paradigm permits subjects to interact or not, as they choose, and allows them considerable freedom in determining the form, nature, and extent of their interaction. At the same time, however, the spatial and temporal limits that the paradigm imposes on the subjects' behavior make it amenable to precise scientific measurement and analysis.

4. *Unobtrusive measurement*. One of the strongest advantages of the dyadic interaction paradigm, relative to other observation methodologies, is that it permits all the behavioral data of interest to be recorded unobtrusively. In doing so, it effectively circumvents the problem of subjects behaving reactively to the knowledge that they are being observed.

5. *Naturalistic interaction*. The paradigm provides a context for the emergence of spontaneous, naturalistic interaction behavior that contrasts sharply with behavior observed in 'fixed confederate' paradigms or in paradigms in which subjects are instructed to interact with the prior knowledge that their behavior during the interaction will be recorded and subsequently analyzed.

6. *Freedom from traditional sources of bias*. The paradigm is relatively free from the traditional sources of subject (awareness, self-presentation) bias, experimenter (expectancy) bias, or bias due to other demand characteristics. This advantage is attributable to features such as (a) the unobtrusive measurement of the subjects' behavior, (b) the deliberately minimal cover story they

are given, (c) the deliberately minimal amount of contact between the experimenter and the subjects, and (d) efforts to keep the experimenter blind, insofar as possible, with respect to any predictor or independent variables.

7. *Internal and external validity*. Because it facilitates naturalistic interaction and is relatively free from traditional sources of bias, the paradigm can be expected to yield results that are both internally and externally valid.

8. *High data yield*. The paradigm enables the researcher to record and analyze a wide range of both individual behaviors (e.g. body orientation, frequency of directed gazes) and dyadic behaviors (e.g. interpersonal distance, frequency of mutual gazes). In addition, it enables the collection of data reflecting (a) the dyad members' own thoughts and feelings, (b) their inferences about the thoughts and feelings reported by their interaction partners, and (c) their posttest impressions of the interaction. The availability of all of these sources of data makes it possible to 'map' the influence of an independent or predictor variable across an unusually large range of cognitive and behavioral measures.

9. *Objective, multiple-act measures*. The primary behavioral measures of interactional involvement are objective, easy to score, and represent the aggregation of the relevant behaviors over the entire observation period. For these reasons, interrater reliabilities are consistently high and the error of measurement associated with these summary measures is likely to be low.

10. *Time-logged events*. If more fine-grained measures are desired, they, too, are available. Due to a recent modification in the DYAD DYNAMICS software (Ickes and Trued, 1985) used to code the subjects' dynamic behaviors, the exact time location of each occurrence of a particular behavior (speaking turn, directed gaze, smile, gesture, etc.) can now be printed as hard copy as well as stored on diskette for subsequent analysis. Because the time location of each thought–feeling entry is also available, it is currently possible to (a) compute trend analyses for both types of data, and (b) examine the linkages between specific thoughts and feelings and specific antecedent and consequent behaviors in extremely fine detail.

11. *Dyad-level cognitive phenomena*. The paradigm enables the study of dyad-level cognitive phenomena such as intersubjectivity and empathic accuracy. This is one of the unique advantages of the dyadic interaction paradigm. It is particularly important in its implications for the study of communication and social cognition.

12. *Integrated, holistic view of social interaction*. Because social behavior and social cognition are both studied as they naturally occur, and in the same 'real time' frame, it is possible to explore their empirical relations in a way that facilitates a more integrated, holistic view of social interaction. This holistic view should also enhance our understanding of how social behavior and social cognition are related to such classes of 'external variables' as (a) traits and dispositions (e.g. Ickes and Barnes, 1977; Rajecki, Ickes and Tanford, 1981). (b) the role relations of the dyad members (e.g. Ickes and Barnes, 1978), (c) sociodemographic variables (e.g. Ickes and Turner, 1983), (d) preinteraction expectancies or stereotypes (Ickes, 1984), and (e) environmental/situational variables.

13. *Inductive and heuristic value*. Because of its potential to reveal an array of previously unsuspected, serendipitous relationships, the inductive and heuristic value of the dyadic interaction paradigm must be regarded as another of its strongest advantages. Serendipitous findings have emerged repeatedly in studies employing the dyadic interaction paradigm, to the frequent benefit of theoretical development (for examples, see Ickes, 1982, 1985; Ickes *et al.*, 1982, 1986; Ickes and Turner, 1983).

14. *Ethical safeguards*. The dyadic interaction paradigm is ethically defensible and affords protection to the researcher as well as the subjects. Although it requires the experimenter to defer obtaining subjects' written consent until their behavior has been videotaped, it effectively safeguards the subjects' right to privacy through its provision that they can have the recording erased before anyone (including the experimenter) has seen it.

15. *Practical utility*. The greatest advantage of the paradigm is its practical utility, as demonstrated repeatedly in studies conducted over the past twelve years. Stated simply, it *works*.

Disadvantages

The disadvantages of the dyadic interaction paradigm are essentially the same ones noted in previous papers (Ickes, 1982, 1983). They may be summarized as follows.

1. *Limit on the number of interactants*. There is a practical limit on the number of interactants that can be studied in a single session. The paradigm is exceptionally well suited to the study of dyads, but the study of triads or larger groups would impose so many additional problems that the costs involved (in terms of time, money, space, research personnel, etc.) may be prohibitively high.

2. *Limit on the observation period*. There is a practical limit on the length of time that subjects' behavior can be recorded during the observation period without them becoming suspicious of the experimenter's continued absence. To obtain longer samples of behavior would require a major change in the cover story.

3. *Limits on situational manipulations*. There is a practical limit on the kinds of situational manipulations the paradigm can accommodate. In general, researchers can expect to establish only those treatment conditions that subjects will find credible in the context of a waiting-room situation.

4. *Carryover effects*. The paradigm is not well suited to the study of multiple interactions involving the same participant(s). If successive interactions of this type were scheduled for sessions held at different times, the subjects' experience during the first session would likely influence their behavior in the later one(s). Although it is technically feasible to have the same subject interact with different partners during a single, longer session, it is still likely that 'carryover effects' from the first interaction would be apparent in the later one(s).

5. *'Candid Camera' syndrome*. Requiring two people to wait together before participating in a psychology study may cause one or both of them to consider

the possibility that their behavior is being covertly observed or recorded. About 3–5 per cent of the dyads in our studies have evidenced an active and persistent suspicion that their behavior has been covertly recorded, resulting in the exclusion of their data from the statistical analyses. Fortunately, this rate of subject loss is no higher than that reported in studies employing more traditional laboratory research paradigms.

6. *High cost factors*. Without question, the paradigm's greatest disadvantage is the high cost of conducting research of this type. In addition to requiring a major investment in space and equipment, the paradigm imposes substantial costs in the time required for software development, subject running, data coding, and data analysis. Because a typical study may easily take two years to complete, researchers who use the paradigm can expect to publish less frequently than those who rely on the more traditional paper-and-pencil questionnaire study.

CONCLUSION

We began this chapter by noting the broad range of personal relationships studied and empirical methodologies employed in systematic observational research. We also noted that the common feature of observational studies is the systematic and selective recording of behavior as it naturally occurs in social situations. Whether observations are made in the laboratory or in field settings, the defining feature of the observational method is its emphasis on the overt, naturally occurring behavior of human subjects.

We proposed, however, that the scope of observational research can be expanded to include the study of subjective thoughts and feelings in addition to the study of objectively rated behavior. In our discussion of the dyadic interaction paradigm, we cited empirical support for our claim that the covert thoughts and feelings of subjects engaged in naturalistic interactions can be studied in a reliable and nonreactive way. Our procedures for assessing the actual and inferred thoughts and feelings of interaction partners have opened up several novel lines of inquiry for relationship research. In particular, they enable the study of 'naturalistic social cognition' and can be used to assess phenomena such as metaperspective taking, intersubjectivity, and empathic accuracy.

As the title of this chapter suggests, the observational method can be extended to study the interactions of the 'minds' as well as the 'bodies' of relationship members. By using this method to capture the dynamic interplay of both the overt and covert features of social interaction, researchers may finally be able to disentangle the complex web of public and private events that are the irreducible essence of personal relationships.

Handbook of Personal Relationships
Edited by S. W. Duck
© 1988 John Wiley & Sons Ltd

6

Self-Report Methods in Studying Personal Relationships

JOHN H. HARVEY
University of Iowa, Iowa, USA
SUSAN S. HENDRICK
Texas Tech University, Lubbock, Texas, USA
and
KAREN TUCKER
Ohio State University, Columbus, Ohio, USA

ABSTRACT

Self-report methods in studying personal relationships are reviewed and evaluated. Emphasis is placed on investigators' attempts to understand respondents' attributions of meaning to what occurs in their lives and action related to such attributions. Steps towards refinement of techniques are also suggested.

In Viktor Frankl's (1962) poignant account of his experiences in the Auschwitz concentration camp, he describes how the prisoners tried to create understandable and bearable meanings for their horrifying and unpredictable circumstances. One such approach involved a retreat into one's memories of and mental constructions regarding a former, happier, personal life. Frankl's own experience illustrates this point:

> My mind still clung to the image of my wife. A thought crossed my mind: I didn't even know if she were still alive. I knew only one thing—which I have learned well by now: Love goes very far beyond the physical person of the beloved . . . nothing could touch the strength of my love, my thoughts, and the image of my beloved. Had I known then that my wife was dead, I think that I would still have given myself, undisturbed by that knowledge, to the contemplation of her image, and that my mental conversation with her would have been just as vivid and just as satisfying. (pp. 37–38)

Frankl suggests that the prisoners' construction of meaning that often pertained to the meaning of their personal relationships was essential to their survival. As Klinger (1977) has argued, personal meaning is for most people crucially created by their thinking about personal relationships. This chapter will examine the techniques by which social scientists can tap those meanings.

Overview

One of the most favored approaches to the exploration and assessment of close, personal relationships is that of 'self-report'. For our purposes, self-report refers to the thoughts or feelings, and behavior—reported by a particular subject in a particular study; such thoughts or feelings may concern other thoughts or feelings or overt behavior. In addition to one's own thoughts and feelings, a subject may report his or her perceptions of another person's thoughts or feelings.

In this chapter we will (1) discuss why there has been and probably will continue to be reliance on self-report methods in studying personal relationships, (2) distinguish among types of self-report, (3) discuss some topical areas as well as representative self-report approaches, (4) comment on a number of problems and issues involved in the use of self-report techniques, and (5) note some possible future directions for work focusing on self-report evidence. For all of these topics our coverage will be selective, and the reader is advised to peruse more systematically many of the research studies and instruments that we discuss only briefly.

A primary explanation for why investigators rely so much on self-report methods in studying relationships is that *we seek to understand others' imputation of meaning for what occurs in their lives* (Heider, 1958; Kelley, 1979; Kelly, 1955). It is usually not enough to simply observe others' behaviors. Forms of overt behavior, whether verbal or nonverbal, may have different meanings to people depending on the context of the behavior, the audience, the nature of the ongoing relationship, etc. We want to know and understand the significant but nonobservable thoughts and feelings as well as the more visible behaviors (see Duck and Sants, 1983).

In addition to the general point about assessing meaning, self-report evidence is often easier and more convenient to collect than are other types of evidence. Materials are usually not as costly as are those needed for behavioral observation. Further, people may be more willing to participate in research involving self-report techniques than in work involving some type of observation of them and their actions. For these reasons, varieties of methods have been created for gathering self-report data, and 'self-report' is a genus of approaches rather than one scientific method. These methods differ in many ways, particularly with regard to their focus. We will evaluate different methods as we describe them separately.

Approaches to Self-Report

There are several distinctions among self-administered questionnaires, interviews, and behavioral records kept by participants that should be noted. Questionnaires are usually designed to obtain summary information, frequently about 'macro' rather than 'micro' processes. Participants are often required to generalize over large classes of events in order to report global relationship properties (e.g. intimacy level) or to infer general causal conditions (e.g. personality traits). Because of the complexity and ambiguity of this assessment task, a self-report questionnaire, by itself, may not offer a complete approach to assessing macro processes or causal conditions.

Interviews are unique among these approaches in that they involve the direct participation of a third person or persons (the investigator/s), who becomes to some degree a variable in the research process itself. In all participant report methods, the investigator structures the content and form of the research questions, but only in the interview does this structuring occur interactively. The researcher can probe, and the participant can seek clarification and elaboration.

In contrast to both questionnaires and interviews, behavioral records typically produce specific, molecular evidence about some event or behavior rather than allow the construction of general assumptions. Such records are usually accounts of some type of interaction. Behavioral records are usually obtained immediately after events have occurred and consist of tallies or written descriptions of these events. However, summarized appropriately, such records can provide information on more general relationship properties. For instance, a husband's records of verbal interactions with his wife, if obtained over a long enough period of time, can provide a good picture of their verbal interaction, taken from his perspective (see Olson, 1977, for a useful discussion of these approaches).

A final approach to self-report that will be discussed in this chapter is that of diaries and accounts. These approaches, while often unwieldy in data-analytic terms, offer some of the richest subjective, descriptive information about intimate personal relationships.

GENERAL SELF-REPORT TECHNIQUES

There are numerous methodological approaches and specific assessment instruments employed in the study of close, personal relationships, and a comprehensive treatment of all of them cannot be given here. Therefore we will focus on a few topical areas that are frequently explored with self-report techniques and will then pursue in depth specific examples of questionnaire, interview, behavioral self-report, and diary research endeavors.

Several of the topical areas that could rightfully be addressed in this chapter are discussed very thoroughly in other chapters in this volume. These include such topics as communication (which we touch on only lightly), social support, loneliness, courtship, friendship, gender roles, intimacy, and several related areas. We thus focus briefly on self-report in the areas of personality, love and related constructs, communication, conflict, sexuality, and relationship satisfaction.

Love and Related Constructs

Rubin (1970, 1973) is credited with early theoretical and scaling differentiation of liking and living as well as with an insistence that love is a respectable topic for scientific inquiry. His liking and loving scales (thirteen items each) are still widely used (e.g. Rusbult, Johnson and Morrow, 1986) in couple research. A more recently developed self-report scale to assess love attitudes was developed by the Hendricks and their colleagues (Hendrick *et al.*, 1984), based on a theoretical typology of approaches to love or 'love styles' developed by Lee (1973/1976). This scale will be discussed more fully later as an example of a self-report questionnaire. Braiker and Kelley (1979) developed a measure of love as part of a larger measure that also assessed the constructs of *conflict–negativity*, *ambivalence*, and *maintenance*. Thus love has sometimes been assessed as an independent 'entity' but more often is linked to other related constructs such as intimacy or commitment.

Attempting to develop an instrument to assess intimacy in several types of adolescent and adult relationships, Tesch (1985) built on early intimacy research (e.g. Orlofsky, Marcia and Lesser, 1973; Tesch and Whitbourne, 1982) in creating the Psychosocial Intimacy Questionnaire, a 60-item self-report measure that indicates promising reliability and validity. A construct often considered to be closely associated with both love and intimacy is commitment, and the Relationship Events Scale (King and Christensen, 1983) is a nineteen-item self-report measure of intimacy, commitment, and interdependence in dating relationships. This instrument more generally measures 'courtship progress', which has been a favorite topic for close relationship researchers (e.g. Huston *et al.*, 1981).

Communication

One of the most significant components of any type of personal relationship is communication. A recent programmatic approach to couple communication is Fitzpatrick's (1984) typological approach to marital interaction. Using a carefully developed 64-item, eight-factor self-report instrument, she categorizes couples as *traditional*, *independent*, *separate*, and *mixed types* and assesses similarities and differences between the mixed types on expressivity and instrumentality of communication, sex-role orientation, dyadic adjustment, conflict, control, and additional related dimensions.

Promising new research in the area of self-disclosure (Berg, 1984; Berg and McQuinn, 1986; Miller and Berg, 1984; Miller, Berg and Archer, 1983) has resulted in the development of two brief self-report scales. The ten-item Self-Disclosure Index (Miller, Berg and Archer, 1983) measures an individual's tendency to disclose on general and intimate topics. Construct validity was established by comparing this instrument to the Jourard Self-Disclosure Questionnaire (Jourard, 1964), and internal consistency has been established. The instrument has been used to help predict continuance in both platonic and romantic relationships and to predict degrees of intimacy of self-disclosure in varied situations, with varied target persons. The ten-item Opener Scale (Miller, Berg and Archer, 1983) measures an individual's self-perceived ability to *elicit* self-disclosure from others. Both scales appear to be extremely appropriate for close relationship work (e.g. Berg and McQuinn, 1986; Hendrick, Hendrick and Adler, 1986).

Conflict

Another favored topic for relationship researchers is conflict. Approaches to measuring conflict have included the exploration of partners' attributions about self, the partner, and the relationship through interviews (e.g. Harvey, Wells and Alvarez, 1978) and through questionnaire items assessing the frequency of occurrence of conflict or negative feelings (Braiker and Kelley, 1979). Germane to a discussion of measurement issues is Braiker and Kelley's finding that 'There appears to be no relation between the amount of interdependence and love in a relationship, on the one hand, and the amount of negative affect and open conflict, on the other hand' (p. 152). The researchers have been to some degree freed from an 'either–or' mindset regarding conflict and love and can more freely pursue both simultaneously.

An innovative approach to the assessment of conflict management or problem-solving in close relationships was developed by Rusbult and Zembrodt (1983), who developed a typology of *exit* (separating, distancing), *voice* (discussing, compromising), *loyalty* (waiting, hoping), and *neglect* (ignoring, abusing) as approaches to couple problem-solving. In a recent study, Rusbult and her colleagues (Rusbult, Johnson and Morrow, 1986) employed a 28-item self-report measure based on the typology, and several additional related measures, finding that conflict-management/problem-solving styles were strongly related to couple distress/nondistress. Richardson (1987) has attempted to extend Rusbult's typology by combining it with Rahim's (1983) five-factor Rahim Organizational Conflict Inventory, a self-report instrument assessing one's response to conflict with various target persons. Preliminary findings (Hammock, Richardson and Lubben, 1986) indicate some interesting and promising relationships between Rusbult's (Rusbult and Zembrodt, 1983) four problem-solving approaches, Rahim's (1983) five conflict-management approaches, and the Hendricks' (Hendrick *et al.*, 1984) six love styles.

Sexuality

One area that has been relatively neglected by personal relationship researchers is sexuality, although there are notable exceptions (e.g. Byrne, 1977; Mosher, 1979; Perlman, 1974), particularly in the area of self-report scaling. The Sexual Opinion Survey, a 21-item self-report measure (Fisher *et al.*, 1986), has been widely used to assess subjects' responses to erotica along a dimension of eroto-phobia to erotophilia, and the Revised Mosher Guilt Inventory (Green and Mosher, 1985) is a 114-item scale consisting of subscales measuring sex-guilt, hostility-guilt, and guilty conscience. A measure of more general sexual attitudes is the Sexual Attitudes Scale (Hendrick *et al.*, 1985; Hendrick and Hendrick, 1987b). This 43-item Likert scale assesses a subject's self-reported sexual attitudes across the dimensions of *permissiveness* (referring to a casual, open attitude towards sexuality), *sexual practices* (largely reflecting sexual responsibility and a conventional approach to sex), *communion* (reflecting idealism), and *instrumentality* (referring to a utilitarian, egocentric sexual perspective). The largest and most powerful of the dimensions is permissiveness, and that subscale (21 items) can be used in addition to the other three subscales or singly as a measure of permissiveness, replacing or at least supplementing some of the more established permissiveness measures such as the Reiss Male and Female Premarital Sexual Permissiveness Scale (Reiss, 1964).

As research on romantic dyadic relationships burgeons, we need to recognize that sexuality, along with love, intimacy, commitment, conflict, and other topics, deserves a central place in relationship research.

Relationship Satisfaction

One important area of marital research concerns relationship satisfaction. There are a number of self-report measures which assess thoughts, feelings, or behaviors within the marital relationship—more than 800 were listed in Straus and Brown's (1978) review of marital and family assessment techniques. According to Snyder, Wills and Keiser (1981), few of those meet minimum reliability and validity criteria. The instruments covered in this section are those which enjoy wide usage and/or satisfy reliability and validity requirements.

The Locke–Wallace Marital Adjustment Test (MAT; Locke and Wallace, 1959) is a fifteen-item questionnaire which has been shown to discriminate between well-adjusted and poorly adjusted marital dyads. It assesses degree of satisfaction and agreement within the marital relationship. This instrument is widely used, and has served as the basis for construct validation of more recent marital adjustment instruments (e.g. Spanier's, 1976, Dyadic Adjustment Scale).

The Spouse Observation Checklist (SOC; G. R. Patterson, 1976) is a 400-item inventory listing specific behaviors or events which are categorized as pleasing or displeasing. Spouses check relevant items, and either rate them as to degree of pleasingness or list costs and benefits of giving/receiving stated behaviors. Satisfaction with the relationship is also rated. A technique was devised (Atkinson and McKenzie, 1984) to eliminate items irrelevant to a particular dyad and allow the dyad to determine categories of pleasing or displeasing, resulting in a personalized version of the instrument which is less lengthy. No significant differences were found between results obtained from the original SOC and the revised, personalized SOC. Jacobson and Margolin (1979) consider the SOC to be invaluable to behavioral marital therapy.

A study conducted by Wills, Weiss and Patterson (1974) utilized a portable event recorder in addition to the SOC. Subjects were asked to record pleasing and displeasing affectional spouse behaviors at time of occurrence on the event counters (each subject had two counters), as well as to fill out the SOC daily.

Although not widely used, this technique could be helpful in providing frequency data that are not subject to the pitfalls associated with retrospective data (see Duck and Sants, 1983, for further discussion of these points).

The Dyadic Adjustment Scale (DAS; Spanier, 1976) is a 32-item questionnaire designed to assess adjustment in marital couples and similar dyads. There are four subscales: satisfaction, consensus, cohesion, and affectional expression. This instrument has been used extensively in marital research, and reliability and validity seem to be well established. Sharpley and Cross (1982) found that six of the items differentiated high from low scorers 92 per cent of the time, and another item alone discriminated between 65 per cent of the cases, suggesting that a shorter form of the DAS could be used in selected situations.

The Marital Satisfaction Inventory (MSI; Snyder, 1979) is a 280-item true–false inventory designed to assess marital satisfaction. It contains a validity scale, a global distress scale, and nine scales that assess specific interaction dimensions. Its reliability, validity, and clinical utility have been demonstrated empirically (Snyder, Wills and Keiser, 1981). It has been found to differentiate between levels and sources of distress, and between sexual dysfunction and more general marital complaints, as well as predict outcome for couples entering sex therapy. It also has been shown to have convergent validity with Gottman's (1979) observational coding system. Recent research (D. K. Snyder and Smith, 1986) with the MSI has focused on creating profiles of marital relationships, similar to MMPI profiles. Along with other instruments such as the Kansas Marital Satisfaction Scale (e.g. Schumm et al., 1985), marital/relationship satisfaction measures offer a rich resource to close relationship researchers (see Jacobson, Follette and Elwood, 1984, for further critical analysis of measures of relationship satisfaction).

SPECIFIC EXAMPLES OF SELF-REPORT APPROACHES

It is apparent that there is no shortage of measures available for research on personal relationships, but the quality of the measures varies widely. One useful—and perhaps essential—approach to relationships is programmatic research, research that doesn't use one measure in one study and another measure in a follow-up but rather tries to build knowledge in an incremental fashion. A programmatic emphasis is to some extent characteristic of the examples we offer to illustrate several different approaches to personal relationship research.

Interviews

Although various types of interviewing techniques have long been popular in the social sciences, a recent series of studies by Huston and his colleagues (e.g. Cate, Huston and Nesselroade, 1986; Huston et al., 1981; Lloyd and Cate, 1985a, b) offers some new variations on standard interview techniques. These researchers focused systematically on assessing courtship and resultant marriage or termination experiences. They have utilized the Retrospective Interview

Technique (Fitzgerald and Surra, 1981), which involves separate interviews of each member of a dyad, in which the relationship is graphed over time. The vertical axis is time in months and the horizontal axis is perceived chance of marrying, ranging from 0 to 100 per cent. The graph begins at the first meeting of the couple, and the respondent is asked to judge when the chance of marriage changed; then that new point is graphed. This process continues until the graph of the relationship reaches the point of marriage or termination. Respondents are asked to identify events or causes of changes in perceived chance of marrying. They are also asked to identify stages of casual dating, serious dating, and commitment. For those in a terminated relationship, two additional stages beyond commitment are identified: uncertainty and certainty. This technique has been used to study relationship development, relationship stages, attributions, significant turning points, the components underlying the trajectories of commitment, and dimensions influencing differential movement to marriage.

One basis for the Huston *et al.* research program was Braiker and Kelley's (1979) use of unstructured retrospective interviews of newly-weds to construct a questionnaire that contained content dimensions applicable to several stages of courtships. Four dimensions were identified through principal components analysis: love, conflict–negativity, maintenance, and ambivalence. Scores on each of the dimensions were found to be different for the different stages of courtship, which included casual dating, serious dating, engagement, and the first six months of marriage.

Although interview techniques are extremely useful, they can be cumbersome to implement and to quantify. Thus, attitude questionnaires have been heavily employed.

Attitude Questionnaires

One recently developed instrument that shows promise for close relationship research is the Hendricks' Attitudes About Love and Sex Scale (e.g. Hendrick and Hendrick, 1986a, 1987b; Hendrick *et al.*, 1984; Hendrick *et al.*, 1985). This 102-item Likert self-report scale is composed of a seventeen-item Background Inventory, a 42-item Love Attitudes Scale, and a 43-item Sexual Attitudes Scale. The love scale is of particular interest since it was theoretically based on and empirically developed from a typology of love styles developed by Lee (1973). Lee proposed three primary orientations to intimate heterosexual loving: *eros* (passionate, sensual love), *ludus* (game-playing love), and *storge* (friendship love). These three love styles are conceptually combined to form three secondary styles (each a compound of two of the primaries) that include; *pragma* (pratical, logical love), *mania* (possessive, dependent love), and *agape* (selfless, altruistic love). Based on an earlier true–false measure (Hatkoff and Lasswell, 1979; Lasswell and Lasswell, 1976), the Hendricks conducted a series of scaling studies to develop and refine the present measure (for a more complete description of scale development see Hendrick and Hendrick, 1986a). Although most of the published research on the love scale pertains to its validity and reliability, the scale has recently been employed in more relationship-relevant settings. Research with homosexual and heterosexual male subjects in Texas and New York (Adler, Hendrick and Hendrick, 1986) revealed few differences in love attitudes (and sexual attitudes) between homosexual and heterosexual subjects. Exploratory research with dual-career professional couples (Castaneda, Hendrick and Flanary, 1986) revealed high correlations between marital partners on several of the love styles (eros, storge, and pragma) and prompted exploration of love styles in dating college couples (Hendrick and Hendrick, 1986b). Several significant love style correlations were found for relationship partners, and a number of significant relationships between love attitudes and various measures of relationship satisfaction also appeared. Such pilot work provides the basis for longitudinal couples' research employing the Love Attitudes Scale and related measures.

Behavioral Self-Report

Behavioral self-report approaches are appropriate for many different areas of personal relationship research and may offer much-needed bridging of the gap between questionnaire self-report and behavioral observation. The Rochester Interaction Record (RIR; Nezlek, Wheeler and Reis, 1983; Reis, Senchak and Solomon, 1985; Wheeler and Nezlek, 1977; Wheeler, Reis and Nezlek, 1983) is an extremely promising example of such measures. The RIR is a fixed-format record of social interactions lasting ten minutes or longer. The RIR is filled out daily, usually for a period of one to two weeks, and provides a record of both quantity and quality of interactions. Indexes include intimacy, disclosure, satisfaction, pleasantness, initiation, influence, number of interaction partners, frequency of contact, time spent socializing, length of each contact, and gender of partners. Subjects appear to have little trouble keeping such a record and perceive their record-keeping as accurate (Reis, Senchak and Solomon, 1985). The RIR has been described as reliable and accurate, and in one study, Reis *et al.* assessed external criterion validity of the RIR against external judges' ratings of degree of intimacy present in a videotaped conversation and found the two to be closely correlated. The RIR has been used in studies relating the variables of loneliness, sex roles, intimacy, and physical attractiveness to social interactions. Other researchers have used techniques similar to the RIR (Jones, 1981; McCormack and Kahn, 1980). Such a technique appears to be useful for studying naturally occurring social interactions. Because the instrument is filled out daily, it should not suffer from the effects of memory and other distortions. It also gives specific details of interactions, rather than global summaries, which should encourage examination of more parameters than those contained in global scales. Valuable longitudinal studies employing the RIR have been reported by Duck and Miell (1986) and Baxter and Wilmot (1986).

Diaries and Accounts

Probably no technique for examining people's reflections on their relationships is older than the diary. For centuries, novelists and biographers have studied diaries to learn about the agonies and ecstasies of people's thoughts and feelings about their love lives. Rosenblatt's (1983) brilliant book, *Bitter, Bitter Tears*, illustrates well the type of useful, poignant information about the loss of one's loved one that can be culled from diaries, in this case from the diaries of people living in the nineteenth century. Also, Frankl's (1962) accounts of his thoughts about his wife while he was in concentration camps partially illustrate the diary–account approach. His experiences were not recorded at the time that they occurred—that was not permitted by the guards. They were recorded from more long-term memory at a later point, for the text of his book.

More common ways of using diary and account approaches involve asking people to keep written records of events and feelings at a point in time close to the event or feeling. In the social and behavioral sciences, Weiss (1975) was one of the first investigators to use this procedure in a study of newly separated members of the organization Parents Without Partners. He also provided a theoretical basis for accounts. With the publication of Weiss' seminal analysis, the concept of an account as an individual's explanation for why a key relationship event occurred became a valuable addition to the self-report literature on relationships. Weiss suggested that, in particular, accounts help people make sense out of the loss of close relationships and provide a feeling of personal control regarding the often chaotic experiences surrounding such loss. Accounts have also been studied as they apply to relationship beginnings and successes. Further discussion of the nature and possible importance of accounts in the study of close relationships is provided by Harvey *et al.* (1986) and Weber, Harvey and Stanley (1987).

Accounts may be long or short. Naturalistically, they may appear in diary form or in recordings, letters and notes, and even videotapes. Further, as Harvey *et al.* (1986) argue, accounts may be continuously updated in content over time by the account-maker. Hence, the longitudinal collection of data is of utmost value in this area. The following is an excerpt from an account:

> I had a feeling of utter failure as a wife but could manage to be happy in the circumstances, i.e., insecurity, particularly economic. I could not reconcile myself to what seemed to be poverty . . . I suppose I rationalized that this was the only way it could have ended, and further events seemed to justify my earlier actions. (From a woman in her late sixties, reporting on the ending of a relationship [Weber, Harvey and Stanley, 1987])

Pros and cons of the diary–account approaches

It should be clear that some of the richest data available on relationships derive from diaries and other forms of reported accounts. Clearly, as Rosenblatt's (1983) insightful work shows, there are many archival sources of these data that have not been tapped by relationships investigators. Giving individuals the opportunity to provide accounts offers them a means of extended reflection and report on their relationship(s). Such reflection and report may be more natural and less subject to reactivity than approaches involving more condensed, questionnaire responses. People can respond to diary-type probes at times when their feelings about the relationship in question are most intense and thoughts most penetrating (e.g. awakening heavy with thought and emotion in the early morning hours).

As with other forms of self-report, diary–account approaches are subject to a variety of methodological issues. Response bias, including self-presentation concerns, may be especially problematic when one is asked to report on sensitive thoughts and feelings to a stranger (as the interviewer may be in the respondent's world). The willingness and/or energy needed to engage in the effortful activity of writing in a diary (perhaps over a long period of time) may be a problem. Further, this type of remembering may be quite painful. The respondent's oral fluency or writing literacy may even be an issue. Possibly most important, diary–account approaches require a considerable and frequently taxing degree of observation and coding of records by multiple coders. In such work, it may be difficult to retrieve most of the central meaning intended by the respondent. Each of these possible concerns may be addressed *a priori* by the careful, knowledgeable investigator. Indeed, the stakes are high in diary–account research. A great amount of highly provocative information may be obtained—or loads of difficult-to-analyze/interpret data may be produced. We do, however, recommend these approaches for relationships investigators' greater scrutiny and possible use.

ISSUES IN THE USE OF SELF-REPORT

Although self-report is obviously a popular approach to data-gathering in relationships, it is not without problems. Such problems may relate primarily to the research subjects, to the researcher, or to the interaction between the wo.

Subject-Related Issues

One extremely important factor already mentioned is the cognitive work required of the respondent. It is necessary that the subject understand the investigator's questions; differences in 'meaning' of various constructs or behaviors may seriously bias the subject's responses. Another major concern is the nature of the memory retrieval required by the subject. Harvey, Christensen and McClintock (1983) noted that the accuracy of subject responses is reduced both as a function of the generality of the questions asked and the length of time between the occurrence of an event and its subsequent recall. In addition, subjects tend to recall certain types of information more readily than other types. Egocentric bias, which refers to a subject's tendency to report more of one's own relationship behaviors than the partner's relationship behaviors (e.g. Ross and Sicoly, 1979) is one potential form of bias in relationship research. Of course, the opposite attribution tendency has been shown by various researchers (e.g. Madden and Janoff-Bulman, 1981; Orvis, Kelley and Butler, 1976), who have noted the tendencies of partners to conflict to attribute more blame to the other than to the self. A number of other self-report validity and reliability problems noted by Huston and Robins (1982) include respondent reactivity, memory distortions, errors in calculation of events, questionnaire response biases, and so on. Such problems raise serious questions about subjects' abilities as accurate reporters of their own relationship behaviors, and indeed Jacobson and Moore (1981) found a low degree of consensus between both distressed and nondistressed marital partners on the occurrence of behaviors affecting the relationship. A useful perspective on how many of these subject-related issues may be resolved is provided by Duck and Sants (1983).

Researcher Issues

We make critical choices throughout the relationship research process. The questions asked may vary on the continuum of specificity (molecular to molar) as well as temporality (proximal to distal), and each variation has different implications for the data that are generated.

A question that follows 'which data?' might well be 'whose data?' Much personal relationship research has focused on the *individual* dyad member's perceptions, referred to by Huston and Robins (1982) as the measurement of 'subjective conditions' of the relationship. Although this focus is both legitimate and necessary, we agree with Thompson and Walker (1982) that 'Taken alone, the study of one person's values, love, or commitment does not constitute dyadic research. A property of the dyad must reflect the combination of or interdependence between members' (p. 891). This emphasis on interdependence is echoed by numerous researchers (e.g. Hill and Scanzoni, 1982; Huston and Robins, 1982) and can be variously achieved through assessment approaches and analytically through 'couple' scores such as correlations, discrepancy scores, agreement coefficients, conditional probabilities, ratios, sums, and the like (Thompson and Walker, 1982). A companion question concerns aggregation of data. An important issue is considering how self-report data are to be summed, weighted, or in general aggregated as we draw conclusions and form concepts about relationships. The analysis of the internal dynamics of the dyad often cannot be easily carried out in terms of *specific* cause and effect links. Accordingly, the analysis is often made in terms of aggregate concepts that involve some type of summation of similar events.

What special problems confront the investigator in aggregating over events and causal connections? First, it is necessary that the events and connections that are combined are indeed similar. The discrete events and connections may be clearcut in some instances, but special care must be exercised when the aggregation procedure involves asking the research participants to report in a global fashion. In effect, the investigator is trying to shortcut a detailed observation process by obtaining participants' impressions of aggregate tendencies. This procedure may be necessary but may also be particularly susceptible to some of the problems previously discussed in terms of memory failure, and distortion and divergency in perception and attribution in couples.

Relationship Between Investigator and Participant

The study of close relationships may involve a greater degree of association between the investigator and the participant than does any other type of research. Levinger (1977) described a possible continuum of interaction between the investigator and the participant along what he calls an 'insiderness' dimension. On one extreme, the 'outside' is a situation in which the investigator, or observer, is entirely outside the relationship (as if watching it from the other side of a one-way mirror). Intermediate is a situation in which the contact is superficial, such as when the observer asks questions in a rather impersonal structured interview. At the other extreme, substantially 'inside', the observer and the respondents (as in a study of dyads) interact in an intimate fashion. Such substantial 'insiderness' may occur when the observer is a close friend or relative, or it may obtain in intensive interviews conducted over a period of time.

Clearly, the investigator who uses a self-report methodology and who seeks answers to questions about people's intimacies must strike a balance between achieving rapport with the respondents and becoming so close that the relationship between investigator and respondent substantially affects what is being studied.

In addition, investigators must be extremely cognizant of the fine line between couples' research and couples' counseling (Rubin and Mitchell, 1976). Although the research process may not create problems between partners, it can certainly intensify them. Thus, research participants need to be fully informed before the research begins and closely monitored throughout the process (Harvey, Christensen and McClintock, 1983; Hendrick and Hendrick, 1983).

Why Self-Report?

Why, with all the problems outlined above, is the self-report approach to data-gathering in personal relationships likely to maintain its past and present popularity? This question was answered succinctly by Harvey, Christensen and McClintock (1983), who noted:

> This method has several unique advantages. First, participant verbalizations about subjective experiences are the only currently available means for investigators to tap directly such covert activities as perceptions, feelings, thoughts, expectations, and memories. Second, participants can describe events that, though overt, are usually private to the relationship, such as sexual behavior or conflict. Finally, participant reports are relatively easy to obtain and involve much less inconvenience and expense than observer reports. (p. 452)

All three reasons hold equally well today.

Thus the question becomes not *whether* to do self-report research but rather how best to do it. The clear consensus on the latter is the multimethod approach, difficult to implement but endorsed by numerous scholars (e.g. Harvey, Christensen and McClintock, 1983; Huston and Robins, 1982; Olson, 1977). Some combination of self-report, behavioral self-report, and observational methods, based upon a guiding theoretical structure, would undoubtedly best serve personal relationships research.

THE FUTURE OF SELF-REPORT

Although it will undoubtedly continue and will hopefully improve, what are some of the possible new directions for self-report research?

Self-Report and Physiological Measurement

A recent development in research on relationships is the attempt to link self-report and physiological measurement of reactions to events. In the future, it may become more common to obtain physiological data focusing on couples and their interactions. These data would be less subject to the possible biases in reporting described in the chapter. Such approaches do, however, require expensive instrumentation, a degree of expertise in psychophysiological theory and recording, and a willingness/ability on the part of the respondents to have electrodes hooked to them while they take relationship-relevant actions. In particular, this feasibility requirement may limit the use of this technique. It is likely that future technology will permit more unobtrusive recordings, as well as recordings on a more remote basis (not necessarily in a laboratory). This latter provision now exists for certain measurement techniques.

A focus for this type of research is the link between physiology and reported cognition and affect. One study is highly suggestive at this point. Levenson and Gottman (1985) reported a study (begun in 1980) that involved a low- or high-conflict conversational interaction between spouses in 30 couples while continuous physiological data were obtained. Later, a self-report of affect was made while spouses watched a videotape of the interaction. Nineteen of these couples were recontacted in 1983 to determine the change in their relationship satisfaction over the three-year period. The researchers found that a broadly based pattern of physiological arousal (across spouses and types of conflict interaction) in 1980 predicted decline in marital satisfaction in 1983. The data also showed the predictive merit of reported affect over the three-year period. For example, greater reciprocity of the husband's negative affect by the wife during the 1980 period was highly related to decline in marital satisfaction over the three years.

As we write, the links between physiology, cognition, and affect responses in relationships are topics more of speculation than of intensive investigation. Nevertheless, they comprise a future exciting frontier for the area. Even with a focus on physiology, the need for refined self-report methodologies remains and is enhanced in the context of searches for interrelated patterns of responses.

Objective Measures

Recommendations that go beyond standard multimethod approaches emphasize multiple laboratory and/or naturalistic settings and populations and the development of less reactive measures. In relation to the latter, O'Leary and Turkewitz (1978) suggest that adjunctive measures such as days absent from work, job productivity, and physical well-being should be given more attention. Potentially useful objective measures might even include such things as outstanding debts, legal problems (e.g. traffic citations), or hobbies and community involvements.

Subjective Measures

At the other extreme are the subjective, descriptive measures such as diaries and other accounts, discussed earlier. Literature, including poetry and drama, has historically provided the rich description of relationships that strikes a responsive chord in each of us. Social science has formalized the process of researching personal relationships but often without 'touching' us in the process. Thus, fully subjective, descriptive self-report approaches deserve a place in the research endeavor.

CONCLUSIONS

Many of the issues raised in this chapter are examples of what makes personal relationship research both endlessly fascinating and ceaselessly frustrating. In an elegant review, Rubin (1984) lauds the movement towards a 'science of close relationships' even as he calls for more attention to the subjective, affective richness that provides the *raison d'être* for relationships. We want it all. We want both scientific rigor and generalizable 'meaning' to characterize our research in personal relationships. If both are ever to be achieved, self-report approaches must inevitably be part of the process.

Section Two

Developmental/Life Cycle

Section Editor   *Dale F. Hay*

Overview

Personal relationships are by their very nature developmental; personal development occurs in the context of particular relationships. The contributors to this part of the Handbook have confronted those two facts and asked, exactly how does one go about studying the development of a relationship? In what different sorts of ways do relationships contribute to the development of an individual? These two questions are of course themselves closely related.

Section Two does not provide separate accounts of the different sorts of relationships in which children engage. Numerous other recent reviews and books have summarized information about parent–child relationships (e.g. Bretherton, 1986; Maccoby and Martin, 1983), sibling relationships (e.g. Dunn, 1987), peer relationships (e.g. Hartup, 1983), and so on, and we have not tried to duplicate those efforts. Indeed, the study of particular relationships in isolation in some ways departs from the spirit of the relationships perspective. Rather, each author was asked to consider a classic developmental issue as it would be applied to the study of personal relationships. In taking up this charge, the contributors have therefore identified a number of conceptual and methodological issues that arise when studying the development of any relationship.

In Chapter 7, entitled 'Ontogeny, Phylogeny, and Relationships', Alison Nash was asked to reconsider the classic nature–nurture issue and examine personal relationships from both a biological and psychological point of view. She focused on the question of origins: how do human beings acquire the fundamental ability to form relationships with other members of their species? Is this ability to any large extent an evolutionary legacy, and, if so, what exactly was it that was selected for? How is the evolutionary heritage transformed by the experiences of the developing individual?

Nash has approached these questions by examining the most influential attempt to undertake an evolutionary analysis of a personal relationship, John Bowlby's (1969) theory of the attachment relationship between parent and infant. She has subjected Bowlby's theory to an analysis based on updated evolutionary concepts and concluded that what is required is not a theory of

117

attachment alone, but rather a comprehensive evolutionary and developmental analysis of the infant's general ability to form relationships.

Nash notes that most of the available evidence about early social relations focuses more on general interactive capabilities than on the characteristics of particular sustained relationships. This may be partly a function of investigators' disinclination to believe that young children have relationships, at least with persons other than their parents, but it also reflects a lack of consensus about measurement criteria. When is it possible to say that a relationship has been formed? What are appropriate general dimensions along which to measure the features and functions of developing relationships? Hildy Ross, J. Allan Cheyne and Susan Lollis take up these questions in Chapter 8, 'Defining and Studying Reciprocity in Young Children'.

Ross and her colleagues note the importance of the concept of reciprocity in a number of disparate theories. At the same time, reciprocity is a concept that is variously defined and measured. Ross *et al.* have tried to sort out much of the semantic confusion; in addition, they have proposed a method for determining, first of all, when relationships can be identified at all and, secondly, when such relationships can be said to be reciprocal. They have devised a hierarchical model-fitting procedure for identifying relationships, illustrating their procedure with some reanalyses of classic data on children's social relations collected by Helen Bott in the 1930s. Thus, these authors have introduced a metric for describing relationships that can then provide a basis for examining changes and continuities over time. Development, of course, encompasses both continuity and change; however, some investigators have focused more on the issue of continuity over time, in terms of identifying stable personality traits, whereas others have focused more on change, in terms of what new abilities and ideas are acquired as the result of experience. The next two chapters take up these complementary issues with respect to the study of personal relationships.

In their contribution entitled 'Traits and Relationships in Developmental Perspective', Kathryn Park and Everett Waters have examined relationships from the point of view of personality development and personality from the point of view of relationships. They argue that neither personality traits nor personal relationships should be viewed as explanations of an individual's behavior and development; rather, traits and relationships themselves are developmental phenomena that require explanation. Park and Waters take up three general questions. How does an individual's personality affect the formation and maintenance of relationships? How, in turn, do an individual's relationships shape personality development? Finally, to what extent do different relationships have different personalities? In other words, to what extent is it helpful to try to identify stable and coherent traits possessed by dyadic relationships?

Human development is paradoxical, in that, with the years, humans seem to become both more individual, more distinctly themselves, and at the same time more socialized, conforming to the norms and values of their social groups. Investigators who focus on socialization have tried to identify the processes responsible for a child's eventual adjustment to societal demands; in their chapter, Rosemary Mills and Joan Grusec have examined how much of this task is accomplished in the context of the close personal relationship between parent and child. Mills and Grusec argue that one cannot understand abstract processes of socialization without reference to the hearts and minds of the child who is being socialized and the parent who is serving as agent of socialization. That is, the process and outcomes of socialization are going to be affected by the parent's thoughts and feelings about the child and by the child's thoughts and feelings about himself or herself and the parent. Power relations and conflict in the parent–child relationship, and the attributions about self and other made by both the parent and the child, affect the socialization process. The authors of both chapters emphasize the paramount role of the parent–child relationship in personality development and socialization. It is clear, however, that develop-ment proceeds within a social world that comprises a number of different personal relationships. How do these relationships themselves interrelate? How does one identify links across relationships? What mechanisms are responsible for those links? Judy Dunn takes up these complex issues in her chapter entitled 'Relations among Relationships'. She identifies the conceptual questions that are raised in trying to examine associations between any pair of relationships, and discusses the evidence for three such associations: between parent–child relationships and the parent's other personal relationships, including that with the spouse; between parent–child and child–peer relationships; and between parent–child and sibling relationships. With respect to each topic, Dunn attempts to seek evidence that the association is one between the relationships in question and not simply a function of individual personality manifesting itself across interpersonal contexts.

In examining these connections between relationships, Dunn notes how experiences in one relationship may be associated with problems in another. This of course raises the question of pathology; when can a relationship be said to be deficient or disordered? Do the same principles of development apply to normal and problematic relationships? In the final chapter in this section, entitled 'A Model for Children's Relationships and Relationship Dysfunctions', Terry Adler and Wyndol Furman propose a general scheme for describing children's relationships that can be applied to the study of both normal and pathological development. In devising this model, they have consulted Weiss's (1974) theory of the 'social provisions' afforded by different sorts of relation-ships, but they have also sought the advice of children themselves. Children's descriptions of their relationships with parents, peers, and siblings have been factor analysed; Adler and Furman argue that the general dimensions emerging from these analyses, namely, warmth, power arrangements, conflict, and relations among relationships, provide a standard means of comparing relation-ships in the normal range and classifying dysfunctions.

All of the contributors to this section of the volume have done considerable theoretical work that advances the study of each topic they have taken up. In addition, they have all in their different ways confronted the fundamental issue in the study of relationships and development: relationships are inherently dyadic phenomena, but development is studied at the individual level of analysis. Is it possible to integrate a focus on dyads with a focus on individual development? It is no easy task, but the chapters that follow illustrate a number of rigorous and inventive attempts at integration. By making the attempt, the authors have both advanced the study of personal relationships and contributed to developmental theory.

Handbook of Personal Relationships
Edited by S. W. Duck
© 1988 John Wiley & Sons Ltd

7

Ontogeny, Phylogeny, and Relationships

ALISON NASH
State University of New York at New Paltz, USA

ABSTRACT

The early origins of capacities for forming relationships are examined. In particular, the focus is on infants' abilities to form relationships not only with peers but with a range of individuals. In this chapter, "attachment" is considered to be a dimension of relationships. At present there exists a conceptual framework for viewing the narrower concept of "attachment" in evolutionary and developmental perspective. What is needed is a conceptual framework with which to view the early origins of relationships.

Humans, as members of a social species, have a network of social relationships which are central to their lives. The capacity for such relationships appears to be a fundamental part of human nature. In this chapter I focus on the possible origins of this capacity. The important role social relationships play in our lives is not unique to humans. Social bonds and networks are important for many species of birds and mammals. Therefore, when I examine personal relationships in humans, I look not only at the beginnings in an individual's life but at the legacy from the evolutionary past as well: the ontogeny and phylogeny of personal relationships. In particular, I will focus on the capacities in human infants for forming relationships, not only with a primary caregiver, but with other people in their lives. For infants, like adults, are part of a social network (Lewis and Rosenblum, 1975), and thus may share the potential to form relationships with a variety of individuals. I will explore the ontogeny and phylogeny of their abilities to do so.

THE BIOLOGY OF RELATIONSHIPS

The study of the development of interpersonal relationships in infancy has always operated under the assumption that such relationships are rooted in biology. Freud explained early relationships in terms of 'instincts' (Freud, 1940), using this concept in much the same way, according to R. Fine (1979), as did his contemporary, McDougal, then the leading theorist of innate dispositions, or instincts. Freud believed that instincts, and in particular sexual drives, were the basis for infants' close emotional relationships with their mothers. In the 1930s and 1940s, British analysts such as Fairbairn and Guntrip objected to the emphasis on instincts, and stressed object relations instead. They believed that 'the ego, and therefore the libido, is fundamentally object-seeking' (Fairbairn, 1963). Thus the object-relations school, as this line of thought came to be called, did not believe that infants' early relationships were rooted in sexual and/or aggressive drives, but that the need for relationships themselves was primary. Although Fairbairn, for example, claimed to reject the notion of a biological psychology (Guntrip, 1961), he believed that 'the libido is not primarily pleasure-seeking, but object-seeking' (Fairbairn, 1952, p. v). If Freudians believe the libido to be pleasure-seeking and object-relations theorists believe it to be object-seeking, both believe, nevertheless, that the libido is something infants are born with. In other words, whether the infant is said to be pleasure- or object-seeking, innate predispositions are hypothesized as contributing to the formation of relationships in infancy.

Unlike the other object-relations theorists, who sought to understand the psychology of early relationships, Bowlby (1958, 1969, 1982) focused on the biological aspects and explicated these early relationships in terms of the prevailing biological theory of behavior of that time—ethological–evolutionary theory. When thus anchored to ethology, a more empirically oriented approach to the study of psychological phenomena than is the psychoanalytic approach, relationship formation in infancy began to be studied empirically. Many were at first skeptical of the object-relations view of the infant, including Mary Ainsworth, whose initial reaction to Bowlby's theory was that no new theory was needed to explain babies' attachment to their mothers. 'Some truths are self-evident: Babies become attached to their mothers because their mothers feed them . . . Nursing is gratifying' (Levine, 1986, p. 211). Only when it was made explicit that object-relations theory is rooted in biology, that the need for relationships themselves can be considered a primary, biological drive, did developmental psychologists begin to view social development from this perspective. Thus Bowlby, by examining its phylogeny, opened the way for developmental psychologists to examine its ontogeny.

Attachments and Relationships

Bowlby's phylogenetic discussion referred not to infants' interpersonal relationships in general, but to the particular dimension of the relationship an infant has with his or her primary caregiver that Bowlby termed 'attachment'. According to

Bowlby, infants have an innate predisposition to maintain proximity with familiar caregivers. They are able to maintain this proximity at first through signals, such as crying and smiling, which bring and/or keep an adult nearby, and later through locomotion as well as signals.

Although the behaviors used to effect proximity may change as the infant gets older, their goal remains the same. Infants are assumed to get a feeling of security through proximity. Attachment refers to the dimension of the infant–caregiver relationship that is concerned with the seeking of security by the infant and its provision by the caregiver. Bowlby suggested that the propensity to form attachments evolved through natural selection, as such attachments functioned to protect infants from predation in the human 'environment of evolutionary adaptedness'.

Although Bowlby's theory concerned phylogeny, it inspired much research on the ontogeny of attachments. Attachment researchers (e.g. Ainsworth et al., 1978; Belsky, Rovine and Taylor, 1984; Egeland and Farber, 1984; Grossman et al., 1985; Sagi et al., 1985) then focused on the ontogeny of individual differences in types of attachments. During this time, another group of investigators was conducting studies of other aspects of infants' relationships. These studies did not use evolutionary-attachment theory as a guide. They focused instead on infants' emerging abilities to interact with others, in particular their very early preference for the perceptual and acoustical stimuli of the human face and voice (reviewed by Spelke and Cortelyou, 1981), and their early abilities to engage in behavioral and vocal dialogues (e.g. Brazelton, Koslowski and Main, 1974; Bruner, 1977; Snow, 1977; Trevarthen, 1977; Schaffer, 1984). Although such studies were not guided by ethological-attachment theory, they too assumed phylogeny to be important, and emerged from the biological preparedness for learning paradigm (Seligman, 1970). Infants were found to be biologically prepared to learn a great many things that helped them form relationships. For example, young infants are best able to hear sounds within the register of human speech (e.g. Eisenberg, 1976; Fernald, 1984), and visually, appear to prefer social (primarily facial) stimuli (reviewed by Sherrod, 1981).

The problem with the biological preparedness paradigm is that, unlike attachment theory, it is not a theory of relationships but of individuals. The infants' abilities to respond to other people are discussed in terms of innate or biological propensities. The focus is thus on the infant, and not the relationship. It is clear, however, that infants' interactional abilities mesh with their interactants' abilities to relate to them. Yet there is no biological theory which focuses on relationships in general.

Relationships are not the same as attachments. As Bowlby himself pointed out, much of interaction is not concerned with the attachment system. Attachment, then, can be viewed as a subset of relationship behaviors. Yet, as Sroufe and Fleeson (1986) have suggested, relationships themselves may influence development, in the same way that a particular dimension of some relationships, i.e. attachment, has been found to influence development. We know, through many studies (reviewed by Lamb et al., 1985), that the quality of infants' attachments to their mothers may influence other aspects of behavior, such as later patterns of adjustment and competence. Theoretically, one can speculate about such influences of other aspects of relationships. For example, relationships are the contexts in which much of socialization takes place, and thus in which children acquire communication skills (Hartup, 1986).

However, there are only a few studies which look at the influence of aspects of relationships other than the quality of attachment on subsequent behavior. In one such study, Maslin, Bretherton and Morgan (1986) examined the ways in which mothers help their infants explore and master their environments. A mother may, for example, show an infant how an object works, hold an object while an infant explores it, help the infant work it, etc. The provision of such support, which helps an infant do something he or she could not do alone, has been termed 'scaffolding' (e.g. Bruner and Sherwood, 1976; Ratner and Bruner, 1978). Besides providing such scaffolds, mothers may also provide emotional support for their infants. According to attachment theorists (e.g. Ainsworth *et al.*, 1978), mothers may provide infants with a secure base from which they can explore their environment. Thus, theoretically, Maslin and her colleagues predicted that several aspects of the infant–mother relationship might affect infants' mastery of the environment. They rated mothers' scaffolding abilities with their infants, the security of infants' attachment to their mothers, and infants' abilities to master the environment. They found that certain scaffolding skills, i.e. active maternal teaching and motivating, were better predictors of children's mastery abilities (independent motivation and exploration) than was the sense of security provided by a secure attachment. They also found that a mother's ability effectively to support and assist her child's mastery attempts was not related to the security of her child's attachment. In other words, a completely separate component of their relationship, unrelated to the security of attachment, was found to influence the child's exploratory tendencies.

In another such study, Nash and Lamb (1987) examined how the infant–mother relationship affected infants' abilities to form relationships with others. In this study, each fourteen-month-old infant subject was observed in a playroom along with his or her mother, a peer, and the peer's mother, for five days in a row. On the second through fifth days the mother left the playroom after ten minutes. About half the infants were distressed when their mothers left and could not be soothed by the other peer's mother within a few minutes at least once, so that their mothers were asked to return to the playroom; the other infants were not as distressed and allowed their mothers to leave all four days. The best predictor of whether a child would fall into the high or low distress group was the behavior of the mother before she left. Children in the low distress group had mothers who interacted significantly more with the peer's mother than children in the high distress group. In fact, a mother's behavior with the peer's mother was a better predictor of distress at being left with the peer and peer's mother than was an infant's attachment quality with his or her mother. Once again, an aspect of an infant's relationship with mother, other than attachment, was found to influence his or her behavior. Infants may watch how their mothers behave in social situations. Observing their mothers interact with someone may provide them the opportunity to decide how they themselves should act with that person.

Thus there is some evidence to suggest 'attachment' is not the only dimension of relationships that may affect development. How can we integrate the relationship and the attachment schools of theory and research? Field's (1985) recent discussion of attachment can be considered an attempt at such a synthesis. She points out that attachment has been studied only by its absence, i.e. the absence or separation from an attachment figure. Why not observe the actual relationship itself? She suggests that 'attachment' be viewed as 'psychobiological attunement' between two individuals. In other words, the processes of the synchronization of the behavior and physiology of the two individuals involved should be examined. It is time to shift the focus from the narrower attachment paradigm to that of the larger relationship.

A difficulty in synthesizing the two perspectives is that attachment is viewed through an evolutionary framework, whereas relationships typically are not. Attachments are said to evolve, through natural selection. Arguments (Bowlby, 1969) have been made about the adaptive value of attachment. No such ultimate or evolutionary explanations have been made about relationships. Relationships have been examined only at a proximate level. At this level, the biological influences on capacities for relationships, and not attachments, have been shown. Thus support for the notion of a biological preparedness for relationships is provided by the studies showing infants' readiness to respond to human faces, voices, and behavior.

What is remarkable about infants' abilities to relate to others is that they are, by definition, 'without speech' (Latin: *in-fans* means un-speaking). Yet even without this highly effective mode of exchanging information with others, they are nevertheless still able to communicate, and to form relationships. It seems, then, that relationships must be important for them. An evolutionary analysis of 'attachment' enabled researchers to better understand its importance for the infant. In the next section, I propose an account of *relationships* from an evolutionary point of view. In particular, I reexamine Bowlby's theory in light of contemporary evolutionary constructs to show that it is compatible with an evolutionary explanation not just of attachments, but of close relationships in general. In the subsequent section, I present the evidence of a biological preparedness for relationships at a more proximate level, by reviewing studies which taken together trace the developmental course of infants' capacities to relate to other people.

Evolutionary Attachment Theory

Evolutionary attachment theory was originally proposed to provide scientific support to the notion, derived from psychoanalytic and object-relations theory, that the first relationship, which is usually between infant and mother, is of utmost importance to the infant's well-being. Like the object-relations theorists (e.g. Fairbairn, 1952; Guntrip, 1961), Bowlby believed that infants instinctively sought this relationship: in other words, that they were biologically equipped to form this relationship. He went on to examine this biological predisposition in terms of the current biological theory of behavior of that time, ethological–evolutionary theory. According to Bowlby, the infant has an innate tendency to 'attach himself (*sic*) especially to one figure' (1982, p. 309). He referred to this tendency as monotropy. He suggested that human propensities for such an early relationship, or 'attachment', have evolved through natural selection. To support this view, he explicated the adaptive value of attachment, and used the comparative method to argue that the process of attachment formation in humans is similar to the imprinting process through which other animals form intimate social bonds (Bowlby, 1982, pp. 222–223).

Bowlby attempted to update concepts used to explain infants' social behavior by applying the then recent innovations in bio-evolutionary ways of thinking about social behavior. Since Bowlby's explication, there have been new developments in evolutionary thinking which could be useful in a reexamination of his still widely accepted theory of the development of early social relations.

Background: Group selection vs individual selection

Interest in the evolution of social behavior was stimulated by Wynne-Edwards' (1962) theory of group selection as a mechanism of evolution. He proposed that certain social behaviors were selected for because they enhanced the survival of the species as a whole, even though in some cases they may not have enhanced the survival of a particular individual. For example, the 'suicidal' behavior of a group of lemmings who jump off a cliff to their deaths may have adaptive value to the species as a whole—although particular lemmings may die, the elimination of part of the population may allow the others access to the food supply. If all had attempted to use a limited food supply, the whole population may have starved. In contrast, Hamilton's (1964) theory of 'inclusive fitness' emphasizes individual reproductive success. 'Inclusive fitness' refers to the net increase of an individual's reproductive success. According to Hamilton's theory, a behavior will be selected for only if it increases the reproductive success of those who have the gene for the behavior. Although the behavior may incur a cost (in terms of reproductive success, or the number of surviving offspring) to some individuals carrying the gene for it, it may benefit others carrying the same gene even more. 'Suicidal' behavior in lemmings would be selected for only if individuals who had the genes for this behavior survived and reproduced—if, for example, those who jumped off the cliff, by doing so, increased the number of offspring their kin, who share some of their genes (and in particular the genes responsible for suicidal behavior), produced. As the concept of 'inclusive fitness' is more consistent with Darwin's theory of evolution via natural selection, it subsequently replaced Wynne-Edwards' concept of 'survival of the species'.

Explaining the evolution of various social behaviors in terms of individual reproductive success then became a primary concern of researchers in the field of evolutionary biology. Social behavior by definition involves more than one individual; for a behavior to be considered to be adaptive in evolutionary terms, the benefits to all involved individuals must be elucidated. Theoreticians elucidated the costs and benefits to each individual involved in various kinds of social relationships thought to have evolved through natural selection. For example, Orians (1969) examined the costs and benefits to females, as well as males, of polygyny in red-winged blackbirds (typically thought of as advantageous only to males); Trivers examined the costs and benefits to both parents and young of parental care of offspring (Trivers, 1974) and to each parent in their relationship to one another in regard to care of their young (Trivers, 1972); Emlen and Oring (1977) analyzed strategies used by males and females in their courting and mating relationships with one another; and Chase (1980) and Maynard-Smith (1974) assessed the costs and benefits to both individuals involved in particular cooperative and conflictual encounters.

The shift towards the modern evolutionary perspective on social behavior based on inclusive fitness occurred after Bowlby advanced his evolutionary theory of attachment, which was based on a classical ethological perspective. He acknowledges these 'major developments in the thinking of biologists studying the social behavior of species other than man' in the preface to the second edition of his treatise (Bowlby, 1982, p. xvi). Elsewhere in the text (pp. 53–57), he provides an explanation for the evolution of 'attachment' in terms of the modern concept of 'gene survival' (e.g. Williams, 1966), rather than the now unpopular concept of 'species survival' (Wynne-Edwards, 1962) which he used in his first edition (Bowlby, 1969). Nevertheless, even while acknowledging the recent changes in evolutionary perspectives, the bulk of Bowlby's (1982) revised evolutionary argument is still presented in terms of classical ethological theory. In contrast to the modern evolutionary perspective's cost-benefit analysis for each individual involved in particular kinds of social encounters, the ethological perspective focuses on the form and function of particular behaviors. Bowlby focuses on the form and function of attachment behaviors in the infant. But in order to explain the evolution of 'attachment' in contemporary terms, the costs and benefits to each individual involved in the attachment relationship must be specified.

Does 'attachment' refer to individuals or dyads?

Bowlby does not make explicit whether his evolutionary analysis pertains to particular infant behaviors or to infant–primary caregiver reciprocal behaviors. At the time of his first formulation, this distinction was not essential, as either infant attachment behaviors or infant–primary caregiver reciprocal behaviors could be explained in terms of 'survival of the species'. In other words, in this view, the primary caregiver in particular need not benefit from 'attachment' behaviors, as long as the species as a whole benefitted. This distinction is essential, however, in examining attachment within the contemporary evolutionary framework. To do so, it must be made clear whether innate predispositions for attachment are genotypic characteristics of infants or are found within both infants and primary caregivers.

Although Bowlby does not make explicit whether his evolutionary analysis pertains to particular infant behaviors or to infant–caregiver reciprocal behaviors, an examination of his argument reveals that infant attachment behaviors may be considered adaptive only if they are responded to appropriately by the individual to whom they are directed. Infants who sought proximity to individuals who then failed to protect them from predators would be unlikely to survive. Therefore, if infants' proximity-seeking behaviors are to be viewed as an evolutionary adaptation, adult caregiving behaviors must be viewed so as well. Bowlby thus implied that he was providing an evolutionary account of infant attachment behaviors in conjunction with adult caregiving behaviors.

Passages throughout the text support this reading. For example, he refers to the attachment behaviors on the part of the infant and caregiving behaviors on the part of the primary caregiver as a 'shared dyadic program' (1982, p. 378). Furthermore, in discussing 'the role of the child and mother', he informs us that 'the role of the mother as partner must be considered' (p. 236). In discussing 'attachment behavior and its place in nature' (p. 80), he lists two criteria which denote the presence of 'attachments', i.e. the occurrence of proximity-seeking behaviors of parent and young to one another, and the specificity of these behaviors to one another. Finally, Bowlby posits 'control systems', i.e. the mechanism by which attachment effects itself, in both the child and the parent. 'The behavior of parents that is reciprocal to the attachment behaviors of juveniles is termed "caregiving behavior"' (p. 182). An entire section of the book is devoted to describing this caregiving behavior on the part of parents.

Thus it appears that Bowlby's evolutionary model of attachment refers to an aspect of the infant–caregiver relationship. In other words, both infant care-soliciting behavior towards primary caregivers and its complement in primary caregivers, caregiving behavior towards infants, are the outcome of natural selection.

I have attempted to clarify whether Bowlby is referring to individuals or to dyads in his view of attachment as a biological adaptation, as this distinction is crucial in viewing attachment through contemporary evolutionary theory. Others (Cairns, 1972; Hinde, 1982; Lamb *et al.*, 1985) have also interpreted Bowlby's argument as referring to innate predispositions in both infants and primary caregivers to respond to one another in particular ways. Hinde and Stevenson-Hinde (1986), for example, discuss Bowlby's concept of attachment in terms of the 'behavioral systems that *each partner* brings to the interactions' (p. 28). If, then, an evolutionary account of attachment–caregiving behaviors is being proposed, the identity of 'caregivers' must be specified. Only then can we discuss the co-evolution of attachment–caregiving behaviors.

Identity of caregivers

Bowlby does not specify who falls into the category of caregivers. Although throughout his treatise he discusses the concept of 'attachment' in terms of infants and mothers, early in his text he informs the reader, through a footnote, that when he uses the term 'mother' he is in fact referring to a 'mother-figure', or primary caregiver (Bowlby, 1982, p. 29). This implies that an attachment can be formed between an infant and whomever primarily cares for the infant, whether biologically related to the infant or not. In fact, the only restriction Bowlby places on the 'attachment' figure is that he or she is 'older and wiser' than the infant. The issue of whether or not the caregiver is related to the infant is of primary importance in viewing attachment through a contemporary evolutionary framework. As discussed earlier, if attachment were selected for, there must be a benefit to both individuals involved in the 'attachment' relationship. Bowlby, still using the classical ethological perspective, only discusses the adaptive value to the infant and not to the primary caregiver.

Bowlby's proposed benefit to the infant, protection from predation, would be the same no matter who fulfilled the caregiver role. In contrast, benefits to parents or kin of providing care for their infants are not the same as benefits to non-related individuals who provide care. In the case of parents being caregivers, the benefit is obvious—survival of their offspring, and therefore of their genes (however, see Hinde, 1982 and Lamb et al., 1985, for a discussion of how it is not necessarily always in parents' best interests to provide care for their young).

The benefits to non-parent caregivers are not as obvious and are best viewed in terms of the more recent explanatory concepts of kin selection (Hamilton, 1964) and/or reciprocal altruism (Trivers, 1971). In the case of related kin (grandparents, siblings, aunts, uncles), caring for the young might increase their own inclusive fitness, as the caregiver and young would share some genes (kin selection). In the case of an unrelated individual who cares for the young, he or she may establish a relationship with the young or their parents, who in return might then help that individual in some way which results in an increase in his or her own reproductive success (reciprocal altruism).

Trivers has pointed out that reciprocal altruism can work only in the context of close relationships. If an increase in fitness is to be truly reciprocal, i.e. each individual involved does something to increase the fitness of the other, a close relationship between the two insures the favor to be returned. Indeed, once the concept of reciprocal altruism is invoked, which it must be to explain attachments with non-related individuals, it can be used to explain not only attachments but also close relationships in general. Reciprocal altruism need not distinguish between attachments and close relationships.

The concepts of kin selection and reciprocal altruism can be applied to Bowlby's theory to provide a rationale for non-parent caregiving. Bowlby indicated that infants and individuals other than mothers can form 'attachments', and furthermore suggested that these individuals could be anyone 'older and wiser' than the infant. Thus it seems that Bowlby believes that any conspecific whom the infant knows well could fulfill the role. It appears, then, that the logical extension of Bowlby's theory, when viewed through contemporary evolutionary theory, is that infants and their conspecifics are predisposed towards the formation of relationships with one another.

If the predisposition for relationships is not between infant and one primary caregiver but between infant and conspecifics, there is no reason to assume a tendency for monotropy. Although Bowlby's theory is used to indicate a biological predisposition towards monotropy, i.e. that an infant has an innate tendency to 'attach himself (*sic*) especially to one figure' (Bowlby, 1982, p. 309), there is no logical support for specific attachment or monotropy. The evolutionary theory can just as readily account for a predisposition for infants and their conspecifics to form close relationships with one another. Further support for this view is provided by examining the adaptive value to both infant and caregiver of monotropy and of multiple relationships.

Adaptive value of monotropy versus multiple relationships

Although Bowlby proposed that infants were predisposed to form attachments to one individual, he did not describe what the adaptive value of monotropy in particular might have for the infant. Even if we accept Bowlby's proposal that the adaptive value of the attachment–caregiver relationship to the infant is protection from predation (the validity of this proposal has been questioned by Hay (1980)), there is still no reason to assume that running or calling to one particular caregiver in times of danger provides better protection than running to any one of a number of individuals. Examination of incidents of threats to infants among extant primate species supports this view. Although incidents of predation of primates, and the primates' responses to it, are difficult to observe in the field (see Washburn, Jay and Lancaster, 1965), field researchers have witnessed threats to infants by conspecifics. When threatened by other troop members, infants have been observed to run not to their mothers but to an individual who is close by (e.g. Japanese macaques, Kawamura, 1963; baboons, Hall and Devore, 1965). Hrdy (1980) had the opportunity to observe near fatal attacks on infant hanuman langurs. In this species, new males coming into a group may attack or kill the infants already in the group. Hrdy observed that several females, not just the infants' mothers, protected the infants and threatened the attacker. In fact, in one such attack, the 'mother was the last of these four individuals (other troop members) to reach her infant' (Hrdy, 1980, p. 260).

Thus, at least under some circumstances, primate infants summon individuals other than their mothers to protect them, and individuals other than mothers protect infants from danger. There is some evidence that human infants, too, approach whomever is available when alarmed. Rosenthal (1967) found that when infant subjects were presented with a frightening stimulus, they tended to seek proximity to whomever was available in the test room, sometimes their mother and sometimes an unfamiliar adult. Similarly, Ipsa (1981) found that infants' distress at being left alone in an unfamiliar room was decreased by the presence of a peer or unfamiliar adult.

Monotropic attachments, then, do not appear to protect infants from danger better than do multiple relationships. It would seem that the infant would receive better protection from several individuals looking out for him or her than from just one. Furthermore, in addition to offering no explanation of the adaptive value of monotropy for infants, Bowlby attempted no such explanation for the primary caregiver. Would it not be helpful to caregivers to receive help in caring for infants? Tronick, Winn and Morelli (1985) speculated about the adaptive value of multiple relationships to infants, mothers, and other caregivers in their discussion of multiple caregiving among the Efe of Zaire. First, the infant would have an increased chance of adoption if the mother died, which, as Margaret Mead (in Schaffer, 1971) has pointed out, was probably a likely event among our human ancestors. Second, the overall quality of received care would increase, since fresh replacements are brought in rather than one person doing all the caregiving. Third, the mother herself may be a better and healthier caregiver when given some relief from the infant and help with the chores. Finally, the infant is given wider and more varied social exposure. Mothers benefit by having free time to engage in work and by getting some respite from the demands of caring for a young infant. The other caregivers may benefit by incurring some reciprocal obligation to be redeemed from the mother in the future and by learning how to care for infants.

The caregiving dimension of relationships with infants is not the only dimension which may have adaptive value. Social relationships are helpful for a variety of reasons. Infants are members of a social species, and must learn the rules of their culture in order to eventually raise children of their own (which is, of course, the ultimate measure of adaptive value or 'reproductive success'). Recent studies have shown that the enculturation process begins in interactions during infancy (see Field et al., 1981). Additionally, humans relate to others all their lives. Experience in doing so may be quite helpful to infants and to their social partners.

Thus, it appears that at an ultimate level of explanation, support is provided for the notion of a biological predisposition for infant capacities to form relationships. Examination at a proximate level gives support to a biological preparedness view as well. We know that very young infants are particularly attracted to social stimuli—to human faces and voices (not just the mother's). This initial attraction focuses infants' attention on people, and can provide a foundation upon which to develop communicative and relational skills. From birth, infants are exposed to a wide variety of individuals (see Lewis and Rosenblum, 1975), in addition to a primary caregiver. They are then given the opportunity to form relationships with people other than their parents. How do they react to the new people they meet? In the next section I examine infants' capacities for interacting with new people.

INFANTS' INTERACTIONS WITH NEW PEOPLE

Prior to the 1970s it was commonly believed that infants were uninterested in their peers and afraid of adult strangers (see Ross and Goldman, 1977). Studies conducted since then, considered alongside earlier studies conducted in the 1930s (e.g. Bridges, 1933; Buhler, 1933; Maudry and Nekula, 1939), indicate otherwise. These studies found infants to be both interested and competent in their interactions with new people, both peers and adults.

In the following review of infants' social behaviors with peers and with adults, I present findings which indicate infants' interest in new people and infants' abilities to relate to others. Two difficulties should be noted at the outset. First, the problem of assessing intentionality in preverbal infants makes it difficult to define social behaviors; it is hard to decide whether a particular act is intentionally directed towards someone else. A solution to this problem has been offered by Hay, Pedersen and Nash (1982), in their review of peer interaction in the first year of life. They suggest that by performing conventional acts (i.e. acts considered social by adult standards such as smiles, vocalizations, touches, and conventional gestures such as offering objects), infants indicate that they recognize another as human beings, and in this sense these behaviors can be viewed as social. Thus although we may not know whether or not an infant is intentionally trying to communicate with someone else, the enactment of conventional behaviors can still be considered social in some sense. It is in this sense that we view the studies presented below which assume such acts to be social.

The second difficulty in assessing infants' capacities for relationships is that the development of interactional skills does not necessarily parallel the development of the capacity for relationships. As infants become older, they do of course become more skilful at interacting with others. But no one would be likely to argue that a one-year-old who cannot talk has less of a relationship with his or her mother than a two-year-old who can talk. In examining infants' social skills we are not directly looking at their abilities for relationships. But interest in others, responsivity to others, and the ability to maintain interactions with others does provide a foundation upon which relationships can be built. Infants are assumed to have relationships, or attachments, to primary caregivers; we would like to present evidence for similar interest and abilities in relating to others as well.

Infant–Peer Interactions

Even newborns are responsive to their peers. They respond to the distress of their peers by becoming distressed themselves (Sagi and Hoffman, 1976; Martin and Clark, 1982). Two- and three-month-olds attend to the activities of their peers (Bridges, 1933) and increase their own activity level in a peer's presence (Field, 1979; Fogel, 1979). By six months of age, peers do not simply elicit responses in infants, as in previous months. At this age, they respond to one another in a more socially complex way. They initiate interactions by touching, vocalizing, and/or smiling at a peer (Vandell, Wilson and Buchanan, 1980; Hay, Nash and Pedersen, 1983). Their increased sensitivity to social cues is indicated by their tendencies to continue an interaction when a peer is responsive and to stop when he or she is not (Hay, Nash and Pedersen, 1983). Additionally, six-month-olds do not automatically cry in response to their peers' cries as do newborns, but attend to a peer's distress, and if it is prolonged, then they become distressed themselves (Hay, Nash and Pedersen, 1981). Adjusting one's mood to that of a partner is of course quite important in the formation of relationships. Further evidence of this ability in children as young as six months of age is seen in another finding of Hay, Nash and Pedersen (1983).

When infants were paired with agemates and placed near one another in a playroom containing toys, they adjusted their social overtures to those of their partners; significant intraclass correlations indicated that the partners' rates of touching one another were more similar to each other than either individual's rates of touching were to the other infants in the sample.

Between six and twelve months of age, infants increase the amount of behaviors they direct toward peers (Maudry and Nekula, 1939; Jacobson, 1981; Vandell, Wilson and Buchanan, 1980), although the amount of physical contact decreases (Vandell, Wilson and Buchanan, 1980). The decrease in the amount of touching may reflect the emergence of a greater reliance on distal rather than proximal modes of interacting. For example, during the second half of the first year infants begin to use conventional acts (gestures, such as pointing and offering objects, and words) to communicate with their peers (Bakeman and Adamson, 1986). The structural complexity of peer-directed acts also increases, until by nine months infants can synchronize several behaviors such as looking at and gesturing towards a peer at the same time (Becker, 1977: Vandell, Wilson and Buchanan, 1980). In addition, they become better able to attend simultaneously to objects and their peers, thus engaging in joint play (Bakeman and Adamson, 1984). They express affect more during such periods of joint engagement with a peer than when alone (Adamson and Bakeman, 1985). Also during this period, infants begin to distinguish between familiar and unfamiliar peers (Jacobson, 1981; Dontas et al., 1985).

At the start of the second year of life, both cooperation and conflict can be identified in interactions between peers. Interactions which in general proceed harmoniously and may involve compliance, turn-taking, and/or games have been documented (Eckerman and Whatley, 1977; Goldman and Ross, 1978; Nash, 1986). The ability to engage in conflicts over toys and personal space, not present among six-month-olds (Hay, Nash and Pedersen, 1983), is found among thirteen- to fifteen-month-olds (Nash, 1986). The social nature of such early conflicts is suggested by Hay and Ross (1982), who found that 21-month-olds did not simply grab toys from one another, but used communicative acts such as gestures and vocalizations in order to resolve disputes. Additionally, when a child yielded possession of an object to a peer, the winner would often then turn away from the object and fix attention elsewhere, as though the interaction itself, and not a desire for the object, was important. Furthermore, duplicates of all toys were provided, so that many struggles occurred over objects of which duplicates were nearby. Thus Hay and Ross concluded that it is not the case that infants are simply interested in obtaining certain toys and view a peer merely as an obstacle. Instead, they appear interested in the dispute itself over the toy, i.e. the interaction is as, or more, salient than the object being fought over. Thus at an early age infants are interested in one of the basic problems of relationships—how to resolve disputes. Moreover, they are interested in the problem of resolving disputes with their agemates, indicating the potential for forming relationships with peers at this young age. It should also be mentioned that such conflicts did not predominate in their interactions with one another; Hay and Ross found that only 5 per cent of infants' interactions with one another contained conflicts.

Thus infants seem to have the skills necessary for forming relationships with their peers. The biological readiness for forming relationships may apply to peers as well as to parents. The similarity in the development of interactional abilities with peers and parents has been pointed out by Hay (1985), who, in synthesizing the separate attachment and peer interaction literatures, concluded that 'children's attainments in forming attachments to parents parallel the steps they take in relating to their peers' (p. 122). Perhaps, then, there is no reason to assume different underlying mechanisms in infants' capacities to relate to parents and peers. A biological preparedness to form relationships with others could apply to both.

The similarity in abilities to relate to parents and peers is apparent from studies in which infants' interactional abilities with their mothers and peers are directly compared. It appears that infants use whatever social competencies they have in their interactions with their peers and mothers alike. Vandell and her colleagues conducted longitudinal studies comparing infants' behavior with mothers and peers when infants were six, nine, and twelve months of age. Vandell (1980) examined particular social behaviors found in the repertoires of young infants, including looking, smiling, vocalizing, and touching, and Vandell and Wilson (1982, 1987) examined both the above behaviors and the frequency and structure of interactions, and reported that cross-lagged correlations indicated no evidence for social skills emerging first with mothers and later with peers.

Other studies of the emergence of particular social skills found no evidence for skills first emerging with mothers and only later with peers. Bakeman and Adamson (Bakeman and Adamson, 1984; Adamson and Bakeman, 1985; Bakeman and Adamson, 1986) examined the ability to coordinate attention to both people and objects, the expression and coordination of affect and attention to others, and the use of conventionalized acts (gestures and words). They observed the same infants with their mothers and with peers every three months when infants were from six to eighteen months of age. For the majority of their subjects, skills first appeared with both mothers and peers at the same age. Additionally, Nash (1986) examined infants' use of social skills previously found to emerge at the start of the second year of life and found that infants who could take turns with another, protest another's actions, and comply with another did so with both mothers and peers. Furthermore, significant correlations in the use of these skills with mother and peer indicated that as infants acquire new skills, they use them to the same extent with both partners.

Thus it appears that as infants develop new interactional skills, they use them with mothers and peers alike. If the early appearance of these skills results from a biological readiness for learning the skills necessary for forming relationships, then this readiness would seem to apply to both types of social partners. Furthermore, infants' interest in forming relationships with individuals other than their mothers is also highlighted by studies in which infants' interactions with mothers and peers were directly compared. Several studies of infants of ages ranging from ten to nineteen months indicated that when given the choice between mother and peer, interactions were more frequent with peers than with their mothers when both were present (Eckerman, Whatley and Kutz, 1975; Rubenstein and Howes, 1976; Rubenstein, Howes and Pedersen, 1982; Nash, 1986). In this situation, infants' interest in peers is not simply due to mothers' minimal social participation. Nash (1986) found that mothers of thirt- een- to fifteen-month-olds initiated more interactions to their infants than their infants did to them, and an equal number as did a peer. Thus infants were not interested in their peer partner because the peer was active and the mother was not; when given the opportunity to interact with equally responsive mothers and peers, infants prefer the latter. The preference found for interacting with an unfamiliar peer over the mothers may reveal an interest in interacting with new people as opposed to the familiar person with whom they interact daily. In this vein, Vandell, Wilson and Hendersen (1985) found that twins engaged in more interactions with unfamiliar peers (who were also twins, but not each subject's own twin) than with their own twin. This preference for interacting with new individuals may indicate a propensity for forming new relationships.

Does this propensity extend to new adults as well as peers? When given a choice, infants seem to prefer new peers to new adults. Studies in which infants were given the opportunity to interact with peers, mothers, and unfamiliar adults consistently show that infants interact more frequently with peers than with unfamiliar adults (Eckerman, Whatley and Kutz, 1975; Lewis et al., 1975; Nash and Lamb, 1987). Thus the preference for peers over adults shown in later childhood may begin in infancy.

However, infants' preference for socializing with peers over adults does not mean that they are uninterested in, or wary of, unfamiliar adults. Indeed, the results from a variety of studies indicate that they are quite adept in their social relations with new people, adults as well as peers.

Infant–Adult Interactions

When infants are about eight months of age, they begin to distinguish between unfamiliar and familiar people by showing signs of apprehension towards the former (Bronson, 1972; Emde, Gaensbauer and Harmon, 1976). This wariness was at one time termed 'fear of strangers' and was treated as a developmental milestone. More recent studies have shown that in many situations infants do not show such wariness. The infant's response to a stranger depends to a large extent on the behavior of the stranger. When an unfamiliar adult approaches an infant in a warm, friendly manner, the infant usually responds in kind (Rheingold and Eckerman, 1973; Bretherton, 1978; Clarke-Stewart, 1978; Bretherton, Stolberg and Kreye, 1981). The parent's behavior, too, can affect the infant's response: infants whose mothers talked to them in a happy tone about a stranger were friendlier towards the stranger than infants whose mothers talked about her in a neutral tone (Feinman, Roberts and Morissette, 1986). Thus when placed in a situation conducive to socializing (i.e. when those present act in a friendly manner), infants respond accordingly. A variety of studies have indicated that infants are quite interested in and able to interact with new people.

Rheingold and Eckerman (1973) found that nearly all the eight- to twelve-month-olds in their study looked and smiled at strangers and appeared comfortable in their presence. Many let the stranger pick them up while their mothers were out of the room. With both their mothers and a friendly, interactive stranger present, twelve-month-old infants approached the stranger, and spent more time with her than with their mothers (Ross and Goldman, 1977). Furthermore, nine- to twelve-month-old infants are as likely to follow an unfamiliar woman as their mothers into another room (Hay, 1977). Not only do infants approach and follow unfamiliar people, they also actively interact with them. Infants share objects with unfamiliar adults, both men and women (Hay and Murray, 1982; Rheingold, Hay and West, 1976; Ross and Goldman, 1977). Eighteen-month-olds imitate an unfamiliar adult's actions towards another person to the same extent as they imitate actions modeled by their mothers (Hay *et al.*, 1986). One-year-olds engage in cooperative play (Bretherton, 1978; Bretherton, Stolberg and Kreye, 1981) and games (Ross and Goldman, 1977) with unfamiliar adults, and eighteen-month-olds were found to help unfamiliar women and men with the household task of shelving groceries (Rheingold, 1982). Younger infants request help from adults by effectively communicating to them their desire for working a particular toy (Rogoff, Malkin and Gilbride, 1984).

Not only are infants interested in new people and able to interact with them, they are able both to understand emotional cues given by a person they have known only a few minutes and to match their own emotions to those of that person. This phenomenon, termed social referencing, was originally defined as 'the tendency of a person of any age to seek out emotional information from a significant other person in the environment and to use that information to make sense of an event that is otherwise ambiguous or beyond the person's own intrinsic appraisal capabilities' (Klinnert *et al.*, 1983, p. 64). However, it now appears that the person whom an infant references need not be 'a significant other' but can be a person whom he or she has just met. One-year-olds were found to look at and be influenced by the facial expressions of an unfamiliar adult experimenter whom the infant had played with for only ten minutes (Klinnert *et al.*, 1986). As has been found in social referencing studies with mothers, infants approached an ambiguous stimulus, in this study a toy robot, more often or more quickly when the adult smiled than when she showed a fearful face.

Infants can thus respond emotionally to the emotional cues of people they have known only a short time. Does this emotional involvement enable a relatively unfamiliar person to provide emotional security for the infant? Using situations similar to that in which infants' attachment behaviors towards parents have been elicited, studies have shown that infants can show such attachment behavior towards people they have known for only a short while. Ten- to fourteen-month-olds who were cared for by an unfamiliar adult for two and a half hours during each of three consecutive days formed attachments to this caregiver. They consistently approached her, and cried when she left them alone in a room with a person they had seen for only a few minutes (Fleener, 1973). One-year-olds who had interacted with a stranger for eight minutes either did not cry when left alone with her or were more effectively soothed by her than were infants who had interacted with a stranger for only one minute (Bretherton, 1978). Furthermore, infants cry when a stranger whom they have only just met departs, leaving them alone in an unfamiliar room (Ipsa, 1981).

Their interest, social competency, emotional involvement, and feelings of security with new people are precisely what is needed to form new close relationships. A variety of studies on infants' relationships with familiar caregivers other than parents indicates that infants form attachments with these people as well as with their parents. Infants were found to form attachments to caregivers both in daycare centers (Ricciuti, 1974; Ainslie and Anderson, 1984) and in Israeli kibbutzim (Fox, 1977; Sagi et al., 1985). Moreover, as with their parents, the type of attachments infants formed with caregivers were found to affect aspects of their personality several years later. Oppenheim, Sagi and Lamb (1986) found that kibbutz infants who had been securely attached to their metaplot (caregivers) at one year of age were more assertive and independent in the preschool setting at five years of age than infants who had been insecurely attached to their metaplot. This was the first study which looked at the influence of infants' relationships with individuals other than their parents on later development. The findings indicate that like parents, relationships with others can have an impact on development.

It appears, then, that there is no reason to assume that the process of attachment to parents is basically different from the process of relationship formation with other kinds of individuals. The way evolutionary-attachment theory has typically been presented, and the separate literatures on attachment and other relationships, imply that separate processes are involved. What is now needed is a unified theory of relationship formation, rather than separate theories for different categories of individuals (parents, peers, strangers, etc.).

This theory should be concerned with both phylogeny and ontogeny. I have discussed phylogeny or biological components of relationships in both ultimate and proximate terms. In the final section I shall discuss the need for a theoretical account of infants' capacities to form relationships which integrates phylogeny and ontogeny.

ONTOGENY AND PHYLOGENY; INDIVIDUALS AND DYADS

Much of the descriptive work on relationships, i.e. infants' abilities to synchronize their behavior with others and engage in behavioral and vocal dialogues (reviewed by Schaffer, 1984), has been at the level of the dyad. These studies have clearly shown the capacities of young infants to form relationships. Yet they reveal little about the processes involved in their formation. The problem, as with Bowlby's evolutionary explanation of attachments, is again one of the level of analysis. Just as evolutionary explanations of dyadic phenomena must rely on processes involving individuals, and not dyads, so must developmental explanations. The only mechanisms of behavioral change envisioned by psychologists, (1) evolution via natural selection and (2) learning, are processes which operate at the level of the individual. The popular transactional approach to relationships (Sameroff and Chandler, 1975) assumes that the two involved individuals are continually influencing each other's behavior, yet, at this time at least, the mechanism of change must be specified on an individual basis.

The importance of providing both a phylogenetic or evolutionary analysis and an ontogenetic or developmental analysis of the behaviors of each individual involved in dyadic encounters is illustrated by West and King's studies of song acquisition in birds (King and West, 1983; West and King, 1984, 1985). Unlike many other investigators of song acquisition, West and King examined not only the song-learning process in the singer, but the role played by the listener as well. To understand an interaction or dyadic encounter or relationship, the processes involved in both individuals must be understood. Through a series of experiments, they discovered that male juvenile brown-headed cowbirds (the singers) will learn to sing the songs of any subspecies to which they are exposed, whereas females (the listeners), no matter what they hear as juveniles, always prefer the song of their own subspecies.

Because juvenile males, in nature, typically hear the songs of their own subspecies, this is what they sing as adults. Furthermore, West and King (1985) also found that females are able to influence the development of male songs; the song development of juvenile males housed only with females (who themselves do not sing), and who had never heard males sing, was influenced by the particular subspecies of females with whom they were housed. In another study, Eastzer, King and West (1985) found that cowbirds engage in assortative mating, i.e. males and females prefer, on the basis of song type, to mate with a member of their own subspecies over a member of another subspecies. Thus, although males typically sing what females like to hear, the developmental pathways by which each sex arrives at this harmony differ. The outcome, which has adaptive significance on an evolutionary level, is the same for both; males and females of the same subspecies mate selectively with one another.

The work of West and King illustrates the importance both of a synthesis of evolutionary and developmental perspectives (phylogeny and ontogeny) and of separating individuals' behaviors from dyadic constructs in both. Although a more precise analysis can be made of song acquisition in birds than of human social behavior, these issues concern research on relationships involving human subjects as well. For example, Schaffer's monograph (1984) on infants' developing capacities for relationships synthesizes the research to date and illuminates the changes in the dyadic relationship over the course of infancy. Yet, as pointed out by Hay (1986), the mechanisms involved are not specified. Hay suggests that Schaffer neglected the importance of learning processes in his analysis.

The recent emphasis on infants' biological preparedness for forming relationships has led developmental research somewhat away from the ontogenetic or learning processes involved. West (1983) recently reminded us that saying that a biological predisposition for a particular behavior exists does not explain it, just as Gottlieb (1979) cautioned researchers to remember that 'the pathway from genes to behavior is a developmental one!' (p. 170). On the other hand, Schaffer (1986) has criticized the construct of 'learning' in the same way:

> In the first place, learning has too often been regarded as an *explanatory* concept, as though the very fact that environmental influence can be demonstrated means that we understand the processes at work . . . Learning can justifiably only be regarded as an umbrella term to cover a vast array of different kinds of environmental influences that bring about effects in ways about which we are still extraordinarily ignorant. The present usage of the term *learning* cloaks that ignorance. We are, for instance, in possession of a vast body of knowledge regarding the many kinds of relationship between parental 'influence' and child 'outcome', but that knowledge is almost entirely correlational in nature and tells us nothing about *how* socialization actually works. (p. 119)

Because of the lack of a paradigm with which to study the biological and experiential processes together, theorists may both believe the workings of the two together to be important but focus on one or the other in their explanations. For example, Schaffer (1984) proposes that in the infant–mother dyad 'the speed of interpersonal synchronization is in fact so great that a stimulus-response model could not account for all interactive sequences. It seems rather that the temporal integration one sees within a dyad may be based on a shared programme . . . This sharing may be brought about because both participants— indeed all human beings—have in common a particular way of functioning in social interactions that is based on some universal, wired-in characteristics' (pp. 54–55). Thus Schaffer focuses on a biological preparedness in this situation. In contrast, Malatesta and Haviland (1985), in describing the face-to-face interactions of young infants and their mothers, reported that mothers on average changed their facial expressions eight times per minute. From this they estimated that mothers change their expression 362 times per day in face-to-face play, 32 580 times over the three-month period of peak face-to-face play. The investigators remarked, 'this is not a trivial learning opportunity for the infant' (p. 104). They thus implicated observational learning in the development of infants' emotional expressiveness.

Recently, Petrovich and Gewirtz (1985) have attempted a synthesis of learning and biological models of attachment. They suggest that the operant learning model for the acquisition of behavioral attachment of mother to infant and of infant to mother 'is open to the operation of unconditioned stimuli (releasers) for species-specific responses' (p. 277). Unfortunately, it has been difficult to identify the specific releasers and learning processes involved in the formation of infants' attachments with others.

Thus, although it is generally agreed that infants are biologically prepared to form social relationships or attachments, the processes involved are seldom specified. A biological readiness to learn certain associations is usually assumed when learning takes place rapidly (as in Schaffer's example of a readiness for infants and mothers each to modify their own behavior so as to synchronize it with that of the other). In fact, Sameroff and Cavanagh (1979) argued that the most direct means of empirically distinguishing learned from prepared stimulus-

–response combinations is by examining the speed of association: prepared associations should occur rapidly, whereas learned associations should take more time.

When the processes involved in the development of capacities for interactions and/or relationships are directly examined, constraints on learning are indicated. Hay *et al.* (1985) examined the process of modeling in an interpersonal context. Models directed unusual behaviors (chosen as ones that infants were unlikely to have in their repertoires) towards another individual. The identity of the model and the recipient of the acts were varied, so that either infants' mothers or an unfamiliar adult modeled the acts and the model directed the acts towards either the infants themselves or another unfamiliar adult. The results indicated that infants did not imitate acts modeled by their mothers more often than ones modeled by an unfamiliar adult (as would be predicted by social learning theory). The variable that most strongly influenced imitation was the recipient of the modeled act; infants who had seen the model direct an act towards an unfamiliar adult were more likely to direct the imitated act towards the same unfamiliar adult.

Thus the learning process, in this case social learning, was constrained. Infants did not automatically imitate a model, nor was the mother a more salient model than an unfamiliar person. Rather, infants imitated as a means of relating to an unfamiliar person. They observed how someone else behaved with that person, and then they followed suit. The principles of social learning were constrained, perhaps due to a biological preparedness to learn how to relate to new individuals. The infants did not automatically imitate the new acts, they used them as a means to interact with a particular person towards whom they had seen another interact in this way. The social nature of the modeled act was salient to the infants.

There is some evidence to support the notion of a biological preparedness to learn from others, via imitation, how to interact with particular individuals. The same process was found to operate in other species as well. In brown-headed cowbirds, males sing a variety of song types, and Nash, West and King (1983) were interested in how young males selected their song type. Did they simply copy what they heard? They found that young males did not copy the songs they heard the most but rather those of the males who had frequent matings with females. Thus, the young males picked up successful courtship songs. Young cowbirds, like human infants, use information about how someone else is acting towards a particular individual to decide how they should themselves act with that individual.

Thus similar constraints on the social learning process were observed in two very different species, but two species in which social relationships are very important. In each species, individuals are able to rapidly learn from how others relate to certain individuals how they themselves can behave with those individuals. This may indicate a biological preparedness to learn how to relate to others.

In summary, theorists of relationships in infancy, from Freud until the present, recognize that a theory of relationships must encompass both phylogenetic and ontogenic processes:

> It will be observed that, for all their fundamental difference, the id and the super-ego have one thing in common: they both represent the influences of the past—the id the influence of heredity, the super-ego the influences essentially of what is taken over from other people—whereas the ego is principally determined by the individual's own experience. . . . (Freud, 1940, p. 4)

> . . . the investigation of attachment acquisition would proceed, in the same way as would inquiries into development of all classes of behavior, by analyses of (1) contemporaneous, *proximate* processes with their controlling variables; and (2) remote, *ultimate* processes of the evolutionary past. (Petrovich and Gewirtz, 1985, p. 259)

The present chapter shows the need for an integration of phylogeny and ontogeny, individual and dyadic levels of analyses, and the relationship and attachment approaches to the study of interpersonal relations in infancy.

Handbook of Personal Relationships
Edited by S. W. Duck
© 1988 John Wiley & Sons Ltd

8

Defining and Studying Reciprocity in Young Children

HILDY S. ROSS, J. ALLAN CHEYNE and SUSAN P. LOLLIS
University of Waterloo, Ontario, Canada

ABSTRACT

We consider the concept of reciprocity as it has been studied among young children, placing particular emphasis on a dyadic focus of analysis, comparisons with various baselines and mutuality of reciprocation. Procedures for establishing the existence of a relationship and for evaluating relational reciprocity are demonstrated with illustrations of emergent and reciprocal relationships among young children.

Analyses of interpersonal processes in terms of reciprocity pervade the social and behavioral sciences. Reciprocity is a sufficiently strong principle to form the keystone of a variety of central theoretical approaches (e.g. Axelrod, 1984; Gouldner, 1960; Hinde, 1979; Mauss, 1925; Piaget, 1948; Trivers, 1971). Even young children seem to regard reciprocity as a feature of social behavior and relationships. By kindergarten age children consider the impact of reciprocity in assessing blame or merit (Berndt, 1977; Peterson, Hartmann and Gelfand, 1977; Peterson, 1980), and the possibility of future reciprocation in offering help (Dreman and Greenbaum, 1973; Peterson, 1980). Young children may also justify wrongdoing with the reciprocity defense: 'He hit me first!' (Walton, 1985), and account for reciprocal helping by reference to the obligation to return favors (Peterson, 1980). Given the belief of both scientists and young children in the importance of reciprocation, we thought it appropriate to examine more closely studies involving the early development of reciprocation; if children can articulate the principle by six years of age, it may be a clear feature of their behavior at an even earlier age.

RECIPROCITY: AN ANALYSIS OF THE CONSTRUCT

Early in our investigations we discovered serious inconsistencies and confusions in the use of the term reciprocity. Unfortunately, it is a construct that has been laden with much surplus meaning (Cairns, 1979). Recently, a number of researchers have begun to formulate systematic definitions of reciprocity, often accompanied by critical comments on those of their predecessors (e.g. Cairns, 1979; Gottman, 1983; Hinde, 1979). Out of respect for tradition, we conform to this pattern. Our basic definition of reciprocity is the return of like behavior between partners. This seemingly simple definition requires that we consider both qualitative and quantitative symmetry as well as the social directedness of behavior to distinguish reciprocity from related constructs of complementarity and imitation.

Reciprocity and Complementarity

We begin with Hinde's (1976, 1979) distinction between reciprocity and complementarity. In a complementary interaction the behavior of each participant differs from, but completes, that of the other (Hinde, 1979, p. 79). Complementary actions stand in some relation to one another, making a whole. By contrast, in a reciprocal interaction two individuals act in a similar fashion either simultaneously or alternately. Hinde's definition of reciprocity seems underspecified to us, in that there is no requirement that the actions have any functional relation. We prefer a definition that requires that similar actions of two participants be *directed* to one another such that the action of B to A would return or requite the action of A to B. In the same way that complementary actions are a subset of all actions that are different, so are reciprocal actions a subset of all actions that are similar.

However, whether the socially directed actions within a dyad are reciprocal or complementary is often determined by the investigator whose theory dictates *a priori* the relevant actions in a particular context. A conversation may be viewed either as reciprocal (the event *talk* is relevant for both participants) or complementary (the event *talk* is relevant for some participants and the event *attend* is relevant for others). Moreover, the specificity of the categories of behavior in question can also affect the determination of whether social actions are reciprocal or complementary. The breadth of categories is an issue faced in all research and is decided on theoretical grounds. This decision will then have implications for whether actions will be described as being reciprocal. The work of Brazelton and his colleagues illustrates how the breadth of categories used to examine reciprocity between mothers and infants can influence the research findings. In their early work, reciprocity was defined in terms of tandem increases in the *total* number of behaviors that mother and child directed to one another (Brazelton, Koslowski and Main, 1974) or in terms of joint participation in a meaningful phase of interaction (Brazelton *et al.*, 1975; Tronick *et al.*, 1978); in neither case was the qualitative similarity of actions of mother and infant considered. All socially directed acts were part of a very broad behavioral category. Action sequences, such as the initiation of interaction with maternal vocalization and infant attention, that might otherwise be described as complementary would be considered as reciprocal. More recently, Brazelton and his colleagues have included the criterion of similarity of actions between partners (Als, Tronick and Brazelton, 1979; Brazelton *et al.*, 1979; Tronick, Als and Brazelton, 1980). Thus, interactions that earlier would have given evidence of reciprocity would be excluded by this later definition.

Reciprocity and Symmetry

The contrast between reciprocity and complementarity is a qualitative one, based on the relation of the actions of the partners. A further distinction must be made related to the *quantitative* symmetry in the contributions of interactive partners. Exchanges are symmetrical when social agents make equal contributions to social exchanges whether they be reciprocal or complementary. That is, partners A and B may engage in equivalent amounts of talking, helping or fighting with one another, or partner A may listen as much as B talks, help as much as B requests help, or submit as much as B attacks. There may also be a significant degree of asymmetry in both reciprocal and complementary interchanges. The issue of symmetry is, in our view, orthogonal to the qualitative distinction of reciprocity and complementarity but must also be included in our definition. Thus reciprocity denotes a quantitative symmetry in qualitatively similar socially directed actions.

Reciprocity and Imitation

We do not include all cases of imitation as instances of reciprocation. Imitative behaviors that are not mutually socially directed are not regarded as reciprocal. In contrast, Cairns' (1979) definition of reciprocity includes actions that are not socially directed. For example, Hall and Cairns (1984) compared the influences of modeling and social reciprocity on the aggressive responding of six- and seven-year-old boys. Reciprocity effects were evaluated by examining the similarity in amount of aggressive behavior between pairs of boys observed together after one or both boys saw one of a set of films. This included similarity in impersonal aggression (hitting a BoBo doll), indirect aggression (hitting the partner's doll), as well as interpersonal aggression (using the doll as a weapon against the partner). Similarity in impersonal aggression, and arguably in indirect aggression as well, seem best considered as imitation but not as reciprocation, whereas similarity in interpersonal aggression is clearly reciprocity.

This distinction between imitation and reciprocity does not preclude the possibility that some reciprocal actions that are mutually socially directed arise out of mutual imitation. Examples of such abound in the literature on mother-- infant games. Hay and Murray (1982) further distinguish reciprocity from imitation by requiring for the former the sequential reversal of the actor and target roles. When giving is reciprocated the actor and the target exchange roles; when giving is imitated the actor shifts but the target does not.

In evaluating reciprocity in the social interaction of young children, investigators have used a variety of research designs and analyses. We next turn our attention to the logic and outcomes of these demonstrations.

RECIPROCITY IN EARLY SOCIAL INTERACTION

Both conceptual and operational definitions of reciprocity depend on the level of analysis selected. We will examine four different levels of analysis that underlie empirical work on reciprocity with young children: (1) an individual reciprocity that reflects the balance of behavior given and received by *individuals*, (2) a dyadic reciprocity that is the symmetry of behavior given and received within *dyads*, (3) temporal reciprocity in which there are immediate returns of like behavior between partners in *interactions*, and (4) relational reciprocity, that constitutes the mutuality of special *relationships*.

Individual Reciprocity: Balance between Behavior Given and Received

The earliest and still most frequent investigations of reciprocity in young children focus on the symmetry of children's output of certain behavior and their receipt of similar behavior from their peers. To evaluate such individual reciprocity the frequencies of behavior given to and received from a variety of peers are correlated. For example, Bott (1934) found correlations for nursery school children's verbal, motor and combined verbal–motor behavior that ranged from 0.81 to 0.93. She interpreted these as evidence of balance in social interaction. 'These correlations indicate that the give and take of social intercourse are nicely balanced; that the child who is active towards others is the one who received most from them' (p. 75).

More recent researchers have also generally reported strong positive correlations between behavior given and received among preschool children. The overall rates of initiation, of constructiveness (the proportion of positive initiations), of agreement, and of help directed to others were correlated with the rates of such actions received from others (Kohn, 1966; Leiter, 1977; Marcus and Jenny, 1977). Three forms of reinforcement, giving attention, affection, and submission, were each found to be positively related to the receipt of like behavior from peers (Charlesworth and Hartup, 1967). The number of children to whom reinforcement was given was also positively correlated with the number from whom it was received. Individual reciprocity of negative behavior has been examined less frequently, but Dodge (1986) has reported a positive correlation between the frequency with which seven-year-old boys initiated aggression and the frequency with which they were the targets of peer aggression.

There is a subtle difference among investigators in their explanations of similar findings of individual reciprocity. For example, Kohn (1966) entitled his article 'The Child as Determinant of His Peer's Approach to Him' and stated that his results 'suggest that both with respect to quantity and quality, the child gets what he puts out; that, in other words, *the child creates his own environment*' (p. 99, our italics). Charlesworth and Hartup, on the other hand, considered the child's output to be a function of reinforcement received. 'The results on the giving and the receiving of reinforcement indicate that these are reciprocal activities. Those who give the most get the most, and *vice versa*, . . . it suggests that reinforcement giving is an operant which comes *under the control of generalized social reinforcers of other children* at very early ages' (p. 1000, our italics). These conflicting perspectives on the symmetry of input and output should alert us to the interdependencies within the peer group; change in one individual may be predicated upon and have ramifications for the behavior of others.

Finally, we should point out that the symmetry between behavior given and received does not describe the reciprocity of dyadic interchanges but merely the behavioral symmetry of the individual as actor and target. To analyze behavior that each child directs towards a peer, researchers have collapsed across all partners and assessed the child's individual score as an actor and as a target. The observed balance between input and output *may* arise because individuals are reciprocating behavior with specific partners, but dyadic reciprocation is not the only process that might account for these results. Another possibility is that children are displacing behavior received; for example, children reinforced by some members of the peer group may, in turn, reinforce other peers; they may be punished by some peers and, in turn, punish others. To examine dyadic reciprocity, interchanges between specific individuals must be investigated. Masters and Furman (1981) took a step in that direction by studying liked and disliked peers; they found that liked peers both gave and received more reinforcing and neutral responses than disliked peers. Similarly, Marcus and Jenny (1977) found that help given to and received from liked peers was more strongly associated than that from disliked peers, although both correlations were significant. However, in both cases researchers examined several liked and disliked peers for each child, and thus their studies did not provide evidence of reciprocation between specific individuals.

Dyadic Reciprocity and Interpersonal Influence

Dyadic reciprocity refers to the symmetry of behavior that two individuals direct to one another. Dyadic reciprocity can arise from two processes: the first involves interpersonal influence, in which one partner matches his or her behavior with that of the other; the second involves selection, in which people who are already alike form relationships (Cairns, 1979; Gottman, 1979). When self-selected or intact pairs are studied in unconstrained interactions, it is not possible to differentiate these two potential sources of reciprocity. However, in some studies children have been randomly assigned to dyads while in other studies experimental procedures have eliminated the possibility of selection (Cairns, 1979). For example, the study by Hall and Cairns gave evidence that interpersonal aggression was reciprocated between randomly matched pairs provided that one or both children had seen a film depicting similar interpersonal aggression. Additional studies using either random assignment to pairs or other experimental techniques to establish dyadic reciprocity will be reviewed in this section.

Anderson (1937, 1939) examined the symmetry of behavior within pairs of preschool and of kindergarten children. Altogether his sample contained 177 children each of whom was generally paired with five others. His two measures were of domination (all aggressive and negative behaviors) and integration (all positive interactive behaviors). Rather than using intraclass correlations, Anderson designated the higher and lower score within each pair and correlated these across pairs; the correlations were all quite high, ranging from 0.68 to 0.83. While the large number of pairs of children and the high correlations make this early demonstration of dyadic reciprocity intriguing, the method of computing the correlations would tend to inflate the estimates of the association.

Two more recent studies have shown reciprocation of communicative behavior between young children (Garvey and Ben Debba, 1974; Ross, Lollis and Elliot, 1982). Garvey and Ben Debba observed three-and-a-half- to five-and-a-half-year-olds, each with two peer partners in a play setting. They found a strong relation between the number of utterances used by the two members of a pair while they interacted with one another. Interestingly, no relation was found between the frequency of utterances that each child directed to his or her two partners within the different sessions. They argue, therefore, that the 'number of utterances is not a stable characteristic of the individual but rather a dynamic feature of the interaction process itself' (p. 1161). Ross et al. found similar relations in the verbal and nonverbal communication of toddler peers. Children who were paired matched one another in total number of communicative acts and in the proportion of communicative requests that met with compliance. In addition, half of the individual categories of communication were reliably related for the two members of the dyad; these included showing or giving an object to the peer, attempting to join the play of a peer, and inviting a peer to join play.

Attempts to demonstrate balance in dyadic reciprocation of peer-directed action with even younger children have met with only partial success. Hay, Pedersen and Nash (1982) studied social influence between six-month-old infants by examining dyadic reciprocity in physical contact. Intraclass correlations indicated symmetry between the two infants within a dyad but only when toys were available; correlations were not reliable when toys were absent. Vandell and Wilson (1982) studied six- and nine-month-old infants and found reciprocity for only some measures of peer-directed behavior (i.e. the number of simple or object-related acts); most socially directed behaviors of these children were unrelated to those of the peer.

Additional experimental approaches have been used for investigations of reciprocity of helping or sharing among young children. Peterson, Hartmann and Gelfand (1977) studied kindergarten and grade three children who played a marble-dropping game to earn prizes. They were led to believe that another child was playing the same game in the next room. Periodically, a marble got stuck and if a penny were inserted into the apparatus by the unseen 'partner', the marble was released and the child could continue to play. Children typically helped their 'partners' when the latter were in need. When subsequently led to believe that their 'partners' either always helped them or never did so, children whose 'partners' had refused to help reciprocated strongly, by offering very little help themselves; reciprocation was especially strong among kindergarten children, who offered nearly no aid to their needy but stingy 'partners'. In later work, Peterson (1980) extended her observations of reciprocation to a situation in which positive behaviors were the focus. In this study reciprocating for help received was contrasted with helping someone in greater need. Older children were more likely than younger children to reciprocate, but only when the beneficiary might have a later opportunity to return the help; when no such opportunity was evident, reciprocation occurred less often and did not change with age.

Levitt et al. (1985) examined reciprocity of sharing among two-year-olds using a design introduced earlier by Staub and Sherk (1970). The earlier study involved pairs of fourth-grade friends; one child was given candies by the experimenter before the second arrived to watch a movie but could share that candy if he or she pleased. After the movie the children were asked to color, but only the second child received a crayon. Crayon-sharing by the second child was related to the receipt of candy from the first. In Levitt et al.'s adaptation of this procedure for toddlers, two children played on either side of a barrier, with only one child being given toys on a first trial. Although the deprived toddler often requested that his or her more privileged peer share the toys, none did until urged to do so by their mothers. In the second trial the previously bereft toddler received all of the toys; in all but one case the second child's sharing was dependent on whether the partner had previously shared. The sensitivity of children this young to the generosity of their peers is striking; this procedure might potentially be used to study the conditions for reciprocation in young children.

Experimental procedures have also been used to explore dyadic reciprocity in mother–child interaction. Parpal and Maccoby (1985) manipulated maternal responsiveness by asking mothers to comply with suggestions and to refrain from questioning, commanding or criticizing their three- to four-year-old children during free play. The children of responsive mothers were more compliant in cooperating with their mothers' subsequent requests during a clean-up period. The children thereby reciprocated their mothers' compliance during the play session.

Thus experimental techniques employing random assignment have been used with young children to study dyadic reciprocity. A variety of behaviors has been examined including domination, compliance, aggression, and sharing. Some investigators have adopted fairly broad categories of behavior; others rather narrow categories. In all but the youngest age group evidence of dyadic reciprocation seems strong. Moreover, assignment procedures allow us to attribute the similarities between children to processes of interpersonal influence. Nonetheless, we know little of how such processes create similarity between interacting peers. One basic issue that is not resolved in these studies is whether the influence is unilateral or mutual. At least one member of the pair changed his or her actions in response to similar behavior by the partner, but we do not know that both participants were influenced by one another (Cairns, 1979). In the case of parent–child interaction, where the capabilities of the interacting partners are unequal, the mutuality of adjustment is a central issue. Is the child adjusting to the behavior of the parent or only parent to child? In the case of peer interaction, where the capabilities of the interacting partners are more equal, it is meaningful to ask whether behavioral characeristics determine which of two children modify their behavior and to what extent. Does a more aggressive child become less aggressive when paired with a passive peer, or does the latter adjust his or her behavior to a greater extent? Does the more social child become less active, or is the change limited to the behavior of the quieter partner? Questions such as these require that we examine the shifts in behavior of each child against some baseline that will illuminate the potential mutality of interpersonal influence.

Temporal Reciprocity and a Baseline of Comparison

Reciprocity, in the studies examined so far, has involved the return of like behavior within a longer or shorter time period, depending on the period of observation. Studies of the balance of behavior given and received were often conducted in preschools over periods of several months; studies of randomly assigned pairs of children generally have been carried out in laboratory settings and lasted for fifteen or 30 minutes. Typically, data collected over the total period of observation were summed to examine reciprocity. Far briefer time periods are critical to a third approach to reciprocity: researchers have considered whether each behavior of one child is immediately returned in kind by the partner. For example, Leiter (1977) found that friendly initiations by one child were followed by agree responses by peers, whereas demanding initiations often received coercive responses or complementary submissive reactions. Hartup (1974) reported that when derogation produced a hostile response among preschoolers, the reaction was equally likely to involve hitting or reprocation of derogation; among first and second graders the preponderance of reactions reciprocated the derogation. Similarly, preschool children were more likely to match the happy affect displayed by their peers than the sad or hurt affect (J. Strayer, 1980). But note that all of these demonstrations involved the behavior of individual children with a variety of partners, rather than within a particular dyad.

   What evidence is there for the immediate reciprocation of socially directed actions within particular relationships? Gottman (1983) has examined the role of immediate reciprocation in the formation of friendships of young children. His definition of reciprocation and suggestions of methods to evaluate reciprocity are particularly instructive. Behavior is reciprocal if the prior socially directed actions of one person increase the probability of the same behavior by the partner. He placed particular emphasis on the examination of contingency, which could establish the influence of one person's behavior on the other. In Gottman's work a baseline, consisting of one individual's unconditional probability of a particular behavior, regardless of the prior action of the partner, is compared with that person's rate of behavior given the same socially directed action by the partner. Gottman used the term *temporal reciprocity* to describe this contingency; it emphasizes the fact that the timing of the actions of the partners is of importance. The action of one participant must *immediately* follow the action of the partner to be considered conditional on the partner's prior action. Thus the child's actions in the context of the partner's immediately preceding behavior are compared to the child's actions regardless of context.

Investigators of early mother–child interactions have demonstrated temporal reciprocity very early in life. For both three-day-old and three-month-old infants the onset of infant vocalizations was influenced by preceding maternal vocalizations; at three months, but not at three days, mothers' vocalizations were similarly affected by those of the infants (Anderson, Vietze and Dokecki, 1977; Rosenthal, 1982; Stern *et al.*, 1975). Further, Martin *et al.* (1981) investigated the contingencies of positive and negative behavior in the interaction of 18-month-old children and their mothers. Their findings suggested that mothers and children reciprocate in kind to one another; although behavior opposite to that of the partner did at times serve as a response, positives from the partner were most likely to be responded to with positives and negatives with negatives. These studies are taken as evidence of the influence of the partner on the individual's behavior. In addition, the studies with three- and eighteen-month-old infants provide evidence of the mutuality of influence between partners.

Gottman (1983) studied the formation of friendships in children from three to nine years of age as they played together in pairs in one of their homes. One group of thirteen children played with their best friend and with a stranger, and a second group of eighteen children played with a new child over three daily sessions. Positive reciprocation was one of a set of process variables for the formation of friendship and was indexed by three specific behavioral measures, the reciprocation of gossip, joking and fantasy. In addition, the extent to which disagreement led to disagreement may be regarded as a measure of negative reciprocity. For each measure, two z-scores were derived; one indexed the extent to which one child's behavior was affected by the prior behavior of the peer, and the second focused on the other child. Thus reciprocation of behavior by one child was evaluated independently of reciprocation by the partner.

Unfortunately for our purposes, Gottman did not report coefficients of reciprocity observed among the children. Rather, he reported the associations of the z-scores with several outcome criteria of how well the children 'hit it off' and with the age of the children. Results relating reciprocation to the criteria and to age were inconsistent; different relations were found depending on the sample considered, the particular criterion selected, the day of observation, and whether the host or guest child was the target. Even Gottman's guarded conclusion that positive reciprocation is more important early in a relationship seems equivocal. Perhaps part of the problem was the relatively small sample sizes used for the correlations. Additionally, however, temporal reciprocity requires that children act immediately after the partner acts, and this may be an overly restrictive limitation. The rationale for this limitation was not presented. Gottman justified his procedure in terms of the necessity of a baseline for establishing the influence of one person on the other, but did not discuss the fact that the comparison with baseline involved the immediate succession of like behaviors for the partners. Holmes (1981) discussed this issue in relation to Gottman's (1979) similar analyses of reciprocation between married couples. Holmes argued that reciprocation that is immediate, explicit, and that involves a return of precisely the same behavior may indicate a relationship with a limited future. Rather, reciprocation in the long term, that is both more subtle and more tolerant with respect to the commodity returned, is taken as a sign of trust within a relationship; partners meet one another's needs, trusting that when they are similarly needy in the future, their partners will respond in kind. Reciprocity of the latter sort may also be more clearly related to the quality of relationships between young children.

In Gottman's work no examination of the mutuality of reciprocity took place. In many instances where relations to friendship criteria were found for host children, similar relations were not found for guests. This leads us to suspect that reciprocation between the two partners might also be unrelated. It could have been possible to evaluate the association between the reciprocity of the two children in a pair, or to derive measures of mutual temporal reciprocity. In the mother–infant work, mutuality was a focus; in contrast, when reciprocation is examined using intraclass correlations, the mutuality of influence cannot be assessed. It is interesting that processes of reciprocation, defined with reference to interpersonal influence, are so often evaluated when mutuality of influence either cannot be or is not established.

Relational Reciprocity and the Interpersonal 'Baseline'

While we agree with Gottman's focus on a baseline of comparison, we would add that more than one type of comparison is possible. Gottman used a temporal baseline consisting of an individual's rate of behavior regardless of the behavior of the partner; however, this type of baseline is but one technique for solving the broader problem of evaluating the effects of context. Here we will develop procedures for the determination of relationships in comparison with an *interpersonal* baseline and of reciprocity in these relationships. Such an interpersonal baseline consists of the socially directed behavior of an individual examined across many social partners which can then be contrasted with behavior with a specific partner. For temporal reciprocity, social actions in the context of the immediately prior behavior of the partner are compared to a temporal baseline. For relational reciprocity, behavior in the context of a specific partner is compared to an interpersonal baseline. Hinde and Stevenson-Hinde (1986) have argued that investigations of the influence of relationships on individuals require assessment of individual characteristics outside of that relationship. The interpersonal baseline is one method of doing so.

In examining the evidence for reciprocation in relation to an interpersonal baseline we return to the work of Helen Bott (1928; 1934). Recall that Bott (1934) reported strong positive associations between behavior children received from and directed to their peers. She cited this as evidence for *balance* at the individual level. Bott then went on to consider the special relationships formed within her group and the reciprocity of these relationships.

Bott's data were divided into both verbal and motor responses in direct observations (when the child was a target of observation) and in indirect records (when the child acted on a peer who was the target). For each of these four measures, the first and second choice companion for each child was determined, and, if the selected partner returned the choice, the relationship was considered reciprocal. Thus mutuality in selection was an essential feature of this definition of reciprocity. The strength of the reciprocal relationship could vary from 1 to 4, depending on the number of measures for which reciprocation of preference was found. Twenty-nine such reciprocal relationships were present in the group of 28 children; only one child was not involved in at least one such relationship. Reciprocal relationships varied in strength from 1 (ten relationships) to 4 (ten relationships involving sixteen children). Most relationships were between children of similar age, but neither the number nor the strength of reciprocal relationships was related to the age of the children involved.*

The implicit baseline in Bott's evaluation of reciprocity was the behavior of each child to each other potential companion who was not selected as first or second choice. While Bott's general approach seems sound, a more general method is required to evaluate the extent to which each child reliably differentiates among companions. We will develop and illustrate a procedure using data from Bott's earlier study (Bott, 1928). To do so, we must make explicit a model of social relationships, based on consideration of characteristics of children as individuals in contrast to characteristics that emerge within relationships.

A model of social relationships

The basic units underlying interactions and relationships are socially directed actions, which incorporate actor, action, and target. Knowledge of these three components of socially directed actions is sufficient and necessary for the study of relationships. Hinde (1979) conceptualized sociality as a hierarchical progression from actions to interactions to relationships. In our model interactions are not an intermediate step between actions and relationships but a separate and conceptually independent organization of socially directed actions. Relationships are relatively protracted and enduring; they may be revealed in stable, stationary patterns of socially directed behaviors. In studying relationships, it is necessary to demonstrate that characteristics of the dyad or group are emergent, that is, not reducible to characteristics of the individuals who comprise that group. The behavior of the dyad must be shown not to be determined by the independent additive effects of each member as actor and target. In this way our definition of special relationships parallels that for a system in that both possess the property of nonadditivity. Knowledge of an individual component of a system is insufficient to predict its behavior within the system, as components behave differently within a given system than they do in isolation or within another system (e.g. von Bertalanffy, 1967; P. Weiss, 1969).

---

*Although interference and resistance were included along with other more positive behavior in this evaluation, Bott was impressed 'that quarreling among young children is part of the social pattern as a whole rather than antagonistic to it' (p. 80). The reciprocal relationships that she found she took to indicate predominantly friendly and cooperative play.

Socially directed actions may be determined, potentially, by at least three orthogonal factors. Two of these, actors and targets, are characteristics of individuals and the third is the emergent relationship factor (see Kenny and LaVoie, 1985, for a similar view employing different analytic techniques and Kenny's chapter, this volume).

Determining relationships and reciprocity

Bott's (1928) study was one of the earliest examinations of young children's social play. She recorded the socially directed actions in a group of eleven preschoolers. Bott discussed her findings solely in terms of what we have called socially directed activity and made no attempt to assess relationships except to note one particularly active and reciprocal pair. Although Bott reported five different categories of behavior, we have simplified her matrix by combining across categories and deriving a single index of socially directed actions (Figure 1). If one considers either the row or column marginals, it will be obvious that

Actor \ Target	1 (26)	2 (29)	3 (31)	4 (36)	5 (37)	6 (38)	7 (40)	8 (45)	9 (52)	10 (53)	11 (54)	Total
1		6	7	3	0	0	2	27	1	1	2	49
2	7		8	6	2	7	1	14	7	1	6	59
3	9	14		16	1	3	10	12	15	10	14	104
4	0	2	6		6	1	3	0	8	4	23	53
5	2	4	2	3		5	1	11	13	4	10	55
6	1	7	5	3	6		0	6	6	5	1	40
7	8	1	22	2	0	0		4	25	11	13	86
8	9	3	5	4	9	0	3		31	4	5	73
9	0	4	3	4	3	0	1	10		3	41	69
10	11	5	7	14	13	1	11	9	8		25	104
11	3	3	6	13	2	1	5	5	77	28		143
Total	50	49	71	68	42	18	37	98	191	71	140	

Figure 1. Matrix of socially directed behavior (from Bott, 1928)

there are apparent individual differences among children in the extent to which they engage in socially directed actions as either actors or targets. The variation among individual cells of the matrix may be a result of random variation, individual actor differences, individual target differences, or any additive combination of these. To the extent that individual cell values cannot be explained by such factors, we must invoke an emergent relationship component. One may formulate a hierarchical series of models and test them sequentially.

Level I model (chaos). Socially directed actions occur at random in the group. All children treat all others essentially alike.

Level II model (individual). Socially directed actions result from individual differences among actors *or* among targets. Either actors differ from one another in how they treat particular targets or targets differ from one another in the treatment they receive from different actors.

Level III model (additive). Socially directed actions are determined by the additive effects of individual differences among actors *and* targets. Actor and target effects combine to determine the way any child treats any other child.

Level IV model (relational). Socially directed actions are determined by unique relationships among individuals considered as dyads or in groups. Knowledge of general actor and target characteristics is not sufficient to predict how any one child treats another.

These models are hierarchical in the sense that higher-order models incorporate lower-order models and correspond to log-linear models for a two-dimensional matrix. Each model may be used to generate expected values for individual cells. An overall test of each of these models may be made using chi-square estimates to test the significance of deviations of cell values from those predicted by the model. A significant chi-square may be interpreted as indicating a poor fit of the model to the data and leads to the rejection of the model. Model I uses only the grand mean to derive an expected value for each cell. Model II is really two parallel models which employ the marginal totals for either actors (rows) *or* targets (columns) to determine expected cell values. Model III simultaneously employs actor *and* target marginals to generate expected values.* If each of these models is rejected in turn then one can accept the sole surviving model, one that *includes* a component that represents the unique relationships that exist between individuals within the group.† A failure to find significant chi-square values for models II and III implies that socially directed actions within the group may be adequately accounted for by individual factors. Thus there would be no justification for invoking higher-order processes, such as relationships, to explain the patterning of socially directed actions.

---

*See Castellan (1979) for procedures for generating expected values with structural zeros on the major diagonal of the matrix.

†Additionally, it is possible to derive and test specific Level IV models that include a particular relational component in the calculation of expected values. If such a model were not rejected, then it could provide a more specific description of the pattern found in the data than does this more general Level IV model.

When the above analyses were applied to the Bott data in Figure 1, Models I–III all proved inadequate to explain the internal structure of the matrix. Therefore, it appears that it is necessary to invoke special relationships within the group to fully describe the patterning of socially directed activity.

One may further investigate the details of the nature of the inadequacy of models by examining the cell residuals from the inadequate models. The residuals are simply a quantitative index of the degree of deviation of the data from values predicted by the model and have the general form, $z(\text{residual}) = (O-E)/SQRT(E)$, where O is the observed value and E is the value expected by the model; these may be interpreted as normal z-scores. In Figure 2 the adjusted residuals (Haberman, 1973) from the application of Model III to the Bott data are given. A number of cells have very large residuals. Such cells may be said to reveal an accommodation between the actor and target in as much as the socially directed behaviors of the actor show adjustment that is unique to the partnership. It should be noted also that each dyad makes two potential accommodations, that of actor A to target B and that of actor B to

Actor \ Target (Child)	1	2	3	4	5	6	7	8	9	10	11
Age (months)	26	29	31	36	37	38	40	45	52	53	54
1		1.9	1.3	-0.5	-1.7	-1.2	-0.1	9.4	-3.7	-1.8	-2.8
2	2.0		1.2	0.6	-0.6	5.4	-1.1	2.8	-2.2	-2.0	-1.8
3	1.1	3.3		2.7	-2.1	0.5	2.5	-0.3	-2.6	0.1	-1.8
4	-1.9	-0.7	0.5		2.1	-0.1	0.3	-2.8	-1.6	-0.5	4.3
5	-0.7	0.4	-1.4	-0.7		3.7	-1.0	1.9	0.0	-0.5	-0.2
6	-0.9	3.3	0.8	-0.1	3.0		-1.4	0.7	-1.2	0.8	-2.7
7	1.4	-2.0	5.6	-2.1	-2.2	-1.4		-2.2	1.2	1.3	-1.0
8	2.2	-0.8	-0.9	-1.0	2.7	-1.4	-0.3		3.4	-1.3	-3.0
9	-2.4	-0.5	-1.8	-1.2	-0.7	-1.4	-1.6	-0.1		-1.8	6.9
10	2.0	-0.6	-1.0	1.9	3.5	-0.9	2.9	-1.3	-4.2		1.0
11	-2.5	-2.5	-2.7	-0.2	-2.5	-1.5	-1.1	-3.9	7.5	3.8	

Figure 2. Residuals from additive model (Bott data: see Figure 1)

target A. There may or may not be symmetry between the accommodations of the two members of the dyad. Hinde (1976) has noted that relationships 'may be mutual' (p. 5), and hence, by implication, they may not. Thus it is possible for accommodations, and hence for relationships, to be one-sided. It is also important to realize that relationships are evaluated in the context of the *group* and may be produced by higher-order dynamics within the group beyond the dyad.

Levels of reciprocation of accommodation in relationships may be assessed by the degree of symmetry of the residuals from the additive model. This symmetry may be determined from Figure 2 by comparing the entries in corresponding cells (i.e. A to B and B to A) above and below the major diagonal. One may consider simple difference scores (Colvin and Tissier, 1985) or, as we prefer, correlations among these corresponding cells (Kenny and Nasby, 1980). Positive correlations would indicate symmetrical accommodations of the children to one another. A negative correlation would indicate reliable asymmetry; one partner might increase and the other decrease frequencies of socially directed actions to the other. This, in turn, could result in rates of activity that are fairly equivalent (as when the more active child decreases and the less active child increases socially directed behavior in the pair). These accommodations might result in dyadic reciprocity; however, on the relational level, such patterns of accommodation would be characterized as asymmetrical adjustments, as the partners alter behavior in opposite directions. In this way it is possible to find dyadic symmetry and, at the same time, relational asymmetry.

At the dyadic level, reciprocity may be evaluated by directly correlating corresponding cells of a behavioral matrix, such as that shown in Figure 1. This *dyadic* reciprocity is related, though not identical, to that considered when intraclass correlations are used within pairs (e.g. Hall and Cairns, 1984). *Relational reciprocity* can be examined by considering the association of residuals as outlined above. There is also *individual* reciprocity, discussed earlier, for which one may examine associations between the marginals of Figure 1 and determine if there is a correlation between A's total socially directed actions and all socially directed actions to A as target. In addition, these three levels of reciprocity are related to one another: dyadic reciprocity consists of the combination of relational and individual reciprocity (Kenny and Nasby, 1980). Thus, conceptually, dyadic reciprocity is a complex entity including both individual and relational components which may have opposing influences.

We examined these three levels of reciprocity for the Bott data presented in Figure 1. At the level of the individual, the balance of behavior given and received was rather modest as reflected in a correlation of 0.44. The intraclass correlations for dyadic and relational reciprocity were somewhat higher at 0.60 and 0.63 respectively. Interestingly, the correlation for relational reciprocity among the five youngest children was only 0.32, whereas among the five oldest children the correlation was 0.69. The relational reciprocity found for Bott's older children is very similar to parallel coefficients reported for grade six children (Whitley, Snyder and Schofield, 1984) and for adults (Kenny and Nasby, 1980). In summary, Bott's data reveal considerable relational reciprocity among preschoolers and a large difference between older and younger preschoolers in relational reciprocity.

F. F. Strayer (1980; Strayer and Trudel, 1984) has also examined relational reciprocity for affiliative behavior in twelve preschool classrooms of children from one to six years. Strayer's procedures come closest to demonstrating relational reciprocity in young children; nonetheless, they fall short in that relational and individual reciprocity are combined. Strayer's analyses examined deviations from predictions based on knowledge of the actor's behavior with no account taken of either target effects or the possible joint action of actor and target effects. Therefore emergent components due to relationships between individuals were not isolated. To examine reciprocation, Strayer determined the number of significant preferences that were returned between partners. This procedure differs from the correlational analyses used here in that it excludes consideration of children who receive less attention than might be expected according to the model tested and in that it dichotomizes (into significant and nonsignificant) what is otherwise a continuous variable (the degree of deviation from expected). Using these procedures, F. F. Strayer (1980) found that within the older groups observed, a majority of the children were involved in reciprocal relationships. Preschool groups tended to be organized into cliques with strong reciprocal preferences within but not between subgroups. Popular children were often chosen by many others within a subgroup. Moreover, both the frequency of significant preferences for other children and the reciprocation of these preferences increased with age (Strayer and Trudel, 1984).

RECIPROCITY AND DEVELOPMENT: EXTENSIONS AND CAUTIONS

We have undertaken this methodological clarification of reciprocity to provide a vehicle for more definitive examinations of hypotheses regarding the role of reciprocity in social life. We can illustrate how this may be accomplished using an example of work within developmental psychology. Youniss (1986) has considered developmental changes in the role of reciprocity in children's friendships. This work is selected because of its simultaneous focus on relationships and reciprocity, and because evidence related to hypotheses about social interchanges has come only from the self-reports of the subjects. Youniss's ideas build on earlier conceptualizations of Sahlins (1965), who suggested that literal tit-for-tat reciprocity is an important *starting mechanism* for group formation prior to the establishment of formal rules of conduct. Extending this notion, Youniss (1986) suggested that early relationships, between six-year-olds for example, are similarly characterized by literal reciprocity. Relationships in this age group would not be consistently differential, but merely build on the initial overture of one partner through the process of immediate reciprocation of like behavior by the other which would continue throughout the interchange. Later, by the age of nine or ten years, friendships become 'selective' and governed by a superordinate principle of fairness. The practice of literal reciprocation is abandoned in the interchanges of older friends; friendship entails reciprocity in providing aid conditional on the need of the partner but not the *immediate* return of aid to a helpful friend. Moreover, the practice of this principle of reciprocity is selective, in that children must select from their peers particular friends and develop new notions of fairness while accommodating to the individual character of their partner.

These hypotheses may be examined in a variety of ways using data on the social activities of children. Literal reciprocity may be tested by examining the interaction of children in comparison with a temporal baseline. Do children return like behavior to a partner? Literal reciprocity should be influenced by the friendship status of the children involved, and should decrease with age. It should apply to prosocial as well as aggressive actions, depending on how the sequence of interaction happened to begin. Gottman's (1983) examination of temporal reciprocity did not show the consistent relations with friendship or with age that Youniss's hypotheses prescribe, but perhaps a focus on different or broader category systems will provide a more appropriate test of these hypotheses. The proposal that reciprocation should be conditional on need could be examined using more experimental procedures such as those of Peterson and her colleagues (Peterson, Hartmann and Gelfand, 1977; Peterson, 1980) or of Staub and Sherk (1970). In these studies the need of the partner was created and so reciprocation was not an automatic reaction to receiving aid but was made conditional on the need of the partner. Youniss predicts greater reciprocation of help among friends and among children who are nine or ten compared with younger children. Interestingly, Staub and Sherk found more sharing among mutual friends but the reciprocation of sharing was greater among nonmutual friends, consistent with Sahlins' (1965) notion of literal reciprocity as a starting mechanism. Also, Peterson (1980) found increased reciprocation of helping over this age period, but only in the case where the beneficiary would have an opportunity to return the favor; with no future expectation of help, there were no differences with age and a lower overall level of reciprocation.

The selectivity of relationships and of 'adapting to the data of individual difference' (Youniss, 1986, p. 100) rather than abandoning reciprocity as Youniss suggests is one of reciprocity of accommodation to the idiosyncracies of one with whom a special relationship has been formed. The procedures for determining the existence of special relationships and relational reciprocity might serve Youniss well in testing his formulations. On the basis of the findings of F. F. Strayer and his colleagues (Strayer, 1980; Strayer and Trudel, 1984) and the analyses of Bott's observations presented here, it is likely that the hypothesized transformation to relational reciprocity may be evident much earlier in development than Youniss' interview data might lead him to believe.

Within developmental psychology, reciprocity has proven to be a protean construct. Considerable variability in operational and conceptual definitions of reciprocity exists in the literature focused on young children. Nonetheless, most definitions used share a minimal set of common features essential to the consideration of reciprocity. These are the return of qualitatively and quantitatively similar, socially directed actions or accommodations between individuals.

These minimal features indicate some form of interpersonal influence and are generally part of the definitions of reciprocation used. Most dangerous, in our view, are other rather holistic uses of the term reciprocity by certain investigators that ignore even these features. Belsky, Taylor and Rovine (1984), for example, defined reciprocity as 'contingently responsive, mutually positive and stimulating social exchange' (p. 707), which they operationalized with a heterogeneous set of social behaviors including some that were neither contingent, responsive, mutual nor stimulating (e.g. 'maternal undivided attention to baby', p. 710). In the works of such investigators reciprocity comes to stand for all that is harmonious, creative and positive in interaction. Belsky and colleagues defend vigorously a pragmatic research strategy that attempts to bypass a detailed analysis of process in favor of global judgements about state. Indeed such global assessments of the overall quality of 'goodness' of relationships may be justified in certain research. However, in such cases care should be taken not to be misled by one's overly specific terminology. Reciprocity is too slender a vehicle on which to heap such an unwieldy hodgepodge of conceptual baggage. Lewis and Feiring (1982) exemplify the use of such definitions with respect to relational reciprocity. They present data for 'reciprocal dyads' about which they comment: 'by reciprocal dyad we mean to indicate the total amount of interaction engaged in by two individuals regardless of which individual is the speaker or the recipient of the action' (p. 131). That is, the measure of 'reciprocity' is achieved by adding together the amount each individual speaks to the other. It is difficult for us to reconstruct the implicit linking constructs between this operationalization of reciprocity and any fruitful theoretical construal of reciprocity. It is because we are of the opinion that reciprocity is potentially a key construct in the understanding of interpersonal dynamics that we are disturbed by attempts to use the term as a generic description of everything that occurs within a dyad.

Handbook of Personal Relationships
Edited by S. W. Duck
© 1988 John Wiley & Sons Ltd

9

Traits and Relationships in Developmental Perspective

KATHRYN A. PARK* and EVERETT WATERS
State University of New York at Stony Brook, New York, USA

ABSTRACT

In this chapter we present parallel definitions of personality and interpersonal relationships as summaries rather than explanations of an individual's or dyad's behavior. Relationships are viewed as a context in which much of interpersonal behavior must be understood. Personality and relationships both modify and are modified by one another. An understanding of how they influence one another's development is complicated by the fact that each is continually undergoing change.

The greatest part of personality-descriptive language in English refers to interpersonal behavior (Wiggins, 1979). It is paradoxical therefore that traditional personality theory and research never evolved towards studying the relationship contexts in which interpersonal behavior occurs.

Historically, personologists have dismissed relationships as the province of sociology or social (as opposed to personality) psychology. In doing so, they have forced a wide range of dyadic phenomena, such as bonds of affection, into the mold of trait concepts and trait measurement models (Waters, 1981). In retrospect it seems evident that personality psychology sowed the seeds of its own decline by overlooking the relationship contexts in which interpersonal behavior occurs. Unfortunately the situationist and interactional perspectives which seek to replace it (Mischel, 1968; Magnusson and Endler, 1977) are no more likely to comprehend the importance of relationships.

Our goal in this chapter is to present parallel definitions of personality and relationships as summaries rather than explanations of behavior. In addition,

* Kathryn Park is now at the University of Denver, Colorado, USA.

we suggest that personal relationships are the contexts in which much of inter-personal behavior must be understood. From this perspective, neither person-ality nor relationship concepts are well defined or amenable to broadly valid assessment until the interconnections between them are defined. These intercon-nections are clearest when we examine the effects of personality on personal relationships and the effects of personal relationships on personality over time.

PERSONALITY

Traditionally, the term *trait* refers to stable differences among individuals. Indeed, one of the goals of personality research has been to identify and measure the most salient ways in which people differ. Personality refers to coherence, as opposed to stability, in an individual's behavior (Block, 1977). Coherence implies that a person's behavior can be understandably different across contexts. A mother may punish an eight-year-old who breaks a house rule but not punish the three-year-old sibling for the same transgression. At the same time, the mother may be described as 'alert' or 'vigilant' if she always responds in some way to her children's transgressions. In this chapter, we define personality as consistency or coherence in affect, cognition, and behavior through which one recognizes different individuals and develops economical models that allow us to predict behavior and coordinate our behavior with theirs.

This definition helps to clarify what should be included under the rubric of personality. The consistency criterion distinguishes affective personality traits from moods, which are transient changes in affective state. It is also useful to distinguish between different types of stable characteristics. One class of traitlike behavior, called mental predicates (Wiggins, 1979), includes individual differ-ences in speech, perception, and thought. In the cognitive domain, constructs such as intelligence and creativity are considered traitlike. Differences in cogni-tive style may account for coherence in an individual's behavior in nonsocial settings.

Stylistic and interpersonal constructs have been the coin of the realm in personality psychology from its inception. Individual differences in behavioral styles have traditionally been conceptualized in terms of temperament traits (Buss and Plomin, 1975). Although differences in behavioral style are considered relevant in the context of social interaction, they are not inherently interactive. That is, temperament theorists construe quickness to anger in social situations as manifestations of the same reactivity construct that underlies reac-tions to hitting a finger with a hammer.

Although temperament theory is perhaps the purest example of trait-oriented research, the bulk of personality theory has been concerned with traits that are more specifically social in their referents and significance and more obviously sensitive to different situational determinants. The largest number of trait descriptors refer to an individual's interpersonal behavior (Wiggins, 1979). Constructs such as sociability, dominance, dependency, and aggressiveness are familiar centerpieces in personality theory and in multidimensional self-report batteries. Interpersonal trait descriptors are those most relevant to the study of personal relationships.

Traits were originally conceptualized as stable and unchanging attributes of individuals which explain differences in people's behavior. Beginning with Freud (1949), personality traits were assumed to be determined by early experiences. One result of this hypothesis is that traits are conceptualized as stable, enduring attributes, with little discussion of how traits develop beyond early childhood. What is the developmental function for different personality traits? Perhaps initially there is plasticity in development, but traits become more highly canalized as environmental influences (e.g. social roles) constrain developmental pathways (Allport, 1961). That is, an individual's traitlike behavior may become less variable and more predictable with age. This model would suggest that personality development does stabilize at some point, unless extreme forces push the individual onto a new developmental (i.e. trait) trajectory (Allport, 1961).

Trait theorists have traditionally spoken of traits as underlying causes of behavior (e.g. Allport, 1961). Unfortunately neither temperament nor personality data have revealed the kind of coherence across situations or stability envisioned in the metatheory of the trait perspective (Mischel, 1968). In addition, the notion that traits are underlying causes of behavior is problematic in itself. In particular, it is unclear what trait language refers to other than the behavior it is proposed to explain. It is manifestly circular to note that a child clings to its mother more than others and then to propose that the clinging is explained by clinginess. This is little more than restating the premise. Moreover, even if trait constructs could be identified with some sort of cognitive structures quite apart from their behavioral referents, we would still need to identify the mechanism through which these structures influenced and thereby explained behavior.

More recently, personality theorists (Mischel, 1973; Buss and Craik, 1983; Wiggins, 1973; Zuroff, 1986) have reconceptualized the meaning of trait. Wiggins' (1973) long unpublished paper entitled 'In Defense of Traits' presents a careful analysis of the epistemological status of trait concepts. In brief, he argues that trait language is appropriate only as a device for summarizing behavior. Trait descriptions are probabilistic statements (Loevinger, 1984; Wiggins, 1973). That is, to say that someone is dependent is simply to say that over the course of your observations 'dependent' is the best word to describe the person's typical behavior. When we say that someone is dependent we might well imply that independent behavior would be atypical, that dependent behavior is predicted in the future, or that this person has also been dependent in the past. But in Wiggins' analysis, traits remain lost causes. Consistency in behavior is a phenomenon to be explained, not an explanation. This analysis will prove useful throughout this chapter.

The fact that personality language is so heavily interpersonal underscores the importance of personality for social relationships. Likewise, a relationship perspective leads to a better understanding of personality. The relationship perspective has its origins in two important insights. First, behavior is often more consistent and coherent within a circumscribed domain, for example in the context of a particular partner (Ross, 1982), than it is in general. Describing the relationships in which a person operates, then, can be viewed as a way of parsing the interpersonal contexts across which or within which individual behavior can be understood.

Second, trait descriptions and explanations notwithstanding, it is evident that the same person will interact differently with different partners as a function of experience with them (e.g. Brody, Graziano and Musser, 1983; Gottman, 1983). That is, in addition to the influences of prevailing contingencies and traitlike consistencies, it is important to identify the influences of behavior that lie in the past whenever individuals have a history of interaction.

PERSONAL RELATIONSHIPS

Hinde (1979) defines a personal relationship as a series of interactions between two people occurring over an extended period of time. *Interaction* emphasizes that relationships can be described with reference to the behavior of the participants. *Series of interactions over time* means that relationships follow a developmental course and have a history. The interaction history shared by the partners distinguishes relationships from initial encounters. *Between two people* implies relationships are the byproduct of the interactions between two people, and as such may involve more than summaries of each individual's behavior. For example, to say a mother–infant pair coordinates its movements is to summarize the behavior of the pair, rather than the specific looks of the infant or the following of the mother.

Viewing each relationship as a context helps to explain consistencies in an individual's behavior. Just as a person may behave differently at home and at work, the person may be different when around a friend versus a stranger, or even when around friend A versus friend B. A person may display only a subset of his or her traits within the context of a particular relationship (Hinde, 1979), and thus different traits are displayed in different relationships. As a result, a person's behavior would look more traitlike within rather than across relationships. For example, throughout childhood children may seek support more often from parents than from friends.

Alternatively, a person may display the same set of traits across relationships but the probability of the behavior occurring and the intensity with which it occurs may vary by the type of relationship. In Magnusson and Endler's (1977) terms, there may be relative rather than absolute consistency in an individual's behavior across situations. An individual who is assertive with friends may be relatively but not absolutely assertive when dealing with his or her boss.

Hinde (1979) has proposed two aspects of relationships to be described. First, relationships can be described by the *content* of the interactions of the participants. For example, in early childhood there is more fantasy play between friends than between acquaintances (Roopnarine and Field, 1984; Vespo, 1985). Relationships can also be described by the *qualities* of the interactions of the participants. 'Qualities' refers to different ways the same action can be performed (and in this way is analogous to the application of temperament descriptors to individuals). For example, children may laugh intensely or meekly. Different types of relationships can be discriminated by their content and qualities. For example, there may be more instances of instruction in parent–child compared to peer relationships (content difference); and within instructional sessions, children may play a subordinate role with their mothers but an equal role with their peers (qualitative difference).

As with personality, there has been a tendency to reify the notion of relationships. Relationships have been discussed as causes, rather than summaries, of behavior. We find it useful to extend Wiggins' analysis of personality to descriptions of relationships. Relationship language summarizes the coherence of expectations about a partner, expectations communicated or engendered in the partner, and the extent to which the behavior of the partners is interdependent across time and situations. If a relationship is 'close', then it would be atypical if one partner felt indifferent, thought the other was unavailable, or refused to disclose information. Descriptions of relationships do not explain dyadic behavior but summarize consistencies which themselves require explanation.

This chapter is, therefore, divided into three main sections. The first section discusses how consistencies and tendencies in an individual's behavior are important in the initiation and maintenance (or dissolution) of relationships. Next, we consider the role of relationships in shaping the consistency and coherence of an individual's behavior. The chapter concludes with a discussion of the personality of relationships and the consistencies in any one individual's relationships.

THE ROLE OF PERSONALITY IN THE DEVELOPMENT OF RELATIONSHIPS

Relationships affect the developmental course of individuals. Relationships are not, however, static influences on development; they are rather developmental phenomena in their own right (Duck, 1983; Hay, 1985; Levinger, 1977; Morton and Douglas, 1981). Relationships have a developmental history just as do individuals. The point in the development of a relationship is one constraint on an individual's behavior. Few people would criticize or argue with a person they are trying to get to know but might feel comfortable doing so with a good friend. In the following section, we will discuss how an individual's personality influences the initiation and maintenance of relationships.

Personality and Initiating Relationships

Individuals often use others' behavior as selection criteria for entering a relationship (Marlowe and Gergen, 1969). This has involved the study of attraction and the process of getting acquainted. For example, Duck (1983; Duck and Craig, 1978) has proposed a filter theory to explain adult acquaintanceship. According to this theory, we begin new relationships by trying to gather information about the other person. Next, we construct a model of our partner's personality. Finally, we assess the degree to which our partner can support our personality. Thus, as we get to know others we apply stricter criteria and 'filter out' people with whom we are unlikely to develop close relationships.

Gottman's (1983) model of friendship formation is similar in its emphasis on information exchange and compatibility. Gottman developed his model after observing three- to nine-year-old best friends and previously unacquainted children. In his model, children begin by exchanging information and establishing a common ground. Next, they explore their similarities and differences. At this point, the relationship may end if the children are unable to resolve their differences. Finally, they engage in mutual play and become more responsive to one another.

Hay (1985) has developed a model of relationship formation designed to apply to children's earliest parent and peer relationships. The model outlines the steps that individuals follow in forming relationships. First, individuals must identify potential social partners. Next, the individual tries to signal the partner. Then, the partners engage in mutual interaction. In the next step, partners modify one another's behavior. Then, the pair establishes unique and idiosyncratic patterns of interaction. Finally, each partner develops an understanding of the mutual relationship. The progression, then, is from individual actions to increasingly coordinated and meshed actions and cognitions.

The models just presented were intended to describe relationship development at different ages (infancy, childhood, and adulthood) and the development of different types of relationships (friendships, parent–child relationships). The similarities among the models suggest a general script for the development of relationships. First, there is an initial attraction between the partners. Next, the partners exchange information and begin reciprocal interaction. At this point, personality similarities and differences between the partners become apparent. Finally, the partners achieve coordinated and mutual interaction. The last step depends on the compatibility of the partners' personalities. All the models would be improved if there were more emphasis on delineating when relationships will *not* progress and how individuals assess personality similarities (Delia, 1980).

The same factors—liking, similarity, compatibility—may be important for the development of relationships at different ages. The criteria which individuals use for assessing the factors may change with age. For example, preschool friends may share similar activity preferences, whereas for adults similarity in attitudes is important.

Personality and Relationship Maintenance

Once begun, relationships can follow several courses. Not all ongoing relationships are close ones; relationships may be at different levels of closeness (Levinger, 1977). Casual but continuous relationships are less often studied. They may, in fact, be governed by different rules and norms (Argyle, Henderson and Furnham, 1985). For instance, children behave differently towards acquaintances than friends: they are less socially responsive (Foot, Chapman and Smith, 1980; Newcomb and Brady, 1982) and less likely to engage in fantasy play (Doyle, 1982; Vespo, 1985) when playing with acquaintances. Casual relationships may be governed by different equity norms. Clark and Mills (1979) suggest that individuals in casual or *exchange* relationships exchange goods in the expectation of receiving a reward or in response to having received a reward. By contrast, individuals in closer, or *communal*, relationships give resources to meet their partners' desires or needs.

In addition to following different equity rules, close relationships may be maintained by factors such as similarities in attitudes and behavioral patterns (Thibaut and Kelley, 1959; Duck, 1973). One personality variable which has received attention recently is the extent to which individuals monitor and alter their behavior to adapt to situational cues and to conform to others' expectations (Snyder, 1974; Snyder, Gangestad and Simpson, 1983). This personality trait has been termed self-monitoring. Individuals high on self-monitoring compartmentalize their relationships and behave differently in different relationships (Snyder, Gangestad and Simpson, 1983). For example, the high self-monitoring individual may play tennis with John but only go shopping with Jill. By contrast, individuals low on self-monitoring tend to engage in a wide range of activities with the same people. In addition, their friendship selections are often based on attitude similarity rather than activity preferences. It may be difficult for a high and a low self-monitoring individual to develop a close friendship, in that the two individuals have different goals and expectations for friendship (Snyder and Smith, 1986). Compatibility between partners is critical for the maintenance of friendships.

Relationships can be disrupted without ending. For example, friendships can endure over long periods of time without the partners interacting. The relationship can be continued upon reunion as long as the partners' expectations and behavior towards each other still mesh. It may be easier to maintain disrupted relationships in adulthood, when individuals undergo less personality change. During childhood and adolescence, and later points in the lifespan when individuals experience developmental change, disrupted relationships are more likely to end.

Not all relationships pass the compatibility test. When the personalities (i.e. the organization of affect, cognition, and behavior) of the two individuals are too dissimilar, the relationship may end. Decisions about ending relationships are determined, in part, by the rewards the partners provide one another (Berg and Clark, 1986; Rusbult, 1983). Individuals are willing to tolerate the costs of a relationship as long as they are still receiving rewards (Hays, 1985; Rusbult, 1983). If an individual's behavior patterns shift during the relationship, one partner's needs may no longer be met and the relationship may end.

Of course, decisions to terminate a relationship may also be based on pragmatic considerations such as an individual's alternatives (Rusbult, 1983). In addition, there is some evidence that individuals decide very early in a relationship, while they are still becoming acquainted, whether to work to maintain a particular relationship (Berg, 1984; Hays, 1985). For example, self-report measures of satisfaction administered after five dates were able to predict, with 80 per cent correct classification, which couples would still be dating four months later; measures of satisfaction administered at four months correctly classified 90 per cent of the cases (J. H. Berg, 1983, cited in Berg and Clark, 1986). In a short-term longitudinal study of roommates, measures of satisfaction administered two weeks into the fall semester and again in the spring semester predicted equally well which adults chose to room together in the following year (Hays, 1985). Given that nonbehavioral factors such as physical attractiveness are related to attraction (e.g. Murstein, 1972), it is easy to *overestimate* the extent to which personality variables determine the relationships that individuals enter or exit.

In sum, personality is one influence on the development of relationships. The compatibility of the partners' personalities may be more important in some stages of a relationship than others. For instance, physical attractiveness rather than personality may influence initial liking and attraction. Personality may play a bigger role once the relationship is established. In addition, individuals may need fewer personal similarities to maintain casual, as compared to close, relationships. Personality factors may be most important in long-term, close relationships which partners have the option of terminating. Incompatible personalities may lead to conflict rather than relationship dissolution in the case of kinships. Finally, the extent to which individuals use personality as a criterion for evaluating relationships may change with age. For young children, whose personalities are still developing, personality similarity may be less important than for adults, who must mesh their established patterns of affect, cognition, and behavior.

RELATIONSHIP CONTRIBUTIONS TO PERSONALITY

One angle on the study of relationships and personality development is to try and answer the following question: how do relationships contribute to the development of a person's characteristic patterns of behavior? In answering this question, the distinction between social interaction and social relationships must be maintained. As Hartup (1985) notes, often what is studied is how opportunities for social interaction affect development; the challenge is to demonstrate that relationships, and not just social interaction, influence development. For example, is it opportunities for peer play or the development of friendships *per se* which affect the development of children's social skills? Presumably a child's relationships with social partners influence social interaction. For example, friends working together on a task may work harder because they feel a sense of commitment to one another.

Different types of relationships may contribute differently to personality development. Weiss (1986) has suggested a typology for classifying relationships by function. For example, security is provided primarily by parent–child relationships, whereas companionship and helping are provided primarily in peer relationships. His view recently received some empirical support (Furman and Buhrmester, 1985). The basis for maintaining a relationship also varies with the type of relationship. For example, in kin relationships individuals are bound together by mutual obligation, although unlike friendships there need not be a high degree of interpersonal liking for the relationship to continue (Weiss, 1986). Thus, in evaluating how relationships affect personality development, it may be necessary to maintain distinctions between different types of relationships.

Different types of relationships may be more or less important at different ages. In infancy and childhood, parent–child relationships are primary. In childhood and adolescence, peer relationships are increasingly important. In adulthood, love relationships may supersede parent–child or peer relationships. Familial and kin relationships may be important across the lifespan as secondary sources of support.

Qualitative differences among relationships will mediate the effect of the relationship on the individual's development. For example, one dimension of relationships is the degree of liking between two individuals. Relationships characterized by a high degree of mutual liking, such as friendships, are frequently studied, but little is known about 'enemyships' (Harré, 1977; Allen, 1981) or relationships characterized almost exclusively by negative affect. The absence of relationships can also affect the individual's affect, cognition, and behavior. For example, children rejected by their peers are more often aggressive and hostile (e.g. Dodge, 1983), inappropriate in social situations (e.g. Putallaz and Gottman, 1981; Putallaz, 1983), more likely to make negative attributions about others (e.g. Dodge, 1980; Dodge and Frame, 1982; Dodge et al., 1986), and more likely to drop out of school or suffer psychological problems (Cowen et al., 1973; Roff, Sells and Golden, 1972) than children who are not rejected (see also Hartup, 1983). Either a lack of relationships or maintenance of relationships characterized by negative affect may have detrimental effects on a child's development.

The contribution of relationships can be assessed by examining their functions. Relationships serve two important functions: they can provide support and a sense of security; and they can mediate socialization and later competence. Ongoing, positive relationships serve an individual's development by providing support and serving as socializing influences.

Relationships as Sources of Support

The parent–child relationship is the developing child's primary source of emotional support (Weiss, 1986). Beginning with Bowlby (1969), the notion of support has been captured in the concept of a child's attachment to mother. According to Bowlby, infants develop attachments to their parents in the first year of life. In expanding on Bowlby's ideas, Ainsworth (1972; Ainsworth, Bell and Stayton, 1972) introduced the notion of the quality of the mother–child tie and the descriptors secure and anxious to describe good versus poor quality mother–child attachments. Securely attached children have a history of responsive, sensitive caretaking (Ainsworth et al., 1978). These social experiences lead them to expect that others will be sensitive and responsive to their needs and to use the mother as a secure base from which to explore (Ainsworth et al.,

1978). Securely attached infants use their mothers as a source of support when distressed; anxiously attached infants do not.

One index of the mother–infant relationship, security, has a number of external correlates, all of which suggest that secure children are exposed to a richer social environment. Children who are securely attached more thoroughly explore objects in their environment and are more socially competent with peers. Clearly, secure attachment to mother is related to the development of a child's characteristic pattern of behavior. Less clear, however, is what causal role attachment might play in shaping a child's pattern of behavior. Why, for instance, are securely attached infants more positive with their peers than are anxiously attached infants?

Bowlby (1973) proposed that children develop a working model of relationships based on experiences with their caregivers (see also Main, Kaplan and Cassidy, 1986; Ricks, 1986; Sroufe, 1987). A child's working model contains expectations about how others are likely to behave; this working model of relationships serves as a guide for the child's behavior. For example, if a child's model of relationships says people are unresponsive and uncaring, that child may be hesitant to initiate social interaction with others. The child's model is initially developed from the child's experience with the mother or primary caretaker(s), but it can be modified by later relationships (Main, Kaplan and Cassidy, 1986).

Sroufe (1987; Sroufe and Fleeson, 1986) has used the concept of working models to explain how the quality of the mother–child relationship can be related to the quality of the child's subsequent peer relationships. According to Sroufe, in forming new relationships children seek to recreate patterns of interaction which occurred in previous relationships. For example, a child who has been exploited in the parent–child relationship has learned the social relationship exploiter–exploited and is likely to assume one of the roles in subsequent relationships. Both early behavior patterns organized in the infant–caregiver system and expectations about relationships are carried forward into new relationships (Sroufe and Fleeson, 1986; Main, Kaplan and Cassidy, 1986).

A few studies support Sroufe's (1987; Sroufe and Fleeson, 1986) hypothesis. In interactions with previously unfamiliar peers, secure children engage in more reciprocal interaction (Pastor, 1981; Lieberman, 1977) and receive more positive interaction bids from peers (Jacobson and Wille, 1986). In addition, insecure children engage in more hostile or negative behavior when with familiar (Lieberman, 1977) or unfamiliar (Sroufe, 1987) peers. Secure children are also more competent and affectively positive around preschool classmates (Waters, Wippman and Sroufe, 1979). Finally, secure children are less dependent around preschool teachers (Sroufe, Fox and Pancake, 1983). As a group, the studies suggest insecurely attached children exhibit social interaction deficits, but more data are needed on how the *relationships* of securely and insecurely attached children differ.

Not only do children have working models of relationships, they also develop working models of the self. Epstein (1973) has recently restated the view of the self as a self-theory. Briefly, Epstein argues that individuals develop a theory that contains several postulates about themselves, many of which are derived from experiences in social interaction. Epstein places more importance on the first postulates an individual develops. Following from this, it could be argued that the mother–child relationship, as a child's first relationship, lays the foundation of a child's self-theory.

Sroufe (1987) emphasizes that information about our self is drawn from experiences in relationships, particularly the mother–child relationship. Children who develop positive, secure attachments view themselves as effective actors on their environment. For example, secure children try to master tasks (Matas, Arend and Sroufe, 1978). By contrast, anxiously attached children incorporate in their model of self the notion that they are unworthy and incompetent. Sroufe (1987) provides an excellent example. In one preschool classroom, an anxiously attached child approached a peer and was rebuffed. Discouraged, the child walked to a corner of the room. Later, a securely attached child was turned down by a playmate. Rather than sulking, the secure child continued to approach children and eventually found a play partner.

This is not to suggest that children's working models of relationships and self are fixed upon conception. Children's working models are most likely to be modified within the context of other relationships (Sroufe and Fleeson, 1986). For instance, peer relationships can also influence a child's self-esteem (Buhrmester and Furman, 1986a). If a child has had a poor relationship with a parent, but subsequently developed good relationships with peers or kin, that child may modify his or her models of relationships and self.

The quality of the mother–child tie impacts on the child's personality development. If attachments fulfill the function of providing security, the child is likely to be confident in exploring the environment, performing tasks, and initiating interaction with others. A lack of security, and expectations that self is unworthy and others are unresponsive, may lead a child to withdraw from social interaction or to utilize inappropriate interaction strategies.

The parent–child relationship has been discussed at length because Freud (1949) and others (Bowlby, 1969; Hinde, 1979) have emphasized the influence of the child's first relationships, particularly the mother–child relationship, on personality development. Other relationships do, however, modify personality across the lifespan. For example, friendships (Asher and Renshaw, 1981; Buhrmester and Furman, 1986a; Duck, 1983; Hartup, 1983) can provide emotional support. Just the presence of agemates (Ipsa, 1981; Schwarz, 1972) can provide support in stressful situations. It is uncertain, however, whether friends provide support in addition to or in place of parental support (Hartup, 1986). In adulthood, dating and spouse relationships presumably take over this function.

When relationships end, the amount of turmoil and disruption caused may depend on the closeness of the relationship. Berscheid (1986) has recently proposed that reactions to separation, rather than intensity of emotion displayed to the partner, provide the clearest indicator of the closeness of a relationship. According to Berscheid, the behavior of two individuals in a close relationship becomes highly interdependent. When one partner permanently withdraws from interaction (i.e. separation), the other partner becomes distressed now that familiar interaction patterns have been disrupted. A corollary of this view is that partners in a close relationship whose behaviors are well meshed and noninterfering may actually display little emotion to each other. The more interdependent the behaviors of the partners—and consequently the closer the relationship—the more distressed the partners will be upon separation. Situational factors, such as the availability of alternative partners, may mediate the intensity of the separation response. Although the theory may prove useful in predicting reactions to permanent separations, its ability to predict temporary separations is more problematic. For example, would securely attached children show more separation protest than insecurely attached children when left at preschool? Reactions to temporary separation are likely influenced by cognitive factors such as judgements about the partners' likelihood of returning. For this reason, it may be useful to assess reunion behavior as well as separation responses when measuring the closeness of a relationship.

Relationships as Mediators of Socialization and Later Competence

Relationships function as a context in which learning occurs (Hay, 1985). Hartup (1985) has suggested several reasons why positive relationships create a favorable learning environment. First, the partners have knowledge about each other's capacities and limitations, which facilitates learning. Vygotsky (1962) suggested optimal learning occurs when instruction is slightly more advanced than the child's current level of thinking, that is when teaching is directed towards the 'zone of proximal development' (Vygotsky, 1962). Mothers may be particularly good at teaching their children because of indepth knowledge of their children's abilities. In addition, partners may be more motivated to exert cognitive effort when working together. Finally, it may be easiest for children to practise 'cognitive regulation' and to learn problem-solving skills within the context of a reciprocal relationship (Matas, Arend and Sroufe, 1978).

Relationships are also a source of knowledge about social roles. Different types of relationships demand different sets of behavior (Buhrmester and Furman, 1986?). For example, a teacher–student relationship operates under different rules and norms than friendships (Argyle, Henderson and Furnham, 1985). A child may associate obedience with authority figures but autonomy with peer relationships (Hartup, 1984). The developing child must learn to distinguish between different types of relationships and to enact the appropriate roles (Duck, Miell and Gaebler, 1980). The way children conceptualize the norms for different types of relationships will constrain their behavior in a relationship.

Finally, relationships modify an individual's attitudes and beliefs. People are not only attracted to others with similar attitudes, but attitudes of individuals in a positive relationship become more similar over time (Newcomb, 1961). This may result from the partners reinforcing aspects of one another's personalities (Thibaut and Kelley, 1959). The opposite may be true for individuals in antagonistic relationships; their views might become more polarized over time as they attempt to create distance from one another.

In addition to influencing current behavior, relationships also serve to mediate socialization outcomes (Waters, Hay and Richters, 1986; Waters and Sroufe, 1983). The general question is whether the quality of a child's relationships is related to socialization outcomes such as adherence to parental standards, development of morality, compliance, and acceptance of obligations. Most often, the parent–child relationship has been linked to socialization outcomes. For example, children who are securely attached to their mothers exhibit fewer behavior problems (Erickson, Sroufe and Egeland, 1986; Lewis *et al.*, 1984) and are more compliant to parental directives (Stayton, Hogan and Ainsworth, 1971; Londerville and Main, 1981). The problem has been how to explain why a secure attachment to parents would lead a child to comply with parental requests or to refrain from engaging in antisocial behaviors.

Most theories of socialization posit that good outcomes result when parents use punitive control techniques to modify their children's behavior. For example, children obey their parents because they wish to avoid punishment or fear withdrawal of parental love (cf. Maccoby and Martin, 1983: see also Mills and Grusec, this volume). By contrast Richters and Waters (in press), in building on current attachment theory and data, propose that good socialization outcomes are the result of parental practices which lead children to adopt a prosocial disposition, including the formation of secure attachment and a prosocial style of exchange. Children receive sensitive, responsive, and appropriate care from parents and in return adopt and comply with parental and societal values. Thus, parents and their children become committed to a prosocial system of exchange which benefits both, and the system is maintained as long as the participants' benefits outweigh the costs.

This is not to suggest, of course, that negative control techniques play no role in socialization; to do so would mean ignoring the research of the past two decades showing the effectiveness of these techniques. The two types of parental strategies may play complementary roles in the socialization process. Negative control techniques such as punishment may be most successful in inducing immediate or situational compliance (Richters and Waters, in press). Strategies which lead children to operate in a system of prosocial exchange may be more related to long-term compliance; because they have invested heavily in the system, children will continue to comply with the rules of the system to ensure a return on their investment.

Peer relationships provide another context in which socialization occurs. Unlike parent–child and sibling relationships, peer relationships are voluntary (Hartup, 1983). Thus, it is through developing peer relationships that children develop the skills for entering, maintaining, and exiting relationships. In friendships, children learn that relationships are negotiable (Corsaro, 1981; Mannarino, 1980) and that they require cooperation and mutual respect (Smollar and Youniss, 1982). Through friendships children also learn generosity, sharing, and sociability (Foot, Chapman and Smith, 1980). A great deal of socialization occurs within peer as well as parent–child relationships.

In sum, relationships are a source of personality change. Connectedness to another person's behavior can stimulate exploration of new interests and give security to explore or undertake more difficult tasks. Similarly, new relationships provide opportunities for new interests and activities. Relationships are also a conservative influence which can have a stabilizing effect on an individual's behavior. For example, partners' expectations for each other may constrain an individual's behavior within the context of the relationship. As such, relationships are responsible for both continuities and discontinuities in an individual's behavior.

The preceding discussion is not intended to imply that relationships are causal mechanisms which determine a dyad's behavior. For example, it is not that a good mother–child relationship causes good outcomes, but that the same factors which lead to good parent–child relationships are also precursors of later competence (Waters, Hay and Richters, 1986). The fact that security of attachment is related to later competence is not the explanation, but the empirical relationship to be explained. Just as trait language serves as summaries of behavior in need of an explanation, relationship language summarizes but does not explain the behavior of a dyad.

PERSONALITY OF RELATIONSHIPS

As yet, there is no study of the personality of relationships. That is, what are the individual differences among relationships? Can relationships be described by the same personality traits which are applied to individuals? For example, are parent–child relationships more controlling than peer relationships? Are male relationships more aggressive than female relationships?

In part, psychology has failed to apply an individual-differences approach to the study of relationships because individuals and not relationships are typically the focus of study. Relationships, however, are dyadic phenomena, and their study requires moving to a different level of description. That is, the study of relationships must be, at least in part, the study of dyads (Maccoby, 1982; Hinde, 1979, 1981; Mannarino, 1980; Levinger, 1977). Taking the dyad as the unit of description captures the bidirectionality of relationships.

Dyads, triads, and other groups represent units of analysis that are quite different from individual assessment (Hinde, 1979; Milardo, 1986). Most importantly, it is unlikely that we can make valid inferences about the behavior of social groups from generalizations about their constituent members (Allen, 1981; Shaw, 1971), particularly if the members differ on a socially relevant variable such as age or sex. For example, the fact that individual boys are generally more aggressive than girls does not necessarily imply that male–male dyads would be more aggressive than male–female or female–female dyads.

One reason for adopting a dyadic level of analysis is that some relationship variables can be described only with reference to the dyad. For example, to say that friendship is more intimate and cohesive than acquaintanceship is to say that *pairs* of friends are more cohesive together than *pairs* of acquaintances. Similarly, although mother–child attachment is assessed by observing the child's behavior to the mother, the major variable assessed, security, describes the pair. This is why a child may be securely attached to mother but anxiously attached to father (Main and Weston, 1981); attachment is not a traitlike characteristic of the individual, but a description of one child–parent relationship (Sroufe, 1985).

This brings up the question of whether or not it is possible for behavior to look traitlike when the relationship rather than the individual is the focus of study. Given that two different individuals are producing each relationship, what is the upper bound on consistency within and across relationships that we can expect to find?

We are really asking two distinct questions. The first is whether relationships can be described along the same traitlike dimensions which are used to describe individuals. A priori, there seems to be no reason to believe this is not possible. Surely aggressive dyads can be distinguished from passive ones, just as aggressive individuals are distinguishable from passives. A more critical question, however, is whether current trait language describes all the ways in which dyads differ. In addition to terms applied to individuals, descriptions of dyads and groups would have to include descriptors such as cohesiveness, security, commitment (Levinger, 1977), and competition and dependency (Sears, 1972).

The second question is whether or not there is traitlike consistency within or across relationships. For example, if we are studying marital dyads, how consistent is that dyad's behavior across time and situation? In fact, dyadic variables and measures of relationships are likely to be more stable than measures of individual behavior. For example, Waters (1978) assessed the stability of mother–infant attachment classification, a dyadic variable, with the Strange Situation when the infants were twelve and eighteen months old. The infants' interactive behaviors during the Strange Situation episode were also scored. Attachment classification was quite stable over the six-month period; ratings of individual interactive behaviors were not. The stability of dyadic behavior has rarely been assessed, but it may prove more stable than an individual's behavior because the partners in a pair constrain one another's behavior.

Perhaps most important for the trait perspective is the question of whether there is any similarity to the descriptions of all the relationships individual A enters. It would be interesting to know the extent to which individual A acts the same with friend A, friend B, a parent, the boss, and the milkman. In one study (Waldrop and Halverson, 1975), sociability with peers at age two was found to predict sociability with peers at age seven.

In studies of conflict between toddlers, there are both consistencies and inconsistencies in behavior across social partners. In two studies (Hay and Ross, 1982; Ross, 1982) a toddler's tendency to initiate conflict was consistent across play partners; a toddler who initiated conflict with child A was likely to initiate conflict with child B. By contrast, a toddler's tendency to yield (or not yield) to a partner during conflict was relationship-specific, suggesting that patterns of control and power develop within a particular relationship. Perhaps examining consistency in behavior across relationships will provide the strongest test yet of the degree to which human behavior can ever be described as traitlike.

CONCLUSIONS

In this chapter, we have tried to highlight some of the issues in the study of personality and relationships. One problem discussed was that of definition. Personality refers to the organization of affect, cognition, and behavior of an individual, whereas relationship refers to the description of a pair's cognitions and feelings about each other and their behavior towards one another. The language of 'personality' and 'relationships' does not afford explanations of developmental change, but instead represents or summarizes what developmental theories must explain.

Two other factors complicate the study of how personality and personal relationships are related. First, both personality and relationships continually undergo change. Relationships and traits will be better understood when both are treated as developmental rather than static entities. This implies that both have antecedents, both follow a beginning to end progression, and both are continually evolving.

Second, the study of relationships should be the study of dyads rather than the study of individuals. Relationships are conceptualized as dyadic, yet what is usually measured is the behavior of one or both partners in a relationship (but see Kenny, this volume). Taking dyads rather than individuals as the focus of study and description will allow assessment procedures to parallel our conceptualization of relationships. Just as individuals should not be looked at in isolation, focusing on a single relationship will fail to illuminate the multiple influences on a child's personality development.

Handbook of Personal Relationships
Edited by S. W. Duck
© 1988 John Wiley & Sons Ltd

10

Socialization from the Perspective of the Parent–Child Relationship

ROSEMARY S. L. MILLS
University of Waterloo, Ontario, Canada
and
JOAN E. GRUSEC
University of Toronto, Scarborough, Ontario, Canada

ABSTRACT

The attempt to understand parental influence as a bidirectional rather than merely a unidirectional process has led developmental researchers to delve beneath the observable chain of actions and reactions between parent and child to uncover the thoughts and feelings believed to mediate their behavior.

Close relationships are defined as those in which the participants have frequent and strong influence on one another across a wide range of activities and over a relatively long period of time (Berscheid and Peplau, 1983). The burgeoning literature seeking to understand how close relationships form, function, and change has most frequently been concerned with adults and heterosexual relationships in particular. Another important relationship, indeed one that may be critical in shaping all others (e.g. Erikson, 1950; Freud, 1933; Sroufe and Fleeson, 1986), is that between parent and child. Two aspects of this relationship have been of special interest: the establishment of an attachment between the pair (see Nash, this volume; Park and Waters, this volume) and the contribution of the relationship to the socialization of the child. This chapter focuses primarily on the latter.

The study of socialization is concerned with how parents influence children to develop socially appropriate modes of thought, feeling, and behavior. We will focus on the cognitive and affective mediators of the process, arguing that how parents think and feel about the child's behavior determines how children socialize. Similarly, the way in which the child responds to the parent's influence attempts is a function of how the child interprets them.

Potentially, almost anything parents do or say has some direct or indirect influence on the child's socialization. However, because it is parents' assigned responsibility to transmit society's values, standards, and rules of conduct to the child, because they have considerable powers of influence at their disposal, and because they often make deliberate efforts to train the child, developmental psychologists have been concerned primarily with the influence parents exert through the use of persuasion and of discipline techniques which are intended to modify the child's subsequent behavior, i.e. with reactive modes of influence (Radke-Yarrow and Zahn-Waxler, 1986). Where possible, however, we shall also deal with another mode of influence which is equally important, i.e. the modeling of socially appropriate behavior. Thus parents provide examples of behavior which children are highly prone to emulate, both prosocial and anti-social. They are particularly potent in this respect because they have an affectionate relationship with their children as well as possessing, in the eyes of those children, such characteristics as power and control of resources which are all effective facilitators of imitation (Bandura, Ross and Ross, 1963; Grusec, 1971; Yarrow, Scott and Waxler, 1973).

POWER AND CONFLICT

The parent–child relationship is like other authority relationships in that one member has more power over the other. The parent not only has more resources available for exerting influence, but also exercises this power more intentionally and purposefully than the child, particularly in the beginning. The extent to which the child accepts and responds to the parent's authority is largely determined by how the parent uses power. This, in turn, is a product of factors in both parent and child. How these factors contribute to the quality of the authority relationship between parent and child, and the effects of this relationship on the socialization of the child, constitute the main focus of this chapter. Whether and how parents choose to exercise their authority depends on the values they hold, the attributions they make about the child's behavior, and the emotional reactions they have to the behavior. In turn, the way in which the child responds to the parent's influence attempts depends on such variables as how the parent's use of power is evaluated by the child and how the parent's behavior influences the child's self-perceptions.

Another feature of the parent–child relationship having implications for socialization is conflict. Conflict is inherent in all interpersonal relationships. An important source of conflict in the parent–child relationship is the socialization process itself, which often puts parental demands directly at odds with the impulses of the child. The disparity in ages and hence in the ways each construes a given situation is another potential source of conflict between parent and child. Conflicting needs and interests provide an essential impetus to developmental change. If conflict is managed constructively the outcome will be positive. When the parent uses forms of power perceived as punitive or exercises authority in areas where it is not considered legitimate, the quality of the affectional tie as well as the parent's effectiveness as a socializing agent are threatened.

Given their centrality in the parent–child relationship, it is not surprising to find that power and conflict are perceived as salient features even by the younger member of the dyad. In a demonstration of this point, Wish, Deutsch and Kaplan (1976) had college students rate various kinds of relationships they had had on a variety of bipolar scales. Parent–child and teacher–child relationships were perceived as far less equal in power than relationships with siblings and close friends, and intermediate in the amount of conflict present in the dyad. When rating adolescent relationships, subjects perceived the relationship between parent and child as particularly high in conflict.

These retrospective perceptions of college students are consistent with the perceptions of a sample of fifth- and sixth-graders who were asked by Furman and Buhrmester (reported in Furman, 1984) to rate the characteristics of several of their current personal relationships. These children considered their parents to be more dominant over them than anyone else (grandparents, siblings, close friends) save their teachers. As well, they perceived more conflict in their sibling relationships than in their relationships with parents, but more conflict with parents than with their closest friend.

Interestingly, then, children are less aware of conflict than they are of power in their relationship with parents. We will review evidence suggesting that the child's acceptance of parental authority is one factor contributing to the reduction of conflict, a factor which may in turn depend on how the parent uses power. Coercive power, for example, generates resistance in the child, escalation of conflict and hostility between parent and child, and ultimately the loss of parental authority.

APPROACHES TO THE STUDY OF PARENTAL INFLUENCE

The Unidirectional Approach

The parent's goal is to transmit society's values, standards, and rules to the child (on the assumption that the parent himself or herself has been successfully socialized). Some are particularly difficult for the child to adopt and can therefore be a source of considerable strain on the parent–child relationship. In the beginning the child's compliance with such rules and prohibitions is externally motivated. Eventually compliance becomes internalized, that is, it is observed to occur even in the absence of overt parental control. Now the child's behavior can be said to be self-governed and the parent's influence can be said to extend beyond specific situations to general patterns of behavior and below the level of overt compliance to underlying values and attitudes.

Partly as a result of this conceptualization, socialization processes have been studied predominantly from a unidirectional perspective in which the child is assumed to be a passive recipient of the parent's influence. The roots of this approach lie in psychoanalytic theory as well as in behaviorism and its environmental explanation of behavior. Observing that conditioning occurs early in life, John Watson (1913), for example, became convinced that most of the infant's innate responses become attached to new stimuli through conditioning. Parents should attempt to avoid the disastrous consequences of accidental conditioning by controlling the child's environment as much as possible. As eliciting stimuli in themselves, parents must also be careful to manage their own behavior. The possibility that the child's behavior could also elicit parental behavior was not considered.

This same principle guided early research on socialization (e.g. Sears, Maccoby and Levin, 1957; Sears, Rau and Alpert, 1965), research which was inspired by a combination of learning and psychoanalytic theory. Psychoanalytic theory, in placing major emphasis on the role of the parent in the young child's social and emotional development, did nothing to militate against the unidirectional approach. (It should be noted that Sears, as early as 1951, urged that researchers develop methods for studying the 'dyad'—the two people involved in any social exchange—and their interaction. These methods, however, did not emerge until much later.)

Instrumental learning theories (Bijou and Baer, 1965; Skinner, 1953), without the overlay of psychoanalytic theory, examine almost the same slice of the interaction chain as did behaviorism. They focus, however, on the causal role of response consequences. In principle, parents and children are equally subject to response consequences. However, the fact that parents have access to a wider range of reinforcers and manipulate them more intentionally than children do is assumed to give the parents greater power to influence behavior. Like other stimulus–response theories, contemporary social learning theory also assumes that the balance of power in parent–child interaction resides with the parent (Bandura, 1977), both directly through the administration of response consequences and indirectly by making the parent an influential model. By observing their parents, children obtain information about response consequences that helps them to predict the outcomes of their own behavior more accurately. Thus children are subject to both intentional and unintentional forms of parental power.

Nevertheless, children do have effects on their parents' behavior. Through their compliance as well as through their failure to comply, children reinforce certain behaviors in their parents. Congenital and other characteristics of children also influence parental behavior. This idea became more acceptable as psychologists began to view the child as spontaneously active, an image promoted by Piagetian theory as well as by modifications of psychoanalytic theory which depicted the ego as developing autonomously rather than emerging from the id (Hartmann, 1952). In an influential paper, Rheingold (1969) reminded developmental psychologists of the impressive power of the young infant to manipulate its caretaker by the simple but very effective device of crying. No one exposed to the piercing cries of an unhappy baby could fail to note that even these very young creatures wield a mighty influence in the process of socialization, with a behavior so aversive that parents will do almost anything to stop it. Much of the recent attention to the issue of the 'direction of effects' in parent–child relations (e.g. Bell, 1968; Bell and Chapman, 1986;

Bell and Harper, 1977) represents an attempt to understand the strength and diversity of the child's influences with a view to correcting the unidirectional model.

Influence of the Child on the Parent

The first step towards an interactional model of the parent–child relationship was to identify some of the ways children influence parent behavior. In the study of socialization, the child's influence on parental disciplinary practices is of particular interest. Various sources of influence have been considered.

Temperament

Bell (1968) attributed a number of correlations found between parent behavior and child outcomes to congenital characteristics of the child. For example, a consistent finding (Hoffman, 1963) was that maternal warmth combined with the use of disciplinary techniques involving reference to the implications of the child's behavior for other people (other-oriented induction) was positively related to moral internalization in the child. Bell suggested that this finding, which was previously interpreted as an indication that parental behavior produces the child's moral internalization, could just as easily be due to the fact that children congenitally high in 'person orientation' elicit more affection and other-oriented reasoning from their mothers. Thus Keller and Bell (1979) found that nine-year-old female confederates who enacted high person orientation by attending to the adult's face and answering promptly elicited more other-oriented induction and less power assertion (bargaining) from female college students encouraging them to be considerate than those who enacted low person orientation by attending to objects and giving delayed responses.

Age

Parents use different tactics depending on the age of the child. Thus Clifford (1959) found, in a study of maternal disciplinary practices with three-, six-, and nine-year-olds, that physical methods such as forced compliance were used more frequently with younger children than they were with older children, while cognitive techniques such as humor and appeals to self-esteem were used more often with older children. One might say that, in general, parents' methods of influencing the child shift from physical to cognitive in approach and from strong to mild in force in part at least because cognitive approaches may be difficult for the young child to comprehend and physical approaches may be more likely to elicit opposition from the older child.

Attractiveness

Dion (1972) reports that female college students given brief descriptions of a child's transgression and shown a picture of the perpetrator evaluate the transgression as more undesirable when the child is unattractive than when the child is attractive. Unattractive transgressors are also rated more 'dishonest' and 'unpleasant' than their attractive counterparts as well as being perceived as more antisocial in disposition in the case of severe transgressions (e.g. injuring a dog by throwing stones). In a second study (Dion, 1974) college students monitored the task performance of an attractive or an unattractive child via videotape, and administered penalties for incorrect responses. Women were more lenient in their administration of penalties with an attractive boy than they were with either an attractive girl or an unattractive boy. Men, on the other hand, were not influenced by either the gender or the attractiveness of the child. We do not know whether this differential responsiveness to attractiveness and gender in a learning situation would also be found in disciplinary situations, or whether attractiveness is a factor in parents' responses to their own children.

Nature of the misdeed

The nature of the transgression itself also influences disciplinary reactions. Grusec and Kuczynski (1980) found that mothers of four- and seven-year-olds reported they would use different disciplinary practices from one situation to the next. Responses to five types of misdeeds were assessed: simple disobedience (e.g. ignoring or refusing to comply with requests), disobedience leading to damage to physical property (e.g. breaking a vase playing ball), disobedience leading to possible harm to self (e.g. running into the street after a ball), disobedience causing physical harm to another (e.g. fighting), and disobedience causing psychological harm to another (e.g. making fun of an elderly man).

Misdeeds typically elicited the use of more than one technique. There was some variation in the types of techniques used across different kinds of misdemeanor. Acts causing physical harm to self or psychological harm to others prompted mothers to use reasoning, i.e. to describe rules or explain the physical or emotional consequences of the child's behavior for others. Most other misdemeanors elicited power-assertive techniques such as physical punishment, withdrawal of privileges, and making the child engage in the appropriate behavior, often followed by the description of rules or a statement of norms. It appeared that mothers might be using reasoning when they felt it was important to promote the long-term objective of internalization, and power-assertive tactics when their goal was to establish immediate control over the child's behavior.

Consistent with these findings, Zahn-Waxler and Chapman (1982) reported that transgressions against people (e.g. pinching the baby in one- to two-and-a-half-year-olds) elicited parental reasoning about the meaning or consequences of the misdeed for the other person or dramatic enactments of their distress (dramatizing the harm caused by highlighting expressions of distress). Transgressions involving property destruction (e.g. drawing on the couch with a pen) or lack of self-control (e.g. spitting in milk) elicited both power assertion (e.g. physical punishment or restraint) and withdrawal of love (e.g. sending the child away). These investigators suggested that psychological harm to others may elicit inductive techniques partly because the parent wishes to impress upon the child the negative consequences such acts have for others, and partly because the alternative of power assertion is believed to transmit a contradictory message about the acceptability of aggression towards others. Acts involving destructiveness or lack of self-control may be associated with power assertion and love withdrawal in combination because the latter allows the parent to gain control over the anger aroused by the aversiveness of such acts.

In yet another study addressed to the issue (Grusec, Dix and Mills, 1982), mothers of seven- to nine-year-olds were asked to describe how they would discipline their children if they engaged in described misdeeds involving either the commission of an antisocial act (lying, stealing, physical aggression) or the failure to be prosocial (not helping, not sharing, not showing concern for others). Antisocial acts were dealt with more punitively than prosocial failures, i.e. with physical punishment, withdrawal of privileges, or isolation, particularly when they were regarded as serious. Prosocial failures were more likely than antisocial misdeeds to elicit empathy training (reasoning which referred to the feelings of others), but only with girls.

Why do mothers use more firm control with antisocial acts than with prosocial omissions? They may be sure about the appropriateness of suppressing antisocial acts but somewhat conflicted about how much prosocial behavior is desirable, hence more willing to be punitive in the former case. Perhaps displays of negative emotion in the child, which would more frequently accompany antisocial acts, are particularly aversive to parents and hence are likely to evoke aggressive counter-reactions (G. R. Patterson, 1982; Zahn-Waxler and Chapman, 1982).

In summary, the literature on child effects demonstrates that the child's age, attractiveness, and actual behavior make a strong contribution to the parent's choice of influence technique. Parents' reactions are probably influenced by a number of factors, including knowledge of the child's maturity, the meaning the parent attaches to the act itself, and interpretations and attributions the parent makes about the child as a function of the act. In the next section, therefore, we describe attempts to uncover some of the thoughts, feelings, and values which influence the ways in which the parent responds to the child in disciplinary encounters. Since the child's reaction to the parent is undoubtedly mediated by the same types of subjective events, we then proceed to consider the internal events influencing the child's response to the parent's behavior.

Interactional Approach

Much current research on the nature of parental influence is predicated on an interactional view of the parent–child relationship. Like other close relationships, the interdependence between parent and child can be conceptualized as occurring on three levels: action, thought, and feeling. Events on all these levels are causally related both within and between the two participants in the relationship. Viewed from this perspective, the chain of interaction is multilayered and temporally dynamic. Six-year-old Mary's failure to pick up her toys after her father sternly asks her to do so may reflect reactance aroused by the gruff tone of his request, defiance originating from a conflict occurring earlier in the day, a judgement from past experience that she can afford to ignore this request, or some combination of these. Father's tone of voice may result from an unrelated marital conflict, annoyance with the disarray produced by Mary's toys, a belief that a threatening tone will gain Mary's compliance, or anger that she has not yet learned to put her toys away without being asked.

Some of the links in the chain of events occurring within and between parent and child are beginning to be assessed (e.g. Sigel, 1985).

Parent Perceptions as Mediators of their Behavior

Parent attributions about behavior

Two fundamental assumptions of attribution theory are that people have a basic need to understand the causes of feelings, attitudes, and behaviors in themselves and others, and that their actions depend on the inferences they make about these causes (Heider, 1958; Jones and Davis, 1965; Kelley, 1971). Parenting behavior may, therefore, often be guided by inferences about the reasons for the child's behavior. Several characteristics of the child and of the parent–child relationship are likely to influence the nature of these inferences (Dix and Grusec, 1985). For one, much of the child's behavior reflects developmental limitations and hence is beyond the child's control. The way in which the child's behavior is interpreted will likely depend on the parent's estimate of the child's age-related level of knowledge and ability. Moreover, such estimates must continually be adjusted in keeping with the child's growth and development. The relative power of parent and child is another factor influencing attributions. Given the child's lesser power, external forces are more likely than internal ones to figure as causes of the child's behavior. Finally, the parent's love for and emotional investment in the child mean that parent attributions are likely to vary depending on the quality of the emotional bond and its significance in the parent's personal identity.

Information on the nature of parental attributions about child behaviors is just beginning to emerge (Dix et al., 1986; Sobol, Ashbourne and Earn, 1986). In one study (Dix et al., 1986), parents of four-, eight-, and twelve-year-olds were read brief vignettes depicting a child of the same age and sex as one of their own children and asked to make causal inferences about the child's behavior. The vignettes described either the commission of an antisocial act (fighting, stealing, lying), failures to be prosocial (not helping, not sharing, being insensitive to others), or positive acts of altruism (sharing, helping, comforting). Parents viewed all types of behavior as increasingly intentional and attributable to personality dispositions, as opposed to being caused by external or situational factors, with the age of the child. As children develop, parents are increasingly likely to infer that they have the necessary knowledge and ability to control their behavior and hence that their actions reflect stable underlying traits and dispositions.

At the same time, parents make inferences about their children's behavior with some generosity. Positive behaviors are more likely to be perceived as intentional and reflective of dispositional characteristics than are negative behaviors (Dix et al., 1986). This positivity bias also extends to parents' inferences about their own role in the child's behavior, as Sobol, Ashbourne and Earn (1986) found when they asked parents of hyperactive and nonhyperactive children for their attributions about compliant and noncompliant behaviors. Both groups of parents (but mothers even more than fathers) rated noncompliance as less due to themselves (the parents) than compliance.

Parents may be reluctant to assign personal responsibility for negative behavior to themselves or their children because they want to think well of themselves and those they love. This seems to be true for other sorts of relationships as well (Hymel, 1986; Regan, Straus and Fazio, 1974; Taylor and Koivumaki, 1976). Also, parents believe that desirable characteristics in their children will last and undesirable ones will change (Goodnow et al., 1984). A positive bias in the interpretations parents make of their children's behavior undoubtedly helps them to maintain a positive self-image. At the same time, there is a good deal of similarity between the attributions people make about others and those they make about themselves (Markus, Smith and Moreland, 1985; O'Mahony, 1984). We suspect, then, that the degree of generosity parents show in interpreting their children's behavior is likely to depend on how generous they are with themselves. It is not surprising, therefore, that maltreating mothers, many of whom begin with a low self-image (Schneider, Hoffmeister and Helfer, 1976), make more stable and internal attributions about *negative* than about positive behavior in their children (Larrance and Twentyman, 1983). We will discuss another source of attribution bias—the development of conflict in a relationship—in a later section of the chapter. For the moment, the important point to note about the phenomenon of attribution bias is that parents' feelings about the child are closely associated with the inferences they make about the causes of the child's behavior.

Parent feelings about behavior

Some types of child behavior are more upsetting to parents than others. Mothers reported, for example, that they would be more angry about antisocial acts than about failures to act prosocially (Grusec, Dix and Mills, 1982). Dix et al. (1986) found that both these types of behavior, however, were increasingly upsetting with the age of the child, and increasingly upsetting the more parents thought them to be intentional, caused by a disposition in the child, and known to be wrong. Although one cannot be certain from these data about the exact role played by emotional reactions to the child's behavior, since affect was age-related and dispositional attributions are known to intensify emotions (Abramson, Seligman and Teasdale, 1978; Weiner, 1979), parents' negative emotional reactions to misdeeds may have been mediated by causal inferences.

How do feelings and inferences about the child influence the parent's behavior? We are, after all, interested in how perceptions and interpretations of the behavior of one member of the dyad, the child, affect how the other member, the parent, behaves towards that child. In addition to measuring parents' attributions about and emotional reactions to child behavior, Dix *et al.* (1986, Study 2) asked parents how they would respond to misconduct. The more upset parents were by their child's misdeeds, the more important they thought it was to respond to the behavior. No relationships were found, however, between the inferences parents made about misdeeds, or the degree to which they were upset by them, and the ways in which they said they would intervene.

The tendency for family members to respond in kind when aversive behavior occurs (G. R. Patterson, 1982) suggests that inferences of intentionality may affect the intensity rather than the mode of the parent's response to misconduct, at least at the moment they first occur. Alternative techniques may be attempted only after inferences have accrued over a period of time, and perhaps only when the child's pattern of behavior is believed to be modifiable. It is not yet clear how changeable parents believe intentional and dispositional behavior to be, how much influence they believe they can have over such behavior, or how their reactions at the moment may differ from the strategies they adopt over the longer term.

Parental values

How and whether parents respond to the child's behavior also depends on the values they hold. Some skills and behaviors are considered more important than others. Moreover, these values appear to vary depending on the sex of the child, and to be different for mothers and fathers. Grusec (1986) asked parents of five-, eight-, and eleven-year-olds to listen to stories about children who engaged in a desirable behavior, to pretend that the child in the story was theirs, to rate the importance of each of the behaviors, and to role-play how they would respond in the situation and how they would feel. The stories involved different kinds of desirable behavior, including maturity, honesty, self-control, helping, and self-sacrifice. Maturity and honesty were considered to be more important than self-control, helping, and self-sacrifice. Self-sacrifice (putting the other person's needs above one's own), while it was rated the least important of the behaviors, was felt to be more important in girls than in boys. Self-control, on the other hand, was thought to be more important in boys than in girls. It is possible that parents value self-sacrifice more in girls than in boys because they consider it more important to promote this behavior in their daughters than in their sons. One source of the high value placed on self-sacrifice may be a gender stereotype in the domain of altruism favoring females over males (Senneker and Hendrick, 1983; Shigetomi, Hartmann and Gelfand, 1981; Zarbatany *et al.*, 1985). Self-control, on the other hand, may be highly valued in boys because it is believed to be more difficult to promote in boys than in girls. Thus the importance placed on desirable behaviors may be a function both of ideals and of expectations.

Consistent with their values, parents indicated that they would respond differentially to acts of self-sacrifice in girls and boys, i.e. they would be more likely to praise girls for self-sacrifice than they would boys. Acts of self-control, on the other hand, were reportedly dealt with similarly in the two sexes.

Child Perceptions as Mediators of Responses to Parent Behavior

Just as the parent is believed to be guided by thoughts and emotions associated with the behavior of the child, so is the child assumed to be guided by thoughts and feelings about the parent's behavior. Parental influence techniques, therefore, are thought to have differential effects depending on how the child perceives these modes of influence.

Evaluation of parent

From an early age children recognize and respect parental authority, i.e. they consider that the parent has a legitimate right to direct their behavior and that it is their obligation to comply (Damon, 1977). Indeed, children appear to prefer parents who exercise some authority to those who do not. Thus mothers who intervene after a child's misbehavior are rated 'good' and are preferred relative to those who allow the behavior to continue (Siegal and Rablin, 1982, Studies 2 and 3).

Children's judgements of parental intervention as 'right' and 'good' clearly reflect their acceptance of parental authority. Several motives may underlie this acceptance, including desire for parental approval and acceptance for behaving appropriately, defense against fear and resentment of the parent's power, desire to possess the parent's powers and abilities, and need for external control.

While children want and accept the legitimacy of parental authority, they regard some uses of authority as more legitimate than others. For example, children consider that the exercise of power is more legitimate in a situation involving a moral transgression (stealing) than in one involving transgression against a convention (not doing a family chore) or transgression against a rule pertaining to a personal matter (playing with a forbidden friend) (Tisak, 1986).

Children also consider some modes of influence to be more acceptable than others. In a study comparing children's evaluations of three parental influence techniques, Siegal and Cowen (1984) found that, for most transgressions (specifically disobedience, causing physical or psychological harm to another, and damaging a material object), mothers using induction or physical punishment were rated as more correct for their response than mothers using love withdrawal or reacting permissively. Induction was considered to be the most correct response to acts causing physical harm to the self.

Children's evaluations of and willingness to accept parental control have obvious implications for their responsiveness to these attempts at control. Children believe that parents are entitled to use punitive or coercive modes of influence to a greater or lesser degree and depending on the circumstances. Nevertheless, when coercion is salient, as we will see in the next sections internalization frequently fails to occur. There is some evidence that such failure is mediated by effects on self-perception.

Perception of self

To promote the internalization of socially appropriate modes of behavior parents first must apply sufficient pressure or firmness to obtain their children's compliance. Just what constitutes optimal firmness is a matter of some controversy (Baumrind, 1983; Lepper, 1981, 1983; Lewis, 1981; Perry and Perry, 1983). From the perspective of attribution theory (e.g. Lepper, 1981, 1983), socialization pressures promote internalization when they are strong enough to obtain compliance but not so strong that they prevent children from attributing their actions to intrinsic motives such as their own wishes, standards, or values. Superfluous amounts of pressure lead children to discount such motives in favor of extrinsic ones such as fear of disapproval or hope of reward.

The impact on children's behavior of socializing techniques that manipulate the salience of their motives is demonstrated in a study by Grusec *et al.* (1978). Seven- and eight-year-olds were induced to donate some of their winnings from a game by having them observe a model donate, by being instructed to donate, or by a combination of the two. Subjects' causal attributions for sharing were then manipulated by attributing their behavior to an external cause (because they thought they were expected to) or an internal disposition (because they are the kind of person who likes to help others). When sharing was induced by observation of a model—a relatively subtle influence—children who received an internal attribution subsequently shared more in tests of internalization than did those who received an external attribution. However, when sharing was induced by more coercive procedures—instruction or modeling combined with instruction—attributions had no effect on internalization. With more coercive influence techniques, then, it was more difficult to promote internal attributions.

Children do appear to attribute their actions to different motives, depending on the mode of influence to which they are exposed. Thus Smith *et al.* (1979) found that children given social reinforcement for helping were more likely to say they had shared because of intrinsic motives (e.g. 'It's nice to share') while those who received material reinforcement attributed it to that external reward. With age, however, all modes of influence are increasingly likely to elicit external causal attributions (Cohen, Gelfand and Hartmann, 1981; Peterson and Gelfand, 1984).

Parental influence attempts appear to have an impact not only on the motives but also on the more enduring dispositions to which children attribute their behavior. In a study whose findings were interpreted in terms of change in self-concept, Grusec and Redler (1980) compared the effects of two forms of praise for altruism—dispositional praise (the application of a trait label) and social reinforcement (praise which was specific to the child's behavior)—on subsequent altruism in seven- and eight-year-olds. Both forms of praise led to an increase in immediate altruism, but only dispositional praise enhanced generalized altruism during and beyond the testing session. Grusec and Redler suggested that dispositional praise produced a stable self-attribution to intrinsic motives, i.e. a change in the child's self-concept, and that this in turn produced an increase in actual intrinsic motivation which was reflected in general, long-lasting effects on subsequent behavior. Nondispositional praise, on the other hand, may have had more specific behavioral effects than those of dispositional praise because its effects on self-perception were more specific.

There have been several attempts to test a self-perception interpretation of the behavioral effects of parental influence attempts (Dix and Grusec, 1983; Lepper, 1973; Mills, 1986; Smith et al., 1979). In one study (Dix and Grusec, 1983), subjects were read stories about characters who helped either spontaneously or under the influence of either maternal power assertion or modeling occurring with or without reasoning. Subjects were then asked to make causal attributions for the story actor's behavior and to rate the actor on the trait of helpfulness. Children were more likely to attribute the actor's behavior to an external cause when helping occurred under power assertion than when it occurred spontaneously or after modeling. Consistent with the earlier findings of Grusec et al. (1978), modeling was not associated with external attribution. Not only was behavior occurring under coercion more likely to be attributed to external conditions, it was also less likely to be attributed to an altruistic trait by all but the youngest children (who were five and six years of age). It would appear that children are sensitive to coercion from a young age, and by eight or nine years of age they begin to perceive it as reflecting on the dispositions of those to whom it is directed. Moreover, they appear to make similar attributions when they themselves are the object of parental influence attempts (Lepper, 1973; Mills, 1986).

One may conclude from these findings that the way in which the parent exerts pressure on the child alters the child's self-concept. While the studies described here demonstrate that coercion is incompatible with making certain internal attributions about the self, it may also promote certain other internal attributions. For example, children who attribute their compliance to external pressure may not only fail to perceive themselves as possessing certain positive traits (e.g. generosity), they may also see themselves as having certain negative traits (e.g. stinginess). In this way modes of parental influence may have far-reaching effects on both self-concept and self-esteem, as correlational studies linking parental control with the child's self-esteem suggest (Coppersmith, 1967; Loeb, Horst and Horton, 1980). As the symbolic interactionists Mead (1934) and Cooley (1902) originally postulated in their theory of the 'looking-glass self', children may see themselves reflected in the way others behave towards them.

In essence, the ways in which parent and child react to each other's behavior depend on how these behaviors are perceived and interpreted by each participant in the relationship. The interpretations and reactions of one participant modify the subsequent interpretations and reactions of the other participant, and so on. Some developmentalists have gone on to study the actual chains of influence between parent and child (e.g. Lytton, 1980; Maccoby and Jacklin, 1983; G. R. Patterson, 1982). The work of Patterson and his colleagues (G. R. Patterson, 1980, 1982, 1984a, 1986), described in the next section, demonstrates the behavioral complexities and temporal dynamics of this chain of interaction. It also illustrates the effects which the excessive use of parental power can have on the outcome of socialization and the quality of the emotional relationship between parent and child.

Coercive Process: The Escalation of Conflict and Loss of Power

While almost any act of interpersonal influence sets up resistance in the person acted upon (French and Raven, 1959), we have seen that some modes of influence produce more resistance to internalization than others. Coercive methods in particular appear to hinder socialization. This is most clearly demonstrated in G. R. Patterson's (1980, 1982, 1984a, 1986) sequential analyses of parent–child interaction in the families of oppositional children. In these families, aggressive or coercive behavior—for example threats, scolding, hitting in the parent and yelling, hitting, and defiance in the child—occurs at high rates (G. R. Patterson, 1982). Both mothers and fathers of aggressive boys are significantly more likely than parents of normal boys to start a conflict with their child (G. R. Patterson, 1982). Aggressive boys often respond in kind to these attacks; indeed, they are significantly more likely than normal boys to counterattack and to continue the conflict (G. R. Patterson, 1982).

What promotes the escalation of conflict in these families? According to Patterson's (1980) coercion theory, small increases in the intensity of one person's attack are matched by the other person. These increases in intensity occur in order to get the other person to comply. When the effort succeeds, the coercive member of the dyad is reinforced by the partner's compliance and the compliant member is reinforced by the cessation of aversive behavior.

Another possible contributor to the escalation of conflict in aggressive families is negatively biased parental attributions about the causes of the child's behavior, i.e. the attribution of behavior to undesirable traits or dispositions. Such attributions have been found to accompany the escalation of interpersonal conflicts in close relationships between men and women (Kelley, 1979). It has been reported (G. R. Patterson, 1986) that in aggressive families parental irritability (e.g. scolding, threatening) towards the problem child is associated with overinclusiveness in classifying behaviors as antisocial. When parents of normal and oppositional children were asked to read vignettes describing parent–child interaction and to classify child behaviors as prosocial or antisocial, the parents of oppositional children were much more likely than those of normal children to include neutral events in the antisocial category. If such overinclusiveness can be equated with the attribution of hostile intentions to the child, then there would appear to be some relationship in these families between the escalation of conflict and the parent's development of a negative attitude towards the child. This could mean either that a negative bias makes the parent overreact (irritably) to the child's behavior, or that the hostility accompanying conflict escalation fosters the development of a negative bias. Quite likely the causal relationship is bidirectional.

It is also probable that the parent's negative attitude contributes to further escalation of the conflict. The child's resistance to parental demands increases, the parent responds with even stronger methods, and the child's resistance and hostility deepen further until eventually the parent loses power altogether. G. R. Patterson (1986) has presented evidence suggesting that this loss of disciplinary control may contribute to eventual parental rejection of these oppositional children. In a sample of mother–son dyads, maternal rejection (measured using child reports of parental labeling, child and parent ratings of how well the two get along, and interviewer ratings of the mother's enjoyment of her role and acceptance of the child) was found to covary significantly with the difficulty and frequency of disciplinary confrontations, the child's irritability to siblings (i.e. the likelihood of starting a conflict, counterattacking when the other initiates, and persisting in irritable behavior), and the mother's reports of daily child problem behaviors. Again, the causal relation is no doubt bidirectional. What does seem clear is that the emotional and power dynamics of the parent–child relationship are closely associated with one another.

CONCLUSION

In the study of socialization in the context of the parent–child relationship, the influence process has been reconceptualized. The assumption that influence occurs in one direction from parent to child has largely given way to the view that it is a product of the interaction between parent and child. At the same time, the behavioral chain of actions and reactions between parent and child is increasingly recognized to be the observable tip of the relationship while the underlying thoughts and feelings of each participant are its substance.

In the shift to this new conceptualization, developmental researchers have emphasized somewhat different mediating events in parent and child. In what may reflect the continuing attraction of the unidirectional view, attention has been paid predominantly to parents' interpretations of the child's behavior as a mediator of parental behavior. Less attention has been given to the question of how the child's behavior may influence the parent's self-perceptions. Conversely, research provides us with some insight into how parental behavior influences the child's self-perceptions, but the child's attributions and feelings about the parent have received somewhat less attention. Since in a relationship as close as that between parent and child one might expect self- and other-perceptions to be highly interdependent, more information about these neglected aspects of the relationship between parent and child would seem essential to a deeper understanding of its nature and contribution to the socialization of the child.

Handbook of Personal Relationships
Edited by S. W. Duck
© 1988 John Wiley & Sons Ltd

11

Relations among Relationships

JUDITH DUNN
Pennsylvania State University, Pennsylvania, USA

ABSTRACT

Evidence on the connections—both concurrent and overtime—between children's relationships with their parents and other relationships is discussed, with a focus on the question of what kinds of *processes* may be involved in the links. Three topics are considered: First, connections between parents' relationships with their children and their other relationships, with emphasis on the evidence from intergenerational studies; second, links between parent–child and peer relationships in early childhood; third, links between parent–child and sibling relationships. It is argued that a number of different processes are implicated in these connections, and our methods and theoretical approaches should be sensitive to this range and its developmental significance.

There are many firmly held beliefs about the effects of particular relationships upon other relationships within the social world in which children grow up. The idea that a child's early relationships affect the relationships that he or she forms later in life is, for instance, an important theme in the grand theories of psychological development (Freud, 1933; Erikson, 1950), and it has wide currency today. It is often suggested that how a mother was herself 'mothered' will affect her own parental behavior, indeed all her intimate relationships as an adult. The child's early relationship with the mother serves, according to this view, as a template in the construction of later relationships. The possibility that there are systematic links between concurrent relationships that affect children's development is also increasingly widely considered. The ideas of family systems theorists are for example now frequently discussed by psychologists (see Kaye and Furstenberg, 1985; Hinde and Stevenson-Hinde, 1987), and within a very different framework the importance of the interconnections between different family relationships within the family is highlighted by developmental behavioral geneticists (Plomin and Daniels, 1987). In the past fifteen

years we have gained much empirical evidence on the links between relationships, both concurrent associations and connections over time, and in this
chapter I will discuss the nature of this evidence and its implications for our
beliefs about the influence of relationships upon relationships.

A consideration of this evidence brings us to a number of central developmental issues. Perhaps the most intractable is the question of what kinds of
mechanism might mediate the connections between relationships. Is it, for
instance, that the personality, self-concept or self-esteem of an individual is
affected by a particular relationship, and this effect on the individual constrains
or influences the nature of the relationships he or she forms in the future? Or
is it that the individual incorporates a 'model' for relationships which then
influences his or her later relationships with others? It should be said at the
outset that we cannot yet answer this question with any clarity, though we have
gained some insights into how to address it.

This issue brings us immediately to a second—one that centrally affects the
kind of answer we find to the first. This is that the level of abstraction and the
nature of the framework that is chosen to describe relationships will profoundly
affect the inferences we make about the processes involved in the connections
between those relationships. This issue of what dimensions are appropriate for
the description of relationships is one that is examined throughout this book.
Here we simply emphasize that the theoretical background of a particular
psychologist will inevitably influence the assumptions made about the significance of the different features of a relationship, and thus the dimensions chosen
to describe it, and inevitably the account given of the developmental processes
linking this relationship to others.

It is important to acknowledge at the outset two other central conceptual
points that must be borne in mind in considering relations among relationships,
even though we are very far from understanding how to assess their implications.
First, the processes linking relationships may well change as children grow up.
We should then consider the developmental significance of any connections that
we find. At what stage of the lifecourse is the link important, and how significant
is it likely to be over time? Second, the connections between relationships exist
not simply in pairs but beyond the dyad. For simplicity of presentation I will
consider pairs of relationships in this chapter. Yet although this division is
useful, it is essentially artificial. Pairs of relationships are not isolated but exist
within a network of other relationships. There may well be indirect links
between any pair of relationships, mediated by other relationships within the
network.

Finally, I will note the limits within which the topic of relations among
relationships—a huge one—will be considered. I shall discuss, primarily,
relationships in early childhood; much of the empirical work on the *developmental* significance of the effects of relationships upon relationships has focused
on early childhood. The question of how far general principles elucidated by
considering early childhood can be usefully applied to adult relationships is an
important one, but will not be pursued here (see, however, Reis and Shaver,
this volume). Three general topics will be considered. First, *links between*

parents' relationships with their children and their other relationships will be discussed; the focus will be upon links between parent–child relationships and the parents' marital and supportive relationships, and their relationships in childhood with their own parents. Discussion of the processes involved in the connections between parents' own experience of being mothered and their later parenting behavior is frequently couched within an attachment framework, and draws heavily upon evidence for links between parent–child attachment and later peer relationships. Our second topic therefore is *links between parent–child and peer relationships*. Thirdly, we consider evidence for *links between parent–child and sibling relationships*. This material highlights a number of different kinds of processes involved in connections between close relationships and brings us to the final section, in which these processes are discussed.

LINKS BETWEEN PARENTS' RELATIONSHIPS WITH THEIR CHILDREN AND THEIR OTHER RELATIONSHIPS

Three themes have been explored in recent research into the influence of the parents' own relationships upon parent–child relationships: the links between the marital and parent–child relationships, the role of other intimate supportive relationships in a mother's relationship with her child, and the possibility of intergenerational effects on maternal behavior. There is a growing literature on each of these; rather than reviewing these studies in detail I shall focus upon the *nature* of the evidence available, and raise the issue of what kinds of processes may be involved in the links between these relationships.

Connections between Marital and Parent–Child Relationships

Within a family systems perspective, it is taken as a given that marital and parent–child relationships are interdependent (Minuchin, 1985). Yet the nature, direction or mechanisms of these connections between marital and parent–child relationships are by no means clear *a priori*. It could be that under the stress of a conflict-ridden or unsatisfactory marriage parents will be less emotionally available for their children, while a warm and supportive marital relationship helps both parents to cope with their children with affection, enjoyment, and relaxation. Indeed, it is usually assumed that a 'good' marriage will be associated with 'good' relations between parent and child. However, it might also be the case that a stressed or unsatisfactory marriage could lead to a parent seeking to satisfy a need for love and affection within his or her relationship with a child—the 'compensatory' hypothesis—while partners within a happy marriage might be so absorbed with each other that they are less emotionally available for their children. Alternatively, the delight of parents in their children could be a shared source of joy that in itself contributes to their positive relationship, while an extremely difficult child could conceivably contribute to stress and conflict between parents. A plausible case can be made for each of these patterns of association. Which is supported by the empirical evidence, and what kinds of processes linking the relationships are suggested by the data?

The bulk of research findings have been interpreted as support for the view that good marital relations are associated with a secure and easy parent–child relationship, while poor marital relations are associated with difficulties in the parent–child relationship. Studies of the transition to parenthood, for instance, have demonstrated that mothers' competence and expressed affection to their babies are linked to the quality of their marriages (Easterbrooks and Emde, 1987). A warm and supportive marital relationship has been found to be associated with a high probability of security of attachment between child and mother, while in families with low marital adjustment more insecure child–mother attachments are reported (Belsky, 1984; Goldberg and Easterbrooks, 1984); conflict between mother and child (in the sense of a lack of compliance by the child in a laboratory situation) is reported to be negatively correlated with the quality of the marital relationship (Meyer, 1987); marital harmony is found to be associated with affection between child and parent and child compliance, while fathers who feel that they have happy marriages report themselves to be warmer and less aggravated by their children than do other men (Easterbrooks and Emde, 1987). In one of the few studies of school-age children in this domain, fathers with marital problems are found to be intrusive and unsupportive in teaching tasks with their children as compared with fathers who have happier marriages (Brody, Pillegrini and Sigel, 1986). Studies of divorce, moreover, have shown that with the lack of the support of a spouse, mothers' relationships with their children deteriorate (Hetherington, Cox and Cox, 1982).

Perhaps the most striking evidence of all for the positive association between a supportive spousal relationship and good parent–child relationships is found in the study by Rutter and his colleagues of a group of mothers who were themselves studied as children being reared in institutions (Quinton and Rutter, 1987). The quality of parenting shown by these women was dramatically linked to whether or not they had a supportive spouse. Of those who lacked marital support, none showed good relationships with their children, but of those who had such support, about half were relating well to their children. The same pattern of association with marital support (though much less marked effects) was found in the control group of women from the general population. Roughly two-thirds of those without support were having problems with parenting, as compared with half of those who had marital support.

However, the links between marital and parent–child relationships within families who are not under social, emotional or psychological stress are not as straightforward, consistent or clear as might at first be concluded from these findings. For instance, in the Goldberg and Easterbrooks study, security of attachment was not related to marital adjustment for the 'middle range' of marriages and attachment to mother was not related to the index of marital harmony, although attachment to father was. In the Easterbrooks and Emde study, the measure of marital adjustment was not related to any of the measures of positive interaction between parent and child. In the study by Meyer and his colleagues, if criterion variables for the mother–child relationship other than child compliance were included, such as affective sharing or referencing, the results of the path models linking marital and parent–child relations were very different.

There is also some evidence in support of the 'compensatory' hypothesis. Happily married men have been reported, for instance, to interact less with their infants (Goth-Owens *et al.*, 1978); mothers in conflict-laden or distressed marital relationships are reported to describe their relationships with their babies in terms of 'role reversal'—as a compensatory source of comfort, love, and affection—or to feel anxiously overprotective of their babies (Engfer, 1987); and in Brody's study of teaching interactions between parents and school-aged children, mothers in 'slightly distressed' marriages used more positive feedback, asked more questions and intruded less on their children, who were themselves more responsive than the children in nondistressed marriages. (In contrast, the fathers in families with many marital problems used *less* positive feedback and intruded more (Brody, Pillegrini and Sigel, 1986).)

The complexity of the patterns of findings from these different studies suggest a number of general lessons to be learnt by the researcher hoping to understand the links between marital and parent–child relationships. First, the nature of the connections may be different for mothers and for fathers (see the results of Easterbrooks and Emde, 1987; Brody, Pillegrini and Sigel, 1986); second, the links may depend upon *how* distressed or poor the marital relation is (Goldberg and Easterbrooks, 1984); third, the links may depend on the particular indices of the marital relationship or parent–child relationship selected (all the studies report inconsistencies in this respect). Finally, the limitations of the samples studied so far—in terms of size, SES, ethnic and cultural groups, and the age of the children, as well as in terms of the limited range of measures used—should be noted. Until we know more about how far these connections are indeed different for fathers and for mothers, for those in extremely poor or conflictual marriages as compared with the 'normal' range, and how far they are evident only with respect to particular dimensions of the marital or parent–child relationship, drawing inferences about the *processes* involved in such connections remains fairly hazardous. In the discussion of processes that follows these caveats should be remembered.

Processes Linking Marital and Parent–Child Relationships

One possible explanation for an association between supportive marital relations and a harmonious parent–child relationship is that both are the consequence of some personal attribute of the parent. A second is that a good spousal relationship enhances a mother's well-being, her sense of self-esteem and of being valued, thus enabling her to feel confident in her relations with her child. One version of this hypothesis suggests that there is a direct 'carryover' from one emotional relationship to another: that the qualities of affection and communication between husband and wife directly affect the way in which a mother relates emotionally to her child. An alternative view is that a good spousal relationship affects the parent–child relationship in a much less specific manner—not through its *relationship* qualities but as one aspect of the mother's environment. Other possible mechanisms linking marital and parent–child relationships are that marital support affects a parent's behavior with his or her child through instrumental help with the tasks of parenthood, or through the provision of a model for parenting.

The study by Rutter and his colleagues provides us with some evidence with which to assess the plausibility of these different possible explanations for the sample of institution-reared women and the control families. The results indicate that the first possible mechanism was unlikely to account alone for the effects of a supportive marital relationship. It was not, for instance, the case that the girls who had supportive spouses were themselves better functioning as children or as adolescents; second, log-linear modeling showed that although choice of spouse was linked to some aspects of the girls' personalities and functioning (summarized as a propensity to 'plan' by Rutter and his colleagues), the effects of marital support were stronger and held after controlling for these 'planning' effects. Thirdly, the functioning of the spouses before meeting the women was linked to the quality of the women's parenting, indicating that it was unlikely that the effects of marital support were attributable solely to the effects of the wife on her husband. It remains of course highly likely that the two adults did influence each other, and that patterns of influence were two-way.

On commonsense grounds it seems likely that the second possibility—that marital support contributes positively to parenting by effects on self-esteem and emotional availability—is important. It also appears important to consider very seriously the second version of this hypothesis. There is a great deal of evidence that the 'protective' effects of marital support are associated with a wide range of adult functioning and are not solely or necessarily mediated through the consequences of one relationship for another. And the 'negative' side of this coin is that poor parenting is more likely when women are living under poor circumstances; stresses that affect parenting come from a wide range of sources, not solely via the marital relationship.

This evidence for the impact on parent–child relationships of a wide range of broad environmental stresses, such as poor housing, suggests that instrumental help with the task demands of parenting may well be part of the explanation of links between supportive spousal and good parent–child relationships. The task demands of bringing up small children under difficult circumstances are very real and far from trivial. However, in discussions of what constitute effective features of 'support', the conclusion is that while there may be instrumental, social status and motivational as well as emotional aspects of support, and that each of these can be important, it is emotional support that is most influential in terms of mental health. How far this is so for the demands and stresses of parenting remains to be explored.

One further point needs consideration. It may be important to examine separately on the one hand the links between marital and parent–child relationships in terms of the *support* that a good marital relationship provides to *protect* a mother from the difficulties of life, including the stress of looking after a child, and on the other hand the *stress* that a poor marriage adds to the burdens of a mother. Rutter has argued from the findings on those mothers from the institution-reared sample who were without a spouse that the effects of support *versus* not support on parenting should be considered separately from the effects of stressful marital relationships, and points out that the same conclusion derives from the evidence on the protective effect on parent–child relationships of nonspousal adult friendships.

Support from Other Relationships

It now appears well established that supportive, confiding, personal relationships can mitigate the effects of stressful life events on adults, and that the lack of such supportive relationships can increase the adverse consequences of such stress. Brown and Harris' research (Brown and Harris, 1978) has shown that intimate friendships with other adults serve to protect mothers who are coping with the everyday stresses of life with young children against depression; thus in an indirect way such intimate adult relationships have an important influence on the parent–child relationship. [See also chapters in Section 0 of this volume, and the findings of studies of the relations between social support and the course of the puerperium (Paykel *et al.*, 1980), complications of pregnancy (Nuckolls, Cassel and Kaplan, 1972), illness, and the life course.] The effects of supportive relationships on the parent–child relationship are not only evident in extremely disadvantaged populations: Crockenberg (1981) studying a sample of young mothers half of whom were middle-class showed that the social support a mother experienced (including here support from husband) was the *best predictor* of the security of a child's attachment to the mother, especially for mothers who had difficult babies. It could be that such connections reflect differences between women in their propensity to establish good relationships with others—including their own babies. The point to be stressed is that such supportive adult friendships are likely to be of particular importance for the relationships of children and parents who are living under social stress or disadvantage. For example, Vaughn and his colleagues (Vaughn *et al.*, 1979), working with a low-income group, documented changes in the nature of children's attachment to their mothers that accompanied increases in stress on their mothers. High life stresses for the mothers during the children's second year were associated with changes in the quality of their children's attachment to them, from secure to insecure.

The processes by which adult supportive relationships affect the parent–child relationship are, as already noted in the context of supportive marital relationships, not clear. It is plausible to infer that mothers with such supportive friendships are as a consequence more emotionally available for their children. The findings are also compatible with the general theory that altruistic behavior, awareness of others' needs, and responsiveness to those needs are higher when a person's own needs are met (Berkowitz, 1972; Hoffman, 1976). It is also possible, however, that the quality of a mother's personality contributes both to the likelihood that she will have supportive adult friendships and to the nature of her responsiveness or sensitivity to her child. Crockenberg's analyses suggest, however, that in her sample it was unlikely that a woman's 'unresponsiveness' *per se* elicited the low levels of support experienced by some mothers. Yet there is power in the argument that it is not the availability of potentially supportive relationships that accounts for differences in protection experienced by individuals, but rather the use that these individuals make of those relationships (Cohen and Syme, 1985). The issue of the origins of differences in those aspects of adults' personalities that are linked to their abilities to form intimate confiding relationships is then crucial, and it is in relation to this issue that intergenerational studies are of particular interest.

Intergenerational Continuities

The idea that an individual's own experiences of childhood relationships with a parent will influence his or her subsequent parental relationships is widely held. For one extreme on the continuum of parent–child relationships—the case of child abuse—there do indeed appear to be strong links between the experience of being abused at the hands of a parent and disturbed or inadequate parenting (for reviews see Belsky, 1978; Friedrich and Wheeler, 1982; Kaufman and Zigler, 1986). How far are such intergenerational continuities evident within the more normal range of parent–child relationships, and what processes might be involved?

These questions have been investigated with two research methodologies: first, prospective longitudinal studies that follow groups of individuals from childhood to adulthood and include studies of their experiences as children and their parenting behavior as adults, and second, retrospective examination of the accounts of their own childhood experiences given by individuals who are studied as parents with their children. The prospective methodology is clearly the most powerful; two recent studies illustrate the strengths of such an approach, and both report clear intergenerational continuities.

The first is a study by Elder and his colleagues (Elder, 1979; Caspi and Elder, 1987) of the individuals taking part in the Berkeley Growth Study. Using initially retrospective reports from the parents of the first children studied, the investigators found that growing up in families in which the parental care was seen as unaffectionate, controlling and hostile was associated with the development of personal instabilities that were reflected in tension in the marital relationship and extreme and arbitrary discipline shown towards their own children. The children of these individuals (the third generation) themselves were likely to develop problems as adults, the women being described by their own children (the fourth generation) as ill-tempered and by their husbands as explosive in child-rearing.

The second study revealing intergenerational continuities is the study of women reared in institutions already referred to in relation to the issue of the connections between marital support and parenting (Quinton and Rutter, 1987). Of these 89 women who had spent much of their early and middle childhood in residential institutions, a third had experienced serious breakdown in parenting when they were traced as adults as compared with none of the control mothers (from the same neighborhood but reared at home). What is more, currently poor parenting at the time of follow-up was much more frequent in the institution group when compared with the control group (40 per cent as compared with 11 per cent). Although it was notable that nearly a third of the institution-reared women had *good* relationships with their children, the evidence for continuities between an institutional upbringing in which specific attachments were discouraged and later problems in the parent–child relationship was striking. The women brought up in institutions had experienced a broad range of problems and adversities, many of which could have contributed to their later difficulties as parents; Rutter and his colleagues showed that one of the most important predictors was whether the girls had experienced disruptive parenting during their first four years. The proportion of women who were themselves inadequate parents was higher in the subgroup who had suffered this disruption in early parenting than in the remainder of the sample. As Rutter comments: 'The implication is that early disruption of parenting may be particularly damaging to the development of those aspects of personality concerned with social relationships; such damage may include ill effects on parenting but parenting difficulties may arise in other ways as well' (Rutter, 1987).

The retrospective research on intergenerational continuities in parent–child relationships has chiefly been conducted within an 'attachment' paradigm. Mothers of children categorized as securely or insecurely attached are asked to recall their own childhood experiences. Such studies reveal that mothers of securely attached one-year-olds describe significantly more acceptance and less rejection from their own mothers than do the mothers of insecurely attached infants (Ricks, 1985), identify positively with their mothers and perceive them as nurturant and emotionally available (Morris, 1980, 1981), recall readily and with coherence their own attachment history and its influence (Main, Kaplan and Cassidy, 1985), and have rich memories of their own attachment relationships with their parents in childhood (Grossmann, Fremmer-Bombik and Rudolph, 1987).

Continuities in the qualities of mother–child relationships across generations are suggested too by a number of other studies. Cox and her colleagues' (Cox et al., 1985) observational and interview study reported that mothers who recalled in pregnancy that their own parents were supportive of their individuality rather than intrusive or controlling were themselves sensitive, responsive and delighted by their own three-month-olds; Heinicke and colleagues (Heinicke et al., 1983) found mothers who reported little conflict in their relations with their own parents when they were growing up were more responsive to their own one-month-old babies than mothers who described more conflict in their childhood relationships. Minde (1980) reported for a sample of premature babies that the mothers who interacted in the least sensitive and responsive way with their infants described poorer relationships with their own mothers in childhood than the mothers who were more sensitive.

Processes of Transmission between Generations

The problems with making inferences about the processes of transition involved
in these cross-generational effects from retrospective data are obvious: it could
be that the mothers who are *currently* happy in their emotional relationships
with child or with spouse look back on their earlier experiences in a positive
manner. Their perceptions of their childhood relationships may be highly
colored by their present circumstances and moods. Such rosy perceptions are
in themselves important and interesting, of course; however, we cannot
conclude from these data alone that at the earlier point their relationships with
their parents were distinctively different from those of the women who give a
less positive account of their earlier relationships. For that inference we need
longitudinal data, such as those from the studies of Elder and Rutter. Yet with
each of these studies there are also problems in drawing clear conclusions
about the processes linking early relationship experiences to later parent–child
relationships.

In the study of institution women, for example, the possibility that the associations arise from genetic influences rather than from the effects of early experience has to be examined. The placement of the girls in institutions in many cases
happened because their own parents were suffering from psychiatric disorder or
were persistent criminals. Rutter (1987) reports that when account was taken
of this parental deviance (as a proxy for genetic risk), there was still a major
effect of disrupted parenting upon later parent–child relationships. There were
some genetic effects in terms of the personality disorders of the women, but
the parenting effects could not be explained in terms of genetic effects.

A second point—one of major developmental significance—is that for many
within this group of women, the adverse experiences of infancy continued
through childhood, adolescence and adulthood. Thus the disturbed relationships
between the women as adults and their own children could be attributable to
a continuing set of troubling experiences, including current difficulties, rather
than to the experiences of relationships in *infancy* alone. The results indicate
that indeed almost none of the girls who had suffered disrupted parenting in
infancy left the institution to return to a *nondiscordant* family. This raises the
question of whether the connections with adult problems in parenting arose from
the lack of attachment relationships in infancy *per se* or from the experiences of
a discordant family. A tentative answer to this question is provided in the
findings on the relationships of those women who had been admitted to the
institution before they were two and had remained in the institution. That is,
they had had very little opportunity to form attachment relationships as very
young children yet had suffered the shortest period of family discord in the
sample as a whole. It is striking that this small group included the highest
proportion of poor parent–child relationships as adults of any of the subgroups
of the total sample.

Such findings indicate that the lack of attachment relationships in infancy was
a major factor in the development of difficulties in parenting as an adult. It
should be noted that in other studies of the long-term consequences of insti-

tutional upbringing, successful late adoptions show that deprivation of early attachment experiences does not necessarily preclude the development of affectionate relationships with a parent figure (Tizard and Hodges, 1978). But the findings face us with the issue of how we should interpret this link between relationships spanning a generation.

The accounts offered by psychologists range from notions of effects on personality conceived in very general terms to propositions that invoke complex cognitive mechanisms, that maintain that the continuity is one of internalized models of relationships. These accounts draw on evidence from the connections between early child–parent attachment relationships and the relationships between children and their peers, and before discussing the various mechanisms invoked to explain connections between relationships we will therefore consider the evidence for links between child–parent, child–peer and child–sibling relationships.

LINKS BETWEEN PARENT–CHILD AND CHILD–PEER RELATIONSHIPS

It has been generally assumed that the emotional security and social skills that children develop in their relationships with parents provide the foundation on which subsequent relationships with peers are based (Sroufe, 1983). Empirical studies of the connections can be grouped into three broad categories: those examining the peer relationships of children who have suffered disrupted parenting or institution experiences, those relating parental behavior and attitudes in 'normal' populations to children's relationships with their peers, and studies within the attachment paradigm. In each of these research traditions, connections between parent–child and peer relations have been demonstrated.

A particularly striking example of the links between the early experiences of institution-reared children and later peer relations is reported by Tizard and Hodges (1978; Hodges and Tizard, 1987a, b). Children who spent their early years in institutions but were then adopted were compared with children who remained in institutions, and with children who were restored to their parents after early institutional experience—usually families who were socially disadvantaged and discordant—and with a control group of family-reared children. The follow-up of these children at eight and at sixteen showed the institution-reared children, adopted, restored and those who remained in institutions, to have difficulties of various sorts in their relations with other children—findings that echoed those of other studies of institution-reared children (see e.g. Roy, 1983). The particularly notable feature of these results is that the adopted children had mostly formed *successful*, deep attachment relationships with their adoptive parents. As eight-year-olds they were described by their adoptive mothers as strikingly affectionate and cuddly. Yet they, in common with the other groups who had spent their early years in the institutions that specifically discouraged attachments, were by sixteen more likely to have trouble in peer relationships, were less likely to have a special friend, were less likely to confide in a friend, and were more likely to be indiscriminately friendly. The puzzle presented by these results is why their peer relationships should be relatively unrelated to their *current* good attachments to their parents yet associated with the much earlier lack of an attachment relationship.

On the basis of attachment theory, it has generally been expected that the quality of early attachment relationships would be linked to later relationships outside the family. Most studies addressing the issue report findings supporting this general proposition. For instance, individuals who were as toddlers securely attached have been reported to be rated by adults, when older, as more sociable, attentive to and interested in other children than individuals who were anxiously attached as toddlers (Pastor, 1981), to engage in more reciprocal interaction and show less negative affect in play with peers (Lieberman, 1977), to show more leadership, less withdrawal and hesitation with peers (Waters, Wippman and Sroufe, 1979), and to be rated by their preschool teachers as higher on peer competence than less secure children (La Frenier and Sroufe, 1985). Conflicting evidence is also reported (Jacobson *et al.*, 1983; Lamb *et al.*, 1985); however, the accumulation of findings demonstrating connections between secure attachment and competence in peer interaction at the preschool stage is impressive. The limitations of the data lie, yet again, in the paucity of studies of relationships between fathers and their children, the limited range of measures of relationships employed, the narrowness of the contexts in which the children are studied, the short-term nature of the follow-ups, and the limited age range studied. In one of the very few studies that has included fathers, MacDonald and Parke (1984) report results that suggest there may well be important differences in the nature of the connections between father–child and mother–child relationships and behavior with peers, and that these links may also differ for boys and girls. The methodological implications are clear: we need to expand our focus from mothers to include other family members. [Studies of parent–child and peer relationships in older children suffer from two other limitations—they are in the main cross-sectional in nature, and their measures of peer relations are frequently simply indices of popularity. The associations that are reported in general support the notion that 'good' parent–child relations are associated with peer popularity, and less aggressive behavior (see for example Baumrind, 1967, 1971; Winder and Rau, 1962).]

The problems entailed in making inferences about the processes involved in these associations bring us to the same issues raised by the research on the connections between marital and parent–child relationships. Are the processes involved in the connections between a discordant, aggressive parent–child relationship and aggressive relations with peers different from those linking a secure parent–child relationship with cooperative and competent peer relations? Are the connections between relationships for children in families within the normal range similar in nature to those for children in families suffering from psychosocial disadvantage? Is it appropriate to move beyond a description of the connections in terms of broad personality or self-esteem dimensions towards inferring more complex cognitive mechanisms, such as internal working models? These issues will be addressed in the final sections of the chapter; meanwhile some relevant lessons are to be learnt from a consideration of one other set of relations between relationships—the connections between parent–child and sibling–child relationships.

LINKS BETWEEN PARENT–CHILD AND SIBLING–CHILD RELATIONSHIPS

A consideration of the evidence for connections between parent–child and sibling–child relationships brings to the fore a principle central to understanding the relations between different relationships: that many different processes are probably involved in such connections. These different kinds of connection between the three family relationships in the mother–sibling triad are discussed in detail elsewhere (Dunn, 1987) and will be only briefly summarized here.

First, studies of the arrival of a sibling show that this event is accompanied by sharp changes in the relationship between mother and firstborn child, and that some children respond to these changes with a general emotional reaction of disturbance. The children whose reaction was one of extreme withdrawal, and whose relationship with their mothers was marked by a particularly sharp drop in communicative interaction, were one year later particularly hostile and negative to their younger siblings, and their siblings were very hostile to them (Dunn and Kendrick, 1982). One possible interpretation of these findings is that the process linking mother–child and sibling–child relationships is a connection mediated by the children's general emotional reaction—their emotional insecurity and anxiety engendered by the changes in their relationships with their parents. Such an interpretation would suggest that these children had difficulty in a number of their important social relationships after the sibling birth: with peers and with fathers and grandmothers, for example.

Other findings from the sibling studies suggest more specific connections between mother–child and sibling–child relationships. In families with firstborn girls in which there had been particularly close relationships between mother and firstborn, a particularly hostile relationship developed between the siblings in the ensuing year. In families in which there had been a relatively high degree of confrontation between mother and firstborn girl before the sibling birth the children were one year later particularly friendly towards their siblings. Interview findings indicated a similar pattern of connections between father–firstborn and later child–sibling relationships (Dunn and Kendrick, 1982).

Such results suggest two interpretations of the links between the family relationships: first, that those children who had been very close to their mothers developed a hostile relationship with their sibling as a result of their emotional reaction to being supplanted; second, that in families in which children had a detached or conflicted relationship with their parents, a warm and friendly relationship with the sibling developed—suggesting that a need for affection is sometimes met within the sibling relationship for those children whose relationships with their parents are rather distant or difficult. Other findings from the first sibling study support such an interpretation, for instance the data showing that in families in which the mothers were depressed after the sibling birth, the relationship between the siblings developed as a strikingly warm one.

A different kind of process linking the parent–child and sibling relationships is suggested by other data from the sibling studies. For some children, the development of a hostile relationship with a secondborn sibling is associated with a particularly warm and affectionate relationship between the mother and the secondborn child. There are both correlations over time between the frequency of mother–secondborn play and the later hostile behavior of both siblings towards each other, and evidence that children respond with promptness (and often hostility) to interaction between their mother and sibling (Kendrick and Dunn, 1983). Similar results are reported by Howe (1986), who showed that the greater the maternal involvement in play and attention to either of two siblings, the less friendly the interaction between the siblings.

This evidence for the vigilance with which children monitor the relationship between their siblings and their mothers suggests a further process that links the three family relationships. This is that differences in the behavior that a mother shows towards her different children are closely monitored by them, and that *relative differences* in her affection, control, punitiveness, and so on matter very much to the children, and affect their feelings about each other. Several studies of siblings have shown that *differential* maternal behavior is systematically linked to differences in the relationship between the siblings (Bryant and Crockenberg, 1980; Brody, Stoneman and McKinnon, 1987; Hetherington, 1987).

Finally, yet another process linking mother–child and sibling–child relationships was suggested by the evidence for the close monitoring by even very young children of the relationships between their parents and their siblings, and by the differences between mothers in their 'management' of the sibling relationship—the ways in which they discussed the feelings and actions of each child with the other, and supported or promoted their relationship. Such differences were associated with later differences in the sibling relationship. The process suggested by such findings is that communication about and discussion of other family members—the interpretation of others' behavior and the articulation of that interpretation—plays an important role in influencing the relationships between family members. At first sight it might seem appropriate to consider such processes relevant for adolescents and children in middle childhood but not for younger children. However, a number of different lines of evidence indicate that even in the preschool period such communication between mother and child is systematically related to differences in the quality of relationship that develops between the siblings (Dunn, 1987). Howe's (1986) research also supports this argument.

INFERENCES ABOUT PROCESSES LINKING RELATIONSHIPS

The studies of siblings and their parents draw our attention to the number of different kinds of process that are involved in linking close relationships—processes that range from general emotional reactions to more focused hostilities or alliances, and to far more cognitive mechanisms involving 'attri-butional style', and the interpretation of others' behavior, motives and relation-ships. The lesson from this discussion of the sibling–mother triad is clear: we should not assume that the mechanisms that link relationships are simple or few. Which we choose to emphasize will depend upon our preferred approach to understanding development, and on the nature of the measures and dimen-sions of the relationships that we chose to employ.

This point is particularly clear when we come to examine the mechanisms that have been invoked to explain the connections between relationships in early childhood and later parent–child relationships, or between the quality of a child's attachment to mother and subsequent peer relationships. Here, as we have noted, psychologists offer accounts that range from reference to broad personality variables to complex cognitive mechanisms. Each extreme of this continuum presents problems. Take, for instance, the interpretation of the links over generations in the Berkeley study (Caspi and Elder, 1987), an account that stresses instability of personality produced by socialization—'ineffective parenting'. Problem behavior, the result of 'unstable relationships' within the family, then results in problem relationships in the next generation. To describe the process by which one relationship affects another as mediated by effects on the personality or problem behavior is so general a redescription that it does not take us very far towards understanding mechanisms. Caspi and Elder acknowledge that such a description fails to specify the processes by which behavioral styles established in childhood are recreated in adulthood in any detail. They move further towards a more detailed description with the specu-lation that one important process may be the tendency for individuals to carry into new relationships the assumptions about self and other learned in previous relationships, suggesting indeed that individuals employ strategies in such new relationships that will confirm their ways of viewing others and themselves.

The grounds for such intentionalist assumptions are not clear, but it is inter-esting that an account that at one level describes the continuity between gener-ations in terms of the individual's personality in very broad terms should also include speculation that the continuity lies in individuals' conceptualization of self, other and relationships, invoking what is presumably a far more complex psychological mechanism. It is this idea that is central to the accounts of links between relationships put forward by those working within the attachment paradigm: the concept of 'internal working models'. Bowlby proposed that children develop increasingly elaborate 'internal working models' of the signifi-cant people in their worlds, and that these internal working models influenced their behavior in subsequent relationships. He noted that this proposal was in fact a reworking of the idea in traditional psychoanalytic theory of the 'internal world' of the individual (Bowlby, 1982).

The usefulness of this notion lies in the help it provides in bringing together data, and in the new ideas it suggests. Bretherton (1985), for instance, draws on the idea of internal working models to urge that those working within the attachment paradigm should try to relate their ideas on children's representation of relationships to the recent work on social cognition in very young children.

However, the limitation of the explanatory power of the internal working model is, paradoxically, that it is so vaguely conceived that it can too easily explain anything. It is sometimes seen as a model of a relationship, sometimes as a model of an individual, sometimes as a model of both sides of a relationship; as self-perpetuating yet as modifiable; as filtering input from the outside world and as directing activity and responses; as a set of rules for organizing information about relationships and as 'a mental representation of an aspect of the world, self, or relationships to others that is of special relevance to the individual' (Main, Kaplan and Cassidy, 1985, p. 68). It is, as Hinde (1987) has pointed out, difficult to avoid the conclusion that properties are added to the 'working model' as new phenomena appear for explanation, and that some of these new properties are identical to the phenomena they are supposed to explain. Moreover, it is very difficult to relate the *complexity* of the cognitive exercise that is involved in representing both sides of a relationship, as Sroufe and Fleeson (1986) suggest, with what we know of the capabilities of a twelve-month-old.

CONCLUSIONS

The exciting research on the links between relationships has, as so often in psychology, raised more questions than it has yet answered. Most striking has been the demonstration from rigorous intergenerational research that early childhood relationships are associated with the quality of later relationships in adolescence and adulthood yet these continuities can be profoundly affected by the spousal relationship, and the accumulating evidence for links between the quality of mother–child attachments and subsequent relationships. The intriguing but intractable issue that remains is the question of how we can best begin to sort out what the *processes* that link relationships may be. But there are certainly lessons in the new research from which we can learn how better to address this matter.

First, the limitations of the data, methodology and theoretical perspectives from which generalizations are confidently made must be acknowledged, as must the dangers of presuming that we have explained a process or revealed a mechanism by redescribing it with a different metaphor. It is most likely that many different mechanisms are involved in the links between relationships. It will be most useful now to set these out with precision, in a manner that is sensitive to the second issue raised in the introduction—that the mechanisms we infer will depend on our descriptive framework. Here the lesson is, surely, that we should describe relationships at different analytic levels, in order not to blinker ourselves to possible processes.

This is a particularly salient issue in relation to the third issue raised in the introduction—that processes linking relationships are likely to change as the child grows up. Our descriptive tools must be sensitive to this. One of the disadvantages of the attachment framework as it is currently employed is that it sets out to categorize in a manner that specifically disregards developmental change in the content of relationships. This is useful for some purposes, yet if we are to understand the developmental significance of particular qualities of a relationship at particular stages of development it clearly is a limitation. Finally, then, there is the obvious lesson that we need to broaden our framework of study. If we are to make progress in understanding the relations among relationships we must draw on the insights of family systems theorists, on the understanding and approaches of developmental psychologists, psychiatrists and developmental behavioral geneticists, and especially build on the strengths of the research strategies of the intergenerational studies that allow us to examine the 'lawful discontinuities' in development over time.

ACKNOWLEDGEMENT

Preparation of this chapter was supported in part by a grant from the National Science Foundation (BNS–8643938).

Handbook of Personal Relationships
Edited by S. W. Duck
© 1988 John Wiley & Sons Ltd

12

A Model for Children's Relationships and Relationship Dysfunctions

TERRY F. ADLER and WYNDOL FURMAN
University of Denver, Colorado, USA

ABSTRACT

In this chapter a model for conceptualizing children's relationships and their dysfunctions is presented. The model emphasizes four main relationship characteristics: warmth, conflict, relative status/power, and comparisons of one relationship with other relationships. These features are applied to both normal and dysfunctional relationships. An emphasis is placed on relationship dysfunctions of dyads rather than on individual children's problems that might lead to social difficulties.

The social world of the child encompasses a wide range of different personal relationships. For most children, interpersonal relationships are a source of support and contribute to personal development. Relationships may also be a source of stress, however, leading to difficulties in development. In other instances still, wide variation may be found. For example, some children may have close relationships with family members but feel ostracized by peers. Alternatively, some children, especially during adolescence, may feel estranged from their parents but have close friendships. Children may also relate differently to members of their families. Some children may have warm relationships with their parents whereas they may experience conflict with their siblings. In other families, siblings may provide the warmth and support that is lacking in parent–child relationships. Social scientists and clinicians alike have been concerned with identifying the sources of children's relationship problems and with developing effective intervention programs to correct them.

Although much research has focused on describing children's relationships and their dysfunctions, it has lacked a common focus. Researchers investigating peer, sibling, or parent–child relationships have focused on different relationship qualities. Moreover, researchers studying normal and dysfunctional relationships have employed different theoretical approaches and different methodological paradigms in their work. This lack of integration has made it difficult to compare different types of childhood relationships or to compare normal relationships and problematic ones.

In the present chapter, we offer a framework that attempts to integrate what is known about children's relationships with parents, peers, and siblings. In developing this framework, we will discuss the advantages and disadvantages of employing such an approach. The framework will also serve to highlight the similarities and differences among children's normal social relationships. The framework will then be applied to children's dysfunctional relationships and will provide a basis for a discussion of the assessment of problems that occur in these relationships.

NORMAL RELATIONSHIPS

Extensive bodies of literature have developed concerning normal relationships with parents (Maccoby and Martin, 1983), siblings (Bryant, 1982; Dunn, 1983) and peers (Hartup, 1983). The different literatures have developed separately from one another, and they have focused on different facets of relationships. For example, investigators studying parent–child relationships have focused on disciplinary techniques, whereas those studying sibling relationships have focused on rivalry. Even when seemingly similar relationship qualities are studied, different terms are used. Social scientists talk about love when discussing parent–child relationships, but they refer to interpersonal attraction in peer relationships. A conceptualization of relationships that allows for generalizations across different types of relationships may allow us to better understand the key dimensions in children's relationships.

One means of developing an integrated framework is to use a common theoretical perspective. For example, Weiss (1974) proposed that individuals seek a series of 'social provisions' or types of social support in their relationships. Weiss proposed a list of six basic provisions: (a) attachment—including affection, security, and intimate disclosure, (b) reliable alliance—a lasting, dependable bond that need not include emotional closeness, (c) enhancement of worth—recognition and affirmation of one's competence or value, (d) social integration—companionship, (e) guidance—tangible aid and advice, and (f) the opportunity for nurturance—taking care of someone else. These provisions can usually be obtained from many people in one's social network, although one may turn to specific people for specific provisions. For example, one may turn to friends for social integration or companionship, whereas one would turn to family members for reliable alliance. With this approach, the same set of constructs—social provisions—can be used to describe different relationships.

Furman and Buhrmester (1985) used Weiss' ideas to understand the similarities and differences among children's personal relationships. To this end, they developed a Network of Relationships Inventory (NRI) to assess social provisions and other characteristics of relationships. The list of ten relationship qualities includes six social provisions: (a) reliable alliance, (b) enhancement of worth, (c) instrumental help (guidance), (d) companionship (social integration), (e) affection, and (f) intimacy (disclosure). Whereas affection and intimacy were both subsumed under attachment in Weiss' theory, the two qualities were distinguished in Furman and Buhrmester's study because of the belief that children may have strong feelings of affection for others without necessarily engaging in intimate disclosure with them. In addition to these social provisions, four other qualities were assessed: (a) relative power of the child and other, (b) conflict, (c) satisfaction with the relationships, and (d) importance of the relationship. In this inventory, children rate how characteristic each of the ten qualities are of their relationships with mothers, fathers, siblings, grandparents, friends, and teachers (Furman and Buhrmester, 1985). Factor analyses of scores for each relationship consistently revealed three dimensions: (1) warmth (i.e. the six social provisions), (2) conflict, and (3) relative power. Thus a common framework can be used to describe children's relationships.

Moreover, one can directly compare and contrast the properties of different relationships because the same qualities are assessed. For example, the questionnaire was initially administered to 198 fifth- and sixth-grade children. Figure 1 depicts the mean ratings of the various characteristics for each relationship. The findings are generally consistent with our intuitions about the similarities and differences among the relationships, and provide support for Weiss' theory (see Furman and Buhrmester, 1985, for further details).

Although the use of a common theoretical perspective to describe relationships has much merit, there are some difficulties with this approach. The approach simply assumes that a common descriptive framework is possible and does not demonstrate that the framework can accurately represent the different relationships. In addition, the unique properties of specific relationships may be simply omitted. There are differences among relationships that make each relationship unique, and these differences need to be understood. For example, disciplinary techniques are important aspects of parent–child relationships that are not seen in peer or many sibling relationships.

An alternative approach is to describe each relationship in its own terms and compare the descriptions that result. In our own research we have derived separate questionnaires for measuring relationships with siblings, friends, and parents. These questionnaires include both qualities thought to be common to all relationships and qualities that may be specific to a particular relationship. For example, conflict is measured in both parent–child and sibling relationships, but disciplinary techniques are measured exclusively in the parent–child relationship and rivalry is measured only in the sibling relationship. Using these questionnaires, we were able to consider whether descriptive frameworks for parent, sibling, and peer interactions correspond to one another. We addressed this issue at each of three levels: (a) the level of underlying dimensions, (b) the level of relationship qualities, (c) the manifestation of these relationship qualities. In methodological terms, these three levels would be equivalent to factors, scales, and items.

We now turn to a discussion of the commonality of the underlying dimensions

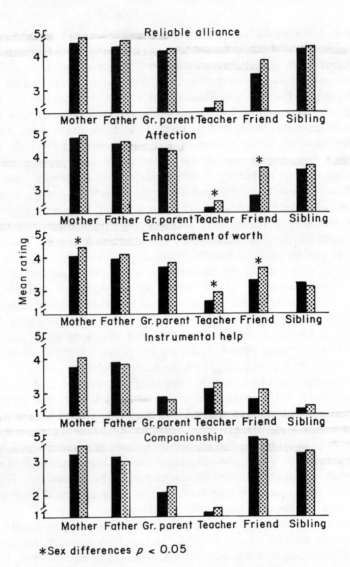

*Sex differences $p < 0.05$

Figure 1. Mean quality scores of each relationship

of children's relationships. We will first examine the individual dimensions of the sibling and peer relationships, and then examine the similarities and differences among these two relationships. Finally, we will discuss the underlying dimensions of the parent–child relationship and compare these dimensions to the dimensions underlying children's friendships and sibling relationships.

The degree of commonality among the dimensions underlying peer, sibling, and parent–child relationships was examined by conducting principal components analyses with oblique rotations. Four main dimensions describe the sibling relationship: warmth/closeness, conflict, rivalry and relative status/power (see Table 1). Representative characteristics of the warmth/closeness dimension

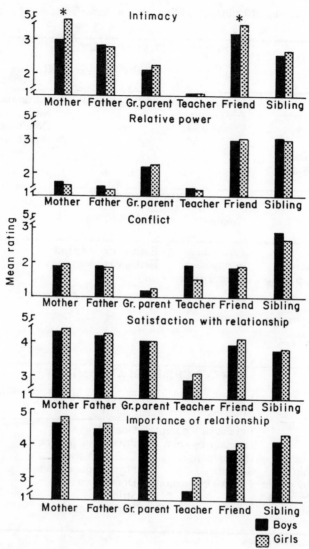

Figure 1 (*continued*)

are intimacy, prosocial behavior, companionship, affection, and admiration. Quarreling, antagonism, and dominance are examples of characteristics of sibling conflict. Rivalry is represented by parent partiality or parental favoritism towards one of the siblings. Relative status/power refers to asymmetry in terms of who dominates or nurtures the other.

Our assessment of peer interactions focuses on children's friendships, rather than peer relationships in general. The principal components analyses revealed that friendships are characterized by three dimensions: warmth/closeness, conflict, and exclusivity (see Table 1). Moreover, the qualities that define these constructs are similar in the two relationships. For example, intimacy, prosocial

Table 1   Dimensions of children's sibling relationships, friendships, and parent–child relationships

SIBLING RELATIONSHIPS

Warmth/ closeness	Conflict	Rivalry	Relative status/power
Intimacy	Quarreling	Parent partiality	Nurturance of sib.
Prosocial behavior	Antagonism		Nurturance by sib. (−)
Companionship	Competition		Dominance of sib.
Similarity			Dominance by sib. (−)
Admiration of sib.			
Admiration by sib.			
Affection			

FRIENDSHIPS

Warmth/ closeness	Conflict	Exclusivity	
Intimacy	Quarreling	Exclusivity of friend	
Prosocial behavior	Antagonism	Exclusivity by friend	−
Companionship	Competition		
Similarity			
Admiration of friend			
Admiration by friend			
Affection			
Acceptance			
Loyalty			

PARENT–CHILD RELATIONSHIPS

Warmth/ closeness	Egalitarian closeness	Power assertion/ conflict	Protectiveness
Nurturance	Intimacy by parent	Quarreling	Protectiveness
Importance	Intimacy by child	Privilege deprivation	
Affection	Egalitarianism	Guilt induction	
Companionship	Similarity	Physical punishment	
Admiration by parent	Positive evaluation	Dominance	
Admiration by child		Strictness	
High expectations		Verbal punishment	
Satisfaction			

(−) negative factor loadings

behavior, companionship, affection, similarity, and admiration define warmth/ closeness in both cases. In no case does a common quality define this dimension for one relationship and not the other. Some warmth/closeness qualities are specific to only one relationship, but they are conceptually similar to the common qualities. For example, loyalty and acceptance are examined only in peer relationships, but these qualities seem similar to other warmth/closeness qualities such as prosocial behavior and admiration.

Conflict in sibling and in peer relationships also seem to be very similar. In both cases, quarreling, antagonism, and competition define this relationship characteristic. Dominance is related to conflict in the sibling relationship, but it was not examined in peer relationships.

Exclusivity in friendships represents the desire to have a singular, exclusive relationship with a peer. Rivalry is similar to exclusivity; it represents the desire to have a special relationship with one's parents. These two dimensions resemble each other in that both represent jealousy in the relationship and comparisons of relationships within a particular system. In our measure of sibling relationships, comparisons are based on children's perceptions of parental behavior towards siblings in the family. In our measure of peer relationships, comparisons are based on children's perceptions of peers' interactions with other children.

An important difference between sibling and peer relationships is that the relative status/power dimension is not found in children's friendships. In previous versions of the questionnaire, we tried unsuccessfully to assess status differences in children's friendships. The vast majority of children report that their friendships are egalitarian in nature. Most of the friendships that children described were same-sex, same-age friendships, and it appears that relative status/power is not a dimension on which these friendships vary. It is possible that the status/power dimension would be salient in mixed-age friendships. On the other hand, a central feature of all friendships (mixed-age or same-age) may be egalitarianism or the lack of status difference. In either case, the status/power dimension does seem to apply to both sibling and peer relationships, but in somewhat different ways. That is, sibling relationships vary on this dimension, but friendships, at least same-age ones, are defined by a certain type of power arrangement.

The patterns of relations among the dimensions representing the two relationships are also similar. In both cases, warmth/closeness and conflict are not correlated. This implies that conflict is not the opposite of warmth/closeness, and that both may occur in the same relationship. There are also moderate positive correlations between conflict and rivalry in sibling relationships and between conflict and exclusivity in friendships. The similarity in the pattern of correlations provides additional support that exclusivity and rivalry are measuring similar qualities of children's relationships. Exclusivity, however, is also moderately correlated with warmth/closeness in friendships whereas rivalry and warmth/closeness are not correlated in sibling relationships. Exclusivity seems to be more socially desirable than rivalry.

Although there are many similarities between the dimensions of sibling relationships and those of friendships, the two relationships differ from those of parent–child relationships. We found that relationships with parents (mother or father) are represented by four dimensions: warmth/closeness, egalitarian closeness, power assertion/conflict, and protectiveness (see Table 1). The first and second dimensions, warmth/closeness and egalitarian closeness, both reflect closeness in the parent–child relationship. The first dimension includes qualities such as admiration, nurturance, and affection and represents aspects of the parent–child relationship that reflect parental love and affection. The second dimension, egalitarian closeness, includes qualities such as egalitarianism and similarity, and represents aspects of the parent–child relationship that reflect friendship and respect of the child. Although researchers have commonly examined warmth in parent–child relationships, we believe we are the first researchers to identify an egalitarian dimension of this warmth. Power assertion/conflict, the second dimension, represents the degree of conflict and use of discipline. Protectiveness represents the degree of parental control and possessiveness.

An examination of the pattern of relations among the dimensions reveals that warmth/closeness and egalitarian closeness are highly correlated. The patterns of correlations for these two dimensions are also similar. Both are negatively correlated with power assertion/conflict and positively correlated with protectiveness.

Despite the fact that sibling relationships and friendships are represented by relatively similar dimensions, the dimensions representing parent–child relationships are different from the others in many respects.* We find that there is not a single dimension of warmth for parent–child relationships, but two. Warmth/closeness appears to represent the parent *qua* parent aspect of the relationship, whereas egalitarian closeness appears to represent the parent *qua* friend aspect of the relationship. Although there is a single dimension of conflict for all three relationships, the parent–child dimension includes types of parental discipline as well as quarreling. Thus, its meaning in parent–child relationships is different from its meanings in friendships or sibling relationships.

Unlike sibling relationships, parent–child relationships do not have a pure relative status/power dimension. The presence of a power differential seems implicit, however, in both the warmth and power assertion/conflict dimensions. Thus, the issue of power and status seems applicable to all three relationships, but the nature of its impact on the descriptions of the three relationships varies.

Finally, protectiveness appears to have some similarities with rivalry or exclusivity, in that it involves comparisons of relationships within a particular social system. The dimension of protectiveness involves comparisons between family and nonfamily relationships. This dimension reflects how much parents prefer that their children interact with family members rather than with outsiders. Protectiveness also includes the quality of possessiveness, and reflects jealousy or the desire for a relationship between parent and child that excludes others.

In addition to comparing the general dimensions of these relationships, we can also consider the similarities and differences among specific qualities. In some respects, we have been examining the issue of similarity at this level by comparing the specific scales that load on various dimensions or factors. One can also compare the three different lists of relationship qualities and see that there are many similarities among the three. For example, affection, companionship, and quarreling would be appropriate descriptors for parent–child, sibling, and peer relationships. At the same time, each relationship has some properties that really apply only to that relationship. Examples of such properties would include loyalty and acceptance for friendships, dominance and parental partiality for sibling relationships, and disciplinary techniques for parent–child relationships. These special properties may help define these

---

* Subsequent analyses of parents' (versus children's) perceptions of parent-child relationships suggest that there may be a fifth factor representing disciplinary aspects of warmth in the parent–child relationship.

relationships and thus help us understand how they can be differentiated from one another.

The differences among the relationships are particularly salient when we consider how relationship qualities are manifested in terms of specific behaviors. This level of analysis would be comparable to the item level in methodological terms. Of course, different qualities (scales) will have different behavioral manifestations, but even the same relationship quality can be manifested differently in various relationships. For example, affection in parent–child relationships may be expressed physically, but few school-aged boys in the United States would be caught dead hugging or kissing their friends. Similarly, self-disclosure is likely to be unilateral in parent–child relationships, but reciprocal in friendships and closely spaced sibling relationships.

Is a common framework a viable means of describing children's relationships? We believe it is. At the very least, we have identified four major elements that must be addressed in describing any of these relationships. These are: (a) the degree of warmth, (b) the degree of conflict, (c) the power/status arrangements, and (d) how the relationship compares with other relationships in the network. These four elements or combinations of them are often reflected in the dimensions of particular relationships. For example, the warmth/closeness dimension in sibling relationships is related to the elements of warmth, whereas egalitarian closeness in parent–child relationships reflects the elements of warmth as well as a particular type of relationship. In the remaining instances, an element may not be reflected in a dimension because it has a fixed or defining value in a relationship. For example, same-age friendships appear to be egalitarian in nature. There is not a dimension of power in the relationship, but obviously a particular power arrangement is an important element of the friendship.

Not only are these four elements important to describe in all relationships but in some cases there may be dimensions common to more than one relationship, particularly for friendships and sibling relationships. Of course, deciding whether we have a common dimension is not straightforward. If we assess the same qualities for all relationships, we are more likely to obtain the same dimensions than if we use different qualities. In fact, the dimensions obtained from the NRI are more similar across relationships than those which were obtained using three different questionnaires. Clearly, one can manipulate the qualities being assessed and thus portray these relationships as more or less similar. Our intent was not to find either similarities or differences. To develop the measures, we asked children or significant others to describe these relationships and used their responses (and existing literature) to develop the lists. Thus, we believe that these results provide a reasonable estimate of the similarities and differences in the relationships.

Although there may be some common dimensions, the differences among relationships become more apparent when one begins to examine qualities and their manifestations. The issues involved in comparing across relationships seem analogous to those raised by comparisons across ages. Kagan's (1969) concepts of phenotypic discontinuity and genotypic continuity are helpful in understanding this comparison. The specific behaviors in which children of different ages engage are likely to differ markedly (phenotypic discontinuity). The different behaviors, however, may represent the same underlying construct (genotypic continuity). When we examine various relationships, we may find that the same general dimension (genotypic similarity) is manifested differently in different relationships (phenotypic dissimilarity). Of course, we need to be cautious about equating relationship dimensions and qualities in different relationships, especially in light of the unique properties of each relationship. There may be geno-typic dissimilarity as well! At the same time, the incorrect assertion of a similarity does not seem to be a worse mistake than the failure to identify an actual similarity. Even when the dimensions are not identical, the emphasis on common properties encourages us to make cross-relationship comparisons and to understand the interrelations among different relationships. For example, we can begin to assess how conflict in parent–child relationships relates to conflict in sibling relationships. Moreover, it can provide a basis for comparing functional and dysfunctional relationships, the topic we turn to next.

DYSFUNCTIONAL RELATIONSHIPS

Our discussion will focus on dysfunctional relationships rather than individual dysfunctions that can lead to relationship problems. We will first review commonly described relationship problems and the different ways they have been conceptualized. We will then discuss specific relationship dysfunctions according to our proposed model.

In the mental health field, there has been a traditional focus on individual psychopathology and relatively little work exists on dysfunctional relationships. This imbalance is reflected in the *Diagnostic and Statistical Manual of Mental Disorders* (DSM-III) of the American Psychiatric Association (1980). In fact, only four DSM-III codes specifically refer to relationship dysfunction: Marital Problem, Parent–Child Problem, Other Specified Family Circumstances, and Other Interpersonal Problem. These codes are very broad and do not provide subcategories for specific types of relationship difficulties. Certainly the DSM-III also has a number of diagnostic codes whose criteria include relationship difficulties. These difficulties are conceptualized, however, as disorders of the *individual* and not as relationship problems. Although etiology and treatment do not have to parallel one another, the two conceptualizations seem to imply different treatments. In the former case, therapeutic intervention would focus on the individual and his or her behaviors. In the latter case, one would focus on the relationship and patterns of interaction. Although many clinicians would choose the latter approach to treatment, the focus on individual psychopathology remains as true as it is inaccurate.

Family theorists have played a particularly important role in shifting the focus from individual psychopathology to relationship dysfunctions. Rather than focusing on delinquent children's individual difficulties, Minuchin *et al.* (1967) explored family patterns of relationships. They found that families of delinquent children were characterized by specific types of family interactions. Similarly, G. R. Patterson (1982) has characterized children's behavioral difficulties in terms of coercive patterns of interactions among family members rather than as instances of individual psychopathology.

Despite the fact that researchers and clinicians have traditionally focused on individual psychopathology, there has been a recent trend towards conceptualizing dysfunction in terms of relationships. For example, researchers have begun to recognize the role that the peer group plays in contributing to difficulties in peer relationships (Hymel, Wagner and Butler, in press). Wright, Giammarino and Parad (1986) have found that the specific bases for peer rejection vary from group to group. Similarly, Bierman and Furman (1984) demonstrated that effective treatment of peer relationship problems may depend on changing both the target child's social skills and the peer group's attitude and behavior towards that child.

To date, the descriptions of relationships have been rather scattered and lack a common framework. Our framework for describing children's relationships may be helpful in categorizing children's dysfunctional relationships. Our dimensions of relationships may characterize dysfunctions as well as normal variations in relationships. Many, although not all, dysfunctions in relationships can be viewed as instances in which the quality of the relationship exceeds normal variation along one or more of these four dimensions. In the subsequent paragraphs, we discuss how our relationship dimensions can be applied to dysfunctions in relationships.

Conflict

One can readily imagine dysfunctions on the conflict dimension. In fact, excessive conflicts with parents, siblings, and peers are all common reasons for seeking psychological services. Of course, the specific issues of conflict differ from relationship to relationship. Excessive quarreling and antagonism often represent difficulties in peer or sibling relationships, whereas discipline and punishment issues are often major problems in parent–child relationships. These differences probably reflect the differences in power distribution. In friendships, the relationships are egalitarian and the issues involve negotiating with each other, whereas in parent–child relationships, the issues are those of parental control. Despite these differences, excessive conflict in all these relationships appears to be a common type of dysfunction.

The research on conflict in one relationship may prove valuable in understanding conflict in the other relationships. For example, we may find that there are patterns to conflictual relationships and that children who have conflictual sibling relationships also have conflictual parent–child relationships. G. R. Patterson's (1982) work on coercive patterns of parent–child interactions supports the importance of examining conflict as a relationship dysfunction rather than simply as the result of individual psychopathology. He has demonstrated that specific patterns of parent–child interactions reinforce conflictual behavior. A coercive cycle develops wherein ineffectual parental disciplinary techniques tend to reinforce negative child behaviors, which in turn produce negative parent behaviors. Resolving such conflict thus requires that parents and children learn more effective patterns of interaction. Patterson's work also highlights the importance of examining the bidirectionality of interactions among parents and children.

Excessive sibling conflict has commonly been conceptualized in individual terms (A. Adler, 1929/1959). For example, conflict may occur if an older child has feelings of anger and displacement because of the birth of another child. In this conceptualization, treatment would be likely to focus on the older child. Although some instances of sibling conflict may very well originate from feelings of displacement, a relationship perspective can shed insights into the nature of the problem and its treatment. G. R. Patterson (1984b) has recently reconceptualized conflictual sibling interactions in terms of coercive family processes. In a study of 60 families, he demonstrated that certain sibling behaviors serve to reinforce conflictual interaction patterns, just as he had found in his earlier research on parent–child interactions. As yet, an intervention program based on the coercive model has not been used to correct excessive sibling conflict, but the idea seems promising. Patterson's work is also important because he has applied his model of coercive interactions to both sibling and parent–child relationships. He is one of the few researchers who has attempted to generalize his understanding of one type of relationship to other relationships. This work is important in developing a framework for children's relationships.

Interestingly, researchers have not focused on children's difficulties with specific friends, but rather have concentrated on children's difficulties with peers in general. Our impression is that parents are also more likely to be concerned about problems in peer relations in general than about problems in specific friendships. In any event, it is clear that excessive peer conflict is dysfunctional. Excessive conflict, aggressiveness, or negative behavior has been repeatedly found to be correlated with peer rejection (see Hartup, 1983) and, in fact, has been shown to lead to being rejected (Coie and Kupersmidt, 1983; Dodge, 1983). Such behaviors have been commonly conceptualized as dysfunctions of the individual, which seems logical because one is describing a person's interactions with many others rather than with a specific individual. At the same time, recent investigators have observed that the peer group can contribute to aggressive or rejected children's difficulties by being more likely to interpret their behavior as aggressive (Dodge, 1980) or by rebuffing their overtures to join in (Putallaz and Gottman, 1981). Thus, even when aggressive children attempt to decrease the degree of conflict in their relationships, their peers may react in ways that maintain conflict.

The past discussion has focused on high levels of conflict in children's relationships. It is unclear if excessively low conflict can be dysfunctional. Children who are very submissive towards peers may be the frequent victims of aggression (Patterson, Littman and Bricker, 1967) and may not have very effective relationships with peers. Similarly, one would be concerned about a family in which the children were never permitted to disagree with their parents. In some parent–child relationships, low conflict may be associated with low warmth. That is, the parents may be uninvolved with their children and indifferent towards them. Our preference is to conceptualize these difficulties as dysfunctions on the other dimensions rather than on the conflict dimension *per se.*

Warmth

Low warmth in the parent–child relationship may be reflected in a number of parenting styles. Baumrind (1971) notes that authoritarian parents discourage verbal give-and-take between parent and child. These parents might thus rank low on our measures of warmth/closeness and egalitarian closeness. Although they are highly involved with their children, and place a number of demands upon them, they are low in their responsivity to them. Interestingly, Baumrind's work also suggests that permissive parents are relatively uninvolved with their children and make few demands upon them. Thus, both authoritarian and permissive parent–child relationships may rate low on the warmth/closeness and egalitarian closeness dimensions. The groups are, however, on opposite ends of the power assertion/conflict dimension.

Low warmth is also characteristic of indifferent or neglecting parents. Maccoby and Martin (1983) characterize uninvolved parents as those who are likely to be motivated to do whatever is necessary to keep their children at a distance and minimize the amount of interaction. Egeland and Sroufe (1981a, b) detailed some of the more extreme implications of low parental involvement. These include physical abuse, verbal abuse, neglect, and psychological unavailability. Parents who were unavailable psychologically tended to be those who were detached, depressed, and uninterested in their children.

We know relatively little about dysfunctions in warmth in sibling relationships, and it is not clear what impact a distant sibling relationship might have. Bank and Kahn (1982) discuss deidentification, a process by which siblings deny any similarities between them and disown the relationship. The sibling relationship is thus characterized as distant and rejecting. These authors state that the rejection between such siblings often results from family identification of one sibling as strong or good and the other sibling as weak or bad. Deidentification thus results in an attempt to avoid any of the weaker sibling's traits. Although deidentification is a normal process, some deidentified relationships may lead to problems in adjustment. The relevant data to assess this hypothesis, however, do not currently exist.

Low warmth in children's friendships is likely to be manifested as a lack of peer relationships. After all, if the interactions between two children were not friendly and warm, it is unlikely that a friendship would develop. It is unclear if social isolation is dysfunctional. Some investigators have argued that it is a serious problem in adjustment (Hops and Greenwood, 1981; Strain, Kerr and Ragland, 1981), whereas others have argued that it is not at all problematic. Intuitively, one might expect social isolation to be problematic, because peer interactions have been found to provide numerous contributions to development (Hartup, 1976). On the other hand, most forms of nonsocial behavior are adaptive (Moore, Evertson and Brophy, 1974), although some are not (Furman and Garcia, 1986; Rubin, 1982). Similarly, social isolation is not usually related to current or subsequent adjustment (Asher, Markell and Hymel, 1981).

The controversy, however, may result from the typical definition of social isolation—low rates of interaction. Some investigators have accurately observed that some forms of interactions are not necessarily more healthy than not interacting at all. Would we want an isolated child to be interacting, but doing so aggressively? Probably not. On the other hand, if we think of 'isolation' in terms of low rates of positive or warm interactions, then most investigators would probably think that isolation, at least in extreme forms, is dysfunctional. In fact, Asher, Markell and Hymel (1981), major critics of the use of low rates of interaction, have reviewed research demonstrating that qualitative indices of interaction, such as frequency of positive interactions, are associated with adjustment.

We do not see a high degree of warmth as being dysfunctional in and of itself. Too much warmth may be detrimental if it occurs along with dysfunctions in other relationship qualities, however. For example, a power dysfunction in a parent–child relationship (with a child taking on a parentified role) might indicate a danger of the parent becoming seductive with the child (Sroufe and Ward, 1980). Seductive parenting is described as behavior which is insensitive and unresponsive to the needs of the child and which tends to draw the child into patterns of interaction that are overly stimulating and inappropriate (Sroufe and Ward, 1980). More generally, high degrees of warmth might also indicate enmeshment of parent and child. In an enmeshed relationship, individuals are overconcerned and overinvolved in each other's lives. We would expect that such enmeshment would be associated with an accompanying lack of closeness in other relationships. The parent and child would be close to the exclusion of other members of the child's social network. Thus, high levels of warmth may be detrimental when associated with other dysfunctions in the relationship. If a relationship is characterized by a normal distribution of power, if warmth is fairly evenly distributed across family members, and if family warmth does not exclude the possibility of interactions with extrafamilial members, high warmth should not be a problem.

Relative Status/Power

The distribution of power between parent and child can be imbalanced in either direction. In the previous section, authoritarian parents and the dysfunctional extreme of rejecting, abusive parents were described. Here, the parent–child relationship is characterized as low in warmth and high in power assertion/conflict. Authoritarian parents may be exerting too much control and are thus not allowing children to develop their own sense of independence. On the other hand, permissive and uninvolved parents may not exert a sufficient amount of control over their children.

Clinicians commonly describe a third kind of distortion in the distribution of power—parentification (Bank and Kahn, 1982; Boszormenyi-Nagy and Spark, 1973; Minuchin, 1974). In this instance, a child has assumed some of the behavioral role characteristics of parents. Of course, some 'parental' responsibilities are normal for older children and adolescents, but in instances of parentification, the child has developmentally inappropriate responsibilities. As a consequence of having responsibilities for the welfare of another family member, the child may miss the support derived from a consistent parenting relationship and his or her developmental needs may not be attended to sufficiently (Friedrich and Reams, 1985).

Parentification may also affect the quality of sibling relationships. A younger child may resent being primarily cared for by an older sibling rather than by parents. Conversely, although a moderate amount of responsibility for nurturing can be a positive aspect of a sibling relationship, too much responsibility can be resented by the older child and can interfere with his or her own development (Bank and Kahn, 1982; Bossard and Boll, 1956).

Excessive dominance can also be problematic in sibling relationships. Such marked power differences can often result in conflict, and in extreme cases sibling abuse (Straus, Gelles and Steinmetz, 1981). Bank and Kahn (1982) observed that parents often fail to intervene in abusive sibling relationships. This may be because of their own need to avoid conflict or because sibling conflict may satisfy their own aggressive impulses. Bank and Kahn (1982) believe that sibling abuse, engendered by parents who amplify conflicts, is widely underreported. Such parents often rationalize their children's aggression as normal power tactics rather than as abusive.

Since egalitarianism is a defining feature of friendship, differences in power in same-age friendships appear to be unusual. It is unclear if such differences would be considered problematic; certainly, it is not a common clinical problem. What is more likely to be considered problematic are children who are very dominant or submissive. Dominant children may find it difficult to establish or maintain friendships. Very submissive children may primarily seek out younger peers as friends, something that is of concern to many parents.

These problems in friendships not withstanding, the issues of power seem to be of greater concern in family relationships. Problems in the balance of power are commonly addressed in clinical interventions. Treatment of this dysfunctional aspect of the relationships may often include helping family members redefine their roles and responsibilities. Teaching family members effective negotiation skills (Robin, Koepke and Nayar, 1986) or attempting to make structural changes in the family (Minuchin and Fishmen, 1981) are also means by which changes in the family power structure may be achieved.

Comparisons of Relationships

Some of the dysfunctions described in previous sections can reflect problems in the comparisons of relationships. For example, marked conflict may occur when parental partiality is judged to be high by siblings. Children who do not have close relationships with their parents will tend to be jealous of their siblings who have such relationships, and conflict between siblings may result. As noted previously, we found that perceptions of parental partiality were correlated with conflict in sibling relationships (T. Adler, 1985; Furman and Buhrmester, 1985).

The influence of one relationship on another has been a primary emphasis of family therapists (Bowen, 1966; Lidz, 1963; Minuchin, 1974). For example, Minuchin (1974) proposed that each family has a structure—an invisible set of demands that organizes the ways in which members interact with each other. The family system carries out its functions through subsystems, which are differentiated by boundaries. In a healthy family, the boundaries between individuals are clear but flexible. Boundaries that are either too rigid or too diffuse are usually inappropriate. Rigid boundaries may result in disengaged relationships, resembling the low involvement described previously. Diffuse boundaries can result in enmeshed relationships. Although the closeness of extremely enmeshed relationships may seem desirable, these relationships can be dysfunctional either by restricting the autonomy of individual family members or by excluding other relationships. Excessive togetherness and sharing may lead to a lack of privacy and excessive possessiveness and protectiveness by the parent. Both parents and children may have difficulty accepting the idea of another person interfering with the close nature of their relationships. Bowen (1966) also describes a similar phenomenon of the undifferentiated family mass, in which there is a conglomerate emotional oneness and symbiotic relationships.

In healthy families, some boundaries are naturally stronger than others. For example, the family may be divided into spousal, parental, and sibling subsystems. Boundaries between subsystems may, however, be distorted by inappropriate relationships. In some instances of parentification, for example, the parentified child becomes allied with one parent and becomes a pseudoparent, while the other parent is relegated to a subservient, demeaning role (Minuchin and Fishman, 1981). Parentification is one example of triangulation, the act of involving an outsider when two people are in tense situations (Bowen, 1978). Triangulation commonly occurs when family alliances are skewed. For example, Minuchin and Fishman (1981) discuss how disobedient young children often disobey rules and 'tyrannize' their families because they have become inappropriately allied with one of their parents. These authors state that in such families the parents disqualify each other, leaving the triangulated child in a position of power that is frightening to him or her as well as to the family.

Family theorists have also emphasized that problems with any individual or specific relationship reflect system problems. The classic instance of this is scapegoating, in which one person is labeled as having problems when in fact the problems actually exist in other individuals or relationships. For example, when a child is brought to a guidance clinic for emotional problems, in actuality it may be that the marital relationship is seriously strained. In effect, the sick child has been designated as the one who will display the family's pathology, thus permitting the others to believe that they are healthy.

Understanding patterns of family interaction can also help us understand the etiology of individual pathology. Work by Minuchin, Rosman and Baker (1978) indicates that families of children who manifest these psychosomatic problems are characterized by certain patterns of interaction. Specifically, enmeshment is common and family members tend to be overprotective of one another. Such families tend to have a low tolerance for conflict, and conflictual situations are avoided or defused. Often, the sick child in the family is given the role of defusing conflict. The family turns its concern to the sick child and thus avoids difficulties such as marital discord. Parents who cannot deal with their conflicts with one another can avoid conflict by directing their energies towards protecting their sick child.

Although we have emphasized the impact of structural dysfunctions on parent–child relationships, these dysfunctions can also affect sibling relationships. Not only can siblings have marked rivalry, but in some instances the sibling relationships can be enmeshed. Bank and Kahn (1982) have proposed that such extreme bonding can occur when the links with parents are distant. Twins may be particularly prone to problems of diffuse ego boundaries (Bank and Kahn, 1982).

Children compare different friendships, but we have difficulty thinking of dysfunctions in this regard. Some parents may be concerned if their children play exclusively with one child. Similarly, jealousy and competing for friends are annoying and undesirable, but it is unlikely that these phenomena are clinically dysfunctional.

CONCLUSION

The primary intent of this chapter was to propose a model for describing both normal and dysfunctional relationships. Although we believe that the four dimensions we have outlined have promise, several limitations warrant mentioning. Our model is based on school-aged children's perceptions of their relationships; thus, an important topic for future research is to see how these perceptions are manifested in behavior. The model also places an emphasis on the description of relationship properties, not the etiology or treatment of relationship dysfunctions. A relationship may be characterized as high in conflict or low in warmth for any number of reasons. The characteristics of the relationship could reflect problems of the individual or, as we have emphasized here, dyadic problems. Etiological descriptions of the problems will require a different set of frameworks. Social learning theorists would emphasize the role that cognitive beliefs, communication skills, social skills, or contingencies of reinforcement play in the development and maintenance of dysfunctions. Psychoanalytically oriented theorists would emphasize the role of early object relations (Greenberg and Mitchell, 1983), whereas family theorists would stress the role of family structure (Minuchin, 1974). We have alluded to different conceptualizations and treatments throughout this chapter. It is clear, however, that much work remains to be done before we can fully appreciate the contributions different perspectives may provide to the understanding of dysfunctional relationships.

Regardless of the approach, however, it is valuable to develop etiological or intervention frameworks that could be applied to different relationships. Although this has not been done frequently, such frameworks have proven useful. For example, G. R. Patterson's (1984b) coercive model appears to be applicable to both sibling and parent–child interactions. Similarly, we are sure that researchers studying social skills in family relations and researchers studying similar phenomena in peer relations could learn from one another.

Even as a descriptive framework, the present one has a limited scope–dyadic relationship quality. Although we have talked about the importance of considering how one relationship compares to another, our emphasis has been on how such comparisons affect the quality of specific relationships. One would want to supplement descriptions of dyadic relationships with additional descriptions of the structure of the family or peer group as a whole. For example, concepts such as triangulation and enmeshment seem essential.

Additionally, not all dysfunctions are manifested in relationship qualities. The absence of certain relationships, such as friendships, can be dysfunctional as well (Furman and Robbins, 1985; Putallaz and Gottman, 1981). Thus, as either clinicians or researchers, we would want to map out the network and the characteristics of its different components.

Our descriptive framework also tends to emphasize similarities among relationships, and subtle differences are minimized. Our model is useful for a general description of normal and dysfunctional relationships. The model would benefit, however, from more detailed descriptions of these relationships and potential dysfunctions. For example, recent investigators have argued that parenting styles vary from domain to domain, and parental concerns about specific issues can lead to particular dysfunctions (Costanzo and Woody, 1985). When assessing relationships, one would thus want to capture such variation. As we develop more detailed descriptions of relationships, we can begin to identify common problematic patterns. Particularly important would be research on developmental changes in normal and dysfunctional relationships (a striking omission in this chapter). Ultimately we could have a taxonomy of relationship disorders similar to the taxonomy of individual psychopathology found in DSM-III (American Psychiatric Association, 1980).

In addition to providing information about the patterns of specific relationships, our model could stimulate work examining the patterns among different relationships. One would expect children with several dysfunctional relationships to be at greater risk than those with an isolated problem. As yet, however, we know little about the different configurations of relationships. The emphasis on common dimensions should make it possible to make comparisons of relationships and provide information about links among relationships. Other researchers have also begun to investigate links among relationships, especially early parent–child relationships (see Dunn, this volume, for example), but the surface of this topic has just been scratched.

Despite its limitations, we believe that our proposed common framework can be valuable. Research on normal and dysfunctional relationships and on different types of relationships have remained separate from one another. We hope that we have illustrated that they have much in common and much to learn from each other. Moreover, our framework may provide a basis for a comprehensive means to understand the etiology and treatment of relationship dysfunctions.

ACKNOWLEDGEMENT

Portions of the research described in this chapter were supported by a grant from the National Institute of Child Health and Human Development (1R01 HD 16142), and preparation of the manuscript was facilitated by a W. T. Grant Faculty Scholar Award to W. Furman.

Section Three

Communication

Section Editor   *Barbara Montgomery*

Overview

Communication is both the method and the substance of relationships. As method, communication is the vehicle for relating. Any number of distinct individuals are transformed into a social unit, be it a dyad or a group, when they communicate with one another. Moreover, the developmental fate of that relational unit—whether it continues or is ended—is determined by the presence or absence of communication between its members. Communication is much more than just a means for beginning, maintaining and terminating relationships, though. It also provides the substantive material of interpersonal bonds. The meanings connected to partners' communicative acts define relational markers like conflicts, lovemaking, flirtations, play, apologies, and so forth. Markers such as these contribute to the relational identities that distinguish any particular relationship from others. They are the matter and material—the stuff—of all relationships.

These intimate links between communicating and relating account for the presence of a 'Communication' section in this handbook on personal relationships. It is broad, reaching across the field of communication to present a representative sample of its work relevant to personal relationships. Yet while its identity is disciplinary, its content is decidedly interdisciplinary. Colleagues from a variety of sister fields including psychology, sociology, and family studies will be familiar with most of the issues discussed and much of the literature cited. What may be unfamiliar, though, are the particular approaches taken to analyze these issues and literatures. These approaches stem from a unique perspective that communication scholars bring to the study of personal relationships.

A COMMUNICATION PERSPECTIVE

As illustrated in the pages of Section Three, those who call themselves communication scholars are exploring a great many diverse questions about personal relationships. Yet there is a common underpinning to the variety, divergence, and subtlety represented in their work. They all view relationships through lenses attuned to the phenomenon of communication. This underlying

233

communication perspective is grounded in the notions of behavioral interaction, process, and multiple meaning systems, each of which is discussed below.

Focus on Behavioral Interaction

Definitionally, communication involves the exchange of behaviors—action *and* reaction, question *and* answer, request *and* response. It follows, then, that a communication perspective is particularly sensitive to the behaviors of relating between two people. Moreover, those behaviors are viewed within the context of other behaviors. Such concepts, then, as interdependence, reciprocity, behavioral contingency, transaction, and feedback are central. While interpretations of these concepts differ in specific communication theories (see, e.g., review and analysis by Fisher, 1978), the notion of interaction—exchanges of behavior—is paramount to all.

One effect of this bias towards observing interaction as opposed to action is that communication scholars view relationships as the product of a least two people's behavior. Relationships and their nature—whether they be loving or hateful, enjoyable or boring, democratic or tyrannical, liberating or oppressive—are assumed to be the outcome of how *both* partners act with each other.

Focus on Process

A second commonality among communication scholars is the view that communication is a *process*: that is, 'thick with a thousand ingredients' (Smith, 1966, p. v) that react and combine with each other through time. This particular view of process draws attention, first, to the structural organization of communication and, consequently, of relationships. Communication scholars show an interest in studying the traditional 'building blocks' of relationships and how they interrelate. These include individuals with their characterizing demographic, psychological, and sociological profiles and situational and cultural contexts with their attendant roles, rules and scripts that influence behavior.

But also paramount is an effort to understand the temporal organization of relationships. The difference in seeing relationships as temporally vs. structurally organized is akin to the difference between describing something with verbs as opposed to nouns. From a temporal perspective, relationships exist in action. They are, to paraphrase a popular saying, constantly in the state of being *and* becoming; they are dynamic, continuous, ever-unfolding and evolving complexities. They have rhythms and tempos, durations and cycles, pasts, presents and futures. At the microlevel of analysis, the interest is in describing how relationships are changed, reinforced, or affected by the sequences of behaviors enacted between their members. These sequences form patterns that, at the macrolevel of analysis, are investigated for their ability to define conversational stages (e.g. greetings, goodbyes) and types (e.g. persuasion, play) and relationship phases (e.g. initiation, termination) and types (e.g. rigid, flexible).

Focus on Multiple Meaning Systems

Interpersonal communication and relationships are not based upon a one-message–one-meaning system. Rather, from a communication perspective, partners are seen to interact with *multiple levels of meaning*.

One explanation for this multiplex of meanings is that a message is represented in multiple *forms* of observable behavior—a touch, a glance, a statement, a tone of voice—all enacted simultaneously. These various behavioral forms need not, indeed more often do not, convey completely redundant information. Rather, the meanings attached to one behavior have the potential to reinforce, contradict, complement or subtly shade meanings attached to others.

A second explanation is that a message *functions* at multiple levels, providing at minimum referential information about topics of conversation and information about how such referential information is to be interpreted within the particular and present context. For instance, saying 'come here' typically indicates a desire for someone to move closer; but the way 'come here' is said (e.g. loud or soft voice, tense or relaxed posture), the relational context of the statement (e.g. boss to employee or lover to lover), and the situational circumstances (e.g. boardroom or bedroom) suggest whether the statement is an expression of anger or sexual arousal, an assertion of dominance or an invitation for togetherness. These overlaid meanings contribute to interactants' perceptions of each other and their relationship. Thus, messages can have layers of meanings, each functioning differently in the interpersonal context.

A third explanation is that the multiple *perspectives* of those involved in the communication event are likely to result in multiple meanings being assigned to any one message. People attend to and weight behaviors differently, place them in different relational and situational frames, attribute them to different motivational circumstances, draw different logical associations between them. The result is that a single message may mean very different things to all those exposed to it.

The assumption of multiple meaning systems encourages communication scholars to look beyond the superficially discernible, simple interpretations of behavioral exchanges between relationship partners. Rather, contemporary communication theory and research are likely to acknowledge and even celebrate the complexity of negotiating relationships at multiple levels of meanings.

OVERVIEW OF CHAPTERS

Interaction, process, and multiple message systems are permeating themes in the chapters in Section Three, but these concerns are manifest in a variety of ways.

Berger revitalizes the persons-as-intuitive-scientists metaphor to highlight the role of information processing within the context of interpersonal relationships. He describes how partners employ a variety of information-gaining and information-evaluating strategies to reduce uncertainty about each other and the nature of their developing relationship. Certain factors, though, complicate this process. One is that more information can lead, in some cases, to increases in uncertainty (for example learning that a spouse is having an affair). Another is that partners simultaneously value both predictability (because of the relational stability it represents) and uncertainty (because of its attendant excitement). Berger suggests that one key to understanding these and other complexities is to develop a strong theoretical base for explaining how individuals set informational goals and effect plans and strategies for achieving them. Within this frame, he presents a provocative set of researchable questions about the intuitive application of social science methodology by relationship partners in their attempts to gain information about each other.

Like Berger, Baxter is interested in the dynamics of relationship development. She uses a wider-angled analytic lens, though, for considering the complexities of forming, maintaining, and dissolving personal relationships. At the heart of her analysis is the definition of basic contradictions of relational life. These include the simultaneous pulls towards autonomy and connection, the concurrent interpersonal needs for both novelty and predictability, and the desire of partners to be open with each other while at the same time to reduce vulnerability by being closed with each other. Baxter suggests that patterns in the responses to these contradictions reflect dialectical phases of relationship development. Baxter's analysis challenges researchers to incorporate a process perspective to study the ways in which these relational contradictions play themselves out through time. More importantly, perhaps, her analysis provides a theoretical basis for segmenting the history of relationships.

Offering a more delimited consideration of communication, Miller and Boster's essay links the topic of persuasion to personal relationships. The authors submit that these two lines of research, which ought to have many ties to one another, have actually 'largely passed like ships in the night'. In an attempt to rectify this state of affairs, the authors draw our attention to a number of personal relationship factors that constrain both the ways in which partners construct persuasive messages and the impact that those messages have on each other and their relationship. Specifically, Miller and Boster discuss the potential effects of an extended and established relational history, multiple opportunities for response and interaction, and intensified concerns for relational consequences. This essay is rich in suggestions for future research. The authors, consistently solicitous about ecological validity, offer both methodological and content guidelines for extending investigation of persuasion within the context of personal relationships.

Rogers and Millar advance a view of interpersonal communication based upon the assumptions of 'systems thinking'. A basic principle of this view is that social interaction forms relationships. Thus, the focal point of their essay is what occurs *between* social actors—not *within* them—as they establish and develop their relationships. What does happen between partners are sequences of behavioral exchanges that can be organized into temporal patterns. These multiplex patterns are noteworthy more for their relational meanings (i.e. implications about the kind of relationship that two people have) than for their content meanings (i.e. referential information about a particular topic of conversation). Rogers and Millar propose that three major dimensions are represented in these relational meanings in the form of information about the control, trust, and intimacy present in the relationship. The authors illustrate the application of their view to personal relationship investigation by reviewing research related to control—that is, how partners negotiate rights to constrain their action together. Rogers and Millar conclude by suggesting potentially profitable avenues for future study, including suggestions for integrating the study of relational and content meanings.

Norton offers another perspective on the multiplex quality of communication messages. Like Rogers and Millar, he emphasizes that communication between relationship partners exists in the interaction of message (i.e. content) and metamessage (i.e. style). According to Norton, style elements do not function only to help partners interpret the 'here-and-now' content of each other's messages. They also contribute to recognizable patterns, creating expectations that influence interpretations of future messages. Norton presents theoretical propositions about how participants make sense of the gestalt formed by the interaction of style and content. Within this theoretical framework, Norton links communicator style to the concept of marital *quid pro quo*: that is, the essential interdependencies in spouses' behaviors that define their unique relationship. Style is presented as a means to maintain, change, and reflect the *quid pro quo*. Norton concludes by discussing the implications of his ideas for researchers and therapists.

Cappella also considers the association between communication patterns and relationship characteristics. He is concerned specifically with how patterns of interaction (i.e. structural and temporal interdependencies among communication behaviors) are linked to both relationship types (e.g. traditional, independent) and relational outcomes (e.g. attraction, stability). In an analysis of the conceptual and operational characteristics of these concepts, Cappella explicates procedures for fitting them together. He also reviews research that he presents as exemplars for attempting to achieve this fit. Cappella concludes by critically examining potential avenues for future research and identifying the most promising.

Finally my own chapter considers the effects of differing value systems in evaluating interpersonal interaction by asking, 'What makes for good communication in personal relationships?' The answer to this question differs, depending upon whether it is grounded in: (1) the prevailing social ideology for relationships, (2) unique relational standards negotiated by the partners themselves, or (3) individual standards, idiosyncratically developed and maintained by only one of the partners. In practice, most partners apply a standard of judgement that integrates elements from all three sources. The essay considers the implications of this for both the research and repair of personal relationships.

CONCLUSION

Individually, each of the chapters in Section Three challenges the reader with unique observations and fresh questions. Collectively, the chapters provide some notable kernels of insight about the associations between communication and personal relationships. (1) Communicating and relating are interdependent processes. One cannot be done without the other. (2) Communicating in personal relationships is different from communicating in impersonal relationships. The quantity and quality of information available to partners in personal relationships, their memories of past interactions and commitments to future ones, their intensified concerns for the quality of their relationships, and the increased opportunities for establishing unique rules, rituals, and regularities affect differences in their communication compared to that which occurs in more public, less personal relationships. (3) The way partners communicate is at least as important if not more important to their relationships as the content of their communication. Nuances associated with such similar concepts as style, relational meanings, and patterns of verbal and nonverbal behaviors exert powerful metacommunicative force on the process of exchanging messages and defining the nature of relationships. (4) The ways individuals communicate differ as their relationships develop. Not only are topics likely to shift as partners move from initial to intermediate to ending phases, but negotiations over some relational issues may result in different outcomes being linked to different stages. (5) Communication affects and is affected by the quality of personal relationships.

In sum, then, Section Three presents a sample of the unique contributions that taking a communication perspective can make to understanding personal relationships. Each chapter efficiently reviews gains that have been made and provocatively previews advances yet to be realized. Overarching all is the message that communication and personal relationships are intimately bound each to the other in theory, research, and practice.

Handbook of Personal Relationships
Edited by S. W. Duck
© 1988 John Wiley & Sons Ltd

13

Uncertainty and Information Exchange in Developing Relationships

CHARLES R. BERGER
Northwestern University, Evanston, Illinois, USA

ABSTRACT

Uncertainty and its reduction are crucial to the development of personal relationships. Uncertainty reduction theories are reviewed and the roles played by uncertainty in relationship development discussed. Strategies for reducing uncertainty are outlined. The adequacy of persons as intuitive experimenters, samplers and psychometricians is considered.

Uncertainty plays a key role in many spheres of public and private life. Governments spend large amounts of money and other resources to find out what other governments intend to do in both immediate and long-term futures. Corporations try to reduce their uncertainties about developing economic trends so they can make decisions that will enhance their profits and market shares. In order to accomplish these goals, they purchase the advice of economic forecasters, in spite of the fact that forecasters' predictions frequently err. Individual investors also try to maximize their returns by subscribing to various investment newsletters and by seeking information from investment counselors. Add to this the billions of dollars that are spent each year on insurance policies by both corporations and individuals and it becomes obvious that hedging against potential negative outcomes is also a thriving business (A. M. Best, 1984).

Students of organizational behavior have consistently pointed to the importance of reducing uncertainty for the survival of formal organizations (Katz and Kahn, 1978; March and Simon, 1958). The ubiquity of decision-making under uncertainty in political and economic affairs has led some psychologists to study the heuristics that persons employ to make uncertain choices (Hogarth, 1980;

Kahneman, Slovic and Tversky, 1982); however, personal and social relationships researchers have infrequently employed uncertainty as a focal point for
their research. This relative lack of interest is curious since social and personal
relationships can be highly uncertain arrangements, especially during their
beginnings. Even 'established relationships' can be debilitated or enhanced by
events that increase relational uncertainties. A basic assumption undergirding
this chapter is that the uncertainty construct provides considerable purchase
in understanding the growth, maintenance, and decay of personal and social
relationships.

Another important assumption made in the present chapter is that information exchanged between relationship partners is critical to relationship development. Miell and Duck (1986) have pointed to the importance of information
exchange in relationships and Kellermann (1984b) has demonstrated the usefulness of viewing individual conversations as exchanges of information. Information exchanged through both verbal and nonverbal communication channels
serves as the input that persons use to make critical judgements about their
relational partners; moreover, persons may engage in metarelational talk to
clarify their thinking and feelings about their relationships. However, exchanges
of verbal and nonverbal messages may or may not reduce uncertainties (Berger
and Bradac, 1982). Knowingly or unknowingly, persons may send their
relational partners messages that are inconsistent or otherwise ambiguous, thus
raising uncertainty levels. If one assumes that because of physiological, psychological, and social perturbations individuals are in a perpetual state of change,
it follows that uncertainty reduction is a fairly constant concern in relational
life. Although an imperfect tool for so doing, exchanging information is an
important path to reduced uncertainty. Given the importance of the seeking
and provision of information for relational development, it is possible to view
relationships as information exchange systems that can survive only if their
subsystems can maintain requisite coordination through uncertainty reduction.

This chapter will approach the uncertainty–information exchange relationship
from two perspectives. First, since uncertainty has not received a great deal of
attention from personal relationships researchers, a general review of theories
that explicitly or implicitly deal with uncertainty will be presented. This review
will be followed by a more detailed specification of the roles played by uncertainty and information exchange in developing relationships. The final section
of the chapter will be devoted to a discussion of future research possibilities.

UNCERTAINTY REDUCTION THEORIES

For purposes of this chapter, uncertainty is viewed as the product of the number
of alternatives in a given situation and the relative likelihood of their occurrence.
The greater the number of alternatives and the degree to which alternatives are
equally likely are both related to increased uncertainty. Reductions in the
number of possible alternatives and/or large differences in the relative likelihood of their occurrence produce uncertainty reduction. This view of uncertainty is compatible with that of information theorists (Shannon and Weaver,

1949); however, Berger and Calabrese (1975) have suggested that the ability to predict the actions of one's self or others is only one facet of uncertainty reduction. *Explaining* each other's actions is also critical to the reduction of uncertainty; although, accurate prediction is somewhat easier to achieve than is complete explanation (Berger *et al.*, 1976). The following social–psychological theories are based on this view of uncertainty.

Social Comparison Theory

Some social psychologists have argued that reducing uncertainty is a basic social motive (Berkowitz, 1969). This assumption is explicitly made in Festinger's (1954) social comparison theory and continues to be embraced by more recent social comparison researchers (Suls and Miller, 1977). Festinger (1954) postulated that individuals have a drive to reduce their uncertainties about their abilities and opinions. Persons will employ physical standards against which to compare themselves; however, if such standards are not available, they will compare themselves with other persons. His theory predicted that when engaging in social comparison, persons will choose similar others rather than dissimilar others as comparison standards. Schachter's (1959) experiments examining the relationship between anxiety and affiliation supported the similarity hypothesis; however, later work has not unequivocally confirmed this prediction (Suls and Miller, 1977).

Cognitive Consistency Theories

Cognitive consistency theories (Festinger, 1957; Heider, 1958; Newcomb, 1953; Osgood, Suci and Tannenbaum, 1957; Rosenberg and Abelson, 1960) generally argue that inconsistent cognitions give rise to psychological tension that must be reduced by changes in affect, cognitions or behavior. Inconsistencies create uncertainty by subverting predictions and explanations. Unfortunately, these theories rest on the questionable assumption that cognitive inconsistencies are necessarily aversive. In fact, Berlyne (1960) has argued that novelty is frequently predicated upon inconsistency. Persons may find novelty pleasant and something to be sought. Moreover, consider the fact that irony is based upon unpredictability and irony can be either tragic or humorous. Thus, when cognitions do not fit together, persons may seek to redress aversive inconsistencies or they may try to maintain novel inconsistency for their enjoyment. In any case, cognitive consistency theories assume that persons are motivated to make their beliefs about the world and themselves coherent. This assumption is predicated on the notion that persons seek to reduce uncertainties about themselves and others.

Personal Construct Theory

Kelly's (1955) theory of personal constructs explicitly advances a person-as-intuitive-scientist metaphor. Persons gain an understanding of themselves and

others by filtering raw experience through personal constructs or bipolar dichotomies on which judgements about self and others are made. The salience of
constructs may vary across persons; however, interactants usually share enough
constructs so that their intersubjectivity makes coordinated social intercourse
possible. Persons with complex and well-articulated personal construct systems
are better able to make predictions about others' behaviors and have more
plausible explanations available for others' actions.

Personal construct theory has demonstrated its heuristic value in the study
of relationship development. Duck (1973) reported that personal construct
similarity is a better predictor of friendship formation than attitude similarity,
a frequently studied antecedent to attraction (Byrne, 1971). Although not done
under the rubric of personal construct theory, other research has shown that
similarity along dimensions underlying judgements is a better predictor of such
rationally relevant variables as communication efficiency than are similarities in
judgements made using these dimensions (Padgett and Wolosin, 1980; Runkel,
1956).

Attribution Theories

Attribution research also employs the person-as-intuitive-scientist metaphor.
Heider's (1958) seminal work on causal attribution and later extensions of it
(Jones and Davis, 1965; Kelley, 1967, 1971) attempt to explain how social
perceivers arrive at explanations for the actions of others. Heider (1958) argued
that perceivers could attribute others' actions to such internal factors as ability
or motivation or to external factors like chance or task difficulty. Kelley (1967,
1971) extended this analysis by isolating the informational dimensions responsible for producing attributions to stimuli, persons or circumstances. Different
patterns of distinctiveness, consistency and consensus information determine
whether one of the three types of attributions will be made. Distinctiveness
information refers to the degree of variation in responses that the individual
shows across similar stimuli, while consistency information concerns the occurrence of similar responses by the individual to repeated interactions with the
same stimulus. Consensus information is derived from the responses of a group
of persons responding to the same stimulus. The combination of high distinctiveness, high consistency and high consensus information produces stimulus attributions. Low levels of distinctiveness and consensus coupled with high consistency give rise to person attributions.

Jones and Davis' (1965) correspondent inference theory seeks to specify
the conditions under which observers are likely to judge targets' actions
to be representative of their underlying dispositions. Correspondent inferences suggest strong links between actions and dispositions. Jones and
Davis argue that when targets make choices involving few noncommon effects, behave in socially undesirable ways, engage in out-of-role behavior,
adjust their behavior for the benefit of observers, and engage in actions that
have hedonic relevance to observers, observers will tend to make correspondent
inferences.

Attribution theory has been invoked frequently to explain judgements made in conflict situations (Harvey, Wells and Alvarez, 1978; Kelley, 1979; Orvis, Kelley and Butler, 1976; Sillars, 1980a, 1981). These studies generally show that couples attribute their relational difficulties to negative dispositional attributes possessed by their partners (Kelley, 1979). Since dispositions are perceived to be more immutable than behaviors, it is difficult to alter behaviors given such attributions. Sillars (1980a, 1981) has demonstrated that the kinds of attributions that persons make for conflicts influence the strategies they use to deal with them. Persons who saw themselves as at least somewhat responsible for conflicts reported using such integrative conflict resolution strategies as problem-solving. By contrast, persons who attributed responsibility for conflicts to their partners tended to employ avoidance strategies for conflict resolution; that is, they avoided the person or the issue responsible for the conflict.

While all of these attribution models are uncertainty reduction theories, they have limited utility in predicting and explaining a wide range of phenomena in the domain of personal and social relationships because of their intense individual focus. Hewstone and Jaspars (1984) have pointed out that the attribution-making of individuals in isolation is likely to be considerably different from attributions made in social situations. For example, McArthur (1972, 1976) reported that information about an individual's responses to an array of similar stimuli (distinctiveness information) and information about an individual's response to the same stimulus over repeated presentations (consistency information) exerted more influence upon causal attributions for the individual's responses than did information concerning a number of observers' reactions to the same stimulus (consensus information) (McArthur, 1972, 1976); however, in these studies attributions were formed by individual persons responding to hypothetical scenarios. Hewstone and Jaspars (1984) contend that if persons were asked to make attributions in social contexts, in which group identifications were salient, consensus information would assume a more significant role in determining attributions.

Finally, the adequacy of persons as intuitive scientists has been severely questioned. Considerable research has shown that by using various heuristics, persons' social judgements are frequently biased (Hogarth, 1980; Kahneman, Slovic and Tversky, 1982; Nisbett and Ross, 1980; Ross, 1977). The rather lengthy list of these judgemental biases will not be presented here (see Hogarth, 1980; Nisbett and Ross, 1980 for such lists). However, if these biases are as pervasive and powerful as they are alleged to be, one wonders how it is possible for interactants to coordinate their actions at all. Like attribution research, many of the studies examining judgemental biases have asked individuals to respond to hypothetical scenarios in nonsocial situations. Some biases might not occur in the first place or might be corrected for within the context of ongoing social relationships (Dailey, 1985). Of course, social interactions could also act to exacerbate individual biases. We now turn to theory and research more directly concerned with information exchange and uncertainty reduction in personal and social relationships.

UNCERTAINTY, INFORMATION EXCHANGE, AND RELATIONSHIP DEVELOPMENT

The growth and deterioration of personal relationships are frequently explained by recourse to social exchange constructs (Altman and Taylor, 1973; Blau, 1964; Foa and Foa, 1974; Homans, 1961; Thibaut and Kelley, 1959; Walster, Walster and Berscheid, 1978). These theories generally argue that relationships grow to the extent they are rewarding relative to the degree to which they are costly. When the costs of remaining in relationships increase relative to rewards, pressures for relational dissolution grow. Perceptions of one's own rewards and costs as well as perceptions of one's relationship partner's rewards and costs allegedly enter into computations of relational equity. While these theories provide plausible explanations for relationship growth and decline, there are certain subtleties they overlook. In discussing the roles played by uncertainty and information exchange in relationship development, we will have occasion to consider some problems with these models and some potential solutions to them.

Uncertainty and Relationship Development

Several researchers have noted that the beginnings of personal relationships are fraught with uncertainties (Berger and Calabrese, 1975; Berscheid, 1983; Livingston, 1980; Miell and Duck, 1986; Sternberg, 1986; Thibaut and Kelley, 1959). New employees in formal organizations face a similar plight (Jablin and Krone, 1987; Lester, 1987). Common to initial interaction situations is the problem that interactants may behave and believe in a number of alternative ways making prediction difficult; although, Berger (1987a) has observed that initial interaction rituals involving exchanges of nonevaluative, demographic information concerned with hometown, occupation, and family characteristics are a way of providing predictable communication sequences for interactants beleaguered by mutual uncertainties. Furthermore, the information exchanged during these stereotyped communication episodes can serve as a means for reducing uncertainty. Berger (1975) found that background information exchanged early in initial encounters was used to predict attitudes not yet disclosed by interactants. This information was also used by observers to explain later expressed differences and similarities in opinions. Several studies employing different measures of uncertainty have shown that as interactions and relationships progress, uncertainty tends to decline (Clatterbuck, 1979; Gudykunst, Yang and Nishida, 1985; Lalljee and Cook, 1973; Sherblom and Van Rheenen, 1984); although, Ayres (1979) reported that in interactions between dyads consisting of either strangers or friends, the total number of questions asked was about the same. If question-asking rate is related to uncertainty, Ayres' finding suggests that uncertainty levels in relationships between friends may be relatively high, at least initially. This study also revealed that friends asked significantly more evaluative questions than did strangers, indicating that friends did not ask the more neutral, demographic questions that are typical of stranger interactions.

The findings of these studies point to the kind of subtlety overlooked by social exchange models that was alluded to previously. These studies suggest that persons may spend considerable energy trying to determine the kinds of currency they will employ in their social exchanges and the kinds of outcomes they are likely to experience in the future. Estimates of past, present, and future reward–cost ratios require data. Moreover, a prerequisite for making these estimates is the establishment of a common currency of exchange. If a common currency is not agreed upon, then such calculations become meaningless; unless, of course, there is some way to convert from one currency to another through a rate of exchange. In any case, uncertainty reduction is necessary *before* social exchange calculi can be used to compute outcome values.

Although the above findings appear to be both straightforward and supportive, there are several issues that complicate the relationship between uncertainty and relationship development. First, persons not only attempt to reduce their uncertainties about each other, they also try to reduce their uncertainties about the future of their relationships (Baxter and Wilmot, 1984; Duck and Miell, 1986). The concept of relationship uncertainty is similar to Altman and Taylor's (1973) predicted future rewards and costs and Thibaut and Kelley's (1959) uncertain outcomes. Thus, when we speak of reducing uncertainty in the context of personal relationships, we are referring to both individual and relational uncertainty. A second complication, anticipated by Berger and Bradac (1982), is suggested by Planalp and Honeycutt's (1985) work. These investigators found that persons had little difficulty thinking of events that *increased* their levels of uncertainty about persons they thought they knew well. Competing relationships, unexplained loss of close contact, sexual behavior, deception, change in personality and values, and betraying confidence were such events. All of these events influenced cognitive, affective and communication variables relevant to relationship development. Generally, they had the effect of increasing relational distance or fostering relational termination. Unfortunately, the questions used to elicit uncertainty-increasing events in this study most probably prompted persons to think of negative events. It is possible to have one's uncertainty increased by positive events; for example, a husband who has never sent his wife flowers during their 25-year marriage suddenly does so. Ironically, such unpredicted positive events may raise suspicions concerning the reasons for sudden shows of affection.

A final problem complicating the relationship between uncertainty and relationship development concerns the role played by uncertainty in romantic relationships. Livingston (1980) has argued that persons feel the intense emotions associated with romance precisely because there is some measure of uncertainty in their relationships. As persons come to know each other because they are both more predictable and explainable, the levels of emotion in their relationships decline and romance becomes a fond memory. This line of argument is very similar to one advanced by Berscheid (1982). Employing Mandler's (1975) general theory of emotion, she has asserted that emotions occur when expected action sequences are disrupted. Since there are more disruptions during the early stages of relationships because of lack of predictability, the opportunities for the manifestation of strong emotions are more frequent. Sternberg (1986) has used a similar line of reasoning in discussing the intimacy component of his triangular theory of love.

The analyses presented by Berscheid (1983), Livingston (1980) and Sternberg (1986) create a provocative dialectic regarding the role played by uncertainty reduction in the development of close relationships. On the one hand, uncertainty and unpredictability can create excitement, something at least some persons wish they had more of in their close relationships. On the other hand, relationships must have some degree of predictability in order to remain stable. For example, Parks and Adelman (1983) found that persons in romantic relationships who communicated more frequently with and received more support from members of their romantic partners' social networks showed lower levels of uncertainty about their partners and were less likely to experience breakups. One possible way to deal with the potential conflict created by the opposing vectors of predictability and novelty is to insure high levels of predictability in areas that are central to the functioning of the relationship and to encourage higher levels of unpredictability in areas of peripheral concern to the relationship. Thus, relational partners may need to know absolutely that they will mutually support each other in the event of a serious illness or other life crisis. However, in order to keep some 'romance' in the relationship, positively valenced, unpredictable events may be introduced into the mundane flow of relational life to create positive emotional experiences. A similar dialectic conception has been suggested by Altman, Vinsel and Brown (1981).

While the evidence discussed above suggests a complex relationship between uncertainty as an antecedent and relationship development as a consequent, some research supports an inverse relationship between subjective feelings of uncertainty towards others and their levels of attractiveness (Clatterbuck, 1979; Gudykunst, Yang and Nishida, 1985). However, Gudykunst, Yang and Nishida's (1985) study revealed that attraction is most probably a cause of uncertainty reduction: that is, persons gather more information from liked others than from disliked others. This relationship was replicated among persons from Japan, Korea, and the United States. The causal ordering reported in this study led Berger (1987a) to suggest that early in their relationships, persons may experience affective reactions to partners that are not based upon cognitive analysis (Zajonc, 1980, 1984). These initial affective responses determine whether subsequent attempts will be made to reduce uncertainty. If the decision is made to continue to get to know the other person, affective responses to the partner's verbal and nonverbal inputs will then determine the course of uncertainty reduction.

It is not immediately apparent how social exchange theories might deal with the distinction between affect based upon cognitive analysis and affect involving no inferences. Clearly, the explications of most social exchange theories imply a kind of conscious weighing of rewards and costs in order to arrive at judgements of outcomes or equity. Equally clear is the fact that sometimes persons make these judgements, as well as others, on bases other than conscious calcu-lation (Nisbett and Bellows, 1977; Nisbett and Wilson, 1977; Nisbett and Ross, 1980; Zajonc, 1980, 1984). While this particular issue may lie outside of the boundary conditions of social exchange theories, it does not lie outside of the domain of concern to personal and social relationships researchers. In order to arrive at as complete an explanation as possible for relationship growth and decline, it will be necessary to understand the details of how information exchanged during interactions is transformed into judgements about the desir-ability of continuing relationships. Explaining relational growth and decay simply in terms of relative reward–cost ratios does not provide an explanation for crucial information-to-judgement transformations.

Uncertainty Reduction Strategies

Given the importance of uncertainty reduction to relational stability, it is important to gain some understanding of how persons reduce their uncertainties about others and their relationships with them. I will first review research that has focused upon strategies for reducing uncertainty about individual others and then consider the small amount of research that has addressed the issue of assessing relationships themselves.

Assessing individuals

Berger (1979) and Berger and Bradac (1982) have proposed a typology of uncertainty reduction strategies consisting of three general categories. Using *passive strategies*, persons gather information by unobtrusively observing the target person. There is no interaction between the observer and the target. *Active strategies* also involve no direct interaction between the observer and the target; however, the observer takes measures to acquire information indirectly. Asking third party sources about the target and structuring the environment to see how the target responds to these alterations are some examples of active information acquisition strategies. Finally, *interactive strategies* involve direct interactions between the observer and the target. One might speculate that interactive strategies are superior to the other two types since the observer can probe the target based upon feedback the observer receives. However, this argument ignores the possibility that during face-to-face interactions, targets may engage in deception or impression management in order to lead the observer to erroneous conclusions. By contrast, passive and active strategies are considerably less likely to produce such reactivity, assuming, of course, that targets are unaware that they are under scrutiny.

Several studies have revealed a number of information-gathering strategies within each of these three broad categories. Within the passive observation context, a series of multidimensional scaling investigations, employing slide pictures of target persons in various social and solitary situations, found that observers consistently employed a social activity dimension in making judge-ments of the information value of the situations for telling them something about the target persons (Berger and Douglas, 1981; Berger and Perkins, 1978, 1979). These studies demonstrated the observers judge social situations in which the target person is actively involved with others to be more informative than noninteractive social situations or solitary situations. In addition, Berger and Douglas (1981) reported that when observers anticipated interaction with the target person, they showed increased preferences for slides depicting the target in informal as opposed to formal situations. These findings suggest that in passive information-gathering contexts, observers prefer to watch targets in situations where their behavior is likely to be disinhibited and more variable. These observation conditions should tend to maximize uncertainty reduction.

Although the above studies focused upon observational strategies that individuals use to reduce their uncertainties, Berger and Calabrese (1975) suggested that the social context itself might act to reduce uncertainty about the persons present in it. For example, individuals attending a rally for a political candidate might be supporters of the candidate and hold specific opinions on a number of issues. In this context, persons meeting for the first time might circumvent initial interaction rituals and begin a conversation focused upon the political candidate and the issues surrounding the election; under other conditions, such topics would only be discussed after considerable interaction. Rubin (1977, 1979) formally tested these predictions and found that when interacting in an ambiguous context, initial interactants asked more questions and more background questions than initial interactants in a less ambiguous context. Moreover, interactions in the ambiguous context lasted significantly longer than those in a less ambiguous context. These findings demonstrate that attributes of the interaction situation itself can aid in the reduction of uncertainty.

Active strategies involving observations of targets' responses to environmental alterations have received little research attention to date; however, some research has investigated how persons evaluate information about target persons that is provided by third party sources (Doelger, Hewes and Graham, 1986; Hewes et al., 1985; Hewes and Planalp, 1982). Hewes et al. (1985) found that both college and noncollege respondents reported that they obtained approximately 30 per cent of their information about persons in their social networks from third party sources. While the respondents indicated that directly obtained information was generally more useful than information provided by third party sources, indirectly obtained information was judged to be 'somewhat useful'. These respondents also showed a high level of awareness of the possibility that information acquired from third party sources might be biased in some way. Moreover, 71 per cent of the respondents claimed that they could debias the indirectly obtained information. Doelger, Hewes and Graham (1986) reported a typology of cues that might induce consumers of indirectly obtained information to engage in 'second guessing'. They also found that when these cues were presented with messages, receivers became more vigilant for the presence of bias in the message. These studies suggest that under some conditions, persons will prevent themselves from being misled by biased information from third party sources.

Considerable research has attempted to ferret out information acquisition strategies used in interactions between observers and targets. Berger and Kellermann (1983) found that persons employed interrogation, self-disclosure, and relaxing the target as ways of acquiring information. In addition, they suggested that these strategies could be ordered with respect to their *efficiency* and *social appropriateness*. Interrogation is perhaps the most efficient but potentially most intrusive of the three strategies, while relaxing the target is the most appropriate but least efficient. In their study of the relaxation strategy, Kellermann and Berger (1984) found that persons instructed to acquire as much information as they could from their conversational partner used a number of verbal and nonverbal means to present a positive impression of themselves. Their findings suggest that information-seekers may try to counterbalance their intrusive question-asking with more socially appropriate behaviors. Berger and Kellermann (1985) examined the tactics that persons employ to thwart others' information-seeking attempts. They discovered two distinct classes of thwarting tactics: offensive and defensive. Offensive tactics involved dominating the floor in order to keep the conversational focus away from the self. Defensive tactics included making ambiguous statements and increasing hesitations. Finally, Berger and Kellermann (1986) examined how information seekers respond to thwarting from targets. This study revealed that information seekers did not alter their question-asking rates in response to their reticent partners. Rather, they encouraged their evasive partners by interrupting them less, increasing their frequency of backchannel responses, and decreasing the numbers of statements focused on themselves. Thus, strategies were accreted as the interactions progressed rather than being deployed and abandoned in a serial manner.

The research done on individual strategies generally suggests that information seekers have a wide variety of information-gaining tactics available to them and when appropriate cues are present, they can become sensitive to the possibility that information they are receiving is in some way biased. Furthermore, it appears that social information gatherers believe they can debias tainted information. These findings indicate that naive social actors and actresses may be somewhat more sophisticated at acquiring and evaluating information than some have argued (Hogarth, 1980; Nisbett and Ross, 1980).

Assessing relationships

Especially in the early stages of developing relationships, persons may want to know how their partners view their relationships. This information is most likely used to decide whether one wishes to escalate or deescalate one's level of commitment to the relationship. Baxter and Wilmot (1984) have studied the strategies that persons employ to reduce their uncertainties concerning their partner's level of commitment to the relationship. They labeled these strategies 'secret tests' and studied their deployment in opposite-sex relationships. They identified the following types of tests: (1) asking third parties, (2) triangles (jealousy), (3) directness tests (asking direct questions), (4) separation tests (not interacting), (5) endurance tests (testing limits, self-putdown), (6) public presentation (presenting partner to others), and (7) indirect suggestion (joking, hinting). Baxter and Wilmot (1984) found that these secret tests could be classified into the passive, active, and interactive strategy categories discussed earlier. The use of these tests was found to vary in platonic, potentially romantic, and romantic relationships. Moreover, females provided more secret tests than did males, suggesting that females may be more inclined to perform such tests.

Comment

While the work done on information acquisition strategies is useful both theoretically and practically, like much of the research examining communication strategies of various kinds it suffers from *lack of a theoretical perspective*. One can imagine the nightmare of being buried in an avalanche of strategies with little in the way of conceptual machinery to explain why particular strategies are employed over others in different contexts. Moreover, studies of strategies-in-use generally ignore the issue of the mechanisms responsible for the production of strategic communication behavior. This issue, as well as others concerning uncertainty reduction and information exchange, will be considered in the next section dealing with future research directions.

FUTURE RESEARCH DIRECTIONS

In this final section, I first consider theoretical issues surrounding the production of strategic communicative conduct. Attention will then be turned to a reexamination of the person-as-intuitive-scientist metaphor as a guide to uncertainty reduction research and theory development.

Planning and Strategic Communication

Within the context of developing relationships, persons seek to achieve a number of different social goals. In this chapter I have focused upon information acquisition and uncertainty reduction; however, there are several others, including ingratiation (Jones, 1964; Jones and Wortman, 1973), affinity-seeking (Bell and Daly, 1984; Douglas, 1987), relational disengagement (Baxter, 1982), and compliance-gaining (see Berger, 1985 for review). One possible way of developing a conceptual framework to explain the fabrication and deployment of these varied strategies is suggested by the text-processing literature. A number of researchers working in this area have recognized that knowledge structures vital for both text comprehension and production are organized around goals and the plans that persons use to achieve them (Bruce, 1980; Cohen and Perrault, 1979; Hayes-Roth and Hayes-Roth, 1979; Schank and Abelson, 1977; Schmidt, 1976; Wilensky, 1983). Hobbs and Evans (1980) have shown how conversations can be modeled from a planning perspective and Bruce (1980) has argued that plan and goal recognition are critical for story comprehension.

Berger (1987b, 1988) and Berger and Bell (1986) have examined persons' plans for achieving such goals as asking another person for a date and ingratiating one's self to a new roommate. Berger (1988) found that persons with more sophisticated plans for date-requesting showed significantly fewer signs of nervousness (as measured by adaptor durations) when asking for a date than did persons with less well developed date-asking plans. Berger and Bell (1986) reported that males with more sophisticated and effective plans for date-requesting and new roommate ingratiation were significantly less shy than males with less sophisticated plans in these two domains. No relationships between the planning variables and shyness were found for females. These findings indicate that when persons lack the conceptual sophistication in a planning domain, they become uncertain about how they should act when attempting to achieve a goal in that domain, especially when the goal is central to their social life. This lack of certainty is reflected in their overt behavior during particular interactions (nervousness) and the long-term effects of this uncertainty apparently produce feelings of shyness.

Although these initial findings are encouraging, they do not constitute a theory of planning. Wilensky (1983) has begun to develop such a theory and Berger (1987b, 1988) has outlined several phenomena such a theory must explain. First, a planning theory needs to deal with the problem of how goals arise and how they change during the course of ongoing interaction sequences. Second, it must explain how plans are assembled and modified in the face of changing goals and failures to reach goals. Third, a useful planning theory has to deal with the issue of what happens when plans are unavailable for the pursuit of goals. Fourth, such a theory needs to deal with the process of transforming plans into action sequences and how these transformations and action sequences are monitored. A theory explaining these aspects of the planning process would bring considerable order to the arbitrary way in which strategies research is currently being conceived and conducted.

Persons-As-Intuitive-Scientists Revisited

As interest in attribution theory has waned and been replaced by a more skeptical view of persons' abilities to generate veridical judgements of themselves and others (Hogarth, 1980; Kahneman, Slovic and Tversky, 1982; Nisbett and Ross, 1980; Ross, 1977), the person-as-intuitive-scientist metaphor has begun to slip away. In the midst of the 'gold rush' to the lodes of cognitive psychology, it is important to remain mindful of the insights provided by hoary texts. As we have seen, the information acquisition strategies research in general and the 'second guessing' research in particular suggest that persons may be more critical consumers of social information than some have suggested. It appears that persons may be able to adjust their judgements for a variety of potential biases. If one is willing to continue to entertain the person-as-intuitive-scientist metaphor as a heuristic for social and personal relationships research, there are a number of interesting and important research questions that can be asked.

Persons-as-intuitive-social experimenters

In discussing active strategies of information acquisition, it was suggested that persons may perform informal experiments to find out things about their relationship partners. Observers might intentionally shift moods or opinions to see how targets respond, or observers might arrange the physical setting of the interaction to test the reactions of targets. Under this view, observers' actions are independent variables and targets' responses dependent variables. There is the possibility for information seekers to perform quasi-experiments in which their ability to control relevant variables is limited. If this kind of informal experimentation takes place, there are a number of potentially interesting questions that can be asked about it. First, are naive social experimenters sensitive to the issue of experimental control: that is, do they establish stable and meaningful baselines against which they assess change? Are persons sensitive to the differences between baselines provided by within-subjects and between-subjects designs? Second, are persons aware of the possibility that their independent variable manipulations may interact with other variables to produce differential effects under different conditions? Are they sensitive to both main effects and interaction effects? Third, are naive experimenters alert to the possibility that events unknown to them may act to bias targets' responses in a particular direction? Fourth, do social experimenters perform the equivalent of manipulation checks to see whether their partners actually perceived the intended variations in their actions? Fifth, do observers use confederates to help them operationalize their manipulations? Finally, are naive experimenters likely to attach different weights to significant and nonsignificant differences?

Although Kelley's (1967) discussion of attribution principles speaks to the importance of covariation assessment in the process of causal attribution, he does not deal specifically with the kinds of issues raised above. Furthermore, Nisbett and Ross's (1980) review of literature indicating the apparent inabilities of social perceivers to consider all relevant information when making covariation judgements does not directly address the issues raised above. Within the context of relatively uninvolving, paper-and-pencil, problem-solving situations, persons may not make covariation judgements that are based upon all relevant information; however, when persons wish to acquire information about others either directly or indirectly, they may perform the kinds of informal experiments outlined above with useful results.

Persons-as-intuitive-samplers

A cornerstone assumption in the conduct of survey research is that in order to generate potentially accurate estimates of population parameters, one must first have a representative sample of the population to which one wishes to generalize. One way to increase the likelihood of obtaining a representative sample of the population is to sample elements randomly from that population. The parameter estimation problems faced by persons trying to come to know others are similar to those faced by the survey researcher. One point of difference is that the survey researcher is interested in estimating parameters for a group of persons, while individuals want to know specific values of certain critical variables for their relationship partners. For example, persons may wish to know how kind, trustworthy, happy, and considerate their potential long-term relationship partners are.

The problem faced by naive samplers is one of the adequacy of the behavioral samples on which they base their inferences about dispositional characteristics of their relationship partners. This problem is not unlike the one attacked by Jones and Davis (1965) in their correspondent inference theory; however, the present approach to this problem raises a series of questions that differs from those dealt with by Jones and Davis (1965). For example, in sampling the behavior of others, do persons simply focus upon the sheer number of observations as a basis for assessing sample adequacy or are they also concerned with the representativeness of the sample units as well? One can 'know' a person for a long time and take numerous samples of behavior; however, if these samples are all gathered in one social context, for example a job, the representativeness of the samples will be questionable, a situation akin to the 1936 *Literary Digest* poll. Large but unrepresentative behavior samples probably give rise to such comments as, 'I never would have guessed that he/she was like that', that are heard when someone who is 'known well' to others does something out of character.

It is of special importance to persons in the process of forming long-term relationships to gather behavioral samples from their partners in situations where their partners are likely to be at their worst rather than their best. Typically, first meetings have a positivity bias operating in them: that is, persons try to be on their best behavior. Furthermore, when persons begin to date, there is also a tendency for them to try to present themselves in the most favorable light possible. Behavioral samples gathered under these conditions are likely to reflect this positivity bias and thus yield distorted estimates of important underlying dispositional parameters. It is when persons are frustrated in trying to achieve goals or when they receive negative news that their positive self-presentations begin to crumble. Observations made under these conditions, when combined with those made under more positive circumstances, are likely to yield more accurate estimates of the values of important underlying dispositional variables than observations made under only one of the two conditions.

In parameter estimation procedures, one not only wishes to make a point estimate but also seeks to establish a confidence interval around that estimate. As the width of the confidence interval increases, one is more confident that the true population value is somewhere within the interval. Reducing the width of a confidence interval reduces the level of confidence one has that the true population value is bracketed by the confidence interval. Of course, when persons observe the behavior of others over protracted periods of time and across heterogeneous situations, they are likely to see considerable variability in dispositionally diagnostic behaviors. Nevertheless, we assume that persons make a kind of point estimate and attach to it an intuitive confidence interval. These possibilities raise a number of potential questions. Are persons sensitive to the relationship between confidence level and interval width in making personal estimates? Are they aware of the possibility that their confidence interval will not bracket the true dispositional value? Do they take into account the relationship between sample size and interval width? Again, these kinds of questions are related to dispositional attribution issues but go beyond the purview of correspondent inference theory.

Persons-as-intuitive-psychometricians

Classical test theory teaches us that the reliability and validity of measures are two critical indicators of their adequacy. Reliability refers to the consistency with which a measure indexes objects, while validity raises the question of whether the measure actually indexes the construct it is purported to measure. High reliability is a prerequisite for validity; however, high reliability is not a sufficient condition for validity. The question considered here is whether persons informally assess the reliability and validity of their observations of others.

Kelley's (1967) attribution analysis suggests that consistent responses to the same stimulus over time strongly influence observers' causal attributions. While consistency information has been found to be an important determinant of the direction of causal attributions (McArthur, 1972), there are additional questions that can be raised about naive reliability analysis. First, we have already considered the problem of behavior sampling. In assessing behavioral consistency over time it is critical to have data points collected across a large number of heterogeneous situations. If a person is consistently friendly through time and across situations, we should be more certain that the person has a friendly disposition. Second, do indicators of a construct give consistent readings of the attribute being estimated? This question is similar to the one answered when an item analysis of a test is performed. If observers employ such empirical indicators as smiling, gesticulation rate, and talkativeness to estimate a target's friendliness, do these indicators all give similar readings? What happens to estimated friendliness if they do not? Can persons provide intuitive estimates of the internal consistency of indicators?

In a sense, correspondent inference theory (Jones and Davis, 1965) addresses questions similar to those raised in naive validity analysis. Do empirical indicators of assumed dispositions actually measure what they are purported to measure? Jones and Davis' analysis isolates the variables responsible for judgements of correspondence or noncorrespondence. Again, however, there are additional issues that go beyond the bounds of their analysis. Do observers try to validate their measurements of others by performing the equivalent of predictive validity studies? Are observers likely to disregard indices that fail to predict actions? Do observers attempt to validate judgements through a naive version of a construct validation procedure in which they look for theoretically specified relationships among a number of variables? Are observers sensitive to the problems associated with reactivity of measurement? This particular problem should be acute when interactive information acquisition strategies are employed.

CONCLUSION

The acquisition, processing, retention, and retrieval of information is vital to the growth, maintenance, and decline of personal and social relationships. Relationships can be viewed as systems of information exchange that must reduce uncertainty in order to survive. This chapter has outlined how variations in uncertainty influence relational growth. It has also considered several uncertainty reduction theories as well as strategies for reducing uncertainty. As has been pointed out, the recent trend in social cognition research has been to provide demonstrations of the information-processing limitations of social actors and actresses. While such limitations are no doubt real and in some instances dramatic, the abilities of persons to develop and maintain friendships, marriages and other close relationships for protracted periods of time, as well as their abilities to carry out numerous nonintimate interactions in their everyday lives, suggest that the social consequences of these biases have been overestimated considerably.

This chapter has advanced the view that persons have available to them both cognitive and communicative strategies that can help them reduce their uncertainties and overcome some of their information-processing limitations. These communication strategies can be deployed in ongoing social interaction situations, but cannot be used in trying to cope with simulated situations presented on paper. In a very real sense, many of the most powerful strategies for reducing uncertainty are taken away from subjects when they are presented with paper-and-pencil decision-making problems. Passive, active, and interactive information acquisition strategies, 'second-guessing', and the intuitive application of social science methodology are all imperfect methods of gaining and evaluating information. However, the facts of social organization, coordinated social interaction, and enduring social relationships suggest that, more often than not, they work.

A Handbook of Personal Relationships
Edited by S. W. Duck
© 1988 John Wiley & Sons Ltd

14

A Dialectical Perspective on Communication Strategies in Relationship Development

LESLIE A. BAXTER
Lewis and Clark College, Portland, Oregon, USA

ABSTRACT

Dialectical theory provides the framework for discussing the research literature in relationship strategies, i.e. the communicative actions by which parties establish, maintain, and
dissolve their personal relationships. The strategic management of three basic contradictions
(autonomy–connection, novelty–predictability, openness–closedness) is discussed for each of
four dialectical phases of relationship development.

For the last decade, I have been attempting to identify the strategic communicative actions by which personal relationships are constituted, maintained, and
disengaged. I have shared my own research and that of fellow relationship
theorists and researchers in many classrooms during this period of time. Many
of my students react to this body of research and theory as I myself have come
to regard it: a somewhat sterile portrait stripped of many of the complexities
we often experience in our relationships—their paradoxes, inconsistencies, and
contradictions. The purpose of this chapter is to advance a dialectical approach
to the study of personal relationships, a perspective which emphasizes the utility
of studying relationship contradictions. In turn, this dialectical framework will
provide the foundation for examining the relationship strategies research.

Although threads of dialectical thinking have emerged among several
relationship theorists and researchers (e.g. Altman, Vinsel and Brown, 1981;
Bochner, 1984), a whole theoretical cloth has yet to be woven which advances
a dialectical theory of relationships. This essay does not pretend to be such a

theoretical cloth, but it does attempt to bring together disparate threads of dialectical thought in order to examine the relationship strategies literature.

Despite the multiplicity of meanings with which the term 'dialectic' has been used, the two features that are common across various dialectical theories are *process* and *contradiction* (Cornforth, 1968). The centrality of the process concept to dialectical thinking leads to a theoretical interest in development in contrast to a focus on static or stable states of being. Such development is not limited in the instance of relationships to the opening phase of a relationship's history but occurs throughout a relationship's entire history. Change, in turn, is caused by the struggle and tension of contradiction. A contradiction is formed whenever two tendencies or forces are interdependent (the dialectical principle of unity) yet mutually negate one another (the dialectical principle of negation).

A dialectical approach to personal relationships provides a relationship-level perspective to complement the individual-level theories which dominate the personal relationships literature—social penetration (Altman and Taylor, 1973), its parent theory of social exchange (Roloff, 1981), and uncertainty reduction theory (Berger and Bradac, 1982). These latter theories share the assumption that relationship dynamics can be explained adequately by understanding the individuals who comprise the relationship. Theoretical frustration with this atomistic orientation is a frequently expressed complaint in the relationship communication literature; however, the relationships field still displays a paucity of genuine relationship-level theories. Although the dialectical contradictions described below are experienced and acted upon by the individual parties, they are situated *in the relationship* between the parties. These basic dialectical oppositions or tensions form the exigence for communicative action between the parties and constitute the basis of change and development in the relationship.

Given that the dominant theories of relationship development are located at the individual level, it is not surprising that the relationship strategies research commonly conceptualizes a 'strategy' as action by which the individual accomplishes his/her goals. Given this markedly individualistic orientation, relationship strategies researchers assume the burden of understanding and explaining individual motives and how those translate into action plans and interaction procedures (see Berger in this volume). In contrast, from a relationship-level perspective, a 'strategy' is conceived less in terms of individual goal achievement and more in terms of its efficacy in response to situational press, in this instance dialectical contradictions. The difference in perspective is subtle but important. The individualistic perspective heads one down the theoretic path of cognitive psychology, whereas a relationship perspective such as dialectical theory focuses attention outwards on the relational situation.

The remainder of this chapter is organized into four sections. The first posits basic dialectical contradictions that comprise personal relationships. The second presents a typology of strategies that are responsive to dialectical contradictions. Section three examines the relationship strategies research through this dialectical lens. Fourth and finally, implications for future research are presented.

BASIC CONTRADICTIONS IN PERSONAL RELATIONSHIPS

Given that relationships are processes of change produced by the clash of opposing tendencies, what exactly are the basic contradictions of relational life? Three bipolar pairs can be identified which meet the conditions of both unity and negation, thus constituting dialectical contradictions. As discussed below, personal relationships require both autonomy and connection, both novelty and predictability, and both openness and closedness. Further, the poles of a given pair mutually negate one another as logical opposites. Dialectical theorists attempt to identify the basic or principal contradiction around which a web of secondary contradictions coheres. In the context of personal relationships, the principal contradiction is autonomy vs connection, with the two remaining opposing pairs serving as secondary contradictions.

The Centrality of the Autonomy–Connection Dialectic

This contradiction is so central to the essence of relationships on definitional grounds alone that it can be regarded as the principal contradiction. No relationship can exist by definition unless the parties sacrifice some individual autonomy. However, too much connection paradoxically destroys the relationship because the individual identities become lost (Askham, 1976). Simultaneously, an individual's autonomy can be conceptualized only in terms of separation from others. But too much autonomy paradoxically destroys the individual's identity, because connections with others are the 'stuff' of which identity is made (Lock, 1986). The tension between autonomy and connection appears to be phenomenologically real to people as they reflect on their own relationship experiences, surfacing as an underlying theme in recollected relationship turning points (Baxter and Bullis, 1986), in recollected ambivalence about committing to the relational partner (Braiker and Kelley, 1979), and in verbalized reflections about what their relationships are like (Carbaugh, 1984; Rawlins, 1983a). The question for this chapter is how the autonomy–connection dialectic is communicatively managed in relationship development.

The Novelty–Predictability Dialectic

Whether one consults uncertainty reduction theory (Berger and Bradac, 1982) or pragmatic systems theory (Fisher, 1978), the necessity of predictability and pattern in relationships is well recognized. However, equally necessary for relationships is the opposite quality of novelty or unpredictability (see Berger in this volume). Pragmatic systems theorists refer to a dysfunctional condition known as 'schismogenesis', which can occur with overly rigidified, i.e. predictable, interaction (Fisher, 1978). Learning theorists recognize the declining affective arousal and the ultimate emotional deadening of a relationship that can occur when patterns are overly repeated and predictable (Kelvin, 1977). In short, relationships require both novelty and predictability, leaving relationship parties a challenging dilemma with which to cope.

The Openness–Closedness Dialectic

A relationship's need for both information openness and information closedness
has been noted by several relationship theorists (e.g. Altman, Vinsel and
Brown, 1981; Bochner, 1984; LaFollette and Graham, 1986). Open disclosure
between the relationship parties is a necessary condition for intimacy, but
openness creates vulnerabilities either for oneself, the other, or the relationship
that necessitate information closedness (Rawlins, 1983b). This dilemma not
only occurs in the private communication between relationship parties but
surfaces as well in the public presentation of the relationship to others. On the
one hand, the parties require privacy or information closedness from others to
establish intimacy. On the other hand, the relationship requires public recognition, which necessitates information openness (Leslie, Huston and Johnson,
1986). As with the other contradictions reviewed here, the relationship parties
must grapple with this difficult dilemma of openness–closedness through their
strategic communicative choices.

These three contradictions probably do not exhaust the set of dialectical
dilemmas which face relationship parties. Further, they have been discussed
separately from one another for ease of presentation, but in actuality they form
an interdependent web, as becomes evident in the following section.

STRATEGIC RESPONSES TO CONTRADICTION

What constitutes a strategic response to contradiction? The typology of strategies suggested below draws heavily upon two research programs technically
outside the domain of relationships research (O'Keefe and Delia, 1982; Bavelas,
1985). The first strategy is one of *selection*, in which relationship parties repeatedly select actions consistent with one polarity of the contradiction. Strategic
selection produces a dialectical transformation, with the selected polarity
emerging as the dominant condition. Fitzpatrick's (1984) married traditionals,
for example, appear to have employed the selection strategy in favor of connection, in contrast to the married types of separates and independents, who appear
to have employed selection in the direction of autonomy.

The second strategy type, temporal/spatial separation, can take two forms.
Relationship parties can attempt to respond to each polarity of a given contradiction at separate points in time, constituting the strategy of *cyclic alternation*.
Altman, Vinsel and Brown (1981), for example, posit that the openness–closedness dialectic is managed with this strategy, resulting in relationship interaction characterized through time by alternating high disclosure and high privacy.
The second form of this general strategy type is labelled *segmentation*, as the
relationship parties distinguish mutually exclusive activity or content domains,
each of which is responsive to one pole of a given contradiction. The openness–closedness dialectic, for instance, would be managed through segmentation
if the parties targeted certain topics as appropriate for open disclosure and
other topics as inappropriate for disclosure.

The final strategy type, integration, involves the attempt to respond simultaneously to both opposing tendencies in a contradiction. Three forms of this complex strategic type can be identified. The strategy of *integrative moderation* involves the use of neutralized messages which are biased towards neither polarity in a given contradiction. The small talk ritual in initial encounters illustrates nicely the moderation strategy. The strategy of *integrative disqualification* involves ambiguous or indirect communicative acts which avoid the explicit engagement of either polarity. Bavelas and her colleagues (Bavelas, 1985) have identified four dimensions of disqualification: content ambiguity over what is being said; speaker ambiguity concerning whose voice is being represented; target ambiguity over who is addressed in the message; and context ambiguity concerning what in the situation prompted the message. The final form of this general strategy type is *integrative reframing*, in which the parties attempt to redefine the contradiction and thereby transcend it. For example, a couple who redefine autonomy and connection such that the poles are no longer conceived as oppositional have enacted the reframing strategy.

It is difficult for several reasons to look to existing relationship strategies research to determine whether selection, cyclic alternation, segmentation, integrative moderation, integrative disqualification, and/or integrative reframing are present. The first obstacle in existing strategies research is the failure to collect truly dialectical data, i.e. simultaneous data about both polarities. Consider the openness–closedness contradiction as a basis of illustration. As Baxter and Wilmot (1985) have observed in their study of 'taboo topics' in relationships, scores on self-disclosure measures do not necessarily inform us about the dynamics of information closedness. Without dual information on openness and closedness, it is difficult to determine with confidence whether selection, cyclic alternation, and/or segmentation strategies are present. At best, the typical relationship strategies study considers but a single polarity of a single contradiction.

A second dialectically based criticism of extant relationship strategies research is its failure to collect longitudinal strategies data. Instead, 'one-shot' data are collected in which respondents indicate what strategy they would use or have used at a single point in time in order to accomplish some specified goal. The difficulty with this becomes evident in the example of openness–closedness. If a strategy of open disclosure is reported, for example, it might simply be a 'peak' of openness in a larger cyclic pattern in which periods of high openness are followed by periods of high closedness and *vice versa* (Altman, Vinsel and Brown, 1981). Data collected at but a single point in time preclude the researcher from differentiating selection modes of response from cyclic alternation modes.

Admittedly, several studies have collected longitudinal data on openness or self-disclosure (e.g. Hays, 1985). Unfortunately, variation in openness within a given relationship has generally been reduced to grist for the statistical least squares mill. If a best fitting line is fit to a cyclic alternation curve which plots variation in openness, the result will likely be a simple linear relationship stripped of cyclic 'bumps'. Reducing the data in this way ignores the pattern of sequential variations in openness from one encounter to another, or from one strategic choice to another within a single encounter, and thus ignores as well the cyclic alternation response mode.

A third problem with existing research on relationship strategies is the relative crudeness with which strategies are studied. Strategies reduced to descriptors such as 'encourage responsiveness in the other', for example, lack the fine-grained linguistic data which are especially useful in detecting the three integration strategies.

Despite the limitations of existing relationship strategies research, it can be usefully considered from a dialectical perspective. Some of the research is suggestive of how dialectical contradictions are managed, and productive directions for future research can be raised in examining extant work through a dialectical lens.

STRATEGIC ACTION IN DIALECTICAL PHASES OF RELATIONSHIP DEVELOPMENT

I have opted to organize the discussion of the relationship strategies research around what I believe are four phases in the principal contradiction of autonomy–connection. In organizing this discussion around autonomy–connection, I am oversimplifying the whole dialectical dynamic in suggesting that the other contradictions are fully synchronized with changes in the autonomy–connection contradiction. Although my hunch is that this tendency exists, I also suspect that there might be substantial departure from lock-step synchrony from relationship to relationship. Moreover, ordering phases numerically from one to four could suggest that all relationships evolve in this sequential manner; such a suggestion also greatly oversimplifies the dialectical process. Finally, it is important to appreciate that a given phase likely has fuzzy beginning and ending boundaries during which the dialectical change occurs. With these caveats in mind, each dialectical phase can now be turned to in more detail.

Phase 1: Autonomy to Connection

This phase is one of mutual exploration as the parties get to know one another and determine whether they want to form an interdependent relationship. Because the management of the secondary dialectical contradictions directly impacts the progress of the autonomy–connection dialectic, it is useful to organize the discussion around the secondary contradictions.

The novelty–predictability dialectic

The dialectically dominant condition during this period is either novelty or predictability, depending on what facet of the relationship is under consideration. At the individual level of analysis, the dominant condition is novelty or unpredictability given the limited information the parties have about each other. As the uncertainty reduction research documents, the relationship parties have a variety of ways of acquiring information about a new acquaintance (see Berger in this volume). From the perspective of the interaction episode, however, the relationship during this period is characterized by the dominance of predictability, not novelty. This predictability occurs through the enactment of initial interaction scripts, i.e. highly structured interaction routines characterized by stock topics and actions (Douglas, 1984).

Paradoxically, predictability present in the enactment of structured, stock routines is likely to jeopardize uncertainty reduction at the individual level. If all the other party does is follow social scripts, one gains little insight into the other as an individual. If one also follows initial interaction scripts, the very information acquisition strategies necessary to acquire information about the other may not be employed (Kellermann, 1984a). Thus, some novelty in the form of deviation from the narrow scripts of initial interaction seems necessary. But if one does violate scripts and seeks information by excessive questioning or self-disclosure, the other party is likely to regard this as a violation of expected initial interaction routines and become even more hesitant to reveal information. Similarly, if the other departs significantly from initial scripts in revealing information, he or she is likely to be perceived negatively rather than accurately.

Unfortunately, as Kellermann (1984a) has noted, we have too little baseline knowledge about the expected and actual behaviors of initial interaction to understand how relationship parties cope interactively with this dialectical tension between novelty at the level of the person and predictability at the level of the interaction episode. However, existing relationship strategies research is suggestive of some response modes over others. The prevalence of the small talk ritual illustrates creative management of this contradiction through the strategy of integrative moderation. Small talk is ritualized activity, yet the parties have some modest opportunity to reveal unique information about themselves. The strategy of integrative disqualification is employed as well, given the work on indirectness summarized below in reference to the openness–closedness dialectic. In addition, it seems reasonable that relationship parties over time might employ the strategy of cyclic alternation, interspersing novel encounters rich in personality insights with the safety of routinized interaction scripts. Further, relationship parties might employ the strategy of segmentation, freeing up certain domains of their relational life for experimentation while maintaining highly scripted encounters in other domains.

The openness–closedness dialectic

Management of the novelty–predictability dialectic obviously implicates the openness–closedness contradiction. Maximum openness through high self-disclosure, for instance, would achieve uncertainty reduction at the person level during this initial relationship phase while constituting a novel departure from the scripts of initial interaction. In general, the relationship strategies research suggests that relationship parties are hesitant to make openness dominant over closedness in this initial interaction phase. Rather, the dialectical strategies of integrative moderation, segmentation, and integrative disqualification appear evident.

As noted above, initial interaction scripts illustrate the dialectical strategy of integrative moderation in maintaining a delicate balance in the novelty–predictability contradiction. Such scripts also illustrate integrative moderation in managing the openness–closedness dialectic. Relationship parties engage in superficial self-disclosure activity, thereby demonstrating a willingness to be open without jeopardizing the safety of closedness about self.

The dialectical strategy of segmentation also appears to be employed by relationship parties during this phase. Certain topics can be discussed openly, whereas other topics are implicitly left closed. Negatively valenced information about self is left unstated, but so is explicit self-presentation about one's most favorable attributes for fear of reaping a negative reaction to perceived self-promotion (Godfrey, Jones and Lord, 1986). Similarly left unstated is one's liking for the other party as a potential relationship party (Baxter and Bullis, 1986). Although the other party can be encouraged to engage in meaningful self-disclosure, one is also socially limited in the amount and kinds of information which can be directly solicited about the other.

The fact that some information cannot be expressed openly does not mean that parties are prevented from its acquisition. Rather, the parties opt for indirect strategies, i.e. integrative disqualification. Prevented from self-promotion, relationship parties demonstrate indirectly through their actions that they are likeable. So-called affinity-seeking is accomplished by a variety of indirect strategies (Bell and Daly, 1984). For example, through their conversational style alone, parties can demonstrate that they are: trusting of others by engaging in confiding behavior; adaptable to others by keeping to the rules of conversation and granting control to the other as appropriate; similar to the other by expressing agreement; and trustworthy by keeping the other's confidences.

Indirectness is employed as well in signaling one's liking for the other party. A variety of indirect signaling strategies have been noted in the literature, all of which involve either the rendering of explicit reward, efforts to be in the other's physical presence, or displays of concern and supportiveness for the other's wants and needs (Baxter and Philpott, 1982; Bell and Daly, 1984; Brown and Levinson, 1978).

Also subject to indirect strategic action is acquisition of information about what the other party is 'really like'. Information about the other party is sought actively from his or her network associates, constituting one of the most valuable sources of information during this initial dialectical phase (Parks and Adelman, 1983). Paradoxically, however, seeking information from the other party's network may forsake relational privacy through public recognition that one is forming a relationship with the other party. Thus, an attempt to avoid openness internally in the relationship may entail openness externally to others.

If the parties navigate this maze of contradictions and emerge with the desire to become interdependent beyond casual acquaintanceship, the autonomy–connection dialectical contradiction has experienced a transformation to connection as the dominant condition.

Phase 2: Autonomy and Connection

It is one thing for relationship parties to make a mental or social commitment to interdependence and quite another to work out the details of precisely what this interdependence will entail. This second phase reflects the 'working out' of the details of connection, particularly with regard to its implications for the individual selves in the relationship. How much freedom will the individual parties have outside the relationship? What rights and responsibilities will the individuals have to themselves, to one another, and to the relationship?

This phase is often characterized by ambivalence in the relationship parties as they wonder whether or not they are making a mistake in forming a bond with one another (Braiker and Kelley, 1979; Huston *et al.*, 1981; Lloyd and Cate, 1985a). Correlated with this ambivalence is an increase in conflict and instability between the partners. Ambivalence, conflict, and instability set the scene for the two secondary dialectical contradictions to reappear in this phase in somewhat different form than during the initial dialectical phase.

The novelty–predictability dialectic

Ambivalence and its companions of conflict and instability mandate a need for predictability. However, unlike the predictability of knowing the other as an individual which drives phase one, this phase deals with a qualitatively different order of predictability, i.e. certainty about the state of the relationship. Several dialectical strategies are employed by relationship parties in an attempt to realize predictability as the dominant condition over novelty. Integrative disqualification, or indirectness, is probably the foremost way in which parties attempt to gain predictability over the state of the relationship. Because indirectness engages the issue of openness, it is discussed below under the openness–closedness dialectic.

In addition to their indirect efforts, relationship parties in this phase of the autonomy–connection dialectic initiate a variety of symbols and rituals which strategically lend predictability to the relationship. Relationship parties develop a private code of idiomatic expressions, including, among others, nicknames, affection phrases, sexual codewords, and private jokes (Hopper, Knapp and Scott, 1981). But such tokens of the relationship's intimate private culture are not limited to linguistic idioms. In a recent study of friendship and romantic relationship symbols, Baxter (1987a) found a rich domain of physical objects, songs, movies, special memories, special places, and nonlinguistic behavioral rituals which the parties identified as symbolic of their respective relationships. Trivial and insignificant to an outsider, these relationship symbols and rituals segment certain facets of the relationship as sources of predictability (Baxter, 1987a; Bochner, 1984; Oring, 1984). Such symbols and rituals are concrete metacommunicative 'statements' about the nebulous qualities of intimacy, caring, and so forth that the parties are seeking to define. Because symbols and rituals emerge from a time-specific situation in the relationship's history, they are constant reminders of the relationship's past and thus bridge the certainty of the known past with the uncertainty of the unknown present and future. Symbols and rituals also serve as guides for what is valued or expected and thus promote predictability in behavioral actions as well. Many symbols and rituals serve to establish or maintain the boundaries of the relationship through public presentation to others, thereby helping to insure the stability of the relationship as a social unit.

Although the relationship parties are striving to reduce the relational uncertainty which characterizes this second autonomy–connection phase, the relationship at this formative stage also has novelty requirements if it is to survive. Of necessity, relationship parties must break beyond the highly structured scripts of initial interaction if they are to expand their interdependence. Indeed, the presence of some unique, nonscripted episode is often regarded retrospectively by the parties as a significant turning point in their relationship's development (Baxter and Bullis, 1986).

During this dialectical phase, relationships have two primary sources of novelty—symbols/rituals and conflict. Many symbols and rituals are playful in nature, paradoxically providing a constant and predictable source of stimulation, fun, and novelty for the relationship parties (Baxter, 1987a; Oring, 1984). The relationship pair which agrees to 'do something different' once a month thus has the best of both predictability and novelty worlds, a true integrative strategy.

Although conflict can constitute a threat to connection, it is also perhaps the best single source of novelty for the relationship. The relationship parties are forced through conflict to explore new relational terrain heretofore avoided (Braiker and Kelley, 1979).

Early conflicts appear to involve a positivity bias, i.e. the other's faults and incompatibility with the other are not perceived as the causes of early relational conflicts (Kelly, Huston and Cate, 1985; Lloyd and Cate, 1985a). This positivity bias is paradoxically a liability as well as an asset in terms of managing the autonomy–connection tension. On the liability side, Kelly, Huston and Cate (1985) have argued that early relational conflict is 'misattended' by the relationship parties because of this bias. That is, conflict during this period can serve as an informative warning signal about the other person and about compatibility between the parties, but the parties are not likely to attend to such warnings during this phase.

However, the positivity bias also serves as an asset. Because such conflicts are less likely to become attributed to the other, the parties are more likely to employ integrative conflict management strategies, i.e. strategies which display cooperative, prosocial problem-solving as opposed to competitive strategies (Sillars, 1981). However, only so much conflict can occur before it begins to reap negative consequences for the relationship, an issue developed further below under the fourth dialectical phase.

The openness–closedness dialectic

As mentioned above, indirectness, i.e. integrative disqualification, is used by relational parties to reduce their uncertainty about the state of their formative relationship. Open discussion of the relationship is the foremost 'taboo topic' reported by developing relationship parties out of fear that such directness would jeopardize the fragility of the forming connection (Baxter and Wilmot, 1985). Thus, although the parties are probably disclosing more about themselves as individuals during this phase as opposed to the first phase, they appear to segment the state of the relationship as inappropriate for openness.

Parties employ a variety of indirect 'secret test' strategies by which to gain predictability about the state of the relationship (Baxter and Wilmot, 1984). Some of these 'tests' ironically seem quite negative given the growing intimacy between the relationship parties. For example, parties report using so-called endurance tests, i.e. making the relationship costly for the other to determine his or her upper limits of commitment. Relationship parties also report using separation tests designed to determine whether affection can endure physical separation of the parties. Triangle tests are also reported, in which a real or hypothetical rival is introduced to determine whether the other party will become jealous. Yet another testing strategy employs indirect hints which are sufficiently obtuse to test whether the other party is really sensitive and high in empathy.

Two additional 'secret test' strategies sacrifice the closedness of relational privacy by making the relationship's existence publicly known. The public presentation testing strategy, for example, involves the public disclosure that the other is one's relationship partner in order to observe his or her reaction. Last, the interrogation test involves the direct questioning of third parties from the partner's social network about the other's feelings concerning the relationship.

The symbols and rituals which emerge during this phase of development also are relevant to the openness–closedness dialectic. The meanings of symbols and rituals do not reside in the phenomena themselves but rather in the minds of interpreters who rarely engage in explicit sharing of their separate meanings (Baxter, 1987a). Thus, symbols and rituals are wonderfully ambiguous stimuli which constitute integrative strategic management of the openness–closedness contradiction.

It is apparent that the same two secondary contradictions which were present in the first phase emerge in different forms during the second phase of the autonomy–connection dialectic. This pattern of transformed contradictions continues into the third developmental phase, discussed next.

Phase 3: Autonomy–Connection Synthesis

With the continued interaction, intimacy, and interdependence of its parties, a relationship will likely experience a dialectical synthesis in which autonomy and connection are no longer regarded as opposites but have become functionally reinforcing of one another. Of course, as Fitzpatrick's (1984) research on traditional, independent, separate, and mixed couple types makes evident, this synthesis will not take identical form from one relationship to another.

The novelty–predictability dialectic

The major relational problem that faces relationship parties during this developmental phase is how to sustain their particular autonomy–connection synthesis in the face of a dialectical predisposition for change. Paradoxically, two sources of predictability in the relationship serve as the catalysts for this change. First, predictability in the form of the established routines of daily relational life can easily lead to reward satiation, reduced emotional arousal, and progressive emotional deadening of the relationship's emotional life (Berscheid, 1983; Kelvin, 1977).

The second form of predictability, the relationship partners' perception that they know one another well, is a catalyst for cognitive deadening and its consequences for relational stability. As Sillars and Scott (1983) have observed, familiarity breeds overconfidence which in turn can lead to exaggeration of one's knowledge about the other, reduced vigilance in keeping current on information about the other, and idealization about the other's qualities. Of course, the reality of day-to-day interdependence shatters the illusion of full predictability and knowledge about the other, leaving the parties with some uncertainty and reduced relational satisfaction (Huston, McHale and Crouter, 1986).

In short, relationships do not sustain themselves automatically and require substantial relational work from their parties. Such relational work ideally prevents the relationship from experiencing excessive predictability and its consequent emotional/cognitive deading, yet simultaneously, such relationship activity must assure reasonable stability in the parties' constructed autonomy–connection synthesis.

Ethnographers of communication have found the 'work' metaphor salient in people's talk about their relationships (Katriel and Philipsen, 1981; Owen, 1984), for example reference to 'working on' one's relationship or 'making the relationship work'. Recently, relationship strategies researchers have begun to examine the strategies which constitute this work on behalf of the relationship's maintenance (Ayres, 1983; Baxter and Dindia, 1987; Bell, Daly and Gonzalez, 1985; Dindia and Baxter, 1987; Shea and Pearson, 1986). Several of these strategies are clearly preventative in nature, functioning to prevent the onset of emotional or cognitive deadening. For example, through such diverse actions as calling one's partner in midday 'just to say hi', giving the partner a surprise gift, or planning an elaborate joint trip, relationship partners can prevent reward satiation by introducing novel displays of affection towards the other. In addition, relationship partners appear to have several strategies by which to maintain information vigilance and perspective-taking, including such actions as spending increased time with the partner, sharing information about one another's days, and taking care to really listen to what the partner is saying.

Relationship parties have a variety of repair strategies which attempt to restore the relationship once it has deteriorated. Some of these strategies involve an attempt to link the present to the past, for example commemorating an event such as an anniversary or jointly reminiscing about the past. Other strategies attempt to restore the relationship by emphasizing the long-term future of the relationship, for example, a couple's decision to undertake a house purchase. Still other strategies attempt to restore the relationship through antisocial brinkmanship, pushing the relationship to the point of crisis with the hope that it will spring back to the relative security of its prior state. Relationship parties also appear to employ a variety of strategies which attempt to restore the relationship through an increase in rewards to the other, for example favor-doing or interacting in especially thoughtful and caring ways.

To date, the research has reported mixed results on the association between maintenance/repair strategy use and relationship satisfaction (Bell, Daly and Gonzalez, 1985; Dindia and Baxter, 1987). This inconsistency in findings probably reflects the complexity of this phase. As Duck (1984a) has observed, maintenance/repair is not a single monolithic phenomenon but rather a system of actions appropriately matched to particular problems. Thus, for example, the relationship that is dying from excessive predictability needs novelty-enhancing strategies, in contrast to the relationship which has deteriorated to the point where its parties can no longer identify with it.

The openness–closedness dialectic

Although the strategy of open relationship talk is present in people's repertoires of maintenance/repair strategies, it is greatly outnumbered by indirect strategic options (Bell, Daly and Gonzalez, 1985; Dindia and Baxter, 1987). Further, open talk is employed relatively less frequently than these other strategies (Shea and Pearson, 1986). All of the first three developmental phases, then, are characterized by the non-dominance of openness over closedness. However, I suspect that this dialectical tension takes on a different form during this third phase in contrast to the first two phases. Openness in 'established' personal relationships may mean vulnerability just as it does in earlier phases (Noller, 1985; Shimanoff, 1985), but it also appears to be conceived as 'work', i.e. something to be employed only when needed to keep the relationship maintained. In everyday relational life, personal relationship parties apparently do not regard this particular form of 'work' as necessary, displaying instead a tendency to engage in nonverbal 'mindreading' (Gottman, 1979). The perception that open discussion is unnecessary undoubtedly is a manifestation of the perceptual overconfidence which the parties have about their knowledge of one another.

If a researcher were to monitor the day-to-day disclosure levels in personal relationships which were in different phases of development, all of the relationships would probably display limited openness. But fear of vulnerability appears to be the exclusive driving force of closedness in developmental phases 1 and 2, in contrast to the perceived absence of instrumental value in openness which is common to more established relationships. *Why?*

For relationships which cannot sustain their synthesized bond, the autonomy-
-connection dialectic will evolve into a fourth phase of dissolution.

Phase 4: Connection to Autonomy

On the surface, this developmental phase appears to be the mere reversal of
the first phase. However, contrary to the claim by Altman and Taylor (1973)
that dissolution is like a movie of the relationship's growth shown in reverse,
dissolution is a qualitatively different dynamic from the earlier phases (Baxter,
1987b; Duck, 1982a). This difference is evident in examining how the secondary
contradictions are manifested during this phase.

The novelty–predictability dialectic

Altman, Vinsel and Brown (1981) have posited that dissolving relationships
initially feature 'rapid-fire' and dramatic shifts between conflicts and attempts
at repair as the parties grapple with their felt ambivalence and gradually become
transformed in the attenuation of conflict and the waning of responsiveness of
any sort through withdrawal. In dialectical terms, the Altman *et al.* argument
posits two distinct periods within this phase: one dominated by unpredictability
of action and outcome in felt ambivalence and pendular swings between conflict
and repair, and the other dominated by predictability of both action and
outcome in the decline of responsiveness of any kind. In general, the research
appears to support this conception of dissolution.

The ambivalence experienced early in this phase concerns whether to dissolve
the relationship or to attempt its repair from within (Duck, 1982a; Vaughn,
1986). Such felt ambivalence manifests itself in an increase in, or continuation
of, conflict (Lloyd and Cate, 1985a). However, unlike the conflict which
accompanies the ambivalence of phase 2, conflict at this point is likely to be
punctuated with a declining rate of repair attempts (Lloyd and Cate, 1985a).
With continuing conflict comes an attributional shift as one comes to regard the
other's faults and/or irreconcilable incompatibilities between the parties as the
reason for the conflicts (Cupach and Metts, 1986; Lloyd and Cate, 1985a).
In turn, this attributional shift leads to a decreased likelihood of integrative,
cooperative conflict management strategies and an increased likelihood of
competitively based strategies (Sillars, 1981). Thus, the conflict which occurs
during this stage lacks the quality of constructive novelty which characterizes
phase 2 conflict; rather, the conflict of this phase produces the certainty of
dissolution.

Once a relationship party has determined to exit from the relationship, strategic withdrawal occurs; the relationship is perceived now as no longer meriting
even the investment of energy needed to argue. This attenuation of conflict and
responsiveness implicates the openness–closedness dialectic and is discussed
further below.

During the dissolution phase, both of the poles in the novelty–predictability
dialectic function to undermine the bond of connection. The source of predict-

ability in this relationship phase, i.e. the increased sense that conflict is inevitable due to inherent flaws in the other party and/or in the relationship, only escalates the disengager's desire to terminate the relationship. In addition, the source of novelty or unpredictability in this phase, i.e. the substitution of ambivalence and conflict–repair cycles for the established routines, symbols, and meanings built during prior phases, also serves to undermine connection.

The openness–closedness dialectic

Relationship parties seeking dissolution convey their desire to exit in a variety of ways, but the most frequent appear to be indirect: (1) pseudo deescalation (e.g. telling the other that one 'still wants to be friends' although the secret intent is never to see the other again); (2) cost escalation, i.e. increasing the costs to the other so that he or she makes the first formal move towards breakup; and (3) indirect withdrawal through reduced frequency of contact and reduced breadth of disclosure (Baxter, 1985). Of course, if the other party persists in seeking to continue the relationship, the disengager will often resort to penultimate directness, often in the form of a confrontation in which attributional blame is cast (Baxter, 1984).

Throughout this progression of ambivalence–conflict–withdrawal, the poles of openness and closedness jointly contribute to the demise of connection. Open conflict which is destructively managed contributes to the disengager's desire to terminate the relationship. Withdrawal serves to prolong the duration of the dissolution itself, frustrating the parties all the more (Baxter, 1985). Thus, whether through openness or closedness, the relationship's demise is the result.

The openness–closedness dialectic works towards the demise of the relationship not only internally in the interaction between the relationship parties but also externally in what is and is not shared with outsiders. Unlike the role of privacy in prior developmental phases, privacy from others during this fourth phase no longer revitalizes the relationship but only serves to perpetuate the negativity bias which the parties now hold about each other. By the time the relationship's difficulties have been made public to others, it is less for external assistance in the relationship's repair and more for purposes of social support or legitimation of one's dissolution decision (Duck, 1982a; Vaughn, 1986).

The meaning of the openness–closedness dialectic is transformed during this dissolution phase. Prior constructions of the dialectic in terms of vulnerability–safety and instrumental value are supplemented by a third meaning, consummation. Although openness during dissolution may be regarded as both risky and unnecessary, it also performs a consummatory function in its public declaration of the disengager's dissatisfaction and desire to exit. The act of verbalization to the other party and/or to outsiders solidifies the relationship's demise, constituting a form of symbolic spoilage of the relationship from which recovery is exceedingly difficult (McCall, 1982).

SUMMARY AND IMPLICATIONS FOR FUTURE RESEARCH

The first three sections of this chapter have presented a dialectical perspective in which contradictions constitute the exigence for strategic action in personal relationships. The central thesis of the chapter is that one primary contradiction, autonomy–connection, and two secondary contradictions, novelty–predictability and openness–closedness, jointly affect and are affected by the communication strategies which the relationship parties enact. Four basic developmental phases were identified in the autonomy–connection dialectic, and the manifestations of the secondary contradictions were noted within each dialectical phase.

The implications of a dialectical perspective for research on relationship strategies are several in number. *First, the study of single poles of single contradictions leads to a greatly oversimplified view of relationship dynamics.* Existing relationship strategies work has tended to cast strategic work in terms of achieving unitary goals, especially uncertainty reduction about the other party and self-presentation of self to the other through self-disclosure. Repeatedly throughout the chapter, a different portrait of relationship dynamics has been painted, a portrait in which strategic actions deemed responsive to one polarity paradoxically negate an opposite polarity which is equally significant to relationship life. To ignore such dialectical paradoxes is to miss a central feature of people's relational experiences.

Second, the study of contradictions must be conceived in process, not static, terms. Some research has been done which claims to take a dialectical view (e.g. Askham, 1976; Baxter and Wilmot, 1985; Miller and Knapp, 1986; Rawlins, 1983a, b). Although this work does identify basic contradictions of relational life, it collectively fails to examine how these dialectical tensions play themselves out through time. As the discussion of the secondary contradictions evidences, a given contradiction is not the same across a relationship's history. The nature and functions of novelty, for example, are quite different depending on the developmental phase. Similarly, the meaning of openness varies depending on the developmental phase. In contrast to existing relationships research, which largely presents us with a view of stable qualities which vary only in degree through time, a dialectical perspective suggests that the qualities themselves are constructed differently depending on the developmental phase.

Third, a dialectical perspective forces us to rethink the basis of parsing a relationship's history into meaningful stages or phases. As Bochner (1984) has observed, relationships researchers have theoretically arbitrary and perhaps circular criteria for segmenting a relationship into its stages or phases of development. A dialectical perspective affords a theoretical basis for determining stages or phases of development in having researchers determine primary and secondary contradictions and then observing points at which these contradictions change qualitatively.

Fourth, relationship strategies research should employ longitudinal language-in-use data. As explained above in the first section, contradictions can be managed strategically in at least six basic ways. But finer-grained language-use data are needed at multiple points in time. Throughout the chapter, I have noted where existing relationship strategies work is suggestive of certain dialectical strategies over others. However, the topography of dialectical contradiction management in relationships remains largely for future researchers to map.

A Handbook of Personal Relationships
Edited by S. W. Duck
© 1988 John Wiley & Sons Ltd

15

Persuasion in Personal Relationships

GERALD R. MILLER and FRANK BOSTER
Michigan State University, East Lansing, Michigan, USA

ABSTRACT

This chapter considers three characteristics of personal relationships that differentiate them from casual acquaintanceships and encounters between strangers: existence of a relational history, opportunities for interaction, and concern for relational outcomes. Attention is also directed at some of the ways these characteristics influence persuasive transactions.

As one of us has noted elsewhere (Miller, 1987; Miller and Burgoon, 1978), fields such as communication and social psychology have typically been mapped in a piecemeal, operational fashion, not by recourse to some comprehensive conceptual atlas or master plan. Consequently, problem areas have come to be defined inductively, largely in terms of the labels attached to particular research contributions and contributors. Thus, the area of 'persuasion' consists primarily of those literatures generated by persons who call themselves 'persuasion researchers'. The same can be said for the area of 'personal relationships'.

In terms of traditional scientific goals pertaining to parsimony and orderly theoretical integration, this aura of operationalistic nationalism constitutes a sad state of affairs. As it relates to the two major areas of concern in this chapter, the *communicative function* of persuasion and the *communicative context* of personal relationships, it has produced two massive bodies of literature, which, while clearly of great mutual relevance, have largely passed like ships in the night. Stated less metaphorically, instances of persuasion research conducted in close relational settings are extremely rare, and references to the concept of persuasion in the literature on personal relationships are equally unusual. These mutual oversights continue to exist even though no one would dispute the claim that personal relationships necessitate considerable persuasive discourse—or, to state the claim more symbiotically, that persuasion and personal relationships are inextricably bound together.

Even if we possessed the insight and imagination to accomplish the task, we could not fully integrate these two vast literatures in 13 chapters, let alone 13 pages. Our aims are thus much more modest; though if accomplished, we believe they will contribute to linking the two problem areas more closely. Specifically, we focus our major efforts on identifying three characteristics of personal relationships that distinguish them from casual acquaintanceships or transient encounters with strangers, and we consider some of the general ways that these differences affect the processes and the outcomes of persuasive transactions. Having explicated these three important characteristics of this relational context, we comment briefly but explicitly on some promising avenues for future research, comments that underscore some investigational priorities implied in our earlier remarks. Our approach throughout is both selective and critical; our objective is to accomplish a modicum of scholarly integration and to suggest promising routes for future research travels. Those seeking more exhaustive summaries of the persuasion literature may avail themselves of a number of helpful alternatives (e.g. McGuire, 1969, 1985; Miller, Burgoon and Burgoon, 1984).

Before embarking on our primary journey, however, some brief definitional comments regarding our two principal concepts are in order. The term 'persuasion' refers to attempts to modify behavior by symbolic transactions (messages). Those attempts are sometimes, but not always, linked with coercive force (indirectly coercive). Furthermore, they involve appeals to the reason and/or emotions of the intended persuadee(s) (Miller, 1987, esp. pp. 451–2). Since the implications of this definition will become apparent as the chapter progresses, two comments will suffice for now. First, the definition excludes nonsymbolic, directly coercive acts—for example spouse-beating or child-battering—from the domain of persuasion, while at the same time recognizing that in the rough-and-tumble social world, persuasive appeals are often linked with coercive acts—for example *threatening* to beat a spouse or to batter a child. This distinction permits us to retain the exclusively symbolic nature of persuasion while avoiding the kind of overly rational and polite approach that Simons (1974) has critically labeled a 'drawing room controversy' view of persuasion. Second, the thrust of the definition is *relational*, i.e. it implicitly recognizes the centrality of *reciprocal influence*, rather than positing a unidirectional symbolic path from an *actor* to others being *acted upon*. As we emphasize later, this notion of reciprocity is particularly important in personal relationships.

'Personal relationships', as we conceive of the term, places a premium on developmental processes while at the same time granting that the situational context also enters into the definition (Miller, 1978). Such relationships typically involve a relatively small number of participants and are primarily, though not entirely, transacted in face-to-face encounters. Since they are characterized by frequent, extensive contact and by lengthy duration, they allow participants to achieve considerable social penetration (Altman and Taylor, 1973), to mutually 'screen' each other via a series of social filters (Duck, 1973), and eventually to relate to each other as individuals, rather than undifferentiated cultural entities or role occupants (Miller and Steinberg, 1975; Miller and Sunnafrank, 1982). Finally, as the preceding remarks imply, because participants invest considerable physical and psychic energy in personal relationships, they usually value them highly, and as a result, conflict in or dissolution of such relationships is particularly painful.

THREE RELEVANT CHARACTERISTICS OF PERSONAL RELATIONSHIPS

Most persuasion research [relies] on a one-to-many situational context. In the traditional persuasion study, a relatively large aggregate of receiver/persuadees— a classroom of students, the members of a PTA, and so forth—is exposed to a message attributed to an individual or an institutional source. With few exceptions[a] linear, unidirectional view of the 'transaction' is enforced by the fact that the message is not even presented live. Instead, the persuadees read it, or see and/or hear it on video or audiotape, a procedure that prevents any meaningful reciprocal influence by the audience. After message exposure the persuadees respond to some measure of persuasive effect, usually a paper-and-pencil assessment of attitude change. Thus, the entire enterprise closely resembles a public speaking or mass media setting, though even here the fit is far from perfect, since there is little opportunity for the kinds of audience social facilitation effects one would expect in real-life communicative settings. (Miller and Burgoon, 1978, p. 33).

This characterization of the procedures used in most persuasion research is as apt today as it was in 1978. Clearly, the traditionally dominant setting for persuasion studies bears little or no resemblance to the state of affairs in personal relationships. Although numerous differences are apparent, we will focus on three characteristics of personal relationships that are missing from the investigational milieu of prior persuasion research, characteristics that exert potentially strong influences on the persuasive exchanges of relational partners.

Relational History

We view the inevitability of conflict in personal relationships as axiomatic. Furthermore, when conflict arises in a personal relationship, there are likely to be strong pressures to resolve it quickly, since its existence has both emotional and behavioral consequences for the relational partners.

Persuasion is a commonly employed method of conflict resolution, yet most persuasion studies evidence no vestige of a relationship between persuader and persuadee(s). Indeed, in many instances, actual relationships are an impossibility because the persuasive agent is a figment of the researcher's imagination. By contrast, a relational history is both an empirical and a definitional fact of personal relationships, and since social and behavioral sciences rest largely on the assumption that past behavior affects present and future behaviors, the impact of relational history on persuasive transactions emerges as a given. We will consider some of the particulars of this impact, using as a point of contrast two divergent ways to conceive of such human symbolic activities as persuasion.

The prevalent stance taken by communication researchers, and to a lesser extent by social psychologists, views communication as a process involving considerable cognitive activity and awareness—in the more metaphorical terms of Langer (1978; Langer, Blank and Chanowitz, 1978), as a highly *mindful* activity. Though this commitment is seldom stated in so many words, it is implicit in the kinds of research questions pursued and the practical advice offered. For example, much of the recent work dealing with the use of compliance–gaining message strategies by persuasive communicators (e.g. Miller *et al.*, 1987; Seibold, Cantrill and Meyers, 1985; Wheeless, Barraclough and Stewart, 1983) seems to assume considerable awareness regarding the wide range of possible available strategies and a good deal of studied reflection about which ones to employ in specific situations. Indeed, the very term 'strategy' connotes at least some level of conscious awareness and deliberate choice.

Acceptance of this mindful view of persuasion implies that persons involved in personal relationships will be able to bring much more information to bear when selecting persuasive strategies. Because of their extensive relational history, parties to personal relationships are likely to have more idiosyncratic information about their partners, as well as considerable prior experience in exchanging persuasive messages. By contrast, casual acquaintances and strangers must largely 'commence from scratch' in their attempts to identify optimal persuasive strategies. Choosing and rehearsing of strategies relies primarily on recourse to cultural and sociological generalizations (Miller and Steinberg, 1975; Miller and Sunnafrank, 1982), prior experience in similar situations, and seat-of-the-pants intuition. Granted, writers such as Milgram (1977) have noted that individuals in urban settings often fantasize extensively about the peculiar properties of 'familiar strangers'—i.e. people whom they frequently encounter physically but with whom they do not speak. Though such 'relationships' are an intriguing aspect of urban culture, any individual inferences that occur must, of necessity, be based on cultural and sociological conclusions gleaned from observation of the stranger's nonverbal and verbal demeanor when interacting with others or from direct communicative exchanges with the stranger.

At first glance, this added informational grist for the cognitive-processing mill suggests that persuaders in personal relationships should be more effective in achieving desired persuasive outcomes, for their greater knowledge about their partners should enhance their mindful quest for optimal strategies. Upon considering the matter reciprocally, the situation is not this simple because the partners, in turn, possess greater knowledge about the persuaders, thus enhancing the likelihood of successful resistance to persuasion or of effective counterpersuasive measures. Regardless of precisely how the situation is analyzed in terms of persuasive processes and outcomes, the fact remains that personal relationships offer a richer informational fabric to guide strategy selection and use.

An alternative approach to conceptualizing persuasion rests on the assumption that many persuasive exchanges are routinized, relatively *mindless* activities

(Berger and Douglas, 1982; Miller, 1977). This alternative implies that parties to personal relationships may fall into habitual patterns of persuasive exchange; rather than devoting considerable conscious efforts to crafting effective messages, they may develop scripts (Abelson, 1981; Schank and Abelson, 1977) that are routinely invoked when persuasive messages are being transacted. When casual acquaintances and strangers communicate persuasively, such habitual message patterns are, of course, absent.

There is reason to believe that much interpersonal persuasion is, indeed, relatively mindless. For example, one consequence of relational conflict is that the conflicting parties are certain to experience heightened arousal. Contemporary theory and research indicates that when arousal increases, behavior becomes increasingly habitual (Bond and Titus, 1983; Zajonc, 1965). Under these conditions the conflicting parties can be expected to exhibit routine, scripted persuasive message behavior. When both parties perform in this relatively mindless way, the interaction may be described as a *scripted performance* (Abelson, 1981). Sometimes, particularly in cases when a cooperative attitude dominates the interaction, these performances contribute to a successful resolution of conflict (e.g. Brechner, 1977); in other instances, when a competitive stance dominates, scripted performances fail abjectly (e.g. Deutsch and Krauss, 1962). It is possible that the presence or absence of opportunities for the parties to save face (Goffman, 1955) is an important predictor of whether a cooperative or competitive position is adopted (e.g. J. Z. Rubin, 1980).

Some recent investigations have reported evidence of habitual, or mindless, compliance-gaining message behavior (Boster and Lofthouse, 1986; Boster and Stiff, 1984; Lofthouse, 1986). In each of these experiments participants were placed in a situation requiring them to seek compliance by another and their persuasive messages were recorded. In every instance the participants exhibited a limited repertoire of compliance-gaining message strategies. Although it is tempting to attribute this finding to the restrictiveness of the persuasive situation—participants were trying to persuade confederates to participate in a survey—alternative explanations abound. For example, most persons may have a relatively small repertoire of compliance-gaining message strategies that are learned and then used habitually. Alternatively, they may have relatively large repertoires, but the anxiety generated by seeking compliance from another may result in the habitual use of only one or two message strategies. Yet a third possibility is that arousal and the situation interact to affect persuasive message behavior. Specifically, the pairing of high arousal with available situational cues may heighten the salience of certain messages (Kahneman and Tversky, 1973) while reducing the salience of others.

We suspect that something of this nature occurred in the Boster and Lofthouse (1986) experiment. In this study the telephone calls used to solicit survey participation were placed to confederates who provided standard responses to each call. In one condition participants were told that the confederates were poor students badly in need of money. In this condition monetary appeals were used almost exclusively, with all other appeals being used infrequently. Other conditions that did not contain references to the economic need of the confederate produced a more varied set of appeals.

Even though the Boster and Lofthouse study was not conducted using parties involved in personal relationships, it suggests some factors that may be relevant in such situations. In personal relationships, a persuasive communicator might choose to use a limited range of strategies either because the issue of concern mandates certain strategies *or* because the relational partner is known to be particularly vulnerable to these strategies. Conversely, if a relational partner were known to respond moderately positively to a wide variety of strategies, all of these strategies might be utilized in the persuasive fray.

The preceding analysis suggests several important unresolved questions for persuasion researchers. How do relational partners go about gathering information about each other, and how does the relative availability of such information influence selection of persuasive strategies? What range of strategies is actually used by participants in personal relationships, and how does it compare with the range of strategies used in encounters between acquaintances and strangers? Do individual differences exist in range of strategy use, both in personal and impersonal relationships? Are *persuasive scripts* a fact of personal relationships, and if so, to what extent do they contribute to or detract from the effectiveness of persuasive transactions? Given the amount of prior attention devoted to the study of persuasion, it may seem that answers to such questions as these should be readily available. Unfortunately, examination of the current literature indicates that they have yet to be earmarked for systematic empirical study.

Interaction Opportunities

As indicated previously, the lion's share of existing persuasion research focuses on the effect of a single persuasive message transmitted in an interactional vacuum. Nothing could be more diametrically opposed to the way communication functions in personal relationships, where many messages are exchanged over time and the immediate opportunity exists for evaluative feedback, counterpersuasive messages, and compliance-resisting responses. The two situations are so dissimilar that generalization of findings from the first to the second situation is fraught with hazards. Indeed, the circumstances that prevail in personal relationships permit patterns of communicative exchange and incremental communicative strategies that are impossible to achieve in the typically designed persuasion investigation.

Consider the mundane example of a persuasive exchange between spouses regarding the plans for their next vacation. Assume that the last several vacations have been spent in the same locale and that one spouse hungers for a change of scenery. Although the discontented spouse may conceivably blurt out a demand for a new vacation site, she or he will probably seek to achieve the persuasive goal more subtly. The seeds of the idea may be sown by initiating a conversation regarding the 'grand time' some friends had at an alternative vacation spot, by 'reminiscing' about calamities the couple experienced during last year's vacation, by calling attention to an article in the travel section of the *New York Times*, or by a host of other opening communicative gambits. Once the matter has been broached, the discontented spouse is likely to proceed through a series of messages, with the aim of the entire sequence being to achieve consensus about the desirability of choosing a new spot for the next vacation.

The ease with which such consensus is achieved will largely depend, of course, on the attitudinal posture of the partner. If he or she is quite pleased with the customary site and wishes to continue vacationing there, attempts to gain a recreational change of venue will be met with resistance. This resistance may take such forms as feigning ignorance about the underlying persuasive goal of the discontented spouse, countering negative reminiscences with positive memories, offering specific inducements to tempt the spouse to return to the familiar vacation haunt, or angrily threatening to forego a vacation if it is not spent at the traditional locale—to mention but a few of the many possibilities.

Even though we have explored this example in some detail, we have not begun to capture the richness of the persuasive dialogue associated with it. Nowhere in the current persuasion literature can one find a concerted attempt to come to scientific grips with such exchanges. The closest that scholars have come to studying them is captured by recent research in the uses of sequential strategies. These techniques create the impression that the persuasive communicator has offered a concession, yet they are effective in obtaining the other's compliance. Furthermore, all the persuasive transactants are able to maintain face rather easily.

One such sequential technique is the door-in-the-face or the reject-then-retreat technique (e.g. Cialdini *et al.*, 1975; Even-Chen, Yinon and Bizman, 1978; Mowen and Cialdini, 1980; Shanab and O'Neill, 1979). The results of studies examining this technique indicate that if persons do not conform with an initial large request, they become more susceptible to subsequent smaller requests. Although there are disagreements concerning the most feasible explanation for this result, the finding is consistently robust (Dillard, Hunter and Burgoon, 1984).

Recently, Lofthouse (1986) reported an interesting application of the door-in-the-face technique. In her study, students wrote a paper and were then required to discuss its evaluation with their professor. The professor opened all discussions by asking what grade the students felt they deserved. After they had given their responses, the professor replied that she or he had read the paper and believed that it deserved a grade one level below the marks suggested by the students. Several students accepted the grade specified by the professor without argument. Subsequent interviews revealed that in a substantial proportion of these cases, the participants had employed a door-in-the-face strategy. They began with the belief that their paper deserved a 'B', but when asked, they opined that the paper merited a grade of 'A'. When the professor suggested that the paper deserved a 'B' grade, the students created the illusion of making a concession and accepted, thus receiving the grade they felt all along they deserved.

Not only is this sequential strategy effective, it produces little or no negative affect. The other party has apparently been given her or his way, and is thus happy. Moreover, the strategy renders rebuttal almost impossible. Having suggested initially that the paper merited a 'B', it would have been quite difficult for the professor to change that position and to argue for a lower grade. Cialdini likens such processes to jujitsu—a martial art in which one uses an opponent's strength to one's own advantage:

> This last feature of the process gives the profiteers an enormous additional benefit—the ability to manipulate without the appearance of manipulation. Even the victims themselves tend to see their compliance as due to the action of natural forces rather than to the designs of the person who profits from that compliance. (Cialdini, 1985, pp. 11–12)

Clearly, the door-in-the-face is not the only technique that makes rebuttal difficult. Such sequential strategies as the foot-in-the-door (Baron, 1973; Beaman *et al.*, 1974; Foss and Dempsey, 1979; Freedman and Fraser, 1966; Rittle, 1981), in which compliance with an initial small request makes one more susceptible to a subsequent larger request, low balling (Cialdini *et al.*, 1978), in which the persuader induces persuadees to perform the desired action and then increases the cost of the action, the legitimization of paltry favors (Cialdini and Schroeder, 1976), in which compliance is enhanced by reducing the perceived size of the complying act, and the that's-not-all technique (Burger, 1986), in which compliance is induced by making the complying behavior more lucrative, have all been shown to be effective in increasing compliance above base rates.

Though these studies represent a step forward from the single messages common to most prior studies, they still fall far short of capturing the persuasive give-and-take occurring in personal relationships. Generally, no prior relationship exists between persuaders and persuadees; a typical procedure involves experimental confederates carrying research participants through a series of persuasive requests of ascending or descending magnitude. Such sequential techniques are undoubtedly common to personal relationships, but the interactive details are considerably more intricate.

To rectify this investigational shortcoming, persuasion researchers will need to depart radically from the procedural habits that have guided most of their research to date. Such a departure will not be simple, for it creates numerous practical and ethical problems foreign to prevailing research practices. Though the desirability of observing actual persuasive exchanges in ongoing personal relationships is easily endorsed, the process is not so readily studied in these environs, particularly if the researcher is concerned about realizing a level of control that permits relatively unambiguous isolation of independent variables. 'To seat 50 undergraduate students in a classroom and measure the impact of a written or spoken message is one thing, to "shadow" each student [or any two students in a personal relationship] as persuasive messages are exchanged in dormitory rooms, cafeterias, [and] bars—to mention but a few possible settings for such exchanges—is quite another, both pragmatically and ethically'

(Miller, 1987, p. 449). Nevertheless, eventual understanding of the complex message exchanges occurring in personal relationships demands this kind of ingenuity and commitment; appreciation of the role of interaction in shaping persuasive processes and outcomes cannot be achieved by studying persuasion in interaction-free environments. Although the preceding assertion probably strikes readers as banal and commonplace, its implications remain relevant to today's persuasion researchers.

Concern for Relational Outcomes

Although there are substantial individual differences in argumentativeness (Infante and Rancer, 1982), we believe that most people are reluctant persuaders, and that they are especially reluctant to persuade those with whom they have personal relationships. Several social forces exert an influence on this reticence to persuade. For example, when we are successful in persuading others, they may capitalize on the norm of reciprocity (Gouldner, 1960) to enlist our compliance at some later date.

Generally speaking, persuasive transactions may be evaluated in terms of at least two broad outcomes: first, the relative success or failure in achieving the immediate persuasive objective; second, the effect of the transaction itself on the subsequent relationship between the persuader and the persuadee(s). Thus, a persuader may be successful in achieving an immediate persuasive objective but incur definite relational costs in doing so, such as when a parent's threats result in a child cleaning up the garage but also produce considerable hostility towards the parent. In a similar vein, Whyte (1949) discusses the frustration and tension produced when waitresses attempt to persuade countermen to speed orders.

One of our favorite examples is found in the Woody Allen film *Annie Hall*. Despite her reticence to do so, Allen hectors Diane Keaton to return to school. When she at last complies with his wish, she immediately begins to have an affair with one of her professors, at which point Allen launches an intense, humorous campaign to convince her to drop out of school:

A: 'It's only mental masturbation.'
K: 'Now there's a topic you know something about.'
A: 'Don't knock it; at least I'm making it with someone I love.'

This argument escalates quickly, and the relationship is terminated temporarily.

Conversely, a persuader may fail to realize an immediate persuasive objective but contribute to relational solidarity in the process—for example, because a person uses temperate, 'low-pressure' persuasive appeals, a close friend develops a more favorable opinion of the person's tact, sensitivity, and concern for others, even though the friend is not swayed by the persuasive message. When both broad outcomes are considered, messages that accomplish the immediate persuasive objective without polluting the relational waters are maximally effective; messages that fail in their immediate persuasive objective while concomitantly poisoning the relational waters are maximally ineffective.

A dramatic example of the latter situation was pointed out to us recently by Michael Burgoon (1987). An employee of a large chemical firm contacted a fatal, job-related disease. Interviews obtained from the employee and his family revealed three important items of information: first, despite his illness, the employee remained very committed to both his job and the company; second, other members of the employee's family expressed strong negative feelings towards both the job and the company; and third, the employee and his family were not on the best of terms. Taken together, these three items of information may seem odd, but subsequent questioning clarified them by revealing the following segment of relational history.

For years the employee's relatives attempted to persuade him to resign and to find a less hazardous job. Placed in the position of having to defend his daily departure to work, the employee contended that he held an excellent position at the chemical company and that he intended to keep working there. When he became ill, members of the family increased the frequency and intensity of their persuasive attacks. Accustomed to defending the company, the employee increased the intensity of his own messages. It was at this point that the interviewers uncovered the information summarized in the preceding paragraph.

Students of persuasion will recognize immediately that the family had put the employee in a natural counterattitudinal advocacy experiment (Festinger, 1957; Miller, 1973; Miller and Burgoon, 1973). Quite probably the employee was not so positive towards the chemical company initially, but because he was placed in the long-standing role of company advocate, he persuaded himself to adopt more strongly pro-company attitudes. Conversely, the employee's family engaged in a similar self-persuasion exercise and developed more negative attitudes towards the company. Finally, the constant conflict engendered by their persuasive exchanges produced ill-will between the employee and his family.

This anecdote illustrates several of the previously discussed features of persuasion in personal relationships. First, the communicators are concerned with persuading their target(s); second, their persuasive exchanges have consequences for the development of their relationship; and third, each of the communicators must be prepared to respond to messages from their persuasive target(s). Each of these features has important implications for the generation, selection, and production of persuasive messages, and we shall next briefly consider some of these implications.

If persuasive messages affect relational outcomes, it is reasonable to contend that the partners will both experience and develop an awareness of this process. This argument provides the justification for several experiments examining the impact of relational intimacy and the duration of relational consequences on compliance-gaining message choices (e.g. Cody, McLaughlin and Schneider, 1981; Kaminski, McDermott and Boster, 1977; Lustig and King, 1980; Miller et al., 1977; Roloff and Barnicott, 1978, 1979; Sillars, 1980b). Generally, these studies have reported nonsignificant findings, and when the results have been statistically significant, the effect sizes have been relatively small (Hunter and Boster, 1979; Jackson and Backus, 1982). It should be stressed, however, that all of these studies asked respondents to role-play persuaders in hypothetical situations and to indicate the likelihood that they would use particular strategies. For reasons that we will detail later, we believe that hypotheses about actual use cannot be tested fairly and powerfully using this role-playing procedure.

Not only may relational outcomes be influenced by the kinds of persuasive message strategies that are employed, the escalation and deescalation of personal relationships may themselves emerge as immediate persuasive objectives. Personal relationships grow at least partly because the parties are mutually oriented towards persuading each other to invest more commitment and resources to the relationship. Conversely, a number of researchers (e.g. Baxter, 1979, 1982; Baxter and Philpott, 1982; Cody, 1982; Miller and Parks, 1982; Wilmot, Carbaugh and Baxter, 1985) have conceived of the dissolution of personal relationships as a persuasive process and have examined the effectiveness of various kinds of persuasive strategies in furthering this process. Seldom are relational outcomes themselves a primary persuasive aim of persuaders in impersonal settings; at most, the persuasive communicators may seek to create the *illusion* of relational escalation or deescalation in order to further other immediate persuasive objectives.

Indeed, in terms of the two broad persuasive outcomes identified above, people will assign differing values to them depending upon the nature of the particular relationship. Though it would be inaccurate to portray casual acquaintances and strangers as totally unconcerned about the relational consequences of their persuasive exchanges, it seems fair to say that such concerns usually are much greater in personal relationships. As noted earlier, personal relationships involve major investments by the participants. From a social exchange perspective (Blau, 1967; Homans, 1961; Thibaut and Kelley, 1959) these relationships normally yield greater endogenous rewards than impersonal encounters, and relational friction or breakdown can result in substantial endogenous and exogeneous costs—for example, a troubled marriage often exacts its toll both in the increased stress encountered in the relationship itself and the social disapproval communicated by significant others, the latter frequently being sufficiently threatening that the troubled parties strive valiantly to 'keep up a good front' even though they are experiencing great discord.

By contrast, persuasive communicators in casual acquaintanceships and transient encounters with strangers are more likely to perceive that they have little to lose relationally by marshaling all the persuasive weapons at their disposal in order to achieve their immediate persuasive objective. Hence, they will probably be less reluctant to use punishment-oriented strategies (Miller et al., 1977; Miller and Parks, 1982), to communicate deceptively (Miller, Mongeau and Sleight, 1986), and to use other aversive and unethical strategies. Indeed, in such extreme relational circumstances as blackmail and confidence games, the persuasive means employed to achieve the immediate objective of economic gain manifest utter contempt for the potential relational implications.

While the preceding discussion makes good theoretical and intuitive sense, it is couched in conditional language because of the dearth of empirical evidence bearing on the issues. Most persuasion studies are concerned solely with assessments of relative success in achieving some immediate persuasive objective: attitudinal and/or behavioral conformity with message recommendations is the stock-in-trade dependent measure of persuasion researchers. Given that these studies have been conducted largely in a relational vacuum, this focus is hardly surprising; it makes no sense to be concerned with relational outcomes in the absence of viable relationships. To return to a familiar lament, however, it also seems foolhardy to place much trust in the generalizability of findings obtained in such a setting when seeking to explain and to understand how persuasion functions in personal relationships.

Once the importance of considering relational outcomes has been established, it becomes obvious that credibility may often be an important persuasive *end* in itself, rather than merely a functional *means* to some immediate persuasive objective. Because of the lack of any ongoing relational context, most prior persuasion research has treated credibility as 'an antecedent, independent variable which influences subsequent persuasive outcomes, rather than a *persuasive outcome* worthy of study in its own right' (Miller and Burgoon, 1978, p. 34, their italics). In personal relationships, many transactions aim primarily at enhancing the credibility of the communicators—or, to invoke a conceptual label more common to the study of personal relationships, such exchanges seek to enhance the communicators' *interpersonal attractiveness*. To acknowledge this fact does not deny the frequent instrumental value of being perceived positively in personal relationships. As with their impersonal counterparts, highly credible communicators in personal relationships are likely to be more successful in achieving their persuasive objectives. Nevertheless, in most personal relationships, communicators devote considerable persuasive energy to *selling themselves* (Miller and Burgoon, 1978), and while there have been some useful lines of research dealing with factors influencing credibility formation in impersonal settings (e.g. Baker, 1965; Giles and Powesland, 1975; Giles and Street, 1985; Jones, 1964; Miller and Hewgill, 1964; Norton, 1983a; Sereno and Hawkins, 1967), much work remains to be done on this process of self-advocacy, particularly as it is practiced in personal relationships.

Taken together, the three characteristics of personal relationships discussed above illustrate the need for bold methodological and procedural departures in future persuasion research. If researchers hope to solve the puzzle of persuasion in personal relationships, they must begin to scrutinize actual persuasive exchanges in these relational settings instead of relying on results based on single-message, large-audience settings, or on the use of hypothetical scenarios that ask respondents to *act* as persuasive *role-players* rather than to *behave* as persuasive *communicators*. Though such an investigational change of course will not be accomplished easily, its achievement is of crucial import for students of persuasion in personal relationships.

IMPLICATIONS FOR FUTURE RESEARCH

As we have stressed repeatedly, few studies have probed the processes and outcomes of persuasion in personal relationships. Although studies have examined, albeit usually indirectly, such issues as the persuasiveness of various message characteristics and strategies, the effect of message choices on relational development, and the effect of message strategies on rebuttal, we are not aware of any study that has investigated this entire set of issues. Furthermore, many studies dealing with these issues are designed and executed inadequately. Because of these limitations, we shall sketch some alternative directions for future studies of persuasive exchanges between persons involved with personal relationships.

To begin with, we have already noted that most studies examining the effects of such variables as relational intimacy and duration of relational consequences on selection of message strategies have employed self-report, role-playing measures. Although we believe that such measures often provide useful information, caution must be exercised in this instance. Hunter and Boster (1987) have shown that ratings obtained for the Marwell and Schmitt (1967) strategies, the typology employed most frequently by researchers studying strategy selection, are unidimensional. Several authors have argued that the single dimension tapped by the strategies is verbal aggression (Boster, 1985; Dillard and Burgoon, 1985; Hunter and Boster, 1987). If so, past research may be reinterpreted to suggest that relational intimacy and duration of relational consequences have little impact on people's verbal aggressiveness in persuasive transactions. Notwithstanding this possibility, verbal aggression is only one dimension of persuasive message behavior, and relational intimacy and duration of relational consequences may well exert effects on other relevant dimensions.

A powerful test of this possibility necessitates an experiment that controls for relational intimacy, duration of relational consequences, or both, while observations of persuasive messages are being made. Whether these observations are made in a controlled or a natural setting, they are necessary before it will be possible to make informed statements about the effects of relational intimacy or duration of relational consequences on actual selection and use of persuasive message strategies.

Scudder (1986) offers a clue regarding how such an experiment might be performed. He varied the power of participants in a car buying/selling simulation, observed the frequency of various types of threats, and arrived at the impact of the various threats on economic outcomes. An extension of this study that controls for relational intimacy and adds a measure of relational affect would provide useful data for examining issues associated with strategy selection. Even if the persuasive situations were simulated, it would be helpful if the participants consisted of partners in personal relationships.

Alternatively, discourse-analytic techniques could be used to examine transcripts of the persuasive exchanges of persons in compatible and incompatible relationships so as to determine what differences, if any, exist in the persuasive appeals and strategies that are employed. This approach has proved useful in uncovering differences between effective and ineffective negotiations (Donohue and Diez, 1985). Of course, such data must be interpreted cautiously, since causal order is always questionable; the question can be raised as to whether persuasive message behavior causes or is caused by relational development.

Third, as the Burgoon example illustrates, traditional persuasive research concerns are not entirely irrelevant to persuasion in personal relationships. Just as Hovland (1959) underscored with regard to experimental and survey studies of attitude change, there are important differences between passive and active communicative contexts, and we have emphasized several of them. One important additional difference is that actual exchanges typically result in much shorter messages than the kinds of message stimuli that have been employed in passive communicative context studies; when interaction is permitted, long messages are apt to be interrupted. This feature of persuasive message-making in personal relationships may lessen, or even negate, the import of message variables such as certain aspects of organization. Nevertheless, numerous other variables, including fear appeals, logical appeals, humor, and message discrepancy, are excellent candidates for investigational scrutiny.

A CONCLUDING DISCLAIMER

As we reflect on the tone of this chapter, we realize that some readers may conclude we have a pessimistic view of the current state of persuasion scholarship. Nothing could be further from the truth; indeed, we believe that the knowledge generated by persuasion researchers constitutes one of the more useful bodies of literature in communication and social psychology. Moreover, the early research on persuasion was purposefully designed to be conducted in large audience settings (Miller, 1987); one is hard pressed to criticize researchers for not solving problems they did not set out to solve.

Two issues do, however, give us cause for concern. First, as noted earlier, our scrutiny of persuasion research and research dealing with interpersonal communication reveals little overlap to the present time. It is no exaggeration to suggest that many view these two areas as conceptually distinct, if not as opposite ends of a continuum. If this chapter succeeds in causing readers to modify this viewpoint and to begin investigating persuasive transactions in interpersonal contexts, then it will have served a useful purpose.

Second, we are less than sanguine about the ecological validity of persuasion experiments conducted primarily in passive communicative contexts, at least as the issue of validity relates to personal relationships. The complexities generated by interaction and by the transactants' relationship render suspect the assumption that the findings of prior persuasion studies can be translated directly to face-to-face, intimate settings. While our position on this issue may be a source of gloom for some readers, we assume a more optimistic posture. Persuasion in personal relationships is a topic ripe for study, and one which, in our opinion, seems certain to yield an abundant harvest.

Handbook of Personal Relationships
Edited by S. W. Duck
© 1988 John Wiley & Sons Ltd

16

Relational Communication

L. EDNA ROGERS
University of Utah, Salt Lake City, Utah, USA
and
FRANK E. MILLAR
University of Wyoming, Laramie, Wyoming, USA

ABSTRACT

A relational approach focuses on the structuring processes and patterned redundancies of communicative behaviors that characterize interpersonal relationships. A system for indexing relational-level dimensions of communication is presented with accompanying research results. The theoretical importance of the synthesis of cognitive and behavioral descriptions of social relations is discussed.

Relational communication is founded on an epistemology of form (Ellis, 1981) which accords primary importance to the study of interaction rather than individual acts. Although the terms 'relationship' and 'social interaction' have been used extensively in the literature, the vast majority of studies have focused on individuals 'engaged in social interaction, not on social interactions *per se*' (Hartup, 1979, p. 27). A relational approach centers on the formative nature of social interaction (Blumer, 1969) by focusing on the communicative patterns that constitute interpersonal relationships (Bateson, 1972).

Increasingly, studies in communication are attending to the socialness of human actors and thereby explicitly focusing on their interdependence and intersubjectivity. For instance, investigators have concentrated on the relational implications of nonverbal messages (Burgoon and Hale, 1984; Burgoon, Coker and Coker, 1986), on developing relational typologies of interspousal perceptions (Fitzpatrick, 1977, 1984), on the relational schemata (Planalp, 1985) and relational knowledge (Hewes and Planalp, 1982) of social actors that effect communicative dynamics. However, because the study of interaction *per se* is of a different level of analysis than either social acts or an actor's subjective knowledge about actions, no amount of analyzing individual messages and/or individuals' information-processing abilities (Hewes *et al.*, 1985; Doelger, Hewes and Graham, 1986) will describe the jointly produced nature of social interaction. 'Social relationships, accordingly, are not the consequences of previously developed selves' communicating; they are the emergent products of the process of interaction' (Kendon, 1982, p. 445).

In playing out relational dramas, each person's behaviors influence and constrain the behaviors of other, but they do not, nor cannot (L'Abate, 1984), unilaterally 'cause' the other's actions. Individual actions are embedded in interactional sequences which are themselves encompassed in larger social and ecological systems. By analogy, words are embedded in sentences, which are embedded in paragraphs, which are encompassed in sections, chapters and larger descriptive units. Just as analyses of words give different information from analyses of sentences even though the levels are interdependent, so do analyses of social acts provide different insights from analyses of sequentially organized interactions. Different levels of analysis provide different types of understandings and require different methodological procedures. Stratified orders of communication structures manifest different properties such that each level of analysis 'cannot be reduced to, nor predicted from, the lower level' (Koestler, 1978, p. 32).

A primary thrust of the relational approach is the development of a model that theoretically and empirically focuses on the 'communication properties that exist only at the dyadic or system level; relational variables do not lie within interactors, but rather exist between them' (Rogers and Farace, 1975, p. 222). Admittedly, analyses of what occurs within social actors and what occurs between them in social interaction are both necessary for more adequate theories of interpersonal relationships. As Simmel (1950) points out, interpersonal relationships 'develop upon the basis of relational knowledge, and this knowledge upon the basis of actual relations'; social interaction is the condition 'where being and conceiving make their mysterious unity empirically felt' (p. 309). This 'mysterious unity' of social interaction is synthetically whole, yet analyses of this unity require that 'relational knowledge' and the 'actual relations' be methodologically closed off in ways that are incompatible. To attribute more validity to one level of description than another is to indulge in misleading theoretical illusions (Bateson, 1979).

In sum, a relational communication approach assumes that mind is an explanatory principle (Bateson, 1977) in human relationships because the receiver is the context for message construction (Bateson, 1979). However, the individual is contextualized by the interactive dynamics within which s/he participates, even while the individual influences the evolving shape of these dynamics. Further, since processes within the individual actor as message constructor are inherently unobservable, a relational approach insists that an adequate *inter*personal model must be grounded in the momentarily visible and empirically known actions manifested in interactive processes. This insistence requires a conceptual shift from describing individual acts or actors to descriptions of the 'temporal form' (Gottman, 1982a) of interactional units. Empirical attention is, therefore, centered on the structuring processes and patterned redundancies immanent in communicative behaviors conceived of as messages that characterize human relationships.

The purposes of this chapter are to: (1) describe in brief the epistemological and conceptual background of the relational approach, (2) outline three basic dimensions of interpersonal relationships, (3) present selected research on the dimension of control, and (4) discuss implications of this approach for future investigations.

EPISTEMOLOGICAL AND CONCEPTUAL BACKGROUND

The development of the relational communication approach is based in the multiple lines of thought currently revolutionizing Western philosophy and science (Maruyama, 1975). Although several authors have discussed the characteristics of this revolution (Bohm, 1980; Koestler, 1978; Bronowski, 1978), Bateson's writings on the 'new order of communication' (1951, p. 209) have most directly influenced our own efforts. Bateson's work, in turn, was heavily influenced by the aesthetics of systems thinking and the language of cybernetics. The relevance of the abstract principles of systems thinking to the study of communicative dynamics has been discussed elsewhere (Watzlawick, Beavin and Jackson, 1967; Buckley, 1967; Penman, 1980; Krippendorf, 1977, 1984; Fisher, 1978) and will not be reviewed here except to remind the reader of the following general notions.

Systems thinking involves looking 'at the world in terms of relationships and integration' (Capra, 1982, p. 266); it is process thinking where 'form becomes associated with process, interrelation with interaction, and opposites are unified through oscillation' (p. 267). A systems orientation offers a fundamentally different way of thinking about 'reality' than the positivistic, deterministic world view that has dominated Western thought for the past four centuries. The empirical focus of this newer world view is on identifying the principles of organization that integrate component parts into coherent, self-regulating wholes. Living systems are thought of as self-organizing (Prigogine and Stengers, 1984) and scientific attention is centered on describing the form of self-regulating patterns which are the evolutionary explanation of the system's current state.

Bateson (1972) chastized the majority of the social and behavioral sciences for concentrating on the wrong half of the ancient substance–form dichotomy. By modeling classical Newtonian physics, we have been concerned with substance, with objects and forces, more than form and process. However, 'mental process, ideas, communication, organization, differentiation, patterns and so on, are matters of form rather than substance' (Bateson, 1972, p. xxv). Thus, the principles of organization that unify parts into wholes are manifested in communication processes.

The work in relational communication has been guided by Bateson's (1979) use of 'double description' and the 'zigzag ladder of dialectic between form and process' for merging actions into interactions, interactions into relational patterns, and relational patterns into still more abstract levels of organization. Each ascending level, what Bateson called 'orders of recursiveness', is contextualized by the others and provides a broader description of the organizing principles underlying different relationships.

Tied to the proposition that relational form resides in the ongoing cycles of messages that interrelate parts into wholes is the logical distinction of the report–command duality of messages. Bateson (1951) asserts that two types of meaning are instantiated in messages, a referential (report) meaning which is simultaneously encompassed within the logically 'higher' relational (command) meaning (pp. 179–180). Messages provide both content information and instructions about the relationship between the participants. The relational meaning, i.e. the implied definitions of the interactants *vis à vis* one another, is of central concern in depicting the codefined patterns of interrelatedness. The combination of relational meanings by which interactants define self in relation to other are the 'patterns that connect' (Bateson, 1979) and constitute the ongoing nature of the relationship.

Bateson's formulation of the concepts symmetry and complementarity represents two basic patterns of social relationships. In a symmetrical pattern the participants' communicative behaviors mirror one another. Symmetry refers to 'those forms of interactional sequences that could be described in terms of competition, mutual emulation and so on' (Bateson, 1979, p. 192). In a complementary pattern the participants' behaviors are maximally different, but mutually fit together (e.g. assertiveness–submissiveness or giving–receiving). These two patterns may be fused to create patterns of pattern: for instance, reciprocal complementarity or a 'parallel' (Lederer and Jackson, 1968) mix of symmetry and complementarity. The patterns of symmetry and complementarity have served as prototypes of the paradigmatic shift from single messages to transactional and larger levels of analysis that underlie the study of relational form (Rogers, 1981).

This brief exploration into Bateson's work reflects the epistemological underpinnings of the relational approach and provides a backdrop for the development of basic dimensions of interpersonal relationships suggested in the next section.

DIMENSIONS OF RELATIONSHIPS

Essential to the study of interpersonal relationships is a theoretical framework for distinguishing various types of human interaction. Although both classificatory and dimensional constructs are necessary for differentiating human relationships, the theorist is more concerned with the continuous dimensions that undergird classification than with the nominal classes *per se* (Hage, 1972).

The development of measurement schemes indicating dimensions of communicative relationships allows research findings to be compared in conceptually meaningful ways. In this manner, investigatory results can be contrasted, theoretical linkages evidenced, and understandings of human relationships accrued.

The model of relationships proposed here is not based on static role descriptions nor individual attributes, but is grounded in the complex structuring of communication patterns that bind system members into relational wholes. As even a casual review of the literature attests, few typologies of social relationships have been based on communication characteristics. However, the work of McCall and Simmons (1966) and Kantor and Lehr (1975) has been particularly helpful in our efforts to formulate basic relational dimensions enacted in message performances.

Basic to our thinking is the spatial metaphor utilized by Kantor and Lehr in the development of their model of family processes. Kantor and Lehr (1975) assume that the family, like all interpersonal systems, is 'primarily an information-processing system and the information it processes is distance regulation in nature' (p. 222). These authors emphasize that social systems are 'continually informing their members what constitutes a proper or optimal distance' (p. 222) between themselves and/or between themselves and external events. They further assume that family systems are goal-oriented or purposeful and propose three dimensions which represent fundamental 'distances' between members— power, affect and meaning (pp. 46–52).

McCall and Simmons (1966) emphasize that an individual's identity is created and sustained through repetitive interactions with others. Individuals are also assumed to be symbolic and purposeful in developing situational plans of action; in any interactional episode the most basic constructs to be negotiated are the identities of each interactant. An individual's identity is not thought of as a personal, idiosyncratic construction, but as a 'social object' (p. 62) created and maintained in interactions with particular others who become inherent components of one's view of self. The socialness of self-identity prompts people to seek out dependable sources of role-identity support. McCall and Simmons assert that reward dependability is the most fundamental of their suggested 'interpersonal ties' that integrate and bind relational members together.

Building on these ideas, we propose a 'distancing' model of relational dimensions for conceptualizing the ways persons move in, around and away from one another in establishing the interpersonal ties that characterize their relationship. Interpersonal relationships are viewed as self-regulating systems that are continually structuring themselves and their members in and through distancing ties manifested in communicative behavior. Three generic 'distances' characterizing this structuring process are control, trust and intimacy. Expanded explications of these dimensions have been given elsewhere (Millar and Rogers, 1976) and are only highlighted here. Table 1 from Millar and Rogers (1987) summarizes these explications and serves as a guide for this review.

Table 1   Summary of relational dimensions (Millar and Rogers, 1987)

	Control	Trust	Intimacy
Spatial distance	Height	Width	Depth
Temporal relevance	Present	Future	Past
Structural identification	Pattern of constraints	Pattern of predictions	Pattern of sentiments
Functional significance	Regulation of definitional rights and constructive efficacy	Regulation of commitments and uncertainties	Regulation of personal identities and enmeshment
Felicity judgements	Freedom Equity	Sincerity Empirical veracity	Affection Understanding
Suggested indices	Redundancy Dominance Power	Vulnerability Reward dependability Confidence	Transferability Attachment Knowledge

Control

In the communication process, presentations of self are continually 'given off' (Goffman, 1959) and simultaneously imply particular actions for the other through 'altercasting' imputations (McCall and Simmons, 1966). Explicitly or implicitly, the communication behaviors of interactants offer definitions of self in relation to other (egocasting) and reciprocal definitions of other in relation to self (altercasting) (Weinstein and Deutschberger, 1964). Relational control definitions concern 'expected acts of deference and demeanor' (Denzin, 1970, p. 71) or the rights and privileges that collectively compose the patterns of constraint which regulate interactive dynamics (Danziger, 1976).

Within the pragmatic perspective to human communication (Fisher, 1978), an interpersonal relationship is emergent in the behaviors as messages that 'pass between' participants (Bateson, 1972, p. 275). In the pragmatic sense, control is synonymous with constraint; it refers to the ordering of communicative behaviors that characterize the structuring of interactive processes. Unequal probabilities of behavioral events indicate an interdependency, a 'systemness'. Control, although only one of the generic dimensions of human relationships, is the predominant organizing dimension (Weick, 1979) that regulates interactional performances. Differential patterns of relational control index different relational forms. The concepts of symmetry and complementarity, then, can be thought of as the interactional poles of relational control.

Conceptually, the control dimension represents the vertical distance between participants. The temporal focus of control is the present, since the rights to define the system's actions are in flux varying with topic and context. In this sense, control is the most dynamic of the three dimensions. Functionally, control patterns affect the 'constructive efficacy' (Kantor and Lehr, 1975, p. 49) of the system's capacity to accomplish desired goals.

The phenomenological importance of this dimension to the interactants is reflected in the felicity criteria of freedom and equity. These subjective judgements center on whether their contributions 'counted', on whether each is respected by other and equitably rewarded in the relationship. Our everyday concerns for the control dimension are indicated in such comments as: 'You can't talk to me like that'; 'He doesn't have the right to tell me what to do'; 'It's not fair that she can go out and I can't'; and 'This relationship is too confining.'

Trust

Relational dynamics are continually in flux and played out in uncertainty. There is an inherent fragility to relational dramas, with vulnerability the price of participation (Simmel, 1950). By definition, system members are interdependent; their actions mutually affect one another, with each member's meanings and reward/cost ratios contingent upon the other's actions. There is no guarantee that the other will behave in what is proposed as an appropriate and competent manner. The trust dimension concerns the inherent uncertainty of human systems and represents the horizontal distance between persons.

Conceptually, trust involves the predictability and obligatory nature of limitations on future choices. It concerns the participants' attempts to establish boundaries (through commitments, rewards, rules, promises, etc.) that constrain alter's subsequent behaviors. Structurally, trust is identified by the patterns of predictions made by ego and alter about the other's probable actions relative to themselves. These predictions function to produce a sense of certainty about future actions and outcomes so that relational commitments and investments can be facilitated.

The time orientation of trust is the future, although probability estimates are obviously based on previous experiences and/or present external factors. The felicity criteria of sincerity and empirical veracity refer, respectively, to judgements about the other's intentions relative to self and the other's competence to carry out these intentions. The relevance of this dimension in our everyday lives is suggested by such comments as: 'You can depend on her'; 'He's not reliable'; 'Don't take her into your confidence'; and 'You won't admit your own vulnerability so you keep pushing me away.'

Intimacy

The intimacy dimension concerns the sentiments associated with the connecting and separating currents of relational dynamics. Intimacy centers on the strength of members' 'attachments', on the extent to which specific others are built into one's self-identity and thereby become 'crucial to the legitimation and enactment of those identities' (McCall and Simmons, 1966, p. 173). This dimension is most central in distinguishing interpersonal relationships from other social relationships (e.g. husband–wife from colleagues). When increased degrees of attachment to a particular other characterize both participants, the more one's identity depends on that particular other for support, the less replaceable other becomes, and the more intimate the relationship.

Structurally, the intimacy dimension refers to the pattern of sentiments characterizing a relationship's history. This pattern functions to define the exclusivity or uniqueness of the relationship and the self-identities known within its bonds. The temporal relevancy of intimacy is, therefore, the past, for feelings of 'closeness' are based on what, how, and how often uniqueness has been shared with a particular other. Clearly, these experienced sentiments influence the evolving shape of messages-in-circuit, but they originate in what has happened. Primary felicity criteria are affection and understanding. Judgements of affection are tied to the belief that other likes/loves us as we are. Understanding is the belief that other knows us from our point of view.

The phenomenological importance of this dimension is illustrated in everyday comments like: 'I can't live without her'; 'He knows me as I really am'; 'I need you more than you need me'; 'I never thought I could feel this way until I met you'; and 'No one else allows me to be the real me.'

In sum, the three dimensions of control, trust and intimacy create a conceptual framework guiding the construction of a communication-based theory of interpersonal relationships. If reliable measures of these three can be developed at the relational level, then a more useful way of differentiating social relationships other than noun-pair classifications can be developed and more finely tuned theories of communicative dynamics can emerge. In order to pursue this long-range goal, we initially turned our efforts towards investigating the control dimension because it is the most basic in describing the various forms of interpersonal relations.

RELATIONAL COMMUNICATION RESEARCH

As discussed previously, Bateson's propositions about the duality of messages, the evolution of relationships within the messages-in-circuit, and the two general types of relationships, symmetry and complementarity, constitute the conceptual base to the study of control. Sluzki and Beavin (1965) proposed that the symmetrical and complementary nature of the relationship in the interactants' discourse would specifically be manifested in the grammatical and response form of sequential messages. Based on these premises, the relational communication coding system was designed to index these aspects of conversation (Rogers and Farace, 1975). The scheme was developed to describe the control implications of the relational aspects (Watzlawick, Beavin and Jackson, 1967) of verbalizations. This technique indexes the form of conversation rather than content. We assume that messages provide not only information about objects and events but also instructions about how persons define and redefine their relational rights. The relational coding scheme focuses on how messages function as pragmatic instructions, on how messages are constrained by the preceding, and in turn constrain the following, messages.

The coding procedures move from the individual message unit to the transact (a structure of contiguous messages) to sequential patterns of interactions. Each individual utterance is assigned a three-digit code. The first number designates the speaker. The second designates the grammatical form as (1) assertion, (2) question, (3) talkover, (4) noncomplete, and (5) other. The third digit describes the response function of the message relative to the other's immediately preceding message as (1) support, (2) nonsupport, (3) extension, (4) answer, (5) instruction, (6) order, (7) disconfirmation, (8) topic change, (9) initiation–termination, or (10) other. For instance, in relation to a preceding message of asserted instruction, the response, 'I don't think we can do that' is coded 212, where the speaker (coded 2) made an assertion (coded 1 for grammatical form) that does not support the previous speaker's utterance (coded 2 for nonsupport). In this manner, an entire conversation can be represented by a series of sequentially ordered three-digit codes.

Each of the 50 possible message types is then categorized according to how it defines the nature of the relationship: an attempt to assert a definition of the relationship is called a one-up movement ($\uparrow$), a request for or acceptance of the other's definition of the relationship is called a one-down movement ($\downarrow$), and a nondemanding, nonaccepting, least-constraining movement is called a one-across maneuver ($\rightarrow$). The nonsupportive assertion described above would be a one-up maneuver.

Do not be lured into thinking that a one-down movement is not constraining. There is nothing noncontrolling about one-down movements, as anyone can attest who has received persistent queries for information and/or assistance. But the constraining nature of a one-down move such as 'Will you help me with this?' is qualitatively different from the one-up move that says 'You get in here and help me!' In neither case is the speaker 'in control' of the other nor of the relational dynamics, but each statement does influence (constrain) the probable relational forms that will evolve.

Finally, by combining the control directions of contiguous messages, the minimum unit for describing relationships is created; this smallest unit is called a transact. In a *complementary* transact, the control directions are opposite, i.e. $\uparrow \downarrow$ or $\downarrow \uparrow$. The definition of the relationship offered by one interactant is accepted by the other. In a *symmetrical* transact ($\uparrow \uparrow$, $\downarrow \downarrow$ or $\rightarrow \rightarrow$), the control directions are the same. Each conversant behaves towards the other as the other has behaved towards them. In *transitory* transacts ($\uparrow \rightarrow$, $\rightarrow \uparrow$ and $\downarrow \rightarrow$, $\rightarrow \downarrow$), the directions are different but not complementary, with one conversant choosing the least-constraining one-across maneuver.

This scheme can be applied to distinguish larger patterns; for example, a double transact of competitive symmetry ($\uparrow \uparrow \uparrow$) defines a minimal unit of conflict as three consecutive one-up moves (Millar, Rogers and Bavelas, 1984). One interactant attempts to define the relationship; this is rejected by an opposing claim from the other which, in turn, is opposed by the initial speaker. The conflict pattern then represents the first step towards symmetrical escalation. The coding system and a graphing of temporal form are exemplified in Table 2.

Table 2 An interspousal conflict

| Dialogue segment | Relational control codes | | Transact | Double |
	Message type	Control direction		transact
W: What did you expect of me when we got married?	W: 123	↓		
H: Well, uh, . . . I really didn't have any expectations of you.	H: 214	↑	↓ ↑	
W: I expected you to take care of me.	W: 113	→	↑→	↓ ↑→
H: Haven't I? (asked challengingly)	H: 222	↑	→↓	↑→↑
W: Yes. Have I complained?	W: 111/ 122*	↓ ↑	↑ ↓ ↓ ↑	→↑ ↓ ↑↓ ↑
H: Yeah.	H: 214	↑	↑ ↑	↓ ↑ ↑
W: No! No.	W: 112	↑	↑ ↑	↑ ↑ ↑
H: Silently!	H: 212	↑	↑ ↑	↑ ↑ ↑
W: No. No, no, . . . no.	W: 112	↑	↑ ↑	↑ ↑ ↑

Graphing of Control Pattern

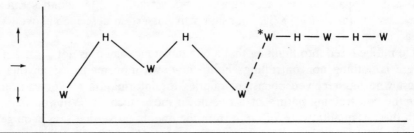

*Messages may be double-coded with the Rogers–Farace system.

Relational Control Measures

The relational coding scheme provides the basis for a rich set of operationalizations of control patterns. (See Rogers-Millar and Millar, 1979; Courtright, Millar and Rogers, 1979, 1983; Rogers, Courtright and Millar, 1980.) As Menzel (1979) emphasizes, the primary methodological problems in coding social interaction are the development of a reliable coding system and the clarification of how these categories are combined into higher-order constructs. To illustrate how we have combined the Rogers–Farace codes into higher-order descriptors of verbal interaction, three measures will be defined: domineeringness, a tabular index of an individual's one-up acts; dominance, a dyadic score representing the minimal unit of relational structure; and transactional redundancy, a measure of the variability in conversational dynamics.

The monadic measure of domineeringness is operationally defined as the number of one-up control moves made by an interactant during the conversation (domineeringness = ↑/total number of messages). Dominance is a relational measure (Van Hooff, 1982) in which the asserted definitional rights of one interactant are accepted by the other; it is operationalized as the number of one-up moves responded to with a one-down message by the other (dominance = given ↑, %↓). Domineeringness and dominance ratios, created by dividing one member's score by the other's, provide relationally specific control indices. For example, a dominance ratio of one indicates equivalency in the negotiation of relational rights; the greater the divergence from one, the more one person is said to be dominate.

Transactional redundancy refers to the amount of alteration in the participants' pattern of constraints; it indexes the amount of oscillation in their interactions over definitional rights. The more limited the transactional types manifested within and across topics, episodes and situated conversations, the more redundant or rigid the control pattern; the less redundant, the more flexible the pattern. Operationally, redundancy is computed by summing the absolute deviations from random use of the nine possible transacts. This measure can range from maximally chaotic (a score of zero) to maximally rigid (a score of 177).

These three measures exemplify a span of analytic levels from acts to transacts to the entire conversation. The multiple types of operationalized concepts available with this scheme are a clear advantage for describing verbal interactions.

Relational Control Research

The reported research represents a small sampling of the results that have been accumulating over the past decade or so and will center on the three control measures defined above. The results illustrate the types of analysis possible; they are not a thorough summary of the work that has been done. Simply, this section is fairly general in nature. (See the cited research for more detailed descriptions of measures, statistical procedures, and results.)

In large part, the results were generated from the analyses of tape-recorded husband and wife discussions of family-related topics gathered in two separate studies. Both samples consist of randomly selected midwestern, middle-social-class American couples in the child-rearing stage of the family-life cycle. The first sample included 45 marital dyads and the second 87. In total, about 80 hours of marital conversation were observed; lengthy questionnaires were also completed by each of the 264 respondents. (See Rogers-Millar and Millar, 1979; Millar, Rogers and Courtright, 1979; Courtright, Millar and Rogers, 1979, 1980.)

Analysis of approximately 24 000 messages (over 10 000 in the first study and over 13 000 in the second) found almost half of the messages were one-across movements with one-up and one-down each accounting for about 25 per cent. Twelve per cent of the transacts were complementary, 33 per cent were symmetrical and 55 per cent were transitory transacts. By comparison, a study of 45 manager–subordinate dyads based on over 11 000 messages found a similar 12 per cent of the transacts to be complementary, but a mirrored reversal of symmetrical (52 per cent) and transitory (35 per cent) transactions (Fairhurst, Rogers and Sarr, 1987). The marital dyads demonstrated considerably more flexibility in their communication patterns; the average redundancy score across the marital dyads was 54 while the manager–subordinate average was 83.

The manager–subordinate discussions resulted in 49 per cent of all transacts being one-across symmetry ($\rightarrow\rightarrow$); in the marital discussions, this type accounted for only 20 per cent of all transacts. One-across or neutralized symmetry depicts a 'safe', low-risk maintenance type of interaction; however, in both the marital and organizational settings large amounts of one-across symmetry were directly related to negative evaluations of the relationship by the participants.

Marital dyads with high role strain (perceived dyadic inequity) were found to have slightly higher proportions of competitive one-up symmetry and more one-across symmetry than low-strain dyads (L. E. Rogers, 1972). The more frequent occurrence of neutralized symmetrical transacts suggests an avoidance pattern that periodically erupts into a competitive struggle. High-strain couples also manifested fewer husband one-down transitory transacts, a structure found to be associated with more conversational harmony. In addition, high role strain couples reported spending less time together, talking less with one another, talking about fewer topics (particularly more personal topics) and indicated less satisfaction with their communication and marital relationship than couples with low marital strain.

Research using the marital typology developed by Fitzpatrick (1976) demonstrated that the different marital types (i.e., traditional, independent and separate) exhibited different relational control patterns (Fitzpatrick, 1984). Traditional couples were characterized as the most cohesive of the three types and had the highest degree of consensus, affection and satisfaction. In contrast, independent couples scored lowest on these three aspects of dyadic adjustment and in particular, lowest on satisfaction. An analysis of 43 couple's discussions of high and low salient conflict topics found that the independents, regardless of topic salience, engaged in more competitive symmetry than the other marital types, while the separates manifested the least amount of one-up symmetry and the highest proportion of complementary transacts. The traditionals demonstrated the most flexibility in their control patterns across topics; these couples decreased the proportion of competitive symmetry and increased their complementarity with low salient topics, and reversed this pattern in high salient topic discussions. The higher transactional variability and marital satisfaction of the traditionals in comparison to the higher redundancy and lower satisfaction of the independents evidences the functionality of flexible control patterns.

A recent study of Spanish marital dyads adds some cross-cultural evidence for the more frequent use and longer sequences of competitive symmetry in conflict situations (Escudero and Gutierrez, 1987). In nonconflict discussions, these couples enacted more complementary and one-down transitory transacts. A study of the control dynamics of couples in therapy (Manderscheid *et al.*,

1982) found that one-up control moves as well as one-down moves led to sequences of competitive symmetry. However, one-up assertions resulted in stronger competition, while yielding responses resulted in more gradual escalation. In contrast, one-across statements decreased the potential for competitive sequences.

At the individual level of analysis, the research by Rogers and her colleagues found that a higher proportion of wife one-up control maneuvers characterized the high role strain dyads. Wife domineeringness was also associated with lower levels of marital and communication satisfaction for both spouses. To gain information about specific styles associated with these distinctions, several other behaviors have been examined. For instance, wives who manifested higher proportions of one-up messages asserting definitional rights offered fewer support statements to their husbands. In contrast, when husbands asserted one-up messages, they tended to also support their wives.

Analyses of talkovers showed that the proportion of both total talkovers and successful talkovers made by husbands and wives was associated with their domineering behavior but not their dominance scores. Interrupting clearly characterized a domineering style. Research on gender language differences showed interruptions to be more of a male characteristic (Zimmerman and West, 1975; Henley, 1977); perhaps this style is an added irritant of wife domineeringness, but not of husband domineeringness.

Of further interest concerning the dynamics of transactional patterning is the negative correlation between domineeringness and transactional redundancy. Our studies indicate that the fewer one-up messages made by the husband, the more rigid the couple's transactional patterns. Apparently, the assertion of definitional rights, especially on the part of the husband, stimulates more variability in the structuring of the couple's conversations. However, if wives are too domineering, the benefits of more transactional flexibility are offset by the associated negative evaluations of the relationship. These results seem to parallel those of Gottman (1982b), although the measures are not directly comparable.

Turning to the dominance index, we find that husband dominance was associated with slightly higher levels of marital and communication satisfaction and lower levels of role strain than was wife dominance. With husband dominance, there was a stronger correlation of wife giving support than the husband giving support when the wife was comparatively more dominant. However, the greater the inequality of the dominance outcome, the lower the reported marital satisfaction and the lower the partners' knowledge indices. With high inequalities of dominance, both partners reported lower understanding, but the more dominant member exhibited lower levels of understanding than the less dominant member (Millar, Rogers and Courtright, 1979).

A similar set of results was found in the organizational setting where manager dominance was negatively related to understanding, perceived subordinate involvement in decision-making processes, and subordinate performance ratings. Thus within the manager–subordinate dyads, the more dominant the manager, the poorer the subordinate's performance evaluation, the less the subordinate was perceived to be involved in decisions, the lower the understanding of the subordinate and, in line with the marital findings, the higher the level of understanding of the subordinate compared with the manager (Fairhurst, Rogers and Sarr, 1987).

To summarize, the following interconnections are suggested by these findings: the more equivalent the dominance ratio, the more flexible the interaction, the more frequent discussions about various topics, the more conflict potential in the dyad's conversations but the more 'in tune' members' expectations and understandings of one another. In contrast, the more discrepant the dominance structure, the more redundant the transactional pattern, the less frequent discussions about fewer topics, the more apparent 'harmony' in the interaction, but the less accurate and up-to-date the dyad's expectations of each other and the greater the avoidance and/or rebellion potential. These findings appear to evidence the functionality of reciprocal complementarity (Bateson, 1972) and the mutually enhancing aspects of parallel relationships (Lederer and Jackson, 1968).

FUTURE IMPLICATIONS

The empirical work to date has focused on operationalizing the control aspects of symmetry and complementarity. The Rogers–Farace scheme has been useful in that quest. However, given that symmetry and complementarity are thought of as the metaphoric poles of interactive processes that can be characterized by differentiated patterns of control, trust and intimacy, future endeavors must enlarge and enrich our descriptions of these dimensions in order to evidence their explanatory potential. Explanations of social relationships are limited by the available descriptions of communicative dynamics; thus, if useful theories of social order and orderings are to be constructed, work must center on the development and refinement of indexing these dimensions. Future efforts will investigate several issues simultaneously; but, for stylistic convenience, the suggested directions are mentioned in order of their level of abstraction.

At the operational level, the control coding procedures need to be refined and expanded. The coding of message types has been slightly modified in current studies. The response mode of 'initiates–terminates' has been replaced with a 'self-instruction' category making the scheme more internally consistent and more finely differentiating one-across movements. The coding rules for 'answer' have also been modified in order to describe more specifically the pragmatic functions of responses to questions. The early returns on these modifications indicate that they do more adequately describe pragmatic functions without loss of reliability.

In the initial research using the relational coding system, L. E. Rogers (1972) suggested two additional measures for increasing the descriptive value of the scheme, a message intensity and a message duration score. The intensity measure (Rogers, Courtright and Millar, 1980) was developed to capture more precisely the 'distancing' implications of messages. It indexes the within-category control variations of one-up, one-down, one-across messages. As an illustration, an assertion coded as an order is a more heavily weighted (intense) one-up control move than an instruction. Future research will continue to explore the utility and refinement of the intensity measures. Potential modifications will involve assessing the representative validity (Folger and Poole, 1982) of the intensity weights so that more detailed depictions of controlling processes can be attained and more subtle nuances of interpersonal relationships can be described. The inclusion of message duration measures provides an expanded description of a dyad's relational 'rhythm'. Message duration is a straightforward clocktime measure of an utterance's length. Case studies employing the temporal length of verbalizations clearly illustrate the descriptive utility of this measure. The inclusion of intensity weightings and message duration measures in turn provides for more expanded analyses of control patterns and patternings of patterns. In general, control researchers have not adequately dealt with larger units of sequential messages. Our own work, for instance, has predominately focused on the transact, but operational means of comparing double transacts and larger chains of messages are necessary to evidence the 'tyranny of pattern' (Bateson, 1979) manifested in communicative dynamics. Refinements of the intensity weights and inclusion of message duration indices will aid such comparisons.

Other high-priority tasks are the development of behaviorally based indices of trust and intimacy. The construction of such measures requires the inclusion of communicative variables explicitly excluded by the Rogers–Farace procedures, i.e. nonverbal behaviors, content analyses and subjective meanings.

The use of process-oriented methodologies (Rogers, Millar and Bavelas, 1985) to characterize nonverbal cues would greatly expand the descriptive utility of the Rogers–Farace procedures and allow for investigation of the relative importance of verbal and nonverbal actions in regulating relational distances. Nonverbal process descriptions will necessarily depict the speaker's and listener's movements simultaneously, and thereby indicate relational-level enactments. Although our conceptualizations of the trust and intimacy dimensions involve subjective judgements which, by definition, are unobservable, our epistemological assumptions assert that these judgements are 'signaled' (Scheflen, 1974) in observable performances. Thus, reliable ways of describing the width (trust) and depth (intimacy) implications of behaviors-as-messages are needed. The work of Burgoon and her colleagues cited earlier will be useful in this regard. Once developed, trust and intimacy indices can be integrated with the vertical distancings of control so that empirically grounded theories of relational dynamics can be constructed and falsified.

We assume that people relate in talk (Duncan, 1967) and have attempted to describe the shapes of relationships as manifested in talking. But this assumption also implies that the content of talk, i.e. what people talk *about*, also influences the shape of evolving forms of relationships. Most content-based schemes (e.g., Bales, 1950; Gottman, 1979; Fisher, Drecksel and Werbel, 1979) do not deal with content as subjective meaning but classify content by function. Exceptions to this functional emphasis exist; for instance, Stiles (1981) attempts to code the interpersonal intent of verbalizations and Bernal and Baker (1979) classify content by metacommunicational levels. However useful these approaches to content are, they do not capture the subjective meanings of verbalizations.

What we envision by content analysis might be called a metaphorical depiction and is consistent with work on relational schemata and relational knowledge. The questions we are concerned with are what pattern of interconnected symbols constitutes the experiential meaning of the expressed content for the speaker, and how is that indicated in observable relational distancings? For example, if a wife states that her marriage is like a zoo, what images does she associate with the zoo metaphor? Cleaning cages, sleeping captives, feeding and breeding animals, policing onlookers, collecting entrance fees are all activities that take place at a zoo. Are these experientially descriptive of her marriage? If so, are her own actions in that marital relation reflective of her meaning? Further, if such connections can be described for one individual, are different primary metaphors of marriages (e.g. zoo vs insane asylum vs floral garden vs castle vs army barracks) systemically associated with different distancing patterns across individuals? If subjective meanings 'cause' actions, then such systematic associations are expected and need to be delineated. However, it may be the case that people's metaphorical descriptions are so general that no direct predictive association with redundant behavioral patterns is possible. If so, then such meanings exert little influence over behaviors, are not empirically falsifiable causes of behaviors, and, therefore, are to be abandoned as theoretical explanations of interpersonal systems. If, however, such metaphorical interpretations are thought of as 'post hoc commentaries' (Scheflen, 1974) on previous events, they might indirectly influence behavior by limiting probable choices in subsequent episodes in self-fulfilling ways. If this latter view is accepted, then clusters of behavioral patterns should be associated with different metaphorical schematas. If such associations are evidenced, then discrediting an individual's retained metaphors and crediting a different metaphorical framing (Weick, 1979) might lead to different behavioral patterns and/or the performance of different behaviors might lead to different interpretations. (Effects affect effects to affect effects.)

The general issue, then, is how to evidence the expected self-fulfilling interconnections between individuals' cognitive meanings and interactional redundancies? The most theoretically important direction for future efforts in relational communication is the synthesis of cognitive (semantic) and behavioral (pragmatic) descriptions of social relationships (Montgomery, 1984c). The 'new order of communication' (Bateson, 1951) consists of both types of propositions. Although no sharp line can be drawn between these two general types of descriptions in human systems, they can be analytically distinguished and they must be methodologically separated, for each requires a different unit of analysis. Their synthesis is crucial since both sets of descriptions are necessary for the construction of theories that provide a sense of understanding about humans *communicating* and of *human* communication.

The coordinated management of meaning (CMM) research (Pearce and Cronen, 1980; Cronen, Pearce and Harris, 1982; Cronen, Johnson and Lannaman, 1982; Cronen, Pearce and Tomm, 1985) seems especially promising for integrating the reflexive form of cognitive meanings with the recursive form of behavioral patterns. Their work, like ours, has developed out of a 'cybernetic epistemology' (Bateson, 1972). The CMM approach assumes that realities are social constructs; it offers a rigorous means of describing the reflexive circuits of subjective meanings and, without unreasonably stretching the contents of these meanings, seems interpretable in terms of the dimensions of control, trust and intimacy.

The simultaneous application of the coordinated management of meaning and the communication control coding procedures, particularly when combined with nonverbal process descriptions, will more thoroughly explicate the messages-in-circuit that are interpersonal relationships from a relational communication point of view. Visualizing how such studies might be conducted and their probable theoretical benefits is not difficult; doing them is. We have offered this chapter in the hope that such synthetic investigations will be initiated.

Handbook of Personal Relationships
Edited by S. W. Duck
© 1988 John Wiley & Sons Ltd

17

Communicator Style Theory in Marital Interaction: Persistent Challenges

ROBERT W. NORTON
Memphis State University, Tennessee, USA

ABSTRACT

This chapter relates communicator style as a construct in its own right to marital interaction. The theoretical argument is lodged in the marital *quid pro quo* or the metaphorical contract upon which marriage is based. The way couples communicate, their communicator style, serves two functions. First, it reflects the quality of the marriage; second, it provides a means to repair dysfunctional marital interaction.

This chapter highlights the essential research issues which relate 'style of communication' to marital interaction. It identifies the persistent challenges marital researchers provoke investigating metamessages. Also, it invites the researcher to gravitate towards a unified theory grounded in the marital *quid pro quo* (Jackson, 1965). With this framework, communicator style theory centers on pragmatic consequences inherent in couple communication.

The first section presents the construct of communicator style. The basic theoretical structure is introduced to establish communicator style as a construct in its own right. The chapter introduces the definitions, assumptions, and axioms which organize the framework of the style construct. This section explicates both a microsense and macrosense of style which are inextricably a function of each other.

The second section argues that the compelling criteria for extending communicator style theory in the marital domain should be based on the *quid pro quo*. Jackson (1965) calls this notion the metaphorical bargain upon which marriages are based. Fish and Fish (1986) provide elegant extensions of the concept.

The third section discusses the research which most directly relates style work to the quality of the marital context. Although few studies use a communicator style frame as a concept in its own right, examples are drawn from a wide range of couple research to illustrate how the criteria generated in the first section can be used to evaluate the respective approaches.

Finally, the fourth section identifies three problems that limit marital research of communicative processes. This section discusses definitional problems, issues of reactivity, and sampling errors which impinge upon research of communicative processes in general and research examining metamessages in particular.

COMMUNICATOR STYLE AS A CONSTRUCT

The degree that the data are relatively dependent on social judgements distinguishes the many ways to classify style research. Data range from types which can be mechanically generated once set up by the researcher to types which require intricate training of many coders to establish reliable judgements. Data for style research run a similar range.

Generic Communication Style Research

Some researchers examine the way individuals communicate by focusing on features of speech. This work requires few assumptions about the social context. In fact, effort often is made to overcome personal effects in the speech. Jassem and Demenko (1985), for instance, reduce voices to a common pitch, equalize individual voice ranges, normalize tempo, and attempt to eliminate linguistic effect to determine the precise relationship between function and form of communication. These types of data are frequently generated mechanically or electronically instead of depending on trained coders.

With this approach, a person's style of communication might, for example, be characterized as excessively low in pitch accompanied by a hoarseness and a slowed tempo. A researcher with this perspective rarely relates the data of speech characteristics to a pragmatic consequent, although some work (Atkinson, 1984; Ladd, Scherer and Silverman, 1986) exemplifies cases to the contrary. It is unlikely, for instance, anyone would expect that a person with an excessively low pitch would be perceived to be a poor husband because of the way he communicated.

Nonverbal communication represents a transition area of research which ranges from investigations that simply tabulate frequency of nonverbal movements to studies which depend upon inferences from a social context. Hewes' (1957) identification of over 1000 different steady postures of man, including the one-legged Nilotic stance found in the Sudan and Venezuela, typifies the first type of research. The taxonomists usually record behavior which may be contingent on understanding only minimal aspects of the culture. Although issues of reliability are enhanced by understanding the context, Morris *et al.* (1979), for example, do not need to know very much about the Greek culture to catalogue that the 'cheek stroke' means 'thin and ill' about one third of the time.

With much nonverbal research, it is usual to talk about the 'way individuals communicate' or 'styles of communication'. Certain deception (Zuckerman, DePaulo and Rosenthal, 1986) can be detected by attending to the person's nonverbal way of communicating; rapport is established by the doctor's nonverbal style (Harrigan and Rosenthal, 1986); an individual's style of communication reflects his or her coronary type (DiMatteo, Prince and Hays, 1986).

However, the notion of 'style of communication' functions at a generic level. There is no commitment to treat the 'manner, mode, or way a person communicates' as a necessary component of the communication gestalt. The notion of 'communication style' is not presented as a construct in its own right. The phrases 'style', 'way', 'mode', 'manner', and 'fashion' are broadly used to report phenomena which are part of the communicative process, but they are not presented within a framework which is articulated as part of a theoretical structure. The following paragraphs elaborate.

A Concept in Its Own Right

Transforming communication style research from the generic to 'name brand' requires precise theoretical commitments. Communication research at this level puts a premium on understanding the 'what' and 'how' of the communicative process. The 'what' is at a semantic level rather than a linguistic level. It makes a difference whether the content is 'I love you', 'I like you', or 'I am thinking about it'. The 'how' is at a style level that inextricably helps to make sense out of the content. Saying 'I love you' in a detached way is a different communicative gestalt from saying 'I love you' in a licentious way.

How and what people say to each other affects them and the relationship. To do work at this level, *it is assumed that every communicative gestalt entails at least two elements, a literal message and a stylistic message which instructs, in at least one way, how to process the literal message.*

Ruesch and Bateson (1951) first introduced the notion that any communication has two operations, what they labeled 'report' (corresponding to content) and 'command' (corresponding to style). Then in 1967, Watzlawick, Beavin and Jackson revived and amplified the notion. In 1983, Norton provided a theoretical structure with which to extend the notion further.

Norton (1983a) begins with two definitions: (1) a message system provides information, and (2) a communication 'gestalt' is the interaction of information from the respective message systems, that is, content and style. Because every communication gestalt entails information from at least two components (by definition), each component has the potential to provide either ambiguous or unambiguous information.

If both the content and style components provide unambiguous information, then the gestalt is synchronous, there is an isomorphic match between message systems, there is low entropy, and redundancy is likely. If either the content or style component provides ambiguous information, then the gestalt is nonsynchronous, 'best' information must be distinguished, and entropy may be high. In the case of nonsynchronous gestalts, the person is pressured to resolve the ambiguity, especially if the following conditions are met.

If one assumes that the person is not communicatively inept and that the stylistic message is nonrandom, then the communicative gestalt must be analyzed in terms of its pragmatic effect to unravel the intrinsic intentionality. If a person says 'I love you' in a licentious way, this communicative gestalt is different from saying the same sentence in an indifferent, hateful, or disgusting way and it is even different from almost synonymous ways such as a racy, sultry, prurient, or romantic declaration. Saying 'I love you' in a hateful way prods the person to understand and resolve the ambiguous gestalt.

On the other hand, if one assumes that the way the person frames the content is nonrandom and nonintentional, then the researcher is looking at extraordinary, pathological, or capricious utterances, in which case the communicative gestalt provides another kind of pragmatic evidence.

In general, communicator style can be defined as 'the way one verbally, nonverbally, and paraverbally interacts to signal how literal meaning should be taken, interpreted, filtered, or understood' (Norton, 1983a, p. 58). The key to the definition is that a *signal or a set of signals* provides the framework with which to process content.

All definitions of style, whether discussing clothing, music, government, or leadership, etc., can be reduced to two senses—a micro sense and a macro sense. Furthermore, both are inextricably related as will be shown later.

In the first sense, style is the way or manner something is done. Style in the micro sense refers to the form-giving signals that are typically in the here and now of the specified situation and context. It is that set of messages which shapes the literal content usually at the specified moment in the designated context. Because style elements function hierarchically, however, a style element can interact in the framing of the gestalt at any point in time (Norton, 1983a).

A communicator has many ways to signal how the literal message should be filtered, taken, understood, or processed. A person can, for example, manifest a dramatic, open, nervous style or any other combination of attributes, including any of 90 style traits Deethardt and McLaughlin (1976) have identified.

Style in the macro sense refers to the consistently recurring patterns one creates by repeatedly communicating in a similar way. If a wife regularly tags her leavetaking messages to her husband with loving and caring signals, then it creates an expectation that is idiosyncratically associated with her by the husband. This association becomes one of many which functions as a norm about the way she communicates, in this case messages about later contact.

Furthermore, the norms are not random; they function like major premises which organize themselves into patterns, which, in turn, create expectations, which, in turn, frame every communicative interaction. The remembered pattern helps the person to monitor the interaction and helps the person classify and evaluate another. The remembered pattern, like a mental template, gives form to the interaction (Norton, 1983a). Not to have a remembered pattern relegates the person to an unconnected and unconnecting life with no sense of time or continuity. Sacks (1985) describes many cases like this in his book *The Man Who Mistook His Wife for a Hat and Other Clinical Tales*.

Accordingly, style in this sense is an accumulation of 'microbehaviors' giving form to literal content that add up to a 'macrojudgement' about a person's style of communicating. *Style as a consistently recurring pattern of association is form giving at the macrolevel because expectations about the way one communicates become increasingly robust.*

Accordingly, if the investigator assumes that every communication gestalt is the inextricable interaction of a content component and a style component, that style components function hierarchically, that the consistently recurring associations of style behaviors create expectations which impact upon processing every interaction, then it is incumbent on the researcher to make appropriate distinctions concerning the exact phenomenon he or she is studying, to attend to hierarchical dynamics, and to respect the histories of communicative interaction which powerfully shape the behavior of the respondents. The principles established here for style theory are applicable across all interactive phenomena, but they are especially apropos to the marital context because of the nature of the *quid pro quo*.

STYLE WORK INEXTRICABLY RELATED TO THE MARITAL *QUID PRO QUO*

Two assumptions must mark the beginning of style work in a marital context. First, the *context* itself affects communicative behavior. Second, the *quality of the context* necessarily modifies communicative behavior in an attempt to maintain or renegotiate the *quid pro quo*.

Marital Context Influencing Behavior

Three characteristics prominently mark the marital context: (1) the sense of being a team, (2) indeterminate time, and (3) institutionalization. Being together pressures the couple to act like a team over an indeterminate time period. Both 'teamness' and the time frame have consequences for the way individuals communicate with each other. Moreover, being together is institutionalized. As such, it reifies togetherness by powerful external forces, including legal, spiritual, and cultural influences.

The researchers (Burns, 1973; Ekeh, 1974; McDonald, 1981) who express the analysis in terms of exchange theory (Homans, 1958, 1961; Blau, 1964; Gergen, Greenberg and Willis, 1980) argue that within the marital context two basic types of exchanges can be distinguished: institutionalized and interpersonal reciprocity. This perspective can easily be integrated into a *quid pro quo* framework.

Being a team

Feeling like part of a team in a marriage is highly correlated with perceiving that one has a good marriage, a very stable relationship with one's partner, a strong marriage, a relationship which makes the individual happy, and a marriage that makes both spouses happy (Norton, 1983b).

Feeling like a team entails the *quid pro quo* that Jackson (1965a) first described:

> *Quid pro quo* (literally 'something for something') is an expression of the legal nature of a bargain or contract, in which each party must receive something for what he [or she] gives and which, consequently, defines the rights and duties of the parties in the bargain. Marriage, too, can be likened to a bargain which defines the different rights and duties of the spouses, each of whom can be said to do X if and because the other does Y. *Quid pro quo*, then, is a descriptive metaphor for a relationship based on differences and expressions of redundancies which one observes in marital interaction. (pp. 591–592)

Fish and Fish (1986) point out that *quid pro quo* describes the overarching pattern of roles played, interactional sequencing, and rules followed which define the marital relationship or interaction. They argue that 'the *quid pro quo* is the "meta" marital rule which gives shape and coherence to the more specific relationship rules' (p. 372). *This means that one of the form-giving messages that constantly interpenetrates every communication gestalt in a marriage is the* quid pro quo. It is an essential part of every communicative process in the marital context—it cannot not be. To ignore the *quid pro quo* in marital communication research is tantamount to missing the essence of the phenomenon.

The *quid pro quo* dictates theoretical expectations. Fish and Fish postulate that when the *quid pro quo* is not balanced, interactional forces work to reestablish the reciprocity. Support for this fundamental notion is found in the works of Bowen (1978), Scanzoni and Polonko (1980), Madanes (1981), and Whitaker (1982). Three issues are pertinent to couples forming and reforming the *quid pro quo*: (1) inclusion, (2) control, and (3) support.

Inclusion. What is to be *included* in the form-giving contract? To answer this question establishes what Bateson (1972) calls a psychological frame in interaction. The dual function of such a frame both excludes and includes certain messages.

Bateson treats psychological frames as 'premises' which are metacommunicative. He asserts that 'any message, which either explicitly or implicitly defines a frame, *ipso facto* gives the receiver instructions or aids in his attempt to understand the messages included in the frame' (p. 188). To reiterate, the *quid pro quo* is a frame which is metacommunicative and necessarily a part of the communication gestalt.

Fox (1974) and later McDonald (1981) point to the unobtrusive dynamic of inclusion. They argue that normatively prescribed roles which favor the male initially are included as part of the *quid pro quo*. In fact, if couples conform to the 'form-giving norm' of their culture, whatever it is, then they will feel normal and avoid the guilt intrinsic to norm violation. The problem is that cultural norms often contribute to external, inequitable weighting within the *quid pro quo*. Unfortunately, little work has been done concerning how couples interactively establish core elements for inclusion in the metaphorical contract.

Control. The second question that couples must address either tacitly or explicitly is one of control: who is in charge of the relationship? Fish and Fish (1986) contend that 'marital partners struggle for equal control of the relationship in varied ways. Just as some couples struggle over who will dominate, others struggle over who will be taken care of' (p. 378).

Control is an inherent issue because it determines the rules for how rules are to be established, maintained, and evaluated. Accordingly, initial control creates metarules for adjudicating issues of inclusion and intimacy. Once the *quid pro quo* is sufficiently shaped and accepted by the couple, interaction then reflects the stamp of the metaphorical contract.

For example, part of a *quid pro quo* in which the wife dominates may entail the tacit understanding that the husband can manifest more dominance messages in inconsequential contexts such as making minor financial decisions, choosing the day the children will be baptized, or participating in experiments to help doctoral students.

The sundry ways to control one's spouse range from the brutally violent to the subtly psychological, but each way suggests some type of 'one-up, one-down' relationship (Rogers and Farace, 1975; Fisher and Drecksel, 1983; Williamson and Fitzpatrick, 1985). Rogers, Millar and Bavelas (1985) provide an exceptional review of this literature.

The act of interactive control implies the right to call into account. Stylistically, a person who calls another into account often manifests an assurance of being right, acts as though he or she possesses superior judgement, and indicates an ability to impose discipline, and possibly inspires fear.

Most of the literature (e.g. Roach, Frazier and Bowden, 1981; Spiro, 1983; Cunningham, Braiker and Kelley, 1982) suggests that equitable control relates strongly to a high-quality marriage. Not to know the *quid pro quo* of a couple is to do interaction research in a vacuum.

Support. The third question relates to support or intimacy. Fish and Fish (1986) suggest that the negotiation for intimacy strikes a balance between the need for autonomy and the need to belong:

> Even if both partners in the marital dyad feel comfortable at the same level of emotional intimacy, the couple still needs to struggle with how they will accommodate it in their relationship. Who will be the pursuer and who will be pursued, who will crave affection and who will wish to be left alone, and are these roles static or is there enough freedom in the relationship to negotiate flexibly of their respective and mutual intimacy needs? (p. 379).

This theme is reminiscent of Sennett's (1980) *Authority*.

Supporting interaction has been positively related to a good relationship in many studies (Hinchliffe *et al.*, 1978; Cheung and Hudson, 1982; Matthews and Clark, 1982; Sullaway and Christensen, 1983; Thompson and Spanier, 1983). Lack of supporting behavior is among the top complaints by both married and cohabiting couples (Cunningham, Braiker and Kelley, 1982; Eidelson, 1983).

The nature of the *quid pro quo* implies that mutual support will be given. Walster and Walster (1978) argue that supporting behavior in the form of validation provides an important antidote for feelings of boredom and stagnation which infest a long-term intimate relationship once the romantic glow begins to fade.

Supporting communication shows that there is a willingness to sustain the other, to contribute to the other's morale or physical being, metaphorically to hold the other up or to help bear the weight. The metamessage of supporting communication is 'I am giving to you'. The pragmatic consequence is confirmation or validation. To know what the other needs or wants in the *quid pro quo* in itself is a partial indication of caring, and then to act on the assessment completes the demonstration.

Indeterminate time frame

The longer the team is together, the greater chance each participant has to know, understand, and foster unique and idiosyncratic means of communicating. The more one knows another person, the better chance one has of accurately predicting that person's behavior. *To the extent that the associations are specific to context, situation, or time, the knowing will seem more salient, consistent, and valid.*

Several researchable questions are embedded in this assumption. For instance, marriages on the verge of disintegrating might have partners who 'know' aspects of each other's style too well or the opposite may be the case—the marriage is in trouble because at least one partner does not 'know' critical aspects of the other's style, the partner no longer can 'read' the other in an adequate way.

Two communicator style postulates are relevant to marital interaction. First, expectations about consistently recurring patterns in style become increasingly stable as a function of more association with the communicator. Without the memories of each other, spouses would not have a sense of history about the couple. An important part of the memories is what individuals say to each other and the way they say it.

Second, style expectations in the macrosense can influence the literal message more powerfully than the immediate style exhibited (Norton, 1983a). If a spouse's consistently recurring pattern has been to communicate in a dramatic and open way, then deviation from that pattern signals something interesting. To ignore the macrojudgement templates is to ignore the communicative 'ground' (Perls, Hefferline and Goodman, 1965) in which any given message is sent.

Institutionally constrained

The best indications of what institutional constraint means are comparisons of: (1) married couples with cohabiting couples or (2) marital interaction with nonmarital interaction for the same couple.

Cohabitation vs marriage. Most cohabitation research asks whether cohabitation leads to a good marriage. Although the popular notion is that cohabitation provides a compatibility test before formalizing the situation, most studies (Clayton and Voss, 1977; Glick and Spanier, 1980; Newcomb, 1980) find that cohabitation has no effect on subsequent marital quality.

DeMaris and Leslie's (1984) work, however, found that having cohabited premaritally was associated with lower perceived quality of communication for wives and lower marital satisfaction for both spouses. They argue that the experience of cohabiting itself is not the reason for the poorer quality of communication or lower marital satisfaction; they maintain that the kinds of people who choose to cohabit already are predisposed to report low satisfaction and poorer communication relating to marriage.

Blumstein and Schwartz (1983) provide the most ambitious and impressive study, comparing 642 cohabiting couples with 3774 married couples. Their findings show that the institution of marriage *per se* alters interaction in sexual, economic, and mundane activity, especially for the woman.

Although Blumstein and Schwartz do not focus on communication variables, it is reasonable to expect that communicative behaviors might also differ because of the constraints of the institution of marriage. However, no research has been done along these lines.

Marital vs nonmarital context. It is a natural expectation that individuals will communicate with their spouses in a different way from with persons who are in a 'one-up' or 'one-down' position, friends, acquaintances, or strangers (Honeycutt, Wilson and Parker, 1982). Norton (1986), for example, found that spouses report communicating in a more relaxed, friendly, open, expressive, attentive, and precise style with their partners than in general. The intriguing questions are 'What is there about the marital context that fosters different ways of communicating?' and 'What are the consequences of communicating in different styles?'

Implications of Style Theory

To focus on style patterns as a determinant of communication gestalts invites the researcher to make more precise analyses of interactive processes. The initial tendency to conclude that bad communication goes with a bad marriage is replaced by the notion that a couple in a bad marriage may be communicating clearly, concisely, intensely, and decisively. The consequent of the messages may be painful, disabling, intolerable, mean, and ugly. The marriage may break apart, but not because the communication *per se* was bad!

In like manner, a good marriage might entail a communicative pattern that is equivocal, vague, and ambiguous, especially if the couple has fostered family myths, useful fictions, or a private language (Raush *et al.*, 1974; Watzlawick, Beavin and Jackson, 1967; Watzlawick, Weakland and Fisch, 1974). In this case, the marriage may stay intact, but not because the communication *per se* is good. Joanning (1982), for example, warns that interrupting a couple's normative pattern of communication which seems 'poor' to the expert but 'works' for the couple poses 'a severe risk to relationship continuity' (p. 467).

The consistently recurring pattern that each partner associates with the other creates a powerful template with which to judge ambiguity in the communicative process. Three principles operate (Norton, 1983a). First, whenever a communication gestalt is ambiguous, one style component in the hierarchy moves more to the center of attention and is valued more. Second, whenever the gestalt deviates from normal expectations, one style component in the hierarchy commands more attention and operates with greater leverage. Third, an ambiguous gestalt motivates the receiver to interactively and inferentially supply premises that alleviate ambiguity.

QUALITY OF MARITAL CONTEXT COVARYING WITH STYLE BEHAVIOR

Generally, researchers assume that the person's style of communication does two kinds of work in a marriage. First, it provides a *means to maintain the* quid pro quo. As such, it can be a means to repair or enhance a relationship (Stein, 1975; Adam and Gingras, 1982; Mitchell, 1982). Second, it *reflects* what is going on in the relationship (Ferreira and Winter, 1974; Feldman and Jorgensen, 1974; Miller, Nunnally and Wackman, 1976; Fineberg and Lowman, 1975).

Communicator style maintaining quid pro quo. The style component always has consequences for the relationship. This notion is an inherent part of Reusch and Bateson's (1951) early conceptualization, later amplified by Watzlawick, Beavin and Jackson (1967, p. 52): 'The command aspect [style component] . . . refers to what sort of message it [content] is to be taken as, and, therefore, ultimately to the *relationship* between communicants.'

Or reiterating Norton's (1983a) definition, communicator style signals how literal meaning should be taken, interpreted, filtered, or understood. If one assumes that the signals are nonrandom and apt, then to determine 'how' signals are to be sent is very close to knowing 'why' they are sent. If one assumes that the signals are competently intentional, then the 'how' inevitably has consequences for the *quid pro quo*. It cannot be otherwise. Furthermore, *if communication gestalts consistently recur enough times, the pattern which shapes the* quid pro quo, *in turn, functions in a form-giving capacity.*

For example, if a spouse can count on her husband to tease her every time she mentions one of his idiosyncratic, personally private habits (e.g. praying before lunch), then she has expectations that her 'X' (mentioned habit) will trigger his 'Y' (retaliatory tease). These expectations which are part of their *quid pro quo* frame the anticipated interaction. To deviate from the expected form is a signal that something is wrong. The partner may be sick, disinterested, preoccupied, or unhappy with that particular scenario.

Repairing the quid pro quo. Necessarily, a marital therapist, counselor, therapeutic friend, or a 'born again' spouse uses communication to attempt repair in the relationship. *The telling question is, 'What is inherent in the process of communicating that will bring about change?'* Sometimes just the effort may be a sufficient signal that things can get better. In this case, communication *per se* functions both reflectively and existentially without entailing a complex strategy for intervention.

Style behavior as a reflector. Style components relate to marital quality in two ways. First, the way individuals communicate with each other provides each partner a way to access the ongoing quality of the relationship, unless intense and successful masking is being done by one or both individuals. Second, the way individuals communicate with each other has consequences for the physical and mental health of each partner.

The patterns of style are the most consistent indicators of the other's disposition. For instance, Paolino and McCrady (1978) identify four patterns of communication which reflect difficulties in a marriage: (1) not having appropriate problem-solving discussions, (2) having difficulty interpreting each other's statements, (3) not sharing positive feelings, and (4) not expressing feelings.

Style components provide clues for partners and, as a consequent, allow a means to diagnose the quality of a marriage by analyzing the interactive behavior in a marriage. It is assumed that changing a 'hurtful' style of communication changes the relationship.

This suggests that if distressed couples are particularly affected and responsive to negative interactional behavior, then even a small reduction in the rate of negative interactions might lead to significant and enduring marital satisfaction. Bornstein *et al.* (1983) found support for this notion.

Other marital researchers (Roy, 1985a; Dinkmeyer and Carlson, 1985) increasingly relate communicative processes to mental health. For example, Moffitt, Spence and Goldney (1986) found that the mental health of wives is more relationship-related than that of husbands. They argue that because wives have a higher need for affiliation and a greater sensitivity to rejection, they have higher internal conflict, which has implications for their mental well-being. If the relationship is confounded by joblessness, career tension, child problems, or dysfunctional habits, then the internal conflict might be exacerbated.

In addition to affecting relationship health, it generally is not surprising that physical health intrudes on the way a person communicates with a spouse. Roy (1985b), for example, shows that chronic pain of a spouse leads to marital difficulties manifested by deterioration of communication patterns. Jamuna and Ramamurti (1984) found that communication problems often are associated with hormonal changes accompanying menopause.

Alcoholic partners communicate in dysfunctional ways. The interaction is asymmetrical and dominant, which exacerbates the high internal conflict of one partner (Uhlig, Schneider and Meyer, 1982; Frankenstein, 1985; Frankenstein, Hay and Nathan, 1985; Steinglass, Tislenko and Reiss, 1985).

Also, certain mental states such as anxiety or depression diminish the quality of communication (Raush *et al.*, 1974). Hinchliffe *et al.* (1978), for instance, demonstrated that depressive symptoms not only limit careful listening to the content and style of a partner, but retard idiosyncratic responsiveness to the partner.

In brief, the communicative perspective offers much to the researcher and diagnostician of couple interaction. It has the dual capacity to reflect the quality of the relationship and, in turn, be a tool in enhancing or repairing a dysfunctional relationship.

FACTORS WHICH JEOPARDIZE COMMUNICATION RESEARCH IN THE MARITAL CONTEXT

Communication research within marital or couple context is still difficult to complete because of the extraordinary flexibility of a couple's communication, the private nature of the *quid pro quo*, and the incapacity to self-monitor. Consequently, marital researchers must take unusual care in attending to the many factors which jeopardize communication research in general and style work in particular.

The following three components are common obstacles. First, the failure to define 'communication' adequately diminishes the clarity of work. Imprecise definitions or definitions which lead to contradictions are forms of this difficulty.

Second, reactivity contaminates the validity of the data. If the phenomenon is significantly altered in the process of studying it—like killing the cat to find the purr—the findings must be presented in language about the transmuted form, substance, interaction, or species, although often this is not the practice.

Third, sampling errors severely weaken generalizations. Like the drunk looking for his or her keys under the lamp-post because that is where the light is, many communication researchers look at the most convenient sample of people or sample of behaviors. The mistake occurs when they generalize to the nonconvenient samples of people or behaviors.

Definitional Problems

There are two kinds of definitional problems which debilitate studies centering on metamessages in general or communication style in particular. The first difficulty occurs when the researcher who investigates communicative phenomena fails to define 'communication'. For example, in an article provocatively titled 'Marital satisfaction: Positive regard *versus* effective communications as explanatory variables', Barnes *et al.* (1984) set up a false dichotomy which reflects little understanding of the hierarchical nature of communicative processes. They capriciously select parts of the Relationship Inventory developed by Barrett-Lennard (1962) which was intended initially to investigate therapist response as a causal factor in therapeutic change.

They arbitrarily stipulate that two parts from the Relationship Inventory will be used to measure marital communication—namely, components evaluating empathy and congruence. They designate a third part from the same inventory to be the phenomenon contrasted to 'effective communications' (empathy + congruence). The authors never define 'communication' or 'effective communication' in any of their work (Schumm, Bollman and Jurich, 1981; Schumm *et al.*, 1983).

If the authors want empathy to represent 'effective communication', it is incumbent upon them to make the argument. If they want congruence to represent 'effective communication', the burden of advocacy must be part of their rationale. In fact, in the original report of the Relationship Inventory, Barrett-Lennard (1962) maintains that for congruence, 'No positive conditions for overt communication of the individual's conscious perceptions are implied in this concept' (p. 4). In short, congruence relates to a covert process; it is not a manifested behavior.

The second difficulty occurs when the researcher acquiesces to a definition which leads to an untenable position or incorporates shifting definitions of communicative phenomena. Noller's (1978, 1980b, 1981, 1982) work, best represented with her 1984 book *Nonverbal Communication and Marital Interaction*, has made an impressive contribution to the marital literature.

However, she never defines 'communication' in her book. Furthermore, she embraces a communicative axiom which leads to semantic difficulties. Noller (1984) does not sufficiently restrict what constitutes the concept of 'communication'; it is anything and everything for her:

> In the marital situation, as in most others, it is impossible to 'not communicate'—communication can continue to occur, either nonverbally, or through the situation, long after the last word has been spoken . . . communication is going on whenever we are in the presence of someone else, even if we are only communicating that we want to have nothing to do with them. (p. 1)

With this perspective, it does not matter whether the person who was just asked about his marriage contorts his face because of a gas pain, an unconscious Freudian reaction, a studied, well-controlled and deliberately false signal, a reaction reflecting a hatred for his wife, a reaction reflecting dislike of the person asking the question, or a random tic—the contorted face is treated as communication.

With this perspective, what constitutes inherently bad communication? Noller (1984) says:

> Undoubtedly when communication proves unsatisfactory, the amount of time spent in communication is likely to decrease. The more often the process of communication proves to be unpleasant or ineffective, the less likely it becomes that the couple will attempt to communicate about, or talk through, similar situations in the future; that is, unsatisfactory communication has a punishing effect . . . there is often a circular effect, in that unsatisfactory communication leads to less communication and lower marital satisfaction, and the more that marital satisfaction drops, the less likely is the communication to be positive, rewarding and effective. (pp. 12–13)

If one cannot not communicate, what does it mean to say there is less communication? The analysis works only if one assumes that the notion of 'communication' is synonymous with 'information'.

In an earlier work, Noller (1980b) stipulates good communication in the marital situation as that which can be decoded by both the spouse and others. In short, unambiguous, agreed upon, and publicly accessible information is treated as good communication. This stance precludes the complexity of interaction. If a wife looks her spouse in the eye and delivers a well-crafted and unambiguous lie in which there is no disagreement about the content, then Noller might call this good communication.

Noller (1984) lists behaviors that lead to effective and ineffective marital communication. It is a bothersome list given the acceptance of the notion that one cannot not communicate. Behaviors that lead to effective marital communication include self-disclosure, being sensitive to each other's feelings, listening and responding, confirmation, and expressing respect and esteem. Behaviors that lead to ineffective marital communication include criticism, arguing, and nagging, faulty behavior change operations, lack of listening, and lack of responsiveness.

'Lack of responsiveness', for example, given Noller's assumption, must be treated as an instance of communication. 'Lack of responsiveness' could be a very accurate, precise, and mutually understood message between a couple. The message of a wife, for instance, signaling that she is not going to be responsive in a particular situation, could be perspicuous in form and content to both parties.

The spouse who is not adaptable, affectionate, empathetic, or accommodating at the moment might be struggling to balance an unequal overt power structure. If there is not a socially satisfying way to equalize the *quid pro quo*, then pathological ways will be found. Fish and Fish (1986) say that 'triangulating a third party such as a child, developing morbid symptoms, and infantilizing one's partner are all ways to increase one's power base' (p. 373). Given this perspective, it is nonsensical to call lack of responsiveness 'ineffective marital communication'.

To be precise about this example, it should be said that here is a couple, for whatever reason, providing a mutually understood message that may or may not have 'hurtful' consequences. But, it is not the case that this message is *inherently* ineffective marital communication.

This is not to say that there may be instances in which lack of responsiveness might be inadvertent or unconscious on one person's part. In which case, the argument should be that one partner gets what seems to be a clear signal that the spouse is not adaptable, affectionate, empathetic, or accommodating at the moment.

The communication of lack of responsiveness should be considered dysfunctional communication only if it can be established that this is not the message that the person intends or it is not the message the person would send if in control. Even at this point, the investigator needs to be careful and should make a distinction in treating the behavior as 'ineffective communication' or 'information which may have hurtful consequences'.

Reactivity Alters Phenomena

To do style research among couples, the researcher must address the issue of reactivity. This means that communication studies done in the laboratory must be treated as extraordinary events. Communication in the sanitized laboratory, often designed to look like a nice living room, is what might be called 'lab com'. It is conversation exchanged by individuals who are sharply aware of the demands of a 'study', an 'experimenter', and a 'situation'.

The knowledge of being part of a study creates a willingness to help the investigator with the effect. Knowing that they are in a university laboratory is an extraordinary context for couples. The situation dictates heightened politeness. Knowing they are going to be videotaped and scrutinized in minute detail cues them to put on their best face. Sometimes researchers even shape the interaction further by telling the couple that interaction is the focus of the study. If Clever Hans, the horse, was bright enough to respond to almost imperceptible and unconscious nonverbal cues to dazzle his investigators with apparent understanding of verbal language (Pfungst, 1911), surely couples in the laboratory are bright enough to figure out partially what the researcher wants.

Consider a recent study by Gaelick, Bodenhausen and Wyer (1985) in their attempt to understand emotional communication. They describe their procedure this way:

> The first session was conducted in a large pleasant room. Couples sat around a coffee table positioned so that each person's face would be visible to a TV camera that was mounted unobtrusively in a corner. They were reminded that the study's purpose was to understand how people interact and how they interpret one another's behavior during their interactions and that they would be asked to engage in three discussions concerning (a) the events of the day, (b) a conflict they were having in their relationship, and (c) the things they liked best about living together. They were also reminded that their discussions would be videotaped and that they would later view the tapes and be asked to interpret them. They were assured of the confidentiality of both the tapes and their ratings of them.

In addition, each couple was told that they would be paid $30 for participating.

How can reactivity not be a issue with this procedure, especially when tracking an aspect of communication style? *The setting contaminates validity from the beginning and probably creates a data set of 'controlled' or 'carefully studied' behaviors.*

'Lab com' cannot capture the day-to-day variations of the most typical style behaviors. Even if the researcher asks the couples to interact in a typical way, the couple is relegated to role play what will pass for a typical interaction, discussed in the privacy of a pleasant living-room facsimile with an objective researcher hovering out of sight. Many couples can adapt—most lab animals can—by deviating from their own habitual style pattern.

Sampling Errors

Two types of sampling errors are seen in the literature trying to relate style components to marital interaction. First, the marital population is not adequately sampled. Many research reports (Gottman, Markman and Notarius, 1977; Marciano, 1974; Jarrett and Nelson, 1984) have such a small sample of couples that their conclusions cannot be used to generalize. In addition, most 'lab com' studies recruit volunteers. This issue plagues most marital research.

It is more likely that a couple which already gets on well volunteers for this kind of study. What this means is that the quarrelsome, brawling, feisty, and/ or contentious couple is not likely to get together with an academic researcher so that they can videotape a little chat. It is also likely that the researcher will miss the indifferent, antisocial, or introverted couple. The problem is that variance of communication style outside the lab is not represented.

Second, as indicated above in the reactivity section, the population of communicative behaviors is not adequately sampled. Only a narrow range of communicative behavior can be seen in 'lab com'. In fact, some researchers (Gottman, 1979; Gottman and Porterfield, 1981) speculate that couples may develop a 'private meaning system' which they use to interpret one another's behavior, and these interpretations may often differ substantially from those of even highly trained observers. This speculation reflects the pull of the *quid pro quo*.

CONCLUSIONS AND FUTURE DIRECTIONS

The task is twofold. First, the *quid pro quo* should be treated as the dependent variable because it is the core of the relationship. Second, the pragmatic impact of communicative processes should be related to understanding the metaphorical contract between couples.

Adopting a Suitable Method To Measure the *Quid Pro Quo*

It is unlikely that a couple could articulate the exact *quid pro quo* working in their marriage. Some elements are ineffable and are relegated to the tacit domain. Some aspects are ambiguous and difficult to monitor. Nevertheless, a couple should be able to appraise the contract even if they cannot detail every aspect.

The assessment would require each person to center on 'we', 'my relationship with X', 'the team (my partner and I)', or the 'whole (both of us)'. Furthermore, each person should provide a normative judgement about the 'individuals as a couple'.

Norton's (1983b) Quality Marriage Index provides a highly reliable and efficient instrument to reflect the *quid pro quo*. It consists of six items: (1) We have a good marriage, (2) My relationship with my partner is stable, (3) Our marriage is strong, (4) My relationship with my partner makes me happy, (5) I really feel like *part of a team* with my partner, and (6) My marriage, everything considered, makes me happy. If the researcher uses the evaluations from both individuals, a dependent variable with strong properties reflecting the *quid pro quo* is created.

It is inappropriate to use a scale which treats context-specific items as the dependent variable to reflect the *quid pro quo*. Spanier's (1976) Dyadic Adjustment Scale (DAS), for example, in addition to other critical flaws outlined by

Norton (1983b), mostly taps into couple agreement and frequency of doing things together. A well-adjusted couple, for instance, could have a *quid pro quo* which allows for a large amount of disagreement and time apart. In this case, the DAS would misclassify the couple.

In short, any instrument measuring the *quid pro quo* must minimally evaluate the relationship as a whole in such a way that context-specific or situation-specific biases about what ought to be part of a couple's *quid pro quo* are eliminated. If a mutual pathology holds a relationship together and the couple maintains that they have a good marriage, the researcher should initially accept the testimony at face value. Otherwise, the researcher functions as an interventionist.

The second task is to generate units of analysis such that both the content and style elements of the communicative process are integrated. When the researcher attends to the communication gestalt, increased precision and sophistication are introduced. In addition, the researcher must attend to the pragmatic intent embedded in the style components. This understanding depends not only upon the couple's sensitivity to their *quid pro quo*, but the researcher's astuteness to implicit and explicit indications of the *quid pro quo*.

There are many ways to investigate the influence of communication gestalts. Hawkins, Weisberg and Ray (1977, 1980) illustrate a method in which content and style are used to create nominal variables—namely, types of communicators. The content is designated as being either low or high in the amount of disclosiveness and the style is designated as being either open or closed. As a result, four categories are constructed: (1) a conventional communicator (low disclosure, closed style), (2) a speculative communicator (low disclosure, open style), (3) a controlling communicator (high disclosure, closed style), and (4) a contactful communicator (high disclosure, open style).

Two categories represent the situation in which the verbal and nonverbal interactions are synchronized. A person who signals an openness to communicate and actually discloses creates little ambiguity. On the other hand, a person who signals an openness to communicate and does not disclose creates ambiguity which calls for resolution. As indicated earlier, the person does more inferential work dealing with an ambiguous gestalt because he or she must supply additional premises to interpret the messages and what they portend for the relationship.

Harris (1980) exemplifies another approach to this orientation which values the content and hierarchical style influences in the communicative process. She conducted a case study of a normally functioning married couple to investigate the relation between their logic and their communication patterns. She found paradoxical rules associated with restricted episodes in which the couple could not obtain their goal of eliminating conflict. She reports:

. . . they were quite skilled at metacommunication. In fact, they had institutionalized the 'confrontation' episode for the purpose of eliminating the undesirable 'personality flaws' of nagging and lack of physical attention. They were aware that the master contract of their relationship consisted of cyclical patterns of conflict, followed by confrontation/resolution. (p. 25)

A researcher cannot do this type of analysis unless content and style components are appreciated within a hierarchical model.

In conclusion, this genre of research is most useful if it can be used to improve the quality of relationships. What is *not* known from most of this work is whether the bad marriage is marked by a poor predisposition or a skills deficiency. For example, the problem relating to not having problem-solving discussions may be a difficulty because the person does not want to have them—it is a matter of motivation. Warmbrod (1982), for example, found that communication skill training did not enhance creativity in generating alternatives for marital problems. On the other hand, the person may not have the skill to engage in a problem-solving discussion (Pierce, 1973; Wieman, Shoulders and Farr, 1974).

The rival explanations make a difference to the marital therapist. The first problem would be treated as an attitudinal one, the second problem as a skills deficiency. If the diagnosis indicates that attitude is the problem, the intervention centers on the *quid pro quo*, usually taking the form of motivation or reframing. If the diagnosis shows that skills are deficient, the intervention focuses on changing aspects of content or style, usually taking the form of teaching a particular skill or practicing a specific behavior.

The linkage of style theory to the *quid pro quo* invites the researcher to treat communicative processes in marital interaction as complex behavior continually influencing and being influenced by hierarchical forces. Even though the light is not bright in this area yet, the promise of discovery warrants the work of confronting the persistent challenges.

Handbook of Personal Relationships
Edited by S. W. Duck
© 1988 John Wiley & Sons Ltd

18

Personal Relationships, Social Relationships and Patterns of Interaction

JOSEPH N. CAPPELLA
University of Wisconsin, Madison, Wisconsin, USA

ABSTRACT

The study of interpersonal relations is intimately concerned with the interaction patterns which create, maintain, and destroy these relationships. This chapter takes up conceptual and definitional problems for interaction pattern (as opposed to the distribution of behaviors) and for relational states. Exemplary research is reviewed and speculations about possible linkages between interaction pattern and relational outcomes are offered.

Although human relationships could not exist without interactions between the people who make up these relationships, research and theory has often proceeded as if the two phenomena were independent. A very little social experience and commonsense tell us that relationships are formed, maintained, and dissolved in interactions with partners. At the same time, interactions can reflect the kind of relationship that exists between the partners. Certainly, no one interaction can be said to be fully representative of a complex relational history nor can it represent completely the role relationships institutionalized within the society. Yet, in the same way that economic indicators carry information about the economy and, over the long haul, are representative of that economy, so too can individual human interactions represent the relationships whose status they indicate. This chapter is about this linkage between human relationships and human interactions.

The chapter considers a particular class of questions concerning interpersonal communication. These questions were derived from an interactionally based definition of interpersonal communication (Cappella, 1987). A review of previous definitions led me to argue that a new definition must be broad enough to avoid excluding a particular set of interpersonal relationships *a priori*, avoid a bias towards reciprocal interactions, focus upon communication patterns rather than relationships, and define interchanges so that they are truly interactional. In brief, this definition set forth three conditions. The first condition held that the probability of person A's behavior given a prior behavior by B is nonzero. Second, this same probability must be significantly different from A's baseline probability of action. Third, the first two conditions must hold with the roles of A and B reversed.

The arguments in favor of this definition need not be of concern here; they are spelled out elsewhere (Cappella, 1987). However, this definition does suggest four classes of questions about interpersonal communication. I have labeled them zero- through third-order questions. Zero-order questions are concerned with the set of behaviors enacted by persons in interpersonal communication. These questions include issues of observation and coding, time units, the meanings or functions of behaviors, the covariation or grouping among behaviors, and so on. First-order questions are questions of behavioral production and behavioral reception, sending and receiving in ordinary language. On the sending side, fundamental questions include the psychological and situational mechanisms, but not interactive mechanisms, that predict baseline probabilities. On the receiving side, is the perception of the other's behavior veridical or filtered through some distorting perceptual mechanism? Second-order questions are unique to the interpersonal level and are concerned with interaction patterns themselves. These are questions of behavioral responsiveness of one person to the other and are sharply separated from questions about the mere amounts of behavior given off (such as mean duration, frequency, total duration, and so on). None of the three types of questions above is the focus of this chapter.

Third-order questions are the focus of this chapter. These questions actually step outside the boundaries of the proposed definition of interpersonal communication to include relationship factors. This category focuses upon the bidirectional linkage, first, between interaction patterns and relational outcomes and second, between relational types and interaction patterns. Let us consider some issues which this category of questions brings into our ken.

The first issue concerns the distinction between pattern of interaction and some distributional measure of behavior. Third-order questions are not concerned with how much of this or that response a given relational state is associated with, but rather how a response pattern is associated with a given relational state. The reason for the switch from distribution to pattern is to match variable types. Just as a relational outcome or relational type is concerned with person A in the context of person B (and *vice versa*), an interaction pattern is concerned with person A's response to B (and *vice versa*) and not just what A does without regard to B's action. Consider an analogy. In Byrne's (1971) work on interpersonal attraction (a relational outcome), the key predictor turned out to be attitudinal similarity and not, for example, the other's attitudes alone. The types of variables were matched conceptually: A's attraction to B with B's similarity of attitude to A's. In the same way, we should expect relational types and outcomes to be associated with patterns of responsiveness and not simply with the distribution of behavior exhibited by the other. (In a later section, I will want to modify this claim somewhat.)

There is a second reason for focusing upon interaction patterns and that is the concept of skill. Whether unfounded or not, a belief permeates the interpersonal literature that better relationships exhibit more skilled interaction and that more skilled interaction can lead to more satisfied relationships (Birchler, 1979; Montgomery, 1981a; Noller, 1984). Unfortunately, most studies of social competence and social skill are based on conceptions of skill which are barren. Most studies treat communicative skill in terms of the emission of this or that amount of behavior rather than the more complex conception involving appropriateness, timing, and sensitivity to context. The concept of skill demands the latter rather than the former, whether we are discussing social interaction or musical virtuosity. Skilled musicianship in no way depends on the frequency and duration of notes of this or that type but rather on their timing, appropriateness, and sensitivity to context. Similarly, skilled interaction depends upon these same factors. Hence, we should expect that interaction patterns would be a more fruitful avenue for studying social skill than would measures of distribution.

Third-order questions also raise significant practical, methodological, and theoretical issues. On the practical side, these questions are located squarely in the tradition of research as social action promoted by Argyris, Putnam and Smith (1985). This view holds that our responsibilities as social scientists are not only to describe social and behavioral realities but to create them. This tradition would encourage researchers to develop and teach interaction patterns observing their outcomes on relational states of partners. On the methodological side, third-order questions present us with labor-intensive and difficult hypotheses. Not only must reliable and valid measures of outcome and relational types be obtained, but costly and time-consuming observational codings must be carried out as well. Methods for establishing interaction patterns are also not well known and not a part of the packaged statistical software used by researchers (Kenny, this volume). On the theoretical side, the sociological view of a relationship as a reality somehow different from the sum of the individual perceptions of the relationship is an issue that has received little attention. If a relationship can exist apart from the separate cognitions of the partners, then how can that relationship arise and how can it be treated operationally?

RELATIONAL STATES

Two important distinctions need to be made concerning the class of variables that I will here call relational states. The first concerns the substantive types of variables which are to be included as subclasses of relational states: relational outcomes and relational types. The second concerns the character of 'relational state variables': group variables and individual variables. The importance of these distinctions both for statistical analysis and for theory and speculation will be considered.

Subclasses of Relational States

'Relational state variables' is the overarching phrase that I adopt here to refer
to the common classes of variables studied in research on social relationships,
namely relational types and relational outcomes. By relational types is meant
a relatively stable pattern of expected response, value, ideology, or attitude
with regard to social and personal relationships. The emphasis is on expectation
and stability so that a relational type is held as a part of the individual or
collective memories of persons within a society. Typically, relational types can
include role relationships (such as doctors and their patients, clergy and their
flock, etc.) and personal relationships (such as traditionals, separates, etc.
(Fitzpatrick, 1984). Note that a relational type is not indexed by a response
pattern but only by an expected response pattern so that there is no tautology
between interaction pattern and relational type. Note further that just because
a particular relationship fulfills a certain (even infrequent) slot within a relational
schema does not mean that the relationship is not a 'type'. A particular and
infrequent instance within a schema is just as much a relational type as is the
relational prototype.

By relational outcome is meant a relatively transient affective or cognitive
judgement about the relationship between self and other, about self in relation
to the other, or about the other in relation to the self. The emphasis is on
relative transience and relational judgements. Note that changes in a person's
expectations about heterosexual relationships among teenagers gleaned from a
television documentary are not changes in a relational outcome variable but
changes in a relational type. Typically relational outcome variables include
measures of interpersonal attraction, satisfaction (Locke and Wallace, 1959),
relational stability, and the like.

Relational outcomes and relational types are really quite analogous to a
fundamental distinction among types of beliefs and values made by Rokeach
(1968). In his hierarchy of beliefs and values, central beliefs and values were
common within cultural groups and relatively unchanging even though these
central beliefs and values might differ markedly from one cultural group to
another. The more peripheral beliefs, opinions, and attitudes were more transient and susceptible to influence from external messages. A similar set of
features would characterize relational types and relational outcomes.

There are several important reasons to make the above distinctions between
relational types and outcomes. First, the literature on third-order questions can
be usefully categorized into work with relational types (e.g. Williamson and
Fitzpatrick, 1985) and work with relational outcomes as the focus (Street, 1986).
Second, the issue of transience and stability would seem to imply that with
respect to interaction patterns, outcomes would primarily play the role of effect
rather than causal variable and that types would play the role of causal rather
than effect variable. In fact, J. A. Davis (1985), in a very useful guide to the
development of causal models, makes just such a suggestion in general.
Although such a claim makes some sense in the short run and in limited
contexts, I want to argue that in general such an assumption breaks down and,

more importantly, that such an assumption places theoretical blinders on us. Concerning the former issue, relational outcomes, though often transitory, can be stable enough to exert a feedback effect on interaction patterns. Certainly, the dissolution of a relationship or the movement towards relational disengagement (Baxter and Wilmot, 1985) can introduce significant changes in interaction patterns. Similarly, the relatively stable relational types could be affected in the long run by a series of interaction patterns. For example, unreciprocated verbal intimacy might lead a person to alter his or her prototypical relationship from emotionally interdependent to emotionally distant. More common, perhaps, is the observation that persons acquire concepts of self and role on the basis of the patterns of interaction which others direct towards them in imputing a specific role or self (Farina, Allen and Saul, 1968; Farina *et al.*, 1971). These counterclaims leave us with the position that it would be a mistake to assume in general that causality flows *from* fixed relational types and *to* relatively transient relational outcomes.

The final observation to make concerns the theoretical blinders that implicit assumptions about causal direction can impose. If researchers and theoreticians assume that relational types produce interaction patterns but not *vice versa*, then what is never asked is how social and individual expectations about relationships arise in the first place. We would then make the same error that has plagued sociological theorists (Berger and Luckman, 1967), namely, relational ideologies and relational institutions would be treated as givens and never subject to the question 'How do they arise?' Failing to ask this latter question is significant because absence of knowledge about how socially shared ideologies of relationships arise is at the same time absence of knowledge about how to change these ideologies when they are in need of change. An interventionist social science would not then be performing its function.

Character of Relational State Variables

The measurement of relational state variables is significant certainly in terms of the usual issues of reliability and validity. After all, the study of third-order questions is quite meaningless without reliable and valid measures of relational state. However, I do not consider that question in this chapter but leave it to other chapters in this Handbook. What is considered is the individual or group character of relational state variables.

Although relational state variables are focused by definition upon the state of a pair or group of persons in relation to one another, the measurement of this relational condition is not at all obvious. In particular, it would seem odd to obtain information about a relational state from the perspective of a single person. Of course, much research measures relational states by obtaining individual scores as judgements on some self-report instrument. Typically, measures of attraction, satisfaction, and relational ideology are obtained from the reports of individuals in the relationship. These are categorized here as individual measures of relational state.

Group measures of relational state cannot be obtained from the assessment of a single person but rather apply to the pair (or group) as a whole simultaneously and are usually established by the consensual judgements of third parties or some objective criterion. For example, in group research, productivity, in terms of either time to solve a series of problems or number of unique ideas, is a group measure of outcomes. In personal relationships, maladjustment as determined by self-selection for counseling and therapy and satisfaction as determined by divorced and separated *versus* cohabiting are examples of group measures of outcome. Relational types such as interviewee and interviewer, doctor and patient are simple examples of role relationships established by social norms. These measures can be described as natural group measures because their application to the group or dyad as a whole is a natural consequence of their definition.

Created group measures, on the other hand, apply to the group or dyad because the researcher has created a group definition from a combination rule applied to the individual measures. For example, a group measure of satisfaction may be obtained from a sum or average of individual satisfaction scores. With regard to relational types, Fitzpatrick (1984) has used the interesting strategy of labeling a type of relationship as, say, separate when both persons agree independently that their own view of the relationship is that it is separate. When the partners disagree as to the type, then they are treated as one of the mixed types. Created group measures should not be confused with the natural group measures because there is a certain *ad hoc* character to the rule used to combine the individual scores. Although created group measures seem to offer an assessment of the relational state *in toto* rather than individual evaluations of the state, that appearance is illusory. Rather, a simple and too often unjustified combination rule is masking real and potentially important differences in individual scores. For example, simply averaging the scores of persons on satisfaction to create a dyadic measure of satisfaction, a common strategy, may hide strong within-dyad variance in satisfaction. Such variation should not be assumed away.

The distinctions above are made to draw attention to certain implications about our measurement of relational state variables. First, when natural variation in individual-level data exists, this natural variation should be a cause for exploration and not an excuse to bypass the variation in favor of a simpler data set. Unfortunately, analysis of individual scores when they are embedded in group context so that they are not necessarily independent can wreak havoc with the validity of significance tests (Kenny and Judd, 1986). Nevertheless, methods for handling this person-within-group problem exist (Kenny, this volume) even though they may not be well known to social scientists. Second, natural group variables have an important and unique theoretical function. Most of the research in social and personal relationships is psychological in orientation, focusing upon the individual's behavior. Natural group variables represent what can only be called sociological states because their existence is ratified by social consensus outside of the particular relationship or by some objective state of affairs which does not depend upon the reports of the individuals themselves. The theoretical questions which are raised by this class of variables are how the behaviors (and behavioral patterns) of individuals can bring about relational states not attributable to one or the other person or their simple combination. One can readily hypothesize how a person's relational states predict or are the result of interaction patterns: individual states are predicted by individual interaction patterns. But how can we understand the evolution of natural group-level variables? This question is a challenge for research and theory in personal and social relationships but a minimal answer would include a conceptual matching between the character of the relational state variable and the character of the interaction pattern associated with it. Put in more straightforward terms, individual relational state variables should be predicted from and predict to individual interaction patterns and group relational state variables should be linked to group interaction patterns. Let us next consider types of interaction patterns.

INTERACTION PATTERNS

Message Patterns and Adaptive Patterns

There are at least two ways to keep track of interactional sequences. The first, labeled here as message patterns, ignores who generates a message or a behavioral event in an interaction and only keeps track of the sequence of messages regardless of their source. Such studies can reveal patterns of interaction but the patterns are contingencies between messages, not contingencies between people. The second, labeled here as adaptive patterns, keeps track not only of the message but who generates the message. Thus, contingencies are established (in the dyadic context) between A's message and B's response and *vice versa*. The message pattern approach has been employed in much of the group interaction research within communication studies (Fisher and Drecksel, 1983; Ellis and Fisher, 1975; Hawes and Foley, 1973). The adaptive pattern approach has been advocated by Hewes (Hewes, 1979; Folger, Hewes and Poole, 1984) and by Cappella (1987).

In general, adaptive patterns are better suited to the study of third-order questions than are message patterns. Message patterns are more appropriate to the study of issues in language pragmatics concerning the structure of dialogues in various linguistic communities. If the linguistic communities differ in terms of their relational states, then different message patterns may reflect or be the result of these different relational states. In this context, message pattern research might be conceptually more congruent with relational states which are natural group variables. However, when one wishes to make connections to the relational states of individuals, message patterns are not appropriate. In this case, one must keep track of who says what so that the contingent responsiveness of persons can be tied back to the individual involved. To summarize, the sociological character of message patterns should be associated with the more sociological relational states; the individualistic character of adaptive patterns should be linked to the more psychological relational states.

Dynamic versus Static Patterns

Interaction patterns can be studied in various ways and still be considered to be studies of responsiveness. But these ways represent a continuum from the dynamic to the static. Dynamic patterns are based upon the observation of who says what at each observational unit and the summary of these observations in appropriate terms (such as contingent probabilities or lagged cross-correlations for more continuous variables). What is important about these patterns is that the measures of contingency are based upon actual temporal patterns of response to prior actions. Contrast this with static patterns, which are pseudo-patterns at best. One of the common ways of obtaining a measure of the pattern of interaction for a group of dyads is to calculate the amount of some behavior (say latency to respond) for each person and correlate the scores (adjustments are necessary, see Kenny and LaVoie, 1985) between persons across dyads. The degree and sign of the covariation is taken as an indication of the pattern of interaction in the groups. However, the nature of this measure of interaction pattern is quite different from that of more dynamic measures (Cappella and Planalp, 1981; Duncan and Fiske, 1985). In particular, one could not conclude from these static measures that the persons in the dyads were temporally responsive to one another. One could only conclude that some mean or total duration was similar (or different as the case may be) across the persons within dyads. Such information is useful for comparing across groups but certainly carries no information about sequential contingency and cannot be used to obtain information about interaction patterns for individual dyads. The obviously useful comparison of temporal responsivity and relational responsivity has not yet been carried out (but see Montgomery, 1984c).

Of course, certain types of analysis of interaction patterns fall between the extreme poles represented above. For example, experimental designs which employ confederates usually observe responses to scripted behavior enacted by the confederate. In this case, the response is contingent upon the confederate's behavior but there is usually no repetition of response. Designs of this type do provide some information about temporal contingency but usually within a relatively limited domain of action.

Static and dynamic measures of interaction pattern provide different information about temporal responsiveness, with static measures being inappropriate for drawing conclusions about temporal responsiveness. Dynamic measures can be used to provide information about individual adaptation within a dyad (when the number of time-series data points are sufficient), and so can be readily linked to individual relational state measures. (They can also be linked to group relational states in ways to be described below.) Static measures provide information about group differences but not information about individual dyadic patterns.

One caveat should be offered here about static measures of interaction patterns. Certain designs (Kenny and La Voie, 1984) allow researchers to obtain individual adaptation information while observing only static data. The social relations model provides measures of the degree to which a particular person adapts to a particular other person over and above their baseline levels of behavior and over and above their typical adjustment to others in interaction. Although this information does not represent temporal contingency, it does represent contingency of another sort, that is relational contingency—how the person responds depends upon who his or her partner is. Such a measure of responsiveness could be linked to individual relational state data.

Types of Interaction Patterns

The types of interaction patterns to be discussed here are not specific to message or adaptive patterns, nor restricted to dynamic or static patterns. However, for the sake of economy of expression I will use the vocabulary of adaptive, dynamic interaction patterns. The types of interaction patterns that can be obtained depend upon the type of variable one is using. The major distinction is between continuous variables which have some form of metric and categorical variables which are not ordered in any way. Of course, by artfully manipulating one's data one can turn categorical data into continuous probability data and continuous data into arbitrary levels such as on and off. Examples of continuous variables include studies of speech latencies, durations, and pauses (Cappella and Planalp, 1981), distance and gaze (Argyle and Dean, 1965), positivity and negativity (Gottman, 1979), and literally dozens of others (Cappella, 1981, 1985b). Categorical variables have included relational control (Manderscheid *et al.*, 1982), gaze patterns (Natale, 1976), accusations and repairs (McLaughlin, Cody and Rosenstein, 1983), and many others.

The types of patterns that one can observe with continuous variables are convergence, divergence, and no change. By convergence is meant that the behavior of one of the persons is changing in the direction of that of the other person. Divergence means that the behavior is changing away from that of the other person. No change does not necessarily mean that a person's behavioral level is unchanging, only that the nature of the overall change is neither towards convergence or divergence. Even very complicated time-series transfer functions, which may include many lagged cross-correlations, can be categorized as convergent or divergent. In point of fact, though, such complex models are not usually observed (Cappella and Planalp, 1981; Cappella and Street, 1986; Thomas and Martin, 1976).

Methods for assessing interaction patterns with continuous variables include in the static case common analysis of variance, correlation, intraclass correlation, various adjusted correlational procedures, and Kenny's newly developed social relations model (see Kenny, this volume, for a summary and some useful advice in applying these techniques). In the dynamic case, the procedures are primarily time-series analysis (McCleary and Hay, 1980), time-series regression (Cappella, 1980; Hibbs, 1974), spectral analysis (Gottman, 1981), and modifications of these techniques (Gottman and Ringland, 1981).

Whenever the data are sufficient to conduct analyses of interaction pattern at the level of individual dyads, then one can assess the divergence and convergence of each person separately (e.g. Cappella and Planalp, 1981). On the basis of these individual measures, it is also possible to establish whether the dyad is converging or diverging in its manifest behaviors. The rules for doing so are perfectly straightforward but will not be laboriously spelled out here (they are related to whether two variables are converging to or diverging from one another over time). The upshot is that a group measure of interaction patterns, such as dyadic convergence or divergence, is available from the individual measures and this group measure can be linked to group measures of relational state.

The types of patterns that can be observed with categorical variables are called matching, mismatching, and no change. They are analogous to the continuous case. They differ in the sense that with categorical variables matching results from person A's behavior X predicting the probability of B's behavior Y above the baseline (or expected probability) of B's behavior. Mismatching results when A's behavior depresses B's behavior below baseline. No change finds A's behavior not significantly predicting B's behavior.

The methods for assessing interaction patterns with categorical variables include log-linear procedures for the static and dynamic cases (Feick and Novak, 1985), and Markov (Hewes, 1975, 1980) and lag sequential procedures (Dumas, 1986; Sackett, 1978, 1979) in the dynamic case. The same kinds of claims hold for categorical variables as hold for their continuous counterparts.

In order to avoid excessive complexity of terminology, I will refer to convergence and matching as reciprocity and to divergence and mismatching as compensation in the remainder of this chapter.

REPRESENTATIVE RESEARCH

Studies of Relational Outcome

In informal social interaction settings, Street and his colleagues (Putman and Street, 1984; Street, 1982, 1984) have been active in assessing the effects of speech convergence on social attractiveness (as well as other perceptions). Using an unstructured interview context, Street (1984) coded various speech behaviors for the interviewer and interviewee in one-minute units. The speech rates, turn durations, and speech latencies were submitted to time-series regression analyses to determine if reciprocity between the partners would be related to positive relational judgements. He found that speech rate reciprocity by one partner was positively related to judgements of social competence of that partner by others, and *vice versa*. Convergence in latency to respond showed a similar trend for interviewees. Reciprocity on other speech behaviors did not predict relational outcomes and no reciprocity measures were related to judgements of social attractiveness.

Other studies in the informal context have shown that dyadic partners who exhibited greater similarity on speech latency were rated by judges to be higher on warmth than partners who exhibited less similarity on speech latency (Welkowitz and Kuc, 1973). Giles and Smith (1979) constructed audiotapes in which there was convergence on speech rate, content, and pronunciation and tapes where there was no convergence. Judges rated the persons with converging patterns as more likeable, more effective, and more willing to cooperate. Only Street's work, however, has seriously assessed whether dynamic patterns of interaction in the informal context are correlated with relational outcomes.

Research on communication patterns in the marital and family contexts has been more productive than the same lines of inquiry in informal contexts in part because of the traditions of skill training as an intervention tactic in distressed marriages (Azrin, Nastor and Jones, 1973; Weiss, Birchler and Vincent, 1974). Pike and Sillars (1985) studied satisfied and dissatisfied married couples as determined by a median split for husbands and wives' summed scores on Spanier's (1976) measure of satisfaction. The couples discussed a variety of topics (ranging from high to moderate importance), taperecording their own conversations. These conversations were analyzed turn by turn for positive, negative, and neutral vocal affect as measured by Gottman's (1979) Couples' Interaction Scoring System and for various verbal tactics related to conflict resolution strategies. Pike and Sillars used a four-way log-linear analysis with marital satisfaction by topical importance by prior act by subsequent act to assess whether satisfaction and reciprocity of action interacted. They found that the less satisfied couples had more reciprocity of negative vocal affect on important topics than did the more satisfied couples, even in the face of strong overall reciprocity for all types of vocal affect for all couples. With regard to verbal conflict strategies, again a strong tendency towards reciprocity was observed for all couples on all topics, with only minor differences in reciprocity of distributive acts (that is, acts which are competitive and individualistic). The surprising finding here was that more satisfied couples tended to reciprocate these acts more than did less satisfied couples.

Pike and Sillars' (1985) research is both interesting and useful. It does adopt the typical strategy of summing husbands and wives' scores ignoring the potential variability within the couple. But once having done so, it adopts a message pattern approach to establishing patterns of interaction predictive of relational state.

Pike and Sillars' findings on reciprocity of negative affect are actually a replication of earlier findings by Gottman (1979). In the first of Gottman's studies, fourteen clinical and fourteen nonclinical couples were subjects. All of these couples were measured on the Marital Relationship Inventory (MRI) for their relational satisfaction (Burgess, Locke and Thomes, 1971). A subgroup of the clinical couples with the lowest MRI scores and a subgroup of the nonclinical couples with the highest MRI scores were selected for special treatment as distressed and nondistressed subgroups respectively. Distressed couples were those in which at least one of the partners had a MRI score of less than 85 and nondistressed were those in which both had MRI scores above 102. All couples interacted over three issues which they had identified as common problems in their marriage. Their interactions were videotaped and coded into eight categories of content and three categories of vocal affect (positive, neutral, and negative) at each thought unit. These temporal data for all 28 couples were analyzed via lag sequential techniques using the husband's behavior as a criterion and then using the wife's behavior as a criterion. The most important, and most widely cited, finding from this research was that clinical couples were more likely to reciprocate negative affect than were nonclinical couples. These findings have been replicated in a reanalysis of data from Raush *et al.* (1974) reported in Gottman (1979) and replicated across a variety of improvisational tasks by Gottman and his colleagues (1979). Other researchers have obtained supportive results (Margolin and Wampold, 1981; Schaap, 1982).

Noller (1984) used rather different procedures and different variables to investigate the relationship between interaction pattern and relational outcome. In her studies, 48 couples were assessed on the Short Marital Adjustment test (Locke and Wallace, 1959). Couples in which both members scored above 120 were placed in the satisfied group; couples in which one of the members scored 95 or less were in the low satisfied group; couples who failed these extremes were in the moderate group. All 48 couples also filled out a questionnaire on areas of change in the relationship and were asked to discuss their responses with one another. These discussions were videotaped and various behaviors were coded at each thought unit. One of the behaviors coded and assessed for reciprocity was face-directed gaze. The percentage of time that each spouse looked at the other while listening and while speaking was calculated. These percentages were correlated across dyads within each of three levels of adjustment. In general, very high positive correlations were obtained for the high and moderate adjustment groups and low positive correlations were obtained for the low adjustment group. Unlike the data from Pike and Sillars and from Gottman, one cannot tell whether there is any temporal reciprocity of face-directed gaze in these couples. However, reciprocity was again found to discriminate satisfied from dissatisfied couples but in a direction opposite to that reported by Gottman. Of course, the behaviors involved are quite different and it would indeed be surprising if the pattern of interaction alone (regardless of the behavior) discriminated relational states.

Relational Type

Although little research has been conducted (to my knowledge) on interaction patterns and relational types, the study by Williamson and Fitzpatrick (1985) is exemplary in every respect. Fitzpatrick (1977, 1984) has developed a typology of relationships which is both theoretically based and extensively replicated and validated. The typology is based on the assumption that three dimensions of relationships are significant: interdependence (or the degree to which the relationship emphasizes autonomy versus connectedness), ideology (the values concerning marriage and family life), and conflict (strategies for dealing with conflict). These dimensions have led to the empirical discovery of three pure relational types: traditionals (interdependent, high in conflict, conventional ideology), separates (autonomous, conflict avoiders, conventional ideology), and independents (autonomous, high in conflict, unconventional ideology). These types suggest that certain patterns of control would be manifest in the particular categories of couples.

To study this issue, 40 couples were randomly selected from lists of married couples in a church organization and in a university department. Couples discussed an issue related to a recent serious conflict and a neutral issue. These were taperecorded. At the conclusion of the discussion, couples filled out the Relational Dimensions Instrument (Fitzpatrick, 1977, 1984) separately. Twenty-one of the couples agreed on their relational type and the other nineteen fell into the mixed couple type. The audiotapes were coded for strong and weak one-up, one-down, and one-across remarks (Ellis *et al.*, 1976). The one-up and one-down codes represent attempts to control or be controlled in the interaction. Tests of transition probability matrices built up from adjacent pairs of control codes indicated that (a) the interaction patterns of the pure couple types differed from the mixed, (b) the three pure types differed from one another, and (c) the sequential structure of control codes was a first-order Markov process. The data were next submitted to a lag sequential analysis which tended to verify the predicted patterns across couple types. Although the results are too complex to reproduce here, one of the interesting differences showed that separate couples who were conflict avoiders did not exhibit reciprocity in dominance while both traditional and independent couples did, especially when discussing conflict-inducing topics.

This is an exemplary piece of research because the predicted association between relational types and interaction patterns was motivated theoretically by the underlying dimensions of the typology. Furthermore, the researchers were careful to use a message pattern format to link to a group-level relational state.

SPECULATIONS

Three questions about the linkage between interaction patterns and relational outcomes will be posed. First, are patterns of interdependence of behavior expected to be associated with relational outcome so that more interdependent partners experience more beneficial relational outcomes than partners who are more independent in their interaction patterns? Second, is some interactional pattern *per se* more likely to be related to relational outcome than another interactional pattern *regardless of the behavior*? For example, should we expect reciprocity of behavior to be associated with valued (or non-valued) relational outcomes regardless of the behavior which partners are reciprocating? Third, should we expect the association between interaction patterns and relational outcome to depend upon the behaviors involved and, if so, in what way?

Interdependence vs Independence

The first issue in studying the association between relational outcomes and interaction pattern is concerned with how necessary interdependent patterns of action are as opposed to patterns of independent action.

The answer is trivial and borders on the definitional. In order for a relationship to even exist, the patterns of action between the participants must be interdependent. Although not all writers who concern themselves with defining interpersonal communication emphasize the role of interaction (Miller and Steinberg, 1975; Berger and Bradac, 1982), others have made interdependence through interaction the defining characteristic of interpersonal relationships. Thus, in this trivial sense, without interdependence in interaction relational outcomes could not exist because a relationship would not exist.

In a nontrivial study related to this observation, Davis and Perkowitz (1979) manipulated the degree of responsiveness which confederates gave to subjects in two different ways: the probability of a response and the proportion of relevant responses. They were also able to control the content of responses across trials. The authors found that as both proportion and probability of responsiveness went up, so did subjects' attraction to the confederate, perceptions of the confederates' attraction to them, and felt acquaintanceship. Thus, the presence of a responsive other seems to be crucial to the formation of an initial relationship.

A less obvious question than the presence of interdependence or not is the association between the degree of interdependence and relational outcomes. Degree of interdependence may sound like an unusual construct but, in fact, it derives quite naturally from the analytic procedures for assessing interaction patterns which have been discussed and referenced in earlier sections. For example, time series, time-series regression, lag sequential procedures, and log-linear techniques all provide parameter estimates which are essentially measures of predictability for A's behavior on B's behavior or behavior X on behavior Y, as the case may be. Thus, when Gottman (1979) describes the association between degree of predictability in interaction and relational outcome, he is considering the same question that is being considered here.

Gottman's (1979) review of this literature makes two claims. First, on empirical grounds alone, he claims that the more predictable interaction patterns are associated with more distressed couples and families. In more informal relational settings, we might expect greater predictability of interaction patterns with less established pairs than with better established pairs. There is some evidence for this with self-disclosure reciprocity (Won-Doornink, 1979) and with choices of persuasive strategies (Fitzpatrick and Winke, 1979).

Gottman's second claim is that asymmetry in predictability in dyadic interactions is more characteristic of distressed than nondistressed couples. Thus, if the husband's behavior predicts the wife's subsequent behavior to a much larger extent than the wife's predicts the husband's, then such a couple is more likely to fall in the category of distressed couples than a couple more symmetric in predictability.

Gottman (1979) does provide some evidence for the second of these claims. The vocal affect of husbands in clinical couples tends to predict that of wives in high-conflict tasks, while there is a more equal predictability of affect between partners for nonclinical couples.

These positive findings, however, should not lead researchers to an unwarranted generalization that predictability or asymmetry in predictability is linked to non-valued relational outcomes. For example, such a proposition would lead us to hypothesize that interactions between infants and their primary caretakers result in more positive outcomes when there is symmetry of predictability. Such a prediction would not be sensible in that particular relational context. Rather, one would expect the moment-to-moment changes in behavior by the infant to be predictive of the mother's response and that such an asymmetry would be healthy. Similarly, Davis' (1982) work on responsiveness in initial encounters would suggest the opposite of Gottman's work in established couples.

Rather, in continuing our study of the linkage between degree of interdependence and relational outcomes, researchers must expect that the behaviors involved, the type of relationship being studied, and, perhaps most importantly, the meaning of the behaviors being studied will determine the way that predictability is related to outcomes.

Reciprocity, Compensation, and Synchrony

The reliability and reproducibility of Byrne's (1971) work on the similarity–attraction relationship had a directive influence on the study of interpersonal relations for many years. It took researchers a long time to ask about other factors affecting attraction and to ask about the conditions under which dissimilarity might itself be attractive. I do not think that researchers should expect to find such powerful and simple associations between interaction patterns and relational outcomes. For example, to find that reciprocity discriminated pairs and groups who differed on some relational outcomes regardless of contexts and behaviors would be a powerful finding but not one with a high probability of generalizability. Several lines of reasoning argue against this simple but powerful hypothesis.

Evidence from human interaction

Evidence reviewed earlier from Gottman (1979) and from Pike and Sillars (1985) indicates that reciprocity on negative affect is associated with less satisfied couples. At the same time, Street and his colleagues (Putman and Street, 1984; Street, 1982, 1985) found that convergence in certain speech variables was positively associated with the attractiveness of the person who converged. Obviously, the behavior and the relational context make a significant difference in the association between reciprocity and relational outcomes. Similarly, Davis and Perkowitz' (1979) findings on responsiveness and attraction must be modified for different behaviors and relationships. Davis and Martin (1978) found that when dating couples provided pleasurable shocks one to the other, more responsive partners were treated more positively than unresponsive partners. However, when the partners were switched from dating partners to strangers, the responsive strangers were treated less positively than unresponsive strangers. Thus, the relational context and the behaviors made a significant difference in the implications that responsiveness had for positive social reactions.

Overall, simple reciprocity, compensation, or behavioral synchrony is unlikely to be uniformly related to relational outcome. Rather, the effect of these patterns will have to be moderated by relational situations and the behaviors under investigation.

Theories of human interaction

In recent years a great number of theories have arisen to explain patterns of human social interaction. These theories have differed in many respects. The mechanisms driving them have included approach and avoidance forces (Argyle and Dean, 1965; Knowles, 1980), arousal factors (Cappella and Greene, 1982; M. L. Patterson, 1976), reward and cost mediators (Burgoon, 1978; Burgoon and Jones, 1976), salience (Andersen, 1985), goals and functions (M. L. Patterson, 1982a), and face (Brown and Levinson, 1978), among others. Despite significant differences among the mechanisms presumed to be driving the interactional give-and-take, all explanations seem ultimately to appeal to some pairing of competing forces. Although these forces are labeled and discussed in significantly different ways, they can be described as representing, on the one hand, mechanisms driving the person towards interdependence, closeness, and responsiveness to the other's needs and, on the other hand, mechanisms driving the person towards autonomy, independence, and responsiveness to one's own needs.

One is tempted to argue at this point that valued relational outcomes are a result of interaction patterns which strike a balance between these competing forces. After all, the argument would go, the person who completely gives up self-interest in favor of complete other-interest, who gives up all autonomy in favor of dependence on the other, will not in the long run be satisfied with the relationship established on those grounds. The other pole of the argument would maintain that total self-interest, autonomy and independence assure that interpersonal relationships cannot exist, let alone produce valued outcomes.

But I do not wish to make this argument because it is based essentially on an ideological position which, I fear, is too culture-specific to be upheld across groups within our own cultural milieu, let alone other cultures. Rather, I believe, the relative balance of forces towards interdependence and independence depends upon personal and cultural dispositions towards these values. Cultures and groups which value autonomy and independence should not exhibit interaction patterns with high degrees of interdependence and predictability. Cultures in which the partners are not assumed to be equal but rather asymmetrically dependent should exhibit patterns in which the powerful partner is independent interactionally (that is, not predictable from the other's behavior) and the less powerful partner is dependent (that is, predictable from the other's behavior). In short, the pattern of interaction alone does not carry sufficient information to indicate its plausible association with relational outcomes. If the patterns have any meaning for relational outcomes, they must represent something deeper than themselves, something embedded within the cultural or personal value system.

Directions for the Study of Third-order Questions

In the paragraphs above I have hoped to dismiss what I believe will be unprofitable lines in the investigation of third-order questions. Directions for the study of such questions are implicit. Let me try to make them explicit. First, there is no question that the greatest need is for more of the high-quality research in the tradition of Gottman (1979) and Williamson and Fitzpatrick (1985). Second, in making hypotheses for and generalizations from available research, theorists must take into account the meanings or functions of the behaviors (Cappella and Street, 1985; M. L. Patterson, 1982b) and the cultural and individual values which represent the ideological context in which the patterns are enacted. Unless we are studying behaviors whose meanings are in some ways representative of underlying cultural and individual relational values, then the patterns enacted through those behaviors will have no predictive force for relational outcomes. Subsequent research should expect to find an interaction between relational types (when those types are ideologically based as in Fitzpatrick (1984)) and interaction patterns in predicting relational outcomes. When interactional patterns are at odds with relational ideologies and values, then those patterns should be associated with nonvalued outcomes; the same patterns should be associated with valued outcomes when they are supportive of relational ideologies and values.

CONCLUSION

This chapter has been addressed to conceptual and research issues concerning what have been labeled as 'third-order questions', questions about the association between patterns of interaction and relational states. This class of questions has practical significance in the study of social and personal relationships because it links how people respond to one another to the causes and effects of these patterned responses; theoretical significance derives from the long-held belief that social interaction and social reality create one another. The domain of social and personal relationships provides a valuable context in which these aspects of society can be studied.

Conceptually, both the patterns of interaction and the classes of relational states can be studied at the individual and at the group levels of analysis. Carefully done research and subtle theory-building will be conscious of the levels of both, being careful to match levels or to specify the process which bridges between levels.

Although available research is limited probably as a result of the cost of conducting this research and the unfamiliarity of the methods, some excellent exemplars have appeared. This work shows the importance of responsiveness in establishing relational links, provides seductive hints about the predictive value of emotional reciprocity for relational outcomes, and ties relational ideologies and values to interactive patterns of control.

However, we must resist the attempt to generalize prematurely from this work to other hypotheses about relational states and patterns of interaction.

The history of the scientific study of interpersonal relationships is marred by a blindness to the ideological base of many of its hypotheses (Bochner, 1982; Parks, 1982; Sennett, 1977). In speculating about the possible associations between interaction patterns and relational states, we should not be surprised to find that the prevailing ideologies and values of partners will determine which patterns will be linked to valued and which to nonvalued outcomes. To expect otherwise would be to assume that relationships and interactions did not participate in the cultures which spawned them.

Handbook of Personal Relationships
Edited by S. W. Duck
© 1988 John Wiley & Sons Ltd

19

Quality Communication in Personal Relationships

BARBARA M. MONTGOMERY
University of Connecticut, Storrs, Connecticut, USA

ABSTRACT

Study of personal relationships is complicated by a pluralistic standard for judging communication quality. The prevailing social ideology values expressions of positiveness, intimacy, and control. Additionally, partners negotiate creative relational criteria. Finally, individuals develop idiosyncratic ideals. At issue is how to accommodate the resulting pluralistic standard in research and therapy.

What makes for good communication in personal relationships? Such a question about quality can challenge the social scientific tradition of objectivity. At issue is not how something is done, but *how well* it is done. Thus, a value-laden standard of judgement is required to answer the question. And herein lies a problem for social scientists who study communication in personal relationships. For while most accept that partners are in search of quality in their communication, there is considerably less agreement about what constitutes quality. This lack of consensus may be explained, in part, by an unmindful concern with the bases for criticizing communication in personal relationships. This chapter, therefore, examines three distinct criteria systems for judging quality: social ideologies, creative relational standards, and individual idiosyncrasies. The chapter concludes by considering how these three systems interact with reference to the overall quality of relationships. First, though, potential links between good communication and good relationships are explored.

The association between good communication and good relationships can be conceptualized in a number of ways. First, some assume a *constitutive* association by specifying that the communication process is the observable manifestation of a relationship. The consequence is to stipulate that certain communication patterns (e.g. often laughing together, rarely quarreling) constitute a good relationship (see, e.g., Spanier, 1976). As Levenson and Gottman (1985, p. 91) explain, 'Interaction seems to us to be the litmus test of a marriage. On a day to day basis, the quality of interaction defines the quality of a marriage.' Second, the association can be conceptualized as *coincidental* in that both good relationships and good communication can be deemed the products of some third factor or set of factors (e.g. love, compatible astrological profiles, similar backgrounds). Third, some assume a *causal* link in expecting that good communication leads to good relationships. Investigators working from this premise have found that teaching couples certain communication skills has positive effects on their happiness together for months after the training has ended (Gottman, 1979; Wampler and Sprenkle, 1980). Although rarely argued, the direction of the causal link could be reversed by suggesting that good communication is the product of good relationships. It seems likely that the more partners respect, care for, and value one another and their relationship, the more apt they are to invest the energy that effective communication requires. Communication is work and good communication is hard work. Without some basic motivation and commitment towards a relationship, partners have no need to communicate well.

All of these conceptualizations—constitutive, coincidental, and causal—presume a positive association between relationship quality and communication quality. They differ only in their explanation of that positive association. Neither the quality nor the quantity of existing research allows a rational choice of one explanatory model over the others. Moreover, I suspect that pursuit of the research evidence required to falsify two models, thereby justifying a choice, would be futile. It seems more likely that the positive association between relationship quality and communication quality is systemic in nature, reflecting forces represented by all three explanatory models. For these reasons, no more (or no less) than a positive association between good communication and good relationships is assumed throughout this chapter.

Thus, good communication is deemed to be that which is positively related to the happiness and satisfaction that partners experience in their relationship. At issue in this chapter, though, is which explicit characteristics and patterns of communication should be labeled good for relationships. The answer to this question varies, depending upon who is asked to provide the judgement. It seems that society, partnerships, and individuals apply different criteria and, therefore, can reach different conclusions about the quality of communication in any one relationship.

SOCIAL IDEOLOGIES

There is little doubt that societies have a vested interest in the quality of their constituents' relationships. A society's ethical, political, and economic well-being is inextricably tied to its social well-being. Moreover, a society's 'personality' grows out of the day-to-day interpersonal transactions of its citizens. It is in these often mundane exchanges with friends and family that a person develops a sense of the rights and responsibilities attendant on social citizenship. In the interests of self-protection, therefore, a society—the people in collective—is motivated to evaluate communication in relationships and to advocate certain kinds over others.

The criteria system for doing both is a direct extension of the society's ideology of relationships. As with other ideologies, this one brings together the society's beliefs, values, and attitudes into a cohesive body of knowledge about what is good and what is not. At issue for those of us in the scholarly community is how to deal with such a value-laden public standard for communication that is based partly on facts and partly on myths. One option, the most popular one, is to scientifically test the validity of ideologic tenets and to argue for their rejection if they fail our tests. To this end, considerable research attention has been directed towards society's notions about quality communication in personal relationships. This attention has focused primarily on three standards: the ideals of positiveness, intimacy, and control.

The Ideal of Positiveness

Our social world is a contrast of positively and negatively signed entities. And, as far as communication is concerned, the positives are valued over the negatives. The interaction rule for all is 'Be polite' (corollary: 'If you can't say or do anything nice, don't say or do anything'). This sentiment is also at the heart of the ideology for personal relationships. People in good relationships are to be supportive, cheerful, and agreeable in word and deed.

This ideal of positiveness also dominates social scientists' hypotheses about the links between communication and relationship quality. Studies have centered on such positivity concepts as agreement (Riskin and Faunce, 1970), confirmation (Cissna and Sieburg, 1981), integration (Ting-Toomey, 1983), constructive problem-solving (Rusbult, Johnson and Morrow, 1986), pleasing behaviors (Wills, Weiss and Patterson, 1974), and positive nonverbal behavior (Gottman, 1979). In general, the findings have confirmed a link between positively valenced behaviors and higher-quality relationships. Particularly, two trends in this literature deserve special attention since they signify advancements consistent with prevailing theoretical assumptions about communication.

The first is interest in how the *exchange* of positive behaviors relates to quality. Communication exists more in the dynamic process of passing messages back and forth between people and less in the messages themselves. Therefore, it follows to question whether the exchange of positive messages is conducted differently in high-quality versus low-quality relationships.

Research addressing this question suggests that it is less important to exchange positive behaviors than it is to not exchange negative behaviors. Specifically, the findings indicate that: (1) valenced (positive or negative) nonverbal behaviors are more strongly related to quality than valenced verbal behaviors (Gottman, 1979; Pike and Sillars, 1985); (2) the prevalence of negative behaviors is more strongly related to quality than the prevalence of positive behaviors, with more negative behaviors being associated with lesser quality relationships (Gottman, 1979; Rusbult, Johnson and Morrow, 1986); (3) negative behaviors are more likely to be reciprocated in relationships of lower quality than in relationships of higher quality (Billings, 1979; Gottman, 1979; Pike and Sillars, 1985); (4) reciprocity of negative behaviors is a better discriminator between high- and low-quality relationships than reciprocity of positive behaviors (Gottman, 1979; Rusbult, Johnson and Morrow, 1986).

At first glance, the emphasis on negative behaviors in these findings may seem inconsistent with a relationship ideology that stresses positiveness. However, the very existence of the ideology may reduce, to some extent, the benefits of following it exactly (Rusbult, Johnson and Morrow, 1986). This is because the ideology sets expectations. Positive behaviors are anticipated; therefore, their actual performance may not seem terribly dramatic or noteworthy. However, a direct challenge to the ideology in the form of negative behavior is likely to be seen as a very dramatic and dissatisfying act.

A second notable trend consistent with advances in communication theory is the increased attention being given to relational expressions of positiveness. Relational meanings are presumed to emerge implicitly from *patterns* in behavioral exchanges rather than from any one, explicit behavior. They evolve as two people develop an interaction history together. Relational meanings are distinguished from content meanings, which emerge from the literal translation of discrete behaviors into culturally shared, standardized meanings.

A result of merging the idea of relational meanings with the ideal of positiveness has been the concept of confirmation (Laing, 1961; Watzlawick, Beavin and Jackson, 1967). Cissna and Sieburg (1981, p. 259) provide a detailed definition:

> . . . the behavior of one person toward another is confirming to the extent that it performs the following functions in regard to the other's self-experience: (1) It expresses recognition of the other's existence; (2) It acknowledges a relationship of affiliation with the other; (3) It expresses awareness of the significance or worth of the other; (4) It accepts or 'endorses' the other's self-experience (particularly emotional experience).

These functions are presumed to be accomplished primarily through relational meanings as opposed to content meanings. Thus, while a partner is not likely to confirm the other by saying, 'I recognize your existence in our world', he or she might well look up, smile, and say 'hello' when the other walks into the room.

The overriding assumption is that confirmation relates positively to the quality of personal relationships (Beebe and Masterson, 1986; Montgomery, 1981a; Sieburg, 1985). The more confirming two people are towards each other, the happier, more satisfied, they are presumed to be. As can happen with ideologic assumptions, this one persists despite a lack of strong empirical support. Few data-based studies have been conducted; fewer still have reached publication. Research findings testing the assumption are sporadic at best and behavioral observation studies generally have been nonsupportive (see, e.g., Goldberg, 1984; Leth, 1977).

A variety of reasons for this poor research showing are possible. The measurement of confirmation is fraught with reliability and validity problems (Cissna, 1986). As a result, researchers are as occupied with developing better assessment schemes as with testing theoretical assumptions. In addition, the key to linking quality with valenced relational messages may not rest with confirmation, but rather with its negative counterpart disconfirmation. Studies involving clinic samples, for instance, have found that certain patterns of disconfirming messages typify 'ill' relationships (Sluzki, Beavin and Tarnopolsky, 1977). Finally, the basic assumption may be at fault. Confirmation and disconfirmation, *per se*, may be neither good nor bad for relationships. Quality may be more related to *what* is being confirmed or disconfirmed. For example, endorsing a partner's self-proclaimed perceptiveness may bode better for a relationship than endorsing a partner's self-proclaimed stupidity. In the latter case, disconfirmation may be a more competent and satisfying choice for both partners. Despite these reservations, belief in the value of confirmation endures because, simply, it 'seems quite sensible' (Cissna, 1986, p. 20). That is, it is consistent with the ideal of positiveness.

The Ideal of Intimacy

The last 30 years have seen a gradual but progressive shift in what determines a person's sense of well-being. In the late 1950s people's happiness depended upon fulfilling their societal roles by being, for example, good teachers, good doctors, good wives, or good husbands. By the late 1970s people were placing more importance on interpersonal sources of happiness like being close to their children, 'really' getting to know their friends, and having 'meaningful' romances (Sennett, 1977; Veroff, Douvan and Kulka, 1981). Brehm (1985) predicts that this 'search for intimacy' will gain even more strength throughout the 1980s.

As sure as intimacy is the goal of this search, communication is its method. For it is through verbally and nonverbally sharing, disclosing, revealing, and expressing themselves that two people become intimate. Society considers this to be 'real communication' as opposed to 'mere talk' (Katriel and Phillipsen, 1981). It is not surprising, therefore, that the ideal of intimacy has become a major theme in the scholarly study of interpersonal communication. A number of theories assert that relationships develop and grow to the extent that partners share information about themselves, i.e. become intimate (Altman and Taylor, 1973; Altman, Vinsel and Brown, 1981; Berger and Calabrese, 1975; Knapp, 1984). Intimacy variables like self-disclosure, expressiveness, and openness are in the mainstream of communication research (see, e.g., Chelune *et al.*, 1979; Noller, 1980a; Norton, 1983a). A few writers go so far as to assert that interpersonal communication exists only when two people act and react based upon intimate knowledge of each other (Miller and Steinberg, 1975; Stewart, 1986).

The cornerstone for this structure of scholarship is the assumption that high levels of intimacy expression are found in good personal relationships. Research findings appear to warrant this assumption with some important qualifications.

First, the nonverbal mode of expression appears to be more closely linked to relationship quality than the verbal mode. In general, people tend to rely more on nonverbal than verbal cues to interpret messages (Archer and Akert, 1977; Argyle, Alkema and Gilmour, 1971; Seay and Altekruse, 1979). While some have estimated that as much as 90 per cent of the meaning in interpersonal exchanges comes from nonverbal channels (Mehrabian and Wiener, 1967), more empirically defensible estimates are from 60 to 65 per cent (Burgoon, 1985). The nonverbal behaviors that typically communicate about intimacy include: proximity, body lean, body orientation, touch, gaze, vocal variation, gesturing, and time spent together. These kinds of nonverbal behaviors have been found to better predict relationship quality than do verbal expressions of intimacy (Chelune *et al.*, 1984; Gottman, 1979). This may be because nonverbal behaviors are viewed as less strategic, more spontaneous and, therefore, more honest than verbal behaviors. Thus, Bateson (1972, pp. 412–413) suggests:

> When boy says to girl, 'I love you,' he is using words to convey that which is more convincingly conveyed by his tone of voice and his movements; and the girl, if she has any sense, will pay more attention to those accompanying signs than to the words. . . . From an adaptive point of view, it is important that [this type of emotional expression] be carried on by techniques which are relatively unconscious and only imperfectly subject to voluntary control.

A second qualification to the intimacy doctrine is that the association between quality and expressions of intimacy may vary considerably over time. Altman, Vinsel and Brown (1981) make this point in a revision of social penetration theory. They suggest that even in the healthiest relationship, partners naturally cycle between being open and accessible and being closed and inaccessible. This cycling helps meet situational needs for both privacy and togetherness, for both differentiation and integration. Analyses of the interaction between friends confirm this explanation (Wiseman, 1986; Rawlins, 1983b). Rawlins (1983b, pp. 12–13) concludes:

> . . . communicating private information about self and making personal observations regarding other are necessary for friendship to develop. But in revealing confidential thoughts and feelings, self becomes susceptible to hurt, and in making candid comments, self discovers other's vulnerabilities. As a result, there is continuous dialectical interplay between the expressive and protective functions of communication in such enduring bonds. Openness often solicits restraint, thereby creating conditions for closedness.

A third qualification is that partners may not equally contribute to the association between expressions of intimacy and quality relationships. At least in heterosexual relationships, women are more likely to carry the major responsibility for expressing intimacy (Dosser, Balswick and Halverson, 1986). For example, while Rubin *et al.* (1980) found that disclosiveness was positively related to dating partners' reported love for each other, the women tended to be more disclosive than their male counterparts. The researchers explain their findings by suggesting that there are two competing ideals concerning intimacy. The first values 'full disclosure' in personal relationships. The second values behavior consistent with stereotypical sexual roles which specify that males are unemotional and restrained and females are emotional and expressive.

A fourth qualification is that the style of intimacy expression may affect its association with relationship quality. That is, *how* intimacy is expressed may be as important to the relationship as the fact that it is expressed. Berg (1987), for instance, notes the importance of such responsive behaviors as addressing the same topic as the partner, matching the intimacy level of a self-disclosure, and various 'listener cues' like eye contact, smiles, head nods, and backchannel behaviors. He reviews research indicating that levels and kinds of responsiveness discriminate between high-quality and low-quality friendships and marital relationships.

Norton and Montgomery (1982) include the notion of responsiveness within the broader concept of open communicator style. An open style signals that a message is representative of a person's felt emotions, beliefs, or opinions. Open styles are typically manifested in intensified nonverbal, emotional, valenced, and receptive behaviors. Chelune (1979) discusses somewhat similar behaviors which he labels 'affective manner of presentation'. Stylistic behaviors are found to be more closely linked to the perception that one's partner is being open and expressive than are verbal behaviors like topic choice and verbal immediacy cues (Montgomery, 1984a). Moreover, an open style has been found to predict quality characteristics of relationships (Montgomery, 1986; Honeycutt, 1986).

The final qualification to the ideal of intimacy is that not all expressive messages are equally linked to quality relationships. Consistent with the ideal of positiveness, the expression of positive as opposed to negative facts and feelings is more indicative of good relationships (Chelune *et al.*, 1984; Levinger and Senn, 1967). This was underscored by a recent study of how individuals deal with the revelation of unexpected, significant information from friends or romantic partners (Planalp and Honeycutt, 1985). The researchers found that learning that a partner had lied, cheated, or the like increased the uncertainty subjects felt about their relationships, resulted in negative emotional reactions towards the partners, and, for about 60 per cent of the subjects, led to decreases in the quality of the relationship. Apparently, to know a person is to love a person *as long as what we know is positive*.

The Ideal of Control

This ideal is not concerned with partners' desires to control or be controlled by each other so much as it is with partners' desires to be *in control* of their relationship. Members of our society prize personal relationships in which they actively shape their own futures, direct their own destinies, and manage their own fates (Miller *et al.*, 1986). Partners value the notion of 'working' on their relationships (Katriel and Phillipsen, 1981). The assumption is that good relationships are not the product of luck, chance, or happenstance; they do not happen by accident. Rather, good relationships result from the abilities and efforts of their members.

To be in control, partners must be able to accurately anticipate future happenings and they must be able to intervene to affect those future happenings. These two processes of prediction and management are at the center of social scientific study related to the ideal of control. Research has investigated how social rules, roles, scripts, and norms, to name a few examples, help partners predict each other's behavior and manage their relationshiis (see, e.g., Argyle, Furnham and Graham, 1981).

Prediction and, especially, management are inextricably associated with the communication process as well. The process of interacting is simultaneously the process of relating. What partners say and do with each other (or, at least, perceive they say or do with each other) are the fundamental facts of their relationship. Successfully managing their interactions, therefore, is an aspect of successfully managing their relationship. In this regard, the ideal of control specifies that in good relationships partners control their communication rather than letting their communication control them.

One sign of this control is the production of coherent conversations: comments are cogent, clear, and concise; topics are introduced smoothly and expanded appropriately; norms for sequencing comments are observed (see Craig and Tracy, 1983). In short, partners cooperate to construct an orderly conversation. Partners in lower-quality relationships do not seem to do these things well. For instance, Gottman (1979; Gottman et al., 1976a) reports that conversations of couples in distressed marriages as opposed to nondistressed ones are characterized more by: (1) kitchen sinking or introducing a number of topics into the conversation at the same time; (2) cross-complaining sequences in which partners exchange a series of criticisms rather than focus their comments on one issue at a time; (3) interruptions; and (4) stagnating repetitions of the same ideas.

Another aspect of managing interactions is coordinating nonverbal behavior. Coordination requires that partners mutually adjust to each other's interaction-regulating behaviors like speech rate, pause length, eye gaze, body orientation, and physical distance (Cappella, 1984). In well-managed interactions partners' regulating behaviors mesh to produce a smoothly synchronized exchange of messages. Uncoordinated interactions, in which behaviors do not mesh, may signal relationship problems and dissatisfactions (Cappella, 1985b; Noller, 1980b).

An additional communication factor often associated with controlling interactions and relationships is metacommunication. In the boradest sense, metacommunication refers to any message, verbal or nonverbal, that has impact on the way other messages are interpreted. Thus, it can be equated with many of the communication characteristics discussed in this chapter (e.g. open style, responsiveness, structuring nonverbal behaviors, relational messages). In a more narrow sense, metacommunication has been defined as explicit, verbalized comments about a conversation's messages (Gottman, 1979). This reflexive talk or 'talk about talk' might sound like: 'I'm trying to tell you how sorry I am', or 'What I hear you telling me is . . .'. It is this form of metacommunication that has not met expectations for helping partners manage their interactions. Gottman (1979), for instance, found no difference in the frequency with which distressed and nondistressed married couples explicitly metacommunicate. Moreover, he observed that distressed couples became much more absorbed with their metacommunication, chaining such messages together at the expense of the original topic of conversation. Apparently, too much talk about talk stymies conversational progress. Partners 'stand in place' by cycling their comments around one idea: 'What you seem to be saying is . . .'; 'What I meant to say was . . .'; 'No, I heard you say that . . .'; 'Well, what I really meant was . . .'. Preoccupation with this kind of metacommunication is more likely to result in mismanaged interactions.

The extent to which partners concur in their interpretations of messages is a fourth management factor related to relationship quality. Shared meanings traditionally have been associated with quality personal relationships (Laing, Phillipson and Lee, 1966; Lewis and Spanier, 1979). And, with few exceptions, research has corroborated this association (see review by Sillars and Scott, 1983). For example, dissatisfied marital partners exhibit more discrepancies between the message one spouse attempts to send and the message the other spouse receives. Moreover, this discrepancy is biased towards assigning negative interpretations to messages with neutral or positive intent (Kahn, 1970; Gottman, 1979). A recent study by Noller and Venardos (1986) adds one more bit of disquieting information. Not only are partners in lower-quality relationships more likely to misinterpret each other's messages, they also more confidently assume that their interpretations are accurate. Thus, 'couples low in marital adjustment are both less accurate in their communication than are other couples and also less aware of that lack of accuracy' (p. 40).

While the link between agreement in message interpretations and relationship quality appears to be fairly robust, two qualifications deserve mention. First, there is probably a threshold in the positive association between agreement and quality. Complete agreement, seeing everything as one's partner sees it, would result in the loss of individuality and sense of self. So it seems likely that partners in quality relationships must reach a *relatively* high level of agreement, but one below levels that would cause them to lose all sense of their personal identities. Second, in some cases it may be more important to the quality of a relationship that partners *think* they share meanings as opposed to actually sharing meanings. Levinger and Breedlove (1966) found this to be so for a sample of married couples. They concluded that shared meanings may be more important on some issues than on others, although their research was not successful in identifying those issues. Cronen, Pearce and Harris (1982) make a similar point when they stress that the bottom line in managing interactions is coordination, not agreement. That is, as long as partners act and react to each other in ways that make sense to them, are responsive, and produce desirable outcomes, it may not be necessary for them to actually share the same meanings for their behaviors.

Understanding The Influence of Relationship Ideology

As the previous paragraphs illustrate, the prevalent scholarly treatment of ideologic standards is to test their validity. This approach has yielded critical information about whether or not certain communication patterns are associated with high-quality relationships for the masses. On the basis of these tests, scholars have argued that some ideals should be modified and some should be abandoned (see, e.g., Bochner, 1982; Parks, 1982).

This standard course of action, however, ignores some important points. One is that *what is good for a relationship cannot be considered apart from what people think is good for a relationship*. The prevailing ethic proclaims that good people are not necessarily people who do good; they are people who try to do good. In other words, the mere *struggle* for goodness helps to distinguish the good from the bad, as witnessed by the appeal of tragic heroes. Similarly, if intimacy, positiveness, and control are valued, then the mere act of trying to be intimate, positive, and in control may bring a sense of satisfaction to relationship partners.

Moreover, we have to be cautious when advocating scientific research as a test of an ideology's worth. Scientists are not immune from the biasing effects of society's ideology. As critics have repeatedly argued, a researcher's tests— what is hypothesized and what is accepted as data and evidence—are inextricably knotted together with the researcher's context—his or her community's current world view (e.g. Kuhn, 1962; Gergen, 1976). The inescapable conclusion is that the outcomes of our studies are as likely to stem from the politics of belief as the 'realities' of relationships.

Additionally, critiquing the prevailing ideology with empirical evidence is not likely to persuade the public nor, perhaps, even social scientists, to modify or abandon it. Ideologies rest more on faith (e.g. 'gut feelings', 'good hunches', 'intuitive hypotheses') than fact. People develop that faith not from what relationships are like, but from what they think relationships should be like (cf. McCall's chapter, this volume). Empirical research is only one source of evidence among many on matters of faith and values. Other even more powerful sources are the mass media, the church, historical tradition, even the economy. This does not make scholarly research aimed at testing ideologic tenets irrelevant; but such tests will not provide the pivotal criteria for accepting or rejecting an ideologic belief.

Thus, researchers may not have much effect on society's relationship ideals by merely shunning those aspects that fail their tests. It may be more productive to consider alternative reactions. One possibility is to devote more energy to investigating how relationship ideologies emerge and are maintained. This suggestion is based on the premise that the more one understands how something works, the better the odds for successful intervention. The few studies along these lines hint at the possibilities. For example, recent analyses of popular literature (Kidd, 1975; Hubbard, 1985; Ulrich, 1986) provide insights about how magazine articles and novels affect the public's idealizations about personal relationships and how those ideals change in relation to other cultural changes. Studies of other social institutions' effects on relationship ideals are few, but equally as pertinent (see, e.g., Bellah *et al.*, 1985). Increased study along these lines promises to suggest powerful schemes for developing, maintaining and changing ideals.

A second alternative, though, may be to affirm rather than try to change 'false ideologies'. Many of us are not completely averse to perpetuating myths or untruths when we think some good can come from it. Falsehoods are often justified by emphasizing utility over truthfulness, a kind of 'ends justifies means' reasoning. Perhaps we should think about relationship ideologies in the same way. Their oversimplified, sometimes mythical tenets could provide 'leverage' for exacting the change partners want in their relationship. Imagine two partners who are trying to end their relationship for whatever reasons. If those reasons are judged too difficult to share with each other or with their social network—perhaps they are extremely abstract, ambiguous, or personally painful—the partners may find it useful to substitute reasons based upon society's ideology: 'We just didn't share enough of ourselves with each other' or 'He was always putting me down'. In other words, ideological tenets may provide useful pseudo-explanations for intensifying, terminating, or maintaining relationships when partners are unable or unwilling to share real explanations.

The communication standards embodied in relationship ideology are tightly woven together with other beliefs and values in the fabric of society. Thus, they are perpetuated in their consistency with the cultural, economic, political, and ethical contingencies of a society. This interdependent framework makes the empirical validation of the assumed links between these communication standards and relationship quality relatively anticlimactic. Most certainly, such tests are not likely to be pivotal in deciding a standard's worth. More fruitful and, perhaps, interesting endeavors for social scientists would be to ask how ideological standards evolve, to what extent couples believe in them, and how they are used by couples to affect and to justify their relationships.

PARTNERSHIPS AND CREATIVE RELATIONAL STANDARDS

Not only do societies develop communication standards for personal relationships; so also do relationship members. Partners have the ability to establish their own system of beliefs about, and behaviors for, relating well to each other. This system has been called an 'epistemic community' (Thayer, 1975), an 'ideoculture' (Fine, 1979), a 'relationship world view' (Stephen, 1984a), and 'creative adjustment' (Tseng, 1977). Both Peplau (1983) and Jackson (1965b) suggest that this system is composed of 'relationship rules', unique formulae for how to act well within the context of a particular relationship. Thus, while the social-level ideology specifies 'Be open', a dating couple within that society might find that they do better by modifying that standard: 'Be open only when it will not hurt the other's feelings.'

Relational standards are distinguished by some key characteristics. First, they are the products of *negotiation*. In day-to-day interaction, partners make claims and counterclaims about the way they should conduct their relationship. This negotiation process continues until some consensus is achieved. Second, these claims and counterclaims are more often communicated at *relational levels of meaning* rather than content levels. They are communicated *implicitly* rather than explicitly. Thus, while a friend is not likely to actually say, 'Flirting is good for our relationship; so we should do it often', two friends might well arrive at that very same conclusion through repeatedly flirting with each other and encountering positive responses. Third, relational standards are phenomenologically *unique* for each partnership. They are developed entirely within the confines of a particular relationship. Fourth, relational standards can *contradict, add to, and substitute for* social ideologies. By definition, relational standards are different from ideological standards. But that difference may be slight, as when friends are happy being open about everything except their incomes. Or the difference may be extreme, as when spouses defy the ideal of positiveness by counting insults as signs of the high quality of their relationship (see Masheter and Harris, 1986).

Evidence for Creative Relational Standards

A growing body of research indicates that partners do develop unique standards for determining the quality of their relationships. For example, I have previously reported that unique bonds of liking develop within groups of college students working together on a month-long project (Montgomery, 1984b). Some students more than others are generally liked by everyone, suggesting that criteria for liking are shared to some extent. However, any one pair's liking bond is measurably different from those developed by other pairs, indicating that some aspects of those bonds are uniquely negotiated.

The study of marital types (Fitzpatrick, 1977) provides further support for creative standards. This work distinguishes among traditional, independent, and separate couples. Briefly, *traditionals* espouse conventional beliefs and values concerning marriage; in other words, their views are most closely aligned with the current relationship ideology. *Independents* value intimacy *and* personal freedom, control *and* change, positiveness *and* confrontation. Theirs seems to epitomize the complex 'modern marriage'. *Separates* are most noted for their emphasis on independence. They value being physically and emotionally detached from each other. Comparisons of the relationship quality for the three couple types indicate that traditional couples tend to be the most satisfied (Fitzpatrick and Best, 1979; Noller and Hiscock, 1986). However, differences within couple types also have been found. These differences are related to the behavioral patterns uniquely valued by the three couple types (Sillars *et al.*, 1983). For example, more satisfied separates are more likely than less satisfied separates to communicate less emotionally and be less talkative during conflict episodes. Thus, these couples defy society's ideals about what makes for good communication in good relationships.

However, the specific communication standards that partners apply may not be as important to relationship quality as simply that the couple has developed some unique standards (Kahn, 1970; Sabatelli, Buck and Dreyer, 1980, 1982;

Stephen, 1984a). Gottman (1979), for example, found that observers and dissatisfied spouses tended to interpret the spouses' nonverbal behaviors in similar ways. However, he found much less agreement between observers and satisfied spouses. He attributed this discrepancy to a 'private message system' developed by those in high-quality relationships.

The Power of Creative Relational Standards

Negotiating a shared and unique standard for communication—a private message system—is undoubtedly very rewarding for partners. Simply sharing in the same meaning system is a positive experience for most. Interactions are coordinated and interpretations are confirmed. Additionally, creating a unique standard helps partners realize a specialness in their relationship. Not only is their standard different from those used to judge the quality of other relationships, but it is specifically tailored to accommodate their relational circumstances.

Besides being rewarding, though, a creative communication standard is a source of tremendous relational power. Partners are not constrained to act as everyone else does. They have the power to apply any judgement criterion they wish, as long as it is mutually acceptable. Masheter and Harris (1986) suggest that this power stems from the distinction between behaviors and interpretations. They give the following example:

> . . . interpretation of the remark, 'your cooking smells', as a compliment is what becomes the fact of compliment. Interpretation of the same remark as an insult brings about the fact of insult. . . . However, a resourceful recipient can define a message along a new dimension of meaning, e.g. s/he can treat an intended insult as 'teasing' or a 'joke'. The 'insult' then is not only ineffective, it can become 'affection' or 'humour' in the particular interaction. In repeated encounters, some relationship partners even create a private language. What may appear to be insults to outsiders may be 'terms of endearment' between the partners themselves. In fact 'affectionate insults' may express a special intimacy in which the partners 'take license' with one another in ways that would estrange most other people.

In this way, couples exercise the freedom to define 'what counts' within the confines of their relationship. They decide which patterns of behavior are acceptable and unacceptable, rewarding and costly, satisfying and unsatisfying. In short, they set the standards for determining the quality of their communication and, ultimately, their relationship.

There appear to be very few constraints on this process. One, which I have already discussed, is that the standard must be the product of negotiation and agreement. It must be mutually acceptable to both partners. Another is that the standard must not adversely affect those outside the relationship. Otherwise, social pressure is likely to be brought to bear on the couple to more closely conform to society's relationship ideology.

Considerable freedom exists within these bounds. Partners may count arguing as caring, rejection as teaching, lying as saving face for the partner, or put-downs as attentiveness. A good relationship may be one which requires little of one's physical and emotional resources; or a good relationship may be one which requires the commitment of vast resources.

Whatever emerges as the creative standard for communication, however, emerges through the communication process itself. Moreover, the requisite negotiating is conducted more often subtly and implicitly at relational levels of meaning than overtly and explicitly at verbalized content levels. Standards are set more by example than by decree. They develop over time rather than emerge fully formed. Their acceptance is signaled more by reciprocation than by formal consent. In short, the partners' standards *for* communication are embodied *in* their communication.

INDIVIDUAL IDIOSYNCRASIES

Besides societal and relational units, individuals also develop communication standards for quality relationships. These individual standards are idiosyncratic in that they are peculiar and unique to a specific person. They are custom made and different from the standards advocated by the society or negotiated by the relational unit. For instance, society's intimacy ideal advises dating couples to be open, share feelings, and disclose information about themselves. A particular dating couple, though, may have found that they are happier if they exclude some topics from this general expectation for expressiveness, say his drinking and her past loves. This discovery might have come through repeated arguments, hurt feelings, misunderstandings, or awkward silences. No matter how it developed, it represents a relational standard of communication that affects the quality of their relationship: if they both avoid the drinking and past loves topics, both are happier and more satisfied with the relationship. In addition, though, both partners may have developed idiosyncratic notions about expressiveness that are not shared but do affect each individual's happiness. For instance, he may most value infrequent but long, late-night, soul-searching, open discussions in which they 'tackle the problems of the world'. She may most value the fifteen-minute chats they have while fixing dinner in which they share synopses of their respective days. The couple may engage in both kinds of intimacy expressions. But since they are not similarly valued, neither probably happens as often or as well as the partner who prizes that particular kind would like. The crucial aspect of these two individual preferences for intimacy expression is that each carries meaningfully different weights in affecting each partner's satisfaction in the relationship. This is the essential characteristic of idiosyncratic standards.

Idiosyncratic standards differ from ideologies and relational standards in other, less fundamental, ways as well. First, idiosyncratic standards tend to be more *diversified*. Since there are no social constraints on their existence—they exist merely at the whim of one person—they can include virtually any aspect of relating that a person counts as important. Second, while they make perfectly good sense to the person who holds them, idiosyncratic standards are more likely to be considered *outlandish or unworkable* by a partner. Dryden (1981), for example, shows how the standards of depressed persons can be so unfathomable to their friends or spouses that the relationships suffer. Third, idiosyncratic standards can be kept completely *secret*; furtively applied unbeknownst to a partner or anyone else. They may exist, for instance, as 'secret tests' which if passed prove a partner's commitment and love but if failed prove just the opposite (see Baxter and Wilmot, 1984).

While clinical ramifications of idiosyncratic communication standards have been explored (see, e.g., Duck and Gilmour, 1981c), their relevance to 'normal', more typical kinds of personal relationships has received scant attention. Yet, there is some evidence that idiosyncratic standards exist and are applied by people in the general population. For example, Sabatelli (1984) argues that individuals differ in their expectations for marriage and, as a result, different ways of relating make them happy. He suggests that social exchange theory, particularly its notion of comparison level, can shed light on these individual differences. Comparison level refers to a standard for judging relationships that emerges from a person's past relational experiences and knowledge about other relationships. As part of his project to create a measure of marital quality based upon these ideas, Sabatelli asked spouses to rate a number of behaviors and experiences for their importance to marital quality. A comparative examination of the means and standard deviations he obtained hints at the existence of some idiosyncratic standards in the sample. For instance, relatively little variability was associated with the strongly endorsed item, 'The amount of respect you experience'. Evidently, most spouses tended to agree that communicating consideration and regard for each other was important to their marital satisfaction. In contrast, variability was more pronounced in the ratings given the item, 'The amount of jealousy your partner expresses'. Moreover, the mean rating for this item fell at the midpoint of the rating scale, halfway between 'very important' and 'not very important'. These parametric characteristics suggest that some view expressions of jealousy on the part of their spouses as an important communication aspect related to quality while others do not. That is, the statistics suggest the existence of idiosyncratic standards related to expressions of jealousy.

Sternberg and Barnes (1985) also reference social exchange theory in discussing how individual standards concerning the behavioral expression of love affect judgements of relationship quality. They contrast 'absolute', population-wide standards with individual standards by introducing the notion of relationship ideals:

> Consider, for example, two individuals in two different romantic relationships who happen to experience a given level of romantic love for their respective partners. If only absolute level of romantic love matters to satisfaction, then, all things equal, these two individuals should be equally satisfied in their relationships. If, however, ideal comparison levels play a role in satisfaction, then it may be the distance from the individual's experienced level of love to the individual's ideal level of love, rather than the absolute level of love, that matters more (or at all). (p. 1587)

The researchers found support for both effects. That is, absolute levels of expressed love and differences between expressed and ideal levels of love predicted satisfaction in romantic relationships. These findings support the notion that both social-level standards, i.e. ideological, and individual-level standards, i.e. idiosyncratic, are associated with judgements of relationship quality.

INTEGRATING IDEOLOGIES, RELATIONAL STANDARDS, AND IDIOSYNCRASIES

These three criteria systems codetermine partners' judgements of how good their communication is. It is hard to imagine the exclusive application of any one system. Relying only on ideologic standards would require seeing one's own relationship as equivalent to all others. It would necessitate denying any unique self and relationship circumstances that might mitigate the effects of society's prescription for good communication. Everyone's ideal would be the same. Conversely, relying only on relational standards would deny any consistency and similarity across relationships. The partners would have to accept responsibility for negotiating anew every standard with which to evaluate their communication. Finally, relying only on idiosyncratic standards would indicate that a person had no sense of self as affected by context. Moreover, it would deny any similarity in communication goals between partners or across partnerships.

A more likely scenario is that partners integrate aspects of society's ideology with relationally negotiated criteria and their own personal idiosyncratic criteria to form a pluralistic standard for good communication. Contemplating this possibility suggests some interesting questions for future research. For instance, what, if any, communication issues are more likely to fall under the influence of one criterion system over the others? What factors affect the development of the various criterion systems? How are they maintained and how are they changed? Do their relative weights in determining what is good communication remain stable, or do they fluctuate? If the latter is the case, is the fluctuation systematic, perhaps explained by developmental stages or personal maturity?

IMPLICATIONS FOR MAKING QUALITY JUDGEMENTS

Regardless of where future research on this topic takes us, the pluralistic definition of good communication offered in this chapter has implications for current work in the area of personal relationships. First and foremost, while good communication is linked to good relationships, the defining characteristics of good communication are not preordained. Good communication is not the product of a formula in which all terms are set and defined. Some members of the formula may change value, drop out, or be added from one couple to the next, from one partner to the next, and from one time to the next. To assume otherwise is to deny the individuality of people and their power to adapt to each other and their unique relational circumstances. So, for example, while society values expressions of intimacy, it would be shortsighted to assume that every couple in society values expressions of intimacy.

The problem for social scientists, then, becomes how best to assess the quality of a couple's communication when the appropriate criteria may be unique and unknown. The solution is to choose a metric that supersedes social, relationship, and individual standards. For instance, Levenson and Gottman (1985) demonstrate that measures of physiological functioning such as heart rate, pulse transmission time, skin conductance level, and general somatic activity are exceptionally powerful indicators of a married couple's appraisal of the quality of their interactions and their relationship. They explain that such physiological measures assess the *result* of the partners' application of their judgement scheme or schemes, whatever they might specifically be. Basically, the more aroused the partners, as indicated by the various physiological variables, the less favorably they view their interactions and their relationships.

Another measure that supersedes societal, relational, and individual standards is an 'impact' report provided by the partners themselves. In effect, partners are asked to provide quality judgements of their on-going message exchanges, either as they actually take place (e.g. Gottman, 1979), while watching a videotape (e.g. Montgomery, 1980), or as the partners assess a reconstructed script of the interaction (e.g. Harris and Sadeghi, 1987). The purpose is similar to that for using physiological measures. Partners' impact reports represent the *output* of an evaluation process that they themselves have conducted by applying their own, unique judgement criteria.

Finally, the recognition of a pluralistic standard for quality communication has implications for therapy. It would be a mistake to assume that every couple in society should be encouraged to communicate intimately, or positively, or with control just because these represent society's ideals. What works for the masses—or, more accurately, what the masses think works for them—may not work for any one couple or any one individual. Ideologic standards are like averages: they describe nothing in particular very well. Without acknowledgement of a pluralistic standard for good communication, couples who seek therapeutic advice risk being encouraged to conform to others' notions of what will make them happy rather than their own.

Section Four

Social Psychology/Sociology

Section Editor   *Steve Duck*

Overview

The previous section, Communication, ends with consideration of quality communication in personal relationships. The present section, on social psychology, starts with consideration of intimacy as it represents both a quality of relationships and a source of quality experiences. Like communication scientists, social psychologists and sociologists who study personal relationships focus on several kinds of questions. Traditionally these have been most attentive to the early stages of attraction. Such questions as 'What influences reactions to others as social stimuli?' have led to a wealth of research into the effects of physical attractiveness on initial attraction, and into the effects of attitude similarity on responses to strangers, for example. Others, such as 'What is the nature of social influences on social emotions?', have led to research on the influence of self-esteem on liking, or the creation of feelings of passionate love. More recently added to this list are new versions of the old questions as researchers have explored self-presentation in acquaintance and recently have looked at loneliness, at embarrassment or at shyness or at communicative incompetence in interaction, for instance. New questions have been added, such as 'What social processes influence the experience and development of relationships?' and 'What influences from the surrounding culture and social context impinge upon the relationships that persons form between themselves?'. The chapters in Section Four deal with such issues.

Proverb tells us that 'The longest journey begins with a single step'. Some major themes of this present section represent the recent single steps made in the progressive shift of interest and attack on both the traditional and the new questions. It is clear from the chapters here that one major issue for researchers now is the matter of *process* in relationships. I have argued earlier that untested but speciously plausible views were previously rampant in the field, for instance the unwise view 'that the development of relationships is smooth, not jerky; that it takes place steadily, not by periods of activity followed by inactivity; that it is continuous, not discontinuous. Perhaps this is an error and acquaintance is really a process characterised by steps and plateaux rather than smooth curves of growth' (Duck, 1977, pp. 19–20). Although such early objections to the prevailing view were largely ignored, the more recent claim that relationships

363

are not states but processes has clearly struck the mark (Duck and Sants, 1983). Almost every chapter in this section now takes that line.

The interesting fact about these views is that they are not concerned, as social psychology often is, with social cognitive process stripped of its everyday content: rather they are focused clearly on the issue of the content that comprises the process. Thus chapters look at the activities that occupy partners in everyday relationships, whether they be courtship, role management or activities in organizations. Another part of this theme is a concern over the influence of time on relationships, such that researchers now examine carefully the changes that take place as relationships develop and are not merely looking for the factor that predicts that progress (usually measured in simple terms as a mere growth in liking or expressed friendship). Workers now clearly act as if relationships are dynamic across time and are not to be treated as if they run themselves like automobiles without drivers once the ignition key has been found, inserted and turned. The chapters here are now extending the view that relationships are processes in many unexpected and valuable ways not merely restricted to the development of friendship.

In the first chapter of this section, Harry Reis and Phil Shaver consider previous formulations of the concept of intimacy—central to social psychologists' conceptualizations of growth and change in close personal relationships—and they review the underlying themes inherent in several different approaches. Their thoughtful and intriguing review leads them to propose an interpersonal process model of intimacy. They view intimacy as composed of several simultaneously operative processes of perception, self-presentation and interpretation that have detailed interdependencies whose interaction is the process that 'creates' the intimacy. In the view of Reis and Shaver, the process of intimacy begins with the expression of personally revealing feelings or information. The process continues with the empathic or supportive response of the partner and proceeds to true intimacy with the discloser's feelings of being understood, validated and cared for.

While the chapter draws some of its major concepts from existing theory, it is provocative and unique in its binding of the major concepts into one whole and in its planting of the whole into a process orientation. Their new and exciting suggestion—one that will clearly stimulate much research in the future—is that 'intimacy is a dynamic process whose operation is best observed in the pattern of communication and reaction between people'.

The next chapter, by Robert Hays, also takes a process orientation and applies it to the nature and development of friendship. Hays gives a skilful review of the extensive and disparate work on friendship. Eternally an enigma and a fascination to observers from ancient times, friendship has come under close scientific inspection only quite recently and its surface has been only scratched by such work. Hays explores this recent work on the friendship bond and then works through the expanding literature on the evolution and development of friendship.

The earliest work on the nature of friendship undoubtedly provided some building blocks for future work, but friendship is not just about a concept and its sophisticated analysis: rather it is a living and growing entity. Using language familiar to those who have just completed reading the previous chapter, Hays thus conceptualizes friendship as 'a highly flexible, dynamic, multidimensional process'. He argues that the changes that occur during the development of friendship are inexorably bound up with several interacting issues, such as the context, the level of intimacy in the friendship, and the characteristics of the two individuals involved. Hays calls for a significant move away from research on the characteristics of friends and their choices of partners: instead we need more work on the dynamics of their evolving relationship.

Rod Cate and Sally Lloyd, in their impressive chapter reviewing research on courtship, also consider the importance of dynamics in the relationship, stressing the significance of interactional processes as influences on the quality of the ultimately resultant marriage. These authors, also, emphasize the relevance and significance of communicative patterns in courtship, noting the importance of patterns that are low in anger and resentment, even if a certain amount of conflict occurs.

Their analysis of the literature leads Cate and Lloyd to argue that incremental change in courtship is strongly associated with qualitative change which leads to redefinitions of the relationship in a cyclical, interactive way. The authors conclude that 'from the interpersonal process perspective, there is need to move toward the broader context in which development and dissolution [of courtship] take place'.

Such contextual issues are well represented in Clyde Hendrick's masterful chapter on 'Roles and Gender in Relationships'. His approach is one based on an analysis suggesting that relationships 'are best viewed as interactional processes within role structures', an argument that has proved both stimulating and provocative to those who have been privileged to read the early drafts. Searching for a conception of social structure that is compatible with notions of process, Hendrick adopts an approach to social structures that captures their nature as enduring patterns whilst also being entities that can be impacted and transformed by the processes of human action.

In that context, Hendrick sees relationships as a set of processes included in the social structure and something that can be likewise transformed and modified by the agency of the participants. Within that argument, Hendrick then proposes a new way to explore the nature of gender and roles in relationships, giving them a dynamism and reality that allows for change in the social structure. He concludes, after reviewing the literature on the sex and gender differences already known to attach to relationships, that 'in time most of the gender differences reviewed in [this] paper would disappear', a hope that will be shared by many observers, not least those who deal with the relationships *between* the sexes.

As Jim Dillard and Katherine Miller indicate in their provocative chapter on 'Intimate Relationships in Task Environments', the study of organizational romance is increasingly important as a fact of today's business world. Whereas previous work and analysis of the issue has been based on speculation or even prejudice, the Dillard and Miller review carefully documents the research on the topic, originating as it does from several different research contexts. They focus on those relationships at work that 'transcend the task roles specified by the organisation . . . those relationships which might, in some sense, be termed "romantic"'.

It is clear from the Dillard and Miller chapter that this new area of research needs integration with other work on relationships for, as the authors note, 'romantic relationships at work are no less complex and meaningful than those in other settings'. It is, perhaps, the fact that they occur in public but are often disguised that makes them so intriguing, and also renders them the object of organizational interference both on the level of the abstract 'corporate management' and at the more mundane level of interaction with other colleagues in the organization.

The final chapter, by George McCall, deals with 'The Organizational Life Cycle of Relationships'. The main theme of McCall's inspiring and cogent representation of a sociology of the dyad is the belief that a dyadic relationship is a species of social organization, which, like other social organizations, has a life over and above the two partners in it. From this it follows that the dyad will and does organize itself in ways comparable to those of other organizations, with role differentiation, objectified forms, a sense of collectivity, and creation of a shared culture.

In this framework, McCall offers an interpretation of the conduct of relationship partners that take us far beyond the usual intrapsychic explanations offered by social psychologists and reviews different models of the development and decline of relationships in terms of the 'organizational life cycle'. He concludes that an organismic analogy for dyads would help us to reorient our approach to relationship development, while a move away 'from "internal locus of control" to a greater recognition of vital environmental influences—especially the variety of interorganizational relationships' can only be good for the field. As such, his chapter provides a neat bridge between this section and the next on community and clinical issues.

Taken as a whole Section Four emphasizes the role of time and process in relationships along with the negotiative interplay of individual cognitions and behaviours in the broader context of the social environment. As such, it reifies the dramatic new direction for the field and points our empirically itchy feet along the most productive road for our continuing long journey of research development.

Handbook of Personal Relationships
Edited by S. W. Duck
© 1988 John Wiley & Sons Ltd

20

Intimacy as an Interpersonal Process

HARRY T. REIS
University of Rochester, New York, USA
and
PHILLIP SHAVER*
University of Denver, Colorado, USA

ABSTRACT

In this chapter, we propose a model of the intimacy process. The process begins when one person expresses personally revealing feelings or information to another. It continues when the listener responds supportively and empathically. For an interaction to become intimate, the discloser must feel understood, validated, and cared for.

'Intimacy' and 'intimate'—from the Latin words *intimus* (innermost) and *intimare* (to make the innermost known) (Partridge, 1966)—are elusive terms for social scientists. They can be used to refer to feelings, to verbal and nonverbal communication processes, to behaviors, to people's arrangements in space, to personality traits, to sexual activities, and to kinds of long-term relationships. What, if anything, do these phenomena have in common? Do all of them relate in some way to making one's innermost qualities known?

In a recent overview of intimacy research entitled 'Intimacy as the proverbial elephant', Acitelli and Duck (1987) observe that 'It is a necessary and valuable part of the research enterprise that some researchers must feel some parts of the creature whilst others probe other areas. We will . . . remain blind only if we fail to relate the different reports to one another or if we see them as exclusive or competitive rather than compatible or complementary' (pp. 306–307). Employing the same metaphor in an analysis of research on communication in intimate relationships, Montgomery (1984b) observed that 'at this point in our progress toward understanding intimates' communication, we are

* Now at the State University of New York at Buffalo.

probably fortunate to have a variety of perspectives which contribute unique information. However, seeing the proverbial elephant in different ways does not negate any one way. Moreover, a comprehensive understanding comes with the ultimate integration of viewpoints, however diverse' (p. 322). Our goal in the present chapter is to begin to assemble the intimacy elephant, so to speak, by juxtaposing and interweaving elements from a variety of theoretical and empirical perspectives. It is too early, no doubt, to create a complete and lifelike creature from the parts that have been identified so far. But it may not be too early to attempt a useful and reliable sketch, a kind of elephant map that can be used to guide future exploration. At the center of this map, we maintain, is a core social psychological process with distinct communicative and emotional features.

The chapter includes four major sections. First, we provide a highly selective overview of theories, concepts, and approaches that we believe are essential for construction of a model of intimacy, given that intimacy is to be conceptualized as an interpersonal, transactional *process*. As Duck and Sants (1983) have noted, the major problem with previous research and theorizing about personal relationships is that phenomena such as attraction and intimacy are treated as 'timeless states and rootless events' rather than dynamic processes affected by the participants' goals and relationship history. As we intend to show, the different everyday and social scientific meanings of the term 'intimacy' make sense when viewed in relation to a process of emotional communication. It is this process, and not a static condition, that marks interactions as intimate.

In the second section of the chapter we present a model of the intimacy process and attempt to clarify its components and stages. This section is, in effect, our sketch of the intimacy elephant, our integration of existing knowledge and speculation. Third, having examined intimacy as an interactive process, we consider how intimate interactions are situated within the context of ongoing relationships. We draw a distinction between intimate interactions and intimate relationships. Finally, we consider why intimacy matters, why it has become a focus of both professional and popular concern, and why learning more about it may prove useful.

THEORY AND RESEARCH: A SELECTIVE REVIEW

Our model will be assembled from existing theories, research findings, and personal observations. The goal is not to provide an exhaustive summary or review of existing approaches but rather to select important and relevant components that fit together to form a coherent model. We consider a broad range of approaches: clinical, communicational, developmental, personological, and social. Each offers unique insights and strengths, and all but the clinical approach are based on the study of naturally occurring relationships. Clinically based theories, we should note at the outset, are largely founded on therapeutic relationships which, though atypical because of their relative one-sidedness, special aims, and narrow range of activity (Duck, 1977), contain a fairly pure form of one important part of the intimacy process: the client's self-revelation in the presence of a sympathetic and attentive listener. This component of the process is easily obscured by other activities and motives in naturally occurring and more diversified relationships.

We assume that researchers and theorists who use the intimacy concept are talking about separate facets of a single complex process, and that because of different intellectual and clinical goals, different theoretical traditions, different methods, different target age groups, and different languages, the central process has remained somewhat concealed. The repeatedly occurring concepts and issues include: approach and avoidance motives related to intimacy, verbal and nonverbal disclosure of self-relevant information and feelings that in other kinds of interaction remain private or hidden, attentiveness and responsiveness on the part of an interaction partner (spouse, friend, therapist), validation of important aspects of one or both interaction partners' self-concepts or identities, and feelings of being understood, cared for, and approved of. In the following subsections we indicate how these components of the intimacy process, each central to the model we propose, are derivable from existing theories and research. Once the necessary elements have been gathered together, we will be ready to present our model.

Psychodynamic Building Blocks

Harry Stack Sullivan. From Sullivan (1953) we borrow two observations. (1) The need for intimacy emerges between childhood and adolescence, when one's closest peer relationships are likely to be with same-sex partners. According to Sullivan, 'Intimacy is that type of situation involving two people which permits validation of all components of personal worth' (p. 246). Intimacy is a collaboration in which both partners reveal themselves, and seek and express validation of each other's attributes and world views. Close friends (or 'chums') generally resemble each other, so collaboration in establishing shared understandings and a mutual sense of worth and security is relatively straightforward. (2) The onset of puberty induces a wish to form a comparable bond with a member of the opposite sex, motivated by 'lustful needs'. For Sullivan, however, intimacy and lust are independent factors which may combine or become opposed in complex ways. Presaging current analyses of sex differences in intimacy (e.g. Rubin, 1983), he suggests that the different socialization and cultural experiences of females and males leave the two sexes somewhat ill-prepared to establish intimate (i.e. mutually validating) relationships with each other.

Research supports Sullivan's claim that intimacy becomes salient during preadolescence, primarily within the context of same-sex friendships. At that point in development, children's descriptions of friendship begin to emphasize sharing of intimate thoughts and feelings (e.g. Berndt, 1981; Buhrmester and Furman, 1987; Furman and Bierman, 1984). Moreover, sophisticated perspective-taking, a prerequisite for adult-like empathy and validation, becomes an important component of social skill during this period (Selman, 1980). Other research, involving adults, has demonstrated the importance of validation as a goal for social interaction. For example, Goethals (1986; Goethals and Darley,

1977) suggested that self-validation is a major motive for social comparison processes, and Gottman (1979) has shown that an important difference between distressed and nondistressed married couples is that the latter exhibit mutual validation to a greater extent in their problem-focused communications.

Erik Erikson. Erikson (1950, 1968), in an effort to conceptualize psychosocial development across the lifespan, went beyond Sullivan while continuing to rely on compatible concepts. Erikson used the term intimacy primarily to describe a quality of mature adult heterosexual relationships. He defined intimacy as a counterpointing and fusing of identities, and argued that it becomes a major developmental issue early in adulthood, after the establishment of a secure identity and before the attainment of 'generativity'. Just as Sullivan noted that same-sex validation of beliefs and feelings is impossible before preadolescence, Erikson observed that genuine commitment to an adult romantic relationship (which to him meant heterosexual marriage) requires the existence of relatively stable and self-acknowledged identities. Identities are what adult lovers share, compare, and ultimately intertwine. Sexuality, an important component of adult intimacy, ideally involves a coordinated mutuality of pleasure between people who know and care deeply about each other, symbolized for Erikson by mutual and satisfying orgasm.

Erikson's portrayal of intimacy as a form of heterosexual relatedness attained only in adulthood conflicts, at first glance, with Sullivan's focus on same-sex friendship during preadolescence. The conflict is more apparent than real for two reasons. First, the earlier form of intimacy that Sullivan described is important to the construction of a stable self-concept. His notion of self is similar to what Erikson called identity, a prerequisite to adult intimacy, so Sullivan was writing about a process by which same-sex chums contribute to identity development. Second, Erikson agreed with Sullivan that same-sex friends are naturally better suited than opposite-sex friends to share understandings and provide validation, owing to their common experiences. However, because a combination of sexuality with trust and commitment ultimately leads to the most satisfying form of relationship according to both Sullivan and Erikson, and because parenthood is an essential part of later stages of development, Erikson maintained that true intimacy is best exemplified by committed heterosexual relationships.

Research based on interviews and questionnaires generally supports Erikson's claim that identity precedes intimacy, although this pattern is typically more common for men than women (Orlofsky, 1987). By and large, existing studies contrast intimacy (i.e. establishment of a committed, integrated heterosexual relationship) with various forms of its absence: for example, preintimacy (involved but not yet committed), stereotyped (uncommitted and superficially involved), pseudointimacy (committed to a superficial relationship), and isolation (Tesch and Whitbourne, 1982). Unfortunately, few studies in this relatively new research area have focused on the emotional and communicative processes involved in comparing identities, establishing sexual mutuality, becoming committed, and so forth; instead, intimacy is treated as a state to be attained. We know relatively little about the dynamics of the intimacy process pointed to by Erikson.

Carl Rogers. From Rogers (1961) we derive an emphasis on the role of unconditional positive regard in fostering open communication, intimacy, lowered defensiveness, and enhanced self-esteem. The intimate partners that Rogers originally had in mind were patients and psychotherapists, and parents and children, but he later extended his thinking to the realms of marriage (Rogers, 1972) and encounter groups (Rogers, 1970), arguing that similar processes are evident in all close relationships. According to Rogers, unconditional positive regard (empathic, nonjudgemental, supportive listening) encourages a person to become more self-accepting and better integrated, which in turn facilitates interpersonal openness and trust. Rogers' ideas fit well with Sullivan's, in that both see validation as a major component of intimacy.

Research from both therapy and nontherapy situations supports Rogers' assertions. For example, he contended that 'organismic experiencing' (authentic emotional expression and acceptance of feelings) encouraged by a therapist's sympathetic listening is at the heart of constructive personal change, and this has been documented in numerous studies (see summaries in Greenberg and Safran, 1987, and Orlinsky and Howard, 1975). One consequence of increased security and self-acceptance is reduction in the feelings of vulnerability and fear of exploitation that can preclude or interfere with intimacy (Hatfield, 1984; Kelvin, 1977). Turning to laboratory findings: being liked is one of the strongest elicitors of liking (Berscheid, 1985b); it encourages self-disclosure, whereas even mild social rejection inhibits disclosure (Taylor, Altman and Sorrentino, 1969); and listener responsiveness leads to increased liking for the listener and a sense that the speaker and listener have become better acquainted (Davis and Perkowitz, 1979).

Attachment and object relations theories. Many psychodynamic theorists begin their analysis of intimacy with the mother–infant relationship. Bowlby's (1969, 1973, 1980) attachment theory, for example, focuses on the infant's need for security, which is satisfied by proximity to a reliable and responsive caregiver. He claims that the infant's sense of security is a prerequisite for normal curiosity and sociability with peers. Ainsworth's empirical extensions of Bowlby's ideas (Ainsworth *et al.*, 1978; see Bretherton, 1985, for a recent review) reveal connections between specific styles of parenting and specific patterns of security and insecurity in young children. Recently, attachment researchers have extended these ideas to adult relationships (e.g. Hazan and Shaver, 1987; Levitz-Jones and Orlofsky, 1985; Main, Kaplan and Cassidy, 1985; Ricks, 1985).

Bowlby contends that cross-age continuity in attachment style is largely due to cognitive structures (comprising expectations, beliefs, and defenses) which he called 'inner working models' of self and relationship partners. This is similar to object relations theorists' notion that social cognition involves representations of self and others, referred to somewhat awkwardly as 'objects', 'part objects', etc., following the terminology of Freud's instinct theory (Greenberg and Mitchell, 1983; Winnicott, 1965). Unfortunately, the working models construct is currently defined so vaguely that different researchers employ rather different measures of it (e.g. Hazan and Shaver, 1987; Main, Kaplan and Cassidy, 1985; see critical analysis by Dunn, this volume). The Hazan and Shaver interpret working models as beliefs about self and relationship partners that can be measured by self-report questionnaires; in contrast, Main *et al.* assess defensiveness and information-processing distortions evident in transcripts of clinical interviews. In addition, there is still no longitudinal study that provides direct evidence for continuity of attachment style between early childhood and adolescence or adulthood. The longest longitudinal studies span only the period from infancy to middle childhood (e.g. Main, Kaplan and Cassidy, 1985; Sroufe, 1987). Attachment–theoretic studies of adults use retrospective questioning about parent–child relationship history, and this method is obviously problematic.

Despite such drawbacks, existing studies do suggest that concepts from Bowlby's theory, designed originally to characterize infant–caregiver relationships, apply meaningfully to adult intimate relationships and to the emotions inherent in them—for example falling in love and grieving for a lost partner (Parkes and Weiss, 1983; Shaver, Hazan and Bradshaw, 1988). For present purposes it is of interest that the process Bowlby delineated, involving a young child's security (or insecurity) produced in relationships with caregivers who are (or are not) emotionally available, sensitive, and responsive, is compatible in spirit with the theories and observations of Sullivan and Rogers, who used concepts such as validation, sensitive listening, and positive regard. This similarity suggests that central components of intimacy appear, perhaps in somewhat different forms, across the lifespan.

Building Blocks from Communication and Exchange Research

Self-disclosure. Sidney Jourard's writings were seminal in calling attention to the topic of self-disclosure and in introducing an objective, easily administered, and face-valid measure of disclosure (Jourard, 1964, 1971; Jourard and Lasakow, 1958). His main contention, supported by much subsequent research, was that disclosure of inner feelings and experiences to another person fosters liking, caring, and trust, thereby facilitating the deepening of close relationships (see Chelune, Robinson and Kommor, 1984; Cozby, 1973; and Levinger and Snoek, 1972, for reviews). Although most self-disclosure theories acknowledge that the act of revealing information about oneself is only one aspect of intimate communication, the lion's share of empirical studies concern the exchange of self-relevant facts, in part, no doubt, because of the simplicity and demonstrated theoretical and predictive utility of existing questionnaires, all of which focus on the depth, interpersonal riskiness, or normative privacy of facts revealed about oneself (e.g. Chelune, 1976; Jourard, 1964; Taylor and Altman, 1966).

As Montgomery (1981b) notes, the 'tacit assumption in the literature . . . that "intimacy" as applied to topics corresponds to "intimacy" as applied to relationships' (p. 29) is too simple. A growing number of studies demonstrate that self-disclosure is a complex multidimensional process characterized by numerous features over and above the simple act of revealing personal facts. For example, Morton (1978) showed that evaluative self-disclosure (revealing personal feelings about various life topics) was more closely associated than descriptive self-disclosure (revealing self-relevant facts) with relationship closeness. More recently, Montgomery (1981b, 1984b) proposed a comprehensive model of open communication which includes such style components as verbal immediacy (e.g. 'I' statements, speaking in the active voice, referring to the here-and-now, and omitting probability qualifiers), relationship relevance, emotional openness, and receptive openness (willingness to receive others' open communication), in addition to the more traditional category of topic intimacy. Montgomery's (1984a) research indicates that whereas observers base their judgements of openness almost equally on content and style, communicators themselves rely primarily on style. In our process model, therefore, we will consider both topical and stylistic components of intimacy.

Nonverbal communication. A noteworthy feature of Montgomery's work is that it portends an integration of verbal and nonverbal approaches to the assessment of intimacy. Until now, the literatures on self-disclosure and nonverbal communication have remained largely distinct despite the fact that both include the term 'intimacy' and contain frequent allusions to each other. Nonverbal communication researchers describe as intimate a variety of behaviors that indicate heightened involvement in interactions (e.g. eye contact, proximity, touch; Argyle and Dean, 1965). These factors are dynamically interrelated; if other parameters remain unchanged, increased eye contact tends to heighten the perceived intimacy of an interaction, for example. If the current degree of involvement is uncomfortable, either interactant may reduce intimacy in several ways—for example by averting gaze, increasing physical distance, shifting body orientation, or steering clear of intimate topics.

Nevertheless, nonverbal behaviors, like verbal statements, must be interpreted in context; the same nonverbal behavior is capable of serving very different functions (Patterson, 1982a, 1984). Rather than possessing inherent meaning, nonverbal cues contribute to intimate interaction in two ways: (1) they communicate specific emotional messages when considered in the light of other available information; and (2) they sometimes intensify the emotions experienced during an interaction (e.g. Argyle and Dean, 1965; Ellsworth, 1975; Patterson, 1982a). Given our earlier suggestion that primitive aspects of intimacy are evident in infant–caregiver interactions (before the infant is verbally proficient), the prominence of touching, gazing, etc., in adult romantic interactions, and the importance of nonverbal factors in communicating openness (Montgomery, 1981b), nonverbal components of intimacy are especially central in a process model meant to apply, at least in certain respects, across the lifespan.

Exchange and interdependence theories. Recent social psychological research on interaction processes is heavily influenced by equity theory (Walster, Berscheid and Walster, 1973). According to this theory, intimate relationships, like most other kinds of relationships, are satisfying to the extent that participants' contributions (inputs) and outcomes (rewards minus costs) are perceived to be balanced (Hatfield, 1982). Contributions and outcomes must be construed broadly, however, so that qualities specific to intimacy are included—loving and jealous feelings, support and rejection, sex, and security, for example. Further, because intimate relationships involve long-term interdependence in diverse kinds of activities, perceptions of equity and inequity must be considered not just relative to a single interaction but also across resource classes and periods of time (Perlman and Fehr, 1987; Reis, 1986).

An alternative point of view has been elaborated by Mills and Clark (1982), who assert that exchange rules apply only to relatively casual or economically oriented interactions. In communal interactions, which are more likely to include intimacy, benefits are instead given and received in response to interaction partners' needs. In research on the communal/exchange distinction (Clark, 1986), the causal arrows are bidirectional. That is, not only do communal relationships involve attending to partners' needs (rather than to equity considerations), the act of meeting another person's needs may foster development of a communal relationship. More important for our purposes, when these needs pertain to self-definitions and self-relevant emotions, responding to needs rather than adhering to equity rules is likely to engender feelings of being understood and cared for (Clark, 1985). Consequently, one way in which interaction partners can increase or decrease the intimacy of a given interaction is to regulate their responsiveness to each other's expressed or inferred needs. Given that individuals frequently seek to increase the intimacy level of their relationships (Miell and Duck, 1986), interpersonal exchange processes often follow a needs rule rather than an equity rule.

Lay and Psychometric Conceptions of Intimacy

One final source of ideas and information regarding the components and dimensions of intimacy is the literature on everyday conceptions of intimacy, and the translation of these and more formal conceptions into measures with research and clinical utility.

Waring and his collaborators (Waring et al., 1980) asked a sample of adults what intimacy meant to them and derived eight categories from their answers. In a second study (Waring et al., 1980), married couples spontaneously mentioned these categories in the following order of importance: affection, expressiveness (including self-disclosure), sexuality, cohesion (commitment), compatibility, autonomy (from parents), conflict (not arguing or criticizing), and identity (knowing oneself, knowing one's needs, and enjoying adequate self-esteem). Helgeson, Shaver and Dyer (1987) extracted prototypes from college students' open-ended accounts of personal instances of intimacy and distance in same-sex and opposite-sex relationships. At the heart of both sexes' prototypes of intimacy were feelings and expressions of closeness, appreciation, and affection; evident but less prominent were informational self-disclosures. In contrast, prototypes of distance centered on felt and expressed dissatisfaction and disapproval. These studies call attention to the importance of emotions, particularly affection, in everyday conceptions of intimacy.

Questionnaire measures reflect more formal conceptions of intimacy. For example, the Personal Assessment of Intimacy in Relationships questionnaire

(PAIR) developed by Schaefer and Olson (1981) assesses five aspects of intimacy: emotional, social, sexual, intellectual, and recreational. Tesch's (1985) questionnaire, examined by factor analysis, seems to tap three domains: romantic love, supportiveness, and communication ease. Guerney's (1977) questionnaire assesses a combination of intimacy and interpersonal trust. The scale designed by Miller and Lefcourt (1982) measures the maximum level of intimacy currently experienced in a respondent's closest relationship. Eriksonian intimacy status can be assessed with a questionnaire designed by Ochse and Plug (1986). McAdams (1982a; this volume) developed a TAT measure of intimacy motivation, which he defines as a 'preference or readiness for experiences of closeness, warmth, and communication' (p. 134). (See Chelune and Waring, 1984, for a review of intimacy measures.)

Taken together, the available measures reveal some of the issues to be considered when constructing a process model of intimacy. When combined with the foregoing theoretical summaries, it is apparent that intimacy is an interpersonal process that involves communication of personal feelings and information to another person who responds warmly and sympathetically. This response validates the first person's experiences, and thereby deepens the relationship and encourages returned affection and support.

A MODEL OF THE INTIMACY PROCESS

All of the theories and research reviewed in the previous section are, we would argue, compatible with the model of intimacy shown in Figure 1. The model is intended to be transactional: intimacy occurs between two people, A and B, who influence each other's feelings and behavior over time. For convenience,

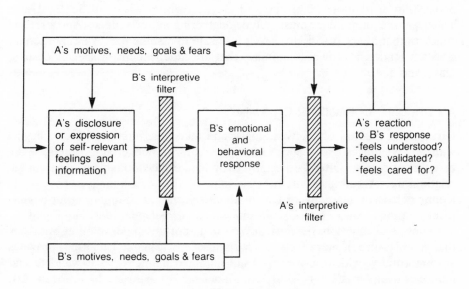

Figure 1

we present a single episode in which A serves as discloser or expresser and B serves as responder, but in many situations the two participants freely exchange roles. The process can commence at any of several points, but we begin our analysis with participants' motives, fears, and goals. Included in the model are both participants' actions (e.g. comments, expressions), emotions, and interpretations.

A's Motives, Fears, and Goals

As Mehrabian and Ksionzky (1974) have shown, approach and avoidance motives independently determine affiliative behavior, and the same is likely to be true for intimate behavior. Intimacy may be sought because a person desires affection, self-understanding, or self-validation; wishes to share feelings; feels lonely; wants guidance; feels sexually attracted—the list of incentives is virtually endless. In conflict with approach tendencies are a host of fears that make people reluctant to become intimate, including, for example, fear of exposure, fear of abandonment, fear of angry attacks, fear of loss of control, fear of one's own destructive impulses, and fear of engulfment (Hatfield, 1984). The roots of many of these desires and fears can be traced to earlier relationship experiences, some reaching as far back as early childhood. A partner's response can substantially alter the relative impact of these approach and avoidance tendencies, which, regardless of personal history, everyone experiences in some mixture at the beginning of potentially intimate encounters.

Besides having needs that relate specifically to intimacy, a person in A's position can presumably regulate self-disclosure and expression of feelings strategically—to test a partner's responsiveness, for example; to define a relationship in a certain way (e.g. as communal or exchange-oriented); or to restrict or intensify a relationship (Miell and Duck, 1986; Snyder and Smith, 1986). Thus, a model of intimacy must include fluctuating motives, needs, and strategic concerns that affect A's disclosure. It is unsafe to assume that A has perpetual, constant tendencies towards intimacy that are independent of specific desires, fears, and goals.

A's Disclosure or Emotional Expression

Given some mixture of motives, goals, and fears, the intimacy process begins with A revealing some aspect of self, verbally or nonverbally, intentionally or unintentionally. Often, especially early in the development of an intimate relationship, A reveals something in spite of (or, occasionally, because of) feeling defensive, guarded, or fearful about rejection, manipulation, or engulfment. In our conceptualization, disclosure of personal desires, fantasies, anxieties, and emotions is generally more important to developing intimacy than is disclosure of mere facts. Such disclosure is valuable because it provides an opportunity, which may or may not be acted upon, for B to validate and indicate caring for A's 'inner self'. This inner self, as discussed by Emde (1983), is an affective core that persists, with increasing complexity and depth, across the lifespan, despite substantial changes in external roles, relationships, appearance, and settings:

> Because our affective core touches upon those aspects of experience which are most important to us as individuals, it also allows us to get in touch with the uniqueness of our own (and others') experience. . . . Once we are in touch with another's emotional life, we are in touch with his or her humanity; this kind of understanding then becomes a basis for going further and appreciating that individual as a unique human being. (p. 180)

A related point is made by Markus and Nurius (1986). They suggest that a person's self-knowledge encompasses not only who one is, but also who one might become, who one would like to become, and who one is afraid of becoming. These 'possible selves' link self-knowledge and motivation; they are 'the cognitive components of hopes, fears, goals, and threats' (p. 954). Revealing these possible selves and other affectively laden, self-relevant information provides the material to which B responds.

An example may clarify the distinction between facts and feelings. Consider this factual disclosure: 'My sixth-grade teacher made fun of me in front of the entire class one day.' From this statement, the listener knows relatively little about the speaker. Emotional elaborations give the event personal meaning, and hence intimacy potential. Contrast 'I was humiliated and am still afraid to speak in front of audiences' with 'That made me the hero of the class from then on'. The two pictures of the inner emotional self differ considerably.

Recent studies in two specialized research areas also highlight the importance of emotional self-disclosure. First, Fitzpatrick (1986) has argued that in marriage, once partners come to know each other, communication of feelings rather than facts is the key determinant of relationship satisfaction. Second, studies of therapeutic interactions demonstrate that emotional processes—such as elaborating emotional expression, accessing previously unacknowledged feelings, and restructuring emotions—are better predictors of therapy outcome than are simple informational disclosures (Greenberg and Safran, 1987).

Communication of feelings obviously need not be verbal. Extensive research indicates that there are identifiable facial, gestural, and paralinguistic cues associated with human emotions (Ekman, Friesen and Ellsworth, 1972; Hornstein, 1985; Izard, 1977; Scherer and Ekman, 1982). Even when people intentionally suppress affect, autonomic markers of emotional states are clearly identifiable (Buck, 1984; Cacioppo, 1986). Facial expressions of emotion can be recognized beyond chance in the absence of other information (Wagner, MacDonald and Manstead, 1986); when contextual cues and prior knowledge about the person expressing the emotion are added, nonverbally transmitted information greatly enhances communication of emotions.

Because people are familiar with the typical components and patterns of the basic emotions (Schwartz and Shaver, 1987; Shaver et al., 1987), they do not require complete information to understand an interaction partner's emotion-related motives, appraisals, action tendencies, and self-regulatory efforts. For example, anger occurs when a person perceives that someone or something is unfairly interfering with attainment of a valued goal. An interaction partner's implicit understanding of anger allows him or her to infer unobserved portions of an anger scenario, such as the underlying desires or values being blocked, or the appraisal linking motives and reactions. Therefore, emotional expression, even without much verbal elaboration, permits interaction partners to respond supportively. In fact, people often feel revealed to others even when little or no intentional communication has taken place—for example when interacting with an insightful therapist, an old friend who knows how one feels, or a stranger with whom one happens to 'click'.

The key aspect of disclosure, then, is the expression of feelings and experiences that characterize the discloser's inner self. Because language and nonverbal cues can be revealing in the absence of intentional disclosure, we rely on the term 'expression' to signify transmission of self-relevant information through any channel.

B's Motives and Interpretive Filter

B, occupying the role of responder, is influenced by a mixture of momentarily active concerns, positive and negative, just as A is. B may want to be a good friend or partner, may have an unusually high need for nurturance, may be strategically interested in creating a feeling of obligation on A's part, and so on. Once again, the list is virtually endless. At the same time, B may fear commitment, dread A's dependency, worry about hurting A, etc. As B interprets A's disclosures and expressions, and prepares to respond, a complex array of motives and goals is at work.

Also influential are B's dispositionally and situationally induced interpretive tendencies, which in Figure 1 are summarized by the term 'interpretive filter'. A large body of social psychological research (reviewed by Markus and Zajonc, 1985) indicates that expectations and schemas profoundly influence interpretations of interaction partners' behavior. For example, A's touch might be construed as spontaneous or manipulative, affectionate or sexist, depending on B's proclivities. Crying may be considered endearing or maudlin, anger seen as justified or immature, and an intimate disclosure received as welcome or presumptuous. There are several legitimate perspectives on such an interchange: A may intend one thing, B perceive another, and outside observers see something different. What matters for B's response is B's construal of A's expression.

Bowlby's ideas about inner working models, as well as the writings of various social–cognitive theorists (Fiske and Taylor, 1984; Kelly, 1955; Mischel, 1973), are relevant to B's interpretive filter. Based on past experiences, people develop general expectations about the manner in which their intimacy-seeking behavior will be received. For example, repeated rejection may lead to an expectation of rejection and humiliation, and thereby to a justifiable fear of self-exposure (Kelvin, 1977). The tendency of mental representations of social experiences to perpetuate themselves by reinforcing certain views of relationships established early in life has been discussed by Sroufe and Fleeson (1985). Some of these representations probably influence adult friendships, romances, and parenting experiences.

Hazan and Shaver (1987) found, for example, that avoidant lovers—those with a history of rejection by primary attachment figures—were especially likely to fear intimacy, believe that romantic love rarely lasts, and doubt that other people are well intentioned and good hearted. Anxious, clingy lovers—those with a history of inconsistent, unpredictable relationships—reported that they fell in love quickly and frequently, experienced intense jealousy, and believed that others were reluctant to commit themselves to a long-term relationship. In contrast, secure lovers expressed positive views about both self and others, and said that lasting, satisfying love was attainable. Most likely, these kinds of beliefs, perhaps founded in early childhood and then confirmed repeatedly via self-fulfilling prophecies (Darley and Fazio, 1980), affect responses to conversational leads, disclosure efforts, and expressions of emotions in potentially intimate interactions.

B's Response to A's Self-Expression

In our model, B's response to A's expression is as important as A's initial disclosure in determining whether an interaction will become intimate. Appropriate responses enhance feelings of connectedness, whereas inappropriate responses or deliberate nonresponsiveness keep interactants at a distance (Kurth, 1970). The role of the listener's response in self-disclosure has been documented in a number of studies. For example, Miller, Berg and Archer (1983) found that the amount of self-disclosure was a function of both the speaker's and the listener's predispositions. Their questionnaire, the Openers Scale, assesses self-reported ability to elicit intimate disclosures from others. More generally, Davis (1982) has noted that responsiveness, which she defines as verbal and nonverbal elaboration by a listener that is matched and relevant to the speaker's comments, plays an important role in facilitating communication and interpersonal attraction. Nonresponsive listeners are perceived as uninterested or uncomprehending (Davis and Perkowitz, 1979), two characteristics antithetical to intimacy (Miller and Berg, 1984).

Of the theorists discussed earlier, Rogers placed the most emphasis on the listener's role in intimate interactions. He thought it critical that a listener communicate unconditional acceptance and warm regard if the goal was to help the speaker feel understood, valued, and intimately connected. Responsiveness of this sort is important even to infants. Stern (1986) has shown that infants develop strong feelings of security and attachment when caregivers communicate that they are aware of, and responsive to, the infant's needs and feelings— by soothing the infant when it appears to feel irritable, for example, or playing boisterously when the infant seems to prefer activity. Such responsiveness engenders a deeply reassuring sense of interpersonal trust and fosters an intimate tie with the caregiver. Nonresponsiveness, in contrast, produces in the infant a sense of alienation and withdrawal from others. In the manner of

Bowlby's inner working models, this orientation may interfere with close relationships later in life.

We do not wish to imply that the bulk of the variance in disclosure and responsiveness resides in individual dispositions. Everyone has interactions in which he or she discloses a lot or a little and responds warmly or coolly, depending on context, partner, mood, and interaction goals. Miller and Kenny (1986), in a study of disclosure among members of a sorority, demonstrated that reciprocity of self-disclosure is overwhelmingly a function of the unique relationship between two people, above and beyond trait-like dispositions to disclose and be disclosed to. This points to the importance of a transactional perspective on the intimacy process.

Finally, we should mention briefly the positive, rewarding emotions that often accompany the listener's role. Both therapists and parents of infants often describe intense feelings of intimacy in interactions with their clients and offspring, respectively, even though the interactions are clearly nonreciprocal: therapists rarely disclose as much as their clients do, and infants are incapable of understanding or deliberately validating their parents' identities. Yet therapists and parents experience warm feelings in these special relationships which they readily label as 'intimate', 'touching', and 'special' in ways corresponding closely to lay conceptions of intimacy. In other words, both A and B may feel intimate even when only A discloses.

A's Interpretive Filter and Reactions to B's Response

Although B's response has features that can be objectively described, what matters most is A's interpretation of and reaction to B's behavior. After all, if A perceives B to be unsupportive or overly intrusive, perhaps because of A's insecurity or because B's good intentions have been poorly realized, an intimate interaction is unlikely to occur. This is why Figure 1 includes an interpretive filter for A. Our earlier discussion of B's interpretive filter also applies to A.

According to the model, for an interaction to be experienced as intimate by A, he or she must register three qualities in B's response: understanding, validation, and caring. Understanding refers to A's belief that B accurately perceives A's needs, constructs, feelings, self-definition, and life predicaments. This is an important part of the intimacy process for at least three reasons. First, the concept of intimacy implies that formerly private aspects of the self have been communicated (Chelune, Robison and Kommor, 1984). One cannot respond contingently to another person's inner qualities if these qualities remain unknown. Second, the provision of relevant and helpful support and advice, a key component of intimate relationships, requires shared knowledge; without it, the offered support may prove inappropriate to A's needs. Third, and most important, to feel validated, A must believe that B values and appreciates A's inner self as A himself or herself understands it. Otherwise, B's response, no matter how well intentioned and seemingly sympathetic, cannot be received as validating inasmuch as it is irrelevant, perhaps even antithetical, to A's self-understanding.

For several reasons, we (and Derlega, 1984) focus on understanding primarily as a precursor of validation. Recall Sullivan's (1953) observation that mature self-esteem and sociability develop in large part through the 'validation of all components of personal worth' (p. 246) which an intimate chum provides. Once A has experienced such intimacy and its attendant gratifications, it becomes a salient goal for subsequent relationships. Social comparison processes, which are motivated partly by the desire for validation (Goethals, 1986; Goethals and Darley, 1977), influence selective affiliation. In other words, people generally choose to interact with others who are likely to confirm their views of themselves and the world (Schlenker, 1984; Wheeler, 1974). As mentioned earlier, the importance of validation has also been documented in studies of marital communication and satisfaction (Gottman, 1979).

Early self-disclosure theorists (Altman and Taylor, 1973; Jourard, 1964) portrayed the act of self-revelation not as an automatic stimulus to interpersonal closeness but as a catalyst that allows interaction partners to express similarity, support, and liking for each other. In fact, empirical studies indicate that self-disclosure does not consistently lead to enhanced liking and trust (Berscheid, 1985b). Rather, 'the reward or nonreward from disclosing [derives] from the reaction of a recipient to a disclosure' (Altman and Taylor, 1973, p. 52). Positive, validating reactions to self-disclosure are the discloser's main reward.

The third important component of A's reaction to B's response is feeling cared for. Many cognitively oriented models of the acquaintance process (e.g. Byrne, 1971; Chelune, Robison and Kommor, 1984) focus on the partners' shared understandings and expectations, slighting the role of affect. (For example, Chelune et al. define intimacy as 'a subjective appraisal, based on interactive behaviors, that leads to certain relational expectations' [Chelune, Robison and Kommor, 1984, p. 13].) There are several reasons why an intimate relationship is necessarily affectionate. Human infants have probably been primed by evolution to feel positive emotions when safely in contact with others and negative emotions (especially anxiety and anger) when these ties are disrupted (Bowlby, 1969; Sroufe and Waters, 1977). Good feelings reinforce the infant's proximity-seeking and the caregiver's nurturance, both of which promote the infant's survival (Bowlby, 1969). It may also be the case that the most secure adult relationships are those that engender comparable feelings of acceptance and being cared for, either because the underlying mechanism is the same (Konner, 1982) or because adult interactions echo past emotional experiences.

The significance of feeling well liked has been demonstrated in many studies of interpersonal attraction and relationship development (Berscheid, 1985b; Burgess and Huston, 1979). Prevailing theories of affiliation and social exchange are based on the principle that satisfying interactions are likely to be continued, a general tendency that undoubtedly applies specifically to intimate interactions. The role of caring in intimacy goes beyond its immediate emotional impact, however. Individuals who are unsure about a partner's esteem are unlikely to disclose personal feelings that might lead to rejection, ridicule, or embarrassment (Altman and Taylor, 1973). Reticence in such situations likely precludes validation of some of the most personal aspects of self—fears, vulnerabilities, socially undesirable traits, and regrettable past actions (Archer, 1980; Kelvin, 1977). Consequently, as Rogers (1961) pointed out, the remaining parts of the intimacy process are unlikely to arise in the absence of caring.

Self-disclosure that oversteps normative limits may also be related to caring. Interaction partners and neutral observers generally attribute negative characteristics, such as immaturity, insecurity, and excessive needs for friendship, to individuals who reveal more than is situationally and relationally appropriate (Wortman et al., 1976). In our model, such disclosure is interpreted as an exaggerated (and usually ineffective) search for intimacy that disregards typical hesitations about displaying vulnerability (Kelvin, 1977), and ignores strategic consideration of B's potential response. A study by Prager (1986) provides support for this explanation. Whereas subjects in her study who had attained an intimate relationship (in the Eriksonian sense) disclosed more personal information to their closest friend than to a stranger, subjects who had not attained an intimate relationship did not distinguish between close friends and strangers, disclosing equally and extensively to both.

If intimacy depends on A's reaction to B's response, it might be asked how closely A's reaction corresponds to B's intention. To some extent, this process involves perceptual bias. Reis, Senchak and Solomon (1985) found that persons who typically engage in more intimate interaction also perceive greater intimacy in videotapes of other people's conversations. Studies of marital interaction have shown greater discrepancies between the intent and impact of a communication in unhappy marriages than in happy marriages, presumably because underlying negative affect provides an interpretive context in which a given message is evaluated more negatively (e.g. Gottman, 1979; Noller, 1987). Similar processes have been demonstrated in non-distressed couples' emotional communication. Gaelick, Bodenhausen and Wyer (1985) found that in the case of love, emotional reactions were based largely on the listener's perceptions, independent of the amount of love the speaker intended to convey. On the other hand, both perceptions and intentions affected reactions to expressed hostility. Clearly, A's reaction to B's response depends on more than the objective or consciously intended features of B's behavior.

Finally, it is important to note that the substance of intimate interaction need not be limited to revealing conversations or nonverbal communication. Interaction partners also establish, intensify, and maintain intimacy in the manner in which they respond to each other's needs (Mills and Clark, 1982). As Kelley (1979, 1984) notes, emotions and attributions within a relationship derive from the habitual patterns by which partners respond to each other's needs and desires, and integrate them with their own needs and desires. When these patterns, however they may be displayed, are perceived to be understanding, validating, and caring, intimacy is heightened. For example, a husband's staying home on his poker night to prepare a candlelight dinner for his wife's birthday might be perceived as a responsive and intimate act. Especially in the context of satisfying, long-term close relationships, people may know their partners well enough to engender in them a validating and affectionate reaction without explicit self-relevant communication.

Feedback

Given what we have already said, it is possible to indicate briefly how intimate interactions can promote both personal development and willingness to enter into subsequent intimate interactions. B's understanding and validation of A's expression may help A become somewhat less defensive and fearful, and may incline A to like and trust B. If no restrictions preclude A's exchanging roles with B, the first step towards intimacy may be followed by a second step in which B discloses and A responds sensitively and supportively. Of course, if an interaction episode fails, for any of numerous possible reasons, to move towards greater intimacy, the effect may be to increase defensiveness and decrease approach motives, thereby diminishing the likelihood that two people will develop an intimate relationship.

FROM INTERACTIONS TO RELATIONSHIPS

In our model we have focused on the intimacy process as it occurs in a single interaction. This approach is consistent with our view that intimacy is a dynamic process whose operation is best observed in the pattern of communication and reaction between two people. Nevertheless, intimate interactions typically, but by no means exclusively, take place in the context of ongoing intimate relationships. Therefore, we now consider how the process itself affects, and is affected by, relationship factors.

Although it may be tempting to see an intimate relationship as a simple aggregation of many intimate interactions between two people, the need for a more complex conception has been noted in prior writings. Hinde (1981), for example, points out that 'just as interactions involve emergent properties not relevant to the behavior of individuals in isolation, so also do relationships involve properties not relevant to their component interactions' (p. 3). Interactions and relationships require different levels of analysis, each with its own focus and each capable of supplying insights to the other (Acitelli and Duck, 1987). In our view, it makes most sense to conceptualize intimate relationships as 'digested' products (Duck and Sants, 1983) of past interactions: that is, as dyadic connections that possess special properties deriving from, but extending beyond, the content of individual intimate episodes. Six specific issues seem important to the 'digestion' process:

(1) Relationships embody a temporal perspective, including a history and an imagined future (Hinde, 1981; Kelley *et al.*, 1983). Reconstructions of past encounters (such as fond or hurtful memories) and anticipations of future events affect the interaction process by influencing goals, motives, and the readiness of partners to be mutually open and responsive. Moreover, early experiences provide a standard against which later outcomes can be evalu-

ated. Because intimate relationships generally span long time periods, and because needs and fears may be especially potent in shaping people's impressions of emotionally laden communications and interactions, feelings and judgements that encompass temporal perspectives may reveal important features of intimate relationships.

(2) In an intimate relationship, partners generally feel committed to their association with each other, over and above momentary variation in positive or negative feelings (Kelley *et al.*, 1983). Commitment arises from many sources—love, moral or legal obligation, fear of being alone, and especially, the emotions engendered in intimate interaction. Whatever its origin, commitment implies stability, security, and readiness to attempt to maintain the relationship in spite of inevitable conflict. Committed partners should also be more likely to play a responsive and supportive listening role for each other.

(3) Intimate partners usually develop metaperspectives on their relationship: that is, a sense of 'we-ness' that arises from awareness of their mutual bond (Acitelli and Duck, 1987; Levinger and Snoek, 1972; McCall, this volume). Two factors are involved here: first, mutuality, in that each partner can, at least to some extent, share the other's experiences; and second, recognition of common assumptions and understandings about the relationship.

(4) Intimate relationships are typically reciprocal and mutual, although certain special cases, such as therapy and parenting, appear more one-sided. The feedback loops in our model indicate how the experience of validation and caring in one interaction episode may predispose partners to respond similarly in a subsequent episode. Moreover, in communal relationships, both partners respond to each other's needs and expect that their own needs will be addressed (Mills and Clark, 1982).

(5) Intimate relationships often involve public recognition of the association between two people. Not all intimate relationships are public, of course, but many are—those between spouses, best friends, and close siblings, for example (Hays, 1985; Wheeler and Nezlek, 1977). As a result, and perhaps also because perceivers tend to link individuals who like each other (Heider, 1958), intimate friends may be treated as a social unit by others. Common experiences with the external world are therefore likely, enhancing shared activities and perspectives but perhaps also making individuation somewhat problematic (cf. Rook, this volume).

(6) Because intimate relationships develop from a history of largely favorable experiences, relatively positive stable expectations and patterns of interdependence tend to emerge (Chelune, Robison and Kommor, 1984; Kelley *et al.*, 1983). Such stability engenders confidence, security, dependability, and trust, all of which facilitate further intimacy by building appropriate predispositions and fostering self-expression and supportive responding. The trust-building process goes beyond predictability. In Rempel, Holmes and Zanna's (1985) analysis, faith—confidence in a partner over and above predictions rooted in prior experience—is the key defining feature of interpersonal trust. Of course, conflict is rarely absent in intimate relationships.

Disagreements, misunderstandings, and areas of incompatibility are bound to arise, and when they do, they can be extremely self-revealing. When handled sensitively and responsively, disclosures of discomfort, disappointment, and anger can be an important part of the intimacy process. Moreover, sharing personal or relational difficulties can contribute to intimacy (Braiker and Kelley, 1979).

In short, relationships that result from the psychological 'digestion' of intimate interactions clearly, and often quickly, become more than the sum of individual episodes from which they are built. Viewed from the relationship side of the interaction–relationship system, intimate relationships create a framework of trust, stable expectations, and practices within which intimate interactions are more likely, and thereby increase feelings of being understood, validated, and cared for. When partners sense that they mutually foster these feelings in each other, they become more aware that their relationship is intimate and typically become more committed to it.

DOES INTIMACY MATTER?

Some authors seek to justify the study of intimacy by pointing to its beneficial personal and relational consequences. This approach is sensible if it is not unduly defensive: that is, if it does not obscure the fact that intimacy is intrinsically rewarding. As we have indicated in our model, intimacy involves feeling understood, validated, cared for, and closely connected with another person. It inherently entails lowering defenses and reducing self-doubts and self-reproach. It includes enjoyment of caring for another, of fostering his or her increased self-insight and personal growth. (Of course, intimate relationships have a dark side too, which is explored by other authors in this Handbook [cf. Gotlib and Hooley, Gottlieb, Hobfoll and Stokes, Dillard and Miller, and Rook].) Nevertheless, because examination of intimacy's positive consequences helps locate it within a broader conception of human well-being, we will briefly discuss three research areas in which it plays a central role.

Social Goals and Loneliness

The demands and structures of everyday work and social activity dictate that most interactions not be intimate (Delia, 1980; Hays, 1985). Many surveys and studies, however, demonstrate that when asked what they most want in their social lives, people generally mention close relationships of an intimate sort (e.g. Astin, 1985; Caldwell and Peplau, 1982; Veroff, Douvan and Kulka, 1981; Weiss, 1974). Absence of intimate interaction consequently may be expected to produce a sense of personal failure in the social realm. Studies of loneliness support this contention. Loneliness, defined as a negative discrepancy between actual and desired social relations (Peplau and Perlman, 1982), has numerous detrimental consequences, including anxiety, depression and helplessness, and self-deprecation. These discrepancies can and do involve dissatisfaction along many different dimensions of social participation, one of which is intimacy. Wheeler, Reis and Nezlek (1983) found that lack of intimacy was a better predictor of loneliness than were other dimensions of interaction quality and an assortment of quantitative indices, such as frequency of interaction, time spent socializing, and number of partners. Cutrona (1982) and Williams and Solano (1983) also showed that interaction quantity predicted loneliness less well than did satisfaction and intimacy. It seems appropriate therefore to view absence of intimate interaction as a cause of loneliness.

The desire for intimacy may be on the rise in American society. In a comparison of survey data collected in 1957 and 1976, Veroff, Douvan and Kulka (1981) concluded that the appeal of intimacy, across domains as diverse as work, family, friendship, and personal growth, had increased dramatically. One might ask why self-validation, close sharing of feelings and experiences, and affection are more attractive now than they were 30 years ago. The human potential movement of the late 1960s and early 1970s may have sensitized Americans to the benefits of intimacy, and thereby enhanced its appeal. In a more dispiriting vein, Perlman and Fehr (1987) suggest that increases in urbanism, divorce, and single-parent families contribute to loneliness and inability to satisfy existing needs for intimacy. We would add to this list trends towards greater geographic mobility, lesser reliance on extended families, and growing career pressures. These factors imply that the heightened interest in intimacy noted by Veroff *et al.* may partly reflect failures in the traditional sources of intimate bonds.

Intimacy and Social Support

Social support is the focus of much current research. Many studies indicate that the perception of social support buffers the impact of stress and facilitates psychological and physical health (Cohen and Syme, 1985). The roots of social support in personality and interaction processes have remained elusive to date. Although studies demonstrating necessary levels of discriminant validity are rare, recent research implicates intimacy as a central determinant of certain forms of social support. For example, Reis (1987) found that interaction intimacy was the best predictor of appraisal support (feeling that useful advice and guidance is available) and group belonging support (feeling integrated in a community of friends). Both of these dimensions of support have been shown to have substantial health benefits. Similarly, although many authors have assumed incautiously that marriage *per se* provides social support, Gove, Hughes and Style (1983) demonstrated that only high-quality marriages—which in our model include intimacy—produce this effect.

Other social support theorists who give priority to intimacy include Brown and Harris (1978) and Hobfoll, Nadler and Lieberman (1986). Miller and Lefcourt (1982), in one of the few studies explicitly linking intimacy and health, showed that high levels of intimacy were effective in buffering the impact of stress. Pennebaker and Beale (1986) found that disclosure of deeply emotional material (e.g. rape episodes) led to improved mental and physical health in a

longitudinal follow-up. Findings such as these led one of us to conclude elsewhere that feelings of social support derive more from intimacy than from any
other feature of social interaction (Reis, 1984).

Psychological Well-Being and Personal Adjustment

In addition to having social value, intimacy also influences individual psychological health. McAdams and Vaillant (1982), for example, found better
psychosocial adjustment in a sample of middle-aged men who had shown higher
levels of intimacy motivation during their early twenties. Other studies demonstrate positive associations between intimacy and various dimensions of psychological maturity (e.g. ego development; Loevinger, 1976) and subjective well-
being (e.g. positive mood; Reis, 1987). Intimacy problems are also closely
linked to many mental health disorders (see Fisher and Stricker, 1982, for a
review).

Intimate relationships can, in certain circumstances, affect individual growth
and development adversely, by stifling independence, discouraging role flexibility, and inducing feelings of engulfment or vulnerability (see chapters in this
Handbook by Hobfoll and Stokes, and Rook). In the majority of instances,
however, the intimacy process facilitates psychological health. The process
begins in the attachment relationship between infants and their caregivers. In
favorable cases, caregivers serve as a secure base from which infants confidently
explore their environment and thereby develop a sense of competence, mastery,
and self-esteem (Ainsworth et al., 1978). During adolescence, intimacy with
a same-sex chum promotes identity development (Sullivan, 1953). Intimate
relationships attained in early adulthood foster productivity, creativity, and
emotional integration later in life (Erikson, 1950). Moreover, throughout the
lifespan, intimacy is an important, if not the most important, component of
interaction in successful therapeutic interventions (Fisher and Stricker, 1982;
Greenberg and Safran, 1987; Rogers, 1961). As a social process, then, intimacy
plays a prominent role in individual psychological growth and well-being.

CONCLUSION

In our opening paragraph, we mentioned that the terms 'intimate' and 'intimacy'
refer to a vast array of phenomena: feelings ('feeling intimate'), styles of verbal
and nonverbal communication, behaviors, arrangements in space, personality
traits, sexual activities, and kinds of long-term relationships. We asked: What,
if anything do these different phenomena have in common? Do all of them
relate in some way to making one's innermost qualities known? It should now
be possible to suggest answers.

Intimacy is an interpersonal process within which two interaction partners
experience and express feelings, communicate verbally and nonverbally, satisfy
social motives, augment or reduce social fears, talk and learn about themselves
and their unique characteristics, and become 'close' (psychologically and often
physically: touching, using intimate names and tones of voice, perhaps having

sex). Under certain conditions, repeated interactions characterized by this process develop into intimate relationships. Within an intimate relationship, some interactions will be intimate in the sense of our process model and many will not. If the frequency and quality of intimate interactions decline below some level which is probably unique to different couples and individuals, the relationship will no longer feel and be perceived as intimate by one or both partners. It will, to use Levinger's (1983) apt term, become 'hollow'. If enjoyment of intimacy was a major reason for establishing and maintaining the relationship, the partners may begin to mourn its death, feel lonely, and consider separation.

Looking back at the theories reviewed in the first section of this chapter, we see that they all map onto the process model presented in the second section. For example, Bowlby's attachment theory states, in essence, that an infant with inborn needs for proximity to a caregiver and with inborn fears of isolation, pain, strange noises, etc., is capable of feeling relaxed, secure, and attached if provided with a reliable, emotionally available, and responsive caregiver. Provided with security-inducing social experiences, the infant becomes a confident explorer of the environment and a more competent interactor with peers. Eventually, such an infant becomes a more empathic and responsive friend, lover, and parent: in other words, a good candidate for subsequent intimate interactions and relationships. Sullivan's theory centers on intimacy between same-sex friends during preadolescence. During this time, children become increasingly aware of their internal psychological states and capable of discussing and comparing them with the newly discovered states and traits of same-sex chums. This is a risky process, one fraught with opportunities for exposure and rejection. When it works, however, it enhances identity development. Erikson's statements about intimacy concern the establishment of a committed heterosexual relationship in the early adult years. We know from both research and personal experience that such relationships can be frightening and challenging, yet when they go well—i.e. when the balance of intimacy over discord and disappointment is positive—they provide some of life's greatest rewards.

Because the intimacy process has been repeatedly rediscovered in all of the social sciences that deal with close relationships, it deserves careful study. One of today's most influential clinical theorists, Heinz Kohut (1978), has developed a 'self psychology' with many features similar to the theories of Bowlby, Sullivan, Erikson, and especially Rogers (cf. Kahn, 1985). The periodic rediscovery of central insights into the process by which intimate interactions reduce defensiveness, increase self-insight and self-integration, and contribute to self-esteem and social development clearly indicates that the intimacy process modeled in Figure 1 will not go away. Rather than continuing to recloak the process in new (and sometimes obfuscating) theoretical language, it would behoove social scientists to examine and attempt to clarify the persistent core that repeats itself almost regardless of an investigator's starting point.

Just as the proverbial elephant has many parts, intimacy is a multicomponent process. But the elephant has certain coherently organized features that make it a unique creature, and so does intimacy. We have attempted to identify and describe the coherently organized components of the intimacy process and indicate how this process is embedded in intimate relationships. Intimacy has been shown to be important to people's health and well-being, and to be a worthy goal in its own right. Its repeated appearance in the literatures on friendship, marriage, childrearing, communication, psychotherapy, and personality development lead us to believe that it will remain an essential focus of theories of interpersonal relations.

ACKNOWLEDGEMENTS

We are grateful to Steve Duck, Gail Goodman, Ellen Nakhnikian, and Judith Schwartz for valuable discussions and helpful comments on earlier drafts of this chapter.

Handbook of Personal Relationships
Edited by S. W. Duck
© 1988 John Wiley & Sons Ltd

21

Friendship

ROBERT B. HAYS
George Washington University, Washington DC, USA

ABSTRACT

This chapter reviews the properties associated with the friendship bond, then discusses the development, evolution, and effects of friendship. Friendship is conceptualized as a highly flexible, dynamic, multidimensional process, the structure and functioning of which will vary depending on characteristics of the individuals involved, the environmental context, and the developmental stage of the friendship.

The term 'friend' is used very loosely and idiosyncratically, by both the general public and social scientists, to describe a diverse range of relationships. A 'friend' may be a casual companion with whom we play racquetball once a week, an intimate confidant with whom our most private thoughts and feelings are shared, someone we interact with every day, someone who lives across the country and we only exchange letters with several times a year, someone we just met a few days ago, or someone we've known all our lives. Further, the nature and structure of friend relationships varies greatly for individuals at different points in the life cycle (Bigelow and La Gaipa, 1975; Dickens and Perlman, 1981), of different sociocultural backgrounds (Allan, 1979; Brain, 1976), and, to some extent, of different sexes (Winstead, 1986), as well as at different developmental stages of the friendship (Hays, 1985; LaGaipa, 1977).

The protean quality of friendship presents a definitional problem for investigators that has impeded the development of a coherent body of knowledge on friendship. On the one hand, researchers often ask respondents to identify friends without specifying or examining the criteria employed in deciding whom to include, making generalizations across studies difficult. On the other hand, when researchers do impose their own definitions of friendship, several prob-

lems arise. First, the definition may not match the respondent's phenomenological meaning of friendship or be appropriate to the particular respondents
or contexts. Second, one investigator's definition of friendship may differ from
that of another. Third, researchers' definitions often impose requirements, such
as frequent contact, same sex, or 'closeness', that exclude particular types
of friends (e.g. long-distance, cross-sex, nonintimate) and so friendship's full
spectrum is not represented in the literature.

Friendship can be considered a social institution in that it is a symbolically
recognized system that provides a dependable source of rewards for a large
number of people (Suttles, 1970; see also McCall's chapter in this volume), yet
clearly friendship is a peculiar institution. Described as the 'least programmed
of all social relations' in Western society (Suttles, 1970), there are no formalized
duties, obligations, or legal bases for the friendship bond (Hess, 1972; Kurth,
1970). Nor are there any public ceremonies or rituals to mark the initiation or
progression of friendships, or honor and celebrate a friendship's existence. As
anthropologist Robert Brain (1976) discusses, many non-Western cultures treat
friendship very differently; some take it as seriously as marriage in terms of
formal role requirements and public legitimacy. For example, in the African
Bangwa society, community elders assign children best friends and that relationship carries with it well-understood rights and rituals, for 'having a best friend
was as important as having a wife or a brother—possibly more important'
(Brain, 1977, p. 94). In Western cultures, however, friendship remains a 'nonin-
stitutionalized institution'.

In order to achieve a valid understanding of friendship, the task of the social
scientist is therefore to develop theoretical models and research methodologies
that take into account the flexible and idiosyncratic quality of friendship. An
essential first step is establishing a comprehensive definition of friendship.

WHAT IS FRIENDSHIP?

The basis of friendship, as with all interpersonal relationships, lies in an interdependence between individuals, meaning that the behavior of each participant
is to some degree coordinated with and influenced by the behavior of the other
(Kelley, 1979). Hinde (1979) further states that for a relationship to truly be
said to exist, the individuals' interactions must occur over an extended period
of time and there must be some degree of continuity between successive interactions. In other words, a relationship between two people is a dynamic process,
with each interaction affected by the dyad's past interactions. It is the nature
of the interdependence between friends that distinguishes friendship from other
interpersonal relationships. In contrast to kin or work relationships, the interdependence between friends is *voluntary*. As Allan (1979) points out, friendship
is never a necessary consequence of role positions. This aspect of friendship
has been noted in virtually all theoretical conceptualizations of friendship
(Kurth, 1970; Reisman, 1981) and has been most clearly articulated by Wright
(1974), who proposes 'voluntary interdependence' as the key behavioral
criterion of friendship: 'Two people are friends to the degree that the plans,

activities and decisions of one of them are contingent upon those of the other in the absence of constraints toward interaction that are external to the relationship itself' (p. 93). Likewise, Hartup (1975) defines friends as 'people who spontaneously seek the company of one another; furthermore, they seek proximity in the absence of strong social pressure to do so' (p. 11).

The primary goal of the interdependence between friends is social–emotional rather than instrumental, meaning that friends derive satisfaction from their interactions themselves (e.g. in the form of companionship, stimulation, belongingness, emotional support) rather than engaging in interaction primarily to achieve an ulterior motive. In a survey of over 1000 adults, Fischer (1982b) found that sociability (i.e. interactions such as discussing pastimes and engaging in recreational activities) was the main criterion used in labeling someone a 'friend'. Likewise, the enjoyment of each other's company consistently emerges as a key property of friendship in studies that asked respondents to define friendship (Crawford, 1977; Davis and Todd, 1982; Weiss and Lowenthal, 1975). Similarly, in a study comparing the preferred activities of friends, kin, and colleagues, Argyle and Furnham (1982) found that friends' interactions were the least task-oriented and tended to revolve around leisure activities such as eating, drinking, and talking. The social–emotional basis of friendship certainly does not exclude the possibility of friendship serving instrumental purposes (e.g. friends helping each other study, get a job, repair a car, etc.); the critical factor lies in the primary motivation for the individuals' involvement. In Allan's (1979) words, 'individuals can be useful because they are friends, but not friends because they are useful' (p. 43).

Friendships vary greatly in the number and types of goals the participants seek in a particular relationship. Reisman (1981) has distinguished between 'reciprocal friendships' which are emotionally close, committed long-term friendships and more casual 'associative friendships' that are based on shared roles and propinquity. This distinction parallels Hess' (1972) description of diffuse, highly involving, intimate friendships versus more narrowly differentiated and compartmentalized friendships such as bowling friends or drinking buddies. Clear examples of diffuse, reciprocal friendships can be seen in the best-friend relationships of adolescents described by Richey and Richey (1980):

> the best friend is more or less a constant companion, a confidant with whom one can share very private information, a critic/advisor whose counsel is acceptable, a standard against which to measure oneself, an ego support whose affection and respect for one are known and reliable, an understanding ally, and a moral support in times of crisis. (p. 537)

In contrast, an excellent case of compartmentalized friendship is provided by Rosecrance's (1986) description of 'racetrack buddies' whose interaction is limited to occasional afternoons enjoying horse races together, yet nonetheless is experienced as a satisfying friendship. The types of goals attained in particular friendships will be influenced by a number of factors. Hess (1972) notes that while preadults can afford the time demands posed by diffuse friendships, middle-aged adults tend to form more compartmentalized friendships. McCall and Simmons (1966) suggest there is a 'strain toward totality' in relationships such that as a friendship develops, more and more areas of the friends' lives are brought into it.

Implicit in the social–emotional nature of friendship is what Wright (1974) refers to as the 'person *qua* person' component of friendship: friends perceive and respond to each other as unique, genuine, and irreplaceable. In other words, friends interact in such a way that they reveal to each other at least part of their 'real' versus 'role' selves (Kurth, 1970). Both Argyle and Henderson (1984) and Davis and Todd (1982) have found that an expectation of intimacy underlies the friendship bond. With increasing intimacy comes an increasing mutual understanding between friends (Davis and Todd, 1982; LaGaipa, 1977). The degree and types of personal knowledge shared between friends can vary from narrow and superficial to broad and highly intimate (Altman and Taylor, 1973) and will depend on an interplay of individual, dyadic and environmental factors. For example, women's friendships tend to involve higher degrees of intimate disclosure than men's friendships (Winstead, 1986). Close friends are more self-disclosing than casual friends (LaGaipa, 1977) and physical proximity has been found to influence the types of information friends know about each other (Rubin and Shenker, 1976).

Given the voluntary nature of friendship, some degree of positive affective bond is necessary to hold a friendship together. This aspect of friendship is included in virtually all theoretical conceptions of friendship (Kurth, 1970; Hess, 1972; Reisman, 1981; Davis and Todd, 1982; LaGaipa, 1977). Indeed, Webster's dictionary definition of a friend as 'one attached to another by affection or esteem' places its sole emphasis on this dimension. The degree and components of two friends' affection can range from the positive regard one may feel for a casual friend, akin to Rubin's (1973) description of 'liking', to a more intense emotional experience between close friends that can genuinely be called love in the sense that the friends deeply care for and depend on each other. Since friends know each other's 'real selves', a friend's positive regard also communicates a sense of acceptance (Davis and Todd, 1982; LaGaipa, 1977; Rose, 1985) that contributes to feelings of trust and spontaneity within the relationship— the security to relax and 'be completely yourself' (Crawford, 1977; Davis and Todd, 1982).

The emotional bond between friends is not necessarily all positive, however. Analyzing friendship from a psychoanalytic perspective, Rangell (1963) notes that any relationship as intense as friendship also brings with it a residue of ambivalence and negative feeling. Likewise, Wright (1974) notes that 'maintenance difficulty' is a potential by-product of interdependence in friendship. Longitudinal studies of friendship have shown ambivalence and conflict to be predictable consequences of increasing friendship intensity (Eidelson, 1980; Hays, 1985) and Duck and Miell (1986) have found that feelings of uncertainty and doubt often underlie college students' friendships.

Friendship can also entail what Kurth (1970) refers to as a sense of 'mutual obligation' between partners: friends help each other. When asked to describe what friendship means, this characteristic of a friend as a source of support, 'someone I can call on for help', consistently emerges (Crawford, 1977; Davis and Todd, 1982; LaGaipa, 1977; Tesch and Martin, 1983; Weiss and Lowenthal, 1975). For example, in a survey of Soviet adolescents' conceptions of friendship, Kon and Losenkov (1978) found 'mutual aid and loyalty' to be one of the most frequently mentioned expectations of a friend. Similarly, four of the friendship rules identified by Argyle and Henderson (1984) reflect this theme (volunteer help in time of need, show emotional support, strive to make him/her happy, stand up for the other in their absence). Importantly, a fifth rule states that friends should 'repay debts and favors', emphasizing the need for a reciprocal 'give and take' between partners in a friendship (Allan, 1979). A degree of equality between individuals on key dimensions such as age and socioeconomic background is often cited as a precondition for friendship (Brain, 1976; Button, 1979), partly because it insures the potential for equity in the social exchange (Jackson, 1977). Friendship is also an 'equalizer' in the sense that if individuals who are disparate on a significant dimension such as age, sex or status do become friends, it is assumed that they will respond to each other symmetrically, as if the status differential were irrelevant. For this reason, some organizations such as military or work settings often actively discourage friendships between individuals of different statuses so as to not threaten the organization's hierarchy.

Interestingly, even though the respondents in Weiss and Lowenthal's (1975) survey of friendship overwhelmingly regarded mutual supportiveness as the most valued characteristic of an ideal friendship, they also reported that it was not often realized in their actual friendships. The degree to which friends help and support one another varies greatly depending on characteristics of the individuals and level of friendship. For example, mutual support is more frequently mentioned in descriptions of women's friendships than men's (Crawford, 1977; Weiss and Lowenthal, 1975). Bigelow and LaGaipa (1975) have found that the view of one's friend as a receiver of help is not prominently mentioned by children until around grade six (i.e. the age of 11–12). In addition, helping and emotional support are more characteristic of close than of casual friendship (Hays, 1985; LaGaipa, 1977).

Having reviewed the characteristics most typically associated with friendship in the theoretical and empirical literature, I will now suggest the following definition of friendship: *voluntary interdependence between two persons over time, that is intended to facilitate social–emotional goals of the participants, and may involve varying types and degrees of companionship, intimacy, affection, and mutual assistance.* Embodied in this definition are several key premises. First, individuals are seen as active and goal-directed in pursuing friendships (Miell and Duck, 1986; Ginsburg, 1986). Those goals, however, will vary in kind and number for a particular friendship depending on characteristics of the individuals (e.g. age, sex, personality), the developmental stage of the friendship (e.g. casual versus close friendship), and environmental factors (e.g. existing social networks, environmental opportunities). Thus there is no universally 'right' type of friendship or ideal endpoint that friendships are assumed to lead to (Altman, Vinsel and Brown, 1981). Second, friendship is a multidimensional phenomenon (LaGaipa, 1977; Wright, 1974), expressed simultaneously on behavioral, cognitive and emotional levels, and every friendship will show a unique pattern of interactional properties. Third, friendship is a dynamic process rather than a state; thus the properties that characterize a friendship dyad are continually evolving as the dyad progresses (Duck and Sants, 1983; Hays, 1985). Finally, since the friendship bond lies in the interrelation between individuals, the appropriate unit of analysis is the dyad as a holistic system rather than the individuals themselves (Ginsburg, 1986). Since situational and developmental factors influence the structure and patterning of the dyad's interdependence, the environmental and temporal contexts must be considered integral components of that system. In sum, friendship can best be understood as a dynamic, multidimensional process that unites individuals and contexts.

FRIENDSHIP MOTIVATIONS AND OPPORTUNITIES

The initial formation of a friendship represents the convergence of individual, environmental and dyadic factors. At an individual level, personal characteristics such as friendship motivation (McAdams and Losoff, 1984), loneliness (Solano, 1986), marital status (Blau, 1961), and position in the life cycle (Hess, 1972; Shulman, 1975) have all been found to influence an individual's motivation to seek friendship. For example, people who are single, young or elderly direct more energy into cultivating friendships than do married or middle-aged adults (Shulman, 1975). In addition, personal characteristics such as social skills (Cook, 1977), friendship schemas (Young, 1986), and shyness (Zimbardo, 1977) will influence an individual's ability to successfully initiate friendships.

Environmental factors create the opportunity for friends to meet and provide situational conditions that can foster or inhibit their developing a friendship. An abundance of research demonstrates that physical proximity contributes to friendship formation (Festinger, Schachter and Back, 1950; Nahemow and Lawton, 1975; Berscheid and Walster, 1978) in that it increases the likelihood two individuals will meet as well as the frequency with which they interact. Equally important, but less investigated, are environmental factors that influence the *quality* of the interactions between acquaintances. Particular environmental factors such as organizational climates, job designs, time schedules and interior design may promote friendly interaction more so than others. For example, the 'jigsaw classroom' described by Aronson et al. (1978) illustrated one way of structuring elementary school classroom activities so as to promote cooperation and the development of friendship between students of different ethnic backgrounds. In an interview study concerning friendship and work, Parker (1964) found that the nature of the respondents' work was associated with the extent to which they made friends with coworkers. Those employed in service occupations were more likely than business employees to have friends in the same line of work. Further, those who had positive attitudes towards their jobs and those whose jobs most encroached on their free time were most likely to draw friends from their work settings. In a survey of over 900 men living in metropolitan Detroit, the most common sources of the men's closest friendships were found to be work (26 per cent), neighborhood (23 per cent), childhood (20 per cent), voluntary associations (7 per cent), and family involvements (7 per cent).

Some degree of mutual liking is an essential condition for friendship formation. Research on interpersonal attraction suggests that at initial encounter, perceptions of another's attitude similarity, physical attractiveness, competence, positive responsiveness, and apparent liking for us will cause us to be attracted to some individuals over others (Berscheid and Walster, 1978; Huston and Levinger, 1978). Investigations of naturally occurring friendships show that friends tend to be more similar to one another than nonfriends in virtually every examined dimension, including age, sex, marital status, race, religion, attitudes, interests, personality traits, and intelligence (Verbrugge, 1983b; Huston and Levinger, 1978; Jackson, 1977). Interestingly, in contrast to laboratory research, which emphasizes attitude similarity (e.g. Byrne, 1971), studies of real friendships have found similarity in behavioral preferences to be more highly associated with friendship (Kandel, 1978; Werner and Parmelee, 1979).

At initial acquaintance, characteristics of the other person serve as stimuli from which to make predictions about the potential rewardingness of the other as a friend (Altman and Taylor, 1973). As a friendship begins to develop, however, assessments of *actual* rewardingness become critical. Knapp and Harwood (1977) asked college students to rate the importance of a variety of characteristics in the formation of a close same-sex friendship and found attitudinal agreement, intimate accessibility, and reciprocal candor to be the most desired qualities.

The critical determinants of attraction for any friendship will depend on the goals the individuals have for the friendship. For example, shared values may be important for a confidant, but not for a bridge partner. Likewise, the evaluative criteria will vary with the developmental stage of the friendship. LaGaipa (1977) found that authenticity (openness and honesty; being real, genuine and spontaneous) was perceived to be important at all levels of friendship, whereas helping and self-disclosure were considered less important until the development of close friendship. In a longitudinal study of friendship development, Duck and Craig (1978) found that value similarity was correlated with friendship ratings at three months of acquaintance, whereas at eight months a more subtle personality characteristic, personal construct similarity, emerged as more associated with friendship ratings. In addition, the individual's existing social network will influence the types of attributes one finds attractive in a potential friend. For example, Lea and Duck (1982) found a tendency for friends to be similar in those relatively unique personal values for which it was uncommon for them to find similarity with others. Thus, the ability of a new acquaintance to provide rewards not currently available in one's social network may increase one's motivation to initiate a friendship with him or her.

THE DEVELOPMENT OF FRIENDSHIP

Assuming two mutually interested individuals meet under circumstances conducive to personal interaction, the stage is set for the development of friendship. The beginning of a friendship is denoted by interaction that goes beyond that required by the individuals' formal roles, for example having lunch together, talking about one's personal life, playing a practical joke on another, etc. Duck (1983) points out that the desire to become closer is usually not directly stated, rather it is indicated by one's behavioral style. Kurth (1970) explains that initial moves towards friendship may be tentative and deliberately ambiguous, given risks of rejection plus uncertainty about the desirability of the other as a friend. Social exchange theorists (Huston and Burgess, 1979) suggest that when individuals find superficial interaction to be unusually rewarding, or when they feel the other has the potential to be rewarding in ways not currently available, they begin to deepen and develop the relationship.

Several general theories of relationship development have been proposed (Altman and Taylor, 1973; Levinger and Snoek, 1972; Murstein, 1970) though a number of them are framed more with regard to courtship couples than platonic friendships. Given the qualitative differences between friendships and romantic relationships (Davis and Todd, 1982), one cannot assume the process of development to follow identical patterns. For example, Purdy (1978) asked college students to draw graphs of relationship development for same-sex friendships and heterosexual romantic relationships. Involvement in friendships was reported to increase more gradually, level off at a lower magnitude, and include fewer fluctuations than romantic relationships. Altman and Taylor's (1973) social penetration theory is the most thoroughly elaborated and researched model of relationship development that is applicable to friendship. According to social penetration theory, interpersonal exchange in a developing relationship operates on two dimensions—breadth (the content areas of exchange) and depth (the intimacy level of exchange). Relationship development is seen as proceeding in an orderly sequence from superficial interaction in narrow areas to increasingly intimate interaction in broader areas. Progression along the breadth and depth dimensions is governed by a process of dyadic exploration, evaluation and forecasting: an individual samples the rewards and costs of interacting with a potential friend and then decides whether to increase or decrease the level of involvement based on perceptions of the probable reward-ingness of future interactions. Support for social penetration theory has been found in a number of studies (Altman and Taylor, 1973; Hays, 1984, 1985). For example, in two longitudinal studies of friendship development among college students, Hays (1984, 1985) asked first-term university students to complete an extensive behavioral checklist of the types of interactions they had engaged in within newly forming friendships at three-week intervals during their first semester. Analysis of responses during the first three weeks of acquaintance showed that the initial interactions of new friends corresponded to a Guttman-scale progression from superficial interaction (e.g. watching television, discussing local events, telling jokes) to increasingly intimate levels of behavioral exchange (e.g. discussing personal problems, visiting each other's relatives, giving gifts). At early stages of the friendships (three and six weeks), the quantity of behaviors the dyads engaged in accounted for most of the variance in attitudinal ratings of friendship intensity; however, as the friendships progressed, the intimacy level of the interaction accounted for an increasing percentage of the variance. Other investigators have also found increasingly intimate interaction between friends as their relationship progresses. Berg (1984), for example, in a longitudinal study of college roommates, found greater self-disclosure in the spring semester than the fall. Likewise, in a longitudinal diary study, Duck and Miell (1986) found that intimate 'sharing' conversations between new college friends increased in frequency over the course of the school year, and that the settings of their interactions shifted from public to more private locations.

Berg and Clark (1986) have recently questioned the assumption that friendship development follows as *gradual* a process as is implied by social penetration theory, suggesting instead that some decisions about the nature of the relationship and corresponding behavioral differences may occur quite early following initial acquaintance. For example, in a series of laboratory investigations with college students, Clark (Berg and Clark, 1986) manipulated participants' expectations that a fellow college student was a potential friend or not and found that subjects showed *immediate* differences in their responses to the target individual, in that they were more likely to follow 'communal' than 'exchange' norms (Clark and Mills, 1979) with a potential friend. In addition, in Hays' (1984, 1985) longitudinal studies, the dyads progressed to close friendship surprisingly quickly. After only six weeks, the dyads had reached their peak in number of intimate behaviors performed and the friendships had begun to stabilize (ratings of friendship closeness at six weeks were correlated 0.78 with friendship ratings five months later). These findings do not contradict the social penetration view that friendship development follows a systematic 'unfolding' of increasing intimacy levels, but do show that the rate of that process can be quite quick in some cases. Individual and situational characteristics will certainly be determining factors. For example, the friendships of college students who are roommates progress more quickly than friends who are not roommates (Hays, 1985). Likewise, the friendships of highly self-disclosing students may develop faster than those of more reticent individuals (Taylor, 1968).

Berg and Clark's (1986) analysis highlights the catalytic role that often overlooked cognitive factors such as friendship scripts, goals and strategies can play in the development of friendship. Through in-depth interviews with university students concerning the communication strategies they used in developing friendships, Miell and Duck (1986) found that self-disclosure is often offered and elicited purposively as a means of gathering information about a potential friend or strategically channeling the flow of communication to intensify or restrict the growth of a friendship. Their work nicely complements Altman and Taylor (1973) by suggesting cognitive strategies that might guide the process of social penetration.

In addition to increases in the depth and breadth of interaction, a number of other changes characterize the transition from initial acquaintance to close friendship. One assumption of social exchange approaches to relationship development (Huston and Burgess, 1979) is that the value of the resources exchanged increases as a relationship progresses. Evidence for this with regard to friendship was found in Hays' (1985) previously described longitudinal study: ratings of the amount of benefits received from interacting with one's friend were highly correlated with ratings of friendship closeness at all assessment times. Moreover, the benefit ratings of dyads which successfully progressed to close friendship by the end of the school term showed a linear increase over time, in contrast to the declining ratings of the dyads which did not progress. Content analyses of free-response questions which asked participants to list the types of benefits received from their friendships identified the following benefits of friendship: companionship, having a confidant, emotional support, information exchange, material or task assistance, self-esteem, and general value of having a friend. Interestingly, whereas companionship was the benefit of friendship most frequently cited by all dyads, the greatest differences between close and nonclose friends appeared in reports that the other person was a confidant and that one received emotional support from the friend, suggesting that those are the critical ingredients that make a friendship 'close'. Similarly, in a diary study in which college students kept records of their interactions with close friends and casual friends for one week (Hays, 1988), close and casual friendships did not differ in the amounts of fun, task assistance or intellectual stimulation experienced but close friends provided more emotional and informational support than did casual friends. Likewise, LaGaipa's (1977) examination of friendship expectations for varying levels of friends found that helping and self-disclosure distinguished close friendship from more casual friendships.

The increasing emphasis on mutual support and confiding as a friendship evolves from a casual to a close friendship highlights the qualitative changes that occur at different stages of friendship development. Kelley (1979) has described the development of a close relationship as marked by a transformation in the partners' motivations, shifting from a focus on one's immediate reward--cost outcomes towards an increasing responsiveness to the joint outcomes of oneself and one's partner. The norms of exchange operating within a friendship are thus altered as the friendship increases in closeness. O'Connell (1984), for example, interviewed individuals whose friends had helped them build their own homes. Though the friends were typically given no payment for their help, this 'one-sided giving' tended not to result in dissatisfaction or a weakening of the friendship ties; indeed many interviewees felt the experience served to strengthen the friendships. Respondents felt the 'friendship licence' bestowed a right to request help without imposing an obligation to reciprocate. In a 'communal' relationship (Clark and Mills, 1979), friends respond to each other's needs and helping the other is in itself personally satisfying. Further, close friends do not expect immediate 'tit for tat' reciprocation, but assume an eventual balance will be reached in the long term (Levinger, 1980). Similar patterns have been found in self-disclosure between close friends (Derlega, Wilson and Chaikin, 1976).

The emergence of unique pair norms in the dyads' communication and inter-actional styles also characterizes the development of close friendship. For example, in an analysis of naturally occurring telephone conversations, Hornstein (1985) found that when speaking with close friends, females used a highly implicit conversational style compared to when speaking with casual acquaintances or strangers. Similarly, Rands and Levinger (1979) found that 'norm regulation' (e.g. dropping by unannounced, using other's things without permission) was perceived as more likely to occur between close friends than more casual friends. Knapp (1978) suggests that as a relationship successfully progresses, the partners' communication patterns become increasingly personal-ized, synchronized and efficient. In support of this, Baxter and Wilmot (1985) found in a diary study of college students that dyads in growing friendships reported more satisfaction, effectiveness, and personalized communication than nonprogressing dyads. In a similar vein, McCall (1970) suggests that a 'private culture' emerges within a friendship and becomes increasingly elaborated as the friendship progresses. This very interesting aspect of friendship development (see McCall's chapter, this volume) has received very little empirical examin-ation, however.

A number of investigators have noted that ambivalence and conflict tend to accompany increases in dyadic involvement (Braiker and Kelley, 1979; Eidelson, 1980; Hays, 1985). In Thibaut and Kelley's (1959) words, 'To enter a new relationship is to abandon an old adaptation . . . some degree of conflict may be inevitable' (p. 66). In two longitudinal studies, Eidelson (1980) asked college freshmen to evaluate newly developing friendships at two-week intervals over the course of their first semester. Reports of interpersonal satisfaction increased during the early stages of friendship, then declined at approximately six weeks when the friendships had reached intermediate levels of involvement, and subsequently rose again with greater involvement. The drop in satisfaction was interpreted as the friends' reactions to the accumulation of restrictive costs that inevitably arise in a growing friendship. In Hays' (1985) longitudinal study, the most frequently mentioned costs in college students' friendships were: time expenditure, added responsibilities, emotional aggravation, loss of indepen-dence, negative influence of friend on self, and negative effects of friendship on other relationships. The consistent positive correlations between ratings of costs and attitudinal ratings of friendship closeness suggested that increasing costs accompanied friendship progression. In particular, reports of emotional aggravation experienced in the friendships, which were fairly infrequent at early stages of friendship, sharply increased at nine and twelve weeks of acquaintance, with one-third of all dyads mentioning instances of aggravation or conflict. The participants' comments suggested that the increase in emotional aggravation resulted from increased knowledge and familiarity between friends. Thus, increasing self-disclosure and interdependence not only are the mechanisms by which friendships are built, but also open up the potential for increased disagreement and disenchantment within friendships.

Braiker and Kelley (1979) point out that conflict and negativity can play a potentially positive role in interpersonal relationships by offering the dyad an opportunity to grow by 'thrashing out their differences' and thus achieving a more satisfying interpersonal adaptation. Insight into how the negotiation of potentially negative aspects of interaction can serve to help a friendship grow is provided by Rawlins' (1983a, b) dialectical analyses of friendship communication. Through in-depth interviews with ten pairs of close friends, Rawlins (1983a) identified the dialectic of expressiveness–protectiveness that is inherent in the development of friendship. Through their expressiveness or self-disclosure, two friends open up their areas of vulnerability to each other. In achieving this openness, however, the dyad also creates the conditions for closedness (protectiveness), for the friends must thereafter strategically manage their communications so as to protect the other's discovered vulnerabilities. According to Rawlins, the appropriate management of this dialectical tension contributes to the development of trust between the friends. In a similar manner, by successfully negotiating the freedom to be simultaneously independent and dependent within the friendship, a friendship becomes more secure and valued by the participants (Rawlins, 1983b). Investigations into the processes by which friends handle relationship dissatisfactions and tensions would greatly increase our understanding of friendship.

FRIENDSHIP MAINTENANCE AND EVOLUTION

Friendships are continually evolving. Specific friendships may stabilize at a particular level of intimacy or within a circumscribed range of activities, but a friendship cannot be static. To continue to exist, a friendship requires ongoing interaction between the partners. Each interaction between friends can be seen as not only expressing the degree and type of friendship the two individuals have (cf. Watzlawick, Beavin and Jackson, 1967) but also *impacting* their friendship—serving to maintain, strengthen or weaken the dyad's bond. Baxter and Wilmot (1986) have also discussed the need for conceptualizing friendships as 'in process' (i.e. growing closer or more distant). There has been very little research, however, on the processes by which established friendships are maintained and evolve (see Duck and Sants, 1983).

The day-to-day functioning of friendships will obviously vary greatly depending on individual, dyadic and situational factors. In terms of the frequency of contact between friends, sociological surveys of social participation (Jackson, 1977; Verbrugge, 1983b) show that the young and elderly interact with their closest friends more often than do the middle-aged. Single people see their friends more than do married people; students more than professionals and self-employed; and neighbours more than friends who live further apart. As Verbrugge (1983b) concludes, convenience may be the primary determinant of interaction frequency between friends. For example, in a study of black urban wives, Feagin (1970) found that friendship contact varied inversely with the distance between friends' residences. Consequently, Jackson (1977) found the somewhat paradoxical result that the urban men in his survey tended to have the most frequent contact with their least intimate friends (neighbors and coworkers), while the most intimate friends were seen the least often.

If situational factors permit it, close friends tend to interact more frequently than casual friends (Hays, 1985; Verbrugge, 1983b). For example, in Hays' (1988) diary study of college students, close friends reported interacting about six times during a week whereas casual friends averaged between three and four interactions. Once a friendship has reached a certain degree of closeness, however, friends may not need to interact very frequently to maintain their friendship. As Hays (1985) found, at advanced stages of friendship development, the quality of a dyad's interaction becomes more important than simply the quantity. Thus, the friendship bond between friends with very limited interaction, as in the case of long-distance friends, can endure if the rewards of their periodic contacts are sufficiently valued. An examination of the processes by which long-distance friendships are maintained would be a valuable area of future research.

When friends do get together, Argyle and Furnham (1982) have found their interactions typically center around joint leisure and recreational activities, personal conversations, eating and drinking. *Psychology Today*'s (Parlee, 1979) friendship survey of over 40 000 respondents found that the activities most frequently engaged in with friends were: having an intimate talk, helping each other, eating a meal together, attending a movie or sports event, shopping, and playing sports. In contrast to notions of friendship as a highly intimate relationship, Duck and Miell (1986) found that superficial conversation was the most frequently occurring interaction between college friends. Similarly, casual communication and superficial companionship were the behavior categories most highly endorsed by college friends in Hays' (1984, 1985) longitudinal studies.

Several investigators have examined in depth the content of conversation between close friends. In a questionnaire study of middle-aged adults, Aries and Johnson (1983) found the most common topics of conversation to be daily activities, community affairs, family activities, family problems, reminiscences, and work. Interestingly, a similar study with college students (Aries and Johnson, 1983) showed that college friends' conversations were much more often personally focused, dealing with their intimate relationships and family issues. In both studies, female friends discussed personal topics more often and in greater depth than did male friends, who more frequently discussed sports. Davidson and Duberman (1980) examined reports of conversations between best friends and found that the women's conversations included a broader range of topics, particularly with regard to personal and relationship-oriented issues, than did the men's conversations, which emphasized external topics.

The findings cited above illustrate the consistent gender differences which emerge in studies of friendship interaction (see Hendrick, this volume). Females tend to emphasize emotional sharing, trust and confiding in their interactions with friends more so than males, whose friendship interactions often revolve around shared activities (Caldwell and Peplau, 1982; Crawford, 1977; Weiss and Lowenthal, 1975). Females are more likely than males to get together 'just to talk' (Caldwell and Peplau, 1982; Baxter and Wilmot, 1986). Personality characteristics can also be expected to influence the patterning of friendship, yet these have received little examination by researchers. One exception is the finding that high self-monitoring individuals are more likely to choose activity partners on the basis of a friend's skill in the particular activity, whereas the low self-monitor's choice is made more on the basis of general liking for one's friends (Snyder, Gangestad and Simpson, 1983).

CROSS-SEX FRIENDSHIP

Platonic friendships between men and women have received very little attention by researchers. As Booth and Hess (1974) discuss, social and occupational structures tend to be sex-typed, making it less likely that individuals of different sexes will meet, especially under conditions of equal status. Further, social norms often discourage cross-sex friendship, considering it a threat to marital relationships. In a survey of 800 middle-aged Midwesterners, close cross-sex friendships were reported by only 28 per cent of the respondents (Babchuk, 1965). Interestingly, the cross-sex friendships that did form were structurally similar to same-sex friendships in that they tended to be homogeneous with respect to age, education and social class. Qualitatively, however, cross-sex friendships appear to differ from same-sex friendships. Seventy-three per cent of the respondents in *Psychology Today*'s friendship survey (Parlee, 1979) agreed cross-sex friendships were unlike same-sex friendships, citing as reasons sexual tensions, social discouragement, and the fact that opposite-sex friends have less in common. K. E. Davis (1985) found that cross-sex friendships were viewed as including less sharing of confidences and assistance and less tendency to 'give the utmost' than same-sex friendships, and were also perceived as less stable. Similarly, in an interview study comparing the functions of same-sex and cross-sex friendships (Rose, 1985), both women and men described their cross-sex friendships as including less communication and providing less help than same-sex friendships. Further, less active strategies were reported in the formation of cross-sex friendships. Whereas same-sex friendship formation was seen as instigated by expressions of mutual affection, communication and acceptance, cross-sex friendships were more often characterized as being initiated by 'no strategy', developing gradually through the passage of time, or stimulated by an initial sexual attraction that eventually settled into being 'just friends'. With the societal relaxation in sex roles and increase of women in the workforce, the incidence of cross-sex friendships will surely increase, and their functioning perhaps change (cf. Dillard and Miller, this volume). The unique value of cross-sex friendship as a significant contributor to greater understanding and equality between the sexes should not be underestimated, and merits investigation.

FRIENDSHIP DISSOLUTION

The end of a friendship can be precipitated by factors at an individual level (e.g. death, change in marital status), environmental level (e.g. moving to separate cities, changing jobs) or dyadic level (e.g. change in reward–cost ratio of the friendship). Factors at each level may be interrelated and may in combination bring about a friendship's dissolution (cf. McCall's chapter, this volume). Rose (1984) points out that one factor (e.g. change in reward level) may weaken the friendship bond, making it more vulnerable to other factors (e.g. moving). Kurth (1970) notes that a sense of relief may be felt when situational changes 'gracefully' end a less than satisfying friendship. As Duck (1982a) emphasizes, the dissolution of a personal relationship is not an 'event' but a process and cannot be viewed as simply a reversal of the developmental process since the partners' relationship experience (e.g. intimate knowledge of the other, shared memories) cannot be withdrawn. In contrast to romantic relationships and marriages, which often end with an emotional, protracted 'break-up', the dissolution of a friendship is more likely to be characterized as a gradual 'fading away'. Since there are no formal ties to be severed nor public announcements to be made, there is little need for negotiation in ending a friendship. It may also be difficult to distinguish temporary downswings in a friendship from absolute declines. Consequently, the dissolution of a friendship many times is only realized in hindsight and often regretted (Rose, 1984).

Rose (1984) asked 155 undergraduates to write essays describing reasons for the decline of a close, same-sex friendship. The main causes identified were: physical separation, new friends replacing old ones, growing to dislike characteristics of the friend's behavior or personality, and interference from dating or marriage relationships. Few friendships ended due to an internal 'breakdown', but were more likely disrupted by external factors.

Argyle and Henderson's (1984) research on friendship rules provides insight into dyadic factors that can contribute to friendship dissolution. They asked individuals to think of a specific friendship that had lapsed because of something about the relationship and to rate the extent to which failure to keep various rules had contributed to the breakdown. The rule violations found to be most critical included jealousy or criticism; lack of tolerance for a third-party relationship; disclosing confidences; not volunteering help when needed; nagging or criticizing the person publicly; and not showing trusting, confiding, positive regard or emotional support. In her conceptualization of relationship dissolution, Rodin (1982) refers to such violations of one's expectations of what a friend should be like as one friend meeting the other's 'dislike criteria'. Alternatively, Rodin (1982) suggests that a friendship can end because either partner's 'like criteria' change, that is, one begins to look for different things in a friend. What an individual expects, desires or needs from a friendship will vary with experience and lifespan changes (Bigelow and LaGaipa, 1975; Dickens and Perlman, 1981), therefore some friends may no longer provide the satisfactions they once did. Likewise, as individuals enter new situations, their comparison level for alternatives changes and they may encounter new acquaintances who are more rewarding than their current friends. From this perspective, letting go of particular friendships is a necessary and potentially growth-enhancing aspect of the individual's own developmental process. Hays and Oxley (1986), for example, found that the most adaptive social networks for first-term university students were those which were permeable, in that they brought in new friends who were also college students, rather than holding on completely to one's old high school or neighborhood friends who did not also enter college. Thus individuals must continually restructure their friendship networks to fit their changing identities and life situations. Enduring friendships may be those in which both partners grow in ways that continue to be mutually stimulating and satisfying.

In an interview study of college students, Rose and Serafica (1986) found that the processes responsible for keeping and ending friendships varied with friendship level. Casual friendships were described as likely to end due to decreased proximity, whereas close and best friends could withstand decreases in contact, assuming degrees of affection within the friendships did not change. Jackson, Fischer and Jones (1977) have made the distinction between 'friends of convenience' and 'friends of commitment'. Friends of convenience result primarily from situational factors that hold the friends together and are easily replaced when one moves on to a new situation. One's attachment to friends of commitment, however, is such that one holds on to them despite changes in external factors. A valuable direction for future research is the identification of characteristics of the friendship bond which contribute to a friendship's durability throughout the individuals' respective life changes.

THE EFFECTS OF FRIENDSHIP

An individual's friendships can have a profound impact—both facilitative and disruptive—on other aspects of the individual's life. The burgeoning literature on social support documents the potentially beneficial consequences of friendship, demonstrating that friends can significantly contribute to one's happiness and life satisfaction, ability to cope with stress, and vulnerability to illness (Fleming and Baum, 1986; Duck, 1983; Gottlieb, this volume).

Friends provide a multitude of functions for individuals, serving both as preventive resources (contributing to positive personal adaptation, thereby making stress and adjustment problems less likely to occur) and as buffers (mediating the effects of stresses that do occur). As Cicero wisely observed, 'A friend multiplies our joys and divides our sorrows'. Although the mechanisms by which friendships produce their positive outcomes are not fully understood (Fleming and Baum, 1986), Solano (1986) discusses three types of important resources that friendships can provide: (1) *emotional* (e.g. intimacy, support, acceptance, belongingness, self-esteem, status), (2) *cognitive* (e.g. stimulation, social comparison, information), and (3) *material* (task assistance, tangible support).

Friendship has long been recognized as an important contributor to an individual's personality development and socialization throughout the lifespan (Berndt, 1982; Hess, 1972; Sullivan, 1953). Sullivan (1953) postulated that the experience of intimacy and acceptance with a close, same-sex 'chum' during preadolescence provided a 'consensual validation' critical for individuals' developing a sense of personal worth. There are a number of aspects of the friendship process that can contribute to an individual's sense of self-esteem, including the recognition that one's friend knows, accepts and likes your 'real self' (Kurth, 1970); perceives the world the same way you do (Duck, 1973); and supports your view of yourself (Bailey, Finney and Helm, 1975). In addition, one's friend provides an opportunity to help, nurture or influence someone else (Z. Rubin, 1980; Candy, Troll and Levy, 1981).

Friendship plays an important role in an individual's socialization process by providing sources of social comparison and a safe setting for trying out new roles and gaining feedback and support (Hess, 1972; Weiss and Lowenthal, 1975). As Rangell (1963) says, 'friends serve as a giant projection screen or sounding board against which one can measure and check [one]self' (p. 20). For this reason, friends have been found to be especially critical during periods of role transition such as adolescence, young adulthood, and retirement (Dickens and Perlman, 1981; Hess, 1972). As peers, friends are able to furnish invaluable information and validation in a way family members are rarely able to. For example, Tokuno (1983) found that college females preferred to discuss developmental issues such as personal values and relationships with friends rather than family members. Similarly, Millen and Rolls (1977) found that adolescent males felt their closest friends were the people who understood them the best; fathers and teachers were seen as the least understanding.

Friendship has often been placed in a sort of 'competition' with other personal relationships, particularly kin and romantic relations, with the expectation that all an individual's needs could or should be met within the nuclear family. Thus friendships have often been viewed as unnecessary or interfering (Bell, 1981a; Brain, 1976). Brain (1977) emphasizes that such unrealistic assumptions—aside from their disservice to friendship—place an unfair burden on marital and family relationships. Weiss' (1973) research on loneliness demonstrated that a spouse provides a sense of emotional attachment whereas friends provide a sense of belongingness and social integration, thus each type of relationship fills unique and complementary needs for the individual. Kon and Losenkov (1978) found that adolescents regarded their best friends as those who understood them best and with whom they would most likely share intimate, confidential information. However, for advice on complicated life situations, both boys and girls reported they would turn to their parents first. Litwak and Szelenyi (1969) suggest that individuals tend to turn to their friends for help on issues in which a degree of similarity and affection is important, whereas family are turned to for problems of a more serious or long-term nature.

In a similar vein, different types of friends will serve different functions for individuals. In a study of foreign students' adaptation to the University of Hawaii, foreigners reported having two kinds of friends: Hawaiians and 'compatriots'. The Hawaiian friends were useful in helping them get settled and 'learn the ropes' in the new culture, while with their compatriots they could share familiar activities and personal conversation (Bochner, McLeod and Lin, 1977). In a comparison of the functions of cross-sex and same-sex friends (Rose, 1985), women reported that their women friends provided them with more acceptance and intimacy than did men friends. Similarly, Hays and Oxley (1986) found that both male and female college students reported receiving more emotional support from female friends than from male friends.

The level of a friendship will greatly influence the resources it offers. The intimacy, mutual concern and ease of communication that characterize close friendships may enable close friends to provide more emotional and information support than casual friends (Hays, 1988), thus close friends are perceived as more therapeutic than casual friends (Davidson and Packard, 1981). On the other hand, the high degree of interdependence and familiarity associated with close friends may interfere with their ability or motivation to provide effective support in some instances. Several studies have shown that close-knit friendship networks are not likely to encourage change or provide the resources needed for coping with situations that are unfamiliar (Hirsch, 1980; Walker, MacBride and Vachon, 1977). As Granovetter (1973) has emphasized, the 'strength of weak ties' such as casual friends and acquaintances lies in the fact that they *are* more distant, and thus able to provide access to new information and perspectives one may not normally encounter.

Clearly, however, there are limits to friends' abilities to help in some situations. An important focus for future research is in identifying the types of problems for which friends can be effective sources of support, and more fully explicating the interactional processes and contextual factors that contribute to their effectiveness. Also in need of investigation are the potential negative consequences of friendship. For example, the desire to be liked and accepted by one's friends or to help one's friends can cause individuals to behave in ways that may go against personal or societal standards and thus work against their best interests. Friendship groups can be particularly vulnerable to social psychological dynamics such as 'groupthink' (Janis, 1972) or deindividuation (Zimbardo, 1970), in which group involvement contributes to members engaging in actions that are more risky, impulsive or ill advised than would the individuals by themselves.

CONCLUDING REMARKS

In terms of a scientific understanding of friendship, the surface has only been scratched. Investigators have described properties associated with the friendship bond, identified factors that precipitate the formation of a friendship, outlined at a general level some of the changes that occur as a friendship develops, and suggested a number of beneficial consequences friendship can have. Very little is known about the actual process of friendship: how friendship is maintained, why and how it grows and evolves, what mechanisms underlie the positive and negative functions friendship can serve, and how a friendship interrelates with the social and physical context in which it is embedded. Most research has focused on the casual and close same-sex friendships of college students. More attention needs to be given to different varieties of friendship (e.g. cross-sex friends, long-distance friends, friendship cliques, 'best' friends, specialized friends, cross-generational friends) among diverse populations and environmental settings. Only then will a valid understanding of friendship be attained.

Handbook of Personal Relationships
Edited by S. W. Duck
© 1988 John Wiley & Sons Ltd

22

Courtship

RODNEY M. CATE
Washington State University, Pullman, Washington, USA
and
SALLY A. LLOYD
University of Utah, Salt Lake City, Utah, USA

ABSTRACT

This chapter presents a selective review and analysis of the literature on courtship development and dissolution. The review organizes this literature according to various predominant theoretical frameworks: the compatibility framework, exchange framework, and interpersonal process framework. In addition, future research directions are suggested.

The institution of marriage is very popular in most all societies. In the United States, over 95 per cent of the population enters marriage at some point in the lifespan. In virtually all societies, marriages are preceded by the institution of *courtship*, the process by which unmarried individuals interact to select a marriage partner. From a societal standpoint, courtship is important because it brings together individuals who will nurture the infants that constitute the citizens of the next generation (Reiss, 1980). Additionally, at the more micro level, it is generally assumed that courtship can play an important role in later satisfaction of married individuals and the quality of their marriages within a society. This assumption has resulted in current research and theorizing focusing on the processes of development of personal commitment (feeling of personal dedication), rather than commitment that is induced by constraints external to the relationship (structural commitment) (Johnson, 1982). The purpose of this chapter is to examine courtship at this more micro level. The chapter will: (a) present evidence that courtship is an important phase of the life cycle; and (b) review research and frameworks for examining courtship and premarital relationship development, as well as examining the dissolution of such relationships. Consequently, as each framework is discussed, we will first look at how and why partners move closer to marriage (the development aspect) and secondly, we will examine what predicts actual continuance or discontinuance of the relationship.

THE IMPORTANCE OF COURTSHIP

Certainly, the nature of courtship has changed remarkably since the turn of the century. The switch from a supervised system, with parents, neighbors, etc., serving as monitors of premarital relationship interaction, to the 'participant-run' system wherein the premarital partners themselves regulated their behavior served as a catalyst for fundamental changes in the nature and purpose of courtship (Murstein, 1976). No longer was the choice of a mate heavily dependent upon parental approval; rather, such choice became a matter of partners assessing their 'compatibility'. In addition, the nature of 'marital compatibility' itself changed over time, with less emphasis placed upon social and economic considerations and more emphasis on emotional gratification and relationship quality. One factor has remained stable with regard to courtship, however: the belief that what transpires premaritally has implications for the quality of the subsequent marriage.

Several dated studies have shown that the length of acquaintance and engagement before marriage is positively related to later marital quality (Locke, 1951; Spanier, 1971). Length of courtship was later conceptualized by Lewis and Spanier (1979) as a premarital resource, which along with level of education, age at marriage, and emotional health leads to higher marital quality. These findings certainly support the speculation that there are premarital processes that operate during this period to promote later marital quality. Unfortunately, these studies do not give solid clues as to which processes are important. Much of the discussion concerning the key functions of courtship has focused on the speculation that premarital couples gain needed information about the partner during dating and engagement, thus helping them assess likely marital compatibility. However, this assumption of compatibility testing is tenuous at best (Robins, 1985), especially when considering that a sizeable proportion of those who marry seriously dated only one person—their spouse. Despite the questioning of compatibility testing as a framework for understanding courtship, recent evidence suggests there are significant dimensions of premarital relationships which influence marital quality. These dimensions are positivity of premarital communication and premarital conflict.

The first line of research has examined the power of premarital communication in predicting marital distress over a five-year period (Markman, 1979, 1981). In this longitudinal study, couples planning marriage were followed over a five-and-a-half-year period. At initial assessment, these couples discussed five tasks in a laboratory. As they discussed each task, the partners rated the impact of their communications on a five-point scale from (1) super negative to (5) super positive. Additionally, the couples completed self-report assessments of their satisfaction with their relationships and the intensity of problems in the relationship. At the three followups (one year, two and a half years, and five and a half years), couples reported on their relationship status (divorced, separated, etc.) and their current satisfaction with the relationship. At the first followup, problem intensity and initial satisfaction were significant predictors of current satisfaction with the relationship, but positivity of premarital communication did not predict. However, at the next two followups, *only* positivity of premarital communication was predictive of current marital satisfaction.

Second, Kelly, Huston and Cate (1985) have reported results of a longitudinal study that supports the idea that conflict is important during courtship. In this interview and questionnaire study, couples who had been married less than twelve months provided detailed time-ordered descriptions of their courtships as well as restrospective questionnaire assessments of love, ambivalence, maintenance behaviors, and conflict/negativity at different stages of the courtship. Approximately two years later they completed these same scales, as well as measures of marital satisfaction and adjustment. Conflict/negativity during the later stages of courtship was significantly related to conflict/negativity two and a half years into the marriage. Additionally, conflict/negativity during the premarital phase was negatively related to satisfaction or adjustment in the marriage. The results of this study clearly demonstrate the importance of conflict/negativity (i.e. expression of negative feelings, intensity of problems, and frequency of arguments) in predicting later marital quality.

The results of these two studies converge to portray the importance of certain interactional processes during courtship in predicting later marital quality. The picture that emerges is that maritally adjusted and satisfied couples are characterized premaritally by positive communication patterns which are relatively low in anger and resentment, as well as by relatively low rates of arguing and communication of negative feelings.

FRAMEWORKS FOR EXAMINING COURTSHIP AND PREMARITAL RELATIONSHIP DEVELOPMENT

Frameworks for establishing premarital relationships may be roughly divided into three types: compatibility, exchange, and interpersonal process models. We have used these three general categories to organize the following discussion of both the development and dissolution of premarital relationships.

Compatibility Frameworks

The major frameworks for examining courtship and premarital relationship development during the past 30 years have posited that mate selection is comprised of compatibility testing by partners. Traditionally, compatibility testing models assume that the choice of a marital partner comes about due to partners assessing the degree of match between their various stable psychological or demographic attributes (Robins, 1985). Such matching of global qualities implies that compatibility is induced at the more micro level of relationship interaction. Matching has been suggested as important in such areas as personality (Winch, 1958), values (Kerckhoff and Davis, 1962; Lewis, 1973; Murstein, 1976), roles (Lewis, 1973; Murstein, 1976), and demographic aspects (Burgess and Wallin, 1953; Hendrick, 1981; Hill, Rubin and Peplau, 1976). Some researchers (Kerckhoff and Davis, 1962; Lewis, 1973; Murstein, 1976) have elaborated on the basic compatibility models to suggest that matching takes place on different attributes at different time points during the premarital relationship. In the remainder of this section, we will discuss these compatibility models, along with criticisms of the framework. In addition, we will discuss how these models relate to research on the dissolution of premarital relationships.

Complementarity

One of the earliest compatibility models postulated that complementarity of personality needs was important in the selection of a mate (Winch, 1958). The basic hypothesis of this complementarity model is: 'In mate-selection each individual seeks within his or her field of eligibles that person who gives the greatest promise of providing him or her with maximum need gratification' (Winch, 1974, p. 400). Such hypothesized gratification is seen to result from two types of complementariness. *Type I* complementarity exists when the same need is gratified in both partners, but at different levels of intensity. For example, *Type I* complementarity exists when one partner has a high need to be dominant and the other partner a low need to be dominant. *Type II* complementarity exists when different needs in the partners are gratified. For example, *Type II* complementarity exists when one partner is high on the need to be dominant and the other partner is high on the need to be submissive.

Winch (1955a, b; Winch, Ktsanes and Ktsanes, 1954) conducted a series of studies designed to test his theory. Basically, the assessment of need complementarity was conducted by a panel of psychoanalysts working together to derive information from content analyses of need interviews and interviewee answers to the Thematic Apperception Test. Winch reported support for complementarity as a process in mate selection. However, several criticisms of the complementarity hypothesis have been leveled. First, most studies have not replicated the Winch findings (Levinger, Senn and Jorgensen, 1970). Winch (1974) noted that most replicative attempts have not been *true* replications, in that all replication studies have utilized paper and pencil measures of needs, rather than analytic assessments. On the other hand, it should be expected that a 'strong' theory or framework should withstand replicative attempts with multiple methods and measures.

A second criticism is that Winch (Winch, Ktsanes and Ktsanes, 1954) may have 'overinterpreted' his data. Tharp (1963) has suggested that the 388 correlations hypothesized to be related to each other are not independent. Consequently, one would need many more correlations to be significant than were reported to claim strong support for the complementarity hypothesis. Third, there are conceptual problems with the complementarity hypothesis. Much of this criticism focuses on the degree to which personality constructs are predictive of observable behavior in relationships. Seyfried (1977) has suggested that interaction is selective, in that married partners have alternative relationships and situations available that allow them to express their needs, thus obviating the necessity of expressing their needs only in the marital relationship. Additionally, it is likely that complementarity interacts with other important variables. For example, theorists (Seyfried and Hendrick, 1973; Tharp, 1963; Winch, 1974) have postulated that complementarity may be facilitative of relationships only in certain role relationships. For example, if cultural norms dictate that men should be dominant over their wives, the pairing of a submissive man with a dominant woman may not lead to attraction.

Similarity

A competing hypothesis to complementarity has been one stating that individuals select marital partners on the basis of similarity. Similarity between premarital or marital partners has been found to exist in various demographic characteristics such as family background, religion, ethnic background, intelligence, etc. (Burgess and Wallin, 1953; Hendrick, 1981; Hill, Rubin and Peplau, 1976), as well as in personality (Antill, 1983; Skolnick, 1981), attitudes (Burgess and Wallin, 1953), values (Schellenberg, 1960), and physical attractiveness (Murstein and Christy, 1976; Price and Vandenberg, 1979). Huston and Levinger (1978) have outlined four explanations for why similarity may induce compatibility in relationships. They suggest that: (a) similarity may be directly reinforcing; (b) similarity may confirm individuals' sense of esteem, worth, etc.; (c) similarity implies that the partner is likely to provide rewarding future experiences; and (d) similarity is important only because it is correlated with the affective value of the partner's characteristics.

Despite the numerous studies demonstrating that premarital and marital partners are similar in various attributes, several criticisms have been leveled against the hypothesis. First, Kerckhoff (1974) has questioned whether people use similarity as an explicit choice factor in mate selection, since individuals usually live rather circumscribed lives that limit their contact with others whose attitudes and values might be drastically divergent. Consequently, the opportunity to select dissimilar others may be quite limited. Second, some studies (Leslie and Richardson, 1956; Coombs, 1962) show that when the influence of social network members declines, people are less likely to pair with similar partners, suggesting that external factors may be more potent in inducing partner similarity than the personal choice of the individual. Third, recent evidence (Stephen, 1985) suggests that the similarity of couples in relationships may be a result of their interaction over time, rather than a result of individuals' preferences for a similar mate. In this longitudinal study, couples were found to become significantly more similar over time in beliefs, attitudes, and values. Fourth, recent studies have found that attitude similarity did not differentiate over time between intact and dissolved couples (Hill, Rubin and Peplau, 1976), nor did it differentiate five groups of couples varying in level of involvement

(Centers, 1975). Finally, an interesting critique of compatibility models comes from Robins (1985). He argues that if testing for similarity (or complementarity) operates in mate selection, then the extent to which people seriously dated many partners before marriage should be related to the degree of compatibility of married couples (to the extent that it increases the probability that a compatible partner will be found). Robins (1985), in a study of young married couples, found no support for this hypothesis.

Sequential filter models

After the development of notions of similarity and complementarity, several sequential models of mate selection were proposed (Kerckhoff and Davis, 1962; Lewis, 1973; Murstein, 1976). The impetus for the development of the earliest 'filter' model of Kerckhoff and Davis (1962) was that most previous studies of similarity and complementarity in mate selection did not examine the effect of these variables on movement to marriage over time. These models propose that individuals assess compatibility using different criteria over time in the courtship. The most prominent model (Kerckhoff and Davis, 1962), developed from a longitudinal study of dating couples, proposes that people first 'filter' partners on the basis of social similarity, followed by value similarity, and finally on the basis of personality complementarity. A similar model has been developed by Murstein (1976), positing that filtering takes place first on stimulus characteristics (physical attractiveness, etc.), later on values, and lastly on role fit of the partners. Additionally, Lewis (1973) has further elaborated the above models by more explicitly delineating pair processes (perceiving similarities, achieving pair rapport, etc.) that might operate sequentially in the developmental course of premarital relationships. Despite the empirical basis on which these models were developed, several weaknesses have been suggested.

A major weakness of the Murstein (1976) and Lewis (1973) models relates to methodological and statistical shortcomings (cf. Rubin and Levinger, 1974). Murstein's (1976) supposed confirmation in many cases rests on cross-sectional data that are insufficient to establish the sequential operation of the proposed factors. Lewis's (1973) confirmation of his model is also questionable, given that his use of the analysis of variance is not sufficient to demonstrate the operation of sequential processes.

A second criticism of the sequential models is that no studies have been able to replicate these models. Levinger, Senn and Jorgensen (1970) attempted to replicate the Kerckhoff and Davis (1962) study. In the replication, neither value similarity nor need complementarity predicted courtship progress, nor was the effect of these variables mediated by length of the relationship.

A third weakness of the sequential models, as well as compatibility models in general, is that the assumption that dating partners are aware of their partners' attitudes, values, and personalities may not be valid. Duck and Sants (1983) have aptly pointed out that at present we know little about the interpersonal processes that may lead to discovery of similarity or complementarity. Some studies lead us to question whether people very accurately discern their partners' attributes. For example, the classic study by Cuber and Harroff (1966) indicated that many marital relationships are *nonintimate* from the beginning. The 'passive–congenial' couples in this study did not engage in the type of interaction that would lead to accurate discovery of partner attributes, at least for some couples. Rubin (1976) has also reported that for working-class couples, the movement to marriage is characterized by rather nonintimate events, suggesting again that accurate assessment of partner attributes is not likely.

In addition to the above criticisms, some sequential filter models suffer from conceptual weaknesses. For example, Murstein (1976) posits that role considerations are important in the later stages of the mate-selection process. This assertion is contrary to convincing theoretical arguments (Levinger and Snoek, 1972) which hold that role factors are salient much earlier in a relationship. Levinger and Snoek (1972) argue that during the early stages of a relationship individuals rely on socially defined roles to guide their behavior and that adequate fulfilment of these roles is important in relationship continuation. An additional conceptual weakness of these models concerns the definition of 'stage'. Sequential models postulate that 'stages' are defined by different factors, at different time points, predicting some end state such as courtship progress or marriage. This would appear to be a rather 'weak' definition of stage, in that to discern the stage one has to look to a future end state or event to occur. A stronger stage model would postulate that the important variables in courtship would interrelate differently at different points in time, thus suggesting qualitative differences by stage. For example, Lloyd and Cate (1985a) found that love was not related to conflict during the developing stage of premarital relationships, but was negatively related to conflict as the relationship deteriorated. This suggests that there are *qualitative* differences that may define stages in premarital relationships. In addition, quantitative changes occur; Braiker and Kelley (1979) and Huston *et al.* (1981) present evidence of incremental change over time in several dimensions of courtship (love, ambivalence, maintenance behaviors, conflict). It would seem likely that such incremental change can lead to redefinitions of a premarital relationship (i.e. qualitative change).

Dissolution From a Compatibility Perspective

As with attempts to explain 'who will marry whom', compatibility models are prevalent in the dissolution literature. Of course, the ultimate compatibility models of dissolution are the theories of mate selection. They indirectly are theories of relationship dissolution, to the extent that it is possible to use them to describe the 'incompatible characteristics' of couples whose relationships terminated. Thus, relationship dissolution is a function of incompatible social similarity, value consensus or need complementarity (Kerckhoff and Davis, 1962), failure to achieve one of the stages of stimulus, value or role (Murstein, 1976), or lack of dyadic crystallization (Lewis, 1973).

Many other studies directly address 'incompatibility' as a factor in premarital dissolution. Unequal levels of involvement have been repeatedly cited as a factor in dissolution (Burgess and Wallin, 1953; Hill, Rubin and Peplau, 1976).

Disparate ages of partners, educational aspirations, intelligence and physical attractiveness were all factors related to relationship breakup in the longitudinal Boston Couples Study (Hill, Rubin and Peplau, 1976). However, matching factors may be weak predictors of dissolution. In a partial replication of Hill *et al.*, Stephen (1984b), using multiple regression, found the best predictors of dissolution to be commitment level, geographic vicinity, and relationship satisfaction. Age discrepancy, value similarity, and unequal status did not contribute significantly to the prediction of breakup.

In terms of a traditional definition of 'compatibility testing', only a few studies have directly assessed matching, similarity, complementarity, etc. However, Levinger and Rands (1985) argue that the essence of compatibility has changed remarkably over the years, from an assessment of social characteristics and value orientations to an assessment of relationship satisfaction, communication, and commitment. Basically, partners are indeed testing compatibility when they assess their ability to communicate, form a mutual definition of the relationship, and gain satisfaction. Several longitudinal studies have outlined the role of such compatibility factors as love and commitment in premarital relationship dissolution.

Berg and McQuinn (1986) noted that couples who broke up showed lower correlations between partners' ratings of conflict, self-disclosure and comparison level than couples whose relationships continued. Relationship dissolution has also been predicted on the basis of low involvement, dissatisfaction with the relationship, degree of uncertainty (inability to predict partner's behavior and feelings, and lack of knowledge of partner), lack of support from partner's network, lack of communication with partner, and lower perceived similarity with partner (Lloyd, Cate and Henton, 1984; Parks and Adelman, 1983).

One interesting question not fully addressed by compatibility models is the issue of when does the incompatibility of the partners become apparent, and when does this awareness lead to dissatisfaction with the relationship and eventual dissolution. Obviously, if incompatibility is based on characteristics of social similarity, awareness may occur very early in the relationship. Do partners simply ignore such incompatibility until dissatisfaction with other aspects of the relationship occurs (e.g. unhappiness over the amount of time spent together), so that social dissimilarity becomes a form of sour grapes ('well, he never was good enough for me anyway'), or does social incompatibility itself spark dissatisfaction with the relationship that eventually leads to its deterioration?

Fortunately, Stephen (1985) presents a very innovative analysis of the compatibility question, in that he has tested whether actual attitude similarity evolves as the relationship develops, or whether actual similarity predates involvement (see previous discussion of similarity). He found strong support for the former view, emphasizing that relationship development is best viewed as a 'circular–causal' model rather than a 'fixed-sequence' one. However, while there was clear evidence that a shared view of the world evolved between premarital partners over time, such attitude similarity was not predictive of relationship dissolution versus continuation (Stephen, 1984b, 1985). As previously noted, other factors such as commitment were stronger predictors of relationship outcome.

In essence, Berg and McQuinn (1986) addressed the incompatibility question, albeit from the opposite direction. Berg and McQuinn assert that relationships differentiate early on, that is, it is possible to tell even after a limited relationship history which relationships will continue (and grow closer together) and which relationships will terminate. They were able to differentiate, with a high degree of accuracy, on the basis of love and maintenance between continuing and noncontinuing relationships soon after these relationships had begun. Berg and McQuinn's (1986) work supports the view that certain types of compatibility (love and commitment) are important very early in relationships.

Perhaps the most interesting question that remains to be answered is what differentiates 'incompatible' relationships that terminate from 'incompatible' relationships that continue, for certainly not all incompatible relationships automatically dissolve. Obviously, many other factors, from dyadic characteristics to circumstantial events, have an impact on relationship dissolution. Some of these factors will be outlined in the following sections.

Exchange Frameworks

Social exchange models have sparked a great deal of courtship-related research. These exchange frameworks assume that the development of a relationship is based on the satisfactory exchange of rewards between partners (Huston and Cate, 1979). However, most of the research and theorizing using these frameworks has focused on identifying rather static variables that discriminate between courtships that are stable versus unstable or satisfying versus dissatisfying, rather than examining the cognitive and interpersonal exchange processes by which partners become committed to each other.

Huston and Cate (1979) have outlined how the exchange process might operate in the development of commitment to a particular partner. In this exchange framework, initial attraction to a partner is seen to involve the assessment of the likelihood that the other will provide rewards. This assessment of capability to reward is usually based on the level of physical attractiveness of the other person, with highly physically attractive individuals seen as potentially providing high rewards. However, the likely rewardingness of the other person is not the sole factor in initial attraction. Initial attraction also involves an assessment of how likely the other person is to reciprocate our attraction (Shanteau and Nagy, 1976). According to this framework, once initial attraction has occurred, deeper involvement is induced when the partner provides rewards that are not easily available elsewhere and the level of rewards is high enough to motivate the partners to intensify their involvement (Altman and Taylor, 1973; Huesmann and Levinger, 1976). At this point, individuals may 'forecast' the likelihood that rewards will be available in the future, and thus further increase their involvement in the relationship (Altman and Taylor, 1973; Huesmann and Levinger, 1976). However, the unique availability of rewards, the level of rewards, and positive forecasts are not the only considerations in deciding to continue a relationship. People may also be motivated to continue relationships because the rewards have been steadily increasing over time (i.e. the slope of rewards) (Huesmann and Levinger, 1976), because the social network supports the relationship (Ridley and Avery, 1979), or because they do not want to lose their previous investment (Johnson, 1985).

Other social exchange oriented researchers (Hatfield, Utne and Traupmann, 1979) have attempted to explain relationship growth by focusing on how rewards are allocated in relationships. Hatfield and her colleagues (Hatfield, Utne and Traupmann, 1979) have posited that people become more intimate when they perceive that they have been treated equitably, that is, when their outcomes equal what they deserve based on their inputs, their partners' inputs, and their partners' outcomes. In other words, this equity model of relationship development holds that people make overt decisions about increasing their involvement based on the perceived fairness of the relationship. However, these equity models of development have recently begun to be questioned.

Although equity has been shown to predict satisfaction with premarital relationships (Walster, Walster and Traupmann, 1978), it has not been found to successfully predict relationship attributes indicative of movement to marriage, such as involvement or commitment. Cate, Lloyd and Long (1988) demonstrated that the absolute perceived reward level, as compared to equity, is the best predictor of relationship involvement over time. Additionally, some equity theorists fail to recognize that other norms of fairness, such as equality (partners receiving equal rewards, regardless of inputs), may be important in relationships. More importantly, it has recently been demonstrated that people may not differentiate between equity and equality norms (Cate *et al.*, 1982). In other words, equity and equality can exist side by side (Huston and Burgess, 1979). A further problematic issue concerning equity models is that its proponents do not recognize that equity may play different roles at different times in a relationship; there is both cross-sectional (Lloyd, Cate and Henton, 1982) and longitudinal (Cate, Lloyd and Long, 1988) evidence that over time equity becomes less predictive of relationship involvement.

Rusbult (1980, 1983) has developed an investment model of relationship development that utilizes social exchanges concepts. This framework proposes that commitment to a partner is developed when satisfaction with the partner is high, costs are low, alternatives are low, and investments into the relationship are high. Rusbult (1983) has tested and found support for this model longitudinally with dating individuals. She found that satisfaction and investments were positively related to the development of commitment over a nine-month period, while the level of alternatives was negatively related. These relations were found for individuals in both stable and unstable pairings. Despite the strong empirical support for this model (Rusbult, 1983), Johnson (1985) has noted two conceptual problems: the operationalization of commitment does not effectively differentiate between *personal* and *structural* commitment, and the operationalization of alternatives taps only alternative *relationships*, thus ignoring that there are other *nonrelationship* alternative considerations that are important in commitment decisions. Also, since Rusbult (1983) asks people to assess their alternatives relative to their current relationship, Johnson (1985) suggests that the alternatives measure is confounded with satisfaction with the relationship, a variable also included in the test of her model.

Dissolution from an Exchange Perspective

The issue of relationship stability is central to social exchange models of relationships. In the early writings on exchange theory, Thibaut and Kelley (1959) outlined the role of comparison level for alternatives as a mediator of stability in relationships. According to the theory, when the best available alternative (a new partner, gaining independence, etc.) is perceived to be better than the current relationship, dissolution is likely to occur.

Levinger (1976, 1979) added the concept of barriers to the exchange view of relationship dissolution. Barriers are those constraining forces which prevent dissolution of the relationship; in many cases, barriers are not recognized until an individual contemplates terminating the relationship. In his commitment model, Johnson (1973, 1982) has elaborated the manner in which the concept of barriers fits into an exchange framework. Structural commitments (conditions which constrain an individual to remain and thus prevent dissolution) may consist of irretrievable investments, termination procedures, social pressures, and attractiveness of available alternatives (Johnson, 1985). Johnson (1985) very carefully points to one of the foibles of trying to measure exchange concepts—factors which mediate personal commitment at one point in time (e.g. the fact that partners share a great many positive memories) may easily become structural constraints at another point in time (i.e. these shared memories make the cost of termination extremely high).

Investments similarly may mediate relationship stability. In a longitudinal test of the investment model, Rusbult (1983) demonstrated that individuals who had terminated their premarital relationships had evidenced a decrease in satisfaction, commitment, rewards, and investment, and an increase in costs and alternative quality. At first glance, Rusbult's (1983) longitudinal test of the investment model seems to lend strong support to the idea that irretrievable investments mediate relationship stability; however, as there is some conceptual confusion in her measure of investments, these results are equivocal (Johnson, 1985).

A final exchange concept that has been emphasized as a key to relationship stability is that of equity (see earlier definition). Walster, Walster and Traupmann (1978) reported that equitable premarital relationships are more likely to remain intact, whereas inequitable relationships are unstable. However, the manner in which the predictive ability of equity was tested is unclear, as it is difficult to determine whether Walster, Walster and Traupmann (1978) tested actual stability (i.e. continuance versus discontinuance) versus the intent to remain together. Later research, however, has not supported this finding; Berg and McQuinn (1986), Cate, Lloyd and Henton (1986) and Lujansky and Mikula (1983) all found that equity scores at one point in time were not predictive of relationship stability at a later date. Rather, other exchange concepts, such as absolute level of rewards, were significant predictors of relationship continuation/dissolution (Cate, Lloyd and Henton, 1986).

Interpersonal Process Frameworks

The current thrust in the area of mate-selection theorizing and research is to move beyond looking solely at such static factors as similarity, complementarity, rewards, investments, etc., as they covary with increased involvement, commitment, or other relationship outcomes. Current theorizing and research is focusing on the development of 'interpersonal process' frameworks of mate selection (Robins, 1983). The interpersonal process framework acknowledges the importance of factors associated with the compatibility (similarity, etc.) and exchange frameworks (rewards, alternatives, etc.), but posits that the interaction between individuals in relationships to a large extent shapes the development of the relationship and choice of mate (cf. Duck and Sants, 1983). Another important facet of this framework is that it acknowledges that the interpersonal processes within couples are affected by and also affect individual attributes, relationship characteristics, and the social and physical environment (Kelley *et al.*, 1983). In summary, this framework (a) focuses on describing relationships in terms of their interactive and psychological characteristics, (b) assumes these characteristics change over time, and (c) assumes a variety of forces influence relationships.

The focus on interpersonal process in this framework assumes that the interaction of partners determines the pathway the couples take to marriage, and because no two couples' interactions are identical there are multiple trajectories to marriage. Several years ago, Bolton (1961), from a small study of newly married couples, suggested that the development of commitment is influenced by many different factors, thus leading to different pathways to marriage. Currently, only three studies (Cate, Huston and Nesselroade, 1986; Surra, 1985, 1987) have used the interpersonal process framework to guide their studies of the mate-selection process. The Cate, Huston and Nesselroade (1986) study will be described somewhat in depth.

In the first study using this framework, Cate, Huston and Nesselroade (1986) retrospectively examined the evolution of 50 newlyweds' courtships to marriage. The evolution of marriage was charted by each partner independently on a 'chance of marriage' graph beginning with the time the couple met until the marriage day. The partners then filled out questionnaires tapping conflict, relationship maintenance behaviors, ambivalence, and love at casual, serious, and committed levels of involvement. In addition, a questionnaire that tapped various other factors more external to their courtship was filled out (how much they had dated previously, parental objections to marriage, etc.).

The graphic data were structured into a set of three references curves that represented the variation in the paths to marriage, with each partner receiving a score indicating how closely their individual graph resembled one of the reference curves. These scores were then correlated with the measures of conflict, maintenance behaviors, ambivalence, love, and the measures of the external factors.

These analyses showed that scores on path 1, which is a slow, rocky ascent to asymptote, were positively correlated with conflict at all three premarital phases and with ambivalence at seriously dating. Scores on path 1 also were negatively correlated with age at time of meeting the spouse and with perceived parental eagerness for the participant to wed.

Path 2 has a shape that accelerates rapidly to asymptote then drops off somewhat. Scores on this path were negatively correlated with conflict and marginally negatively correlated with maintenance at seriously dating. In contrast to path 1, higher scores on path 2 were associated with older age at time of meeting the spouse and a stronger perception that parents were eager for the respondent to wed.

Path 3 takes an initially slow movement to asymptote with a later progression that falls midway between the remaining paths. The higher the scores on path 3, the less conflict reported at all three premarital phases. Moreover, there was a tendency for path 3 scores to be negatively related to ambivalence at seriously dating. The number of prior dating relationships, serious involvement with others at the time participants met the spouse, and age at time of meeting the spouse also were positively associated with path 3 scores.

Although the Cate, Huston and Nesselroade (1986) study took a descriptive perspective, the results do suggest how various interpersonal processes (conflict, relationship maintenance behaviors), properties of individuals (ambivalence), and extradyadic factors (age at meeting partner, number of previous partners, etc.) all may influence courtships to differ in their progression to marriage. The more similar an individual's graph to path 1, the greater the interpersonal conflict and ambivalence. These factors may partially contribute to the turbulent progression to commitment characteristic of this path. In addition, certain individual attributes, namely being relatively young when meeting the spouse and perceiving parents to be less eager for marriage to occur, may directly retard the development of commitment. An alternative possibility is that individual characteristics indirectly affect commitment through their impact on dyadic interaction; for example, perceiving parents to be against marriage may induce higher levels of interpersonal conflict.

Having a courtship similar to path 2, with a rapid acceleration, is linked to lower levels of conflict and maintenance at seriously dating. These results indicate that, in contrast to courtships like path 1, it is the relative absence of conflict and maintenance that facilitates a smooth, quick progression to marriage. Being older when the courtship began and perceiving parents to be eager for marriage may help set the stage for quickly developing courtships to require little interpersonal negotiation.

Similar to the findings for path 2, having a courtship like path 3 is associated with lower levels of conflict. Yet the shapes of paths 2 and 3 are distinct, such that low levels of conflict are associated with *rapid* progression in the case of path 2 but an *initially delayed* progression for path 3. Moreover, there was less ambivalence about getting involved for partners who had courtships similar to path 3. It may be that other forces interfere with the evolution of courtships represented well by path 3, even under conditions (e.g. low conflict) that ordinarily induce commitment quickly. This interpretation is supported by the results indicating that similarity to path 3 is related to a greater number of prior relationships and serious involvement in an alternative relationship prior to meeting the spouse.

Surra's (1985, 1987) studies further demonstrate the utility of examining courtship from an interpersonal process perspective. In these studies, couples again provided retrospective portrayals of their courtships over time, with these data being used to generate courtship pathways. In contrast to the Cate, Huston and Nesselroade (1986) study, data were gathered concerning the partners' affectional activities with each other, instrumental activities performed alone and with each other, and leisure activities performed alone, with partner, and the social network. Additionally, data were gathered concerning perceived reasons (intrapersonal/normative, dyadic, social network, or circumstantial) for why the turning points in the relationship occurred. Surra (1985, 1987) found similar pathways to the Cate, Huston and Nesselroade (1986) study. Individuals following these pathways did differ in their activities with each other and their networks, as well as in the reasons they gave for changes in commitment over time. For example, Surra found that relationships that accelerate rapidly to marriage show greater interdependence than those which move to marriage at an intermediate rate, as well as the participants reporting more intrapersonal/normative reasons for turning points in the relationship. Additionally, Surra found that in prolonged relationships the participants' interaction with the social network was important in promoting and maintaining commitment, while these participants were more likely than others to give circumstantial reasons for changes in commitment.

A recent study by Leslie, Huston and Johnson (1986) illustrates more specifically how the interpersonal process framework can be used to illuminate the role of the social network in the development of premarital relationships. In this study, respondents were asked about their feelings of closeness to their parents, their involvement with a dating partner, and attempts by parents to influence their thinking about their dating relationships. The respondents were contacted four months later concerning their present level of involvement with the same dating partner. Interestingly, the extent and nature of parents' attempts to influence the respondents concerning their dating partners were not related to changes in level of involvement four months later. However, the results did show that respondents and parents do engage in activity designed to influence each other concerning the dating partner.

The results of the above studies suggest that courtships differ in their progression to marriage. It appears that this differential progression to marriage might be accounted for by: (a) the interpersonal processes that occur between partners, (b) interaction between partners and their networks, (c) intrapsychic factors, and (d) circumstantial or environmental factors.

Dissolution from an Interpersonal Process Perspective

Both the compatibility and the exchange studies previously discussed treat relationship dissolution as a discrete event, around which antecedents and consequences can be discovered. Our knowledge of premarital relationship termination is not complete, however, without an examination of dissolution as process (Duck, 1982b). Process studies of dissolution have described both the ways in which premarital partners 'accomplish their unbonding' and the sequencing of events, emotions, and turning points along the pathway to disengagement (Baxter, 1985).

Duck (1982a) has proposed a conceptual model of the process of relationship dissolution. Stage 1, intrapsychic, involves the internal turmoil caused by individual dissatisfaction with the relationship. Stage 2, dyadic, encompasses mutual negotiation of the breakup with the partner. Stage 3, social, represents the presentation of the breakup to family and friends. Stage 4, grave-dressing, focuses on 'getting over' the breakup and coming to terms with past memories.

The longitudinal study of Hill, Rubin and Peplau (1976) has some process elements to it. These researchers examined relationships early in their formation, and then followed them for two to three years. When breakups occurred, individuals recounted why the dissolution of the relationship had taken place. Interesting descriptions of relationship dissolution abound from this study, including the tendency for women to be initiators more often than men, the differences in reasons given by men and women for the breakup (men were much more external than women in their explanations), and the fact that the couple was reported to have remained friends more often when the male partner had been the least interested party in the relationship. Circumstantial factors played a role as well; breakups were most likely to occur at the time of school breaks.

Baxter (1985) offers a series of studies which describe various aspects of the dissolution process. She draws several conclusions from her work, the most important of which is her contention that dissolution is not merely the reversal of development (Baxter, 1983). Rather, multiple pathways and strategies for disengagement are delineated. Partners may use withdrawal, avoidance, positive tone or open confrontation in their attempts to dissolve their relationships (Baxter, 1982). These strategies do vary as a function of relationship characteristics; for example, direct disengagement strategies (e.g. a state-of-relationship talk) are used more often when the relationship was very intimate and when partners anticipate future interaction (Baxter, 1983).

Work by Lloyd and Cate (1985a, b) further corroborates the assertion (Duck, 1982a; Baxter, 1984) that relationship dissolution is fundamentally different from a reversal of relationship development. Conflict emerges as a key variable in the process of development and decline. Interestingly, conflict and love are not related during developmental stages of the relationship, but they are negatively related during dissolution stages. Maintenance evidences a similar 'flip'; maintenance behaviors (self-disclosure, discussing the good and bad points of the relationship) are positively related to conflict levels during the development of the relationship, yet maintenance and conflict are unrelated during dissolution (Lloyd and Cate, 1985a).

Similarly, when describing reasons for changes in their relationships, individuals give different types of reasons for changes during development of the relationship versus dissolution of the relationship. More dyadic reasons (attributions that are rooted in the interaction of the pair) are given for relationship turning points that occur as the relationship is developing, while more individual (attributions that flow from one partner's belief system) and network (the impact of interaction with others) reasons are offered to explain changes in the relationship during dissolution phases (Lloyd and Cate, 1985b).

One thing these studies of relationship dissolution have in common is a clear retrospective element to their process descriptions. Indeed, three additional studies (Baxter, 1984; Lee, 1984; Lloyd and Cate, 1983) which describe the process and sequencing of relationship dissolution are completely retrospective, reflecting the difficulty of conducting research on low-frequency events which last for variable amounts of time and which are emotionally laden. The use of retrospective data places some limits on the results of these studies, for as Harvey *et al.* (1982) point out, any study of a relationship that has broken up is affected by the fact that the search for meaning and causes continues long after the demise of the relationship. Such ongoing attribution may indeed color the retrospective description of the relationship. Despite the limitations inherent in retrospective data, it is indeed fortunate that three process studies of premarital relationship dissolution have been completed. These three studies assume that interpersonal processes induce differential pathways to dissolution.

Lee (1984) outlined five stages in relationship dissolution based on descriptions of the course of dissolution: discovery of dissatisfaction, exposure of the dissatisfaction to the partner, negotiation of issues, resolution by one or both partners to take action, and transformation of resolution into action. These five stages are fitted together in various patterns to form four breakup 'formats'. Simple format dissolutions contain all five stages, omission formats leave one or more stages out (usually exposure and negotiation), extension formats repeat one or more stages, and mixed formats represent combinations of mixed and extended.

These four types of formats (or trajectories to dissolution) did vary in both pre- and postdissolution characteristics. For example, partners who omitted discussion of dissatisfaction were more likely to have been involved in short, less intense relationships; their breakups were more likely to occur quickly. Individuals who 'scaled down' their relationships (characteristic of mixed and extension formats) felt that the breakup had been more confusing; their relationships had been more intense, cooperative, socioemotional and intimate prior to the dissolution.

Baxter (1984) has constructed a flow chart of disengagement based on a retrospective free-response task. She identified six 'critical features' of the dissolution process—gradual versus sudden onset, unilateral versus bilateral desire to terminate, direct versus indirect termination strategy, short versus long length of negotiation, presence versus absence of attempts to reconcile, and termination versus continuation. While this framework allows a multiplicity of disengagement patterns, a more limited subset of common patterns was noted. Most commonly, relationship dissolutions were unilateral and indirect with no attempts at repair. Other patterns included 'swift, explicit mutuality' and 'mutual ambivalence' (Baxter, 1984).

A third process study of disengagement was conducted by Lloyd and Cate (1983). Using the RIT developed by Huston et al. (1981), the development and dissolution of broken serious relationships was outlined over time. These relationship trajectories were analyzed so as to identify distinct patterns; five relationship types were noted. Accelerated relationships were characterized by rapid development to high levels of involvement, a high perceived chance of marriage, and rapid dissolution. Low-level relationships were quite different from accelerated relationships—low-level relationships developed more gradually, reached only a moderate chance of marriage, and dissolved rapidly. Moderate relationships were highly symmetrical—they rose gradually to a moderately high level of involvement, and dissolved at the same gradual pace.

There were two prolonged types of broken relationships. Prolonged–turbulent relationships were characterized by numerous ups and downs, gradual and prolonged movement to a high chance of marriage, and rapid relationship dissolution. Prolonged–smooth relationships were the slowest to develop and dissolve. These relationships reached a very high level of involvement with few or no downturns; their breakups lasted on average twelve months.

Ultimately, retrospective process studies of premarital relationship dissolution have highlighted common factors—the most important of these being that there is a great deal of variability in relationship dissolution. We have moved well beyond the early conceptualization of dissolution as sudden death versus fading away (cf. Knapp, 1978) to a realization that developmental characteristics set the stage for the key issues of relationship breakdown and dissolution (Duck, 1987b; Graziano and Musser, 1982). Indeed, one of the most important future needs for research on broken relationships is assessment of the process of dissolution in the context of relationship development (Lee, 1984; Lloyd and Cate, 1985a).

Future Directions for Research

It is the opinion of the present authors that the interpersonal process framework will most fruitfully guide future research endeavors in the area of courtship and premarital relationships. The framework acknowledges the complexity of these relationships, but more clearly delineates the multiple levels of causality that must be accounted for in order to better understand the development and dissolution of courtships. However, the acknowledged complexity of courtship from this perspective requires that several areas be addressed in future research.

According to proponents of the interpersonal process framework, the basic data of interaction are patterns of events (Kelley et al., 1983), which become the basis for the subjective and relatively stable feelings, attributions and meanings attached to the partner and the relationship. Thus, rather than simply studying partners' feelings towards one another (e.g. love, satisfaction), the emphasis has shifted towards the study of behavioral interactions (events) that lead to the development of love and commitment, as well as the ways in which feelings of love in turn affect relationship interaction. It is evident from this chapter that event-level data are scarce in the study of courtship. Although some laboratory observation studies have been performed (Markman, 1979, 1981), little has been done to examine events occurring in the natural setting. Several innovative data collection techniques are now being developed to examine events in courtship. Such techniques include diary methods to track ongoing interaction and episodes of conflict (Baxter, 1985; Lloyd, unpublished; Milardo, Johnson and Huston, 1983) and the use of telephone interviews to record the occurrence of specific positive and negative behaviors in marriage (Atkinson and Huston, 1984). These techniques also allow for tracking of day-to-day interaction, rather than sampling a single point in time which may not adequately represent the character of the partners' interaction.

The multiple levels of causation posited by the interpersonal process framework require that researchers make explicit decisions concerning the manner in which relationships are measured. One problematic issue concerns the measurement of dyadic or relationship properties (Thompson and Walker, 1982). For example, a measurement device that assesses the extent to which one premarital partner communicates negative feelings to the other is not a measure of conflict, a relationship property. Such a measure is an assessment of an individual property. In order to tap a relationship property, the researcher must examine the pattern between partners on some variable, although the informant may be one partner, both partners, or an outside observer (Thompson and Walker, 1982). In other words, to assess the level of conflict in a relationship, the researcher would need to know the degree to which the partner reacted behaviorally to the expression of negative feelings by the other partner.

Those adhering to the interpersonal process framework are also concerned with the linkages between various levels of relationships (Kelley *et al.*, 1983). Many previous studies, such as those testing compatibility models, have assumed that various attributes, attitudes, attributions, perceptions, and other individual-level variables affect event-level interaction in courtships. However, the manner in which these variables influence interaction between partners is largely unspecified (Duck, 1987b). For example, a researcher might examine differences in relationship satisfaction between blacks and whites, but never look at what interactional differences exist between couples of different races that might lead to varying levels of satisfaction. Complicating the examination of linkages between causal levels is the acknowledgement by the interpersonal process framework that the influence between levels is likely reciprocal in many cases. Present statistical techniques are not well suited to handling this problem of reciprocal causality. However, Huston and Robins (1982) have noted that technological advances in unobtrusive video and audio recording may allow research participants to provide researchers with *post hoc* analyses of the causal direction between their behaviors and subjective experiences in particular interaction sequences.

From the interpersonal process perspective, there is a need to move towards examination of the broader context within which development and dissolution take place (for an example, see Leslie, Huston and Johnson, 1986). Indeed, Surra (1987) emphasizes that changes in relationship involvement are affected by much more than dyadic interaction alone; circumstantial happenings, network influences, and other external events all affect relationships as they develop and dissolve. Indeed, according to Johnson (1982), relationships are so embedded in a larger context that 'even the seemingly most individual and psychological aspects of relationship(s) . . . are supremely social in character' (p. 73).

A final area for future research from an interpersonal process perspective is that of individual factors which affect development and dissolution. Huston and Levinger (1978) observed that researchers know little about how individual factors influence interpersonal relationships. Specifically, past research has shown that standard personality measures are not very useful in understanding behavior (Huston and Levinger, 1978). More recently, it has been demonstrated that some individual factors such as predispositions and standards for a partner or a relationship are related to the differential development of premarital relationships (Surra, 1987). These findings suggest that if individual factors are to be expected to explain interpersonal behavior, it is necessary to examine factors that are more logically connected to specific behaviors occurring between people.

In summary, there is much to be learned about courtship development and dissolution. Recent trends that acknowledge the complexity of the process should lead to the involvement of many disciplines (social psychology, clinical psychology, developmental psychology, sociology, family science, communications, etc.) in furthering knowledge in this important area.

ACKNOWLEDGEMENTS

The authors would like to express their appreciation to Dr Catherine Surra for her helpful comments on an earlier draft of this chapter and to Dr Ted Huston for stimulating many of the ideas presented.

Handbook of Personal Relationships
Edited by S. W. Duck
© 1988 John Wiley & Sons Ltd

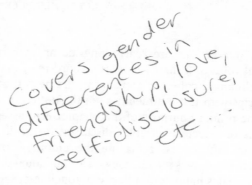

Covers gender
differences in
friendship, love,
self-disclosure,
etc ...

23

Roles and Gender in Relationships

CLYDE HENDRICK
Texas Tech University, Lubbock, Texas, USA

ABSTRACT

This chapter considers gender differences within relationships. A conceptual analysis suggests that relationships are best viewed as interactional processes within role structures. Gender differences on several variables are reviewed, including love, sexual attitudes, self-disclosure, jealousy, loneliness, friendship, power strategies, mate selection, social support, and shyness. A small number of prototype variables are hypothesized to underlie many gender differences.

The study of roles and gender in relationships is a complex enterprise because it involves different levels of analysis across different academic disciplines, posing formidable difficulties in understanding and integrating disparate concepts into a coherent pattern. Restricting the focus primarily to gender roles within heterosexual relationships hardly relieves the difficulty. One might assume that the 'basic fact' of biological sex and resulting differences would provide a secure conceptual foundation. Such is not the case: indeed, the importance of biological sex in explaining heterosexual relationships has been hotly debated (see e.g. Fausto-Sterling, 1985). Concepts such as sex roles (or more recently, gender roles), only loosely linked to biological sex, are claimed by many to be more important than biological sex in explaining gender relationships and gender differences. The notion of gender role is complex in itself, but doubly so when one realizes that role has meaning only within the context of another complex concept, that of a human *relationship*. Thus, within one brief paragraph one may move from concrete male and female persons with their differing anatomies to the abstract conception of complementary gender roles defined within an even more abstract notion of a relationship. The existence of an extreme psychological approach to relationships (only persons and their interactions are real) alongside an extreme sociological approach (only social roles and their relationships are real) makes apparent the difficulties in developing a coherent explanatory framework; yet this chapter seeks to come to grips with those difficulties via the notion of roles in relationships.

The primary purpose of this chapter is to assess heterosexual relationships in terms of selected variables discussed in the literature. The main focus is on gender differences, reflecting the emphasis of the literature. Some of the selected variables may be viewed as individual difference factors on which males and females happen to differ (e.g. loneliness, self-disclosure, shyness), and such differences may in turn affect diverse aspects of male–female relationships. Other variables pertain directly to male–female relationships (e.g. love attitudes, sexual attitudes, jealousy), possibly leading to patterned behavior differences within a relationship.

In order to make some sense of gender differences in the various relationship variables, it seems necessary to grapple first with the concept of *relationship*. A successful outcome requires that one understand that the meaning of *relationship* varies widely, and that the roots of this variation might be pursued right down to the bedrock of one's philosophy of science and construal of the nature of reality.

Two broad metaphilosophical approaches to social/behavioral science are currently emerging as competitors for the 'proper' construal of reality. Social constructionism (Gergen, 1985), a movement based on diverse areas such as symbolic interaction, ethnomethodology, phenomenology, existentialism, etc., construes reality as based on the active structuring and creation of the world by persons. Realism (Bhaskar, 1978; Manicas and Secord, 1983), the traditional approach to science, construes the world as existing apart from persons and having an objective reality ascertainable by objective methods. On the former view, reality is constructed; on the latter, reality is discovered.

These differing philosophies suggest different theoretical approaches to gender. Social constructionism implies that gender attributes and differences are as changeable as the shifting circumstances of culture and history. On this view, even the 'basic' category of sexuality emerges from discourse (Foucault, 1980; Tiefer, 1987) and not from biology. Sexuality is not a need or biological urge to be shaped or repressed, but only a potential for consciousness and physical experience shaped into cultural 'scripts' (Gagnon, 1977) by the realms of discourse in a particular society at a particular time. Indeed, some have urged that there are no intrinsic biological reasons for only two genders; three or more are viable if a culture defines it as so (e.g. Kessler and McKenna, 1978).

In contrast, realism proposes different accounts of gender. Sociobiology, as one example, suggests that gender differences are partially rooted in the differing morphology and sexual functions of males and females, which are based in turn on slightly differing evolutionary tasks of the two sexes. Sex difference is the rule among mammals (Kenrick, 1987), and many such differences seem to follow from a concept of inherent sex differences in parental investment. Females can produce few offspring relative to males. From such a structural difference may follow females' presumed greater selectivity in choosing a mate and males' presumed greater interest in diversity of sexual experience (Hinde, 1984).

The contrasts of realism and constructionism suggest very different approaches to the meaning of biological sex and gender. One should expect that consideration of gender roles within relationships will be no less complex.

GENDER AND RELATIONSHIPS

At least four different approaches to gender and relationships can be identified. A traditional psychological approach views gender and related gender differences in relationships as caused by traits within persons. Masculinity and femininity have served as basic explanatory categories for such a trait approach. In contrast, a traditional sociological approach views relationships as social structures and gender differences as governed by role expectations that differ for males and females. This static structural approach may be contrasted with a third viewpoint that construes relationships as social processes. I will suggest a fourth approach that combines the previous two approaches, construing relationships as processes occurring within social structures. Each approach is considered briefly.

Relationships as Expressions of Traits

When psychology developed as a science at the end of the nineteenth century, there was hope that it would develop a comprehensive, objective knowledge of the two sexes and explain the 'obvious' psychological differences between them. However, the obvious proved to be elusive. The presumed sex differences either did not occur, or were trivial in magnitude or inconsistent from study to study (Morawski, 1987). By the 1920s this early research tradition faltered.

Because this early research was based on a philosophy of realism and because everyday life suggested many sex differences, the conclusion of 'no difference' was not drawn by researchers. Instead, research design was faulted and sex differences were presumed to have a 'deep structure' beyond the reach of typical laboratory experiments (Morawski, 1987). Based on such assumptions, Terman and Miles (1936) developed their famous measure of masculinity (M) and femininity (F) that set a research tradition for the next 40 years. Many other scales were developed during this period, but all shared a common set of assumptions: MF was a bipolar dimension, reflected a deep-seated and pervasive aspect of one's inner nature (i.e. a trait), and determined many differences between the sexes. These assumptions reinforced cultural stereotypes about males and females and the scientific ideology that gender was a real, substantive entity (Morawski, 1985).

These assumptions persisted until Constantinople (1973) suggested that MF is neither bipolar nor a single dimension. Constantinople's paper appeared concurrently with the upsurge in modern feminist thinking and protest, and political aspects of previous MF research soon became apparent. Within the previous MF research tradition, 'masculine' had been associated with dominance and power and, because M and F were deemed, in that tradition, to be mutually exclusive, 'feminine' had been associated, conversely, with dependency and powerlessness. Constantinople alerted us to the fact that the time was ripe for a new conception that addressed the inequities of the old social order. The concept of 'androgyny' emerged as the new hero/heroine to address the task.

Bem (1974), among others (e.g. Spence and Helmreich, 1978), proposed the notion of an androgynous individual, one who combines both M and F. On this view, and the scales were designed accordingly, M and F are independent, not bipolar. As was true of earlier scales, M presumably measures instrumental, agentic behavior and F measures expressive, communal behavior. Being high on both (i.e. androgynous) was viewed as a desirable human condition. One implication of this approach was that, psychologically, M and F were detached from their biological base. Presumably, cultural conditioning, and not biological sex, determined the mix of M and F that one possessed, as reflected in psychological measurement. Therefore gender differences, if considered undesirable, could be eliminated by altering the cultural conditioning.

The vast industry spawned by the notion of androgyny is beyond the scope of this chapter. Many conceptual problems have been discussed, and it is now clear that the concept of androgyny will not solve social problems, or even stimulate new theoretical advances. Basically the concept was an attempt to transform a fixed personality trait (M or F) into a more flexible set of behavioral categories. If 'M and F' could be combined in ways that 'M or F' cannot, quite possibly gender differences could be changed drastically through socialization. This agenda is still person-centered, and relatively ignores social structure.

Relationships as Social Structures

In shifting the focus of attention from personality traits to the notion of relationship, we soon note that it is caught between the philosophical pulls of realism and constructionism. A relationship is not a material entity and is therefore in some sense abstract (Hendrick and Hendrick, 1983). The abstract notion is made empirical by defining a specific relationship operationally as 'patterned interaction'. However, as Duck and Perlman (1985) correctly noted, defining a relationship in terms of interaction alone is impoverished. The issue is to account for the manner in which relationships are created from 'strings of interactions' and from the cognitions individuals have about their interactions.

Role is the primary concept for a structural approach to relationships. 'A role is a socially defined set of expectations with rules for permissible and obligatory behavior that govern the relationship' (Hendrick and Hendrick, 1983, p. 18). Roles often come in complementary pairs, such as teacher–student, counselor–client, husband–wife, or in non-complementary sets, such as friends or acquaintances. Common roles are reasonably well understood by people socialized in a particular society. Roles provide behavioral niches by which people organize their behaviors, including overt interaction patterns as well as beliefs and emotions related to their roles. Roles may be tightly or loosely prescribed.

Clerk–customer, for example, is circumscribed closely. The joint interactions of clerk and customer can usually 'run off' without much cognitive/affective involvement by either party. Such roles do not require much knowledge of the other person. Therefore they are considered nonintimate. Other role pairings are broader in scope, encompassing a wide range of one's life. Lovers, friends, and husband–wife are typical examples. Such roles do require substantial knowledge of and affective involvement with the other person, and therefore tend to be intimate in nature, carrying both psychological and physical closeness as part of their definitions. However, even though uniqueness of knowledge of the other person is important and people often believe that their own relationship is a free meshing of partners, there remains a general role framework within which they must operate. Argyle and Henderson (1985), for instance, gathered substantial cross-cultural data showing that relationships follow rules, in a manner analogous to the rules of a game. Rules serve as a guide to behavior. When a rule is broken, a game stops. A relationship tends to stop also, and must be 'repaired'. Although they found some cultural variation, Argyle and Henderson identified several 'universal rules'. As one might expect, such rules are commonly known—make eye contact, respect privacy, keep confidences, be faithful, repay obligations, avoid public criticism. Despite the feeling of freedom from such rules, personal relations are obviously bound by them. Thus, intimate relations do not escape the net of rule governance shared by more formal role relationships.

The role approach tends to be encompassing, locking role partners into relatively fixed behavior patterns based on socially derived role expectations, and operating by means of rules and norms. Following this approach, gender role differences are based on different societal expectations for the two sexes, differing expectations as to proper apparel, interests, sexual interactions, and the like. The role approach has little to say about the original causes of expectations or why they might differ between the sexes, nor can the role concept easily account for social change. It tends to be static in approach, ignoring the flow of time.

Relationships as Social Processes

As a parody on Wittgenstein (1958), one might ask whether a meaningful relationship is possible in one second. To phrase the question is to reveal the time-dependent nature of relationships. To begin to construe relationships as flowing in time is to conceive of them as processes rather than as fixed structures. The process conception of relationships has been developed cogently by Duck and Sants (1983). In their view, relationships are composed of continuously interacting components, evolving as events in time, and changing even while threads of continuity endure. Duck and Sants clarify the process aspects of relations through four delightful metaphors, described as unwanted conceptual heirlooms.

1. *Relationships as the chemistry of partner attributes.* Similarity of attributes

does not create a relationship; only active social processes do—fighting, communicating, disclosing, jointly behaving, and the like.

2. *Relationships as undigested interactions.* The raw fact of interaction does not define a relationship. People define it, both inside and outside of ongoing interaction, with cognition and desire, appeals to third parties, etc. A relationship is more than a sum of interactions.

3. *Relationships as pots of gold at the rainbow's end.* There is no fixed object that is the relationship. There are as many perspectives as there are perceivers. The primary 'insiders' may differ from each other in their perspectives, as well as from all 'outsider' perspectives. As the relationship endures through time, it may be reconstructed differently at each different temporal vantage point.

4. *Relationship participants as air traffic controllers.* It is a fallacy to assume that people are perfectly definite in their awareness of a relationship and their expectations for it. More often, people do not know what they are doing, are uncertain of where they stand in the relationship, and may even be uncertain of their own feelings.

These four metaphors clearly suggest our tendencies towards reification of the concept of a relationship. As Duck and Sants (1983) make clear, the debunking of these objectifications makes transparent the nature of a relationship as a transient, intangible, fluid process in time.

When the notion of relationship is viewed as a structure, it is difficult at best to also view relationship as a process. Upon reflection, however, it is clear that both approaches, suitably melded, are necessary for full understanding of the subtle, complex concept of relationship. Thus relationship as reified static structure is alien to the flow of daily life as we know it. Process without social content is also in danger of reification. The process of a relationship must flow within a broader context, and that context may be viewed as a social structure of which the relationship is a part.

Relationships as Processes Within Structures

What is needed is a conception of social structure that is compatible with notions of process. Such an approach was provided by Manicas (1980). In Manicas' theory social structures are constituted by the actions of persons and exist solely in virtue of those constitutive activities. Social structures do not exist independently of people's conceptions of what they are doing; however, it does not follow that people must therefore understand what the social structures are. Social structures are real because they have real effects, such as constraining, limiting and enabling actions.

One critical consideration is that we inherit a host of social structures because we are born into an ongoing social order. Therefore we do not *create* social structures; we *reproduce* and *transform* them by our actions. This notion of reproduction and transformation, rather than creation, has been called 'structuration' (Giddens, 1976), and it captures well both the quality of social structures as enduring patterns and the process of human action impacting and transforming those structures.

Given this conception, it is relatively easy to view a relationship as a set of processes within a social structure. As children are socialized into a social order, their observation and active learning of ongoing social forms—of role relationships—provide guides to their understanding of how many different kinds of social relating are done. Vast arrays of norms, rules, and associated sentiments are learned. But 'learning about' and 'living through' a relationship are two very different things. The rules and norms must be applied in the process of relating, and in that process the rules and norms will be adapted, reproduced, and transformed, sometimes slightly, sometimes greatly. The living through of the transformations grants to actors a measure of agency. They are neither role puppets nor revolutionaries of a new social order, but rather persons—coping, changing and reconstruing their relationships. Because of the transformative process, each relationship develops its own unique history while at the same time remaining statistically comparable to other relationships on selected structural features.

This joint approach to structure and process makes social change more readily understandable. Because each relationship reproduces and transforms the rules and norms that govern it, change is always possible. When some relationship feature becomes a bone of contention (e.g. husbands are the head of the family) across a great many relationships, the relevant rules may be transformed into a new set of rules (e.g. husbands and wives are coequals). In time, the relevant social structure will have changed by virtue of the fact that people now define that particular relationship differently than was the case in previous generations.

Gender Roles and Relationships

The approach to relationships as processes within structures provides one means for construing gender roles, particularly changes in gender role conceptions. It seems clear that masculinity and femininity (or their hybrid, androgyny), as trait attributes of persons, cannot account for differences in gender roles, especially for historical changes in gender roles. As Duck and Sants (1983) might caution, gender roles are not fixed entities. For example, Deaux (1985) pointed out that over the last 20 years, females have made significant gains in mathematical, spatial, and verbal abilities, relative to males. Such changes suggest that one cannot assume immutable sex differences, even in supposed basic cognitive abilities.

It is clear that gender differences for relationship variables do currently exist, and that for several variables such differences may possibly be in transition. The concept of a relationship as process within structure is an attempt to provide an ideologically neutral framework for the analysis of gender roles. Gender differences, as they exist, are neutrally accepted. Changes in gender role, in whatever directions, are equally permissible. This general conception does not, however, provide specific causal accounts for gender differences. Specific theories oriented to the relevant domain are required.

An example will prove useful. One result of the feminist movement is pressure towards equality of males and females, in employment, payment for services, value as persons, etc. Previous social differences, now called discrimination, may have seemed perfectly 'natural' to previous generations of both men and women. The movement towards equality is thus ideological, reflecting strong value shifts of many women and men. One may ask why such value shifts occurred. Different theoretical analyses, using varying historical perspectives, may be proposed. For example, a psychologist might propose that access to modern media sensitized women to their social inequality and activated their desire to be included, along with men, under a norm of reciprocity. One result might be the development of equity in relationships in most areas of social life. This psychological approach would thus provide one answer for some of the recent changes in gender roles (e.g. fathers sharing in child care).

A different kind of conceptual question may be posed. Why were women generally treated as unequal to men in the first place? Equity theory cannot answer this question. Some other specific approach, such as sociobiology, might suggest that male dominance is based on our evolutionary heritage. Perhaps men initially held power over women simply because they were bigger and coerced obedience. Such power differences then reproduced themselves 'naturally' and with moral justification when humans evolved to the point of creating social orders.

The conclusion is that specific sociological, linguistic, or psychological hypotheses are necessary to account for specific gender differences and changes in gender roles. However, such hypotheses will be most productive within the generic framework of gender relationships as ongoing processes within social structures. With this approach in mind, gender differences in specific relationship variables are considered.

GENDER DIFFERENCES IN RELATIONSHIP VARIABLES

Males and females may differ on a host of variables relevant to heterosexual relationships. Such variables include conceptions of love, role norms about courtship, patterns of friendship, sexual attitudes and behavior, self-disclosure and communication styles, loneliness, general interaction strategies, approaches to conflict resolution, jealousy, styles of relationship formation, and many others. Several reviews of selected portions of the literature are available (e.g. Ashmore and Del Boca, 1986; Brehm, 1985; Dion and Dion, 1985; Eagly, 1987; Peplau and Gordon, 1985). An entire volume would be required to discuss all of the variables in detail. This review is restricted to love, selected aspects of sexuality, self-disclosure, jealousy, loneliness, and selected aspects of heterosexual interactions.

Gender Differences in Love

One must distinguish love as a set of emotions and attitudes held for one or more other persons from generic conceptions about love widely shared in a society. The latter constitutes an ideology about the nature of love. In Western societies, the prevailing ideology has been dubbed 'romanticism', and it was researched relatively early, primarily by sociologists.

Romanticism

This ideology contains two major components, 'love conquers all' and 'one should marry for love' (Brehm, 1985, p. 99). One cultural myth holds that men are more practical and unsentimental about love than women, possibly because of the association of instrumentality with males and expressivity with females. However, several investigators constructed scales to measure romanticism and generally found the opposite of the myth to be closer to the truth. With few exceptions (e.g. Cunningham and Antill, 1981), males subscribe to the romantic ideology more than females (e.g. Fengler, 1974; Hobart, 1958; Knox and Sporakowski, 1968; Rubin, 1973; Spaulding, 1970). This effect is most pronounced in young males of high school and college age. In fact, romanticism tends to decrease with age, although it may increase again later in marriage (Knox, 1970) or after children have left home (Munro and Adams, 1978), suggesting a curvilinear relation between romanticism and age (Brehm, 1985). Some of the data even suggest that only in youth are males more romantic; in later life females may surpass males in romanticism.

The most common explanation for romanticism stresses a type of functionalism (Buehler and Wells, 1981). Gender differences might be explained in terms of the need for females to pick mates more carefully because they are at the same time choosing a 'provider and protector'. Therefore young females should be less susceptible to the romantic ideology. However, in later married life, romanticism might help protect them against the dependency and boredom often associated with the housewife role. Whatever the causes of romantic ideology, its importance diminishes when one considers the complexities of love in actual relationships.

Theories of love

There are a great many theories about love and its relevance to heterosexual relationships. One classic approach views love as an exchange of rewards and costs, analogous to other types of exchange in social life (Blau, 1964). Love has been identified with passion (Berscheid and Walster, 1974), pragmatic commitment (Kelley, 1983), a general 'factor' consistent across several types of close relationships (Sternberg and Grajek, 1984), and limerence (Tennov, 1979), an obsessive preoccupation with the loved one. Polarities have been popular: liking versus loving (Rubin, 1970), exchange versus communal love relations (Clark and Mills, 1979), romantic versus conjugal love (Munro and Adams, 1978), and companionate versus passionate love (Walster and Walster, 1978).

The ferment of theorizing eventually led to more complex constructions. Dion and Dion (1973) proposed five concepts (or styles) of love, named volatile, circumspect, rational, passionate, and impetuous. Lee (1973) proposed a circumplex model analogous to the color wheel. This model contains three primary love styles: eros (romantic, passionate love), ludus (manipulative, game-playing love), and storge (friendship love). Three secondary styles occur by compounding primaries: mania (possessive, dependent love), pragma (logical, computer-mating love), and agape (selfless love). Each of the six love styles logically relates to the others, but each style is also qualitatively independent. In Lee's view, these styles are different but equally valid ways of loving that different people have chosen.

Lee's theory is one of the most sophisticated statements on love to date. One of its advantages is that most of the single-factor or bipolar theories can be translated into one or more of Lee's love styles. Another advantage is that the theory suggests a powerful multidimensional approach to the measurement of love. Lasswell and Lasswell (1976) developed a 50-item true–false scale to measure the six love styles (see also Hatkoff and Lasswell, 1979; Rosenman, 1978). The Lasswells' scale was reformulated in Likert format, and in a substantial research program relatively pure measures of the six love styles emerged (Hendrick and Hendrick, 1986a; Hendrick et al., 1984). A more complete description of details of the scale's construction and validation may be found in Harvey, Hendrick and Tucker (this volume).

Gender differences

Few studies have found gender differences on Rubin's (1970) love scale, although several have found that females like their partners more than their partners like them (Brehm, 1985). Dion and Dion (1973), using bipolar adjectives as a rating form, found that college women were less idealistic and more pragmatic than men about love. Within the Lee (1973) tradition, Hatkoff and Lasswell (1979) found that men were more ludic and erotic, and women were slightly more manic, storgic, and pragmatic. Hendrick et al. (1984) found strong sex differences. Males differed from females on 29 of 54 individual items. Males were more erotic and ludic, and females were more storgic, pragmatic, and manic. The same pattern of results was replicated in two large studies (Hendrick and Hendrick, 1986a), except for eros.

Love lived out within a relationship shows gender differences consistent with results from the individual rating instruments. The Boston Couples Study (e.g. Hill, Rubin and Peplau, 1976; Rubin, Peplau and Hill, 1981) found that men fell in love more easily than women (eros), who were more cautious about entering relationships (pragma). Once involved in a love relationship, men were less likely than women to break it off, and it was easier for women to remain friends after the breakup (storge). The consistency with which women report higher mania may be true only early in the relationship, when they are more uncertain of where they stand and are more dependent on the etiquette of male initiative for dates. The greater ludic qualities that males manifest may occur mostly prior to entering committed relationships. A strong tendency to play the field increases the probability that a suitable relationship will eventually be found.

The data on gender differences are relatively consistent across a variety of studies. Young males appear more romantic, seek greater partner variety, and fall in love more readily. Females show a streak of pragmatism and are more oriented to friendship aspects of the relationship. Females also report more 'physical symptoms' of love; however, this tendency may reflect a more general pattern of greater female willingness to report physical symptoms (Mechanic, 1978).

Gender Differences in Sexual Expression

A tremendous literature on sexuality has developed since Kinsey's early work (Kinsey, Pomeroy and Martin, 1948). Much of the research is concerned with premarital intercourse and the concept of sexual permissiveness (Reiss, 1964, 1967). Traditionally, it has been assumed that women were more conservative in sexual attitudes and behavior than men, an assumption backed by data (Jurich and Jurich, 1974; Luckey and Nass, 1969; Mercer and Kohn, 1979). However, somewhere along the way a sexual revolution presumably occurred (Hendrick and Hendrick, 1983). A large number of studies suggest that Western societies have shifted in a more permissive direction (Hunt, 1974) and that women have shifted faster than men (Bell and Chaskes, 1970; Curran, 1975), leading towards a convergence of male and female sexual standards (DeLamater and MacCorquodale, 1979; King, Balswick and Robinson, 1977; Mahoney, 1978; Perlman, 1974; Walsh, Ferrell and Tolone, 1976). Some even proclaimed that the double standard was dead, or nearly so (e.g. Curran, 1975).

The situation is complicated, as most types of social change usually are. Peplau, Rubin and Hill (1977) found that the majority of their Boston couples engaged in intercourse. However, males were the initiators, but females controlled the onset and timing of intercourse. In addition, females were less favorable than males towards casual sex. Other studies indicate that women continue to remain more conservative (e.g. Medora and Woodward, 1982). Still other work, using panel analyses over a decade (Ferrell, Tolone and Walsh, 1977), suggests support for a single *attitudinal* standard of sexual permissiveness but with suspicion that the double standard endures for sexual *behavior*.

An additional complication, described by Robinson and Jedlicka (1982), is that the old double standard might be endangered by a new double standard wherein both males and females impose stricter standards on the other sex than on their own. A tendency was also noted for both males and females to endorse more conservative sexual attitudes than had been reported in previous studies. This hint of a conservative regress in sexual attitudes is congruent with Helmreich, Spence and Gibson's (1982) report that male sex-role attitudes recently stabilized while female sex-role attitudes have actually shown a slight conservative shift.

The confusion in the literature stimulated a recent research program on sexual attitudes (Hendrick and Hendrick, 1987a; Hendrick et al., 1985). We generated over 100 Likert rating items, with the intention of covering a wide range of sexual attitude topics, including permissiveness. One objective of the work was to assess gender differences in attitudes. In the initial effort (Hendrick *et al.*, 1985), males differed from females on 73 of 102 items, including all 29 of the permissiveness items. In every case, males were more permissive. Females, more than males, endorsed items pertaining to responsible sexual practices, conventional behavior, and communion (sex as the merging of two souls, etc.). Males, however, were more instrumental (sex is a bodily function, like eating).

Final revisions of the scale (Hendrick and Hendrick, 1987a) retained four subscales: permissiveness, sexual practices, communion, and instrumentality. Gender differences were reported for two large samples. For both samples, males were more permissive and instrumental in attitude. Females endorsed communion and sexual practices more in one study but not in the second study. One research question was the relation, if any, between love and sexual attitudes. A factor analysis of scores for the six love scales and the four sex scales yielded interesting results. Sexual permissiveness and instrumentality loaded on the same factor with ludus (game-playing) and negatively with agape (selfless love). On a second factor sex practices and communion loaded with eros, mania and agape.

These results suggest that attitudes about love and sex are rather closely linked. The results of our research program also suggest that gender differences in sex attitudes are even more pervasive than the differences found for love attitudes. Males are consistently more permissive and instrumental in their sexual attitudes. The sexes have not converged in this aspect of relationships. Of course, it is possible that males and females were even more disparate a generation ago.

Gender Differences in Self-Disclosure

Gender differences occur on a variety of communication dimensions (Brehm, 1985). One facet of communication, self-disclosure, has received extensive study. Based on Jourard's (e.g. 1971) concept that some degree of intimate self-disclosure is necessary for human relatedness and mental health, many studies have explored aspects of self-disclosure as it pertains to relationship formation and satisfaction. Until recently, this literature unreflectingly followed Jourard's assumption that self-disclosure is good. Recent commentators (e.g. Gilbert, 1976) have noted a possible conflict between needs for security and privacy and a need for intimacy. Self-disclosure may foster intimacy and threaten security. If so, self-disclosure should be related to other aspects of relationships, such as relative power, conflict potential, stage of the relationship, and the like. Therefore complex results for self-disclosure might be expected, depending upon the particulars of a research project. The literature is not disappointing in this regard. Complexity abounds.

When the sexes are compared, most reports have indicated that females are more self-disclosing than males (e.g. Chelune, 1977; Cozby, 1973; DeForest and Stone, 1980; Stokes, Fuehrer and Childs, 1980), although a few studies (e.g. Komarovsky, 1974) did not find a sex difference.

This general gender effect is qualified in several ways. Females tend to disclose more personal feelings, such as feelings about parents, friends, etc., but males tend to disclose more about political views, things liked about the partner, etc. (Rubin et al., 1980). Spouses differ in the areas in which they do not disclose. For example, one study (Burke, Weir and Harrison, 1976) found that wives did not want to bother their husbands regarding home problems and husbands wanted to keep work and home affairs separate.

Males appear to disclose less than females in same-sex encounters, but not necessarily in cross-sex interactions (Derlega et al., 1985; Reis, Senchak and Solomon, 1985). Indeed, under high intimacy conditions, males may be more emotionally invested in their disclosure than females if they expect future interaction (Shaffer and Ogden, 1986). Males can disclose readily in a prospective romantic encounter with females. However, females rate themselves as better at eliciting disclosure from others (Miller, Berg and Archer, 1983).

Much self-disclosure research studying pairs of strangers suggests that strangers follow a reciprocity principle of disclosures with level of disclosure approximately matched. Some (e.g. Komarovsky, 1967) have found such reciprocity among long-standing relationships (e.g. spouses), but others (e.g. Morton, 1978) have found that spouses were less reciprocal in disclosure than strangers.

It is clear that self-disclosure correlates positively with relationship satisfaction. Hendrick (1981) found such a positive relationship; further, the relation held between each spouse's level of self-disclosure and the other's marital satisfaction, as well as for couples as units. However, level of self-disclosure was negatively related to length of marriage. Several other studies have also found a positive relation between communication effectiveness/self-disclosure and satisfaction with the relationship (Bienvenu, 1970; Burke, Weir and Harrison, 1976; Miller, Corrales and Wackman, 1975; Navran, 1967). It is not clear that males and females differ in the linkage between self-disclosure and satisfaction. In one interesting study of taboo topics, Baxter and Wilmot (1985) found that nearly all relationships involved at least one taboo topic (most frequently, metacommunication about the relationship); however, males and females did not generally differ in frequency or type of taboo topic named.

Self-disclosure has been recently linked to romantic attitudes. Adams and Shea (1981) suggested one possible sex difference. Using a cross-lagged panel investigation, they suggested that for females romantic affect precedes self-disclosure, but for males self-disclosure precedes romantic affect. However, Hendrick and Hendrick (1987b), using Miller, Berg and Archer's (1983) scales, found similar patterns of correlations for males and females between self-disclosure and Lee's (1973) love styles.

It is clear that some gender differences in self-disclosure exist. However, defining the boundaries and meaning of such differences is not yet possible. In general, the literature has focused on verbal communication. Research on nonverbal communication should be pursued (cf. Patterson's chapter, this volume).

Gender Differences in Jealousy

The green-eyed monster has a long history, but a short research life. Solid research data accumulated only during the past decade. Clanton and Smith (1977) summarized past research, mostly clinical studies. That work suggested that jealous males are more likely than jealous females to deny feelings of jealousy, to exhibit rage and violence, to focus more on sexual activity of the partner as opposed to emotional involvement, to externalize the cause of their jealousy, and to display competitive behavior towards a rival.

Everyone knows what jealousy means! Therefore it is very difficult to define it precisely for scientific purposes. Jealousy may perhaps best be considered as a complex, aversive reaction due to a partner's real or imagined extradyadic relationship (Bringle and Buunk, 1985). Jealousy appears to be universal, although it is modulated by cultural variation (Hupka, 1981). Sexual exclusivity or its lack may be a critical variable (Brehm, 1985). Even in marriages that are explicitly open, jealousy commonly occurs (Buunk, 1981), with women in such marriages experiencing jealousy somewhat more frequently than men.

White (1981) proposed that romantic jealousy is based on two kinds of losses, loss of relationship rewards and loss of self-esteem, and support has been provided for the theory (Mathes, Adams and Davies, 1985). White also found a sex difference in type of jealousy response. Female jealousy depended relatively more upon availability of alternative male relationships, but male jealousy depended more on his dependency on the partner for self-esteem fulfilment. In general, females seem more interested than males in preserving a relationship. One consequence is that females may attempt to induce partner jealousy more than males (White, 1980) to bolster a male's flagging interest in the relationship. Buunk's (1981) finding of more frequent jealousy by wives in open marriages may have been due to the possibility that they perceived more threat to the marital relationship. Because males tend to focus more on sexual threats and females more on other relationship threats, wives in open marriages should experience jealousy more frequently.

In a provocative analysis of sexuality, Reiss (1986) firmly connected sexuality to marital jealousy and gender role power. Jealousy serves as a boundary maintenance mechanism, and in one form or another is universal, according to Reiss. On this view, jealousy is a form of territorial behavior. Those with the most territory (or social power) should react most violently to its threatened loss. Because males tend to be dominant in most societies, they should react more aggressively as a response to jealous emotions, whereas females should react more self-punitively, such as by feeling depressed. Because sexuality is highly valued, it will tend to be acquired and 'hoarded'. The more powerful male should, therefore, have a stronger tendency towards sexual jealousy than females, but jealousy towards sexuality as property rather than about relationships *per se*. Interestingly, however, this orientation towards hoarding sexual property may result in more permissive male attitudes, results found previously (e.g. Hendrick and Hendrick, 1987a). One interesting hypothesis is that permissive, instrumental attitudes are functional for males in satisfaction of the territorial imperative to acquire as much sexuality as possible. However, once sexual partners are acquired, jealousy, following Reiss, is a protective means to retain the services of those partners. The greater the territorial urge, the greater the potential for jealousy. Therefore permissive, instrumental attitudes should, in males, be correlated with jealousy towards actual partners. This hypothesis should be easily testable.

Gender Differences in Loneliness

Several scales have been devised to measure loneliness. The UCLA Loneliness Scale has been most popular (Russell, Peplau and Cutrona, 1980). It does not ask directly whether one is lonely, and the earlier research with this scale found few sex differences. However, gender appears to interact with marital status. Among married couples, women report more loneliness, but when the relationship is disrupted by separation, death or divorce men report greater loneliness (Rubenstein and Shaver, 1982b).

The bulk of the reported research has been conducted with college students. The more recent research suggests that college males are more lonely than females (e.g. Solano, 1980; Schmidt and Sermat, 1983; Schultz and Moore, 1986). However, this conclusion is tempered by a review of two kinds of data by Borys and Perlman (1985). First, a meta analysis of 28 studies using the UCLA Loneliness Scale indicated that males report more loneliness than females. Second, a review of survey studies indicated that females, more often than males, label themselves as lonely. Borys and Perlman (1985) also provided evidence that males who admit to loneliness suffer more rejection than lonely females, suggesting that females are freer than males to admit their loneliness directly. The indirect nature of the UCLA Loneliness Scale presumably allows males to express their underlying loneliness more freely than on the direct questions of survey studies.

Schultz and Moore (1986) suggested that loneliness is more highly related to affect and social risk-taking in males than in females. Loneliness may be linked more tightly to negative self-evaluations and internal attributions for males as compared to females. If true, loneliness should show relatively more trait as compared to state manifestations in males than in females.

After Peplau and Perlman's (1979) work, loneliness is usually defined in terms of the difference between the kind of social relationships we have and the kind we want. Males are expected to lead in initiating heterosexual relationships. Therefore the quality of their relationships should be relatively more attributable to their personal characteristics. It is reasonable, then, that loneliness may be more strongly related to personality characteristics and internal attributions in males than in females. If these conjectures are correct, the best explanation would seem to be the sex-role norm of male initiative. In societies, if they exist, where females are equally free to initiate relationships, no gender differences in loneliness would be expected.

Other Gender Differences

The literature indicates gender differences on many other relationship variables. The relative recency of research efforts precludes definitive conclusions. A small sample of variables and studies is described below.

Friendship

Several studies have found that male same-sex friendships differ from female same-sex friendships (summarized in Brehm, 1985). In general, males are more oriented towards engaging in joint activities, whereas females are more oriented towards sharing emotional activities. Wright (1982) summarized this difference in terms of males having side-by-side relationships and females having face-to-face relationships.

Gender differences have also been found in the ways friendships end (Rose, 1984). Physical separation is the most frequent reason for the ending of male friendships; dating or marriage is the most frequent reason for females.

Social power and influence strategies

Several studies have examined gender differences in power strategies in dating and married couples. Among dating couples, males accrue more power the more dating alternatives they have available, but females base their power more on control of reciprocation of affect within the relationship (Sprecher, 1985). This result fits other data showing that females tend to use 'weak' (supplication, manipulation) as opposed to 'strong' (bullying, autocracy, disengagement, bargaining) influence tactics within their relationships (Howard, Blumstein and Schwartz, 1986). Both of these studies are in turn consistent with results (Gaelick, Bodenhausen and Wyer, 1985) suggesting that males interpret their partners' failure to express love as hostility, whereas females interpret lack of hostility as an indication of love. Among heterosexual couples, males report more direct and bilateral (e.g. bargaining) power strategies than females (Falbo and Peplau, 1980). However, these differences did not hold for lesbian or male homosexual couples, indicating that male–female sex roles are involved.

Because males are expected to initiate intimate relationships, females are at an initial disadvantage. We would expect *sub rosa* influence strategies by females in order to gain relationship equality, perhaps bolstered by a strong value orientation of equality. Cochran and Peplau (1985) found that females showed a stronger preference than males for 'egalitarian autonomy'. Similarly, a review by Gray-Little and Burks (1983) demonstrated that egalitarian marriages have the highest levels of satisfaction. Interestingly, marriages with dominant wives were most unhappy, and the wives tended to be most unhappy, possibly because their husbands were perceived as low in competence.

Preferences in mate selection

In an interesting research program, Buss (e.g. Buss and Barnes, 1986) has found several gender differences in mate selection preferences. Males, more than females, want a spouse who is attractive, a good cook, and frugal. However, females show a stronger preference for attributes such as considerateness, honesty, kindness, dependability, understanding, fondness for children, ambition for a career, good family background, and tallness. Apparently, traditional gender stereotypes about marriage are still alive and well.

Social support and interaction

Using a standardized instrument to measure individual differences, the Social Support Questionnaire, Sarason *et al.* (1983) found that females reported greater perceived social support in their lives than did males, and greater satisfaction with the available support. In a later study (Sarason *et al.*, 1985) same-sex pairs of subjects interacted in a brief acquaintance exercise. Males were rated lower than females in tendency to give social support and in social skills.

Some sex differences in interaction may be due to sex-role considerations. Ickes (1985) summarized a research program that found that traditional sex-typed dyads (masculine male, feminine female) had less rewarding interactions than couples in which one or both partners were androgynous. However, Antill (1983) found that marital satisfaction was related to the femininity of one's partner. It may be that social stereotypes dictate that males will be more task oriented and females will be more socially oriented. Such a result was found by Wood and Karten (1986) using mixed-sex groups of four people. However, a second study manipulated perceived status of group members and was able to eliminate gender differences. Apparently, many of the reported gender differences in interaction style depend heavily on subjects' norms for gender-appropriate behavior.

Shyness

Very recent summaries of research on shyness (e.g. Cheek *et al.*, 1986; Jones and Carpenter, 1986) suggest that adolescent girls are shyer than boys, although patterns of correlations between shyness and other variables are similar for both sexes. This result is not what would be expected from the review of the loneliness literature. It may be that males perceive more strongly that they are not supposed to be shy; hence, the ratings reflect this norm. It is too soon to form a firm conclusion.

EXPLAINING GENDER DIFFERENCES

In attempting to explain gender differences one should not try to explain more than needs explaining. Because this chapter has focused on differences, similarities between males and females have been ignored. The similarities may be greater than the differences, but human cognition treats similarities as nonproblematic, whereas differences require explanation.

We tend to view current cultural norms as fixed, perhaps a necessary consequence of the shortness of an individual life in comparison to the history of a culture. However, it seems clear that male–female relations have undergone historical changes. The concept of human relationships as processes within social structures offers a descriptive framework for understanding such historical change, but does not provide a specific causal account. Functionalism is one general approach to causal explanation (Dion and Dion, 1985). For example, it might be argued that romantic love serves a bonding function. Romantic love perhaps arose as a functional substitute when previous bonding mechanisms, such as economic interdependence, became weak or disappeared (e.g. Rosenblatt, 1974). Sociobiological explanations also have a functionalist flavor, but are unable to account for historical changes in sex differences.

Another approach to explanation is an attempt to conceptualize a small number of *prototype variables* that underlie and hopefully account for a wide range of surface differences (e.g. see Davis and Todd's 1985 use of the concept). The prototype variables are presumed to be linked contextually to form a system of variables, and change in one variable may qualitatively change and transform the entire system. Functional, sociobiological, and other types of explanations can be used to explain the linkage of a prototype variable to its surface variables and the expected effects of change in a prototype on surface variables. For example, in the course of the review of gender differences, *male initiative* in relationships emerged several times as a probable variable of considerable importance. Males initiate more than females: in courtship, in sexual relations, in communication, in self-disclosure (e.g. Davis, 1978), and in power strategies. This descriptive fact of initiation may be relevant to other gender differences. For example, ludic love attitudes and permissive sexual attitudes function to promote the initiation of sexual encounters. The need to initiate poses greater performance pressures on the self and may lead to stronger self-defenses. Low self-disclosure, except possibly when courting, would generally protect one's self from external attacks, but would lead to greater loneliness. Another functional effect of the tendency to initiate relationships would be the construction of consistent self-attributions that one is agentic, active, and instrumental. If the social norm that males initiate relationships ceased to exist, the major reason for differences between males and females on typical measures of masculinity and femininity would cease to exist, and that particular gender difference might well disappear.

It may be conjectured therefore that relationship initiation is a prototype variable that ramifies broadly across many gender-related attributes, resulting directly or indirectly in several gender differences. Of course, why males initiate more than females is not thereby explained. Perhaps the best approach to theorizing is to specify the initiation variable as contextually and mutually determined by a small set of other prototype variables. Any proposed set of prototypic variables to explain gender differences must be speculative at this time. My proposed set follows.

1. *Physical size.* Sex differences in body size and strength have ongoing implications for human relationships. Social and behavioral scientists have not been very adept at linking such 'crass variables' to the warm variables of intimate relationships. But the physical differences exist, will not go away, and are most likely of constant though unseen relevance to relationship variables.

2. *Sexual morphology.* Anatomy may not be destiny, but neither is it totally unrelated to human relationships. In particular, sex differences in the structure of the sexual organs, and associated hormonal differences, suggest many possible effects on relationship variables. The implications of the basic fact that only females give birth often seem to be overlooked by social scientists. The potential for rape, surely based ultimately on anatomical structure, is another pervasive aspect of male–female relationships. This morphological potential must of course be elaborated into sociological possibility. The possibility of rape depends on a concept of an autonomous self (see 3 below), a concept of free will and its limits (or lack of limits) with respect to others, beliefs about others as property, and complex social rules granting relatively less sexual autonomy to females than to males. Other biological differences also may have many and indefinite relationship ramifications. In truth, we are at the earliest stages in attempting to link our physical characteristics and their differences to social relations.

3. *An autonomous self.* The meaning of masculinity and femininity should differ in societies with an undeveloped sense of self, relative to the individualism of Western societies. The notion of being an agent implies an acting self. Concept of self in turn affects basic relationship notions. For example, the notion of rape implies a self who can be violated. It is unlikely, for example, that our current concept of the meaning of rape was the same concept held by humans at the dawn of civilization.

4. *Self as initiating agent.* This prototype was discussed previously. At this point, one must presume that this variable, in interaction with the other three variables, serves to explain why males initiate more relationship activities.

There probably are other prototype variables, but this list will serve our current purposes. I should stress that the list is not conservative in precluding social change. For example, the concept of an autonomous self could eventually be linked to a value that all selves are morally equal and have equal rights. If such a value were fully internalized by all members of the species, rape would become a rarity, largely neutralizing the prototype variable of anatomy. Full equality would also suggest that males and females would have equal rights to initiate relationship activities. In time, most of the gender differences reviewed in this chapter would disappear.

ACKNOWLEDGEMENTS

I am indebted to Bram Buunk, Margaret S. Clark, Val Derlega, Alice H. Eagly, Judith A. Hall, John H. Harvey, Susan S. Hendrick, Marylyn Rands, Jack Shaffer, Cookie White Stephan, Walter G. Stephan, as well as the Editor, Steve Duck, for their comments on an earlier draft of the chapter.

24

Intimate Relationships in Task Environments

JAMES P. DILLARD
University of Wisconsin, Madison, Wisconsin, USA
and
KATHERINE I. MILLER
Michigan State University, East Lansing, Michigan, USA

ABSTRACT

The focus of this chapter is on romantic relationships at work. Because there is such a tiny empirical base, our orientation is necessarily broad rather than deep. We attempt to show why the study of organizational romance is important and how this issue ties into better established areas of inquiry in the study of personal relationships.

Many years ago, Allport (1933) introduced the concept of partial inclusion. He argued that organizations, like any social grouping, capture only a portion of any individual. Typically, work organizations want only that segment of the person which is necessary to carry out the production-related tasks of the organizational role. What organizations get is considerably more. Individuals come equipped with many needs and desires which may be superfluous to organizational functioning or may push the individual to behave in ways that are viewed as counterproductive to the social aggregate.

The focus of this chapter is on relationships which significantly transcend the task roles specified by the organization. Rather than dealing with all types of close, personal relationships, the more modest aim of our chapter is to examine only those relationships which might, in some sense, be termed 'romantic'. For our present purposes, romantic relationships are considered to be intimate relationships between employees of the same organization which are characterized by some substantial degree of mutual sexual attraction. Because of the absence of data (to our knowledge) on gay and lesbian involvement, we limit our review to heterosexual relationships.

A HISTORICAL PERSPECTIVE ON ORGANIZATIONAL ROMANCE

In the past, and to a lesser extent in the present, there has been a great deal of effort expended towards preventing close relationships among workers. This has sometimes taken the form of a formal policy, but more often than not it exists as an informal norm with the status of folk wisdom. Burrell (1984) suggests that several forces have made standard this desexualization of the workplace. In his historical analysis, he traces the influence of moral and religious beliefs on the suppression of sexuality at work. This dynamic took the form of a desire to 'civilize' workers and to save them from their 'baser animal instincts' (p. 113). Operating in conjunction with this complex of forces was the push of puritanical notions of efficiency. If time is money, money is lost whenever employees' thoughts turn from labor to lust.

Individually and in the aggregate, these forces are weakening. One recent development that ensures greater opportunity for romantic attachment is the sexual integration of the workforce. Women are not only entering the labor market in record numbers, but they are staying in it (US Bureau of the Census, 1984). This virtually guarantees increased male–female interaction. Since it is well established that interaction produces attraction (Berscheid, 1985b; Huston and Levinger, 1978), it seems reasonable to expect that this change alone will counteract the sexual separatist dynamics identified by Burrell (1984) to some extent. Another source of change is in societal norms concerning sexual activity (Bradford, Sargent and Sprague, 1975, p. 54). There is greater tolerance for sexual behavior and increased recognition that sex is a stable feature of human existence. One additional reason to suspect that the forces of desexualization are going to meet increased resistance in the future is the changing nature of organizations themselves. To a larger extent than ever before, organizations are becoming central to the lives of individual members. In an effort to build a cohesive corporate culture, organizations are attempting to provide the members with services which bring their people together.

For all of these reasons, it seems plausible that romantic involvement among members of the same organization will become more matter-of-course. Unfortunately, the corpus of social scientific knowledge presently available on this topic may be conservatively characterized as embryonic. While several writers have decried this paucity of information (e.g. Burrell, 1984; Chatov, 1981, pp. 498–499; Mainiero, 1986), the number of studies focusing directly on organizational romance remains quite small. For example, Mainiero found only nineteen studies in her review of the organizational romance literature, and only two of these considered a sample of more than fifteen cases.

The increasingly commonplace nature of organizational romance, and corresponding lack of information about it, is not the only compelling reason to undertake inquiry in this area. As several recent publications point out, romance in the workplace may cause decrements in organizational effectiveness. Quinn and Judge (1978) suggest that gossip and suspicion may undermine a leader's ability to get the job done. Collins (1983) contends that the very structure of an organization may be endangered by love between managers. While these writers appear quite willing to make clear policy-oriented statements about organizational romance, the data are somewhat sparse. Because individuals' livelihoods hang in the balance, it would seem most prudent to proceed on the basis of data rather than assertion.

Finally, there is the issue of the relationship itself and the persons who comprise it. Clawson and Kram (1984) note that married persons who become involved with a fellow employee must contend with guilt and perhaps separation or divorce. Even for uncommitted persons the relationship may suffer from the strains imposed by secrecy if the couple attempts to maintain the appearance of noninvolvement. In addition, tension undoubtedly runs high between those persons who decide to terminate the romantic portion of their relationship but find it necessary to continue to interact with one another frequently at work.

A CURRENT PERSPECTIVE ON ORGANIZATIONAL ROMANCE

In the following sections we examine what is known about romantic relationships between employees of the same organization. Let us again emphasize that the database on such relationships is woefully small. However, this small database springs from a variety of areas. At one end of the spectrum are journalists who offer conclusions based on informal interviews or on their own system of values (e.g. Goodman, 1983). At the other pole are empirically oriented social scientists who prefer more systematic forms of data collection (e.g. Quinn, 1977). While we have attempted to provide a synthetic blend highlighting the strengths of both approaches, we have no illusions that the account we offer is a balanced one.

Formative Influences

Although we prefer to think of relationship formation as under the control of individuals, it is unquestionable that features of the social and physical environment influence behavior (Kram, 1984). One observation we might make about any structured social aggregate is that communication activity is unevenly distributed among members and, to some extent, channeled by macrofeatures of organization and work group. Coupled with the now classic finding that interaction (usually) produces attraction, it becomes evident that we must examine those aspects of organizations and work groups which influence the nature of that interaction.

Many researchers point to the importance of the ratio of males to females in jobs, occupations, and work groups as a fundamental determinant of social—sexual behavior (e.g. Fairhurst and Snavely, 1983; Kanter, 1977). In an explication of the forces which shape sexual communication at work, Gutek (1985) outlines the consequences of imbalanced sex ratios. Her data show clear effects for the composition of groups such that the number of opposite-sex persons in the work environment is positively associated with the amount of verbal and nonverbal social–sexual behavior.

In addition, her data underscore the important role the supervisor plays in promoting or inhibiting such behavior. Women with male supervisors reported significantly more sexual comments, both complimentary and insulting, more complimentary sexual looks and gestures, as well as more sexual and nonsexual touching, than did women with female supervisors. A similar, but nonsignificant, pattern was obtained for males with female supervisors compared to male supervisors. Gutek's (1985) findings, while intriguing, must be viewed cautiously in the context of this chapter. Since the focus of her work was sexual harassment, and many of the respondents considered the behaviors described above as sexual harassment, it is not clear that such behaviors lead to relational formation. However, two surveys of members of the American Psychological Association showed that a substantial minority of educator–student romantic relationships were viewed by the female partner as coerced (Glaser and Thorpe, 1986; Pope, Levenson and Schover, 1979).

Not only is the balance of males and females in an organization important to understanding relational development, but so also is the absolute number of employees. Data from one study suggest a curvilinear relationship between likelihood of involvement and organizational size (Dillard and Witteman, 1985). It seems probable that there is an optimal balance between size of the field of eligibles (the larger the organization, the more potential partners to choose from) and the forces of cohesion (the smaller the organization, the more likely a person is to be exposed to the remaining individuals and to spend time interacting with them). In addition to the size of the organization, formalization can also play a key role in encouraging and discouraging organizational romance. LoVette and Canary (1987) found a significant relationship between the level of formalization reported by employees and the degree to which they believed there was both a small field of eligibles and more constraints on the development of romantic relationships.

The effect of proximity on attraction is well established. Since Festinger, Schachter and Back's (1950) study of informal relationships in housing units, researchers have noted that we tend to like people we are close to and we tend to increase proximity with those we like. Huston and Levinger (1978) describe the complex and reciprocal nature of this relationship: 'proximity heightens the probability of interaction, which tends to enhance familiarity and liking, which again may further proximity; continuing nearness, in turn, is found to promote attraction' (p. 129). Clearly, work organizations are social structures which typically require the proximity of members (Monge et al., 1985). Though early research dealt primarily with the relationship between proximity and attraction in initial interaction, it is not unreasonable to expect that high levels of proximity and interaction over time in the workplace could lead to the development of interpersonal—and possibly romantic—relationships. Anderson and Hunsaker's (1985) study of organizational romance supports the role of proximity in developing relationships. In their study, 94 per cent of romantic partners worked in the same building, 68 per cent of romantic partners shared an office or had adjoining offices.

Proximity in the organizational hierarchy also influences the amount of communication which may take place between two individuals. There is evidence that a negative association exists between distance in the formal status hierarchy and likelihood of romantic involvement (Dillard and Witteman, 1985).

New directions

Because research has been so successful at examining the role that proximity plays in relational development, the more intriguing questions may now center around relational de-escalation. What happens if the romance goes sour? Arousal models of interpersonal attraction suggest that proximity acts as an 'amplifier' of affect, intensifying the feelings that are already present (Burgoon, 1978; Cappella and Greene, 1982; Patterson, 1982, and this volume). Thus, negative feelings about failed relationships could become particularly detrimental in the closed field of the organization.

Who Becomes Involved?

The claim that similarity between individuals breeds attraction (and *vice versa*) has become a truism. Byrne and his associates (see Byrne, 1971, for review) have demonstrated this link repeatedly using the 'bogus stranger' experimental paradigm. In addition, there is also sociological evidence of the similarity between engaged couples (Burgess and Wallin, 1943) and married couples (Kerchkhoff, 1974).

Given that organizations both select and attract persons who are similar to their members (Oldham and Hackman, 1981), a relatively high degree of homogeneity of personnel within organizations is likely. Such similarities should act to increase the overall level of interpersonal attraction within organizations. If we can take attraction as a necessary condition for the formation of a relationship, romantic relationships among members of the same organization may be more common than relationships between members of different organizations.

While this reasoning is flawed to the extent that much of courtship and marriage occurs prior to organizational entry, it nonetheless implies that romantic relationships may be quite common. In fact, a sample-size weighted average of five studies (Anderson and Hunsaker, 1985; Dillard and Witteman, 1985; LoVette, 1987; Miller and Ellis, 1987; Quinn, 1977) supports this observation: 71 per cent of the combined samples report having observed at least one romantic relationship at work. A sample-size weighted average of three studies (Dillard and Witteman, 1985; LoVette, 1987; Miller and Ellis, 1987) indicates that 31 per cent of persons surveyed had themselves been involved in a relationship with someone at work.

While it is evident that a great many persons who are employed under similar circumstances, i.e. in the same organization, become involved with one another, it is also apparent that relational partners are far from identical. Participants tend to differ in rank. A sample-size weighted average of four studies (Anderson and Hunsaker, 1986; Dillard and Witteman, 1985; Miller and Ellis, 1987; Quinn, 1977) showed that in 60 per cent of the relationships studied the male was of higher organizational rank than the female. The female superior relationship occurred only 16 per cent of the time. Some 35 per cent of the pairings involved persons of equal status.

Participants also differ in terms of age and education (Dillard and Witteman, 1985). Education tends to be positively associated with involvement for males, while age is negatively associated with involvement for females.

In sum, it appears that, in a number of ways, organizations act as a conduit for relational entry. However, similarity and proximity alone are not sufficient to bring about romantic attraction. Individuals must also be motivated to enter the relationship. The next two sections explore the substance of those motivations.

Rank and Attractiveness

The fact that men are often the older, better educated and higher-status partner in organizational romance implies that there may be some differences in the relative social worth of the two persons. Prior research (Murstein, 1974) suggests that individuals attempt to achieve relational equity by selecting a partner who is of comparable social value. Elder (1969) reports that attractive girls parlayed their good looks into a relationship with a male of higher social status and greater mobility potential. Harrison and Saeed (1977), in a study of 'lonely hearts' advertisements, found that women are more likely to 'offer' attractiveness while men are more likely to 'offer' financial security. Is it possible that participants in organizational romances trade on their status and appearance to secure a desirable partner?

Respondents in the Dillard and Witteman (1985) study were asked to rate each romantic partner's physical attractiveness on a scale of 1 (very unattractive) to 10 (very attractive). The difference between male and female attractiveness scores was then correlated with the difference between the male and the female's rank in the organizational hierarchy. For relationships in which the male was the high-status partner the coefficient was $r (118) = -0.01$. For relationships in which the female was high status the coefficient was $r (25) = 0$. Thus, it does not appear that physical attractiveness is a commodity exchanged for organizational status.

Obviously, these findings do not rule out the possibility that equity may be maintained along other dimensions. One simple way of balancing the relational accounting sheet is to pair with an individual whose physical attributes are roughly equal to one's own. Support for this version of the matching hypothesis has been found by several researchers (Murstein, 1972; Silverman, 1971). In the Dillard and Witteman (1985) data, male and female attractiveness scores were correlated $r (207) = 0.44$, $p < 0.001$. Thus, these data show support for the matching hypothesis within the realm of physical attractiveness, but not across commodities such as attractiveness and status.

Motives

Motives may be considered to be specific goals which an individual seeks to obtain through a relationship with a fellow employee. Using exploratory methods, Quinn (1977) empirically isolated three motives underlying organizational romance. The first, love, is described as the sincere desire to find a long-term companion or spouse. The ego motive is predominant in persons who view the relationship as a means to personal gratifications such as excitement, adventure, and sexual experience. Additionally, an individual may develop a relationship with a fellow employee for job-related reasons such as greater job security or power. Confirmatory factor analysis was used in a later study to replicate Quinn's findings (Dillard, 1987).

The Covariation of Male and Female Motives

Given that both males and females possess motives for forming and maintaining relationships, the question arises as to how they covary. Quinn (1977) addressed that question by forming a correlation matrix of male and female motives. His findings, which are presented in panel A of Table 1, reveal the existence of three statistically significant pairings. In his data male and female love motives were correlated (yielding the sincere love relationship), ego motives were correlated (yielding the fling relationship), and male ego and female job motives were correlated (yielding the utilitarian relationship).

Table 1   Correlations Among Motives for Engaging in Organizational Romance

Male's motives	Female's motives		
	Ego	Job	Love
Panel A: Quinn's (1977) Participant data ($N = 126$)			
Ego	0.61**	0.23**	−0.09
Job	a	a	a
Love	−0.15	0.00	0.50**
Panel B: Dillard's (1987) Participant data ($N = 77$)			
	Ego	Job	Love
Ego	0.53**	0.20**	−0.01
Job	0.19	0.53**	−0.06
Love	−0.20*	0.28**	0.44**
Panel C: Dillard's (1987) Observer data ($N = 97$)			
	Ego	Job	Love
Ego	0.62**	0.20**	0.10
Job	0.28**	0.32**	0.21**
Love	−0.01	−0.12	0.44**

[a]This portion of the matrix was not provided in the original.
*$p < 0.10$
** < 0.05

Data of the same sort from a more recent study (Dillard, 1987) are given in panels B and C of the same table. Two general points are apparent from inspection of the table as a whole. First, it appears that there is substantial, but not total, agreement between the second and third matrices. Second, it is also evident that the latter two matrices show a much greater variety of motive pairings than does the first. Let us examine each of those observations in turn.

The consistency in panels B and C is probably not remarkable, as the data are drawn from the same study. But, it is important to note that the matrices are constructed from the responses of relational participants (panel B) and relational observers (panel C). Thus, agreement between the two sets of correlations indicates that these perceptions of relational motives are robust across participants and observers.

However, there are several discrepancies between these matrices, particularly involving the covariation of job and love motives. Participants see love-seeking males pairing with job-motivated females, while observers believe that just the opposite occurs. The positive male job–female love correlation in the observer matrix (panel C) implies that persons who view relationships from the outside tend to see men exploiting women for job-related reasons.

The actor–observer literature suggests two ways of accounting for these findings. On the one hand, these differences may be a function of the perceptual vantage point of the individual. Behavior which is indicative of the love motive in males and the job motive in females may be more salient to participants than to observers. Further, behavior which is seen as revealing the job motive in the male and the love motive in the female may be more salient to observers than to participants.

On the other hand, participants may have more accurate information about the goals of the partner than do the observers. Since the male is typically the high-status partner, participants may be more realistic about the nature of their relation. Observers, in contrast, may rely more on traditional sex stereotypes for interpreting the behavior they see.

The second major observation to be made concerning Table 1 is the relative lack of similarity when comparing panel A with B and C. In contrast to Quinn's (1977) data, which showed only three instances of statistically reliable covariations among motives, Dillard's (1987) data paint a more catholic picture of relationships in organizations. Across panels B and C there are five significant correlations beyond those reported by Quinn.

For example, Dillard's study suggests the existence of relationships in which the male is seeking to further his job-related goals in a relationship with an ego-motivated female. Moreover, observers and participants agree that the occurrence of the job motive in one partner is likely to correspond to the same motive in the other.

How might this greater variety in motivations be accounted for? One candidate is regional differences: Quinn's (1977) sample was drawn from travelers in two eastern airports, while Dillard's (1987) was the result of random-digit dialing in a mid-sized, midwestern city. Another somewhat more appealing interpretation is that sufficient time elapsed between the two studies that a greater diversity of motivational associations now exists. Whatever the case, it is clear that these differences merit further investigation.

RELATIONAL TYPES

The two studies examined in the previous section claim that relationships may be defined by the motives of the participants. They infer the existence of various types of relationships on the basis of covariation between individual motives. Such an approach is valid only to the extent that individuals are driven by single motives. It is quite possible, however, that individuals are motivationally complex and have more than a single reason for entering relationships with others at work.

This issue was addressed in a recent study by Dillard and Segrin (1987). In that investigation, 128 observers were interviewed concerning the motivations of the two relational partners as well as other features of their relationship. A nonhierarchical cluster analysis of the motive data yielded a five-cluster solution which was then validated on additional variables. Descriptions of each of the relational types are provided below.

The Passionate Love Relationship

Males and females in the first and largest cluster (36 per cent of the sample) were seen as possessing both love and ego motives in relatively equal amounts. This suggested a type of pairing in which both partners emphasize gratifications such as excitement and sexual experience and view these things as necessary components of a long-term relationship. This type of relationship appeared to resemble what other researchers have referred to as 'passionate love' (Driscoll, Davis and Lipetz, 1972; Berscheid and Walster, 1978).

Persons representative of all levels of age, education, income, and power were present in this group. In 20 per cent of these relationships one or both participants were married.

The Companionate Love Relationship

Persons in this type of relationship are driven only by the desire for sincere affection and long-term companionship. Very low scores on the ego motive suggest a relationship that is more controlled and pragmatic than the passionate love described above. This cluster seemed to be consistent with what Berscheid and Walster (1978) have referred to as 'companionate love' and Quinn (1977) has called 'sincere love'.

Only 14 per cent of the companionate love relationships in this sample involved at least one married partner. Thus, persons very high in the love motive were unlikely to enter into a relationship which compromised the marital fidelity of themselves or their partners. In this sample, 23 per cent of the examined relationships fell into the companionate love category.

The Fling Relationship

This type of relationship was characterized by a simple motivational structure for both participants: each was seeking ego gratifications exclusively. Over half (54 per cent) of the fling relationships had at least one married participant. Further analyses showed that high-power males are unlikely to become involved in a fling, but females enter into this type of relationship regardless of their rank or informal power. Flings comprised 19 per cent of the sample.

The Male-Dominated Utilitarian Relationship

This relatively rare relational type (8 per cent of the sample) is composed of a female who is above average on both love and job motives and a male who is above average on the ego motive and very high on the job motive. The extremely high job motive score for the male implies that this motivation is central to the relationship. This speculation is corroborated by the positive association between cluster membership and female power.

The overall picture which emerges regarding this relational type is that of a predatory male who seeks out a female of greater organizational power than himself for the purpose of controlling his job environment. The female in the relationship apparently feels genuine affection for him, but perhaps has a job-related agenda of her own. Only 10 per cent of the male utilitarian relationships involved married partners.

The Female-Dominated Utilitarian Relationship

In some ways the gender inverse of the male utilitarian pairing, this relational type included a female who was above average on the ego motive and very high on the job motive. Her partner, however, was in the relationship for ego-related reasons. This category of relationships comprised 14 per cent of the sample.

Of all the relational types, this one was the most distinctive. It showed a positive correlation with male power and a negative association with female power. Thus, it appears that lower-power females form relationships with higher-power males. The males in the female utilitarian cluster tended to be older, better educated, and better salaried than males in the other relationships. Many (50 per cent) of the female utilitarian relationships violated traditional morality regarding marital fidelity.

Motivationally Simple and Complex Relationships

This analysis provides evidence that in many cases people are seeking more than one thing from a close relationship with a fellow employee. The motivationally complex passionate love, male and female utilitarian relationships together constituted 58 per cent of the sample in the study described above. The motivationally simple fling and companionate love relational types comprised the remaining 42 per cent. Of course, those findings are qualified by the fact that the data were drawn from observers only.

New Directions

As noted previously, Quinn (1977) uncovered three motives for organizational romance: love, ego, and job. His work stimulated other studies in which motives figured very prominently. While this developing body of research may have enriched our understanding of the dynamics of close relationships at work, it is important to remember that all of the studies including motive variables rest upon Quinn's essentially atheoretic scheme.

Related work on attributions in close relationships suggests that further investigation in a context of discovery may be called for. From the perspective of attribution theory all three motives (love, ego, and job) place the locus of causality in the individual participants: they are variants of dispositional attributions. Of course, attribution theory specifies the existence of situational attributions which might also bear on organizational relationships (e.g. they had to travel together a great deal). Moreover, other researchers have advanced cogent arguments for the need to consider categories of attributions which locate causality between the two persons or in their surrounding social network (Newman, 1981a, b). Since existing data seem to support the validity of these proposals (Baxter and Bullis, 1986; Lloyd and Cate, 1985b), it may be the case that research on organizational romance would benefit from a temporary return to exploratory modes of inquiry.

INSIDE AND OUTSIDE THE RELATIONSHIP

When a pair of employees develop a close relationship with one another, actually two relationships are formed: one between the participants and one between the pair and the organization. Clawson and Kram (1984) refer to these as the internal and external relationships. Although their conceptual distinction referred to mentor–protege relationships, it is equally applicable to romantic relationships.

The Internal Relationship

By definition, organizational romances are relationships which have their start in task-prescribed roles. At some later point the limited relationship delineated by the organization grows into something which substantially exceeds the work activities of the two persons. At that time, the involved individuals are faced with juggling a new and complex set of potentially conflicting role demands.

Although we know of no existing research on how these problems are dealt with in organizational romances *per se*, the body of research on dual-career couples offers some likely parallels. Intraindividual sources of stress for working persons include their work role, their couple role, and the interaction between the two. In addition, individuals in dual-career relationships face sources of interindividual stress: they must contend with the interaction of their partner's work and couple roles with their own work and couple roles (Gupta and Jenkins, 1985; Pleck, 1977). When one considers the number of possible interactions, it quickly becomes apparent that the potential for stress rises exponentially in dual-career relationships. It is likely that this complex situation is exacerbated for persons who see one another on the job as well as off.

In light of this potential for cognitive overload, it is surprising that dual-career relationships seem to fare so well. A recent review of the area concludes that dual-career status may actually enhance the productivity of the couple, although career growth may be somewhat inhibited (Gupta and Jenkins, 1985). In addition, the preponderance of evidence seems to indicate that members of dual-career relationships are more affectively positive towards their relationships than are persons in one-career families (Gupta and Jenkins, 1985).

The External Relationship

Apparently, most participants make a concerted effort to minimize others' awareness of their relationship (Anderson and Hunsaker, 1985; Quinn, 1977). Reasons for deception include fear of criticism from fellow employees, concern about formal censure by management, and, in those instances where one or both partners are married, fear that family members may become aware of the affair.

In spite of the efforts by the involved couple to maintain the appearance of relating through work roles only, participants unknowingly provide behavioral cues alerting coworkers to the existence of the relationship. Some of the most common tipoffs include being seen together away from work, spending excessive amounts of time together at work, and taking extended lunches (Anderson and Hunsaker, 1985; Quinn, 1977).

New Directions

One area which may prove particularly ripe for future research is that of the communication behaviors associated with maintaining the secret of the relationship. While little is known about secrecy in organizations (Zander, 1977, pp. 23–35), there is a rapidly growing literature on deception which would certainly be applicable to this problem (e.g. Zuckerman, DePaulo and Rosenthal, 1981). The 'no relationship illusion' may be an ideal phenomenon for deception researchers since it involves both factual and emotional deceit, the participants are presumably motivated to maintain the illusion, the opportunity for slipping up is ever present, and the nature of the deception may change as others begin to suspect the existence of the relationship from concealment to evasion to outright lying (or confession).

THE CONSEQUENCES OF RELATIONSHIPS AT WORK

An organizational romance may have a considerable impact on the job-related behavior of the participants, as well as repercussions for their coworkers, subordinates, and superiors, and the organization as a whole. This section will consider two major consequences of organizational romance. First, perceptions regarding the effects of the romance on the participants will be assessed. Second, the reactions of coworkers and the organization towards the romance will be reviewed.

The Job Performance of Relational Participants

A major concern regarding intimate relationships in organizations is the degree to which the job performance of the participants is affected. As Feinberg and Levenstein (1982) note of executives, 'their primary concern is the impact on work performance and company reputation'.

A wide variety of behavioral changes in the participants are reported by observers of organizational romance (Quinn, 1977). Negative changes in job performance included preoccupation, arriving late and leaving early, doing less work, missing commitments and meetings, producing lower-quality work, making costly errors, and becoming incompetent. The behavioral changes noted were relatively consistent for males and females, though women were seen as becoming preoccupied somewhat more than men. Although many changes were reported, Quinn's overall assessment seems to be that the relationships produce more undesirable than desirable outcomes for the organization (see also Quinn and Judge, 1978).

More recent research has generally echoed his conclusion. Anderson and Hunsaker (1985) also found judgements of both negative behavioral changes (e.g. lower-quality work, costly errors) and positive changes (e.g. easier to get along with, more productive). More general judgements indicate that the relationships had some positive impacts in 21 per cent of the cases studied and negative impacts in 79 per cent.

Finally, Dillard (1987) considered overall estimates of performance during the relationship as compared to before the relationship began. For male participants, performance was seen to have declined in 8 per cent of the cases, stayed the same in 64 per cent of the cases, and improved in 28 per cent of the cases. For females, performance was seen to have declined in 15 per cent of the cases, stayed the same in 48 per cent of the cases, and improved in 37 per cent of the cases. Hence, these data suggest somewhat more beneficial consequences than either Quinn (1977) or Anderson and Hunsaker (1985).

Efforts to explain alterations in task behavior have revolved around the motives thought to underlie the relationship. Surprisingly, this work has yielded very little evidence that the job motive produces effects which are detrimental to the host organization, though one study shows a significant relationship between the job motive and absenteeism (Dillard and Broetzmann, 1986). In contrast, data suggest that love-motivated individuals (especially women) may actually show an upturn in overall performance, job involvement (Dillard, 1987), and enthusiasm (Dillard and Broetzmann, 1986).

Several explanations have been offered for the link between love motivations and positive outcomes. First, love-motivated persons may be attempting to impress their partners by increasing their output. Second, if the involved employee believes the management fears that the relationship will result in performance decrements, then performance improvements will demonstrate to management that the relationship in question is the exception to the rule. Third, it is possible that once an individual has met the need for companionship, there is more time and energy available to expend on task requirements. Fourth, individuals in love may simply feel good, and this could make the hassles of the day (including tasks) easier to cope with. Finally, it is possible that observers have a more positive reaction towards love relationships, and a halo effect may account for the positive assessment of work performance changes.

In short, a judicious interpretation of the existing data permits only a guarded conclusion: organizational romance may correspond with positive or negative changes in the performance behavior of the relational participants, though in many instances there are no changes at all. Further, there appears to be some association between particular motives and performance changes but the effect sizes are small.

It merits mention that none of this research deals with objective job performance data, but rather with observers' perceptions of changes in the behavior of participants and, in some cases, with participants' self-reports. Thus, we hesitate to conclude that these reported changes are a true reflection of the behavior of romantic participants. Nonetheless, 'no matter how the relationship has or has not affected the work of partners, the perception of coworkers will be that behaviors have changed, and perceptions are very real' (Butler, 1986, p. 32).

New directions

Clearly, future research should address the causes of performance alterations. One potentially valuable research strategy would contrast organizational with nonorganizational romances. Such an approach would permit the isolation of effects due to general relational involvement versus involvement with an organizational compatriot.

The Alteration of Power Relationships

An equally important concern is the degree to which the romance influences the balance of power in workplace. Favoritism is a common problem, although less so now than a decade ago (cf. Quinn, 1977 with Anderson and Hunsaker, 1985).

Other changes in power relationships reported by these researchers included promotion of the relational partner, becoming inaccessible, isolating the partner from other organizational members, ignoring complaints about the partner, and granting the partner additional power. These changes reportedly occur in well under half of the observed relationships.

Informal Reactions

The most prevalent reaction to knowledge of a relationship seems to be 'hands off'. In over two-thirds of the relationships examined by Quinn (1977) and by Anderson and Hunsaker (1985), the couples' colleagues and subordinates were said to have 'tolerated' their involvement. In about 20 per cent of the cases, approval was expressed by coworkers.

The presence of an intimate relationship at work is likely to affect communication behavior in the work group in a variety of ways. One almost certain outcome is that knowledge of the relationship will cause substantial gossip (Anderson and Hunsaker, 1985; Quinn, 1977). Although the overall amount of gossip appears to be independent of the motives of the participants, the tone of that talk is not. Females viewed as job-motivated generate primarily negative discussion. In sharp contrast, gossip takes on a positive tone when the male is seen as love-motivated (Dillard, 1987). These findings may indicate the operation of a cultural bias favoring males in the workplace.

Attempts to cope with the relationship provoke other sorts of communication. In about half of organizational romances, colleagues or subordinates apparently feel compelled to provide advice to one or both of the participants (Anderson and Hunsaker, 1985; Quinn, 1977). Complaints to management occur in about a third of the cases, and threats or blackmail in only a very small percentage of relationships. Finally, LoVette (1987) found that a wide variety of information-gathering strategies was likely to be used when an individual was suspected of romance—particularly if there was the perception that the individual's work performance had been influenced. The most active information-gathering strategies were used by peers, as opposed to supervisors or subordinates.

Organizational Response

Existing research suggests that the most frequent 'official' reaction of the organization to knowledge of a relationship was complete lack of action (Quinn, 1977). This fact was reflected in responses such as deciding to ignore the situation, not wanting to risk action, not knowing what to do, and feeling that the problem would resolve itself. In light of the very mixed data on the impact of romantic relationships on organizational effectiveness, absence of action may reflect rational managerial policy.

When there is official action, Quinn reports that open discussion and counseling occurred relatively frequently (particularly for the male participant), and that punitive actions such as reprimands, termination, and warnings were less probable. Additional evidence regarding bias against women is suggested by data which indicate that the chances of being fired as a result of becoming involved are twice as high for women (11 per cent) as for men (5 per cent) (Quinn, 1977).

Making Judgements About Intimacy at Work

As noted earlier, all existing data on the behavior of relational participants and the reactions of others to the romance are perceptually based. This suggests two points of concern. First, recall and/or report of the events surrounding the relationship may not correspond perfectly with reality. Second, the expectations of employees, perhaps the respondents, about organizational romance may in some way influence the operation of and outcomes associated with the relationship. Two studies have examined the way in which certain values may color the perception of intimate relationships at work.

One investigation advanced the claim that organizational romances were judged simultaneously on a task dimension and on a social dimension. It was hypothesized that persons who valued the task dimension more would be disapproving of relationships at work and would anticipate more negative consequences for relationships which could potentially interfere with organizational functioning. More positive judgements were expected from persons who gave precedence to the social dimension. The anticipated results comported closely with the actual findings (Dillard, 1986). Analysis of the reasons given for holding either a positive or negative attitude towards organizational romance showed that persons who described their orientation as negative tended to offer justifications centered around the importance of task/organizational requirements. Respondents who gave their attitudes as positive provided a preponderance of socially oriented reasons.

Another investigation which sought to examine the influence of preexisting value structure on judgements about relationships was recently carried out by Miller and Ellis (1987). In that experiment, subjects were presented with hypothetical scenarios which described the participants in an organizational romance. The descriptions varied the attractiveness and status of each of the relational partners.

The results revealed some strong and consistent stereotypes regarding the way individuals and organizations react to romantic participants. Surprisingly, reactions to the romantic partners were not predicted by the hierarchical standing of the participants. That is, romances between coworkers were no more likely to be approved of than those between supervisor/subordinate pairs. The major predictor of reactions to the romance was the relative attractiveness of the participants. Relationships in which the participants were matched in terms of attractiveness were more likely to be approved of and less likely to induce ostracism, sabotage, blackmail, and quitting than relationships where one partner was attractive and one was unattractive. In addition, respondents tended to attribute job or ego motives to the low-status participant in mixed-attractiveness relationships. When partners were matched on attractiveness they were both seen as being in love.

Reactions were also significantly predicted by perceived motives. The most severe reactions were reserved for individuals motivated by job and the most positive reactions were garnered by love-motivated participants. Surprisingly, ego motives were evaluated differently for male and female relational participants. Females motivated by ego were seen as being advised, tolerated and 'stood by', while males motivated by ego were seen as somewhat likely to be obstracized by coworkers.

Taken together, this pair of studies clearly indicates that perceptions of relationships at work may be influenced by factors other than the relationship itself. The task-social distinction seems to exert substantial sway on persons' judgements, but an investigation which directly measures these two values is needed. The Miller and Ellis (1987) study provides evidence that the relative attractiveness of participants is very likely an important determinant of motive attributions and expectations. The extent to which these factors bias retrospective accounts or mold organizational reality is not known.

LOOKING FORWARD

If any one conclusion readily emerges from the set of investigations which comprise this review, it is that romantic relationships at work are no less complex and meaningful than those in other settings. They are distinguished by the fact that they form and operate in particularly public places and by the fact that in a great many instances other parties feel compelled to intervene.

Some writers have sought to institutionalize a policy of intervention. Collins (1983) has argued that organizations should treat love between managers as a conflict of interest. She advises organizations to encourage the couple to seek outside help. But if that is insufficient to convince them that the needs of the organization take precedence over their relationship, one or both must resign or be fired.

Even if it were possible to overlook the moral implications of Collins' (1983) position, it is apparent from the data examined throughout this review that the economic conclusions are far too mixed to offer any support to her point of view. As one observer of a relationship remarked, 'Dress codes are enough. God forbid we should get into living codes' (quoted in Westhoff, 1985, p. 238).

Handbook of Personal Relationships
Edited by S. W. Duck
© 1988 John Wiley & Sons Ltd

25

The Organizational Life Cycle of Relationships

GEORGE J. MCCALL
University of Missouri, St Louis, Missouri, USA

ABSTRACT

The sociological notion of an 'organizational life cycle' affords a distinctive basis for reconceptualizing the course of dyadic relationships. The lively debate within the organizational literature about the aptness of the organismic analogy (birth, development, death, etc.) serves to illuminate the organizational peculiarities of dyads and to reorient theories about relationship development. In addition, the sociological literature on organizational life cycles may at last turn scholarly attention from its fixation on a dyad's supposed 'internal locus of control' to a greater recognition of vital environmental influences—especially the variety of interorganizational relations—upon the course of relationships.

Serious study of the dyadic relationship is generally dated from the pioneering works of Georg Simmel, the maverick sociologist who not only redefined society as a process of social interaction but then reinvented sociology as a kind of abstract topology of the fundamental social forms in and of social interaction. It was Simmel (1908/1950) who first showed that the dyad is itself a fundamental—but quite distinctive—form organizing social interaction. That Simmelian thesis was sustained by his own brilliant followers—in Europe, by Leopold von Wiese, and in America, by the great entrepreneurs of the Chicago school, Albion Small and Robert E. Park. But it fell to a third scholarly generation—through the leadership of two fellow graduate students at the University of Chicago, Howard P. Becker and Willard Waller—to establish a fullblown sociology of the dyad (Waller, 1930, 1938; Wiese and Becker, 1932; Becker and Useem, 1942).

Although closely intertwined and symbiotic with classical sociological work on courtship (Bolton, 1961), marriage (Blood and Wolfe, 1960; Rubin, 1983), divorce (Weiss, 1975; Goode, 1956), and friendship (Lazarsfeld and Merton, 1954; Chambliss, 1965; Rubin, 1985), sociology of the dyad more abstractly strives to understand the 'twoness' of all social and personal relationships (see Allan, 1979; Blumstein and Schwartz, 1983; Davis, 1973; McCall, 1970; Vaughn, 1986).

RELATIONSHIPS AS SOCIAL ORGANIZATIONS

The cornerstone of the sociology of the dyad is the realization that *a dyadic relationship is a species of social organization* (McCall, 1970). That is to say, a marriage, a friendship, or a partnership is—in essence—quite like the local banking firm, the church on the corner, or the neighborhood school. Like these larger cousins, a relationship is properly depicted through the now familiar device of the table of organization, as in Figure 1(a), which graphically conveys the basic Simmelian point that *a relationship is a social unit over and above the two individuals*.

To fully appreciate the point, counterpose this 'organizational' depiction of a relationship (Figure 1(a)) to the more conventional, 'interpersonal' depiction

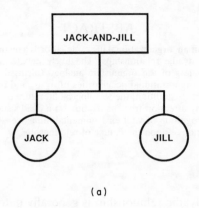

(a)

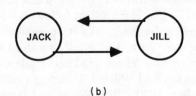

(b)

Figure 1

of the same relationship (Figure 1(b)). In the interpersonal depiction, the two individuals see only one another; in the organizational depiction, the two individuals see not only one another but also their relationship, as a social unit over and above themselves, to which they belong and of which they are members. It is just this difference to which sociologists refer when they insist that social phenomena must be distinguished from the interpersonal.

A relationship, like any social organization, displays aspects both of unity and of diversity—that is, aspects of *collectivity* (the sense of comprising one social unit, to which the participating individuals 'belong' or of which they are 'members') and of *social structure* (a differentiated pattern in which members not only play distinctive parts in a 'division of labor' but also occupy distinct, though interdependent, social positions; McCall and Simmons, 1982). Like any other organization, the flesh-and-blood social reality of a relationship does not show up well in those 'X-ray pictures' we call tables of organization. That is to say, an organization is not only a structured collectivity but also very much a dynamic social *process of organizing* threads of human lives. Indeed, Duck and Sants (1983) contend that personal relationships largely consist in this emotionally involving and expressive process of organizing. Relationships are thus a species of 'joint social action' (Shotter, 1987b), are emergent rather than prefabricated social entities.

Organizational Features of the Dyad

Through the recognition that a relationship is a social unit over and above the two individuals, attention is usefully directed to certain features of relationships that are shared with all other organizations. Four of these features can be developed here.

1. Awareness of objectified, institutionalized social form

The members of a family, a church, or a baseball team ordinarily appreciate that their organization, though it be very much their own local creation, will be apprehended by others—and themselves—as *being* a family, a church, or a baseball team. Similarly, Ginsburg (1986) rightly insists:

A primary relationship is a *social* fact, an entity of social interdependencies that exists over an extended time period and has its own emergent qualities. . . . One basic step in coming to understand primary relationships is to determine how it is that people know that a particular relationship exists and what it is like. (p. 41)

Friendship, for example, is an objectified social form—an *institutionalized* mode of social organization. That is to say:

When persons say they are friends, usually they can point to cultural images, rules of conduct, and customary modes of behavior to confirm their claims. This is likely to be most apparent when one or both parties find their relationship questioned by outsiders. At these times there will be an appeal to standards, rules, or 'facts' by which persons can validate whether or not they are, indeed, 'friends'. (Suttles, 1970, p. 98)

Such objectified, institutionalized social forms of relationships include not only what might be regarded as the master types of dyads (friendship, love, marriage, colleagueship, etc.) but also key subtypes of each—for example conventional marriage and companionate marriage (Burgess and Locke, 1945).

Anthropologists have been interested in these social forms as 'cultural blueprints' for relationships—the more highly institutionalized and ritualized, the better—and have been much less interested in the actual dynamics of specific dyads (Eisenstadt, 1956; Eisenstadt and Roniger, 1984). Attention is focused on discovering similarities and differences among, say, the institution of *compadrazgo* (in Mexico) and that of blood brotherhood (in Africa). As we will see more clearly in a subsequent section of this chapter, sociologists too are interested in why such social forms for relationships emerge, persist, and die out (and certainly their work towards that end should take more seriously the anthropologists' contributions in cultural ecology).

However, sociologists are far more interested in how these forms, or cultural blueprints, come to be enacted (implemented, instantiated, manifested). The heart of the matter here, in Simmelian formal sociology, is the tension between forms and contents (Simmel, 1908/1950). According to Levine (1971, p. xxiv), contents are 'the needs, drives, and purposes which lead individuals to enter into continuing association with one another'. Such contents are given definite identity, structure, and meaning through the imposition of social forms—'those synthesizing processes by which individuals combine into supraindividual unities, stable or transient, solidary or antagonistic, as the case may be'. Once created, forms tend to become rigid and 'incapable of adapting to the continuous oscillations of subjective need. The conflict between established forms and vital needs produces a perpetual tension, a tension which is nevertheless the source of the dialectical development or replacement of social structures and cultural forms throughout history' (Levine, 1971, p. xxxix; compare also the 'structuration theory' of Giddens, 1976, and the 'institutionalization theory' of Zucker, 1983).

As an example of this tension, consider how difficult it is to bring off, or enact, the social form of an 'open marriage'. The 'feeling rules' which are a vital part of that relational form proscribe expressions of sexual jealousy, yet even sustained 'emotion work' may fail to quell those sentiments, leading to guilt and even further turmoil (Hochschild, 1983).

It is in this enactment tension, too, that external parties exert such an important 'audience effect' on relationships by commenting on implementation efforts and criticizing how those efforts measure up against the standards set forth in the cultural blueprints. Because 'relationships are socially accredited entities recognized and responded to by other people' (Duck and Sants, 1983), collective definition (Berger and Kellner, 1964) and social accountability (Scott and Lyman, 1968; Semin and Manstead, 1983; Shotter, 1984) become key factors in the process of enacting any relationship form. Davis and Todd (1982,

1985) have shown how the 'paradigm case formulation' procedures of so-called descriptive psychology can be used to identify the kinds of considerations that people use to explain to others (and themselves) the ways in which the particular relationship does exemplify the social form and the ways in which such relationships can be said to go wrong or to be defective.

2. Sense of collectivity (of membership, belonging)

Interpersonal views of relationships have traditionally been concerned with the cohesiveness of the dyad, and have approached that concern through analyses of 'interpersonal bonding'. Such bonding between members does of course take place within all social organizations (McCall and Simmons, 1966/1978), but more important organizationally is the bond between member and social unit. Social organizations (MacIver, 1937) are concerned (a) to create and sustain among members a sense that they belong within an overarching social entity, and (b) to develop among them the felt importance of membership. Organizational interests include, then, identification, loyalty, morale, and *esprit de corps*.

In any relationship, a sense of 'shared fate' tends to arise as members discover that the surrounding world treats them not so much as separate individuals but rather as a couple, or unit. Married people, for example, are invited to social events not as persons but as couples. Awareness of this sort of 'dual participation' (Waller, 1938) often leads members to appreciate more deeply the extent to which theirs is a shared fate and a common interest. This appreciation in turn reinforces their tendency to collective action, in the form of 'pair-centered interaction' (Waller, 1938). Married couples, friends, and colleagues typically act towards outsiders as *teams*, cooperating to maintain proper fronts of solidarity and to further their joint ventures. In important ways, then, members' awareness of the relationship is enhanced by external impingements that evoke a 'we-feeling'.

3. Creation of shared culture

Interpersonal approaches to the dyad have placed great importance on a 'mutual interpenetration' model, in which two individuals progressively permit one another access to ever deeper and more intimate spheres of their personalities, thereby increasing each party's knowledge and understanding of the other (Altman and Taylor, 1973). This phenomenon does occur too between members within any sort of social organization, but its significance is generally dwarfed by the organizational centrality of culture creation—of socially constructing shared knowledge about an 'us' (Shotter, 1987).

The vital part that 'organizational culture'—the values, beliefs, meanings, heroes and legends, vocabulary, conventions, understandings, rules, rituals that have developed within the membership of an organization—plays in the life and fate of organizations is now widely recognized even in the business world (Ouchi and Wilkins, 1985). Culture is not something that an organization *has* so much as it is part of what an organization *is*. For example, Wilkins (1983) shows how 'organizational stories' function as symbols to effectively control the organization. Even small-group cultures have been fruitfully studied (McFeat, 1974; Fine, 1979; Ridgeway, 1983), thus encouraging scholarly interest in the culture creation process within dyadic relationships. Wood (1982) and Baxter (1987a) not only provide the fullest review of studies of relationship cultures, but also explicitly link these cultures to processes of dyadic communication. Wood (1982, p. 78) views the culture of a relationship as 'the hallmark of intimacy, a privately transacted system of understandings that arises, alters, and dissolves in communication'. According to Berger and Kellner (1964, pp. 13–14):

> The reconstruction of the world in marriage occurs principally in the course of conversation. . . . Each partner ongoingly contributes his conceptions of reality, which are then '*talked through*', usually not once but many times, and in the process become objectivated by the conversational apparatus. . . . In the marital conversation a world is not only built, but it is also kept in a state of repair and ongoingly refurnished. The subjective reality of this world for the two partners is sustained by the same conversation.

Normative expectations arise between them regarding: appropriate activities; the division of labor; the amount, distribution, and priority of time and effort to be contributed; relations to external persons and organizations; patterns of communication and revelation; and the like. The negotiation processes through which such normative expectations are developed, applied, and refined are of great organizational significance. It appears, for example, that dyads tacitly negotiate their unique 'rules of relationship' primarily through remedial episodes (Stokes and Hewitt, 1976; Morris and Hopper, 1980; Morris, 1985).

Private understandings of a less normative nature are also elaborated. Relational symbols take many forms, but together these convey the unique identity of the relationship and therefore serve to guide collective action (Baxter, 1987a). Private terms, or neologisms, bearing on its organizational concerns are frequently invented by the members of a relationship, and almost universally some private meanings are attached to common terms (Hopper, Knapp and Scott, 1981). These private terms and meanings often stem from, or give rise to, private jokes (Oring, 1984). Still another important type of private understanding is the unique calendar provided by the historical development of the relationship. Members frequently date events in relation to significant incidents in the history of the relationship ('it was right after our trip to Yellowstone').

Rituals and ceremonies are a vital component in all organizational cultures (Bossard and Boll, 1950; Trice and Beyer, 1984), but nowhere do they have such significant personal meanings as in a relationship (Maynard and Zimmerman, 1984; Cohen, 1958). Rituals, or 'dyadic traditions' (Oring, 1984), arise from the routinization of any recurring relationship activity—morning coffee at the kitchen table, flipping a coin to see who buys the beer, sex after the Saturday night dance. Other relational symbols (Baxter, 1987a) become incorporated into these rituals, as settings, props, and cues—the table in the back at the rendevous restaurant, the colored scarves for the bicycle ride, a particular nightgown.

4. Role differentiation (division of labor)

In any organization, members' lines of action differ one from the other yet remain interdependent in certain ways. Interpersonal approaches view this phenomenon as resulting from some sort of 'mutual entrainment of behaviors' (as diagrammed, for instance, in Kelley et al., 1983, pp. 20–67). Of course, such interpersonal entrainment does occur within organizations of all types, but the differentiation and coordination of members' lines of action is more usefully viewed as the organizational process of 'role-making' (Turner, 1962; Graen, 1976; McCall and Simmons, 1982). Individuals' organizational participation is determined through recruitment, defined through socialization, implemented through interaction, altered through innovation, and constrained through social control. These five basic processes are dynamically interrelated, through both direct and feedback linkages, to form an endlessly cycling system of social process—'role-making'—which shapes and reshapes the individual's organizational role (McCall and Simmons, 1982, pp. 155–165).

Although no primary relationship is at heart a role relationship, its interactions do take place through performances of informally differentiated roles. The primary social structure of such a relationship is actually the fit between the 'personas' (subsets of role identities) that the members present to one another (McCall and Simmons, 1966/1978; Backman, 1983; Vaughn, 1986). That is to say, an interpersonal relationship is not so much a relationship between two persons as one between two personas. As the members informally differentiate their respective roles, each is guided by his or her own role identities and by the presented persona of the other. This fit between their personas (a) effectively requires them to avoid certain actions that are prescribed by their institutional role relationships but that happen to be inconsistent with a member's presented role identity, and (b) allows them, conversely, to perform actions that deviate from institutional role prescriptions but that happen to be consistent with the presented role identities of the members. For such reasons, it may turn out that neither member of a marital couple will do any cooking, or that in the privacy of their own apartment they speak to each other largely in baby talk.

Peculiarities of the Dyad as Social Organization

Though Simmel did establish that dyadic relationships are indeed social organizations, with all the generic features of these, he was more concerned to demonstrate that the dyad is a *species* of organization, distinct from, for example, the triad or pentad. We turn now to identify some of the distinctive or peculiar features of the dyad as social organization.

Some of these distinctive features pertain to its social structure. Like a few other small, number-defined forms of organization (see Caplow, 1960), the dyad cannot vary in size; but of these, the dyad is irreducibly the smallest. Consequently, internal social differentiation of any kind is absolutely minimal, for there are only two structural positions definable. For the same reason, as in no other organizational form, factional suborganization is necessarily and completely absent.

These structural oddities of the dyad in turn engender some peculiarities in organizational processes. To a degree unmatched in any other organizational form, the process of recruitment gives rise to the entire organization and overshadows all of its subsequent life (McCall, 1970). No internal coalitions are available within the process of ratifying or stigmatizing innovations; although this entails that a member can never be outvoted, it also entails that he or she can never obtain any internal backing in any dispute with another member (McCall and Simmons, 1982).

In Simmel's eyes, however, the feature that most distinguishes the dyadic relationship is its inherent sentimentalism. In his influential analysis of sentiment, Gordon (1981, p. 567) concludes that 'every sentiment is organized around a relationship to a social object, usually another person . . .'. For his part, Simmel would further contend that the dyad is the prime locus not only of sentiment, but more importantly of sentimentalism, as revealed in the membership's:

1. *Sense of uniqueness*. Their feeling that 'there has never been a friendship (a love) quite like ours' emerges through the enactment tension described above, as creative compromises with the institutionalized social form are hammered out and a dyadic culture is created (Baxter, 1987a; compare Martin *et al.*, 1983).
2. *Sense of intimacy*. The sense of giving or revealing certain things only to partner, and to no one else, emerges through the process of creating a shared culture.
3. *Sense of consecration*. Their feeling that each of them must take responsibility for what happens to the relationship—that neither member can hide individual doings or failures behind the organization—emerges through the developing sense of collectivity, described above.
4. *Sense of purity of reciprocity*. Their feeling, further, that such doings or failings cannot be hidden behind another individual member emerges through the process of role differentiation.

Most importantly, in Simmel's view, all this sentimentalism is enormously heightened by:

5. *Sense of mortality of the dyad*

> . . . each of the two feels himself confronted only by the other, not by a collectivity above him. The social structure here rests immediately on the one and on the other of the two, and the secession of either would destroy the whole. The dyad, therefore, does not attain that superpersonal life which the individual feels to be independent of himself. . . . This dependence of the dyad upon its two individual members causes the thought of its existence to be accompanied by

the thought of its termination much more closely and impressively than in [an organization], where every member knows that even after his retirement or death, the group can continue to exist. . . . A dyad, however, depends on each of its two elements alone—in its death, though not in its life: for its life, it needs *both*, but for its death, only one. This fact is bound to influence the inner attitude of the individual toward the dyad, even though not always consciously nor in the same way. It makes the dyad into a [social structure] that feels itself both endangered and irreplaceable, and thus into the real locus not only of authentic sociological tragedy, but also of sentimentalism. (Simmel, 1908/1950, pp. 123–124)

The pathos here lies in the fact that the dyad is the only organization that can *never* expect to outlive *any* of its members.

This early identification of (1) the peculiar vulnerability of the dyad and (2) members' consequent obsession with its mortality is responsible for a second main hallmark of the sociological perspective on relationships, namely, a fully 'life-cycle' perspective—that is, one concerned not only with the birth and the life of a relationship but also with its death. As pointed out by, for example, Duck (1982a), outside this life-cycle perspective the decline and termination of relationships has to date received scant scholarly attention.

ORGANIZATIONAL LIFE CYCLES

The key focus of this chapter is to bring to bear on relationships some recent sociological work (of much more general scope) about the 'organizational life cycle'.

To begin with, there is a considerable social psychological literature on the life cycle of the small group. Lacoursiere (1980), for example, reviews and synthesizes a wide variety of longitudinal studies on *The Life Cycle of Groups*. In his Group Development Stage theory (GDS), most groups are considered as passing through five developmental stages of the group life cycle. In the *orientation* stage, participants' positive expectations are balanced by anxiety and concern as they try to discover something of the situation, nature, purpose, and personal consequences of the nascent group. As discrepancies between participants' expectations and the realities of the group become apparent, the group enters the *dissatisfaction* stage in which negative feelings (frustration, anger, disappointment, sadness) outweigh the earlier hopefulness and eagerness. In the *resolution* stage, there develops some 'rapprochement between expectations and the realities (task, leader, abilities, other members, and so on), and also some increase in skills' (p. 32), which together serve to rebuild positive feelings and task effort. Following on such a resolution, the group enters a *production* stage in which 'members are working well together with satisfactory agreement—implicit or explicit—about the nature of their relationships' (p. 34). If, for whatever reason, the group can at some point no longer continue, a *termination* stage ensues in which member concerns shift to a consideration of accomplishments and to a sense of loss or mourning triggered by the group's impending dissolution. (These same five stages have been alternatively designated (Tuckman and Jensen, 1977) as *forming, storming, norming, performing, and adjourning.*)

This small groups life-cycle literature seems rather a natural choice for application to relationships, since many view dyads as essentially two-person groups. Yet, attempts to apply GDS theory to dyadic relationships have so far proved uninspiring. In perhaps the most sophisticated of these applications, Krain (1975, 1977) found little evidence in dating relationships that conflictual communication shows the predicted midcourse peak followed by a stage of conflict resolution.

The fundamental flaw, I think, in this small groups life-cycle literature *qua* model for the course of relationships lies in the fact that it has tended to mistake the merely interpersonal for the social. Group structure, for example, has been largely equated with what I have termed (McCall and Simmons, 1982) 'secondary social structures'—rankings of individual members in terms of some specific attribute, such as power, leadership, respect, liking, or communication activity (Secord and Backman, 1974). The primary, or role, structure of small groups is an essentially social rather than interpersonal phenomenon, and therefore has received less research attention. The pioneering work on group roles by Benne and Sheats (1948) has been developed only sporadically over the four decades, but the research of Breiger and Ennis (1979) and Mandel (1983) offers promising new tools with which to investigate primary structure. Group process, similarly, has been essentially equated with various interpersonal rather than organizational processes (McCall and Simmons, 1982). That is to say, group process has been analyzed not in the terms of recruitment, socialization, innovation, or social control but rather in terms of such categories as asking for opinion, giving suggestion, disagreeing, or showing tension. Certainly, the processes underlying GDS theory are explicitly interpersonal:

> GDSs depend considerably on an adequate personal and usually interpersonal focus in the group. There will not be much hope developed or frustration experienced with highly impersonal and easily definable tasks that stimulate primarily the more conscious thought processes for their fairly easy accomplishment. Interpersonal aspects will not be a significant part of an experience if the experience is very brief, and if the relationships remain superficial and do not stimulate or elicit deeper, less conscious interpersonal fantasies and feelings. (Lacoursiere, 1980, p. 175)

Fortunately, there is within sociology a much more generalized organizational life-cycle literature, epitomized by the Kimberly and Miles (1980) volume *The Organizational Life Cycle: Issues in the Creation, Transformation, and Decline of Organizations.* For the study of relationships, this generalized literature may prove more instructive because—being focused on large complex organizations—it has not been tempted to confuse the social with the merely interpersonal. Issues of creation, transformation, and decline currently loom large in organizational sociology, and it is the implications of this work for an understanding of relationships that I wish to examine here.

To begin with, the sharp debate within this organizational literature about the usefulness and viability of the *organismic analogy* in its references to birth, death, growth, development, and decline of organizations (see Cafferata, 1982; Kimberly, 1980) can help us to sharpen our terribly vague conceptualizations of what relationships are. In pursuing each aspect of the organismic analogy, the necessity for a distinction between social form and concrete dyad will become quite apparent.

Birth. For relationships, even more than other organizations, there is seldom any marker event comparable to emergence from the birth canal. How can we date the birth of a friendship? Even in the case of a more formal relationship, such as a marriage, it seems somewhat artificial to claim that the wedding ceremony constitutes the birth event, for the couple's relationship may antedate their wedding by a number of years. The imagery of birth entails a distinction between the history and the prehistory of a relationship (Miles, 1980). If the wedding is the historical birth of a marriage, when and how was the marriage conceived? In what sense was there a period of gestation? The point here is that the history–prehistory distinction pertains not to the concrete dyad but to some one social form it has sought to enact. It is only through their becoming wed that the *history* of a concrete male–female dyad becomes the *prehistory* of their marriage.

Death. Whereas all organisms must die, there is nothing inevitable about the demise of a social organization (Kimberly, 1980)—*except* for the dyad, as Simmel has shown us.

The death of a relationship, like its life, is only virtual rather than literal. Thus, there is rarely any marker event that definitely dates its demise. Even for once quite lively relationships, to determine now whether they are dead or alive can be most difficult. Friendships that have undergone years of separation are essentially 'missing in action' and can only be 'presumed dead'. Even continuing relationships may be so moribund that their vital signs prove fugitive. Often, for example, the 'heart' of a relationship may have died but the relationship itself is kept 'alive' by means of artificial support systems, maintaining only the highly attenuated husk of a relationship. Less commonly, a relationship may be declared to be 'brain dead' and is formally or publicly terminated: that is to say, the 'plug is pulled', an event that is more precisely dateable. Yet even in such cases, the notion of death can be quite misleading, for relationships often exhibit a very real 'afterlife'. For example, the relationship between divorced parents never really vanishes; it is only the *social form* of the relationship (viz. marriage) that has died, not the concrete dyad.

Life. How are we to think about what happens with a relationship during that span between its birth and its death? The organismic analogy suggests attention to processes of growth and decline on the one hand and to processes of maturation and development on the other. Growth always implies an increase in size, with or without a change in form; development always implies a change in form, with or without a change in size (Brent, 1984). Both notions have proved somewhat difficult to apply appropriately to organizations (Starbuck, 1971), but especially to relationships.

Growth/decline. After all, dyads have a fixed membership size! The growth of a relationship therefore cannot be reckoned by increases in the number of members, an index often employed in studying the growth of other social organizations. Nor can the organizational decline of a relationship be measured by decreases in its membership, since the loss of even a single member is tantamount to the death of the dyad.

The growth of a relationship is rather a matter of what the members put into it, and the lushness of what they are able to cultivate therein. More appropriate dimensions of growth might then include: quality of its human resources; the degree of members' participation; the number of role identities included (see Ridley and Avery, 1979, on multiplex relations); management skills; desire; richness of dyadic culture (especially in its symbolic and ritual aspects, such as roles, understandings, meanings, definitions, priorities, honor, respect, teamwork). Diminishment of any such features of a relationship might then be regarded as signaling the decline of a relationship. But all shrinkage-based definitions of organizational decline, whatever the size dimensions selected and whatever the organizational type, have been attacked by Greenhalgh (1983) for focusing attention on manifestations of decline rather than on the underlying processes. In Greenhalgh's alternative approach:

> organizational decline is viewed as deterioration in the organization's adaptation to its environment. Decline occurs when the organization fails to maintain the adaptiveness of its response to a stable environment, or when it fails to either broaden or increase its domination of a niche which has a diminishing carrying capacity. The converse of decline, thus defined, is not growth, as is often implied, but adaptation. (p. 232)

This explicitly ecological concept of a relationship's adaptation to its environment will be further discussed below, yet its clear linkage with cultivation and with organizational effectiveness already suggests its utility.

Development. Most theories of relationship development have adopted what Brent (1984) terms the levels-by-stages model:

> A level of organization is a qualitatively distinct form of organization in an ordered series of such forms. A stage of development, on the other hand, is one interval in a temporally ordered series of intervals during which either: (1) There is little internal change in a structure with regard to some function; or (2) one form of organization dominates the others with respect to some particular function, or both. The levels-by-stages model is thus primarily concerned with the relationship between the formal ordering of structures and their temporal order. . . . It is also implicit in the concepts of precocity, retardation, and regression. (p. 165)

Such *progressive stage* theories of relationship development are fundamentally teleological, in the sense that they are framed in terms of how a concrete relationship attains some final social form of interest to the researcher, such as marriage or best friends. The relationships literature contains several varieties of such progressive stage theories (Duck, 1984b). One variety emphasizes 'maturational stages', in an Eriksonian-like sequence of developmental issues or problems; examples include the theories of Lacoursiere (1980) and Lewis

(1972). Another sort of developmental theory (e.g. that of LaGaipa, 1981, or Levinger, 1983) emphasizes 'embryological stages':

> . . . in the *tadpole–frog model* where although it changes in form, and even in 'lifestyle', the relationship retains its recognizable central features; and in the *insect model* where the relationship moves in stages from egg to larva to pupa to adult forms of itself, and where each stage depends on success in the previous form, which is related to past elements but nonetheless bears little resemblance to them. In all of these models the implication is of some relational form that transcends the partners and develops according to some inherent relational principles. . . .
> [In the *horticultural model*] relationships take root, grow, blossom, flourish, wither and fade. The assumption is that while their ideal form is predetermined by inherent features, it can nevertheless be modified by external circumstances (e.g. a relationship fails to flourish because it is starved of support or is inequitable). Whilst partners' actions can influence the health, success or vigour of the relationship, its 'true form' is predetermined and partners merely affect the degree to which it achieves the perfect exemplary form of the ideal. (Duck, 1984b, pp. 510, 509)

In progressive stage theories of whatever kind, a dyad's failure to progress monotonically through the entire sequence of stages is viewed as abnormal—'fixation', 'regression', 'retardation'—and often is tacitly taken to amount to (virtual) death of the relationship. On the other hand, the horticultural model suggests that many social relationships actually die as a result of *organizational success* (see Miles, 1980) in passing through all stages of development. Just as many plants bear their fruit and die, so the relationship between a realtor and his or her client, for example, is likely to terminate when all the details of the house transaction have been completed.

A key conclusion in the general organizational life-cycle literature is its clear-eyed insistence that *social organizations lack any fixed developmental sequence* (e.g. Kimberly, 1980). This conclusion leads to the view of development as *transformation*, looking not at stages but rather *phases*—that is, changes in the social form of a particular dyad, without any necessary concern for the directionality of their sequence. Just as water can pass directly from any of its phases—vapor, liquid, solid—to any other, so a Richard Burton/Liz Taylor relationship can resemble a 'random walk' alternation among a variety of social forms and two young children can be friends, rivals, or enemies on different days of a week. To study the ongoing self-transformation of relationships requires many fewer of those implicit theoretical assumptions that Duck (1984b; 1987a) has shown to trouble the study of the development progress of relationships. Moreover, a transformation view seems to suggest a greater emphasis on the study of relationship processes, as compared to the focus of developmental views on relationship outcomes.

ENVIRONMENTAL INFLUENCES ON ORGANIZATIONAL LIFE CYCLE

Precisely because organizations *do* lack fixed developmental sequences, most of the work on general organizational life-cycle notions has tended to emphasize *environmental influences* rather than internal forces. Historically, organizational sociology had considered mainly the *internal anatomy and dynamics* of organizations, seeking management theories for rationally adapting the strategies and structures of an organization in pursuit of organizational goals. In recent years, however, this emphasis on the 'internal locus of control' of organizations has taken a back seat to consideration of an 'external LOC' reflecting organizations' dependence on externally available resources—even to the point of *environmental determinism* (Aldrich, 1979; Meyer and Scott, 1983; Pfeffer and Salancik, 1978; Bidwell and Kasarda, 1985). Indeed, some scholars (e.g. Meyer and Rowan, 1977; Zucker, 1983) now take this environmental determinism so far as to contend that the fabled internal structure and technology of organizations is in fact largely mythical and ceremonial. To maintain legitimacy within their environment, organizations must adopt the form—though not necessarily the substance—of environmentally institutionalized views on what their type of organization should look like.

> To maintain ceremonial conformity, organizations that reflect institutional rules tend to buffer their formal structures from the uncertainties of technical activities by becoming loosely coupled, building gaps between their formal structures and actual work activities. (Meyer and Rowan, 1977, p. 341)

Somewhat intermediate between these extreme views is what might be called *random transformation theory*, which claims that organizations do change their structures mainly in response to endogenous processes, but that such changes are only loosely coupled with the desires of organizational leaders and with the demands and threats of environments (Cohen, March and Olsen, 1972; March and Olsen, 1976; Weick, 1979).

This is in fact the second potential contribution of the general organizational life-cycle literature I wish to propose—namely, that we have probably overemphasized the role of *rational adaptation* (of strategy and structure) in the trajectory of relationships, at the expense of the role played by *environmental selection*. As noted by Duck (1984b, pp. 508–509), researchers often speak of:

> the track of relationships, or the trajectory of a relationship. This suggests to me a belief in a goal towards which the relational partners are tending, either by prearranged routes (often with 'stages' or 'crossroads')—the freeway model—or by their own devices across uncharted terrain—the prairie model. Such pioneering metaphors . . . suggest that partners have some awareness of where, in broad terms, they are headed; that they might take a course through a range of possible stages which have a recognizable and generally familiar form and which are common—perhaps predetermined—in the culture; that there are many, or at least several, different routes to the same goal, although the goal retains the same character. One strong assumption, then, in these metaphors is that individuals choose their own routes and that partners' choices and behaviour rather than the social form of the relationship are the determinants of relational progress.

This emphasis placed on the role of rational adaptation reflects, I think, the tacit commitment of the relationships field to a model of marriage counseling—

that as a result of our research, partners can be taught adaptive strategies for relationship preservation and repair, so that their relationship can be 'saved'. Often, however, it is environmental influences which fundamentally determine whether the relationship endures or terminates. Even quite apart from the operations of such environmental selection processes, there is clear need to pay much greater attention to environmental influences on relationships.

Environmental influences on a relationship are overwhelmingly the influences of its interorganizational relations (Galaskiewicz, 1985). 'As any organization looks at its environment, it sees not only people, buildings, geographical terrain, and meterological conditions but—most vividly—*other organizations*' (McCall and Simmons, 1982, pp. 62–63; compare Aldrich and Pfeffer, 1976). The current sociological literature affords three principal conceptual views of these interorganizational relations:

1. Larger organizations surround and constrain smaller organizations;
2. Organizations (especially those of equivalent size) comprise a network;
3. Organizations (especially those of similar form) comprise an ecological population.

As we examine how each of these approaches illuminates the organizational life cycle—especially that of the dyad—we will find that each approach is differentially associated with (respectively) the birth, life, and death of organizations.

Embedding/Nesting Approach

Often, one organization may be embedded or nested within another, larger one. A sibling relationship, for example, is embedded within a family group. 'From the standpoint of the embedded organization, the larger organization within which it is lodged is effectively an external organization—perhaps the most immediate and critical feature of the embedded organization's environment' (McCall and Simmons, 1982, p. 63). The many ways in which a larger 'host' organization, such as a school, critically influences embedded dyads, such as childhood friendships, can be seen very clearly in Epstein and Karweit (1983). That study examined a comprehensive range of environmental influences of the school upon the embedded dyads—in their birth, their life, and their death.

The distinctive strength of this approach, however, lies in its accounts of the *birth* of dyads. For many years, relationship formation has been viewed as being driven by some sort of homophily principle, that like seeks like, and birds of a feather flock together. More recently, however, sociologists (Fischer *et al.*, 1977; Fischer, 1982a; Feld, 1981, 1982) have proposed that it is the social structuring of activity that tends to bring similar people into frequent contact with one another and thereby encourages the development of relationships among them.

Although relationships can develop from a single encounter, most relationships originate in activities organized around foci—[objects around which joint activities are organized]. Foci can be formal (e.g. a school) or informal (e.g. a regular hangout), large (e.g. neighborhood) or small (e.g. a household). Most relationships originate in foci of activity that bring together disproportionately homogeneous sets of people. The more homogeneous these sets of people are, the more relationships tend to be with similar others. A sample survey and a study of friendships in one large factory illustrate the importance of the social structuring of activity for age similarity. It is suggested that the neglect of structural factors has led to the overestimation of the extent to which people 'prefer' to associate with similar others. (Feld, 1982, p. 797)

An interesting, earlier study along these lines is Zena Blau's (1961) investigation of structural constraints on friendship in old age.

Network Approach

The social environment may instead be viewed as a structured network of social relationships (Holland and Leinhardt, 1979). Examined from the outside, this web of dyads represents a 'social network'; the surprising extent and manner in which dyadic social networks exert influence on the character and fate of a relationship have been ably surveyed by Ridley and Avery (1979). Examined from the perspective of any individual within it—as is the more common practice (Wellman, 1982)—that web represents a 'personal network'.

Every individual maintains and depends upon a personal network—a set of persons with whom one is knowingly involved and cross-linked through a web of direct and indirect relationships. This personal network constitutes the effective interpersonal environment, the resources from which are derived the necessities and amenities of elementary social life . . . One's network, then, represents a 'personal economy' of relationships to be managed more or less effectively . . . (McCall, 1982, pp. 212–213)

Feger (1981) provides a most useful overview of network theory and network analysis applicable to either social or personal networks—with attention to its distinctive quantiative tools deriving from applications of the mathematical theory of graphs.

Although scholars have well noted the important roles played by social and personal networks in the formation of relationships (Hallinan, 1978; Lewis, 1972) and in their demise (Johnson, 1982; LaGaipa, 1982; McCall, 1982), the network approach to interorganizational relations is most distinctively associated with studies of the *life* of dyads. There is, for example, the 'Romeo and Juliet effect' (Driscoll, Davis and Lipetz, 1972), whereby divergent personal networks are shown to affect the blossoming of romance. Similarly, the 'dyadic withdrawal hypothesis' suggests that the progressive development of, say, a romantic relationship (Lewis, 1973b; Krain, 1977) hinges centrally on success in merging the personal networks of both members:

. . . a close relationship is characterized by the partners' overlapping memories of shared experiences, participation in joint activities, and the disclosure of personal information. These shared experiences, activities, and disclosures will often involve third parties—friends, kin relations, and acquaintances. . . . As a pair becomes further involved with each other their separate networks shrink in size, and a joint network of constituents common to both members of the pair unfolds . . . (Milardo, 1982, p. 163)

This shrinkage in, or withdrawal from, separate networks is quite selective (Johnson and Leslie, 1982). Indeed, as suggested by Parks, Stan and Eggert (1983), 'dyadic realignment' is a more apt description than 'dyadic withdrawal'.

Population Ecology Approach

Construing interorganizational relations as the dynamics of a population of competing organizations (Carroll, 1984; Hannan and Freeman, 1977; Warriner, 1984), the population ecology approach—like the organizational life cycle notion—makes great use of the organismic analogy. Likening social organizations to biological organisms and social forms to biological species (McKelvey, 1982; Aldrich and Mueller, 1982; Hannan and Freeman, 1986), the principles of population ecology are thoroughly Darwinian: variation in (social) form, competition for resources, selection, and persistence. The ecological concepts of 'adaptation' and 'niche', as applied to the problem of organizational resources, pose another interesting challenge to the organismic analogy (Green-halgh, 1983; Freeman and Hannan, 1983; Warriner, 1984). Even the severest critics concede, however, that the concepts and the quantitative tools of ecological analysis—such as Lotka–Volterra equations, for density-dependent selection processes (McPherson, 1983)—bring new potential to the field of organizational studies.

In this Darwinian approach, changes in aggregate organizational features over time are viewed as much less the result of adaptation than of selection processes. The distinctive strength of the population ecology approach is to be found, then, in its selection-process analyses of rates of organizational *death*. These analyses (Brittain and Freeman, 1980; Freeman, Carroll and Hannan, 1983) bring to organizational study intriguing new quantitative tools, including life-table methods such as survivor functions, hazard functions, and Gompertz––Makeham models.

In population ecology models there is, quite naturally, some mutual dependence between assumptions about selection processes and assumptions about the organizational life cycle (Hannan and Freeman, 1984). For instance, a model might assume that developmental anomalies abort, or miscarry, before birth. As applied to organizational populations, interdependent assumptions of this sort have been expressed in terms of various survival 'liabilities' of organizations, especially liabilities of the organizational life cycle. For example, small new organizations tend not to survive. This fact, while enormously significant, poses difficulties for the organizational analyst in separating the liability of size from the liability of newness (Freeman, Carroll and Hannan, 1983); is the selection process more size-dependent or more age-dependent? Subtly distinct from these are the proposed 'liability of uniqueness' (novelty of social form, as distinguished from newness of the concrete dyad) and the 'liability of transformation' (the increased risk sustained by an organization as a result of changing its social form) (see Miles, 1980; Hannan and Freeman, 1984).

These organizational liabilities may cast useful light on the survival or termination of relationships. Indeed, the 'liability of uniqueness' is peculiarly germane, given the demonstrated importance of distinguishing momentary form from concrete dyad. If studies of relationship transformation do begin to displace studies of relationship development, the 'liability of transformation' will likewise become a central concern. With respect to the oft-confounded liabilities of size and of newness, dyads provide a potentially strategic case; because their size cannot vary, newness is not confounded with size. Survival function representations of divorce rates, for example, certainly do suggest a liability of newness among dyads.

Comparison of Approaches

It is, perhaps, remarkable that the leading contemporary approaches to the problem of interorganizational relations should turn out to specialize, respectively, in the birth, life, and death of organizations. Of these three approaches, thus far only the network approach has proved at all popular within the study of relationships. That preference is especially intriguing in view of the fact that the other two approaches claim to account for the emergence and persistence of social networks. Following on the initial work by Peter Blau (1977), the influences of various embedding macrostructures on networks have been shown rather convincingly (Fararo, 1981; Skvoretz, 1983). Similarly, it has been well argued that the selection dynamics of population ecology explain how social networks emerge and endure (Aldrich, 1982; Williamson, 1981). At the very least, such explanatory efforts do indicate that a more integrated approach to environmental influences on the organizational life cycle of relationships appears feasible and potentially more fruitful.

CONCLUSIONS

Sociologists, because they recognize the social organizational nature of relationships, may be expected to reconceptualize the course of relationships in terms of an 'organizational life cycle'. Theory and research on the life cycle of small groups, by conflating the realms of the social and the merely interpersonal, seems to cast little light on dyadic relationships. A more generalized literature on organizational life cycles does not make that same mistake, and seems therefore to provide a more useful guide to the study of relationships. In this chapter I have suggested two main ways in which it does so. First, the whole debate in the organizational literature about the aptness of the organismic analogy (birth, development, death, etc.) does much to clarify the organizational peculiarities of dyads and to reorient developmental theories of relationships. Second, that literature serves to turn scholarly attention from a dyad's supposed 'internal locus of control' to a greater recognition of vital environmental influences—especially the variety of interorganizational relations—upon the course of relationships.

Section Five

Community and Clinical

Section Editor   *Stevan E. Hobfoll*

Overview

Personal relationships have been considered in both clinical and community psychology since the inception of each of these fields. Two dimensions separate the modern study of personal relationships in the context of clinical and community psychology from past viewpoints, namely a focus on *interactive behaviors* and on the *here and now*.

INTERACTIVE BEHAVIORS

In the first case, whereas personal relationships were thought to affect individuals throughout modern thinking in clinical psychology, the focus tended to be either on early relationships, such as between mother and child, or on current relationships viewed as products of tendencies forged on earlier interpersonal interactions. Clinicians typically obtained their knowledge about interactions from adult accounts or inferred them through retorspective psychodynamic interpretations based on adult behavior. In neither case were these formative interactions empirically studied, nor were the interactions the major object of attention. The interaction was secondary to the psyche or personality. This is epitomized by psychoanalytic theories that depicted psychopathology as almost wholly based on dysfunctional personal relationships in early childhood (Freud, 1933; Klein, 1932).

The recent study of personal relationships in clinical psychology, in contrast, is more interested in the actual interpersonal behaviors of individuals. Rather than inferring what these interactions are, attempts are made to study them as directly as possible. As indicated in the chapter by Gotlib and Hooley, this may take the form of individual self-report, self-report by dyads, and observations of actual interactions. Thus, whereas earlier perspectives merely inferred these interpersonal behaviors, recent research on personal relationships attempts to study the behaviors themselves. This belies a related bias of current research, namely an interest in relationships themselves, not merely as a key to subsequent psychopathology. The present biases are products of an environmental viewpoint and a systems-oriented approach to clinical problems not espoused in earlier clinical theories and viewpoints.

Whereas the study of personal relationships in clinical psychology represents a perspective oriented more to systems theory than was the case in earlier approaches, the opposite may be said for community psychology's interest in personal relationships. Community psychology originally brought attention to environmental effects on people and highlighted systems perspectives. Early research was directed, for example, at new approaches to psychiatric treatment, changes in school environments, effects of physical environments (e.g. noise, residential planning) on people, and community organization (Zax and Spector, 1974).

One area of interest which focused on the use of paraprofessional mental health workers in the place of professional mental health personnel may be seen as a progenitor of an increased interest in personal relationships in community psychology (Mitchell and Hurley, 1981). Research on paraprofessional mental health workers showed that they could be as effective as professionals in many instances, and that when targeted towards specific needy populations that they could be even more effective than their professional counterparts (Durlak, 1979). What seemed to be a key to the effectiveness of paraprofessionals was their ability to form therapeutic relationships with their clients. Rather than being selected on the basis of their knowledge and education, they were chosen for their empathy and the fit of their personal characteristics with the needs of the client population (Hobfoll, 1980a, b). So, for example, college students were used successfully with delinquent adolescents, housewives with children displaying early school problems, and widows with newly bereaved women (Durlak, 1979; Jason, 1985; Karlsruher, 1974). In this way, community psychology took a step towards attending to the nature of personal relationships and away from the larger macroenvironmental systems focus.

This led to an interest in other natural (i.e. nonprofessional) health-enhancing factors, factors that continued the interest in personal relationships among community psychologists. In particular, attention focused on social support and its role in effecting positive mental and physical health (Heller and Swindle, 1983). Social support was depicted in two ways. One focus of research envisaged it as the extent of social embeddedness of people in their community or social network. A second direction depicted social support as interpersonal interactions whose intent was to provide help (see Hobfoll and Stokes, this volume; Shumaker and Brownell, 1984).

Both the study of social embeddedness and socially supportive interactions shared a common interest in the interactions of individuals with others in their environment. At first the mere presence of social ties was thought to be health-enhancing, but this romanticized notion of social support quickly gave way to a search for the specific salutary qualities of particular social relationships (Sarason and Sarason, 1985). Indeed, it did not take long before investigators reawakened to the fact that what had been deemed social 'support' was not necessarily supportive and that it could, in fact, have detrimental effects on people (Rook, 1984a; Hobfoll, 1985a). Again, these notions were products of an increasingly intensive study of the actual interactions that people reported, what they received, who they received it from, and the meaning of the receipt for them.

HERE AND NOW

The second common focus of the modern study of personal relationships in clinical and community psychology is the attention afforded to the 'here and now'. Rather than referring to interactions or relationships in early childhood or the distant past, emphasis is assigned to the nature of current relationships. No doubt social interactions occurring during childhood are developmentally related to personal relations in later life and this link may even represent an important focus of future research (cf. Reis and Shaver; Dunn; and Nash, this volume). This perspective, however, has often obscured the importance of examining current or recent personal ties and their effect on well-being and pathology, especially in the field of clinical psychology.

The emphasis on the here and now is related to two factors, one theoretical and one methodological. On the theoretical plane, personal relationships are seen as important in and of themselves. While early theories in psychology spotlighted early childhood relationships as the progenitor of mental health, more recent theories assign importance to contemporary relationships' contribution to mental health. This alternative viewpoint may be seen as a by-product both of behaviorism, on the one hand, and of humanism, on the other hand, as these two very different perspectives share an emphasis on the role of people's present environment in shaping their health. Current relationships are powerful sources of stress as well as potential moderators of other stressors, depending on the qualities of the relationships and the personal characteristics of those involved. Humans are social animals who spend much of their lifetimes involved in interactions with others. Indeed, even people's ability to be alone is, in part, a product of their satisfaction with their relationships (see Rook's chapter in this section).

Methodologically, an emphasis on the here and now is viewed as advantageous because the current look at personal relationships in clinical and community psychology is strongly empirical. Past relationships are lost in history and may not be reliably studied. So, too, prospective studies of relationships beginning in childhood and extending into adulthood are few and far between. Contemporary relationships, in contrast, can be conveniently studied and are available for verification. Even if the self-report method is used, it is more likely that recall of events is accurate when memory of interpersonal interactions is fresh. Hobfoll and Stokes (this volume) and Gotlib and Hooley (this volume) nevertheless underscore the importance of actually observing social interactions and of obtaining verification of reported interactions. Indeed, the processes which are viewed as being of importance in each of the chapters contributing to this section of the book may in many instances be brought into more controlled laboratory situations where people with existing ties are studied. This availability to investigation in a number of contexts via observation, self-report, and report by others offers an inestimably more defensible basis for research and subsequent development of theory.

DIRECTIONS OF THE STUDY OF PERSONAL RELATIONSHIPS

The chapters in Section Five represent a broad cross-section of topics of interest to clinical and community psychologists. The confines of space precluded presentation of all areas of clinical and community psychology that are relevant to this volume, but these were chosen because they are major research directions and because they express an alignment with the movement to study personal relationships.

In the first chapter Joe Stokes joins me in a discussion of the process of social support in stress resistance. We outline a new stress model that depicts stress as being a product of loss of resources or of a lack of gain of resources given investment of other resources. This model differs from previous models in that it views resources as the only things that may be invested or lost by individuals: they are both sources of stress and that which is employed to combat stress. The threat of loss or actual loss of resources is stressful; at the same time resources are also used to restore that which is lost, to offset loss, and to ensure future protection from loss. Specific categories of resources are also introduced in this chapter and the properties of these categories are discussed.

Having defined stress as a function of loss, social support is depicted as a resource that may directly substitute for loss of important resources or that may act as an indirect replacement for lost resources or to forestall additional loss. In this way, social support is seen as being of central importance to stress resistance because it aids the actualization of resources dormant in the recipient of aid (e.g. encouraging sense of mastery or hope) and broadens the array of resources at the recipient's disposal. It is argued that social support provides these functions both through the actual supportive aid that is transferred between the provider and the recipient and via the sense of connectedness that individuals feel as a product of their relationships with intimate others. Both these functions are seen as having functional and symbolic value for individuals as their effect is both to supply aid and to restore a sense of belonging and of being loved.

Adopting these constructs as a theoretical backdrop, the process by which individuals develop a need for, seek, obtain, and exploit social support is outlined. Joe Stokes and I then proceed to examine investigations which directly and indirectly reflect on this assumed process. Specifically, research on factors that determine the receipt of support, on the structure of social networks, and on sex differences in the provision and receipt of social support are evaluated. In addition, the advantage of studying social support as a product of subjective versus objective accounts is considered through a look at investigations that have employed either or both of these perspectives.

These analyses lead to a number of guidelines for interventionists. The importance of fit of social support to lost resources and personal characteristics of the recipient of support follows from a number of studies. In addition, the history of the relationships that are assumed to have a palliative effect and the comfort of the recipient with the receipt of social support are viewed as paramount. These guidelines argue against an overly optimistic or simplistic future for social support interventions, because the most effective transfer of social support can be shown to occur among individuals who possess strong personal resources (e.g. self-esteem, mastery) and who are privy to intimate, positive ties. These individuals are least likely to need artificial attempts to add social support, unless they are situationally distanced from supportive others, say, during a transitional move. On the other hand, those in most need of social support may lack self-esteem, a sense of mastery, intimate ties, and requisite social competencies. These factors may preclude any positive effects of simply grafting new social ties to their environment and point to the need to work on more basic interventions aimed at enhancing capacity for intimacy, self-esteem and other personal resources, and teaching interpersonal competencies.

The next chapter is written by Ben Gottlieb. His earlier typology of social support categories which differentiated between emotional support, instrumental support, material support, and advice (Gottlieb, 1978) was widely adopted and contributed towards a clearer understanding of the active ingredients in social support (see Gottlieb, 1981; Hobfoll, 1985b; Sarason and Sarason, 1985). In the current chapter he presents a new typology for the study of social support interventions. Adopting a commonsense, structural view of support interventions he suggests that supportive interventions may proceed on the individual, dyadic, group, social system, and community levels. He reviews current research on each of these levels and points to directions for future research.

Perhaps most surprising and provocative is the inclusion of the individual level in this typology. He argues, however, that individuals require certain skills, knowledge, and coping repertoires to facilitate both the receipt and the provision of social support. Interventions at this level will help ensure that the provision of social support will be met receptively and exploited to its best advantage. He highlights the importance of beliefs in the efficacy of social support versus self-reliance and of behaviors that encourage or repel the provision of aid. He also underscores how reactions on the part of providers may inhibit the effective commerce of social support.

On the dyadic level, Gottlieb differentiates between naturally occurring relationships and grafted relationships that are artificially provided to individuals in need. In his discussion he also invokes the concept of fit of social support to the particular needs of the individual and emphasizes the role of intimacy in effective provision of support. On the group level, he divides intervention efforts into those focusing on existing ties and those aimed at grafting additional support to the social environment of those in need. He is particularly optimistic about the effectiveness of self-help groups, although he also points out that little controlled research can be called upon to verify the precise way in which participants gain from such efforts and even less to identify the feature of the self-help that is aiding those who report benefiting from it.

Structural interventions on the social systems level are considered in Gottlieb's next category level. These include structural changes in institutions designed to enhance the exchange of social support, for example, where patients are assigned primary care nurses to ensure greater continuity of hospital care. Finally, a few programs that have attempted to enhance the use of social support on the community level are discussed. A fine example of such a program is the work by Jason (1985), who used radio broadcasts to educate the public about the availability of self-help groups and to prompt referral to them. Such attempts may be especially important because they can reach those in undeserved populations.

Gottlieb suggests that the study of social support interventions has important implications for a more complete understanding of the process and mechanics of social support. By studying controlled social support interventions, causative factors may be uncovered and the conditions wherein social support is most effectively transferred may be identified. Model studies may thus bridge the distance between theory and effective applications, enhancing both goals simultaneously.

In the following chapter, Ian Gotlib and Jill Hooley discuss interaction in the marriages of depressed persons. They argue that marriage may buffer depression or increase depression depending on the nature of the interaction between spouses; the greater the marital distress, the greater the depression. They point to research that identifies the possession of an intimate opposite-sex partner as critical to the onset of depression, those who have such a relationship being resistant to depression and those who lack such a tie being especially prone to depression. They further present evidence linking increase in marital discord to the onset of depressive episodes.

Marital relationships are also seen by Gotlib and Hooley as affecting the course and outcome of depressive disorders. They discuss how spouses' tendency to express more extreme emotions, especially rejecting or critical emotions, has been related to increased marital dissatisfaction and relapse of depressive episodes in the depressed partner. Many of the studies which are reviewed, however, are faulted by Gotlib and Hooley on methodological grounds owing to their reliance on self-report, often by a single member of the marital dyad. They go on to suggest that examination of the actual behavioral interactions of depressed individuals and their partners is a more potent direction for future research as this will aid the identification of causative factors and because the reliability of the measures is more often assured.

Investigations which relied upon observations of the actual interactions within marital relationships are reviewed by Gotlib and Hooley, who interpret the findings of these studies as indicating that depressed individuals encourage rejection and distancing by their partners and have inadequate social skills. In addition, they suggest that some evidence points to the rejecting emotional climate cast by the nondepressed partner in the relationship as a major source of depression. Still other studies seem to place the onus not on the interpersonal behavior of the depressed or nondepressed partner but on the hostility and lack of support typical of the shared marital interaction of the two partners.

Given this background, Gotlib and Hooley discuss the prospects for interactional perspectives on marital therapy with depressed individuals. They find such efforts promising and adopt an intra–interpersonal approach that envisages marital interactions as operating, on the one hand, as sources and sustaining factors in depression and, on the other hand, as anti-depressive factors. In order to differentiate between these aspects they suggest the carrying out of longitudinal studies of marital interactions of individuals at high risk for depression and those who already have exhibited signs of depression. They further encourage greater standardization of procedures both for diagnosing depression and for depicting the nature of the marital interaction, as well as the employment of appropriate control groups. Finally, they suggest that data should be obtained from a variety of sources, including direct observation, self-report, and spouse and family reports, as convergence of these separate sources of data may be most illuminating. Overall, their chapter both illuminates the complexity of this area of research and gives some valuable suggestions for unraveling the answers to important questions that are being asked.

Karen Rook looks at research on loneliness and its implications for clinical interventions in the final chapter of this section. It is interesting that much of the work on loneliness has been generated by social psychologists like Rook who have shown an interest in personal relationships, rather than by clinical psychologists. This is despite the fact that loneliness is one of the most common presenting complaints of those seeking psychotherapy. While loneliness is a very personal feeling, previously addressed more by existential philosophers than psychologists, Rook discusses how research on the interaction of lonely individuals illuminates the nature and etiology of loneliness. Rook has shown herself in the past to be an especially creative thinker and her chapter here once again testifies to that fact.

In this chapter Rook begins by discussing the nature of loneliness. She points out that loneliness may be a chronic traitlike characteristic of an individual or a felt state during a circumscribed period of time. She further reminds the reader that even when loneliness is a chronic individual trait it may have both environmental and internal causes. Looking at environmental factors, she argues that lonely individuals may lack certain kinds of nurturant relationships or be without attachment to an adequate social network. This may be due to situational exigencies, their own rejection of support, or their inability to build, maintain, or esteem close ties.

Rook illustrates how loneliness may also follow from problems with existing ties. Citing evidence that lonely individuals do not necessarily have fewer or less frequent social ties, she argues that loneliness may also be the product of difficulty in achieving intimacy, conflicted ties, or rejection. From an interactional perspective, loneliness may follow from inadequate interpersonal skills which act to alienate others. Alternatively, from a cognitive vantage point, lonely people may misinterpret social cues and relationships, tending to be pessimistic, cynical, mistrusting, and denigrating of themselves and others. The cognitive and behavioral facets of loneliness may, in fact, be intertwined in a way that almost ensures isolation and anomie.

Rook also presents as a novel cause of loneliness, deficient solitude skills. Lonely people may be lonely not only owing to deficiencies in relationship skills and negativistic cognitive appraisals of their relationships but also because they may have poorer tolerance for aloneness. Ironically, however, lonely individuals may at the same time be attracted to solitude because of their fears of rejection and the stress they experience in interpersonal contexts. This ambivalence may in itself further exacerbate their plight.

Rook suggests that any intervention with lonely individuals must address environmental, cognitive, and behavioral components of loneliness. Interventions may be applied on both the individual and group levels and following onset of loneliness or on a preventive basis. Teaching social skills working on cognitive styles as Rook advises may also act to remove some of the stigma of traditional psychotherapy. In addition, her identification of the areas of deficit among lonely persons might be applied on all five levels of intervention outlined by Gottlieb in his chapter.

CONCLUSIONS

In inviting contributions for this section we were interested in approaches that emphasized interpersonal interaction and a 'here and now' time perspective. Upon reading these studies, however, some additional commonalities emerge.

Each of these diverse areas of research highlights the importance of intimacy. In this regard, intimacy emerges as being of primary importance in social support, in warding off depression, and in avoiding loneliness. It is also indicated that the achievement of intimacy involves social skills and the capacity to feel comfortable with close ties. As the chapters by Stokes and myself and Rook illustrate, intimacy is also potentially threatening as it heightens the potential cost of rejection; this makes it especially threatening for those with low self-esteem or a pessimistic view about their abilities to sustain relationships.

Each of the chapters also highlights that both cognitions and environmental factors are important in personal relationships. Actual problems in relationships and the passage of objective social support represent one facet of the interpersonal process, realities that exist in the environment. The appraisal of this interpersonal commerce reflects a second facet of the total picture. Researchers have tended to isolate the two components, but the review of these different areas of research clearly underscores the need for the integrated study of objective events and subjective appraisals.

This dual basis of personal relationships, consisting of environmental and internal facets, is related to the concept of *fit* that also emerged as central in this section. Fit implies that certain kinds of environmental resources complement individuals' needs, while others may miss the mark or even prove detrimental. Researchers and interventionists have typically employed a shotgun approach, not addressing the match between personal needs and environmental conditions, but this trend seems to be giving way to a tailored approach. The model of conservation of resources detailed by myself and Stokes offers one way of conceptualizing this matching, suggesting that personal relationships that substitute for losses or that are perceived as preventing future loss may be most efficacious. When individuals feel free of the threat of impending loss they may then be free to employ interpersonal strategies whose goal is to maximize gain, and in so doing adopt a positive, growth-oriented approach.

Finally, the study of personal relationships in clinical and community psychology can be seen as emphasizing a need for the examination of interpersonal process. Early research has tended to assume the nature of interpersonal interactions and focus on outcome. So, for example, social support was envisaged as a stress mediator, not as an object of interest in and of itself. More recently, however, researchers have understood that the full puzzle cannot be solved if the mechanisms by which social support operates are not fully clarified. The same may be said for the interpersonal processes that accompany depression or loneliness or that follow from stressful circumstances. Future research has its task laid out for it as this will require more ecological approaches than have previously been applied, approaches that demand attention to the internal, environmental, and interactive components of the human ecology.

ACKNOWLEDGEMENTS

Work on this volume was conducted, in part, while I was on sabbatical at DePaul University, Chicago, Illinois, USA and thanks are extended to Dr Sheldon Cotler, Department Chair, and Dr Lenny Jason for their hospitality.

Handbook of Personal Relationships
Edited by S. W. Duck
© 1988 John Wiley & Sons Ltd

26

The Process and Mechanics of Social Support

STEVAN E. HOBFOLL
Kent State University, Ohio, USA
and
JOSEPH P. STOKES
University of Illinois at Chicago, USA

ABSTRACT

This chapter discusses the process of social support, including how support is obtained, the costs of support, and how support counteracts the effects of stress. A new definition of stress, based on the concept of loss of resources, is presented. Sex differences in support and the conceptual development of the support concept are considered.

Interest in social support and its relationship to mental health, physical health, and stress resistance has surged recently (Cohen and Syme, 1985; Gottlieb, 1981; Hobfoll, 1986a; Sarason and Sarason, 1985). In general, social support has been linked to lower levels of psychological and physical symptomatology and enhanced stress resistance (Cohen and Wills, 1985; Sarason and Sarason, 1985). Some studies, however, have noted that social support may in some instances be related to poorer adjustment (Hobfoll, 1985a; Hobfoll and London, 1986; Riley and Eckenrode, 1986), and surely not all social ties are supportive (Gotlib and Hooley, this volume). There has also been considerable argument over whether social support is related directly to well-being or whether it buffers the effects of highly stressful circumstances in particular. This latter position has been termed the stress-buffering hypothesis (Wilcox, 1981b).

There have been a few attempts to disentangle the various effects of social support, but most studies have not examined the process that occurs in socially supportive interactions (cf. Cohen and Wills, 1985). By process of support we mean the actual building of supportive ties, seeking and obtaining aid, and the behavioral, cognitive, and emotional reactions to that aid, as well as thoughts, emotions, and behaviors that mediate such reactions. We contend that only by examining the process of social support and factors associated with its acquisition will we enhance our understanding of what actually occurs under the broad umbrella of constructs that constitute social support (see also Gottlieb, this volume). In this chapter we will focus on the relatively few studies that have investigated the *process* of social support. We will also draw from other studies that have not directly examined process, but whose results may be used to speculate about process and to suggest future research directions.

We will begin by defining social support, after which we will make a case for why social support is needed during stressful and nonstressful conditions. We will also develop a new model of stress and examine the results of obtaining support in terms of this model. Having established the need for support, we will look at what social support provides and how it is obtained. How supportive social systems are developed and how they operate will then be discussed in three sections which address the dynamics of social networks, whether support is best envisaged as an objective or a subjective entity, and sex differences in the development and use of social support, respectively. Finally, we will discuss the limitations and negative consequences of social support. In all of this our expressed intent is not only to summarize the work that has been done to date, but to go beyond the data and to speculate, in order to suggest avenues for future research and to invite greater discussion.

DEFINITIONS OF SOCIAL SUPPORT

Social support has been defined in many ways. In one sense, social support is a generic term for that 'right stuff' that is gained by being socially connected. In another sense, social support has come to mean those interactions in which supportive acts occur between people.

Gerald Caplan (1974) was one of the first to discuss the psychological benefits of social support. He suggested that social support aids individuals by providing feedback, validation, and a sense that they can master their environments. He further postulated that social support is important because it provides material resources that individuals may not otherwise obtain. Cobb (1976), another early theorist, suggested that the benefit of social support is derived from the information that it provides to people that they are loved, esteemed, and valued members of a social network.

House (1981) introduced a more action-oriented and specific interpretation of what constitutes social support. He felt that social support involves the actual transaction between two or more people in which emotional concern, instrumental aid, information, or appraisal occurs. Most recently, Shumaker and Brownell (1984), also emphasizing action, defined social support as 'an exchange between at least two individuals perceived by the provider or the recipient to be intended to enhance the well-being of the recipient' (p. 13).

We feel that social integration and socially supportive interactions are both important aspects of social support, and, often, it is difficult to distinguish between the two. We propose that *social integration* should be viewed as *the state of connectedness of individuals to significant others* and that this is a primary element of social support. We further argue that Shumaker and Brownell's definition applies to socially supportive *interactions*, in particular, and not to social support, in general. We combine these two aspects and define social support as *those social interactions or relationships that provide individuals with actual assistance or with a feeling of attachment to a person or group that is perceived as caring or loving*. Social support would then encompass both aspects of social support: social connectedness and supportive interactions. With this definition in hand we can begin to develop an understanding of why social support is important to individuals.

A MODEL OF STRESS

There has been repeated criticism in the literature regarding a lack of theory about how social support aids stress resistance (Sarason and Sarason, 1985; Shumaker and Brownell, 1984). To address this issue one must first have a model of stress that is testable and parsimonious. Stress and stress resistance are two sides of the same coin, and so the models representing them should have compatible qualities. Few attempts have been made in the literature, however, to effect this integration.

Typically, McGrath's (1970) balance model has been adopted to explain stress. According to this model, stress is the state of imbalance between perceived demand or threat and coping capacity in a situation with consequences that are important to the individual. When demand or threat outweighs coping capacity, stress is created. This model implies that stress resistance occurs either by increasing coping capacity or by decreasing demand. Social support might act on either side of this balance to aid stress resistance. Friends might increase our perceived coping capacity by convincing us that we really can master the challenge. Alternatively, they might act directly to attenuate the stressor facing us by, say, intervening to prevent our being fired from the job.

Given this type of formulation, researchers are left with an infinity of ways that social support might act. The response to this in the literature has been to look at social support in many different ways, with no central theoretical formulation. Being married (Eaton, 1978), having relationships that revolve around a number of life concerns (Hirsch, 1980; Hobfoll and Walfisch, 1984), being given a loan (Sarason *et al.*, 1983), and intimacy (Brown, Bhrolchain and Harris, 1975; Hobfoll and Lieberman, 1987; Stokes, 1983) have all been studied as aspects of social support. They probably all are ways of looking at social support, but what is missing is a central defining structure.

In recent writings, Hobfoll (in press) has presented a definition of stress that may help to clarify a central defining structure around which social support can be understood. The general model is termed the *Model of Conservation of Resources*. This model proposes that individuals act to gain resources and to offset loss of resources. Stress is thus defined as (a) *the perception of net loss of resources*, (b) *the perception of threat of loss of resources*, or (c) *the perception of lack of gain of resources following investment of resources. Resources*, in turn, are defined as *those objects, conditions, feelings, and energies that we value, or that enable us to obtain those objects, conditions, personal characteristics, or energies that we value.*

We will apply this model to explain how social support acts to limit stress and to explain why use of social support, itself, contributes to stress. To do this we must first outline how people react to loss of resources and the types of resources proposed by the model.

The model of conservation of resources suggests that individuals act to minimize net loss of resources and to maximize gain of resources. This, in turn, implies that *when individuals are confronted with a potential loss of resources, they invest other resources to offset this loss*. It also implies a very important second notion that does not follow from the balance model of stress. Specifically, *if stress is a product of perceived loss of resources, individuals will act to gain resources that either* (1) *will replace lost resources or* (2) *will intervene to minimize net loss*. Third, the model implies that *during nonstressful periods individuals will act to minimize the chance of future loss of resources and maximize the future gain of resources*. In this way the model also predicts how social support is sought and used during stressful and nonstressful periods.

The model of conservation of resources is more easily testable than the balance model. The difficulty in testing the balance model stems from the fact that it places threat on one side of the balance scales and resources on the other. Thus, to know *a priori* if stress is present, we must be able to operationalize threat and resources in comparable units of measurement; we must know how much threat is equivalent to how much resources, an almost impossible task. A second problem with the balance notion is that what is perceived as threat is influenced by the availability of resources that impact the initial phases of exposure to stressful events. Because resources influence the perception of stress, the balance model has an element of tautology and the two sides of the balance are not truly separate. Indeed, the balance model is more of a conceptual backdrop than a directly testable theory.

By conceptualizing stress as the perception of loss of resources or the actual loss of resources, in contrast, we have a single construct (resources) that can be measured and assigned different values. The measurement may use future, past, and present time frames and subjective or objective indices to yield indications of the degree of stress individuals are experiencing. Whether this is the most valuable way to conceptualize stress is an empirical question, but at least the model is given to validation, modification, or rejection.

The model of conservation of resources is also more comprehensive than the balance model. The conservation model predicts behavior during stressful and everyday circumstances, in anticipation of stress, and long after confrontation with traumatic events. The balance model, in comparison, predicts outcome only at the time of confrontation with stressors. Another way in which the model of conservation of resources is more comprehensive than the balance model is that the concept of fit is integral to the former. In contrast, the notion of fit must be applied as an addendum to the balance model, which merely implies that stress is counteracted by the presence of resources in general.

The need to consider resources in terms of their fit to the situational demands has gained increasing currency. Cohen and McKay (1984), for example, suggested that the effectiveness of social support will depend to a large part on its fit with the particular needs of the individual. However, they do not detail the determinants of fit. Hobfoll (1985b, 1986b) has outlined a more complex fit model that suggests that the fit of any resource will depend on the nature of the environmental demand on individuals, individuals' needs, their tendencies to react with certain kinds of strain (e.g. tendency to drink, to experience lower back pain, or to become depressed), time (in the person's own life and *vis à vis* the event), values (of the individual and society), and perceptions (trait and situational biases). Finally, and this is a very important point, fit of social support to needs will depend on the person's other resources, both internal (e.g. hardiness) and external (e.g. money, insurance). Consequently, one may not speak of fit of social support to needs without considering the other resources (or the lack thereof) available to the individual.

TYPES OF RESOURCES

In the model of conservation of resources the term resources implies those objects, feelings, conditions, and energies that are *valued* by the individual. Some resources may possess properties relevant to more than one category, but this is the exception rather than the rule. The value of the resource is ultimately an individual perception, but socialization ensures a large degree of consistency in the values that are assigned to resources within a given culture (Rokeach, 1973; Williams, 1979).

Objects are the first type of resources. Objects are resources when their innate or implied physical nature is valuable. An automobile is an innately valuable resource because it provides transportation. A sexy Italian sports car is valued both because it provides transportation and because it has implied value— status. Shelter, clothing, and a personal computer are all object resources.

Conditions are the second category of resources. Psychologists have been loth to examine conditions, but sociologists have envisaged conditions as important resources and have integrated them into their thinking about stress (Pearlin, 1983; Menaghan, 1983). Conditions are valued resources when they are central to our identity and are the means of achieving other valuable resources. They may also be resources when they act to offset loss of resources. Examples of resource conditions include marriage, parenthood, seniority, tenure, employment, being vice president of the company, and the title Doctor or Professor. They suggest attainment of roles esteemed by society. It is also typical of resource conditions that they are difficult to obtain and sustain, and, indeed, they often require a lifetime of investment of resources for achievement.

Personal characteristics are the third category of resources. Feelings are valued when they are stable states that are positively experienced or when they are stable states that facilitate achievement of desired goals. In this way, a general sense of hope (Breznitz, 1983) is a valued resource for many. Mastery (Hobfoll and London, 1986), internal locus of control (Lefcourt, Martin and Saleh, 1984), hardiness (Kobasa and Puccetti, 1983), self-esteem (Hobfoll and Lieberman, 1987), and a sense of coherence (Antonovsky, 1979) are examples of personal resources that are typified by their provision of a positive feeling about the self and their facilitation of an outlook that aids achievement of desired goals.

Personal characteristics can be especially valuable resources because they are carried with the individual. Consequently, they require no recruitment time and are easily accessible (Hobfoll, 1985a). We emphasize that we are implying trait not state characteristics. Individuals who possess traits do not always experience thoughts or feelings associated with the trait, but they do tend to experience such thoughts or feelings more often and with greater intensity than those who are low on the trait (Spielberger, 1972). So, whereas persons with high hardiness may at a given time feel out of control and alienated, they are more likely than persons low in hardiness to feel in control and to experience a sense of commitment (Kobasa and Puccetti, 1983).

Energies are the last type of resources. Energies are resources if they enable the achievement of other resources. They have no innate value. Examples of this type of resource include money, credit, being owed favors, social skills, and knowledge. So, whereas knowledge is valued, it is valued only because it is a means to an end. It is also characteristic of energy resources to lose value when they are converted to meet goals. A new automobile, for instance, immediately loses value when driven from the dealer, and knowledge is less valuable for producing power if the knowledge is shared. The value of energy resources, in part, lies in their being convertible to a variety of resources.

We should point out that this schema categorizes resources according to their functional properties. People for instance, are not resources *per se*, but may provide resources based on their functional significance. The concept of social support is so promising because it suggests a broad set of valuable functional roles that people fulfill. When we say that our colleague or spouse is valuable to us, we are really referring to functions that they fulfill, say, in helping us complete work reports, providing us important feedback, and/or giving us a sense of being loved and appreciated.

WHAT SOCIAL SUPPORT PROVIDES

Social support may be seen as providing, bolstering, or facilitating the provision of each of the four types of resources. Social support is so valuable because *it extends the self and what the self can achieve alone*. In this regard, individuals are limited by their own set of resources, however rich. By obtaining social support, however, individuals may obtain additional resources that they themselves do not possess or cannot actualize. In the former case, one may be given money that one didn't previously possess. In the latter case, one may, for instance, be helped in moving a couch. One could lift half the couch alone, yet without help in lifting the other half one's own strength has no value. Help lifting the couch, then, actualizes one's own resources.

In environmental terms, the four types of resources may each be enriched, enhanced, or provided outright by social support. This is objectively what social support provides. However, the effect of social support is mediated by the perception of meaning that the recipients of support assign to what they receive. In this regard, a number of researchers have noted that what is important is not so much what is provided in terms of aid, but the perception of being supported (Barrera, 1981; Henderson, Byrne and Duncan-Jones, 1981; Hobfoll, Nadler and Leiberman, 1986; Stokes, 1983).

This point may be illustrated by an everyday example. A friend wants to comfort you after you have experienced a failure. Being uncomfortable with intimacy, he doesn't know what to say, so he comes over to help fix your car. The car may not even require repair, but you recognize his actions as his way of showing he cares. This recognition makes you feel better.

Emphasizing perceived support suggests that the provision of energies, conditions, and objects may all be translated in terms of feelings on the perception level. This point appears central to understanding the effects of social support. You may receive a gift from your father-in-law of a large sum of money, but feel that he offers it as a way of gaining control. This may cause you to disregard or denigrate his gesture. Thus, attributions are made not to the face value of what social support provides, but to the combination of the face value and the intent we perceive behind the provision of support.

The real social support, as we will discuss in detail later, may be neither the objective (environmental) provision of the resource nor the perception of the value of what is received, but a combination of the two. This point underscores the importance of intimacy, because in intimate relationships, one is likely to receive actual provision of resources when they are required, and one is likely to make the attribution that the aid signifies love or deep caring. In other words, both aspects of social support, social integration and supportive transactions, are likely to occur within intimate relationships.

Hobfoll, Nadler and Leiberman (1986) also found that it is not mere intimacy that is important. Rather, they suggest that it is important that such intimacy be present in healthy relationships. Intimacy in troubled or enmeshed relationships may lead to negative attributions as to the intent of aid (Minuchin, 1974). In conflicted relationships social support may be disregarded or have adverse effects because the underlying motivation is suspect.

Trying to weigh the relative contributions of perceived intent and actual support is difficult. We would speculate, however, that when people have extreme feelings, positive or negative, about the provider of support, they will make attributions based not on what resources are provided, but on who is providing it and why. That which a loved intimate offers is viewed as a gift and leaves one with a feeling of being loved. On the other hand, anything offered by a vindictive colleague is viewed as manipulative. In contrast, what is actually provided by people towards whom we have less polarized feelings is more likely to be viewed in terms of the actual properties of the resource provided.

OBTAINING SOCIAL SUPPORT

In this discussion we have implied that social support is something that exists in people's social environment. How is this valuable commodity obtained? Surprisingly little research has been directed at determining the receipt of social support. Sarason and Sarason (1985) have begun some preliminary work in this area by examining the correlates of social support. As one might expect, they found social support to be correlated positively with extroversion and negatively with neuroticism. From this they surmized that those who seek social contacts are more likely than those who do not to receive social support. They also suggested that neurotics may be unattractive to others and may be unsuccessful at creating or sustaining the kinds of stable relationships that will foster social support.

The Sarasons also noted that social support is negatively related to loneliness. Due to the correlational nature of this research, no causal statement can be made about the direction of this relationship. However, it would be consistent with theoretical notions about loneliness that individuals who are lonely lack the skills to elicit social support or to sustain the kinds of relationships that are likely to provide support (Hansson, Jones and Carpenter, 1984; Jones, 1985). Most likely there is also a feedback loop, such that those who do not then receive support become increasingly lonely and isolated. One might argue that the lack of social support and loneliness are one and the same. However, it has not been found that merely lacking social support leads to loneliness, nor even that gaining social support will necessarily diminish loneliness (Rook, 1985, and this volume).

Kahn and Antonucci (1981) suggested that early childhood experiences in the obtaining and observing of supportive relationships affect individuals throughout their lives. According to their model, 'a close accounting of early interpersonal interactions and the role transactions of an individual will provide insights into individuals' present and future course of interpersonal relationships and social support' (Antonucci, 1985, p. 23). So, either through modeling of behaviors or acquisition of personal traits that affect interpersonal behavior, Kahn and Antonucci are suggesting that individuals learn if, how, and when to seek social support.

Cutrona (1986a) also adopted a lifespan approach in her study of the determinants of social support. She found that social network variables modestly predicted loneliness and perceived adequacy of social support among an elderly sample, but not among mothers of one-year-old children. She ascribed this difference to developmental factors that are reflected in the environment. Specifically, elderly people's networks were very much affected by whether the individual was married or single, many elderly being widowed. Consequently, some elderly were very isolated, while others had intact relations. Mothers of one-year-olds, in contrast, almost always had a close relationship with their spouse. For them, the quality of that relationship was interpreted as being more important than the quantity of social network ties.

Cutrona also suggested that stress levels may moderate the amount of social support people receive. In a second study Cutrona (1986b) supported this contention when she found that behaviors reflecting emotional and informational support occurred as a specific response to stressful events. Hobfoll and Lerman (1986), however, found that stress plays a more complex role in terms of acquisition of social support. In a one-year, prospective study they found that mothers of well children and children who had been acutely ill and were now recovered received greater levels of social support if they had more intimate ties and felt more comfortable seeking support. These qualities were not, however, related to acquisition of social support among mothers of chronically ill children. It would seem that the demands of continued stress determine social support levels to a greater degree than do social and personal characteristics for this latter group. Perhaps mothers of chronically ill children who previously received high levels of support find their support reservoirs depleted, while those who would not normally have the social characteristics related to the acquisition of support are pressed to obtain the minimum of support required to adjust to the chronic stress situation. The sum effect of these two forces may explain the intermediary levels of support that were found among the mothers of chronically ill children. This is the first study, to our knowledge, that has examined how attitudes towards seeking support affect support acquisition, and we think this is a promising direction for future research (see also Nadler and Mayeless, 1983).

Possessing personal resources that are themselves associated with stress resistance has also been found to be related to receipt of social support. Using a combined measure of self-esteem and mastery, Hobfoll and Lehrman (1986) found that those who possessed these qualities receive greater levels of social support. This suggests that one reason these resources aid stress resistance is that they are related to the rallying of social support during stressful episodes. Mastery, for example, not only may directly limit distress by providing a feeling that one can master the present challenge, but also may indirectly limit distress because it facilitates developing social relationships so that they can be mobilized successfully during crises.

Future investigations will want to examine how personal, social, and environmental factors are related to seeking and obtaining of social support (see also Wortman and Lehman, 1985). The pioneering studies that have been reported are encouraging but should be viewed cautiously because they have examined only a limited number of antecedents and have not been replicated. One important aspect of these investigations, nonetheless, is that they attempt to tie social support research to a broader lifespan approach that considers individuals and their needs in person–situation contexts. This approach may help integrate the generally atheoretical study of social support with more firmly founded developmental, social, and personality constructs.

SOCIAL NETWORK DENSITY AND THE SUPPORTIVE PROCESS

One approach to studying social support involves analyzing the social networks that provide support (cf. Gottlieb, this volume). Such social network analysis may provide a kind of social X-ray that yields process information. Originally developed by sociologists and social anthropologists (see Mitchell and Trickett, 1980), network analysis focuses on quantitative description of social networks. A number of variables can be used to describe networks. In this chapter we will focus on one variable, the density of the network. A network is dense to the degree that network members have relationships with one another. In a low-density network, the network members tend not to interact with or even know one another. Density, then, refers to interconnections among network members, not to the number of connections of the focal member.

There are data that suggest lower-density networks may be more helpful and satisfying than high-density networks. Hirsch (1980) found that with younger widows and mature women returning to college, lower-density networks were associated with more satisfying support and better mental health. Similarly, Wilcox (1981a) found that lower density facilitated adjustment following divorce. Both Hirsch and Wilcox mentioned some reasons why their subjects, all of whom were undergoing some kind of transition, would benefit from low-density networks. Lower-density networks can be associated with lower normative pressure and a greater variety of roles for the focal person. During periods of transition when major life changes have occurred, having relatively little normative pressure from one's network and having a wide variety of roles *vis-à-vis* others in the networks may facilitate adjustment. Wilcox also suggested that the relation between low density and high adjustment among his sample of recently divorced women was mediated by a third variable, the percentage of relatives in the network. Obviously, networks composed largely of relatives will tend to be dense, since relatives usually have personal relationships with one another. The lack of satisfaction with social support and the relatively poor adjustment of respondents with dense networks may be attributable not to high density *per se* but to a high percentage of relatives. Other researchers have suggested that family support is a mixed blessing, yielding both support and stressful obligations (Hobfoll, Nadler and Leiberman, 1986; Stein and Rappaport, 1986). Investigators studying network density need to be sensitive to the inevitable confounding of the density of the network and percentage of relatives in it.

Hirsch (1979) further asserted that high-density networks have a higher potential for intranetwork conflict than do low-density networks. If persons A and B are in conflict, and if A seeks support or guidance from C, the support C gives may depend on C's relationship with B. In a dense network, when C and B are likely to interact, C may be cautious and ambiguous in supporting A, for fear of offending B. Heider's (1958) balance theory gives a similar explanation for why the density of a network might correlate negatively with satisfaction and/or supportiveness. According to balance theory, if I have positive relationships with person A and with person B, but A and B do not like each other, the three-person system will be out of balance and likely to cause conflict and distress. Similarly, if I like A and dislike B, a friendship between A and B might put strain on my relationship with A.

In short, low-density networks may be most helpful when one is experiencing

Do low density networks tend to be larger (have more people in them)?

a major life transition and when one needs the freedom to explore new roles. Lower-density networks may also be helpful when one needs referrals or information, such as when one wants to find a new apartment or a new job. In such cases low-density networks would probably provide more different, weak ties (Granovetter, 1973), which could provide more information or contacts from more different groups than would highly dense networks. Particularly during periods of transition, people may adjust more easily because of the increased information or contacts that low-density networks can provide.

In contrast, there are probably times when a dense network is best able to provide support. In the period immediately following the death of a loved one, a close-knit network might provide feelings of belonging that are comforting. The young widows Hirsch studied, however, were more satisfied with support from low-density networks. Perhaps earlier in the grief process (these widows were not contacted until at least three months after their husband's death) support from high-density networks would have been especially helpful. When one requires intense, almost constant support, as when recuperating from serious illness or surgery, a dense network of friends might best be able to coordinate their efforts so as to provide continuous assistance to the invalid.

Dense networks may also provide beneficial support when stressors are chronic. Potasznik and Nelson (1984), for instance, found a positive relation between network density and satisfaction with support for parents of a mentally ill person. Having a family member with a mental illness is a chronic condition that requires continuous coping. Potasznik and Nelson hypothesized that their subjects who were coping successfully had a small group of friends and relatives with whom they could speak intimately and on whom they could depend. These friends and relatives typically formed a small, rather dense network that provided a lot of support. In contrasting their finding with those of researchers who found negative correlations between density and satisfaction with support, Potasznik and Nelson emphasized the notion of the 'fit' between the particular situation and the density of the social network.

Dense networks may also limit feelings of loneliness, as noted by Stokes (1985). He speculated that networks in which the members are interconnected and are important in each other's lives provided a sense of community, a sense of belonging to a group, which tempers loneliness. Stokes and Levin (1986) reported that this relation of density and feelings of loneliness is stronger for men than for women, a finding they attributed to men's being more group oriented in their friendships and in their criteria for evaluating loneliness. Stokes and Levin also found evidence that the density–loneliness relation is mediated by social support. Perhaps, for male subjects at least, higher density leads to increased levels of socially supportive behaviors, which in turn lead to less loneliness.

These results highlight the importance not only of studying the ability of structural variables to predict satisfaction and adjustment but of understanding the mechanisms involved. Do network structures differences influence satisfaction with support or adjustment directly, or by affecting the nature of behavioral exchanges, which in turn influence satisfaction? Rook (1983) has argued that researchers need to control for the effects of specific behavior exchanges in order to demonstrate the independent effects of network structure. Although controlling the content of social support is probably not feasible, researchers certainly need to examine specific behavioral exchanges in order to understand the relation of density and other structural variables to satisfaction with support and to psychological adjustment.

SUBJECTIVE VERSUS OBJECTIVE MEASURES OF SOCIAL SUPPORT

The degree to which measures of social support tap objective transactions versus subjective perceptions implies assumptions about the process of supportive interactions and social support. Measures of social support can be placed on a dimension from objective to subjective. Studies that observe or record transactions in a way that could be called truly objective are rare indeed (see Glidewell et al., 1983, for an example where trained observers rated interactions). Relatively objective self-report measures include those that require subjects to keep a diary of interactions or support received (e.g. Hirsch, 1979, 1980; Wheeler and Nezlek, 1977) and those that ask respondents to indicate how frequently they have received specific supportive behaviors (e.g. ISSB; Barrera, Sandler and Ramsay, 1981). Hobfoll and Lerman (1986) have also attempted to get second-party assessments of social support received instead of merely relying on self-report. Most of the other measures of social support in the literature are thoroughly subjective, calling for evaluations of satisfaction with, perceived adequacy of, or perceived availability of, support.

Gottlieb (1985a) pointed out that social support was originally thought of as an environmental resource, a conception that dictates measuring either social networks or supportive transactions. The natural partnership of the studies of social support and close relationships, he argued, has been undermined by the tendency of research on social support to take a psychological rather than a transactional perspective. The psychological sense of support tapped by most measures of social support, he wrote, is 'a cognitive representation of the phenomenon whose correspondence with social reality is uncertain' (Gottlieb, 1985a, p. 356). According to Gottlieb, this focus on a psychological sense of support, whose measures must necessarily be subjective, has limited understanding of the helping behavior that transpires within close relationships.

Gottlieb (1985a) recognized, nonetheless, that perceptions of available support are important because they affect appraisals of contextual threat. The appraisal of stress will be relatively benign if people think they have social support resources that will combat the stress effectively. Feeling deficient in social support, in contrast, will exacerbate psychological distress in response to stress. The belief that social support is available when needed is 'psychologically nourishing and uplifting, mainly because it conditions a positive self-image, contributes to a sense of control through help-seeking, and instils self-confidence' (Gottlieb, 1985a, p. 360). Gottlieb went on to argue that this sense of support cannot substitute for actual supportive transactions when coping is necessary after the initial appraisal of the stressor has been made. We agree that actual supportive actions are needed sometimes, but the positive self-image, sense of control, and self-confidence that accompany perceptions of available support are powerful allies, even in the actual coping that follows appraisal. Nevertheless, it is hard to argue with Gottlieb's suggestion that measuring perceived support cannot serve as a substitute for measuring actual supportive exchanges.

Others maintain that subjective, perceived support is of utmost importance. Cobb's (1976) important paper emphasizes the subjective nature of social support as *information* that leads the subject *to believe* that s/he (1) is cared for and loved, (2) is esteemed and valued, and/or (3) belongs to a network of communication and mutual obligation. By this definition, social support occurs only to the degree that it influences the recipient's beliefs. For Cobb social support is intrinsically linked to a cognitive process that is, to some degree at least, subjective. What others do for me or say to me becomes social support only when it changes my beliefs on one of three relevant dimensions. Wethington and Kessler (1986) emphasized the importance of perceived support by suggesting that the influence of actual support received is mediated by perceived support: that is, supportive transactions are helpful mainly because they influence perceptions of support.

Although some types of supportive behaviors could be measured objectively (e.g. statements that you are held in esteem, provision of material aid), the subjective experience of the recipient defies measurement in any objective sense. As we stated in the section on how social support operates, the recipient's sense of the provider's intention is critical. Transactions will not be viewed as supportive if the recipient thinks the provider acted solely out of a sense of obligation or for the purpose of producing a sense of obligation in the recipient.

Research has demonstrated with some consistency that the objective, quantitative measures of social support are not very strongly related to more subjective measures like satisfaction or to outcome measures like health or adjustment (Hirsch, 1979; Sandler and Lakey, 1982). Studies that have tried to predict satisfaction with social support from network variables have not been very successful (Hobfoll, Nadler and Leiberman, 1986; Oritt, Behrman and Paul, 1982; Stokes, 1983). Subjective appraisals of the adequacy of or satisfaction with support are, in contrast, almost always associated with measures of psychological disorder like anxiety and depression (Barrera, 1981; Cohen et al., 1984; Fiore et al., 1986; Henderson et al., 1980; Hirsch, 1980; Sandler and Barrera, 1984), and subjective assessments regarding social ties have been found to be related to satisfaction with support (Hobfoll, Nadler and Leiberman, 1986; Stokes, 1983). In studies that used both objective and subjective support measures (Barrera, 1981; Cohen et al., 1984; Sandler and Barrera, 1984), the more objective measure was at best weakly related to psychological disorders, and, in every case, it was substantially less predictive of psychological disorder than were the measures tapping satisfaction with support.

One interpretation of these findings that measures of perceived availability and adequacy of support are the best predictors of disorder is that subjective appraisals of support are what really matter in preventing symptomatology. Another, probably more parsimonious, explanation suggests the relation of subjective satisfaction with support and psychological disorder reflects intrapersonal cognitive processes. More specifically, some people may hold a pervasive negative view of themselves and of the world in general that predisposes them to evaluate themselves as relatively anxious, depressed, *and* unsupported. Consistent with this interpretation, Watson and Clark (1984) suggested that trait anxiety, neuroticism, depression, and other personality variables can be viewed as reflecting aspects of an overriding, integrative construct which they call negative affectivity (NA). People high in NA tend to be distressed and to dwell on their failures and shortcomings. Because they focus on the negative side of themselves and of others, they tend to hold unfavorable views of themselves and of others and are generally dissatisfied with themselves and with life. People high in NA would tend to appear anxious, depressed, and neurotic on self-report measures of these constructs, and they would be relatively dissatisfied with the social support they received. Perhaps dissatisfaction with social support reflects intrapersonal cognitive processes as much as or more than objective deficiencies in socially supportive transactions.

Hobfoll and his colleagues (Hobfoll and Leiberman, 1987; Hobfoll and Walfisch, 1984) have shown that part of the effect of social support on outcome can be attributed to personal characteristics like self-esteem and sense of mastery (see also Henderson, Byrne and Duncan-Jones, 1981; Wethington and Kessler, 1986). This aspect of their findings supports the interpretation that dissatisfaction with social support and psychological disorder reflect a single intrapersonal cognitive process. They also indicated, however, that subjective social support is predictive of more healthy outcome even after controlling for certain personal characteristics that reflect intrapersonal cognitive processes.

The Sarasons and their colleagues at the University of Washington have also published several articles that have implications for the idea that intrapersonal cognitive processes determine to a large degree perceptions of and satisfaction with social support. Sarason and Sarason (1982) found that subjects high in social support held 'more benign and hopeful views of mental illness' (p. 338) than did subjects low in social support. Those high in social support tended to have low scores on an Anomie Scale which measured a 'negative, despairing, alienated view of life' (p. 340). In general the subjects who perceived themselves as having a lot of social support available and who were rather satisfied with that support seemed happy, hopeful, and optimistic. That is, they were low in negative affectivity. Sarason et al. (1983) reported that subjects low in social support tended to be anxious, depressed, hostile, and, to a lesser degree, introverted and neurotic. Based on these and other results, Sarason et al. concluded that people low in social support are more emotionally labile and more pessimistic about both the present and the future than are people high in social support. In an article titled 'Social support as an individual difference variable', Sarason, Sarason and Shearin (1986) went further in support of the idea that ratings of available support and satisfaction with that support are determined at least in part by individual differences. They demonstrated the stability of their measures of support over a period of three years, a finding that is consistent with viewing support as a personal trait. In fact, the stability of the measures of social support was greater than that of the affective variables of anxiety, depression, and hostility.

Cohen *et al.* (1985) also reported high test–retest correlations for their measure of perceived support and speculated that stable personality factors may cause the correlations of ratings of social support and psychological outcomes. Gottlieb (1985a) commented that the 'high reliability of perceived support ratings may be better testimony to the influence of stable organismic variables than of the stability of the social processes occurring in the individual's trans-actions with his/her social network' (p. 357). Hobfoll and Lerman (1986), however, did find that second-party assessments (subjects' spouses) of social support correlated with self-assessments, suggesting some validity for self-report measures of social support.

Although assuming that social support is itself a personality variable is an extreme view, certainly researchers need to be aware of the interaction of personality and social support and need to include personality variables in their research. Even if they conceive of social support as an environmental factor, researchers should recognize that people vary in their ability to mobilize and use the social environment, and in the way they perceive and interpret supportive transactions. Increasingly researchers are including characterological variables in their research or in their models of social support. DePue and Monroe (1986) stressed the importance of considering personality differences in research predicting psychological disorder, and Heller and Swindle (1983) wrote that 'social support is most profitably viewed in terms of an interaction between environment and person variables occurring across time' (p. 91). Similarly, Lefcourt, Martin and Saleh (1984) concluded that 'interactions between personal proclivities and milieu characteristics should always provide better predictions of criteria such as mood disturbance than should simpler, unifactor models' (p. 389).

In summary, traitlike individual difference variables like negative affectivity may be responsible, in part, for the correlations of measures of social support and psychological disorder. To the degree that subjective appraisals of social support can be accounted for by negative affectivity, the usefulness of subjec-tively perceived constructs like satisfaction with support must be questioned. More research should include measures of personality variables like negative affectivity so that the *unique* contribution of appraisals of social support in predicting disorder or in buffering the stress–disorder relation can be evaluated. Further, the interaction of personality variables and social support should be considered in predicting disorder.

SEX DIFFERENCES IN SUPPORT

The study of sex differences may provide further insights into the development and use of social support. Very little research has focused on the differential distribution of supportive resources between men and women, as most research in social support has used only male or only female subjects, and studies with both men and women have not always reported data separately by gender. There are, however, data to support the idea that women are more involved in social interaction and receive more support than do men.

Using a methodology where subjects completed an interaction diary daily, Hirsch (1979) found that female college students reported spending more time interacting with others in their social networks than did males during an exam period. Women also reported spending more time than men exchanging emotional support, defined as sharing feelings and personal concerns with others. Although this measure of emotional support is clearly confounded with openness or willingness to self-disclose, being open with personal information and emotions is one aspect of the process of social support. Hirsch's results are consistent with the notion that women have more social contact and receive more social support than men do. Burke and Weir's (1978) results with adolescents show similar sex differences, with females more willing than males to discuss personal problems with peers. The study has been cited as evidence supporting sex differences in social support, although its measures, like Hirsch's, seem more closely related to willingness to self-disclose than to social support per se.

Other studies using measures more clearly focused on social support provide evidence that women receive more support, especially emotional support, than do men. Cohen et al. (1984) found that women reported being recipients of significantly more socially supportive acts than did men. Women also scored higher than men on measures of perceived support. Stokes and Wilson (1984) found that women reported receiving more emotional support than did men. Burda, Vaux and Schill (1984) also found that females reported receiving more emotional support than did males, but they found no sex differences in cognitive guidance, material aid, and socializing. Rich, Sullivan and Rich (1986) reported sex differences in several measures related to social support from family. Among college-student subjects, women reported more contact with family (visits, phone calls, letters) than did men. Women also rated their families higher than did men on cohesiveness and expressiveness.

Several studies have reported that women have larger social networks than men. Lootens and Strube (1985) measured the size of networks associated with particular supportive functions (e.g. positive feedback, physical assistance). In each category of support except giving advice and information, the women in their study listed significantly more people than the men did. Similarly, Burda, Vaux and Schill (1984) found that, compared to men, women reported larger social networks.

The Sarasons and their colleagues have collected a lot of data with the Social Support Questionnaire (SSQ: Sarason et al., 1983). For each item in the SSQ (e.g. 'whom can you really count on to listen to you when you need to talk'), respondents list who might be available to fill that function and rate how satisfied they are with the help available. In the Sarasons' studies with the SSQ, 'women consistently have reported greater perceived support [number of supporters] and greater satisfaction with the support available than men' (Sarason *et al.*, 1985, p. 478).

A fair amount of evidence, then, suggests that women may have greater social support resources than men have. Different patterns of socialization for men and women may help explain this difference. Socialization for males traditionally has emphasized autonomy and independence. The stereotypic male may be reluctant to acknowledge difficulties or to ask for help or support. Other writers (Fausteau, 1974; Lewis, 1978) have suggested that men are uncomfortable with intimacy and that their friendships tend to be shallow and superficial.

The stereotypic feminine role, on the other hand, emphasizes warmth, supportiveness, and comfort with intimacy. Women, relative to men, are encouraged to acknowledge personal difficulties and to seek support. If these stereotypes reflect reality to even a moderate degree, women should be more comfortable seeking social support. The feminine sex role also emphasizes interpersonal competence, which can lead to more satisfactory relationships and broader social support. Consistent with these notions, several studies have found that women are more effective interpersonally and more skilled socially than men are (Sarason *et al.*, 1985; Sarason, Sarason and Shearin, 1986).

If women are especially comfortable with and eager to achieve intimacy and interpersonal closeness, then emotional support might also be more helpful to them than to men, at least under certain conditions. Following a similar line of thought, Cohen and Wills (1985) speculated that women show more benefit from confidant support than do men. Empirical support for these contentions may be found in a number of studies. In one such study, Henderson *et al.* (1980) reported data showing the association of the availability and adequacy of close relationships with psychological disorders was stronger for women than for men. In a second investigation, Husaini *et al.* (1982) found that among married couples measures of social support from spouses correlated with symptoms of depression more strongly for women than for men. In a large-scale epidemiological study, Berkman and Syme (1979) looked at the relationship between social contact and mortality over a nine-year period. Being married, having relatively frequent contact with friends and relatives, and belonging to churches and other formal or informal groups reduced mortality rates after initial level of health had been controlled. These effects were true for both men and women but were more pronounced for women at all age groups.

One other sex difference involves the ability of social network structure variables (e.g. network size, density) to predict perceptions of support or satisfaction with support. Stokes and Wilson (1984) found that the number of confidants in a network predicted support received for males but not for females. Similarly, Sarason, Sarason and Shearin (1986) reported that the number of supporters and satisfaction with support are more closely related for men than for women. Stokes and Levin (1986) found that network structure variables were more highly correlated with self-reported loneliness for men than for women. These researchers reviewed evidence that suggested that men are more group oriented in their friendships than are women. Women focus more than men on intimate, close dyadic ties. It seems likely that men and women use different standards for evaluating relationships and that certain socially supportive behaviors have different meanings for men and women. Perhaps men evaluate social support more in terms of the quantity of relationships available to them rather than the quality or depth of ties. Reis, Senchak and Solomon (1985) noted that men limit the intimacy of their social ties, even though they are capable of interacting intimately when they choose to do so. This suggests a more complex possibility, that men prefer one or two close ties combined with attachment to a large group of less intimate buddies, whereas women prefer greater numbers of intimate ties. Obviously, the scant data on hand can only point the way for future research.

In summary, there is enough evidence to suggest that sex differences in the quantity and types of social support received, as well as in the mechanisms underlying the effectiveness of such support, are worthy of study. This section has focused on sex differences in three areas. Women consistently report receiving more support, especially emotional support, than men do. There is also some evidence that women benefit more than men from support that stems from close, intimate relationships. Perhaps support focusing on socializing and more group-oriented activities is especially helpful to men. Overall, however, women's socialization enhances the possibility that supportive ties will provide them resources and the probability that they will positively evaluate such provisions. Finally, measures of network structure seem more highly correlated for men than for women to perceived social support, satisfaction with support, and to related variables like loneliness. Overall network structure is especially salient for men; for women, the number and nature of close, intimate relationships may be more important.

THE COST OF CARING

We have been discussing process issues involved in the acquisition of social support and its relation to adjustment. In this discussion we have assumed that if social support meets individuals' needs, then its effects will be beneficial. There are, however, two indirect costs of caring that need to be considered.

First, by possessing close supportive ties, people expose themselves to the pain of others' tragedies. Kessler, McLeod and Wethington (1985) argued that the difference in the rate of depression for women as compared to men (women being up to twice as likely to be depressed as men) may be attributable to the greater attachment of women to others. The argument follows that since women have a larger number of others with whom they feel close ties, then they also have increased vulnerability to stress. They are exposed to more stressors than men, who have more limited numbers of intimates and, thus, more limited concerns regarding others' problems. Thus, the higher rates of depression among women may not be a sign of psychological weakness but the consequence of their larger number of intimate ties.

In addition to this increased vulnerability, there may be another cost of caring. If stress is defined as the perceived loss of resources, and if people offset this loss by investing other resources, then investing resources both attenuates and produces stress. Schönpflug (1985) made this point in his astute behavioral economics approach to stress when he stated that all modes of coping consume external and internal resources, and thereby are costly. Tapping supportive ties involves expending resources and incurring associated costs, such as using up owed favors, alienating friends by overburdening them, or risking rejection. Accepting support also begets social debts which entail future costs.

This analysis probably applies more accurately to superficial relationships than to relationships with intimates (Clark, 1983). In this regard, Clark provided evidence to buttress her contention that within intimate relations communal principles operate and exchange principles are less relevant. In intimate relationships no careful accounting of who owes whom occurs; instead partners assess the general status of their relationships. Consequently, by seeking and receiving aid intimates are not taxing reserves.

Paradoxically, requesting and receiving social support may increase intimacy in close relationships and not only avoid a cost but achieve a gain. Often after family tragedies the one positive outcome is that the need to help one another made family members closer and resulted in their appreciating each other more.

If using social support in intimate relationships both attenuates the negative effects of stress and increases intimacy, it is no wonder that intimacy has been found repeatedly to be the key to effective social support (Brown, Bhrolchain and Harris, 1975; Hobfoll, Nadler and Leiberman, 1986; Reis, 1984; Stokes, 1983). This is not to say that individuals will increase intimacy only by taking social support; they will, of course, also need to give and to do other things to sustain love, caring, and closeness.

The ultimate payoff for using social support is not clear. What can be said is that employing social support engenders costs that are not immediately obvious, and that these costs might even outweigh benefits in superficial relationships. In intimate relationships the cost of caring is increased vulnerability, but the rewards are great. Support provided by intimate ties is the most satisfying kind of support and the use of support within intimate relationships often leads to greater intimacy.

One might ask why people risk exposure to the pain of others and expend resources in order to gain social support. According to the proposed model of conservation of resources, *risk* and *investment* of resources are necessary in order to gain more valued resources or offset the loss of more valued resources. It would appear that those who employ social support feel they have more to gain than to lose by tapping sources of support. Those who have obligated social relationships, however, may be pressed into exchanges of social support that entail more risks and costs than benefits. This may help explain why obligated relationships are often perceived as stressful, despite intimacy or supportive exchanges (Hobfoll, Nadler and Leiberman, 1986; Stein and Rappaport, 1986).

CONCLUSIONS AND IMPLICATIONS FOR INTERVENTION

In this chapter we have reviewed, critiqued, and expanded on some areas of social support research that are relevant to an understanding of the process of social support. We began by reviewing various definitions of social support that reflect some of the best research to date. We settled on a definition that emphasizes the value of social support as the provider of both a sense of social embeddedness and functional assistance. Thus social support was defined as *those social interactions or relationships that provide individuals with actual assistance or with a feeling of attachment to a person or group that is perceived as caring or loving.*

Examination of the process of social support suggests the importance of considering elements found in the self and elements found in the environment. Consequently, whether targeting individuals or groups, interventionists will need to be cognizant of qualities of the objective environment, of individuals' perceptions of the environment, and of how individuals translate the consequences of support into personally meaningful contexts (see Gottlieb, this volume). In addition to this general caveat, four themes emerge from the study of the process of social support that may aid efforts to effect support interventions.

First, the concept of fit between resources and needs may be critical to the effectiveness of social support. When fit is inappropriate, attempts at aid may prove unhelpful or even detrimental. The resources which are offered or enhanced by social support must meet the needs of individuals. The model of conservation of resources outlines a mechanism by which the general concept of fit may be applied. Specifically, researchers and clinicians are directed to attend to those resources that have been lost by the individual or that the individual wants to increase. Exact replacement may not be possible, but substitution efforts will be most successful when providers understand the loss on the level of feelings and in terms of its meaning for the individual.

The second theme to emerge from a study of the process of social support is that the ability to use support is developmentally based. The socialization of individuals who make use of attempts to aid them appears to include encouragement of self-disclosure and intimacy, some degree of dependency on others, and perhaps the willingness to appear vulnerable. Women are more likely to be socialized in this way and may have an advantage over men in both establishing and benefiting from close relationships. This observation may be discouraging to interventionists, because it implies that intensive efforts to alter basic personality traits or ways of coping may be required if individuals who do not normally rely on social support are to benefit from it. Interventions may be most successful among people who are only situationally without support due, say, to a period of transition. These individuals are most likely to respond positively and comfortably to offers of social aid. Those who are characterologically low in social support may not benefit from efforts aimed at providing support.

The third theme that may be derived from a study of the process of support is that the receipt of social support involves both gains and losses. This conclusion is consistent with the data. It also follows from the model of conservation of resources, which indicates that resources may be used to counteract the effect of loss, but that the application of resources often results in their depletion. Clinical and community intervention efforts will have to judge carefully whether the implied costs in accepting support are so great as to nullify any positive effect of the provision of support.

Finally, intimacy emerges as central to effective support. Intimate ties are most likely to be the kind that provide a valid substitute when important losses occur. Attempts by nonintimate others may provide some replacement for losses but are unlikely to provide the underlying feelings of attachment, caring, and love that intimate support engenders. Furthermore, the costs of sharing and appearing vulnerable may be too great to allow an openness to social support if the help provider is not viewed as invested in the well-being of the recipient of aid. This conclusion further complicates the issue of intervention and suggests that more superficial attempts at aid may prove inadequate. Clinicians, however, should be encouraged to examine the degree of intimacy their clients have with family and friends. The capacity of intimacy is central to the ability to develop supportive relationships. Early intervention designed to encourage intimacy and openness in families and in close social settings may also have long-term impact on individuals.

Overall, any application of social support must acknowledge the ecological nature of the support process. This indeed may be the greatest theoretical contribution of social support, as it provides one of the first topics of study in which aspects of the self, environment, and culture mix to affect the individual. Furthering knowledge in this area will require a corresponding openness to different disciplines and methods of study if the fullest depiction of the support phenomenon is to be achieved. The study of social support may not only increase our knowledge of social support but widen the method by which social scientists approach interpersonal behavior.

ACKNOWLEDGEMENTS

This chapter was prepared while the first author was on sabbatical at the Department of Psychology, DePaul University, Chicago, Illinois, USA. Thanks are extended to Sheldon Cotler, Department Chair, and Lenny Jason, both of DePaul, for making the sabbatical possible.

Handbook of Personal Relationships
Edited by S. W. Duck
© 1988 John Wiley & Sons Ltd

27

Support Interventions: A Typology and Agenda for Research

BENJAMIN H. GOTTLIEB
University of Guelph, Ontario, Canada

ABSTRACT

This chapter presents a definition and typology of social support interventions, distinguishing between interventions at the individual, dyadic, group, social system, and community levels. Relevant research is critically reviewed leading to a discussion of the causes and process of social support and recommendations for improving the impact of support interventions.

As research on the topic of social support accumulates, adding greater precision to our knowledge of the contribution to health made by personal relationships, more attention is being paid to practical applications of this knowledge on behalf of distressed clinical and community populations (Gottlieb, 1983; Rook and Dooley, 1985; Shumaker and Brownell, 1985). Heralded as a critical moderator of stress and as a key social provision sustaining human attachments, informal support is being marshaled both to improve coping in the face of a variety of life adversities and transitions and to shore up close relationships, especially when they are jeopardized by threatening external events. Moreover, the mobilization of social support is owed only in small part to the efforts of professional practitioners; for the most part it reflects the impulses and natural activities of ordinary citizens striving to secure the resources they need to grapple with changing life circumstances. It is reflected in the ingenious ways that people enlist the aid of family members and workmates when they try to quit smoking or moderate their drinking, in the ways that teachers use their lunch hours to swap strategies of managing student misconduct in the classroom, in the ways that couples undergoing the transition to first-time parenthood reweave their networks and recruit other new parents, and in the numerous initiatives taken by citizens to create mutual aid groups for fellow sufferers with addictions, noxious habits, medical afflictions, and other acute and chronic life problems. In fact, the knowledge that can be gained from observing the spontaneous activities of people engaged in the process of giving and getting social support in the natural environment can guide the design of professionally engineered interventions.

Support interventions have a special appeal to practitioners, policy-makers, and their intended beneficiaries for several reasons. First, many practitioners recognize that dispositional characteristics implicated in the coping process, such as personality attributes and cognitive responses, are much less mutable than environmental resources for resisting stress. While they also recognize that individual differences in social skills affect people's abilities to initiate and maintain relationships, and ultimately to gain social support from them, practitioners are more sanguine about the prospects for improving these interpersonal skills than they are about the likelihood of changing basic personality attributes. Moreover, they are more attracted to a *social intervention* than to a *person-centered intervention* because of its potential ecological and preventive impacts, the creation of a more responsive and durable personal community yielding longer-term benefits. Practitioners also realize that person-centered interventions which conflict with the values and norms of the client's social network will be neutralized or discredited by its members. Therefore, interventions aimed to directly alter the structure, composition, and/or supportive exchanges of the client's social network, or even its norms about help-seeking and giving, carry greater ecological validity (see Hobfoll and Stokes chapter, this volume).

Policy-makers share the practitioners' interest in mounting interventions that are sensitive to the social context, especially among historically unserved and underserved populations at risk. The burgeoning social support literature offers them persuasive evidence of the influence that cultural blueprints have on help-seeking, the sources and types of support that are utilized and proscribed, the structural properties of social networks, and the very meanings that support takes on (see, for examples, Valle and Vega, 1980; Vaux, 1985; Vega and Miranda, 1985). Moreover, support interventions are appealing to policy-makers on economic grounds as well. In this era of financial retrenchment in the human services and decentralization, the concept of community support systems is invoked by conservatives bent on the privatization of health and welfare programs and by liberals seeking to weave voluntary and private supportive arrangements into the social safety-net of government and publicly funded services (Froland et al., 1981).

Finally, support interventions are particularly attractive to their intended beneficiaries and to the public at large because they embrace widely held norms favoring self-reliance, collective action, and a more recent ideology of empowerment. The popularity of self-help groups in North America is testimony to this ethic as are the multitude of local, grassroots family support and education programs which have recently banded together under the umbrella of the Family Resource Coalition. Especially in these times when people are being wrenched from their familiar social contexts due to marital disruption, cyclical economic dislocations, and geographic relocations, mutual aid has become a scarce commodity in great demand. Moreover, the social solidarity and psychological sense of community gained from mutual aid activities are welcome antidotes to the loneliness, grief, and anxiety attending modern life. Ultimately, their empowering effect stems from the sense of confidence and competence they instill, and from the dignity restored to people when they experience change at their own hands rather than at the hands of professionals.

The appeal of social support to these three audiences not only reflects their respective values and priorities but also the different images they have of what the mobilization of support entails. These images arise from numerous sources including interventions reported in the literature, existing human service programs, media accounts of self-help advocacy and support groups, and compelling if romantic accounts of the old-fashioned ways in which kin and kith rallied mutual aid on one another's behalf. The very fact that so many different images are conjured up betrays how ill defined the boundaries of support interventions actually are. To date, no one has circumscribed the terrain covered by support interventions, leaving only a broad expanse encompassing all efforts to improve the quality of people's lives by augmenting the resources they give to and get from lay associates. In the absence of criteria for assigning the label support intervention to any of these efforts, there is no basis for arbitration between the claims of parties disputing the genuine article. What yardsticks can be invoked to determine whether or not prenatal classes for expectant parents constitute a support intervention? Is social support the 'active ingredient' of home visitor programs to the frail elderly or to unwed teenage mothers? Is it chiefly responsible for the moderation of stress among hospitalized children whose parents are allowed to room-in? Does an increase in the level of support account for improved morale, less tardiness and absenteeism, and improved grades among high school students whose classes were reorganized so that the same set of students could stay together for all their core courses?

To dispel the ambiguity surrounding this subject, I begin by presenting a preliminary typology of support interventions, organized simply according to their level of intervention. I have adopted the following working definition of support interventions: *efforts to optimize the psychosocial resources which individuals proffer and/or receive in the context of relations with their primary social field.* The typology presents examples epitomizing this definition at the individual, dyadic, group, social system, and community levels. While detailed descriptions of each illustrative intervention are beyond this chapter's purposes and scope (detailed descriptions of many support interventions appear in Gottlieb, 1983, 1987; Roback, 1984; and Shumaker and Brownell, 1985), key issues deserving attention at each level are discussed in the context of the wider literature on social support. Next, the chapter presents an agenda for research aimed to improve our understanding of the conditions conducive to the expression of social support and of its mechanisms of action. The chapter concludes with several suggestions for improving the conduct and impact of support interventions.

A PRELIMINARY TYPOLOGY OF SUPPORT INTERVENTIONS

In generating the typology of support interventions that appears in Table 1, I drew on many sources, applying the working definition to published reports of interventions, initiatives in the planning or implementation stage, ongoing agency programs, and even to suggestions for interventions offered by those investigating more basic issues related to the mobilization of support or failed efforts to marshal support (e.g. Lehman, Ellard and Wortman, 1986; Peters-Golden, 1982). Aiming for comprehensiveness, I have also included examples that were not conceived or labeled by their designers as support interventions (e.g. lowering levels of 'expressed emotion' among schizophrenics' key network members), but nevertheless conform to the working definition. Finally, I had hoped to restrict the examples to interventions that were rigorously evaluated, using control or comparison groups, incorporated psychometrically sound

Table 1   A preliminary typology of support interventions

Level of intervention	Examples
Individual	
Support provider	Promoting a network orientation to coping
	Promoting ways of coping that invite support
Support recipient	Controlling distress during supportive exchanges
Dyadic	
Support from key network member	Consultation to informal community caregivers
	Spouse-coach in the Lamaze method of childbirth
	Enlisting close associate in health habit change
	Lowering levels of expressed emotion (EE)
Introduction of new tie	Home visitor programs, including companions and friendly visitors
	Therapeutic partnerships between 'fellow sufferers'
	Lay helping alliances such as buddies, coaches, mentors, and preceptorships
Group	
Support from set of network members	Cultivation of natural helping networks
	Network therapy and its variants
	Network/support assessment and development
Grafting on a set of new ties	Creation of support groups
	Family support programs such as Extend-a-Family and Family Clusters
	Psychosocial rehabilitation programs such as Fountain House and Lodge society
Social system	
Role redefinitions	Expanded role for the primary nurse and high school homeroom teacher
Organizational policy/structural changes	Workplace day-care programs
	Network members room-in and assume care responsibilities in hospital
	Students in first year of high school stay together for core courses
Community	California's 'Friends Can Be Good Medicine' campaign
	Radio talk/phone-in shows featuring self-help groups

outcome measures, and illuminated the processes contributing to the optimiz-ation of support. I found few instances of the former and none of the latter. This discovery alone reveals that intervention research on social support is in a state of chrysalis, its further development depending on closer scrutiny of the conditions giving rise to and hampering the expression of support and on stronger outcome evaluation designs.

The Individual Level

Turning to the typology itself, the inclusion of interventions at the individual level may at first seem surprising, because it is difficult to conceive of an intervention as supportive in the absence of any transactions with members of the primary social field. Indeed, interventions at this level do not involve actual commerce among the parties to a helping exchange as do interventions at the dyadic and group levels. Nevertheless, as the working definition states, they are aimed to optimize the psychosocial resources individuals proffer or receive in their interactions with lay associates by equipping them with the knowledge, skills, and attitudes potentiating the receipt or donation of support. Three recent papers in particular and other discussions of the modifiable dispositional factors constraining and enabling the expression of support highlight the import-ance of interventions at the individual level.

Calling on Tolsdorf's (1976) speculation that differences in people's 'network orientation' may account for differential mobilization of peer support, Ecken-rode (1983) administered an 'efficacy of help-seeking scale' to a large sample of women who had experienced a number of stressful life events. He found that beliefs in the efficacy of seeking and accepting support from others distinguished between those women reporting more and fewer supportive exchanges with peers. Hence, if people are exposed to persuasive messages from credible peer or professional sources aimed to increase their confidence in the potential productivity of consulting lay persons within or outside their networks, they may overcome their inhibitions about seeking social support. This possibility is borne out in Gottlieb's (1982) study of 87 members of diverse mutual aid groups. Specifically, 15 per cent of the members reported that a professional in the health or human services field was most influential in their decision to attend their first group meeting, 36 per cent nominated someone who was already a member of the group, and 9 per cent nominated a family member or friend. The remaining 40 per cent joined through their own initiative. Parenthetically, it is noteworthy that the two mass media interventions falling at the community level are both aimed in part to foster such a network orientation to coping (see Table 1). For example, by listening to the interactions of members of mutual aid groups on a radio talk show and by actually calling in and talking to the members, the audience's convictions about the superiority of self-reliance may be disrupted. Of course, interventions aimed to condition beliefs in the legit-imacy and efficacy of giving and receiving informal support (e.g. Schilling, Gilchrist and Schinke, 1984) must neither condemn beliefs in self-reliance nor ignore the circumstances under which network reliance is unrealistic or even damaging. For example, people are unlikely to disclose such shameful or embarrassing stressors as spouse abuse or incest to any network members, including those they are closest to. Moreover, recent research suggests that such disclosures would not elicit support because of the feelings of helplessness and threat these kinds of events arouse in others (Wortman and Conway, 1985).

Two other empirical studies shed light on the interaction between individual differences and both the expression and receipt of social support, thereby spotlighting additional foci for intervention at the individual level. The first points to the relationship between individual coping and the extent and types of support gained from the network, while the second underscores the importance of teaching would-be support providers how to regulate their own emotions when responding to distressed network members. In the former study, Dunkel-Schetter, Folkman and Lazarus (1987) discovered that the coping strategies practised by individuals provide important clues to their associates about whether or not support is needed and about the types of support needed. Specifically, they found that problem-solving modes of coping (making a plan of action and following it) elicited more support of all types than did palliative modes (distancing oneself from the problem or from feelings about it), that specific strategies such as squarely confronting the problem elicited informational rather than emotional or tangible aid, and that strategies such as positive reappraisal (focusing on 'the silver lining') invited expressions of support.

The latter finding closely converges with the conclusions of the second study revealing that when would-be providers of support experience heightened tension in their interactions with the distressed, by and large their support attempts failed (Lehman, Ellard and Wortman, 1986). Notably, they did not fail because the providers intended to offer inappropriate types of support, a possibility eliminated on the basis of data revealing that prospective helpers planned to offer types of support desired by the distressed. They failed because their anxiety interfered with their ability to translate their knowledge into action in face-to-face interactions with the distressed, in this instance the bereaved. The implication drawn by the authors offers another focus for intervention at the individual level of the typology: 'This suggests that instead of teaching support providers about specific strategies, it may be more important to teach them how to manage and control the anxiety inherent in their interactions with the victim' (p. 444). In addition, by showing that the amount and types of support provided and the ease or difficulty of tendering it are governed by the recipient's manner of coping, Dunkel-Schetter, Folkman and Lazarus (1987) highlight another focus for individual intervention: alerting individuals to the ways their coping strategies affect the likelihood of their receipt of support and then encouraging them to adopt coping strategies that are less socially alienating and more inviting.

It is noteworthy that both of the preceding studies call for interventions at the individual level that are based on fine-grained analyses of the interpersonal processes and cues affecting the expression of support. Although it is also possible that certain deficiencies in people's social skills (viz. Heller, 1979) or in their knowledge of the substance of informal help (viz. D'Augelli *et al.*, 1981) detract from the quantity and quality of their supportive exchanges, these two studies draw attention to the ways the ongoing commerce between the recipient and provider attenuates or spurs the expression of support (see also Rook chapter, this volume). Hence, potential donors can discern which if any social provisions are most germane by more carefully scanning the cues elicited by the coping behaviors of the recipient. In addition, by learning how to regulate their emotions when they interact with distressed associates, potential donors can do a better job of actually providing the support that they know is needed. Conversely, potential support recipients can improve their chances of receiving appropriate types of support which are effectively communicated if they learn to cope in ways which invite support, while controlling their own expressions of distress. These process-oriented interventions at the individual level together with a broader focus on conditioning a network orientation to coping promise to improve people's preparation for and receptivity to supportive exchanges.

The Dyadic Level

Interventions at the dyadic level involve the mobilization of support either from a member of the existing social network or from a lay person who is grafted onto the recipient's personal community. The former typically entail efforts to augment or intensify particular kinds of support from a key network member, either on a short- or long-term basis. The latter entail a more complicated process of matching and introducing an outsider to the recipient and then taking steps to optimize the likelihood of the two parties forming a supportive alliance, again on a short- or long-term basis. As the examples reveal, interventions that bring to bear the resources of a key network member differ from those introducing a new tie by virtue of the following three features. First, in the former the support provider is usually not experiencing the same stressful circumstances as the recipient, while in the latter 'fellow sufferers' often form a partnership. Second, interventions among network members are as frequently directed towards uprooting conflictual interactions between the parties as they are towards intensifying supportive exchanges. In contrast, interventions involving a grafted tie place exclusive emphasis on the augmentation of support. Third, as noted earlier, the extra work entailed in determining the basis for pairing strangers for the purpose of mobilizing support is unnecessary in interventions involving two parties who already have an ongoing relationship. Those conducting the latter intervention will still need to discern who among the beneficiary's associates is best equipped to render the support that is called for, but they do not need to take the extra steps involved in the process of sponsoring a new tie on the beneficiary's behalf.

In both of the types of dyadic interventions the programs' designers have provided considerable guidance regarding the kinds of support that should be delivered. The spouse-coach assisting at childbirth is instructed how to render support (Wideman and Singer, 1984), the schizophrenic patient's mother is led to engage in a low expressed emotion (EE) style of interaction with her adult son (Goldstein, 1981), 'buddies' who are initially strangers attempting to quit smoking are told to contact each other every day for five weeks and help each other maintain their resolve and their gains (Janis, 1983), and home visitors are told what types of support to render in order to shore up the parenting skills of unwed, teenage mothers (Halpern and Covey, 1983). These *directed* support interventions at the dyadic level have even offered behavioral training and written instructions prescribing the supportive activities of the helping partner. For example, in the context of smoking cessation, Malott *et al.* (1984) developed a seventeen-page partner support manual as part of a multicomponent intervention in the workplace, and McIntyre-Kingsolver, Lichtenstein and Mermelstein (1986) offered training, encouragement, and feedback to the spouses of persons trying to quit smoking regarding their supportive efforts.

In contrast to these directed support interventions, a minority of the dyadic strategies entail the provision of (undirected) *diffuse* support. Examples include the assignment of a Big Brother/Sister to children from single-parent families, 'Friendly Visitor' programs for the isolated elderly, 'companionship therapy' (Goodman, 1972; Skirboll and Pavelsky, 1984) offered by volunteers to mental patients through such programs as Compeer, and the Extend-A-Family program in which a physically or mentally handicapped child is matched to a 'host family', receiving care and companionship during periodic visits. Essentially, the support that is delivered by the grafted tie amounts to befriending; it consists of diffuse social stimulation offered during *episodes* of companionship. Accordingly, the beneficiaries are viewed as suffering from social isolation and a general deficiency of support due to their deviant or exceptional personal characteristics or their isolating circumstances. In contrast, the beneficiaries of the directed support interventions are seen as lacking specific supportive provisions required to improve their coping with the particular demands imposed by stressful life events or transitions or by the challenge of changing such noxious health habits as smoking, drinking, and overeating. In effect, directed support interventions marshal the partner's specialized supportive resources while diffuse interventions compensate for a generally impoverished social field.

The basic research on social support contains a cluster of studies revealing that one intimate, confiding relationship is vital to health protection, thereby providing the theoretical and empirical grounds for dyadic support interventions. On the one hand, there is evidence, less relevant to these interventions, that loss of a close relationship through death or divorce predisposes to morbidity (Osterweis, Solomon and Green, 1984), and on the other hand, evidence more germane to these interventions suggests that 'attachment providing relationships' (Weiss, 1974) protect and promote health and morale (Brown and Harris, 1978; Lowenthal and Haven, 1968; Waring and Patton, 1984). Moreover, more recent research, and particularly refinements in the measurement of social support, point to the importance of identifying particular persons who are uniquely capable of providing the supportive provisions called for in the face of different stressors or as the demands of a given stressor change over time (House and Kahn, 1985; Oritt, Paul and Behrman, 1985; Pearlin, 1985; Procidano and Heller, 1983; Sarason *et al.*, 1983; Tardy, 1985). As Pearlin

(1985) states: '. . . two dimensions of specialization [of support] . . . can be recognized. One concerns the fact that supports may be drawn from different sources for different problems; the other pertains to the shifts in supports that occur between the onset of a problem and its final resolution' (p. 46). Evidence for such specificity with respect to the most appropriate and effective types of support rendered by particular sources comes from Brown and Harris' (1978) research on the unique protective impact (against depression) afforded by a husband or boyfriend, from Levitt, Weber and Clark's (1986) finding that spousal support and marital quality, above all other close relationships, contributed to maternal well-being, from Dunkel-Schetter's (1984) discovery of the specialized supportive functions that family members and friends on the one hand and professionals on the other fulfill for cancer patients, and from research on workplace relationships revealing the differential impact of co-worker and supervisor support on different job stressors (House, 1981). It appears that help providers in the network cannot be substituted for one another largely because of their specialized personal and role relationships with the focal individual, each relationship conferring special significance and impact on the supportive provisions they extend.

Taken as a whole, the basic research on social support therefore offers a strong theoretical and empirical foundation for efforts to mount dyadic interventions that carefully assess who in the beneficiary's present network is best suited to proffer the supportive resources called for or the type of grafted relationship that promises to deliver the most appropriate level and types of support. In directed dyadic support interventions, the partner can either be encouraged to intensify the expression of his/her specialized but natural supportive behaviors or, through training, to adopt those deemed most conducive to the relationship and to effecting desired changes. In diffuse support interventions typically involving a grafted tie, the speed and success of relationship development, *which is its own end*, can be optimized either by simply capitalizing on the partners' existing social skills or by upgrading them through training.

The Group Level

Interventions at the group level are also partitioned according to their focus on optimizing the support offered by the beneficiary's existing social orbit or mobilizing the support of a set of ties grafted onto the social field. Here too, relationship initiation and development constitutes a part of the extra work entailed in the latter type of group intervention because group cohesion, productivity, and expressions of support are in part predicated on the participants' attraction to one another. However, one-to-one relationships in a grafted group intervention need not receive as careful scrutiny as in dyadic interventions, because it is the group dynamics that give rise to its supportive functions. Certain members of the group may be attracted to one another and even develop a close friendship outside the group or after it terminates, but it is the properties of the group as a whole, including its composition, leadership, structure, norms, and frequency and duration of meeting, which chiefly determine the supportive processes that unfold or fail to materialize. In short, because group interventions are dedicated to creating more robust and durable support *systems* on behalf of one or more of their members, both those which aim to optimize support in an ongoing network and those designed to create a new set of supportive ties must carefully analyze and subsequently modify the *systemic* properties of the social aggregate.

In ongoing or natural networks composed of various mixes of family members, friends, workmates, and neighbors, the systemic properties subject to modification include their morphological, interactional, and functional characteristics. Morphological variables include the network's size, density, and clustering, while interactional variables relate to the character of the focal individual's ties to others, including their intimacy, duration, and dimensionality (uniplex versus multiplex). The functional dimension can involve changes in any patterns of social influence among the actors, but with respect to social support it concerns the flow of resources through the network (Wellman, 1981). These resources include various types of social support such as tangible aid, emotional, appraisal, and esteem support, cognitive guidance, and support involving socializing and sheer companionship (Tardy, 1985). Accordingly, network interventions can optimize support by teaching members how to expand their repertoire of supportive behaviors (D'Augelli *et al.*, 1981), by effecting changes in the size, composition, or density of the network (Cohen and Adler, 1986; Gottlieb and Coppard, 1987; Morin and Seidman, 1986), or by altering relationships the focal individual maintains with key associates (Goldstein, 1981; Rook, 1984b).

Because of the interdependence among these network dimensions and especially because so little is presently known about how the network's structure and the attachments therein allocate resources and constrain behavior, interventions in natural networks have been relatively rare. Those attempted have had mixed success. For example, Chapman and Pancoast (1985) recently reported on three largely unsuccessful efforts to strengthen the informal helping networks of elderly clients through such tactics as altering the network's size, changing the content of the members' exchanges, reinforcing existing ties, and directly modifying the network's structure. Equally important, they cite client resentment towards the intrusion on their private social world among the barriers to this type of group intervention.

Two bodies of literature promise to inform the nascent craft of planning and effectively executing interventions in natural networks. The first, an extension of family therapy, addresses the application of network analysis to clinical populations. The second issues directly from the basic research on social support. Those in the forefront of the former work include a group of 'network therapists' striving to achieve such clinically relevant goals as improving the stability and flexibility of the networks which chronic mental patients inhabit (Hammer, Makiesky-Barrow and Gutwirth, 1978; Morin and Seidman, 1986), and reconstituting the networks of psychiatric outpatients during times of crisis

(Beels, 1981; Rueveni, 1979; Schoenfeld et al., 1985). Neither principles nor guidelines for network intervention have yet emerged from this work.

Similarly, piecemeal suggestions rather than a coherent framework for network-centered interventions aimed to strengthen the fabric of support have come from researchers attending to the complex patterns of interaction among network properties. Network-analytic approaches to the study of the recently widowed (Hirsch, 1980; Walker, MacBride and Vachon, 1977), the divorced (Daniels-Mohring and Berger, 1984; Wilcox, 1981b), teenagers expecting a child (Barrera, 1981; Unger and Wandersman, 1985), and other populations facing stressful life events and transitions have yielded abundant insights into the interplay between structure, interaction, and function, but collectively they offer precious little guidance for intervention. The kaleidoscopic view of the social field afforded by network analysis is at once its greatest virtue and its liability. Moreover, the prospects for identifying principles of network intervention dim further in the face of evidence suggesting that people's requirements for and satisfaction with support fluctuate over the life course (Schulz and Rau, 1985), in relation to different stressors, and even according to different stages of coping with a given stressor (Jacobson, 1986).

Initiatives aimed to optimize support by supplementing the focal individual's network with a set of new peer ties are far more numerous than those which attempt to restructure the relationships that already exist. In their modern incarnation they consist of support groups convened and often led by professionals who assemble persons facing the same stressful events, transitions, or circumstances, or sharing the same affliction, noxious habit, or problems in living, for the purpose of mutual aid (Gottlieb, 1983). But the healing and restorative powers of self-help groups have been recognized for decades; only recently has their formal study and evaluation commenced (Katz, 1981). Kropotkin's (1955) treatise on the topic of mutual aid documents its genesis and various forms and functions, embracing religions, brotherhoods, guilds, 'secret societies', trade unions, Freemasons, friendly societies, and fellowships of the persecuted. The second half of the twentieth century has seen a rapid proliferation of self-help groups whose *raison d'être* shifted from fraternal, religious, and political bases of solidarity to social and health-related affinities. With the formation of Alcoholics Anonymous (AA), the best known of these self-help groups, came many other small communities of fellow sufferers, some adapting the principles of AA to meet their own ends and some inventing helping practices of their own.

Professionally initiated support groups have in turn borrowed methods from self-help groups, blending them with ideas drawn from the professional lore on therapy groups, psychoeducational groups, and group dynamics. This hybrid is typically composed of 8–10 members who meet in an agency or institutional setting for a fixed number of sessions, guided by a professional who supplements the participants' experiential knowledge with expertise about the group's process, the stressors members face, and the coping strategies that may be germane. Unlike many self-help groups that have a dual focus on coping and advocacy, support groups tend to focus exclusively on the former. Examples include support groups for the bereaved (Vachon *et al.*, 1980), for new parents (McGuire and Gottlieb, 1979; Wandersman, 1982), for the divorced (Bloom, Hodges and Caldwell, 1982; Warren and Amara, 1984) and their children (Stolberg and Garrison, 1985; Kalter, Pickar and Lesowitz, 1984), and for persons who experienced two or more recent life changes of any sort (Roskin, 1982). It is noteworthy that several novel forms of support systems also consisting of a set of grafted ties have been engineered by those working with deinstitutionalized mental patients, including Lodge societies (Fairweather *et al.*, 1969), psychosocial rehabilitation settings such as Fountain House (Beard, 1978), and halfway houses designed to offer a 'psychosocial kinship system' to their residents (Budson and Jolley, 1978). However, they offer an altogether different venue for social support than do time-limited support groups.

The systemic properties of support groups differ dramatically from those of natural networks and, surprisingly, have received scant attention. Published reports of support groups typically *describe* their leadership, composition, activities, number and duration of sessions, and even the content of the expert input and member-to-member dialogue, without explaining why these choices were made and how the decisions may have influenced the supportive processes that unfolded or failed to materialize. The best analytic work, based on multiple methods of inquiry across several groups, has illuminated the behavioral and cognitive processes occurring in support groups (Levy, 1979) and their mechanisms of change (Lieberman, 1979), but has not yet revealed how variations in their systemic properties affect these supportive processes and mechanisms. Moreover, because there are no published reports of support groups that failed—instances when the graft did not take hold—it is impossible to learn about the systemic properties implicated in the group's collapse. To this extent, support group interventions and natural network interventions share the status of a 'black box', appealing strongly to practitioners but leaving obscure the pathways to support afforded by different features of the natural and engineered social surround.

The Social System Level

Interventions at the individual, dyadic, and group levels respectively revolve around the dispositional, interpersonal, and systemic determinants of social support. At the social system level, interventions aim to influence the physical and sociocultural contexts in which people are enveloped. Specifically, changes in the structure and supportive functions of networks and the patterning of dyadic relations can be effected by altering policies, norms, role definitions, physical design features, and other macrosystem variables. This proposition is borne out both in empirical research and in everyday experience.

For example, in a fascinating set of careful observational and interview studies, Glidewell *et al.* (1982) discovered that the norms that teachers subscribed to, namely norms of equal status and autonomous decision-making, constrained them from overtly requesting or offering advice to one another. Direct appeals for help with teaching problems, even in a resource center explicitly established for the purpose of assisting teachers, were virtually absent as were direct acts of help-giving on the part of the center's staff. Instead, the expression of support was disguised in ways that neither undermined the help-seeker's status and autonomy nor conferred superiority on the donor. They consisted of 'experience swapping' among teachers, modeling, and in the resource center, recommendations for 'autonomous experimentation' offered by the staff. These forms of support proved to be highly adaptive alternative means of meeting teachers' needs because they did not violate professional norms. Moreover, the researchers observed overt exchanges of help and support only among those teachers who were involved in team teaching, suggesting that this structural anomaly supplanted their commitment to the norms that constrained direct channels of helping. That is, by introducing new forms of interdependence among teachers such as team teaching, collegial helping became legitimized.

Other research in schools, hospitals, the workplace, neighborhood, and other residential settings underscores the impact of the social and physical ecology on opportunities for and actual expressions of supportive exchanges. The design of the built environment has powerful effects on patterns of interaction and, in turn, on the formation of friendships (Festinger, Schachter and Back, 1950; Holohan *et al.*, 1978). Conversely, residential relocation can lead to the loss of the displaced residents' sense of spatial and social continuity, aside from rupturing stable, long-term networks of mutual aid (Fried, 1963). In hospitals, new policies have been introduced which remove barriers to interaction between patients and their family members and close friends, allowing a parent to room-in with a hospitalized child, a spouse or other close associate to attend at childbirth, and even encouraging spouses to assume the role of 'care partners', living with the patient in the hospital and performing many tasks traditionally handled by nurses (Berg, 1983). In addition, the roles of hospital personnel have been redefined to enlarge patients' and their families' access to support as well as the staff's. For example, the advent of primary nursing (Ciske, 1974) promises to give patients access to a single continuous caregiver throughout their stay, while new formulations of the neonatal nurse's role expand the intensity and duration of her involvement with the family. Team-building is a prominent organizational development strategy in hospitals and other work-places, partly because of its contribution to the improved coordination of work activities, and partly because of the premium it places on mutual aid as an antidote to burnout. Furthermore, a 'new wave' of employee assistance programs has shifted their emphasis from individual counseling for alcohol and other personal problems to the design of structural changes in employment and managerial practices, and the introduction of such novel corporate benefits as worksite day care, subsidies for physical exercise classes attended by employees, and work/life discussion groups composed of representatives from several levels of the organizational hierarchy (Galinsky, 1986).

Rigorously designed interventions aimed to mobilize support by effecting more distal structural variables in a given social system have been scarce. They pose numerous evaluative challenges because of ongoing changes occurring both inside and outside the system, and they require a long time perspective for their effects to surface. Nevertheless, these system-centered interventions have a special appeal because of their potential contribution to primary prevention, augmenting the supportive resources available to all the members of the setting. One prominent example is the initiative taken by Felner, Ginter and Primavera (1982), who restructured the homeroom teacher's role and partially reorganized the social system in a large urban high school in order to increase peer and teacher support during the critical first year. Specifically, the homeroom teacher's role was expanded to include many guidance and administrative duties, including maintaining contact with the students' parents. At the same time, to establish more stable relations among the students themselves, the same set of students attended all four core academic classes together rather than following the customary procedure whereby students find themselves in a different social matrix in each class. By bringing greater stability and consistency to the peer social system and by giving students a multidimensional relationship with one teacher, the intervention designers hypothesized that they would generate greater peer and adult support, thereby smoothing the students' transition and adaptation to this new social system. Their findings revealed that, relative to a matched control group of students in another urban school, the students participating in the intervention achieved significantly better academic and attendance records, developed more positive self-concepts, and viewed the school milieu more favorably, perceiving its expectations and structure more clearly and assigning higher ratings to the level of teacher support offered.

The Community Level

Community-wide interventions aimed to promote greater public reliance on informal sources of support and to spur the expression of support in everyday life range from California's massive public education program called 'Friends Can be Good Medicine', to the widespread dissemination of bumper stickers reading 'Have you hugged your kid today?', to various public service announcements exhorting family members to show greater sensitivity to one another's feelings and needs, and to a series of radio shows and self-help fairs spotlighting local mutual aid groups. The California campaign to promote a network orientation to coping is particularly impressive because it used the mass media, attractive print materials targeted to specific ethnic and age groups, the public schools, and community organizations and businesses to reach the public. It carried messages about the general health benefits accruing from the establishment of close peer relationships, urging citizens to improve their relationships with peers as a basis for intensifying supportive exchanges (Hersey et al., 1984). In addition, at the local level it took a 'community-driven approach' involving the creation of steering committees whose members were trained to adapt the project materials to their own needs and culture, and then to disseminate them through existing communication networks.

In Chicago, Jason (1985) recently mounted a less ambitious and less costly public education intervention designed to familiarize the public with the helping processes occurring in self-help groups and to prompt referrals to them. He persuaded the manager of a far-reaching radio station to allow him to host a show featuring a half-hour discussion among three members of a self-help group followed by the fielding of calls from the audience for the second half hour. Members of Toughlove, Abusers Changing Themselves, and LaLeche League each spent an hour a week for two weeks on the show, each broadcast ending with information about how to contact the group's local chapter. Jason then monitored the number of referral calls received by each group for several weeks before and after its broadcast, finding a sizeable increase for each. Moreover, he was approached by six additional self-help groups clamoring to participate on the show. Finally, mindful of the potential criticism that the show might receive on ethical grounds, Jason also convened a panel of twelve mental health professionals from different disciplines who listened to the call-in portions of the broadcasts, judging the advice to callers as neither incorrect nor harmful or unethical.

Generally, these and other public education programs are of uncertain benefit to those actually exposed to their messages. Because they do not specifically target populations at risk of deficient support due to social isolation or exposure to stressful life events and because they do not adopt a more behavioral focus involving intensive face-to-face instruction in ways of forming and improving supportive relationships, their impact may be minimal. On the other hand, if they aim only to inform the public about informal helping resources, demystifying self-help groups and calling attention to the support residing in people's personal communities, they may prove to be cost-effective advertisements for mutual aid. In order to spur the public to get involved in mutual aid activities, these media messages must conclude with practical information about local resources that can be tapped. The self-help clearinghouses that have recently been established in many regions of the United States and Canada are engaged in this kind of brokerage, while also educating professionals about mutual aid and offering technical assistance to local self-help groups (Borck and Aronowitz, 1982).

PROMINENT ISSUES ARISING FROM THE INTERVENTION TYPOLOGY

Before addressing several priorities for research on support interventions, I wish to offer two sets of observations about the typology itself. First, although I have separately reviewed the interventions at each level of the typology, it should be recognized that some support strategies entail sequencing two or more initiatives, either intentionally or inadvertently. For example, in Vachon et al.'s (1980) 'self-help intervention for widows', a support group was convened only after each new widow had established a relationship with a veteran widow who offered practical help and emotional support. Indeed, customary practice often entails preparing prospective support group members for the group by first establishing a comfortable relationship between one or more group members or between a member and the leader, especially when the candidates have no backlog of group experience and lack confidence in their group skills. Moreover, dyadic and group support are often rendered to members concurrently rather than sequentially when two members become friends outside the group. Elsewhere (Gottlieb, 1985b), I have described such a pattern of combined support arising serendipitously among adolescents who joined a support group following their parents' separation. I showed that each social context (the dyadic and the group) served a unique supportive function, complementing the other's.

The typology also suggests another way in which different support interventions arise sequentially, namely by interventions at one level having radiating effects on the support expressed at other levels. An axiom of systems theory is that changes at one level of a complex organization create changes at other levels due to their interdependence. Applied to the social network or to the support group, this axiom underscores the importance of monitoring both desirable and undesirable, anticipated and unanticipated consequences of support interventions at several levels. For example, system-level changes (in policies, roles, and routines) in a hospital must be made in order to introduce the dyadic support of the spouse during childbirth, and conversely, the introduction of a Big Brother can create significant dislocations in the wider network of relationships a child maintains with family members and friends. In short, the typology not only presents practitioners with a set of options regarding the level of intervention, but also reminds them to gauge the impact of intervention at one level on others.

A second set of observations about the typology concern its inherent limitations. Aside from portraying the kaleidoscopic nature of support interventions, the typology provides guidance neither about the conditions calling for one or another level of intervention nor about the psychosocial provisions which should be optimized within a given level of intervention. The latter shortcoming may at first appear particularly troublesome in light of the working definition of support interventions as efforts to optimize the psychosocial resources which individuals proffer and/or receive in the context of relations with their primary social field. However, the typology cannot prescribe which type or combination of supportive provisions ought to be delivered at a given level of intervention. That depends on the nature of the relationship between the recipient and provider of support, if this distinction applies to the parties, the type and duration of the stressor, and the ways the actors involved communicate and interpret messages about the supportive requirements. Further, except at the individual level, the typology does not specify whether the focus of the intervention is on preparing the recipient or provider of support, or both, for the delivery of the psychosocial resources that are needed. That decision is also predicated on careful assessment of the two parties' personal assets and liabilities, situational factors constraining or facilitating exchanges between them, and, especially in interventions involving members of an ongoing network, the character of the past and present relationship between the two. For example, dyadic support programs aimed to mobilize the daily care and aid of daughters on behalf of their elderly dependent parents must take account of both parties' past relationship, their respective personality resources, and the wider constraints imposed by other household members as well as their resources, in order to determine the appropriate foci for intervention. In effect, the typology only spotlights the diverse points of entry to intervention, not the precise elements subject to change nor the processes entailed in changing them.

Learning about Support's Causation

One avenue for gaining a deeper understanding of the social conditions that animate support involves first the germination of a support intervention in a given locale and then its transplantation in other community contexts. For example, the blueprint of a home visitor program for unwed teenage mothers will contain a guiding set of assumptions and techniques of intervention based on the culture in which it germinated. However, in its application to other ecological contexts it is likely to spawn numerous hybrids depending on the nutrients available in the host setting and other environmental conditions, and may even fail to 'take' altogether. Thus, what was originally conceived as a uniform support intervention is transmuted into many different interventions, and it is precisely those conditions that altered the forms of the interventions or that proved too inhospitable which inform our knowledge of the ecological underpinnings of such support interventions.

By the same token, there is an urgent need for intervention research that varies the systemic properties of support groups because each of their design elements has a potential impact on the supportive processes arising among the members. Here, social psychological theory can be invoked to shed light on the interpersonal and group dynamics that unfold in response to changes in the design elements of a support group. Social comparison theory (Festinger, 1954) yields predictions about the ways that similarities and differences among members in the severity of their problems, in their apparent mastery of the problem, and in their life circumstances affect both their attraction to one another and their feelings and cognitions about their own relative well-being. By altering the group's composition and even its leadership to optimize opportunities for upward comparisons with members who can model productive coping behaviors and for private downward comparisons with members who are not coping as well or who have a more serious affliction, participants can gain reassurance, a sense of optimism about their own prospects for recovery, and knowledge of effective coping strategies (viz. Wood, Taylor and Lichtman, 1985).

Attribution theory is also apposite since both the receipt and expression of support are contingent on the parties' beliefs about the causes of the help-seeker's predicament. Like self-help groups (Antze, 1976), support groups can generate ideologies that help members to reattribute their problems to factors outside or within their control and to reassign the responsibility for change to themselves or to situational or societal forces. At present there is moot evidence about the effect that these causal and control attributions have on affect, behavior, and self-perceptions. For example, Bulman and Wortman (1977) argue that causal attributions of self-responsibility are adaptive because they heighten feelings of control, and others disagree (e.g. Taylor, Lichtman and Wood, 1984). The topic begs for more systematic study. Experts making presentations at the meetings of support groups can emphasize causal information about the members' predicament that either blames or exonerates them, while feelings of helplessness or agency can be promoted by the testimony that the leader, experts, or other members provide about the possibility of assuming control over the problem's trajectory and impact.

These and other social psychological theories such as equity theory, reactance theory, and emergent theories about the nature and extent of emotional ventilation intensifying or attenuating negative mood states such as depression (Coates and Winston, 1983; Pennebaker and O'Heeron, 1984) offer predictions that can be systematically tested in support groups and in 'grafted' dyadic interventions to discern more clearly how features of the social context affect the expression of support. Practice that is grounded in these theories can also help us to learn more about the parameters of matchmaking in the grafted types of interventions such as home visitor programs, directed helping partnerships among smokers, alcoholics, and overeaters, and spontaneously arising partnerships among support group members who meet outside the group sessions. Moreover, in the context of support interventions aimed to change self-injurious health behaviors, settings such as the workplace offer opportunities to take advantage of natural affinities among people. For example, by organizing teams among co-workers, their members can be allocated proportional shares of a monetary prize awarded to the team on the basis of its collective weight loss or reduction in cigarette consumption. By structuring incentive systems in a way that places a premium on cooperation, either by offering a group financial reward or by pitting a team from one workplace against a team from another, supportive exchanges among the team members can be fostered and the group morale boosted (Cohen, 1988).

The forces contributing to support's causation in relationships among members of an ongoing social network are much different from those animating support in grafted types of interventions, although they are certainly as complex. Earlier, I called attention to the importance of carefully examining the 'goodness of fit' between the source of support, the types of support called for in the face of a given stressor, the character of the past and present relationship between the parties, and the situational impediments or enabling factors operating. In addition, I drew attention to recent process-oriented research revealing that the expression of support is hindered when either or both parties are unable to control their distress and when the potential recipient of support copes in a manner which signals to the provider that support is not required. In emphasizing *the contingent nature of social support*, these latter studies open a window onto other equally important communication dynamics leading to the failure or miscarriage of social support in personal relationships. Some of them have been described by Coyne, Wortman and Lehman (1988) and by Wortman and Conway (1985). They include: feelings of threat and helplessness that are often experienced by the help-seeker in response to the very nature of the problem the potential support recipient is saddled with; feelings of anger and resentment towards the latter for showing little gratitude or progress in recovering; overprotectiveness and emotional overinvolvement on the part of the helper which only compound the recipient's problems in coping; and a variety of socially alienating behaviors and verbalizations expressed by potential support beneficiaries many of which reflect their distorted views of themselves and the world that are shaped by their present affective state.

Coyne (1976a) has paid particularly close attention to the interactional sequences occurring between depressed persons and members of their social environment, describing how would-be helpers mask their censure and their guilt with false reassurances and avoidant behavior while the depressed party responds with greater distress to gain further support from and control over his/her associates. The result is an even more depressive social process, marked by exacerbation of the depressed party's symptoms and an induction of negative mood states among the associates, sometimes culminating in their rejection of the depressed person. In short, the twin challenges involved in improving the expression of support between the parties to a close relationship are to achieve greater synchrony in their coping efforts and to protect, if not enhance, the relationship between the two. Since both parties have a stake in the relationship, in the outcomes of their transactions regarding the problem at hand, and in protecting their own self-concepts, interventions must attend to the needs of both the recipient and the provider of support.

Another feature of support's causation that complicates interventions in ongoing relationships concerns the norms that family and network members subscribe to regarding the expression of support. Whether or not they are conscious of them, family members and network associates adhere to norms about preferred sources of support, the occasions when it should be mobilized, and the forms it should take. These norms are not only passed from one generation to another, but are also rooted in the family's broader social network and in the sociocultural milieu of those networks, whether defined along ethnic or age lines. Hence, interventions in networks or among members thereof must respect these norms or directly impact upon them without alienating the actors from the host culture in which they are embedded. Moreover, since there are established patterns of coping in families and repeated interactional sequences in which family and network members influence and are influenced by one another's coping behaviors and appraisals, intervention must focus on uprooting destructive patterns of support, reinforcing productive exchanges, and teaching new practices that are ecologically sound. The ethical dictates of engineering support in the natural environment call for much caution in this enterprise of normative and behavioral change.

Support's Mechanisms of Action

In attempting to understand how and why social support accomplishes its much-heralded stress-moderating function, Cohen and Syme (1985) argue that '. . . significant advances . . . will occur only if future studies focus on the *process* by which support is linked to well-being . . .' (p. 15), adding that its impact on health may be '. . . mediated by behavioral change, physiological change, perceptual change, or some combination of these three' (p. 15). The broad generative base of research on social support provides abundant leads about these intervening processes but because so much of it is correlational in nature, causal relations have not been empirically established. Carefully planned intervention research is therefore particularly well suited to the task of testing hypothetical behavioral, cognitive, and psychological processes implicated in social support's mechanisms of action.

What are these potential intervening processes? Certainly they are bound to vary according to the conditions prevailing at each level of intervention and in relation to the supportive requirements aroused by a given stressor, transition, or coping challenge. For example, Pearlin et al.'s (1981) prospective inquiry into the process whereby social support cushioned the impact of job loss on depression revealed that its protective effect stemmed from the preservation of the unemployed men's self-esteem. Coates and Winston's (1983) analysis of the supportive processes mitigating feelings of deviance and depression in peer support groups for victims led them to conclude that emotional ventilation and validation had a normalizing effect that was typically not produced in interactions with network members who were not similarly victimized. Hirsch (1981) and Thoits (1985) also invoke the notion of validation, but refer to a different meaning, namely the affirmation of valued roles and identities that is gained from ongoing social relationships, particularly during role transitions. In fact, Swann and Predmore (1985) have offered experimental evidence supporting this mechanism, revealing that '. . . people's relationships exert a powerful stabilizing influence on their self-conceptions' (p. 1614), protecting them from self-discrepant feedback. Other mechanisms underlying social support's beneficial psychological impact include the sense of control and personal efficacy gained from the process of giving testimony and assuming the role of helper in support groups (Arntson and Droge, 1987), social support's more general contribution to the reduction of uncertainty in novel circumstances (Albrecht and Adelman, 1987), and the positive effect that sheer emotional ventilation has on mood states, particularly in confiding relationships marked by empathic understanding (Pennebaker and O'Heeron, 1984).

Directed support interventions involving behavioral changes conducive to improved physical health can test another set of hypotheses about support's mechanisms of action. According to Berkman (1985), social networks might influence health by: (a) providing advice and influence leading to improved self-care behaviors or medical care; (b) directly offering care; (c) serving as models of good health care and placing pressure on individuals to abandon risky health behaviors; and (d) extending the psychologically supportive provisions purported to augment general immunity to disease through their effect on the neuroendocrine control system. Of course, the last of these hypotheses begs the question regarding the provisions that do reduce susceptibility to disease.

Finally, two tentative leads about social support's mechanisms of action come from accounts of the benefits that self-help group members derive from their 'fellowship', and from Wortman and her colleagues' research among people who suffered fateful tragedies such as the loss of a close family member in a motor vehicle accident (Bulman and Wortman, 1977; Lehman, Wortman and Williams, 1987; Silver and Wortman, 1980). The former concerns the frequent reports contained in the 'soft' consumer satisfaction measures completed by self-help group members testifying to the sense of hope and optimism they gained from their group experience. Many come away with a more sanguine life outlook, with less apprehension about the future, and with a sense of coherence as Antonovsky (1979) defines it: '. . . a global orientation that expresses the extent to which one has a pervasive, enduring though dynamic feeling of confidence that one's internal and external environments are predictable and that there is a high probability that things will work out as well as can reasonably be expected' (p. 123). In effect, the group process conditions more benign appraisals of present and future life prospects perhaps because new members see veteran sufferers who have surmounted or at least accepted the same adversity or because they learn new rules to live by.

Wortman's collaborative research points to a second potential mechanism of action at the cognitive level which is also conditioned in part by communications among close associates. She found that fateful events involving important social losses trigger a search for meaning among many, though not all of their victims. For example, she found that 85 per cent of spouses and 90 per cent of parents whose loved ones had died in a car accident had asked themselves the question 'Why me?' or 'Why my spouse/child?' Fifty-eight per cent of both groups reported being unable to answer the question, even several years after the accident, and a large majority of the spouses and parents reported some level of distress about having been unable to find meaning in the death (Lehman, Wortman and Williams, 1987).

While religious beliefs and life philosophies may provide the meaning that most people search for in the face of such tragic events, the events themselves are often so impactful because they nullify fundamental assumptions about the world. Therefore, part of the contribution that social ties and support group ideologies can make to the process of coping with adversity is to restore faith in those assumptions or to substitute new world views for them, thereby moderating distress and allowing people to resume life, albeit on different grounds. Moreover, in light of recent evidence suggesting that the negative psychological consequences of a stressful event are mitigated when people derive positive meaning from adversity (Thompson, 1985), support interventions can attempt to condition such positive reevaluations. Indeed, the very act of joining a self-help group, creating a new one, or working for an organization dedicated to helping other victims of the same misfortune may instill positive meaning.

All of the preceding mechanisms of action point to potential mediating processes implicated in support interventions and therefore deserve attention in their empirical evaluation. By examining changes in the parties' causal and control attributions, their self-esteem and self-conceptions, feelings of deviance, and their sense of hopefulness and meaning attached to their predicaments, significant advances can be made in our understanding of the pathways whereby social support promotes adaptation and impacts on health.

Conclusion

The myriad of support interventions included in the typology in part reflects the creative efforts of individuals who have translated the findings of basic research on social support into practical strategies of augmenting and mobilizing support or into ideas about ways of preparing individuals to use and deliver support more effectively. However, many of the interventions are not grounded in the theoretical or empirical literature on social support; they were conceived either by practitioners who embraced other theoretical heuristics or by intervention-minded researchers whose empirical data implicated the immediate social environment in the cause or maintenance of a particular disorder. In addition, some were conceived by persons outside the scientific community whose observations and experiences formed an inductive basis for such programs of dyadic support as Big Brothers/Sisters and for support group interventions. Many of the interventions took shape long before the dawn of research on social support while others have adopted the language of that research but do not obtain instruction from it.

In addition to acknowledging the foreign origins of many of these interventions and their early genesis, we must also recognize that *there is presently no coherent theory of social support that accounts for both its mechanisms of action on human functioning and its causation*. In its absence, it is impossible to follow Kurt Lewin's dictum that 'There is nothing as practical as a good theory', making the planning of support interventions a somewhat chaotic enterprise built upon fragments of empirical data, intuition, and intelligent hunches. However, another foundation for support interventions could be laid down by accruing knowledge based on practice itself, so long as practice is conducted in a manner which illuminates how systematic variations in the elements of intervention affect the expression of support, *the causation issue*, and how the support that materializes impacts on proximal and distal outcomes, *the mechanisms of action issue*.

Despite the voluminous generative base of empirical research on social support, my review of interventions reveals how little is presently known about the forces that give rise to social support, the forms it takes in actual experience, and the meanings it has for different people in different sociocultural contexts. Although there are various schemes for classifying and subdividing this global construct, ranging from the three broad categories of aid, affirmation, and affect proposed by House (1981) to Gottlieb's (1978) empirically derived scheme consisting of 27 discrete types of 'informal helping behaviors', they nevertheless bear an uncertain correspondence to people's experience of support. Moreover, the basic research consistently documents the fact that it is the quality of support, not its frequency or duration, that bears the strongest relationship to whatever outcomes are of interest (Porritt, 1979; Tardy, 1985), suggesting that the manner of its expression is critical to its impact. In our zeal to measure social support for the purpose of empirical inquiry we may have lost sight of its holistic character, resulting in both a surfeit of reductionism and a loss of the actors' perspectives in their various ecological niches.

But there are remedies at hand which can penetrate the phenomenology of social support, including naturalistic studies of the process of network formation, observational and interview studies probing the meaning of support among various ethnic and age groups, and natural history studies which carefully document how people capitalize on the resources of the social environment to avert or cope with life events and transitions. On the latter score, studies are only now beginning to identify how alcoholics, smokers, and overeaters kicked their respective habits and maintained their resolve by arranging the social environment or their interactions with members of it in a manner conducive to their goals. Furthermore, in order to gain a deeper understanding of the style and substance of the communications that people interpret as supportive, we need to examine both the perceptions and the behaviors of people engaged in spontaneous dialogues about their private concerns and ambitions and their vulnerabilities. At present, we seem to have only a dim understanding of the reasons why some people are such graceful supporters, adopting a manner and language that lifts the spirits and promotes constructive changes in self-perspective and life outlook. Particularly in transactions among the most intimate network members, the character of supportive communications is bound to be influenced by the nature and stage of the parties' relationship, their skills in offering comfort and consolation, and, above all, by each party's dominant coping responses. Supportive exchanges among intimates so often go awry because they become contests concerning the superiority of coping styles, contests that can only be won by damaging the bonds of affection and trust that undergird all close relationships. Hence, the enterprise of building supportive ties and networks of mutual aid is inextricably tied to the larger challenge of learning to nurture and be nurtured by our human attachments.

Handbook of Personal Relationships
Edited by S. W. Duck

28

Depression and Marital Distress: Current Status and Future Directions

IAN H. GOTLIB
University of Western Ontario, London, Ontario, Canada
and
JILL M. HOOLEY
Harvard University, Cambridge, Massachusetts, USA

ABSTRACT

Following a review of pertinent literature, we introduce a multiprocess model of marital distress and depression that highlights possible causal pathways between these two constructs. We discuss critical methodological and theoretical issues in the study of depression and marital distress, and offer fruitful directions and strategies for future research.

Depression is by far the most common of psychiatric disorders, accounting for 75 per cent of all psychiatric hospitalizations. Each year more than 100 million people worldwide develop clinically recognizable depression, an incidence ten times greater than that of schizophrenia. Furthermore, during the course of a lifetime, it is estimated that 25 per cent of the general population will experience at least one debilitating affective episode (Weissman, Myers and Harding, 1978). For a significant proportion of these individuals, the depressive episode will result in suicide. A recent report from the National Institute of Mental Health, for example, indicates that of the 22 000 suicides committed annually in the United States, upwards of 80 per cent can be traced to a precipitating depressive episode. Indeed, the mortality risk from all causes appears to be considerably elevated in depressed individuals. Lehmann (1971), for example, has observed that depressed males and females have premature death rates that are two and three times that of their nondepressed counterparts, respectively. When one considers the various medical and diagnostic categories of which depression is an integral part or with which it is frequently associated, together with the number of individuals who may manifest depression in a masked or subclinical form, it is clear that the problem of depression is considerable, and its consequences potentially lethal.

While no single set of factors can adequately explain the full range of phenomena associated with depression, there is a growing appreciation of the significance of interpersonal aspects of this disorder (e.g. Brown and Harris, 1978; Cane and Gotlib, 1985; Coyne, 1976b; Coyne, Kahn and Gotlib, 1987; Gotlib, 1982; Gotlib and Colby, 1987; Hooley, 1986; Hooley, Orley and Teasdale, 1986). This recent focus on interpersonal functioning has led researchers to begin to investigate the role of close relationships in the etiology, course, and treatment of depression; in addition, the potentially negative impact of depression on close relationships is also beginning to receive attention. Within this context, it is not surprising that the marriages of depressed persons have now become a major focus of interest.

Our purpose in writing this chapter is to examine the current state of knowledge concerning the relationship between depression and marital distress, and to highlight what we consider to be a number of key issues that must be addressed if future research in this field is to advance significantly.* We begin with a summary of empirical studies that document the pervasiveness of this association and that provide the impetus and rationale for current research and theory in this field. We then introduce a multiprocess model of marital distress and depression that highlights possible causal pathways between these two constructs and serves as an organizing theme and frame of reference for our summary and discussion of the remaining literature. Although this presentation is not intended to be exhaustive, it is representative of the research in this area and, in addition, includes a discussion of studies currently in progress in our own laboratories. Finally, we conclude by emphasizing a number of the more pressing unresolved methodological and theoretical issues in the study of depression and marital distress, and offer what we believe are fruitful directions and strategies for future research.

DEPRESSION AND MARITAL DISTRESS: CURRENT STATUS

The Link Between Marital Distress and Depression

In the early 1970s the results of studies from a number of diverse areas converged to underscore the clinical promise and potential theoretical importance of adopting an interpersonal perspective in the study of depression. Epidemiological investigations, for example, demonstrated not only that women were 1.6–3 times more likely to be depressed than were men (Weissman and Boyd, 1983; Weissman and Klerman, 1977), but that married women were

*Throughout the literature on marriage and marital interaction, the terms 'marital distress', 'marital conflict', and 'marital dissatisfaction' are used synonymously. For ease of presentation, we too will use these terms interchangeably.

particularly at risk relative to their unmarried counterparts (Overall, 1971). In a finer-grained analysis, Renne (1971) reported that both males and females who were unhappily married were more depressed than were those who were separated and divorced. Further evidence of a link between marital distress and depression was provided by Ilfeld's (1977) finding that more than 25 per cent of the variance in depression scores in a community survey could be accounted for by the stresses of marriage and parenting.

An association between depression and marital distress is also suggested by self-reports and interviews with depressed psychiatric patients. Coleman and Miller (1975) and Crowther (1985), for example, both reported significant positive correlations between depressive symptomatology and self-report measures of marital distress in psychiatric samples. Working with a broader population of affectively disordered patients, Hoover and Fitzgerald (1981) found that both bipolar (manic depressive) and unipolar patients reported greater conflict in their marriages than did nondepressed controls. Similar findings were also reported by Weissman and her colleagues (e.g. Bullock, Siegel and Weissman, 1972; Rounsaville et al., 1979; Weissman and Paykel, 1974), who conducted structured interviews with 40 moderately to severely depressed female outpatients over the course of their treatment. The responses of these women were compared with those of 40 matched nondepressed, nonpatient controls. Although the depressed women reported impairment in all social roles, impairments were most marked in marital functioning. Indeed, Weissman and Paykel observed that

> Marital relationships become an arena for the depression and are characterized by friction, poor communication, dependency, and diminished sexual satisfaction. The depressed woman feels a lack of affection towards her husband, together with guilt and resentment. Communication is poor and hostility overt. (p. 211)

Their findings led Weissman and Paykel to conclude that, '. . . the marital relation was a significant barometer of clinical status' (p. 94).

The poor communication reported by depressed individuals in their marriages is further highlighted by the results of Freden's (1982) interview study of 91 depressed men and women in Sweden. Comparisons made with 109 nondepressed controls provide evidence of a link between depression and a lack of marital intimacy. Specifically, whereas 40 per cent of the depressed subjects in Freden's sample reported that they were unable to talk to their spouse about almost anything, only 7 per cent of the nondepressed controls reported having a similar communication problem.

The results of these investigations clearly underscore the pervasiveness of the relationship between depression and marital disturbance. We must note, however, that because these data are essentially correlational, it is difficult to make strong statements concerning the causal nature of this relationship. In the following section, we consider this issue of causality more closely, and discuss a number of possible directions of influence. Our purpose in presenting this discussion is to alert the reader to the likely complexity of the relationship between marital distress and depression. At the same time, we will attempt to isolate those causal pathways that have received particular theoretical and empirical attention. We will then utilize these pathways as an organizing theme in reviewing the relevant literature in this area.

A Multiple-Entry Model of Depression

The simple 'snapshots' of the marriages of depressed persons that we have discussed thus far belie the complexity of underlying causal linkages between depression and marital distress. As indicated in Figure 1, the paths of influence linking these two variables are likely to be manifold. It is possible, for example, that the experience and impact of a depressive episode may cause subsequent marital distress. Similarly, marital distress might lead one or both spouses to exhibit symptoms of depression. A final possibility to be discussed here is that underlying characterological disorders may place individuals at increased risk for the development of both marital distress and depression. We will briefly outline these three possibilities below, and will then consider the empirical support for each.

A depressive episode leads to marital distress

Assuming no prior marital difficulties and a patient's first episode of depression, marital distress may represent the result of a spouse's inability and/or unwillingness to cope with the stresses of living with a depressed partner. Within this formulation, marital distress is viewed as being caused by a spouse's episode of depression that is itself a result of other internal and/or external factors. For example, the occurrence of a negative life event may trigger a depressive episode that then disrupts a previously harmonious marital relationship. It is important

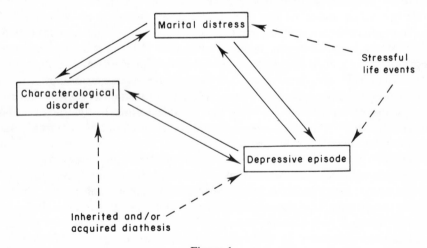

Figure 1

to note that the 'event' may also be internal (e.g. biochemical changes) or may interact with internal factors (e.g. maladaptive cognitions) in a diathesis–stress relationship to produce depression. The resulting marital distress may be transient and last only as long as the depressive episode persists. Or, for any of a number of reasons, this secondary distress may engender more enduring patterns of interaction that eventually take a toll on the fabric of the marriage. In such cases marital distress may represent a scar that persists after the depressive symptoms have remitted.

Marital distress leads to a depressive episode

An alternative model of influence maintains that marital distress is implicated directly in the development of a depressive episode. One can imagine, for example, a marriage in which neither partner has a history of depression, but which nevertheless sours and leads to a depressive episode in one of the spouses. Stressful life events may be implicated in this model as well, and may function either as direct or as indirect causes of marital distress; moreover, they may also function either additively or interactively with the domestic tension in leading to a depressive episode. For example, financial strains may cause a direct increase in marital discord, which may in turn trigger the onset of depressive symptoms in one of the spouses. Alternatively, poor marital relationships may interact with negative life events to produce depression, either by increasing the total level of stress experienced or by failing to provide an adequate buffer against the impact of the events (Hobfoll and Lieberman, 1987).

The role of character disorders

Imputing causality to marital distress, however, poses the question of why marriages go wrong in the first place. Although it is clear that otherwise stable marriages may be damaged by external factors, intra- and interpersonal characteristics of the spouses must also be considered. For example, using stringent DSM-III criteria, the NIMH collaborative study of depression recently reported that 35 per cent of a large sample of depressed outpatients had at least one personality disorder, while an additional 40 per cent exhibited sufficient personality problems to warrant probable diagnosis (Shea et al., 1987). These data suggest the possibility that underlying characterological disorders may be a vulnerability marker, placing individuals at increased risk for developing depressive episodes. It is also possible that personality disorders may lead the individuals to become involved in poor quality marriages (e.g. through assortative mating), or to engender problematic relationships with spouses, children, and/or peers (e.g. through dysfunctional interactions). In such cases both marital disharmony and depression may be viewed as consequences of an underlying character disorder. In statistical terms, one implication of this formulation is that the relationship between marital distress and depression should be attenuated when controlling for personality characteristics of one or both of the partners.*

Obviously, we have only scratched the surface: there are also hybrids of each of these formulations that warrant consideration. Our present purpose, however, is not to delineate each of these models in detail, but instead, to sensitize the reader to the wide range of possible explanations for the link between marital distress and depression. Furthermore, it is likely naive to consider these models as *competing* explanations of the relationship between depression and marital distress. Certain of these formulations may apply differentially to particular subgroups of individuals or couples, and not to others (cf. Gotlib and Colby, 1987). Indeed, it is likely that all of these formulations are applicable in some cases, and these models may best be considered to be *complementary* in accounting for the association between depression and marital distress. Therefore, we should guard against bringing premature closure to any of these avenues of inquiry.

In the sections that follow, we summarize the results of studies with respect to their relevance to the three formulations described above. We begin with studies that indicate that depressive behavior can engender problems within relationships. In this context, we also consider studies that have evaluated the extent to which levels of marital distress decrease following symptomatic improvement. We then turn to studies demonstrating that marital problems frequently predate the onset of a depressive episode, and/or are associated with relapse. Following this, we review evidence concerning the role of personality disorders in the development of both marital distress and depression. Finally, we consider studies that have included a marital therapy component for the treatment of depression. Because the impetus for these clinical trials was derived in part from the studies we review, their findings provide a strong feedback loop, resulting in a dynamic interplay among theory, research, and application.

Do Depressive Episodes Cause Marital Difficulties?

As indicated in Figure 1, depression in one spouse may lead to marital distress, even in those cases in which the premorbid marital relationship is sound. Living with a depressed individual, for example, may strain the coping resources of the nondepressed partner to such an extent that marital tension results. Furthermore, a vicious cycle may develop, in which these marital difficulties then exacerbate or prolong the depressive symptomatology. Unfortunately, the kind of data needed to provide an adequate test of this causal linkage are not available. In this section, therefore, we discuss studies demonstrating that depressed individuals may induce tension and negative affect and behavior in others with whom they interact. We then consider studies examining the extent to which marital tensions dissipate as depressive symptoms remit.

---

*Although it is beyond the scope of this discussion, we should note that it is also possible for depressive episodes to affect the severity of the underlying personality disorder (cf. Shea *et al.*, 1987). Thus, we have also included an arrow in Figure 1 leading from depressive episode to characterological disorder.

Interactions with strangers

The vast majority of interactional studies have been conducted with depressives in one-time encounters with strangers. The results of these studies indicate that depressed individuals are less socially skilful in interpersonal interactions than are their nondepressed counterparts. Compared to nondepressed controls, depressed persons have been found to maintain less eye contact (Gotlib, 1982; Hinchliffe *et al.*, 1978), to be less verbally productive (Hinchliffe *et al.*, 1978), to speak more softly, more slowly, and more monotonously (Gotlib, 1982; Gotlib and Robinson, 1982; Hinchliffe *et al.*, 1978), and to take longer to respond to the verbalizations of others (Libet and Lewinsohn, 1973; Youngren and Lewinsohn, 1980). Depressives' conversational behavior is frequently self-focused and negatively toned (Jacobson and Anderson, 1982), and in interpersonal situations they tend to communicate self-devaluation, sadness, and helplessness (Blumberg and Hokanson, 1983).

Given these behavioral patterns, it is not surprising to find that many of these studies have further demonstrated that depressed individuals elicit a variety of negative reactions from those with whom they interact (e.g. Coyne, 1976a; Gotlib and Robinson, 1982; Howes and Hokanson, 1979), although this is not invariably the case (cf. King and Heller, 1984). Persons interacting with depressed individuals, compared to controls, have been found to emit a greater number of negative statements and fewer positive statements (Gotlib and Robinson, 1982; Howes and Hokanson, 1979), to report experiencing more negative affect (Coyne, 1976a; Marks and Hammen, 1982), to perceive themselves as less skilful (Gotlib and Meltzer, 1987), and to be less willing to interact again with the depressed individual (Coyne, 1976a; Howes and Hokanson, 1979). Although these studies are useful in examining the social skills of depressives and the reactions they engender from strangers, they tell us little about the extent to which the obtained results can be generalized to the interactions of depressed persons with more intimate partners, such as spouses. It is to this issue that we now turn.

Interactions with spouses

Earlier, we reviewed the results of a number of self-report studies that suggested that the marital relationships of depressed individuals are problematic. One difficulty with these data is that the investigators relied almost exclusively on the self-reports of depressed persons. A number of theorists have postulated that, congruent with their mood, depressed individuals demonstrate negatively distorted perceptions of their environments (cf. Beck *et al.*, 1979; Johnson and Magaro, 1987). Several studies, in fact, have found that negative mood states facilitate the recall of negatively toned information (e.g. Bower, 1981; Derry and Kuiper, 1981; Gotlib, 1981, 1983). Therefore, studies based on data derived from self-report are at risk of being influenced by response or recall biases, as well as by situational demand characteristics (cf. Blaney, 1986; Coyne and Gotlib, 1983, 1986).

A number of investigators have addressed this issue by conducting direct observations of the marital interactions of depressed persons. In one of the earliest of these studies, Hinchliffe, Hooper and Roberts (1978) examined 20-minute interactions of eight male and twelve female depressed inpatients and their spouses while in the hospital, and again after recovery. These interactions were compared with the 'in-hospital' interactions of ten male and ten female nonpsychiatric surgical patients and their spouses, and with the interactions of the 20 depressed patients with opposite-sex strangers. Compared with the interactions of the nondepressed controls, Hinchliffe *et al.* found that the conversations of couples with a depressed spouse were marked by greater conflict, tension, and negative expressiveness. Their interactions were also characterized by high levels of disruption, negative emotional outbursts, incongruity between verbal messages and nonverbal behavior, and a greater frequency of interruptions and pauses.

Interestingly, the interactions of depressed patients and their spouses differed in a number of respects from the patients' interactions with strangers. On almost every dimension measured, interactions between the depressed patients and their spouses were more negative and uneven than were their interactions with strangers.* The depressed patients demonstrated more negative expressiveness, more negative tension, and a greater number of disruptions with their spouses than with strangers. As Hinchliffe, Hooper and Roberts (1978) state, the patterns of depressive behavior are 'created and sustained by the couple so that the internal world of the patient and the interpersonal world of the couple become fused together into a system . . . What we saw between spouse and stranger was interaction free of this system constraint' (p. 74).

These results lend support to Weissman and Paykel's (1974) and Gotlib and Colby's (1987) contention that the interpersonal difficulties of depressed persons are more pronounced in close relationships. That interactions with depressed individuals take a toll on their spouses is also suggested by data reported by Arkowitz, Holliday and Hutter (1982). These investigators found that following interactions with their wives, husbands of depressed women reported feeling more hostile than did husbands of psychiatric and nonpsychiatric control subjects. In a similar study, Kahn, Coyne and Margolin (1985) reported that compared with nondepressed couples, couples containing a depressed spouse were angrier following their interactions with each other, and reported experiencing each other as more negative, hostile, competitive, and inhibited, as well as less agreeable, nurturant, and affiliative.

These data, juxtaposed with those concerning the responses of strangers to depressed individuals, provide tentative support for a causal arrow leading from depressive symptomatology to marital distress. Depressive behavior does seem to be experienced by others as aversive, and can lead to dysfunctional interac-

---

*Even though depressed patients' interactions with strangers were more positive than were their discussions with their spouses, it is important to remain cognizant of the findings reviewed earlier demonstrating that depressed individuals are less positive in their interactions with strangers than are nondepressed subjects. Thus, Hinchliffe's findings should not be interpreted as indicating that depressed individuals demonstrate *no* skills deficits with strangers, but rather, that their interactions with strangers, while disturbed, are less problematic than are their marital interactions.

tions. Precisely what it is about depressive behavior that makes it so aversive, however, remains to be investigated. Hooley and her colleagues are currently examining the association between specific verbal and nonverbal behaviors of depressed inpatients and the extent to which they are rejected by others. The results of this investigation may begin to illuminate the factors associated with the poor interpersonal relationships of affectively disordered individuals.

Do relationships improve when depressive episodes end?

Figure 1 suggests that depression may be both a consequence and a cause of marital distress. Thus, one might expect studies that have examined changes in the marital relationship across illness and recovery periods to have generated a mixed pattern of results. In cases in which marital distress results solely from the stresses associated with living with a depressed individual, remission of symptoms should, in the simplest of models, lead to a corresponding increase in marital quality. On the other hand, if an individual's depression is a consequence rather than a cause of marital distress, symptom remission should not be associated with a concomitant improvement in marital satisfaction, in the absence of interventions targeted specifically at enhancing the quality of the marital relationship.

Available data essentially support both of these hypothesized models. For example, in a four-year follow-up of Weissman and Paykel's (1974) depressed women, whose reported marital difficulties were described earlier, Bothwell and Weissman (1977) found that marital problems persisted, even though the women were no longer severely depressed and had improved in the other areas of functioning. Consistent with this finding, Schless et al. (1974) found that the vulnerability demonstrated by depressed patients to marriage- and family-related stresses persisted after symptomatic recovery.

On the other hand, interactional data from the Hinchliffe, Hooper and Roberts (1978) study revealed a number of significant changes in the interactions of the depressed patients and their spouses between hospitalization and recovery. In couples in which the depressed patient was *male*, behavior patterns became less negative following recovery and, in fact, resembled the interactions of the surgical controls. In contrast, however, and consistent with Weissman and Paykel's (1974) interview data, the depressed *women* and their spouses continued to demonstrate high levels of tension and negative expressiveness following hospital discharge.

Preliminary results from a recent study by Gotlib (1986) further serve to highlight the potential importance of gender to an understanding of the differences in patterns of marital satisfaction across periods of hospitalization and symptom remission. Twenty depressed inpatients (ten male; ten female), 20 nondepressed medical inpatients, and 20 nondepressed, nonpsychiatric community control subjects completed measures of marital satisfaction and also participated in three interaction sessions with their spouses: the first within a week of hospitalization; the second within a week following discharge; and the third approximately six months later. All community control subjects were time-matched with the patients. Gotlib found that at hospitalization, the depressed females demonstrated greater marital dissatisfaction than did either the depressed males or the nondepressed controls. Their husbands, on the other hand, reported even lower levels of marital satisfaction. Although all depressed patients demonstrated successively less depressive symptomatology at discharge and at follow-up, different patterns of changes in marital satisfaction were observed for males and females. Whereas the depressed males demonstrated a significant improvement in their levels of marital satisfaction from hospitalization to follow-up, the depressed females did not move from their initially low level of marital satisfaction and, interestingly, neither did their husbands. As before, the wives of the depressed husbands were more satisfied with their marriages than were the husbands of the depressed wives, who still demonstrated the lowest scores of all the subjects at follow-up. Thus, at the six-month follow-up session the depressed males and their wives were indistinguishable from the nondepressed controls with respect to levels of both depression and marital distress. In contrast, the depressed females, although no longer depressed, still reported high levels of marital dissatisfaction, a perception also shared by their spouses. These data suggest that the marital concerns and dissatisfactions of the female patients are not simply a function of their levels of depression, and further, serve to underscore the importance of examining the effects of gender in future studies of depression and marital functioning.

Do Marital Difficulties Cause Depressive Episodes?

Thus far, we have considered those studies that suggest that depressive episodes may lead to marital difficulties. It is also possible, of course, that marital distress may in some cases be a cause rather than a consequence of the disorder. In this context, we will first examine literature indicating that marital dysfunction may precede the onset of depressive symptoms, and will then turn to studies suggesting that level of marital distress can predict the occurrence of subsequent episodes of depression.

Onset of depressive episodes

Data from several studies suggest that a disturbance in the marital relationship may precede the onset of a depressive episode in some individuals. Paykel et al. (1969), for example, found that the most frequent life event reported by depressed women preceding the onset of their depression was an increase in arguments with their spouses. From a somewhat different perspective, Rounsaville et al. (1979) reported that over half of their sample of depressed women presented with marital problems. The majority of the depressed women in Weissman and Paykel's (1974) study also presented to treatment with marital problems and, consistent with Paykel et al.'s finding, an increase in marital disputes was the most frequently reported event in this sample prior to requesting treatment.

Data from a major epidemiological study conducted by Brown and Harris

(1978) are also relevant here. Brown and Harris interviewed two separate random samples of 458 community-living women and a group of 114 depressed patients and their relatives. Although their data are complex and have been criticized on both conceptual and methodological grounds (e.g. Everitt and Smith, 1979), Brown and Harris essentially identified four factors that were associated with women becoming depressed in the face of the 'provoking agents' of life events and chronic difficulties. These were: having three or more children under the age of fourteen, being unemployed, losing one's mother before the age of eleven, and particularly important with reference to the present discussion, lack of a confiding, intimate relationship with a spouse or boyfriend. The potential importance of not having an intimate spousal relationship to the onset of depressive episodes has also been suggested in more recent reports from Costello (1982), Roy (1978), and Freden (1982), whose data concerning marital intimacy were described earlier. In addition to finding that depressed individuals experienced difficulties talking to their spouses, Freden also found that they perceived their spouses as being excessively demanding and burdensome, particularly during the period prior to the onset of their depressive episodes.

Expressed emotion and the course of depressive episodes

In addition to focusing on the potential role of psychosocial factors in the etiology of depressive episodes, investigators are now recognizing that interpersonal difficulties may also affect the course of depressive disorders. For example, Sims (1977) and Rounsaville et al. (1979) both found that those psychiatric patients whose symptoms appeared to be precipitated by marital difficulties evidenced the poorest outcomes in treatment. Furthermore, resolution of these marital disputes resulted in both a decrease in depressive symptoms and a reduced likelihood of relapse.

The importance of family relationships in the course of both depressive and schizophrenic illnesses has also been highlighted by Vaughn and Leff (1976) in a study that involved interviewing the family members of schizophrenic and depressed patients at or around the time of the patients' hospitalizations. Whereas the majority of the schizophrenic patients were living with parents, most of the depressed patients were living with spouses. On the basis of the extent to which they expressed critical, hostile, or emotionally overinvolved attitudes to the researcher when talking about the patient, relatives were classified as high or low in expressed emotion (EE; see Hooley, 1985, for a recent review of this construct). Vaughn and Leff found that patients who returned from the hospital to live with high EE relatives were significantly more likely to relapse during a nine-month follow-up period than were patients who returned home to live with low-criticism family members.

The association between spouses' high levels of EE and relapse in their unipolar depressive spouses was recently replicated by Hooley, Orley and Teasdale (1986). Interestingly, although the spouses of depressed patients were just as critical of their patient-partners as were the relatives of the schizophrenics in Vaughn and Leff's (1976) study, the depressed patients relapsed at lower rates of relatives' criticism than did schizophrenic patients: both Vaughn and Leff and Hooley *et al.* found that the level of spouses' criticism associated with depressed patients' nine-month relapse rates was much lower than the levels of criticism typically associated with relapse in studies involving schizophrenic samples (e.g. Brown, Birley and Wing, 1972).

Collectively, these results suggest that depressed patients may be more vulnerable to criticism from family members than are individuals suffering from schizophrenia. The precise reasons for this increased vulnerability, however, are unclear. Vaughn and Leff (1976) have suggested that depressed individuals are more sensitive to criticism than are schizophrenics. Hooley, Orley and Teasdale (1986), on the other hand, note that the source of the criticism may be an important variable. Whereas almost all of the depressed patients in Vaughn and Leff's study, and all of the 39 depressed patients in Hooley *et al.*'s replication sample, were being criticized by spouses, the majority of the schizophrenic patients were being criticized by parents. The depressed and schizophrenic patients differed from each other, therefore, not only in terms of their formal psychiatric diagnoses, but also with respect to the type of relative (spouse vs parent) who was criticizing them. Hooley *et al.* hypothesized that depressed patients relapsed at lower rates of criticism than did schizophrenic patients because criticism from a spouse may have a greater psychological impact than does disparagement from a parent. While parents rarely disengage from relationships with their children, for example, marital relationships frequently end in divorce. Criticism from a spouse may therefore be more threatening than criticism from a parent because it triggers fears about possible termination of the relationship. Again, however, in the absence of empirical data capable of evaluating these two alternative explanations, it is not yet clear to what extent the increased vulnerability of depressed patients to lower levels of relatives' criticism is a function of the disorder itself, the nature of the patient–relative relationship, or some as yet unidentified third variable.

Even though marital interaction research and EE research have, to date, generated two distinct bodies of literature, it is now apparent that the two constructs have much in common. Hooley and Hahlweg (1986), for example, have recently demonstrated that spouses' criticism is negatively correlated with their own self-reported levels of marital satisfaction (measured using the Dyadic Adjustment Scale; Spanier, 1976) as well as with the reports of their patient-partners. Analyses currently in progress on this sample further indicate that both EE and marital satisfaction scores predict relapse in depressed patients subsequent to hospital discharge. Moreover, these two variables appear to be functionally equivalent in terms of relapse variance explained: entry of one variable into a regression equation obviates the need for the other. Because the construct of expressed emotion is clearly measuring an important aspect of the relationship between depressed patients and their spouses, and because it appears to overlap to a degree with the construct of marital satisfaction, it is likely that EE research will become an area of increased focus in future years among those interested in the link between marriage and depression.

These studies suggest, then, that marital difficulties may predate the onset of depressive symptoms, and may affect the course of a depressive episode. As such, they offer tentative support for a model that views some forms of depression as being caused or influenced by interpersonal difficulties. The interpretability of these studies, however, hinges upon whether the depressive episode in question is a patient's first affective disturbance or is one in a series of depressive problems. Unfortunately, no information is typically given regarding the proportion of first-onset patients in a sample. Because of this shortcoming, it is difficult to assess the causal role of marital difficulties directly. This issue should be borne in mind throughout our discussion of the remaining literature.

The Role of Characterological Factors

In the previous section we considered studies suggesting that marital distress may influence the onset and course of depressive disorders. This formulation, however, raises obvious questions about the etiology of marital distress and high levels of expressed emotion. Estimates of the co-morbid presence of personality disorders in depressed inpatients range from 37 per cent (Charney, Nelson and Quinlan, 1981), to 53 per cent (Pfohl, Stangl and Zimmerman, 1984), to a high of 87 per cent (Friedman *et al.*, 1983); moreover, comparable figures have been found for depressed outpatients (Shea *et al.*, 1987). Compared with depressed patients without character disorders, patients with personality problems have been shown to have an earlier age of onset of first depressive episode (Charney, Nelson and Quinlan, 1981; Pfohl, Stangl and Zimmerman, 1984; Shea *et al.*, 1987) and a poorer response to antidepressants (Akiskal *et al.*, 1980; Charney, Nelson and Quinlan, 1981; Pfohl, Stangl and Zimmerman, 1984; Tyrer, Casey and Gall, 1983); their episodes of depression also last longer (Shea *et al.*, 1987). Finally, the long-term outcomes of depressed patients with personality disorders appear to be less favorable (Akiskal *et al.*, 1978; Weissman, Prussoff and Klerman, 1978).

These studies, then, provide strong evidence for a link between the frequency and severity of a patient's episodes of depression and more enduring, maladaptive personality characteristics. Therefore, those investigators who have examined *only* the link between depressive episodes and marital distress may have neglected an important third variable. This link may to a considerable extent be spurious; the correlation may derive entirely from the associations these variables share with the patient's underlying personality dysfunctions. Even though marital distress may predate the onset of a first depressive episode, the marital distress itself may be a product of the patient's (or spouse's) preexisting character disorder. Obviously, the same caution should be applied to interpretations of studies in which depressive episodes appeared to predate marital difficulties. Given the paucity of available data, there is unfortunately no empirical basis for an extended discussion of this issue. Hooley and her colleagues are currently collecting data designed to examine the associations between schizophrenic patients' and their relatives' personality disorders and measures of EE, relationship quality, and clinical outcome; we urge depression researchers to follow this lead and consider the potential mediating role of personality factors in their future investigations.

Isolating Sources of Influence

Although the findings of the studies discussed thus far are provocative, the absence of appropriate control groups in many studies limits the conclusions that can be drawn concerning the specificity to depression of the obtained communication deficits. For example, it is possible that deviant communication patterns observed in couples with a depressed spouse are not unique to depression, but rather, are characteristic of couples with a spouse who is suffering from *any* psychiatric condition. Thus, a group of nondepressed but otherwise impaired subjects might also have problematic marital relationships. An important factor to consider in future studies, therefore, is the use of control groups that will allow hypotheses concerning the specificity of particular communication patterns or deficits to depression to be addressed.

In a similar vein, it is also possible that the interpersonal difficulties found in the relationships of depressed persons are characteristic of *all* couples who are distressed in their marriages. In this context, it is interesting to note that the communication patterns of depressed couples are similar to those found more generally in problematic marriages. Both depressed and distressed couples, for example, have been characterized by higher rates of negative behavior (e.g. Birchler, Weiss and Vincent, 1975; Bullock *et al.*, 1972; Jacobson, Waldron and Moore, 1980; Jacobson, Follette and McDonald, 1982; Weissman and Paykel, 1974), greater negative reactivity to recent negative events (e.g. Jacobson, Waldron and Moore, 1980; Jacobson, Follette and McDonald, 1982; Rounsaville *et al.*, 1979), greater hostility and more frequent criticism (e.g. Arkowitz, Holliday and Hutter, 1982; McLean, Ogston and Grauer, 1973; Navran, 1967), greater levels of coercion (e.g. Biglan *et al.*, 1985; Raush *et al.*, 1974), more rejection (e.g. Birchler, Weiss and Vincent, 1975; Hautzinger, Linden and Hoffman, 1982), and more inhibited communication (e.g. Kahn, 1970; Navran, 1967; Rounsaville *et al.*, 1979).

Communication difficulties are also present in interactions involving high EE spouses. Compared with their low EE counterparts, for example, high EE spouses have been found to be more critical, less accepting, and more likely to disagree with what their depressed partners say to them. Furthermore, these behaviors in high EE spouses are accompanied by low levels of self-disclosing behavior on the part of the individuals with whom they interact (Hooley, 1986; see also Hooley and Hahlweg, 1986). To address the issue of specificity to depression, therefore, it will be important for future researchers to include measures of marital distress and 'nondepression' psychopathology in their assessment batteries. It should also be recognized that depression and marital distress may combine to provide additive or interactive effects that are not evident when only one of these constructs is present.

One way in which the influences of depression and marital distress can be separated statistically is through analyses of covariance. Such procedures require that marital distress be measured in depressed and nondepressed subjects, and that subsequent group analyses be conducted both with and without level of marital distress as a covariate. Group differences that are significant in analyses conducted without using marital distress as a covariate, but that disappear when distress is covaried, may be due as much to the disruptive effects of marital distress as to the negative impact of depression.

Such covariance techniques have recently been utilized by Ruscher and Gotlib (in press) in examining the interaction patterns, postinteraction mood, and marital satisfaction levels of 22 community-living couples, in half of whom at least one spouse was depressed. All couples participated in a marital interaction task, following which their mood was assessed. In addition, videotapes of their interactions were coded with respect to the spouses' verbal and nonverbal behaviors. Preliminary analyses indicated that couples containing a depressed spouse reported more negative affect following the interactions than did nondepressed couples. In addition, the interactions of couples with a depressed spouse were more negative than were those of nondepressed couples with respect to both verbal and nonverbal behavior. When the effects of marital distress were partialled out, however, using scores on the Marital Adjustment Test (Locke and Wallace, 1959) as a covariate, these group effects were no longer significant: the two groups of subjects and their spouses did not differ with respect to either postinteraction mood or verbal and nonverbal behavior. At least in some samples, then, it appears that the findings of depression-associated patterns of marital communication may be attributable as much to marital distress as to depression.

An alternative approach to differentiating the effects of depression from those of marital distress is represented by studies that have used high and low levels of marital distress and/or depression to form independent groups of subjects. Hautzinger, Linden and Hoffman (1982), for example, examined the interactions of 26 couples seeking marital therapy, in half of whom one spouse was depressed. The two groups of couples were then matched with respect to severity of marital problems. Hautzinger *et al.* found communication in maritally distressed couples with a depressed partner to be more disturbed than in distressed couples without a depressed spouse. Specifically, conversations in couples with a depressed partner more frequently concerned psychological well-being, particularly emotional difficulties, and tended to be more uneven, negative, and asymmetrical than was the case in distressed but not depressed couples. Spouses of depressed partners seldom agreed with the depressive, offered help in an ambivalent manner, and evaluated the depressed spouse negatively. The depressed spouses, in contrast, spoke positively of their partners but emitted a high proportion of negative self-statements. These data suggest, therefore, that depression has a negative impact on spousal communication beyond that of marital distress.

Biglan *et al.* (1985) also used an independent groups approach in their effort to separate the disruptive effects of depression from those of marital distress, and came to a similar conclusion. The problem-solving interactions of 'normal' (i.e. nondistressed–nondepressed) marital dyads were compared with those of two groups of couples in which the wife was clinically depressed. In one of these two groups the couples were experiencing marital distress, while the level of marital distress in the other depressed group, although higher than in the normal group, was lower than in the distressed group. Biglan *et al.* found that both depressed groups emitted a lower rate of self-disclosures than did the nondepressed couples, and that the depressed–distressed couples emitted a lower rate of facilitative behaviors than did couples in the two nondistressed groups. Regardless of their level of marital distress, the depressed women exhibited higher rates of depressive behavior and lower rates of problem-solving behavior than did either their husbands or the nondepressed control spouses.

It appears, therefore, that the findings of studies that have attempted to separate the effects of depression on dyadic interactions from those of marital distress have yielded results that are not entirely consistent. For example, whereas Ruscher and Gotlib (in press) found that covarying the effects of marital distress statistically attenuated the effects of depression, Hautzinger, Linden and Hoffman (1982) and Biglan *et al.* (1985) found couples in which one spouse was both distressed and depressed to differ from couples in which spouses were either depressed or distressed, but not both. Although these differences may be an artifact of the type of covariation method employed, it is also possible that they reflect real differences between the samples in terms of the models of influence discussed earlier. Because of the lack of information concerning the affective history of the depressed individuals studied, however, little closure can be brought to this issue at present. As we noted earlier, it is important in future studies of depression and marital functioning that psychiatric history be assessed.

Marital Therapy for Depression

The consistent link between depression and marital distress has understandably led investigators to examine the efficacy of marital therapy in the treatment of depression. Because the concept of treating depression from a marital perspective is relatively new, there is not a large body of outcome studies in this area. The few studies that have been reported, however, highlight the need to treat not only the symptoms of depression, but the marital relationship as well.

Based on a series of case studies, Lewinsohn and his colleagues have suggested that providing patients and their spouses with feedback about their interpersonal behaviors in the home can lead to a decrease in depression and an improvement in their marital and family relationships. Lewinsohn and Atwood (1969) and Lewinsohn and Schaffer (1971) presented cases in which feedback about the interpersonal behavior between depressed women and their husbands was used in combination with individual and marital therapy to effect behavior change. Their results indicated significant decreases in the women's MMPI— Depression scores and improvement in communication between the women and their husbands.

McLean, Ogston and Grauer (1973) examined the effects of behaviorally oriented conjoint marital therapy on the valence of marital communications in 20 depressed outpatients and their spouses. Prior to treatment, their interactions were characterized by high levels of negative exchanges. Therapy consisted of training half of the couples to give each other positive and negative feedback at home. At three-month follow-up, McLean *et al.* found that, compared with control couples who received antidepressant medication and/or individual psychotherapy, depressed couples receiving the conjoint marital treatment demonstrated a significant reduction in depressed mood and a reduction in the frequency of their negative interchanges.

Friedman (1975) also described encouraging results of a twelve-week therapy program for depression designed to assess the separate and combined effects of amitriptyline and 'marital and family oriented psychotherapy'. Depressed patients were randomly assigned to treatment groups and were assessed with respect to depression symptom severity, global symptomatic improvement, and marital and family relations. Friedman reported that both drug and marital therapy showed substantial advantages over their respective control conditions (placebo drug and minimal individual contact). However, whereas drug therapy was associated with early improvement in clinical symptoms, marital therapy was associated with longer-term improvement in patients' participation and performance in family role tasks, as well as with a reduction in family hostility and improvement in patients' perceptions of marital quality.

Positive results for marital therapy are also reported by Beach and O'Leary (1986) in preliminary findings from their study of the relative efficacies of conjoint behavioral marital therapy, individual cognitive therapy, and a waiting list control condition for the treatment of depression. Because their report is based on only eight subjects, it is clearly too early to draw any firm conclusions about the differential effectiveness of these intervention approaches. Beach and O'Leary did report, however, that whereas the three wives who received behavioral marital therapy and the three women who received individual cognitive therapy all showed clinically significant reductions in depressive symptomatology, only the wives who received conjoint marital therapy also showed a marked reduction in marital discord. Interestingly, the results of both Friedman's (1975) and Beach and O'Leary's (1986) studies are consistent with Weissman's (1979) observations that while antidepressant medication combined with intrapsychic individual psychotherapy can reduce depressive symptoms, it seems to have little effect on interpersonal difficulties and social adjustment. Indeed, Weissman and Klerman (1973) reported that, despite symptomatic improvement, marital difficulties represented the problem area discussed most frequently by depressed women in maintenance therapy.

Finally, Gotlib and Colby (1987) have presented an interpersonal systems approach to understanding depression and have outlined explicit strategies and procedures to be used for assessing and treating depressed patients and their families. Gotlib and Colby delineate circumstances under which the spouses or relatives of depressed individuals should be involved in therapy, and describe the effective use of such therapeutic procedures as joining, enactment, reframing, restructuring, and altering family boundaries. Although additional empirical work is required to further validate the efficacy of this intervention and to refine the techniques described, the results of initial studies utilizing this interpersonal approach to the treatment of depression are promising.

Summary

The results of the studies reviewed thus far clearly demonstrate that all is not well within the marital relationships of depressed persons. Their interactions are characterized by poor communication, negative affect, friction, tension, overt and covert hostility, and a tendency for positive verbal messages to be delivered with negative nonverbal affect. Moreover, disturbed marital relationships have been found not only to precede the onset of depressive episodes, but to be associated with the course of the depression and, in some cases, to persist following symptomatic recovery.

There is also evidence that depressed individuals interact more politely and positively with strangers than they do with their spouses, suggesting that their communication deficits may be particularly exacerbated when interacting with intimates. Finally, there is evidence to suggest that while individual therapy may be effective in reducing levels of depressive symptomatology, it tends not to ameliorate difficulties in interpersonal functioning; therapies that include a focus on the marriages of depressed persons may be necessary to achieve both symptom relief and a reduction in the high level of marital discord.

Although there is a consistent association between depression and marital distress, we have seen that the nature of the link is complex. Available data suggest that a number of causal pathways are likely to be operating, all of which deserve scrutiny in future investigations. In the following section we raise a number of issues that warrant particular attention, and discuss ways in which they might be addressed empirically.

DEPRESSION AND MARITAL DISTRESS: FUTURE DIRECTIONS

The Issue of Causality

One of the most serious limitations to our understanding of the nature of the association between marital relationships and depression involves the lack of data regarding premorbid levels of marital satisfaction. Typically, the marital relationships of depressed persons are assessed only after one spouse is already symptomatic. This methodological shortcoming, combined with a general paucity of data concerning marital satisfaction levels subsequent to symptomatic improvement, makes it virtually impossible to separate the disruptive effects of depression from those of marital distress.

Prospective studies of depression and marital distress that are capable of testing competing models of causality are clearly needed. One possible research design that we have already discussed involves assessing the quality of the marital relationships of individuals when they become depressed and following these subjects with repeated measurements over the course of their depression (e.g. Gotlib, 1986). By examining the extent to which the quality of marital functioning covaries with level of depressive symptomatology, this type of study has the potential to yield important information about the temporal relationship between marital distress and depression. Unfortunately, it is not possible to determine whether increased marital friction in remitted depressives is a consequence or scar of the depressive episode, or alternatively, is a stable characteristic that preceded the depression.

This issue can be examined more directly by assessing the marital relationships of individuals *before* they become clinically depressed. Although such an undertaking is simply not feasible with a randomly selected community sample, there are specific populations that are at elevated risk for depression. For example, epidemiological studies have demonstrated that approximately 15 per cent of women who are pregnant develop clinically significant depression in the postpartum period. In fact, postpartum depression likely represents the highest incidence of emotional disturbance temporally associated with one specific life event. The use of pregnant women as subjects in studies examining the relationship between marital distress and depression thus provides a sample of subjects who not only experience the same major life event, but who are also at high risk for depression in the months after delivery. By assessing the marital relationships of these women both before and after they give birth, and by comparing the premorbid characteristics of women who become clinically depressed with the characteristics of those who do not, investigators would be able to examine more directly the temporal nature of the relationship between depression and marital distress.*

Gotlib and his colleagues are currently collecting and analyzing extensive interview, self-report, and observational data from a large sample of pregnant women and their spouses over the course of the women's pregnancy and subsequent postpartum period. Measures of depression, psychiatric history, marital adjustment, social support, stress, and coping resources are being obtained from 1000 women and their husbands on four separate occasions: at the beginning of the second trimester of pregnancy, one month before the delivery date, one month postpartum, and again at a six-month follow-up. Based on epidemiological findings, it is expected that between 120 and 150 of the women in this study will meet DSM-III criteria for Major Depressive Episode following the birth of their children. In addition, a subsample of 200 initially nondepressed women and their spouses are also participating in videotaped marital interaction sessions during the second trimester of their pregnancies. Again it is expected that between 20 and 30 of these women will develop diagnosable depression following the birth of their children. These women and their husbands will be brought into the laboratory to participate in a second interaction session, as will an equal number of matched nondepressed

*An important assumption of this research strategy is that the factors implicated in the etiology and maintenance of postpartum depressions are also relevant to an understanding of the processes involved in depressions arising outside the puerperium. Fortunately, there is some evidence to suggest that this assumption is warranted (cf. Cutrona, 1983; Hobfoll and Lieberman, 1987; O'Hara, Rehm and Campbell, 1982; O'Hara, Neunaber and Zekoski, 1984; Paykel *et al.*, 1980).

couples from the original subsample. Finally, these couples will participate in a six-month follow-up session, at which time some of the women who were depressed postpartum will presumably no longer be symptomatic. It is hoped that a comparison of the quality of the depressed women's marital interactions before, during, and after their depressive episode, combined with a consideration of their stress levels, coping, and social support at these three times, will provide valuable information concerning the causal nature of the relationship between depression and marital distress.

Although we have outlined two possible methodologies for examining the issue of causality, the types of studies we have described are certainly not the only alternatives available. In the discussion that follows, we continue with a review of other issues that warrant consideration and guidelines that might be followed in undertaking such an enterprise.

The Role of Cognitive and Perceptual Factors

Although the increased focus of researchers on face-to-face interactions of depressed individuals promises to yield important data concerning the interpersonal context of depression, the most significant advances in our understanding of the link between marital distress and depression are likely to come from a utilization of multiple and convergent sources of data in the measurement of these constructs. For example, given our knowledge about selective bias in the information processing of depressed persons, it is important that data be obtained not only from depressed patients, but from their spouses and, if possible, from independent observers as well. Researchers must also recognize that information about cognitive and perceptual factors may be valuable in interpreting behavioral data. Couples' perceptions of their interactions and their attributions of responsibility for its quality, for example, may prove to be more fundamental determinants of its process and outcome than is the observer-rated quality of their interactions. In this context, Jacobson and his colleagues (Jacobson, Waldron and Moore, 1980; Jacobson, Follette and McDonald, 1982) have demonstrated that distressed couples are more reactive to both positive and negative behavioral events than are nondistressed couples; negative events in particular were found to have a different meaning for distressed couples with respect to the way they process and interpret what happens within their relationships.

Jacobson's findings highlight the importance of relationship history as a powerful influence on the ways in which spouses' behaviors are interpreted: *behaviors that may appear neutral or even positive to an outside observer may function as powerful negative signals for a spouse whose knowledge of the information value of the behaviors is more extensive.* Because the meaning of behaviors may vary from couple to couple, studies that include both observer- and self-ratings of marital interaction, as well as data concerning both behavioral and cognitive functioning, may be particularly valuable for our understanding of the marital relationships of depressed persons.

The importance of considering cognitive and perceptual factors is illustrated in separate studies conducted by the authors. Kowalik and Gotlib (1987) examined the relative contributions of depression, global psychopathology, and marital distress to the quality of the interactions of depressed individuals. Depressed and nondepressed psychiatric outpatients and nondepressed non-psychiatric controls participated in videotaped low- and high-conflict interactional tasks with their spouses. As partners interacted, each spouse coded on a 'talk table' (Gottman et al., 1976b) both the intended impact of their own behavior and their perception of their spouse's communications. The talk table is an apparatus that allows speakers to register on a five-point scale, from very negative to very positive, the intended impact of each message they send, and allows their spouse to simultaneously code the perceived impact of that message. In addition, each message was also coded by observers. Thus, the data consisted not only of the couples' observer-rated behaviors, but of their own perceptions of their behaviors, *while they were interacting*, on a message-by-message basis.

The results of this study underscore the importance of examining cognitive and perceptual factors in the marital interactions of depressed persons. The marital relationships of depressed psychiatric outpatients were found to be characterized by negative interactions; moreover, this negative quality was specific to depression. In the absence of coding differences among the three groups of spouses, the depressed patients coded their spouses' statements more negatively and less positively than did the nondepressed controls, and in addition, intended fewer positive messages for their spouses than did the nondepressed psychiatric patients. Interestingly, the observer ratings did not discriminate among the three groups of subjects, supporting our earlier contention of the importance of relationship history. Although it is tempting to conclude that the depressed patients were negatively distorting their spouses' interactional behaviors, it is also possible that their spouses' behaviors held different signal value or meaning for patients as a function of their relationship histories. An ostensibly supportive statement such as 'I'll do all I can to help you', for example, may justifiably be interpreted as insincere or patronizing when spoken by an unsupportive or critical spouse.

One strategy for examining this possibility would be to ask patients and control subjects to review and interpret their videotaped interactions with their spouses. This would allow the investigator to determine whether the patients' attributions were systematically related to independently assessed characteristics of either the spouse or the marital relationship. An elaboration of this design would require patients and control subjects to evaluate each other's videotaped interactions as well as their own, allowing the investigator to assess the extent to which the patients' negative interpretations generalized beyond their own relationships. Although neither of these designs alone is capable of bringing closure to the issue of whether patients' perceptions are a function of depression *per se* or of the relationship history, systematic inquiry along these lines does hold considerable promise for illuminating the nature and origins of depressed patients' cognitions and perceptions.

A recent study conducted by Hooley (1986) also illustrates the benefits of measuring constructs both behaviorally and from the perspectives of each marital partner. In this study, which focused on the relationship between EE and relapse in depressed patients, spouses' criticism was assessed in a number of different ways. First, the number of critical comments made by spouses about their depressed partner during the first hour of an interview were recorded. Some days later, couples were videotaped while discussing topics on which they disagreed, and a frequency count of their criticism was obtained from these interactions. Spouses' criticism was thus assessed behaviorally in two different situations, using two different methods. Finally, using a self-report questionnaire, all spouses rated the degree to which both they and their partners were critical about each other.

Intercorrelations among these four measures of criticism indicated that, as expected, the frequency of critical comments spouses made about their depressed partner during interview was significantly related to their critical behavior toward their patient-partners during face-to-face interactions. The data thus provided concurrent validity for the EE construct in a depressed sample. Of particular interest with respect to the present discussion, however, was the finding that the self-ratings of the spouses were *not* significantly related to their critical behavior, either during the interview or during discussions with their patient-partner. The self-reports of the high and low EE spouses of depressed patients do not, therefore, provide the same kind of information as that obtained from an interview or from a focus on their behavior. Finally, although the criticism ratings assigned to the spouses by their depressed partners did not predict their spouses' behavior either during interview or during direct interaction, the patients' ratings of perceived spouse criticism *were* strongly predictive of their own nine-month relapse rates.

Because the severity of patients' depression and perceptions of spouses' criticism were not significantly associated, it is unlikely that the perceptions of spouse criticism obtained from these patients merely serve to mark those individuals who are most severely ill and are therefore at the highest risk for relapse. The data do suggest, however, that depressed patients who feel criticized, relative to those who do not, are more likely to suffer another depressive episode in the months subsequent to discharge from hospital. Precisely why some patients feel criticized while others do not remains to be investigated. Some patients may feel criticized with good reason: they may quite simply be living with more critical spouses. Other patients, however, may be living in critical family environments and yet be unaware, or unconcerned, about the high ambient levels of criticism, while still others may be living with uncritical or low EE partners. Nevertheless, the *perception* of criticism, even if unjustified on the basis of their partners' behaviors, may place a depressed patient at the same risk as living in a high EE household.

A related line of research focuses on the role of causal attributions in close interpersonal relationships (e.g. Berley and Jacobson, 1984; Doherty, 1981a, b; Fincham and O'Leary, 1983; Holtzworth-Monroe and Jacobson, 1985; Jacobson *et al.*, 1985). Results of these studies have recently led Hooley *et al.* (1987) to hypothesize that the attributions spouses make about the causes of symptomatic behavior in their patient-partners may be important in understanding their marital relationships. Specifically, Hooley *et al*. hypothesized that a patient's psychiatric symptoms are more likely to be considered by the spouse to be caused by genuine illness if they are perceived as not being under the patient's control. Symptoms that are perceived to have a volitional component, on the other hand, may be less likely to be evaluated in this way. Therefore, if symptoms that are generally viewed as having a controllable component dominate the clinical picture, the patient, rather than the illness, is at risk of being blamed by the spouse for any disruptive behavior that is experienced. This controllability model predicts that florid symptom behaviors, such as hallucinations and delusions (which are generally perceived by others as involuntary, see Hooley, 1987), are likely to be attributed to 'illness' and consequently will be associated with relatively good patient–spouse relationships. In contrast, negative symptoms, such as apathy, anergia, self-neglect, and depressed mood, will be associated with more disturbed patient–spouse relationships. In the face of such symptoms, spouses are more likely to blame the patient, rather than the illness, for noxious behaviors. To the extent that this happens, marital difficulties are predicted to result.

In a recent test of this model based on a large sample of schizophrenic and affectively disordered patients, Hooley *et al*. (1987) found that the psychiatric patients' predominant symptom profiles were more strongly related to the marital satisfaction scores reported by their spouses than were their DSM-III psychiatric diagnoses. Consistent with the controllability model, spouses of patients whose symptoms were more likely to be perceived as illness related and involuntary reported higher levels of marital satisfaction than did spouses of patients whose predominant symptom profiles were more readily interpretable within a volitional or intentional framework. These findings are all the more interesting in light of the fact that the former group of patients was rated by independent observers as being more severely impaired in their overall functioning than were the patients whose marriages were more troubled. A simple behavioral model, therefore, cannot easily account for these findings.

Although it is not yet clear to what extent spouses' and patients' perceptions and attributions mediate the association between depression and marital distress, the data from these three studies illustrate the importance and promise of obtaining, self-, partner-, and observer-rated measures of the constructs in question. Indeed, they also suggest that cognitive and perceptual factors may help to explain both the high levels of marital dissatisfaction reported by the spouses of depressed patients and the observation that the divorce rates of depressed patients two years postdischarge are eight times higher than the expected rate for the general population (Merikangas, 1984). Depressed patients are not easy to live with, and the reports of their spouses certainly suggest that they (the spouses) feel burdened; many, in fact, indicate regret at having married their depressed partners (Coyne *et al*., 1987). With the inclusion of multiple sources of information and a focus on the meaning of behavioral interactional data from the perspectives of patient and spouse we may begin to gain a better understanding of why this is so.

Standardized Measures and Procedures

It is evident from our review that one of the areas of greatest neglect in the study of depression and marriage concerns the standardization of measures and procedures. While we are not advocating that researchers restrict their measures to those instruments that are already widely cited in the depression and marital interaction literatures, we should note that there are significant benefits to be derived from incorporating a standard set of widely used instruments into the assessment batteries of future studies of depression and marital functioning. Not only would these instruments provide a basis for evaluating new measures, but they would also encourage dialogue among researchers by facilitating comparisons of otherwise diverse studies.

Depression

In this regard, studies that diagnose subjects according to currently accepted diagnostic criteria (e.g. DSM-III, RDC, or ICD-9), using standardized assessment techniques, will be particularly valuable (see Gotlib and Colby, 1987, for a review of various diagnostic procedures and instruments). Wherever possible, diagnosis should be based on structured clinical interviews for which adequate levels of reliability have been demonstrated (e.g. the Structured Clinical Interview for DSM-III, Spitzer, Williams and Gibbon, 1986 revision; the Schedule for Affective Disorders and Schizophrenia, Endicott and Spitzer, 1978; and the Present State Examination, Wing, Cooper and Sartorius, 1974). These can be administered not only to clinical samples (e.g. inpatients or outpatients), but with minor modifications, to nonclinical or community populations as well. This is an important advantage, because it permits a clinical evaluation not only of the patients, but of their spouses as well. Indeed, if the marital relationship is considered to be important in the development and prognosis of depression, both partners in the marriage must be assessed (cf. Gotlib and Colby, 1987). At the very least, some screening instrument such as the General Health Questionnaire (GHQ; Goldberg and Hillier, 1979), the Beck Depression Inventory (BDI; Beck *et al.*, 1961), or the Center for Epidemiological Studies Depression Scale (CES-D; Radloff, 1977) for the assessment of spouses of depressed individuals is essential.

Structured psychiatric interviews have additional advantages for researchers examining the marriages of depressed persons. They increase diagnostic reliability by minimizing information variance, and they generate detailed symptom data for each subject. Although this information is potentially important, it has not yet become a significant focus for investigators interested in the interpersonal context of depression. However, clinicians and researchers alike recognize that married depressives are a heterogeneous group, and that interpersonal factors may not play a significant role in all subtypes of depression. There are differences in marital distress that seem to be associated with the onset and course of depressive episodes, as well as gender differences both in recovery and in marital satisfaction following remission. It may be necessary, then, to consider this and other forms of heterogeneity in attempts to describe the marital adjustment of depressed persons. By collecting data concerning patients' symptomatology, researchers retain the option of regrouping patients in a number of different ways that may reflect possible subtypes of depression. Information about the presence or absence of discrete symptoms also allows patients to be reclassified or rediagnosed if, at some future date, diagnostic criteria change, or another system for classification appears to be particularly promising. The Hooley *et al.* (1987) study concerning symptom controllability, for example, would not have been possible on the basis of DSM-III diagnostic classifications alone.

Marital satisfaction

Depression researchers have employed a variety of measures to assess the association between depression and marital functioning. For example, whereas Weissman and Paykel (1974) had depressed women complete the Social Adjustment Scale, Merikangas (1984) used divorce rates as a measure of marital functioning, and Gotlib (1986) had couples complete the Marital Adjustment Test (MAT). Although diversity in measurement is important, it obviously makes comparison across studies very difficult. In this regard it is worth noting that a number of easily administered self-report marital satisfaction questionnaires are available. The MAT and the Dyadic Adjustment Scale (DAS), for example, have demonstrated reliability and validity and have been widely used by marital interaction researchers. Furthermore, they can be completed by most couples in a matter of minutes. Because the DAS incorporates all of the MAT questions and provides the investigator with both a DAS and an MAT score, and because it is more psychometrically sophisticated than is the MAT, there is much to gain from an inclusion of the DAS in standard assessment batteries for the measurement of marital distress.

Marital interactions

In addition to using standardized measures of depression and marital distress, it is also important for researchers examining the marital interactions of depressed persons to use common and standardized procedures. These commonalities should extend to the structure of the marital interactions. It is possible to use either structured tasks, such as the Inventory of Marital Conflict (Olson and Ryder, 1970) or the Revealed Differences Questionnaire (Strodtbeck, 1951), or unstructured tasks, such as having the couple discuss pleasurable activities (Gottman, 1979) or how they spent their day (Levenson and Gottman, 1983). Regardless of the procedure selected, however, researchers must remain aware that the type of task chosen may affect the nature of the obtained data.

Coding systems

A number of coding systems have now been developed for use in scoring and analyzing the interactional behavior of spouses. The Couples Interaction Scoring

System (CISS; Gottman, 1979), the Marital Interaction Coding System (MICS; Hops et al., 1972), and the Kategoriensystem fur Partnerschaftliche Interaktion (KPI; Hahlweg and Conrad, 1983), for example, have all been standardized for use in coding marital interaction data, and, with only minor modifications, can be profitably utilized by depression researchers. In addition, by providing investigators with simple frequency counts of behaviors, these coding systems preserve the temporal order of the codes, thereby permitting an examination of sequences of behavior. Although other potentially valuable coding systems have been developed (e.g. The Living in Familial Environments Coding System; Biglan et al., 1985), further proliferation of coding systems will make strong comparisons of results across studies increasingly difficult. The point of diminishing returns may fast be approaching and, for the present at least, the time and energies of depression researchers may well be spent more productively assessing the marital interactions of depressed patients with one of the existing coding systems, or with some modification thereof.

Reactivity

In recent years it has become increasingly apparent that couples react in predictable ways to being videotaped in a laboratory setting. Markman et al. (1980) and Vincent et al. (1979), for example, found that husbands react more positively when they are aware of being videotaped, and Gottman (1979) similarly demonstrated that couples tend to be more positive when interacting in the laboratory than at home. One implication of these findings is that the degree of negative affect and negative reciprocity present in these relationships may be underestimated when the interactions are videotaped in the laboratory. It may therefore be valuable to examine home interactions (e.g. Lewinsohn and Schaffer, 1971), or, if this is not possible, to consider having couples engage in warm-up discussions prior to the collection of interactional data. Multiple or extended interactions (e.g. Hautzinger, Linden and Hoffman, 1982) are also recommended. In any case, it is clear that in the absence of reactivity data, findings from the laboratory should be generalized to real-life situations only with considerable caution.

Sample descriptions

Many investigators fail to report relevant subject characteristics that may be integral to an accurate interpretation of their findings. This shortcoming also hampers generalization across studies. As a final point in this section, therefore, we would like to reiterate O'Leary and Turkewitz's (1978) recommendation that the following information be included in empirical research reports: subjects' ages, education, socioeconomic status, length of current and previous treatment (if any), length of marriage, number of children, and number of previous marriages. As indicated earlier, we would add to this list information concerning the past and current psychological functioning of both spouses. Also, with respect to depressed subject selection, the specific inclusion and exclusion criteria should be reported, as should the total number of patients screened.

CONCLUDING COMMENTS

In this chapter we have focused on the well-documented link between depression and marital functioning, and have offered a review of literature pertaining to possible causal connections between these two variables. Although a considerable amount of work has already been done, it is clear that the study of marriage and depression is still in its infancy; much remains to be learned. We have raised a number of issues that must be addressed in future work, but in doing so, have also tried to make it clear that many of these issues do not lend themselves to an easy resolution. On a more optimistic note, however, we hope that we have provided the reader with a number of constructive suggestions concerning directions in which future research in this area might profitably move.

Although it is clear that researchers must address issues of causality if we are significantly to advance our understanding in this area, we must also begin to appreciate the importance of focusing as much on depressive *episodes* as on depressed *individuals*. Depressive episodes are discrete periods of illness in individuals who may or may not have underlying characterological disorders and/or previous histories of depression. Choosing simply to study depressed individuals and ignoring their psychiatric histories and personality profiles makes it impossible to determine which of the many arrows present in the model outlined in Figure 1 are viable. We are calling, therefore, for an increased focus on the marital relationships of recent onset patients with and without a significant history of depression.

There is also a pressing need for more information concerning personality disorders in both the depressed patients and their (ostensibly) well spouses. It is clear from our review that many depressed patients have co-morbid personality disorders, and a more negative course of illness. Whether this reflects a stronger underlying diathesis or is due more directly to the association between characterological factors and marital difficulties (or both), however, is by no means clear. With respect to the spouses, the responses of these individuals to their partners' depressive episode are likely to be influenced to some degree by their own personality characteristics. An assessment of these characteristics would aid in clarifying this issue and, in addition, might help researchers understand why their partners are depressed.

Also worthy of consideration in this regard are the possible functional roles of depression within relationships, and the differential effects of gender. Sequential analyses of the interactional data collected by Biglan *et al.* (1985), for example, indicated that husbands' aversive behavior decreased following their wives' depressive displays. Determining exactly what role depressive behavior plays within the relationship, therefore, would seem to represent a productive topic of inquiry. Biglan's data also highlight the need for a more specific examination of gender differences—both in the expression and possible function of depressive symptomatology, and in recovery. The vast majority of the studies reviewed in this chapter have examined the marriages of depressed women. Consequently, we know very little about the marital relationships of depressed men. Although it is possible that the relationship between depression and marital distress is more complex for women than it is for men, much more research examining the marriages of depressed males is required in order to address this issue more explicitly.

Our final comments concern the lack of theory underlying many investigations of marital interaction and depression. Virtually all of the studies in this area have been essentially exploratory and descriptive in nature. Although to some extent this is to be expected, given that the study of marriage and depression is a relatively recent endeavor, it is now time to begin the process of integrating the findings of these studies in the service of developing and testing a comprehensive theory (or theories) of the relationship between depression and marital distress. Progress in this area will rest heavily on the extent to which researchers are able to generate specific and falsifiable hypotheses and predictions. To this end, we would like to conclude this chapter with a plea for greater communication among researchers working in fields that, although appearing to be distinct, are strongly interrelated. We encourage researchers interested in the study of marriage and depression to become more familiar with the methodologies and findings of marital research that has focused more narrowly on distressed and nondistressed relationships. Similarly, studies that have examined levels of expressed emotion in spouses are also worthy of further exploration.

Understanding precisely what happens in depressed relationships, and why, will not be an easy task. Investigations that adequately address the issues we have raised will undoubtedly be time-consuming, and the coding, analyses, and interpretive efforts will be exacting work. These caveats notwithstanding, however, we believe that the study of the relationship between depression and marital distress holds great promise to contribute significantly to our understanding of the etiology and maintenance of depression, and to the empirically based development of programs designed for the treatment and, ultimately, the prevention of this disorder.

ACKNOWLEDGEMENTS

Preparation of this chapter was facilitated by Grant MA-8574 from the Medical Research Council of Canada to the first author. The authors wish to express their appreciation to John E. Richters, whose insightful comments on an earlier version of the chapter contributed substantially to its final form.

29

Toward a More Differentiated View of Loneliness

KAREN S. ROOK
University of California, Irvine, California, USA

ABSTRACT

In recognition of the diversity of causes and manifestations of loneliness, researchers have increasingly urged a shift away from a global, undifferentiated view of loneliness towards a more differentiated view. This chapter reviews work on this newer focus, emphasising variations in the duration of loneliness, specific interpersonal deficits, motivational and behavioral causes of loneliness, and the manner of coping with loneliness. Implications for further research and clinical interventions are highlighted.

Loneliness is a term that has an intuitive meaning to most people. For example, when people are asked in large-scale surveys whether loneliness is a problem for them or how often they feel lonely, most readily respond without needing to have these terms clarified (Peplau and Perlman, 1982). Yet it would be a mistake to assume that the meaning of loneliness is the same for all people. Like depression, loneliness is a vague concept with multiple meanings. Not surprisingly, both researchers and clinical theorists alike have struggled to define loneliness (see reviews by Applebaum, 1978; Peplau and Perlman, 1982; Sadler, 1978). Although several definitions have had enormous value from the standpoint of stimulating empirical work and theory development (e.g. Peplau and Perlman, 1982; Weiss, 1973), a single, universally accepted definition of loneliness has not been adopted by scholars. Partly in response to this definitional impasse, researchers have increasingly urged a shift away from a global, undifferentiated view of loneliness toward a more differentiated view that recognizes distinctions among types of loneliness (e.g. Shaver, Furman and Burhmester, 1985; Wittenberg and Reis, 1986). A more differentiated conception of loneliness has been cited as a prerequisite to the design of appropriate therapeutic interventions (Applebaum, 1978) and to further theoretical advances (Shaver, Furman and Burhmester, 1985; Weiss, 1973; Wittenberg and Reis, 1986). This chapter examines previous efforts to identify different kinds of loneliness.

A variety of theoretical distinctions have been invoked as a basis for decomposing the global concept of loneliness. These have included the duration of loneliness, the nature of the social deficit involved, the cause of loneliness, and the manner of coping with loneliness (Peplau and Perlman, 1982). These theoretical distinctions are discussed in the following four sections of the chapter. Research needs and clinical implications are highlighted throughout the chapter.

Two caveats are in order before turning to the first section. First, most research on loneliness has focused on white, middle-class college students (Perlman and Peplau, 1984). This chapter accordingly emphasizes loneliness among these groups, and it is important to bear in mind that the conclusions may not generalize readily to other populations (cf. Sears, 1986). Other researchers offer useful information about loneliness among children (e.g. Asher, Hymel and Renshaw, 1983; Foot, Chapman and Smith, 1980; Rubin, 1982), adolescents (Brennan, 1982; Franzoi and Davis, 1985), older adults (Berg et al., 1981; Jones, Hansson and Cutrona, 1984; Peplau et al., 1982; Perlman, Gerson and Spinner, 1978; Revenson and Johnson, 1984; Schultz and Moore, 1984), low-income groups (e.g. Fischer and Phillips, 1982), the psychiatrically impaired (Fromm-Reichmann, 1959; Schein, 1974), and highly stressed populations (Solomon, Mikulincer and Hobfoll, 1986).

Second, by discussing the implications of existing research for clinical interventions, I do not wish to imply that lonely individuals need psychotherapy or that psychotherapy necessarily represents the best means of helping them. Nor do I wish to minimize the very real structural and environmental factors that cause or aggravate loneliness for some people (Peplau and Perlman, 1982). Without 'blaming' lonely individuals for their difficulties (Perlman and Peplau, 1984), it is also important to recognize that personal characteristics do predispose some people to severe loneliness and that some form of psychotherapy may be beneficial in such cases (cf. Shaver, Furman and Buhrmester, 1985). Approaches to preventing or alleviating loneliness through community-based programs and educational interventions have been discussed elsewhere (e.g. Jones, Hansson and Cutrona, 1984; Rook, 1984b). Finally, it is important to emphasize that most suggestions for intervention, whether clinical or community-based, have been derived from a largely social psychological literature and should therefore be viewed as tentative rather than empirically established.

DURATION OF LONELINESS

Most discussions of the duration of loneliness have centered on the distinction between chronic loneliness and short-term (or situational) loneliness. Although situationally induced loneliness may be quite painful, evidence suggests that most people recover without professional help as they form new social bonds (Cutrona, 1982; Rook and Peplau, 1982). For example, many college freshmen suffer from loneliness at the start of the school year because contacts with high school friends and family members are often curtailed. Yet Cutrona (1982) found that roughly 80 per cent of the freshmen in her study who suffered from loneliness in the fall term were no longer lonely by the spring term.

Trait versus State Loneliness

The greatest conceptual and empirical contributions to understanding differences between situational and chronic loneliness have been made by Shaver and his colleagues (Rubenstein and Shaver, 1982a; Shaver and Rubenstein, 1980; Shaver, Furman and Buhrmester, 1985). Shaver, Furman and Buhrmester (1985) recently proposed that for some people loneliness resembles an enduring personality trait, whereas for others it is a time-limited state. Not only are trait-lonely individuals apt to be lonely for long periods of time, they are also likely to suffer from loneliness in many different settings. Thus, Shaver *et al.* cite both cross-situational generality and chronicity as critical features that distinguish trait loneliness from state loneliness.

Empirical evidence

Consistent with this view, in a study of entering college freshmen, Shaver, Furman and Buhrmester (1985) found that students who scored high on a measure of trait loneliness were unable to take advantage of the opportunities on campus to meet others and form friendships. These trait-lonely students had suffered from loneliness before entering college and remained lonely in the new setting. State-lonely students, in contrast, had not been lonely in high school and did manage to make a successful social adjustment to college after an initial period of loneliness.

Individuals for whom loneliness persists (or recurs frequently) are believed to have deficient social skills (Jones, 1982), dysfunctional cognitive schemata (Young, 1982), and/or atypical social needs (Shaver, Furman and Buhrmester, 1985). Trait loneliness was found in Shaver *et al.*'s study to be inversely correlated with measures of social skill that tapped social initiative, self-disclosure, and assertion. Deficient skill in encoding others' nonverbal communications was similarly found to characterize the loneliest individuals in a study by Gerson and Perlman (1979). Cutrona (1982) found that attitudinal factors distinguished initially lonely college freshmen who recovered from loneliness during the school year from those who remained lonely. The students who recovered were less likely to attribute their loneliness to undesirable, unchangeable aspects of their own personalities. Little research has specifically examined the possibility that the chronically lonely may have atypical social needs, although Shaver, Furman and Buhrmester (1985, p. 219) suggested that "trait-lonely individuals seem to want something from relationships that they cannot obtain' even when objective features of their relationships 'are about the same as everyone else's".

The extent to which trait loneliness can be changed represents another important research issue, particularly if the trait-lonely are least able to overcome relational deficits on their own.

Methodological implications of the trait–state distinction

The distinction between trait and state loneliness has several important methodological implications. Shaver, Furman and Buhrmester (1985) note that the use of global loneliness scales which do not differentiate trait and state loneliness may lead to erroneous conclusions about 'lonely people' in general. For example, previous findings that appear to have documented deficient social skills or dysfunctional cognitive patterns among 'the lonely' may actually have been due to the responses of a small subgroup of trait-lonely individuals in the sample (Shaver, Furman and Buhrmester, 1985). Moreover, if college students are studied, the proportion of the sample suffering from state versus trait loneliness is likely to be a reflection of the time of the academic year (Shaver, Furman and Buhrmester, 1985). Studies conducted in the fall term are likely to yield a large proportion of state-lonely students, whereas studies conducted in the spring term are likely to yield a large proportion of trait-lonely students because most of the formerly state-lonely students will have recovered. Thus, if generic measures of loneliness are used, the dissimilar natures of the lonely samples identified in the fall and spring terms will be masked. Because the attitudes and behaviors of the two kinds of lonely students differ in many respects, this unrecognized sampling problem could cause researchers' findings to appear less replicable than they really are (Shaver, Furman and Buhrmester, 1985). These kinds of problems point to the need to develop more differentiated measures of loneliness.

NATURE OF THE SOCIAL DEFICIT

In addition to distinguishing between enduring and situation-specific loneliness, theorists have differentiated among types of loneliness on the basis of the kind of social relationships that the lonely person *lacks* or the kind of problems that tend to occur within *existing* relationships. These two different approaches to understanding the nature of the social deficit underscore the fact that loneliness is not inevitably caused by social isolation but can result from deficiencies in existing relationships (Greene and Kaplan, 1978; Peplau and Perlman, 1982). It is also important to recognize that the research base for both approaches is largely cross-sectional in nature and that definitive statements about the kinds of relational deficits that contribute to loneliness are likely to require prospective studies.

Loneliness that Reflects the Absence of Specific Kinds of Relationships

Emotional versus social loneliness

Weiss (1969, 1973, 1974) was one of the first theorists to argue that different kinds of loneliness result from specific relational deficits. Weiss hypothesized that all people need an intimate relationship with an attachment figure (such as a spouse) as well as ties to a cohesive social group (such as a network of friends or a neighborhood organization). Failure to meet these two inherent needs results in emotional loneliness and social loneliness, respectively. Weiss argued, moreover, that each kind of loneliness is characterized by distinct feelings and behaviors.

An interesting feature of Weiss's analysis is that a relationship with an attachment figure and ties to a social group are believed to serve complementary rather than interchangeable functions. That is, even a highly satisfying relationship with an attachment figure cannot compensate for the absence of group ties, and *vice versa*. In a similar line of reasoning, Margulis, Derlega and Winstead (1984) suggested that intense involvement in a primary relationship does not guarantee protection from loneliness and sometimes even increases vulnerability to loneliness, although their analysis does not rest on assumptions about universal social needs. Rather, Margulis *et al.* argued that as members of a couple increase their emotional involvement and interdependence, they often curtail efforts to maintain other social ties and may even erect informal barriers to preserve their privacy as a couple. Research suggests that such dyadic withdrawal is fairly common (e.g. Johnson and Leslie, 1982). It makes the members of the couple highly vulnerable to loneliness, however, if the relationship turns sour and may additionally place unwanted pressures on the relationship itself (cf. Weissman and Paykel, 1973). Weiss (1973) and Margulis, Derlega and Winstead (1984) thus converge in predicting that excessive dependence upon a primary attachment figure can increase vulnerability to loneliness, even if the relationship is highly satisfying.

Empirical evidence

Few studies have investigated whether different relational deficits produce different kinds of loneliness. In a recent exception, Russell *et al.* (1984) demonstrated that measures of social and emotional loneliness were linked to a lack of friendships and a lack of intimate relationships, respectively. Social and emotional loneliness appeared to share a common core of distress but also had some unique elements of subjective experience. Correlations between measures of the two types of loneliness and individual items from the UCLA Loneliness Scale (Russell, Peplau and Cutrona, 1980) suggested that social loneliness was particularly related to feeling that one has little in common with others and that one is not part of a group of friends. Emotional loneliness, in contrast, was more strongly related to feeling close to no one and misunderstood by others. The pattern of findings from this study is generally consistent with Weiss's (1973, 1974) predictions, although less support was found for the hypothesized affective correlates of the two types of loneliness. For example, social loneliness, rather than emotional loneliness, was associated with anxiety, and both kinds of loneliness were strongly related to depression.

Alternative frameworks

A variety of other frameworks for conceptualizing social needs have been proposed (e.g. Buhrmester and Furman, 1986b; Hogan, Jones and Cheek, 1985; McAdams, 1984, 1985c; Murray, 1938; Perlman and Peplau, 1982; Shaver and Buhrmester, 1983). Although these approaches cannot be discussed in detail here (see McAdams' and Reis and Shaver's chapters in this volume), they are similar to Weiss's in that they postulate universal social needs against which an individual's existing social relationships can be evaluated. It seems likely that most clinicians similarly embrace explicit or implicit criteria by which they evaluate clients' interpersonal goals and relationships. Lonely individuals who seek professional help can also be expected to have ideas of their own about their most pressing interpersonal needs.

Clinical implications and cautions

Several cautions stem from these observations. First, empirical support for theoretical models of social needs is just beginning to emerge (e.g. Buhrmester and Furman, 1986b; McAdams, 1984, 1985c; Russell *et al.*, 1984), and practitioners and researchers should accordingly be modest about assuming that their preferred social need schemata are substantiated or relevant to all groups. To consider just one example, the idea that people have an inherent need for ties to a social group (Weiss, 1969, 1974) may be more applicable to men than to women. Developmental research indicates that young boys tend to socialize in groups to a much greater extent than do young girls. Girls, in contrast, are more likely to form strong dyadic attachments (e.g. Eder and Hallinan, 1978; Waldrop and Halverson, 1975). Similar gender differences have been documented in adulthood (e.g. Bell, 1981b; McAdams, 1984). In addition, membership in a cohesive social network increases not only the opportunities for social support but also the responsibilities and work necessary to maintain relationships (Margulis, Derlega and Winstead, 1984). This has led some researchers to argue that there may be an optimal network size beyond which the costs outweigh the available rewards (Stokes, 1983). Recent research suggests, moreover, that the responsibilities associated with social network involvement may be greater for women than for men. As compared with men, women appear to be more distressed by adverse events that affect their friends, are more likely to be aware that such events have occurred, and are more likely to assume caretaking responsibilities (Kessler and McLeod, 1984; Kessler, McLeod and Wethington, 1985). The toll taken by empathizing with and rendering care to others is not trivial. Analyses by Kessler and his colleagues (e.g. Kessler, McLeod and Wethington, 1985) suggested that such network-related strains are of sufficient magnitude to help explain the well-established finding that women have higher rates of psychological distress than do men. This example illustrates one way in which even a very popular and intuitively appealing model of complementary social needs (Weiss, 1969, 1973, 1974) may need to be qualified or at least adapted thoughtfully in actual clinical practice.

A second caution stems from the idea that clients and practitioners frequently may have different views about the best way to alleviate loneliness or about what constitute reasonable interpersonal goals. Lonely young adults, for example, substantially underestimate the value of a friendship in alleviating loneliness and overestimate the value of a romantic relationship (Cutrona, 1982). Without rejecting clients' own goals or values, it may sometimes be necessary for practitioners and lonely clients to negotiate treatment goals that differ from (or supplement) those that the clients initially expressed (Young, 1982).

A similar point has been made with respect to lonely individuals' needs for status (Rook and Peplau, 1982). Like most people, the lonely may strive to establish relationships that will afford them a certain amount of status in the eyes of others. Indeed, one might expect the lonely to have comparatively strong concerns about public acceptance because loneliness itself is widely viewed as a stigmatizing condition (Perlman and Peplau, 1981); lonely people tend to be seen as 'losers' (Gordon, 1976; Parmelee and Werner, 1978). Status strivings are therefore understandable but nonetheless problematic if they lead lonely individuals to reject potentially rewarding relationships simply because they do not appear to afford sufficient social status (Rook and Peplau, 1982). It seems most appropriate in such cases for the practitioner to empathize with the lonely client's frustrated status needs while at the same time structuring therapy to reduce the client's self-defeating preoccupation with issues of image maintenance and public approval.

Loneliness that Reflects Problems within Existing Relationships

The approaches discussed thus far differentiated among types of loneliness on the basis of the kind of relationships that the person lacks. Yet studies indicate that the lonely do not inevitably have fewer social ties or less frequent social contact than the nonlonely (Jones, 1982; Stokes, 1985; Williams and Solano, 1983). Such findings suggest that dissatisfaction with existing social relationships, rather than the lack of relationships *per se*, contributes to feelings of loneliness for some people.

Lack of intimacy

Consistent with this alternative view, the social relationships of lonely individuals have been found to be characterized by lower levels of intimacy and reciprocity than are the relationships of nonlonely individuals (see reviews by Shaver and Hazan, 1985; Solano, 1986). This pattern emerges from self-report data in which lonely people evaluate their relationships (e.g. Cutrona, 1982; Jones, 1981; Rook, 1987; Wheeler, Reis and Nezlek, 1983) as well as from independent ratings made by their friends (Williams and Solano, 1983) and by people who have spent a limited time interacting with them in acquaintanceship studies (Solano, Batten and Parish, 1982). Although some lonely people may avoid intimacy for reasons of self-protection (Horowitz, 1983; Rook, 1984b) or as a result of ingrained modes of interacting (e.g. Bowlby, 1977a, b, see also

Reis and Shaver, this volume), many lonely people express a strong desire for greater closeness to others (Perlman, Gerson and Spinner, 1978). Indeed, research (Solano, Batten and Parish, 1982) and clinical observations (Weiss, 1973; Young, 1986) suggest that loneliness is sometimes linked to efforts to achieve intimacy too quickly, which may cause others to feel uncomfortable or to withdraw.

Interpersonal conflict

Conflict and other negative events within existing relationships also contribute to feelings of loneliness. Jones *et al.* (1985) asked people to write descriptions of the kinds of life situations and events that caused them to feel lonely. Experiences of separation from or rejection by others proved to be the most common experiences that triggered loneliness, but interpersonal conflict was also mentioned by 25 per cent of the participants. Rook (1984a) similarly found that the number of people with whom elderly widowed women had conflictual relationships was significantly associated with greater loneliness.

Studies that document such difficulties in achieving intimacy or managing interpersonal conflict serve as an important reminder that, for some lonely people, relationship development is more problematic than relationship initiation (Rook and Peplau, 1982; Young, 1986). Young (1986) offers a number of recommendations for tailoring work with the lonely to address issues of relationship development versus initiation.

CAUSES OF LONELINESS

Researchers have cited many factors as potential causes of loneliness. Most discussions distinguish between internal causes, such as deficient social skills or dysfunctional cognitive patterns, and external causes, such as inadequate financial resources or environmental obstacles (cf. Jones *et al.*, 1985; Peplau and Perlman, 1982). Because this chapter focuses on research that is most relevant to clinical interventions, external causes are not discussed here (see Jones *et al.*, 1985 for a review of external causes).

Loneliness undoubtedly often results from the *interaction* of person factors and situational constraints, and an understanding of how such interactions contribute to loneliness would prove valuable both to clinicians and to researchers. For example, Guttentag (1983) presented provocative historical data on sex ratios in different societies to argue that the relative proportions of men and women in a society strongly influence a person's prospects for marriage and many other important outcomes. Echoing Guttentag's ideas, much media attention has focused recently on an alleged 'marriage crunch' experienced in this country (e.g. Salhoz, 1986), or the claim that the prospects of finding an appropriate marriage partner decline much more dramatically for women than for men after their mid-twenties. Given the societal importance attached to marriage (Gordon, 1976), such demographic constraints may make many women vulnerable to loneliness, and women who are shy or otherwise socially inhibited are apt to be the most vulnerable. Unfortunately, few studies have attempted to examine how situational and personal factors jointly affect vulnerability to loneliness (see Shaver, Furman and Buhrmester, 1985; Jones *et al.*, 1985 for exceptions), and this section accordingly does not address such interactions.

This section also reflects the tendency in the existing research literature to emphasize contemporary (or maintaining) causes of loneliness rather than precipitating causes (Perlman and Peplau, 1984). For example, dysfunctional cognitive patterns have frequently been cited as contributing to loneliness, but the developmental origins of such patterns have not been documented. Clinical theorists have speculated about the developmental antecedents of loneliness (e.g. Fromm-Reichmann, 1959; Sullivan, 1953) but researchers are just beginning to test these ideas (e.g. Shaver and Rubenstein, 1980). The causes discussed in this section are those that have received the greatest empirical attention— deficient solitude skill, deficient social skill, and dysfunctional cognitive patterns.

Deficient Solitude Skill

It is but one of many ironies evident in the literature on loneliness that both difficulties in relating to others and difficulties in spending time alone have been cited as contributing to loneliness. Arguments that link loneliness to the way that an individual deals with solitude have tended to take two forms: 'avoidance of solitude' and 'retreat into solitude'.

Avoidance of solitude

One version suggests that lonely people have little tolerance for aloneness (Greene and Kaplan, 1978; Winnicott, 1958), that they actually fear being alone (Young, 1982). Thus, aloneness is a more aversive condition for the lonely than it is for others (Young, 1982), and the intense distress caused by being alone is assumed to have 'driving power' (Sullivan, 1953) in that it motivates lonely people to seek social contact. Sullivan (1953) regarded this driving power as desirable because it ensures that lonely people will eventually make efforts to break out of their isolation. Other theorists (e.g. Young, 1982; Weiss, 1973) consider such driving power to be dangerous if desperation about being alone leads people to launch relationships too hastily or to select inappropriate partners; loneliness is merely aggravated when these relationships fail. The clinical recommendation that stems from this latter view is to help lonely people learn how to engage in satisfying solitary activities (to increase their 'solitude skill'). This presumably makes them less dependent on others for experiencing enjoyment, thereby reducing the urgency with which they seek relationships (Rook and Peplau, 1982; Rook, 1984b; Shaul, 1982; Young, 1982).

Retreat into solitude

A second and quite different version of the link between loneliness and solitude suggests that solitude offers protection from interpersonal threats and demands and therefore might be particularly appealing to lonely people (e.g. Larson, Cziksentmihalyi and Graef, 1982; Satran, 1978). Clinical observations (Fromm-Reichmann, 1959; Weiss, 1973) and empirical data (Cheek and Busch, 1981; Jones, Freemon and Goswick, 1981) portray the lonely as highly self-conscious and acutely sensitive to imagined or real rejections. Moreover, limited assertion skills make it difficult for some lonely individuals to resist others' demands and expectations (Satran, 1978). Withdrawal into solitude, therefore, offers protection from a variety of interpersonal stresses (Jones *et al.*, 1985) and potential threats to self-esteem (Horowitz, 1983; Rook, 1984b), although it also serves to perpetuate loneliness. The clinical recommendations that stem from this perspective are to help bolster lonely clients' self-esteem and to assist them in finding ways to make interactions with others less threatening.

Empirical evidence

These two versions clearly make different predictions about how lonely people regard solitude and have different implications for clinical intervention. Although much has been written about solitude and loneliness, little empirical work provides a basis for evaluating these different predictions. Evidence that is consistent with the second version described above emerged in a study of relational stress and loneliness among college students by Jones *et al.* (1985). The researchers found that students who had experienced numerous interpersonal stresses exhibited both an increased desire to affiliate with others and, paradoxically, an increased tendency to avoid others. Shaver, Furman and Buhrmester (1985) found that trait-lonely individuals appear to have intense social needs but nonetheless engage in coping strategies that do not include other people. The idea that solitude may afford comfort to lonely people received support in an innovative time-sampling study of how people feel when they are alone versus with others (Larson, Cziksentmihalyi and Graef, 1982). In this study, the people who reported the most positive moods when they were alone also tended to report discomfort being with others and, not surprisingly, tended to be most lonely. In preliminary analyses of data collected from college students at the University of California, Irvine, we have found evidence of distinctly ambivalent feelings about solitude (Rook and Thuras, 1987). On the one hand, lonely students' responses to scales that were designed to measure attitudes toward solitude indicated that they disliked engaging in activities by themselves and were critical of others who did so. On the other hand, their responses also indicated that they wished they could more easily protect their privacy and that they derived some benefits from being alone, such as feeling 'freer to be myself'.

Unresolved issues

The findings from these different studies suggest that lonely individuals' attitudes towards solitude are neither unidimensional nor static. Indeed, such attitudes are likely to shift over time as lonely individuals struggle to balance

[handwritten marginal note: Maybe both theories are valid - are valid - different types of lonely people]

change paper

needs for intimacy and privacy. Larson, Cziksentmihalyi and Graef (1982) similarly hypothesized that the meaning of solitude and the motivation to use solitude productively may vary across the life cycle. More research is needed regarding such temporal and developmental shifts. Research is also needed regarding the clinical efficacy of recommendations to help lonely individuals develop solitude skills. In a study of coping with loneliness, Rubenstein and Shaver (1982a) reported that respondents who made active and constructive use of their time alone were less likely to suffer from loneliness, but such data do not demonstrate the clinical soundness of encouraging solitary activities among individuals who are sufficiently lonely to seek professional help. Greater clarity is also needed regarding what is meant by constructive solitude. For some theorists, this seems to be synonymous with 'keeping busy', (Rubenstein and Shaver, 1982a; Shaul, 1982), whereas for others it seems to refer to periods of withdrawal that are necessary for self-discovery, artistic development, or other creative activity (Suedfeld, 1982). Although these two views are not necessarily incompatible, they suggest somewhat different conclusions about the functions of solitude and about the reasons for recommending solitary activity to lonely individuals.

Deficient Social Skill

Loneliness has frequently been linked to deficient social skill (see reviews by Jones, 1982; Jones, Hansson and Cutrona, 1984; Solano, 1986). Lonely college students report greater difficulty than nonlonely students in introducing themselves to others, making phone calls to initiate social contact, participating in groups, enjoying themselves at parties, asserting themselves, and taking social risks (Horowitz, French and Anderson, 1982; Jones, 1982; Moore and Sermat, 1974). Lonely people also describe themselves as shy and self-conscious in social situations (Cheek and Busch, 1981; Jones, Freeman and Goswick, 1981; Solano, Batten and Parish, 1982). Lonely older adults report similar interpersonal difficulties (Perlman, Gerson and Spinner, 1978).

Laboratory studies of acquaintanceship have documented differences in both the verbal and nonverbal behavior of lonely college students. For example, lonely students have been found to make self-disclosures that are ill-matched with those of their interaction partners in terms of intimacy (Solano, Batten and Parish, 1982), ask fewer questions of their interaction partners, talk more about themselves, and change the topic of conversation more arbitrarily (Jones, 1982; Jones, Hobbs and Hockenbury, 1982). Lonely older adults have been found to be unskilled at encoding others' expressive nonverbal communications (Gerson and Perlman, 1979). Jones (1982) summarized these differences in social behavior as indicating that the lonely are self-absorbed and less responsive in their interactions with others.

The findings from these different studies converge in many respects. Nonetheless, they leave unanswered several important methodological and substantive questions about the relationship between social skills deficits and loneliness.

Methodological issues

At a methodological level, it is unclear whether the differences observed in these studies represent causes or consequences of loneliness (Jones, 1982). In addition, as noted earlier, findings of inadequate social skill among 'the lonely' may actually have been due to the presence of a small subgroup of trait-lonely individuals in these studies (Shaver, Furman and Buhrmester, 1985). Consistent with this, Spitzberg and Canary (1985) trichotomized a sample of college students on a measure of loneliness chronicity and found that the low and medium chronicity groups did not differ from each other with respect to self-rated competence and competence as judged by an interaction partner, whereas the high chronicity group differed from both groups on these measures. If the high chronicity group contained many trait-lonely students, then their distinctiveness in this study supports the views of Shaver and his colleagues.

Differential importance of specific skills

At a conceptual level, previous studies do not indicate whether specific social skill deficits are differentially related to loneliness. Although previous studies have documented skill deficits in a variety of areas, it is unclear whether these different problems contribute equally to loneliness or whether certain problems are singularly important. For example, perhaps difficulties in initiating social contact are most strongly related to loneliness. Alternatively, perhaps knowing how to foster intimacy or to provide emotional support in a close relationship represent more serious stumbling blocks for the lonely. Few studies have sought to determine which social skill deficits are most strongly related to loneliness.

An exception in this regard is a study by Wittenberg and Reis (1986). These researchers examined the association between loneliness and seven dimensions of social skill: initiation of social contact, self-disclosure, dating skills, provision of advice and guidance, general assertiveness, assertiveness about negative situations and feelings, and conflict resolution. Correlational analyses revealed that greater skill in each area was associated with less loneliness. Factor analyses indicated that these seven skills tended to cluster into two important categories that were equally important predictors of loneliness: relationship-forming skills (e.g. initiation, assertiveness) and relationship-deepening skills (e.g. disclosure, providing guidance, conflict resolution). Although this study did not provide evidence that specific kinds of interpersonal skills are differentially linked to loneliness, it does underscore the importance of skills that go beyond relationship initiation *per se*. Relationships must be rewarding and mutually enjoyable in order to succeed, yet social skills researchers have paid relatively little attention to such potentially important skills as the ability to be playful, nurturant, and emotionally supportive. Research by Leary *et al.* (1986) illustrates nicely, for example, that people who are perceived to be boring are rated negatively by others on nearly all dimensions that would be important to interpersonal success. Perhaps the social inhibition that many lonely people exhibit simply fails to spark others' interest and invites attributions of aloofness (Burgoon and Koper, 1984; Leary *et al.*, 1986).

Competence, performance, and motivation

Another important issue that has received relatively little attention is whether the deficient social skills exhibited by lonely individuals in previous studies reflect underlying problems of competence or performance or motivation (Horowitz *et al.*, 1982; Leary, 1983). For example, interpersonal deficits could reflect either a true lack of competence (as in 'I don't know how to start a conversation') or inhibiting factors such as anxiety or self-consciousness that mar the individual's performance (as in 'My nervousness causes me to start conversations in a awkward manner') or motivational deficits (as in 'I don't like small talk and don't want to start superficial conversations'). Few studies have been designed to distinguish these three different kinds of deficient interpersonal skill (see Horowitz *et al.*, 1982 for an exception).

Some of the atypical interpersonal responses that have been found to characterize lonely individuals in previous studies may reflect motivational factors rather than social skill deficits *per se*. For example, the motivation to protect fragile self-esteem may at times be more potent than the motivation to deepen a developing relationship with another person through self-disclosure or some other potentially risky form of interaction (Arkin, Lake and Baumgardner, 1986; Horowitz, 1983; Schlenker and Leary, 1982). The reticence exhibited among such lonely people accordingly could be due to motivation rather than to a deficit in conversational skill *per se*. Unfortunately for such individuals, research suggests that reticence is often misperceived by strangers as unfriendliness, although friends of reticent persons do not make this mistake (Burgoon and Koper, 1984). Other social motives might similarly lead some lonely individuals to behave in a way that is judged unattractive by others. For example, the desire to appear generous and caring might lead some people to shower gifts on others or to render unsolicited and perhaps unwanted support (see Bowlby's discussion of excessive caretaking, 1977a,b). Some lonely people may engage in self-deprecation to convey an impression of modesty or to signal their aproachability, yet research suggests that such self-deprecation often fails to kindle others' enthusiasm (Arkin, Lake and Baumgardner, 1986).

Research should be undertaken to contrast the interpersonal motivations and strategies of lonely versus nonlonely people. For example, lonely and nonloney people may be motivated by fundamentally different goals. Alternatively, they may endorse similar interpersonal goals but use different strategies in pursuit of these goals. Recent work by McAdams (1984, 1985c) offers an interesting empirical example of how social motives can be linked to friendship patterns and satisfaction. Miell and Duck (1986) present a useful analysis of the strategies that people use, with varying degrees of conscious deliberation, to intensify or restrict the development of new friendships. In a similar vein, shyness has recently been analyzed from the perspective of self-handicapping and strategic self-presentation (Snyder and Smith, 1986). Such approaches might be adapted by loneliness researchers to shed light on how motivational factors, either separately or in combination with actual skill deficits, contribute to loneliness.

Reactions of others to lonely people

Implicit in this emerging literature on the social behavior of the lonely is the idea that the distinctive interpersonal responses of the lonely alienate others or in some other way serve to perpetuate loneliness. Jones (1982, p. 241) suggested, for example, that nonnormative interpersonal behaviors 'may put the lonely person in a position of social marginality'. Perlman and Peplau (1981) offered several reasons why the lonely might be more prone to rejection than the nonlonley, including the possibility that interaction with lonely people may provide fewer rewards and entail more costs. Rubenstein and Shaver (1982b) reported anecdotally that they personally reacted with feelings of frustration and, indeed, depression to a subset of the lonely people with whom they conducted in-depth interviews. Clinical theorists have similarly noted that lonely clients sometimes evoke troubling reactions in therapists (Greene and Kaplan, 1978; Satran, 1978) and that it can be difficult for therapists to empathize with lonely clients (Satran, 1978).

Yet the empirical evidence regarding others' reactions to lonely individuals is sparse and inconsistent (Jones, 1982). In some studies, peers perceive the lonely to have deficient interpersonal skills (e.g. Spitzberg and Canary, 1985), whereas in other studies they do not (e.g. Chelune, Sultan and Williams, 1980). Lonely college students were not rated more harshly by their partners than were nonlonely students in two dyadic interaction studies (Jones, Freemon and Goswick, 1981). In a study by Sloan and Solano (1984), the interaction partners of lonely male college students did not find their conversations to be less satisfying than did the partners of nonlonely students. Another interaction study (Solano, Batten and Parish, 1982), however, found that lonely students were rated by their interaction partners as more difficult to get to know. Williams and Solano (1983) similarly found that the friendship choices of lonely students were less likely to be reciprocated than were the friendship choices of nonlonely students, although there was no difference between lonely and nonlonely students in the degree of reciprocation by those regarded as best friends.

In light of such contradictory findings, further work is clearly needed to determine how the distinctive interpersonal behaviors of the lonely serve to perpetuate loneliness. A variety of pathways other than overt rejection by others might be involved. For example, doubts about their own interpersonal effectiveness may lead the lonely to avoid social situations that entail both potential risks and benefits (Arkin, Lake and Baumgardner, 1986; Jones *et al.*, 1985; Pietromonaco and Rook, 1987). Jones (1982) also suggested that even relatively minor differences in the way that lonely and nonlonely people are perceived might decrease the probability that friendship would develop from initial contacts. Consistent with this, research suggests that the depressed often receive feedback from others that is ambivalent rather than overtly negative (Coyne, 1976a; Howes and Hokanson, 1979). Indeed, theories regarding the interpersonal aspects of depression (e.g. Coates and Wortman, 1980; Coyne, 1976a; Horowitz *et al.*, 1982) and studies of the social responses to depressed persons (e.g. Gotlib and Robinson, 1982; Howes and Hokanson, 1979) offer a number of insights that might apply to the lonely.

Dysfunctional Cognitive Patterns

Dysfunctional cognitive patterns have also frequently been cited as contributing to loneliness (Peplau and Perlman, 1982; Perlman and Peplau, 1984; Young, 1982). These dysfunctional cognitions concern the self, other people, and events (Young, 1982).

Views of self

Lonely individuals have been found to suffer from low self-esteem in numerous studies (see review by Peplau, Miceli and Morasch, 1982). Goswick and Jones (1981) found that loneliness was associated with negative perceptions of one's body, sexuality, health, and appearance. Similarly, in the acquaintanceship studies described earlier, lonely students evaluated themselves critically and expected others to reject them, although they were not differentially evaluated by nonlonely students (Jones, 1982).

Views of others

Ironically, evidence suggests that some lonely individuals view others negatively as well. In scales that elicit ratings of people in general, the lonely report greater cynicism and mistrust than do the nonlonely (Brennan and Auslander, 1979; Jones, Freemon and Goswick, 1981; Moore and Sermat, 1974; Wittenberg and Reis, 1986). Lonely students rated their interaction partners more negatively and expressed less desire for continued contact with them (Jones, 1982). As compared with nonlonely college students, lonely college students have been found to rate their roommates more negatively (Wittenberg and Reis, 1986). The empirical evidence does not uniformly document critical views of others, however. Chelune, Sultan and Williams (1980) and Spitzberg and Canary (1985) found that subjects' loneliness was not significantly related to ratings of their interaction partners.

Additional research suggests that the lonely may misperceive the degree of intimacy in their interactions with others. Solano, Batten and Parish (1982) found in a dyadic interaction study that partners of lonely subjects described their interactions as relatively low in intimacy and indicated that they did not know the lonely subjects well, whereas the lonely subjects characterized their interactions as more intimate and reported greater familiarity with their partners. Yet despite this apparent 'overestimation' of intimacy by lonely subjects in an initial encounter with a stranger, research described earlier indicates that lonely people characterize their actual, ongoing relationships with others as comparatively low in intimacy. These discrepant findings might mean either that something prevents the growth of further intimacy following initially promising relationships with new acquaintances, or that the intimacy that does develop is not sufficient to satisfy lonely individuals. It is also possible that the greater intimacy reported by lonely subjects in structured acquaintanceship exercises (Solano, Batten and Parish, 1982) is to some extent artifactual and does not generalize to actual initial encounters with others (an idea that is discussed more fully later).

Views of events

Less research has focused on lonely individuals' interpretations of events, but pessimistic and self-defeating interpretations are also believed to contribute to loneliness (e.g. Young, 1982). Hanley-Dunn, Maxwell and Santos (1985) found that lonely women offered more negative interpretations of hypothetical interaction scenarios. Research by Peplau, Russell and Heim (1979) suggests that the lonely tend to blame themselves for their interpersonal difficulties. Young (1982, 1986) presented numerous examples from clinical cases that illustrate how negative interpretations of events may perpetuate loneliness.

As was noted earlier in the discussion of social skills, it is unclear whether the negativity documented in these studies is a cause or a consequence of loneliness. The extent to which particular subgroups, such as the trait-lonely, account for these patterns of negativity also remains unclear. In addition, it is unclear whether the negativity documented in previous studies should be viewed as evidence of cognitive distortions.

The issue of distortion

There appears to be an implicit contradiction in the tendency to characterize lonely individuals' perceptions as distorted or inaccurate while at the same time characterizing their interpersonal skills as deficient. Young (1986) argued, for example, that the cognitive schemata of the lonely have realistic origins in childhood (e.g. harshly critical parents), but become self-perpetuating and unrealistic in adulthood. Yet if lonely people have objectively limited social skills, then some degree of pessimism about the probable outcome of encounters with others would appear to represent a realistic rather than a distorted response. Similarly, the finding that lonely subjects in acquaintanceship studies perceive their interactions to be more intimate than their partners do (Solano, Batten and Parish, 1982) does not in itself indicate that the lonely are inaccurate in judging intimacy. Rather, a half-hour interaction that is structured by a researcher to encourage mutual disclosure may indeed be a fairly intimate experience for some lonely people if, as research suggests (e.g. Wheeler, Reis and Nezlek, 1983), most of their naturally occurring interactions with others are low in intimacy. Given such a personal baseline, the social perceptions of lonely subjects in the experimental situation could be characterized as fairly accurate rather than inaccurate. The negativity that characterizes lonely individuals' interpretations of events (e.g. Hanley-Dunn, Maxwell and Santos, 1985) could similarly represent a fairly realistic extrapolation from their own personal experiences rather than cynicism or mistrust *per se*.

This uncertainty about how to view the greater negativity exhibited by lonely people has parallels in research on depression. Like the lonely, the depressed have been found to have negative perceptions (see reviews by Beck, 1976; Teasdale, 1983) and these negative perceptions were originally viewed as inaccurate distortions. However, recent research on depression has challenged this idea (see review by Kuiper and Higgins, 1985). Indeed, some studies suggest that nondepressed individuals make unrealistically positive and self-enhancing inferences, whereas depressed individuals make comparatively accurate inferences (e.g. Alloy and Abramson, 1982; Lewinsohn *et al.*, 1980).

It is difficult to evaluate the accuracy of lonely individuals' social perceptions without more information about the kind of responses that they actually tend to elicit from others. They may be fairly accurate, for example, in detecting ambivalence in others' responses, or in sensing that others' overt behaviors and private sentiments are not entirely consistent. Complicating this issue, and underscoring the need for further research, is the difficulty of knowing from whose perspective 'accuracy' should be gauged—that of the lonely person, that of the lonely person's partner, or that of the researcher (cf. Acitelli and Duck, 1987; Duck and Sants, 1983).

More research is also needed regarding the interpersonal goals and expectations of the lonely. The popular definition of loneliness as the response to a perceived discrepancy between one's desired relationships and one's actual relationships (Peplau and Perlman, 1982) clearly invites research on both kinds of judgements, yet most research has focused only on lonely people's judgements of their existing relationships. Much less is known about their relationship aspirations, although it is plausible that highly idealized aspirations contribute to loneliness as much or more than does dissatisfaction with existing relationships (cf. Solano, 1986; Young, 1986).

MANNER OF COPING WITH LONELINESS

Considerable diversity appears to exist among lonely individuals with respect to how they attempt to cope with loneliness. At the most basic level, people differ in their readiness to recognize or admit that they are lonely (Booth, 1983; Rook and Peplau, 1982). Feared stigma, for example, may lead some lonely individuals to avoid the label 'lonely' even when seeking professional help. Fromm-Reichmann suggested that 'Even mild . . . states of loneliness do not seem to be easy to talk about' (1959, p. 6). Some people may guard against the pain of loneliness by denying the experience. H. E. Peplau (1955, p. 67) suggested, 'Often loneliness is not felt; instead the person has a feeling of unexplained dread, or desperation, or of extreme restlessness. These feelings [precipitate] automatic actions that force other persons to come into contact with the lonely individual.' She offered the example of a patient whose severe drinking required nursing care, thus providing the social contact that was actually needed. Clinical theorists have accordingly argued that clinicians must be prepared to infer the presence of loneliness that clients are either reluctant to admit or that is experienced at a genuinely unconscious level (Booth, 1983; Fromm-Reichmann, 1959).

Although little research has directly addressed this idea of denial of loneliness, indirect evidence suggests that men and women may differ in their willingness to admit that they are lonely. In a review of gender differences in loneliness, Borys and Perlman (1985) noted that women tend to have higher scores on measures that make explicit references to loneliness, whereas men tend to have higher scores on measures that avoid explicit references to loneliness. Borys and Perlman offered several explanations for this difference, including the possibility that men are more reluctant to label themselves as lonely. The researchers presented empirical evidence, moreover, that this reluctance may stem from a greater societal stigma attached to loneliness among men. College students were asked to read a description of a lonely man or woman (the descriptions were identical in other respects) and to make ratings of the stimulus person. Both male and female subjects rated the lonely man more harshly. Thus, reluctance to admit loneliness may sometimes reflect a person's realistic appraisal of the critical judgements that such an admission would elicit from others.

Apart from differences in willingness to acknowledge their loneliness, people also appear to differ in the specific actions that they take to cope with loneliness. Rubenstein and Shaver (1982a) identified four major coping strategies in a factor analytic study of reactions to loneliness: (1) sad passivity—a 'state of lethargic self-pity' (p. 215) in which lonely individuals report that they overeat, watch television, sleep, take tranquilizers, consume alcohol, or merely sit and do nothing, (2) active solitude—an effort to cope with loneliness by finding constructive ways to spend time alone, such as working on a hobby, reading, or exercising, (3) spending money—an apparent effort to alleviate or distract oneself from the negative feelings associated with loneliness, and (4) social contact—an effort to reduce loneliness by seeking contact with others, such as calling a friend or visiting someone. Individuals who engaged in activities characteristic of the sad passivity factor were the loneliest, and Rubenstein and Shaver (1982a) speculated that such a style of coping contributes to a vicious cycle of low self-esteem and social isolation.

CONCLUSION

Loneliness is a form of distress that has many roots and manifestations. Recognition of the multidimensionality of loneliness has grown in recent years and, as the overview in this chapter suggests, existing research has identified several bases for distinguishing among different kinds of loneliness. Important differences have been documented among lonely individuals with respect to the duration of their loneliness, the nature of their relationship deficiencies, the causes of those deficiencies, and the manner of coping with loneliness. Moreover, as the preceding discussion indicated, there is emerging evidence of consistent relationships among some of these different dimensions. For example, the duration of loneliness appears to be associated with the choice of specific coping strategies. Similarly, certain personal characteristics that contribute to loneliness appear to cluster together, such as limited interpersonal confidence, heightened sensitivity to social disapproval, and a tendency to retreat to solitary activities.

More work is needed to uncover the how different features of loneliness tend to covary. Although it may be unrealistic to hope for a tidy typology of loneliness, it seems worthwhile to attempt to learn how various elements of the loneliness experience cluster together. In a series of innovative studies, Horowitz and his colleagues (Horowitz, French and Anderson, 1982; Horowitz et al., 1982) have drawn upon the concept of prototypes to illustrate how the characteristics of lonely people form organized and thematically coherent clusters. Their work suggests that the prototype of a lonely person is a subset of the broader prototype of a depressed person. Thus, knowing that a person is lonely allows one to predict that significant symptoms of depression are also likely to be present. Because depression is a larger prototype with more varied features, knowledge of a person's depression does not in itself imply problems with loneliness. Perhaps the prototype approach or a similar approach could be pursued to identify subsets that may be nested within the general category of loneliness. This would allow attributes and experiences that most lonely people share to be distinguished from those that are unique to different subgroups of the lonely.

Finally, it would seem useful to extend this sort of analysis to include a comparison of the similarities and differences between loneliness and other conditions that involve interpersonal deficits. The literatures on shyness (e.g. Jones, Cheek and Briggs, 1986), social anxiety (e.g. Schlenker and Leary, 1982; Leary, 1983), introversion–extraversion (e.g. Green, 1986), self-consciousness (e.g. Fenigstein, 1979; Fenigstein, Scheier and Buss, 1975), and the interpersonal aspects of depression (e.g. Cane and Gotlib, 1985; Coates and Wortman, 1980; Coyne, 1976a) provide ample evidence for identifying points of convergence and divergence in underlying cognitive, behavioral, affective, and motivational processes. In addition, these literatures provide a rich source of hypotheses that could be examined by loneliness researchers. For example, vigilance to interpersonal threats has been emphasized as a hallmark of both loneliness and introversion, and studies of introversion offer interesting clues that this vigilance may be traced to physiological (Eysenck, 1967; Green, 1986; Gray, 1972) as well as cognitive factors (Graziano, Feldesman and Rahe, 1985). Similarly, shyness researchers have broken ground in areas that have received less attention from loneliness researchers, such as the childhood antecedents of social inhibition (e.g. Plomin and Daniels, 1986; Kagan and Reznick, 1986) and the strategic function of social reticence in self-presentation (Arkin, Lake and Baumgardner, 1986; Snyder and Smith, 1986). Synthesis and extension of findings from these diverse literatures is likely to contribute not only to a more sophisticated view of loneliness but to a more complex understanding of the processes that underlie interpersonal difficulties more generally.

References

Abelson, R. jr. (1981). Psychological status of the script concept. *American Psychologist*, **36**, 715–729.

Abramson, L. Y., Seligman, M. E., and Teasdale, J. (1978). Learned helplessness in humans: Critique and reformulation. *Journal of Abnormal Psychology*, **87**, 49–74.

Acitelli, L. K. (1986). The influence of relationship awareness on perceived marital satisfaction and stability. Doctoral dissertation, The University of Michigan, Ann Arbor.

Acitelli, L. K., and Duck, S. W. (1987). Intimacy as the proverbial elephant. In D. Perlman and S. W. Duck (Eds) *Intimate Relationships: Development, Dynamics, and Deterioration*. Beverly Hills: Sage, pp. 297–308.

Adam, D., and Gingras, M. (1982). Short- and long-term effects of a marital enrichment program upon couple functioning. *Journal of Sex and Marital Therapy*, **8** (2), 97–118.

Adams, G. R., and Shea, J. A. (1981). Talking and loving: A cross-lagged panel investigation. *Basic and Applied Social Psychology*, **2**, 81–88.

Adamson, L. B., and Bakeman, R. (1985). Affect and attention: Infants observed with mothers and peers. *Child Development*, **56**, 582–593.

Adler, A. (1927). *The Practice and Theory of Individual Psychology*. New York: Harcourt Brace.

Adler, A. (1929/1959). *Understanding human nature*. New York: Premier Books.

Adler, N., Hendrick, S. S., and Hendrick, C. (1986). Male sexual preference and attitudes toward love and sexuality. *Journal of Sex Education and Therapy*, **12**, 27–30.

Adler, T. F. (1985). Parental influences on sibling relationships. Unpublished master's thesis, University of Denver, Denver, Colorado.

Ainslie, R., and Anderson, C. (1984). Daycare children's relationships to their mothers and caregivers. In R. C. Ainslie (Ed.) *Quality Variations in Daycare*. New York: Praeger.

Ainsworth, M. D. S. (1972). Attachment and dependency: A comparison. In J. L. Gewirtz (Ed.) *Attachment and Dependency*. Washington, DC: Winston, pp. 97–137.

Ainsworth, M. D. S., Bell, S. M., and Stayton, D. J. (1972). Individual differences in the development of some attachment behaviors. *Merrill-Palmer Quarterly*, **18**, 123–143.

Ainsworth, M. D. S., Blehar, M. C., Waters, E., and Wall, S. (1978). *Patterns of Attachment: A Psychological Study of the Strange Situation*. Hillsdale, NJ: Erlbaum.

Akiskal, H. S., Bitar, A. H., Puzantian, B. R., Rosenthal, T. L., and Walker, P. W. (1978). The nosological status of neurotic depression. *Archives of General Psychiatry*, **35**, 756–766.

Akiskal, H. S., Rosenthal, T. L., Haykel, R. S., Lemmi, H., Rosenthal, R. H., and Scott-Strauss, A. (1980). Characterological depression: Clinical and sleep EEG

591

findings separating 'subaffective dysthymics' from 'character spectrum disorders'. *Archives of General Psychiatry*, **37**, 777–783.

Albrecht, T., and Adelman, M. B. (1987). Communicating social support: A theoretical perspective on process and functions. In T. Albrecht and M. B. Adelman (Eds) *Communicating Social Support*. Beverly Hills: Sage, pp. 18–39.

Aldrich, H. E. (1979). *Organizations and Environments*. Englewood Cliffs, NJ: Prentice-Hall.

Aldrich, H. E. (1982). The origins and persistence of social networks: A comment. In P. V. Marsden and N. Lin (Eds) *Social Structure and Network Analysis*. Beverly Hills: Sage.

Aldrich, H. E., and Mueller, S. (1982). The evolution of organizational forms: Technology, coordination, and control. *Research in Organizational Behavior*, **4**, 33–87.

Aldrich, H. E., and Pfeffer, J. (1976). Environments of organizations. *Annual Review of Sociology*, **2**, 79–105.

Alger, C. F. (1966). Interaction in a committee of the United Nations General Assembly. *Midwest Journal of Political Science*, **10**, 411–447.

Allan, G. A. (1979). *A Sociology of Friendship and Kinship*. London: Allen & Unwin.

Allen, V. L. (1981). Self, social group, and social structure: Surmises about the study of children's friendships. In S. R. Asher and J. M. Gottman (Eds) *The Development of Children's Friendships*. New York: Cambridge University Press, pp. 182–203.

Allison, P. D., and Liker, J. K. (1982). Analysing sequential categorical data in dyadic interaction: A comment on Gottman. *Psychological Bulletin*, **91**, 393–403.

Alloy, L. B., and Abramson, L. Y. (1982). Learned helplessness, depression and the illusion of control. *Journal of Personality and Social Psychology*, **42**, 1114–1126.

Allport, F. H. (1933). *Institutional Behavior*. Chapel Hill, NC: University of North Carolina Press.

Allport, G. W. (1961). *Pattern and Growth in Personality*. New York: Holt, Rinehart, & Winston.

Als, H., Tronick, E., and Brazelton, T. B. (1979). Analysis of face-to-face interaction in infant–adult dyads. In M. E. Lamb, S. J. Suomi and G. R. Stephenson (Eds) *Social Interaction Analysis*. Madison: University of Wisconsin Press.

Altman, I., and Taylor, D. A. (1973). *Social Penetration: The Development of Interpersonal Relationships*. New York: Holt, Rinehart, & Winston.

Altman, I., Vinsel, A., and Brown, B. B. (1981). Dialectic conceptions in social psychology: An application to social penetration and privacy regulation. In L. Berkowitz (Ed.) *Advances in Experimental Social Psychology*. New York: Academic Press, pp. 107–160.

American Psychiatric Association (1980). *Diagnostic and Statistical Manual of Mental Disorders*, 3rd end. Washington, DC: APA.

Andersen, P. A. (1985). Nonverbal immediacy in interpersonal communication. In A. W. Siegman and S. Feldstein (Eds) *Multichannel Integrations of Nonverbal Behavior*. Hillsdale, NJ: Erlbaum, pp. 1–36.

Anderson, B. J., Vietze, P., and Dokecki, P. R. (1977). Reciprocity in vocal interactions of mothers and infants. *Child Development*, **48**, 1676–1681.

Anderson, C. A., and Hunsaker, P. L. (1985). Why there's romancing at the office and why it's everybody's problem. *Personnel*, February, 57–63.

Anderson, H. H. (1937). Domination and integration in the social behavior of young children in an experimental play situation. *Genetic Psychology Monographs*, **19**, 341–408.

Anderson, H. H. (1939). Domination and integration in the social behavior of young children in an experimental play situation. *Genetic Psychology Monographs*, **21**, 287–385.

Angyal, A. (1941). *Foundations for a Science of Personality*. New York: Commonwealth Fund.

Antill, J. K. (1983). Sex role complementarity versus similarity in married couples. *Journal of Personality and Social Psychology*, **45**, 145–155.

Antonovsky, A. (1979). *Health, Stress and Coping*. San Francisco: Jossey-Bass.

Antonucci, T. C. (1985). Social support: Theoretical advances, recent findings, and pressing issues. In I. G. Sarason and B. R. Sarason (Eds) *Social Support: Theory, Research and Applications*. The Hague: Martinus Nijhoff, pp. 21–37.

Antze, P. (1976). The role of ideologies in peer psychotherapy organizations. *Journal of Applied Behavioral Science*, **12**, 232–346.

Applebaum, F. (1978). Loneliness: A taxonomy and psychodynamic view. *Clinical Social Work Journal*, **6**, 13–20.

Archer, D., and Akert, R. (1977). Words and everything else: Verbal and nonverbal cues in social interpretation. *Journal of Personality and Social Psychology*, **35**, 443–449.

Archer, R. L. (1980). Self-disclosure. In D. M. Wegner and R. R. Vallacher (Eds) *The Self in Social Psychology*. New York: Oxford University Press, pp. 193–205.

Argyle, M. (1972). Non-verbal communication in human social interaction. In R. A. Hinde (Ed.) *Non-Verbal Communication*. Cambridge, MA: Cambridge University Press, pp. 243–269.

Argyle, M. (1986). The skills, rules, and goals of relationships. In R. Gilmour and S. W. Duck (Eds) *The Emerging Field of Personal Relationships*. Hillsdale, NJ: Erlbaum, pp. 23–39.

Argyle, M., and Dean, J. (1965). Eye contact, distance, and affiliation. *Sociometry*, **28**, 289–304.

Argyle, M., and Furnham, A. (1982). The ecology of relationships: Choice of situations as a function of relationship. *British Journal of Social Psychology*, **21**, 259–262.

Argyle, M., and Henderson, M. (1984). The rules of friendship. *Journal of Social and Personal Relationships*, **1**, 211–237.

Argyle, M., and Henderson, M. (1985a). The rules of relationships. In S. W. Duck and D. Perlman (Eds) *Understanding Personal Relationships: An Interdisciplinary Approach*. London: Sage, pp. 63–84.

Argyle, M., and Henderson, M. (1985b). *The Anatomy of Relationships*. London: Methuen.

Argyle, M., Alkema, F., and Gilmour, R. (1971). The communication of friendly and hostile attitudes by verbal and non-verbal signals. *European Journal of Social Psychology*, **1**, 385–402.

Argyle, M., Furnham, A., and Graham, J. A. (1981). *Social Situations*. Cambridge, MA: Cambridge University Press.

Argyle, M., Henderson, M., and Furnham, A. (1985). The rules of social relationships. *British Journal of Social Psychology*, **24**, 125–139.

Argyle, M., Lalljee, M., and Cook, M. (1968). The effects of visibility on interaction in a dyad. *Human Relations*, **21**, 3–17.

Argyris, C., Putnam, R., and Smith, D. M. (1985). *Action Science*. San Francisco: Jossey-Bass.

Aries, E. J., and Johnson, F. L. (1983). Close friendship in adulthood: Conversational content between same-sex friends. *Sex Roles*, **9**, 1183–1197.

Arkin, R. M., Lake, E. A., and Baumgardner, A. H. (1986). Shyness and self-presentation. In W. H. Jones, J. M. Cheek and S. R. Briggs (Eds) *Shyness: Perspectives on Research and Treatment*. New York: Plenum, pp. 189–203.

Arkowitz, H., Holliday, S., and Hutter, M. (1982). *Depressed Women and Their Husbands: A Study of Marital Interaction and Adjustment*. Paper presented at the Annual Meeting of the Association for the Advancement of Behavior Therapy, Los Angeles.

Arntson, P., and Droge, D. (1987). Social support in self-help groups: The role of communication in enabling perceptions of control. In T. Albrecht and M. B. Adelman (Eds) *Communicating Social Support*. Beverly Hills: Sage, pp. 148–171.

Aronson, E., Blaney, N., Stephan, C., Sikes, J., and Snapp, M. (1978). *The Jigsaw Classroom*. Beverly Hills: Sage.

Asher, S. R., and Gottman, J. M. (1981). *The Development of Children's Friendships*. New York: Cambridge University Press.

Asher, S. R., and Renshaw, P. D. (1981). Children without friends: Social knowledge and social skill training. In S. R. Asher and J. M. Gottman (Eds) *The Development of Children's Friendships*. New York: Cambridge University Press, pp. 273–296.

Asher, S. R., Hymel, S., and Renshaw, P. D. (1983). Loneliness in children. *Child Development*, **52**, 1239–1245.

Ashmore, R. D., and Del Boca, F. K. (Eds) (1986). *The Social Psychology of Female–Male Relations: A Critical Analysis of Central Concepts*. Orlando, FL: Academic Press.

Askham, J. (1976). Identity and stability within the marriage relationship. *Journal of Marriage and the Family*, **38**, 535–547.

Astin, A. (1985). *The American Freshman: National Norms*. Los Angeles: UCLA Graduate School of Education.

Atkinson, B. J., and McKenzie, P. N. (1984). The Personalized Spouse Observation Checklist: A computer–generated assessment of marital interaction. *Journal of Marital and Family Therapy*, **10**, 427–429.

Atkinson, J. and Huston, T. L. (1984). Sex role orientation and division of labor early in marriage. *Journal of Personality and Social Psychology*, **41**, 330–345.

Atkinson, M. (1984). *Our Masters' Voices: The Language and Body Language of Politics*. London: Methuen.

Axelrod, R. (1984). *The Evolution of Cooperation*. New York: Basic Books.

Ayres, J. (1979). Uncertainty and social penetration theory expectations about relationship communication. *Western Journal of Speech Communication*, **43**, 192–200.

Ayres, J. (1983). Strategies to maintain relationships: Their identification and perceived usage. *Communication Quarterly*, **31**, 62–67.

Azrin, N. H., Nastor, B. J., and Jones, R. (1973). Reciprocity counselling: A rapid learning-based procedure for marital counselling. *Behavior Research and Therapy*, **11**, 365–382.

Babchuk, N. (1965). Primary friends and kin: A study of the association of middle-class couples. *Social Forces*, **43**, 483–493.

Backman, C. W. (1983). Toward an interdisciplinary social psychology. *Advances in Experimental Social Psychology*, **16**, 220–261.

Bailey, R. C., Finney, P., and Helm, B. (1975). Self-concept support and friendship duration. *Journal of Social Psychology*, **96**, 237–243.

Bakan, D. (1966). *The Duality of Human Existence: Isolation and Communion in Western Man*. Boston: Beacon Press.

Bakeman, R. (1983). Computing lag sequential statistics: The ELAG program. *Behavior Research Methods & Instrumentation*, **15**, 530–535.

Bakeman, R., and Adamson, L. B. (1984). Coordinating attention to people and objects in mother–infant and peer–infant interaction. *Child Development*, **55**, 1278–1289.

Bakeman, R., and Adamson, L. B. (1986). Infants' conventionalized acts: Gestures and words with mothers and peers. *Infant Behavior and Development*, **9**, 215–230.

Bakeman, R., and Dabbs, J. M., Jr (1976). Social interaction observed: Some approaches to the analysis of behavior streams. *Personality Social Psychology Bulletin*, **2**, 335–345.

Bakeman, R., and Gottman, J. M. (1986). *Observing Interaction*. New York: Cambridge University Press.

Baker, E. E. (1965). The immediate effects of perceived speaker disorganization on speaker credibility, and audience-attitude change in persuasive speaking. *Western Journal of Speech Communication*, **29**, 148–161.

Bales, R. F. (1950). *Interaction Process Analysis: A Method for the Study of Small Groups*. Reading, MA: Addison-Wesley.

Bandura, A. (1977). *Social Learning Theory*. Englewood Cliffs, NJ: Prentice-Hall.

Bandura, A., Ross, D., and Ross, S. A. (1963). A comparative test of the status envy, social power, and secondary reinforcement theories of identificatory learning. *Journal of Abnormal and Social Psychology*, **67**, 527–534.

Bank, S. P., and Kahn, M. D. (1982). *The Sibling Bond*. New York: Basic Books.

Barker, R. G. (1968). *Ecological Psychology: Concepts and Methods for Studying the Environment of Human Behavior*. Stanford: Stanford University Press.

Barker, R. G., and Gump, P. V. (1964). *Big School, Small School: High School Size and Student Behavior*. Stanford: Stanford University Press.

Barnes, H., Schumm, W., Jurich, A., and Bollman, S. (1984). Marital satisfaction: Positive regard *versus* effective communications as explanatory variables. *The Journal of Social Psychology*, **123**, 71–78.

Baron, R. A. (1973). The 'foot-in-the-door' phenomenon: Mediating effects of size of first request and sex of requestor. *Bulletin of the Psychonomic Society*, **2**, 113–114.

Barrera, M., Jr (1981). Social support in the adjustment of pregnant adolescents: Assessment issues. In B. H. Gottlieb (Ed.) *Social Networks and Social Support*. Beverly Hills: Sage, pp. 69–96.

Barrera, M., Jr, Sandler, I. N., and Ramsay, T. B. (1981). Preliminary development of a scale of social support: Studies on college students. *American Journal of Community Psychology*, **9**, 435–447.

Barrett-Lennard, G. (1962). Dimensions of therapist response as causal factors in therapeutic change. *Psychological Monographs: General and Applied*, **76** (43), Whole No. 562.

Bartlett, F. C. (1932). *Remembering: A Study in Experimental and Social Psychology*. Cambridge, MA: Cambridge University Press.

Bateson, G. (1937). *Naven*. Cambridge, MA: Cambridge University Press.

Bateson, G. (1951). Information and codification: A philosophical approach. In J. Ruesch and G. Bateson (Eds) *Communication: The Social Matrix of Psychiatry*. New York: Norton, pp. 168–211.

Bateson, G. (1972). *Steps to an Ecology of Mind*. New York: Ballantine Books.

Bateson, G. (1977). Afterword. In J. Brockman (Ed.) *About Bateson*. New York: E. P. Dutton, pp. 235–247.

Bateson, G. (1979). *Mind and Nature: A Necessary Unity*. New York: E. P. Dutton.

Baumrind, D. (1971). Current patterns of parental authority. *Developmental Psychology Monograph*, **4**, (1, Pt 2).

Baumrind, D. (1967). Childcare practices anteceding three patterns of preschool behavior. *Genetic Psychology Monographs*, **75**, 43–88.

Baumrind, D. (1983). Rejoinder to Lewis's reinterpretation of parental firm control effects: Are authoritative families really harmonious? *Psychological Bulletin*, **94**, 132–142.

Bavelas, J. B. (1985). A situational theory of disqualification: Using language to 'leave the field'. In J. P. Forgas (Ed.) *Language and Social Situations*. New York: Springer-Verlag, pp. 189–211.

Baxter, L. A. (1982). Strategies for ending relationships: Two studies. *Western Journal of Speech Communication*, **46**, 223–241.

Baxter, L. A. (1983). Relationship disengagement: An examination of the reversal hypothesis. *Western Journal of Speech Communication*, **47**, 85–98.

Baxter, L. A. (1984). Trajectories of relationship disengagement. *Journal of Social and Personal Relationships*, **1**, 29–48.

Baxter, L. A. (1985). Accomplishing relationship disengagement. In S. W. Duck and D. Perlman (Eds) *Understanding Personal Relationships: An Interdisciplinary Approach*. London: Sage, pp. 243–265.

Baxter, L. A. (1986). Gender differences in the heterosexual relationship rules embedded in break-up accounts. *Journal of Social and Personal Relationships*, **3**, 289–306.

Baxter, L. A. (1987a). Symbols of relationship identity in relationship cultures. *Journal of Personal and Social Relationships*, 4, 261–280.

Baxter, L. A. (1987b). Self-disclosure and relationship disengagement. In V. Derlega and J. Berg (Eds) *Self-Disclosure: Theory, Research and Therapy*. New York: Plenum.

Baxter, L. A., and Bullis, C. (1986). Turning points in developing romantic relationships. *Human Communication Research*, 12, 469–493.

Baxter, L. A., and Dindia, K. (1987). Marital partners' perceptions of strategies to maintain and repair their relationship. Paper presented at the International Communication Association Convention, Montreal, May.

Baxter, L. A., and Philpott, J. (1982). Attribution-based strategies for initiating and terminating relationships. *Communication Quarterly*, 30, 217–224.

Baxter, L. A., and Wilmot, W. (1984). Secret tests: Social strategies for acquiring information about the state of the relationship. *Human Communication Research*, 11, 171–201.

Baxter, L. A., and Wilmot, W. (1985). Taboo topics in close relationships. *Journal of Social and Personal Relationships*, 2, 253–269.

Baxter, L. A., and Wilmot, W. W. (1986). Interaction characteristics of disengaging, stable, and growing relationships. In R. Gilmour and S. W. Duck (Eds) *The Emerging Field of Personal Relationships*. Hillsdale, NJ: Erlbaum, pp. 145–159.

Baxter, R. A. (1979). Self-disclosure as a relationship disengagement strategy. *Human Communication Research*, 5, 215–222.

Beach, S. R. H., and O'Leary, K. D. (1986). The treatment of depression occurring in the context of marital discord. *Behavior Therapy*, 17, 43–49.

Beaman, A. L., Svanum, S., Manlove, S., and Hampton, C. (1974). An attribution theory explanation of the foot-in-the-door effects. *Personality and Social Psychology Bulletin*, 1, 122–123.

Beard, J. H. (1978). The rehabilitation services of Fountain House. In L. I. Stein and M. A. Test (Eds) *Alternatives to Mental Hospital Treatment*. New York: Plenum, pp. 201–208.

Beck, A. T. (1976). *Cognitive Therapy and the Emotional Disorders*. New York: International Universities Press.

Beck, A. T., Rush, A. J., Shaw, B. F., and Emery, G. (1979). *Cognitive Therapy of Depression*. New York: Guilford Press.

Beck, A. T., Ward, C. H., Mendelson, M., Mock, J., and Erbaugh, J. (1961). An inventory for measuring depression. *Archives of General Psychiatry*, 4, 561–571.

Becker, E. (1973). *The Denial of Death*. New York: Free Press.

Becker, H., and Useem, R. H. (1942). Sociological analysis of the dyad. *American Sociological Review*, 7, 13–26.

Becker, J. M. T. (1977). A learning analysis of the development of peer-oriented behavior in 9-month-infants. *Developmental Psychology*, 13, 481–491.

Beebe, S., and Masterson, J. (1986). *Family Talk: Interpersonal Communication in the Family*. New York: Random House.

Beels, C. C. (1981). Social support and schizophrenia. *Schizophrenia Bulletin*, 7, 58–72.

Beier, E. G., and Sternberg, D. P. (1977). Marital communication: Subtle cues between newlyweds. *Journal of Communication*, 27, 92–103.

Bell, R. A., and Daly, J. A. (1984). The affinity-seeking function of communication. *Communication Monographs*, 51, 91–115.

Bell, R. A., Daly, J., and Gonzalez, C. (1985). Affinity-maintenance in marriage. Paper presented at the Speech Communication Association Convention, Denver, November.

Bell, R. Q. (1968). A reinterpretation of the direction of effects in studies of socialization. *Psychological Review*, 75, 81–95.

Bell, R. Q., and Chapman, M. (1986). Child effects in studies using experimental or brief longitudinal approaches to socialization. *Developmental Psychology*, 22, 595–603.

Bell, R. Q., and Harper, L. V. (1977). *Child Effects on Adults*. New York: Wiley.

Bell, R. R. (1981a). Friendships of women and men. *Psychology of Women Quarterly*, **5**, 402–417.

Bell, R. R. (1981b). *Worlds of Friendship*. Beverly Hills: Sage.

Bell, R. R., and Chaskes, J. B. (1970). Premarital sexual experience among coeds, 1958 and 1968. *Journal of Marriage and the Family*, **32**, 81–84.

Bellah, R., Madsen, R., Sullivan, W., Swidler, A., and Tipton, S. (1985). *Habits of the Heart: Individualism and Commitment in American Life*. Berkley: University of California Press.

Belsky, J. (1978). Three theoretical models of child abuse: A critical review. *International Journal of Child Abuse and Neglect*, **2**, 37–49.

Belsky, J. (1984). The determinants of parenting: A process model. *Child Development*, **55**, 83–96.

Belsky, J., Rovine, M., and Taylor, D. (1984). The Pennsylvania Infant and Family Development Project III: The origins of individual differences in infant–mother attachment: Maternal and infant contributions. *Child Development*, **55**, 718–728.

Belsky, J., Taylor, D. G., and Rovine, M. (1984). The Pennsylvania Infant and Family Development Project II: The development of reciprocal interaction in the mother––infant dyad. *Child Development*, **55**, 706–717.

Bem, S. (1974). The measurement of psychological androgyny. *Journal of Consulting and Clinical Psychology*, **42**, 155–162.

Benne, K. D., and Sheats, P. (1948). Functional roles of group members. *Journal of Social Issues*, **4**, 41–49.

Berg, B. (1983). A touch of home in hospital care. *The New York Times Magazine*, Section 6, November 27.

Berg, J. H. (1984). The development of friendship between roommates. *Journal of Personality and Social Psychology*, **46**, 346–356.

Berg, J. H. (1987). Responsiveness and self-disclosure. In V. Derlega and J. Berg (Eds) *Self-Disclosure: Theory, Research, and Therapy*. New York: Plenum.

Berg, J. H., and Clark, M. S. (1986). Differences in social exchange between intimate and other relationships: Gradually evolving or quickly apparent? In V. J. Derlega and B. A. Winstead (Eds) *Friendship and Social Interaction*. New York: Springer-Verlag.

Berg, J. H., and McQuinn, R. D. (1986). Attraction and exchange in continuing and noncontinuing dating relationships. *Journal of Personality and Social Psychology*, **50**, 942–952.

Berg, S., Mellstrom, D., Persson, G., and Suanborg, A. (1981). Loneliness in the Swedish aged. *Journal of Gerontology*, **36**, 342–349.

Berger, C. R. (1975). Proactive and retroactive attribution processes in interpersonal communication. *Human Communication Research*, **2**, 33–50.

Berger, C. R. (1979). Beyond initial interaction: Uncertainty, understanding, and the development of interpersonal relationships. In H. Giles and R. St. Clair (Eds) *Language and Social Psychology*. Oxford: Blackwell, pp. 122–144.

Berger, C. R. (1985). Social power and interpersonal communication. In M. L. Knapp and G. R. Miller (Eds) *Handbook of Interpersonal Communication*. Beverly Hills: Sage, pp. 439–499.

Berger, C. R. (1987a). Communicating under uncertainty. In M. E. Roloff and G. R. Miller (Eds) *Interpersonal Processes: New Directions in Communication*. Newbury Park, California: Sage.

Berger, C. R. (1987b). Planning and scheming: Strategies for initiating relationships. In R. Burnett, P. McGhee and D. Clarke (Eds) *Accounting for Relationships: Social Representations of Interpersonal Links*. London: Methuen.

Berger, C. R. (1988). Planning, affect, and social action generation. In L. Donohew, H. Sypher and E. T. Higgins (Eds) *Communication, Social Cognition and Affect*. Hillsdale, NJ: Erlbaum, pp. 99–116.

Berger, C. R., and Bell, R. A. (1986). Plans and the initiation of social relationships.

Unpublished paper, Department of Communication Studies, Northwestern University, Evanston, Illinois.

Berger, C. R., and Bradac, J. J. (1982). *Language and Social Knowledge: Uncertainty in Interpersonal Relations*. London: Edward Arnold.

Berger, C. R., and Calabrese, R. J. (1975). Some explorations in initial interaction and beyond: Toward a developmental theory of interpersonal communication. *Human Communication Research*, **1**, 99–112.

Berger, C. R., and Douglas, W. (1981). Studies in interpersonal epistemology III: Anticipated interaction, self-monitoring and observational context selection. *Communication Monographs*, **48**, 183–196.

Berger, C. R., and Douglas, W. (1982). Thought and talk: 'Excuse me, but have I been talking to myself?' In F. E. X. Dance (Ed.) *Human Communication Theory: Comparative Essays*. New York: Harper & Row, pp. 42–60.

Berger, C. R., and Kellermann, K. A. (1983). To ask or not to ask: Is that a question? In R. N. Bostrom (Ed.) *Communication Yearbook 7*. Beverly Hills: Sage, pp. 342–368.

Berger, C. R., and Kellermann, K. A. (1985). Personal opacity and social information gathering: Seek, but ye may not find. Paper presented at the annual convention of the International Communication Association, Honolulu.

Berger, C. R., and Kellermann, K. A. (1986). Goal incompatibility and social action: The best laid plans of mice and men often go astray. Paper presented at the annual convention of the International Communication Association, Chicago, Illinois.

Berger, C. R., and Perkins, J. (1978). Studies in interpersonal epistemology I: Situational attributes in observational context selection. In B. Ruben (Ed.) *Communication Yearbook 1*. New Brunswick: Transaction, pp. 171–184.

Berger, C. R., and Perkins, J. (1979). Studies in interpersonal epistemology II: Self-monitoring, involvement, facial affect, similarity and observational context selection. Paper presented at the annual convention of the Speech Communication Association, San Antonio, Texas.

Berger, C. R., Gardner, R. R., Parks, M. R., Schulman, L., and Miller, G. R. (1976). Interpersonal epistemology and interpersonal communication. In G. R. Miller (Ed.) *Explorations in Interpersonal Communication*. Beverly Hills: Sage, pp. 149–171.

Berger, P. L., and Kellner, H. (1964). Marriage and the construction of reality: An exercise in the microsociology of knowledge. *Diogenes*, **46**, 1–25.

Berger, P. L., and Luckman, T. (1967). *The Social Construction of Reality*. Garden City, NJ: Doubleday.

Berkman, L. F. (1985). The relationship of social networks and social support to morbidity and mortality. In S. Cohen and S. L. Syme (Eds) *Social Support and Health*. Orlando, FL: Academic Press, pp. 242–262.

Berkman, L. F., and Syme, S. L. (1979). Social networks, host resistance, and mortality: A nine-year follow-up study of Alameda County residents. *American Journal of Epidemiology*, **109**, 186–204.

Berkowitz, L. (1969). Social motivation. In G. Lindzey and E. Aronson (Eds) *Handbook of Social Psychology*. Reading, MA: Addison-Wesley, pp. 50–135.

Berkowitz, L. (1972). Social norms, feelings, and other factors affecting helping and altruism. In L. Berkowitz (Ed.) *Advances in Experimental Social Psychology*, Vol. 6. New York: Academic Press.

Berley, R. A., and Jacobson, N. S. (1984). Causal attributions in intimate relationships: Toward a model of cognitive-behavioral marital therapy. In P. C. Kendall (Ed.) *Advances in Cognitive-Behavioral Research and Therapy*, Vol. 3. Orlando, FL: Academic Press, pp. 1–60.

Berlyne, D. (1960). *Conflict, Arousal, and Curiosity*. New York: McGraw-Hill.

Bernal, G., and Baker, J. (1979). Toward a metacommunicational framework of couple interactions. *Family Process*, **18**, 293–302.

Bernard, H. R., and Killworth, P. D. (1973). On the social structure of an ocean-going research vessel and other important things. *Social Science Research*, **2**, 145–184.

Berndt, T. J. (1955). Effects of friendship on prosocial intentions and behavior. *Child Development*, **52**, 636–643.

Berndt, T. J. (1977). The effect of reciprocity norms on moral judgment and causal attribution. *Child Development*, **48**, 1322–1330.

Berndt, T. J. (1981). Relations between social cognition, nonsocial cognition, and social behavior. In J. H. Flavell and L. D. Ross (Eds) *Social Cognitive Development*. New York: Cambridge University Press, pp. 176–199.

Berndt, T. J. (1982). The features and effects of friendship in early adolescence. *Child Development*, **53**, 1447–1460.

Berscheid, E. (1983). Emotion. In H. H. Kelley *et al.* (Eds) *Close Relationships*. San Francisco: Freeman, pp. 110–168.

Berscheid, E. (1985a). Compatibility, interdependence, and emotion. In W. Ickes (Ed.) *Compatible and Incompatible Relationships*. New York: Springer-Verlag.

Berscheid, E. (1985b). Interpersonal attraction. In G. Lindzey and E. Aronson (Eds) *Handbook of Social Psychology*, Vol. 2, 3rd edn. New York: Random House, pp. 413–484.

Berscheid, E. (1986). Emotional experience in close relationships: Some implications for child development. In W. W. Hartup and Z. Rubin (Eds) *Relationships and Development*. Hillsdale, NJ: Erlbaum, pp. 135–166.

Berscheid, E., and Peplau, L. A. (1983). The emerging science of relationships. In H. H. Kelley, E. Berscheid, A. Christensen, J. H. Harvey, T. L. Huston, G. Levinger, E. McLintock, L. A. Peplau and D. R. Peterson (Eds) *Close Relationships*. New York: W. H. Freeman, pp. 1–19.

Berscheid, E., and Walster, E. H. (1974). A little bit about love. In T. L. Huston (Ed.) *Foundations of Interpersonal Attraction*. New York: Academic Press, pp. 355–381.

Berscheid, E., and Walster, E. H. (1978). *Interpersonal Attraction*, 2nd edn. Reading, MA: Addison-Wesley.

Best, A. M., Inc. (1984). *Best Aggregates and Averages: Property and Causality*.

Bhaskar, R. (1978). *A Realist Theory of Science*, 2nd edn. Atlantic Highlands, JN: Humanities Press.

Bidwell, C. E., and Kasarda, J. D. (1985). *The Organization and its Ecosystem: A Theory of Structuring in Organizations*. Greenwich, CT: JAI Press.

Bienvenu, M. J. (1970). Measurement of marital communication. *The Family Coordinator*, **19**, 26–31.

Bierman, K. L., and Furman, W. (1984). The effects of social skills training and peer involvement on the social adjustment of preadolescents. *Child Development*, **55**, 151–162.

Bigelow, B. J., and LaGaipa, J. J. (1975). Children's written descriptions of friendship: A multidimensional analysis. *Developmental Psychology*, **11**, 857–858.

Biglan, A., Hops, H., Sherman, L., Friedman, L. S., Arthur, J., and Osteen, V. (1985). Problem-solving interactions of depressed women and their husbands. *Behavior Therapy*, **16**, 431–451.

Bijour, S. W., and Baer, D. M. (1965). *Child Development II: Universal Stage of Infancy*. New York: Appleton-Century-Crofts.

Billings, A. (1979). Conflict resolution in distressed and nondistressed married couples. *Journal of Consulting and Clinical Psychology*, **47**, 368–376.

Birchler, G. R. (1979). Communication skills in married couples. In A. S. Bellack and M. Hersen (Eds) *Research and Practice in Social Skills Training*. New York: Plenum.

Birchler, G. R., Weiss, R. L., and Vincent, J. P. (1975). Multimethod analysis of social reinforcement exchange between maritally distressed and nondistressed spouse and stranger dyads. *Journal of Personality and Social Psychology*, **31**, 349–360.

Blaney, P. H. (1986). Affect and memory: A review. *Psychological Bulletin*, **99**, 229–246.

Blau, P. M. (1964). *Exchange and Power in Social Life*. New York: Wiley.

Blau, P. M. (1977). *Inequality and Heterogeneity*. New York: Free Press.

Blau, Z. S. (1961). Structural constraints on friendship in old age. *American Sociological Review*, **26**, 429–439.

Block, J. (1977). Advancing the psychology of personality: Paradigmatic shift or improving the quality of research. In D. Magnusson and N. S. Endler (Eds) *Personality at the Crossroads*. Hillsdale, NJ: Erlbaum.

Blood, R. O., and Wolfe, D. N. (1960). *Husbands and Wives: The Dynamics of Family Living*. New York: Free Press.

Bloom, B. L., Hodges, W., and Caldwell, R. (1982). A preventive program for the newly separated: Initial evaluation. *American Journal of Community Psychology*, **10**, 251–264.

Blumberg, S. R., and Hokanson, J. E. (1983). The effects of another person's response style on interpersonal behavior in depression. *Journal of Abnormal Psychology*, **92**, 196–209.

Blumer, H. (1969). *Symbolic Interactionism: Perspective and Method*. Englewood Cliffs, NJ: Prentice-Hall.

Blumstein, P., and Schwartz, P. (1983). *American Couples: Money, Work, Sex*. New York: William Morrow.

Bochner, A. P. (1982). On the efficacy of openness in closed relationships. In M. Burgoon (Ed.) *Communication Yearbook 5*. New Brunswick, NJ: Transaction, pp. 109–124.

Bochner, A. P. (1984). The functions of human communication in interpersonal bonding. In C. Arnold and J. Bowers (Eds) *Handbook of Rhetorical and Communication Theory*. Boston: Allyn & Bacon, pp. 544–621.

Bochner, B., McLeod, B. M., and Lin, A. (1977). Friendship patterns of overseas students: A functional model. *International Journal of Psychology*, **12**, 277–294.

Bohm, D. (1980). *Wholeness and the Implicate Order*. London: Routledge & Kegan Paul.

Bolton, C. D. (1961). Mate selection as the development of a relationship. *Marriage and Family Living*, **23**, 234–240.

Bond, C. F., Jr, and Titus, L. J. (1983). Social facilitation: A meta-analysis of 241 studies. *Psychological Bulletin*, **94**, 265–292.

Booth, A., and Hess, E. (1974). Cross-sex friendship. *Journal of Marriage and the Family*, February, 38–47.

Booth, R. (1983). Toward an understanding of loneliness. *Social Work*, **28**, 116–119.

Borck, L. E., and Aronowitz, E. (1982). The role of the self-help clearinghouse. *Prevention in Human Services*, **1** (3), 121–129.

Bornstein, P., Hickey, J., Schulein, M., Fox, S., and Scolatti, M. (1983). Behavioural-communications treatment of marital interaction: Negative behaviours. *British Journal of Clinical Psychology*, **22**, 41–48.

Borys, S., and Perlman, D. (1985). Gender differences in loneliness. *Personality and Social Psychology Bulletin*, **11**, 63–74.

Bossard, J. H. S., and Boll, E. S. (1950). *Ritual in Family Living*. Philadelphia: University of Pennsylvania Press.

Bossard, J. H. S., and Boll, E. S. (1956). *The Large Family System*. Philadelphia: University of Pennsylvania Press.

Boster, F. J. (1985). Argumentation, interpersonal communication, persuasion, and the process(es) of compliance gaining message use. In J. R. Cox, M. O. Sillars and G. B. Walker (Eds) *Argument and Social Practice: Proceedings of the Fourth SCA/AFA Conference on Argumentation*. Annandale, VA: Speech Communication Association, pp. 578–591.

Boster, F. J., and Lofthouse, L. J. (1986). Determinants of the persistence and content of compliance gaining behavior. Paper presented at the annual meeting of the International Communication Association, Chicago, Illinois.

Boster, F. J., and Stiff, J. B. (1984). Compliance-gaining message selection behavior. *Human Communication Research*, **10**, 539–556.

Boszormenyi-Nagy, I., and Spark, G. M. (1973). *Invisible Loyalties: Reciprocity in Intergenerational Family Therapy*. New York: Harper & Row.

Bothwell, S., and Weissman, M. (1977). Social impairments four years after an acute depressive episode. *American Journal of Orthopsychiatry*, **47**, 231–237.

Bott, H. McM. (1928). Observation of play activities in a nursery school. *Genetic Psychology Monographs*, **4**, 44–88.

Bott, H. McM. (1934). *Personality Development in Young Children*. Toronto: University of Toronto Press.

Bowen, M. (1966). The use of family theory in clinical practice. *Comprehensive Psychiatry*, **7**, 345–374.

Bowen, M. (1978). *Family Therapy in Clinical Practice*. New York: Aronson.

Bower, G. H. (1981). Mood and memory. *American Psychologist*, **36**, 129–148.

Bower, G. H., Black, J. B., and Turner, T. J. (1979). Scripts in memory for text. *Cognitive Psychology*, **11**, 177–220.

Bowlby, J. (1958). The nature of the child's tie to his mother. *International Journal of Psychoanalysis*, **39**, 350–373.

Bowlby, J. (1969). *Attachment and Loss: Vol. 1. Attachment*. London: Hogarth.

Bowlby, J. (1973). *Attachment and Loss: Vol. 2. Separation: Anxiety and Anger*. New York: Basic Books.

Bowlby, J. (1977a). The making and breaking of affectional bonds. I. Aetiology and psychopathology in the light of attachment theory. *British Journal of Psychiatry*, **130**, 201–210.

Bowlby, J. (1977b). The making and breaking of affectional bonds. II. Some principles of psychotherapy. *British Journal of Psychiatry*, **130**, 421–431.

Bowlby, J. (1980). *Attachment and Loss: Vol. 3: Loss: Sadness and Depression*. New York: Basic Books.

Bowlby, J. (1982). *Attachment and Loss: Vol. 1. Attachment*, 2nd edn. New York: Basic Books.

Bradford, D. L., Sargent, A. G., and Sprague, M. S. (1975). The executive man and woman: The issue of sexuality. In F. Gordon and M. Strober (Eds) *Bringing Women into Management*. New York: McGraw-Hill.

Braiker, H. B., and Kelley, H. H. (1979). Conflict in the development of close relationships. In R. L. Burgess and T. L. Huston (Eds) *Social Exchange in Developing Relationships*. New York: Academic Press, pp. 135–168.

Brain, R. (1976). *Friends and Lovers*. New York: Basic Books.

Brain, R. (1977). Somebody else should be your own best friend. *Psychology Today*, October, 83–86.

Brandt, R. M. (1972). *Studying Behavior in Natural Settings*. New York: Holt, Rinehart, & Winston.

Brazelton, T. B., Koslowski, B., and Main, M. (1974). The origins of reciprocity: The early mother–infant interaction. In M. Lewis and L. Rosenblum (Eds) *The Effect of the Infant on its Caregiver*. New York: Wiley.

Brazelton, T. B., Tronick, E., Adamson, L., Als, H., and Wise, S. (1975). Early mother–infant reciprocity. In *Parent–Infant Interaction* (Ciba Foundation Symposium, 33). New York: Associated Scientific Publishers.

Brazelton, T. B., Yogman, M. W., Als, H., and Tronnick, E. (1979). The infant as a focus for family reciprocity. In M. Lewis and L. A. Rosenblum (Eds) *The Child and Its Family*. New York: Plenum Press.

Brechner, K. C. (1977). An experimental analysis of social traps. *Journal of Experimental Social Psychology*, **13**, 552–564.

Brehm, S. S. (1985). *Intimate Relationships*. New York: Random House.

Breiger, R. L., and Ennis, J. G. (1979). Personae and social roles: The network structure of personality types in small groups. *Social Psychology Quarterly*, **42**, 262–270.

Brennan, R., and Auslander, N. (1979). *Adolescent Loneliness: An Exploratory Study of Social and Psychological Predispositions and Theory*, vol. 1. Washington, DC:

National Institute of Mental Health, Juvenile Problems Division (ERIC Document Reproduction Service No. ED 194822).

Brennan, T. (1982). Loneliness at adolescence. In L. A. Peplau and D. Perlman (Eds) *Loneliness: A Sourcebook of Current Theory, Research, and Therapy*. New York: Wiley, pp. 269–290.

Brent, S. B. (1984). *Psychological and Social Structures*. Hillsdale, NJ: Erlbaum.

Bretherton, I. (1978). Making friends with one-year-olds: An experimental study on infant–stranger interaction. *Merill-Palmer Quarterly*, **24**, 29–51.

Bretherton, I. (1985). Attachment theory: Retrospects and prospect. In I. Bretherton and E. Waters (Eds) Growing points of attachment theory and research. *Monographs of the Society for Research in Child Development*, **50**, (1–2, Serial No. 209), pp. 3–35.

Bretherton, I., Stolberg, U., and Kreye, M. (1981). Engaging strangers in proximal interaction: Infants' social initiative. *Developmental Psychology*, **17**, 746–755.

Breznitz, S. (1983). The noble challenge of stress. In S. Breznitz (Ed.) *Stress in Israel*. New York: Van Nostrand-Reinhild, pp. 265–274.

Brickman, P. (1978). Is it real? In J. H. Harvey, W. Ickes and R. F. Kidd (Eds) *New Directions in Attribution Research*, Vol. 2. New York: Springer-Verlag.

Bridges, K. M. B. (1933). A study of social development in early infancy. *Child Development*, **4**, 36–49.

Bringle, R. G., and Buunk, B. (1985). Jealousy and social behavior: A review of person, relationship, and situational determinants. In P. Shaver (Ed.) *Review of Personality and Social Psychology: Vol. 6. Self, Situations, and Social Behavior*. Beverly Hills: Sage, pp. 241–264.

Brittain, J., and Freeman, J. (1980). Organizational proliferation and density-dependent selection. In J. Kimberly and R. Miles (Eds) *The Organizational Life Cycle*. San Francisco: Jossey-Bass.

Brody, G. H., Graziano, W. G., and Musser, L. M. (1983). Familiarity and children's behavior in same-age and mixed-age peer groups. *Developmental Psychology*, **19**, 568–576.

Brody, G., Pillegrini, A. D., and Sigel, I. (1986). Marital quality and mother–child and father–child interactions with school-aged children. *Developmental Psychology*, **22**, 291–296.

Brody, G. H., Stoneman, Z., and McKinnon, C. (1987). Contributions of maternal childrearing practices and interactional contexts to sibling interactions. *Journal of Applied Developmental Psychology*.

Bronowski, J. (1978). *The Common Sense of Science*. Cambridge, MA: Harvard University Press.

Bronson, G. (1972). Infants' reactions to unfamiliar persons and novel objects. *Monographs of the Society for Research in Child Development*, **32** (4, Serial No. 112).

Brown, G. W., and Harris, T. (1978). *Social Origins of Depression: A Study of Psychiatric Disorder in Women*. London: Tavistock.

Brown, G. W., Birley, J. L. T., and Wing, J. K. (1972). Influence of family life on the course of schizophrenic disorders: A replication. *British Journal of Psychiatry*, **121**, 241–258.

Brown, G. W., Bhrolchain, M., and Harris, T. (1975). Social class and psychiatric disturbance among women in an urban population. *Sociology*, **9**, 225–253.

Brown, P., and Levinson, S. (1978). Universals in language usage: Politeness phenomena. In E. N. Goody (Ed.) *Questions and Politeness: Strategies in Social Interaction*. Cambridge, MA: Cambridge University Press, pp. 74–289.

Brown, R., and Fish, D. (1983). The psychological causality implicit in language. *Cognitive Psychology*, **14**, 237–273.

Bruce, B. C. (1980). Plans and social actions. In R. L. Spiro, B. C. Bruce and W. F. Brewer (Eds) *Theoretical Issues in Reading Comprehension*. Hillsdale, NJ: Erlbaum, pp. 367–384.

Bruner, J. S. (1977). The organization of early skilled action. *Child Development*, **44**, 1–11.

Bruner, J. S., and Sherwood, V. (1976). Peek-a-boo and the learning of rule structures. In J. Bruner, A. Jolly and K. Silva (Eds) *Play: Its Role in Evolution and Development*. Harmondsworth: Penguin, pp. 277–285.

Bryant, B. K. (1982). Sibling relationships in middle childhood. In M. E. Lamb and B. Sutton-Smith (Eds) *Sibling Relationships: Across the Lifespan*. Hillsdale, NJ: Erlbaum.

Bryant, B. K., and Crockenberg, S. (1980). Correlates and dimensions of prosocial behavior: A study of female siblings and their mothers. *Child Development*, **51**, 529–544.

Buber, M. (1970). *I and Thou*. New York: Scribner.

Buck, R. (1984). *The communication of Emotion*. New York: Guilford Press.

Buckley, W. (1967). *Sociology and Systems Theory*. Englewood Cliffs, NJ: Prentice-Hall.

Budson, R. D., and Jolley, R. E. (1978). A crucial factor in community program success: The extended psychosocial kinship system. *Schizophrenia Bulletin*, **4**, 659–662.

Buehler, C. J., and Wells, B. L. (1981). Counseling the romantic. *Family Relations*, **30**, 452–458.

Buhler, C. (1933). The social behavior of children. In C. A. Murchison (Ed.) *Handbook of Child Psychology*. New York: Russell & Russell, pp. 374–416.

Buhrmester, D., and Furman, W. (1986a). The changing functions of friends in childhood: A Neo-Sullivanian perspective. In W. W. Hartup and Z. Rubin (Eds) *Relationships and Development*. Hillsdale, NJ: Erlbaum, pp. 41–62.

Buhrmester, D., and Furman, W. (1986b). Theories of friendship: The analysis of interpersonal attraction. In V. J. Derlega and B. A. Winstead (Eds) *Friendship and Social Interaction*. New York: Springer-Verlag, pp. 41–62.

Buhrmester, D., and Furman, W. (1987). The development of companionship and intimacy. *Child Development*, **58**, 1101–1113.

Bullock, R. C., Siegel, R., Weissman, M., and Paykel, E. S. (1972). The weeping wife: Marital relations of depressed women. *Journal of Marriage and the Family*, **34**, 488–495.

Bulman, R. J., and Wortman, C. B. (1977). Attributions of blame and coping in the 'real world': Severe accident victims react to their lot. *Journal of Personality and Social Psychology*, **35**, 351–363.

Burda, P. C., Jr, Vaux, A., and Schill, T. (1984). Social support resources: Variation across sex and sex role. *Personality and Social Psychology Bulletin*, **10**, 19–126.

Burger, J. M. (1986). Increasing compliance by improving the deal: The that's not all technique. *Journal of Personality and Social Psychology*, **51**, 277–283.

Burgess, E. W., and Locke, H. (1945). *The Family: From Institution to Companionship*. New York: American Book.

Burgess, E. W., and Wallin, P. W. (1943). Homogamy in social characteristics. *American Journal of Sociology*, **49**, 109–124.

Burgess, E. W., and Wallin, P. W. (1953). *Engagement and Marriage*. Philadelphia: Lippincott.

Burgess, E. W., Locke, H. J., and Thomes, M. M. (1971). *The Family*. New York: Van Nostrand.

Burgess, R. L., and Huston, T. L. (1979). *Social Exchange in Developing Relationships*. New York: Academic Press.

Burgoon, J. K. (1978). A communication model of interpersonal space violations: Explication and initial test. *Human Communication Research*, **4**, 129–142.

Burgoon, J. K. (1985). Nonverbal signals. In M. Knapp and G. R. Miller (Eds) *Handbook of Interpersonal Communication*. Beverly Hills: Sage.

Burgoon, J. K., and Hale, J. L. (1984). The fundamental topoi of relational communication. *Communication Monographs*, **51**, 193–214.

Burgoon, J. K., and Jones, S. B. (1976). Toward a theory of personal space expectations and their violations. *Human Communication Research*, **2**, 131–146.

Burgoon, J. K., and Koper, R. J. (1984). Nonverbal and relational communication associated with reticence. *Human Communication Research*, **10**, 601–626.

Burgoon, J. K., Coker, D. A., and Coker, R. A. (1986). Communicative effects of eye gaze. *Human Communication Research*, **12**, 495–524.

Burgoon, M. (1987). Personal communication with Miller and Boster as chapter authors.

Burke, R. J., and Weir, T. (1978). Sex differences in adolescent life stress, social support, and well-being. *Journal of Psychology*, **98**, 277–288.

Burke, R. J., Weir, T., and Harrison, D. (1976). Disclosure of problems and tensions experienced by marital partners. *Psychological Reports*, **38**, 531–542.

Burnett, R., and Clarke, D. (1988). *Thinking About Relationships*. London: Methuen.

Burnett, R., McGhee, P., and Clarke, D. (1987). *Accounting for Relationships: Explanation, Representation and Knowledge*. London: Methuen.

Burns, T. (1973). A structural theory of social exchange. *Acta Sociologica*, **16** (3), 188–208.

Burrell, G. (1984). Sex and organizational analysis. *Organizational Studies*, **5**, 97–118.

Buss, A. H. (1980). *Self-consciousness and Social Anxiety*. San Francisco: W. H. Freeman.

Buss, A. H., and Plomin, R. (1975). *A Temperament Theory of Personality Development*. New York: Wiley.

Buss, D. M., and Barnes, M. (1986). Preferences in human mate selection. *Journal of Personality and Social Psychology*, **50**, 559–570.

Buss, D. M., and Craik, K. H. (1983). The act frequency approach to personality. *Psychological Review*, **90**, 105–126.

Butler, K. (1986). When cupid wears pinstripes. *Grand Rapids Magazines*.

Button, L. (1979). Friendship patterns. *Journal of Adolescence*, **2**, 187–199.

Buunk, B. (1981). Jealousy in sexually open marriages. *Alternative Lifestyles*, **4**, 357–372.

Byrne, D. (1971). *The Attraction Paradigm*. New York: Academic Press.

Byrne, D. (1977). Social psychology and the study of sexual behavior. *Personality and Social Psychology Bulletin*, **3**, 3–30.

Cacioppo, J. T. (1986). Social psychophysiology. Invited address, American Psychological Association, Washington, DC.

Cacioppo, J. T., and Petty, R. E. (1981). Social psychological procedures for cognitive response assessment: V. Thought listing technique. In N. T. Merluzzi, C. Glass and M. Genest (Eds) *Cognitive Assessment*. New York: Guilford, pp. 309–342.

Cafferata, G. L. (1982). The building of democratic organizations: An embryological metaphor. *Administrative Science Quarterly*, **27**, 280–303.

Cairns, R. B. (1972). Attachment and dependency: A psychobiological and social learning synthesis. In J. L. Gewirtz (Ed.) *Attachment and Dependency*. Washington, DC: Winston.

Cairns, R. B. (1979). *Social Development: The Origins and Plasticity of Interchanges*. San Francisco: W. H. Freeman.

Caldwell, M. A., and Peplau, L. A. (1982). Sex differences in same-sex friendship. *Sex Roles*, **8**, 721–732.

Candy, S. G., Troll, L. E., and Levy, S. G. (1981). A developmental exploration of friendship functions in women. *Psychology of Women Quarterly*, **5**, 456–472.

Cane, D. C., and Gotlib, I. H. (1985). Implicit theories of psychopathology: Implications for interpersonal conceptualizations of depression. *Social Cognition*, **3**, 341–368.

Cantor, N., Mischel, W., and Schwartz, J. C. (1982). A prototype analysis of psychological situations. *Cognitive Psychology*, **14**, 45–77.

Caplan, G. (1974). *Social Support and Community Mental Health: Lectures on Concept Development*. New York: Behavioral Publications.

Caplow, T. (1960). *Two Against One: Coalitions in Triads*. Englewood Cliffs, NJ: Prentice-Hall.

Cappella, J. N. (1980). Structural equation modeling: An introduction. In P. R. Monge and J. N. Cappella (Eds) *Multivariate Techniques in Human Communication Research*. New York: Academic Press, pp. 57–110.

Cappella, J. N. (1981). Mutual influence in expressive behavior: Adult–adult and infant–adult dyadic interaction. *Psychological Bulletin*, **1981**, 101–132.

Cappella, J. N. (1984). The relevance of the microstructure of interaction to relationship change. *Journal of Social and Personal Relationships*, **1**, 239–264.

Cappella, J. N. (1985a). Controlling the floor in conversation. In A. W. Siegman and S. Feldstein (Eds) *Multichannel Integrations of Nonverbal Behavior*. Hillsdale: Erlbaum, pp. 69–103.

Cappella, J. N. (1985b). The management of conversations. In M. L. Knapp and G. R. Miller (Eds) *The Handbook of Interpersonal Communication*. Beverly Hills: Sage, pp. 393–438.

Cappella, J. N. (1987). Interpersonal communication: Fundamental questions and issues. In C. R. Berger and S. Chaffee (Eds) *The Handbook of Communication Science*. Beverly Hills: Sage.

Cappella, J. N., and Greene, J. O. (1982). A discrepancy-arousal explanation of mutual influence expressive behavior for adult–adult and infant–adult interaction. *Communication Monographs*, **49**, 89–114.

Cappella, J. N., and Planalp, S. (1981). Talk and silence sequences in informal conversations III. Interspeaker influence. *Human Communication Research*, **7**, 117–132.

Cappella, J. N., and Street, R. L. Jr (1985). A functional approach to the structure of communicative behavior. In R. L. Street, Jr and J. N. Cappella (Eds) *Sequence and Pattern in Communicative Behavior*. London: Edward Arnold, pp. 1–29.

Cappella, J. N., and Street, R. L., Jr (1986). Speech adaptability in children's interactions with adults. Unpublished paper, Department of Communication Arts, University of Wisconsin, Madison.

Capra, F. (1982). *The Turning Point: Science, Society and the Rising Culture*. New York: Simon & Schuster.

Carbaugh, D. (1984). What's in a relationship? Code and community in an American speech event. Paper presented at the Speech Communication Association Convention, Denver, November.

Carroll, G. R. (1984). Organizational ecology. *Annual Review of Sociology*, **10**, 71–93.

Caspi, A., and Elder, G. H. (1987). Emergent family patterns: The intergenerational construction of problem behavior and relationships. In R. A. Hinde and J. Stevenson-Hinde (Eds) *Relations Between Relationships*. Oxford: Oxford University Press.

Castaneda, G. G., Hendrick, S. S., and Flanary, R. (1986). Housework allocation, role conflict, and coping strategies in dual-career couples. Paper presented at the Annual Convention of the Southwestern Psychological Association, Fort Worth, Texas, April.

Castellan, N. J. (1979). The analysis of behavior sequences. In R. B. Cairns (Eds) *The Analysis of Social Interactions: Methods, Issues, and Illustrations*. Hillsdale, NJ: Erlbaum.

Cate, R. M., Huston, T. L., and Nesselroade, J. R. (1986). Premarital relationships: Toward the identification of alternative pathways to marriage. *Journal of Social and Clinical Psychology*, **4**, 3–22.

Cate, R. M., Lloyd, S. A., and Henton, J. M. (1986). The effect of equity, equality and reward level on the stability of students' premarital relationships. *Journal of Social Psychology*, **125**, 715–721.

Cate, R. M., Lloyd, S. A., Henton, J. M., and Larson, J. H. (1982). Fairness and reward level as predictors of relationship satisfaction. *Social Psychology Quarterly*, **45**, 177–181.

Cate, R. M., Lloyd, S. A., and Long, E. (1988). The role of rewards and fairness in developing premarital relationships. *Journal of Marriage and the Family*.

Centers, R. (1975). Attitude similarity–dissimilarity as a correlate of heterosexual attraction and love. *Journal of Marriage and the Family*, **37**, 305–314.

Chambliss, W. J. (1965). The selection of friends. *Social Forces*, **43**, 370–380.

Chapman, N. J., and Pancoast, D. L. (1985). Working with the informal helping networks of the elderly: The experiences of three programs. *Journal of Social Issues*, **41**, 47–64.

Charlesworth, R., and Hartup, W. W. (1967). Positive social reinforcement in the nursery school peer group. *Child Development*, **38**, 993–1003.

Charney, D. S., Nelson, C. J., and Quinlan, D. M. (1981). Personality traits and disorder in depression. *American Journal of Psychiatry*, **138**, 1601–1604.

Chase, I. D. (1980). Cooperative and noncooperative behavior in animals. *The American Naturalist*, **115**, 827–857.

Chatov, R. (1981). Cooperation between government and business. In P. C. Nystrom and W. H. Starbuck (Eds) *Handbook of Organizational Design*, Vol. 1. New York: Oxford University Press, pp. 487–502.

Cheek, F. E., and Anthony, R. (1970). Personal pronoun usage in families of schizophrenics and social space utilization. *Family Process*, **9**, 431–448.

Cheek, J. M., and Busch, C. K. (1981). The influence of shyness and loneliness in a new situation. *Personality and Social Psychology Bulletin*, **7**, 572–577.

Cheek, J. M., and Buss, A. H. (1981). Shyness and sociability. *Journal of Personality and Social Psychology*, **37**, 12–24.

Cheek, J. M., Carpentieri, A. M., Smith, T. G., Rierdan, J., and Koff, E. (1986). Adolescent shyness. In W. H. Jones, J. M. Cheek and S. R. Briggs (Eds) *Shyness: Perspective on Research and Treatment*. New York: Plenum, pp. 105–115.

Chelune, G. J. (1976). Self-disclosure situations survey: A new approach to measuring self-disclosure. *Catalog of Selected Documents in Psychology*, **6**, 111 (ms 1367).

Chelune, G. J. (1977). Sex differences, repression-sensitization and self-disclosure: A behavioral look. *Psychological Reports*, **40**, 667–670.

Chelune, G. J. (1979). Measuring openness in interpersonal communication. In G. J. Chelune *et al.*, *op. cit.*

Chelune, G. J., and Waring, E. M. (1984). Nature and assessment of intimacy. In P. McReynolds and G. J. Chelune (Eds) *Advances in Psychological Assessment*, Vol. 6. San Francisco: Jossey-Bass, pp. 277–311.

Chelune, G. J., Robison, J. T., and Kommor, M. J. (1984). A cognitive interactional model of intimate relationships. In V. J. Derlega (Ed.) *Communication, Intimacy, and Close Relationships*. New York: Academic Press, pp. 11–40.

Chelune, G. J., Sultan, F. E., and Williams, C. L. (1980). Loneliness, self-disclosure, and interpersonal effectiveness. *Journal of Consulting Psychology*, **27**, 462–468.

Chelune, G. J. *et al.* (1979). *Self-Disclosure: Origins, Patterns, and Implications of Openness in Interpersonal Relationships*. San Francisco: Jossey-Bass.

Chelune, G. J., Waring, E., Yosk, B., Sultan, F., and Ogden, J. (1984). Self-disclosure and its relationship to marital intimacy. *Journal of Clinical Psychology*, **40**, 216–219.

Cheung, P., and Hudson, W. (1982). Assessment of marital discord in social work practice: A revalidation of the index of marital satisfaction. *Journal of Social Service Research*, **5** (1/2), 101–119.

Christie, R., and Geis, F. L. (Eds) (1970). *Studies in Machiavellianism*. New York: Academic Press.

Cialdini, R. B. (1985). *Influence: Science and Practice*. Glenview, IL: Scott, Foresman.

Cialdini, R. B., and Schroeder, D. A. (1976). Increasing compliance by legitimizing paltry contributions: When even a penny helps. *Journal of Personality and Social Psychology*, **34**, 599–604.

Cialdini, R. B., Cacioppo, J. T., Bassett, R., and Miller, J. A. (1978). Low-ball procedure for producing compliance: Commitment then cost. *Journal of Personality and Social Psychology*, **36**, 463–476.

Cialdini, R. B., Vincent, J. E., Lewis, S. K., Catalan, J., Wheeler, D., and Darby, B.

L. (1975). Reciprocal concessions procedure for inducing compliance: The door-in-the-face technique. *Journal of Personality and Social Psychology*, **31**, 206–215.

Ciske, K. L. (1974). Primary nursing: Evaluation. *American Journal of Nursing*, **74**, 1436–1438.

Cissna, K. (1986). On observing confirmation and disconfirmation: A review, critique, and proposal. Paper presented at the Speech Communication Association Convention, Chicago, Illinois.

Cissna, K., and Sieburg, E. (1981). Patterns of interactional confirmation and disconfirmation. In C. Wilder-Mott and J. Weakland (Eds) *Rigor & Imagination: Essays from the Legacy of Gregory Bateson*. New York: Praeger.

Clanton, G., and Smith, L. G. (Eds) (1977). *Jealousy*. Englewood Cliffs, NJ: Prentice-Hall.

Clark, H. H. (1985). Language use and language users. In G. Lindzey and E. Aronson (Eds) *The Handbook of Social Psychology*, 3rd end, Vol. 2. New York: Random House, pp. 179–231.

Clark, M. S. (1983). Reactions to aid in communal or exchange relationships. In B. M. DePaulo, A. Nadler and J. D. Fisher (Eds) *New Directions in Helping, Vol. 1: Recipient Reactions to Aid*. New York: Academic Press, pp. 281–304.

Clark, M. S. (1985). Implications of relationship type for understanding compatibility. In W. Ickes (Ed.) *Compatible and Incompatible Relationships*. New York: Springer-Verlag, pp. 119–140.

Clark, M. S. (1986). Evidence for the effectiveness of manipulations of communal and exchange relationships. *Personality and Social Psychology Bulletin*, **12**, 414–425.

Clark, M. S., and Mills, J. (1979). Interpersonal attraction in exchange and communal relationships. *Journal of Personality and Social Psychology*, **37**, 12–24.

Clark, R. E., and Halford, L. J. (1978). Going . . . going . . . gone: Some preliminary observations on 'deals' at auctions. *Urban Life*, **7**, 285–307.

Clarke, D. D., Allen, C. M. B., and Dickson, S. (1985). The characteristic affective tone of seven classes of interpersonal relationship. *Journal of Social and Personal Relationships*, **2**, 117–120.

Clarke-Stewart, K. A. (1978). Recasting the lone stranger. In J. Glick and K. A. Stewart (Eds) *The Development of Social Understanding*. New York: Gardner, pp. 109–176.

Clatterbuck, G. W. (1979). Attributional confidence and uncertainty in initial interaction. *Human Communication Research*, **5**, 147–157.

Clawson, J. G., and Kram, K. E. (1984). Managing cross-gender mentoring. *Business Horizon*, May–June, 22–32.

Clayton, R., and Voss, H. (1977). Shacking up: Cohabitation in the 1970s. *Journal of Marriage and the Family*, **39** (May), 273–283.

Clifford, E. (1959). Discipline in the home: A controlled observational study of parental practices. *Journal of Genetic Psychology*, **85**, 45–82.

Coates, D., and Winston, T. (1983). Counteracting the deviance of depression: Peer support groups for victims. *Journal of Social Issues*, **39**, 169–194.

Coates, D., and Wortman, C. B. (1980). Depression maintenance and interpersonal control. In A. Baum and J. E. Singer (Eds) *Advances in Environmental Psychology*, Vol. 2. Hillsdale, NJ: Erlbaum, pp. 149–181.

Cobb, S. (1976). Social support as a moderator of life stress. *Psychosomatic Medicine*, **38**, 300–314.

Cochran, S. D., and Peplau, L. A. (1985). Value orientations in heterosexual relationships. *Psychology of Women Quarterly*, **9**, 477–488.

Cody, M. J. (1982). A typology of disengagement strategies and an examination of the role intimacy, reactions to inequity and relational problems play in strategy selection. *Communication Monographs*, **49**, 148–170.

Cody, M. J., McLaughlin, M. L., and Schneider, M. J. (1981). The impact of relational consequences and intimacy on the selection of interpersonal persuasion tactics: A reanalysis. *Communication Quarterly*, **29**, 91–106.

Cohen, C. I., and Adler, A. (1986). Assessing the role of social network interventions with an inner-city population. *American Journal of Orthopsychiatry*, **56**, 278–288.

Cohen, E. A., Gelfand, D. M., and Hartmann, D. P. (1981). Causal reasoning as a function of behavioral consequences. *Child Development*, **52**, 514–522.

Cohen, L. H., McGowan, J., Fooskas, S., and Rose, S. (1984). Positive life events and social support and the relationship between life stress and psychological disorder. *American Journal of Community Psychology*, **12**, 567–587.

Cohen, M. D., March, J. G., and Olsen, J. P. (1972). A garbage can model of organizational choice. *Administrative Science Quarterly*, **17**, 1–25.

Cohen, P. R., and Perrault, C. R. (1979). Elements of a plan-based theory of speech acts. *Cognitive Science*, **3**, 177–212.

Cohen, R. Y. (1988). Mobilizing support through competition in worksite health promotion. In B. H. Gottlieb (Ed.) *Marshalling Social Support: Formats Processes and Effects*. Beverly Hills: Sage.

Cohen, S., and McKay, G. (1984). Social support, stress, and the buffering hypothesis: A theoretical analysis. In A. Baum, J. E. Singer and S. E. Taylor (Eds) *Handbook of Psychology and Health*, Vol. 4. Hillsdale, NJ: Erlbaum, pp. 253–267.

Cohen, S., and Syme, S. L. (1985). Issues in the study and application of social support. In S. Cohen and S. L. Syme (Eds) *Social Support and Health*. Orlando, FL: Academic Press, pp. 3–22.

Cohen, S., and Wills, T. A. (1985). Stress, social support, and the buffering hypothesis. *Psychological Bulletin*, **98**, 310–357.

Cohen, S., Mermelstein, R., Kamarch, T., and Hoberman, H. (1985). Measuring the functional components of social support. In I. G. Sarason and B. R. Sarason (Eds) *Social Support: Theory, Research and Applications*. The Hague: Martinus Nijhoff, pp. 73–94.

Cohen, Y. A. (1958). Some aspects of ritualized behavior in interpersonal relationships. *Human Relationships*, **11**, 195–211.

Coie, J. D., and Kupersmidt, J. B. (1983). A behavioral analysis of emerging social status in boys' groups. *Child Development*, **54**, 1400–1416.

Coleman, R. E., and Miller, A. G. (1975). The relationship between depression and marital maladjustment in a clinical population: A multi-trial, multi-method study. *Journal of Consulting and Clinical Psychology*, **43**, 647.

Collett, P. (1977). The rules of conduct. In P. Collett (Ed.) *Social Rules and Social Behavior*. Oxford: Blackwell, pp. 1–27.

Collins, E. G. C. (1983). Managers and lovers. *Harvard Business Review*, **83**, 142–153.

Colvin, J., and Tissier, G. (1985). Affiliation and reciprocity in sibling and peer relationships among free-ranging immature male rhesus monkeys. *Animal Behavior*, **33**, 959–977.

Cone, J. D., and Hawkins, R. P. (Eds) (1977). *Behavioral Assessment: New Directions in Clinical Psychology*. New York: Brunner Mazel.

Constantinople, A. (1973). Masculinity–femininity: An exception to a famous dictum. *Psychological Bulletin*, **80**, 389–407.

Cook, E. P. (1985). *Psychological Androgyny*. New York: Pergamon.

Cook, M. (1977). The social skill model and interpersonal attraction. In S. W. Duck (Ed.) *Theory and Practice in Interpersonal Attraction*. New York: Academic Press.

Cooley, C. H. (1902). *Human Nature and the Social Order*. New York: Charles Scribner.

Coombs, R. H. (1962). Reinforcement of values in the parental home as a factor in mate selection. *Marriage and Family Living*, **24**, 155–157.

Coopersmith, S. (1967). *The Antecedents of Self-Esteem*. San Francisco: W. H. Freeman.

Cornforth, M. (1968). *Materialism and the Dialectical Method*. New York: International Publishers.

Corsaro, W. A. (1981). Friendship in the nursery school: Social organization in a peer environment. In S. R. Asher and J. M. Gottman (Eds) *The Development of Children's Friendships*. New York: Cambridge University Press, pp. 207–241.

Costanzo, P. R., and Woody, E. Z. (1985). Domain-specific parenting styles and their impact on the child's development of particular deviance: The example of obesity proneness. *Journal of Social and Clinical Psychology*, 3, 425–445.

Costello, C. G. (1982). Social factors associated with depression: A retrospective community study. *Psychological Medicine*, 12, 329–339.

Courtright, J. A., Millar, F. E., and Rogers, L. E. (1979). Domineeringness and dominance: Replication and expansion. *Communication Monographs*, 46, 179–192.

Courtright, J. A., Millar, F. E., and Rogers, L. E. (1980). Message control intensity as a predictor of transactional redundancy. In D. Nimmo (Ed.) *Communication Yearbook 4*. New Brunswick, NJ: Transaction Books, pp. 199–216.

Courtright, J. A., Millar, F. E., and Rogers, L. E. (1983). A new measure of interactional control patterns. *Communication*, 12, 47–68.

Cowen, E. L., Pederson, A., Babigan, H., Izzo, L. D., and Trost, M. A. (1973). Long-term follow-up of early detected vulnerable children. *Journal of Consulting and Clinical Psychology*, 41, 438–446.

Cox, M. J., Owen, M. T., Lewis, J. M., Riedel, C., Scalf-Michler, L., and Susta, A. (1985). Intergenerational influences on the parent–infant relationship in the transition to parenthood. *Journal of Family Issues*, 6, 543–564.

Coyne, J. C. (1976a). Depression and the response of others. *Journal of Abnormal Psychology*, 85, 186–193.

Coyne, J. C. (1976b). Toward an interactional description of depression. *Psychiatry*, 39, 28–40.

Coyne, J. C., and Gotlib, I. H. (1983). The role of cognition in depression: A critical appraisal. *Psychological Bulletin*, 94, 472–505.

Coyne, J. C., and Gotlib, I. H. (1986). Studying the role of cognition in depression: Well-trodden paths and cul-de-sacs. *Cognitive Therapy and Research*, 10, 695–705.

Coyne, J. C., Kahn, J., and Gotlib, I. H. (1987). Depression. In T. Jacob (Ed.) *Family Interaction and Psychopathology*. New York: Plenum.

Coyne, J. C., Kessler, R. C., Tal, M., Turnbull, J., Wortman, C. B., and Greden, J. (1987). Living with a depressed person. *Journal of Consulting and Clinical Psychology*, 55, 347–352.

Coyne, J. C., Wortman, C. B., and Lehman, D. R. (1988). The other side of support: Emotional overinvolvement and miscarried helping. In B. H. Gottlieb (Ed.) *Marshalling Social Support: Formats, Processes and Effects*. Beverly Hills: Sage.

Cozby, P. C. (1973). Self-disclosure: A literature review. *Psychological Bulletin*, 79, 73–91.

Craig, R., and Tracy, K. (Eds) (1983). *Conversational Coherence: Form, Structure, and Strategy*. Beverly Hills: Sage.

Crawford, M. (1977). What is a friend? *New Society*, 20, 116–117.

Crockenberg, S. (1981). Infant irritability, mother responsiveness and social support influences on the security of infant–mother attachment. *Child Development*, 52, 857–865.

Cronbach, L. J. (1955). Processes affecting scores on 'understanding of others' and 'assumed similarity'. *Psychological Bulletin*, 52, 177–193.

Cronbach, L. J., Gleser, G. C., Nanda, H., and Rajaratnam, N. (1972). *The Dependability of Behavioral Measurements: Theory of Generalizability for Scores and Profiles*. New York: Wiley.

Cronen, V. E., Johnson, K. M., and Lannaman, J. W. (1982). Paradoxes, double binds, and reflexive loops: An alternative theoretical perspective. *Family Process*, 21, 91–112.

Cronen, V. E., Pearce, W. B., and Harris, L. M. (1982). The coordinated management of meaning. In F. E. X. Dance (Ed.) *Human Communication Theory*. New York: Harper & Row, pp. 61–89.

Cronen, V. E., Pearce, W. B., and Tomm, K. (1985). A dialectical view of personal change. In K. Gergen and K. Davis (Eds) *The Social Construction of the Person*. New York: Springer-Verlag, pp. 203–224.

Crowther, J. H. (1985). The relationship between depression and marital maladjustment: A descriptive study. *Journal of Nervous and Mental Disease*, **173**, 227–231.

Cuber, J. F., and Harroff, P. B. (1966). *Sex and the Significant Americans*. New York: Penguin.

Cunningham, J. D., and Antill, J. K. (1981). Love in developing romantic relationships. In S. W. Duck and R. Gilmour (Eds) *Personal Relationships 2: Developing Personal Relationships*. New York: Academic Press, pp. 27–51.

Cunningham, J., Braiker, H., and Kelley, H. (1982). Marital status and sex differences in problems reported by married and cohabiting couples. *Psychology of Women Quarterly*, **6** (4), 415–427.

Cupach, W., and Metts, S. (1986). Accounts of relational dissolution: A comparison of marital and non-marital relationships. *Communication Monographs*, **53**, 311–334.

Curran, J. P. (1975). Convergence toward a single sexual standard? *Social Behavior and Personality*, **3**, 189–195.

Cutrona, C. E. (1982). Transition to college: Loneliness and the process of social adjustment. In L. A. Peplau and D. Perlman (Eds) *Loneliness: A Sourcebook of Current Theory, Research and Therapy*. New York: Wiley-Interscience, pp. 291–309.

Cutrona, C. E. (1983). Causal attributions and perinatal depression. *Journal of Abnormal Psychology*, **92**, 161–172.

Cutrona, C. E. (1986a). Objective determinants of perceived social support. *Journal of Personality and Social Psychology*, **50**, 349–355.

Cutrona, C. E. (1985b). Behavioral manifestations of social support: A microanalytic investigation. *Journal of Personality and Social Psychology*, **51**, 201–208.

D'Augelli, A. R., Vallance, T. R., Danish, S. J., Young, C. E., and Gerdes, J. L. (1981). The Community Helpers Project: A description of a prevention strategy for rural communities. *Journal of Primary Prevention*, **1**, 209–224.

Dabbs, J. M., Jr, and Ruback, R. B. (1987). Dimensions of group process: Amount and structure of vocal interaction. In L. Berkowitz (Ed.) *Advances in Experimental Social Psychology*, Vol. 21. Orlando, FL: Academic Press.

Dailey, W. O. (1985). The effects of discussion on debiasing judgment: Two pilot studies. Paper presented at the annual convention of the Speech Communication Association, Denver, Colorado.

Damon, W. (1977). *The Social World of the Child*. San Francisco: Jossey-Bass.

Daniels-Mohring, D., and Berger, M. (1984). Social network changes and the adjustment to divorce. *Journal of Divorce*, **8**, 17–32.

Danziger, K. (1976). *Interpersonal Communication*. New York: Pergamon.

Darley, J. M., and Fazio, R. H. (1980). Expectancy confirmation processes arising in the social interaction sequence. *American Psychologist*, **35**, 867–881.

Davidson, L. R., and Duberman, L. (1980). Friendship: Communication and interactional patterns in same-sex dyads. *Sex Roles*, **8**, 809–822.

Davidson, S., and Packard, T. (1981). The therapeutic value of friendship between women. *Psychology of Women Quarterly*, **5**, 495–510.

Davis, D. (1982). Determinants of responsiveness in dyadic interaction. In W. I. Ickes and E. S. Knowles (Eds) *Personality, Roles, and Social Behaviors*. New York: Springer-Verlag, pp. 85–139.

Davis, D., and Martin, H. J. (1978). When pleasure begets pleasure: Recipient responsiveness as a determinant of physical pleasuring between heterosexual dating couples and strangers. *Journal of Personality and Social Psychology*, **36**, 767–777.

Davis, D., and Perkowitz, W. T. (1979). Consequences of responsiveness in dyadic interaction: Effects of probability of response and proportion of content-related responses on interpersonal attraction. *Journal of Personality and Social Psychology*, **37**, 534–551.

Davis, J. A. (1985). *The Logic of Causal Order*. Beverly Hills: Sage.

Davis, J. D. (1978). When boy meets girl: Sex roles and the negotiation of intimacy in an acquaintance exercise. *Journal of Personality and Social Psychology*, **36**, 684–692.

Davis, K. E. (1985). Near and dear: Friendships and love compared. *Psychology Today*, February, 22–30.

Davis, K. E., and Todd, M. J. (1982). Friendship and love relationships. In K. E. Davis (Ed.) *Advances in Descriptive Psychology*, **2**, 79–122. Greenwich, CT: JAI Press.

Davis, K. E., and Todd, M. J. (1985). Assessing friendship: Prototypes, paradigm cases and relationship description. In S. W. Duck and D. Perlman (Eds) *Understanding Personal Relationships: An Interdisciplinary Approach*. London: Sage, pp. 17–38.

Davis, M. S. (1973). *Intimate Relations*. New York: Free Press.

Dawe, H. C. (1934). An analysis of two hundred quarrels of pre-school children. *Child Development*, **5**, 139–157.

Deag, J. M. (1977). Aggression and submission in monkey societies. *Animal Behaviour*, **25**, 465–474.

Deaux, K. (1985). Sex and gender. *Annual Review of Psychology*, **36**, 49–81.

Deethardt, J., and McLaughlin, M. (1976). A pilot study of communicator types and styles. Paper presented at the meeting of the International Communication Association, Berlin.

DeForest, C., and Stone, G. L. (1980). Effects of sex and intimacy level on self-disclosure. *Journal of Counseling Psychology*, **27**, 93–96.

DeLamater, J., and MacCorquodale, P. (1979). *Premarital Sexuality: Attitudes, Relationships, Behavior*. Madison: University of Wisconsin Press.

Delia, J. G. (1980). Some tentative thoughts concerning the study of interpersonal relationships and their development. *Western Journal of Speech Communication*, **44**, 97–103.

DeMaris, A., and Leslie, G. (1984). Cohabitation with the future spouse: Its influence upon marital satisfaction and communication. *Journal of Marriage and the Family*, February, 77–84.

Denzin, N. K. (1970). Rules of conduct and the study of deviant behavior: Some notes on the social relationship. In G. J. McCall, M. M. McCall, N. K. Denzin, G. D. Suttles and S. E. Kurth (Eds) *Social Relationships*. Chicago: Aldine, pp. 62–94.

DePaulo, B. M., Kenny, D. A., Hoover, C., Webb, W., and Oliver, P. V. (1987). Accuracy in person perception: Do people know what kind of impressions they convey? *Journal of Personality and Social Psychology*, **52**, 303–315.

DePue, R. A., and Monroe, S. A. (1986). Conceptualization and measurement of human disorder in life stress research: The problem of chronic disturbance. *Psychological Bulletin*, **99**, 36–51.

Derlega, V. J. (1984). Self-disclosure and intimate relationships. In V. J. Derlega (Ed.) *Communication, Intimacy, and Close Relationships*. New York: Academic Press, pp. 1–9.

Derlega, V. J., and Winstead, B. A. (1986). *Friendship and Social Interaction*. New York: Springer-Verlag.

Derlega, V. J., Wilson, M., and Chaikin, A. L. (1976). Friendship and disclosure reciprocity. *Journal of Personality and Social Psychology*, **34**, 578–582.

Derlega, V. J., Winstead, B. A., Wong, P. T. P., and Hunter, S. (1985). Gender effects in an initial encounter: A case where men exceed women in disclosure. *Journal of Social and Personal Relationships*, **2**, 25–44.

Derry, P. A., and Kuiper, N. A. (1981). Schematic processing and self-reference in clinical depression. *Journal of Abnormal Psychology*, **90**, 286–297.

Deutsch, M., and Krauss, R. M. (1962). Studies of interpersonal bargaining. *Journal of Conflict Resolution*, **6**, 52–76.

Dickens, W. J., and Perlman, D. (1981). Friendship over the life-cycle. In S. W. Duck and R. Gilmour (Eds) *Personal Relationships 2: Developing Personal Relationships*. New York: Academic Press.

Dillard, J. P. (1986). Close relationships in task environments: The basis for evaluation. Unpublished manuscript, Department of Communication Arts, University of Wisconsin, Madison, Wisconsin.

Dillard, J. P. (1987). Close relationships at work: Perceptions of the motives and performance of relational participants. *Journal of Social and Personal Relationships*, **4**, 179–193.

Dillard, J. P., and Broetzmann, S. M. (1986). Romantic relationships at work: Changes in job-related behaviors as function of participant's motive, partner's motive, and gender. Manuscript submitted for publication.

Dillard, J. P., and Burgoon, M. (1985). Situational influences on the selection of compliance-gaining messages: Two tests of the predictive utility of the Cody–McLaughlin typology. *Communication Monographs*, **52**, 289–304.

Dillard, J. P., and Segrin, C. (May, 1987). Intimate relationships in organizations: Relational types, illicitness, and power. Paper presented at the annual meeting of the International Communication Association, Montreal.

Dillard, J. P., and Witteman, H. (1985). Romantic relationships at work: Organizational and personal influences. *Human Communication Research*, **12**, 99–116.

Dillard, J. P., Hunter, J. E., and Burgoon, M. (1984). Sequential-request persuasive strategies: Meta-analysis of foot-in-the-door and door-in-the-face. *Human Communication Research*, **10**, 461–487.

DiMatteo, M., Prince, K., and Hays, R. (1986). In P. Blanck, R. Buck and R. Rosenthal (Eds) *Nonverbal Communication in the Clinical Context*. University Park: Pennsylvania State University Press, pp. 74–98.

Dindia, K. (1987). The effects of sex of subject and sex of partner on interruptions. *Human Communication Research*, **13**, 345–371.

Dindia, K., and Baxter, L. A. (1987). Maintenance and repair strategies in marital relationships. *Journal of Social and Personal Relationships*, **4**, 143–158.

Dinkmeyer, D., and Carlson, J. (1985). TIME for a better marriage. *Individual Psychology: Journal of Adlerian Therapy and Research and Practice*, **41** (4), 444–452.

Dion, K. K. (1972). Physical attractiveness and evaluation of children's transgressions. *Journal of Personality and Social Psychology*, **24**, 207–213.

Dion, K. K. (1974). Children's physical attractiveness and sex as determinants of adult punitiveness. *Development Psychology*, **10**, 772–778.

Dion, K. K., and Dion, K. L. (1985). Personality, gender, and the phenomenology of romantic love. In P. Shaver (Ed.) *Review of Personality and Social Psychology: Vol. 6. Self, Situations, and Social Behavior*. Beverly Hills: Sage, pp. 209–239.

Dion, K. L., and Dion, K. K. (1973). Correlates of romantic love. *Journal of Consulting and Clinical Psychology*, **41**, 51–56.

Dix, T. H., and Grusec, J. E. (1983). Parental influence techniques: An attributional analysis. *Child Development*, **54**, 645–652.

Dix, T. H., and Grusec, J. E. (1985). Parental attribution processes in the socialization of children. In I. E. Sigel (Ed.) *Parental Belief Systems: The Psychological Consequences for Children*. Hillsdale, NJ: Erlbaum, pp. 201–233.

Dix, T. H., Ruble, D. N., Grusec, J. E., and Nixon, S. (1986). Social cognition in parents: Inferential and affective reactions to children of three age levels. *Child Development*, **57**, 879–894.

Dodge, K. A. (1980). Social cognition and children's aggressive behavior. *Child Development*, **51**, 162–170.

Dodge, K. A. (1983). Behavioral antecedents of peer social status. *Child Development*, **54**, 1386–1399.

Dodge, K. A. (1986). Social information-processing variables in the development of altruism and aggression in children. In C. Zahn-Waxler, E. M. Cummings and R. Iannotti (Eds) *Altruism and Aggression*. Cambridge, MA: Cambridge University Press.

Dodge, K. A., and Frame, C. L. (1982). Social cognitive biases and deficits in aggressive boys. *Child Development*, **53**, 620–635.

Dodge, K. A., Pettit, G. S., McClaskey, C. L., and Brown, M. M. (1986). Social competence in children. *Monographs of the SRCD*, **51** (Serial No. 213).

Doelger, J. A., Hewes, D. E., and Graham, M. L. (1986). Knowing when to 'second-guess': The mindful analysis of messages. *Human Communication Research*, **12**, 301–338.

Doherty, W. J. (1981a). Cognitive processes in intimate conflicts: I. Extending attribution theory. *American Journal of Family Therapy*, **9**, 5–13.

Doherty, W. J. (1981b). Cognitive processes in intimate conflict: II Efficacy and learned helplessness. *American Journal of Family Therapy*, **9**, 35–44.

Donohue, W. A., and Diez, M. E. (1985). Directive use in negotiation interaction. *Communication Monographs*, **52**, 305–318.

Dontas, C., Maratos, O., Fafoutis, M., and Karangelis, A. (1985). Early social development in institutionally reared Greek infants: Attachment and peer interaction. In I. Bretherton and E. Waters (Eds) *Growing Points of Attachment Theory and Research. Monographs of the Society for Research in Child Development*, **50**, 136–146.

Dosser, D., Balswick, J., and Halverson, C. (1986). Male inexpressiveness and relationships. *Journal of Social and Personal Relationships*, **3**, 241–256.

Douglas, W. (1984). Initial interaction scripts: When knowing is behaving. *Human Communication Research*, **11**, 203–220.

Douglas, W. (1987). Affinity-testing in initial interaction. *Journal of Social and Personal Relationships*, **4**, 3–15.

Doyle, A. (1982). Friends, acquaintances, and the strangers: The influence of familiarity and ethnolinguistic background on social organization. In K. H. Rubin and H. S. Ross (Eds) *Peer Relations and Social Skills in Childhood*. New York: Springer-Verlag.

Dreman, S. B., and Greenbaum, C. W. (1973). Altruism or reciprocity: Sharing behavior in Israeli kindergarten children. *Child Development*, **44**, 61–68.

Driscoll, R., Davis, K. E., and Lipetz, M. E. (1972). Parental interference and romantic love: The Romeo and Juliet effect. *Journal of Personality and Social Psychology*, **24**, 1–10.

Dryden, W. (1981). The relationship of depressed persons. In S. W. Duck and R. Gilmour (Eds) *Personal Relationships 3: Personal Relationships in Disorder*. London: Academic Press, pp. 191–214.

Duck, S. W. (1973). *Personal Relationships and Personal Constructs: A Study of Friendship Formation*. Chichester: Wiley.

Duck, S. W. (1977). Inquiry, hypothesis and the quest for validation: Personal construct systems in the development of acquaintance. In S. W. Duck (Ed.) *Theory and Practice in Interpersonal Attraction*. London: Academic Press, pp. 379–404.

Duck, S. W. (1982a). A topography of relationship disengagement and dissolution. In S. W. Duck (Ed.) *Personal Relationships 4: Dissolving Personal Relationships*. London: Academic Press, pp. 1–30.

Duck, S. W. (1982b). *Personal Relationships 4: Dissolving Personal Relationships*. London & New York: Academic Press.

Duck, S. W. (1983). *Friends for Life*. Brighton: Harvester.

Duck, S. W. (1984a). A perspective on the repair of personal relationships. In S. W. Duck (Ed.) *Personal Relationships 5: Repairing Personal Relationships*. New York: Academic Press, pp. 163–184.

Duck, S. W. (1984b). A rose is a rose (is a tadpole is a freeway is a film) is a rose. *Journal of Social and Personal Relationships*, **1**, 507–510.

Duck, S. W. (1984c). *Personal Relationships 5: Repairing Personal Relationships*. London & New York: Academic Press.

Duck, S. W. (1986). *Human Relationships*. London: Sage.

Duck, S. W. (1987a). Adding apples and oranges: Investigators' implicit theories about personal relationships. In R. Burnett, P. McGhee and D. Clarke (Eds) *Accounting for Relationships*. London: Methuen.

Duck, S. W. (1987b). How to lose friends without influencing people. In M. Roloff and G. R. Miller (Eds) *Explorations in Interpersonal Communication*. Newbury Park: Sage.

Duck, S. W., and Craig, G. (1978). Personality similarity and the development of friendship: A longitudinal study. *British Journal of Social and Clinical Psychology*, **17**, 237–242.

Duck, S. W., and Gilmour, R. (1981a). *Personal Relationships 1: Studying Personal Relationships*. London: Academic Press.

Duck, S. W., and Gilmour, R. (1981b). *Personal Relationships 2: Developing Personal Relationships*. London: Academic Press.

Duck, S. W., and Gilmour, R. (1981c). *Personal Relationships 3: Personal Relationships in Disorder*. London: Academic Press.

Duck, S. W., and Miell, D. E. (1986). Charting the development of personal relationships. In R. Gilmous and S. W. Duck (Eds) *The Emerging Field of Personal Relationships*. Hillsdale, NJ: Erlbaum, pp. 133–143.

Duck, S. W., and Perlman, D. (1985). The thousand islands of personal relationships: A prescriptive analysis for future explorations. In S. W. Duck and D. Perlman (Eds) *Understanding Personal Relationships Research: An Interdisciplinary Approach*. London: Sage, pp. 1–15.

Duck, S. W., and Sants, H. K. A. (1983). On the origin of the specious: Are personal relationships really interpersonal states? *Journal of Social and Clinical Psychology*, **1**, 27–41.

Duck, S. W., Miell, D. K., and Gaebler, H. C. (1980). Attraction and communication in children's interactions. In H. C. Foot, A. J. Chapman and J. R. Smith (Eds) *Friendship and Social Relations in Children*. Chichester: Wiley, pp. 89–115.

Dumas, J. E. (1986). Controlling for autocorrelation in social interaction analysis. *Psychological Bulletin*, **100**, 125–127.

Duncan, H. D. (1967). The search for a social theory of communication in American sociology. In F. E. X. Dance (Ed.) *Human Communication Theory*. New York: Holt, Rinehart, & Winston, pp. 236–263.

Duncan, S. D., Jr (1969). Nonverbal communication. *Psychological Bulletin*, **72**, 118–137.

Duncan, S. D., Jr (1972). Some signals and rules for taking speaking turns in conversations. *Journal of Personality and Social Psychology*, **23**, 283–292.

Duncan, S. D., Jr, and Fiske, D. W. (1977). *Face-to-Face Interaction: Research, Methods, and Theory*. Hillsdale, NJ: Erlbaum.

Duncan, S. D., Jr, and Fiske, D. W. (1979). Dynamic patterning in conversation. *American Scientist*, **67**, 90–98.

Duncan, S. D., Jr, and Fiske, D. W. (1985). *Interaction Structure and Strategy*. New York: Cambridge University Press.

Duncan, S. D., Jr, and Niederehe, G. (1974). On signaling that it's your turn to speak. *Journal of Experimental Social Psychology*, **10**, 234–247.

Dunkel-Schetter, C. (1984). Social support and cancer: Findings based on patient interviews and their implications. *Journal of Social Issues*, **40**, 77–98.

Dunkel-Schetter, C., Folkman, S., and Lazarus, R. S. (1987). Social support received in stressful situations. *Journal of Personality and Social Psychology*, **53**, 71–80.

Dunn, J. (1983). Sibling relationships in early childhood. *Child Development*, **54**, 787–811.

Dunn, J. (1987). Connections between relationships: Implications of research on mothers and siblings. In R. A. Hinde and J. Stevenson-Hinde (Eds) *Relations between Relationships*. Oxford: Oxford University Press.

Dunn, J., and Kendrick, C. (1982). *Siblings: Love, Envy and Understanding*. Cambridge, MA: Harvard University Press.

Durlak, J. A. (1979). Comparative effectiveness of paraprofessional and professional helpers. *Journal of Consulting and Clinical Psychology*, **86**, 80–92.

Eagly, A. H. (1987). *Sex Differences in Social Behavior: A Social-role Interpretation*. Hillsdale, NJ: Erlbaum.

Easterbrooks, M. A., and Emde, R. N. (1987). Marital and parent–child relationships:

The role of affect in the family system. In R. A. Hinde and J. Stevenson-Hinde (Eds) *Relations between Relationships*. Oxford: Oxford University Press.

Easterbrooks, M. A., and Lamb, M. E. (1979). The relation between quality of infant–mother attachment and infant competence in initial encounters with peers. *Child Development*, **50**, 380–387.

Eastzer, D. H., King, A. P., and West, M. J. (1985). Patterns of courtship between cowbird subspecies: Evidence for positive assortment. *Animal Behavior*, **33**, 30–39.

Eaton, W. W. (1978). Life events, social supports, and psychiatric symptoms: A reanalysis of the New Haven data. *Journal of Health Social Behavior*, **19**, 230–234.

Eckenrode, J. (1983). The mobilization of social supports: Some individual constraints. *American Journal of Community Psychology*, **11**, 509–528.

Eckerman, C. O., and Whatley, J. L. (1977). Toys and social interaction between infant peers. *Child Development*, **48**, 1645–1656.

Eckerman, C. O., Whatley, J. L., and Kutz, S. L. (1975). The growth of social play with peers during the second year of life. *Developmental Psychology*, **11**, 42–49.

Eder, D., and Hallinan, M. T. (1978). Sex differences in children's friendships. *American Sociological Review*, **43**, 237–250.

Edinger, J. A., and Patterson, M. L. (1983). Nonverbal involvement and social control. *Psychological Bulletin*, **93**, 30–56.

Edwards, A. L. (1959). *The Edwards Personal Preference Form*. New York: The Psychological Corporation.

Egeland, B., and Farber, E. A. (1984). Infant–mother attachment: Factors related to its development and changes over time. *Child Development*, **55**, 753–771.

Egeland, B., and Sroufe, L. A. (1981a). Attachment and early maltreatment. *Child Development*, **52**, 44–52.

Egeland, B., and Sroufe, L. A. (1981b). Developmental sequelae of maltreatment. *Child Development*, **11**, 77–92.

Eidelson, R. J. (1980). Interpersonal satisfaction and level of involvement: A curvilinear relationship. *Journal of Personality and Social Psychology*, **39**, 460–470.

Eidelson, R. J. (1983). Affiliation and independence issues in marriage. *Journal of Marriage and the Family*, August, 683–688.

Eisenberg, R. B. (1976). *Auditory Competence in Early Life: The Roots of Communicative Behavior*. Baltimore: University Park Press.

Eisenstadt, S. N. (1956)Ritualized personal relations: Blood brotherhood, best friends, compadre, etc. Some comparative hypotheses and suggestions. *Man*, **96**, 90–95.

Eisenstadt, S. N., and Roniger, L. (1984). *Patrons, Clients and Friends*. London: Cambridge University Press.

Ekeh, P. (1974). *Social Exchange Theory*. Cambridge, MA: Harvard University Press.

Ekman, P., and Friesen, W. V. (1969). The repertoire of nonverbal behavior: Categories, origins, usage and coding. *Semiotica*, **1**, 49–97.

Ekman, P., Friesen, W. V., and Ellsworth, P. C. (1972). *Emotion in the Human Face*. New York: Pergamon.

Elder, G. H. (1969). Appearance and education in marriage mobility. *American Sociological Review*, **34**, 519–533.

Elder, G. H. (1979). Historical change in life patterns and personality. In P. B. Baltes and O. G. Brim (Eds) *Lifespan Developments and Behavior*, Vol. 2. New York & London: Academic Press.

Ellis, D. G. (1981). The epistemology of form. In C. Wilder-Mott and J. H. Weakland (Eds) *Rigor and Imagination: Essays for the Legacy of Gregory Bateson*. New York: Praeger, pp. 215–230.

Ellis, D. G., and Fisher, B. A. (1975). Phases of conflict in small group development: A Markov analysis. *Human Communication Research*, **1**, 195–212.

Ellis, D. G., Fisher, B. A., Drecksel, G., Hoch, D., and Werbel, W. (1976). Codebook for relational control scheme. Unpublished manuscript, Department of Communication, University of Utah.

Ellsworth, P. C. (1975). Direct gaze as a social stimulus: The example of aggression. In L. Krames, T. Alloway and P. Pliner (Eds) *Nonverbal Communication of Aggression*. New York: Plenum.

Emde, R. (1983). The prerepresentational self and its affective core. *Psychoanalytic Study of the Child*, **38**, 165–192.

Emde, R. N., Gaensbauer, T. J., and Harmon, R. J. (1976). Emotional expression in infancy: A biobehavioral study. *Psychological Issues*, **10** (whole No. 1).

Emlen, S. T., and Oring, L. W. (1977). Ecology, sexual selection, and the evolution of mating systems. *Science*, **197**, 215–223.

Endicott, J., and Spitzer, R. L. (1978). A diagnostic interview: The schedule for affective disorders and schizophrenia. *Archives of General Psychiatry*, **35**, 837–844.

Engfer, A. (1987). The interrelatedness of marriage and the mother–child relationship. In R. A. Hinde and J. Stevenson-Hinde (Eds) *Relations Between Relationships*. Oxford: Oxford University Press.

Epstein, J. L., and Karweit, N. (Eds) (1983). *Friends in School: Patterns of Selection and Influence in Secondary Schools*. New York: Academic Press.

Epstein, S. (1973). The self-concept revisited. *American Psychologist*, **28**, 404–416.

Epstein, S. (1979). The stability of behavior: I. On predicting most of the people much of the time. *Journal of Personality and Social Psychology*, **37**, 1097–1126.

Erickson, M. F., Sroufe, L. A., and Egeland, B. (1986). The relationships between quality of attachment and behavior problems in preschool in a high-risk sample. In I. Bretherton and E. Waters (Eds) *Monographs of the SRCD*, **50** (Serial No. 209).

Erikson, E. (1950). *Childhood and Society*. New York: Norton.

Erikson, E. H. (1968). *Identity: Youth and Crisis*. New York: Norton.

Erlebacher, A. (1977). Design and analysis of experiments contrasting the within- and between-subjects manipulation of the independent variable. *Psychological Bulletin*, **84**, 212–219.

Escudero, V., and Gutierrez, E. (1987). Una perspectiva secuencial de la dimension replacional de la communicacion: Control interpersonal y conflicto. Unpublished manuscript, Departamento de Psicologia y Psicobiologia, University de Santiago de Compostela, Santiago de Compostela, Spain.

Even-Chen, M., Yinon, Y., and Bizman, A. (1978). The door in the face technique: Effects of the size of the initial request. *European Journal of Social Psychology*, **8**, 135–140.

Everitt, B. S., and Smith, A. M. R. (1979). Interaction in contingency tables: A brief description of alternative explanations. *Psychological Medicine*, **9**, 581–583.

Eysenck, H. J. (1967). *The Biological Basis of Personality*. Springfield, IL: Charles C. Thomas.

Fairbairn, W. R. D. (1952). *Psychoanalytic Studies of Personality*. London: Tavistock.

Fairbairn, W. R. D. (1963). An object relations theory of the personality. *International Journal of Psychoanalysis*, **44**, 224–25.

Fairhurst, G. T., and Snavely, B. K. (1983). Majority and token minority group relationships: Power acquisition and communication. *Academy of Management Review*, **8**, 292–320.

Fairhurst, G. T., Rogers, L. E., and Sarr, R. A. (1987). Manager–subordinate interactions and self-reported relational states. In M. L. McLaughlin (Ed.) *Communication Yearbook 10*. Beverly Hills: Sage.

Fairweather, G. W., Sanders, D. H., Maynard, H., and Cressler, D. L. (1969). *Community Life for the Mentally Ill: An Alternative to Institutional Care*. Chicago: Aldine.

Falbo, T., and Peplau, L. A. (1980). Power strategies in intimate relationships. *Journal of Personality and Social Psychology*, **38**, 618–628.

Fararo, T. J. (1981). Biased networks and social structure theorems. *Social Networks*, **3**, 137–159.

Farina, A., Allen, J. B., and Saul, B. B. (1968). The role of the stigmatized in affecting social relationships. *Journal of Personality*, **36**, 169–182.

Farina, A., Gliha, D., Boudreau, L. A., Allen, J. G., and Sherman, M. (1971). Mental illness and the impact of believing others know about it. *Journal of Abnormal Psychology*, **77**, 1–5.

Fausteau, M. F. (1974). *The Male Machine*. New York: McGraw-Hill.

Fausto-Sterling, A. (1985). *Myths of Gender: Biological Theories about Women and Men*. New York: Basic Books.

Feagin, J. R. (1970). A note on the friendship ties of black urbanites. *Social Forces*, **49**, 303–308.

Feger, H. (1981). Analysis of social networks. In S. W. Duck and R. Gilmour (Eds) *Personal Relationships 1: Studying Personal Relationships*. London: Academic Press.

Feick, L. F., and Novak, J. A. (1985). Analyzing sequential categorical data on dyadic interaction: Log-linear models exploiting the order in variables. *Psychological Bulletin*, **98**, 600–611.

Feinberg, M. R., and Levenstein, A. (1982). Sex and romance in the office and plant. *The Wall Street Journal*, 29 November.

Feinman, S., Roberts, D., and Morissette, L. (1986). The effect of social referencing on 12-month-olds' responses to a stranger's attempts to 'make friends'. Paper presented at the International Conference on Infant Studies, Beverly Hills, California.

Feld, S. L. (1981). The focused organization of social ties. *American Journal of Sociology*, **86**, 1015–1035.

Feld, S. L. (1982). Social structural determinants of similarity among associates. *American Sociological Review*, **47**, 797–801.

Feldman, R., and Jorgensen, D. (1974). Communication and marital conflict. *Journal of Applied Communications Research*, **2** (2), 53–66.

Feldstein, S., and Welkowitz, J. (1978). A chronography of conversation: In defense of an objective approach. In A. W. Siegman and S. Feldstein (Eds) *Nonverbal Behavior and Communication*. Hillsdale: Erlbaum, pp. 329–378.

Felner, R. D., Ginter, M. A., and Primavera, J. (1982). Primary prevention during school transitions: Social support and environmental structure. *American Journal of Community Psychology*, **10**, 277–290.

Fengler, A. P. (1974). Romantic love in courtship: Divergent paths of male and female students. *Journal of Comparative Family Studies*, **5**, 134–139.

Fenigstein, A. (1979). Self-consciousness, self-attention, and social interaction. *Journal of Personality and Social Psychology*, **37**, 75–86.

Fenigstein, A., Scheier, M. F., and Buss, A. H. (1975). Public and private self-consciousness: Assessment and theory. *Journal of Consulting and Clinical Psychology*, **43**, 522–527.

Fernald, A. (1984). The perceptual and affective salience of mothers' speech to infants. In L. Feagans, C. Garvey, R. Golinkoff, M. T. Greenberg, C. Harding and J. N. Bohannon (Eds) *The Origins and Growth of Communication*. Norwood, NJ: Ablex.

Ferreira, A., and Winter, W. (1974). On the nature of marital relationships: Measurable differences in spontaneous agreement. *Family Process*, **13** (3), 355–369.

Ferrell, M. Z., Tolone, W. L., and Walsh, R. H. (1977). Maturational and societal changes in the sexual double-standard: A panel analysis (1967–1971; 1970–1974). *Journal of Marriage and the Family*, **39**, 255–271.

Festinger, L. (1954). A theory of social comparison processes. *Human Relations*, **7**, 117–140.

Festinger, L. (1957). *A Theory of Cognitive Dissonance*. Stanford, CA: Stanford University Press.

Festinger, L., Schachter, S., and Back, K. (1950). *Social Pressures in Informal Groups: A Study of a Housing Community*. New York: Harper & Row.

Field, T. (1979). Differential behavioral and cardiac responses of 3-month-old infants to a mirror and a peer. *Infant Behavior and Development*, **2**, 179–184.

Field, T. (1985). Attachment as psychobiological attunement: Being on the same wavelength. In M. Reite and T. Field (Eds) *The Psychobiology of Attachment and Separation*. Orlando, FL: Academic Press, pp. 415–454.

Field, T. M., Sostek, A. M., Vietze, P., and Leiderman, P. H. (1981). *Culture and Early Interactions*. Hillsdale, NJ: Erlbaum.

Fienberg, S. E., and Wasserman, S. S. (1981). Categorical data analysis of multiple sociometric relations. In S. Leinhardt (Ed.) *Sociological Methodology 1981*. San Francisco: Jossey-Bass.

Fincham, F., and O'Leary, K. D. (1983). Causal inferences for spouse behavior in maritally distressed and nondistressed couples. *Journal of Social and Clinical Psychology*, **1**, 42–57.

Fine, G. A. (1979). Small groups and culture creation: The idioculture of Little League baseball teams. *American Sociological Review*, **44**, 733–745.

Fine, G. A., Stitt, J. L., and Finch, M. (1984). Couple tie-signs and interpersonal threat: A field experiment. *Social Psychology Quarterly*, **47**, 282–286.

Fine, R. (1979). *A History of Psychoanalysis*. New York: Columbia University Press.

Fineberg, B., and Lowman, J. (1975). Affect and status dimensions of marital adjustment. *Journal of Marriage and the Family*, **37** (1), 155–160.

Fiore, J., Coppel, D. B., Becker, J., and Cox, G. B. (1986). Social support as a multifaceted concept: Examination of important dimensions for Adjustment. *American Journal of Community Psychology*, **14**, 93–111.

Fischer, C. S. (1982a). *To Dwell among Friends: Personal Networks in Town and City*. Chicago: University of Chicago Press.

Fischer, C. S. (1982b). What do we mean by 'friend'? An inductive study. *Social Network*, **3**, 287–306.

Fischer, C. S., and Phillips, S. L. (1982). Who is alone? Characteristics of people with small networks. In L. A. Peplau and D. Perlman (Eds) *Loneliness: A Sourcebook of Current Theory, Research and Therapy*. New York: Wiley, pp. 21–39.

Fischer, C. S., *et al.* (1977). *Networks and Places: Social Relations in the Urban Setting*. New York: Free Press.

Fish, R., and Fish, L. (1986). *Quid Pro Quo* revisited: The basis of marital therapy. *American Journal of Orthopsychiatry*, **56** (3), 371–384.

Fisher, A., and Drecksel, G. (1983). A cyclical model of developing relationships: A study of relational control interaction. *Communication Monographs*, **50**, 66–78.

Fisher, B. A. (1978). *Perspectives on Human Communication*. New York: Macmillan.

Fisher, B. A., and Drecksel, G. L. (1983). A cyclical model of developing relationships. *Communication Monographs*, **50**, 66–78.

Fisher, B. A., Drecksel, G. L., and Werbel, W. S. (1979). Social information processing analysis (SIPA): Coding ongoing human communication. *Small Group Behavior*, **10**, 3–21.

Fisher, M., and Stricker, G. (Eds) (1982). *Intimacy*. New York: Plenum.

Fisher, W. A., Byrne, D., White, L. A., and Kelley, K. (1986). Erotophobia–erotophilia as a dimension of personality. Unpublished manuscript.

Fiske, S. T., and Taylor, S. E. (1984). *Social Cognition*. Reading, MA: Addison-Wesley.

Fitzgerald, N. M., and Surra, C. A. (1981). Studying the development of dyadic relationships: Explorations into a retrospective interview technique. Paper presented at the National Council on Family Relations Pre-Conference Workshop on Theory and Methodology, Milwaukee, Wisconsin.

Fitzpatrick, M. A. (1976). A typological approach to communication in relationships. Unpublished PhD dissertation, Temple University, Philadelphia, Pennsylvania.

Fitzpatrick, M. A. (1977). A typological approach to communication in relationships. In B. Rubin (Ed.) *Communication Yearbook 1*. New Brunswick: Transaction Books, pp. 263–275.

Fitzpatrick, M. A. (1984). A typological approach to marital interaction: Recent theory and research. In L. Berkowitz (Ed.) *Advances in Experimental Social Psychology*, Vol. 18. New York: Academic Press, pp. 2–47.

Fitzpatrick, M. A. (1986). Marriage and verbal intimacy. In V. J. Derlega and J. Berg (Eds) *Self-Disclosure: Theory, Research and Therapy*. New York: Plenum.

Fitzpatrick, M. A., and Best, P. (1979). Dyadic adjustment in traditional, independent, and separate relationships: A validation study. *Communication Monographs*, **46**, 167–178.

Fitzpatrick, M. A., and Winke, J. (1979). You always hurt the one you love: Strategies and tactics in interpersonal conflict. *Communication Quarterly*, **27**, 1–11.

Fleener, D. E. (1973). Experimental production of infant–maternal attachment behaviors. Paper presented at the meeting of the American Psychological Association, Montreal.

Fleming, R., and Baum, A. (1986). Social support and stress: The buffering effects of friendship. In V. J. Derlega and B. A. Winstead (Eds) *Friendship and Social Interaction*. New York: Springer-Verlag.

Foa, U., and Foa, E. (1974). *Societal Structures of the Mind*. Springfield, IL: Charles Thomas.

Fodor, E. M., and Smith, T. (1982). The power motive as an influence on group decision making. *Journal of Personality and Social Psychology*, **42**, 178–185.

Fogel, A. (1979). Peer- vs. mother-directed behavior in 1- to 3-month-old infants. *Infant Behavior and Development*, **2**, 215–226.

Folger, J. P., and Poole, M. S. (1982). Relational coding schemes: The question of validity. In M. Burgoon (Ed.) *Communication Yearbook 5*. New Brunswick: Transaction Books, pp. 235–247.

Folger, J. P., Hewes, D. E., and Poole, M. S. (1984). Coding social interaction. In B. Dervin and M. Voight (Eds) *Progress in Communication Sciences*. New York: Ablex, pp. 115–161.

Foot, H. C., Chapman, A. J., and Smith, J. R. (1980a). Patterns of interaction in children's friendships. In H. C. Foot, A. J. Chapman and J. R. Smith (Eds) *Friendship and Social Relations in Children*. Chichester: Wiley, pp. 267–289.

Foot, H. C., Chapman, A. J., and Smith, J. R. (1980b). *Friendship and Social Relations in Children*. Chichester: Wiley.

Forgas, J. P. (1982). Episode cognition. In L. Berkowitz (Ed.) *Advances in Experimental Social Psychology*, **15**. New York: Academic Press, pp. 59–101.

Foss, R. D., and Dempsey, C. B. (1979). Blood donation and the foot-in-the-door technique: A limiting case. *Journal of Personality and Social Psychology*, **37**, 580–590.

Foucault, M. (1980). *The History of Sexuality: Vol. 1. An Introduction* (R. Hurley, trans.). New York: Vintage (original work published 1976).

Fox, A. (1974). *Beyond Contract: Work, Power and Trust Relations*. London: Faber & Faber.

Fox, N. (1977). Attachment of kibbutz infants to mother and metapelet. *Child Development*, **48**, 1228–1239.

Frankenstein, W. (1985). Asymmetry of influence in alcoholics' marital communication: Alcoholics' effects on interaction dominance. *Journal of Marital and Family Therapy*, **11** (4), 399–410.

Frankenstein, W., Hay, W., and Nathan, P. (1985). Effects of intoxication on alcoholics' marital communication and problem-solving. *Journal of Studies on Alcohol*, **46** (1), 1–6.

Frankl, V. E. (1962). *Man's Search for Meaning*. Boston: Beacon Press.

Franzoi, S. L., and Davis, M. H. (1985). Adolescent self-disclosure and loneliness: Private self-consciousness and parental influences. *Journal of Personality and Social Psychology*, **48**, 768–780.

Freden, L. (1982). *Psychosocial Aspects of Depression*. Chichester: Wiley.

Freedman, J. L., and Fraser, S. C. (1966). Compliance without pressure: The foot-in-the-door technique. *Journal of Personality and Social Psychology*, **4**, 195–203.

Freeman, J. (1982). Organizational life cycles and natural selection processes. *Research in Organizational Behavior*, **4**, 1–32.

Freeman, J., and Hannan, M. T. (1983). Niche width and the dynamics of organizational populations. *American Journal of Sociology*, **88**, 1116–1145.

Freeman, J., Carroll, G. R., and Hannan, M. T. (1983). The liability of newness: Age dependence in organizational death rates. *American Sociological Review*, **48**, 692–710.

French, J. R. P., Jr and Raven, B. (1959). The bases of social power. In D. Cartwright (Ed.) *Studies in Social Power*. Ann Arbor, MI: Institute for Social Research, pp. 150–167.

Freud, S. (1900/1953). The interpretation of dreams. In J. Strachey (Ed.) *The Standard Edition of the Complete Psychological Works of Sigmund Freud*, Vols. 4–5. London: Hogarth.

Freud, S. (1920/1955). Beyond the pleasure principle. In J. Strachey (Ed.) *The Standard Edition*, Vol. 18. London: Hogarth.

Freud, S. (1933). *New Introductory Lectures in Psychoanalysis*. New York: Norton.

Freud, S. (1940). *An Outline of Psycho-analysis*. New York: Norton (translated and reprinted 1949).

Freud, S. (1949). *An Outline of Psychoanalysis*. New York: Norton.

Fried, M. (1963). Grieving for a lost home. In L. Duhl (Ed.) *The Urban Condition*. New York: Basic Books.

Fried, M. L., and DeFazio, V. J. (1974). Territoriality and boundary conflicts in the subway. *Psychiatry*, **37**, 47–59.

Friedman, A. S. (1975). Interaction of drug therapy with marital therapy in depressive patients. *Archives of General Psychiatry*, **32**, 619–637.

Friedman, R. C., Aronoff, M. P., Clarkin, J. F., Corn, R., and Hurt, S. W. (1983). History of suicidal behavior in depressed borderline patients. *American Journal of Psychiatry*, **140**, 1023–1026.

Friedrich, W., and Reams, R. (1985). Parentification of young children: Assessment of a clinical phenomenon. Unpublished manuscript, University of Washington.

Friedrich, W., and Wheeler, K. (1982). The abusing parent revisited: A decade of psychological research. *Journal of Nervous and Mental Diseases*, **170**, 577–587.

Froland, C., Pancoast, D. L., Chapman, N. J., and Kimboko, P. (1981). *Helping Networks and Human Services*. Beverly Hills: Sage.

Fromm-Reichmann, F. (1959). Loneliness. *Psychiatry*, **22**, 1–15.

Furman, W. (1984). Some observations on the study of personal relationships. In J. C. Masters and K. Yarkin-Levin (Eds) *Boundary Areas in Social and Developmental Psychology*. Orlando, FL: Academic Press, pp. 15–42.

Furman, W., and Bierman, K. (1984). Children's conceptions of friendship: A multidimensional study. *Developmental Psychology*, **96**, 925–931.

Furman, W., and Buhrmester, D. (1985). Children's perceptions of the personal relationships in their social networks. *Developmental Psychology*, **21**, 1016–1022.

Furman, W., and Garcia, D. M. (1986). An examination of the concurrent and predictive relations of different types on nonsocial behavior. Unpublished manuscript.

Furman, W., and Robbins, P. (1985). What's the point? Issues in the selection of treatment objectives. In B. Schneider, K. Rubin and J. Leddingham (Eds) *Peer Training*. New York: Springer-Verlag.

Fusso, T. E. (1985). The situational analysis of the rehabilitative experience of the spinal cord injured. PhD dissertation, Interdisciplinary PhD Program in Social Psychology, University of Nevada, Reno.

Gaelick, L., Bodenhausen, G. V., and Wyer, R. S., Jr (1985). Emotional communication in close relationships. *Journal of Personality and Social Psychology*, **49**, 1246–1265.

Gagnon, G. H. (1977). *Human Sexuality*. Glenview, IL: Scott, Foresman.

Gagnon, G. H., and Simon, W. (1973). *Sexual Conduct*. Chicago: Aldine.

Galaskiewicz, J. (1985). Interorganizational relations. *Annual Review of Sociology*, **11**, 281–304.

Galinsky, E. (1986). Family life and corporate policies. In M. W. Yogman and T. B. Brazelton (Eds) *In Support of Families*. Cambridge, MA: Harvard University Press, pp. 109–145.

Garvey, C. (1977). *Play*. Cambridge, MA: Harvard University Press.

Garvey, C., and Ben Debba, M. (1974). Effects of age, sex, and partner on children's dyadic speech. *Child Development*, **45**, 1159–1161.

Geen, R. G. (1986). Physiological, affective, and behavioral implications of extraversion–introversion. In W. H. Jones, J. M. Cheek and S. R. Briggs (Eds) *Shyness: Perspectives on Research and Treatment*. New York: Plenum, pp. 265–278.

Gergen, K. J. (1976). Social psychology, science, and history. *Personality and Social Psychology Bulletin*, **2**, 373–383.

Gergen, K. J. (1985). The social constructionist movement in modern psychology. *American Psychologist*, **40**, 266–275.

Gergen, K. J., Greenberg, M., and Willis, R. (1980). *Social Exchange: Advances in Theory and Research*. New York: Plenum.

Gerson, A. C., and Perlman, D. (1979). Loneliness and expressive communications. *Journal of Abnormal Psychology*, **88**, 258–266.

Gibson, J. J. (1966). *The Senses Considered as Perceptual Systems*. Boston: Houghton-Mifflin.

Giddens, A. (1976). *New Rules of Sociological Method*. London: Hutchinson.

Gilbert, S. (1976). Self-disclosure, intimacy and communication in families. *The Family Coordinator*, **25**, 221–231.

Giles, H., and Powesland, P. F. (1975). *Speech Style and Social Evaluation*. New York: Academic Press.

Giles, H., and Smith, P. M. (1979). Accommodation theory: Optimal levels of convergence. In H. Giles and R. N. St Clair (Eds) *Language and Social Psychology*. Oxford: Blackwell, pp. 45–65.

Giles, H., and Street, R. L., Jr (1985). Communicator characteristics and behavior. In M. L. Knapp and G. R. Miller (Eds) *Handbook of Interpersonal Communication*. Beverly Hills: Sage, pp. 205–261.

Gilligan, C. (1982). *In a Different Voice: Psychological Theory and Women's Development*. Cambridge, MA: Harvard University Press.

Gilmour, R., and Duck, S. W. (1986). *The Emerging Field of Personal Relationships*. Hillsdale, NJ: Erlbaum.

Ginsburg, G. P. (1986). The structural analysis of primary relationships. In R. Gilmour and S. W. Duck (Eds) *The Emerging Field of Personal Relationships*. Hillsdale, NJ: Erlbaum, pp. 42–62.

Glaser, R. D., and Thorpe, J. S. (1986). Unethical intimacy: A survey of contact and advances between psychology educators and female graduate students. *American Psychologist*, **41**, 43–51.

Glick, P., and Spanier, G. (1980). Married and unmarried cohabitation in the United States. *Journal of Marriage and the Family*, **42** 19–30.

Glidewell, J. C., Tucker, S., Todt, M., and Cox, S. (1982). Professional support systems: The teaching profession. In A. Nadler, J. P. Fisher and B. M. DePaulo (Eds) *Applied Research in Help-Seeking and Reactions to Aid*. New York: Academic Press.

Godfrey, D., Jones, E., and Lord, C. (1986). Self-promotion is not ingratiating. *Journal of Personality and Social Psychology*, **50**, 106–115.

Goethals, G. R. (1986). Social comparison theory: Psychology from the lost and found. *Personality and Social Psychology Bulletin*, **12**, 261–278.

Goethals, G. R., and Darley, J. (1977). Social comparison theory: An attributional perspective. In J. Suls and R. Miller (Eds) *Social Comparison Processes: Theoretical and Empirical Perspectives*. Washington, DC: Hemisphere, pp. 259–278.

Goffman, E. (1955). On face-work: An analysis of ritual elements in social interaction. *Psychiatry*, **18**, 213–231.

Goffman, E. (1959). *The Presentation of Self in Everyday Life*. Garden City, NJ: Doubleday.

Goffman, E. (1963). *Behavior in Public Places*. New York: Free Press.

Goffman, E. (1967). *Interaction Ritual*. Garden City, NJ: Anchor.

Goffman, E. (1971). *Relations in Public*. New York: Basic Books.

Goldberg, D. P., and Hillier, V. F. (1979). A scaled version of the General Health Questionnaire. *Psychological Medicine*, **9**, 139–145.

Goldberg, J. (1984). Relationship of family cohesiveness and confirmation/disconfirmation, non-immediacy, and perceived confirmation. Unpublished doctoral dissertation, University of Denver (University Microfilms No. 81-3846).

Goldberg, W. A., and Easterbrooks, M. A. (1984). Role of marital quality in toddler development. *Developmental Psychology*, **20**, 504–514.

Goldman, B. D., and Ross, H. S. (1978). Social skills in action: An analysis of early peer games. In J. Glick and K. A. Clarke-Stewart (Eds) *The Development of Social Understanding*. New York: Gardner, pp. 177–212.

Goldstein, M. J. (Ed.) (1981). *New Directions for Mental Health Services: New Developments in Interventions with Families of Schizophrenics*, No. 12. San Francisco: Jossey-Bass.

Goldstein, M., Kilroy, M., and Van de Voort, D. (1976). Gaze as a function of conversation and degree of love. *Journal of Psychology*, **92**, 227–234.

Goode, W. J. (1956). *After Divorce*. New York: Free Press.

Goodman, E. (1983). In an office love affair, woman is usually the loser—of job. *Milwaukee Sentinel*, 19 September, Section 1, p. 10.

Goodman, G. (1972). *Companionship Therapy: Studies in Structured Intimacy*. San Francisco: Jossey-Bass.

Goodnow, J. J., Cashmore, J., Cotton, S., and Knight, R. (1984). Mothers' developmental time tables in two cultural groups. *International Journal of Psychology*, **19**, 193–205.

Gordon, S. (1976). *Lonely in America*. New York: Simon & Schuster.

Gordon, S. L. (1981). The sociology of sentiments and emotion. In M. Rosenberg and R. H. Turner (Eds) *Social Psychology: Sociological Perspectives*. New York: Basic Books.

Goswick, R. A., and Jones, W. H. (1981). Loneliness, self-concept and adjustment. *Journal of Psychology*, **107**, 237–240.

Goth-Owens, T. L., Stollak, G. A., Messe, L. A., Peshkess, I., and Watts, P. (1982). Marital satisfaction, parenting satisfaction, and parenting behavior in early infancy. *Infant Mental Health Journal*, **3**, 187–197.

Gotlib, I. H. (1981). Self-reinforcement and recall: Differential deficits in depressed and nondepressed psychiatric inpatients. *Journal of Abnormal Psychology*, **90**, 521–530.

Gotlib, I. H. (1982). Self-reinforcement and depression in interpersonal interaction: The role of performance level. *Journal of Abnormal Psychology*, **91**, 3–13.

Gotlib, I. H. (1983). Perception and recall of interpersonal feedback: Negative bias in depression. *Cognitive Therapy and Research*, **7**, 399–412.

Gotlib, I. H. (1986). Depression and marital interaction: A longitudinal perspective. Presented at the Third International Conference on Personal Relationships, Tel Aviv, Israel.

Gotlib, I. H., and Colby, C. A. (1987). *Treatment of Depression: An Interpersonal Systems Approach*. New York: Pergamon.

Gotlib, I. H., and Meltzer, S. J. (1987). Depression and the perception of social skill. *Cognitive Therapy and Research*, **11**, 41–54.

Gotlib, I. H., and Robinson, L. A. (1982). Responses to depressed individuals: Discrepancies between self-report and observer-rated behavior. *Journal of Abnormal Psychology*, **91**, 231–240.

Gottlieb, B. H. (1978). The development and application of a classification scheme of informal helping behaviours. *Canadian Journal of Behavioural Science*, **10**, 105–115.

Gottlieb, B. H. (Ed.) (1981). *Social Networks and Social Support*. Beverly Hills: Sage.

Gottlieb, B. H. (1982). Mutual-help groups: Members' views of their benefits and of roles for professionals. *Prevention in Human Services*, **1** (3), 55–68.

Gottlieb, B. H. (1983). *Social Support Strategies: Guidelines for Mental Health Practice*. Beverly Hills: Sage.

Gottlieb, B. H. (1985a). Social support and the study of personal relationships. *Journal of Social and Personal Relationships*, **2**, 351–375.

Gottlieb, B. H. (1985b). Theory into practice: Issues that surface in planning interventions that mobilize support. In I. G. Sarason and B. R. Sarason (Eds) *Social Support: Theory, Research and Applications*. The Hague: Martinus Nijhoff, pp. 417–438.

Gottlieb, B. H. (Ed.) (1987). *Marshalling Social Support: Formats, Processes and Effects*. Beverly Hills: Sage.

Gottlieb, B. H., and Coppard, A. E. (1987). Using social network therapy to create support systems for the chronically mentally ill. *Canadian Journal of Community Mental Health*.

Gottlieb, G. (1979). Comparative psychology and ethology. In E. Hearst (Ed.) *The First Century of Experimental Psychology*. Hillsdale, NJ: Erlbaum, pp. 147–173.

Gottman, J. M. (1979). *Marital Interaction: Experimental Investigations*. New York: Academic Press.

Gottman, J. M. (1981). *Time-Series Analysis*. Cambridge, MA: Cambridge University Press.

Gottman, J. M. (1982a). Temporal form: Toward a new language for describing relationships. *Journal of Marriage and the Family*, **44**, 943–962.

Gottman, J. M. (1982b). Emotional responsiveness in marital conversations. *Journal of Communication*, **32**, 108–120.

Gottman, J. M. (1983). How children become friends. *Monographs of the Society for Research in Child Development*, **48** (3, Serial No. 201).

Gottman, J. M., and Parker, J. G. (1986). *Conversations of Friends*. New York: Cambridge University Press.

Gottman, J. M., and Porterfield, A. (1981). Communicative competence in the nonverbal behavior of married couples. *Journal of Marriage and the Family*, **4**, 817–824.

Gottman, J. M., and Ringland, J. T. (1981). The analysis of dominance and bidirectionality in social development. *Child Development*, **52**, 393–412.

Gottman, J. M., and Roy, A. K. (1987). *Sequential Analysis: Temporal Form in Social Interaction*. New York: Cambridge University Press.

Gottman, J. M., Markman, H., and Notarius, C. (1977). The topography of marital conflict: A study of verbal and nonverbal behavior. *Journal of Marriage and the Family*, **39**, 461–477.

Gottman, J. M., Notarius, C., Gonso, J., and Markman, H. (1976a). *A Couple's Guide to Communication*. Champaign, IL: Research Press.

Gottman, J. M., Notarius, C., Markman, H., Bank, S., Yoppi, B., and Rubin, M. E. (1976b). Behavior exchange theory and marital decision making. *Journal of Personality and Social Psychology*, **34**, 14–23.

Gouldner, A. W. (1960). The norm of reciprocity: A preliminary statement. *American Sociological Review*, **25**, 161–178.

Gove, W. R., Hughes, M., and Style, C. B. (1983). Does marriage have positive effects on the psychological well-being of the individual? *Journal of Health and Social Behavior*, **24**, 122–131.

Graen, G. (1976). Role-making processes within complex organizations. In M. D. Dunnette (Ed.) *Handbook of Industrial and Organizational Psychology*. Chicago: Rand McNally.

Granovetter, M. S. (1973). The strength of weak ties. *American Journal of Sociology*, **78**, 1360–1380.

Gray, J. (1972). The psychophysiological nature of introversion–extraversion: A modification of Eysenck's theory. In V. O. Nebylitsyn and J. A. Gray (Eds) *Biological Basis of Individual Behavior*. London: Academic Press, pp. 182–205.

Gray-Little, B., and Burks, N. (1983). Power and satisfaction in marriage: A review and critique. *Psychological Bulletin*, **93**, 513–538.

Graziano, W. G., and Musser, L. M. (1982). The joining and parting of the ways. In S. W. Duck (Ed.) *Personal Relationships 4: Dissolving Personal Relationships*. London: Academic Press, pp. 75–106.

Graziano, W. G., Feldesman, A. B., and Rahe, D. F. (1985). Extraversion, social cognition, and the salience of aversiveness in social encounters. *Journal of Personality and Social Psychology*, **49**, 971–980.

Green, S. E., and Masher, D. L. (1985). A causal model of sexual arousal to erotic fantasies. *Journal of Sex Research*, **21**, 1–23.

Greenberg, J. R., and Mitchell, S. A. (1983). *Object Relations in Psychoanalytic Theory*. Cambridge, MA: Harvard University Press.

Greenberg, L. S., and Safran, J. D. (1987). *Emotions in Psychotherapy*. New York: Guilford.

Greene, M., and Kaplan, B. L. (1978). Aspects of loneliness in the therapeutic situation. *International Review of Psychoanalysis*, **5**, 3321–3330.

Greenhalgh, L. (1983). Organizational decline. *Research in the Sociology of Organizations*, **2**, 231–276.

Grossmann, K., Fremmer-Bombik, E., and Rudolph, J. (1987). Maternal attachment representations as related to child–mother attachment patterns and maternal sensitivity and acceptance of her infant. In R. A. Hinde and J. Stevenson-Hinde (Eds) *Relations Between Relationships*. Oxford: Oxford University Press.

Grossmann, K., Grossmann, K. E., Spangler, G., Suess, G., and Unzner, L. (1985). Maternal sensitivity and newborns' orientation responses as related to quality of attachment in northern Germany. In I. Bretherton and E. Waters (Eds) *Growing Points in Attachment Theory and Research. Monographs of the Society for Research in Child Development*, **50** (1–2, Serial No. 209), 233–256.

Grusec, J. E. (1971). Power and the internalization of self-denial. *Child Development*, **42**, 93–105.

Grusec, J. E. (1986). The socialization of self-sacrifice in boys and girls. Paper presented at XXIst Committee on Family Research Conference of the International Sociological Association, Jerusalem.

Grusec, J. E., and Kuczynski, L. (1980). Direction of effect in socialization: A comparison of the parent vs. the child's behavior as determinants of disciplinary techniques. *Developmental Psychology*, **16**, 1–9.

Grusec, J. E., and Redler, E. (1980). Attribution, reinforcement, and altruism: A developmental analysis. *Developmental Psychology*, **16**, 525–534.

Grusec, J. E., Dix, T. H., and Mills, R. (1982). The effects of type, severity, and victim of children's transgressions on maternal discipline. *Canadian Journal of Behavioural Science*, **14**, 276–289.

Grusec, J. E., Kuczynski, L., Rushton, J. P., and Simutis, Z. M. (1978). Modeling, direct instruction, and attributions: Effects on altruism. *Developmental Psychology*, **14**, 51–57.

Gudykunst, W. B., Yang, S. M., and Nishida, T. (1985). A cross-cultural test of uncertainty reduction theory: Comparisons of acquaintances, friends, and dating relationships in Japan, Korea, and the United States. *Human Communication Research*, **11**, 407–457.

Guerney, B. G., Jr (1977). *Relationship Enhancement: Skill-Training Programs for Therapy, Problem Prevention, and Enrichment*. San Francisco: Jossey-Bass.

Guilford, J. P. (1959). *Personality*. New York: McGraw-Hill.

Guntrip, H. (1961). *Personality Structure and Human Interaction*. New York: International Universities Press.

Gupta, N., and Jenkins, C. G. (1985). Dual career couples: Stress, stressors, strain, and strategies. In T. A. Beehr and R. S. Bhagat (Eds) *Human Stress and Cognition in Organizations: An Integrated Perspective*. New York: Wiley, pp. 141–176.

Gutek, B. A. (1985). *Sex and the Workplace*. San Francisco: Jossey-Bass.

Guttentag, M. (1983). *Too Many Women: The Sex Ratio Question*. Beverly Hills: Sage.

Haberman, S. J. (1973). The analysis of residuals in cross-classified tables. *Biometrics*, **29**, 205–220.

Hage, J. (1972). *Techniques and Problems of Theory Construction in Sociology*. New York: Wiley.

Hahlweg, K., and Conrad, M. (1983). Coding manual for the Interaction Coding System (KPI). Unpublished manuscript, Max-Planck-Institute, Germany.

Hall, K. R. L., and DeVore, I. (1965). Baboon social behavior. In I. DeVore (Ed.) *Primate Behavior*. New York: Holt, Rinehart, & Winston, pp. 53–110.

Hall, W. M., and Cairns, R. B. (1984). Aggressive behavior in children: An outcome of modeling or social reciprocity? *Developmental Psychology*, **20**, 739–745.

Hallinan, M. T. (1978). The process of friendship formation. *Social Networks*, **1**, 193–210.

Halpern, R., and Covey, L. (1983). Community support for adolescent parents and their children: The parent-to-parent program in Vermont. *Journal of Primary Prevention*, **3**, 160–173.

Hamilton, W. D. (1964). The genetical evolution of social behavior, I, II. *Journal of Theoretical Biology*, **7**, 1–16, 17–52.

Hammer, M., Makiesy-Barrow, S., and Gutwirth, L. (1978). Social networks and schizophrenia. *Schizophrenia Bulletin*, **4**, 522–545.

Hammock, G., Richardson, D. R., and Lubben, T. (1986). Lovestyles and the dissolution of relationships. Paper presented at the Annual Convention of the Eastern Psychological Association, New York, April.

Hanley-Dunn, P., Maxwell, S. E., and Santos, J. F. (1985). Interpretation of interpersonal interactions: The influence of loneliness. *Personality and Social Psychology Bulletin*, **11**, , 445–456.

Hannan, M. T., and Freeman, J. (1977). The population ecology of organizations. *American Journal of Sociology*, **82**, 929–964.

Hannan, M. T., and Freeman, J. (1984). Structural inertia and organizational change. *American Sociological Review*, **49**, 149–164.

Hannan, M. T., and Freeman, J. (1986). Where do organizational forms come from? *Sociological Forum*, **1**, 50–72.

Hansson, R. O., Jones, W. H., and Carpenter, B. N. (1984). Relational competence and social support. In P. Shaver (Ed.) *Review of Personality and Social Psychology*, Vol. 5. Beverly Hills: Sage, pp. 265–284.

Harlow, H. F. (1958). The nature of love. *American Psychologist*, **13**, 673–685.

Harré, R. (1977). Friendship as an accomplishment. In S. W. Duck (Ed.) *Theory and Practice in Interpersonal Attraction*. London: Academic Press.

Harré, R., and Secord, P. F. (1972). *The Explanation of Social Behaviour*. Oxford: Blackwell.

Harrigan, J., and Rosenthal, R. (1986). ???. In P. Blanck, R. Buck and R. Rosenthal (Eds) *Nonverbal Communication in the Clinical Context*. University Park: Pennsylvania State University Press, pp. 36–73.

Harris, L. (1980). Analysis of a paradoxical logic: A case study. *Family Process*, **19**, 19–33.

Harris, L., and Sadeghi, A. (1987). Realizing: How facts are created in human interaction. *Journal of Social and Personal Relationships*, **4**, 480–495.

Harrison, A. A., and Saeed, L. (1977). Let's make a deal: An analysis of revelations and stipulations in lonely hearts advertisements. *Journal of Personality and Social Psychology*, **35**, 257–264.

Harrison, R. P. (1973). Nonverbal communication. In I. S. Pool, W. Schramm, N.

Maccoby, F. Fry, E. Parker and J. L. Fern (Eds) *Handbook of Communication*. Chicago: Rand McNally, pp. 93–115.

Hartmann, H. (1952). The mutual influences in the development of ego and id. *The Psychoanalytic Study of the Child*, **7**, 9–30.

Hartup, W. (1974). Aggression in childhood: Developmental perspectives. *American Psychologist*, **29**, 336–341.

Hartup, W. W. (1975). The origins of friendships. In M. Lewis and L. A. Rosenblum (Eds) *Friendship and Peer Relations*. New York: Wiley.

Hartup, W. W. (1976). Cross-age vs. same-age peer interactions: Ethological and cross-cultural perspectives. In V. Allen (Ed.) *Children Teaching Children: Theory and Research in Tutoring*. Madison: University of Wisconsin Press.

Hartup, W. W. (1979). Levels of analysis in the study of social interaction: An historical perspective. In M. E. Lamb, S. J. Suomi and G. R. Stephenson (Eds) *Social Interaction Analysis: Methodological Issues*. Madison: University of Wisconsin Press, pp. 11–32.

Hartup, W. W. (1983). The peer system. In E. M. Hetherington (Ed.) *Handbook of Child Psychology: Vol. 4. Socialization, Personality, and Social Development*, 4th edn. New York: Wiley, pp. 103–196.

Hartup, W. W. (1984). Commentary: Relationships and child development. In M. Perlmutter (Ed.) *Minnesota Symposia on Child Psychology*, vol. 17. Hillsdale, NJ: Erlbaum.

Hartup, W. W. (1985). Relationships and their significance in cognitive development. In R. A. Hinde, A. N. Perret-Clermont and J. Stevenson-Hinde (Eds) *Social Relationships and Cognitive Development*. New York: Oxford University Press, pp. 66–82.

Hartup, W. W. (1986). On relationships and development. In W. W. Hartup and Z. Rubin (Eds) *Relationships and Development*. Hillsdale, NJ: Erlbaum, pp. 1–26.

Harvey, J. H., Christensen, A., and McClintock, E. (1983). Research methods. In H. H. Kelley, E. Berscheid, A. Christensen, J. H. Harvey, T. L. Huston, G. Levinger, E. McClintock, L. A. Peplau and D. R. Peterson (Eds) *Close Relationships*. New York: W. H. Freeman, pp. 449–485.

Harvey, J. H., Weber, A. L., Galvin, K. S., Huszti, H. C., and Garnick, N. N. (1986). Attribution and the termination of close relationships: A special focus on the account. In R. Gilmour and S. W. Duck (Eds) *The Emerging Field of Personal Relationships*. Hillsdale, NJ: Erlbaum, pp. 189–201.

Harvey, J. H., Weber, A. L., Yarkin, K. L., and Stewart, B. E. (1982). An attributional approach to relationship breakdown and dissolution. In S. W. Duck (Ed.) *Personal Relationships 4: Dissolving Personal Relationships*. London: Academic Press, pp. 107–126.

Harvey, J. H., Wells, G. L., and Alvarez, M. D. (1978). Attribution in the context of conflict and separation in close relationships. In J. H. Harvey, W. Ickes and R. F. Kidd (Eds) *New Directions in Attribution Research*, Vol. 2. Hillsdale, NJ: Erlbaum, pp. 235–260.

Hatfield, E. (1982). Passionate love, companionate love, and intimacy. In M. Fisher and G. Stricker (Eds) *Intimacy*. New York: Plenum, pp. 267–292.

Hatfield, E. (1984). The dangers of intimacy. In V. J. Derlega (Ed.) *Communication, Intimacy, and Close Relationships*. New York: Academic Press, pp. 207–220.

Hatfield, E., and Traupmann, J. (1981). Intimate relationships: A perspective from equity theory. In S. W. Duck and R. Gilmour (Eds) *Personal Relationships 1: Studying Personal Relationships*. London: Academic Press, pp. 165–178.

Hatfield, E., Traupmann, J., Sprecher, S., Utne, M., and Hay, J. (1985). Equity and intimate relations: Recent research. In W. Ickes (Ed.) *Compatible and Uncompatible Relationships*. New York: Springer-Verlag, pp. 91–117.

Hatfield, E., Utne, M. K., and Traupmann, J. (1979). Equity theory and intimate relationships. In R. L. Burgess and T. L. Huston (Eds) *Social Exchange in Developing Relationships*. New York: Academic Press, pp. 93–133.

Hatkoff, S., and Lasswell, T. E. (1979). Male–female similarities and differences in conceptualizing love. In M. Cook and G. Wilson (Eds) *Love and Attraction: An International Conference*. Oxford: Pergamon, pp. 221–227.

Hautzginer, M., Linden, M., and Hoffman, N. (1982). Distressed couples with and without a depressed partner: An analysis of their verbal interaction. *Journal of Behavior Therapy and Experimental Psychiatry*, **13**, 307–314.

Hawes, L. C., and Foley, J. M. (1973). A Markov analysis of interview communication. *Speech Monographs*, **40**, 208–219.

Hawkins, J., Weisberg, C., and Ray, D. (1977). Marital communication style and social class. *Journal of Marriage and the Family*, **39**, 479–490.

Hawkins, J., Weisberg, C., and Ray, D. (1980). Spouse differences in communication style: Preference, perception, behavior. *Journal of Marriage and the Family*, August, 585–593.

Hay, D. F. (1977). Following their companions as a form of exploration for human infants. *Child Development*, **48**, 1624–1632.

Hay, D. F. (1980). Multiple functions of proximity-seeking in infancy. *Child Development*, **51**, 636–645.

Hay, D. F. (1985). Learning to form relationships in infancy: Parallel attainments with parents and peers. *Developmental Review*, **5**, 122–161.

Hay, D. F. (1986). Learning to be social: Some comments on Schaffer's 'The Child's Entry into a Social World'. *Developmental Review*, **6**, 107–114.

Hay, D. F., and Murray, P. (1982). Giving and requesting: Social facilitation of infants' offers to adults. *Infant Behavior and Development*, **5**, 301–310.

Hay, D. F., and Ross, H. S. (1982). The social nature of early conflict. *Child Development*, **53**, 105–113.

Hay, D. F., Murray, P., Cecire, S., and Nash, A. (1985). Social learning of social behavior in early life. *Child Development*, **56**, 43–57.

Hay, D. F., Nash, A., and Pedersen, J. (1981). Responses of six-month-olds to the distress of their peers. *Child Development*, **52**, 1017–1075.

Hay, D. F., Nash, A., and Pedersen, J. (1983). Interaction between six-month-old peers. *Child Development*, **54**, 557–562.

Hay, D. F., Pedersen, J., and Nash, A. (1982). Dyadic interaction in the first year of life. In K. H. Rubin and H. S. Ross (Eds) *Peer Relationships and Social Skills in Childhood*. New York: Springer-Verlag, pp. 11–39.

Hayano, D. M. (1980). Communicative competency among poker players. *Journal of Communication*, **30**, 113–120.

Hayes, S. C., Brownstein, A. J., Haas, J. R., and Greenway, D. E. (1986a). Instructions, multiple schedules, and extinction: Distinguishing rule-governed from schedule-controlled behavior. *Journal of the Experimental Analysis of Behavior*, **46**, 137–147.

Hayes, S. C., Brownstein, A. J., Zettle, R. D., Rosenfarb, I., and Korn, Z. (1986b). Rule-governed behavior and sensitivity to changing consequences of responding. *Journal for the Experimental Analysis of Behavior*, **45**, 237–256.

Hayes-Roth, B., and Hayes-Roth, F. (1979). A cognitive model of planning. *Cognitive Science*, **3**, 275–310.

Haynes, S. N., and Wilson, C. C. (1979). *Behavioral Assessment: Recent Advances in Methods, Concepts, and Applications*. San Francisco: Jossey-Bass.

Hays, R. B. (1984). The development and maintenance of friendship. *Journal of Social and Personal Relationships*, **1**, 75–98.

Hays, R. B. (1985). A longitudinal study of friendship development. *Journal of Personality and Social Psychology*, **48**, 909–924.

Hays, R. B. (1988). The day-to-day functioning of casual versus close friendship. *Journal of Social and Personal Relationships*, **5**.

Hays, R. B., and Oxley, D. (1986). Social network development and functioning during a life transition. *Journal of Personality and Social Psychology*, **50**, 305–313.

Hazan, C., and Shaver, P. (1987). Romantic love conceptualized as an attachment process. *Journal of Personality and Social Psychology*, **52**.

Head, H. (1926). *Aphasia and Kindred Disorders of Speech*. Cambridge, MA: Cambridge University Press.

Heider, F. (1958). *The Psychology of Interpersonal Relations*. New York: Wiley.

Heinicke, C., Diskin, S., Ramsey-Klee, D., and Given, K. (1983). Prebirth parent characteristics and family development in the first year of life. *Child Development*, **54**, 194–208.

Helgeson, V. S., Shaver, P., and Dyer, M. (1987). Prototypes of intimacy and distance in same-sex and opposite-sex relationships. *Journal of Social and Personal Relationships*, **4**, 195–233.

Heller, K. (1979). The effects of social support: Prevention and treatment implications. In A. P. Goldstein and F. H. Kanfer (Eds) *Maximizing Treatment Gains: Transfer Enhancement in Psychotherapy*. Orlando, FL: Academic Press.

Heller, K., and Swindle, R. W. (1983). Social networks, perceived social support, and coping with stress. In R. D. Felner, L. A. Jason, J. N. Mortisugu and S. S. Farber (Eds) *Preventive Psychology: Theory, Research and Practice*. New York: Pergamon, pp. 87–103.

Helmreich, R. L., Spence, J. T., and Gibson, R. H. (1982). Sex-role attitudes: 1972–1980. *Personality and Social Psychology Bulletin*, **8**, 656–663.

Henderson, S., Byrne, D. G., and Duncan-Jones, P. (1981). *Neurosis and the Social Environment*. Sydney: Academic Press.

Henderson, S., Byrne, D. G., Duncan-Jones, P., Scott, R., and Adcock, S. (1980). Social relationships, adversity and neurosis: A study of associations in a general population sample. *British Journal of Psychiatry*, **136**, 354–583.

Hendrick, C., and Hendrick, S. S. (1983). *Liking, Loving, and Relating*. Monterey, CA: Brooks/Cole.

Hendrick, C., and Hendrick, S. S. (1986a). A theory and method of love. *Journal of Personality and Social Psychology*, **50**, 392–402.

Hendrick, C., and Hendrick, S. S. (1986b). Love attitudes and satisfaction in dating couples. Unpublished manuscript.

Hendrick, C., Hendrick, S. S., Foote, F. H., and Slapion-Foote, M. J. (1984). Do men and women love differently? *Journal of Social and Personal Relationships*, **1**, 177–195.

Hendrick, S. S. (1981). Self-disclosure and marital satisfaction. *Journal of Personality and Social Psychology*, **40**, 1150–1159.

Hendrick, S. S., and Hendrick, C. (1987a). Love and sexual attitudes, self-disclosure, and sensation seeking. *Journal of Social and Personal Relationships*, **4**, 281–297.

Hendrick, S. S., and Hendrick, C. (1987b). Multidimensionality of sexual attitudes. *Journal of Sex Research*.

Hendrick, S. S., Hendrick, C., and Adler, N. (1986). Love, disclosure, and sensation seeking: Validation of the love styles. Paper presented at the Annual Convention of the Southwestern Psychological Association, Fort Worth, Texas, April.

Hendrick, S. S., Hendrick, C., Slapion-Foote, M. J., and Foote, F. H. (1985). Gender differences in sexual attitudes. *Journal of Personality and Social Psychology*, **48**, 1630–1642.

Henley, N. M. (1977). *Body Politics: Power, Sex and Nonverbal Communication*. Englewood Cliffs, NJ: Prentice-Hall.

Hersey, J. C., Klibanoff, L. S., Lam, D. J., and Taylor, R. L. (1984). Promoting social support: The impact of California's 'Friends Can Be Good Medicine' campaign. *Health Education Quarterly*, **11**, 293–311.

Hess, B. (1972). Friendship. In M. W. Riley, M. Johnson and A. Foner (Eds) *Aging and Society*, Vol. 3. New York: Russell Sage.

Hetherington, E. M. (1987). Parents, children and siblings six years after divorce. In R. A. Hinde and J. Stevenson-Hinde (Eds) *Relations Between Relationships*. Oxford: Oxford University Press.

Hetherington, E. M., Cox, M., and Cox, R. (1982). Effects of divorce on parents and children. In M. E. Lamb (Ed.) *Nontraditional Families: Parenting and Child Development*. Hillsdale, NJ: Erlbaum, pp. 233–288.

Hewes, D. E. (1975). Finite stochastic modeling of communication processes. *Human Communication Research*, **1**, 271–283.

Hewes, D. E. (1979). The sequential analysis of social interaction. *Quarterly Journal of Speech*, **65**, 56–73.

Hewes, D. E. (1980). Finite stochastic modeling of communication processes. In P. R. Monge and J. N. Cappella (Eds) *Multivariate Techniques in Human Communication Research*. New York: Academic Press, pp. 393–427.

Hewes, D. E., and Planalp, S. (1982). There is nothing as useful as a good theory . . .: The influence of social knowledge on interpersonal communication. In M. E. Roloff and C. R. Berger (Eds) *Social Cognition and Communication*. Beverly Hills: Sage, pp. 107–150.

Hewes, D. E., Graham, M. L., Doelger, J. A., and Pavitt, C. (1985). 'Second-guessing': Message interpretation in social networks. *Human Communication Research*, **11**, 299–334.

Hewes, G. (1957). The anthropology of posture. *Scientific American*, **196**, 123–132.

Hewstone, M., and Jaspars, J. (1984). Social dimensions of attribution: A European perspective. In H. Tajfel (Ed.) *The Social Dimension: European Developments in Social Psychology*. Cambridge/Paris: Cambridge University Press/Maison des Sciences de l'Homme.

Hibbs, D. A. (1974). Problems of statistical estimation and causal inference in time series regression models. In H. L. Costner (Ed.) *Sociological Methodology 1974*. San Francisco: Jossey-Bass, pp. 252–308.

Hill, C. T., Rubin, Z., and Peplau, L. A. (1976). Breakups before marriage: The end of 103 affairs. *Journal of Social Issues*, **32**, 147–168.

Hill, W., and Scanzoni, J. (1982). An approach for assessing marital decision-making processes. *Journal of Marriage and the Family*, **44**, 927–941.

Hilton, D. J., and Slugoski, B. R. (1986). Knowledge-based causal attribution: The abnormal conditions focus model. *Psychological Review*, **93**, 75–88.

Hinchliffe, M., Hooper, D., and Roberts, F. J. (1978). *The Melancholy Marriage*. New York: Wiley.

Hinchliffe, M., Vaughan, P., Hooper, D., and Roberts, F. (1978). The melancholy marriage: An inquiry into the interaction of depressives. III. Responsiveness. *British Journal of Medical Psychology*, **51**, 1–13.

Hinde, R. A. (1976). Interactions, relationships and social structure. *Man*, **11**, 1–17.

Hinde, R. A. (1979). *Towards Understanding Relationships*. London: Academic Press.

Hinde, R. A. (1981). The bases of a science of interpersonal relationships. In S. W. Duck and R. Gilmour (Eds) *Personal Relationships. 1: Studying Personal Relationships*. London: Academic Press, pp. 1–22.

Hinde, R. A. (1982). Attachment: Some conceptual and biological issues. In J. Stevenson-Hinde and C. M. Parkes (Eds) *The Place of Attachment in Human Behavior*. New York: Basic Books, pp. 60–76.

Hinde, R. A. (1984). Why do the sexes behave differently in close relationships? *Journal of Social and Personal Relationships*, **1**, 471–501.

Hinde, R. A. (1987). Continuities and discontinuities: Conceptual issues and methodological considerations. In M. Rutter (Ed.) *Proceedings of the ESF Workshop on Risk and Protective Factors in Psychosocial Development*.

Hinde, R. A., and Stevenson-Hinde, J. (1986). Relating childhood relationships to individual characteristics. In W. W. Hartup and Z. Rubin (Eds) *Relationships and Development*. Hillsdale, NJ: Erlbaum, pp. 27–50.

Hinde, R. A., and Stevenson-Hinde, J. (Eds) (1987). *Relations Between Relationships*. Oxford: Oxford University Press.

Hirsch, B. J. (1979). Psychological dimensions of social networks: A multimethod analysis. *American Journal of Community Psychology*, **7**, 263–277.

Hirsch, B. J. (1980). Natural support systems and coping with major life changes. *American Journal of Community Psychology*, **8**, 159–172.

Hirsch, B. J. (1981). Social networks and the coping process: Creating personal communities. In B. H. Gottlieb (Ed.) *Social Networks and Social Support*. Beverly Hills: Sage, pp. 149–170.

Hobart, C. W. (1958). The incidence of romanticism during courtship. *Social Forces*, **36**, 362–367.

Hobbs, J. R., and Evans, D. A. (1980). Conversation as planned behavior. *Cognitive Science*, **4**, 349–377.

Hobfoll, S. E. (1980a). Personal characteristics of the college volunteer. *American Journal of Community Psychology*, **8**, 503–506.

Hobfoll, S. E. (1980b). Inter-racial commitment and involvement of undergraduate tutors in an inner-city preschool. *Journal of Community Psychology*, **8**, 80–87.

Hobfoll, S. E. (1985a). The limitations of social support in the stress process. In I. G. Sarason and B. R. Sarason (Eds) *Social Support, Theory, Research and Applications*. The Hague: Martinus Nijhoff, pp. 391–414.

Hobfoll, S. E. (1985b). Personal and social resources and the ecology of stress resistance. In P. Shaver (Ed.) *Review of Personality and Social Psychology*, **6**, 265–290. Beverly Hills: Sage.

Hobfoll, S. E. (Ed.) (1986a). *Stress, Social Support, and Women*. Washington, DC: Hemisphere.

Hobfoll, S. E. (1986b). The ecology of stress and social support among women. In S. E. Hobfoll (Ed.) *Stress, Social Support, and Women*. Washington, DC: Hemisphere, pp. 3–14.

Hobfoll, S. E. (1988). *The Ecology of Stress Resistence*. Washington, DC: Hemisphere.

Hobfoll, S. E., and Lerman, M. (1986). Predicting receipt of social support: A longitudinal study of parents' reactions to their child's illness. Unpublished manuscript, Tel Aviv University.

Hobfoll, S. E., and Lieberman, Y. (1987). Personality and social resources in immediate and continued stress resistance among women. *Journal of Social Psychology*, **52**, 18–26.

Hobfoll, S. E., and London, P. (1986). The relationship of self-concept and social support to emotional distress among women during war. *Journal of Social and Clinical Psychology*, **4**, 189–203.

Hobfoll, S. E., and Walfisch, S. (1984). Coping with a threat to life: A longitudinal study of self concept, social support, and psychological distress. *American Journal of Community Psychology*, **12**, 87–100.

Hobfoll, S. E., Nadler, A., and Leiberman, Y. (1986). Satisfaction with social support during crisis: Intimacy and self-esteem as critical determinants. *Journal of Personality and Social Psychology*, **52**, 296–304.

Hochschild, A. R. (1979). Emotion work, feeling rules, and social structure. *American Journal of Sociology*, **85**, 551–575.

Hochschild, A. R. (1983). *The Managed Heart*. Berkley: University of California Press.

Hodges, J., and Tizard, B. (1987a). IQ and behavioral adjustment of ex-institutionalized adolescents. *Journal of Child Psychology and Psychiatry*.

Hodges, J. and Tizard, B. (1987b). Social and family relationships of ex-institutional adolescents. *Journal of Child Psychology and Psychiatry*, in press.

Hoffman, C., Lau, I., and Johnson, D. R. (1986). *Journal of Personality and Social Psychology*, **51**, 1097–1105.

Hoffman, M. L. (1963). Childrearing practices and moral development: Generalizations from empirical research. *Child Development*, **34**, 295–318.

Hoffman, M. L. (1976). Empathy, role taking, guilt, and development of altruistic motives. In T. Lickona (Ed.) *Moral Development and Behavior*. New York: Holt, Rinehart, & Winston.

Hoffman, M. L. (1981). Is altruism part of human nature? *Journal of Personality and Social Psychology*, **40**, 121–137.

Hogan, R. (1982). A socioanalytic theory of personality. In M. Page (Ed.) *Nebraska Symposium on Motivation*. Lincoln, NE: University of Nebraska Press, pp. 58–89.

Hogan, R., Jones, W. H., and Cheek, J. M. (1985). Socioanalytic theory: An alternative to armadillo psychology. In B. Schlenker (Ed.) *Self and Identity: Presentations of Self in Social Life*. New York: McGraw-Hill, pp. 175–198.

Hogarth, R. (1980). *Judgement and Choice: The Psychology of Decision*. New York: Wiley.

Holdaway, S. (1980). The police station. *Urban Life*, **9**, 79–100.

Holland, P. W., and Leinhardt, S. (1979). *Perspectives on Social Network Research*. New York: Academic Press.

Holmes, J. G. (1981). The exchange process in close relationships. In M. J. Lerner and S. C. Lerner (Eds) *The Justice Motive in Social Behavior*. New York: Plenum.

Holohan, C. J., Wilcox, B. L., Burnam, M. A., and Culler, R. E. (1978). Social satisfaction and friendship formation as a function of floor level in high-rise student housing. *Journal of Applied Psychology*, **63**, 529–531.

Holtzworth-Monroe, A., and Jacobson, N. S. (1985). Causal attributions of married couples: When do they search for causes? What do they conclude when they do? *Journal of Personality and Social Psychology*, **48**, 1398–1412.

Homans, G. (1958). Social behavior as exchange. *American Journal of Sociology*, **63** (May), 597–606.

Homans, G. (1961). *Social Behavior: Its Elementary Forms*. New York: Harcourt, Brace and World.

Honeycutt, J. (1986). A model of marital functioning based on an attraction paradigm and social-penetration dimensions. *Journal of Marriage and the Family*, **48**, 651–667.

Honeycutt, J., Wilson, C., and Parker, C. (1982). Effects of sex and degrees of happiness on perceived styles of communication in and out of the marital relationship. *Journal of Marriage and the Family*, **44** (2), 395–406.

Hooley, J. M. (1985). Expressed emotion: A review of the critical literature. *Clinical Psychology Review*, **5**, 119–139.

Hooley, J. M. (1986). Expressed emotion and depression: Interactions between patients and high- versus low- expressed-emotion spouses. *Journal of Abnormal Psychology*, **95**, 237–246.

Hooley, J. M. (1987). The nature and origins of expressed emotion. In K. Hahlweg and M. J. Goldstein (Eds) *Understanding Major Mental Disorder: The Contribution of Family Interaction Research*. New York: Family Process Press.

Hooley, J. M., and Hahlweg, K. (1986). Interaction patterns of depressed patients and their spouses: Comparing high and low EE dyads. In M. J. Goldstein, I. Hand and K. Hahlweg (Eds) *Treatment of Schizophrenia: Family Assessment and Intervention*. Heidelberg: Springer.

Hooley, J. M., Orley, J., and Teasdale, J. D. (1986). Levels of expressed emotion and relapse in depressed patients. *British Journal of Psychiatry*, **148**, 642–647.

Hooley, J. M., Richters, J. E., Weintraub, S., and Neale, J. M. (1987). Psychopathology and marital distress: The positive side of positive symptoms. *Journal of Abnormal Psychology*, **96**, 27–33.

Hoover, C. F., and Fitzgerald, R. G. (1981). Marital conflict of manic-depressive patients. *Archives of General Psychiatry*, **38**, 65–67.

Hopper, R., Knapp, M. L., and Scott, L. (1981). Couples' personal idioms: Exploring intimate talk. *Journal of Communication*, **31**, 23–33.

Hops, H., and Greenwood, C. R. (1981). Social skills deficits. In E. J. Mash and L. G. Terdal (Eds) *Behavioral Assessment of Childhood Disorders*. New York: Guilford.

Hops, H., Wills, T., Patterson, G. R., and Weiss, R. L. (1972). Marital interaction coding system (MICS). University of Oregon and Oregon Research Institute (NAPS Document No. 02077). Eugene, Oregon.

Hornstein, G. A. (1985). Intimacy in conversational style as a function of the degree of closeness between members of a dyad. *Journal of Personality and Social Psychology*, **49**, 671–681.

Horowitz, L. M. (1983). The toll of loneliness: Manifestations, mechanisms and means of prevention. Prepared for the National Institute of Mental Health, Office of Prevention.

Horowitz, L. M., French, R. S., and Anderson, C. A. (1982). The prototype of a lonely person. In L. A. Peplau and D. Perlman (Eds) *Loneliness: A Sourcebook of Current Theory, Research and Therapy*. New York: Wiley, pp. 183–205.

Horowitz, L. M., French, R. S., Lapid, J. J., and Weckler, D. A. (1982). Symptoms and interpersonal problems: The prototype as an integrating concept. In J. C. Anchin and D. J. Kiesler (Eds) *Handbook of Interpersonal Psychotherapy*. New York: Pergamon, pp. 168–189.

House, J. S. (1981). *Work Stress and Social Support*. Reading, MA: Addison-Wesley.

House, J. S., and Kahn, R. L. (1985). Measures and concepts of social support. In S. Cohen and S. L. Syme (Eds) *Social Support and Health*. Orlando, FL: Academic Press, pp. 83–108.

Hovland, C. I. (1959). Reconciling conflicting results derived from experimental and survey studies of attitude change. *American Psychologist*, **14**, 8–17.

Howard, J. A., Blumstein, P., and Schwartz, P. (1986). Sex, power, and influence tactics in intimate relationships. *Journal of Personality and Social Psychology*, **51**, 102–109.

Howe, N. (1986). Socialization, social cognitive factors and the development of the sibling relationship. Unpublished doctoral dissertation, University of Waterloo.

Howes, M. J., and Hokanson, J. E. (1979). Conversational and social responses to depressive interpersonal behavior. *Journal of Abnormal Psychology*, **88**, 625–634.

Hrdy, S. B. (1980). *The Langurs of Abu*. Cambridge: Harvard University Press.

Hubbard, R. (1987). Relationship styles in popular romance novels, 1950 to 1983. *Communication Quarterly*, **33**, 113–125.

Huesmann, L. R., and Levinger, G. (1976). Incremental exchange theory: A formal model for progression in dyadic social interaction. In L. Berkowitz and E. Walster (Eds) *Advances in Experimental Social Psychology*. New York: Academic Press, pp. 193–229.

Hunt, M. (1974). *Sexual Behavior in the 1970s*. Chicago: Playboy Press.

Hunter, J. E., and Boster, F. J. (1979). Situational differences in the selection of compliance-gaining messages. Paper presented at the annual meeting of the Speech Communication Association, San Antonio, Texas.

Hunter, J. E., and Boster, F. J. (1987). A model of compliance-gaining message selection. *Communication Monographs*, **54**, 63–84.

Hupka, R. B. (1981). Cultural determinants of jealousy. *Alternative Lifestyles*, **4**, 310–356.

Husaini, B. A., Neff, J. A., Newbrough, J. R., and Moore, M. C. (1982). The stress-buffering role of social support and personal competence among the rural married. *Journal of Community Psychology*, **10**, 409–425.

Huston, T. L., and Burgess, R. (1979). Social exchange in developing relationships: An overview. In R. Burgess and T. L. Huston (Eds) *Social Exchange in Developing Relationships*. New York: Academic Press, pp. 3–28.

Huston, T. L., and Cate, R. M. (1979). Social exchange in intimate relationships. In M. Cook and G. Wilson (Eds) *Love and Attraction*. London: Pergamon, pp. 263–269.

Huston, T. L., and Levinger, G. (1978). Interpersonal attraction and relationships. In M. R. Rosenzweig and L. W. Porter (Eds) *Annual Review of Psychology*. Palo Alto: Annual Reviews, pp. 115–156.

Huston, T. L., and Robins, E. (1982). Conceptual and methodological issues in studying close relationships. *Journal of Marriage and the Family*, **44**, 901–925.

Huston, T. L., McHale, S., and Crouter, A. (1986). When the honeymoon's over: Changes in the marriage relationship over the first year. In R. Gilmour and S. W.

Duck (Eds) *The Emerging Field of Personal Relationships*. Hillsdale, NJ: Erlbaum, pp. 109–132.

Huston, T. L., Surra, C. A., Fitzgerald, N. M., and Cate, R. M. (1981). From courtship to marriage: Mate selection as an interpersonal process. In S. W. Duck and R. Gilmour (Eds) *Personal Relationships 2: Developing Personal Relationships*. New York: Academic Press, pp. 53–88.

Hutt, S. J., and Hutt, C. (1970). *Direct Observations and Measurement of Behavior*. Springfield, IL: Charles C. Thomas.

Hymel, S. (1986). Interpretations of peer behavior: Affective bias in childhood and adolescence. *Child Development*, **57**, 431–445.

Hymel, S., Wagner, E., and Butler, L. J. (1987). Reputational bias: View from the peer group. In S. R. Asher and J. D. Coie (Eds) *Peer Rejection in Children: Origins, Consequences, and Intervention*. Cambridge, MA: Cambridge University Press.

Ickes, W. (1981). Sex-role influences in dyadic interaction: A theoretical model. In C. Mayo and N. Hanley (Eds) *Gender and Nonverbal Behavior*. New York: Springer-Verlag, pp. 95–128.

Ickes, W. (1982). A basic paradigm for the study of personality, roles, and social behavior. In W. Ickes and E. S. Knowles (Eds) *Personality, Roles, and Social Behavior*. New York: Springer-Verlag.

Ickes, W. (1983). A basic paradigm for the study of unstructured dyadic interaction. In H. Reis (Ed.) *New Directions for Methodology of Social and Behavioral Science*. San Francisco: Jossey-Bass.

Ickes, W. (1984). Compositions in black and white: Determinants of interaction in interracial dyads. *Journal of Personality and Social Psychology*, **47**, 330–341.

Ickes, W. (1985). Sex-role influences on compatibility in relationships. In W. Ickes (Ed.) *Compatible and Incompatible Relationships*. New York: Springer-Verlag, pp. 187–208.

Ickes, W., and Barnes, R. D. (1977). The role of sex and self-monitoring in unstructured dyadic interactions. *Journal of Personality and Social Psychology*, **35**, 315–330.

Ickes, W., and Barnes, R. D. (1978). Boys and girls together—and alienated: On enacting stereotyped sex roles in mixed-sex dyads. *Journal of Personality and Social Psychology*, **36**, 669–683.

Ickes, W., and Teng, G. (1987). Refinement and validation of Brickman's measure of internal–external correspondence. *Journal of Research in Personality*,

Ickes, W., and Trued, S. (1985). A system for collecting dyadic interaction data on the Apple II computer. *Electronic Social Psychology*, Article No. 8501012, **1**, 1–13.

Ickes, W., and Turner, M. (1983). On the social advantages of having an older, opposite-sex sibling: Birth-order influences in mixed-sex dyads. *Journal of Personality and Social Psychology*, **45**, 210–222.

Ickes, W., Patterson, M. L., Rajecki, D. W., and Tanford, S. (1982). Behavioral and cognitive consequences of reciprocal versus compensatory responses to pre-interaction expectancies. *Social Cognition*, **1**, 160–190.

Ickes, W., Reidhead, S., and Patterson, M. L. (1986). Machiavellianism and self-monitoring: As different as 'me' and 'you'. *Social Cognition*, **4**, 58–74.

Ickes, W., Robertson, E., Tooke, W., and Teng, G. (1986). Naturalistic social cognition: Methodology, assessment, and validation. *Journal of Personality and Social Psychology*, **51**, 66–82.

Ickes, W., Schermer, B., and Steeno, J. (1979). Sex and sex-role influences in same-sex dyads. *Social Psychology Quarterly*, **42**, 373–385.

Ickes, W., Tooke, W., Baker, V. L., and Teng, G. (1987). Intersubjectivity in initial, unstructured dyadic interactions. Manuscript in preparation, University of Texas at Arlington.

Ilfeld, F. W. (1977). Current social stressors and symptoms of depression. *American Journal of Psychiatry*, **134**, 161–166.

Infante, D. A., and Rancer, A. S. (1982). A conceptualization and measure of argumentativeness. *Journal of Personality Assessment*, **46**, 72–80.

Ipsa, J. (1981). Peer support among Soviet day care toddlers. *International Journal of Behavioral Development*, **4**, 255–269.

Irwin, D. M., and Bushnell, M. M. (1980). *Observational Strategies for Child Study*. New York: Holt, Rinehart, & Winston.

Izard, C. E. (1977). *Human Emotions*. New York: Plenum.

Jablin, F. M., and Krone, K. J. (1987). Organizational assimilation and levels of analysis in organizational communication research. In C. R. Berger and S. H. Chaffee (Eds) *Handbook of Communication Science*. Newbury Park, CA: Sage.

Jaccard, J. J. (1974). Predicting social behavior from personality traits. *Journal of Research in Personality*, **7**, 358–367.

Jackson, D. (1965a). Family rules: Marital *quid pro quo*. *Archives of General Psychiatry*, **12**, 589–594.

Jackson, D. (1965b). The study of family. *Family Process*, **4**, 1–20.

Jackson, D. N. (1967). *Personality Research Form Manual*. Goshen, NY: Research Psychologists Press.

Jackson, R. M. (1977). Social structure and process in friendship choice. In C. S. Fischer (Ed.) *Networks and Places*. New York: Free Press.

Jackson, R. M., Fischer, C. S., and Jones, L. M. (1977). The dimensions of social networks. In C. S. Fischer (Ed.) *Networks and Places*. New York: Free Press.

Jackson, S., and Backus, D. (1982). Are compliance-gaining strategies dependent on situational variables? *Central States Speech Journal*, **33**, 469–479.

Jacobs, J. B. (1974). Participant observation in prison. *Urban Life Culture*, **3**, 221–240.

Jacobson, D. E. (1986). Types and timing of social support. *Journal of Health and Social Behavior*, **27**, 250–264.

Jacobson, J. L. (1981). The role of inanimate objects in early peer interaction. *Child Development*, **52**, 618–626.

Jacobson, J. L., and Wille, D. E. (1986). The influence of attachment pattern on developmental changes in peer interaction from the toddler to the preschool period. *Child Development*, **57**, 338–347.

Jacobson, J. L., Wille, D. E., Tianen, R. L., and Aytch, D. M. (1983). The influence of infant–mother attachment on toddler sociability with peers. Paper presented to the Society for Research in Child Development, Detroit.

Jacobson, N. S., and Margolin, G. (1979). *Marital Therapy*. New York: Brunner/Mazel.

Jacobson, N. S., and Moore, D. (1981). Spouses as observers of the events in their relationship. *Journal of Consulting and Clinical Psychology*, **49**, 269–277.

Jacobson, N. S., Follette, W. C., and Elwood, R. W. (1984). Outcome research on behavioral marital therapy: A methodological and conceptual reappraisal. In K. Hahlweg and N. Jacobson (Eds) *Marital Interaction: Analysis and Modification*. New York: Guilford, pp. 113–129.

Jacobson, N. S., Follette, W. C., and McDonald, D. W. (1982). Reactivity to positive and negative behavior in distressed and nondistressed married couples. *Journal of Consulting and Clinical Psychology*, **50**, 706–714.

Jacobson, N. S., McDonald, D. W., Follette, W. C., and Berley, R. A. (1985). Attributional process in distressed and nondistressed couples. *Cognitive Therapy and Research*, **9**, 35–50.

Jacobson, N. S., Waldron, H., and Moore, D. (1980). Toward a behavioral profile of marital distress. *Journal of Consulting and Clinical Psychology*, **48**, 697–703.

Jacobson, R. H., and Anderson, E. (1982). Interpersonal skills deficits and depression in college students: A sequential analysis of the timing of self-disclosure. *Behavior Therapy*, **13**, 271–282.

Jaffe, J., and Feldstein, S. (1970). *Rhythms in Dialogue*. New York: Academic Press.

Jamuna, D., and Ramamurti, P. (1984). Age, adjustment and husband–wife communication of middle aged and old women. *Journal of Psychology Researches*, **28** (3), 145–147.

Janis, I. L. (1972). *Victims of Groupthink*. Boston: Houghton Mifflin.

Janis, I. L. (1983). The role of social support in adherence to stressful decisions. *American Psychologist*, **38**, 143–160.

Jarrett, R., and Nelson, R. (1984). Reactivity and unreliability of husbands as participant observers. *Journal of Behavioral Assessment*, **6** (2), 131–145.

Jason, L. A. (1985). Using the media to foster self-help groups. *Professional Psychology*, **16**, 455–464.

Jassem, W., and Demenko, G. (1985). Extracting linguistic information from FO traces. In C. Johns-Lewis (Ed.) *Intonation in Discourse*. San Diego: College-Hill Press.

Joanning, H. (1982). The long-term effects of the Couple Communication Program. *Journal of Marital and Family Therapy*, October, 463–468.

Johnson, M. H., and Magaro, P. A. (1987). Effects of mood and severity of memory processes in depression and mania. *Psychological Bulletin*, **101**, 28–40.

Johnson, M. P. (1973). Commitment: A conceptual structure and empirical application. *Sociological Quarterly*, **4**, 359–406.

Johnson, M. P. (1982). Social and cognitive features of the dissolution of commitment to relationships. In S. W. Duck (Ed.) *Personal Relationships 4: Dissolving Personal Relationships*. London: Academic Press, pp. 51–74.

Johnson, M. P. (1985). Commitment, cohesion, investment, barriers, alternatives, constraint: Why do people stay together when they really don't want to? Paper presented at the Theory Construction and Research Methodology Workshop, National Council on Family Relations Annual Meeting, Dallas, Texas.

Johnson, M. P., and Leslie, L. (1982). Couple involvement and network structure: A test of the dyadic withdrawal hypothesis. *Social Psychology Quarterly*, **45**, 33–43.

Jones, E. E. (1964). *Ingratiation*. New York: Appleton-Century-Crofts.

Jones, E. E., and Davis, K. E. (1965). From acts to dispositions: The attribution process in person perception. In L. Berkowitz (Ed.) *Advances in Experimental Social Psychology*, Vol. 2. New York: Academic Press, pp. 219–266.

Jones, E. E., and Wortman, C. B. (1973). *Ingratiation: An Attributional Approach*. Morristown, NJ: General Learning Press.

Jones, R. R., Reid, J. B., and Patterson, G. R. (1975). Naturalistic observations in clinical assessment. In P. McReynolds (Ed.) *Advances in Psychological Assessment*, Vol. 3. San Francisco: Jossey-Bass.

Jones, S. E., and Yarbrough, A. E. (1985). A naturalistic study of the meanings of touch. *Communication Monographs*, **52**, 19–56.

Jones, W. H. (1981). Loneliness and social contact. *Journal of Social Psychology*, **113**, 295–296.

Jones, W. H. (1982). Loneliness and social behavior. In L. A. Peplau and D. Perlman (Eds) *Loneliness: A Sourcebook of Theory, Research and Therapy*. New York: Wiley, pp. 238–252.

Jones, W. H. (1985). The psychology of loneliness: Some personality issues in the study of social support. In I. G. Sarason and B. R. Sarason (Eds) *Social Support: Theory, Research and Application*. The Hague: Martinus Nijhoff, pp. 225–241.

Jones, W. H., and Carpenter, B. N. (1986). Shyness, social behavior, and relationships. In W. H. Jones, J. M. Cheek and S. R. Briggs (Eds) *Shyness: Perspectives on Research and Treatment*. New York: Plenum, pp. 227–238.

Jones, W. H., and Perlman, D. (1987). *Advances in Personal Relationships*, Vol. 1. New York: JAI Press.

Jones, W. H., and Russell, D. (1982). The social reticence scale: An objective measure of shyness. *Journal of Personality Assessment*, **46**, 629–631.

Jones, W. H., Briggs, S. R., and Smith, T. G. (1986). Shyness: Conceptualization and measurement. *Journal of Personality Assessment*, **46**, 629–631.

Jones, W. H., Cavert, C. W., Snider, R. C., and Bruce, T. (1985). Relational stress: An analysis of situations and events associated with loneliness. In S. W. Duck and D. Perlman (Eds) *Understanding Personal Relationships: An Interdisciplinary Approach*. London: Sage, pp. 221–242.

Jones, W. H., Cheek, J. M., and Briggs, S. R. (Eds) (1986). *Shyness: Perspectives on Research and Treatment*. New York: Plenum.

Jones, W. H., Freemon, J. R., and Goswick, R. A. (1981). The persistence of loneliness: Self and other determinants. *Journal of Personality*, **49**, 27–48.

Jones, W. H., Hansson, R. O., and Cutrona, C. E. (1984). Helping the lonely: Issues of intervention with young and older adults. In S. W. Duck (Ed.) *Personal Relationships 5: Repairing Personal Relationships*. London: Academic Press.

Jones, W. H., Hobbs, S. A., and Hockenbury, D. (1982). Loneliness and social skill deficits. *Journal of Personality and Social Psychology*, **42**, 682–689.

Jöreskog, K. G., and Sörbom, D. (1986). *LISREL VI*. Mooresville, IN: Scientific Software.

Jourard, S. M. (1964). *The Transparent Self*. New York: Van Nostrand.

Jourard, S. M. (1971). *Self-Disclosure: An Experimental Analysis of the Transparent Self*. New York: Wiley.

Jourard, S. M., and Lasakow, P. (1958). Some factors in self-disclosure. *Journal of Abnormal and Social Psychology*, **56**, 91–98.

Jung, C. G. (1961). *Memories, Dreams, Reflections*. New York: Vintage.

Jurich, A. P., and Jurich, J. A. (1974). The effect of cognitive moral development upon the selection of premarital sexual standards. *Journal of Marriage and the Family*, **36**, 736–741.

Kagan, J. (1969). The three faces of continuity in human development. In D. A. Goslin (Ed.) *Handbook of Socialization Theory and Research*. Chicago: Rand McNally.

Kagan, J., and Reznick, J. S. (1986). Shyness and temperament. In W. H. Jones, J. M. Cheek and S. R. Briggs (Eds) *Shyness: Perspectives on Research and Treatment*. New York: Plenim, pp. 81–90.

Kahn, E. (1985). Heinz Kohut and Carl Rogers: A timely comparison. *American Psychologist*, **40**, 893–904.

Kahn, J., Coyne, J. C., and Margolin, G. (1985). Depression and marital disagreement: The social construction of despair. *Journal of Social and Personal Relationships*, **2**, 447–461.

Kahn, M. (1970). Nonverbal communication and marital satisfaction. *Family Process*, **9**, 449–456.

Kahn, R. L., and Antonucci, T. C. (1981). Convoys of social support: A life-course approach. In J. G. March, S. B. Kiesler, J. N. Morgan and N. K. Oppenheimer (Eds) *Aging, Social Change*. New York: Academic Press.

Kahneman, D., and Tversky, A. (1973). On the psychology of prediction. *Psychological Review*, **80**, 237–251.

Kahneman, D., Slovic, P., and Tversky, A. (1982). *Judgment under Uncertainty: Heuristics and Biases*. Cambridge: Cambridge University Press.

Kalter, N., Pickar, J., and Lesowitz, M. (1984). School-based developmental facilitation groups for children of divorce: A preventive intervention. *American Journal of Orthopsychiatry*, **54**, 613–623.

Kaminski, E. P., McDermott, S. T., and Boster, F. J. (1977). The use of compliance-gaining strategies as a function of Machiavellianism and situation. Paper presented at the annual meeting of the Central States Speech Association, Southfield, MI.

Kandel, D. B. (1978). Similarity in real-life adolescent friendship pairs. *Journal of Personality and Social Psychology*, **36**, 306–312.

Kanouse, D. E. (1971). *Language, labeling, and attribution*. Morristown, NJ: General Learning Press.

Kanter, R. M. (1977). Some effects of proportions in group life: Skewed sex ratios and response to token women. *American Journal of Sociology*, **2**, 965–990.

Kantor, D., and Lehr, W. (1975). *Inside the Family*. San Francisco: Jossey-Bass.

Karlsruher, A. E. (1974). The nonprofessional as a psychotherapeutic agent: A review of the empirical evidence pertaining to his effectiveness. *American Journal of Community Psychology*, **2**, 61–77.

Katriel, T., and Philipsen, G. (1981). 'What we need is communication': 'Communication' as a cultural category in some American speech. *Communication Monographs*, **48**, 301–317.

Katz, A. H. (1981). Self-help and mutual aid: An emerging social movement? *Annual Review of Sociology*, **7**, 129–155.

Katz, D., and Kahn, R. L. (1978). *The Social Psychology of Organizations*, 2nd edn. New York: Wiley.

Kaufman, J., and Zigler, E. (1986). Do abused children become abusive parents? Unpublished MS: Yale Univ.

Kawamura, S. (1963). The process of sub-culture propagation among Japanese macaques. In C. H. Southwick (Ed.) *Primate Social Behavior*. Princeton: Van Nostrand.

Kaye, K., and Furstenberg, F. F. (Eds) (1985). *Child Development*, **55**, 279–501.

Kegan, R. (1982). *The Evolving Self: Problem and Process in Human Development*. Cambridge, MA: Harvard University Press.

Keller, B. B., and Bell, R. Q. (1979). Child effects on adult's method of eliciting altruistic behavior. *Child Development*, **50**, 1004–1009.

Kellermann, K. (1984a). The negativity effect and its implication for initial interaction. *Communication Monographs*, **51**, 37–55.

Kellermann, K. A. (1984b). A formal model of information exchange in initial interaction. Unpublished dissertation, Department of Communication Studies, Northwestern University, Evanston, Illinois.

Kellermann, K. A., and Berger, C. R. (1984). Affect and the acquisition of social information: Sit back, relax, and tell me about yourself. In R. N. Bostrom (Ed.) *Communication Yearbook 8*. Beverly Hills: Sage, pp. 412–445.

Kelley, H. H. (1967). Attribution theory in social psychology. In D. Levine (Ed.) *Nebraska Symposium on Motivation*, Vol. 15. Lincoln, NB: University of Nebraska Press, pp. 192–238.

Kelley, H. H. (1971). *Attribution in Social Interaction*. Morristown, NJ: General Learning Press.

Kelley, H. H. (1979). *Personal Relationships: Their Structures and Processes*. Hillsdale, NJ: Erlbaum.

Kelley, H. H. (1983). Love and commitment. In H. H. Kelley, E. Berscheid, A. Christensen, J. H. Harvey, T. L. Huston, G. Levinger, E. McClintock, L. A. Peplau and D. R. Peterson (Eds) *Close Relationships*. New York: Freeman, pp. 265–314.

Kelley, H. H. (1984). Affect in interpersonal relations. In P. Shaver (Ed.) *Review of Personality and Social Psychology*, Vol. 5. Beverly Hills: Sage, pp. 89–115.

Kelley, H. H., *et al.* (1983). *Close Relationships*. San Francisco: Freeman.

Kelley, H. H., *et al.* (1971). *Attribution in Social Interaction*. Morristown, NJ: General Learning Press.

Kelly, C., Huston, T. L., and Cate, R. M. (1985). Premarital relationship correlates of the erosion of satisfaction in marriage. *Journal of Social and Personal Relationships*, **2**, 167–178.

Kelly, G. A. (1955). *The Psychology of Personal Constructs*. New York: Norton.

Kelvin, P. (1977). Predictability, power and vulnerability in interpersonal attraction. In S. W. Duck (Ed.) *Theory and Practice in Interpersonal Attraction*. London: Academic Press, pp. 355–378.

Kendon, A. (1967). Some functions of gaze-direction in social interaction. *Acta Psychologica*, **26**, 22–63.

Kendon, A. (1982). The organization of behavior in face-to-face interaction: Observations on the development of a methodology. In K. R. Scherer and P. Ekman (Eds) *Handbook of Methods in Nonverbal Behavior Research*. Cambridge: Cambridge University Press, pp. 440–505.

Kendrick, C., and Dunn, J. (1983). Protest or pleasure? The response of firstborn children to interaction between their mothers and infant siblings. *Journal of Child Psychology and Psychiatry*, **23**, 117–129.

Kenny, D. A. (1985). The generalized group effect model. In J. Nesselroade and A. von Eye (Eds) *Individual Development and Social Change: Explanatory Analyses.* Orlando, FL: Academic Press.

Kenny, D. A. (1986a). Measuring interpersonal processes: Characteristics of dyads and groups. In W. D. Crano and M. B. Brewer (Eds) *Principles and Methods of Social Research*. Boston: Allyn & Bacon.

Kenny, D. A. (1986b). SOREMO: A FORTRAN program for multivariate round robin data sets. Unpublished paper, University of Connecticut.

Kenny, D. A. (1986c). BLOCKO: A FORTRAN program for multivariate block designs. Unpublished paper, University of Connecticut.

Kenny, D. A. (1987). *Statistics for the Social and Behavioral Sciences*. Boston: Little, Brown and Co.

Kenny, D. A. (1988a). Person perception: A social relations analysis. *Journal of Social and Personal Relationships*, **5**, 220–248.

Kenny, D. A. (1988b). What makes a relationship special? In T. Draper (Ed.) *Family Variables: Conceptualization, Measurement and Use*. Beverly Hills: Sage.

Kenny, D. A., and Acitelli, L. K. (1987). How marital pairs view their relationships: A round robin analysis. Unpublished paper, University of Connecticut.

Kenny, D. A., and Albright, L. (1987). Accuracy in interpersonal perception: A social relations analysis. *Psychological Bulletin*, **102**, 390–402.

Kenny, D. A., and Harackiewicz, J. M. (1979). Cross-lagged panel correlation: Practice and promise. *Journal of Applied Psychology*, **64**, 372–379.

Kenny, D. A., and Judd, C. M. (1986). The consequences of violating the independence assumption in analysis of variance. *Psychological Bulletin*, **99**, 422–431.

Kenny, D. A., and LaVoie, L. (1982). Reciprocity of attraction: A confirmed hypothesis. *Social Psychology Quarterly*, **45**, 54–58.

Kenny, D. A., and LaVoie, L. (1984). The social relations model. In L. Berkowitz (Ed.) *Advances in Experimental Social Psychology*, Vol. 18. New York: Academic Press, pp. 141–182.

Kenny, D. A., and LaVoie, L. (1985). Separating individual and group effects. *Journal of Personality and Social Psychology*, **48**, 339–348.

Kenny, D. A., and Nasby, W. (1980). Splitting the reciprocity correlation. *Journal of Personality and Social Psychology*, **38**, 249–256.

Kenny, D. A., and Stigler, J. (1983). LEVEL: A FORTRAN program correlational analysis of group-individual data. *Behavior Research Methods and Instrumentation*, **15**, 606.

Kenrick, D. T. (1987). Gender, genes, and the social environment: A biosocial interactionist perspective. In P. Shaver and C. Hendrick (Eds) *Review of Personality and Social Psychology: Vol. 7. Sex and Gender*. Beverly Hills: Sage.

Kerckhoff, A. C. (1974). The social context of interpersonal attraction. In T. L. Huston (Ed.) *Foundations of Interpersonal Attraction*. New York: Academic Press.

Kerckhoff, A. C., and Davis, K. E. (1962). Value consensus and need complementarity in mate selection. *American Sociological Review*, **27**, 295–303.

Kessler, A. C., and McLeod, J. D. (1984). Sex differences in vulnerability to undesirable life events. *American Sociological Review*, **49**, 620–631.

Kessler, R. C., McLeod, J. D., and Wethington, E. (1985). The costs of caring: A perspective on the relationship between sex and psychological distress. In I. G. Sarason and B. R. Sarason (Eds) *Social Support: Theory, Research and Application*. The Hague: Martinus Nijhoff, pp. 491–506.

Kessler, S. J., and McKenna, W. (1978). *Gender: An Ethnomethodological Aporoach*. New York: Pergamon.

Kidd, V. (1975). Happily ever after and other relationships styles: Advice on interpersonal relations in popular magazines, 1951–1972. *Quarterly Journal of Speech*, **61**, 31–39.

Kimberly, J. R. (1980). The life cycle analogy and the study of organizations: Introduction. In J. Kimberly and R. Miles (Eds) *The Organizational Life Cycle*. San Francisco: Jossey-Bass.

Kimberly, J. R., and Miles, R. H. (Eds) (1980). *The Organizational Life Cycle: Issues in the Creation, Transformation, and Decline of Organizations*. San Francisco: Jossey-Bass.

King, A. P., and West, M. J. (1983). Epigenesis of cowbird song—A joint endeavour of males and females. *Nature*, **305**, 704–706.

King, C. E., and Christensen, A. (1983). The Relationship Events Scale: A Guttman scaling of progress in courtship. *Journal of Marriage and the Family*, **45**, 671–678.

King, D. A., and Heller, K. (1984). Depression and the response of others: A re-evaluation. *Journal of Abnormal Psychology*, **94**, 477–480.

King, K., Balswick, J. O., and Robinson, I. E. (1977). The continuing premarital sexual revolution among college females. *Journal of Marriage and the Family*, **39**, 455–459.

Kinsey, A. C., Pomeroy, W. B., and Martin, C. E. (1948). *Sexual Behavior in the Human Male*. Philadelphia: Saunders.

Klein, M. *The Psychoanalysis of Children*. London: Hogarth.

Kleinke, C. L. (1977). Compliance to requests made by gazing and touching experimenters in field settings. *Journal of Experimental Social Psychology*, **13**, 218–223.

Kleinke, C. L. (1980). Interaction between gaze and legitimacy of request on compliance in a field setting. *Journal of Nonverbal Behavior*, **5**, 3–12.

Kleinke, C. L., Meeker, F. B., and LaFong, C. (1974). Effects of gaze, touch, and use of name on evaluation of 'engaged' couples. *Journal of Research in Personality*, **7**, 368–373.

Klinger, E. (1977). *Meaning and Void: Inner Experience and the Incentives in People's Lives*. Minneapolis: University of Minnesota Press.

Klinnert, M. D., Campos, J. J., Sorce, J. F., Emde, R. N., and Svejda, M. (1983). Emotions as behavior regulators: Social referencing in infancy. In R. Plutchick and H. Kellerman (Eds) *Emotions in Early Development: Vol. 2. The Emotions*. New York: Academic Press.

Klinnert, M. D., Emde, R. N., Butterfield, P., and Campos, J. (1986). Social referencing: The infant's use of emotional signals from a friendly adult with mother present. *Developmental Psychology*, **22**, 427–432.

Knapp, C. W., and Harwood, B. T. (1977). Factors in the determination of intimate same-sex friendships. *Journal of Genetic Psychology*, **131**, 83–90.

Knapp, M. L. (1978). *Social Intercourse: From Greeting to Goodbye*. Boston: Allyn & Bacon.

Knapp, M. L. (1984). *Interpersonal Communication and Human Relationships*. Boston: Allyn & Bacon.

Knowles, E. S. (1980). An affiliative conflict theory of personal and group spatial behavior. In P. B. Paulus (Ed.) *Psychology of Group Influence*. Hillsdale, NJ: Erlbaum, pp. 133–188.

Knowles, P. L., and Smith, D. L. (1982). The ecological perspective applied to social perception: Revision of a working paper. *Journal for the Theory of Social Behavior*, **12**, 53–78.

Knox, D. H., and Sporakowski, M. J. (1968). Attitudes of college students toward love. *Journal of Marriage and the Family*, **30**, 638–642.

Knox, D., Jr (1970). Conceptions of love at three developmental levels. *The Family Coordinator*, **19**, 151–156.

Kobasa, S. C. O., and Puccetti, M. C. (1983). Personality and social resources in stress-resistance. *Journal of Personality and Social Psychology*, **45**, 839–850.

Koestler, A. (1978). *Janus: A Summing Up*. New York: Vintage Books.

Kohn, M. (1966). The child as a determinant of his peer's approach to him. *Journal of Genetic Psychology*, **109**, 91–100.

Kohut, H. (1978). *The Restoration of the Self*. New York: International Universities Press.

Komarovsky, M. (1967). *Blue-Collar Marriage*. New York: Vintage Books.

Komarovsky, M. (1974). Patterns of self-disclosure of male undergraduates. *Journal of Marriage and the Family*, **36**, 677–686.

Kon, I. S., and Losenkov, V. A. (1978). Friendship in adolescence: Values and behavior. *Journal of Marriage and the Family*, **40**, 143–155.

Konner, M. (1982). *The Tangled Wing: Biological Constraints on the Human Spirit*. New York: Holt, Rinehart, & Winston.

Kowalik, D. L., and Gotlib, I. H. (1987). Depression and marital interaction: Concordance between intent and perception of communication. *Journal of Abnormal Psychology*, **96**, 127–134.

Kraemer, H. C. (1975). On estimation and hypothesis testing problems for correlation coefficients. *Psychometrika*, **40**, 473–485.

Kraemer, H. C., and Jacklin, C. N. (1979). Statistical analysis of dyadic social behavior. *Psychological Bulletin*, **86**, 217–224.

Kraemer, H. C., Hole, W. T., and Anders, T. F. (1984). The detection of behavioral state cycles and classification of temporal structure in behavioral states. *Sleep*, **7**, 3–17.

Krain, M. (1975). Communication among premarital couples at three stages of dating. *Journal of Marriage and the Family*, **37**, 609–618.

Krain, M. (1977). A definition of dyadic boundaries and an empirical study of boundary establishment in courtship. *International Journal of Sociology of the Family*, **7**, 107–123.

Krain, M. (1983). Communication as a process of dyadic organization and development. *Journal of Communication*, **23**, 392–408.

Kram, K. E. (1984). How organizations shape the dynamics of cross-gender relationships. Paper presented at the annual meeting of the National Academy of Management, Boston, August.

Krippendorf, K. (1977). Information systems theory and research: An overview. In B. Rubin (Ed.) *Communication Yearbook 1*. New Brunswick, NJ: Transaction Books, pp. 149–171.

Krippendorf, K. (1984). An epistemological foundation of communication. *Journal of Communication*, **34**, 21–36.

Kropotkin, P. (1955). *Mutual Aid: A Factor in Evolution*. Boston: Extending Horizon Books.

Kuhn, T. (1962). *The Structure of Scientific Revolutions*. Chicago: University of Chicago Press.

Kuiper, N. A., and Higgins, E. T. (1985). Social cognition and depression: A general integrative perspective. *Social Cognition*, **3**, 1–15.

Kurth, S. B. (1970). Friendship and friendly relations. In G. J. McCall, M. M. McCall, N. K. Denzin, G. D. Suttles and S. B. Kurth, *Social Relationships*. Chicago: Aldine, pp. 136–170.

L'Abate, L. (1984). Beyond paradox: Issues of control. *The American Journal of Family Therapy*, **12**, 12–20.

Lacoursiere, R. B. (1980). *The Life Cycle of Groups: Group Developmental Stage Theory*. New York: Human Sciences Press.

Ladd, D., Scherer, K., and Silverman, K. (1986). An integrated approach to studying intonation and attitude. In C. Johns-Lewis (Ed.) *Intonation in Discourse*. San Diego: College-Hill Press.

LaFollette, H., and Graham, G. (1986). Honesty and intimacy. *Journal of Social and Personal Relationships*, **3**, 3–18.

LaFrance, M., and Ickes, W. (1981). Postural mirroring and interactional involvement: Sex and sex-typing effects. *Journal of Nonverbal Behavior*, **5**, 139–154.

LaFreniere, P., and Sroufe, L. A. (1985). Profiles of peer competence in the preschool: Interrelations between measures, influence of social ecology, and relation to attachment history. *Developmental Psychology*, **21**, 56–68.

LaGaipa, J. J. (1977). Testing a multidimensional approach to friendship. In S. W. Duck (Ed.) *Theory and Practice in Interpersonal Attraction*. New York: Academic Press.

LaGaipa, J. J. (1981). A systems approach to personal relationships. In S. W. Duck and R. Gilmour (Eds) *Personal Relationships 1: Studying Personal Relationships*. London: Academic Press.

LaGaipa, J. J. (1982). Rules and rituals in disengaging from relationships. In S. W. Duck (Ed.) *Personal Relationships 4: Dissolving Personal Relationships*. London: Academic Press.

Laing, R. D. (1961). *The Self and Others*. New York: Random House.

Laing, R. D., Phillipson, H., and Lee, A. R. (1966). *Interpersonal Perception: A Theory and Method of Research*. New York: Harper & Row.

Lalljee, M., and Cook, M. (1973). Uncertainty in first encounters. *Journal of Personality and Social Psychology*, **26**, 137–141.

Lalljee, M., Brown, L. B., and Ginsburg, G. P. (1984). Attitudes: Disposition, behaviour or evaluation? *British Journal of Social Psychology*, **23**, 233–244.

Lamb, M. E., and Gilbride, K. E. (1985). Compatibility in parent–infant relationships: Origins and processes. In W. Ickes (Ed.) *Compatible and Incompatible Relationships*. New York: Springer-Verlag.

Lamb, M. E., Thompson, R. A., Gardner, W. P., and Charnov, E. L. (1985). *Infant–Mother Attachment: The Origins and Developmental Significance of Individual Differences in Strange Situation Behaviour*. Hillsdale, NJ: Erlbaum.

Lamb, M. E., Thompson, R. A., Gardner, W. P., Charnov, E. L., and Estes, D. (1984). Security of infantile attachment as assessed in the 'strange situation'. *The Behavioral and Brain Sciences*, **7**, 127–147, 167–171.

Langer, E. J. (1978). Rethinking the role of thought in social interaction. In J. H. Harvey, W. Ickes and R. F. Kidd (Eds) *New Directions in Attribution Research*, Hillsdale, NJ: Erlbaum, pp. 35–58.

Langer, E. J., Blank, A., and Chanowitz, B. (1978). The mindlessness of ostensibly thoughtful action: The role of 'placebic' information in interpersonal interaction. *Journal of Personality and Social Psychology*, **36**, 635–642.

Larrance, D. T., and Twentyman, C. R. (1983). Maternal attributions and child abuse. *Journal of Abnormal Psychology*, **92**, 449–457.

Larson, R., Cziksentmihalyi, M., and Graef, R. (1982). Time alone in daily experience: Loneliness or renewal? In L. A. Peplau and D. Perlman (Eds) *Loneliness: A Sourcebook of Theory, Research and Therapy*. New York: Wiley, pp. 40–53.

Lasswell, M., and Lobsenz, N. M. (1980). *Styles of Loving*. New York: Ballantine.

Lasswell, T. E., and Lasswell, M. E. (1976). I love you but I'm not in love with you. *Journal of Marriage and Family Counseling*, **38**, 211–224.

Lazarsfeld, P. F., and Merton, R. K. (1954). Friendship as a social process. In M. Berger, T. Abel and C. Page (Eds) *Freedom and Control in Modern Society*. Princeton: Van Nostrand.

Lea, M., and Duck, S. W. (1982). A model for the role of similarity of values in friendship development. *British Journal of Social Psychology*, **21**, 301–310.

Leary, M. R. (1983). *Understanding Social Anxiety: Social, Personality and Clinical Perspectives*. Beverly Hills: Sage.

Leary, M. R., Rogers, P. A., Canfield, R. W., and Coe, C. (1986). Boredom in interpersonal encounters: Antecedents and social implications. *Journal of Personality and Social Psychology*, **51**, 968–975.

Lederer, W. J., and Jackson, D. D. (1968). *The Mirages of Marriage*. New York: Norton.

Lee, J. A. (1973). *The Colors of Love: An Exploration of the Ways of Loving*. Don Mills, Ontario: New Press (popular edition, 1976).

Lee, L. (1984). Sequences in separation: A framework for investigating endings of the personal (romantic) relationship. *Journal of Social and Personal Relationships*, 1, 49–74.

Lefcourt, H. M., Martin, R. A., and Saleh, W. E. (1984). Locus of control and social support: Interactive moderators of stress. *Journal of Personality and Social Psychology*, 47, 378–389.

Lehman, D. R., Wortman, C. B., and Williams, A. F. (1987). Long-term effects of losing a spouse or child in a motor vehicle crash. *Journal of Personality and Social Psychology*, 52, 218–231.

Lehman, D. R., Ellard, J. H., and Wortman, C. B. (1986). Social support for the bereaved: Recipients' and providers' perspectives on what is helpful. *Journal of Consulting and Clinical Psychology*, 54, 438–446.

Lehmann, H. E. (1971). Epidemiology of depressive disorders. In R. R. Fieve (Ed.) *Depression in the 70's: Modern Theory and Research*. Princeton: Excerpta Medica.

Leiter, M. P. (1977). A study of reciprocity in preschool playgroups. *Child Development*, 48, 1288–1295.

Lepper, M. R. (1973). Dissonance, self-perception, and honesty in children. *Journal of Personality and Social Psychology*, 25, 65–74.

Lepper, M. R. (1981). Intrinsic and extrinsic motivation in children: Detrimental effects of superfluous social control. In W. A. Collins (Ed.) *Minnesota Symposia on Child Psychology*, Vol. 14. Minneapolis: University of Minnesota Press, pp. 155–214.

Lepper, M. R. (1983). Social-control processes and the internalization of social values: An attributional perspective. In E. T. Higgins, D. N. Ruble and W. W. Hartup (Eds) *Social Cognition and Social Development: A Sociocultural Perspective*. Cambridge, MA: Cambridge University Press, pp. 294–330.

Leslie, G. R., and Richardson, A. H. (1956). Family versus campus influences in relation to mate selection. *Social Problems*, 4, 117–121.

Leslie, L. A., Huston, T. L., and Johnson, M. P. (1986). Parental reactions to dating relationships: Do they really make a difference? *Journal of Marriage and the Family*, 48, 57–66.

Lester, R. E. (1987). Organizational culture, uncertainty reduction, and the socialization of new organizational members. In S. Thomas (Ed.) *Communication—Methodology, Behavior, Artifacts and Institutions*. Norwood, NJ: Ablex, pp. 105–113.

Leth, S. (1977). Interpersonal response: Confirmation, rejection, and disconfirmation in established friendships. Unpublished doctoral dissertation, Purdue University (University Microfilms No. 77–7492).

Levenson, R. W., and Gottman, J. M. (1983). Marital interaction: Physiological linkage and affective exchange. *Journal of Personality and Social Psychology*, 45, 587–597.

Levenson, R. W., and Gottman, J. M. (1985). Six physiological and affective predictors of change in relationship satisfaction. *Journal of Personality and Social Psychology*, 49, 85–94.

Leventhal, H., and Sharp, E. (1965). Facial expressions as indicators of distress. In S. S. Tomkins and C. E. Izard (Eds) *Affect, Cognition, and Personality*. New York: Springer.

Levine, A. (1986). Profile: Mary D. Ainsworth. In S. Scarr, R. A. Weinberg and A. Levine (Eds) *Understanding Development*. San Diego: Harcourt Brace Jovanovich, pp. 210–213.

Levine, D. N. (Ed.) (1971). *Georg Simmel on Individuality and Social Forms: Selected Writings*. Chicago: University of Chicago Press.

Levinger, G. (1976). A social-psychological perspective on marital dissolution. *Journal of Social Issues*, 31, 21–47.

Levinger, G. (1977). Re-viewing the close relationship. In G. Levinger and H. L. Raush (Eds) *Close Relationships*. Amherst, MA: University of Massachusetts Press.

Levinger, G. (1979). A social exchange view on the dissolution of pair relationships. In R. W. Burgess and T. L. Huston (Eds) *Social Exchange in Developing Relationships*. New York: Academic Press, pp. 169–193.

Levinger, G. (1980). Toward the analysis of close relationships. *Journal of Experimental Social Psychology*, **16**, 510–544.

Levinger, G. (1983). Development and change. In H. H. Kelley *et al.* (Eds.) *Close Relationships*. San Francisco: Freeman.

Levinger, G., and Breedlove, J. (1966). Interpersonal attraction and agreement: A study of marriage partners. *Journal of Personality and Social Psychology*, **3**, 367–372.

Levinger, G., and Rands, M. (1985). Compatibility in marriage and other close relationships. In W. Ickes (Ed.) *Compatible and Incompatible Relationships*. New York: Springer-Verlag, pp. 309–331.

Levinger, G., and Senn, D. (1967). Disclosure of feelings in marriage. *Merrill-Palmer Quarterly*, **13**, 237–249.

Levinger, G., and Snoek, J. D. (1972). *Attraction in Relationships: A New Look at Interpersonal Attraction*. Morristown, NJ: General Learning Press.

Levinger, G., Rands, M., and Talaber, R. (1977). *The assessment of involvement and rewardingness in close and casual pair relationships* (National Science Foundation Technical Report DK). Amherst, MA: University of Massachusetts.

Levinger, G., Senn, D. J., and Jorgensen, B. W. (1970). Progress toward permanence in courtship: A test of the Kerckhoff–Davis hypotheses. *Sociometry*, **33**, 427–443.

Levitt, M. H., Weber, R. A., and Clark, M. C. (1986). Social network relationships as sources of maternal support and well-being. *Developmental Psychology*, **22**, 310–316.

Levitt, M. J., Weber, R. A., Clark, M. C., and McDonnell, P. (1985). Reciprocity of exchange in toddler sharing behavior. *Developmental Psychology*, **21**, 122–123.

Levitz-Jones, E. M., and Orlofsky, J. L. (1985). Separation-individuation and intimacy capacity in college women. *Journal of Personality and Social Psychology*, **49**, 156–169.

Levy, L. H. (1979). Processes and activities in groups. In M. A. Lieberman and D. L. Borman (Eds) *Self-Help Groups for Coping with Crisis*. San Francisco: Jossey-Bass, pp. 234–271.

Lewinsohn, P. M., and Atwood, G. E. (1969). Depression: A clinical research approach. *Psychotherapy: Theory, Research, and Practice*, **6**, 166–171.

Lewinsohn, P. M., and Schaffer, M. (1971). The use of home observations as an integral part of the treatment of depression: Preliminary report of case studies. *Journal of Consulting and Clinical Psychology*, **37**, 87–94.

Lewinsohn, P. M., Mischel, J., Caplin, K., and Barton, R. (1980). Social competence and depression: The role of illusory self-perceptions. *Journal of Abnormal Psychology*, **90**, 213–219.

Lewis, C. C. (1981). The effects of parental firm control: A reinterpretation of findings. *Psychological Bulletin*, **90**, 547–563.

Lewis, M., and Feiring, C. (1982). Some American families at dinner. In L. M. Laosa and I. E. Siegel (Eds) *Families as Learning Environments for Children*. New York: Plenum.

Lewis, M., and Rosenblum, L. (Eds) (1974). *The Effect of the Infant on its Caregiver*. New York: Wiley.

Lewis, M., and Rosenblum, L. (1975). Introduction. In M. Lewis and L. Rosenblum (Eds) *Friendship and Peer Relations*. New York: Wiley, pp. 1–9.

Lewis, M., Feiring, C., McGuggog, C., and Jaskir, J. (1984). Predicting psychopathology in six-year-olds from early social relations. *Child Development*, **55**, 123–136.

Lewis, M., Young, G., Brooks, J., and Michalson, L. (1975). The beginning of friendship. In M. Lewis and L. Rosenblum (Eds) *Friendship and Peer Relations*. New York: Wiley, pp. 27–66.

Lewis, R. A. (1972). A developmental framework for the analysis of premarital dyadic formation. *Family Process*, **11**, 17–48.

Lewis, R. A. (1973a). A longitudinal test of a developmental framework for premarital dyadic formation. *Journal of Marriage and the Family*, **35**, 16–25.

Lewis, R. A. (1973b). Societal reaction and the formation of dyads. *Sociometry*, **36**, 409–418.

Lewis, R. A. (1978). Emotional intimacy among men. *Journal of Social Issues*, **34**, 108–121.

Lewis, R. A., and Spanier, G. B. (1979). Theorizing about the quality and stability of marriage. In W. Burr, R. Hill, F. Nye and I. Reiss (Eds) *Contemporary Theories about the Family*, Vol. 1. New York: Free Press, pp. 268–294.

Libet, J., and Lewinsohn, P. M. (1973). The concept of social skill with special reference to the behavior of depressed persons. *Journal of Consulting and Clinical Psychology*, **40**, 304–312.

Lidz, T. (1963). *The Family and Human Adaptation*. New York: International Universities Press.

Lieberman, A. F. (1977). Preschoolers' competence with a peer: Relations with attachment and peer experience. *Child Development*, **48**, 1277–1287.

Lieberman, M. A. (1979). Analysing change mechanisms in groups. In M. A. Lieberman and D. L. Borman (Eds) *Self-Help Groups for Coping with Crisis*. San Francisco: Jossey-Bass, pp. 194–233.

Lindblom, D. E., and Cohen, D. K. (1979). *Usable Knowledge*. New Haven: Yale University Press.

Litwak, E., and Szelenyi, I. (1969). Primary group structures and their functions: Kin, neighbors and friends. *American Sociological Review*, **34**, 465–481.

Livingston, K. R. (1980). Love as a process of uncertainty reduction—cognitive theory. In K. S. Pope and Associates (Eds), *On Love and Loving*. San Francisco: Jossey-Bass, pp. 133–151.

Lloyd, S. A., and Cate, R. M. (1983). A typological description of premarital relationship dissolution. Paper presented at the Rocky Mountain Psychological Association Meeting, Snowbird, Utah, April.

Lloyd, S. A., and Cate, R. M. (1985a). The developmental course of conflict in premarital relationship dissolution. *Journal of Social and Personal Relationships*, **2**, 179–194.

Lloyd, S. A., and Cate, R. M. (1985b). Attributions associated with significant turning points in premarital relationship development and dissolution. *Journal of Social and Personal Relationships*, **2**, 419–436.

Lloyd, S. A., Cate, R. M., and Henton, J. (1982). Equity and rewards as predictors of satisfaction in casual and intimate relationships. *The Journal of Psychology*, **110**, 43–48.

Lloyd, S. A., Cate, R. M., and Henton, J. M. (1984). Predicting premarital relationship stability: A methodological refinement. *Journal of Marriage and the Family*, **46**, 71–76.

Lock, A. J. (1986). The role of relationships in development: An introduction to a series of occasional articles. *Journal of Social and Personal Relationships*, **3**, 89–100.

Locke, H. J. (1951). *Predicting Adjustment in Marriage*. New York: Holt, Rinehart, & Winston.

Locke, H. J., and Wallace, K. M. (1959). Short marital-adjustment and prediction tests: Their reliability and validity. *Marriage and Family Living*, **21**, 251–255.

Loeb, R. C., Horst, L., and Horton, P. J. (1980). Family interaction patterns associated with self-esteem in preadolescent girls and boys. *Merrill-Palmer Quarterly*, **26**(3), 205–217.

Loevinger, J. (1976). *Ego Development*. San Francisco: Jossey-Bass.

Loevinger, J. (1984). On the self and predicting behavior. In R. A. Zucker, J. Aronoff and A. I. Rabin (Eds) *Personality and the Prediction of Behavior*. London: Academic Press, pp. 43–68.

Lofthouse, L. J. (1986). An empirical investigation of individual and situational differences in compliance-gaining. Unpublished master's thesis, Department of Communication, Arizona State University, Tempe, Arizona.

Londerville, S., and Main, M. (1981). Security of attachment, compliance, and maternal training methods in the second year of life. *Developmental Psychology*, **17**, 289–299.

Lootens, A. L., and Strube, M. J. (1985). Daily hassles, social support, and psychological well-being. Paper presented at the Annual Meeting of the American Psychological Association, Los Angeles, California, August.

LoVette, S. (1987). Applying uncertainty reduction theory to organizational romance: An empirical investigation. Paper presented at the annual convention of the Western Speech Communication Association, Salt Lake City, Utah, February.

LoVette, S., and Canary, D. J. (1987). Beliefs and communication strategies associated with organizational romance. Unpublished manuscript, Department of Communication Arts and Sciences, University of Southern California, Los Angeles, California.

Lowe, G. R. (1969). *Personal Relationships in Psychological Disorders*. Harmondsworth: Penguin.

Lowenthal, M. F., and Haven, C. (1968). Interaction and adaptation: Intimacy as a critical variable. *American Sociological Review*, **33**, 20–30.

Luckey, E. B., and Nass, G. D. (1969). A comparison of sexual attitudes and behavior in an international sample. *Journal of Marriage and the Family*, **31**, 364–379.

Lujansky, H., and Mikula, G. (1983). Can equity theory explain the quality and stability of romantic relationships? *British Journal of Social Psychology*, **22**, 101–112.

Lustig, M. W., and King, S. W. (1980). The effect of communication apprehension and situation on communication strategy choices. *Human Communication Research*, **7**, 74–82.

Lytton, H. (1980). *Parent–Child Interaction: The Socialization Process Observed in Twin and Singleton Families*. New York: Plenum.

Maccoby, E. E. (1982). Commentary: Organization and relationships in development. In W. Collins (Ed.) *Minnesota Symposia on Child Psychology*, Vol. 15. Hillsdale, NJ: Erlbaum.

Maccoby, E. E., and Jacklin, C. N. (1983). The 'person' characteristics of children and the family as environment. In D. Magnusson and V. L. Allen (Eds.) *Human Development: An Interactional Perspective*. New York: Academic Press, pp. 75–91.

Maccoby, E. E., and Martin, J. A. (1983). Socialization in the context of the family: Parent–child interaction. In E. M. Hetherington (Ed.) *Handbook of Child Psychology: Vol. 4. Socialization, Personality, and Social Development*, 4th edn. New York: Wiley.

MacDonald, K., and Parke, R. D. (1984). Bridging the gap: Parent–child play interaction and peer interactive competence. *Child Development*, **55**, 1265–1277.

MacIver, R. M. (1937). *Society*. New York: Farrar & Rinehart.

MacKay, D. M. (1972). Formal analysis of communicative processes. In R. A. Hinde (Ed.) *Non-Verbal Communication*. Cambridge, MA: Cambridge University Press, pp. 3–25.

Madanes, C. (1981). *Strategic Family Therapy*. San Francisco: Jossey-Bass.

Madden, M. E., and Janoff-Bulman, R. (1981). Blame, control, and marital satisfaction: Wives' attributions for conflict in marriage. *Journal of Marriage and the Family*, **43**, 663–674.

Magnusson, D., and Endler, N. S. (1977). Interactional psychology: Present status and future prospects. In D. Magnusson and N. S. Endler (Eds) *Personality at the Cross-roads: Current Issues in Interactional Psychology*. Hillsdale, NJ: Erlbaum, pp. 3–31.

Mahoney, E. R. (1978). Age differences in attitude change toward premarital coitus. *Archives of Sexual Behavior*, **7**, 493–501.

Main, M., and Weston, D. R. (1981). The quality of the toddler's relationship to mother and to father: Related to conflict behavior and the readiness to establish new relationships. *Child Development*, **52**, 932–940.

Main, M., Kaplan, N., and Cassidy, J. (1985). Security in infancy, childhood, and adulthood: A move to the level of representation. In I. Bretherton and E. Waters

(Eds) *Growing Points of Attachment Theory and Research*, pp. 66–104. *Monographs of the SRCD*, **50** (1–2, Serial No. 209).

Main, M., Kaplan, N., and Cassidy, J. (1986). Security in infancy, childhood, and adolescence: A move to the level of representation. In I. Bretherton and E. Waters (Eds) *Monographs of the SRCD*, **50** (Serial No. 209).

Mainiero, L. A. (1986). A review and analysis of power dynamics in organisational romances. *Academy of Management Review*, **11**, 750–762.

Malatesta, C. Z., and Haviland, J. M. (1985). Signals, symbols, and socialization: The modification of emotional expression in human development. In M. Lewis and C. Saarni (Eds) *The Socialization of Emotions*. New York: Plenum, pp. 89–116.

Malloy, T. E., and Kenny, D. A. (1986). The Social Relations Model: An integrative method for personality research. *Journal of Personality*, **54**, 101–127.

Malott, J. M., Glasgow, R. E., O'Neil, H. K., and Klesges, R. C. (1984). Co-worker social support in a worksite smoking control program. *Journal of Applied Behavior Analysis*, **17**, 485–495.

Mandel, M. J. (1983). Local roles and social networks. *American Sociological Review*, **48**, 376–386.

Manderscheid, R. W., Rae, D. S., McCarrick, A. K., and Silbergeld, S. (1982). A stochastic model of relational control in dyadic interaction. *American Sociological Review*, **47**, 62–75.

Mandler, G. (1975). *Mind and Emotion*. New York: Wiley.

Manicas, P. T. (1980). The concept of social structure. *Journal for the Theory of Social Behavior*, **10**, 65–82.

Manicas, P. T., and Secord, P. E. (1983). Implications for psychology of the new philosophy of science. *American Psychologist*, **38**, 399–413.

Mannarino, A. P. (1980). The development of children's friendships. In H. C. Foot, A. J. Chapman and J. R. Smith (Eds) *Friendship and Social Relations in Children*. Chichester: Wiley, pp. 45–63.

March, J. G., and Olsen, J. P. (1976). *Ambiguity and Choice in Organizations*. Bergen: Universitetsforlaget.

March, J. G., and Simon, H. A. (1958). *Organizations*. New York: Wiley.

Marciano, T. (1974). Middle-class incomes, working-class hearts. *Family Process*, **13** (4), 489–502.

Marcus, R. F., and Jenny, B. (1977). A naturalistic study of reciprocity in the helping behavior of young children. *The Alberta Journal of Educational Research*, **23**, 195–206.

Margolin, G., and Wampold, B. E. (1981). Sequential analysis of conflict and accord in distressed and nondistressed marital partners. *Journal of Consulting and Clinical Psychology*, **49**, 554–567.

Margulis, J. T., Derlega, V. J., and Winstead, B. A. (1984). Implications of social psychological concepts for a theory of loneliness. In V. J. Derlega (Ed.) *Communication, Intimacy, and jclose Relationships*. Orland, FL: Academic Press, pp. 133–160.

Markman, H. J. (1979). The application of a behavioral model of marriage in predicting relationship satisfaction of couples planning marriage. *Journal of Consulting and Clinical Psychology*, **47**, 743–749.

Markman, H. J. (1981). Predicting marital distress: A 5-year follow-up. *Journal of Consulting and Clinical Psychology*, **49**, 760–762.

Markman, H. J., Ferraro, B., Wells, J., Kotanski, K., Baccuss, G., Sullivan, M., and Floyd, F. (1980). The reactivity of marital interaction in videotape versus nonvideotape conditions. Unpublished manuscript, Bowling Green State University.

Marks, T., and Hammen, C. L. (1982). Interpersonal mood induction: Situational and individual determinants. *Motivation and Emotion*, **6**, 387–399.

Markus, H., and Nurius, P. (1986). Possible selves. *American Psychologist*, **41**, 954–969.

Markus, H., and Zajonc, R. B. (1985). The cognitive perspective in social psychology. In G. Lindzey and E. Aronson (Eds) *Handbook of Social Psychology*, 3rd edn, Vol. 1. New York: Random House, pp. 137–230.

Markus, H., Smith, J., and Moreland, R. L. (1985). Role of the self-concept in the perception of others. *Journal of Personality and Social Psychology*, **49**, 1494–1512.

Marlowe, D., and Gergen, K. J. (1969). Personality and social interaction. In G. Lindzey and E. Aronson (Eds) *The Handbook of Social Psychology*, Vol. 3. Reading, Mass: Addison-Wesley.

Martin, G., and Clark, R. (1982). Distress crying in neonates: Species and peer specificity. *Developmental Psychology*, **18**, 3–10.

Martin, J., Feldman, M., Hatch, M., and Sitkin, S. (1983). The uniqueness paradox in organization stories. *Administrative Science Quarterly*, **28**, 438–453.

Martin, J. A., Maccoby, E. E., Baran, K. W., and Jacklin, C. N. (1981). The sequential analysis of mother-child interaction at 18 months: A comparison of microanalytic methods. *Developmental Psychology*, **17**, 146–157.

Maruyama, M. (1975). The post-industrial logic. In A. A. Spekke (Ed.) *The Next 25 Years: Crisis and Opportunity*. Washington, DC: The World Future Society, pp. 43–50.

Marwell, G., and Schmitt, D. R. (1967). Dimensions of compliance-gaining behavior: An empirical analysis. *Sociometry*, **30**, 350–364.

Masheter, C., and Harris, L. (1986). From divorce to friendship: A study of dialectic relationship development. *Journal of Social and Personal Relationships*, **3**, 177–190.

Maslin, C. A., Bretherton, I., and Morgan, G. A. (1986). The influence of attachment security and maternal scaffolding on toddler mastery motivation. Paper presented at the International Conference on Infant Studies, Beverly Hills, California, April.

Masling, J. (1986). Orality, pathology, and interpersonal behavior. In J. Masling (Ed.) *Empirical Studies of Psychoanalytic Theories: 2*. New York: Academic Press, pp. 73–106.

Maslow, A. (1968). *Toward a Psychology of Being*. New York: Van Nostrand–Reinhold.

Masters, J. C., and Furman, W. (1981). Popularity, individual friendship selection, and specific peer interaction among children. *Developmental Psychology*, **17**, 344–350.

Matas, L., Arend, R. A., and Sroufe, L. A. (1978). Continuity of adaptation in the second year: The relationship between quality of attachment and later competence. *Child Development*, **49**, 547–556.

Mathes, E. W., Adams, H. E., and Davies, R. M. (1985). Jealousy: Loss of relationship rewards, loss of self-esteem, depression, anxiety, and anger. *Journal of Personality and Social Psychology*, **48**, 1552–1561.

Matthews, C., and Clark, R. (1982). Marital satisfaction: A validation approach. *Basic and Applied Social Psychology*, **3** (3), 169–186.

Maudry, M., and Nekula, M. (1939). Social relations between children of the same age during the first two years of life. *Journal of Genetic Psychology*, **54**, 193–215.

Mauss, M. (1925). *The Gift*. London: Cohen & West.

Mayer, J. D., and Bower, G. H. (1986). Learning and memory for personality prototypes. *Journal of Personality and Social Psychology*, **51**, 473–492.

Maynard, D. W., and Zimmerman, D. H. (1984). Topical talk, ritual and the social organization of relationships. *Social Psychology Quarterly*, **47**, 301–316.

Maynard-Smith, J. (1974). The theory of games and the evolution of animal conflicts. *Journal of Theoretical Biology*, **47**, 209–221.

McAdams, D. P. (1980). A thematic coding system for the intimacy motive. *Journal of Research in Personality*, **14**, 413–432.

McAdams, D. P. (1982a). Intimacy motivation. In A. J. Stewart (Ed.) *Motivation and Society*. San Francisco: Jossey-Bass, pp. 133–171.

McAdams, D. P. (1982b). Experiences of intimacy and power: Relationships between social motives and autobiographical memory. *Journal of Personality and Social Psychology*, **42**, 292–302.

McAdams, D. P. (1984). Human motives and personal relationships. In V. J. Derlega (Ed.) *Communication, Intimacy, and Close Relationships*. New York: Academic Press, pp. 41–70.

McAdams, D. P. (1985a). *Power, Intimacy, and the Life Story: Personalogical Inquiries into Identity*. Chicago: Dorsey.

McAdams, D. P. (1985b). The 'imago': A key narrative component of identity. In P. Shaver (Ed.) *Self, Situations, and Social Behavior: Review of Personality and Social Psychology*, Vol. 6. Beverly Hills: Sage, pp. 115–141.

McAdams, D. P. (1985c). Motivation and friendship. In S. W. Duck and D. Perlman (Eds) *Understanding Personal Relationships: An Interdisciplinary Approach*. Beverly Hills: Sage, pp. 85–105.

McAdams, D. P. (1987). *The Person: An Introduction to Personality Psychology*. San Diego: Harcourt Brace Jovanovich.

McAdams, D. P., and Constantian, C. A. (1983). Intimacy and affiliation motives in daily living: An experience sampling analysis. *Journal of Personality and Social Psychology*, **45**, 851–861.

McAdams, D. P., and Losoff, M. (1984). Friendship motivation in fourth and sixth graders: A thematic analysis. *Journal of Social and Personal Relationships*, **1**, 11–27.

McAdams, D. P., and Powers, J. (1981). Themes of intimacy in behavior and thought. *Journal of Personality and Social Psychology*, **40**, 573–587.

McAdams, D. P., and Vaillant, G. E. (1982). Intimacy motivation and psychosocial adjustment: A longitudinal study. *Journal of Personality Assessment*, **46**, 586–593.

McAdams, D. P., Healy, S., and Krause, S. (1984). Social motives and patterns of friendship. *Journal of Personality and Social Psychology*, **47**, 828–838.

McAdams, D. P., Jackson, R. J., and Kirshnit, C. (1984). Looking, laughing, and smiling in dyads as a function of intimacy motivation and reciprocity. *Journal of Personality*, **52**, 261–273.

McAdams, D. P., Lester, R., Brand, P., McNamara, W., and Lenski, D. B. (1987). Sex and the TAT: Are women more intimate than men? Do men fear intimacy? Unpublished manuscript.

McArthur, L. A. (1972). The how and what of why: Some determinants and consequences of causal attribution. *Journal of Personality and Social Psychology*, **22**, 171–193.

McArthur, L. A. (1976). The lesser influence of consensus than distinctiveness information on causal attributions. *Journal of Personality and Social Psychology*, **33**, 733–743.

McArthur, L. Z., and Baron, R. M. (1983). Toward an ecological theory of social perception. *Psychological Review*, **90**, 215–238.

McCall, G. J. (1970). The social organization of relationships. In G. J. McCall *et al. Social Relationships*. Chicago: Aldine.

McCall, G. J. (1974). A symbolic interactionist approach to attraction. In T. L. Huston (Ed.) *Foundations of Interpersonal Attraction*. New York: Academic Press.

McCall, G. J. (1982). Becoming unrelated: The management of bond dissolution. In S. W. Duck (Ed.) *Personal Relationships 4: Dissolving Personal Relationships*. New York: Academic Press, pp. 211–232.

McCall, G. J., and Simmons, J. L. (1966/1978). *Identities and Interactions*. New York: Free Press (Second Edn, 1978).

McCall, G. J., and Simmons, J. L. (1982). *Social Psychology: A Sociological Approach*. New York: Free Press.

McCleary, R., and Hay, R. A. (1980). *Applied Time Series Analysis for the Social Sciences*. Beverly Hills: Sage.

McClelland, D. C. (1961). *The Achieving Society*. New York: Free Press.

McClelland, D. C. (1975). *Power: The Inner Experience*. New York: Irvington.

McClelland, D. C. (1985). *Human Motivation*. Glenview, IL: Scott, Foresman & Company.

McClelland, D. C., Davis, W. N., Kalin, R., and Wanner, E. (1972). *The Drinking Man*. New York: Free Press.

McClintock, E. (1983). Interaction. In H. H. Kelley, E. Berscheid, A. Christensen, J.

H. Harvey, T. L. Huston, G. Levinger, E. McClintock, L. A. Peplau and D. R. Peterson. *Close Relationships*. New York: Freeman, pp. 68–109.

McCormack, S. H., and Kahn, A. (1980). Behavioral characteristics of lonely and nonlonely college students. Paper presented at the Annual Convention of the Midwestern Psychological Association, St Louis, MO.

McDonald, G. (1981). Structural exchange and marital interaction. *Journal of Marriage and the Family*, November, 825–839.

McDougall, W. (1908). *Social Psychology*. London: Methuen.

McFeat, T. (1974). *Small-Group Cultures*. New York: Pergamon.

McGrath, J. E. (1970). A conceptual formulation for research on stress. In J. E. McGrath (Ed.) *Social and Psychological Factors in Stress*. New York: Holt, Rinehart, & Winston, pp. 10–21.

McGuire, J. C., and Gottlieb, B. H. (1979). Social support groups among new parents: An experimental study in primary prevention. *Journal of Child Clinical Psychology*, **8**, 111–116.

McGuire, W. J. (1969). The nature of attitudes and attitude change. In G. Lindzey and E. Aronson (Eds) *Handbook of Social Psychology*, 2nd edn, Vol. 3. Reading, MA: Addison-Wesley, pp. 136–314.

McGuire, W. J. (1985). Attitudes and attitude change. In G. Lindzey and E. Aronson (Eds) *Handbook of Social Psychology*, 3rd edn, Vol. 2. New York: Random House, pp. 233–346.

McGuire, W. J., and McGuire, C. (1986). Differences in conceptualizing self versus other people as manifested in contrasting verb types used in natural speech. *Journal of Personality and Social Psychology*, **51**, 1135–1143.

McIntyre-Kingsolver, K. O., Lichtenstein, E., and Mermelstein, R. J. (1986). Spouse training in a multicomponent smoking cessation program. *Behavior Therapy*, **17**, 67–74.

McKelvey, B. (1982). *Organizational Systematics: Taxonomy, Evolution, Classification*. Berkeley: University of California Press.

McLaughlin, M. L., Cody, M. J., and Rosenstein, N. E. (1983). Account sequences in conversations between strangers. *Communication Monographs*, **50**, 102–125.

McLean, P. D., Ogston, L., and Grauer, L. (1973). Behavioral approach to the treatment of depression. *Journal of Behaviour Therapy and Experimental Psychiatry*, **4**, 323–330.

McPherson, M. (1983). An ecology of affiliation. *American Sociological Review*, **48**, 519–532.

Mead, G. H. (1934). *Mind, Self, and Society*. Chicago: University of Chicago Press.

Mechanic, D. (1978). *Medical Sociology*, 2nd edn. New York: Free Press.

Medin, D. L., and Schaffer, M. M. (1978). Context theory of classification learning. *Psychological Review*, **85**, 207–238.

Medora, N., and Woodward, J. C. (1982). Premarital sexual opinions of undergraduate students at a midwestern university. *Adolescence*, **17**, 213–224.

Mehrabian, A., and Ksionzky, S. (1974). *A Theory of Affiliation*. Lexington, MA: Lexington Books.

Mehrabian, A., and Wiener, M. (1967). Decoding of inconsistent communications. *Journal of Personality and Social Psychology*, **6**, 109–114.

Menaghan, E. G. (1983). Individual coping efforts: Moderators of the relationship between life stress and mental health outcomes. In H. B. Kaplan (Ed.) *Psychosocial Stress Trends in Theory and Research*. New York: Academic Press, pp. 157–191.

Mendoza, J. L., and Graziano, W. G. (1982). The statistical analysis of dyadic social behavior: A multivariate approach. *Psychological Bulletin*, **92**, 532–540.

Menzel, W. (1979). General discussion of the methodological problems involved in the study of social interaction. In M. E. Lamb, S. J. Suomi and G. R. Stephenson (Eds) *Social Interaction Analysis: Methodological Issues*. Madison: University of Wisconsin Press, pp. 291–309.

Mercer, G. W., and Kohn, P. M. (1979). Gender differences in the integration of conservatism, sex urge, and sexual behaviors among college students. *Journal of Sex Research*, **15**, 129–142.

Merikangas, K. R. (1984). Divorce and assortative mating among depressed patients. *American Journal of Psychiatry*, **141**, 74–76.

Meyer, H. J. (1987). Marital and mother–child relationships: The impact of developmental history, parental personality characteristics and child's difficulties. In R. A. Hinde and J. Stevenson-Hinde (Eds) *Relations Between Relationships*. Oxford: Oxford University Press.

Meyer, J. W., and Rowan, B. (1977). Institutionalized organizations: Formal structure as myth and ceremony. *American Journal of Sociology*, **83**, 340–363.

Meyer, J. W., and Scott, W. R. (Eds) (1983) *Organizational Environments: Ritual and Rationality*. Beverly Hills: Sage.

Miell, D. E., and Duck, S. W. (1986). Strategies in developing friendships. In V. J. Derlega and B. A. Winstead (Eds) *Friendship and Social Interaction*. New York: Springer-Verlag, pp. 129–143.

Milardo, R. M. (1982). Friendship networks in developing relationships: Converging and diverging social environments. *Social Psychology Quarterly*, **45**, 162–172.

Milardo, R. M. (1986). Personal choice and social constraint in close relationships: Applications of network analysis. In V. J. Derlega and B. A. Winstead (Eds) *Friendship and Social Interaction*. New York: Springer-Verlag.

Milardo, R. M., Johnson, M. P., and Huston, T. L. (1983). Developing close relationships: Changing patterns of interaction between pair members and social networks. *Journal of Personality and Social Psychology*, **44**, 964–976.

Miles, R. H. (1980). Findings and implications of organizational life cycle research: A commencement. In J. Kimberly and R. Miles (Eds) *The Organizational Life Cycle*. San Francisco: Jossey-Bass.

Milgram, S. (1977). The familiar stranger: An aspect of urban anonymity. In S. Milgram *The Individual in a Social World: Essays and Experiments*. Reading, MA: Addison-Wesley, pp. 51–53.

Millar, F. E., and Rogers, L. E. (1976). A relational approach to interpersonal communication. In G. R. Miller (Ed.) *Explorations in Interpersonal Communication*. Beverly Hills: Sage, pp. 87–103.

Millar, F. E., and Rogers, L. E. (1987). Relational dimensions of interpersonal dynamics. In M. E. Roloff and G. R. Miller (Eds) *Interpersonal Processes: New Directions in Communication Research*. Nebury Park, CA: Sage.

Millar, F. E., Rogers, L. E., and Bavelas, J. B. (1984). Identifying patterns of verbal conflict in interpersonal dynamics. *Western Journal of Speech Communication*, **48**, 231–246.

Millar, F. E., Rogers, L. E., and Courtright, J. A. (1979). Relational control and dyadic understanding: An exploratory predictive regression model. In D. Nimmo (Ed.) *Communication Yearbook 3*. New Brunswick, NJ: Transaction Books, pp. 213–224.

Millen, L., and Rolls, S. (1977). Adolescent males' ratings of being understood by fathers, best friends, and significant others. *Psychological Reports*, **40**, 1079–1082.

Miller, G. R. (1973). Counterattitudinal advocacy: A current appraisal. In C. D. Mortensen and K. K. Sereno (Eds) *Advances in Communication Research*. New York: Harper & Row, pp. 105–152.

Miller, G. R. (1977). On the pervasiveness and marvelous complexity of human communication: A note of skepticism. *Journal of the Annual Fresno Conference in Communication*, **4**, 1–18.

Miller, G. R. (1978). The current status of theory and research in interpersonal communication. *Human Communication Research*, **4**, 164–178.

Miller, G. R. (1987). Persuasion. In C. R. Berger and S. H. Chaffee (Eds) *Handbook of Communication Science*. Newbury Park, CA: Sage, pp. 446–483.

Miller, G. R., and Burgoon, M. (1973). *New Techniques of Persuasion*. New York: Harper & Row.

Miller, G. R., and Burgoon, M. (1978). Persuasion research: Review and commentary. In B. D. Ruben (Ed.) *Communication Yearbook 2*. New Brunswick, NJ: Transaction Books, pp. 29–47.

Miller, G. R., and Hewgill, M. A. (1964). The effect of variations in nonfluency on audience ratings of source credibility. *Quarterly Journal of Speech*, **50**, 36–44.

Miller, G. R., and Parks, M. R. (1982). Communication in dissolving relationships. In S. W. Duck (Ed.) *Personal Relationships 4: Dissolving Relationships*. New York: Academic Press, pp. 127–154.

Miller, G. R., and Steinberg, M. (1975). *Between People: A New Analysis of Interpersonal Communication*. Chicago: Science Research Associates.

Miller, G. R., and Sunnafrank, M. J. (1982). All is for one but one is not for all: A conceptual perspective of interpersonal communication. In F. E. X. Dance (Ed.) *Human Communication Theory: Comparative Essays*. New York: Harper & Row, pp. 220–242.

Miller, G. R., Boster, F., Roloff, M., and Seibold, D. (1977). Compliance-gaining message strategies: A typology and some findings concerning effects of situational differences. *Communication Monographs*, **44**, 37–51.

Miller, G. R., Boster, F. J., Roloff, M. E., and Seibold, D. R. (1987). MBRS rekindled: Some thoughts on compliance gaining in interpersonal settings. In M. E. Roloff and G. R. Miller (Eds) *Interpersonal Processes: New Directions in Communication Research*. Newbury Park, CA: Sage.

Miller, G. R., Burgoon, M., and Burgoon, J. K. (1984). The functions of human communication in changing attitudes and gaining compliance. In C. C. Arnold and J. W. Bowers (Eds) *Handbook of Rhetorical and Communication Theory*. Newton, MA: Allyn & Bacon, pp. 400–474.

Miller, G. R., Mongeau, P. A., and Sleight, C. (1986). Fudging with friends and lying to lovers: Deceptive communication in interpersonal relationships. *Journal of Social and Personal Relationships*, **3**, 495–512.

Miller, K. I., and Ellis, B. H. (1987). Stereotypical views of intimate relationships in organizations. Paper presented at the annual meeting of the International Communication Association, Montreal, May.

Miller, L. C., and Berg, J. H. (1984). Selectivity and urgency in interpersonal exchange. In V. J. Derlega (Ed.) *Communication, Intimacy, and Close Relationships*. New York: Academic Press, pp. 161–205.

Miller, L. C., and Kenny, D. A. (1986). Reciprocity of self-disclosure at the individual and dyadic levels: A social relations analysis. *Journal of Personality and Social Psychology*, **50**, 713–719.

Miller, L. C., Berg, J. H., and Archer, R. L. (1983). Openers: Individuals who elicit intimate self-disclosure. *Journal of Personality and Social Psychology*, **44**, 1234–1244.

Miller, P., Lefcourt, H., Holmes, J., Ware, E., and Saleh, W. (1986). Marital locus of control and marital problem solving. *Journal of Personality and Social Psychology*, **51**, 161–169.

Miller, R. S., and Lefcourt, H. M. (1982). Social intimacy: An important moderator of stressful life events. *American Journal of Community Psychology*, **11**, 127–139.

Miller, S., Corrales, R., and Wackman, D. B. (1975). Recent progress in understanding and facilitating marital communication. *The Family Coordinator*, **24**, 143–152.

Miller, S., Nunnally, E., and Wackman, D. (1976). A communication training program for couples. *Social Casework*, **57** (1), 9–18.

Miller, V., and Knapp, M. (1986). Communication paradoxes and the maintenance of living relationships with the dying. *Journal of Family Issues*, **7**, 255–275.

Mills, J., and Clark, M. S. (1982). Communal and exchange relationships. In L. Wheeler (Ed.) *Review of Personality and Social Psychology*, Vol. 3. Beverly Hills: Sage, pp. 121–144.

Mills, R. S. L. (1986). Praising children: Effects on behaviour, self-perception, and affect. Paper presented at the Annual Meeting of the Canadian Psychological Association, Toronto.

Minde, K. (1980). Bonding of parents to premature infants: Theory and practice. In P. M. Taylor (Ed.) *Parent–Infant Relationships*. New York: Grune & Stratton.

Minuchin, S. (1974). *Families and Family Therapy*. Cambridge, MA: Harvard University Press.

Minuchin, S. (1985). Families and individual development: Provocations from the field of family therapy. *Child Development*, **56**, 289–302.

Minuchin, S., and Fishman, H. C. (1981). *Family Therapy Techniques*. Cambridge, MA: Harvard University Press.

Minuchin, S., Montalvo, B., Guerney, B. G., Jr, Rosman, B. L., and Schumer, F. (1967). *Families of the Slums: An Exploration of their Structure and Treatment*. New York: Basic Books.

Minuchin, S., Rosman, B. L., and Baker, L. (1978). *Psychosomatic Families: Anorexia Nervosa in Context*. Cambridge, MA: Harvard University Press.

Mischel, W. (1968). *Personality and Assessment*. New York: Wiley.

Mischel, W. (1973). Toward a cognitive social learning reconceptualization of personality. *Psychological Review*, **80**, 252–283.

Mitchell, C. (1982). Recognizing and accommodating different communication styles in marriage. *Family Therapy*, **9** (3), 227–230.

Mitchell, R. E., and Hurley, D. J. (1981). Collaboration with natural helping networks: Lessons from the study of paraprofessionals. In B. H. Gottlieb (Ed.) *Social Neworks and Social Support*. Beverly Hills: Sage.

Mitchell, R. E., and Trickett, E. J. (1980). Social networks as mediators of social support: An analysis of the effects and determinants of social networks. *Community Mental Health Journal*, **16**, 27–44.

Moffitt, P., Spence, N., and Goldney, R. (1986). Mental health in marriage: The roles of need for affiliation, sensitivity to rejection, and other factors. *Journal of Clinical Psychology*, **42** (1), 68–76.

Monge, P. R., Rothman, L. W., Eisenberg, E. M., Miller, K. I., and Kirste, K. K. (1985). The dynamics of organizational proximity. *Management Science*, **31**, 1129–1141.

Montgomery, B. M. (1980). Reliability and validity of self, spouse, and observer assessments of open communication in marriage. Unpublished doctoral dissertation, Purdue University.

Montgomery, B. M. (1981a). The form and function of quality communication in marriage. *Family Relations*, **30**, 21–30.

Montgomery, B. M. (1981b). Verbal immediacy as a behavioral indicator of open communication content. *Communication Quarterly*, **30**, 28–34.

Montgomery, B. M. (1984a). Behavioral characteristics predicting self and peer perceptions of open communication. *Communication Quarterly*, **32**, 233–240.

Montgomery, B. M. (1984b). Communication in intimate relationships: A research challenge. *Communication Quarterly*, **32**, 318–323.

Montgomery, B. M. (1984c). Individual differences and relational interdependencies in social interaction. *Human Communication Research*, **11**, 33–60.

Montgomery, B. M. (1986). Interpersonal attraction as a function of open communication and gender. *Communication Research Reports*, **3**.

Montgomery, B. M., and Kenny, D. A. (1987). Relational effects over time. Unpublished paper, University of Connecticut.

Moore, J. A., and Sermat, V. (1974). Relationship between self-actualizing and self-reported loneliness. *Canadian Counsellor*, **8** (3), 194–196.

Moore, N. V., Evertson, C. M., and Brophy, J. E. (1974). Solitary play: Some functional reconsiderations. *Developmental Psychology*, **10**, 830–834.

Morawski, J. G. (1985). The measurement of masculinity and femininity: Engendering categorical realities. *Journal of Personality*, **53**, 196–223.

Morawski, J. G. (1987). The troubled quest for masculinity, femininity, and androgyny. In P. Shaver and C. Hendrick (Eds) *Review of Personality and Social Psychology: Vol. 7. Sex and Gender*. Beverly Hills: Sage.

Morin, R. C., and Seidman, E. (1986). A social network approach and the revolving door patient. *Schizophrenia Bulletin*, **12**, 262–273.

Morris, D. (1980). Infant attachment and problem solving in the toddler: Relations to mother's family history. Unpublished doctoral dissertation, University of Minnesota.

Morris, D. (1981). Attachment and intimacy. In G. Stricker (Ed.) *Intimacy*. New York: Plenum, pp. 305–323.

Morris, D., Collett, P., Marsh, P., and O'Shaughnessy, M. (1979). *Gestures: Theor Origins and Distribution*. London: Jonathan Cape.

Morris, G. H. (1985). The remedial episode as a negotiation of rules. In R. L. Street, Jr, and J. N. Cappella (Eds) *Sequence and Pattern in Communicative Behaviour*. London: Edward Arnold.

Morris, G. H., and Hopper, R. (1980). Remediation and legislation in everyday talk: How communicators achieve consensus on rules. *Quarterly Journal of Speech*, **67**, 266–274.

Morton, T. L. (1978). Intimacy and reciprocity of exchange: A comparison of spouses and strangers. *Journal of Personality and Social Psychology*, **36**, 72–81.

Morton, T. L., and Douglas, M. A. (1981). Growth of relationships. In S. W. Duck and R. Gilmour (Eds) *Personal Relationships 2: Developing Personal Relationships*. New York: Academic Press, pp. 3–26.

Mosher, D. L. (1979). Sex guilt and sex myths in college men and women. *The Journal of Sex Research*, **15**, 224–234.

Mowen, J. C., and Cialdini, R. B. (1980). On implementing the door-in-the-face technique in a business context. *Journal of Marketing Research*, **22**, 253–258.

Munro, B., and Adams, G. R. (1978). Love American style: A test of role structure theory on changes in attitudes toward love. *Human Relations*, **31**, 215–228.

Murray, H. A. (1938). *Explorations in Personality*. New York: Oxford University Press.

Murstein, B. I. (1970). Stimulus-value-role: A theory of marital choice. *Journal of Marriage and the Family*, **32**, 465–481.

Murstein, B. I. (1972). Physical attractiveness and marital choice. *Journal of Personality and Social Psychology*, **22**, 8–12.

Murstein, B. I. (1974). *Love, Sex, and Marriage Through the Ages*. New York: Springer.

Murstein, B. I. (1976). *Who Will Marry Whom?* New York: Springer.

Murstein, B. I., and Christy, P. (1976). Physical attractiveness and marital adjustment in middle-aged couples. *Journal of Personality and Social Psychology*, **34**, 537–542.

Nadler, A., and Mayeless, O. (1983). Recipient self-esteem and reactions to help. In J. D. Fisher, A. Nadler and B. M. DePaulo (Eds) *New Directions in Helping, Vol. 1: Recipient Reactions to Aid*. New York: Academic Press.

Nahemow, L., and Lawton, M. P. (1975). Similarity and propinquity in friendship formation. *Journal of Personality and Social Psychology*, **32**, 205–213.

Nash, A. (1986). A comparison of infants' social competence with mother and peer. Paper presented to the American Psychological Association, Washington, DC, August.

Nash, A., and Lamb, M. E. (1987). Becoming acquainted with unfamiliar adults and peers in infancy. Paper presented to the Society for Research in Child Development, Baltimore, MD, April.

Nash, A., West, M. J., and King, A. P. (1983). Song sharing in Brown-headed Cowbirds. Unpublished manuscript.

Natale, M. (1976). A Markovian model of adult gaze behavior. *Journal of Psycholinguistic Research*, **5**, 53–61.

Navran, L. (1967). Communication and adjustment in marriage. *Family Process*, **6**, 173–184.

Neisser, U. (1976). *Cognition and Reality: Principles and Implication of Cognitive Psychology*. San Francisco: Freeman.

Newcomb, A. F., and Brady, J. E. (1982). Mutuality in boys' friendship relations. *Child Development*, **53**, 392–395.

Newcomb, T. M. (1953). An approach to the study of communicative acts. *Psychological Review*, **60**, 393–404.

Newcomb, T. M. (1961). *The Acquaintance Process*. New York: Holt, Rinehart, & Winston.

Newman, H. M. (1981a). Interpretation and exploration: Influences on communicative exchanges within intimate relationships. *Communication Quarterly*, **29**, 123–132.

Newman, H. M. (1981b). Communication within ongoing intimate relationships: An attributional perspective. *Personality and Social Psychology Bulletin*, **7**, 59–70.

Nezlek, J., Wheeler, L., and Reis, H. T. (1983). Studies of social participation. In H. T. Reis (Ed.) *Naturalistic Approaches to Studying Social Interaction*. San Francisco: Jossey-Bass, pp. 57–73.

Nisbett, R. E., and Bellows, N. (1977). Verbal reports about causal inferences on social judgments: Private access versus public theories. *Journal of Personality and Social Psychology*, **35**, 613–624.

Nisbett, R. E., and Ross, L. (1980). *Human Inference: Strategies and Shortcomings of Social Judgment*. Englewood Cliffs, NJ: Prentice-Hall.

Nisbett, R. E., and Wilson, T. D. (1977). Telling more than we can know: Verbal reports on mental processes. *Psychological Review*, **84**, 231–259.

Noller, P. (1978). Sex differences in the socialization of affectionate expression. *Developmental Psychology*, **14**, 317–319.

Noller, P. (1980a). Misunderstandings in marital communication: A study of couples' nonverbal communication. *Journal of Personality and Social Psychology*, **39**, 1135–1148.

Noller, P. (1980b). Gaze in married couples. *Journal of Nonverbal Behavior*, **5**, 115–129.

Noller, P. (1981). Gender and marital adjustment level differences in decoding messages from spouses and strangers. *Journal of Personality and Social Psychology*, **39**, 1135–1148.

Noller, P. (1982). Channel consistency and inconsistency in the communications of married couples. *Journal of Personality and Social Psychology*, **43** (4), 732–741.

Noller, P. (1984). *Nonverbal Communication and Marital Interaction*. Oxford: Pergamon.

Noller, P. (1985). Negative communications in marriage. *Journal of Social and Personal Relationships*, **2**, 289–301.

Noller, P. (1987). Nonverbal communication in marriage. In D. Perlman and S. W. Duck (Eds) *Intimate Relationships: Development, Dynamics, and Deterioration*. Beverly Hills: Sage, pp. 149–175.

Noller, P., and Hiscock, H. (1986). Fitzpatrick's typology: An Australian replication. Paper presented at the Third International Conference on Personal Relationships, Herzlia, Israel, July.

Noller, P., and Venardos, C. (1986). Communication awareness in married couples. *Journal of Social and Personal Relationships*, **3**, 31–42.

Norton, R. (1983a). *Communicator Style: Theory, Applications, and Measures*. Beverly Hills: Sage.

Norton, R. (1983b). Measuring marital quality. *Journal of Marriage and the Family*, February, 141–151.

Norton, R. (1986). Communicator style profiles within the marital context. Paper presented at the meeting of the Speech Communication Association, Boston, November.

Norton, R., and Montgomery, B. (1982). Style, content, and target components of openness. *Communication Research*, **9**, 399–431.

Nuckolls, K. B., Cassel, J., and Kaplan, B. H. (1972). Psychosocial assets, life crises and the prognosis of pregnancy. *American Journal of Epidemiology*, **95**, 431–441.

O'Connell, L. (1984). An exploration of exchange in three relationships: Kindship, friendship and the marketplace. *Journal of Social and Personal Relationships*, **1**, 333–345.

O'Hara, M. W., Neunaber, D. J., and Zekoski, E. M. (1984). Prospective study of postpartum depression: Prevalence, course, and predictive factors. *Journal of Abnormal Psychology*, **93**, 158–171.

O'Hara, M. W., Rehm, L. P., and Campbell, S. B. (1982). Predicting depressive symptomatology: Cognitive-behavioural models and postpartum depression. *Journal of Abnormal Psychology*, **91**, 457–461.

O'Keefe, B., and Delia, J. (1982). Impression formation and message production. In M. Roloff and C. Berger (Eds) *Social Cognition and Communication*. Beverly Hills: Sage, pp. 33–72.

O'Leary, K. D., and Turkewitz, H. (1978). Methodological errors in marital and child treatment research. *Journal of Consulting and Clinical Psychology*, **46**, 247–258.

O'Mahony, J. F. (1984). Knowing others through the self—Influence of self-perception on perception of others: A review. *Current Psychological Research & Reviews*, **3**(4), 48–62.

Ochse, R., and Plug, C. (1986). Cross-cultural investigation of the validity of Erikson's theory of personality development. *Journal of Personality and Social Psychology*, **50**, 1240–1252.

Oldham, G. R., and Hackman, J. (1981). Relationships between organizational structure and employee reactions: Comparing alternative frameworks. *Administrative Science Quarterly*, **26**, 66–83.

Olson, D. H. (1977). Insiders' and outsiders' views of relationships: Research studies. In G. Levinger and H. L. Raush (Eds) *Close Relationships: Perspectives on the Meaning of Intimacy*. Amherst: University of Massachusetts Press, pp. 115–135.

Olson, D. H., and Ryder, R. (1970). Inventory of marital conflicts (IMC): An experimental interaction procedure. *Journal of Marriage and the Family*, **32**, 443–448.

Olweus, D. (1977). Aggression and peer acceptance in adolescent boys: Two short-term longitudinal studies of ratings. *Child Development*, **48**, 1301–1313.

Oppenheim, D., Sagi, A., and Lamb, M. E. (1986). Classifications of infant–adult attachment on Israeli kibbutzim in the first year of life and their relation to socio-emotional development four years later. Paper presented at the International Conference on Infant Studies, Beverly Hills, April.

Orians, G. H. (1969). On the evolution of mating systems in birds and mammals. *American Naturalists*, **103**, 589–603.

Oring, E. (1984). Dyadic traditions. *Journal of Folklore Research*, **21**, 19–28.

Oritt, E. J., Behrman, J., and Paul, S. C. (1982). Social support: Conditions related to satisfaction with received support. Paper presented as part of a symposium at the annual convention of the American Psychological Association, Washington, DC, August.

Orritt, E. J., Paul, S. C., and Behrman, J. A. (1985). The perceived support network inventory. *American Journal of Community Psychology*, **13**, 565–582.

Orlinsky, D. E., and Howard, K. I. (1975). *Varieties of Psychotherapeutic Experience*. New York: Teacher's College Press.

Orlofsky, J. L. (1987). Intimacy status: Theory and research. Manuscript submitted for publication, Univ. of Missouri, St. Louis.

Orlofsky, J. L., Marcia, J. E., and Lesser, I. M. (1973). Ego identity status and the intimacy versus isolation crisis of young adulthood. *Journal of Personality and Social Psychology*, **27**, 211–219.

Orvis, B. R., Kelley, H. H., and Butler, D. (1976). Attributional conflict in young couples. In J. H. Harvey, W. Ickes and R. F. Kidd (Eds) *New Directions in Attribution Research*, Vol. 1. Hillsdale, NJ: Erlbaum, pp. 353–368.

Osgood, C. E., Suci, G. J., and Tannenbaum, P. H. (1957). *The Measurement of Meaning*. Urbana, IL: University of Illinois Press.

Osterweis, M., Solomon, F., and Green, M. (1984). *Bereavement: Reactions, Consequences, and Care*. Washington, DC: National Academy Press.

Ouchi, W. G., and Wilkins, A. L. (1985). Organizational culture. *Annual Review of Sociology*, **11**, 457–483.

Overall, J. (1971). Associations between marital history and the nature of manifest psychopathology. *Journal of Abnormal Psychology*, **78**, 213–221.

Owen, W. (1984). Interpretive themes in relational communication. *Quarterly Journal of Speech*, **70**, 274–287.

Padgett, V. R., and Wolosin, R. J. (1980). Cognitive similarity in dyadic communication. *Journal of Personality and Social Psychology*, **39**, 654–659.

Paine, R. (1969). In search of friendship: An exploratory analysis in middle-class culture. *Man*, December, 505–524.

Paolino, T., and McCrady, B. (1978). *Marriage and Marital Therapy*. New York: Brunner/Mazel.

Parker, S. R. (1964). Type of work, friendship patterns and leisure. *Human Relations*, **17**, 215–219.

Parkes, C. M., and Weiss, R. S. (1983). *Recovery from Bereavement*. New York: Basic Books.

Parks, M. R. (1982). Ideology in interpersonal communication: Off the couch and into the world. In M. Burgoon (Ed.) *Communication Yearbook 5*. Beverly Hills: Sage, pp. 79–108.

Parks, M. R., and Adelman, M. B. (1983). Communication networks and the development of romantic relationships: An expansion of uncertainty reduction theory. *Human Communication Research*, **10**, 55–79.

Parks, M. R., Stan, C. M., and Eggert, L. L. (1983). Romantic involvement and social network involvement. *Social Psychology Quarterly*, **46**, 116–131.

Parlee, M. B. (1979). The friendship bond. *Psychology Today*, October, 42–54.

Parmelee, P., and Werner, C. (1978). Lonely losers: Stereotypes of single dwellers. *Personality and Social Psychology Bulletin*, **4**, 292–295.

Parpal, M., and Maccoby, E. E. (1985). Maternal responsiveness and subsequent child compliance. *Child Development*, **56**, 1326–1334.

Parsons, T., and Bales, R. F. (1955). *Family, Socialization, and Interaction Processes*. New York: Free Press of Glencoe.

Partridge, E. (1966). *Origins: A Short Etymological Dictionary of Modern English*. New York: Macmillan.

Pastor, D. L. (1981). The quality of mother–infant attachment and its relationship to toddlers' initial sociability with peers. *Developmental Psychology*, **17**, 232–335.

Patterson, G. R. (1976). Some procedures for assessing changes in marital interaction patterns. *Oregon Research Bulletin*, **16** (7).

Patterson, G. R. (1980). Mothers: The unacknowledged victims. *Monographs of the Society for Research in Child Development*, **45** (5, Serial No. 196), 1–64.

Patterson, G. R. (1982). *A Social Learning Approach. Vol. 3: Coercive Family Process*. Eugene, OR: Castalia.

Patterson, G. R. (1984a). Microsocial process: A view from the boundary. In J. C. Masters and K. Yarkin-Levin (Eds) *Boundary Areas in Social and Developmental Psychology*. Orlando, FL: Academic Press, pp. 43–66.

Patterson, G. R. (1984b). Siblings: Fellow travelers in coercive family processes. In J. Blanchard and D. C. Blanchard (Eds) *Advances in the Study of Aggression*, Vol. 1. New York: Academic Press.

Patterson, G. R. (1986). Maternal rejection: Determinant or product for deviant child behavior? In W. W. Hartup and Z. Rubin (Eds) *Relationships and Development*. Hillsdale, NJ: Erlbaum, pp. 73–94.

Patterson, G. R., Littman, R. A., and Bricker, W. (1967). Assertive behavior in children: A step toward a theory of aggression. *Monographs of the Society for Research in Child Development*, **32** (5, Whole No. 113).

Patterson, M. L. (1976). An arousal model of interpersonal intimacy. *Psychological Review*, **83**, 235–245.

Patterson, M. L. (1982a). A sequential functional model of nonverbal exchange. *Psychological Review*, **89**, 231–249.

Patterson, M. L. (1982b). Personality and nonverbal involvement: A functional analysis. In W. J. Ickes and E. S. Knowles (Eds) *Nonverbal Behavior: A Functional Perspective*. New York: Springer-Verlag, pp. 141–164.

Patterson, M. L. (1983). *Nonverbal Behavior: A Functional Perspective*. New York: Springer-Verlag.

Patterson, M. L. (1984). Intimacy, social control, and nonverbal involvement: A functional approach. In V. Derlega (Ed.) *Communication, Intimacy, and Close Relationships*. New York: Academic Press, pp. 105–132.

Patterson, M. L. (1985). Social influence and nonverbal exchange. In S. Ellyson and J. Dovidio (Eds) *Power, Dominance, and Nonverbal Behavior*. New York: Springer-Verlag, pp. 207–217.

Patterson, M. L. (1987). Presentational and affect-management functions of nonverbal involvement. *Journal of Nonverbal Behavior*, **11**, 110–122.

Patterson, M. L., Powell, J. L., and Lenihan, M. G. (1986). Touch, compliance, and interpersonal affect. *Journal of Nonverbal Behavior*, **10**, 41–50.

Paykel, E. S., Emms, E. M., Fletcher, J., and Rassaby, E. S. (1980). Life events and social support in puerperal depression. *British Journal of Psychiatry*, **136**, 339–346.

Paykel, E. S., Myers, J. K., Dienelt, M. N., Klerman, G. L., Lindenthal, J. J., and Pepper, M. P. (1969). Life events and depression: A controlled study. *Archives of General Psychiatry*, **21**, 753–760.

Pearce, W. B., and Cronen, V. E. (1980). *Communication, Action and Meaning: The Creation of Social Realities*. New York: Praeger.

Pearlin, L. I. (1983). Role strains and personal stress. In H. B. Kaplan (Ed.) *Psychosocial Stress: Trends in Theory and Research*. New York: Academic Press, pp. 3–32.

Pearlin, L. I. (1985). Social structure and processes of social support. In S. Cohen and S. L. Syme (Eds) *Social Support and Health*. Orlando, FL: Academic Press, pp. 43–60.

Pearlin, L. I., Lieberman, M. A., Managhan, E. G., and Mullan, J. T. (1981). The stress process. *Journal of Health and Social Behavior*, **22**, 337–356.

Pedersen, F. (Ed.) (1980). *The Father–Infant Relationship: Observational Studies in the Family Setting*. New York: Praeger Special Studies.

Penman, R. (1980). *Communication Processes and Relationships*. London: Academic Press.

Pennebaker, J. W., and Beale, S. K. (1986). Confronting a traumatic event. *Journal of Abnormal Psychology*.

Pennebaker, J. W., and O'Heeron, R. C. (1984). Confiding in others and illness rate among spouses of suicide and accidental death victims. *Journal of Abnormal Psychology*, **93**, 473–476.

Peplau, H. E. (1955). Loneliness. *American Journal of Nursing*, **55**, 1476–1481.

Peplau, L. A. (1983). Roles and gender. In H. H. Kelley, E. Berscheid, A. Christensen, J. H. Harvey, T. L. Huston, G. Levinger, E. McClintock, L. A. Peplau and D. R. Peterson. *Close Relationships*. New York: Freeman, pp. 220–264.

Peplau, L. A., and Gordon, S. L. (1985). Women and men in love: Gender differences in close heterosexual relationships. In V. E. O'Leary, R. K. Unger and B. S. Wallston (Eds) *Women, Gender, and Social Psychology*. Hillsdale, NJ: Erlbaum, pp. 257–291.

Peplau, L. A., and Perlman, D. (1979). Blueprint for a social psychological theory of loneliness. In M. Cook and G. Wilson (Eds) *Love and Attraction: An International Conference*. Elmsford, NY: Pergamon, pp. 101–110.

Peplau, L. A., and Perlman, D. (1982). Perspectives on loneliness. In L. A. Peplau and D. Perlman (Eds) *Loneliness: A Sourcebook of Theory, Research and Therapy*. New York: Wiley, pp. 1–18.

Peplau, L. A., Bikson, T. K., Rook, K. S., and Goodchilds, J. D. (1982). Being old and living alone. In L. A. Peplau and D. Perlman (Eds) *Loneliness: A Sourcebook of Theory, Research and Therapy*. New York: Wiley, pp. 135–151.

Peplau, L. A., Miceli, M., and Morasch, B. (1982). Loneliness and self-evaluation. In L. A. Peplau and D. Perlman (Eds) *Loneliness: A Sourcebook of Theory, Research and Therapy*. New York: Wiley, pp. 135–151.

Peplau, L. A., Rubin, Z., and Hill, C. T. (1977). Sexual intimacy in dating relationships. *Journal of Social Issues*, **33** (2), 86–109.

Peplau, L. A., Russell, D., and Heim, M. (1979). The experience of loneliness. In I. H. Frieze, D. Bar-Tal and J. S. Carroll (Eds) *New Approaches to Social Problems: Applications of Attribution Theory*. San Francisco: Jossey-Bass, pp. 53–78.

Perlman, D. (1974). Self-esteem and sexual permissiveness. *Journal of Marriage and the Family*, **36**, 470–473.

Perlman, D., and Duck, S. W. (1987). *Intimate Relationships*. Beverly Hills: Sage.

Perlman, D., and Fehr, B. (1987). The development of intimate relationships. In D. Perlman and S. W. Duck (Eds) *Intimate Relationships: Development, Dynamics and Deterioration*. Beverly Hills: Sage, pp. 1–29.

Perlman, D., and Peplau, L. A. (1981). Toward a social psychology of loneliness. In S. W. Duck and R. Gilmour (Eds) *Personal Relationships 3: Personal Relationships in Disorder*. London: Academic Press, pp. 31–56.

Perlman, D., and Peplau, L. A. (1982). Theoretical approaches to loneliness. In L. A. Peplau and D. Perlman (Eds) *Loneliness: A Sourcebook of Current Theory, Research and Therapy*. New York: Wiley, pp. 123–134.

Perlman, D., and Peplau, L. A. (1984). Loneliness research: A survey of empirical findings. In L. A. Peplau and S. E. Goldston (Eds) *Preventing the Harmful Consequences of Severe and Persistent Loneliness*. Washington, DC: US Government Printing Office, pp. 13–46.

Perlman, D., Gerson, A., and Spinner, B. (1978). Loneliness among senior citizens. *Essence*, **2**, 239–248.

Perls, F., Hefferline, R., and Goodman, P. (1965). *Gestalt Therapy: Excitement and Growth in the Human Personality*. New York: Dell.

Perry, D. G., and Perry, L. C. (1983). Social learning, causal attribution and moral internalization. In J. Bisanz, G. L. Bisanz and R. Kail (Eds) *Learning in Children: Progress in Cognitive Development Research*. New York: Springer-Verlag, pp. 105–136.

Peters-Golden, H. (1982). Breast cancer: Varied perceptions of social support in the illness experience. *Social Science and Medicine*, **16**, 483–491.

Peterson, L. (1980). Developmental changes in verbal and behavioral sensitivity to cues of social norms of altruism. *Child Development*, **51**, 830–838.

Peterson, L., and Gelfand, D. M. (1984). Causal attributions of helping as a function of age and incentives. *Child Development*, **55**, 504–511.

Peterson, L., Hartmann, D. P., and Gelfand, D. M. (1977). Developmental changes in the effects of dependency and reciprocity cues on children's moral judgments and donation rates. *Child Development*, **48**, 1331–1229.

Petrovich, S. B., and Gewirtz, J. L. (1985). The attachment learning process and its relation to cultural and biological evolution: Proximate and ultimate considerations. In M. Reite and T. Field (Eds) *The Psychobiology of Attachment and Separation*. Orlando, FL: Academic Press, pp. 259–291.

Pfeffer, J. (1982). *Organizations and Organization Theory*. Boston: Pitman.

Pfeffer, J., and Salancik, G. (1978). *The External Control of Organizations: A Resource Dependence Perspective.* Boston: Harper & Row.

Pfohl, B., Stangl, D., and Zimmerman, M. (1984). The implications of DSM-III disorders for patients with major depression. *Journal of Affective Disorders,* **7,** 309–318.

Pfungst, O. (1911). *Clever Hans, the Horse of Mr. Von Osten.* New York: Holt, Rinehart, & Winston.

Piaget, J. (1948). *The Moral Judgment of the Child* (trans. H. Gabin). Glencoe, IL: Free Press.

Pierce, R. (1973). Training in interpersonal communication skills with the partners of deteriorated marriages. *Family Coordinator,* **22** (2), 223–227.

Pietromonaco, P. R., and Rook, K. S. (1987). Decision style in depression: The contribution of perceived risks versus benefits. *Journal of Personality and Social Psychology,* **52,** 399–408.

Pike, G. R., and Sillars, A. L. (1985). Reciprocity and marital communication. *Journal of Social and Personal Relationships,* **2,** 303–324.

Planalp, S. (1985). Relational schemata: A test of alternative forms of relational knowledge as guides to communication. *Human Communication Research,* **12,** 3–29.

Planalp, S., and Honeycutt, J. M. (1985). Events that increase uncertainty in personal relationships. *Human Communication Research,* **11,** 593–604.

Pleck, J. (1977). The work–family role system. *Social Problems,* **24,** 417–427.

Plomin, R., and Daniels, D. (1986). Genetics and shyness. In W. H. Jones, J. M. Cheek and S. R. Briggs (Eds) *Shyness: Perspectives on Research and Treatment.* New York: Plenum, pp. 63–80.

Plomin, R., and Daniels, D. (1987). Why are children within the same family so different from one another? *Behavioral and Brain Sciences,* **10,** 1–59.

Pope, K. S., Levenson, H., and Schover, L. (1979). Sexual intimacy in psychology training: Results and implications of a national survey. *American Psychologist,* **34,** 682–689.

Porritt, D. (1979). Social support in crisis: Quantity or quality? *Social Science and Medicine,* **13A,** 715–721.

Posner, M. I. (1973). *Cognition: An Introduction.* Glenview, IL: Scott, Foresman.

Potasznik, H., and Nelson, G. (1984). Stress and social support: The burden experienced by the family of a mentally ill person. *American Journal of Community Psychology,* **12,** 589–607.

Prager, K. J. (1986). Intimacy status: Its relationship to locus of control, self-disclosure, and anxiety in adults. *Personality and Social Psychology Bulletin,* **12,** 91–110.

Price, R. A., and Vandenberg, S. S. (1979). Matching for physical attractiveness. *Personality and Social Psychology Bulletin,* **5,** 398–400.

Prigogine, I., and Stengers, I. (1984). *Order Out of Chaos: Man's New Dialogue with Nature.* Toronto: Bantam Books.

Procidano, M. E., and Heller, K. (1983). Measures of perceived social support from friends and from family: Three validation studies. *American Journal of Community Psychology,* **11,** 1–24.

Purdy, T. F. (1978). Perceptions of involvement in close relationships. Senior honors thesis, University of Massachusetts, Amherst.

Putallaz, M. (1983). Predicting children's sociometic status from their behavior. *Child Development,* **54,** 1417–1426.

Putallaz, M., and Gottman, J. M. (1981). An interactional model of children's entry into peer groups. *Child Development,* **52,** 986–994.

Putman, W. B., and Street, R. L., Jr (1984). The conception and perception of non-content speech performance: Implications for speech accommodation theory. *International Journal of the Sociology of Language,* **46,** 97–114.

Quinn, R. E. (1977). Coping with Cupid: The formation, impact, and management of romantic relationships in organizations. *Administrative Science Quarterly,* **22,** 30–45.

Quinn, R. E., and Judge, N. A. (1978). The office romance: No bliss for the boss. *Management Review*, **67**, 43–49.

Quinton, D., and Rutter, M. (1987). *Parenting Breakdown: The Making and Breaking of Intergenerational Links*. Aldershot: Gower.

Radke-Yarrow, M., and Zahn-Waxler, C. (1986). The role of familial factors in the development of prosocial behavior: Research findings and questions. In D. Olweus, J. Block and M. Radke-Yarrow (Eds) *Development of Antisocial and Prosocial Behavior: Research, Theories, and Issues*. Orlando, FL: Academic Press, pp. 207–233.

Radloff, L. S. (1977). The CES-D Scale: A self-report depression scale for research in the general population. *Applied Psychological Measurement*, **1**, 385–401.

Rahim, M. A. (1983). A measure of styles of handling interpersonal conflict. *Academy of Management Journal*, **26**, 368–376.

Rajecki, D. W., Ickes, W., and Tanford, S. (1981). Locus of control and reactions to a stranger. *Personality and Social Psychology Bulletin*, **7**, 282–289.

Rands, M., and Levinger, G. (1979). Implicit theories of relationship: An intergenerational study. *Journal of Personality and Social Psychology*, **37**, 645–661.

Rangell, L. (1963). On friendship. *Journal of American Psychoanalytic Association*, **11**, 3–54.

Rank, O. (1936/1978). *Truth and Reality*. New York: Norton.

Ratner, N., and Bruner, J. S. (1978). Games, social exchange, and the acquisition of language. *Journal of Child Language*, **5**, 1–15.

Raush, H. L., Barry, W. A., Hertel, R. K., and Swain, M. A. (1974). *Communication, Conflict and Marriage*. San Francisco: Jossey-Bass.

Rawlins, W. (1983a). Negotiating close friendship: The dialectics of conjunctive freedoms. *Human Communication Research*, **9**, 255–266.

Rawlins, W. (1983b). Openness as problematic in ongoing friendships: Two conversational dilemmas. *Communication Monographs*, **50**, 1–13.

Reed, D., and Weinberg, M. S. (1984). Premarital coitus: Developing and established sexual scripts. *Social Psychology Quarterly*, **47**, 129–138.

Regan, D. T., Straus, E., and Fazio, R. (1974). Liking and the attribution process. *Journal of Experimental Social Psychology*, **10**, 385–397.

Reis, H. T. (1984). Social interaction and well-being. In S. W. Duck (Ed.) *Personal Relationships 5: Repairing Personal Relationships*. London: Academic Press, pp. 21–45.

Reis, H. T. (1986). Levels of interest in the study of interpersonal justice. In H. W. Bierhoff, R. L. Cohen and J. Greenberg (Eds) *Justice in Interpersonal Relations*. New York: Plenum, pp. 187–209.

Reis, H. T. (1987). Where does social support come from? Manuscript in preparation, University of Rochester.

Reis, H. T., Senchak, M., and Solomon, B. (1985). Sex differences in the intimacy of social interaction: Further examination of potential explanations. *Journal of Personality and Social Psychology*, **48**, 1204–1217.

Reisman, J. M. (1981). Adult friendships. In S. W. Duck and R. Gilmour (Eds) *Personal Relationships 2: Developing Personal Relationships*. New York: Academic Press.

Reiss, I. L. (1964). The scaling of premarital sexual permissiveness. *Journal of Marriage and the Family*, **26**, 188–198.

Reiss, I. L. (1967). *The Social Context of Premarital Sexual Permissiveness*. New York: Holt, Rinehart, & Winston.

Reiss, I. L. (1980). *Family Systems in America*, 3rd edn. New York: Holt, Rinehart, & Winston.

Reiss, I. L. (1986). A sociological journey into sexuality. *Journal of Marriage and the Family*, **48**, 233–242.

Reitz, K. P. (1982). Using loglinear analysis with network data: Another look at Sampson's monastery. *Social Networks*, **4**, 243–256.

Rempel, J. K., Holmes, J. G., and Zanna, M. P. (1985). Trust in close relationships. *Journal of Personality and Social Psychology*, **49**, 95–112.

Renne, K. S. (1971). Health and marital experience in an urban population. *Journal of Marriage and the Family*, **33**, 338–350.

Revenson, T. A., and Johnson, J. L. (1984). Social and demographic correlates of loneliness in late life. *American Journal of Community Psychology*, **12**, 71–85.

Rheingold, H. L. (1969). The social and socializing infant. In D. A. Goslin (Ed.) *Handbook of Socialization Theory and Research*. Chicago: Rand McNally, pp. 779–790.

Rheingold, H. L. (1982). Little children's participation in the work of adults, a nascent prosocial behavior. *Child Development*, **53**, 114–125.

Rheingold, H. L., and Eckerman, C. O. (1973). Fear of stranger: A critical examination. In H. W. Reese (Ed.) *Advances in Child Development and Behavior*, Vol. 8. New York: Academic Press, pp. 185–222.

Rheingold, H. L., Hay, D. F., and West, M. J. (1976). Sharing in the second year of life. *Child Development*, **47**, 1148–1158.

Ricciuti, H. (1974). Fear and the development of social attachments in the first year of life. In M. Lewis and L. Rosenblum (Eds) *The Origins of Human Behavior: Fear*. New York: Wiley, pp. 73–106.

Rich, A. R., Sullivan, J. A., and Rich, V. L. (1986). Hardiness, social support, and depression in college students. Paper presented at the annual meeting of the Midwestern Psychological Association, Chicago, Illinois, May.

Richardson, D. R. (1987). Management of interpersonal conflict. *Social Science Newsletter*.

Richey, M. H., and Richey, H. W. (1980). The significance of best-friend relationships in adolescence. *Psychology in the Schools*, **17**, 536–540.

Richters, J., and Waters, E. (1988). Attachment and socialization: The positive side of social influence. In M. Lewis and S. Feinman (Eds) *Social Influences and Development*. New York: Plenum.

Ricks, M. H. (1986). The social transmission of parental behavior: Attachment across generations. In I. Bretherton and E. Waters (Eds) Growing points of attachment theory and research (pp. 211–227). *Monographs of the Society for Research in Child Development*, **50** (1–2, Serial No. 209).

Ridgeway, C. L. (1983). *The Dynamics of Small Groups*. New York: St Martin's.

Ridley, C., and Avery, A. (1979). Social network influence on the dyadic relationship. In R. L. Burgess and T. L. Huston (Eds) *Social Exchange in Developing Relationships*. New York: Academic Press, pp. 223–246.

Riley, D., and Eckenrode, J. (1986). Social ties: Subgroup differences in costs and benefits. *Journal of Personality and Social Psychology*, **51**, 770–778.

Riseman, D., and Watson, J. (1964). The sociability project: A chronicle of frustration and achievement. In P. E. Hammond (Ed.) *Sociologists at Work*. New York: Basic Books.

Riskin, J., and Faunce, E. (1970). Family interaction scales, III. Discussion of methodology and substantive findings. *Archives of General Psychiatry*, **22**, 527–537.

Rittle, R. H. (1981). Changes in helping behavior: Self versus situational perceptions as mediators of the foot-in-the-door effect. *Personality and Social Psychology Bulletin*, **7**, 431–437.

Roach, A., Frazier, L., and Bowden, S. (1981). The marital satisfaction scale: Development of a measure for intervention research. *Journal of Marriage and the Family*, August, 537–546.

Roback, H. D. (Ed.) (1984). *Helping Patients and Their Families Cope with Medical Problems*. San Francisco: Jossey-Bass.

Robin, A. L., Koepke, T., and Nayar, M. (1986). Conceptualizing, assessing, and treating parent–adolescent conflict. In B. B. Lahey and A. E. Kazdin (Eds) *Advances in Clinical Child Psychology*, Vol. 9. New York: Plenum.

Robins, E. J. (1983). An empirical test of the compatibility testing model of marital choice. Unpublished doctoral dissertation proposal, The Pennsylvania State University, State College.

Robins, E. J. (1985). Compatibility, field search, and courtship progress: Examining the compatibility testing model of marital choice. Unpublished manuscript, The University of North Carolina, Greensboro.

Robinson, E., and Price, M. (1980). Pleasurable behavior in marital interaction: An observational study. *Journal of Consulting and Clinical Psychology*, **48**, 117–118.

Robinson, I. E., and Jedlicka, D. (1982). Change in sexual attitudes and behavior of college students from 1965 to 1980: A research note. *Journal of Marriage and the Family*, **44**, 237–240.

Rodin, M. J. (1982). Non-engagement, failure to engage, and disengagement. In S. W. Duck (Ed.) *Personal Relationships 4: Dissolving Personal Relationships*. New York: Academic Press.

Roff, M., Sells, S. B., and Golden, M. M. (1972). *Social Adjustment and Personality Development in Children*. Minneapolis: University of Minnesota Press.

Rogers, C. R. (1961). *On Becoming a Person*. Boston: Houghton Mifflin.

Rogers, C. R. (1970). *Carl Rogers on Encounter Groups*. New York: Harper & Row.

Rogers, C. R. (1972). *Becoming Partners: Marriage and its Alternatives*. New York: Delacorte.

Rogers, L. E. (1972). Dyadic systems and transactional communication in a family context. Unpublished doctoral dissertation, Michigan State University, East Lansing, Michigan.

Rogers, L. E. (1981). Symmetry and complementarity: Evolution and evaluation of an idea. In C. Wilder-Mott and J. H. Weakland (Eds) *Rigor and Imagination: Essays in the Legacy of Gregory Bateson*. New York: Praeger, pp. 231–251.

Rogers, L. E., and Farace, R. V. (1975). Analysis of relational communication in dyads: New measurement procedures. *Human Communication Research*, **1**, 222–239.

Rogers, L. E., Courtright, J. A., and Millar, F. E. (1980). Message control intensity: Rationale and preliminary findings. *Communication Monographs*, **47**, 201–219.

Rogers, L. E., Millar, F. E., and Bavelas, J. B. (1985). Methods for analysing marital conflict discourse: Implications of a systems approach. *Family Process*, **24**, 53–72.

Rogers-Millar, L. E., and Millar, F. E. (1979). Domineeringness and dominance: A transactional view. *Human Communication Research*, **5**, 238–246.

Rogoff, B., Malkin, C. M., and Gilbride, K. (1984). Interaction with babies as guidance in development. *New Directions for Child Development*, **23**, 31–43.

Rokeach, M. (1968). *Beliefs, Attitudes, and Values*. San Francisco: Jossey-Bass.

Rokeach, M. (1973). *The Nature of Human Values*. New York: Free Press.

Roloff, M. E. (1981). *Interpersonal Communication: The Social Exchange Approach*. Beverly Hills: Sage.

Roloff, M. E., and Barnicott, E. F., Jr (1978). The situational use of pro- and anti-social compliance-gaining strategies by high and low Machiavellians. In B. D. Ruben (Ed.) *Communication Yearbook 2*. New Brunswick, NJ: Transaction Books, pp. 193–205.

Roloff, M. E., and Barnicott, E. F., Jr (1979). The influence of dogmatism on the situational use of pro- and anti-social compliance-gaining strategies. *Southern Speech Communication Journal*, **45**, 37–54.

Rook, K. S. (1983). The functions of social bonds: Perspectives from research on social support, loneliness and social isolation. Paper presented at NATO Advanced Research Workshop, France, Banas, September.

Rook, K. S. (1984a). The negative side of social interaction: Impact on psychological well-being. *Journal of Personality and Social Psychology*, **46**, 1097–1108.

Rook, K. S. (1984b). Promoting social bonding: Strategies for helping the lonely and socially isolated. *American Psychologist*, **39**, 1389–1407.

Rook, K. S. (1985). The functions of social bonds: Perspectives from research on social support, loneliness, and social isolation. In I. G. Sarason and B. R. Sarason (Eds) *Social Support: Theory, Research, and Applications*. The Hague: Martinus Nijhoff, pp. 243–267.

Rook, K. S. (1987). Reciprocity of social exchange and social satisfaction among older women. *Journal of Personality and Social Psychology*, **52**, 145–154.

Rook, K. S., and Dooley, D. (1985). Applying social support research: Theoretical problems and future directions. *Journal of Social Issues*, **41**, 5–28.

Rook, K. S., and Peplau, L. A. (1982). Perspectives on helping the lonely. In L. A. Peplau and D. Perlman (Eds) *Loneliness: A Sourcebook of Current Theory, Research and Therapy*. New York: Wiley, pp. 357–378.

Rook, K. S., and Thuras, P. (1987). Attitudes toward solitude, 'solitude skill', and loneliness. Unpublished manuscript, University of California, Irvine, Program in Social Ecology.

Roopnarine, J. L., and Field, T. M. (1984). Play interactions of friends and acquaintances in nursery school. In T. M. Field, J. L. Roopnarine and M. Segal (Eds) *Friendship in Normal and Handicapped Children*. Norwood, NJ: Ablex.

Rosch, E. (1978). Principles of categorization. In E. Rosch and B. B. Lloyd (Eds) *Cognition and Categorization*. Hillsdale, NJ: Erlbaum.

Rose, S. M. (1984). How friendships end: Patterns among young adults. *Journal of Social and Personal Relationships*, **1**, 267–277.

Rose, S. M. (1985). Same and cross-sex friendships and the psychology of homosociality. *Sex Roles*, **12**, 63–74.

Rose, S., and Serafica, F. C. (1986). Keeping and ending casual, close and best friendships. *Journal of Personal and Social Relationships*, **3**, 275–288.

Rosenberg, M. J., and Abelson, R. P. (1960). An analysis of cognitive balancing. In M. J. Rosenberg, C. I. Hovland, W. J. McGuire, R. P. Abelson and J. W. Brehm (Eds) *Attitude Organization and Change*. New Haven: Yale University Press, pp. 112–163.

Rosenblatt, P. C. (1974). Cross-cultural perspective on attraction. In T. L. Huston (Ed.) *Foundations of Interpersonal Attraction*. New York: Academic Press, pp. 79–95.

Rosenblatt, P. C. (1983). *Bitter, Bitter Tears: Nineteenth Century Diarists and Twentieth-Century Grief Theories*. Minneapolis: University of Minnesota Press.

Rosencrance, J. (1986). Racetrack buddy relations: Compartmentalized and satisfying. *Journal of Social and Personal Relationships*, **3**, 441–456.

Rosenfeld, H. M. (1978). Conversational control functions of nonverbal behavior. In A. W. Siegman and S. Feldstein (Eds) *Nonverbal Behavior and Communication*. Hillsdale, NJ: Erlbaum, pp. 291–328.

Rosenman, M. F. (1978). Liking, loving, and styles of loving. *Psychological Reports*, **42**, 1243–1246.

Rosenthal, M. K. (1967). The generalization of dependency behavior from mother to stranger. *Journal of Child Psychology and Psychiatry*, **8**, 117–133.

Rosenthal, M. K. (1982). Vocal dialogues in the neonatal period. *Development Psychology*, **18**, 17–21.

Roskin, M. (1982). Coping with life changes—A preventive social work approach. *American Journal of Community Psychology*, **10**, 331–340.

Ross, H. S. (1982). Toddler peer relations: Differentiation of games and conflicts. *Canadian Journal of Behavioral Science*, **14**, 364–379.

Ross, H. S., and Goldman, B. D. (1977). Establishing new social relations in infancy. In T. Alloway, P. Pliner and L. Krames (Eds) *Advances in the Study of Communication and Affect, Vol. 3: Attachment Behavior*. New York: Plenum, pp. 61–79.

Ross, H. S., Lollis, S. P., and Elliott, C. (1982). Toddler–peer communication. In K. H. Rubin and H. S. Ross (Eds) *Peer Relationships and Social Skills in Childhood*. New York: Springer-Verlag.

Ross, L. (1977). The intuitive psychologist and his shortcomings: Distortions in the attribution process. In L. Berkowitz (Ed.) *Advances in Experimental Social Psychology*, Vol. 10. New York: Academic Press, pp. 173–220.

Ross, M., and Sicoly, F. (1979). Egocentric biases in availability and attribution. *Journal of Personality and Social Psychology*, **37**, 322–336.

Rounsaville, B. J., Weissman, M. M., Prusoff, B. G., and Herceg-Baron, R. L. (1979). Marital disputes and treatment outcomes in depressed women. *Comprehensive Psychiatry*, **20**, 483–489.

Roy, A. (1978). Vulnerability factors and depression in women. *British Journal of Psychiatry*, **133**, 106–110.

Roy, A. (1985a). Depression and marriage. *Journal of the University of Ottawa*, **10** (2), 101–103.

Roy, A. (1985b). Chronic pain and marital difficulties. *Health & Social Work*, **10** (3), 199–207.

Roy, P. (1983). Is continuity enough? Substitute care and socialization. Paper presented at the Spring Scientific Meeting, Child and Adolescent Psychiatry Section, Royal College of Psychiatrists, London, March.

Rubenstein, C. M., and Shaver, P. (1982a). The experience of loneliness. In L. A. Peplau and D. Perlman (Eds) *Loneliness: A Sourcebook of Current Theory, Research and Therapy*. New York: Wiley, pp. 206–223.

Rubenstein, C. M., and Shaver, P. (1982b). *In Search of Intimacy*. New York: Delacorte.

Rubenstein, J. (1973). *City Police*. New York: Ferrar, Strauss, & Giroux.

Rubenstein, J., and Howes, C. (1976). The effects of peers on toddler interaction with mothers and toys. *Child Development*, **47**, 597–605.

Rubenstein, J., Howes, C., and Pedersen, F. A. (1982). Second order effects of peers on mother–toddler interaction. *Infant Behavior and Development*, **5**, 185–194.

Rubin, J. Z. (1980). Experimental research on third-party intervention in conflict: Toward some generalizations. *Psychological Bulletin*, **87**, 370–391.

Rubin, K. H. (1982). Social and social-cognitive developmental characteristics of young isolate, normal, and sociable children. In K. H. Rubin and H. S. Ross (Eds) *Peer Relationships and Social Skills in Childhood*. New York: Springer-Verlag.

Rubin, L. B. (1976). *Worlds of Pain: Life in the Working-Class Family*. New York: Basic Books.

Rubin, L. B. (1983). *Intimate Strangers: Men and Women Together*. New York: Harper & Row.

Rubin, L. B. (1985). *Just Friends: The Role of Friendship in our Lives*. New York: Harper & Row.

Rubin, R. B. (1977). The role of context in information seeking and impressive formation. *Communication Monographs*, **44**, 81–90.

Rubin, R. B. (1979). The effect of context on information seeking across the span of initial interactions. *Communication Quarterly*, **27**, 13–20.

Rubin, Z. (1970). Measurement of romantic love. *Journal of Personality and Social Psychology*, **16**, 265–273.

Rubin, Z. (1973). *Liking and Loving: An Invitation to Social Psychology*. New York: Holt, Rinehart, & Winston.

Rubin, Z. (1980). *Children's Friendships*. Cambridge, MA: Harvard University Press.

Rubin, Z. (1982). Children without friends. In L. A. Peplau and D. Perlman (Eds) *Loneliness: A Sourcebook of Current Theory, Research and Therapy*. New York: Wiley, pp. 255–268.

Rubin, Z. (1984). Toward a science of relationships. *Contemporary Psychology*, **29**, 856–858.

Rubin, Z., and Levinger, G. (1974). Theory and data badly mated: A critique of Murstein's SVR and Lewis's PDF models of mate selection. *Journal of Marriage and the Family*, **36**, 226–231.

Rubin, Z., and Mitchell, C. (1976). Couples research as couples counseling: Some unintended effects of studying close relationships. *American Psychologist*, **31**, 17–25.

Rubin, Z., and Shenker, S. (1976). Friendship, proximity and self-disclosure. *Journal of Personality*, **46**, 1–22.

Rubin, Z., Hill, C. T., Peplau, L. A., and Dunkel-Schetter, C. (1980). Self-disclosure in dating couples: Sex roles and the ethic of openness. *Journal of Marriage and the Family*, **42**, 305–317.

Rubin, Z., Peplau, L. A., and Hill, C. T. (1981). Loving and leaving: Sex differences in romantic attachment. *Sex Roles*, **7**, 821–835.

Ruesch, J., and Bateson, G. (1951). *Communication: The Social Matrix of Psychiatry*. New York: Norton.

Rueveni, U. (1979). *Networking Families in Crisis*. New York: Human Sciences Press.

Runkel, P. (1956). Cognitive similarity in facilitating communication. *Sociometry*, **19**, 178–191.

Rusbult, C. E. (1980). Commitment and satisfaction in romantic associations: A test of the investment model. *Journal of Experimental Social Psychology*, **16**, 172–186.

Rusbult, C. E. (1983). A longitudinal test of the investment model: The development (and deterioration) of satisfaction and commitment in heterosexual involvements. *Journal of Personality and Social Psychology*, **45**, 101–117.

Rusbult, C. E. (1987). Responses to dissatisfaction in close relationships: The exit-voice–loyalty–neglect model. In D. Perlman and S. W. Duck (Eds) *Intimate Relationships: Development, Dynamics, and Deterioration*. Newbury Park, CA: Sage, pp. 209–237.

Rusbult, C. E., and Zembrodt, I. M. (1983). Responses to dissatisfaction in romantic involvements: A multidimensional scaling analysis. *Journal of Experimental Social Psychology*, **19**, 274–293.

Rusbult, C. E., Johnson, D. J., and Morrow, G. D. (1986). Impact of couple patterns of problem solving on distress and nondistress in dating relationships. *Journal of Personality and Social Psychology*, **50**, 744–753.

Ruscher, S. M., and Gotlib, I. H. (in press). Marital interaction patterns of couples with and without a depressed partner. *Behavior Therapy*.

Russell, B. (1945/1972). *A History of Western Philosophy*. New York: Simon & Schuster.

Russell, D., Cutrona, C. E., Rose, J., and Yurko, K. (1984). Social and emotional loneliness: An examination of Weiss's typology of loneliness. *Journal of Personality and Social Psychology*, **46**, 1313–1321.

Russell, D., Peplau, L. A., and Cutrona, C. E. (1980). The revised UCLA loneliness scale: Concurrent and discriminant validity evidence. *Journal of Personality and Social Psychology*, **39**, 472–480.

Rutter, M. (1987). Functions and consequences of relationships: Some psychopathological considerations. In R. A. Hinde and J. Stevenson-Hinde (Eds) *Relations Between Relationships*. Oxford: Oxford University Press.

Ryder, R. G., Kafka, J. S., and Olson, D. H. (1971). Separating and joining influences in courtship and early marriage. *American Journal of Orthopsychiatry*, **41**, 450–464.

Sabatelli, R. (1984). The marital comparison level index: A measure for assessing outcomes relative to expectations. *Journal of Marriage and the Family*, **46**, 651–661.

Sabatelli, R., Buck, R., and Dreyer, A. (1980). Communication via facial cues in intimate dyads. *Personality and Social Psychology Bulletin*, **6**, 242–247.

Sabatelli, R., Buck, R., and Dreyer, A. (1981). Nonverbal communication accuracy in married couples: Relationships with marital complaints. *Journal of Personality and Social Psychology*, **43**, 1088–1097.

Sabatelli, R., Buck, R., and Kenny, D. A. (1986). A social relations analysis of nonverbal communication accuracy in married couples. *Journal of Personality*, **54**, 513–527.

Sabini, J., and Silver, M. (1981). Introspection and causal accounts. *Journal of Personality and Social Psychology*, **40**, 171–179.

Sackett, G. P. (1978). Measurement in observational research. In G. P. Sackett (Ed.) *Observing Behavior*, Vol. 2. Baltimore: University Park Press, pp. 25–44.

Sackett, G. P. (1979). The lag sequential analysis of contingency and cyclicity in behavioral interaction research. In J. P. Osofsky (Ed.) *Handbook of Infant Development*. New York: Wiley, pp. 623–649.

Sacks, O. (1985). *The Man who Mistook his Wife for a Hat and Other Clinical Tales*. New York: Summit Books.

Sadler, W. A., Jr (1978). Dimensions in the problem of loneliness: A phenomenological approach. *Journal of Phenomenological Psychology*, **9**, 1–12.

Sagi, A., and Hoffman, M. (1976). Empathetic distress in the newborn. *Developmental Psychology*, **12**, 175–176.

Sagi, A., Lamb, M. E., Lewkowicz, K. S., Shoham, R., Dvir, R., and Estes, D. (1985). Security of infant–mother, –father, and –metapelet attachments in kibbutz-reared Israeli children. In I. Bretherton and E. Waters (Eds) Growing points in attachment theory and research. *Monograph of the Society for Research in Child Development*, **50** (1–2, Serial No. 209), 257–275.

Sahlins, M. D. (1965). On the sociology of primitive exchange. In M. Banton (Ed.) *Relevance of Models of Social Anthropology*. New York: Praeger.

Salhoz, E., Michael, R., Starr, M., Doherty, S., Abramson, P., and Wing, P. (1986). Too late for Prince Charming? *Newsweek*, June, 54–61.

Sameroff, A. J., and Cavanagh, P. J. (1979). Learning in infancy: A developmental perspective. In J. Osofsky (Ed.) *Handbook of Infant Development*. New York: Wiley.

Sameroff, A. J., and Chandler, M. J. (1975). Reproductive risk and the continuum of caretaking casualty. In F. D. Horowitz (Ed.) *Review of Child Development Research*, Vol. 4. Chicago: University of Chicago Press.

Sandler, I. N., and Barrera, M. (1984). Toward a multidimensional approach to assessing the affects of social support. *American Journal of Community Psychology*, **12**, 37–52.

Sandler, I. N., and Lakey, B. (1982). Locus of control as a stress moderator: The role of control perceptions and social support. *American Journal of Community Psychology*, **10**, 65–80.

Sarason, B. R., Sarason, I. G., Hacker, T. A., and Basham, R. B. (1985). Concomitants of social support: Social skills, physical attractiveness, and gender. *Journal of Personality and Social Psychology*, **49**, 469–480.

Sarason, I. G., and Sarason, B. R. (1982). Concomitants of social support: Attitudes, personality characteristics, and life experiences. *Journal of Personality*, **50**, 331–344.

Sarason, I. G., and Sarason, B. R. (Eds) (1985). *Social Support: Theory, Research, and Applications*. The Hague: Martinus Nijhoff.

Sarason, I. G., Levine, H. M., Basham, R. B., and Sarason, B. R. (1983). Assessing social support: The Social Support Questionnaire. *Journal of Personality and Social Psychology*, **44**, 127–139.

Sarason, I. G., Sarason, B. R., and Shearin, E. N. (1986). Social support as an individual difference variable: Its stability, origins, and relations aspects. *Journal of Personality and Social Psychology*, **50**, 845–855.

Satran, G. (1978). Notes on loneliness. *Journal of the Academy of Psychoanalysis*, **6**, 281–300.

Scanzoni, J., and Polonko, P. (1980). A conceptual approach to explicit marital negotiation. *Journal of Marriage and the Family*, **42** (February), 31–44.

Schaap, C. (1982). *Communication Adjustment*. Lisse, Netherlands: Swets & Zeitlinger.

Schachter, S. (1959). *The Psychology of Affiliation*. Stanford: Stanford University Press.

Schaefer, M. T., and Olson, D. H. (1981). Assessing intimacy: The PAIR inventory. *Journal of Marital and Family Therapy*, **7**, 47–60.

Schaffer, H. R. (1971). *The Growth of Sociability*. Harmondsworth: Penguin.

Schaffer, H. R. (1984). *The Child's Entry into a Social World*. Orlando, FL: Academic Press.

Schaffer, H. R. (1986). Some thoughts of an ordinologist. *Developmental Review*, **6**, 115–121.

Schank, R. C., and Abelson, R. P. (1977). *Scripts, Plans, Goals and Understanding: An Inquiry into Human Knowledge Structures*. Hillsdale, NJ: Erlbaum.

Scheflen, A. E. (1963). Communication and regulation in psychotherapy. *Psychiatry*, **28**, 126–136.

Scheflen, A. E. (1964). The significance of posture in communication systems. *Psychiatry*, **27**, 316–331.

Scheflen, A. E. (1974). *How Behavior Means*. Garden City, NJ: Anchor.

Scheflen, A. E., and Ashcraft, N. (1976). *Human Territories: How we behave in space and time*. Englewood Cliffs: Prentice Hall.

Schein, H. M. (1974). Loneliness and interpersonal isolation: Focus for therapy with schizophrenic patients. *American Journal of Psychotherapy*, **28**, 95–107.

Schellenberg, J. A. (1960). Homogamy in personal values and the 'field of eligibles'. *Social Forces*, **39**, 157–162.

Scherer, K. R., and Ekman, P. (1982). *Handbook of Research in Nonverbal Behavior*. Cambridge: Cambridge University Press.

Schilling, R. F., Gilchrist, L. D., and Schinke, S. P. (1984). Coping and social support in families of developmentally disabled children. *Family Relations*, **33**, 47–54.

Schlenker, B. R. (1984). Identities, identifications, and relationships. In V. J. Derlega (Ed.) *Communication, Intimacy, and Close Relationships*. New York: Academic Press, pp. 71–104.

Schlenker, B. R., and Leary, M. R. (1982). Social anxiety and self-presentation: A conceptualization and model. *Psychological Bulletin*, **92**, 641–669.

Schless, A. P., Schwartz, L., Goetz, C., and Mendels, J. (1974). How depressives view the significance of life events. *British Journal of Psychiatry*, **125**, 406–410.

Schmidt, C. F. (1976). Understanding human action: Recognizing the plans and motives of other persons. In J. S. Carroll and J. W. Payne (Eds) *Cognition and Social Behavior*. Hillsdale, NJ: Erlbaum, pp. 47–67.

Schmidt, N., and Sermat, V. (1983). Measuring loneliness in different relationships. *Journal of Personality and Social Psychology*, **44**, 1038–1047.

Schneider, C., Hoffmeister, J. K., and Helfer, R. E. (1976). In R. E. Helfer and C. H. Kempe (Eds) *Child Abuse and Neglect: The Family and the Community*. Cambridge, MA: Ballinger, pp. 393–407.

Schoenfeld, P., Halevy-Martini, J., Jemley-Van der Velden, E., and Ruhf, L. (1985). Network therapy: An outcome study of twelve social networks. *Journal of Community Psychology*, **13**, 281–287.

Schönpflug, W. (1985). Goal directed behavior as a source of stress: Psychological origins and consequences of inefficiency. In M. Frese and J. Sabini (Eds) *The Concept of Action in Psychology*. Hillsdale, NJ: Erlbaum, pp. 172–188.

Schultz, N. R., and Moore, D. (1984). Loneliness: Correlates, attributions, and coping among older adults. *Personality and Social Bulletin*, **10**, 67–77.

Schultz, N. R., Jr, and Moore, D. (1986). The loneliness experience of college students: Sex differences. *Personality and Social Psychology Bulletin*, **12**, 111–119.

Schulz, R., and Rau, M. T. (1985). Social support through the life course. In S. Cohen and S. L. Syme (Eds) *Social Support and Health*. Orlando, FL: Academic Press, pp. 129–150.

Schumm, W. R., Anderson, S. A., Benigas, J. E., McCutchen, M. B., Griffin, C. L., Morris, J. E., and Race, G. S. (1985). Criterion-related validity of the Kansas Marital Satisfaction Scale. *Psychological Reports*, **56**, 719–722.

Schumm, W., Benigas, J., McCutchen, M., Griffin, C., Anderson, A., and Race, G. (1983). Measuring empathy, regard, and congruence in the marital relationship. *Journal of Social Psychology*, **119**, 141–142.

Schumm, W., Bollman, S., and Jurich, A. (1981). The dimensionality of an abbreviated version of the Relationship Inventory: An urban replication with married couples. *Psychological Reports*, **48**, 51–56.

Schumm, W., Jurich, A., and Bollman, S. (1980). The dimensionality of an abbreviated Relationship Inventory for couples. *Journal of Psychology*, **105**, 225–230.

Schwartz, J., and Shaver, P. (1987). Emotions and emotions knowledge in interpersonal relations. In W. Jones and D. Perlman (Eds) *Advances in Personal Relationships*, Vol. 1. Greenwich, CT: JAI Press, pp. 197–241.

Schwarz, J. C. (1972). Effects of peer familiarity on the behavior of preschoolers in a novel situation. *Journal of Personality and Social Psychology*, **24**, 276–284.

Scott, M. B., and Lyman, S. (1968). Accounts. *American Sociological Review*, **33**, 46–62.

Scudder, J. (1986). Power, threat use, and the formation of agreements: An alternative compliance-gaining approach. Paper presented at the annual meeting of the Speech Communication Association, Chicago, Illinois.

Sears, D. O. (1986). College sophomores in the laboratory: Influences of a narrow data base on social psychology's view of human nature. *Journal of Personality and Social Psychology*, **51**, 515–530.

Sears, R. R. (1951). A theoretical framework for personality and social behavior. *American Psychologist*, **6**, 476–482.

Sears, R. R. (1963). Dependency motivation. In M. R. Jones (Ed.) *Nebraska Symposium on Motivation*. Lincoln, NE: University of Nebraska Press, pp. 25–64.

Sears, R. R. (1972). A theoretical framework for personality and social behavior. In E. P. Hollander and R. G. Hunt (Eds) *Classic Contributions to Social Psychology*. New York: Oxford University Press.

Sears, R. R., Maccoby, E. E., and Levin, H. (1957). *Patterns of Child-Rearing*. Evanston, IL: Row, Peterson.

Sears, R. R., Rau, L., and Alpert, R. (1965). *Identification and Child-Rearing*. Stanford: Stanford University Press.

Seay, M. B., and Kay, E. J. (1983). Three-way analysis of dyadic social interactions. *Developmental Psychology*, **19**, 868–872.

Seay, T., and Altekruse, M. (1979). Verbal and nonverbal behavior in judgments of facilitative conditions. *Journal of Counseling Psychology*, **26**, 108–119.

Sechrest, L. (Ed.) (1979). *Unobtrusive Measurement Today: New Directions for Methodology of Behavioral Science*. San Francisco: Jossey-Bass.

Secord, P. F., and Backman, C. W. (1974). *Social Psychology*, 2nd edn. New York: McGraw-Hill.

Seibold, D. R., Cantrill, J. G., and Meyers, R. A. (1985). Communication and interpersonal influence. In M. L. Knapp and R. G. Miller (Eds) *Handbook of Interpersonal Communication*. Beverly Hills: Sage, pp. 551–611.

Seligman, M. E. P. (1970). On the generality of the laws of learning. *Psychological Review*, **77**, 406–418.

Selman, R. L. (1980). *The Growth of Interpersonal Understanding: Developmental and Clinical Analyses*. New York: Academic Press.

Semin, G. R., and Manstead, A. S. R. (1983). *The Accountability of Conduct: A Social Psychological Analysis*. London: Academic Press.

Senneker, P., and Hendrick, C. (1983). Androgyny and helping behavior. *Journal of Personality and Social Psychology*, **45**, 916–925.

Sennett, R. (1977). *The Fall of Public Man*. New York: Vintage.

Sennett, R. (1980). *Authority*. New York: Alfred A. Knopf.

Serafica, F. C. (1983). Conceptions of friendship and interaction between friends: An organismic-developmental perspective. In F. C. Serafica (Ed.) *Social-Cognitive Development in Context*. London: Methuen, pp. 100–132.

Sereno, K. K., and Hawkins, G. J. (1967). The effects of variations in speakers' nonfluency upon audience ratings of attitude toward the speech topic and speakers' credibility. *Speech Monographs*, **34**, 58–64.

Seyfried, B. A. (1977). Complementarity in interpersonal attraction. In S. W. Duck (Ed.) *Theory and Practice in Interpersonal Attraction*. London: Academic Press, pp. 165–184.

Seyfried, B. A., and Hendrick, C. (1973). When do opposites attract? When they are opposite in sex and sex-role attitudes. *Journal of Personality and Social Psychology*, **25**, 15–20.

Shaffer, D. R., and Ogden, J. K. (1986). On sex difference in self-disclosure during the acquaintance process: The role of anticipated future interaction. *Journal of Personality and Social Psychology*, **51**, 92–101.

Shanab, M. E., and O'Neill, P. (1979). The effects of contrast upon compliance with socially undesirable requests in the door-in-the-face paradigm. *Canadian Journal of Behavioral Science*, **11**, 236–244.

Shannon, C., and Weaver, W. (1949). *The Mathematical Theory of Communication*. Urbana, IL: University of Illinois Press.

Shanteau, J., and Nagy, G. (1976). Decisions made about other people: A human judgment analysis of dating choice. In J. Caroll and J. Payne (Eds) *Cognition and Social Judgment*. Hillsdale, NJ: Erlbaum, pp. 221–242.

Shantz, C. U. (1983). Children's understanding of social rules and the social context. In F. C. Serafica (Ed.) *Social-Cognitive Development in Context*. London: Methuen, pp. 167–198.

Sharpley, C. F., and Cross, D. G. (1982). A psychometric evaluation of the Spanier Dyadic Adjustment Scale. *Journal of Marriage and the Family*, **44**, 739–741.

Shaul, S. (1982). The effectiveness of two counseling strategies for reducing loneliness. Paper presented at the annual meeting of the American Psychological Association, Washington, DC, August.

Shaver, P., and Buhrmester, D. (1983). Loneliness, sex-role orientation, and group life: A social needs perspective. In P. B. Paulus (Ed.) *Basic Group Processes*. New York: Springer-Verlag, pp. 259–288.

Shaver, P., and Hazan, C. (1985). Incompatibility, loneliness, and 'limerance'. In W. Ickes (Ed.) *Compatible and Incompatible Relationships*. New York: Springer-Verlag, pp. 163–184.

Shaver, P., and Rubenstein, C. (1980). Childhood attachment experience and adult loneliness. In L. Wheeler (Ed.) *Review of Personality and Social Psychology: 1*. Beverly Hills: Sage, pp. 42–73.

Shaver, P., Furman, W., and Buhrmester, D. (1985). Aspects of a life transition: Network changes, social skills and loneliness. In S. W. Duck and D. Perlman (Eds) *Understanding Personal Relationships*. London: Sage, pp. 193–219.

Shaver, P., Hazan, C., and Bradshaw, D. (1988). Love as attachment: The integration of three behavioral systems. In R. J. Sternberg and M. Barnes (Eds) *The Anatomy of Love*. New Haven: Yale University Press.

Shaver, P., Pullis, C., and Olds, D. (1980). Report on the LHJ 'Intimacy Today' Survey. Private research report to the *Ladies' Home Journal*.

Shaver, P., Schwartz, J., Kirson, D., and O'Connor, C. (1987). Emotion knowledge: Further exploration of a prototype approach. *Journal of Personality and Social Psychology*.

Shaw, M. E. (1971). *Group Dynamics: The Psychology of Small Group Behavior*. New York: McGraw-Hill.

Shaw, R., and Bransford, J. (1977). Introduction: Psychological approaches to the problem of knowledge. In R. Shaw and J. Bransford (Eds) *Perceiving, Acting, and Knowing*. Hillsdale, NJ: Erlbaum, pp. 1–39.

Shea, B. C., and Pearson, J. C. (1986). The effects of relationship type, partner intent, and gender on the selection of relationship maintenance strategies. *Communication Monographs*, **53**, 352–364.

Shea, M. T., Glass, D. R., Pilkonis, P. A., Watkins, J., and Docherty, J. P. (1987). Frequency and implications of personality disorders in a sample of depressed outpatients. *Journal of Personality Disorders*, **1**, 27–42.

Sherblom, J., and Van Rheenen, D. E. (1984). Spoken language indices of uncertainty. *Human Communication Research*, **47**, 180–200.

Sherrod, L. R. (1981). Issues in cognitive-perceptual development: The special case of social stimuli. In M. E. Lamb and L. R. Sherrod (Eds) *Infant Social Cognition: Empirical and Theoretical Considerations*. Hillsdale, NJ: Erlbaum, pp. 11–36.

Shigetomi, C. C., Hartmann, D. P., and Gelfand, D. M. (1981). Sex differences in children's altruistic behavior and reputations for helpfulness. *Developmental Psychology*, **17**, 434–437.

Shimanoff, S. (1985). Expressing emotions in words: Verbal patterns of interaction. *Journal of Communication*, **35**, 16–31.

Shotter, J. (1984). *Social Accountability and Selfhood*. Oxford: Blackwell.

Shotter, J. (1987). The social construction of an 'us': Problems of accountability and narratology. In R. Burnett, P. McGhee and D. Clarke (Eds) *Accounting for Relationships*. London: Methuen.

Shulman, N. (1975). Life-cycle variations in patterns of close relationships. *Journal of Marriage and the Family*, **37**, 813–821.

Shumaker, S. A., and Brownell, A. (1984). Toward a theory of social support: Closing the conceptual gaps. *Journal of Social Issues*, **40**, 11–36.

Shumaker, S. A., and Brownell, A. (1985). Social support: New perspectives in theory, research and intervention. Part II. Interventions and policy [Special Issue]. *Journal of Social Issues*, **41**.

Sieburg, E. (1985). *Family Communication: An Integrated Systems Approach*. New York: Gardner.

Siegal, M., and Cowen, J. (1984). Appraisals of intervention: The mother's versus the culprit's behavior as determinants of children's evaluations of discipline techniques. *Child Development*, **55**, 1760–1766.

Siegal, M., and Rablin, J. (1982). Moral development as reflected by young children's evaluation of maternal discipline. *Merrill-Palmer Quarterly*, **28**(4), 499–509.

Sigel, I. E. (Ed.) (1985). *Parental Belief Systems: The Psychological Consequences for Children*. Hillsdale, NJ: Erlbaum.

Sillars, A. L. (1980a). Attributions and communication in roommate conflicts. *Communication Monographs*, **47**, 180–200.

Sillars, A. L. (1980b). The stranger and the spouse as target persons for compliance-gaining strategies: A subjective expected utility model. *Human Communication Research*, **6**, 265–279.

Sillars, A. L. (1981). Attributions and interpersonal conflict resolutions. In J. H. Harvey, W. Ickes and R. F. Kidd (Eds) *New Directions in Attribution Research*, Vol. 3. Hillsdale, NJ: Erlbaum, pp. 279–395.

Sillars, A., and Scott, M. (1983). Interpersonal perception between intimates: An integrative review. *Human Communication Research*, **10**, 153–176.

Sillars, A., Pike, G., Jones, T., and Redmon, K. (1983). Communication and conflict in marriage. In R. Bostrom (Ed.) *Communication Yearbook 7*. Beverly Hills: Sage.

Silver, R. L., and Wortman, C. B. (1980). Coping with undesirable life events. In J. Garber and M. Seligman (Eds) *Human Helplessness*. New York: Academic Press, pp. 179–340.

Silverman, I. (1971). Physical attractiveness and courtship. *Sexual Behavior*, **3**, 22–25.

Simmel, G. (1908, 1950). *The Sociology of Georg Simmel* (trans. Kurt Wolff). New York: Free Press.

Simons, H. W. (1974). The carrot and stick as handmaidens of persuasion in conflict situations. In G. R. Miller and H. W. Simons (Eds) *Perspectives on Communication in Social Conflict*. Englewood Cliffs, NJ: Prentice-Hall, pp. 172–205.

Sims, A. (1977). Prognosis in the neurosis. *American Journal of Psychoanalysis*, **37**, 155–161.

Skinner, B. F. (1953). *Science and Human Behavior*. New York: Macmillan.

Skirboll, B. W., and Pavelsky, P. K. (1984). The Compeer Program: Volunteers as friends of the mentally ill. *Hospital and Community Psychiatry*, **35**, 938–939.

Skolnick, A. (1981). Married lives: Longitudinal perspectives on marriage. In D.

Eichorn, J. Clausen, N. Haan, M. Honzik and P. Mussen (Eds) *Present and Past in Middle Life*. New York: Academic Press, pp. 270–298.

Skvoretz, J. (1983). Salience, heterogeneity and consolidation of parameters: Civilizing Blau's primitive theory. *American Sociological Review*, **48**, 360–375.

Slavin, M. O. (1972). The theme of feminine evil: The image of women in male fantasy and its effects on attitudes and behavior. Unpublished doctoral dissertation, Harvard University.

Sloan, W. W., Jr, and Solano, C. H. (1984). The conversational styles of lonely males with strangers and roommates. *Personality and Social Psychology Bulletin*, **10**, 293–301.

Sluzki, C. E., and Beavin, J. (1965). Simetria y complementaridad: Una definicion operacional y una tipologia de parejas. *Acta Psiquiatrica y Psicologica de America Latina*, **11**, 321–330.

Sluzki, C. E., Beavin, J., and Tarnopolsky, A. (1977). Transactional disqualification: Research on the double bind. In P. Watzlawick and J. Weakland (Eds) *The Interactional View*. New York: Norton, pp. 208–227.

Smith, A. (1966). *Communication and Culture: Readings in the Codes of Human Interaction*. New York: Holt, Rinehart, & Winston.

Smith, C. L., Gelfand, D. M., Hartmann, D. P., and Partlow, M. E. Y. (1979). Children's causal attributions regarding help giving. *Child Development*, **50**, 203–210.

Smith, D. L. (1977). An ecological approach to the perception of intention. PhD dissertation, Interdisciplinary PhD Program in Social Psychology, University of Nevada, Reno.

Smith, D. L., and Ginsburg, G. P. (1987). Impact of action structure on impressions of social episodes. Paper presented at the annual meeting of the Western Psychological Association, Long Beach, California.

Smollar, J., and Youniss, J. (1982). Social development through friendship. In K. H. Rubin and H. S. Ross (Eds) *Peer Relations and Social Skills in Childhood*. New York: Springer-Verlag.

Snow, C. E. (1977). The development of conversations between mothers and babies. *Journal of Child Language*, **4**, 1–22.

Snyder, C. R., and Smith, T. W. (1986). On being 'shy like a fox': A self-handicapping analysis. In W. H. Jones, J. M. Cheek and S. R. Briggs (Eds) *Shyness: Perspectives on Research and Treatment*. New York: Plenum, pp. 161–172.

Snyder, D. K. (1979). *Marital Satisfaction Inventory*. Los Angeles: Western Psychological Services.

Snyder, D. K., and Smith, G. T. (1986a). Classification of marital relationships: An empirical approach. *Journal of Marriage and the Family*, **48**, 137–146.

Snyder, D. K., Wills, R. M., and Keiser, T. W. (1981). Empirical validation of the Marital Satisfaction Inventory: An actuarial approach. *Journal of Consulting and Clinical Psychology*, **49**, 262–268.

Snyder, M. (1974). Self-monitoring of expressive behavior. *Journal of Personality and Social Psychology*, **30**, 526–537.

Snyder, M., and Ickes, W. (1985). Personality and social behavior. In G. Lindzey and E. Aronson (Eds) *The Handbook of Social Psychology*, 3rd edn, Vol. 2. New York: Random House, pp. 883–947.

Snyder, M., and Smith, D. (1986b). Personality and friendship: The friendship worlds of self-monitoring. In V. Derlega and B. Winstead (Eds) *Friendship and Social Interaction*. New York: Springer-Verlag, pp. 63–80.

Snyder, M., Gangestad, S., and Simpson, J. (1983). Choosing friends as activity partners: The role of self-monitoring. *Journal of Personality and Social Psychology*, **45**, 1061–1072.

Sobol, M. P., Ashbourne, D. T., and Earn, B. M. (1986). Parental attributions for compliance of hyperactive and nonhyperactive children. Paper presented at the Annual Convention of the American Psychological Association, Washington.

Solano, C. H. (1980). Two measures of loneliness: A comparison. *Psychological Reports*, **46**, 23–28.

Solano, C. H. (1986). People without friends: Loneliness and its alternatives. In V. J. Derlega and B. A. Winstead (Eds) *Friendship and Social Interaction*. New York: Springer-Verlag, pp. 227–246.

Solano, C. H., Batten, P. G., and Parish, E. A. (1982). Loneliness and patterns of self-disclosure. *Journal of Personality and Social Psychology*, **43**, 524–531.

Solomon, Z., Mikulincer, M., and Hobfoll, S. E. (1986). Effects of social support and battle intensity on loneliness and breakdown during combat. *Journal of Personality and Social Psychology*, **51**, 1269–1276.

Solso, R. L., and McCarthy, J. E. (1981). Prototype formation of faces: A case of pseudo-memory. *British Journal of Psychology*, **72**, 499–503.

Solso, R. L., and Raynis, R. A. (1979). Prototype formation from imaged, kinesthetically, and visually presented geometric figures. *Journal of Experimental Psychology (Human Perception and Performance)*, **5**, 701–712.

Solso, R. L., and Raynis, R. A. (1982). Transfer of prototypes based on visual, tactual, and kinesthetic exemplars. *American Journal of Psychology*, **95**, 13–29.

Solso, R. L., Ament, P., Kuraishy, F., and Mearns, C. (1986). Prototype formation of various classes. Paper presented at the 27th annual meeting of the Psychonomic Society, New Orleans, Louisiana.

Sommer, R., and Ross, H. (1958). Social interaction on a geriatric ward. *International Journal of Social Psychology*, **4**, 128–133.

Spanier, G. B. (1971). A study of the relationship between and social correlates of romanticism and marital adjustment. Unpublished master's thesis, Iowa State University, Ames.

Spanier, G. B. (1976). Measuring dyadic adjustment: New scales for assessing the quality of marriage and similar dyads. *Journal of Marriage and the Family*, **38**, 15–28.

Spaulding, C. (1970). The romantic love complex in American culture. *Sociology and Social Research*, **55**, 82–100.

Spelke, E. S., and Cortelyou, A. (1981). Perceptual aspects of social knowing: Looking and listening in infancy. In M. E. Lamb and L. R. Sherrod (Eds) *Infant Social Cognition: Empirical and Theoretical Considerations*. Hillsdale, NJ: Erlbaum, pp. 61–84.

Spence, J. T., and Helmreich, R. L. (1978). *Masculinity and Femininity: Their Psychological Dimensions, Correlates, and Antecedents*. Austin: University of Texas Press.

Spence, J. T., Helmreich, R., and Stapp, J. (1975). Ratings of self and peers on sex role attributes and their relation to self-esteem and conceptions of masculinity and femininity. *Journal of Personality and Social Psychology*, **32**, 29–39.

Spielberger, C. D. (1972). Anxiety as an emotional state. In C. D. Spielberger (Ed.) *Anxiety: Current Trends in Theory and Research*. New York: Academic Press, pp. 23–49.

Spiro, J. (1983). Persuasion in family decision-making. *Journal of Consumer Research*, **9**, 393–402.

Spitzberg, B. H., and Canary, D. J. (1985). Loneliness and relationally competent communication. *Journal of Personal and Social Relationships*, **2**, 387–402.

Spitzer, R. L., Williams, J. B. W., and Gibbons, M. (1986). *Structured clinical interviews for DSM-IIIR (Patient Version) SCID-P 8/1/86*. New York: BRDNYSPI.

Sprecher, S. (1985). Sex differences in bases of power in dating relationships. *Sex Roles*, **12**, 449–462.

Sroufe, L. A. (1983). Infant–caregiver attachment and patterns of adaptation in preschool: The roots of maladaptation and competence. In M. Perlmutter (Ed.) *Minnesota Symposium in Child Psychology*, Vol. 16. Hillsdale, NJ: Erlbaum, pp. 44–81.

Sroufe, L. A. (1985). Attachment classification from the perspective of infant–caregiver relationships and infant temperament. *Child Development*, **56**, 1–14.

Sroufe, L. A. (1987). The role of infant–caregiver attachment in development. In J. Belsky and T. Nezworski (Eds) *Clinical Implications of Attachment*. Hillsdale, NJ: Erlbaum.

Sroufe, A. (1988). An organisational perspective on the self. In D. Cicchetti and R. Eagly (Eds). *Transitions from Infancy to Childhood: The Self*. Chicago: UCP.

Sroufe, L. A., and Fleeson, J. (1985). Attachment and the construction of relationships. In W. W. Hartup and Z. Rubin (Eds) *Relationships and Development*. Hillsdale, NJ: Erlbaum, pp. 57–71.

Sroufe, L. A., and Ward, M. J. (1980). Seductive behavior of mothers or toddlers: Occurrence, correlates and family origins. *Child Development*, **51**, 1222–1229.

Sroufe, L. A., and Waters, E. (1977). Attachment as an organizational construct. *Child Development*, **48**, 1184–1199.

Sroufe, L. A., Fox, N. E., and Pancake, V. R. (1983). Attachment and dependency in developmental perspective. *Child Development*, **54**, 1615–1627.

Starbuck, W. H. (1971). *Organizational Growth and Development*. New York: Penguin.

Staub, E., and Sherk, L. (1970). Need for approval, children's sharing behaviors and reciprocity in sharing. *Child Development*, **41**, 243–252.

Stayton, D. J., Hogan, R., and Ainsworth, M. D. S. (1971). Infant obedience and material behavior: The origins of socialization reconsidered. *Child Development*, **42**, 1057–1070.

Stein, C. H., and Rappaport, J. (1986). In S. E. Hobfoll (Ed.) *Stress, Social Support and Women*. Washington, DC: Hemisphere, pp. 47–66.

Stein, E. (1975). An experiment in marriage enrichment. *Family Coordinator*, **24** (2), 167–170.

Steinglass, P., Tislenko, L., and Reiss, D. (1985). Stability/instability in the alcoholic marriage: The interrelationships between course of alcoholism, family process, and marital outcome. *Family Process*, **24** (3), 365–376.

Stephen, T. D. (1984a). A symbolic exchange framework for the development of intimate relationships. *Human Relations*, **37**, 393–408.

Stephen, T. D. (1984b). Symbolic interdependence and post break-up distress: A reformulation of the attachment construct. *Journal of Divorce*, **8**, 1–16.

Stephen, T. D. (1985). Fixed-sequence and circular-causal models of relationship development: Divergent views on the role of communication in intimacy. *Journal of Marriage and the Family*, **47**, 955–963.

Stern, D. N. (1977). *The First Relationship*. Cambridge, MA: Harvard University Press.

Stern, D. N. (1986). *The Interpersonal World of the Infant*. New York: Basic BKOOKS.

Stern, D. N., Jaffe, J., Beebe, B., and Bennett, S. L. (1975). Vocalizing in unison and in alternation: Two modes of communication within the mother–infant dyad. *Annals of the New York Academy of Sciences*, **263**, 89–100.

Sternberg, R. J. (1986). A triangular theory of love. *Psychological Review*, **93**, 119–135.

Sternberg, R. J., and Barnes, M. (1985). Real and ideal others in romantic relationships: Is four a crowd? *Journal of Personality and Social Psychology*, **49**, 1586–1608.

Sternberg, R. J., and Grajek, S. (1984). The nature of love. *Journal of Personality and Social Psychology*, **47**, 312–329.

Stevenson, M. B., Leavitt, L. A., Thompson, R. H., and Roach, M. A. (1988). Siblings and parents as partners in play. *Child Development*.

Stewart, A. J., and Rubin, Z. (1976). Power motivation in the dating couple. *Journal of Personality and Social Psychology*, **34**, 305–309.

Stewart, J. (1986). *Bridges not Walls*. New York: Random House.

Stiles, W. B. (1981). Classification of intersubjective illocutionary acts. *Language and Society*, **10**, 227–249.

Stokes, J. P. (1983). Predicting satisfaction with social support from social network structure. *American Journal of Community Psychology*, **11**, 141–152.

Stokes, J. P. (1985). The relation of social network and individual difference variables to loneliness. *Journal of Personality and Social Psychology*, **48**, 981–990.

Stokes, J., and Levin, I. (1986). Gender differences in predicting loneliness from social network characteristics. *Journal of Personality and Social Psychology*, **51**, 1069–1074.

Stokes, J. P., and Wilson, D. G. (1984). The inventory of socially supportive behaviors: Dimensionality, prediction, and gender differences. *American Journal of Community Psychology*, **12**, 53–69.

Stokes, J., Fuehrer, A., and Childs, L. (1980). Gender differences in self-disclosure to various target persons. *Journal of Counseling Psychology*, **27**, 192–198.

Stokes, R., and Hewitt, J. P. (1976). Aligning actions. *American Sociological Review*, **41**, 838–849.

Stolberg, A. L., and Garrison, K. M. (1985). Evaluating a primary prevention program of children of divorce. *American Journal of Community Psychology*, **13**, 111–124.

Stotland, E., Sherman, S. E., and Shaver, K. G. (1971). *Empathy and Birth Order*. Lincoln, NE: University of Nebraska Press.

Strack, S., and Coyne, J. C. (1983). Social confirmation of dysphoria: Shared and private reactions to depression. *Journal of Personality and Social Psychology*, **44**, 798–806.

Strain, P. S., Kerr, M. M., and Ragland, E. U. (1981). The use of peer social initiations in the treatment of social withdrawal. In P. S. Strain (Ed.) *The Utilization of Classroom Peers as Behaviors Change Agents*. New York: Plenum.

Straus, M. A., and Brown, B. W. (1978). *Family Measurement Techniques: Abstracts of Published Instruments, 1935–1974* (rev. ed.). Minneapolis: University of Minnesota Press.

Straus, M. A., Gelles, R., and Steinmetz, S. (1980). *Behind Closed Doors*. New York: Doubleday.

Strayer, F. F. (1980). Social ecology of the preschool peer group. In W. A. Collins (Ed.) *The Minnesota Symposia on Child Psychology*, Vol. 13. Hillsdale, NJ: Erlbaum.

Strayer, F. F., and Trudel, M. (1984). Developmental changes in the nature and function of social dominance among young children. *Ethology and Sociobiology*, **5**, 279–295.

Strayer, J. (1980). A naturalistic study of empathic behaviors and their relation to affective states and perspective-taking skills in preschool children. *Child Development*, **52**, 815–822.

Street, R. L., Jr (1982). Evaluation of noncontent speech accommodation. *Language and Communication*, **2**, 13–31.

Street, R. L., Jr (1984). Speech convergence and speech evaluation in fact-finding interviews. *Human Communication Research*, **11**, 139–169.

Street, R. L., Jr (1985). Participant–observer differences in speech evaluation. *Journal of Language and Social Psychology*, **4**, 125–130.

Street, R. L., Jr (1986). Interaction processes and outcomes in interviews. In M. L. McLaughlin (Ed.) *Communication Yearbook 9*. Beverly Hills: Sage, pp. 215–250.

Street, R. L., Jr, and Cappella, J. N. (Eds) (1985). *Sequence and Pattern in Communicative Behavior*. London: Arnold.

Strodtbeck, F. L. (1951). Husband–wife interaction over revealed differences. *American Sociological Review*, **16**, 468–473.

Suedfeld, P. (1982). Aloneness as a healing experience. In L. A. Peplau and D. Perlman (Eds) *Loneliness: A Sourcebook of Current Theory, Research and Therapy*. New York: Wiley, pp. 54–67.

Sullaway, M., and Christensen, A. (1983). Assessment of dysfunctional interactional patterns in couples. *Journal of Marriage and the Family*, August, 653–660.

Sullivan, H. H. (1953). *The Interpersonal Theory of Psychiatry*. New York: Norton.

Suls, J. M., and Miller, R. L. (1977). *Social Comparison Processes: Theoretical and Empirical Perspectives*. New York: Halsted Press.

Surra, C. A. (1985). Courtship types: Variations in interdependence between partners and social networks. *Journal of Personality and Social Psychology*, **56**, 357–375.

Surra, C. A. (1987). Reasons for changes in commitment: Variations by courtship style. *Journal of Social and Personal Relationships*, **4**, 17–33.

Suttles, G. D. (1970). Friendship as a social institution. In G. J. McCall (Ed.) *Social Relationships*. Chicago: Aldine.

Swann, W. B., and Predmore, S. C. (1985). Intimates as agents of social support: Sources of consolation or despair? *Journal of Personality and Social Psychology*, **49**, 1609–1617.

Tardy, C. H. (1985). Social support measurement. *American Journal of Community Psychology*, **13**, 187–202.

Taylor, D. A. (1968). Some aspects of the development of interpersonal relationships: Social penetration processes. *Journal of Social Psychology*, **75**, 79–90.

Taylor, D. A., and Altman, I. (1966). Intimacy-scaled stimuli for use in studies of interpersonal relations. *Psychological Reports*, **19**, 729–730.

Taylor, D. A., Altman, I., and Sorrentino, R. (1969). Interpersonal exchange as a function of rewards and costs and situational factors: Expectancy confirmation–disconfirmation. *Journal of Experimental Social Psychology*, **5**, 324–339.

Taylor, S. E., and Koivumaki, J. H. (1976). The perception of self and others: Acquaintanceship, affect, and actor–observer differences. *Journal of Personality and Social Psychology*, **33**, 403–408.

Taylor, S. E., Lichtman, R. R., and Wood, J. V. (1984). Attributions, beliefs about control, and adjustment to breast cancer. *Journal of Personality and Social Psychology*, **46**, 489–502.

Teasdale, J. D. (1983). Negative thinking in depression: Cause, effect, or reciprocal relationship? *Advances in behavior research and therapy*, **5**, 3–25.

Tennov, D. (1979). *Love and Limerence: The Experience of Being in Love*. New York: Stein & Day.

Terman, M. C., and Miles, C. C. (1936). *Sex and Personality*. New York: McGraw-Hill.

Tesch, S. A. (1985). The Psychosocial Intimacy Questionnaire: Validational studies and an investigation of sex roles. *Journal of Social and Personal Relationships*, **2**, 471–488.

Tesch, S. A., and Martin, J. (1983). Friendship concepts of young adults in two age groups. *Journal of Psychology*, **115**, 7–12.

Tesch, S. A., and Whitbourne, S. K. (1982). Intimacy and identity status in young adults. *Journal of Personality and Social Psychology*, **43**, 1041–1051.

Tharp, R. G. (1963). Psychological patterning in marriage. *Psychological Bulletin*, **60**, 97–117.

Thayer, L. (1975). Knowledge, order, and communication. In B. Ruben and J. Kim (Eds) *General Systems Theory and Human Communication*. Rochelle Park, NJ: Hayden.

Thayer, S., and Schiff, W. (1977). Gazing patterns and attribution of sexual involvement. *Journal of Social Psychology*, **101**, 235–246.

Thibaut, J. W., and Kelley, H. H. (1959). *The Social Psychology of Groups*. New York: Wiley.

Thoits, P. A. (1985). Social support and psychological well-being: Theoretical possibilities. In I. G. Sarason and B. R. Sarason (Eds) *Social Support: Theory, Research and Applications*. The Hague: Martinus Nijhoff, pp. 51–72.

Thomas, A. P., and Bull, P. (1981). The role of pre-speech posture change in dyadic interaction. *British Journal of Social Psychology*, **20**, 105–111.

Thomas, E. A. C., and Martin, J. A. (1976). An analysis of parent–infant interaction. *Psychological Review*, **83**, 141–156.

Thompson, L., and Spanier, G. (1983). The end of marriage and acceptance of marital termination. *Journal of Marriage and the Family*, February, 103–113.

Thompson, L., and Walker, A. J. (1982). The dyad as the unit of analysis: Conceptual and methodological issues. *Journal of Marriage and the Family*, **44**, 889–900.

Thompson, S. C. (1985). Finding positive meaning in a stressful event and coping. *Basic and Applied Social Psychology*, **6**, 279–295.

Tiefer, L. (1987). Social constructionism and the study of human sexuality. In P. Shaver and C. Hendrick (Eds) *Review of Personality and Social Psychology: Vol. 7. Sex and Gender*. Beverly Hills: Sage.

Ting-Toomey, S. (1983). An analysis of verbal communication patterns in high and low marital adjustment groups. *Human Communication Research*, **9**, 306–319.

Tisak, M. S. (1986). Children's conceptions of parental authority. *Child Development*, **57**, 166–176.

Tizard, B., and Hodges, J. (1978). The effect of early institutionalized rearing on the development of eight-year-old children. *Journal of Child Psychology and Psychiatry*, **19**, 99–118.

Tokuno, K. A. (1983). Friendship and transition in early adulthood. *Journal of Genetic Psychology*, **143**, 207–216.

Tolsdorf, C. C. (1976). Social networks, support, and coping: An exploratory study. *Family Process*, **15**, 407–418.

Tomkins, S. S. (1979). Script theory: Differential magnification of affects. In H. E. Howe and R. A. Dienstbier (Eds) *Nebraska Symposium on Motivation*. Lincoln, NE: University of Nebraska Press, pp. 201–236.

Trevarthen, C. (1977). Descriptive analyses of infant communicative behavior. In H. R. Schaffer (Ed.) *Studies in Mother–Infant Interaction*. London: Academic Press, pp. 227–270.

Trice, H., and Beyer, J. (1984). Studying organizational cultures through rites and ceremonials. *Academy of Management Review*, **9**, 653–669.

Trivers, R. L. (1971). The evolution of reciprocal altruism. *Quarterly Review of Biology*, **46**, 35–57.

Trivers, R. L. (1972). Parental investment and sexual selection. In B. Campbell (Ed.) *Sexual Selection and the Descent of Man*. Chicago: Aldine, pp. 136–179.

Trivers, R. L. (1974). Parent–offspring conflict. *American Zoologist*, **14**, 249–269.

Tronick, E., Als, H., Adamson, L., Wise, S., and Brazelton, T. B. (1978). The infant's response to entrapment between contradictory messages in face-to-face interaction. *Journal of American Academy of Child Psychiatry*, **17**, 1–13.

Tronick, E., Als, H., and Brazelton, T. B. (1980). Monadic phases: A structural descriptive analysis of infant–mother face to face interaction. *Merrill-Palmer Quarterly*, **26**, 3–24.

Tronick, E. Z., Winn, S., and Morelli, G. A. (1985). Multiple caretaking in the context of human evolution: Why don't the Efe know the Western prescription for child care? In M. Reite and T. Field (Eds) *The Psychobiology of Attachment and Separation*. Orlando, FL: Academic Press, pp. 293–322.

Tseng, W. (1977). Adjustment in intercultural marriage. In W. Tseng, J. McDermott and T. Maretzki (Eds) *Adjustment in Intercultural Marriage*. Honolulu: University of Hawaii Press.

Tuckman, B. W., and Jensen, M. A. C. (1977). Stages of small group development revisited. *Group and Organizational Studies*, **2**, 419–427.

Turiel, E. (1979). Social convention and morality: Two distinct conceptual and developmental systems. In C. B. Keasey (Ed.) *Nebraska Symposium on Motivation*, **25**. Lincoln, NE: University of Nebraska Press.

Turnbull, W., and Slugoski, B. R. (1987). Conversational and linguistic processes in causal attribution. In D. Hilton (Ed.) *Contemporary Sciences and Natural Explanation: Commonsense Conceptions of Causality*. London: Harvester Press.

Turner, R. H. (1962). Role-taking: Process versus conformity. In A. M. Rose (Ed.) *Human Behavior and Social Processes*. Boston: Houghton Mifflin.

Tyrer, P., Casey, P., and Gall, J. (1983). Relationship between neurosis and personality disorder. *British Journal of Psychiatry*, **142**, 404–408.

Uhlig, G., Schneider, G., and Meyer, A. (1982). Personality interaction in the alcoholic marriage. *Psychology, A Quarterly Journal of Human Behavior*, **19** (2/3), 28–36.

Ulrich, W. (1986). The uses of fiction as a source of information about interpersonal communication: A critical view. *Communication Quarterly*, **34**, 143–153.

Unger, D. G., and Wandersman, L. P. (1985). Social support and adolescent mothers: Action research contributions to theory and applications. *Journal of Social Issues*, **41**, 29–46.

US Bureau of the Census (1984). *Statistical Abstract of the United States, 1982–1983*, 103rd edition. Washington, DC.

USA Weekend (Sunday newspaper supplement), 2–4 January 1987.

Vachon, M. L. S., Layall, W., Rogers, J., Freedman-Letofsky, K., and Freeman, S. (1980). ja controlled study of self-help intervention for widows. *American Journal of Psychiatry*, **137**, 1380–1384.

Valle, R., and Vega, W. (1980). *Hispanic Natural Support Systems: Mental Health Promotion Perspectives*. Sacramento: State of California Department of Mental Health.

Van Hooff, J. A. R. A. M. (1982). Categories and sequences of behavior: Methods of description and analysis. In K. R. Scherer and P. Ekman (Eds) *Handbook of Methods in Nonverbal Research*. Cambridge, MA: Cambridge University Press, pp. 362–439.

Vandell, D. L. (1980). Sociability of peer and mother during the first year. *Developmental Psychology*, **16**, 335–361.

Vandell, D. L., and Wilson, K. S. (1982). Social interaction in the first year: Infants' social skills with peers versus mother. In K. H. Rubin and H. S. Ross (Eds) *Peer Relationships and Social Skills in Childhood*. New York: Springer-Verlag, pp. 187–208.

Vandell, D. L., and Wilson, K. S. (1987). Infants' interactions with mother, sibling, and peer: Contrasts and relations between interaction systems. *Child Development*, **58**, 176–186.

Vandell, D. L., Wilson, K. S., and Buchanan, N. R. (1980). Peer interaction in the first year of life: An examination of its structure, content, and sensitivity to toys. *Child Development*, **51**, 481–488.

Vandell, D. L., Wilson, K. S., and Henderson, K. (1985). Peer interaction in twin and singleton infants: Negative effects of peer familiarity and peer experience. Paper presented to the Society for Research in Child Development, Toronto, Canada, April.

Vaughn, B., Egeland, B., Sroufe, L. A., and Waters, E. (1979). Individual differences in infant–mother attachment at twelve and eighteen months: Stability and change in families under stress. *Child Development*, **50**, 971–975.

Vaughn, C. E., and Leff, J. P. (1976). The influence of family and social factors on the course of psychiatric illness: A comparison of schizophrenic and depressed neurotic patients. *British Journal of Psychiatry*, **129**, 125–137.

Vaughn, D. (1986). *Uncoupling: Turning Points in Intimate Relationships*. New York: Oxford University Press.

Vaux, W. A. (1985). Variations in social support associated with gender, ethnicity, and age. *Journal of Social Issues*, **41**, 89–110.

Vega, W. A., and Miranda, M. R. (1985). *Stress and Hispanic Mental Health* (DHHS Publication No. ADM 85-1410). Washington, DC: US Government Printing Office.

Verbrugge, L. J. (1983a). A research note on friendship contact: A dyadic perspective. *Social Forces*, **61**, 78–83.

Verbrugge, L. J. (1983b). The structure of adult friendship choices. *Social Forces*, **56**, 576–597.

Vermes, G. (1975). *The Dead Sea Scrolls in English*, 2nd edn. Harmondsworth: Penguin.

Veroff, J. (1982). Assertive motivations: Achievement versus power. In A. J. Stewart (Ed.) *Motivation and Society*. San Francisco: Jossey-Bass, pp. 99–132.

Veroff, J., and Feld, S. (1970). *Marriage and Work in America: A Study of Motives and Roles*. New York: Van Nostrand-Reinhold.

Veroff, J., Douvan, E., and Kulka, R. A. (1981). *Mental Health in America: Patterns of Help-Seeking from 1957 to 1976*. New York: Basic Books.

Vespo, J. E. (1985). Children's relationships with friends and acquaintances in preschool classes. Unpublished doctoral dissertation, State University of New York at Stony Brook.

Vincent, J. P., Friedman, L. C., Nugent, J., and Messerly, L. (1979). Demand characteristics in observations of marital interaction. *Journal of Consulting and Clinical Psychology*, **47**, 557–566.

Von Bertalanffy, L. (1967). *Robots, Men and Minds*. New York: Braziller.

Vygotsky, L. S. (1962). *Thought and Language*. Cambridge, MA: MIT Press.

Vygotsky, L. S. (1978). *Mind in Society*. Cambridge, MA: Harvard University Press.

Wagner, H. L., MacDonald, C. J., and Manstead, A. S. R. (1986). Communication of individual emotions by spontaneous facial expressions. *Journal of Personality and Social Psychology*, **50**, 737–743.

Waldrop, M. F., and Halverson, C. F., Jr (1975). Intensive and extensive peer behavior: Longitudinal and cross-sectional analyses. *Child Development*, **46**, 19–26.

Walker, K. N., MacBride, A., and Vachon, M. L. (1977). Social support networks and the crisis of bereavement. *Social Science and Medicine*, **11**, 35–42.

Waller, W. (1930). *The Old Love and the New: Divorce and Readjustment*. New York: Liveright.

Waller, W. (1938). *The Family: A Dynamic Interpretation*. New York: Dryden Press.

Walsh, R. H., Ferrell, M. Z., and Tolone, W. L. (1976). Selection of reference groups, perceived reference group permissiveness, and personal permissiveness attitudes and behavior: A study of two consecutive panels (1967–1971; 1970–1974). *Journal of Marriage and the Family*, **38**, 495–507.

Walster, E. H., and Walster, G. W. (1978). *A New Look at Love*. Reading, MA: Addison-Wesley.

Walster, E. H., Berscheid, E., and Walster, G. W. (1973). New directions in equity research. *Journal of Personality and Social Psychology*, **25**, 151–176.

Walster, E. H., Walster, G. W., and Berscheid, E. (1978). *Equity Theory and Research*. Boston: Allyn & Bacon.

Walster, E. H., Walster, G. W., and Traupmann, J. (1978). Equity and premarital sex. *Journal of Personality and Social Psychology*, **36**, 82–92.

Walton, M. D. (1985). Negotiation of responsibility: Judgments of blameworthiness in a natural setting. *Developmental Psychology*, **21**, 725–736.

Wampler, K., and Sprenkle, D. (1980). The Minnesota couple communication program: A follow-up study. *Journal of Marriage and the Family*, **25**, 577–584.

Wandersman, L. P. (1982). An analysis of the effectiveness of parent–infant support groups. *Journal of Primary Prevention*, **3**, 99–115.

Waring, E. M., and Patton, D. (1984). Marital intimacy and depression. *British Journal of Psychiatry*, **145**, 641–644.

Waring, E. M., Tillman, M. P., Frelick, L., Russell, L., and Weisz, G. (1980). Concepts of intimacy in the general population. *Journal of Nervous and Mental Disease*, **168**, 471–474.

Warmbrod, M. (1982). Alternative generation in marital problem solving. *Family Relations: Journal of Applied Family & Child Studies*, **31**(4), 503–511.

Warner, R. M., Malloy, D., Knoth, R., Schneider, K., and Wilder, B. (1987). Rhythmic organization of social interaction and observer ratings of positive affect and involvement. Unpublished paper, University of New Hampshire.

Warner, R. M., Waggener, T. B., and Kronaver, R. E. (1983). Synchronised cycles in ventilation and vocal activity during spontaneous conversational speech. *Journal of Applied Physiology*, **54**, 1324–1334.

Warren, N. J., and Amara, I. A. (1984). Educational groups for single parents: The Parenting After Divorce programs. *Journal of Divorce*, **8**, 79–96.

Warriner, C. K. (1984). *Organizations and their Environments: Essays in the Sociology of Organizations*. Greenwich, CT: JAI Press.

Washburn, S. L., Jay, P. C., and Lancaster, J. B. (1965). Field studies of Old World monkeys and apes. *Science*, **150**, 1541–1547.

Wasserman, S., and Iacobucci, D. (1986). Statistical analysis of discrete relational data. *British Journal of Mathematical and Statistical Psychology*, **39**, 41–64.

Waters, E. (1978). The reliability and stability of individual differences in infant–mother attachment. *Child Development*, **49**, 483–494.

Waters, E. (1981). Traits, behavioral systems, and relationships: Three models of infant–adult attachment. In K. Immelman, G. Barlow, L. Petrinovitch and M. Main (Eds) *Behavioral Development*. Cambridge, MA: Cambridge University Press.

Waters, E., and Sroufe, L. A. (1983). Social competence as a developmental construct. *Developmental Review*, **3**, 79–97.

Waters, E., Hay, D., and Richters, J. (1986). Infant–parent attachment and the origins of prosocial and antisocial behavior. In D. Olweus, J. Block and M. Radke-Yarrow (Eds) *Development of Antisocial and Prosocial Behavior: Research, Theories, and Issues*. New York: Academic Press.

Waters, E., Wippman, J., and Sroufe, L. A. (1979). Attachment, positive affect, and competence in the peer group: Two studies in construct validation. *Child Development*, **50**, 821–828.

Watson, D., and Clark, L. A. (1984). Negative affectivity: The predisposition to experience aversive emotional states. *Psychological Bulletin*, **96**, 465–490.

Watson, J. B. (1913). Psychology as the behaviorist views it. *Psychological Review*, **20**, 158–177.

Watzlawick, P., Beavin, J., and Jackson, D. (1967). *Pragmatics of Human Communication: A Study of Interactional Patterns, Pathologies, and Paradoxes*. New York: Norton.

Watzlawick, P., Weakland, J., and Fisch, R. (1974). *Change: Principles of Problem Formation and Problem Resolution*. New York: Norton.

Weber, A. L., Harvey, J. H., and Stanley, M. A. (1987). The nature and motivations of accounts in failed relationships. In R. Burnett, P. McGhee and D. Clarke (Eds) *Accounting for Relationships*. London: Metheun.

Wegner, D. M., and Giuliano, T. (1982). The forms of social awareness. In W. Ickes and E. S. Knowles (Eds) *Personality, Roles, and Social Behavior*. New York: Springer-Verlag.

Weick, K. E. (1968). Systematic observational methods. In G. Lindzey and E. Aronson (Eds) *The Handbook of Social Psychology*, 2nd edn. Reading, MA: Addison-Wesley, pp. 357–451.

Weick, K. E. (1979). *The Social Psychology of Organizing*, 2nd edn. Reading, MA: Addison-Wesley.

Weick, K. E. (1985). Systematic observational methods. In G. Lindzey and E. Aronson (Eds) *The Handbook of Social Psychology*, 3rd edn. New York: Random House, pp. 567–634.

Weinberg, M. S., Swenson, R. G., and Hammersmith, S. K. (1983). Sexual autonomy and the status of women: Models of female sexuality in U.S. sex manuals from 1950 to 1980. *Social Problems*, **30**, 312–324.

Weiner, B. (1979). A theory of motivation for some classroom experiences. *Journal of Educational Psychology*, **71**, 3–25.

Weinstein, E. A., and Deutschberger, P. (1964). Tasks, bargains, and identities in social interaction. *Social Forces*, **42**, 451–456.

Weiss, L., and Lowenthal, M. F. (1975). Life-course perspectives on friendship. In M. F. Lowenthal, M. Thurnher and D. Chiriboga (Eds) *Four Stages of Life*. San Francisco: Jossey-Bass.

Weiss, P. (1969). The living system: Determinism stratified. In A. Koestler and J. R. Smythies (Eds) *Beyond Reductionism*. London: Hutchinson.

Weiss, R. S. (1969). The fund of sociability. *Transaction/Society*, **6**, 36–43.

Weiss, R. S. (1973). *Loneliness: The Experience of Emotional and Social Isolation*. Cambridge, MA: MIT Press.

Weiss, R. S. (1974). The provisions of social relationships. In Z. Rubin (Ed.) *Doing unto Others*. Englewood Cliffs, NJ: Prentice-Hall.

Weiss, R. S. (1975). *Marital Separation*. New York: Basic Books.

Weiss, R. S. (1986). Continuities and transformations in social relationships from childhood to adulthood. In W. W. Hartup and Z. Rubin (Eds) *Relationships and Development*. Hillsdale, NJ: Erlbaum, pp. 95–110.

Weiss, R., Birchler, G., and Vincent, J. (1974). Contractual models for negotiation training in marital dyads. *Journal of Marriage and the Family*, **36**, 1–11.

Weissman, M. M. (1979). The psychological treatment of depression. *Archives of General Psychiatry*, **36**, 1261–1269.

Weissman, M. M., and Boyd, J. H. (1983). The epidemiology of affective disorders: Rates and risk factors. In L. Grinspoon (Ed.) *Psychiatry Update*, Vol. II. Washington, DC: American Psychiatric Press.

Weissman, M. M., and Klerman, G. L. (1973). Psychotherapy with depressed women: An empirical study of content themes and reflection. *British Journal of Psychiatry*, **123**, 55–61.

Weissman, M. M., and Klerman, G. L. (1977). Sex differences in the epidemiology of depression. *Archives of General Psychiatry*, **34**, 98–111.

Weissman, M. M., and Paykel, E. S. (1973). Moving and depression in women. In R. S. Weiss (Ed.) *Loneliness: The Experience of Emotional and Social Isolation*. Cambridge, MA: MIT Press, pp. 154–164.

Weissman, M. M., and Paykel, E. S. (1974). *The Depressed Woman: A Study of Social Relationships*. Chicago: University of Chicago Press.

Weissman, M. M., Myers, J. K., and Harding, P. S. (1978). Psychiatric disorders in a U.S. urban community: 1975–1976. *American Journal of Psychiatry*, **135**, 259–462.

Weissman, M. M., Prusoff, B. A., and Klerman, G. L. (1978). Personality and the prediction of long-term outcome of depression. *American Journal of Psychiatry*, **135**, 797–800.

Welkowitz, J., and Kuc, M. (1973). Interrelationships among warmth, genuineness, empathy and temporal speech patterns in interpersonal interaction. *Journal of Consulting and Clinical Psychology*, **41**, 472–473.

Wellman, B. (1981). Applying network analysis to the study of support. In B. H. Gottlieb (Ed.) *Social Networks and Social Support*. Beverly Hills: Sage, pp. 171–200.

Wellman, B. (1982). Studying personal communities. In P. Marsden and N. Lin (Eds) *Social Structure and Network Analysis*. Beverly Hills: Sage.

Werner, C., and Parmelee, P. (1979). Similarity of activity preferences among friends: Those who play together stay together. *Social Psychology Quarterly*, **42**, 62–66.

West, M. J. (1983). Learning by trying and erring. Paper presented to the American Psychological Association.

West, M. J., and King, A. P. (1984). Learning by performing: An ecological theme for the study of vocal learning. In T. D. Johnston and A. T. Pietrewicz (Eds) *Issues in the Ecological Study of Learning*. Hillsdale, NJ: Erlbaum, pp. 245–272.

West, M. J., and King, A. P. (1985). Social guidance of vocal learning by female cowbirds: Validating its functional significance. *Zeitshrift fuer Tierpsychologie*, **70**, 225–235.

Westhoff, L. A. (1985). *Corporate Romance*. New York: Times Books.

Wethington, E., and Kessler, R. C. (1986). Perceived support, received support, and adjustment to stressful life events. *Journal of Health and Social Behavior*, **27**, 78–89.

Wheeler, L. (1974). Social comparison and selective affiliation. In T. L. Huston (Ed.) *Foundations of Interpersonal Attraction*. New York: Academic Press, pp. 309–329.

Wheeler, L., and Nezlek, J. (1977). Sex differences in social participation. *Journal of Personality and Social Psychology*, **35**, 742–754.

Wheeler, L., Reis, H. T., and Nezlek, J. (1983). Loneliness, social interaction and sex roles. *Journal of Personality and Social Psychology*, **45**, 943–953.

Wheeless, L. R., Barraclough, R., and Stewart, R. (1983). Compliance-gaining and power in persuasion. In R. Bostrom (Ed.) *Communication Yearbook 7*. Beverly Hills: Sage, pp. 105–145.

Whitaker, C. (1982). In F. Neill and D. Kniskern (Eds) *From Psyche to System: The Evolving Therapy of Carl Whitaker*. New York: Guilford.

White, G. L. (1980). Inducing jealousy: A power perspective. *Personality and Social Psychology Bulletin*, **6**, 222–227.

White, G. L. (1981). A model of romantic jealousy. *Motivation and Emotion*, **5**, 295–310.

Whitley, B. E., Snyder, H. N., and Schofield, J. W. (1984). Peer preferences in a desegregated school: A round robin analysis. *Journal of Personality and Social Psychology*, **46**, 799–810.

Whyte, W. F. (1949). The social structure of the restaurant. *American Journal of Sociology*, **54**, 302–308.

Wideman, M. V., and Singer, J. E. (1984). The role of psychological mechanisms in preparation for childbirth. *American Psychologist*, **39**, 1357–1371.

Wieman, R., Shoulders, D., and Farr, J. (1974). Reciprocal reinforcement in marital therapy. *Journal of Behavior Therapy & Experimental Psychiatry*, **5** (3–4), 291–295.

Wiese, L. von, and Becker, H. (1932). *Systematic Sociology*. New York: Wiley.

Wiggins, J. S. (1973). In defense of traits. Unpublished manuscript, University of British Columbia.

Wiggins, J. S. (1979). A psychological taxonomy of trait-descriptive terms: The interpersonal domain. *Journal of Personality and Social Psychology*, **37**, 395–412.

Wilcox, B. L. (1981a). Social support in adjusting to marital disruption: A network analysis. In B. H. Gottlieb (Ed.) *Social Networks and Social Support*. Beverly Hills: Sage, pp. 97–115.

Wilcox, B. L. (1981b). Social support, life stress, and psychological adjustment: A test of the buffering hypothesis. *American Journal of Community Psychology*, **9**, 371–386.

Wilensky, R. (1983). *Planning and Understanding: A Computational Approach to Human Reasoning*. Reading, MA: Addison-Wesley.

Wilkins, A. (1983). Organizational stories as symbols which control the organization. In L. R. Pondy, P. M. Frost, G. Morgan and T. C. Dabdridge (Eds) *Organizational Symbolism*. Greenwich, CT: JAI Press.

Willems, E. P., and Raush, H. L. (1969). *Naturalistic Viewpoints in Psychological Research*. New York: Holt, Rinehart, & Winston.

Williams, G. C. (1966). *Adaptation and Natural Selection*. Princeton: Princeton University Press.

Williams, J., and Solano, C. H. (1983). The social reality of feeling lonely: Friendship and reciprocation. *Personality and Social Psychology Bulletin*, **9**, 237–242.

Williams, R. M., Jr (1979). Change and stability in values and value systems: A sociological perspective. In M. Rokeach (Ed.) *Understanding Human Values: Individual and Societal*. New York: Free Press, pp. 15–46.

Williamson, O. E. (1981). The economics of organization: The transaction cost approach. *American Journal of Sociology*, **87**, 548–577.

Williamson, R. N., and Fitzpatrick, M. A. (1985). Two approaches to marital interaction: Relational control patterns in marital types. *Communication Monographs*, **52**, 236–252.

Willis, F. N., and Hamm, H. K. (1980). The use of interpersonal touch in securing compliance. *Journal of Nonverbal Behavior*, **5**, 49–55.

Wills, T., Weiss, R., and Patterson, G. (1974). A behavioral analysis of the determinants of marital satisfaction. *Journal of Consulting and Clinical Psychology*, **42**, 802–811.

Wilmot, W. W., Carbaugh, D. A., and Baxter, L. A. (1985). Communicative strategies used to terminate romantic relationships. *Western Journal of Speech Communication*, **49**, 204–216.

Winch, R. F. (1955a). The theory of complementary needs in mate selection: A test of one kind of complementariness. *American Sociological Review*, **20**, 52–56.

Winch, R. F. (1955b). The theory of complementary needs in mate selection: Final results on the test of the general hypothesis. *American Sociological Review*, **20**, 552–555.

Winch, R. F. (1958). *Mate Selection: A Study in Complementary Needs*. New York: Harper & Row.

Winch, R. F. (1974). Complementary needs and related notions about voluntary mate-selection. In R. Winch and G. Spanier (Eds) *Selected Studies in Marriage and the Family*, 3rd edn. New York: Holt, Rinehart, & Winston, pp. 399–410.

Winch, R. F., Ktsanes, T., and Ktsanes, V. (1954). The theory of complementary needs in mate selection: An analytic and descriptive study. *American Sociological Review*, **19**, 241–249.

Winder, C. L., and Rau, L. (1962). Parental attitudes associated with social deviance in preadolescent boys. *Journal of Abnormal and Social Psychology*, **64**, 418–424.

Wing, J. K., Cooper, J. F., and Sartorius, N. (1974). *Measurement and Classification of Psychiatric Symptoms: An Instructional Manual for the PSE and Catego Program*. New York: Cambridge University Press.

Winnicott, D. W. (1965). *The Maturational Processes and the Facilitating Environment*. New York: International Universities Press.

Winnicott, M. T. (1958). The capacity to be alone. *International Journal of Psychoanalysis*, **39**, 416–420.

Winstead, B. A. (1986). Sex differences in same-sex friendship. In V. J. Derlega and B. A. Winstead (Eds) *Friendship and Social Interaction*. New York: Springer-Verlag.

Winter, D. G. (1973). *The Power Motive*. New York: Free Press.

Winter, D. G., and Stewart, A. J. (1978). The power motive. In H. London and J. E. Exner, Jr (Eds) *Dimensions of Personality*. New York: Wiley, pp. 391–448.

Winter, D. G., McClelland, D. C., and Stewart, A. J. (1981). *A New Case for the Liberal Arts: Assessing Institutional Goals and Student Development*. San Francisco: Jossey-Bass.

Winter, D. G., Stewart, A. J., and McClelland, D. C. (1977). Husband's motives and wife's career level. *Journal of Personality and Social Psychology*, **35**, 159–166.

Wiseman, J. (1986). Friendship: Bonds and binds in a voluntary relationship. *Journal of Social and Personal Relationships*, **3**, 191–212.

Wish, M., Deutsch, M., and Kaplan, S. J. (1976). Perceived dimensions of interpersonal relations. *Journal of Personality and Social Psychology*, **33**, 409–420.

Wittenberg, M. T., and Reis, H. T. (1986). Loneliness, social skills, and social perception. *Personality and Social Psychology Bulletin*, **12**, 121–130.

Wittgenstein, L. (1958). *Philosophical Investigations* (trans. G. E. M. Anscombe). Oxford: Blackwell.

Won-Doornink, M. J. (1979). On getting to know you: The association between the stage of a relationship and reciprocity of self-disclosure. *Journal of Experimental Social Psychology*, **15**, 229–241.

Wood, J. T. (1982). Communication and relational culture: Bases for the study of human relationships. *Communication Quarterly*, **30**, 75–83.

Wood, J. V., Taylor, S. E., and Lichtman, R. R. (1985). Social comparison in adjustment to breast cancer. *Journal of Personality and Social Psychology*, **49**, 1169–1183.

Wood, W., and Karten, S. J. (1986). Sex differences in interaction style as a product of perceived sex differences in competence. *Journal of Personality and Social Psychology*, **50**, 341–347.

Worobey, J., Laub, K. W., and Schilmoeller, G. L. (1983). Maternal and paternal responses to infant distress. *Merrill-Palmer Quarterly*, **29**, 33–45.

Wortman, C. B., Adesman, P., Herman, E., and Greenberg, R. (1976). Self-disclosure: An attributional perspective. *Journal of Personality and Social Psychology*, **33**, 184–191.

Wortman, C. B., and Conway, T. L. (1985). The role of social support in adaptation and recovery from physical illness. In S. Cohen and S. L. Syme (Eds) *Social Support and Health*. Orlando, FL: Academic Press, pp. 281–302.

Wortman, C. B., and Lehman, D. R. (1985). Reactions to victims of life crisis: Support attempts that fail. In I. G. Sarason and B. R. Sarason (Eds) *Social Support: Theory, Research and Application*. The Hague: Martinus Nijhoff, pp. 463–489.

Wright, H. F. (1967). *Recording and Analysing Child Behavior*. New York: Harper & Row.

Wright, J. C., Giammarino, M., and Parad, H. W. (1986). Social status in small groups: Individual-group similarity and the social 'misfit'. *Journal of Personality and Social Psychology*, **50**, 523–536.

Wright, P. H. (1974). The delineation and measurement of some variables in the study of friendship. *Representative Research in Social Psychology*, **5**, 93–96.

Wright, P. H. (1982). Men's friendships, women's friendships and the alleged inferiority of the latter. *Sex Roles*, **8**, 1–20.

Wyer, R. S., Jr, and Bodenhausen, G. V. (1985). Event memory: The effects of processing objectives and time delay on memory for action sequence. *Journal of Personality and Social Psychology*, **49**, 301–316.

Wyer, R. S., Jr, Shoben, E. J., Fuhrman, R. W., and Bodenhausen, G. V. (1985). The temporal organization of social action sequences. *Journal of Personality and Social Psychology*, **49**, 857–877.

Wynne-Edwards, V. C. (1962). *Animal Dispersion in Relation to Social Behavior*. Edinburgh: Oliver & Boyd.

Yarrow, M. R., Scott, P. M., and Waxler, C. Z. (1973). Learning concern for others. *Developmental Psychology*, **8**, 240–260.

Young, J. E. (1982). Loneliness, depression and cognitive therapy: Theory and application. In L. A. Peplau and D. Perlman (Eds) *Loneliness: A Sourcebook of Theory, Research and Therapy*. New York: Wiley, pp. 379–405.

Young, J. E. (1986). A cognitive-behavioral approach to friendship disorders. In V. J. Derlega and B. A. Winstead (Eds) *Friendship and Social Interaction*. New York: Springer-Verlag, pp. 147–276.

Youngren, M. A., and Lewinsohn, P. M. (1980). The functional relationship between depression and problematic behavior. *Journal of Abnormal Psychology*, **89**, 333–341.

Youniss, J. (1986). Development in reciprocity through friendship. In C. Zahn-Waxler, E. M. Cummings and R. Iannotti (Eds) *Altruism and Aggression*. Cambridge, MA: Cambridge University Press.

Zahn-Waxler, C., and Chapman, M. (1982). Immediate antecedents of caretakers' methods of discipline. *Child Psychiatry and Human Development*, **12**, 179–192.

Zajonc, R. B. (1965). Social facilitation. *Science*, **149**, 269–274.

Zajonc, R. B. (1980). Feeling and thinking: Preferences need no inferences. *American Psychologist*, **35**, 151–175.

Zajonc, R. B. (1984). On the primacy of affect. *American Psychologist*, **39**, 117–123.

Zander, A. (1977). *Groups at Work*. San Francisco: Jossey-Bass.

Zarbatany, L., Hartmann, D. P., Gelfand, D. M., and Vinciguerra, P. (1985). Gender differences in altruistic reputation: Are they artifactual? *Developmental Psychology*, **21**, 97–101.

Zax, M., and Spector, G. A. (1974). *An Introduction to Community Psychology*. New York: Wiley.

Zimbardo, P. (1970). The human choice: Individuation, reason, and order versus deindividuation, impulse and chaos. In W. J. Arnold and D. Levine (Eds) *Nebraska Symposium on Motivation*, Vol. 17. Lincoln: University of Nebraska Press.

Zimbardo, P. G. (1977). *Shyness: What it is, what to do about it*. Reading, MA: Addison-Wesley.

Zimmerman, D. H., and West, C. (1975). Sex roles, interruptions, and silence in conversation. In B. Thorne and N. Henley (Eds) *Language and Sex: Difference and Dominance*. Rowley, MA: Newbury House, pp. 105–129.

Zucker, L. G. (1983). Organizations as institutions. *Research in the Sociology of Organizations*, **2**, 1–47.

Zuckerman, M., DePaulo, B. M., and Rosenthal, R. (1981). Verbal and nonverbal communication of deception. In L. Berkowitz (Ed.) *Advances in Experimental Social Psychology*, Vol. 14. New York: Academic Press.

Zuckerman, M., DePaulo, B., and Rosenthal, R. (1986). Humans as deceivers and lie detectors. In P. Blanck, R. Buck and R. Rosenthal (Eds) *Nonverbal Communication in the Clinical Context*. University Park: The Pennsylvania State University Press, pp. 13–35.

Zuroff, D. C. (1986). Was Gordon Allport a trait theorist? *Journal of Personality and Social Psychology*, **51**, 993–1000.

Index of First Authors

Abelson, R. P. 29, 279
Abramson, L. Y. 185
Acitelli, L. K. 69, 367, 383, 384, 587
Adam, D. 316
Adams, G. R. 441
Adamson, L. B. 133, 134
Adler, A. 12, 222
Adler, N. 107
Adler, T. F. 226
Ainslie, R. 137
Ainsworth, M. D. S. 79, 123, 124, 169, 371, 387
Akiskal, H. S. 555
Albrecht, T. 538
Aldrich, H. E. 480, 481, 483, 484
Alger, C. F. 80
Allan, G. A. 391, 392, 393, 395, 468
Allan, V. L. 169, 174
Allison, P. D. 75
Alloy, L. B. 587
Allport, F. H. 449
Allport, G. W. 163
Als, H. 145
Altman, I. 45, 50, 244, 245, 246, 257, 258, 260, 261, 270, 276, 347, 381, 394, 395, 397, 398, 399, 417, 471
American Psychiatric Association 220, 228
Anderson, P. A. 340
Anderson, B. J. 151
Anderson, C. A. 452, 453, 454, 460, 461, 462, 463
Anderson, H. H. 148
Angyal, A. 11, 12
Antill, J. K. 413, 445
Antonovsky, A. 502, 539
Antonucci, T. C. 504
Antze, P. 535
Applebaum, F. 571, 572
Archer, D. 348
Archer, R. L. 382
Argyle, M. 24, 25, 26, 27, 37, 47, 166, 172, 333, 340, 348, 350, 373, 393, 394, 395, 403, 405, 433
Argyris, C. 327

Aries, E. J. 403
Arkin, R. M. 583, 584, 589
Arkowitz H. 550, 556
Arntson, P. 538
Aronson, E. 396
Asher, S. R. 171, 224, 572
Ashmore, R. D. 436
Askham, J. 272
Astin, A. 385
Atkinson, B. J. 104
Atkinson, M. 308, 426
Axelrod, R. 143
Ayres, J. 244, 268
Azrin, N. H. 335

Babchuk, N. 404
Backman, C. W. 473
Bailey, R. C. 406
Bakan, D. 11, 12, 14, 21, 42
Bakeman, R. 74, 76, 133, 134
Baker, E. E. 286
Bales, R. F. 303
Bandura, A. 178, 180
Bank, S. P. 223, 224, 225, 227
Barker, R. G. 80
Barnes, H. 318
Baron, R. A. 282
Barrera, M., Jr. 503, 508, 509, 592
Barrett-Lennard, G. 318, 319
Bartlett, F. C. 33
Bateson, G. 289, 290, 291, 292, 294, 302, 303, 304, 305, 312, 348
Baumrind, D. 188, 204, 223
Bavelas, J. B. 260, 261
Baxter, L. A. 28, 39, 107, 245, 249, 250, 259, 261, 264, 265, 266, 267, 268, 271, 272, 285, 329, 357, 401, 402, 403, 423, 424, 425, 426, 441, 459, 472, 472, 474
Beach, S. R. H. 559
Beaman, A. L. 282
Beard, J. H. 530
Beck, A. T. 549, 566, 587
Becker, E. 12
Becker, H. 467

Becker, J. M. T. 133
Beebe, S. 346
Beels, C. C. 529
Beier, E. G. 51
Bell, R. A. 250, 264, 268, 269
Bell, R. Q. 180, 181
Bell, R. R. 407, 439, 576
Bellah, R. 353
Belsky, J. 123, 160, 196, 200
Bem, S. L. 12, 14, 21, 432
Benne, K. D. 476
Berg, B. 531
Berg, J. H. 102, 103, 167, 168, 349, 399,
    416, 417, 419
Berg, S. 572
Berger, C. R. 240, 241, 244, 245, 246,
    247, 248, 249, 250, 251, 258, 259,
    279, 347
Berger, P. L. 329, 470, 472
Berkman, L. F. 513, 538
Berkowitz, L. 199, 241
Berley, R. A. 564
Berlyne, D. 241
Bernal, G. 303
Bernard, H. R. 80
Berndt, T. J. 66, 143, 369, 406
Berscheid, E. 93, 171, 177, 244, 245, 246,
    268, 371, 381, 396, 397, 437, 450, 457
von Bertalanffy, L. 153
Best, A. M. 239
Bhaskar, R. 430
Bidwell, C. E. 480
Bienvenu, M. J. 441
Bierman, K. L. 221
Bigelow, B. J. 391, 395, 405
Biglan, A. 556, 557, 558, 568, 569
Bijou, S. W. 180
Billings, A. 346
Birchler, G. R. 327, 556
Blaney, P. H. 549
Blau, P. M. 9, 244, 285, 311, 396, 437,
    484
Blau, Z. S. 482
Block, J. 162
Blood, R. O. 467
Bloom, B. L. 530
Blumberg, S. R. 549
Blumer, H. 289
Blumstein, P. 315, 468
Bochner, A. P. 257, 260, 265, 272, 342,
    352, 407
Bochner, B. 407
Bohm, D. 291
Bolton, C. D. 420, 467
Bond, C. F., Jr. 279
Booth, R. 587, 588
Borck, L. E. 532
Bornstein, P. 317

Borys, S. 443, 588
Bossard, J. H. S. 225, 472
Boster, F. J. 279, 287
Boszormenyi-Nagy, I. 224
Bothwell, S. 551
Bott, H. McM. 146, 152, 153, 154
Bowen, M. 226, 312
Bower, G. H. 30, 31, 549
Bowlby, J. 10, 18, 117, 122, 125, 126, 127,
    128, 130, 169, 170, 171, 207, 371,
    381, 583
Bradford, D. L. 450
Braiker, H. B. 26, 31, 102, 103, 106, 259,
    265, 266, 385, 401, 415
Brain, R. 391, 392, 395, 407
Brandt, R. M. 80
Brazelton, T. B. 123, 144, 145
Brechner, K. C. 279
Brehm, S. S. 347, 436, 437, 438, 440, 437,
    442, 444
Breiger, R. L. 476
Brennan, R. 585
Brennan, T. 572
Brent, S. B. 477, 478
Bretherton, I. 117, 135, 136, 137, 207, 371
Breznitz, S. 502
Brickman, P. 90, 91
Bridges, K. M. B. 131, 132
Bringle, R. G. 442
Brittain, J. 483
Brody, G. H. 164, 196, 197, 206
Bronowski, J. 291
Bronson, G. 135
Brown, G. W. 199, 499, 386, 526, 527,
    544, 552, 554
Brown, P. 340, 264
Brown, R. 38
Bruce, B. C. 250
Bruner, J. S. 24, 123, 124
Bryant, B. K. 206, 212
Buber, M. 20
Buck, R. 377
Buckley, W. 291
Budson, R. D. 530
Buehler, C. J. 437
Buhler, C. 131
Buhrmester, D. 171, 172, 369, 576
Bullock, R. C. 545, 556
Bulman, R. J. 535, 539
Burda, P. C., Jr. 512
Burger, J. M. 282, 453
Burgess, E. W. 335, 412, 413, 415, 470
Burgess, R. L. 381
Burgoon, J. K. 289, 340, 348, 453, 583
Burgoon, M. 284
Burke, R. J. 441, 512
Burns, T. 311
Burrell, G. 450

Buss, A. H. 54, 162, 163
Buss, D. M. 445
Butler, K. 462
Button, L. 395
Buunk, B. 442
Byrne, D. 103, 242, 326, 339, 381, 397, 453

Cacioppo, J. 377
Cafferata, G. L. 477
Cairns, R. 128, 144, 145, 147, 149
Caldwell, M. A. 385, 403
Candy, S. G. 407
Cane, D. B. 544, 589
Cantor, N. 34
Caplan, G. 498
Caplow, T. 474
Cappella, J. 46, 49, 325, 326, 331, 332, 333, 340, 341, 350, 453
Capra, F. 291
Carbaugh, D. 259
Carroll, G. R. 483
Caspi, A. 200, 206
Castaneda, G. G. 107
Castellan, N. J. 155
Cate, R. M. 105, 418, 419, 420, 421, 422
Centers, R. 414
Chambliss, W. J. 468
Chapman, N. J. 528
Charlesworth, R. 146
Charney, D. S. 555
Chase, I. D. 127
Chatov, R. 450
Cheek, F. E. 80, 445
Cheek, J. M. 13, 580, 581
Chelune, G. J. 347, 348, 349, 372, 375, 380, 381, 384, 440, 584, 585
Cheung, P. 313
Christie, 12
Cialdini, R. B. 281, 282
Ciske, K. L. 531
Cissna, K. 345, 346, 347
Clanton, G. 442
Clark, H. H. 374
Clark, M. S. 10, 38, 167, 399, 400, 437
Clark, R. E. 80
Clarke, D. D. 38
Clarke-Stewart, K. A. 135
Clatterbuck, G. W. 244, 246
Clawson, J. G. 451, 459
Clayton, R. 315
Clifford, E. 181
Coates, D. 536, 538, 585, 589
Cobb, S. 498, 509
Cochran, S. D. 444
Cody, M. J. 284, 285
Cohen, C. I. 386, 528, 537
Cohen, E. A. 188

Cohen, L. H. 509, 512
Cohen, M. D. 480
Cohen, P. R. 250
Cohen, R. Y. 536
Cohen, S. 200, 497, 501, 511, 513
Cohen, Y. A. 472
Coie, J. D. 222
Coleman, R. E. 545
Collett, P. 24, 25, 37
Collins, E. G. C. 451, 465
Cone, J. D. 80
Constantinople, A. 431
Cook, E. P. 14
Cook, M. 396
Cooley, C. H. 189
Coombs, R. H. 413
Coopersmith, S. 189
Cornforth, M. 258
Corsaro, W. A. 173
Costanzo, P. R. 228
Costello, C. G. 553
Courtright, J. A. 298, 299
Cowen, E. L. 169
Cox, M. J. 201
Coyne, J. C. 536, 537, 544, 549, 565, 584, 585, 589
Cozby, P. C. 372, 440
Craig, R. 350
Crawford, M. 393, 394, 395, 403
Crockenberg, S. 199
Cronbach, L. J. 59
Cronen, V. E. 304, 351
Crowther, J. H. 545
Cuber, J. F. 415
Cunningham, J. D. 313, 437
Cupach, W. 270
Curran, J. P. 439
Cutrona, C. E. 386, 504, 505, 561, 577

D'Augelli, A. R. 525, 528
Dabbs, J. M., Jr. 74
Dailey, W. O. 243
Damon, W. 187
Daniels-Mohring, D. 529
Danziger, K. 294
Darley, J. M. 379
Davidson, L. R. 403
Davidson, S. 408
Davis, D. 338, 339, 371, 379
Davis, J. A. 328
Davis, J. D. 446
Davis, K. E. 24, 27, 33, 37, 39, 393, 394, 395, 398, 404, 446, 470
Davis, M. S. 468
Dawe, H. C. 79, 80
Deag, J. M. 79
Deaux, K. 435
Deethardt, J. 310

DeForest, C. 440
DeLamater, J. 439
Delia, J. G. 166, 385
DeMaris, A. 315
Denzin, N. K. 294
DePaulo, B. M. 72
DePue, R. A. 511
Derlega, V. J. 381, 400, 441
Derry, P. A. 549
Deutsch, M. 279
Dickens, W. J. 391, 405, 407
Dillard, J. P. 281, 452, 453, 454, 455, 456,
    457, 461, 463, 464
DiMatteo, R. M. 309
Dindia, K. 65, 268, 269
Dinkmeyer, D. 317
Dion, K. K. 181, 182, 437, 438, 446
Dion, K. L. 436, 446
Dix, T. H. 184, 185, 186, 189
Dodge, K. A. 146, 169, 222
Doelger, J. A. 248, 290
Doherty, W. J. 564
Donohue, W. A. 287
Dontas, C. 133
Dosser, D. 348
Douglas, W. 250, 263
Doyle, A. 167
Dreman, S. B. 143
Driscoll, R. 457, 482
Duck, S. W. 28, 31, 39, 42, 56, 77, 100,
    105, 107, 110, 165, 167, 171, 172,
    242, 245, 269, 270, 271, 277, 363, 364,
    368, 374, 376, 383, 394, 396, 397,
    398, 399, 402, 403, 406, 414, 420, 423,
    425, 426, 432, 433, 434, 435, 469,
    470, 475, 478, 479, 480, 587
Dumas, J. E. 334
Duncan, H. D. 303
Duncan, S. D., Jr. 25, 49, 50, 58, 74, 77,
    93, 332
Dunkel-Schetter, C. 524, 527
Dunn, J. 117, 205, 206, 212

Eagly, A. H. 436
Easterbrooks, M. A. 196, 197
Eastzer, D. H. 138
Eaton, W. W. 499
Eckenrode, J. 523
Eckerman, C. D. 133, 135
Eder, D. 576
Edinger, J. A. 52
Edwards, A. L. 8
Egeland, B., 123, 223
Eidelson, R. 313, 394, 401
Eisenberg, R. B. 123
Eisenstadt, S. N. 470
Ekeh, P. 311
Ekman, P. 47, 377

Elder, G. H. 200, 454
Ellis, D. G. 289, 331, 337
Ellsworth, P. C. 373
Emde, R. 135
Emlen, S. T. 127
Endicott, J. 566
Engfer, A. 197
Epstein, J. L. 481
Epstein, S. 88, 170
Erickson, E. 177, 193
Erickson, M. F. 173
Erikson, E. H. 369, 387
Erlebacher, A. 67
Escudero, V. 300
Even-Chen, M. 281
Everitt, B. S. 553
Eysenck, H. J. 589

Fairbairn, W. R. D. 122, 125
Fairhurst, G. T. 300, 302, 451
Fairweather, G. W. 530
Falbo, T. 444
Fararo, T. J. 484
Farina, A. 329
Fausteau, M. F. 513
Fausto-Sterling, A. 429
Feagin, J. R. 402
Feger, H. 482
Feick, L. F. 334
Feinberg, M. R. 461
Feinman, S. 135
Feld, S. L. 481, 482
Feldman, R. 316
Feldstein, S. 49
Felner, R. D. 531
Fengler, A. P. 437
Fenigstein, A. 40, 91
Fernald, A. 123
Ferreira, A. 316, 439
Ferrell, M. Z. 439
Festinger, L. 284, 396, 531, 535
Field, T. 125, 131, 132
Fienberg, S. E. 74
Fincham, F. 564
Fine, G. A. 38, 353
Fine, R. 122, 472
Fineberg, B. 316
Fiore, J. 509
Fischer, C. S. 393, 481, 572
Fish, R. 307, 312, 313, 320
Fisher, A. 259, 294, 303, 313, 331
Fisher, B. A. 234
Fisher, M. 387
Fisher, W. A. 103
Fiske, S. T. 28, 29, 31, 33, 378
Fitzgerald, N. M. 106
Fitzpatrick, M. A. 43, 44, 102, 260, 267,

290, 300, 328, 330, 336, 337, 338, 341, 354, 377
Fleener, D. E. 137
Fleming, R. 406
Foa, U. 244
Fodor, E. M. 15
Fogel, A. 132
Folger, J. P. 303, 331
Foot, H. C. 166, 173, 572
Forgas, J. P. 31
Foss, R. D. 282
Foucault, M. 430
Fox, A. 312
Frankenstein, W. 317
Frankl, V. E. 99, 108
Franzoi, S. L. 572
Freden, L. 545, 553
Freedman, J. L. 282
Freeman, J. 483
French, J. R. P., Jr. 190
Freud, S. 7, 11, 12, 122, 141, 163, 171, 177, 193, 487
Fried, M. 80, 531
Friedman, A. S. 559
Friedman, R. C. 555
Friedrich, W. 225
Friedrick, W. 200
Froland, C. 520
Fromm-Reichmann, F. 572, 579, 580, 587, 588
Furman, W. 168, 179, 212, 213, 223, 226, 228, 369
Fusso, T. E. 27

Gaelick, L. 321, 382, 444
Gagnon, G. H. 30, 32, 430
Galaskiewicz, J. 481
Galinsky, E. 531
Garvey, C. 10, 148
Geen, R. G. 589
Gergen, K. J. 311, 352, 430
Gerson, A. C. 573, 581
Gibson, J. J. 39
Giddens, A. 434, 470
Gilbert, S. 440
Giles, H. 286, 334
Gilligan, C. 12
Ginsburg, G. P. 37, 395, 396, 469
Glaser, R. D. 452
Glick, P. 315
Glidewell, J. C. 508, 530
Godfrey, D. 264
Goethals, G. R. 369, 381
Goffman, E. 13, 38, 53, 54, 279, 294
Goldberg, D. P. 566
Goldberg, J. 346
Goldberg, W. A. 196, 197
Goldman, B. D. 133

Goldstein, M. J. 526, 528
Goldstein, M. 51
Goode, W. J. 468
Goodman, E. 451
Goodman, G. 526
Goodnow, J. J. 185
Gordon, S. L. 474, 577, 578
Goswick, R. A. 585
Goth-Owens, T. L. 196
Gotlib, I. H. 548, 549, 550, 551, 557, 559, 566, 567, 558, 561, 585
Gottlieb, B. H. 497, 511, 519, 521, 523, 528, 529, 530, 534, 540
Gottlieb, G. 138
Gottman, J. M. 43, 44, 58, 74, 76, 79, 86, 105, 144, 147, 150, 151, 152, 159, 164, 166, 269, 291, 301, 303, 321, 322, 333, 335, 336, 338, 339, 341, 344, 345, 346, 348, 350, 351, 355, 359, 370, 381, 382, 563, 567, 568
Gouldner, A. W. 143, 283
Gove, W. R. 386
Graen, G. 473
Granovetter, M. S. 408, 507
Gray, J. 589
Gray-Little, B. 444
Graziano, W. G. 425, 589
Greenberg, J. R. 227, 371
Greenberg, L. S. 377, 387
Greene, M. 574, 579, 584
Greenhalgh, L. 478, 483
Grossmann, K. 123, 201
Grusec, J. E. 182, 183, 185, 186, 188, 189
Gudykunst, W. B. 244, 246
Guerney, B. G. Jr. 375
Guilford, J. P. 12
Guntrip, H. 122, 125
Gupta, N. 460
Gutek, B. A. 451, 452
Guttentag, M. 578

Haberman, S. J. 156
Hage, J. 292
Hahlweg, K. 568
Hall, K. R. L. 130
Hall, W. M. 145, 157
Hallinan, M. T. 482
Halpern, R. 526
Hamilton, W. D. 126, 129
Hammer, M. 528
Hammock, G. 103
Hanley-Dunn, P. 586
Hannan, M. T. 483, 484
Hansson, R. O. 504
Harlow, H. F. 10
Harre, R. 25, 169
Harrigan, J. 309
Harris, L. 323, 359

Harrison, A. A. 454
Harrison, R. P. 47
Hartmann, H. 180
Hartup, W. W. 117, 124, 150, 168, 169, 171, 172, 173, 212, 222, 223, 289, 393
Harvey, J. H. 39, 103, 108, 109, 111, 243, 424
Hatfield, E. 43, 371, 373, 376, 418
Hatkoff, S. 106, 438
Hautzinger, M. 556, 557, 558, 568
Hawes, L. C. 331
Hawkins, J. 323
Hay, D. F. 130, 132, 133, 134, 136, 138, 140, 145, 148, 166, 168, 172, 175
Hayano, D. M. 80
Hayes, S. C. 26
Hayes-Roth, B. 250
Haynes, S. N. 80
Hays, R. B. 167, 261, 384, 385, 391, 394, 395, 396, 398, 399, 400, 401, 405, 407, 408
Hazan, C. 371, 372, 379
Head, H. 33
Heider, F. 100, 184, 241, 242, 384, 506
Heinicke, C. 201
Helgeson, V. S. 374
Heller, K. 511, 524
Helmreich, R. L. 439
Henderson, S. 503, 509, 510, 513
Hendrick, C. 9, 10, 102, 103, 104, 106, 107, 111, 432, 438, 439, 440, 441, 442
Hendrick, S. S. 10, 412, 413, 441
Henley, N. M. 301
Hersey, J. C. 531
Hess, B. 392, 393, 394, 396, 406, 407
Hetherington, E. M. 196, 206
Hewes, D. E. 248, 290, 331, 334
Hewes, G. 308
Hewstone, M. 243
Hibbs, D. A. 333
Hill, C. T. 412, 413, 415, 416, 423, 438
Hill, W. 110
Hilton, D. J. 38
Hinchliffe, M. 313, 317, 549, 550, 551
Hinde, R. A. 46, 128, 129, 143, 144, 152, 153, 157, 164, 171, 174, 193, 208, 223, 392, 431
Hirsch, B. J. 408, 499, 506, 508, 509, 512, 529, 538
Hobart, C. W. 437
Hobbs J. R. 250
Hobfoll, S. E. 386, 488–517, 547, 561
Hochschild, A. R. 24, 25, 470
Hodges, J. 203
Hoffman, C. 36
Hoffman, M. L. 10, 181, 199

Hogan, R. 11, 12, 13, 18, 21, 576
Hogarth, R. 239, 243, 249, 251
Holdaway, S. 80
Holland, P. W. 482
Holmes, J. G. 152
Holohan, C. J. 531
Holtzworth-Monroe, A. 564
Homans, G. C. 244, 285, 311
Honeycutt, J. 315, 349
Hooley, J. M. 544, 563, 564, 567
Hoover, C. F. 545
Hopper, R. 265, 472
Hops, H. 223, 568
Hornstein, G. A. 377, 401
Horowitz, L. M. 581, 583, 585, 589
House, J. S. 498, 526, 527, 540
Hovland, C. I. 288
Howard, J. A. 444
Howe, N. 206
Howes, M. J. 549, 584, 585
Hrdy, S. B. 130
Hubbard, R. 352
Huesmann, L. R. 417, 418
Hunt, M. 439
Hunter, J. E. 284, 287
Hupka, R. B. 442
Husaini, B. A. 513
Huston, T. L. 102, 105, 110, 111, 265, 268, 397, 398, 400, 413, 415, 417, 418, 425, 426, 427, 450, 452
Hutt, S. J. 80
Hymel, S. 185, 221

Ickes, W. 6, 13, 14, 18, 21, 67, 81, 82, 86, 88, 89, 90, 91, 92, 93, 94, 95, 96, 445
Ilfeld, F. W. 545
Infante, D. A. 283
Ipsa, J. 130, 137
Irwin, D. M. 80
Izard, C. E. 12, 21, 377

Jablin, F. M. 244
Jaccard, J. J. 88
Jackson, D. N. 8, 307, 312, 353
Jackson, R. M. 395, 397, 402, 406
Jackson, S. 284
Jacobs, J. B. 80
Jacobson, D. E. 529
Jacobson, J. L. 133, 170, 204
Jacobson, N. S. 104, 105, 110, 556, 564
Jacobson, R. H. 549
Jaffe, J. 74
Jamuna, D. 317
Janis, I. L. 408, 526
Jarrett, R. 321
Jason, L. A. 492, 532
Jassem, W. 308
Joanning, H. 315

Johnson, M. H. 549
Johnson, M. P. 30, 32, 409, 418, 419, 427, 482, 483, 575
Jones, E. E. 184, 242, 250, 253, 254, 286, 445
Jones, R. R. 80
Jones, S. E. 50, 51
Jones, W. H. 13, 60, 107, 572, 573, 577, 578, 579, 580, 581, 582, 583, 584, 585, 589
Joreskog, K. G. 69
Jourard, S. M. 102, 372, 381, 440
Jung, C. G. 8
Jurich, A. P. 439

Kagan, J. 219, 589
Kahn, E. 388
Kahn, J. 550
Kahn, M. 351, 354, 556
Kahn, R. L. 504
Kahneman, D. 240, 243, 251, 279
Kalter, N. 530
Kaminski, E. P. 284
Kandel, D. B. 397
Kanouse, D. E. 38
Kanter, R. M. 451
Kantor, D. 293, 294
Katriel, T. 268, 347, 349
Katz, A. H. 529
Katz, D. 239
Kawamura, S. 130
Kaye, K. 193
Kegan, R. 12
Keller, B. B. 181
Kellermann, K. 240, 249, 263
Kelley, H. H. 9, 53, 93, 100, 184, 190, 242, 243, 252, 254, 382, 383, 384, 392, 400, 420, 425, 426, 437, 473
Kelly, C. 266, 411
Kelly, G. A. 8, 10, 241, 378
Kelvin, P. 259, 371, 378, 382
Kendon, A. 47, 49, 50, 290
Kendrick, C. 206
Kenny, D. A. 5, 59, 60, 63, 68, 69, 71, 72, 154, 157, 330, 332
Kenrick, D. T. 430
Kerckhoff, A. C. 412, 413, 414, 415, 453
Kessler, R. C. 514
Kessler, S. J. 430
Kidd, V. 352
Kimberly, J. R. 476, 477, 479
King, A. P. 138
King, C. E. 102
King, D. A. 549
King, K. 439
Kinsey, A. C. 32, 439
Klein, M. 487
Kleinke, C. L. 51, 52

Klinger, E. 3
Klinnert, M. D. 136
Knapp, C. W. 397, 401, 425
Knapp, M. L. 347
Knowles, E. S. 340
Knowles, P. L. 39
Knox, D. H. 437
Kobasa, S. C. O. 502
Koestler, A. 290, 291
Kohn, M. 146
Kohut, H. 388
Komarovsky, M. 441
Kon, I. S. 395, 407
Konner, M. 381
Kowalik, D. L. 563
Kraemer. H. C. 62, 63, 76
Krain, M. 476, 482
Kram, K. E. 451
Krippendorf, K. 291
Kropotkin, P. 529
Kuhn, T. 352
Kuiper, N. A. 587
Kurth, S. B. 379, 392, 398, 405, 406

L'Abate, L. 290
La Gaipa, J. J. 391, 394, 395, 396, 397, 400, 479, 482
Lacoursiere, R. B. 475, 476, 478
Ladd, D. 308
LaFollette, H. 260
LaFrance, M. 50, 86
LaFreniere, P. 204
Laing, R. D. 87, 346, 351
Lalljee, M. 38, 244
Lamb, M. E. 79, 123, 128, 129, 204
Langer, E. J. 278
Larrance, D. T. 185
Larson, R. 580, 581
Lasswell, M. 11, 438
Lasswell, T. E. 106
Lazarsfeld, P. F. 468
Lea, M. 397
Leary, M. R. 582, 583, 589
Lederer, W. J. 292, 302
Lee, J. A. 9, 10, 102, 106, 424, 425, 438, 441
Lee, L. 424
Lefcourt, H. M. 502, 511
Lehman, D. R. 522, 524, 539
Lehmann, H. E. 503, 543
Leiter, M. P. 146, 150
Lepper, M. R. 188, 189
Leslie, G. R. 413, 422, 427
Leslie, L. A. 260
Lester, R. E. 244
Leth, S. 346
Levenson, R. W. 112, 344, 359, 567
Leventhal, H. 80

Levine, A. 122
Levine, D. N. 470
Levinger, G. 111, 165, 166, 174, 175, 349, 351, 372, 384, 388, 398, 400, 412, 414, 415, 416, 419
Levitt, M. 149, 527
Levitz-Jones, E. M. 371
Levy, L. H. 530
Lewinsohn, P. M. 558, 568, 587
Lewis, C. C. 188
Lewis, M. 121, 131, 135, 160, 173
Lewis, R. A. 79, 351, 410, 412, 414, 415, 478, 482, 513
Libet, J. 549
Lidz, T. 226
Lieberman, A. F. 170, 204
Lieberman, M. A. 530
Lindblom, D. E. 80
Litwak, E. 407
Livingston, K. R. 245, 246
Lloyd, S. A. 105, 266, 270, 415, 416, 418, 423, 424, 425, 459
Lock, A. 259
Locke, H. J. 104, 328, 336, 410, 557
Loeb, R. C. 189
Loevinger, J. 163, 387
Lofthouse, L. J. 279, 281
Londerville, S. 173
Lootens, A. L. 512
LoVette, S. 452, 453, 463
Lowenthal, M. F. 526
Luckey, E. B. 439
Lujansky, H. 419
Lustig, M. W. 284
Lytton, H. 190

Maccoby, E. E. 117, 173, 174, 190, 212, 223
MacDonald, K. 204
MacIver, R. M. 471
MacKay, D. M. 47
Madanes, C. 312
Madden, M. E. 109
Magnusson, D. 161, 164
Mahoney, E. R. 439
Main, M. 170, 175, 201, 208, 371, 372
Mainiero, L. A. 450
Malatesta, C. L. 139
Malloy, T. E. 5, 60, 71
Malott, J. M. 526
Mandel, M. J. 476
Manderscheid, R. W. 300, 333
Mandler, G. 245
Manicas, P. T. 430, 434
Mannarino, A. P. 173, 174
March, J. G. 239, 480
Marciano, T. 321
Marcus, R. F. 146, 147

Margolin, G. 336
Margulis, J. T. 575, 576
Markman, H. J. 410, 426, 568
Marks, T. 549
Markus, H. 28, 29, 30, 33, 38, 185, 377, 378
Marlowe, D. 165
Martin, G. 132, 151
Martin, J. 474
Maruyama, M. 291
Marwell, G. 287
Masheter, C. 354, 355
Maslin, C. A. 124
Masling, J. 10
Maslow, A. 8, 9
Masters, J. C. 147
Matas, L. 171, 172
Mathes, E. W. 442
Matthews, C. 313
Maudry, M. 131, 133
Mauss, M. 143
Mayer, J. D. 33, 34, 35, 38
Maynard, D. W. 472
Maynard-Smith, J. 127
McAdams, D. P. 11, 12, 15, 16, 17, 20, 21, 22, 42, 44, 375, 387, 396, 576, 583
McArthur, L. A. 243, 254
McArthur, L. Z. 39
McCall, G. J. 24, 271, 293, 294, 295, 393, 401, 468, 469, 471, 473, 474, 476, 481, 482
McCleary, R. 333
McClelland, D. C. 12, 15
McClintock, E. 24, 25
McCormack, S. H. 107
McDonald, G. 311, 312
McDougall, W. 8
McFeat, T. 472
McGrath, J. E. 499
McGuire, J. C. 530
McGuire, W. J. 38, 276
McIntyre-Kingsolver, K. O. 526
McKelvey, B. 483
McLaughlin, M. L. 333
McLean, P. D. 556, 558
McPherson, M. 483
Mead, G. H. 189
Mechanic, D. 439
Medin, D. L. 33
Medora, N. 439
Mehrabian, A. 348, 376
Menaghan, E. G. 501
Mendoza, J. L. 66
Menzel, W. 298
Mercer, G. W. 439
Merikangas, K. R. 565, 567
Meyer, H. J. 196

Meyer, J. W. 480
Miell, D. E. 240, 244, 374, 376, 395, 399, 583
Milardo, R. M. 174, 387, 426, 483
Miles, R. H. 477, 479, 484
Milgram, S. 278
Millar, F. E. 293, 297, 299, 301
Millen, L. 407
Miller, G. R. 275, 276, 277, 278, 279, 283, 284, 285, 286, 288, 338, 347, 349
Miller, K. I. 453, 454, 464, 465
Miller, L. C. 72, 102, 103, 379, 380, 441
Miller, P. 386
Miller, R. S. 375
Miller, S. 316, 441
Miller, V. 272
Mills, J. 26, 27, 374, 382, 384
Mills, R. S. L. 189
Minde, K. 201
Minuchin, P. 195, 220, 224, 226, 227, 503
Mischel, W. 161, 163, 378
Mitchell, C. 316
Mitchell, R. E. 506
Moffitt, P. 317
Monge, P. R. 452
Montgomery, B. M. 71, 72, 304, 327, 332, 346, 349, 354, 359, 367, 372, 373
Moore, J. A. 581, 585
Moore, N. V. 223
Morawski, J. G. 431
Morin, R. C. 528
Morris, D. 201, 308
Morris, G. H. 472
Morton, T. L. 165, 372, 441
Mosher, D. L. 103
Mowen, J. C. 281
Munro, B. 437
Murray, H. A. 8, 10, 576
Murstein, B. I. 168, 398, 410, 412, 413, 414, 415, 454

Nadler, A. 505
Nahemow, L. 396
Nash, A. 124, 133, 134, 135, 140
Natale, M. 333
Navran, L. 441, 556
Neisser, U. 33
Newcomb, A. F. 166, 172
Newcomb, T. M. 241
Newman, H. M. 459
Nezlek, J. 107
Nisbett, R. E. 243, 247, 249, 251, 252
Noller, P. 43, 44, 269, 319, 320, 327, 347, 351, 354, 382
Norton, R. 286, 309, 310, 312, 314, 315, 316, 322, 323, 347, 349
Nuckolls, K. B. 199

O'Connell, L. 400
O'Hara, M. W. 561
O'Keefe, B. 260
O'Leary, K. D. 113, 568
O'Mahony, J. F. 185
Ochse, R. 375
Oldham, G. R. 453
Olson, D. H. 101, 111, 507
Olweus, D. 12
Oppenheim, D. 137
Orians, G. H. 127
Oring, E. 265, 472
Oritt, E. J. 509, 526
Orlinsky, D. E. 371
Orlofsky, J. L. 102, 370
Orvis, B. R. 109, 243
Osgood, C. E. 241
Osterweis, M. 526
Ouchi, W. G. 471
Overall, J. 545
Owen, W. 268

Padgett, V. R. 242
Paolino, T. 317
Parker, S. R. 396
Parkes, C. M. 372
Parks, M. R. 246, 264, 342, 352, 416, 482
Parlee, M. B. 403, 404
Parmelee, P. 577
Parpal, M. 149
Parsons, T. 14
Partridge, E. 367
Pastor, D. L. 170, 204
Patterson, G. R. 104, 183, 186, 190, 191, 220, 221, 222, 227, 373
Patterson, M. L. 11, 13, 17, 21, 46, 52, 340, 341, 453
Paykel, E. S. 199, 552, 561
Pearce, W. B. 304
Pearlin, K. I. 501, 526, 538
Pedersen, F. 79
Penman, R. 291
Pennebaker, J. W. 386, 536, 538
Peplau, H. E. 385, 436, 587
Peplau, L. A. 26, 353, 439, 443, 572, 574, 578, 585, 586, 587
Perlman, D. 18, 43, 46, 103, 374, 386, 439, 576, 577, 578, 579, 581, 584, 585
Perls, F. 314
Perry, D. G. 188
Peters-Golden, H. 522
Peterson, L. 143, 148, 149, 159, 188
Petrovich, S. B. 139, 141
Pfeffer, J. 480
Pfohl, B. 555
Pfungst, O. 321
Piaget, J. 143

Pierce, R. 324
Pietromonaco, P. R. 584
Pike, G. 335, 339, 345, 346
Planalp, S. 245, 290
Pleck, J. 460
Plomin, R. 193, 589
Pope, K. S. 452
Porritt, D. 540
Posner, M. I. 33
Potasznik, H. 507
Prager, K. J. 382
Price, R. A. 413
Prigogine, I. 291
Procidano, M. E. 526
Purdy, T. F. 398
Putallaz, M. 169, 222, 228
Putman, W. B. 334, 339

Quinn, R. E. 450, 451, 453, 454, 455, 456,
    457, 459, 460, 461, 462, 463
Quinton, D. 196, 200

Radke-Yarrow, M. 178
Radloff, L. S. 566
Rahim, M. A. 103
Rajecki, D. W. 82, 93, 95
Rands, M. 401
Rangell, L. 394, 407
Rank, O. 11, 12
Ratner, N. 124
Raush, H. L. 315, 317, 556
Rawlins, W. K. 259, 260, 348, 402
Reed, D. 30, 32
Regan, D. T. 185
Reis, H. T. 107, 382, 386, 387, 441, 515
Reisman, J. M. 392, 393
Reiss, I. L. 104, 409, 439, 442
Reitz, K. P. 74
Rempel, J. K. 384
Renne, K. S. 545
Revenson, T. A. 572
Rheingold, H. L. 135, 136, 180
Ricciuti, H. 137
Rich, A. R. 512
Richardson, D. R. 103
Richey, M. H. 393
Richters, J. 173
Ricks, M. H. 170, 201, 371
Ridgeway, C. L. 472
Ridley, C. A. 418, 478, 482
Riley, D. 497
Riseman, D. 80
Riskin, J. 345
Rittle, R. H. 282
Roach, A. 313
Roback, H. B. 521
Robin, A. L. 225
Robins, E. J. 410, 411, 414, 420

Robinson, I. E. 439
Rodin, M. J. 405
Roff, M. 169
Rogers, C. R. 8, 371, 382, 387
Rogers, L. E. 290, 292, 296, 298, 300,
    302, 303, 313
Rogers-Millar, L. E. 298, 299
Rogoff, B. 136
Rokeach, M. 328, 501
Roloff, M. 258, 284
Rook, K. S. 508, 519, 528, 572, 573, 577,
    578, 579, 580, 584, 587
Roopnarine, J. L. 164
Rosch, E. 33, 34
Rose, S. M. 30, 39, 394, 404, 405, 406,
    444
Rosenberg, M. J. 241
Rosenblatt, P. C. 108, 446
Rosencrance, J. 393
Rosenfeld, H. M. 49
Rosenman, M. F. 438
Rosenthal, M. K. 130, 151
Roskin, M. 530
Ross, H. S. 131, 136, 148, 164, 175
Ross, L. 251
Ross, M. 109
Rounsaville, B. J. 545, 552, 553
Roy, A. 317, 553
Roy, P. 203
Rubenstein, C. M. 443, 573, 581, 584
Rubenstein, J. 80, 135
Rubin, J. Z. 279
Rubin, K. H. 572
Rubin, L. B. 467, 468
Rubin, R. B. 248
Rubin, Z. 11, 19, 50, 51, 102, 111, 113,
    223, 348, 369, 394, 409, 413, 414,
    437, 438, 441
Ruesch, J. 306, 309
Rueveni, U. 529
Runkel, P. 242
Rusbult, C. E. 14, 19, 102, 103, 167, 345,
    346, 418, 419
Russell, B. 12
Russell, D. 443, 557
Rutter, M. 201, 202

Sabatelli, R. 72, 354, 357
Sabini, J. 25
Sacks, O. 311
Sadler, W. A., Jr. 571
Sagi, A. 123, 132, 137
Sahlins, M. D. 158, 159
Salhoz, E. 578
Sameroff, A. J. 138, 139
Sandler, I. N. 509
Sarason, B. R. 59, 445, 510

Sarason, I. G. 497, 499, 504, 510, 512, 513, 526
Satran, G. 580, 584
Scanzoni, J. 312
Schaap, C. 336
Schachter, S. 55, 241, 452
Schaefer, M. T. 69, 375
Schaffer, H. R. 123, 131, 137, 138, 139
Schank, R. C. 29, 250, 279
Scheflen, A. E. 50, 54, 80, 303, 304
Schein, H. M. 572
Schellenberg, J. A. 413
Scherer, K. R. 377
Schilling, R. F. 523
Schlenker, B. R. 381, 583, 589
Schless, A. P. 551
Schmidt, C. F. 250, 443
Schmidt, N. 443
Schneider, C. 185
Schoenfeld, P. 529
Schonpflug, W. 515
Schultz, N. R. 443, 572
Schultz, R. 529
Schumm, W. R. 105, 318
Schwartz, J. 377
Schwarz, J. C. 171
Scott, M. B. 470
Scudder, J. 287
Sears, D. D. 175, 572
Sears, R. R. 10, 180
Seay, M. B. 66, 348
Seay, T. 348
Sechrest, L. 80
Secord, P. F. 476
Seibold, D. R. 278
Seligman, M. E. P. 123
Selman, R. L. 369
Semin, G. R. 24, 25, 470
Senneker, P. 186
Sennett, R. 313, 342, 347
Serafica, F. C. 33, 37
Sereno, K. K. 286
Seyfried, B. A. 413
Shaffer, D. R. 441
Shanab, M. E. 281
Shannon, C. 240
Shanteau, J. 417
Shantz, C. U. 24
Sharpley, C. F. 105
Shaul, S. 579, 581
Shaver, P. 14, 18, 372, 377, 571, 573, 576, 577, 579, 580, 582
Shaw, M. E. 174
Shea, B. C. 268, 269
Shea, M. T. 547, 548, 555
Sherblom, J. 244
Sherrod, L. R. 123
Shigetomi, C. C. 186

Shimanoff, S. 269
Shotter, J. 25, 469, 470, 471
Shulman, N. 396
Shumaker, S. A. 498, 499, 519, 521
Sieburg, E. 346
Siegal, M. 187
Sigel, I. E. 184
Sillars, A. L. 243, 266, 268, 270, 284, 351, 354
Silver, R. L. 539
Silverman, I. 454
Simmel, G. 290, 295, 467, 470, 475
Simons, H. W. 376
Sims, A. 553
Skinner, B. F. 180
Skolnick, A. 413
Skvoretz, J. 484
Slavin, M. O. 16
Sloan, W. W. 584
Sluzki, C. E. 296, 347
Smith, A. 234
Smith, C. L. 188, 189
Smith, D. L. 39
Smollar, J. 173
Snow, C. E. 123
Snyder, C. R. 376, 583, 589
Snyder, D. K. 104
Snyder, M. 167
Sobol, M. P. 184, 185, 404
Solano, C. H. 396, 406, 443, 577, 578, 584, 585, 586, 587
Solomon, Z. 572
Solso, R. L. 33, 34, 35
Sommer, R. 80
Spanier, G. B. 104, 105, 322, 335, 344, 410
Spaulding, C. 437
Spelke, E. S. 123
Spence, J. T. 14, 432
Spielberger, C. D. 502
Spiro, J. 313
Spitzberg, B. H. 582, 584, 585
Spitzer, R. L. 566
Sprecher, S. 444
Sroufe, L. A. 123, 170, 171, 175, 177, 203, 208, 224, 372, 378, 381
Starbuck, W. H. 477
Staub, E. 149, 159
Stayton, D. J. 173
Stein, C. H. 506, 515
Stein, E. 316
Steinglass, P. 317
Stephen, T. D. 355, 413, 416
Stern, D. N. 79, 151, 246, 379
Sternberg, R. J. 10, 21, 42, 43, 44, 244, 357, 437
Stevenson, M. B. 72
Stewart, A. J. 15, 19

Stewart, J. 347
Stiles, W. B. 303
Stokes, J. P. 441, 499, 503, 507, 509, 512, 513, 515
Stokes, R. 472
Stolberg, A. L. 530
Stotland, E. 93
Strain, P. S. 223
Straus, M. A. 104, 225
Strayer, F. F. 150, 158, 159
Street, R. L. 74, 328, 334, 339
Strodtbeck, F. L. 567
Sullaway, M. 313
Sullivan, H. S. 18, 369 f, 381, 387, 406, 579
Surra, C. A. 422, 427
Suttles, G. D. 392
Swann, W. B. 538

Tardy, C. H. 526, 528, 540
Taylor, D. 371, 372, 399
Taylor, S. E. 185, 536
Teasdale, J. D. 587
Tennov, D. 437
Terman, M. C. 431
Tesch, S. A. 102, 370, 375, 395
Tharp, R. G. 412, 413
Thayer, L. 51, 353
Thibaut, J. W. 26, 167, 172, 244, 245, 285, 401
Thoits, P. A. 538
Thomas, A. P. 50
Thomas, E. A. C. 333
Thompson, L. 110, 313, 426
Thompson, S. C. 539
Tiefer, L. 430
Ting-Toomey, S. 345
Tisak, M. S. 187
Tizard, B. 203
Tokuno, K. A. 407
Tolsdorf, C. C. 523
Tomkins, S. S. 11, 12, 17, 21
Trevarthen, C. 123
Trice, H. 472
Trivers, R. L. 127, 129, 143
Tronick, E. Z. 131
Tseng, W. 353
Tuckman, B. W. 476
Turiel, E. 24
Turnbull, W. 38
Turner, R. H. 473
Tyrer, P. 555

US Bureau of the Census 450
Uhlig, G. 317
Ulrich, W. 352
Unger, D. G. 529

Vachon, M. L. S. 530, 533
Valle, R. 520
Van Hooff, J. A. R. A. M. 299
Vandell, D. L. 132, 133, 134, 148
Vaughan, D. 270, 271
Vaughn, B. 199
Vaughn, C. E. 553, 554
Vaughn, D. 468, 473
Vaux, W. A. 520
Vega, W. A. 520
Verbrugge, L. M. 397, 402, 403
Vermes, G. 23, 25
Veroff, J. 16, 347, 385, 386
Vespo, J. E. 164, 167
Vincent, J. P. 568
Vygotsky, L. S. 10, 172

Wagner, H. L. 377
Waldrop, M. F. 175, 576
Walker, K. N. 408, 529
Waller, W. 467, 471
Walsh, R. H. 439
Walster, E. H. 9, 43, 244, 314, 373, 418, 419, 437
Walton, M. D. 143
Wampler, K. 344
Wandersman, L. P. 530
Waring, E. M. 374, 526
Warmbrod, M. 324
Warner, R. M. 61, 62, 76
Warren, N. J. 530
Warriner, C. K. 483
Washburn, S. L. 130
Wasserman, S. 66
Waters, E. 161, 170, 173, 174, 175, 204
Watson, D. 510
Watson, J. B. 180
Watzlawick, P. 291, 296, 309, 315, 316, 346, 402
Weber, A. L. 108
Wegner, D. M. 87
Weick, K. E. 80, 294, 304, 480
Weinberg, M. S. 30, 32
Weiner, B. 185
Weinstein, E. A. 294
Weiss, L. 168, 169, 393, 395, 403, 407
Weiss, P. 153
Weiss, R. S. 18, 108, 119, 212, 407, 468, 571, 572, 574, 575, 576, 578, 579, 580
Weiss, R. 335
Weissman, M. M. 543, 544, 545, 550, 551, 552, 555, 556, 559, 567, 575
Welkowitz, J. 334
Wellman, B. 528
Werner, C. 397
West, M. J. 138

Westhoff, L. A. 465
Wethington, E. 509, 510
Wheeler, L. 107, 381, 384, 386, 577, 586
Wheeless, L. R. 278, 508
Whitaker, C. 312
White, G. L. 442
Whitley, B. E. 157
Whyte, W. F. 283
Wideman, M. V. 525
Wieman, R. 324
von Wiese, L. 467
Wiggins, J. S. 161, 162, 163
Wilcox, B. L. 497, 506, 529
Wilensky, R. 250, 251
Wilkins, A. 472
Willems, E. P. 80
Williams, G. C. 127
Williamm, J. G. 386, 577, 584
Williams, R. M., Jr. 501
Williamson, O. E. 484
Williamson, R. N. 313, 328, 336, 341
Willis, F. N. 52
Wills, T. 104, 345
Wilmot, W. W. 285
Winch, R. F. 412, 413
Wing, J. K. 566
Winnicott, D. W. 371, 579
Winstead, B. A. 391, 394
Winter, D. G. 12, 16, 17
Wiseman, J. 348

Wish, M. 179
Wittenberg, M. T. 571, 572, 582
Wittgenstein, L. 433
Won-Doornink, M. J. 338
Wood, J. 445, 472
Wood, J. V. 535
Wood, W. 445
Worobey, J. 59, 61
Wortman, C. B. 382, 524, 536, 539
Wright, H. F. 80, 444
Wright, J. C. 221
Wright, P. H. 392, 394, 396
Wyer, R. S., Jr. 30, 31
Wynne-Edwards, V. C. 126, 127

Yarrow, M. R. 178
Young, J. E. 396, 573, 577, 578, 586, 587
Youngren, M. A. 549
Youniss, J. 158, 159

Zahn-Waxler, C. 182, 183
Zajonc, R. B. 246, 247, 279
Zander, A. 460
Zarbatany, L. 186
Zimbardo, P. 396, 408
Zimmerman, D. H. 301
Zucker, L. G. 460, 480
Zuckerman, M. 309, 560
Zuroff, D. C. 163

Subject Index

accountability 470 f
accounts 107 f
adaptation 331, 483
adaptive patterns 331 f
affective manner of presentation 347 f
affinity-seeking 250 f
agape 9, 12
agency, 7, 11, 12, 13
agentic style of friendship 16
agreement 345
altruism 12
ambiguity 316
ambiguous gestalt 310
ambiguous information 309
androgyny, psychological 14, 432
anomie 506
attachment 10, 122 f, 127, 139
attitude questionnaires 106 f
attraction 249
attractiveness 181–182
attributional process 242 f, 562 f
autocorrelagram 76

behavioral samples 253, 254
between-dyad variable 68
biological preparedness 122, 123, 125,
    138, 139
birth order 93
block design 70 f
bonding 471
Book of Discipline 23, 25

'Candid Camera' syndrome 96
caring 385
checkerboard design 70
chum 18
closedness 347
cognitive consistency theories 241
cohabitation 315
COLLECT YOUR THOUGHTS
    computer software 87
collectivity 469
communal love 11
communal style of friendship 20, 374
communication 102, 326

communication gestalt 309
communication management 348
communication patterns 326
communication quality 47 f, 343 f
communication strategies 247 f, 250 f
communion 7, 12
companionate love 9
comparative design 58
compatibility 411 f
competence, personal 510
    relational 502
complementarity 412
compliance-gaining 250, 297 f
confidants 523, 530–531
conflict, 103, 177 f, 190 f, 221 f, 243, 300
consensus information 243
consistency information 254
construct validation 254
constructive problem solving 345
content accuracy 88
content analysis 304, 323
context 311
contradiction 259, 260
control 294 f, 313, 349 f
convergence 333
conversational coherence 350
coordination of behavior 350
coping 503, 538
correlational structure 58, 69 f
correspondent inferences 242, 254
costs 244
courtship 409
culture 340
currency of exchange 245
cycle 76 f

Dead Sea Scrolls 23
decision making 255 f
decline 477
deficiency love 9
definitions of communicative phenomena
    311
depression 543 f, 546, 557, 562 f, 566 ff,
    586, 589
development 477

dialectical theory 262, 402
diary accounts 99, 107 ff
disclosure 348
disconfirmation 347
disengagement 329
dissolution 415 f
distance regulation 293
distinctiveness information 243
divergence 333
divorce 196, 468
dominance 301 f
domineering style 297, 299
Don Juan 15
dyad 467
DYAD DYNAMICS computer software
    95
dyadic interaction paradigm 81 f, 89 f
dyadic reciprocity 147 f, 149, 157
dynamic behaviors 86 f

ecological perception 24
efficiency 249
emotion 245
emotional isolation 18
emotional well-being 501–502
empathy 85, 88
enmeshed relationships 507
environmental influences 479
environmental selection 480
equity 436
eros 9, 12
evolution 125 ff, 128
exchange 9, 417 f
excitement/interest 11, 12, 17
exit 14, 103
Expressed Emotion (EE) 553 ff
expressiveness 347

Family Systems 220–227
feelings, parental 185 f
femininity 16, 18 ff, 431
filter models 414 f
form-giving messages 312, 316
form-giving capacity 316
form-giving contract 312
form-giving norm 312
friendship 395 ff, 401, 404, 406, 444, 468
    and socialization 396
    and work 396
    conversation 401, 403
    cross-sex friendship 404
    definition 395
    episode 16
    in children 21, 212 f
friendships 225 f

gender roles 435 ff
gestalt 309

goals 251
Group Development Stage theory 475
growth 477

hardiness 502
health 499, 503
heuristics 243
hierarchical dynamics 311
histories of communicative interaction 311

'I–Thou' encounter 20
ideologies 344 f, 352 f
impact reports 359
inclusion 312
inclusive fitness 126, 127
independence 59 f, 66
indeterminate time frame 311
indistinguishability 61
individual idiosyncrasies 356
individual reciprocity 146 f
infancy 124, 126, 128, 130, 131 f, 135
information acquisition 47 f, 247, 248, 249
information exchange 240
information gaining tactics 249
information theory 240
ingratiation 243
inner working models 371
institutionalization 311, 470
integrative strategies 345
intentionality 310
interaction 43, 45 f, 46, 47 f, 49 ff, 280,
    297, 326 ff, 331, 332, 339
    patterns 297, 331, 332, 339
    quality 90 f
interactional involvement 90 f
interdependence 336 f
internal consistency 254
interorganizational relations 481
interpersonal influence 147 f
interpersonal process 420
interpreting messages 351
interrogation 249
intersubjectivity 91
intervention (support) 520, 522 ff, 540
interviews 101, 105
intimacy 11, 17 ff, 19 ff, 50, 295 ff, 347 ff,
    369 ff, 503, 515, 517, 577
intraclass correlation 61, 62, 63, 76

jealousy 442
joy/enjoyment 12, 17
judgmental biases 243

kin selection 129
knowledge structures 243, 254
Kraemer–Jacklin design 63 f, 67

lab com 321

levels of analysis 290, 291
liabilities 483
life cycle 201, 202, 475
life events 538, 539
limerence 437
locus of control 502
log linear analysis 73 f, 75
loneliness (state, trait, chronic) 17 ff, 385,
    572 f, 573 f
loss 507
love 9 ff, 102 f, 106, 438
loyalty 19, 103
ludus 9, 12

macrojudgement 311
mania 9, 12
marital distress 544 ff, 546 f, 552 f, 557,
    560 ff
marital interaction 548–551, 564, 567
marital quality 343 f, 354, 357
marital relationship 196 f
marital satisfaction 545, 547, 564, 567
marital therapy 558 f
marital types 354
Markov model 76
marriage 468
masculinity 14, 431
mass media 526
mastery 502, 505
mate-selection 411
mental health 503
mental template 310
message control 296, 299, 331
message duration 303
message intensity 304
message pattern 297, 331
messages systems 309
meta-message 307
meta-perspectives 87, 91
meta-relational talk 250, 312
meta-rules 313
metacommunication 312, 350
metaphor 304, 307
microbehaviors 311
misdeeds, children's 182 f
mismatching 334
multiple partner design 58, 70 f
mutual aid 525, 527 f

naturalistic social cognition 89
naturally-occurring interaction behavior
    94
need for achievement 15 f
need for interpersonal intimacy (Sullivan)
    18
negative affectivity (NA) 510
negative behaviors 345
neglect 14, 19, 103

negotiation 353
networks 482
niche 483
nonindependence 59 f
nonverbal communication 41 ff

observational method 80 f
ontogeny 123, 137 f
openness 347
oral dependency needs 12
organismic analogy 476

parameter estimation 252
parent–child relationship 177 ff, 187 f,
    213, 217 f
parental influence 179 f, 183 f
partner effect 70
passionate love 9
peers 132 f
persona 473
Personal Construct Theory 241 f
personal resources 510, 511
personality
    as summaries 162 f
    defined 162 f
    development of 166
    disorders 555 f
phylogeny 123, 137 f
physiological measures 359
plans 250, 251
pluralistic approach 358
population ecology 483
positive behaviors 343, 345
positivity bias 253
power 7, 14, 15, 16, 17, 21, 178 f, 190 f,
    217, 219, 224
pragma 9, 12
pragmatics 310, 314
predictability 338
predictive validity 254
preinteraction expectancies 90
press 8
private self-consciousness 90, 91
prototypes 33 ff, 446
proximity 348
psychiatric disturbance 504, 513
psychological distress 510, 513
psychological frame 312
psychological well-being 387
public self-consciousness 90

quality communication 47 f, 311, 316, 345
quality marriage 316
quid pro quo 397 f
Qumran community 23, 25, 27

rape 447 f
reactivity 254, 318

realism 430
reciprocal altruism 129
reciprocity 144 f, 145 f, 148, 149, 150, 151,
    158, 297, 339
regulating behavior 49 f
relational control coding 296, 299
relational control findings 299
relational decay 249
relational deterioration 250
relational dimensions 294
relational disengagement 250
relational history 277 f
relational ideologies 329
relational maintenance 249, 250
relational meanings 346
relational messages 281 ff
relational outcomes 329, 330
relational reciprocity 152 f
relational types 336
relationship culture 472
relationship development 45, 258, 268,
    269, 270, 411
relationship satisfaction 104 f
relationships 43, 47 f, 50, 54 f, 153 f, 164,
    165, 166, 167, 171, 173 f, 177 f, 193 f
    children's 203, 212
    developing 45
    dysfunctional 220–227
    intergenerational 200 f, 202 f
    parent-child 177 f, 193, 195, 203
repair 316
report-command message meaning 292 f
responsiveness 349
reward–cost ratios 245
role 432, 473
role strain 300
role-making 473
romance 245, 460
romantic relationships 245, 437, 449, 450,
    451, 453, 455, 456, 457, 460, 461,
    463
romantic relationships in organizations
    449, 450, 451, 455, 460, 461
romanticism 437
round robin design 71
rule knowledge 24 f
rules 24, 25, 26, 28, 353

sampling errors 321
satisfaction 335
Scaffolding 124
scripts 28 f, 29, 30
second guessing 251
secret tests 249–250, 357
self, models of 170
self-concept 189 f, 502
self-disclosure 102, 372
self-esteem 90, 188 f, 198, 584, 585

self-expression 379
self-identity 188
self-monitoring 91, 188
self-report 100 f, 107, 109, 111, 112
sentiments 474
separates 336
sex-roles 91, 92, 439
sexuality 103 f
shared meanings 351
shyness 578, 584, 589
sibling relationship 195, 205 f, 214, 216,
    221
signals 310
similarity 413 f
social anxiety 90, 581
social appropriateness 249
social comparison 241, 370
social competence 581 f, 583, 584
social constructionism 430
social control 7, 11, 13
social exchange 246
social form 474
social information 249
social institutions 353
social integration 499
social interaction 290
social networks 217, 504, 506 f, 513, 514,
    529, 537, 576
social obligations 514
social organization 469
social power 444
Social Relations Model 58 f, 333
social resources 500, 501 f, 505, 516
social roles 512–513
social skills 502, 573, 579, 581 f
social stereotypes 91
social structure 469
social support 498 f, 499, 504, 508 f, 511 f,
    515, 516 f, 520, 522 f
socialization 177 f, 407
socioanalytic theory (Hogan) 13
sociobiology 430
sociology 467
sociometric data 72 f
solitude 579
speech convergence 334
stages 475
standard dyadic design 59 f, 82
static 332
static behaviors 86 f
storge 9, 12
strategic communication 240, 247, 250,
    297
stress 198, 499, 514
structural model of love 10, 11
structuration theory 434, 470
style 307 f, 309, 314, 315, 317
support 198, 313

support groups 199, 529, 530
supporting interaction 198
symmetry 292
Systems Theory 291, 533 f

temperament 181
temporal reciprocity 150 f
text processing 250
Thematic Apperception Test 14, 19
therapeutic relationships 368
thought-feeling assessment 82, 84, 87, 90
time series design 74 f, 76, 333
traditionals 336
traits 162, 163
transactional redundancy 299
transactional types 298

Triangular Theory of Love 246
trust 318 f

uncertainty 239, 240
unit of analysis 57
unobtrusive observation 82 ff

valence accuracy 92–93
values, parental 186 f
videotape data 84 f
voice 19

warmth 217, 223 f
Weiss 212
within-dyad analyses 95
within-dyad variable 57, 66 f